Also by PHILIP TAFT

The A.F. of L. in the Time of Gompers (1957)

The A.F. of L. from the Death of Gompers
to the Merger (1959)

ORGANIZED LABOR
IN AMERICAN HISTORY

ORGANIZED LABOR

IN

AMERICAN HISTORY

PHILIP TAFT

HARPER & ROW, PUBLISHERS

NEW YORK, EVANSTON, AND LONDON

ORGANIZED LABOR IN AMERICAN HISTORY. *Copyright © 1964 by Philip Taft. Printed in the United States of America. All rights reserved. No part of this book may be used or reproduced in any manner whatsoever without written permission except in the case of brief quotations embodied in critical articles and reviews. For information address Harper & Row, Publishers, Incorporated, 49 East 33rd Street, New York 16, N. Y.*

FIRST EDITION

LIBRARY OF CONGRESS CATALOG CARD NUMBER: LC 64-12712

E-O

To the Memory of

ERNEST L. MEYER

Contents

Acknowledgments

A number of friends and colleagues, and several libraries and their staffs have aided me in this study. It is a pleasure to acknowledge their assistance.

Mrs. Claire Brown of the Littauer Library at Harvard University has helped me to discover documents and newspapers and has given freely of her time. The Economics Division of the New York Public Library (the Forty-second Street Branch) has helped me on a number of occasions in finding scarce materials not available elsewhere. Miss Margaret Brickett and her efficient staff in the Library of the U.S. Department of Labor have always been helpful. Dr. David C. Mearns and the staff of the Manuscript Division of the Library of Congress made available materials. The archives of the Catholic University of America allowed me to use the Philip Murray and Terence Powderly papers, and Charles F. Ritter, the assistant archivist, guided me through these collections. The University of Wisconsin Library made available the unpublished manuscript of Father Charles F. Kileen. The National Archives was of assistance. To the staffs of the above institutions, my sincere thanks.

I am especially grateful to the staff of the John Hay Library at Brown University. Miss Helen Kurtz and Mrs. Eva Frankfurt helped with government documents; the Misses Dorothy Day, Sara De Luca, and Mary Vandersea have always answered my sometimes unreasonable requests for aid. I regret my bad temper and thank them for their assistance. The secretarial staff of the Economics Department of Brown University—the Misses Marion Anthony, Claire Carr, Dorothy Heselwood, and Christine Peterson—have struggled with a number of drafts of the manuscript and my illegible writing. For their aid and patience, my most sincere gratitude.

The Library of the American Iron and Steel Institute allowed me to use its publications, and I thank Mr. George S. Rose, secretary, and Mr. Leo Teplow, assistant vice-president, for the opportunity. The Pinkerton's National Detective Agency, Inc., opened its archival material on the Molly Maguires and the Moyer, Haywood, Pettibone cases, and I am grateful for the privilege and thankful to Mr. Bernard F. Boyce and Mr. George F. O'Neill, on the staff of the agency, for their assistance.

A number of active and former union officers have provided assistance. Adolph Germer, a veteran unionist, who was active in the Ludlow coal miners' strike and in the more important early campaigns of the CIO, discussed a number of issues with me. R. J. Thomas, on the staff of the AFL-CIO, read some of the manuscript; Lane Kirkland, administrative assistant to President George Meany, was helpful in a number of matters; Otto Jaeger of the Industrial Union Department gave useful advice; R. J. Corbett of the New York State AFL-CIO allowed me to examine several scarce documents; C. J. Haggerty, president of the Building and Construction Trades Department, granted unrestricted access to the files of the California State Federation of Labor, of which he was secretary; Don Vial was helpful during my work at the offices of the California State Federation of Labor, and Thomas L. Pitts, secretary of the California Labor Federation, allowed me an opportunity to continue examining the records. George W. Johns of the San Francisco Labor Council made available his records for examination; Paul and the late Mrs. Scharrenberg made available information on the California labor movement, the Wheatland hop riot, and the Mooney case. To all who have given freely of their time and knowledge, and who supplied advice and materials, my sincerest gratitude.

A number of friends and colleagues assisted with criticism and advice. Merlyn Pitzele read several chapters and made some helpful suggestions. Professor Harold Roberts of the University of Hawaii directed me to fruitful sources and aided my research during my stay at his institution. Francis Gates of the Extension Division of the University of California in Berkeley gave me sound advice on a number of matters; Mary Gallagher shared her unsurpassed knowledge of the Mooney case with me; Professor Maurice Neufeld of the Cornell University New York State School of Industrial and Labor Relations read a number of chapters and made some helpful criticisms and valuable suggestions. Professor Philip Ross of the University of Pittsburgh discussed most of the problems connected with this study with me, and his suggestions on style and content were invaluable. Professor George W. Taylor of the Wharton School of Finance and Commerce read a large part of the manuscript, and the finished product owes a great deal to his penetrating insights into the history and practice of unionism. Dr. Carlin T. Kindilien helped me with editorial problems. My sincerest thanks to all of them for their patience and generosity.

My colleagues at Brown University, Professors George Borts, Jerome

Stein, and Merton P. Stoltz, have been helpful throughout the study with advice and suggestions.

My wife, as always, was of great assistance. She aided in much of the research, made suggestions on style and content, kept the manuscript in order, and performed the innumerable chores which made this work possible. Without her assistance the study would not have been started, let alone finished. Of course, I alone am responsible for errors.

The volume is dedicated to the late Ernest L. Meyer, a Madison newspaperman and the first friend I found when I went to the University of Wisconsin in 1928. It would indeed be difficult for me to explain the wonderful qualities, the kindness, and help that I, among many, found in Ernie's home. The remembrance is a small mark of the affection which so many Wisconsin students have had for this remarkable man.

PHILIP TAFT

Brown University
Providence, R. I.
January 1, 1964

Introduction

Re-examining the past may yield a better understanding of preceding events and a keener appreciation of existing institutions. The emotions that surround current controversies are likely to be dissolved by time, and the dissipation of excessive hopes and fears they once aroused may make possible a fairer and more accurate reappraisal.

American unionism came on the scene not quite two hundred years ago. The first labor organizations and the central bodies they established in the late eighteenth and early nineteenth centuries were exponents of what is today called "business unionism," a view and practice carried on by all generations of unionists from the founding of the first economic organizations of labor in the late eighteenth century to our own time. The evidence presented will show that the tenets of business unionism were followed by the first unions. In contrast to the ephemeral programs of social and political reform offered to American labor, business unionism has remained the permanent expression of organized workers seeking remedies for the evils and problems arising in the place of employment.

Business unionism stresses limited objectives, immediate improvements and eschews broader programs of social and political change. It depends upon the willingness of workers to organize for mutual help, upon the existence of an expanding economy as well as political freedom and civil rights for special groups to organize for the promotion of their own interests. This view was given greater coherence by the unionists of the 1870's and 1880's, and was later summarized by Gompers as the eternal quest for "more and more." Such a program, while lacking the grandeur of the elaborate programs for the reorganization of society on more correct principles, is highly suitable for enlarging the rights and liberties of the individual and for protecting him against changes in the supply and demand for labor.

Business unionism was a practical program. It is a mark of the genius of its sponsors that they recognized that out of the continually expanding economy of the United States and the increased product generated, workers could obtain more and more.[1] It was a realizable program because no central power could arbitrarily decide the division of the gross product between consumption and investment; and the pressure of organized workmen could not be repressed or ignored.

From time to time other kinds of organizations have been formed. From the vague land nationalization scheme of Thomas Skidmore to contemporary communism, programs of reform and revolution have been offered the workers of the United States. No superior power compelled their rejection. The National Labor Union, for example, failed because it did not address itself to the needs of workers in the plant. Business unionism has not been greeted with open arms by employers. Those who question its idealism tend to forget its struggle to survive; its battles on the picket line; and the violence, fear, and black-list which were the accompaniments of its campaigns of organization. Employers are likely to be indifferent to ideology as the experience of communist dominated unions shows; wage increases and changes in conditions of employment are the employers' chief concern. The annals of labor disputes from 1877 to the Little Steel strike are filled with heroism and sacrifice unmatched in any other industrial nation. In fact, the tendency of labor disputes in some industries to degenerate into violence has led students to describe erroneously the Molly Maguires as a link in the labor movement.

The Knights of Labor offered another alternative to business unionism. Its failure to survive appears to have been caused by its ill-defined purpose rather than the atttacks of the trade unions. The nascent American Federation of Labor, as the record shows, was too weak to injure its more powerful rival. The newly formed AFL could only denounce the invasions of its affiliates' jurisdictions. Words may be weapons, but they must be supplemented by more powerful means. As the dispute between the AFL and the Congress of Industrial Organizations demonstrated, an organization can ride out an attack if it serves its members effectively. The rapid decline and extinction of the Knights of Labor was the result of its own inadequacy, and not of the fatal wounds inflicted by business unions.

Like the unions of the present, those of the past have been favorably or adversely affected by public opinion, the attitude of government, and the policies, tactics, and leadership of the organizations themselves. The severe depression of the 1890's, with its armies of destitute unemployed, softened the public attitude towards organized labor, and reflected itself in the adoption of the labor provisions of the Erdman Act protecting the right of railroad workers to organize and the multiplicity of more general state legislation granting the same rights. While difficult to measure precisely, the more favorable public climate was a great aid to the expansion of unionism in the years from 1897 to 1904. On a much greater scale the experiences of labor during the New Deal followed a similar pattern. Public sympathy shifted to the labor side as a result of the severe unemployment and destitution of the early 1930's, and made it easier to gain congressional consent to the labor legislation and to subsequent campaigns to muster the unorganized into unions.

Public opinion was also a significant factor in the employer campaigns to push back labor organizations to weaker positions. The open-shop drives of the first decade of this century and the American Plan of Employment of the early 1920's were prepared by powerful propaganda barrages designed to dissipate public sympathy for organized labor. Adverse public opinion generated by the spread of labor disputes and the exposure of fiduciary laxity contributed to the enactment of the Taft-Hartley and Landrum-Griffin laws.

Government has always influenced the progress of the labor movement. From the conspiracy trials to the Landrum-Griffin law, government has defined the rights and duties of labor and management; nonintervention is largely a myth. Deputizing sheriffs during strikes and lockouts, granting employers the right to maintain private police forces, limiting picketing, protecting yellow-dog contracts, and aborting organizing campaigns and boycotts by court orders are forms of intervention which were exceedingly effective. Government has in the past been as effective in inhibiting labor organization and collective bargaining as the New Deal labor laws have been in protecting the right to organize.

Intervention is inevitable in a free democratic society, because no government can stand by idly while economic and social life grinds to a halt. A labor dispute which affects the economy seriously will always be an object of governmental attention. There is, however, a difference between compulsion and intervention by which the government seeks to narrow differences and work out compromises. The reserved power of refusal by the parties gives them a voice in the ultimate settlement. From 1886 to the 1963 controversy over work rules on the railroads, the government has intervened whenever the possibility of a serious suspension of operations existed. In the Burlington and Chicago Railroad strikes the government intervened through the courts; Congress settled the 1916 dispute over the eight-hour workday; and Presidential seizure ended the national railroad strike of 1946. The responses of railway management and labor has been influenced by past experience, and both sides are aware that no administration will allow them to fight a battle "to the death."

The reasons for American labor's political tactics have never been adequately explained, because students have directed their attention to the debates on socialism and politics at the conventions of the AFL. The real explanation for the policy of pressure politics, followed for more than one hundred years must be sought elsewhere. Because students have been convinced that the formation of a labor party was a "natural" function of the trade unions, they have ignored the uniqueness of American political life and the significance of American labor's political instrumentalities, the state federations of labor. An examination of the evidence will show that the AFL could never impose its political views on its affiliates, and never sought to do so. Persuasion and influence are not compulsion. Rejection of independent political action was based upon a keen appreciation of the realities of political life: the low discipline and lack of central control of American political parties over officials elected under their labels. Low party discipline has been the greatest force for democracy and for permitting local needs and interests to express themselves in the legislatures and the Congress. State federations of labor and local central bodies have been the political instruments of organized workers. The extensive body of labor and welfare legislation, most of it of vital interest to particular labor groups, has been enacted largely through the influence of these institutions. Sponsorship of independent political action would have imperiled relationships built up at the state capitols, endangered labor's program, and enabled bills favored by anti-union groups to receive a friendlier reception.

Leadership on the management and labor sides have always affected the growth and prosperity of union organization. Labor relations were greatly influenced by the rise, in the 1890's, of the imperious business leader typified by Henry C. Frick and Elbert E. Gary. Even today, a Lemuel Boulware can be a factor in union growth. Equally important is leadership on the union side. Big hearts and noble resolves are not necessarily qualities which make for efficient labor leadership. The lost strikes on the railroads in 1894, the strikes in the steel industry and in the metal trades in the early years of the century show the effect of leadership incapable of gauging accurately the situations facing their organizations. But the maneuvers of an adroit leadership may be too narrowly restricted by the refusal of the membership to make concessions. Fear of unemployment or of the effect upon the position of a skilled group may induce opposition to change, as in the metal trades in the early 1890's, and in some current work rules disputes. Nevertheless, leadership plays an important, and on occasion, a decisive role. In contrast to failure in the railway and steel industries, the tactical skills of John Mitchell shine brightly. Against overwhelming odds he was able to lead 150,000 anthracite coal miners to victory. But even a man of genius might not be able to overcome the limits imposed by the economic environment. With all of his great gifts, John L. Lewis was unable to halt the erosion of his union's power in the 1920's.

Jurisdictional disputes have appeared and reappeared from the 1870's to our own time. Although many can be eliminated today through representation elections of government boards, their persistence is a manifestation of permanent tendencies in American labor. As with the present federation, the AFL sought to avoid involvement in these controversies and was compelled by the demands of its affiliates to seek solutions. Cooperative action among closely related trades was one of the by-products of the attempts to devise methods of settling such differences.

Dual unionism was largely an ideological phenomenon, although breakaway organizations have always existed. Dual unionism culminated in the formation of the Industrial Workers of the World in 1905. Although the IWW espoused a revolutionary program of militant direct action, the greatest opposition to its activities usually came when it sought to organize workers for improving the terms of employment. Even the prosecutions during World War I were largely influenced by organizing campaigns in the lumber and copper mining industries, as were the Everett and Centralia incidents. In fact, the policies of the IWW were evolving towards a pragmatic type of unionism when its activities were undermined by government prosecution.

IWW activity must be distinguished, as is shown, from the efforts of the Communists to dominate the labor scene. In part, the efforts of the IWW were directed to sections of the economy in which traditional unions were not numerous or absent, and where the obstacles to permanent organization were very great. Communist policy ultimately sought to capture the trade unions so that the party might obtain transmission belts for its propaganda and control. When the first campaign of union infiltration failed, the Communists shifted their policy to dual unionism. Later they went back to boring-from-within tactics. The success of the Communists in the 1930's was not due to the greater appeal of their message, but to the formation of new unions without experienced leadership. To the extent that employers contributed to the absence of trained leaders, they aided the Communist successes. As indicated below, employers appear to prefer a tractable Communist-dominated union to a militant conservative one—such a conclusion can be drawn from the Aesopian language of employers who attack with equal impartiality Communist and anti-Communist labor organizations.

The attitudes of organized labor towards immigration and minorities have not been based on racial doctrines or feelings. Whether opposition was expressed to Chinese or southern and eastern European immigrants, the basis of the view was fear of the effect of a constant inflow of new workers upon the supply of labor and wages. The children and grandchildren of the new immigrants of 1880 have not welcomed Negro and Puerto Rican workers into their industries and unions with greater enthusiasm than was shown to their ancestors by the older settlers. The immigration question can be understood by reference to the attitude towards minorities, as they spring from the same fear—increasing the supply of labor.

The great crisis of the 1930's in the ranks of organized labor was the result of a series of errors and the ignoring of the spirit, practice, and constitution of the AFL. The CIO was largely a creation of John L. Lewis, without whose leadership and whose union's finances, the movement would have floundered and expired. In the creation of the CIO and in the early organizing campaigns, the importance of leadership is clearly visible. However, the sympathetic climate of opinion and the policy of the federal government played more than a supporting role. The CIO organized a number of important industries and compelled the discarding of the principle of exclusive jurisdiction, which had governed the theory and practice of the AFL since its founding. With time, the differences dividing the federations narrowed, and separation could no longer be justified. In most respects, the CIO unions resembled closely many of those in the AFL. Differences were likely to be due more to economic environment than to affiliation.

The merged federation, AFL-CIO, is a child of the past. Its limited power, its policies on social and economic problems show the deep traces of earlier labor experience. Of course, labor organizations, like other institutions, must take cognizance of changes in the economy and society, and the new federation is not a pure duplicate of its predecessors. It takes a firmer position on ethical practice and has the right to investigate the behavior of affiliates. It also has more constitutional power in the adjustment of jurisdictional disputes and discrimination. Nevertheless, in all of these areas its influence is predominantly moral. Because the federation is a neutral party with an interest in peaceful settlements, its offices can be useful in difficult jurisdictional disputes. But it has no method by which it can impose its dicta, and the old AFL, despite contrary opinion, was not entirely unsuccessful in settling such differences.

The merged federation also has not mounted many extensive organizing drives. It would appear that a federation is not the most effective instrument for day-to-day organizing. Except for a special campaign in an industry or an area, a federation's role is likely to be complementary to the efforts of affiliates. Contrary to some expectations, the federation has refused the burden of supervising the moral health of its affiliates. No federation can perform such a task effectively, and except for a great scandal such matters are better left to the government and the courts. The fact is that the reports under the Landrum-Griffin law show the level of moral and democratic health of the labor movement to be quite high. Let its critics compare the record under Landrum-Griffin with any other group in the community for honesty. Let critics compare the democracy in unions with that in other institutions—the church, universities, fraternal and philanthropic societies, employer organizations, and local, state, and federal governments. There is no doubt that the democracy within the labor movement is much greater and more broadly based than in most other institutions of the country.

In the last thirty years the American labor movement has vastly expanded its influence on public policy and power in determining the terms of employment in industry. Like millions of its members, it may be facing a multitude of new problems as a result of changes in technology and the labor force. No one can forecast the future with any degree of certainty, but the labor movement has in the past been able to ride out serious storms. Experience in the last decade shows no reasons for believing that the labor movement will not be able to meet the difficulties and problems it may be called upon to face. The effectiveness of American labor organizations has weakened the appeal of reform and revolutionary doctrines among American wage earners. Organized labor has supported the United States in its wars and more limited conflicts with foreign powers. It played an important and constructive role in postwar international relations, and continues to be active, although in a normal period its influence is lessened. The labor movement is not without serious faults, but it can be proud of its achievements on behalf of the workers of the United States, and of the country and its people.

ORGANIZED LABOR
IN AMERICAN HISTORY

CHAPTER 1

The First Organized Action

CONDITIONS IN THE COLONIES

Settlement of the New World brought with it the need for skilled labor. Craftsmen came to the United States as indentured servants. Some resumed their trade at the expiration of their term, and others became farmers. European artisans also arrived on their own and set up shops in which they practiced their trades.[1] The high demand for and short supply of skilled labor in the early period of colonial settlement led to attempts at wage control. In 1633, Massachusetts sought to regulate the returns of master carpenters, sawyers, masons, brickmen, tilers, joiners, wheelwrights, and others; but the common feature of all such legislation was its "instability."[2] Experiments in the impressment of labor for special public and even private tasks were also made, but like wage control, these methods proved inefficient and unworkable.[3]

As colonial society stabilized, a class of artisan tradesmen developed and prospered in the towns and cities. Some bought to sell again, and others offered the fruits of their own labor. Artisans usually maintained in their homes shops which could be identified by a special sign of the craft that was practiced.[4]

Capital was initially provided by British sources, and the property of the colonists was largely in land and improvements. Profits were high, and trading capital was accumulated in Boston, Newport, Philadelphia, and other seaports. English and European capital played an important role in the financing of some industries.[5]

1

The lack of competent craftsmen adversely affected industrial growth, and there existed few opportunities for replenishing the supply by vocational training. Since it was impossible to maintain the English standards of apprenticeship, the level of skill among hired workers declined. Unspecialized household and homespun industries supplied some of the market for goods. Journeymen craftsmen, employing their own tools, worked on custom orders or for the general market. In Massachusetts, Pennsylvania, and Rhode Island shoemaking, coopering, and shipbuilding became active industries. But the colonists did not establish many societies modeled on the English guilds, although a number were organized and thrived.[6]

Although American industry developed slowly, the growth of population and wealth led to industrial expansion. The market widened, and some small tradesmen became merchant capitalists catering to larger markets. The boycott of English manufacture by the colonists, following England's enactment of the revenue laws of 1764 and 1765, helped to stimulate the expansion of American industry which sought to supply the colonial markets. The contest between the colonies and England reached a climax when colonial merchants were called upon in 1774 and 1775 to cease importing goods from England. The nonimportation agreements sought to reduce the demand for English goods and to create a preference for home products. The American Revolution made the colonies largely dependent upon their own industrial ability and increased the demand for many industrial products.

In an effort to increase the supply of skilled labor, voluntary apprenticeships were arranged with the consent of parents, but compulsory indentures were signed by town authorities. The latter type placed orphans and children born out of wedlock under the jurisdiction of a master for instruction in a trade. The supply was inadequate a large part of the time, and many apprentices refused to serve out their full term and ran away to other communities or to farming areas. Consequently, colonial journeymen were very often poorly trained, because the abler and more ambitious could go into business on their own. Hours of labor were long, and many masters were harsh and exacting.

With time, increases in population and the growth of towns and cities led to an expansion of industry and of the number of artisan craftsmen. "The pre-industrial cities," according to Bridenbaugh, "harbored no large resident working class that might be designated as a proletariat. Even humble carters and porters occasionally turned out to be property owners."[7] There were reports of occasional strikes among wage earners, but many apparent strikes were merely efforts by independent craftsmen to raise their prices.[8]

INFLUENCE OF THE REVOLUTION

The revolution against England stimulated the growth of home industry to supply the needs formerly provided by English manufacture. For the twenty-five years after the establishment of the United States, agriculture and the other extractive industries remained the chief source of livelihood. Manufacturing was on the rise, but its gains about matched the increases in population; consequently, no important net per capita increase in manufacturing took place. The cotton industry had been established in 1790 in Rhode Island when the owners hired Samuel Slater, a young Englishman with experience in mill management in his native country, to direct the enterprise. Slater, who had come to the United States in search of opportunity, was able to construct from memory the textile machinery whose export from England had been forbidden. In the next fifteen years several other mills were established, but they faced severe competition from the more experienced English producers. Hampered by competition and the shortage of capital and labor, few mills survived.[9]

The Napoleonic wars played an important if indirect role in stimulating the growth of the cotton textile and other manufacturing industries. Interference with the commerce of the United States caused Congress to enact the Embargo Act of 1807, under which an attempt was made to restrict foreign trade. The Non-Intercourse Act and the War of 1812 had the same effect. While they adversely affected the export of agricultural commodities and shipbuilding, the restraints which the laws and events imposed upon commerce had a buoyant effect upon American manufacture. The shortage of imported cottons increased prices and made the industry attractive to investors who had heretofore placed their monies in commerce. Cotton spindles in the United States increased from 8,000 in 1807 to 130,000 in 1815.[10] Factories first appeared in the textile industries, but changes in other industries helped to transform the economy of the United States and to change the character of American labor-management relations.[11]

LABOR ORGANIZATION

American labor organizations had their beginning in the late eighteenth century before the emergence of the factory. Combinations of businessmen and self-employed in trade associations have existed for a much longer period of time than trade unions. A union of wage earners, whether they be mechanics, semi-skilled, or unskilled workers, aims to affect the terms of the wage bargain and to change conditions under which its members are employed. A trade association, on the other hand, is customarily made up of independent businessmen who might seek to affect prices or in some other way change the terms of sale. A worker is dependent upon a single employer for his orders. In contrast, a self-employed businessman may have a larger amount of capital available and is likely to carry on business with several consumers who purchase his product or service. The household worker is dependent for his raw materials upon his employer who is usually the connecting link between him and his market. Moreover, because the market is separated, in either space or time, the worker depends upon the advances of his employer in the form of wages to maintain him. The establishment of permanent trade unions is likely to take place later than common action among wage earners. A change in pay or the imposition of an unjust penalty might stimulate a walkout,[12] but the formation of a permanent trade union is a later step, one that requires much greater persistence and cohesion.

The first to organize was the skilled artisan, the printer, shoemaker, and building tradesman. According to Professor Commons, changes in the market rather than in technology gave rise to the first combinations of workers. Commons believed that the "two economic factors of largest import are the progress of invention in tools and machinery (the technique of the 'instruments of production') and the extension of markets through growth of population and improved transportation. . . . Perhaps the difference is only one between the immediate and the remote causes of industrial evolution, but, at any rate, so far as concerns the characteristic features of the labor movement as we find them in documents at our command, it is the extension of markets more than the technique of production that determines the origin of industrial classes, their form or organization, their political and industrial policies and demands, and their fate. Even the inventions of machinery follow rather than precede the widening of the markets."[13]

Commons selected the shoe industry to demonstrate his view. Originally, in the colonial period, the cordwainer operated in a custom order market and made shoes and boots to the order of his neighbors at his home shop. A next step was taken when the master cordwainer began to accumulate an inventory of standard sizes and the master became a retail merchant who required a stock of raw material as well as finished goods. The retailer at this stage also employed journeymen to make up work in their homes. With improvement in transportation, some of the masters began to prospect in wider fields for orders. Larger investments, credit, and an increased number of workers were needed to take care of the increased business. Commons calls this period the wholesale order stage.

It was the widening of these markets with their lower levels of competition and quality, but without changes in the instruments of production, that destroyed the primitive identity of master and journeymen cordwainers and split their community of interest into the modern alignment of employers' association and trade union. . . . It was a struggle on the part of the merchant employer to require the same *minimum quality* of work for each of the markets, but lower rates of wages on work destined for the wider and lower markets. It was a struggle on the part of the journeyman to require the same *minimum wage* on work destined for each market, but with the option of a higher wage for a higher market. The conflict came over the wage and quality of work destined for the widest, lowest and newest market.[14]

The conflict was shaped by the attempt of the entrepreneurs to shift part of the risks, because the absence of advanced orders created a possibility of overestimating demand, to the wage earner. Widening of the market also stimulated competition among merchants who attempted to offset their lower prices by reducing wages and working standards. The worker responded by organizing trade societies. According to the *Lancaster* (Pa.) *Journal,* mechanics established unions "to protect themselves and their families against the cupidity of the employers, who not content with taking every advantage of the working men to reduce their wages, carried on a system of encroaching upon their time to such a degree, that they were literally reduced to a state of slavery."[15] The indictment of 1806 against the Philadelphia Journeymen Boot and Shoemakers of Philadelphia claimed the union was not "content to work, and labor in that art and occupation, at the usual prices and rates for which they and other artificiers workmen and journeymen, in the same art and occupation were used and accustomed to work and labour; but contriving, and intending unjustly and oppressively to increase and augment the prices and rates usually paid and allowed to them and other artificiers."[16]

Like their successors, the early trade unions were mainly concerned with holding their wage levels so that they could maintain their standard of life as skilled workers. Proud of their crafts, some of the early organizations claimed that their members were superior workmen; others, that they excluded inferior men.[17]

[The first union, a society of Philadelphia shoemakers, was established in 1792 and lasted less than a year.[18] It did not leave its name. According to Samuel Logan, a witness in the conspiracy trial of 1806 involving a group of their craftsmen, "There was an affirmation introduced, as solemn as the oath I have just taken. It was that I will support such and such wages to the utmost of my power." The society was dissolved, and it was revived "again for the support of wages; as soon as we could agree upon the increase, we raised our wages." The turnout or strike of 1799 "was occasioned by employers attempting to reduce wages."[19]

[In 1794 the shoemakers of Philadelphia established the first permanent union, the Federal Society of Cordwainers, and it conducted a number of strikes and remained active until 1806. The early unions found it difficult to continue functioning.]

Whatever associated effort there was among printers before 1795 was temporary. These efforts had a single purpose and when this was accomplished, the compact was dissolved. It was the custom in all trades to call a "general meeting" of the trade whenever a matter of general importance presented itself.[20] Such meetings were held in private homes where statements were drawn up embodying the views of those attending. All approving the views would sign their names to the document, and if a strike followed, regular meetings would be held. Once the trouble was ended, the organization dissolved.

In 1799 the Franklin Typographical Society of Journeymen Printers of New York was formed. This society formulated the first complete wage scale ever adopted by the printers of New York City, and went on strike to enforce it.[21] This union like its predecessors concerned itself with the terms of employment. The early printers' unions show the same general attitudes as the shoemakers' journeymen organizations. Like their modern offspring, the early unions were primarily concerned with wages and working conditions. In fact, Stewart calls attention to the program of the Typographical Society of Philadelphia which closely resembles many of those believed to have arisen later. This union demanded exclusive employment of union men, a "working card," and a system closely resembling a union hiring hall.[22]

In the years between 1800 and 1810 those trades which had labor organizations attempted to force up wages by strikes. Many of them were started as benevolent societies of workers in one craft in a city or of artisans following a trade. But between 1800 to 1810 many of them changed their objectives. For example, the Federal and Union Society of Journeymen Tailors in Philadelphia complained in 1800 of low wages and declared its members would not work for low-standard employers.[23]

Four years later the journeymen tailors of Baltimore requested a wage increase and struck to enforce the demand. In 1805 the Philadelphia cordwainers struck for higher wages, and the strike led to their indictment for conspiracy to raise wages. A second strike by the Baltimore tailors was called in 1808, and the demand was again for higher wages. The dissatisfaction spread to New York, where the well-organized shoemakers struck against a shop which refused to pay the union rate. When the struck employer transferred his work to other shops, a general strike of shoemakers was called in New York City. A strike of shoemakers in Albany, New York, in 1810 for wage increases was also reported.[24]

Collective Bargaining

As already noted, the early unions engaged in collective bargaining. Before counter organizations were established by employers the union representatives visited each master separately with the price or wage lists which had been accepted at the meeting of the union journeymen. From the beginning labor organizations were concerned about the hiring of men who had not served a full apprenticeship and thereby debased the trade and increased the labor supply. The Typographical Society noted that employers were willing to hire "two-thirders," workmen who had not finished their apprenticeship and were willing to work below scale. A committee appointed to consider this problem reported that to maintain harmony between the society and the master printers it would be desirable to confer with the employers so as to devise a set of prices which will enable employers to give the preference to members of the society or at least to men who have served a regular apprenticeship.[25]

Complaints against a surplus of learners, runaway apprentices, and "half-way" journeymen were frequent among the early trade societies. Indentured boys might leave their employers and obtain work elsewhere at wages slightly above the amount they were earning as apprentices. There were also adults who had not completed their apprenticeships and were willing to accept employment below the scale. In 1809 the New York Typographical Society decided against admitting applicants who had not served a full three-year apprenticeship. In 1811 a committee from the Society, after investigating the question, issued a circular addressed to the Master Printers of the City of New York: "the practices of employing what is usually styled 'half-way' journeymen in preference to those who have served their time, while it holds encouragement to boys to elope from their masters as soon as they acquire sufficient knowledge of the art to be enabled to earn their bread, is a great grievance to the journeyman and almost certain to ruin the boys themselves." The circular complains of the employment of incompetent craftsmen, many of them foreigners, and observes that to "render the art respectable it is indispensably necessary that professors should be perfect masters of their calling, which can only be acquired by serving a proper apprenticeship."[26]

From the custom of setting up a price list and asking each employer for his agreement, it was only a step to group bargaining. The first recorded collective bargaining was the negotiations between the Philadelphia Journeymen Cordwainers and their employers in 1799. It followed a lockout after the workers refused to accept a wage cut. A committee of workers called on the employers who, acting through a group of representatives, were able to compromise the differences. A clear-cut instance of collective bargaining initiated by employees is not found until 1809, when the New York Journeymen printers drew up a price list and submitted it to their employers. The employers met, considered the proposals, and appointed a committee to negotiate with the journeymen. Committees from both groups met several times and evolved a compromise.[27]

Strike Benefits

From the beginning of the labor movement, strike benefits received considerable attention. The Philadelphia printers pledged themselves in

1786 to support all journeymen forced out of work because of their refusal to accept a wage cut. Sums were given to those workers and to their families so that they would stay in line. In some instances, namely one involving the New York printers, money was advanced to individual strikers in need and if the loan could not be repaid, it was financed by a tax upon all members. The practice of financing striking workers was copied from that of employers who financed individual masters who were in difficulty. In the early period only one organization—the New York shoe-makers—set up in 1805 a permanent defense fund. In addition to strike benefits, some of the early unions also paid sick and death benefits, these depending upon the amount of surplus funds the union had.[28]

The early unions were, in the main, organizations for improving wages and working conditions. Strikes were generally peaceful and short lived. But the workers in their early efforts toward cooperation faced several defeats on the industrial front. Following an unsuccessful strike in 1791, the Philadelphia carpenters announced that they would jointly offer their labor below the rates asked by their masters.[29]

Closed Shop

The demand for the exclusion of the unorganized man from employment coincides with the beginning of trade unionism. In fact, control over the supply of labor was characteristic of many of the first organizations. A charge that appears in almost all of the labor conspiracy trials is that trade societies sought to compel all craftsmen to affiliate.[30]

Reversals

The early trade unions were highly unstable. Opposition from employers and government, as well as the loss of interest among many members, were frequently fatal to the more fragile organizations. The opposition was often too powerful. Professor George E. Barnett notes that the period from 1815 to 1830 was unfavorable for the survival of unions of printers. Only the Columbia Society of Washington continued to 1830 to regulate wages, and even this organization's activities were largely of a beneficial kind. Only two trades in the New York construction industry were organized strongly enough in 1815 to make demands upon their employers.[31]

Professor Barnett believes that the inability of the early trade unions, at least in the printing industry, to survive was not the result of hostility of the employer or the prosecutions of the cordwainers under the law of conspiracy. He attributes their demise as protective organizations and their frequent transformation into beneficiary societies to the lack of continuing interest of the journeymen members.[32]

Loss of interest following a successful negotiation of a wage contract seems to have been the experience of the New York Typographical Society.

After the new scale went into effect in 1815, the influence of the society as a trade union began to decline. Dissatisfaction appeared after a proprietor member was expelled; this action was followed by the barring of master printers who had joined the society as journeymen and had retained their membership when they became masters. Because of distress among the members, a proposal for granting assistance was made in 1815 and rejected. The society then sought to organize its benevolent society upon a regular and permanent basis. To protect its assets, it sought a charter from the legislature. It was granted in March 1818 on condition that it cease to interfere with the price of labor, and the New York Typographical Society ceased to function as a trade union.[33] The impermanence of the early printers' unions, whose members appear to have been the most cohesive and conscious of the trade groups, with the possible exception of the cordwainers, reflects the difficulties faced by virtually all early organizations. While Professor Barnett's view is supported by evidence, the general low esteem in which the early trade union was held, even if it was not directly due to employers' hostility, certainly affected the ability of many organizations to remain active. Moreover, the friendly attitude of the master printers was not typical of employers in all trades. At a meeting in Boston on July 20, 1832, the master carpenters adopted the following resolution which clearly gives their view of the organization:

It being understood that the journeymen Carpenters and Caulkers have abandoned their Combination to control the liberty of individuals in the hours of Labour, and considering the extreme warmth of the weeks, and fear of Pestilence that pervades the community, it is the sense of the meeting that the Master Carpenters and Caulkers be authorized to allow the journeymen, two hours intermission at noon during the month of August. It being especially understood that they shall commence the day's work at sunrise, and terminate it at sunset.[34]

The Conspiracy Trials

The conspiracy trials of organized workers dating from 1806 to 1842 not only show the hostility with which the organized activity of workers was greeted in some trades, but reveal the character of the early labor organizations. According to the indictment (*Commonwealth* versus *Pullis*), the eight Philadelphia cordwainers, members of the Journeymen Boot and Shoemakers of Philadelphia, combined and conspired to "prevent by threats, menaces, and other unlawful means, other artificers, workmen, and journeymen in the said art and occupation, but at certain large prices, and rates which they . . . then and there fixed."[35] The defendants, according to prosecuting counsel, were indicted for "undertaking by a combination, to regulate the price of labour of others as well as their own."[36] Moreover, they refused to make a distinction between good and bad workmen. In other words, they took the position of the present-day unions that the standard rate had to be paid to all who are in a particular class or trade.[37] They also refused to work with journeymen who did not belong to the society. The jury found the defendants guilty of a conspiracy to raise wages, and each defendant was fined by Recorder Levy eight dollars and costs.[38]

The Journeymen Cordwainers of the City of New York *People* versus *Melvin* was also prosecuted in 1809–1810 for conspiracy to raise wages and also for insisting upon a closed shop. The indictment of twenty-four members of the union charged the defendants with a conspiracy to establish a closed shop so that none would work for less than the agreed upon prices for the several grades of boots.[39] Evidence was also adduced at the trial that Article IX of the union's constitution allowed members whose wages had been reduced below the scale or were otherwise aggrieved to bring their complaints before the union.[40]

The New York cordwainers were found guilty. The court advised the defendants to modify their rules and behavior, and fined each $1.00 with costs.[41]

The trial of the journeymen tailors in Philadelphia *(Commonwealth versus Moore, et al.)* in 1827 was also "for conspiring to raise their wages, to exact and extort from . . . master tailors, higher wages than were usually paid to journeymen tailors in Philadelphia."[42] The prosecution and defense took their usual positions. In this case, a committee representing the twenty-five defendants claimed that the pay for some of the work was too low. The employer, Robb and Winebrener, temporarily yielded, but as soon as the work upon which the committee was engaged was finished, they were discharged. Thereupon, fourteen other journeymen demanded their reinstatement and when the employer refused to yield, they left their jobs. The defense accepted the definition of conspiracy, but argued that a confederacy is not necessarily criminal if it is designed to resist oppression, to protect rights. Consequently, the tailors did not seek an illegal object, nor were their means illegal.[43] They were, nevertheless, found guilty, but only upon one count out of the eight charged. The case was appealed but no record that it was argued has been found.[44]

In every conspiracy trial, the charge was that the workers conspired to raise their wages. In none of the cases was evidence introduced that the defendants expressed subversive views, that they were interested in any action besides increasing their pay and limiting the supply of labor in their market to members of their society.

Gradually the trade union and its activity became more acceptable, and the conspiracy doctrine as applied to peaceful organized activity received a blow in the Massachusetts courts. In *Commonwealth* versus *Hunt,* rendered by Chief Justice Lemuel Shaw of the Massachusetts Supreme Court, a group of journeymen shoemakers had been convicted of improper conduct in Boston in 1840 under the common law. In reversing the decision, Justice Shaw affirmed that the general rules of the common law were effective in Massachusetts, but he argued that "it must depend upon the local laws of each country to determine, whether the purpose to be accomplished by the combination, or the concerted means of accomplishing it, be unlawful or criminal in the respective countries."

In inducing [he declared] all those engaged in the same occupation to become members of it . . . is not unlawful. It would give them [the union members] a power which might be used for useful and honorable purposes, or for dangerous and pernicious ones. . . . But in order to charge all those who become members of an association with the guilt of a criminal conspiracy, it must be averred and proved that the actual, if not the avowed object of the association was criminal . . . when an association is formed for purposes actually innocent, and afterward its powers are abused by those who have the control and management of it, to purposes of oppression and injustice, it will be criminal in those who thus misuse it, or give consent thereto, but not in the other members of the association. . . . In this state of things, we cannot perceive that it is criminal for men to agree together to exercise their own acknowledged rights, in such a manner as best to subserve their own interests.[45]

For the emerging labor organizations, the decision was a charter and a landmark. It gave voice to the new understanding of the position and significance of labor organizations and their activity. Even though a decision of a Massachusetts court was not controlling in other states, the eminence of its author gave it an influence beyond the borders of Massachusetts.

CHAPTER 2

The First Labor Movement: Business
Unionism in the Second Phase

Economic conditions in the late 1820's and through most of the 1830's provided a favorable backdrop for the growth of labor organizations. The growing complexity of problems occasioned in part by the widening of the markets for labor and products stimulated a variety of plans for cooperation among labor unions. The first labor movement showed the same tendencies to concentrate its major attention upon improvement of wages and other conditions of employment. What has since been described as business unionism is clearly reflected in the decisions and policies of the first labor organizations made up of workers from more than one craft.

William English, a Philadelphia cordwainer and a leader of the first labor movement, the Mechanics' Union of Trade Associations, was opposed to including the word "political" in the description of the purposes of the National Trades' Union of the 1830's, of which he was a founder and secretary. His objection was based upon his experience with the Mechanics' Union of Trade Associations, which he claimed was destroyed because some of its members insisted upon involving the organization in politics. Such principles as exclusive jurisdiction, sacredness of contracts made with the employer, the need for standardizing wages of a trade, limiting hours, regulating apprenticeship, setting up a strike fund, requiring permission of a national board for strike approval if the strike fund is to be drawn upon, and avoidance of direct involvement in politics are repeatedly expressed by the labor organizations of the 1830's. Even the division of available work on the basis of first in first out was practiced by some trades. No member of the Philadelphia Society of Tailors could accept work unless the employer maintained a record of all journeymen who took out work "so that none would work out of turn." Other societies posted lists of their members in tap houses, and none could accept employment before all those who preceded them on the lists had been employed.[1]

While many unions were wiped out by the panic of 1837, labor organizations continued to exist. All traces of the earlier views were not erased. Moreover, the newly formed unions of the succeeding decades show the same propensity for business unionism as their predecessors. American workers in the time of the two Adams, and Jackson, hammered out the cardinal principles of business unionism. These principles were designed for protection at the place of employment. This chapter will demonstrate that business unionism is the oldest labor "ism" in American labor history.

Not that American labor has eschewed politics. Actually, the workers of the United States have always been faced with problems which could only be solved through legislative action. In addition, the worker as citizen may face problems or be confronted by conditions which do not involve the work place. Public policy on education and immigration, industrial safety and housing have always been important to the welfare of the wage earner. Many of these questions confronted the workers' organization as they appeared on the American scene. The first question that the early unions had to answer was the kind of political action they would embark upon. While the answer was not then, or is not even now, unanimous, the early trade unions avoided direct involvement in political activity and carried their demands for political reform to the other parties.

UNIONS IN THE 1820's

The late 1820's witnessed a revival of labor organizations; moreover, the first formal cooperation between organizations of labor took place in this period. The Philadelphia cordwainers, prosecuted for conspiracy in 1809, appealed to the New York Typographical Society for financial assistance. The New York group pleaded inability to make a contribution, but the plea was sympathetically received.[2] The revival of interest in trade unionism was shared by a number of trades. The shoemakers, bakers, and cabinet makers were organized in New York in 1821, and an unorganized strike of one thousand wharfmen was reported in 1825. In the celebration of the opening of the Erie Canal in November 1825, members of twenty labor organizations were among the marchers in the parade. Philadelphia was another city in which a number of unions were established in the 1820's.[3] Gains in organization were made in other towns.

Shorter Hours

The first central labor union—a delegate body composed of representatives of a number of trades—met in Philadelphia in 1827. The meeting followed the unsuccessful attempt of the Journeymen Carpenters to gain a ten-hour day. In a resolution, signed by William Louck, chairman, and Charles Ferris, secretary, the Journeymen Carpenters declared that the "house carpenters, of the city and county of Philadelphia, have for a long time suffered under a grievous and slave like system of labour, which they believe to be attended with many evils injurious alike to the community and the workmen; they believe that a man of common constitution is unable to perform more than ten hours faithful labour in one day, and that men in the habit of labouring from sun rise until dark, are generally subject to nervous and other complaints."[4]

The demand for support of this resolution was made upon the master carpenters, who at their meeting on June 15, 1827, decided it was "inexpedient and altogether improper to comply with the resolutions passed by the Journeymen House Carpenters." The master carpenters regretted the formation of a society which had a tendency to "subvert good order, and coerce and mislead those who have been industriously pursuing their avocation and honestly maintaining their families."[5] A committee of twelve was appointed to solicit the pledges and signatures of masters who were not present at the meeting.

In an address to the public, the Journeymen Carpenters attacked the views of the employers as "improper and untrue." They denied that a ten-hour day would deprive the employers, as was charged, of one-fifth part of the working day. As a rule, the Journeymen Carpenters claimed, they were on the job fifteen hours in the summer, the number of hours "of sun." Two hours a day were taken in the summer for meals, leaving a working day of thirteen hours in the summer. In the shorter days of winter, there were about nine hours of sun and eight hours of work, which averaged about ten and one-half hours of work throughout the year. They now proposed to work ten hours in the summer and as long as they could see in the winter, taking only one hour for meals, and the work day would thus average nine and one-half hours. Employers would thereby lose only one-twelfth of the present workday instead of one-fifth as they claimed.[6]

Following the refusal of the employers, the house carpenters voted to refrain from all labor and to distribute strike benefits among those "poor Journeymen House Carpenters who stand in need of assistance during the stand out."[7] The master carpenters accepted the challenge and advertised for strikebreakers in other cities, promising employment to several hundred at good wages in Philadelphia. The issue remained in doubt for some time, but in the following year the claim was made that the strikers had gained at least part of their objective and others would, if they remained steadfast, gain the shorter workday.[8] The bricklayers and painters also showed an interest in reduced workdays.

Mechanics' Union of Trade Associations

The carpenters' campaign to gain the ten-hour day stimulated a movement for greater unity within labor, and a call was issued for the setting up of a central labor organization as a vehicle for rallying support in an emergency for each trade. Only trade societies were invited. The Mechanics' Union of Trade Associations was established and in its preamble decried the evils which flow from an inequality of wealth and power. The preamble announced that labor was the source of all wealth, and that "all who toil have a natural and unalienable right to reap the fruits of their own industry. . . . The principles upon which the institution shall be founded, are principles, alike, of the strictest justice, and the most extended philanthropy."[9] It argued further that prosperity and demand for goods are influenced by the ability of the masses to consume. "The real object," the preamble announced, "of this association, is to avert, if possible, the desolating evils which must inevitably arise from a depreciation of the intrinsic value of human labor; to raise the mechanical and productive classes to that condition of true independence and equality [sic] which their practical skill and ingenuity, their immense utility to the nation and their growing intelligence are beginning imperiously to demand: to promote, equal, the happiness, prosperity and welfare of the whole community . . . and to assist, in conjunction with such other institutions of this nature as shall hereafter be formed throughout the union, in establishing a just balance of power, both mental, moral, political and scientific, between all the various classes and individuals which constitute society at large."[10]

A clause in the constitution of the Mechanics' Union of Trade Associations excluded all political action, but a number of delegates were convinced that it could not achieve its objectives without political participation. The Working Men's party was organized in 1828. At the time of the formation of the political organization, the Mechanics' Union, according to its leader, William English, had fifteen unions affiliated with it. It steadily lost affiliates until only four remained, and by the end of the year the Mechanics' Union expired, an obvious victim of the political malady.[11] English decided that it was dangerous for a labor union to become directly involved in the promotion of a political party.[12]

Working Men's Party

The political venture led to the formation of the Working Men's party, the first party of labor in the world. At a meeting of Philadelphia working men on August 11, 1828, it was announced that workers were determined to manage their own interests "as a class" and a ticket was selected for Assembly and City Council offices.[13] A committee to solicit the views of candidates to the state legislature was appointed. The appearance of a labor party was not warmly received by the older politicians who hoped to divert the new movement into regular channels. Delegates met at another convention in September 1828, and a committee to direct the campaign was chosen and a headquarters secured. The candidates on the Working Men's ticket polled several hundred votes in the city and county, but none was elected. The candidates on the ticket of President Andrew Jackson who were endorsed by the Working Men's party were, however, successful.[14] The Working Men's party continued its activity, making alliances with other parties, resisting blandishments, fighting against absorption, and, at the same time, denying charges of impiety and subversion. Before it disappeared from the scene after the election of 1831, this party had issued a number of interesting statements which indicate the drift of labor and reform views at the time.

Education

The Working Men's party appointed a committee to examine the educational needs of the community. It found that the elementary schools "throughout the state . . . [were] irresponsible institutions, established by individuals, from mere motives of private speculation or gain, who are sometimes destitute of character, and frequently of the requisite attainments and abilities."[15] The committee reported that many poor families could not afford to send their children to school even if one were available, since the earnings were needed to supplement the family income. Criticism of teaching methods, curricula, and the allocation of large funds for higher education was also made. Finally, the committee believed that liberty rested on a wide diffusion of knowledge, that all citizens should be instructed in their rights and duties as well as in reading, writing, and arithmetic. It therefore proposed that free public schools, controlled and managed by elected representatives, be established throughout the state and that they be supported by taxation and be available to all children. In addition the committee recommended that each county establish one school, which, along with the usual subjects, would teach agricultural and mechanical subjects.[16]

The proposals were not universally welcomed. One editor doubted that such a laudable goal could ever be attained, inasmuch as the leisure necessary was only available to the wealthy.[17]

Other Demands

In the "Address of the City and County Convention to the Working Men of the State," the Working Men's party demanded, along with equal opportunities for education, an end to monopolies and banks which were charged with injuring the people by emissions of currency "fluctuating and easily imitated." Lotteries were attacked as wasteful and immoral, and the compulsory military system was decried for its inconvenience and the promotion of "scenes of debauchery." Imprisonment for debt was denounced as adding "oppression and insult to the wounded feeling of the unfortunate man," and its abolition demanded.[18]

Demand for Ten-Hour Day in New York City

As in Philadelphia, the demand for a shorter workday in New York City led in 1829 to the formation of a political party of labor. In New York mechanics and other tradesmen (not members of a single trade as in Philadelphia) met to demand the shorter workday. Five days after the first meeting, another was held at which a committee of fifty was appointed to devise means for achieving the purposes of the shorter-hour resolution.[19] An important difference should be noted between the shorter hour movements in the two cities. In Philadelphia the demand emanated from a given trade union, and it was directed to a specific group of employers who regularly employed the members of the union making the request. Rejection of the demand was followed by a strike. The New York movement was essentially political, because the demand for reduced hours was directed at all, rather than particular, employers. No economic action was taken to enforce the demand. Since the committee of fifty did not directly represent any workers with a common trade interest, it was inevitable that it would come up with a political program.

The "Report and Resolutions of the Committee of Fifty" was written by Thomas Skidmore—a machinist, teacher, and self-taught intellectual, who published *The Rights of Man to Property*. He was a believer in the fundamental reorganization of society that will "leave behind it no trace of that government which has denied to every human being an equal amount of property on arriving at the age of maturity, and previous thereto, equal food, clothing, and instruction at the public expense."[20] The extreme sentiments of the committee of fifty were repudiated at a meeting on December 29, 1829, at which Skidmore is said to have attempted to speak. Instead a resolution affirmed that "we have no desire or intention of disturbing the rights of property in individuals, or the public. On the contrary, we consider the acquiring of property to soften the asperities of sickness, of age, and for the benefit of posterity, as one of the greatest incentives to industry."[21] As a result, Skidmore and his followers set up a party of their own. A new general executive committee was elected by the reorganized Working Men's party. It advocated the establishment of a system of education that would enable everyone before the age of twenty-one "to acquire a competent knowledge of the language of their country, arithmetic, geography, history, natural philosophy, geometry and chemistry."[22] The address also called upon the legislature to enact a mechanics' lien to assure the protection of earned wages, attacked speculators, advocated the abolition of the compulsory militia system, and called for the end of the system of imprisonment for debt.[23]

State Guardianship

The new Working Men's party, however, was soon split over another issue, that of education. A faction led by Robert Dale Owen, the son of the English Socialist and factory reformer, Frances Wright, champion of labor and women's rights, and George Henry Evans, pioneer labor editor, demanded a more radical system of education.

Owen was born in Glasgow, Scotland, in 1801, and was educated in private schools in Switzerland. He came to the United States with his father in 1825, and lived in New Harmony, Indiana, where he taught school. After the collapse of the colony, he became associated with Frances Wright's ideas on education. Owen served in the Indiana legislature, and for two terms in Congress. He was in the foreign service in the administrations of Presidents Franklin Pierce and James Buchanan. He was an abolitionist, philanthropist, and reformer.

Frances Wright (1795–1852) came to the United States from her native Scotland in 1818. The daughter of a wealthy family, she became interested in social reform. She returned to Europe in 1820, and stayed until 1824. The following year she organized a cooperative colony in Tennessee with the slaves she purchased. The experiment failed. She now devoted herself to espousing advanced educational and reform views. She participated in reform politics in the 1830's.

They favored a system of boarding schools to which children would be sent by their parents at an early age. The boardinghouses would follow a regimen of spartan simplicity, in which children would be similarly dressed, eat the same food, and be taught the same subjects until they were ready for professional education. Nothing "savoring of inequality, nothing reminding them of the pride of riches, or the contempt of poverty, should be suffered to enter these republican safeguards of a young nation of equals. We propose that the destitute widow's child or the orphan boy should share the public care equally with the heir to a princely estate; so that all may become, not in word, but in deed and in feeling, free and equal."[24]

Owen's opponents in the party set up their own executive committee and published the *Evening Journal* to answer Owen's *Daily Sentinel*. Both factions sought to speak in the name of the party. State guardianship was reviled as an attempt to subvert the existing social and political institutions; it was described as "agrarianism" and "infidelity."[25] The differences between the two factions were deep and irreconcilable. In the elections of 1830, two labor tickets were on the ballot. The Democrats, to neutralize some of the labor support, advocated the adpotion of a mechanics' lien law. None of the candidates on the Working Men's party tickets was elected, and both parties disappeared from the scene.

According to Professor Frank T. Carelton, the Working Men's party of New York made an important indirect contribution to future labor tactics. "When in 1833–1837, the strong trade union movement arose, the fate of the Working Men's Party was accepted as a conclusive argument against direct political effort. Hence the trade unions kept aloof from party politics and merely questioned candidates as to their position on measures which were regarded as affecting the interests of labor."[26] In other words, the policy of pressure politics was followed by workers in the early part of the nineteenth century, not because of the acceptance or rejection of an ideology, but because these independent parties had failed to answer the workers' political needs. Indirect political pressure had achieved one of the workers' most important legislative aims: the mechanics' lien law and the abolition of imprisonment for debt.

New England Association of Farmers, Mechanics and Other Workmen

The New England Association of Farmers, Mechanics and Other Workmen seems to have been a general reform organization seeking legislative changes of benefit to wage earners. A meeting of delegates on December 5, 1831, called a convention in Boston for the following February. The "object of the Convention is to mature measures to concentrate the efforts of the laboring classes, to regulate the hours of labor, by one uniform standard, to promote the cause of education and general information, to reform abuses practiced upon them, and to maintain their rights as American Freemen."[27] It should be noted that the particular program is not directly related to the place of employment. The failure to indicate specifically who the delegates were and to whom the demands were directed would indicate that the Association was a reform effort, although it is not unlikely that articulate workers would be represented in such bodies as either delegates from some trade union society or as individuals.

The meeting constitution specified that the "Association was to consist of such persons of good moral character" as accept the constitution. Each person, except those who were farmers, was to agree that he would not work for more than ten hours a day unless he were paid extra compensation at the rate of one tenth of a day for each hour worked above ten.[28] No method for enforcing this objective, aside from the refusal to accept employment, was suggested. No provision was made for support of those who refused to work under the old schedule of hours.

At the convention in Boston in September 1832, delegates from five New England states attended. The New England Association was one of the first groups to demand regulation of the factories. The call to the second convention declared that a "large proportion of the operatives in our factories are and must continue to be a helpless population. It is indispensable that they should be put under the unremitted supervision and protection of the law of the land."[29]

Unlike the movement in Philadelphia which broke up as a result of the machinations of old-line politicians, the one in New York was torn by serious ideological differences. From the beginning the New York movement suffered from Skidmore's presence. Despite his repudiation, the Working Men's party was attacked as a proponent of agrarian radicalism. Nor was the affiliation of Robert Dale Owen an asset; his sponsorship of the state guardianship scheme allowed critics to describe the movement as anarchical.

Reform political movements appeared during this period in Pennsylvania, Delaware, and New England. On the whole these movements had similar attitudes on important public questions. They criticized the credit system and monopolies and favored abolition of imprisonment for debt, a mechanic's lien law, and free public education; but their names notwithstanding, they were not in fact labor parties. The labor historian time and again faces a semantic problem: How much weight should be given to the names of political groups which call themselves Labor and Working Men's parties? The adoption of a labor plank or planks by the Democratic or Republican parties has never been regarded as changing them into spokesmen of labor. Certainly an "interaction" between trade union and reform movements of the 1830's took place, but they were separate and different in purpose and outlook.[30]

REVIVAL OF LABOR ORGANIZATION

Interest in labor organization began to revive in 1830.[31] Professor Barnett found that between 1830 and 1836 thirteen local unions of printers had been established, and eleven more joined them during the next four years. These local unions were spread through northern and southern cities. Ethelbert Stewart has listed the names of fourteen unions whose members marched in a parade in November 1830, celebrating the victory of "correct principles" in the French Revolution. Strikes for wage increases became more common, but by no means popular during the 1830's. The Pianoforte Makers' Union, organized early in 1835, struck in November for the discharge of a foreman. In October of the same year, the Hand-Loom Weavers' Union of Philadelphia struck against a wage reduction. Shoemakers in Philadelphia, saddlers and harnessmakers in New York, Bridgeport, and Hartford, and carpenters in Boston struck for higher wages.[32] The tactics of these unions were not basically different from organizations of a later time.[33]

THE GENERAL TRADES' UNION OF NEW YORK CITY

The General Trades' Union of New York City was a trade union body organized for the purpose of developing closer cooperation of trade societies of the city. This trades' union was the outgrowth of a dispute between the carpenters and their employers over a demand that wages be raised from $1.37½ to $1.50 a day. The printers' organization, which had been actively supporting the demand of the carpenters, voted on June 22, 1833, to call a meeting of the different societies of mechanics to suggest that a trades' association be established. The circular, addressed to the Journeymen Mechanics and Artisans of New York City, called on their societies to elect a delegate authorized to vote for the establishment of a General Union of Journeymen Mechanics and Artisans of every branch in this city.[34]

The purpose of the General Trades' Union was to establish a strike fund by a per capita tax of one cent per week, "which, in case of a strike, shall entitle all paying into such sum, weekly, as the Convention may determine can be afforded from the funds."[35]

If the members of a specified union were aggrieved and sought an increase in wages, the question was to be presented to a meeting of the delegates of the General Trades' Union, who, in the first instance, would determine whether the demand was appropriate. If the demand was held justified, and a strike was necessary to enforce it, "all of this trade who shall have contributed to the funds their regular quota, shall be entitled to receive a specific sum until their difficulties are adjusted."[36] If a combination of employers were to try to reduce wages, the General Trades' Union would be obligated to support the strikers against such an effort.

The General Trades' Union was primarily concerned with supporting its affiliates both morally and financially. As the local unions had at the time no permanent links with labor organizations outside of the city, the sources of mutual support were inevitably the organized journeymen of other crafts. Similar to the policies of subsequently formed national and international unions, financial support was predicated upon approval by a general body not directly concerned with the pending dispute. Nine unions —carpenters, printers, bookbinders, leather dressers, coopers, carvers and gilders, bakers, cabinet makers, and shoemakers—sent delegates, and three others approved the purposes of the meeting. On August 28th the first convention was held and a constitution drawn up. Article XIV specified: "No Trade or Art shall strike for higher wages than they at present receive, without the sanction of the Convention."[37] Ely Moore, a printer, was elected president. In accordance with its principles, the General Trades' Union supported the organized craftsmen whenever they were engaged in sanctioned disputes with their employers. For example, in June 1834, it called for support of the striking bakers. At the same time it approved a proposal "to bestow . . . patronage on those employers and those only, who give their men the full wages."[38] In another instance the per capita of the stonecutters was remitted for the month because they had been on strike.[39]

Exclusive Jurisdiction

The principle of exclusive jurisdiction was first formulated by the New York General Trades' Union. In August 1835 the New York Weavers' Society sought affiliation. During the discussion of this matter, "it appeared that an article of the constitution prohibited the acceptance of two sets of delegates from any one Trade whose interests are so intimately connected. It was on motion resolved, that they have the privilege of withdrawing their credentials." At the same meeting the credentials from the Union Trade Society of Journeymen was rejected because there was "a constitutional objection to receiving two sets of delegates from one Trade or Art."[40]

The meeting on October 7, 1835, congratulated the Sail Makers for their recently successful strikes and appointed a committee "to consider the propriety of erecting a Trades' Union Hall."[41] It also appointed a committee to inquire into the reasons for the refusal by the New York City Common Council of a room for the convention of the National Trades' Union which was held in New York City. The city fathers refused to answer the protest.[42] A proposal was made to establish a penny daily newspaper and after listening to the reports of a committee, a board of directors was appointed to carry out the project. The union hall was not constructed, but the publication of a daily did succeed. In giving its approval to strikes, the Trades' Union declared, "it will always be governed by the maxim 'live and let live' and while it is willing that employers shall have a just and equitable profit from the labor of those they employ, it will always endeavor to obtain for those who labor a just remuneration for their labor." It also hoped, through friendly conference, to do away "with the necessity of those frequent strikes which are alike detrimental to themselves and to the public."[43]

Although the General Trades' Union survived for only a short period, its attitudes on strikes, wages, exclusive jurisdiction, and cooperation with the employer are the same general kind that predominate among later unions. It is true that because of opposition from employers, less community acceptance, and low propensity for staying organized, the trade unions of the early nineteenth century were less stable. What is striking, however, is their pure trade union outlook. Unions occasionally sought, as did the United Trade Society of Journeymen Tailors, to counter the opposition of their employers by organizing a producers' cooperative. The General Trades' Union urged union members to support the venture.[44]

Commenting upon the rise of labor activity, the *New York Journal of Commerce,* in its issue of June 1, 1835, suggested that "the turnouts [strikes] which are taking place among the different classes of mechanics in all our large cities are the legitimate fruits, and no doubt the concerted results, of Trades Unionism."[45] The aggressiveness of the trade unions led to counter organization by the employers in some trades; among them the Curriers and Leather Dealers, which charged the trade unions with conspiracy to gain more wages and injuring trade, threatening violence, and demanding equal wages for mechanics of different abilities. Employers in the manufacturers and retailers branches of the ladies' shoe industry also organized, resolved not to recognize any list of prices submitted by their employees, and vowed to "oppose every injurious combination connected with the Trade Union."[46] The Master Tailors went further and decided to deny employment to any member of the Union Trade Society of Journeymen Tailors in New York City.

THE PHILADELPHIA TRADES' UNION

The Philadelphia venture was initiated by several unions. William C. Doores was chosen president and William English was selected as secretary of the organizing committee which drew up the statement declaring the contemplated organization was "for the purpose of mutual protection."[47] The "Address to Mechanics and Working Men" emphasized the aid a central labor union could provide for the maintenance of a fair wage. It pointed to the danger of wage reductions continually faced by workers. "To avert an evil so afflicting, and to which all workmen are liable, Trades Societies have been formed. But this remedy in many instances has failed. . . . The state of feebleness, therefore, that in the first case suggested a union of the members of a trade into Societies, suggests also, in the second, a union of the Trades Societies.[48] Citizens were assured that the Philadelphia Trades' Union was made up of "mechanics and working men, for the advancement of their interests, individually and collectively, and entirely distinct from, and unconnected with, any political party whatsoever."[49]

Delegates from thirteen locals met and adopted the constitution of the Trades' Union of the City and County of Philadelphia. Its only function was to grant "pecuniary aid" to unions on strike. Apparently the Trades' Union recognized from the beginning the danger to their unity of discussions at its meetings of political and religious questions. Article XIX of the constitution stated: "No party, political, or religious questions shall at any time be agitated in, or acted upon by this Union."[50] This prohibition closely resembles the one enacted by the American Federation of Labor almost seventy years later.

The records available show that the Philadelphia General Trades' Union fulfilled the purpose of its founders. At a meeting on March 10, 1836, it granted $1,000 to the bookbinders and $300 to the hatters in support of their strikes.[51] On March 30, 1837, $1,000 was appropriated to the striking Journeymen Cordwainers. On April 8, $500 was donated to aid the Oak

Coopers, and $300 to the Leather Dressers. The records show the Philadelphia General Trades' Union to have been completely devoted to trade matters, support of strikes, and assistance to specific craft groups. On May 10, 1836, the Day Laborers requested aid in their efforts to improve the conditions of their work, and a committee was appointed to devise methods by which such aid could be provided. When the Day Laborers sought a raise in wages and picketed some of their employers, they were arrested. The Trades' Union was directed to procure counsel for the accused.[52]

The Philadelphia General Trades' Union eventually reached a membership of 48 societies of locals "sovereign and independent in themselves, but bound by ties of honor and interest to support and assist each other in cases of aggression or danger."[53] One of the locals claimed a membership of 900, and four locals each had 700 members. Within less than two years, the Philadelphia General Trades' Union more than trebled its numbers.

Employers in the ladies' branch of the boot and shoemaking trade lamented "the frequent turn-outs of our Journeymen, for an advance of wages and other measures."[54] The employers argued that they could no longer determine the prices to be charged for their goods. They, therefore, decided to resist the demands of their employees and announced that hereafter they would not recognize any list of wages submitted to them.

In Baltimore, seventeen unions set up the Union Trade Society in September 1833; and four unions established a central body in Washington, D.C., in 1836. Extracts from the latter's constitution show it sought to aid its affiliates in disputes with employers over wages or over the rectifying of other grievances, but no "Trade or Art, striking for higher wages or other causes, without the consent of the Convention, will be entitled to support from the Trades' Union."[55]

The records of the other trades' societies show the same characteristics as those in New York, Philadelphia, Boston, and Baltimore. They were established for mutual assistance of particular unions in their disputes with employers. Since some of the trades' unions operated strike funds, control over strikes, to the extent of approving or rejecting financial aid, was placed in the hands of the trades' union.

NATIONAL TRADES' UNION

An invitation by the General Trades' Union of the City of New York and its vicinity for a conference of trades' unions and trade societies in August 1834 led to the formation of the National Trades' Union, the first national trades' organization in the United States. Thirty delegates from Boston, Philadelphia, Newark, Brooklyn, Poughkeepsie, and New York City, representing almost 21,000 members, attended the first convention. It lasted five days. A constitution was adopted and a number of resolutions were passed.

A system of manual schools and a demand for the reduction of work hours were endorsed, and opposition to a reduction in wages was approved. For the "general benefit of the laboring classes," the convention recommended "the formation of Trades' Unions all over the country, thereby promoting a concerted action in every branch of Mechanical business by an interchange of feelings and just understanding of the difficulties under which each may labor."[56] The statement advised that the separate unions "be connected with each other in every section of the country: the result of which will be the dissemination of correct information from one district to another and from one trade to another; preventing a surplus of hands in any department of business, and securing to all steady employment and just wages."[57] Ely Moore, a New York printer, was elected president and William English, a Philadelphia shoemaker, became recording secretary.

The "objects of this Union," according to the constitution, "shall be, to recommend such measures to the various unions represented herein as may tend to advance the moral and intellectual condition and pecuniary interests of the laboring classes; promote the establishment of Trades' Unions in every section of the United States; and also publish and disseminate such information as may be useful to the Mechanics and Working Men generally; and to unite and harmonize the efforts of all the productive classes of our country."[58]

One of the interesting debates at the National Trades' Union convention was devoted to politics. When the committee to draft resolutions on the "social, civil and political condition of the laboring classes" was appointed, a delegate requested the omission of the word "political" from the resolution. He believed that the unions might be injured by arousing the opposition of one of the political parties if the term were included.[59]

Another delegate, Mr. Townsend, opposing affiliation with any political party, believed that the laboring classes should draw up its demands and "each party would be anxious to adopt their measure."[60] The most extended argument against political involvement was made by William English, the leader of Philadelphia labor who had earlier been chosen secretary by the convention. In Philadelphia in 1828, English said, "the first Trades' Union was formed in this country, and one clause of its constitution excluded all political action; but, judging that the objects of the Union could not be obtained without its taking a part in politics, many members diverged from it and established what was called the 'Working Men's Party' and from that moment, as it advanced the Union retrograded, and though at one time it embraced fifteen societies, at the end of the year the number was reduced to four, and the Union adjourned *sine die*." The same cause, he said, "would produce the same effect."[61]

In Philadelphia two societies had refused to send delegates to the convention, and from Baltimore there was not a single delegate. Wilmington and the District of Columbia, too, where unions existed, were unrepresented in the convention. English thought it would be advisable to avoid every-thing that might have "a tendency to prevent a Union of the Trades and he was in favor of striking out" the word "political." The amendment carried, and the word "political" was stricken from the resolution.[62]

Second Convention

Twenty-six delegates attended the second convention in New York in October 1835. New York, New Jersey, Maryland, and Pennsylvania were represented. Seth Luther, a labor leader and reformer from Massachusetts, was invited to take a seat as a corresponding delegate. A ways and means committee was elected to suggest a program for organizing unions through-out the country. A committee was appointed to draft a petition to Congress requesting a reduction of the hours of labor on public works. A request for shortened hours had been made to the Secretary of the Navy by the mechan-ics of Brooklyn and New York. The Secretary appointed a Board of Navy Commissioners to consider the request, and they recommended denial. It was believed that the support of the convention would influence Congress. "For," the delegate sponsoring the proposal said, "Mechanics, we now have a representative [Ely Moore] in the National Legislature who, to use his own words, 'will neither shrink from the task, or despair of success;' and with such an advocate as this, we have little to fear from the aristocracy of the House."[63] The convention claimed that the practice of laboring on gov-ernment works from sunrise to sunset was both inconvenient and difficult. "We are of the opinion, that ten hours a day is fully sufficient for any laboring man to work."[64]

The convention found "that the formation and permanency of Trade Societies and Trades' Unions, presents the only security against the entire degradation of the whole mass of working men in the United States to the level of mere beasts of burthen." It, therefore, resolved to form a board of organizers, who were to be delegated the responsibility of forming trade unions and city central bodies in all cities and towns of the United States on the basis of principles espoused by the National Trades' Union. A com-mittee was appointed to inquire into the extent of prison labor, and the factory system was described as "mental and physical slavery, to which the sons and daughters of freemen ought never to submit."[65] The convention also recommended to the "several Trades' Unions, to adopt such measures as will connect more closely the different associations of each trade or art, for the purpose of equalizing the prices of labor throughout the various places in which such associations are located."

Third Convention

The third and last convention of the National Trades' Union opened in Philadelphia on the last Monday in October 1836. Thirty-three delegates from five states were on hand, and one was seated after the sessions got under way. Committees to report to the convention on trades' unions, co-operation, education, public lands, ways and means, state prison labor, the factory system, and female labor were appointed by President Alexander J. W. Jackson, of Baltimore. He had been chosen to succeed Alexander Ferral, a leading trade unionist of the convention city.

The committee on female labor, the first to report, charged that the system of employing women workers was a disgrace to free men and would lead if not checked to the degradation of future generations. "The physical organizations, the natural responsibilities, and the moral sensibility of women, prove conclusively that her labors should be of a domestic nature."[66] The committee also objected to the employment of women because of the effect upon the wages of men who were forced to compete with women for jobs. The committee pointed to the employment of women in New England in the printing, saddling, brushmaking, tailoring, whipmaking, and other industries and feared that the system would inevitably spread to other parts of the country. Gradual elimination was suggested, but unions were also advised: "All those trades affected by female labor could regulate their laws in such a way as to admit those females in their society, so that in case of difficulty they would be governed by their laws and receive their support—or raise the Society of females, and make one auxilliary to the other."[67]

The committee on education suggested cooperative trade associations to enable the mechanic to control and dispose of the products of his labor. The committee on trades' unions urged energetic action to spread trades' unions through the country. It also asked the trade societies to "open an immediate and extensive correspondence with other societies of the same trade as themselves, in all places where they exist, and where none are formed, to solicit their fellow-workmen to enter into immediate and ener-getic measures for their formation."[68]

The committee on prison labor suggested that members of unions use their influence to reform the systems of prison labor "believing that the employment of convicts upon articles to compete with those manufactured by the honest portion of the community to be manifestly unjust." The com-mittee on the ten-hour day for government works described the efforts made by the National Trades' Union, the Philadelphia Trades' Union, as well as unionists in other communities. In August 1836 a meeting of union-ists and other citizens appealed to the President of the United States for the establishment of the ten-hour workday on government works in Philadel-phia. "Ten hours of labor was and is consequently considered and ac-knowledged a sufficiency for one day, by the government in Philadelphia."[69] But other installations were unaffected by this change. In conclusion, the convention recommended "to the various unions the necessity of using their influence in favor of the ten hour system . . . by requesting of the

President of the United States his interference for the adoption of the system."[70]

The 1836 convention seems to have been the last one of importance, although a notice of sessions of the National Trades' Union appeared in the Philadelphia *Public Ledger,* May 4, 1837. Despite its brief existence, the National Trades' Union is of considerable historical importance, for it expressed all of the attitudes of late nineteenth and twentieth century trade unionism. Exclusive jurisdiction, opposition of direct involvement of unions in politics, limited objectives, equal pay for equal work or the standard rate, and limited commitment were all clearly stated by the early trade unions and the city centrals they established.

ATTEMPTS AT NATIONAL ORGANIZATION IN THE TRADES

The National Trades' Union by bringing leaders of trade organizations from different communities together was the indirect promoter of the first national organizations of trades. Five national unions were established in the 1830's, the first among the cordwainers, and while not one survived for very long, the causes which gave rise to these efforts were in general similar to those which stimulated the movement toward national union in the post-Civil War.

In response to the request of the Philadelphia Cordwainers' Society, the Ladies' Cordwainers' Society of New York agreed in April 1835 not to admit traveling journeymen to its ranks unless they produced a certificate showing that they had conformed to all the obligations of their union in their home community.[71] Soon thereafter, the Cordwainers' unions in New York and Newark invited the locals in the rest of the country to set up a national union of the craft. In the evening of the last day of the convention of the National Trades' Unions, a number of delegates representing local unions voted to send out invitations to all local cordwainers' unions to a meeting of "the several associations of the same trade throughout the United States to form a National compact of the craft."[72]

Forty-five delegates from sixteen cities and towns representing five thousand craftsmen met in New York City on March 1, 1836, and letters endorsing the purposes of the meeting were received from locals in Troy, Albany, Schenectady, and Washington, D.C. A committee of seven was "appointed to draft a plan of cooperation among the various Societies of the Cordwainers of the United States, with a view of sustaining each other in all strikes within their respective limits."[73] Another resolution asked for information on the wage increases gained by each society, the percentage increase, the present wages received, and the plans for increases in the near future.

It was reported that wage rates in the eastern states were lower than those paid in the middle and southern states. The convention therefore recommended the adoption of measures as will "equalize the wages throughout the United States as far as practicable, in proportion to the expense of living." Societies were requested to use their efforts "to procure the adoption of the Standard Bill of Wages agreed upon by the Convention."[74] A resolution offered by William English, and adopted, called for limiting apprentices to two at any one time. Societies were urged to seek adoption of this rule, "provided, that no existing contract shall be impaired."[75]

A resolution that importation of foreign boots and shoes was destructive to the interests of journeymen engaged in their manufacture at home because the lower prices of foreign goods adversely affected wages, and a resolution calling for an investigation of the use of prison labor in the manufacture of boots and shoes so that journeymen might refuse to work at places where prison goods were sold were adopted. The convention drew up rules for the support of strikes of affiliated locals. Whenever a strike for a wage increase or against a decrease was to be called, the local contemplating the strike was to notify all other affiliated societies. If the striking local requested financial assistance, a levy of not less than six and one-quarter cents per week was to be imposed upon every member for aid to the walkout. Whenever local unions were notified that a particular local was on strike, "no certificate shall be granted by any other Society to its members for the purpose of visiting (with the intention of working) the city or town where such strike exists. An infringement of this rule by any member having obtained a certificate, shall be considered an act of scabbing, and shall subject the offender to a fine of not less than five dollars."[76]

Carpenters

The Philadelphia Journeymen House Carpenters succeeded in organizing a convention of unions of its craft. At a meeting on August 19, 1836, a national convention was called for October 4 of that year. Delegates from Albany, Pittsburgh, Baltimore, Washington, and Philadelphia appeared. Committees were appointed to draft a preamble and constitution. The convention favored an annual convention of the organized workers of the trade. It resolved "that the object of this Convention is to establish and secure the ten-hour system, and such other regulations in our trade as may be conducive to the interests of the Journeymen House Carpenters of the United States."[77]

The convention resolved that there should be a "corresponding uniformity of prices throughout the different towns, villages, and cities in the United States. It should be the duty of every member of the trade to concentrate and use all his influence in establishing societies where they do not now exist, in order to consolidate the great body of the trade, and bring them into one solid phalanx which would be immovable."[78]

Hand-Loom Weavers

Similarly, the resolution presented to the special meeting of the New York Hand-Loom Weavers stressed the necessity of increasing wages and "to investigate the evils which affects our trade; whether they be the result from forcing or home competition, or from the product of the power loom, or from all these and other sources; and that a remedy if possible might be devised. Likewise that the Delegates might arrive at a clear knowledge where to fix the standard of prices to be paid for the various fabrics of Hand Loom Weaving throughout the United States."[79]

The Printers

The early printers' unions also show a fully developed trade union attitude. Moreover, because of the lengthy records of local unions in this craft, the influences which led to the formation of the national union as well as information on the views of the early locals can be traced. In 1802 the Franklin Typographical Society of New York proposed to the Philadelphia local that the two unions should jointly seek an increase in the duty on imported books.[80] In the following year, the Baltimore local requested the Philadelphia society to approve a resolution concerning apprentices. Announcements of the election of officers and of price lists were circulated by the printers' unions in the first decade of the nineteenth century. Notice of the existence of strikes and pleas that members of other local unions disregard advertisements by employers for help were also circulated among the early unions in the trade. For example, in October 1809 the New York society appealed to the printing unions of other cities to prevent the recruitment of strike breakers during its strike. According to Professor Barnett, the "societies notified appear in every case to have interested themselves, and to have used every effort to prevent the employers from securing workmen."[81]

The early printers' unions also sought to devise methods of discouraging journeymen from violating the scale and to create a system of membership transfer between local unions, so that journeymen on removing to another city would be admitted immediately in good standing to the union in the community to which he transferred his residence. One of the difficulties in enforcing rules on working at scale was that the wage scales were not the same in all cities, and printers frequently claimed they were governed by the one effective in their home local even if it were below the level of the community in which they were employed. The adoption of an agreement on transfer of members would also enable a journeyman to secure assistance in procuring employment and fraternal aid.

Apprenticeship was another question which agitated the early printers' unions, and "members were held liable to expulsion if it was discovered that there had been irregularities in [their] apprenticeship."[82] Increasingly, the single society found itself appealing for and providing assistance to locals in other communities. In 1824 the Franklin Typographical Society of Boston proposed to the New York printers the establishment of "a more efficient union than at present exists between individual societies in the different towns."[83] The proposal called for each society giving relief to members of other societies and being reimbursed by the one to which the beneficiary belonged. A number of societies provided for the issuance of certificates to traveling members, and Professor Barnett believes that "it is probable that all issued them."[84]

The attempt to restrict the number of apprentices by the Columbia Typographical Society of Washington, D.C., in 1834 was the indirect cause for the establishment of the first national union of printers. General Duff Green, a Washington editor and printer for the House of Representatives, operated the Washington Institute for the training of printers. Green was charged, in a pamphlet issued by the Columbia Society, with cutting wages of printers and replacing trained journeymen with boys who worked for lower pay.[85]

The printers were asked not to come to Washington and act as instructors in the institute.[86]

When Green refused a satisfactory adjustment, a strike against the Institute was called in March 1835 by the Washington unionized printers. "For the first time in its history the Washington society sent out a 'rat circular' [an anti-strikebreaker leaflet]. Philadelphia and New York promised to restrain their members from accepting employment in the Washington establishment, and the Philadelphia association expelled all its members who did so."[87]

It was, however, the Franklin Typographical Society of Cincinnati which issued in November 1835 a call for the formation of a national union of printers. It suggested:

1. That each society in its own district be sustained by all others in the prices it may establish.

2. That journeymen bringing certification of membership in any society, of good standing, receive a preference over all others in the efforts made to procure them employment.

3. That rats, pronounced such by one society, be considered as such by all other societies.[88]

The circular also called for a convention in Washington in the following year with power to draft a constitution, which, after ratification by two-thirds of the locals, would become the law of the organization. The response was favorable, and the first national convention of printers' unions met in Washington on November 7, 1836. Delegates from unions in Baltimore, New York City, Washington, Harrisburg, and Philadelphia were present. The convention called on local unions to adopt uniform rules on apprenticeship: that runaways from one shop not be permitted to work in another; that members expelled by one local should not be admitted in another; that "rat" lists be exchanged; and that societies be advised to organize all journeymen at the trade whether they served or did not serve an apprenticeship, but after a given period the apprenticeship was to be six years. Local unions were authorized to establish the list of prices suitable to their sections of the country. In the case of a strike by one local, the others were to contribute "such sum as may be necessary to sustain them: Provided the Board of Control of the National Society previously sanctions the strike."[89]

The National Typographical Society, at its first convention, worked out a constitution and a rate of contributions to the national organization. A second convention met in New York City in September 1837, with delegates from eight locals and a fraternal delegate from Canada present. The convention of 1838 was scheduled but not held. Although the National Typographical Society existed only a short period, its statements reveal attitudes similar to those held by unions in the printing industry. Like the cordwainers and other craftsmen who sought to set up national organizations in the 1830's, the printers showed a shrewd understanding of the purposes of trade unionism, and as the records show, even when the national organization ceased to exist cooperation among the locals never completely ended.

SCATTERED ACTIVITY

The craftsmen who sought to expand their unions beyond their own communities were the most militant and progressive trade unionists of the 1830's. Scattered strikes took place, and while many did not lead to permanent organization they showed that workers were aware of the methods for redressing their grievances. In 1835 strikes of Boston ship carpenters occurred for a two-hour lunch period and in the following year, the carpenters of the same city struck for the ten-hour workday. Their efforts failed, and T. L. Holmes, in an address to the Boston Mechanical Society, regarded the failure with a sense of gratification.[90]

PANIC OF 1837

The panic which began in 1837 lasted until 1844. It appears to have been caused by speculation induced by an excessive expansion of bank credits, followed by a rapid rise in imports and increases in foreign debts. The demand of English banks for settlement of the adverse balance of payments led to fear that it would cause large exports of specie. Banks began to restrict credit, with the consequent decline in economic activity. The declining level of economic activity made it impossible to sustain projects based on the assumption of continued expansion, and the country became engulfed in a severe crisis which affected labor unions as well as other institutions.[91]

CHAPTER 3

Setbacks and Survival

The panic of 1837 seriously affected the viability of many firms that found the decline in prices and business activity too difficult to surmount. Inevitably many labor organizations suffered. Their positions were not too firm; their acceptance by the community was, at least, unenthusiastic. Moreover, they faced a hostile and determined employer interest which was unaccustomed to having its decisions questioned or its power at the employment place curtailed. Yet the depression did not wipe out all traces of labor organization or turn the workers' interest towards Fourierism—a form of producers' cooperation—or to the consumer variety. Fourierism was largely the concoction of writers, preachers, and teachers, who, shocked by the rising industrialism, sought a sudden and complete way out of the dilemmas of the factory system. Although trade unionism was in the shadows, it reasserted itself for periods during this decade. The trade unions showed the same general characteristics as their forerunners of the 1830's: emphasis upon improvements in wages, shortened hours, and control of the trade.

The fact that a national convention of printers' unions could be called in 1850 is proof that trade union sentiment had never been deeply submerged in the printing trade. The formation of a national union, or an international union as it is called today, is analogous to statemaking in the nineteenth century. The process of unifying a number of scattered local unions into a national organization is usually dependent upon the need to standardize wages so as to eliminate competition in the product market and/or regulate the flow of labor between communities and in that manner exercise more effective control over labor supply.[1] A host of special conditions may also influence the rapidity with which nationalization is accepted.

Such a movement is itself based upon a high level of trade union sophistication, the existence of a number of local unions in a trade or industry, and the recognition of the existence of a problem of assistance and/or control which extends beyond the local labor market. By its very nature, the desire to unify a trade must be directed toward limited objectives. The success of such ventures depends in some measure upon the availability of a trade union leader. The submergence of local interest and personal rivalry, and the willingness to grant a modicum of authority to the central organization are not easily achieved.

The problems that confronted the early national organizations were often simpler than those of today, and the local unions were jealous of their rights and fearful that they might be chipped away by an overreaching national leadership. Such an attitude was an obstacle to geographical extension which overriding need finally overcame. Moreover, the limited resources compelled the newly established organizations to offer modest, if any, stipends to the newly elevated officials. The officers in the United Sons of Vulcan, openly organized in 1861, but formed two years earlier, received no salaries. They did the work at night after a day's work at the mills.[2] But these original movements to unite workers and their unions over a larger geographic area than the local community shows both the changes in the economy and the growth of pure trade consciousness. This evidence is very significant in demonstrating the permanence of trade union attitudes which has been critically and approvingly called business unionism.

THE INTERNATIONAL TYPOGRAPHICAL UNION

The exchange of price and "rat" lists between the typographical associations throughout the 1840's had never ceased and such cooperation led to the eventual formation of a national union in 1852. A stream of communications from local societies asking printers in other communities to discourage members from accepting employment below scale, and circulars on apprentices and the existence of strikes are common among printers' organizations in the 1840's. Many locals did not survive, but frequently they reappeared under another name. As one examines their activities, it is clear that they were primarily engaged in regulating trade matters, or they might accurately be described as business unions.[3]

Increasing cooperation among societies prompted the New York local union to sound a call for a national convention in September 1850; Boston and Philadelphia joined in the call. The convention met on December 2 in New York City, with delegates from six cities present; locals in five other communities sent communications to the meeting. Most of this convention's time was devoted to discussing the apprentice system in the trade, and recommendations were made that local unions undertake to limit the number trained. Printers everywhere in the United States were urged to form unions "and establish connection with each other for the purpose of securing united action upon every question involving the interest of the trade."[4] The convention recommended a number of steps. Local unions were to be organized to regulate scales of prices in order to eliminate conflict among them; traveling journeymen were to be provided with certificates, effective for one year, which would recommend the holders for aid in cities where employment was not available; a registry of "rats" was to be maintained. A stranger unable to produce a certificate of membership from a bona fide society to which he belonged were not to be accepted by other locals. A contribution of at least $10.00 per member for a strike fund was to be established. Transfer rights were automatically to be granted members permanently shifting residence. The convention also urged locals to abolish the benefit system under which members insured themselves against loss arising out of illness or unemployment.

An address to the Journeymen Printers of the United States dealt with more philosophical issues. The convention declared that the remedy for the disparity of power of employers and workers was a "combination for mutual agreement in maintaining wages, [and it] has been resorted in many trades, and principally our own. Its success has abundantly demonstrated its ability."[5] The convention regarded the combination "merely to fix and sustain a scale of prices . . . of minor importance, compared to that combination which looks to an ultimate redemption of labor. Scales of prices, to keep up the value of labor, are only necessary under a continued downward tendency. But when labor determines no longer to sell itself to speculators, but to become its own employer; to own and enjoy itself and the fruit thereof, the necessity for scales of prices will have passed away, and labor will be forever rescued from the control of the capitalist."[6] The practical proposals were, however, much the same as those adopted by the National Union in 1838.

A national executive committee was elected, and a second convention met in Baltimore in September 1851. A constitution, adopted by delegates from eleven cities, was to serve as the basis for the newly established National Typographical Union. A minority of the delegates recommended that the constitution be disapproved, because only a few of the fifty locals functioning throughout the country were represented.[7]

IRON AND STEEL WORKERS

Iron production rapidly expanded during and after the 1830's in Pennsylvania. Throughout the 1840's the railroads constituted an important factor in providing a wider market and also as a direct consumer of the products of the iron furnaces and forges of Pennsylvania. The demand for nails, shovels, axes, plates, and later rails encouraged widespread expansion. Strikes against wage reductions took place in Pittsburgh in 1842, according to John Jarrett, a leader of nineteenth-century unionism.

The strikers were defeated and accepted the lower rate until May 1845, when a demand for an increase was won by a successful strike. In 1848 the puddlers at the Phoenix Rolling Mills in Chester, Pennsylvania, unsuccessfully struck against a rate reduction. "In conducting these strikes some form of organization must have been conducted. It is through such experiences as these that the wage-workers learn the need of trades-unionism.[8]

In January 1850 a strike of the Pittsburgh Iron workers against a sharp reduction of wages was countered by the importation of strikebreakers. Clashes between strikers and their replacements led to arrests and convictions of two men and four women. They were fined and imprisoned but eventually pardoned by Governor Johnson. The men were defeated, and the strike left its bitter mark upon the workers of the trade. Rules were introduced in the Pittsburgh mills which the workers found distasteful, and they reacted with strikes and other acts of disapproval. In the midst of this turbulence the United Sons of Vulcan was organized in the boiling department of the Pittsburgh iron mills in April 1858. While the organization was not made public, a constitution and by-laws were adopted in 1861, and Miles Humphrey was chosen Grand Master. The organization spread to other parts of the country, and the general constitution was adopted in 1862. It provided that only competent practical workmen were to be admitted, and described its object: to maintain the interests of the craft.

The Civil War, with its increased demand for the product of the iron mills, was a favorable occasion for wage increases. Usually, representatives from each side were chosen to adjust the wage rate. In order to avoid frequent meetings, a plan was devised which set the rate of wages in relation to the price of the product. This was the first example of the sliding scale of wages, as the arrangement was called, in the United States. It was reached on February 13, 1865, and tied the scale of wages to be paid for Boiling Pig Iron to Manufacturers' Scale of Prices. It was understood that either side could terminate the arrangement on ninety days' notice.[9] Although the United Sons of Vulcan was established in the 1850's, it is clear that there was no break in the attitude of workers during the 1840's.

The Iron Molders

The iron molding industry came on the scene later than such artisan trades as printing and hatmaking. The historian of the International Molders' Union of North America believes that it cannot be traced much farther back than the 1820's, although a few establishments existed.[10] Wages were low, hours long, and payment was made in part by store orders. While the date of the formation of the first iron molders' unions cannot be ascertained, there are records of their existence in the 1830's. But the elimination of the first organizations in the trade during the panic of 1837 was not followed by the establishment of durable unions of craftsmen in the next decade. A number of strikes took place, and according to Professor Henry S. Hoagland, there exists "some evidence of temporary organizations of journeymen" in 1843–1844.[11] The early 1840's were a period of prosperity, but in 1848 there was a sudden drop in prices as a result of changes in economic activity, which was followed almost immediately by reductions in demand for molders and in wages. At the same time, there was an increase in the supply of labor resulting from the increased immigration of Irish peasants following the potato famine of 1847 and of Europeans fleeing the unsuccessful democratic revolutions in 1848.

When employers in Cincinnati cut the wages of their workmen in 1849, a strike was called; and when it ended in failure, the strikers formed a producers' cooperative, the Journeymen Moulders' Union Foundry. Stock was issued, and a small amount of capital was raised to secure a stock of patters and other needed machinery. Two local philanthropists advanced funds for the purchase of a building, and after the election of a governing board, the cooperative began working in August 1848. This was the first of several ventures in producers' cooperation among the iron molders in the middle of the nineteenth century. These ventures in self-employment did little to solve the problems facing the members of the craft. As a rule, interest in cooperation dwindled, and the factories were taken over as partnerships or individual enterprises.[12]

These ventures in cooperation have been sometimes described as representing a stage in the growth of trade union consciousness; that is, workers turned to trade unionism after they found that producers' cooperation would not work effectively. A sounder explanation is that producers' cooperation was an ephemeral response to special situations. There is no reason to assume that the belief in the efficacy of the trade union to defend the workers' interests had been lost.

During the 1840's the molders also established a number of fraternal benefit societies, limited to trade members, which offered them assistance during illness and paid a death benefit to survivors. These organizations performed no protective functions; they did not deal with wages or other employment terms. In the early 1850's, however, a widespread attempt developed by molders in eastern cities to gain wage increases. These attempts were in many instances immediately followed by the formation of unions concerned only with conditions surrounding employment. In 1853 the molders of Philadelphia established the Journeymen Iron Molders'

Association, *Section No. 1,* which has led Professor Hoagland to conclude that some sort of statewide association existed at this time.[13]

Journeymen appeared to be less interested in fraternal and benevolent activities and "concentrated all their energies on increasing wages and creating better working conditions."[14] Strikes were now carried on in an entire trade in a locality, and negotiations with employers' groups or associations began in the iron molding industry at this time. In 1853–1854 unions in different localities appeared to be in correspondence with each other. By 1858 unions were functioning in thirteen cities in addition to Philadelphia.[15] Many of these organizations were not durable, but the working men seem to be perennially trying to revive their trade organizations. In the latter part of 1858 and early 1859, iron molders' unions tried to recover wage cuts they had suffered the preceding year. Refusal by employers to make concessions was frequently followed by strikes, the most bitter at Albany, New York.

The attacks on the organized molders, along with the friendly relations which existed between the leaders of a number of local unions, finally led to the successful calling of a convention for Philadelphia on July 5, 1859. The call was initiated by the heads of the molders' organization in Philadelphia, President Isaac A. Sheppard and Secretary William H. Sylvis. Representatives from twelve unions attended, and two sent letters approving the venture. A constitution was framed which declared: "In Union There Is Strength and in the formation of a National Organization, embracing every Moulder in the country, a union founded upon a basis broad as the land in which we live, lies our only hope."[16]

The constitution speaks of raising the position of molders as mechanics, the degradation of the trade, and the need for unified action to avert continuing decline in the standards of journeymen. The first national convention created a national executive committee but did not arm it with much power. It was allowed to advise, in case of a strike by one of the affiliated locals, what assistance should be given to the strikers. Provision was also made for a transfer or traveling card system for journeymen who were shifting between communities, as well as for a revenue system to support the national organization.

William H. Sylvis was defeated for president but was chosen national treasurer. Sylvis was a believer in cooperation as a method of rescuing the worker from the evils of the wage system. With the union defeats in 1867 and 1868, he turned to cooperation as the remedy for the ills of labor,[17] and he also became disillusioned with the effectiveness of the strike weapon. Obviously, Sylvis' analysis of problems led him to believe that other remedies were necessary to clear away the injustices that faced the worker. In fact, his disillusion with trade unionism is not dissimilar to the experience of Eugene V. Debs, who in the 1890's found that the limited aims of trade unionism did not afford sufficient scope for his idealistic hopes.[18] The unions continued to arise and alternately to grow and diminish, but the tendencies they embodied appear to have been, despite the continual changes in the fortunes of organized workers, never erased from the consciousness of labor.

HATTERS

Organizations in the hatmaking trade appeared earlier than in the iron industry, but many were wiped out in the panic of 1837. Unions reappeared soon thereafter. There is evidence of a hatters' union in 1841 or 1842, "for they adopted a set of Rules and Regulations of the Trade on March 29th, 1845."[19] The New York hatters were organized in 1845, and they adopted the practice of "going on turn" in looking for work, a form of job sharing common among craft unions and adopted by unions in the maritime trades in our time. The New York hatters' union adopted a policy of "[avoiding] all such measures as are calculated to conflict with the interests of our employers—but such as will prove beneficial to both."[20] This local called upon journeymen in trade to follow the example of its members and establish a union.

A number of locals were organized between 1847 and 1854. Fines were levied against those who violated union rules or went "foul," and the New York local banned its members from working with foul men. By 1854 hat finishers' unions were functioning in a number of cities, and the continual movement of journeymen between hat producing centers in search of employment brought the single locals closer together. In June 1854 twenty-seven delegates from twelve unions in nine states met in Philadelphia, the center of the silk hat trade, and established the United States Hat Finishers Trade Association. The constitution provided for a four-year apprenticeship, the right of each local to set its own scale of wages, and the issuance of a traveling certificate to traveling journeymen. The convention asserted:

We are fully alive to the fact that the interests of both employers and employees are identical and we declare and acknowledge their right to manage and control their business as they see fit but at the same time do claim for ourselves as a body the privilege of agreeing upon any concerted action whereby our interests as mechanics shall not be injured.[21]

The preamble to the constitution announced that the separate locals had to be united in one union if wage rates were to be maintained, good employers aided, and the public protected against inferior merchandise. Moreover, the convention declared that as journeymen they had a right "to resolve what should be the compensation for our labor and in what manner that labor should be performed."[22] These declarations are typical pronouncements of a craft organization, and the attempt of craft unions to impose working rules upon their trade are evident right down to our own time and reflect the view "that the craftsmen have the right to determine the conditions under which he will provide his labor to the employer."[23]

In 1860 the national convention adopted a "three boy rule" under which no factory working under a union arrangement was allowed to employ more than three apprentices to reduce the supply of craftsmen in the trade.

LABOR ORGANIZATION IN GENERAL

Strikes occurred throughout the 1840's and 1850's. Some were spontaneous walkouts in response to a change in wages or working conditions, but others were directed by union organizations toward achieving improvement or preventing changes adversely affecting the particular work force. In 1840 railroad workers struck at Rowley, Massachusetts, against a pay deduction for failing to begin work at a specified hour. There were clashes with the police, and strikers were dispersed. In the same year factory operatives at Lowell, Massachusetts, unsuccessfully struck for higher wages. Reports of strikes during this period appear in every year, sometimes involving a large number of workers. Some of these instances involved more than one plant or community.[24] For example, a strike of weavers over the wages to be paid involved plants at Moyamensing and Kensington, Pennsylvania, and led to serious rioting. The walkout lasted from August 1842 to January 1843. Very likely many more strikes than those which were reported took place. The report of the U.S. Commissioner of Labor for the period prior to 1881 was based largely on the work of the Bureau of Labor Statistics of Massachusetts in its report of 1880 and the Bureau of Industrial Statistics of Pennsylvania for 1881. Although other sources were consulted, it is evident that much information has not been recorded and has eluded investigators.[25] During the 1840's strikes of journeymen took place in a number of cities; journeymen tailors struck several times in Philadelphia during this decade, usually for an increase in wages. Saddlers, furniture makers, rolling mill boilers, hod carriers, weavers, and cotton mill workers also struck during the decade.[26]

According to the *New York State Mechanic* for May 18, 1843, signs of restiveness among mechanics were evident in a number of communities. The *People's Paper* of Cincinnati reported in its July 24, 1844, issue that its advice "that it was impossible, in large cities for mechanics to redress their grievances, unless they formed societies, resolved to firmly adhere to each other, and boldly demand their rights," had been proven correct. The printers led in forming a union, and the example of the printers was followed by shoe makers, tailors and cigar makers, all of whom had formed unions of their craft.[27]

Trade unions were not the only type of organizations that workers established. Many workers' societies in the early period were mutual benefit associations set up by tradesmen to protect each other against the risk of illness and death. But the significance of the organizations espousing pure trade union objectives is that it indicates the persistence of a trade union outlook through this period. According to Professor Sumner Slichter, the 1850's saw the formation of six separate national unions which were still in existence at the end of the decade.[28]

In the first years of the 1850's business activity was light, and severe unemployment in the cotton textile industry existed. About 800,000 of over 2.4 million cotton textile spindles in New England were idle. Employers used the occasion to cut wages; all Fall River corporations except one announced in November 1850 that wages would be reduced. The spinners struck without notice and formed a union. The strikers claimed they had been subjected to many petty tyrannies and their work loads had been recently increased. Employers, on the other hand, insisted that despite the lowering of wages they would remain as high as elsewhere in New England. Unconvinced, the strikers continued their walkout for several months. To aid those without funds, "delegations from the Spinners' Union visited other cities for the purpose of securing subscriptions and relief. They are said to have raised $2,000." In March 1851, *The Trades Union and Fall River Journal* was founded, but the strikers were fighting a losing battle. On June 1, 1851, the strike ended.[29]

Strikes of Pittsburgh iron workers against reduced wages offered by the mills led to violent clashes between the strikers and strikebreakers. Six weeks after the strike had started, on February 18, the mills were sufficiently filled with strikebreakers for the walkout to be regarded as a failure, although many of the strikers did not return to their job until the summer months. A number of the men and women who had been arrested for rioting were fined and sent to jail. Upon petition of the jury which had convicted them and a large number of other citizens, the prisoners were pardoned by the governor.[30]

During 1850 strikes of laborers on the railroad west of Schuylkill, Pennsylvania, were reported. There was also a strike of two hundred employees in a cotton and woolen factory of Philadelphia. In neither of these two strikes is the result known. According to George McNeil:

saddlers, silversmiths, iron and metal workers, steam boiler makers, lady milliners, bookbinders, tanners, lady shoemakers, riggers, sailmakers, watch-case makers, coach painters, sash and blind makers, window-shade painters, carvers, gilders, upholsterers, bakers, laborers, and dry-goods clerks joined forces with the trades already organized. There were many strikes at about this time among the carpenters, the most notable one being that of the carpenters of New York who struck for one dollar and seventy-five cents per day, and marched through the streets in a procession a quarter of a mile long and four deep. . . . Strikes occurred in many of the industries, each success giving renewed hope, and each failure awakening new efforts for organization. The increased immigration of the cheaper labor of Europe to the United States rendered many of the attempts at improvement abortive. When a strike occurred, especially in the factories, foreigners were imported to take the place of the operatives on strike.[31]

CHAPTER 4

In Search of Shorter Hours

Long hours of labor in the new factory towns sparked a reform movement. Pointing to the harmful effects of a prolonged working day upon the health and morals of the thousands of women employed in the textile towns, reformers appealed to the legislature to curb excessive work hours. Among those who participated in the campaign to curtail the hours of labor were some who sought more fundamental remedies for the evils of their day. The reformers, however, were not agreed upon the causes of the social malaise they were seeking to rectify. One group believed that the problem could be traced to the inefficiencies of a competitive economy; a second sought to remedy the evils of the day through systems of consumers' and producers' cooperation; and a third saw relief in the reorganization of the money and credit system so it would protect the worker and farmer against bankers, capitalists, and middlemen. Irrespective of their differences, they were all certain that the adoption of their panaceas would lead to justice, equity, and happiness.

EXECUTIVE ORDER OF PRESIDENT VAN BUREN

One of the more significant steps in the establishment of shorter hours in industry, the ten-hour day order of President Martin Van Buren was taken without the intervention or even influence of the philanthropists and reformers. The executive order of the President establishing the ten-hour day for mechanics and laborers on government works followed an appeal of the National Trades' Union, which had ceased to function when the order was issued. Rebuffed in its plea for a shortened workday by Congress, the National Trades' Union brought its case to the President of the United States. Aside from the effect upon the workday of government employees, the order inferentially supported the reasonableness of the demand of the artisans and factory workers for the ten-hour day. Van Buren's order was a victory for the tactics of trade unionism and not of the reformers.

COTTON TEXTILES

A major source of labor for the cotton textile industry in the 1840's was the thousands of young farm women. Two systems of hiring and employing labor were followed by the early New England textile companies: the Waltham system around Lowell, and the English system in Rhode Island and the middle states. The paternalistic Waltham system provided the women operatives with living quarters and board in company establishments. The young women were required to be in quarters by 10 P.M. They were closely supervised in both their work and leisure time. On the whole, the physical conditions in the mills operated under the Waltham system were regarded as superior to the ones prevalent in Rhode Island.[1]

In contrast to the Waltham system, the plan introduced by Samuel Slater in the last decades of the eighteenth century was unconcerned with the morals of the operatives. It depended for its labor supply upon entire families, including children. The view is generally held that the Waltham system provided more effectively for the material needs of the workers; perhaps it may even have protected the worker's morals. Yet the loss of freedom and the regulation of activities unrelated to the factory were certainly not in harmony with democratic principles. On the other hand, conditions in the factories that followed a laissez faire policy were harsh and the hours of work long. The movement for the ten-hour day in the 1840's was best organized in Massachusetts.[2] In the 1840's a controversy erupted over the optimum length of the work day. Dr. Elisha Bartlett, a writer on labor questions, conceded that the hours were too long but believed that changes should be left to the judgment and altruism of employers. Others insisted that a compulsory ten-hour day should be established in the interests of the employees and the community.[3]

Petitions to the Massachusetts legislature were first presented in 1842 by women workers of Fall River, who claimed that "in many manufacturing establishments more hours of labor are required than can be made consistent with the bodily health and the proper intellectual and moral improvement and well being of adults."[4] In the following year the female employees of Fall River again petitioned the legislature for a reduced working schedule, but the plea was unheeded on both occasions. As a result, the Mechanics' Association of Fall River organized a convention in 1844 at which the New England Working Men's Association was formed. Subsequently it changed its name to the Labor Reform League of New England. The convention of the Working Men's Association opened in Boston in October 1844 with two hundred delegates present. The deliberations were not limited to the hours of labor; in addition to approving the ten-hour workday, the delegates came out for the freeing of the public lands and abolition of monopoly of the soil. Another question considered was the most effective organization of useful labor. This objective was to be achieved, according to the meeting, by the "formation of practical associations, in which working men can use their own capital, work their own stock, establish their own hours, and have their own price."[5]

This resolution, along with other pronouncements, shows that the meeting was not mainly concerned with shortening the hours of labor for the factory girl, but that many delegates believed that relief could be attained by a "system of attractive industry, a system in which every laborer has a direct personal interest in the fruits of labor; in which all the faculties of human nature are called into exercise; and amount of leisure, together with ample means for its wise, orderly and beneficial employment shall be guaranteed to every man, woman and child, such as, under the present arrangement of society is neither practicable nor desirable."[6]

CHARLES FOURIER

Such were the views of Charles Fourier, a French reformer described by Karl Marx in the *Communist Manifesto* as a "utopian socialist." Fourier had published books in France in the early part of the nineteenth century, and his theories were introduced into the United States by Albert Brisbane. Fourier believed that the social, as well as the natural, order was governed by God's Plan, one of harmony. Just as Newton had discovered the principle governing the physical universe, so he had unraveled the principle of attraction governing society.

He was critical of individualism, for it led, in his opinion, to neglect and failed to achieve perfection. It was inefficient and backward; it fostered competition which was injurious to individuals and to society. Fourier, instead, advocated associated labor, the organization of society into cooperative communities of 1,500 to 1,600 people called Phalanstries.

These ideas were brought to the United States by Albert Brisbane, the son of a well-to-do landowner of Batavia, New York, who had received an extensive education and traveled widely. On his return to the United States, Brisbane launched his propaganda in behalf of Fourier's views. He published the *Social Destiny of Man,* which gave a popularized version of the master's thoughts and succeeded in winning to his standard Horace Greeley, who became for a time his leading disciple.[7]

The best known of the associative colonies was organized at Brook Farm, near Boston. George Ripley, William Ellery Channing, Margaret Fuller, Ralph Waldo Emerson, Henry D. Thoreau, and Nathaniel Hawthorne were at least sympathetic to the Brook Farm idea. At first the group met socially for literary and philosophic discussions, soon taking the name, Transcendental Club. Ripley resigned his office as minister in a Unitarian church, and with a few others organized Brook Farm. All members were given employment in accordance with their taste and ability, remunerated at a uniform rate, and worked a maximum of ten hours a day. Amidst mutual work, literary and scientific discussions were conducted. By 1844, Brook Farm became a Fourieristic phalanx, but no change took place except to make it a center of propaganda for associative labor. Differences among the members, a destructive fire, and the successful suit of a creditor put the colony under severe strain. On August 18, 1847, the last meeting of Brook Farm phalanx adjourned.

Cooperation

The views of Fourier and Brisbane had their greatest influence on intellectuals. It was difficult for workers living in an industrialized community to recognize the relationship between a phalanx in the country and their problems in the shop. After Greeley's enthusiasm for associative labor began to wane, he advocated a system of profit sharing; when this idea failed to take hold, he urged producers' cooperation as a way by which the problems of labor could be solved.

Distributive cooperation had a wider appeal. Some advocates did not believe that workers could accumulate a sufficient amount from their savings to establish producers' cooperatives. Consequently, they advised that a cooperative store be organized and that profits be plowed back until sufficient capital was available to launch a productive enterprise. A second group held that workers lacked sufficient managerial ability to operate a producers' cooperative. In their view, however, the worker could escape from the duplicity of trade by organizing a cooperative retail store.[8]

Josiah Warren

A number of programs for revolutionizing the basis of exchange were developed in the 1840's. One of the more original came from Josiah Warren, a pioneer American libertarian or anarchist. Warren, born in Boston in 1798, moved to Cincinnati when a young man. Originally a follower of Robert Owen, he finally rejected socialism, embraced anarchism, and opened a number of "time stores." Goods were presumably sold at labor cost. In addition, the storekeeper was paid for his time in labor notes which required the payer to recompense the storekeeper for the time the latter spent in waiting on customers. In philosophy Warren was an extreme individualist, and his views closely resembled those of the German individualist anarchist, Max Stirner.

Stephen Pearl Andrews

Warren's views were expounded by Stephen Pearl Andrews, who believed that commodities ought to be exchanged for each other on the basis of equal amounts of labor; that is, not the same quantity, but the labor of the same amount of repugnance. This could be brought about by agreeing upon labor of average repugnance and using it as a yardstick to measure other kinds af labor. Despite the problem of individual evaluation, Andrews believed that the estimates would be close to each other. He wanted to bring out a labor note as a new kind of money which retailers could issue against their own and other people's labor, and against their inventories embodying labor. Under this system each person would be independent, and no laws or government would be needed. Voluntary cooperation would spread and the principle of individual sovereignty would rule.

Wilhelm Weitling

The German Socialist, Wilhelm Weitling, also developed a plan of reform based on a bank of exchange. He came to the United States after a career as a revolutionary in Switzerland and Germany. In January 1850 he started his New York journal, the *Republik der Arbeiter,* through which he gained wide influence among German workers. He advocated the establishment of a bank of exchange as a means of creating a new money system. The banks of exchange would receive goods manufactured and issue paper money to their producers based upon the value of the goods. Such an arrangement would abolish unemployment; profits formerly pocketed by the middleman would be retained by the producer; the bank would be able to balance supply and demand.[9] Weitling was for a time active in the New York labor movement, ran into factional difficulties, and after the middle 1850's ceased to be active.

George Henry Evans

Among those who sought to reorganize society upon a more equitable or efficient basis, the pleas of the land reformers appear in a low key. Nevertheless, in view of the importance of the public domain, the question of land reform was of both practical and theoretical importance. George Henry Evans, a leading land reformer, came to the United States from England in 1820, settled in New York, learned the printing trade and operated his own shop. He started the *Working Man's Advocate* in 1829 and *Man* in 1834. He withdrew from journalism for a time and resumed these activities in 1841 with a program for distributing the land in the government's possession to settlers with a limit of one hundred and sixty acres.[10] He was an anti-monopolist, opposed central banks, and advocated the use of pressure politics under the slogan of "vote yourself a farm." The political tactics he proposed were already time-tested in his own day, having been used by organized workers in previous decades.

The Lowell Convention

Meeting in March 1845, the Lowell Convention approved a mechanics' lien law, a reduction of the hours of labor, and such other measures "as will secure to the workingmen of New England their rights." The ballot box was the means to attain these objectives. Resolutions were enacted favoring improved education for children, opposition to prison labor as unjust to the "honest mechanic," representation of labor in the capital of the states, opposition to speculation in public lands, and annual congresses. L. W. Ryckman of Brook Farm pointed out "the necessity of a prompt, immediate, and thorough revolution in industry and the formation of an Industrial Congress analogous to that which fostered the liberties of the American Republic."[11] The meeting approved the calling of a national reform convention for amending the Constitution of the United States. A critical review of the proceedings was given by one of the delegates who claimed that there were only twenty men and women present. He found that the reformers were aware that they did not speak for labor, and accordingly they complained "about the want of interest felt by the workingmen for the cause of reform. I am not the least surprised that the workingmen of Massachusetts," wrote this critical observer, "care nothing for such reforms as were proposed by some of the members. A member . . . made a speech in which he said that Capitalists and Priests had joined hands to put down, grind and oppress the laboring men—that commerce, manufacturing and foreign immigration were killing them—that there were ten times more slavery in Lowell, than on the Southern Plantations—that Lowell manufactured the prostitutes of New York, and that the first thing that must be done to elevate the workingmen, was to collect and burn the Sunday books, which were poisoning the minds of the young. Such sentiments were listened to without rebuke by men calling themselves reformers —the friends of the laboring classes. No wonder the meeting was thinly attended—no wonder the clear-headed, stout-hearted, practical workingmen of Massachusetts, who have been reared in our free schools and Sabbath schools and churches should care nothing for such reforms."[12]

The views of this observer, who wrote that he was a friend of Horace Greeley and attended the convention at the latter's invitation, cannot be dismissed. They show that the reformers neither represented the views of the workers nor found much sympathy in the ranks of labor. In fact, their interest in cooperative enterprises and politics was not shared by workers in any large number.

FIRST LEGISLATIVE INVESTIGATION
OF THE LABOR PROBLEM

In response to the petitions of factory operatives and other citizens, the Massachusetts legislature authorized in 1845 the first investigation of a labor question—the hours of factory workers. Witnesses testified that the hours of labor were excessive. A lady employed as an operative in a Lowell textile mill claimed she went to work at five in the morning during the summer season, and continued working until seven in the evening with a half of an hour for breakfast and three-quarters of an hour for lunch. The air in the room, she testified was unwholesome, since it was lighted by 293 small, and 61 large, lamps. About 130 women, 11 men, and 12 children between the ages of eleven and fourteen years were employed in the same room as she. The children worked nine months a year, and attended school the other three. She also complained about the high incidence of illness among the operatives, especially the women. She said that there was a general desire for the ten-hour day among women workers even if they had to take a wage cut.[13]

In its report, the committee questioned inferentially the ill-effects of factory employment on health, calling attention to the increase in population, of both men and women between 1840 and 1844 at Lowell, and a simultaneous decline in the death rate.

The committee believed that the enactment of a ten-hour law would place Massachusetts industry under a competitive disadvantage with industries in other states. In addition, the committee maintained that it would be impossible to restrict the hours of labor without "affecting materially the question of wages; and that is a matter which experience has taught us can be much better regulated by the parties themselves than by the Legislature."[14] The committee admitted that abuses existed in the employing of labor, and expressed the wish that workers might not be "severely tasked," the hours of labor were shorter, more time was allowed for meals, more attention was paid to ventilating the factories and work shops, and many other improvements which were not specified.

Another investigation of the advisability of shortening the hours of labor was made by the Massachusetts legislature in 1850. The majority was of the same opinion as its predecessor, that it was inadvisable to legislate on the subject. A minority of two submitted a careful and critical review of conditions in the factories of the state.

Legislative investigations of the effect of long hours upon the health of the factory operative were made in New Hampshire several years after Massachusetts, although petitions calling for an inquiry were presented to the legislature of the state in 1845. Two years later, in response to new requests, the legislature appointed a committee to investigate. The majority rejected intervention by the government, but the minority found bargaining between a corporation and a worker, usually a woman, to be unequal. It therefore recommended action to restrict the hours of labor. A law was enacted setting ten hours as the legal day's work, but allowed for longer work schedules by individual contract.

Pennsylvania, after a number of petitions, enacted a law in 1848 that limited the employment in factories of children to those who were more than twelve years of age, and that prescribed "that labor performed during a period of ten hours in any secular day, in all cotton, woolen, silk, paper, bagging, and flax factories, shall be considered a legal day's labor, and thereafter no minor or adult engaged in any such factories shall be holden or required to work more than ten hours in any secular day, or sixty hours in any secular week."[15] The law allowed for special contracts between employer and employee for twelve hours' work.

The proprietors of cotton mills met in Pittsburgh on May 23, 1848, and their reaction to the law is of some interest. They approved "the benevolent action of the legislature in excluding children under twelve years of age from employment in factories, and believe that at no time was it the interest of them or their employers, but that the practice originated through the entreaties of indigent parents, whose wants were supplied by their earnings. We at the same time sympathize with many widows and others, in afflictive circumstances, in being thus deprived of their ordinary supply of the daily necessities of life."[16] The manufacturers further resolved, because competition had reduced their returns on cotton goods to a small profit and because they faced competition from the free and slave states, any attempt to reduce the hours of labor would be harmful to the industry. They therefore felt constrained to adopt special contracts with the operatives for a twelve-hour day.[17]

Many states passed similar laws, but they were equally ineffective because of the escape clauses they contained. The laws must be regarded as expressions of a pious wish rather than effective enactments capable of achieving a desirable social purpose.

CHAPTER 5

The Labor Movement in the 1860's

Expansion of railway building tended to weld the separate parts of the country into a more unified economic whole. The flow of population into the midwestern and the prairie states was gradually filling the empty areas with farms, towns, and villages; some travelers did not stop until they reached the Pacific Coast. The increase in foreign commerce accelerated the expansion of the merchant marine, which had become a principal carrier of cargo around the world. At the same time the copper extracted from Michigan mines and the gold dredged from the California hills were adding to the nation's wealth. The rising curve of prosperity was periodically reversed, but the long-run trend was upward. The Civil War gave a sharp stimulus to economic activity.

"The mines were as notably productive as the farms. The output of coal, iron, copper, salt, gold and silver in most cases surpassed all previous records; many important new mines were opened and the totally new petroleum industry was developed."[1] Progress in iron mining and copper production was proceeding rapidly as a result of improvements in metal refining and the discovery of new sources which could be worked. Prosperity in mining and agriculture stimulated improvements in earnings of the burgeoning railroad transportation system in most parts of the North. New England railroads made the least spectacular progress, since they carried few crops and did not profit greatly from troop movements. On the other hand, the Pennsylvania roads increased their earnings carrying the coal, iron, and petroleum of its mines and mills. Western roads which brought crops to eastern markets also prospered in a larger measure than their promoters had hoped. Even those roads running north and south found the business of hauling crops and soldiers profitable. The transcontinental systems which were soon to span the country were laid during the Civil War.

Availability of raw material and a transportation network, the increases in population through both an excess of births over deaths (except during the war), and the flow of immigrants provided a basis for a great increase in manufacturing. Food processing, woolen manufacture, and after a short relapse the cotton textile industry flourished. The invention of the sewing machine by Elias Howe revolutionized clothing production, and ready-made clothes supplanted the imports from London's East End. The McKay stitcher played a similar role in shoemaking. The clothier and shoemaker moved from the home to the factory.

Consumption of iron increased; and New York, New Jersey, and especially Pennsylvania became booming production centers. Increasing use of the Bessemer process was a stimulant to the growth of the steel industry, and steel rails began replacing the softer ones made of iron.[2]

On the whole, while the worker was not in an unfavorable position, he was facing a number of new problems brought on by changing technology and public policy. Sometimes the employer might transfer some of the work performed by craftsmen to the unskilled, and if the conditions were favorable, the employer might substitute women for men workers. "Immigrants as a class of cheap labor greatly surpassed in numbers and importance any of the classes. . . . Only labor stood apart and took offense at every manifestation of the country's attitude toward the oncoming tide. It was exasperating to the labor leaders to see the many persistent attempts of employers to encourage immigration. Oftentimes shops, against which a strike was declared, sent private agents to Europe to secure help; mines and railroads suffering from want of labor did the same."[3]

LABOR ORGANIZATIONS

Between 1860 and 1869, twenty-four national unions were established. Each of these unions was made up of a number of local organizations, and evidence shows them to have been trade organizations.

American Miners' Union

Unions in the coal mines first appeared in the 1840's and 1850's. The first miners' organization was formed in Schuylkill County, Pennsylvania, in 1848 and was limited largely to that county. The Bates Union, as it was called, was named after John Bates, an English miner and chartist who had settled in the United States. The union reached a membership of about five thousand.[4] In May 1849 a strike against payment by order which could only be cashed in merchandise at certain stores was called. At first the mine owners refused to negotiate, but they acceded after a three weeks' walkout. In July of the same year, the union called a strike to reduce the coal supply. This maneuver failed, and Bates was charged with being in league with the operators. He left the area, and the union disintegrated.[5]

Strikes in the bituminous coal fields of the Monongahela Valley of Pennsylvania were called in the 1840's, although only those involving large numbers of workers are recorded. In September 1848 the Monongahela Valley miners struck against a wage reduction and compelled the operators to cancel part of the decrease. Strikes in the Maryland coal fields have been noted in the 1850's, and strikes in 1859 affected mines in Monongahela, Allegheny, Washington, and Westmoreland counties in Pennsylvania. Wage reduction in St. Clair County, Illinois, in January 1861 was the indirect cause of the formation of the first national miners' union in the United States, the American Miners' Association. A week after the walkout the strikers organized. The strike itself led the legislature to enact a law providing for the measurement of coal in St. Clair County by "coal scalers," who were to be appointed by the county judge.

The American Miners' Association was organized in West Belleville, Illinois, on January 28, 1861. Thomas Lloyd was elected president and Daniel Weaver, secretary. In an address to the miners, Weaver declared that "unity is essential to the attainment of our rights, and the amelioration of our present conditions. Our voices must be heard in the legislative halls of the land. There it is that our complaints must be heard and our rights defined. The insatiable law of capital would devour every vestige of labor's rights, but we must demand legislative protection; and to accomplish this, we must organize."[6] The American Miners' Association spread through the coal producing areas of the United States; and an official newspaper, the *Weekly Miner,* edited by John Hincliffe, was published in Belleville, the headquarters' city. Strikes were to be called against operators who discharged members of the union, and payment of strike benefits was provided to those victimized by dismissal, as well as those who struck in their support. Members were given certificates, or traveling cards, entitling them to admittance to locals in other districts if they shifted their residence. The general association allowed for the admittance of all who worked in and around the mines, and set the dues and penalties for blacklegging or working during strikes. The Association decided that it would "not submit to any reduction of the present prices of mining, under any circumstances whatever, in any of the mines that come under this jurisdiction of the Association."[7]

The American Miners' Association survived only until the end of the decade. Structurally, the American Miners' Association set the pattern for the miners' unions which followed, and its industrial form became a model for later unions in the industry. Dissension, the bane of early labor organizations, put an end to the first national organization in the mines.[8]

The Bricklayers

Unlike the miners, the bricklayers, instead of forming an industrial organization, set up a craft union in 1865. Strikes took place and local unions were established in the 1830's and, like the organizations in other trades, many of them did not survive. "In the spring of 1850 the Bricklayers and Plasterers Benevolent Society united with the newly formed Bricklayers Union of New York under the name of Bricklayers and Plasterers Protective Association for the purpose of gaining higher wages and improved working conditions. 'As to our benevolent features,' said President Cornelius McCloskey, President of the New York Bricklayers Union, 'they are separate and distinct from our primary organization—our protection features remain unchanged and are cherished by us more than any other.' "[9]

In May 1850 the bricklayers and plasterers' organization sought to increase wages to $2.00 per day; for the balance of the year $1.75 and no three-quarter days allowed except where men are prevented from work by inclement weather, or any other justifiable cause.[10] In 1854 the bricklayers sought to establish a national union of all building trades. Although the venture failed, the desire for organization could not be repressed despite the shifts in the fortunes of local unions. After the Civil War, bricklayers' unions were operating in a number of cities. Local unions of bricklayers were functioning in Brooklyn, Albany, Baltimore, Providence, Pittsburgh, St. Louis, and Jersey City. The list appeared in *Fincher's Trade Review* of Philadelphia, and it was obviously only a partial list of unions in the trade.[11]

The demand of the Baltimore Mason Contractors Association in May 1865, that the local union work exclusively for its members, was refused. As a result the association sought to reduce wages from $4.00 to $3.50 a day. When the bricklayers called a strike, the Philadelphia union not only tried to keep its members from replacing the strikers but also provided financial aid. After the strike the two locals in Baltimore and Philadelphia decided to establish a national organization, and at a delegate meeting in Baltimore on October 16, 1865, the Bricklayers' International Union of the United States of North America was founded. A convention was called for the following January, and seven unions sent delegates.[12]

The Bricklayers' Union was able to gain the affiliation of a number of locals, and strikes for increased wages were reported from several cities. In 1867 the union sought to limit the number of apprentices to two per contractor. The rule was designed to prevent filling jobs with partially trained craftsmen. The president was authorized to levy, with the approval of the vice-president, an assessment of from ten cents to fifty cents a day in

support of strikes, and the first assessment was soon imposed for this purpose. It is quite obvious that the local bricklayers' unions in the 1860's
were concerned primarily, if not entirely, with wage and hour questions
and other conditions affecting their employment. In fact, the continual levying of assessments by the national president in support of local strikes led
the convention of 1867 to change the procedure. In the event of a strike,
subordinate locals were required to submit a "Bill of Grievances" setting
forth the reasons for the strike and an estimate of the possibilities of success. The information was then submitted to the membership, and approval
by two-thirds of the locals was needed for levying an assessment.[13]

The movement for nationalization in the bricklayers' trade is perhaps
the best key to the attitudes of the organized workers of the time. The formation of a national union is inevitably the response to the need for greater
cooperation to protect the worker in a particular calling or to increase the
bargaining strength of the local union.

The Knights of St. Crispin

The Knights of St. Crispin was a craft union whose quick rise and
rapid decline can be explained by the desire of skilled shoe craftsmen to
prevent their displacement by unskilled workers using a newly developed
machine.

In 1864, Newell Davis of Milford, Massachusetts, conceived the idea of
organizing the shoemakers and not allowing mechanics to teach the trade
to new hands, without first obtaining the consent of the organization. He
drafted a constitution and with Stephen Onion and Elba Underwood formed
a boot-treers' society.[14] Daniels succeeded in organizing in Milwaukee, Wisconsin, an industrial union of shoemakers with all who worked for one
year at the shoe trade eligible to join. Daniels' constitution was adopted,
and a committee prepared a secret ritual for the new society called the
Knights of St. Crispin.

The first lodge was established in Milwaukee in March 1867, and several others were organized soon afterward. On April 23, 1869, a general
convention was held at Worcester, Massachusetts, and a preamble and
constitution for the International Grand Lodge were adopted. The Crispins
spread rapidly through the shoe-manufacturing areas of the country and
reached a membership, according to Professor Don D. Lescohier, of over
50,000, the largest membership attained by any union of the United States
before 1875.[15] Shoemakers' unions had been formed in the 1860's in several Massachusetts shoe manufacturing communities. A Marlborough shoe
manufacturer testified that his employees had struck "two and a half years before the organization of the Crispins, but when there was a shoemakers' union
in town. The object of the strike was to get more pay."[16] A worker explained that "many of us thought we had got to do something if we ex-

pected living wages. This was before the Crispin Association was thought of. We formed a union of the bottomers and finishers, and got all who would pay the initiation fee, and then admitted the rest free. This was in October. In March we drew up what we thought was a fair list of prices for our work, and chose a committee to put this list in the office of every manufacturer in town. . . . Some sat down and argued with us. The result was we were completely ignored. We got no conference or compromise. They said we had no rights at all in the matter. So we struck in two shops, in different parts of the town. The manufacturers formed an association. . . . They tried every means and used every inducement, but they could not break us up. . . . What drove us into union most, however, was that we could get no money, but were obliged to take store orders." The union was successful and later joined the Crispins.[67]

Before the Civil War shoemaking was a product of highly skilled craftsmen, but slow changes lessened the skill needed and in time was responsible for the ousting of many from the trade. Work began to shift from the small shop to the factory in the latter part of the 1850's after the introduction of the power pegging machine; the onset of the Civil War quickened the trend to factory organization. The increased demand for sewed shoes by the government to supply its armies coincided with the invention of the McKay stitcher in 1862.[18]

Green hands moved into the industry, because there were few unions whose apprenticeship rules could impede entry. Moreover, for a time the high demand during the war hid the effect of the new technology upon the labor market. The end of the war affected workers in the shoe industry in two ways. First, the supply of labor was sharply increased by the re-entry of returned soldiers into the labor markets where shoes were manufactured. Second, demobilization reduced the demand for the product. The shift of work from the small shop to the factory also changed the work cycle for many. Instead of steady employment, workers in the shoe industry were now subjected to alternating periods of employment and unemployment.

The Crispins sought to stem the flow of semi-skilled workers then engulfing the trade. Article X of the constitution for subordinate lodges of the Internatonal Grand Lodge of 1869 stated: "No member of this order shall teach, or aid in teaching, any part or parts of boot and shoe making, unless the lodge shall give permission by a three-fourths vote of those present and voting thereon, when such permission is first asked; *provided,* this article shall not be so construed as to prevent a father teaching his own son."[19]

During its existence, the Knights of St. Crispins was a typical craft union concentrating its major interest upon the most crucial issue affecting its members: technological displacement. The solution it sought, while not an effective one, was typical of skilled workers. Inevitably a policy of this kind cannot succeed because the new technique can be used in nonunion areas, and the Knights of St. Crispin was compelled to engage in a series of disastrous strikes to enforce its policies. The organization declined and almost perished in the first years of the 1870's. Turning to cooperation, it still failed to halt the flow of unskilled workers into its industry.

Locomotive Engineers

One of the more stable labor unions in American labor history has been the Brotherhood of Locomotive Engineers, the first union to be organized on the railroads. An effort to establish a union was made in 1855, following an unsuccessful protest strike against the discharge of sixteen engineers by the Baltimore and Ohio Railroad during the preceding year. About seventy delegates responded to a call for a meeting by engineers of the Baltimore and Ohio Railroad; they came from fourteen states and fifty-five railroads. The meeting organized the National Protective Association of the United States, chose a slate of officers, and drafted a constitution. The association met once more, during the following years, but several local groups continued to exist, although they were not very active.[20]

Wage cutting by the railroads and the imposition in some instances of unfavorable terms of employment kept the spirit of organization alive. An association of railroad employees had been started at Adrian, Michigan, but it included all workers in the operating and mechanical crafts. The more active leaders in the new campaign to form a union believed that a craft organization of engineers was necessary. W. D. Robinson and George Q. Adams, engineers on the Michigan Central Railway, took the lead. At a meeting at Robinson's home in Marshall, Michigan, in April 1863 it was decided to begin correspondence with engineers on the roads running into Detroit with a view to forming a union in the trade. At the same time, it was decided that if anyone was discharged for belonging to the union, the rest of the engineers would refuse to work until his reinstatement.

The correspondence between the engineers on the Michigan Central Railway and workers on other roads led to the convention of May 1863. Representatives of only four roads were asked, and the twelve delegates drew up a constitution and by-laws.

On the 8th of May 1863, twelve engineers, including the delegates, joined hands in a circle, repeated the obligation, which was read by George Q. Adams, thus pledging themselves to support the constitution and by-laws then adopted. Officers were at once selected and Division No. 1, Brotherhood of the Footboard, was fully organized, and stood forth the pioneer in the great work of regeneration and elevation of the locomotive engineers on the continent, eager to extend the hand of fellowship to all worthy members of the craft who had any faith in their rights as a class, a belief that in organized action alone rested a hope for their vindication. In a general way, it may be said that the idea most prominent in the constitution, and which is repeated with emphasis in every annual address of the Grand Chief Engineer, is that members of the Brotherhood shall aim to reach a high standard of ability as engineers and of character as men, well fitted to the important and responsible nature of their occupation, thus entitling them to liberal compensation, which should be insisted upon by all legitimate means.[21]

William D. Robinson was the father of the Brotherhood. His frequent requests for leaves of absences and the hostility which his union activities aroused led to his discharge from his post on the Michigan Central Railway, and he then devoted full time to union work. By the end of the brotherhood's first year, fifty-four divisions, or locals, had been established. At the second convention in August 1864, the name was changed to Brotherhood of Locomotive Engineers, and Charles Wilson of Rochester, New York ,was chosen Grand Chief. The 1866 convention established the *Locomotive Engineers' Journal,* and the next year, the Locomotive Engineers' Mutual Life Insurance Association. In 1872 the convention voted to expel members engaged in unauthorized strikes. But when Grand Chief Engineer Wilson denounced a strike against a wage cut by the engineers on the Pennsylvania Railroad, a special convention voted for his removal and replaced him with P. M. Arthur, who headed the organization for thirty-one years. Brotherhood strikes were usually caused by attempts to cut wages or by attempts to undermine the union. The brotherhood first exhausted all peaceful means of settlement, but when necessary, "stopped the trains at such hours as to cause as little inconvenience as practicable to the traveling and business public. The Brotherhood was generally successful in securing a compliance with their requests without much delay. Sometimes the struggle was more protracted, the officials refusing at first to even recognize the Brotherhood, or Chief Arthur as its representative. But they were eventually compelled to do so. In a few instances the strikes were unsuccessful, owing usually to the assistance rendered by other companies. The companies always paid much more, in the long run, to fight the Brotherhood than it would have cost to have acceded to its requests."[22]

The Locomotive Engineers, like the other unions of the 1860's, attempted to win recognition so as to influence the terms of employment. The importance of the service rendered by its members in the industrial and social life of the community developed a cautious policy among the leaders, who feared the effect of militant action upon public opinion. Nevertheless, its members, while never enthusiastic about walking off their jobs, were willing to use their economic power to win demands they believed justified.

THE NATIONAL LABOR UNION

The 1860's also witnessed an abortive movement to set up a labor federation. As already noted, the National Trades' Union of the 1830's was purely a trade union body, almost syndicalist in character. It refused to allow a discussion of political questions and removed the word "political" from its list of objectives. However, the desire for a wider union of labor was shared not only by trade unionists but also by reformers. A preliminary meeting of eleven trade union leaders in New York City in March 1866 discussed the calling of a national labor convention. The 1864 convention of the Molders' Union endorsed the idea, and the founding convention of the Bricklayers' National Union supported the proposals. The March meeting in New York appointed William Harding, head of the Coach Makers' International Union, John Reed, a Jersey City carpenter, and J. H. Foy, a dry goods clerk of New York, to cooperate with the Baltimore Trades' Assembly in carrying out the plan for calling the convention. It was decided that consideration of the eight-hour question would be the principal business of the meeting.[23]

The convention, meeting in Baltimore on August 20, 1866, was attended by seventy-seven delegates from thirteen states and the District of Columbia. Fifty of the delegates represented local unions, seven came from eight-hour leagues, and three from two international unions. Among the unions, the largest representation came from the nineteen building trades locals; the molders', machinists', and ship carpenters' trades were each represented by seven delegates. In addition, leading trade unionists Jonathan C. Fincher, John White and E. T. Kirby of the Bricklayers' Union, and Alexander H. Troup, secretary of the National Typographical Union, were either delegates or were seated as guests of the convention. A. C. Cameron (1834–1892), a printer and the editor of the *Workingman's Advocate,* came from the Chicago Trades' Assembly. He was active in the Chicago labor movement and favored independent political action at first. He attended the meeting of the International Workingmen's Association in Basle in 1869. At the convention of the Illinois State Labor Association in 1884, Cameron favored a policy of bipartisanship. He opposed a resolution in behalf of the Chicago anarchists on the ground it was not a proper subject before the convention.[24] John Hincliffe, another leading labor publicist of the time was sent by the Miners' Lodge of Illinois and several other unions.[25] Although the convention contained a representative group of labor leaders, Baltimore, the convention city, appears to have been overrepresented by twenty-one delegates. Such heavy representation by local people may mean that unions in other parts of the country were not aware of the meeting, found the expense of sending a delegate too high, or did not believe the proceedings would lead to fruitful results.

The committee on trades' unions and strikes, headed by A. C. Cameron, recommended the formation of unions in "all localities where the same do not now exist, and the formation of an international organization in every branch of industry as a first and most important duty of the hour."[26]

In regard to strikes, the committee believed they were "productive of great injury to the laboring classes; that they have been injudicious and ill-advised, and the result of impulse rather than principle." Such an outright condemnation would indicate the predominance of reformers rather than trade unionists. It further recommended the establishment of arbitration committees to settle disputes between labor and employers.[27]

The National Labor Union was permanently organized with trades' unions, workingmen's associations, and eight-hour leagues entitled to membership. The convention urged the adoption of an eight-hour law by Congress and, on politics, suggested that "each locality should be governed by its own policy." Many delegates favored a different approach to this issue, and the report was later amended to endorse the formation of a national labor party.[28]

An address to the workers of the United States was issued: It pointed to the lack of cooperation among national unions and to the failure to work "for a common end, the want of which has been experienced for many years by every craft and calling."[29] The statement expressed certainty that eight hours would shortly become, by legal enactment, "a day's work in every state in the American Union."[30] The address claimed that far from encouraging the spirit of hostility to employers, "all properly organized unions recognize an identity of interest between and confer as many benefits to the employer as the employed. . . ."[31] Unions, they claimed, insist, "and justly so, that the employee shall have, at least, an equal voice with the employer in determining the value of the labor performed, and knowing that isolation is weakness and combination strength, they prefer trusting to the power and justice of their united claims, than in the magnanimity or generosity of capital."[32]

The report spoke out against the opposition to the employment of women in industry and warned that if labor failed to extend the hand of friendship to the Negro, others would use him to the detriment of all workers. The statement pointed to the importation of Negro strikebreakers from Virginia to Boston to replace ship caulkers. It called on "every union to help inculcate the grand, enobling idea that the interests of labor are one; that there should be no distinction of race or nationality; no classification of Jews or Gentile, Christian or Infidel; that there is but one dividing line—that which separates mankind into great classes." In addition, the disposal of the public domain to land monopolists was opposed. The formation of an independent political party was endorsed. J. S. Whaley of the Washington Trades' Assembly was elected president, and C. William Gibson of the eight-hour association of New Haven, secretary.[33]

The views on trade unionism of the convention show the influence of the labor leaders who were present. But the National Labor Union, aside from issuing a statement, offered only advice, not plans, for their extension and support. It declared that strikes were useful as a final weapon, but it did not seek methods by which strike assistance might be given to a beleaguered group of workers or even suggest a means for disseminating information of the existence of such disputes so that potential strikebreakers might be discouraged from entering the strike area. In a sense, the National Labor Union was unlike the National Trades' Union of 1837. The succeeding five conventions show a continual trend toward politics and away from trade unionism.

The 1867 convention met in Chicago in August with seventy-one delegates representing sixty-four organizations. A. C. Cameron was present as a representative of the Illinois State Workingmen's Convention; Richard Trevellick came from the Detroit Trades' Assembly; John Hincliffe from Illinois; John Bingham represented the American Miners' Association; and William Harding, the Coachmakers' International Union. President Whaley complained of lack of funds and the difficulty of determining who were members since "the constituency . . . had been indistinctly defined and but questionably established."[34]

Whaley suggested that the president and secretary be paid salaries and that the unions pay a per capita tax to support the organization.

The 1867 convention drew up a constitution under which the "National Labor Union shall be composed of such organizations as may now, or hereafter exist, having for their object the amelioration of the condition of those who labor for a living." A scale of contributions of affiliated organizations, as well as the salaries of the president and secretary, was defined. The Committee on Political Organization believed that the time had arrived for the industrial classes to cut themselves loose from party ties "and organize themselves into a National Labor Party, the object of which shall be to secure by proper legislation the labor reforms necessary to the prosperity of the nation."[35]

The convention of 1867—J. C. Whaley was re-elected its president and C. H. Lucker its secretary—also called for an equitable distribution of the public domain and for the sale of land only to actual occupants and not to speculators. A demand for the eight-hour workday was to be achieved through legislation, although the convention recognized that the eight-hour laws enacted by six states were "frauds upon the laboring classes." Therefore, the committee recommended that the workers organize a political party under the auspices of the National Labor Union so that the reduction of hours by statute could be attained.

The Committee on Negro Labor decided it was inexpedient to discuss the subject because of the wide diversity of views among the delegates. Some delegates insisted, however, that the convention take a position; others believed the Negro should be helped; and a third wanted the Negroes to organize themselves. William Sylvis, who was generally unfriendly to the Negro, spoke out for conciliation. He feared the "black vote would be cast against them," and thereby create a fruitful source of strikebreakers. "There is no concealing the fact that the time will come when the 'Negro will take possession of the shop if we have not taken possession of the Negro.' "[36]

The 1868 convention was held in New York City on September 22. Seventy-eight delegates represented seventy-two organizations, and Susan B. Anthony, the suffragette leader of the campaign to gain women the vote, came as a delegate from the Workingmen's Protective Association; Alexander Troup from the National Typographical Union; A. W. Phelps, E. L. Roseman and Andrew Turnbull represented the Carpenters and Joiners' National Union; Samuel R. Gaul, National Bricklayers' Union; and Jonathan C. Fincher, the International Union of Machinists and Blacksmiths. Other delegates represented local unions, workingmen's assemblies, and trade societies. In his report, President J. C. Whaley advised against alliances with particular political parties and suggested that it would be better to work with either party as conditions dictated. A. M. Kennady, the vice-president, reported that in California, where he lived, such legislative gains as a mechanic's lien law and an eight-hour law had been achieved.

In a debate on reaffirming the opposition to strikes, Susan B. Anthony defended the views of the National Labor Union and charged that workingmen who went on strike were tools of "political tricksters." The clause expressing opposition to strikes was stricken, largely because it was believed it might be used against a group of striking bricklayers who had been indicted for conspiracy. The presence of so many friends of labor who did not understand the function of the strike is a commentary on the organization's outlook.[37]

The National Labor Union linked tariff protection to immigration. In the first instance competition between American workers and those abroad takes place through the sale of goods in American producer markets; in the latter instance, by bringing foreign workers to the United States to compete with labor. The convention denounced companies that imported immigrants to the United States and asked the Congress to rescind the charter of the Emigrant Society, which had been organized to import labor from Europe. The convention also endorsed a resolution for the establishment of a department of labor and the monetary system approved by Edward Kellogg; declared the *Workingman's Advocate* of Chicago and the *Arbeiter Union* of New York, national labor organs; and recognized Susan B. Anthany's *Revolution* as entitled to full support. William H. Sylvis was chosen president and A. W. Phelps, treasurer. Sylvis died the following July and his term was finished by C. H. Lucker, the first vice-president.

The convention of 1869—Richard Trevellick was elected president—

was attended by one hundred and ninety-two delegates from eighty-three organizations; it was the largest held by the National Labor Union. Representatives were present from three international unions, and the rest came from the state trade associations and state federations, local unions, and reform and mutual benefit societies. M. R. Walsh of New York Typographical Union No. 6 objected to the seating of Susan B. Anthony on the ground that the Workingwomen's Protective Association she headed was not a bona fide labor organization. A. C. Cameron and Richard Trevellick, among others, defended her seating, and O. B. Daly, president of the Machinists and Blacksmiths National Union, and Conrad Kuhn of Cigarmakers Union No. 90 supported Walsh's motion. Her credentials were rejected.

An unusual feature of the 1869 convention was the attendance of a number of Negro delegates; Robert H. Butler of Maryland thanked the convention on their behalf for the courteous reception they received. He said that they were not interested in "sociabilities, but for the rights of manhood." He deprecated the coolie trade.[39] A resolution for the organizing of colored workers of Pennsylvania was passed.

The congress of 1870 was attended by ninety-six delegates from seventy-six organizations. On the second day of the meeting a motion to grant the floor to H. S. Carry, a pro-labor Congressman, was carried. Thereupon a proposal to admit Professor J. F. Langston, a Negro lawyer and Republican officeholder, was made. It was opposed by Alexander Troup of the New York Labor Union on the ground that Professor Langston wanted to use the colored laboring men in the interests of the Republican party. After a lengthy discussion, Langston was excluded.

President Trevellick pointed to the lack of money to print the proceedings of the last congress and the poor response to the appeal for the Sylvis Fund. Although it was obvious that the organization was getting nowhere, the congress continued on the old road. Opposition to Chinese immigration was reaffirmed and legislation for its restriction endorsed. A resolution by Friedrich Sorge which approved the principles of the International Workingmen's Association [First International] was adopted.

The convention of 1871 reaffirmed the views of the earlier meetings. The executive committee had met in Washington on January 17, 1871, and organized the National Labor party. The political organization was separated from the industrial branch. A convention of the National Labor Reform party met in Columbus, Ohio, on February 21, 1872. The delegates could not agree on a policy and nothing was accomplished.

Only seven persons were present when the Industrial Congress met in Cleveland on September 16, 1872. It appointed a committee to seek the cooperation of the heads of national, state, and local unions for the forming of a national industrial congress to discuss questions of a nonpolitical character.

The National Labor Union could never have become the labor federation of the future, because its basic approach to the solution of economic problems was political. It believed that shorter hours could be best achieved through legislation, and it was suspicious of the efficiency of the strike as a weapon and means of defense. Moreover, its failure to limit membership to unions meant that reformers and reform politicians, usually the more vocal, would dominate the proceedings of its conventions and its policies. It offered little beyond friendly sentiments to the trade union local seeking support. Consequently, it could never rally the majority or even a substantial minority of organized workers. Of the more than twenty international unions which functioned through most of the time the National Labor Union was active, not more than four sent delegates to any of the conventions. The number of unions that were represented was never a large proportion of the total active. Inevitably, the National Labor Union became increasingly committed to political activity, with the ultimate result that it finally expired.

Industrial Congress and Industrial Brotherhood

Writing to President William J. Hammond of the International Typographical Union, William Saffin, president of the International Molders' Union, said: "Many of the discreet and thoughtful men in the trade union movement have canvassed the advisability of forming a national trades assembly or industrial congress, and have decided that such an association must be entirely free from political influences and composed of delegates from *bona fide* trade and labor unions."[40] Not an isolated one, this view was endorsed by the printers' union; similar views had been expressed by the coopers' organizations, which called in 1872 for "more solidarity between the several national and international organizations. . . . a combination of all the disconnected trade organizations in the country; a central medium of communication and cooperation between the several labor associations that are now isolated."[41]

The desire to form a trade union federation independent of political groups led Saffin and John Fehrenback, president of the Machinists' and Blacksmiths' International Union, M. A. Foran of the Coopers' International Union, and John Collins, secretary of the International Typographical Union, to call in 1873 for a convention of organizations built on protective principles, but including cooperative and other associations. An antipolitical sentiment crept into the call and the signers announced that as far as it was within their power the new organization would not deteriorate into a political party, "but shall to all intents and purposes remain a purely Industrial Association."

The convention met in Cleveland on July 15 with seventy delegates present, and delegates from six internationals in attendance. It drew up a twelve-point program. Arbitration was held to be a substitute for strikes, and the contract immigration law was denounced. The convention also proposed the establishment of producers' and consumers' cooperatives, the establishment of bureaus of labor statistics by the state and federal governments, laws to bear equally on capital and labor, and the "prohibition of the importation of all servile races, the discontinuance of all subsidies granted to national vessels bringing them to our shore, and the abrogation, or at least modification, of the Burlingame Treaty."[42] A plan by which unions might assist each other during strikes was suggested. The importance of national and international unions was recognized through the device of giving them three delegates, two to state and local trade assemblies, and one to all other types of labor organizations. Cooperation and financial reform were endorsed, but independent political action was not approved. In fact, the *Coopers' Journal* declared before the meeting: "We do not propose that the proposed Congress should ignore all measures looking towards political action. We are ready to admit that political action can accomplish a great deal if judiciously applied. What we want to avoid is separate independent political action."[43] Robert Schilling of the Coopers' Union was elected president and S. Keefe, a member of the Coopers' Union, secretary.

The decline in business activity and employment was an obstacle to the new organization's activity. Its pronouncements are, however, of some importance as indicators of opinion among the organized craftsmen of the time. A second meeting was held in Rochester, New York, on April 14, 1874. Three national unions were represented by delegates, and John Siney of the Miners' National Association and William Saffin of the Molders' Union were given seats. Several trades assemblies and local unions were represented, and delegates were on hand from a secret organization, the Industrial Brotherhood and the Patrons of Husbandry. A dispute between the trade unionist and the reformist points of view came to the fore during the debate on the constitution. President Schilling wanted an organization with beneficiary features and secrecy, and he did not recoil from political action or from endorsing a monetary program. Under his influence, the second convention endorsed most of the policies that were long the staple of the reform movements which periodically swept across the country. Political parties, however, were given little encouragement, and the convention decided to vote for candidates accepting its principles. Schilling was re-elected president, and after adjournment of the congress he issued an announcement that an organization similar to the Grangers had been founded and invited unions to affiliate. The trade unions, facing serious problems in surmounting the wave of unemployment which spread through the economy, were unable to provide much support.[44]

The congress met again in Indianapolis on April 13, 1875. Twenty-three delegates were present; the International Typographical Union, whose headquarters were in the convention city, was the only international represented.

The congress adopted a number of resolutions, one calling for the establishment of the eight-hour workday by July 4, 1876. This was a pattern for the resolution adopted in 1884 by the Federation of Organized Trades and Labor Unions, but it had even less practical effect. The congress failed to meet again; at least no record of its meeting is available. The views of the printers may indicate the disillusion of trade unionists with the new endeavor. The 1875 convention directed the officers to pay their financial obligations, but to discontinue membership in the Industrial Congress.[45]

CHAPTER 6

The Eruption of Violence

Rapid expansion of fixed investments, especially railroad building which for a time could not be sustained by demand, appears to have been the chief cause of the panic of 1873. Rapid settlement of the public lands increased agricultural output so that the farmers' prices were cut and many farmers could not meet their fixed charges or interest on loans. The decline of agricultural income reduced the market for farm machinery and other manufactured goods which in turn adversely affected commercial and manufacturing enterprises. A serious danger signal was the failure of the Sprague Company, a large New England textile combine.

September was a bad month with a series of business failures culminating with the closing of a major Philadelphia banking house headed by Jay Cooke. Investors heavily committed in railway expansion were in trouble, and the slowing down of railway building affected demand in the iron and steel and other manufacturing industries. The depression lasted, with occasional breaks, for six years and led to wage cuts which aroused unexpected resistance in the ranks of labor. Hard times and suspicion of the growing power of the bankers and businessmen aroused sympathy for the unemployed and the worker subjected to short time and wage cuts. Even police and guardsmen called out to restore order often showed sympathy for the mobs. Labor organization was not completely wiped out during this period.

UNION ORGANIZATION

Twenty international unions were formed during the 1870's, but only five of the twenty were established after 1875. While the depression made the survival of many labor organizations difficult, many trade unions were able to surmount the adversities they faced. The Tenth Census listed 2,440 local and 39 national unions active in 1880. Out of the total, 886 local assemblies in 31 districts were affiliated with the Knights of Labor. However, it would appear that the method used "showing the total number of local or un-attached societies and of the branches of the national societies is not more than [an] approximation. It is simply the best that could be obtained under the circumstances, and in some cases is made up from reports in news-papers and from other nonofficial sources."[1] It is obvious that the under-estimation of the number of local trades' unions would inevitably be substantial, for these organizations might in many instances be unknown outside of their community. Moreover, independent local unions rather than assemblies of the Knights of Labor would more likely be uncounted, be-cause of the formers' nonaffiliation with a regional or national organization.

The unions in 1880 were established in every state except Florida, al-though 1,705 local unions were located in seven states—Pennsylvania, Ohio, Illinois, New York, Missouri, New Jersey, and Massachusetts. Less than ten locals were reported from each of fourteen states. The strike record of 1880 also gives some indication of the magnitude of trade union activity. Joseph D. Weeks reported that 762 strikes and lockouts had taken place in 1880, but he observed that his "report can not claim to include all the strikes or lockouts that occurred. . . . There were, no doubt, a number of which the existence even was not known to me. In addition to those there were some few concerning which no facts could be learned other than that there was a strike or a lockout."[2]

The largest reported number of strikes—304—took place in Pennsyl-vania; New York had 104, and the rest of the states each had less than 100. The strikes, and the number of unions that were in existence in 1880, show that labor organizations carried on a considerable activity during the pre-ceding decade, and that unions were not unaware of the methods of joint settlement of the conditions of employment. Moreover, the strikes of 1880 affected a variety of industries. The largest number were in the iron and steel industries with 236; and each of the following industries reported more than 10: coal mining, 158; textile trades, 28; glass industries, 27; piano making, 14; and boot and shoe making, 11.[3]

The 1870's awakened the public to the seriousness of labor problems within the United States. The violent explosion on the railroads and the vio-lence charged to the Molly Maguires, an alleged secret society in the anthra-cite coal fields of Pennsylvania, brought widespread concern lest the United States become involved in the bitter class war prevalent in European coun-tries.

THE WORKINGMEN'S BENEVOLENT ASSOCIATION

The anthracite coal area, where the Mollies operated, is located mainly in Lackawanna, Luzerne, Carbon, Schuylkill, and Northumberland counties. The one hundred and seventy square mile area is divided into several fields. Use of anthracite coal began in the eighteenth century; later it was found to be usable for domestic fuel and in 1840 for smelting of iron ore. In the 1850's it replaced charcoal. Conditions at the beginning were hard, and wages were low; the miners were mainly of English, Welsh, Scottish, and Irish origin. Strikes in Schuylkill County took place in 1842 and 1844. Wages fluctuated with general economic conditions. Beginning in the 1840's the Philadelphia and Reading Railroad started carrying anthracite from Schuylkill County to Philadelphia, but until the 1850's the railroads were feeders or auxiliaries of the canal network. In the 1850's the railroads extended their power and mileage, and the Delaware and Lackawanna and Western Railroad, the Lehigh Valley Railroad, and the Pennsylvania joined the Philadelphia and Reading Railroad as coal carriers. The railroads also gained control of large areas of coal lands, aided in this endeavor by the laws enacted by the Pennsylvania legislature. Almost simultaneous with the beginning of unionization, the Philadelphia and Reading came under the domination of Franklin B. Gowen—a dynamic, resourceful, domineering, and ruthless entrepreneur. Coal mining in the anthracite became big business during the Civil War, and wages fluctuated with changes in demand and prices of coal. Partly as a consequence of such experiences, workers in the collieries of the Forestville Improvement Company organized a union in 1860, but it lasted for only four years.[4]

Several other organizations were formed, and these were united into the Workingmen's Benevolent Association through the efforts of John Siney, a pioneer organizer of coal miners in the United States. Siney was born in Ireland, one of seven children in a family of tenant farmers in 1830. His parents were evicted in 1835, and it moved to Wigan, a Lancashire manufacturing town in England, where John went to work in the coal mines at the age of seven. He became a bricklayer and joined the union of his craft. Emigrating to the United States in 1863, he worked for a short time in New York and then settled in St. Clair, Schuylkill County, Pennsylvania, where he found employment at the Eagle Colliery. He worked there until he was hired by the newly organized Workingmen's Benevolent Association. He resigned in 1873 to assume leadership of a plan to form a national union. He called the convention in Youngstown, Ohio in October 1873 which formed the National Association. He headed the organization until 1875.[5]

Siney was living in St. Clair near Pottsville, and after a strike at the colliery in which he was employed, he became convinced that permanent organization was necessary if conditions were to be ameliorated. The Workingmen's Benevolent Association was chartered on April 6, 1868, by the Court of Common Pleas of Schuylkill County by sixteen miners. On April 14 the eight-hour mining law was signed by the governor.[6]

The eight-hour law went into effect on July 1, 1868, and the operators who had organized a local association in 1867 and others the following year, insisted upon a corresponding reduction in wages. The men refused to accept a cut, and a strike spread through a large part of the area. The operators were not adverse to the walkout, since the large reserves of coal were being effectively reduced by the strike. At the end of a month, the coal piles had been sufficiently lowered to raise the price. The strike was settled by a 10 per cent wage increase. Organization spread to the entire region, and the Workingmen's Benevolent Association overnight became a powerful union. On March 11, 1869, a general council to coordinate the policies of the locals was formed at Hazelton with each anthracite county represented.

On April 29 the general council ordered a suspension for May 10, 1869. The purpose of the stoppage was to reduce the supply of coal and thereby allow the operators to raise prices, which could be used as a means for raising wages. Only the Pennsylvania Coal Company and the Delaware and Lackawanna and Western Coal Company refused to go along and its workers remained in the pits. On June 4, 1869, the Coal Association of the Schuylkill region proposed a new agreement under which wages were to be based upon the price of coal at Port Carbon and Elizabethport, the shipping points for coal mined in Schuylkill County. When coal sold for $3.00 a ton at Port Carbon and $5.00 a ton at Elizabethport, outside labor would be paid $11.00 a week; platform men, $11.50 a week; inside labor, $12.00 a week; and miners, $14.00 a week. The council asked for changes, and eventually a 5 per cent increase in wages was to be granted for every increase in the price of coal at Port Carbon. Operators in the northern anthracite districts would not accept the sliding scale or basis.

At its meeting on June 9, the association's general council declared: "That, the object of the suspension having been attained by the depletion of the surplus coal in the market, on and after June 16, all districts and branches that can agree with their employers as to basis and condition of resumption do resume work."[7]

The Anthracite Board of Trade, which had been organized in November 1869, proposed a substantial cut in wages for the following year. Rejecting the proposal, the miners struck. The operators insisted that miners' wages should slide down as well as up with prices. The offer of the operators was withdrawn and a new one made that the basis be fixed at $2.50 or that wages would not move below that level. The revised offer was also rejected, and tonnage mined fell below 20,000 tons in the third week of the walkout.

Late in July, Franklin B. Gowen, president of the Philadelphia and Reading Railway, was asked to settle the differences. He conferred with the general council and came out with the "Gowen" compromise under which the men accepted an 8.25 per cent increase in wages for every rise of 25 cents in the price of a ton of coal. In return they agreed to accept a decrease at the same rate if coal fell below $3.00 and as low as $2.00 a ton. The following year coal prices fell sharply and the miners' wages with them. John Siney tried to reopen the wage question, but the operators would have none of it.[8] However, on July 29, 1870, operators and miners signed the first written agreement in the coal industry.

On November 7, 1870, representatives of the union and operators met to arrange for 1871. Both groups were willing to continue with the old agreement if the railroad company would reduce its rates for hauling coal so that coal would be priced at Port Carbon at $2.50 a ton. In the meantime, the companies in the northern district reduced wages, and a strike started. The Schuylkill miners joined the walkout and were silently supported by the operators who were anxious to reduce the large accumulation of unsold coal. Gowen was angered by the action of the Schuylkill miners.

The operators now presented other grievances against the Workingmen's Benevolent Association. Some objected to the union's insistence that all miners join the union and companies reinstate discharged union men. The operators decided to reduce the pretensions of the union, and under the leadership of Gowen the coal-carrying roads raised the freight rates on coal to prevent operators who might wish to deal with the union from successfully shipping to their normal markets. An investigation by the legislature followed, and Gowen proposed that the issues in dispute be submitted to arbitration. Both sides agreed, and Judge William Elwell was chosen arbitrator. In his decision, Elwell ruled that colliery operators had a right to exclusive control and management of their properties, including hiring. He stated that it was against the spirit of the law for the union to refuse to work with those not members of the organization, and operators "ought not in any manner to combine against persons who belong to the Miners' and Laborers' Benevolent Association."[9] He advised that after work was resumed, provisions should be made to adjust differences before they became an impediment to continued production.

Because no settlement of the wage question could be agreed to, the operators directly appealed to the miners of Schuylkill, Northumberland, and Columbia counties to resume work on the scale of wages they proposed. The union thereupon agreed to arbitrate wages, and the offer was accepted by the operators. Judge Elwell was again chosen, and he set the basis at $2.75 at Port Carbon, and wages were to be advanced 1 cent for every 3 cents increase in the price of coal and decline 1 cent for every 3 cents decline in price. Agreements with some changes were made without incident through 1874. At the end of that year, the operators sought to reduce wages ten per cent. The union's refusal and a six-month strike ended the union in the anthracite coal fields.[10] Not for a quarter of a century would a union again function in the region.

Violence had increased as the strike went on, and when "the power of the labor union was completely broken and paralyzed, the Mollies became more desperate and crime commenced."[11]

THE MOLLY MAGUIRES

The Workingmen's Benevolent Association was a peaceful organization seeking to negotiate the terms of employment with the anthracite coal mine operators. There was violence during strikes, and even in normal periods the coal areas may have experienced more assaults and murders than other communities. The Molly Maguires, a secret organization, was said to exist in the anthracite mining area, and much of the violence against persons and property was charged to its members; arson and assault, maiming and murder were its weapons. Societies, secret and open, among Irish immigrant workers employed in constructing canals and railroads in the early decades of the nineteenth century were formed to prevent the exploiting of the defenseless immigrant by the American and Irish contractors who employed him. The "secret society," according to a student of Irish immigration, "had economic objectives: better pay, redress of grievances against unscrupulous contractors."[12]

The first formal organization of the Molly Maguires in the anthracite coal districts of Pennsylvania took place in 1843. Every Molly also belonged to the Ancient Order of Hibernians, a benevolent society operating in the United States and England whose leaders had no connection with the activities of the Mollies. Under the rules of the Molly Maguires, any member might make a formal complaint to the bodymaster—the local head. If it were decided that action against a person was required, members from a distant community would be obtained to assault or kill the offender.[13]

The first crime attributed to the Mollies was the fatal beating of a mine boss by a gang of men during a celebration on July 4, 1862. The following December, two hundred armed men visited the colliery of William Coyne, assaulted several employees and fired a few shots, and departed without taking any property.

In the following years, murders, shootings, and assaults in the anthracite area were attributed to the Mollies.[14] Gowen took the lead in ending the reign of terror. In October 1873 he met Allan Pinkerton, the head of the best-known private detective agency in the United States, and asked his aid in exposing the secret society and its agents. James McParlan, an Irish immigrant and an employee of the Pinkerton Detective Agency, was assigned to the task. Under the name of James McKenna he entered the coal fields, describing himself as an unemployed gold miner from Colorado.[15]

McParlan was born in Ulster, Ireland, in 1844. After working in a chemical plant in Belfast, he came to the United States in 1867. At first he was employed in a dry goods store in New York, and became a private policeman in 1868. He joined the Pinkerton Detective Agency in 1871. He arrived at Port Carbon in October 1873. McParlan was a natural for the job. Physically courageous, a raconteur and a "cold soak," one who could consume large amounts of alcohol and remain sober, he was also a good singer of Irish ballads. Passing himself off as a fugitive from justice, he was, after considerable effort and danger, able to penetrate the wall of secrecy and learn the name of the terrorists.

McParlan reported daily to the superintendent of the Philadelphia agency, Benjamin Franklin. Naturally, the Mollies were suspicious, but McParlan was able to convince them that he was a genuine fugitive and ready to participate in any crimes for which he was delegated. He was initiated into the Ancient Order of Hibernians at the home of Michael Lawler on April 14, 1874, and was present when a number of murders were planned. In fact, McParlan was aware of the plan to kill Thomas Sanger, but was unable to notify the authorities in advance.[16]

According to a "strictly confidential" circular issued by a "vigilance committee," the Mollies were guilty of a number of murders during 1875 beginning with the killing of William (Bully Bill) Thomas on June 28. The names of the victims as well as those of the killers and their addresses were given. The latter were also identified as Mollies.

As a result, a "crowd of masked men . . . entered Mrs. O'Donnell's house at Wiggan Patch and . . . killed James O'Donnell alias Friday, Charles O'Donnell, James MacAlister and also Mrs. MacAlister whom they took out of the house and shot."[17] McParlan, who reported the shooting, was indignant at the assault upon a woman and offered to resign.

The killing of John P. Jones, a foreman for the Lehigh and Wilkes-Barre Coal Company, led to the first break in the wall of silence which had surrounded the deeds of the Mollies. According to plan, Jones was murdered at the railroad station in Lansford, and two gunmen, Edward Kelley and Michael Doyle, were later arrested. The murder was directed by James Kerrigan, who was hidden from view; after he was arrested, he confessed and turned state's evidence.

Michael Doyle was brought to trial at Mauch Chunk on January 18, 1876. Each side was represented by a battery of eminent lawyers. On February 1, 1876, the jury brought in its verdict of guilty. Soon thereafter, seven persons were arrested for various murders committed over the years, and almost simultaneously it became known that Kerrigan was assisting the prosecution by providing evidence. The conviction and arrests, accompanied by reports of betrayal, led to suspicion that McParlan was a detective supplying evidence against the accused, but he was nevertheless, able to maintain his pose. The other defendant in the Jones murder, Edward Kelley, was brought to trial, and Kerrigan's confession along with the identification of witnesses was sufficient for a conviction. Kerrigan charged that the murders and other acts of violence were done at the direction of the Ancient Order of Hibernians. The twenty-four-year-old Kelley was convicted.

The Mauch Chunk trials created remarkable interest in the Mollies and the Ancient Order of Hibernians. The next act in the drama took place in the Pottsville courthouse on May 4, 1876. James Carroll, James Boyle, Hugh McGehan, and James Roarity were brought to trial. A fifth defendant, James Duffy, was allowed a severance; he was also convicted. McParlan now revealed his true name and office and implicated the Ancient Order of Hibernians as the source of the evil infecting the anthracite area. The four were convicted. In the meantime, Alexander Campbell, a leader of the Ancient Order of Hibernians and a saloon keeper, and Thomas Munley were convicted of two murders. Altogether nineteen Mollies paid with their lives; others were convicted for perjury and for being accessories before the fact and sentenced to jail.[18]

The convictions were appealed, but the higher court found no reversible error. On June 21, 1877, several who had been convicted of first degree murder suffered the ultimate penalty. In the Pottsville prison, "Father Daniel McDermott . . . said mass and prayed with the men until their time. . . . At 10:54 a little doorway at the rear of the yard opened, and the sheriff and the prison officials appeared."[19] Six were hanged in Pottsville and another four in Mauch Chunk. Nine others were to hang before the course of bloody vengeance had run itself out; the last Mollie paid with his life on January 16, 1879.

The Molly Maguires had become a popular legend and particularly a labor legend. There is no question that there were criminal elements among the Ancient Order of Hibernians, but the murders committed had no relation to labor difficulties or labor organizations. It may be true that some of the assaults and murders of mine officials were in revenge for harshness and a reaction of men who felt themselves persecuted. Perhaps if a union were allowed to function openly, the grievances would have been redressed and the harshness mitigated. It is, however, unlikely that violence would have completely subsided as labor dissatisfaction appears to have been only a contributing cause. Violence was endemic to the coal fields of the time, and in some instances members of the Molly Maguires were themselves its victims. Hatred between ethnic groups nourished by diverse national origin and religious affiliation were also causes, and robbery and personal vengeance were occasional motives. The Molly Maguires was not a labor organization, nor a forerunner of one, but its members did, at times, seek to punish the harsh and overbearing supervisor and protect its own members from oppression. In hunting down malefactors, it appears the government was not always careful of the innocent and the punishment of some appears to have been too severe.[20]

THE STRIKES OF 1877

The Molly Maguires were active in a small corner of Pennsylvania, but the upheaval of 1877 was a danger signal that serious tensions and dangers existed in other sectors of American industry. It started with a strike which broke out on July 16, 1877, when more than forty firemen and brakemen in the freight division of the Baltimore and Ohio Railroad in Baltimore refused to accept a wage cut, and spread through the country to the Pacific Coast. Before the strike ended, millions of dollars in property had been destroyed and more than one hundred, it is estimated, were dead.[21]

The wage reduction came after four years of depression. Wages had been cut on the Boston and Maine Railroad early in 1876, and the Brotherhood of Locomotive Engineers, seeking to recoup part of the wage loss in January 1877, asked for an increase of ten cents a day. The road refused and was able to replace the engineers who struck to enforce the demand.

In March 1877 the brotherhood sought a 20 per cent increase on the Philadelphia and Reading Railroad, but it did not threaten a strike if its request were rejected. The railroad, on the other hand, ordered the engineers to resign from the union or leave their jobs. Unable to find a compromise, and its existence on the Philadelphia and Reading in danger, the brotherhood called a strike in April 1877. It was fighting a losing battle. Franklin Gowen, who had undermined the Workingmen's Benevolent Association and pursued the Molly Maguires, carried off the victory. The Pennsylvania Railroad Company and the Lackawanna Valley Railroad followed the example of the other roads and cut wages. Recognizing the failures of the other roads, the employees reluctantly acquiesed.[22]

The Strike on the Baltimore and Ohio

The workers on the Baltimore and Ohio were of a different disposition. On July 16, the day the wage reduction was to become effective, "the fireman on Engine 32 deserted his train . . . and other firemen soon joined him. While company agents quickly hired replacements, the strikers remained nearby to persuade their comrades to leave the trains idle."[23] Police rushed to the scene and made arrests, but uncertain of their position they deferred the trials of the accused. Meanwhile the company reaffirmed the order for a wage cut and assured the governor of Maryland that no troops were needed to preserve order. Trains moved out of the city, but in Martinsburg, West Virginia, an important division point, they encountered trouble. Firemen left their engines, and Vice-President John King, in charge of operations, immediately called on Governor Henry Mathews for troops, although at the time no violence had been directed against railroad property.[24]

Governor Mathews dispatched Colonel C. J. Faulkner and the Berkeley Light Infantry Guards to the scene. Upon his arrival, Faulkner attempted to move a westbound freight train, and this led to the killing of a striker who attempted to halt the movement, the wounding of a militiaman guarding the right of way, and the desertion of the engine crew. Faulkner thereupon announced that he had done his duty and withdrew his men to the armory.

At the demand of the officers of the Baltimore and Ohio Railroad, Governor Mathews wired President Rutherford B. Hayes, requesting federal troops "to protect the law-abiding people of the State against domestic violence, and to maintain supremacy of the law."[25] Secretary of War George McCrary immediately replied that the "President is averse to intervention unless it is clearly shown that the State is unable to suppress the insurrection. Please furnish a statement of facts. What force can the State raise?" Mathews replied that the two companies of troops sent to Martinsburg were "in sympathy with the rioters, who are believed to be 800 strong."[26] The governor added that he had few troops to handle the riot. Thereupon, Secretary McCrary, in accordance with the President's direction, ordered General William French with four hundred soldiers to proceed to Martinsburg and report to Governor Mathews' aide, Colonel Delaplaine. Before federal troops had arrived, Delaplaine had asked for additional soldiers and for two pieces of artillery. After General French and his troops arrived, the request was withdrawn on July 19.

In the meantime, the conduct of the federal commander at Martinsburg did not please the officers of the Baltimore and Ohio Railroad. Charging General French with being drunk, the railroad officials insisted upon controlling the movement of trains and refused to provide the general with transportation to trouble spots. Exasperated by the treatment accorded him by the railroad officials, French criticized "the insolence of railroad officials, not only to myself, but to my subordinates. If I cannot act independent of them in the delicate duties which have heretofore been performed by me with satisfaction to the War Department, and without shedding the blood of employees of the Baltimore and Ohio Railroad, it would be preferable to have another officer who would be less objectionable to that corporation."[27] General Getty displaced the officer who was unsympathetic to the use of strong measures against the strikers, posted his troops at prominent places on the line, and succeeded in restoring order and the movement of traffic. By the end of July trains were running from Baltimore to the Ohio River.

Trouble in Pittsburgh

In contrast to the strikes in Maryland and West Virginia, the disturbance in Pittsburgh was not occasioned by a wage cut. In fact, little protest was made when the Pennsylvania Railway Company instituted a 10 per cent reduction on June 1, 1877. However, the attempt of the company to introduce "double headers" on July 19 was deeply resented. Under this system, the length of trains was to be doubled, with a front engine pulling, and one at the rear pushing the train. Moreover, the run was increased from 48 to 116 miles. Road crews refused to obey the orders for the changes, and a yard crew was given the assignment. This crew also refused to obey on the ground that it had been hired for yard duty. When an attempt was made to move the train by a newly recruited crew, it was attacked by pickets. Gradually other trainmen were convinced or compelled to leave their jobs so that not a single train was moving in the area around Pittsburgh the night of July 19.[28]

Pickets would not allow the trains to move. Sheriff R. C. Fife of Allegheny County wired Governor Hartranft that "large assemblages of people . . . upon the railroad, and the movement of freight trains either east or west is prevented by intimidation and violence."[29]

As it was believed that the number of local National Guardsmen was insufficient to handle the mounting threats, the First Division of the Pennsylvania National Guard was ordered to Pittsburgh from Philadelphia. Six hundred men and two Gatling guns arrived in Pittsburgh on the afternoon of July 21. At 3 P.M. the sheriff, accompanied by several brigades of guardsmen, attempted to arrest the leaders. A scuffle led to the wounding of a striker by a bayonet thrust, and the crowd started pelting the soldiers with stones and lumps of coal. When firing started, Pittsburgh troops threw down their arms and joined the strikers. However, the Philadelphia troops held the field until six in the evening, when they were ordered by General Pearson to retreat to the railroad roundhouse.

By 8 P.M. mobs were moving through the streets sacking stores to secure arms. Shut up in the roundhouse, the guardsmen were surrounded by a large crowd that called upon them to surrender. A gun brought up by the rioters and loaded with couplings and broken rails steadily pelted the roundhouse, but the guardsmen held out and marched out only when the pickets had pushed burning oil cars against the building. The retreating troops were fired upon as they moved through the streets, and several fell from revolver and rifle shots.

On Sunday, July 22, thousands of pickets, idlers, and troops were burning freight cars or removing their contents for their own use. A citizens' committee was formed on July 23 to prevent the burning and looting which threatened to reduce the city to ashes.[30] By Monday, July 23, order had been restored in Pittsburgh, but by this time the strike had spread through the entire Pennsylvania Railroad system. The company discontinued all trains.

Violence in Other Parts of Pennsylvania

Governor Hartranft appealed to President Hayes for assistance. In a proclamation, the President called on the mob to disperse and ordered General W. S. Hancock to proceed to Pittsburgh with as many troops as could be spared from Baltimore. Strikers blocked the road at Altoona and refused to allow National Guardsmen to proceed to Pittsburgh. In Harrisburg, on July 23, strikers compelled engineers and firemen to leave their cabs, and the trains ceased to move. Firemen and brakemen also struck in Philadelphia, but the police were prepared and no violence followed. The governor set up headquarters in Philadelphia, assembled troops and set out for Western Pennsylvania, followed by several hundred regular army troops equipped with artillery.

Rioting involving the Philadelphia and Reading started on July 22 with the destruction of considerable amounts of railroad property. Late in the afternoon a regiment of National Guardsmen arrived from Allentown. Taunted by pickets, they emptied their rifles into the crowd, killing ten and wounding forty bystanders and participants. Another regiment of guardsmen arrived and having heard of the killing expressed their indignation at the action of the Allentown troops. Both regiments were asked to leave Reading.[31] In their place, 3,330 regular troops arrived on July 24. Violence then subsided. On August 31 the coroner's jury reported that ten persons has been killed by soldiers and attributed the tragedy to the lawless body.[32]

From Reading the strike spread to the Pennsylvania mining regions. In the Schuylkill district, incipient trouble on July 24 was suppressed. On the following day trainmen on the Lehigh Valley Railroad began a strike and stopped all trains. All traffic was suspended until the end of July. On the last day of the month the company announced that the strikers had left their jobs and would be replaced. In Scranton, the employees of the Lackawanna Iron and Coal Company joined the strike on July 24, tying up the rolling mills, foundry, and steel works. At first the strikers refused to allow the manning of the pumps to prevent flooding, but retreated from their positions in time to prevent serious damage to the mine properties. A clash between pickets and a posse that had been recruited by the mayor of Scranton resulted in the killing of four men and the wounding of several others. Aid was sought from the governor while armed citizens patrolled the city streets. A force of 1,800 men was dispatched and was followed by 2,000 additional troops. The first contingent reached Scranton on August 1. Strong feeling was expressed against what many regarded as needless shooting by the posse, and the coroner's jury returned a verdict of "wilful murder" against several of its members. They were arrested, but before they could be arraigned, they were released by the military.

Strikes in New York

In New York a walkout of firemen and brakemen started on July 19 on the Hornellsville division of the Erie Railroad, where the trains were stopped. Immediately the operating officers of the railroad requested protection from Governor Lucius Robinson. On July 22 the governor in a proclamation demanded an end of interference with train operation. By the evening of July 21 the troops arrived but the strikers, under the leadership of Bernard J. Donahue, were able for a time to prevent the resumption of traffic. The strikers were willing to compromise their demands, but the receiver would neither make the slightest concession nor agree to the rehiring of the committee of strikers who had been dismissed. From Hornellsville, trouble spread to other parts of New York state, and clashes between strikers and their sympathizers and strikebreakers and soldiers took place in Buffalo, Elmira, and Corning.

On July 26 a committee of the strikers and officers of the Erie Railroad reached an agreement under which the discharge of the committee presenting the original demands would be reconsidered, gang bosses would be prohibited from levying a tax of 3 per cent on the wages of the men they directed, and the company would not actively prosecute the leader of the strike, Bernard Donahue, although it would not promise he would be released. He was later sentenced to thirty days in jail for defying an officer of the court—the receiver of the railroad.[33]

On July 23 employees of the New York Central and Hudson River Railroad went out on strike when their demands for a wage increase were refused. President William H. Vanderbilt of the railroad appealed to the men to remain on the job and assured them he would confer with their committee after the excitement had subsided.[34] Railroad shops were compelled to close, and trains were forced to cease running. There was, however, virtually no destruction of property. Troops were ordered to Albany and started traffic moving. By July 26, the strike at Albany had ended. On August 1, President Vanderbilt in a letter to his employees commended their loyalty and orderliness. In recognition of their conduct, Vanderbilt directed that $100,000 be divided among all employees, except executive and departmental officers and the clerical force not directly engaged in operating the road.[35]

On the Long Shore Railroad, a part of the New York Central system, between Buffalo and Toledo, a strike started on July 22, and President Vanderbilt ordered all trains stopped. By July 26 all trains were again moving, and all interference had been stopped.

Events in New York City

While no walkout took place in New York City, the events transpiring elsewhere in the country aroused interest, hope, and fear among many. Fear was sufficiently great for the government to order several regiments of National Guardsmen to remain on the alert. The plans of trade unions to hold a meeting at Tompkins Square to express their sympathy with the striking railroad men aroused what proved to be needless concern. John Swinton, an editor of the New York *Sun* and a student of labor problems, criticized the wage cuts and brutal suppression of the strikers. Resolutions were adopted advising the workers of the country to unite in a political party that would bring about a revolution which would confiscate the ill-gotten wealth of "chartered corporation thieves."[36]

Strikes in the Middle West

In Ohio brakemen and firemen joined the strike of their fellow-workers on the Baltimore and Ohio. On July 18 a strike started in Newark, and four days later employees of the Pan Handle Railroad followed. Trains were stopped against the orders of the sheriff, and Governor Thomas L. Young sent troops to keep the roads open. In the meantime, the strike spread to Columbus, the capital of the state. Workers in a number of steel mills and factories joined the walkout. Other railroad centers in Ohio were also affected. In Cleveland employees on the Michigan and Lake Shore Division of the New York Central Railroad demanded a 20 per cent increase in wages and a promise that those on strike would suffer no discrimination. The demands were rejected, and on July 24 the general superintendent asked that, in accordance with the request of William H. Vanderbilt, all trains be kept running, and as "soon as the excitement is allayed, conferences will be invited with the employees respecting the rates of wages."[37] By the end of July the strike had ended, and the superintendent agreed to correct some local abuses and grant passes to employees.

Trainmen joined the strike on July 21 at Fort Wayne, Indiana. Both the Pittsburgh, Fort Wayne, and Chicago and the Wabash railroads were involved. Demonstrators visited the roundhouses and shops, and workers were compelled to leave their jobs. On July 24 the strike was extended to several industrial establishments. Officers of the Pittsburgh, Fort Wayne, and Chicago Railroad decided not to suspend temporarily the movement of trains, and appealed to the governors of the several states in which the road crossed for protection. On August 2, troops were sent into Fort Wayne and on the pledge that strikers would not suffer discrimination, the men returned to work.[38]

Chicago suffered a more serious outbreak. On July 24 the employees of the Michigan Central Railroad demanded the restoration of a wage cut made earlier in the year. Their demand rejected, the men went on strike. Switchmen employed by the Illinois Central Railroad also requested a restoration of a wage cut and walked off the job when the request was refused. The reduction was not restored. Action to spread the walkout to other roads in Chicago began. At the same time, crowds of pickets began visiting manufacturing plants and either by force or persuasion induced other workers to stop work. In a proclamation on July 24, Mayor M. Heath called on all citizens to maintain order and directed the closing of all liquor stores. Governor Shelby M. Cullom joined in the appeal for peace and cited the untoward action of mobs in other states as a warning against violence. Ignoring these pleas, the crowds clashed with the police, some of the rioters were killed and many others wounded.

On July 25 a strong detachment of regular soldiers arrived in Chicago from the west, and they were reinforced by additional units the following day. Several of the crowd, it was reported, had been killed by police clubbing and gun fire. Order was restored with the arrest of rioters and their leaders. A number of downstate communities experienced some tension, but no outbreaks took place. Trains were started on July 27 under the protection of troops. Governor Cullom, on the same day, called on police officers in the state to prevent interference with the train movement.[39]

St. Louis

The discontent which had seized the railroad men of the country also came to the surface in St. Louis in a meeting on July 22, when a demand for a wage increase was refused. Employees on the Toledo and Wabash Railroad whose wages had not been reduced earlier that year went out in sympathy. On July 24 the strikers extended their walkout to passenger trains which, in the first two days, had been allowed to run unmolested. The strike did not affect the Missouri, Pacific, and St. Louis, Kansas City and northern roads. Troops arrived from the western part of the United States, although there was no sign of trouble.

On July 25 the mayor warned against interference with private property, and announced that a committee of safety had been formed with General A. J. Smith, Judge Thomas T. Gantt, and General S. Marmaduke as members; subcommittees were established in various parts of the city. A crowd of 2,000 marched through the industrial district and demanded that manufacturing establishments close and that their employees join their ranks. There was no trouble, but the mayor ordered all crowds to disperse. By July 27 the union depot was reoccupied, and the strikers were ousted. The police authorities announced that armed guards would be furnished to industrial plants. The railroads resumed operations on July 28 and by the end of the month, Governor Cullom of Illinois arrived in East St. Louis with six companies of National Guardsmen and ordered strikers to cease interfering with train movements. The walkout ended at this point.[40]

The strikes and riots of 1877 awakened the country to the danger of allowing relations between labor and management to deteriorate. The nationwide demonstrations brought the first intervention of the federal government in labor disputes. When first made, the requests for federal troops occasioned surprise among those who were critical of the use of federal troops to impose the will of the central government upon the southern states. The widespread riots shattered the belief that the United States would escape the tensions and conflicts between labor and capital which had been shaking the governments of Europe. Moreover, the worst disturbances were not generally in areas of large concentrations of foreign workers; they were carried on by native Americans. The first federal investigation of labor problems was influenced by the desire to discover the causes and cures for a deep sickness affecting American society.

CHAPTER 7

The Knights of Labor

The return of prosperity in the 1880's had a favorable influence upon organized labor. Sixty-two international unions were established between 1880 and 1889. Many did not survive, but in 1889 there were seventy-nine international unions active, some of which had been established in the 1850's. Carpenters, plumbers, glass workers, seamen, boilermakers, plasterers, miners, bakers, musicians, telegraphers, patternmakers and shoemakers were a few who set up international unions in their trades and callings. Organized labor was also active on another front, the establishment of labor federations. The 1880's witnessed the rise of the Knights of Labor, the beginning of the Federation of Organized Trade and Labor Unions of the United States and Canada, and finally, the emergence of the American Federation of Labor. For many organizations it was a testing time which was to determine whether the union had the stamina and loyalty of workers in its trade or calling to enable it to survive internal dissension and employer opposition.

THE KNIGHTS OF LABOR

For a short time it appeared that the Knights of Labor was destined to consolidate the scattered labor groups. In 1862 a group of Philadelphia garment cutters organized themselves to prevent a wage reduction; they announced they were entitled to a fair day's pay for their labor. Having served its original purpose, it became a beneficial society. To avoid dissolution because of lack of interest, its members decided to reorganize. On December 9, 1869, the association was dissolved; December 28, on the motion of James L. Wright, this society became Assembly No. 1 of the Noble Order of the Knights of Labor.[1] In addition to Wright, six others were present. At the next meeting, Uriah S. Stephens (1821–1822) was elected Master Workman, the highest office in the Order. He was born in Cape May, New Jersey, where he learned the tailoring trade. He also taught school and traveled in Central and South America. Stephens ran for Congress on the Greenback-Labor ticket in 1878, and temporarily retired from his office as Grand Master Workman. Again elected in 1879, he withdrew permanently from the office later that year. Stephens was a strong believer in secrecy, advocated a broad union of all labor, the skilled and unskilled, and the achieving of the cooperative commonwealth through education. His differences with the majority over secrecy led to his withdrawal from the Order in 1881.

The affairs of the assembly, as the local organization was called, ran along without incident. By October 1, it decided "to initiate good men of all callings, and to allow them the benefits of association on the same footing with the garment cutters, except in deciding trade matters. Sojourners were not required to pay any dues until such time as enough of their own calling had been initiated to form a separate Assembly. The sojourner was admitted that he might become a missionary among his fellow-tradesmen; he was to be an instructor and an organizer."[2] This was an important step for, despite its secret ritual, the Knights of Labor was initially only a craft union. By accepting a member from another trade or a sojourner, as he was called, the Order, in Powderly's opinion, became "something in advance and differing from, the exclusive trade union."[3] Before that time the "principles of cooperation and assistance were to be confined to a few who could pass examination as first class workmen."[4]

Cooperation was the fundamental principle upon which the organization was based. It was not

a co-operation of men for the mere purpose of enhancing the value of their combined contributions to any productive enterprise alone, but a co-operation of the various callings and crafts by which men earned the right to remain upon the earth's surface as contributors to the public good. The barriers of trade were to be cast aside; the man who toiled, no matter at what, was to receive and enjoy the just fruits of his labor and exercise of his art whether as a skilled artisan or of the humblest toilers of the earth. Such is but an epitome of the aims and objects of the new Order which had its real beginning when the Garmentcutters' Association voted to admit men of all callings. The old society admitted to membership none but garment cutters, but a radical change was made in the direction by the new one. It recognized the right of all toilers to combine, and, having admitted that they should do so, it was considered best for all that all should be associated in one fold, wherein the actions of all craftsmen would be known to each other and thus avoid the errors of the purely trade society.[5]

In a letter, Stephens said that the purpose of the Order was to "elevate man."[6]

As the Knights of Labor grew in size, the belief that the trade unions were not the most effective vehicle for solving many of labor's problems spread among the ranks. Powderly questioned whether unions had a right to impose hardships upon workers who might be indirectly affected by a walk-out, but who were not given a voice in the decision to strike. An even more important objection, in Powderly's view, was the trade union neglect of the unskilled, "common everyday laborer." Unions failed "to grapple and satisfactorily deal with the labor question on its broad, far-reaching basic principle; the right of all to have a say in the affairs of one.[7]

But the Order was not sympathetic to socialism. Stephens warned: "You must not allow the Socialists to get control of your Assembly. They are simply disturbers, and only gain entrance to labor Societies that they may be in a better position to break them up. . . . If the Socialists ever get control they will kill the work of years."[8]

The Order made slow progress, and it was not until July 18, 1872, that Assembly No. 2 was organized. It was made up of ship carpenters and caulkers from Philadelphia and the surrounding area. The practice was to initiate sojourners in Assembly No. 1, and when a sufficient number of one craft were recruited, to establish a new assembly of their own trade or calling. However, as Powderly explained, the "organization of new Assemblies did not prevent the workers of No. 1 from initiating persons whose crafts were organized. When a member of No. 1 discovered a man who would make a good member, he proposed his name in No. 1, had him initiated and then gave him a card with which to gain admittance to the Assembly of his craft."[9] This practice described by Powderly was to be the principal cause of the difficulties which later arose between the Order and the trade unions.

Local assemblies were the basic unit in the Order. They were made up of workers in single crafts—trade assemblies—or of several trades and callings and even employers—mixed assemblies. Five local assemblies could form a district assembly, whose limits were not clearly defined, nor was it ever specifically determined how much territory a district could cover. Locals had the right to determine whether they wished to send delegates to a district.[10]

The first District Assembly No. 1 was established in Philadelphia on Christmas Day 1873. District No. 2 was established in Reading, Pennsylvania, soon afterward, and in August 1875, District No. 3 was founded in Pittsburgh. The expansion into western Pennsylvania represented a breakthrough, and the Order spread in all directions.[11]

The growth of the Knights of Labor in 1872 and 1873, made the need for the establishment of uniform rules to govern the local and district assemblies imperative. It was tacitly recognized that District No. 1 was the supreme group in the Order. However, the authority of this unit was increasingly challenged. Halting steps for a national organization were made, and some assemblies were especially anxious to have secrecy abolished. After an exchange of views, District Assembly No. 1 called for a convention at Philadelphia for July 3, 1876.

Thirty-five delegates were present when the meeting was opened by James L. Wright of District No. 1. The convention declared itself the executive head of the Knights of Labor and resolved "that no one should be admitted in the Order except he be a man of good moral character, sober and industrious, and thoroughly understanding of the trade which he follows."[12] District Assembly No. 3 of Pittsburgh disapproved of the Philadelphia meeting, and it was in its area where the sentiment for making public the name and activities of the Order predominated. The Philadelphia meeting had failed to act on secrecy. The meeting of the Pittsburgh district agreed that a member of the Order could make his name and activity known to his confessor if he were a communicant of the Roman Catholic church. To overcome the conflict between the two factions, a convention was called in a "neutral city," Reading, on January 1, 1878. The purpose was to form a central assembly, create a "resistance fund," a statistical service and "provide revenue for the work of organization." Thirty-two delegates appeared. The convention was named the General Assembly of the Knights of Labor of North America. Uriah Stephens was elected head of the Order, Grand Master Workman; and the constitution "of the Industrial Brotherhood as far as practicable" was adopted.[13] A fifteen-point program was announced. The first matter was "To bring within the folds of organization every department of productive industry, making knowledge a standpoint for action, and industrial and moral worth, not wealth, the true standard of individual and national greatness."[14]

The Order also sought to secure labor "a proper share of wealth that they create; more of leisure that belongs to them; more societary advantages; more of the benefits, privileges and emoluments of the world." Another point called for the establishment of producers' and consumers' cooperatives, the reserving of the public domain to actual settlers, abrogation of all laws which do not bear equally upon capital and labor, compelling corporations to pay their employees weekly in lawful money, a mechanics' lien law, abolition of the contract system on all government work, substitution of arbitration for strikes, prohibiting the employment of children under fourteen years of age in factories, abolition of the contract system of employing prison labor, equal pay for equal work regardless of sex, the reduction of the hours of labor to eight per day, and the establishment of "a purely national circulating medium, based upon the faith and resources of the nation, and issued directly to the people, without the intervention of any system of banking corporations, which money shall be legal tender in payment of all debts, public and private."[15]

The program of the Knights is one which any labor leader of the time could have accepted without the slightest hesitancy. There was nothing radical in the views or pronouncements of the Order. It used the shibboleths and the anti-monopoly language of the time. As Powderly readily admitted, the "preamble" to the constitution was taken almost entirely from the Industrial Brotherhood.[16]

Secrecy and the Roman Catholic Church

Secrecy was a problem facing the Knights of Labor. Membership had spread through western Pennsylvania, and many communicants of the Roman Catholic faith had joined. Some members of the clergy expressed fear that the Knights of Labor was a secret, oath-bound revolutionary organization. Powderly urged the second convention to grant the district assemblies authority to make the name of the Order public, if such a step were approved by the affiliated local assemblies.[17] The New York convention in 1882 had voted to make the name of the Order public by January 1882, but secrecy continued for some purposes. The American hierarchy was not of one opinion on the attitude to be taken toward the Order. In the end, the view of James Cardinal Gibbons that the Knights of Labor was a labor and not a secret revolutionary society prevailed. In August 1888, Cardinal Gibbons announced that "the Society of the Knights of Labor may be allowed for the time being, provided whatever in its statutes is improperly expressed or susceptible of wrong interpretation shall be corrected. Especially in the preamble of the constitution for local assemblies which seem to savor of socialism and communism must be emended in such a way to make clear that the soil was granted by God to man, or rather the human race, that each one might have the right to acquire some portion of it, by use however of lawful means and without violation of the right of private property."[18] The decision was a victory for the more liberal elements of the church in the United States who opposed condemnation because it would injure an organization of labor, and who also feared that such a step might alienate thousands of loyal members who worked in industry and were influenced by the Knights of Labor. The churchmen whose views were expressed by Cardinal Gibbons were able to prevent a banning of the Order, which was a reversal of the step taken in Canada in 1884 at the request of Archbishop Elzear Taschereau of Quebec.[19]

Second Convention

The Knights of Labor did not make spectacular progress. Its second convention was attended by only twenty-nine delegates. A resistance fund was established which Stephens believed would compel settlement of labor disputes.[20] Like the trade union leaders of the time, he was sure that a large defense fund would lead to the abolition of strikes,[21] however, it was to become a serious point of dispute, for the leaders were not certain for what purposes these monies were to be used.

At the same time, Stephens invited all trade unions to affiliate "with our great brotherhood," so as to eliminate "the weakness and evils of isolated effort or association, and useless and crushing competition resulting therefrom."[22] From the beginning of its history the Knights of Labor advocated a moderate program. It opposed the exclusiveness of the craft unions, and sought to recruit members from all classes and was friendlier towards the unskilled, women, and racial minorities than the trade unions. The brotherhood sought to make the cause of one the common cause of all. The Knights of Labor was not, however, clear on how to proceed in achieving its laudable objectives. There was always a strong element that was favorable to the use of trade union tactics and wanted to encourage their entrance into the Order. The second convention approved a resolution by C. C. Burnett of Pittsburgh District Assembly No. 3, "That trades organized as trades may select an executive officer of their own, who may have charge of their organization, and organize Local Assemblies of the trade in any part of the country, and attach them to the District Assembly controlling said trade, providing all the expense attached to said office shall be paid by said trade."[23]

Cooperation, both producers' and consumers', was a basic principle of the Knights of Labor. At the General Assembly in 1881, A. M. Owens, chosen treasurer that year, proposed that a cooperative fund be established. After July 1, 1882, every male member was to pay ten cents a month into a local fund which was to be used solely for promoting cooperative enterprises. The next year a cooperative board was elected. Not much was accomplished by this board, and another replaced it.[24]

According to Secretary Robert D. Layton, the principal cooperative enterprises operated by units of the Order were "grocery or dry goods stores and country stores." Layton explained that in 1883 there were a number of assemblies building their own lodges with a view to starting a cooperative store. The Knights also operated a pottery at East Liverpool, Ohio, and a coal mine at Cannelburg, Indiana. These enterprises were seldom successful.[25]

Strikes

Stephens was again elected Grand Master Workman at the Second General Assembly, but he did not finish his term. He suggested as his successor either Terence V. Powderly or Richard Griffiths. The convention elected Powderly, a machinist by trade and a politician by instinct.

Terence Vincent Powderly (1849–1924) was born in Carbondale,

Pennsylvania, and attended school until he was thirteen years of age. He then worked as a brakeman, became an apprentice machinist and a journeyman at the age of twenty. He moved to Scranton and joined the Machinists' and Blacksmiths' International Union and, in 1874, the Knights of Labor. His most important achievement as head of the Order was his negotiations with James Cardinal Gibbons over the secrecy oath. He was elected mayor of Scranton in 1878, and served three terms, refusing to be a candidate in 1884. Powderly's principal interests were temperance, land reform, and cooperation. He opposed trade unions, and believed the strike an ineffectual and harmful weapon. He refused to join in the campaign for the eight-hour workday, and would not support the petition for clemency for the Chicago anarchists. After his departure from office in 1893, he studied law, and was active in behalf of the election of William McKinley for President. He was appointed to the U.S. Department of Commerce, and later to the Bureau of Immigration and Naturalization.

The first general assembly voted that a resistance fund be raised by a tax of five cents on each member per month, and that the amount be allowed to accumulate for two years in the local assemblies before it was used. A suggestion that the money accumulated in the resistance fund be used for cooperation and to support strikes was rejected.[26]

Powderly hoped the organization would "embark in a system . . . which will eventually make every man his own master—every man his own employer, a system which will give the laborer a fair proportion of the products of his toil. It is to cooperation, then as the lever of labor's emancipation that the eyes of the workingmen and women are directed, upon cooperation their hopes are centered. . . . There is no good reason why labor cannot, through cooperation, own and operate mines, factories and railroads."[27]

But Powderly's views were not approved by all in the Order.[28] The strike issue was a constant source of discussion within the Order. Trade unions in the Order were following their method of redressing grievances. According to Secretary Charles H. Litchman, the "Officers of the General Assembly have been much embarrassed by the question of strikes. The Constitution being silent upon this matter no authority is given to the Grand Officers. In one or two instances where the need seemed pressing appeals for contributions have been issued. When these appeals appeared they acted seemingly as incentive to every Local and District to go upon a strike and to demand that the Grand Officers should issue appeals in their power. Some of these demands were couched in very offensive language, the writers seeming to think that the General Officers held some magic wand by the touch of which money could be made to flow freely down the hill-side in an inexhaustible stream."[29]

Litchman's statement shows that the activity of the Knights of Labor was also limited by the financial resources made available. The general officers could not draw on the finances of the local or district assemblies, and the Knights of Labor could not always provide assistance to its needy affiliates. The executive board recommended in 1880 that some provision be made to support strikes under certain conditions. It was finally agreed that, in the event of failure to settle a difference between labor and management through negotiations and arbitration, a strike would be supported financially. Each local assembly was to establish an arbitration board to seek settlements of differences between members and their employer. If arbitration failed, the district assembly would intervene and seek a settlement. The next step would be to call for the appointment of one representative from each of the two adjacent districts, and with a third member from the district assembly in which the dispute arose, a final attempt at an agreement would be made. If this effort failed, a report was to be submitted to the executive board which in conjunction with the general officers could order a strike. Unles this procedure was followed, no benefits would be provided to strikers.[30]

It was agreed that 30 per cent of the fifteen cents each member would pay quarterly into the defense fund would be used to support strikes.[31] But Secretary Litchman reported to the 1881 convention that "so far as it has been possible to learn the sentiment of the Order is overwhelmingly in favor of applying the Fund for cooperative purposes."[32] Whatever differences existed within the Order, they were not sufficiently important to interfere with its progress. Membership had started at over 9,200 in 1879, and rose steadily except for one year, 1880. Growth was accompanied by rising differences between the Knights and the unions, some of which had sought to establish a federation in the previous year. "With the prospect of a strike," he wrote, "large numbers flock in . . . only to flock out just as soon as they find that they cannot walk up to the treasurer and demand four dollars a week."[33]

Since the Knights were not a political party or a trade union, it is difficult to determine what its objectives were or how they would be attained. Cooperation, while a principle, did not gain much practical support, although it was generally favored. Undoubtedly finances limited the number of enterprises that could be established on the cooperative principle. Powderly once explained that "we take all men who obey the divine injunction. 'By the sweat of thy brow shall thou eat bread', the machinist, the blacksmith, molders, pattern maker, laborer, miner and clerk. All who labor. No drones. No lawyers, no bankers, no doctors, no professional politicians. By combining all branches of trade in one common brotherhood, a complete system of communicating and receiving intelligence is at once established. . . . We teach the laborer to discuss labor in all its interest at each meeting."[34]

In 1882, in his report to the general assembly, Powderly lashed out at strikes which he wrongfully held could not change basic conditions. Strike funds should be used to "amass a sum sufficient to erect shops and factories to give employment to their idle brethren."[35]

At the next meeting of the general assembly, Powderly reversed himself in part: "If we are to support strikes, notwithstanding our declaration that we do not favor them, let us adopt some means of providing for those engaged in the battle. We cannot avoid lockouts, and it is no time to prepare for strife when we are in the act of dealing with our enemy."[36] Almost at the same time, he wanted to "stick to the original plan of the Order, that of educating the members as to the folly of strikes."[37] A proposal at the 1883 general assembly to levy an assessment for support of strikes was defeated. In fact, the 1883 meeting showed a growing hostility to trade assemblies and voted not to issue charters for trade districts unless it were clear that "such trade could not be effectively organized under the system of Mixed or Territorial Districts as now generally in operation throughout the Order."[38]

Whatever merit the Knights of Labor might possess, it obviously did not answer the need of the trade unions for a trade union federation divorced from other kinds of labor societies. Moreover, the criticism to which trade union tactics were often subjected by leading members of the Order would raise doubts in the minds of trade unionists of the benefits to be derived from joining. Many were not sympathetic to the desire for exclusive jurisdiction so that they might control, or at least influence, the conditions of employment in their trade. Trade union leaders had sought to establish a union federation which would combine the isolated economic organizations and enable them to cooperate together on common problems, while allowing each to pursue its own interests.

FEDERATION OF ORGANIZED TRADES AND LABOR UNIONS OF THE UNITED STATES AND CANADA

Soon after the failure of the Industrial Brotherhood, efforts to set up a trade union federation were renewed. At the direction of the 1878 convention of the Amalgamated Association of Iron and Steel Workers, President Joseph Bishop issued a circular inviting trade unions to send delegates to a conference for devising a plan for a labor federation. William Saffin, chief of the Molders' Union, asked his convention to authorize the sending of delegates to the proposed conference.[39] While many trade union leaders favored a closer alliance, this was no easy task. The International Typographical Union endorsed such a project in 1879 and took the additional step of sounding out the different internationals on their willingness to cooperate in it. Even though the response was unfavorable, the International

Typographical Union went along with its program of uniting the trade unions into some kind of central federation. At its 1880 convention a committee on the Amalgamation of International Trades Unions was organized, and Lyman A. Brant, a vigorous believer in the need for such a union, and W. H. Foster, who was to become the secretary of the planned federation, were among its members. In addition, the corresponding secretary was directed to invite the national and international unions of the United States and Canada to send delegates to a convention to establish a Continental Federation of Trades which was to meet annually.[40]

It is important for an understanding of the forces that shaped the development of the American labor movement to mark the dates. The discussions leading to the establishment of the federation which preceded the formation (and was a direct ancestor) of the American Federation of Labor were going on among trade union leaders in the 1870's; these leaders had always held the view that some kind of national federation of trade unions was necessary. Moreover, there had always been a substantial number among the trade union leadership who believed that such a federation could function only if it were completely divorced from reform and political groups. The chief sponsor, the International Typographical Union, was one of the purest of trade unions, and in the years when the crucial discussions of the need for a trade union federation were going on (1878–1881), the Knights of Labor, while active, presented a minor threat to the organized trade unionists. The Knights of Labor had fewer than 20,000 members in 1881, when the federation was first organized.[41]

Moreover, many trade unionists, including Samuel Gompers, were two-card men, that is, they held membership in a trade union and in an assembly of the Knights of Labor.[42] The trade unions believed that they needed an organization which could unite them, and at the same time exclude organizations that were not strictly trade groups. Despite several failures, the officers of the International Typographical Union persisted, and it was the result of their efforts that twenty-one representatives from thirteen unions in eight cities met at Terre Haute, Indiana, on August 2, 1881, to discuss the setting up of a labor federation. The meeting was opened by E. F. Pagette, secretary of the Amalgamated Labor Union of the host city, and the committee on organization reported "that in view of the small attendance . . . we deem it inexpedient to take steps looking to the framing of a constitution and by-laws for the government of a national Amalgamated Labor Union."[43]

A call for a meeting in Pittsburgh on November 15, 1881, was issued.[44] It pointed to the annual meetings of the labor organizations of England and France, and described the need for examining the conditions of every trade so that "by a combination of forces secure that justice which isolated and separated trade and labor unions can never fully command."[45] The modesty of the aspirations and the emphasis upon the promotion of trade union objectives indicate that the sponsors sought to avoid programs of fundamental reform. The committee hoped that the combination of labor unions would establish a committee to represent labor before Congress patterned after the Parliamentary Committee of the Trades Union Congress in England. Mark W. Moore, the delegate from Terre Haute Typographical Union No. 76, handled the correspondence. He advised that action should be "cool, deliberate, and not too over-reformatory. Grasp one idea, viz., less hours and better pay, and carry into all your work as the first principle."[46]

Several trade unions were seeking to form a central trade union federation which would enable them to support each other and at the same time develop an institution that would represent them before legislative bodies. The limited type of program always had supporters in the ranks of the organized. The mere fact that a number of labor officers responded to the call indicates that the view was not sufficiently novel to arouse suspicion. Moreover, the action indicated that many trade union leaders did not regard the Knights of Labor as suitable for their needs. Two-card men, including Gompers, did not think the Knights fulfilled the narrow function of a trade union federation, even though they might approve of some of its objectives.

The Pittsburgh meeting was not welcomed by Terence Powderly, the leader of the Knights of Labor. His suspicions were aroused by the failure of the sponsoring committee to invite the Order, which he believed represented labor adequately. He advised capture of the new labor federation so that it would not become a rival.[47] Although the Knights of Labor did not control its affiliated trade assemblies too closely, it exercised more influence than a trade union would accept. Moreover, the promoters of the new venture wanted a federation whose activities were primarily centered on the promotion of trade unions and their purposes. The objectives of trade unions were only a few among a larger number the Knights sponsored. In addition, many within the Order were suspicious of trade unionism, its activities, and objectives. Consequently, many trade union leaders would scarcely be attracted to the Knights. Even those who might approve of the general activities of the Order might still believe that a purely trade union federation was necessary. These facts need emphasizing because many have assumed that the campaign for a trade union federation was engineered by Samuel Gompers, Peter McGuire, Adolph Strasser, and a few other trade union plotters. This view is contrary to the facts. The sentiment for a pure trade union federation had never been submerged, and the efforts which eventually led to the formation of the American Federation of Labor were initiated before the Knights of Labor cast its shadow over the labor scene.

Powderly's suggestion that the Knights capture the Pittsburgh meeting produced a large contingent from the Order, almost half of the delegates, but the trade unions had a slight majority—58 out of 108. But the size of the meeting did not reflect its true character, since 68 delegates came from Pennsylvania. There were delegates from fourteen states, and one came from San Francisco. John Jarrett, head of the Amalgamated Association of Iron and Steel Workers and a leading trade unionist of the time, was selected temporary presiding officer. A slight furor among the delegates was caused by the charge in the local press that Samuel Gompers, a delegate from the Cigar Makers' Union, was the spearhead of a Socialist attempt to capture the convention. Gompers denied the allegation. Both Gompers and Richard Powers, the head of the Lake Seamen's Union, withdrew as candidates for permanent chairman, when John Jarrett was nominated for the post from the floor.

The convention sent greetings to Henry Broadhurst and the Parliamentary Committee of the British Trades Union Congress, and then got into the business of trying to set up a labor federation. Gompers was elected chairman on the plan of organization, and his proposal for a "Federation of Trade Unions" touched off a debate. Some delegates believed that the title was too restrictive and that it meant that the new federation would be limited to craftsmen; others defended the name, because "it will keep out of the Federation political labor bodies." In the end, the name "Federation of Trades and Labor Unions of the United States and Canada" was chosen.

The "preamble" started with the declaration that "a struggle is going on in the nations of the civilized world between oppressors and oppressed of all countries, a struggle between capital and labor, which must grow in intensity from year to year and work disastrous results to the toiling millions of all nations if not combined for mutual protection and benefit." Similar sentiments were added, but the language must be regarded as stock expressions of the time. While it appears to imply a criticism of the social system, the recommendations of the preamble are scarcely revolutionary. "Conforming to the old adage, 'in union there is strength,' the formation of a Federation embracing every trade and labor organization in North America, a union founded upon a basis as broad as the land we live in, is our only hope. The past history of Trades Unions proves that small organizations, well conducted, have accomplished great good, but their efforts have not been of that lasting character which a thorough unification of all the different branches of industrial workers is bound to secure."[48]

The program presented called for laws to allow the incorporation of trade unions, restriction of child labor, outlawing of the use of script, payment of wages in lawful money, a mechanic's lien law, uniform apprentice legislation, opposition to contract and Chinese labor, and (at the demand of Jarrett) an endorsement of a protective tariff. W. H. Foster, a printer, was elected secretary, and a legislative committee was chosen to head the organization. Slightly more than $56.00 was donated by the delegates to get the federation started.

From the beginning the federation was hampered by lack of funds and by its failure to attract a substantial number of the international trade unions. While many trade unions favored a federation, few were ready to support it. Some could see no benefit from affiliation, and even the leading sponsors were dissatisfied with the results of the Pittsburgh meeting and the methods of financing the new venture. The second convention was attended by only nineteen delegates, who decided to rescind the endorsement of a protective tariff which had been enacted at the first meeting at the suggestion of John Jarrett. Jarrett subsequently took his union, the Amalgamated Association of Iron and Steel Workers of America, out of the federation. The second convention also allowed district assemblies of the Knights of Labor to be represented.

The outlook for the survival of the federation appeared slightly improved by the third convention. Receipts, which were under $300 in the first year, reached over $700 in the second. Scarcely a staggering sum, it could at least be regarded as progress. Gompers, who had been elected to the legislative committee in 1882, was chosen to preside over the 1883 convention. Yet aside from passing a series of resolutions on conventional labor topics, the federation was inactive. The temper of the delegates at the 1883 meeting is evident in their rejection of a resolution to send a committee to the conventions of the two political parties, but a proposal to endorse government ownership of the telegraph system was approved by a vote of sixteen to eight.

The poor performance of the federation did not greatly discourage some leading supporters. President George Clark of the International Typographical Union reported to his convention that "after many delays, and repeated failures, the project for a Federation of the Trades of the United States has passed the primary stage of existence and taken its place among the organizations of the time."[49] Few unions shared the printers' interest in a labor federation.[50] Gabriel Edmonston, a leading member of the Carpenters' Union, was elected secretary. He sponsored the historic eight-hour resolution. It declared "that eight hours shall constitute a legal day's labor from and after May 1, 1886, and we recommend to labor organizations throughout this jurisdiction that they so direct their laws as to conform to this resolution by the time named."[51]

CHAPTER 8

Strikes of the Knights of Labor

The rapid expansion of membership in the mid-1880's posed both internal and external problems for the Knights of Labor. Many of the new recruits did not join for contemplation of ultimate solutions, but were anxious to find a means by which they could rectify grievances. Such organizations were likely to become embroiled in offensive and defensive conflicts with management, and the Knights' opposition to strikes was scarcely a check upon these tendencies. Moreover, the trade assemblies set up by the Knights of Labor could declare and end strikes without the approval of the general officers of the Order. But the trade assemblies frequently leaned on the Order for financial and other kinds of support.

THE TELEGRAPHERS' STRIKE

In 1883 the Brotherhood of Telegraphers of District Assembly No. 45 went on strike for the eight-hour day. Formed as a branch of the Order in 1882, the brotherhood grew rapidly. On July 16, 1883, Thomas D. Eckert, manager and acting president of the Western Union Telegraph Company, received a demand for wage increases of 15 per cent, the establishment of an eight-hour workday and equal pay for both men and women. The demands were ratified, according to John Campbell, District Master Workman, by two-thirds of the assemblies in the brotherhood, but the Western Union and other telegraph companies refused to "recognize the right of the executive board of the Brotherhood of Telegraphers to present grievances or to speak in behalf of the employees of the Western Union Telegraph Company."[1]

When the brotherhood had been formed in March 1882, it was avowed, according to Campbell, "that the organization was to be for protective purposes—to protect the interests of the craft." While a number of organizations had preceded the brotherhood, none was very important except the Telegraphic Protective League, whose four-day strike in 1870 led to its dissolution.[2] Jay Gould, who was the dominant personality in the Western Union and was to challenge the Order on a larger scale, blamed the strike on "dissatisfied men—the poorest part of your labor generally are at the bottom of a strike."[3] When asked his opinion about unions, Gould replied that he had not paid much attention to the subject. He thought "that anything that tends to elevate the working classes or to educate them, or that provides for those who are in want, provides a fund for the widows and orphans in any particular business, I think anything of that kind is the legitimate object of such societies. But when they get beyond that I think they get into a broad sea that they cannot control, because labor, like everything else, is regulated by the law of supply and demand."[4]

The strike continued, and two of the smaller telegraph companies granted the demands of the workers. The Knights of Labor sent out an appeal for financial assistance to its lodges, but only $1,640.65 was contributed. The Knights "loaned" $2,000 more. The strikers were fighting against overwhelming odds. The 19,000 men on strike had few resources, and by August 19 the strike was ended. Most of the strikers kept their old jobs, and the Western Union Telegraph Company introduced some improvements in the work schedule, that is, abolishing Sunday work without any reduction in pay. Some of the leaders were denied employment.[5]

RAILROAD STRIKES AND THE ORDER

For two years the Knights of Labor was involved in several railroad strikes. In May 1884, Union Pacific shopmen went out on strike after an announcement that wages would be reduced 10 per cent to 25 per cent. The unorganized strikers called on Joseph Buchanan, a Denver labor editor, for assistance in directing the walkout. Under Buchanan's leadership, the strikers agreed "in mass meeting assembled . . . to refuse to do any work under the jurisdiction or upon the premises of said Union Pacific Company until such notice of a reduction in wages is withdrawn."[6] Every shop on the line from Omaha, Nebraska, to Ogden, Utah, was closed down as a result of the announcement, and the men on other divisions of the railroad instructed the Denver committees to act on their behalf. Two days after the order had been issued, it was rescinded. Anticipating further trouble in the future, the strikers set up organizations along the line of those affiliated with the Knights of Labor.

The settlement was only temporary, since the company had not given up the hope of successfully cutting wages. On August 11 a 10 per cent reduction in wages was imposed upon machinists in Ellis, Kansas, and a number of workers active in the last strike were discharged in Denver.

The response was a complete withdrawal of shopmen from service along the entire line. After some negotiations, prolonged because of the company's refusal to reemploy the secretary of the Denver strike committee, the wage cut was rescinded and the discharged workers were reinstated.[7]

Strike of Shopmen on the Missouri Pacific Railroad

In October 1884 wages of shopmen and other employees on the Missouri Pacific Railroad were reduced by 10 per cent. The men submitted; they did not belong to any union. The following February another cut of 5 per cent in wages was ordered. "No labor union organized the strike, but on Saturday, March 7, 1885 . . . at Sedalia, Mo., at a given signal the shopmen laid down their tools and walked out of the shops in a body and proceeded to Smith's hall and organized a secret meeting."[8] After the walkout, the employees formed a permanent organization and forwarded a statement of grievances to H. M. Hoxie, vice-president of the Missouri Pacific Railroad Company. They demanded a restoration of the wage cuts they had suffered during the last two years, and steadier employment than they had been receiving. Many strikers complained that they were employed on short time.

The strike became general on March 9 on all points of the Southwestern System, "and in many places the men had the active sympathy of all citizens."[9] All freight traffic was suspended, and there was no violence, the strikers having appointed a special police force from their ranks to keep order. Citizens and officials intervened and on March 15, Governor John A. Martin of Kansas and Governor John S. Marmaduke of Missouri requested that the "company restore to its striking employees in Missouri and Kansas the same wages paid them in September, 1884, including one and one-half price for extra time worked: and restore all said striking employees to their several employments without prejudice to them on account of said strike."[10] The request was accepted by H. M. Hoxie on behalf of the company and the strike ended the next day.

Difficulties on the Wabash

While the differences on the Missouri Pacific Railway had been settled temporarily, the Knights were confronted by trouble on the Wabash, St. Louis and Pacific (the Wabash) Railroad. The Wabash was operated by A. W. Talmadge, a court-appointed receiver who refused to recognize the Order. The workers on the Southwestern system, controlled by Jay Gould, were concerned over this development, and it was largely at their request that the general executive board of the Knights of Labor met in St. Louis, Missouri, on August 13. In answer to requests for a conference, Talmadge stated that "he saw no reason why he should meet the Knights of Labor for a discussion, friendly or otherwise. The employees of the company were attending to their duties and he was not aware of any dissatisfaction among them."[11] Thereupon the general executive board ordered a strike on the Wabash Railroad for August 18. At the same time Secretary Frederick Turner declared that all members of the Knights of Labor in the employ of the Union Pacific and its branches or any other railroad "must refuse to repair or handle in any manner Wabash rolling stock until further orders from the general executive board, and if this order is antagonized the companies through any of its officials, your executive committee is hereby ordered to call out all Knights of Labor on the above system."[12]

The general executive board tried again to arrange a conference with Talmadge. A meeting was finally held in the office of Jay Gould in New York. Powderly and Secretary Turner were empowered by the general executive board to work out an arrangement. At the end of August 1885, Powderly and Gould reached an agreement, and the strike was called off. It was believed, at least by Powderly, that there would be no discrimination against striking members of the Knights of Labor.[13] It looked like a great victory and the prestige of the Order increased. The Knights of Labor had defeated Jay Gould, an aggressive financier who had become a symbol of the unrestrained uses of economic power. Gould accepted the temporary defeat, and waited for a more favorable time to even the score with Powderly and the Knights of Labor.

The Strike in the Southwest

In 1885 the executive board of the mixed assembly to which the workers of the Gould system belonged met in Denison, Texas, and drew up a statement complaining of the failure of the company to carry out its agreement. The board was unable to present their grievances to Hoxie, who was unavailable. C. A. Hall of Marshall, Texas, a member of the union committee and foreman in one of the shops of the car department of the Texas and Pacific Railroad, was discharged. In September the Gould system employees withdrew from the mixed assembly and established District Assembly No. 101, choosing Martin Irons as Master Workman.[14] The new district assembly faced many difficulties. Its newly organized members were employed by a powerful and resourceful corporation whose initial agreement appears to have been a device for gaining time.

On January 10, 1886, District Assembly No. 101 submitted to the local assemblies a request for approval of two demands to be made on the Southwestern railroad system: recognition of the Knights of Labor, and a minimum wage for unskilled labor of $1.50 a day. In his letter to the members, Irons wrote that the railroad officials insisted that the March agreement covered only mechanics in the shops and, therefore, refused to increase the pay of the unskilled, "Who, from the smallness of their pay, need more protection than shop hands."[15] In the meantime, the Texas and Pacific Railroad, a link in the Gould system, went into bankruptcy, forced into receivership by other roads under the same control because of failure to meet interest payments on its bonds. Naturally, there was a suspicion that the receivership was a legal maneuver by Gould for a favorable position in his oncoming contest with the Knights of Labor. When demands were presented to the receivers of the Texas and Pacific, they refused to discuss them. Irons thereupon wired that unless differences between the district assembly and the railroad were settled by March 1, 1886, a strike would be called. The telegram, like the earlier demands, was ignored. The receivers announced that they had no trouble in their shops, and that Irons had no authority to speak for the employees of the Texas and Pacific.[16]

The strike on the Texas and Pacific started on schedule at Marshall, Texas, on March 1. Irons said that the walkout was not "in the interest of one man but for a principle . . . that the contract between the employers and the railroad made one year ago had been violated; that the contract was that no man should be discharged without due notice and investigation."[17] By March 8 the strike on Gould's Southwestern system had become general and included shopmen, trackmen, switchmen, wipers, and other employees totaling 60,000 workers. On March 10, Irons submitted a proposal for settlement.[18] Hoxie claimed that "committees representing the employees at different points, and also the various labor organizations to which they belonged, were met and all grievances candidly discussed."[19]

On March 18, Powderly intervened again and asked Hoxie whether he would meet with him and a committee to settle the strike. Hoxie denied that his company could reinstate Hall, since he was an employee of the Texas and Pacific Railroad which was in the hands of a receiver and not subject to his orders. He emphasized that the Knights of Labor had "committed the error of striking first, and endeavoring to negotiate afterwards, it has the power to and should end the present troubles by permitting such of our employees and others as desire to work to do so without fear of threats or intimidation, leaving this company free to resume its operations, and adjust with its employees, as it has at all times been ready and willing to do, any grievances that they may have."[20]

In the meantime Powderly visited the Southwest and learned that Irons had opposed the strike but had been forced by armed threats on his life to agree to it. Powderly decided to ask for a conference with Jay Gould, who controlled the Southwestern railroad system, and seek a basis for ending the walkout.[21] William O. McDowell a businessman and member of the Order, acted as an intermediary. A meeting was arranged for March 28 and, in Powderly's opinion, it was agreed that differences would be arbitrated and that the strikers would return without prejudice, unless guilty of violence or damaging railroad property. In regard to this understanding, which Gould denied, Powderly wrote: "I understood you to mean that arbitration would be agreed to; the only method of arbitration that was discused was in line with that suggested in the letter which I sent you in the name of our board the day previous; there was nothing particular agreed upon as you well know. . . . You alone can settle this strike."[22] This letter was written after Powderly realized that Gould had no intention of arbitrating. But the executive board had in the meantime under a misapprehension of the nature of the Gould-Powderly agreement, called off the strike on March 30.

When the board arrived in St. Louis soon afterward, it found that Hoxie would only rehire 50 per cent of the strikers, and those who were active in the strike were not among those re-employed. Thereupon, it rescinded the order ending the strike. Subsequent developments were not favorable. Not knowing what to do, Powderly asked McDowell, who seems to have been a shadowy type of fixer, to enlist the aid of Cyrus W. Field, a leading industrialist and friend of Gould. Powderly believed that it was "unfortunate that this strike did not end two weeks ago. It seems that nothing can be done to hasten the final proceedings."[23] Field called on Gould, who would not negotiate. He was convinced that "the strike was entirely over."[24] It dragged on until May 4, when it was concluded by the order of the general executive board.

Reaction to the Lost Strike

The blame for the loss of the strike fell mainly on Martin Irons, who had in fact opposed the walkout.[25]

Irons was also blamed for not ending the strike in time to salvage a modicum of protection for the workers and hope for the Knights of Labor. On the other hand, others charged the general officers, especially Powderly, with responsibility for the debacle. The newly organized workers in the Southwest were unaccustomed to the slow negotiations which an established union might follow. Irons, while a superb agitator, appears to have lacked the foresight essential to a union leader. It is doubtful, however, if other tactics would have led to different results.

It is even questionable that the lost strike affected membership beyond the areas in which it took place. It demonstrated that there was no magic formula for victory against a powerful employer, and that an entire group of employees of a company might be defeated as readily as particular segments of a company's work force. Also, as Professor Allen believes, it might have encouraged the skilled workers to go it alone and avoid the "one big union" with the unskilled. The strike demonstrated too that sentiments of solidarity were easier to express than to practice. Workers on the Union Pacific Railroad rightfully refused to break their contract and join with their fellow members of the Order in the strike. Such action was not unusual and was regarded as proper by leaders of the Order. Had they done otherwise, they also might have faced defeat and in avoiding a breach of contract, they had perhaps saved their union.

THE STOCKYARDS STRIKE

On May 1, 1886, the employees of the Chicago stockyards struck, in common with thousands of other workers, for the eight-hour workday. They were successful and were able to establish the same pay for the shorter schedule as they had received for ten hours. They "then pushed the work of organization of their craft."[26] The concessions appear to have been in the nature of a "holding operation" until a united front of employers could be established. P. Armour, head of one of the leading companies in the industry, was the leader in the plan to deflate the organizations recently formed by the packinghouse workers. Arguing that they were not able to meet competition from lower-wage plants outside of Chicago, the employers demanded that the pork packers accept a wage cut of 10 per cent. When it was refused by the workers and their unions, the employers decided to reinstall the ten-hour work day by October 11. A strike of 12,000 was the answer.

An appeal for aid to the Richmond general assembly brought T. B. Barry, a member of the general executive board of the Knights of Labor, to the scene. He was dispatched by Powderly with instructions not to involve the Knights in the controversy—an unusual order to a man sent to aid and to lead a strike of 12,000 workers! Barry was able to gain concessions from two small independent packers, but the large ones refused to follow. He, nevertheless, concluded that the strike should be ended on the employer's terms. It was charged that Powderly had ordered an end to the walkout as a result of an appeal from Father P. M. Flannagan, pastor of St. Ann's Church, to which many of the strikers belonged. Flannagan believed that the packers were "importing and [would] continue to import foreign workmen, and unless this matter is settled immediately this immense army of workmen, some of whom have labored for many years, most of whom have their homes and families here, will find themselves replaced by others and never taken back."[27]

This was only the first skirmish in what was to be a battle between the workers and the organized packers. The packers soon announced that the beef butchers would be placed on a ten-hour work schedule. On November 1 another strike was called and when the packers refused to arbitrate, others joined until approximately 25,000 were out, twice as many as the first walkout. Barry was directed to assist but "not to involve the Order in the trouble or make us responsible for it."[28]

In a circular issued on November 10, Powderly defined the views of the Knights of Labor on the Chicago strike and reiterated the orders he had issued in April against members striking for shorter hours. Earlier Powderly charged that "In opposition to that circular the men at the stock yards struck for 8 hours. The Order of the Knights of Labor was not brought into controversy, hence no action was necessary during the session of the General Assembly. Men at the yards struck again. You [Barry] were sent to try and settle, but, in case of failure, the Order was not to be involved or asked for assistance. You settled by ordering the men back at the old hours. They have in violation of law and your order, and without notifying us, again struck for 8 hours. The Board instructed you . . . to settle by putting the men back at the old hours until the Order of the Knights of Labor takes definite action on the 8-hour plan. If the men refuse, take their charter."[29] Barry did not believe the order was genuine and in a wire to Powderly asked if it was "false," and if not, "suppress." Powderly answered: "Order to return not false and must be obeyed," to which Barry replied: "We obey in opposition to our judgment."[30]

A resolution by representatives from the assemblies to which the strikers belonged denounced the general executive board as "guilty of an act of heartless cruelty, as well as incompetency, in ordering 25,000 men and women to return to work, under threat of taking the charters if not obeyed, at a time when the packers demanded by resolution that no one could return to work unless they renounced their allegiance to the Order and similar organizations, thus placing the members in the painful dilemma of choosing between renouncing their membership in the Order for the sake of obtaining work on one hand, or, if they refused to do this, threatened with expulsion by order of the General Executive Board."[31] The resolution was rejected by a vote of 117 to 49, which is an index of the dissatisfaction with the conduct of the national officers. Whatever reason may have existed for the behavior of Powderly and the other members of the executive board, their action again demonstrated that the Order was not more effective in its strike strategy than the pure trade unions.

THE ANTHRACITE STRIKE

The Knights of Labor was also involved in a lost anthracite strike. In 1879 an organization was established in the coal area, the Miners' and Laborers' Amalgamated Association, and it gained a following in the middle and southern districts. Simultaneously, Knights of Labor assemblies were established in the Scranton area. At first membership in the Knights of Labor increased slowly, but it expanded rapidly over the entire region in

1886.[32] In 1886 a joint committee from the Miners' and Laborers' Amalgamated Association and the Knights of Labor succeeded in winning a wage increase from the Reading Coal Company.

In the following year a joint committee from the two organizations proposed a wage increase and a revision of the sliding scale. The Lehigh operators refused to consider the demands or even negotiate. A strike followed in September. In contrast, the operators in the southern area agreed to an advance in wages from September to January 1888 and to continue the higher rate if the Lehigh operators were compelled to meet the same terms. The miners of the southern district supported those on strike in the Lehigh area, and the operators in turn sought to lessen the pressure upon the coal owners in the striking district by supplying them with coal with which to meet their orders. Angered by this stratagem, the strikers regarded the action of their employers as a breach of faith. The miners' protests were ignored and the coal shipments to the strike-bound companies continued. By the end of 1887 the miners tried a new tack. Members of the Knights of Labor refused to load coal produced by union miners for the Reading Company on barges of the Lehigh Company. Those refusing were discharged. Railroad employees also refused to handle the coal of the striking Reading Company and were also dismissed. As a result, a complete tie-up involving 22,000 workers of the Reading properties began on February 6, 1888. The strike lasted until March 1. All pleas for arbitration and negotiation were rejected, and the unions on the railroads as well as in the mines were shattered.[33]

Private Police

The strike led to a congressional investigation of labor conditions in the anthracite coal fields. The congressional committee was critical of the companies' refusal to settle their differences with their employees. It also sharply denounced the private armies of police established by a number of coal, railroad, and iron and steel companies. Every "railroad in 1865 and every colliery, iron furnace, or rolling mill in 1866, was granted by statute liberty to employ as many policemen as it saw fit, from such persons as would obey its behests, and they were clothed with all the authority of policemen in the city of Philadelphia—were paid such wages and armed with such weapons as the corporations determined—usually army revolvers, sometimes Winchester rifles or both—and they were commissioned by the governor. His decision was and is now the only limit upon the number of such policemen to be appointed; and it is believed that the governor seldom refused to commission the number and particular persons asked for. They report to nobody but the heads of the corporations employing them, from whom they get their orders and which they execute generally with a mailed hand. It struck some of your committee as a curious condition of affairs, while walking the streets of Hazeltown and Shenandoah, two mining towns of several thousand inhabitants, that there were three different sets of policemen—one wearing a metallic shield engraved 'Borough Police,' a second, 'Railway Police,' and a third, 'Coal and Iron Police.' "[34]

CHAPTER 9

The American Federation of Labor

CONFLICT BETWEEN THE KNIGHTS
AND THE TRADE UNIONS

As membership of the Knights of Labor expanded, opportunities for conflict between its assemblies and trade and labor unions increased. Powderly and most of the other leaders were unsympathetic to the claims of the unions to control their trade. When J. P. McDonnell, a leading labor editor, complained of the encroachments of a trade assembly upon a trade union, Powderly answered that the "Knights of Labor makes no attempts on trade unions at all. On the contrary they try to show the folly of separate action and endeavor to bring all workingmen into one organization."[1] At first these were isolated conflicts, but gradually many unions found themselves engaged in jurisdictional difficulties with a Knights of Labor assembly.

Powderly's views were shared by many leaders and members of the Order. When Adolph Strasser, as a delegate to the 1884 general assembly, protested against the violation by Progressive Painters Assembly No. 2888 of an understanding with other unions in the trade, a violation which led to a wage reduction, his complaint was rejected.[2] An appeal by a member of a fine imposed by a local assembly for working during a strike was set aside by Powderly who ruled: "Your L.A. has no right to inflict any punishment on its members for disobeying the laws or directions of any other organization or union."[3] Many unions found the encroachments of the Knights a serious problem. President Mark L. Crawford of the International Typographical Union complained in 1884 that "where assemblies of the Knights of Labor are organized, wholly composed of printers, a card authorized by our body is treated secondary to one issued by such assemblies . . . they admit as members men who have not served sufficient apprenticeship, as well as men who have 'ratted' in our own organization . . . men who hold working cards are compelled to work side by side with notorious 'rats' in offices that are called Union offices."[4] He suggested that he be authorized to discuss these issues with Powderly.

The Bricklayers' Union made a survey and found that assemblies of the Knights of Labor had been organized and had competed with locals of bricklayers in a number of places, and that as a rule these assemblies charged lower dues and initiation fees, and worked for lower wages. Thomas A. O'Dea submitted a statement listing the instances in which Knights of Labor assemblies had recently come into conflict with locals of the Bricklayers' Union.[5] The willingness of the Knights to charter locals made up of dissidents from a trade union increased the difficulties between the Knights and labor organizations on the outside. Such action not only created a fissure within a trade, but made it more difficult for trade unions to impose discipline upon warring factions within their midst.

Cigarmakers' Union

The dispute between the Knights of Labor and the Cigarmakers' International Union highlighted the division in the house of labor. Although a large Socialist group had existed within this organization since the middle 1870's, it was unable to gain control over the union's international administration. At the 1877 convention, delegate Frank Hirth proposed the adoption of the following resolution: "Trades unions are utterly incompetent to remove the pressure resting upon them caused by . . . mental and social infirmities, the delegates . . . recommend to and urge upon all local unions to form themselves into labor bodies upon the basis and platform of the Workingmen's Party of the United States." The resolution was promptly tabled.

Two years later, a delegate to the 1879 convention presented proposals whose sentiments were, the delegates believed, too extreme, and they were stricken from the convention minutes. But the Cigarmakers' Union was to be split on another issue, the methods to be pursued to gain legislation outlawing the manufacture of cigars in tenements. Such a law was essential for the survival of the union and for raising the standards of the trade. Moreover, as long as cigars were manufactured in tenements, there was no way of preventing the employment of underage children. A bill to outlaw tenement house work was introduced in the New York legislature by Edward Grosse, a Republican and member of the Printers' Union. When Grosse was a candidate, he was opposed by the Socialist Labor party, which urged its followers to abstain from voting. Such action was resented by the Cigarmakers' International.

In turn, Socialists in Local No. 144, New York, attacked the political tactics pursued by the international and carried their campaign into the local union. The Socialists succeeded in electing their candidate for local president; he was, however, immediately removed by Adolph Strasser, the head of the International Union, on the ground that the victorious Socialist was a manufacturer and therefore ineligible. Strasser's conduct was not completely in accordance with the union's constitution, but it was justified by the delegates to the 1883 convention "by the extraordinary necessities of the case."[6]

The Socialists seceded and formed the Progressive Cigarmakers' Union. Little progress was made by this breakaway group until the fall of 1882, when, fearful that their employment might be adversely affected by the recent enactment of an antitenement house bill, many tenement house workers flocked into the secessionist organization.[7] After a short stay as independents, many of the secessionists returned to the old union. Some of the more belligerent opponents of Strasser and his administration refused to make peace. Weakened by the departure of many of their original members, the opposition secured a charter as Local Assembly 2,814 and affiliated with District Assembly No. 49, the center of antitrade-union sentiment within the Knights of Labor. Now, supported by a powerful Order, the dissident cigarmakers issued a white label to compete with the blue label of the Cigarmakers' International Union used to identify cigars manufactured under union conditions.

The conflict in the cigarmaking industry became widely known because each side sought to rally support around its own label on a product consumed by union members. It epitomized a struggle between the Knights and the trade unions which had been growing in magnitude and virulence in the early 1880's.[8]

STRIKES AND UNIONS

It is true that specific unions represented a single group, while a federation of unions could represent every trade that was able to organize at the place of employment. Unions could also cooperate together and offer assistance to each other in times of need. In addition, the unions of the time understood better than the Knights of Labor the uses of economic power. Although unions have in the past and since, opposed strikes, their views were basically different from those espoused by the Order. Testifying before a Senate committee in 1883, Peter J. McGuire defined his views on strikes and expressed those held by most trade union leaders of the time:

No strike is a loss or a failure to the workers, even if the point sought is not gained for the time being. If naught else, they at least teach the capitalists that they are expensive luxuries to be indulged in. Consequently, we find it proven by facts that in trades where strikes have been most prevalent in the past, the employers are now more ready to listen to the demands of their employees. Very few employers who have passed through the agonies of one or two strikes ever care to enter into any further struggle, and this is a warning to employers generally. Were it not for fear of strikes, employers would be far more exacting than they are. Hence every strike is a *success* [italics in original] to the workers, and is effective in advancing the social interests of the working class.

Viewing the question from another standpoint, we find the result of a strike, if not satisfactory in gaining the point at issue, instead of dampening the ardor of the men, only demonstrates all the more forcibly the importance of organization beforehand and the necessity of accumulating funds to sustain them. More than that, they are an education to the working classes in showing us what we have to expect from the Government when it uses its police and soldiers at the instant bidding of the capitalists to imprison and shoot us down. In proof of my point that wherever strikes have occurred, employers in those occupations are more inclined to treat with their employees.[9]

The views of the trade unionists were basically different from the vague aspirations of the Knights. McGuire was not, at the time he testified, a radical among labor leaders.[10] His position on strikes, however, was shared by the majority of union leaders. He feared that the invasion of trade jurisdictions by the Knights posed a threat to all economic organizations of labor.

In contrast to McGuire, Powderly's attitude fluctuated, and depended in part upon the affiliation of the person he was addressing. To Secretary Fred Turner, he wrote that after "the General Assembly had decided the justice of the claim we make for recognition of the label of the order if it is continued then we should wipe the blue label out of existence, providing Strasser has been selling it as represented."[11] A group of officers from the Cigarmakers' Union met with Powderly and the board in Philadelphia on March 3, 1886. In answer to the charges of Strasser, the executive board agreed to revoke the charters of the assemblies which were guilty of the complaints charged. Then, according to Powderly, the Cigarmakers' Union and its officers bitterly assailed the Knights of Labor at the time when it was engaged in a struggle against the Gould system.[12]

First Steps to Federation

Encroachments upon their jurisdictions created a common interest among the trade unions in the establishment of a federation. On April 26, 1886, a confidential circular was issued by Strasser, McGuire, John Dyer of the Granite Cutters, Paul Fitzpatrick of the Iron Molders, and William H. Foster, a printer who had served as secretary of the Federation of Organized Trades and Labor Unions. It called for a conference of national officers of trade unions at an early date in Philadelphia "to protect our respective organizations from the malicious work of an element who openly boast 'that trade unions must be destroyed.' This element urges our local unions to disband, and it is doing incalculable mischief by arousing antagonisms and dissensions in the labor movement. Under cover of the Knights of Labor, and as far as we can learn, without authority from that body, this element pursues its work. 'Rats,' 'scabs,' and unfair employers are backed up by this element. Suspended and expelled members are welcomed into their ranks. And these elements use the Knights of Labor as an instrument through which to vent their spite against trade unions."[13]

Invitations were sent to forty-three unions but only twenty accepted and sent twenty-two delegates. A number of others expressed sympathy with the views of the sponsors of the conference. A committee was elected which drew up a "treaty" of six points to be presented to the Knights. Under the suggested treaty, the Knights of Labor (1) would not establish a trade assembly in any jurisdiction in which a national or international labor organization was active; (2) no one would be admitted to the Knights who worked for a wage below the scale of wages fixed by the union of his craft, had ever been convicted of scabbing, ratting, or embezzlement or other offenses against his trade or calling, unless he had been exonerated of the charges; (3) charters of Knights of Labor assemblies "having a national or international union shall be revoked," and the members be asked to join a mixed assembly or form a local union of their craft and affiliate with their respective national or international union; (4) organizers of the Knights of Labor who seek to disrupt or disband a local union are to have their commissions revoked; (5) no assembly shall interfere with a strike or lockout; and (6) the Knights of Labor were not to issue any trade mark competing with one issued by a national or international union.[14]

Reaction of the Knights of Labor to the Treaty

If the treaty had been accepted by the Knights of Labor, the organization would have been reduced to carrying on some kind of vague educational work. The Order was not engaged in direct political activity, although some of its officers believed politics was a field the Order might well enter. Secretary Charles H. Litchman deplored the ignoring of politics by trade societies and advocated discussions of political questions but not during meetings of assemblies.[15] Powderly, however, always regretted any attempts to identify the Order with any political party. As far as reform parties were concerned, he expressed the view that the "same agencies that debauched the old parties can and will debauch the new."[16]

Powderly was not consistent in his views on trade unions. Even though he started his labor career as a member of a craft organization, he had little understanding of unions. In fact, he did not want them within the Order, at least, that is what he sometimes said. In 1885 he did not favor "the establishment of any more National Trade Districts; they are a step backward in the direction of the old form of trade unions, they adopt some of the plans of the latter, and among them I cannot find any good points; we should discourage them in future. I have also observed that the Assembly that is composed of men who belong to one calling devote no time to anything but trade topics."[17]

Despite this attitude toward trade unions and trade matters, which was shared by at least a powerful minority of the Order, the leaders of the Knights of Labor were determined to dominate and control the trade unions. Their attitude can only be understood by the success achieved in the middle years of the 1880's. In his reply to the trade union committee, Powderly was conciliatory and expressed the hope "that all of these troubles in the cigar trade will be ended at this session."[18]

At the special meeting of the Knights of Labor in Cleveland on May 25, 1886, the treaty was placed before a committee which included leading trade unionists. The committee suggested that some plan be devised by which both the trade unions and the Knights of Labor would be protected against those who have been expelled or suspended for violating union rules. In addition, uniform systems of wages and hours should be worked out by the organizations of labor in a trade, and working cards exchanged so that members of a craft belonging to different organizations could work in harmony together. The report of the committee aroused prolonged discussion on the floor, because some delegates wanted to placate the trade unions and others to intensify the war against them. The assembly voted to appoint a special committee to confer with the trade unions and report back to the regular assembly scheduled for later that year.

For a time Powderly could not find five members to negotiate and in the end appointed the general executive board to handle the matter. At a conference with the trade union committee, the board suggested that the treaty be considered at the forthcoming Richmond meeting of the general assembly. In the interim, it was agreed that attempts would be made to settle specific differences between the trade unions and the Knights.

The Richmond convention of the Knights of Labor which met on October 4, 1886, was the largest labor body assembled in American history. It was a confident meeting that opened with a welcoming speech by Governor Fitzhugh Lee. But the crucial question of the relation of the Order to the trade unions was not considered. Instead, the general assembly, to Powderly's regret, compounded the difficulty by deciding that members of the Knights of Labor would have to disassociate themselves from the Cigarmakers' International Union or leave the Order.[19]

According to Joe Buchanan, an active member of the Knights of Labor and onetime member of its general executive board:

It was at Richmond that the seal of approval was placed upon the acts of those members who had been bending every energy since the Cleveland special session to bring on open warfare between the order and the trades-unions. . . . While the question at issue was the Knights against the whole trades-union movement, the discussion covering every possible phase of the subject, one trade only was named in the action taken. . . . The General Master Workman desired harmony in the order, and permitted himself to be deceived into the belief that harmony could only be secured by killing the influence of the trades-unionists who were Knights. He lacked the penetrative power that enabled many others to see through the thin veil behind which was hidden the selfishness and the ambition of the anti-unionists.[20]

Home Club

A year later Powderly recognized the error made at the Richmond convention, and he now declared that the outlawing of members of the Cigarmakers' Union was unconstitutional and therefore invalid.[21] The 1887 general assembly rescinded its earlier action, but it was now too late to halt the campaign for closer unity among the trade societies. Rumors had persisted over the years that a strong antitrade-union faction having its center in a secret society, the Home Club, in District Assembly No. 49, was the real power within the Order. The reports were sufficiently widespread for an investigation of the charges to be ordered. The Home Club, however, was absolved and its antitrade-union bias denied.[22]

Columbus Meeting of Trade Unions

The failure to establish an acceptable relationship induced William Weihe, P. J. McGuire, Christopher Evans, P. F. Fitzpatrick, and Adolph Strasser to issue, on November 10, a call for a meeting of trade unions on December 8 at Columbus, Ohio. The congress was necessary to bring about closer unity among the trade unions of America. An annual congress was proposed which would (1) aid in the formation of trade unions and encourage the trade union movement in America; (2) encourage the establishment of trades assemblies, trades councils, or central labor unions; (3) establish "State Trades Assemblies, or State Labor Congresses, to influence State Legislation in the interest of the working masses"; (4) establish "National and International Trades Unions, based upon the strict recognition of the autonomy of each trade"; (5) establish an "American Federation of Labor or an alliance of National and International Trades Unions, to aid and assist each other, and . . . secure national legislation in the interest of the working people, and influence public opinion by peaceful and legal methods in favor of organized labor"; and (6) aid the labor press.

The trade union conference opened with twenty-eight delegates, and two others arrived later. They were joined by twelve delegates from the

Federation of Organized Trades and Labor Unions, which had decided to shift its convention from St. Louis to Columbus, and now joined the meeting of trade unions. The convention was not well attended; only eleven out of forty-five international unions were represented, with an additional seven local unions and five trades assemblies. John McBride of the National Federation of Coal Miners was elected chairman. P. J. McGuire reported on the efforts to reach an understanding with the Knights of Labor, and described his visits to the general assembly in Cleveland on May 25, 1886, and the discussions with the executive board on September 28. A committee from the Knights of Labor, appointed by Powderly, was on hand to discuss differences. It met the trade union group on December 9. Fitzpatrick of the Molders' Union asked whether the Knights of Labor was willing to accept the treaty. John Howes answered that his committee has no proposals to make, "but will consider any proposition coming from your committee. We have no grievances against the Trade Unions."[23] He said that the Knights of Labor was anxious to settle existing differences, and to Fitzpatrick's statement that abundant testimony exists that "suspended and expelled members of Trade Unions, 'rats and scabs,' embezzlers of union funds, and unfair men generally, have been admitted to membership in the K. of L.," Howes assured him: "If such be the case, will it be sufficient if this committee will assure you that they will use their utmost influence to prevent such trouble for the future, and recommend [to] the executive board the adoption of such measures as to prevent their occurrence."[24]

The two committees met again on December 10 and discussed the criteria to be used to determine who is an "unfair" man. Howes observed that "there is likely to be conflict while there is a double jurisdiction of the Knights of Labor and the Trades Union in any occupation. . . . The only remedy is in consolidation with the Knights of Labor."[25] Convinced that the Knights' committee had no power to act, the meeting was adjourned after one-half hour.

The committee of the Order had a different version of events. In its report to the general assembly in 1887, the Knights of Labor negotiators believed that "insincerity surrounding the actions and sayings of some members of that committee [from the trade unions] which erected a barrier that could not be broken down; and our opinion is that the so-called grievances, if they do exist, are rather acceptable to some people in their organizations, and are used by them to accomplish selfish purposes. . . . Much is said by the leadership of the trade organizations of the destruction of their unions by absorption of their members into the Knights of Labor and the necessity on their part to oppose any tendency in that direction that the autonomy of their distinctive trade may be preserved. Such arguments are but an evidence of their ignorance, of those who advance them, of the principles and workings of our Order, which has given opportunity to any trade to organize within the Order and perform its functions as a trade organization when the conditions involved would justify."[26] The Knights of Labor committee clearly did not believe that the complaints of many of the trade unions were valid and recommended no action except issuance of a public statement defining the position of the Order.

THE AMERICAN FEDERATION OF LABOR

At the Columbus meeting of the trade unions, it was decided, after talks by McGuire, Evans, Fitzpatrick, and Strasser, to organize a federation of trade unions. George J. Block of the Bakers' Union wanted a more radical organization; he was overruled. However, the preamble to the constitution had a radical sound. It announced that a "struggle is going on in all of the civilized world between oppressors and oppressed of all countries, between capitalist and laborer which grows in intensity from year to year. . . . It therefore behooves the Representatives of the Trades and Labor Unions of America . . . to adopt such measure and disseminate such principles among the mechanics and laborers of our country as will permanently unite them." After denouncing Chinese immigration, voting a boycott of the *New York Tribune,* the *Cleveland Daily Leader,* and *Evening News,* approving a federal apprentice law applicable to the District of Columbia and the territories, the convention unanimously elected Samuel Gompers (1850–1924), president; Peter J. McGuire (1852–1906), secretary; Gabriel Edmonston, treasurer; and George Harris and J. W. Smith as vice-presidents. A per capita tax of one-half cent per member per month was voted in support of the federation.[27] The convention did not neglect to pay its respects to the Knights of Labor:

The K. of L. have persistently attempted to undermine and disrupt the well established Trades' Unions, organized and encouraged men who have proven themselves untrue to their trade, false to the obligations of their union, embezzlers of moneys, and expelled by many of the unions, and conspiring to pull down the Trades' Unions, which has cost years of work and sacrifice to build; therefore, be it Resolved we condemn the acts above recited, and call upon all workingmen to join unions of their respective trades, and urge the formation of all under one head, the American Federation of Labor.[28]

Gompers was the chief architect of the modern American trade union movement. He was born in London, and came to the United States at the age of thirteen. He joined the Cigarmakers' International Union the following year. He served as president of Local No. 144 from 1876 to 1881, as a vice-president of the Cigarmakers' International Union from 1887 to his death. He was a member of the legislative committee of the Federation of Organized Trades and Labor Unions of the United States and Canada every year of its existence except one; president of the New York State Workingmen's Association in 1886; president of the AFL from 1886 to 1894, and from 1895 to 1924. He was the author of five books, twenty-four pamphlets, and numerous articles for magazines and journals. He edited the *American Federationist* from its founding in 1894 to 1924, except in 1895 when he was out of office.

No man in his time or since has had his pervasive influence upon organized labor in North America. Even more remarkable was his lack of power. Gompers did not directly control any large union, and he always faced opposition to his policies within the AFL. While he was an excellent speaker with a fine voice, he lacked the commanding presence or the size which is frequently an aid to the orator. Gompers' influence was founded upon his intelligence and consuming loyalty to the trade union movement; his ability to devote endless hours in its service; his remarkable capacity for work; his knowledge of the needs of labor and his power to express them in writing; his talent for compromise and negotiation; and, finally, his acceptance of the limited power which he and the federation could exercise upon affiliates. Gompers, after a short flirtation with social radicalism, became convinced that labor in the United States could progress more easily and rapidly by influencing the conditions of employment through trade union pressure. He also perceived that the American economy was an expanding one, and that the possibilities existed for continually raising real wages, and his doctrine of "more and more" epitomized his belief in constant improvement. While he was always aware of the importance of government upon labor and industry, he believed that the social and political conditions in the United States called for avoidance of a class party, and reliance upon a policy of pressure politics. The directions in which he led have not been reversed, even though the movement has grown in size and influence.

Gompers' chief collaborator, Peter J. McGuire, was more closely attached to the radical movement in his youth than Gompers, but gradually he also came to believe that the most effective instrument for improving the lot of the worker was the trade union. He established *The Carpenter* in 1881, and in a true sense he was the founder of the United Brotherhood of Carpenters and Joiners of America, one of the great labor unions. For the first quarter of a century of the union's existence, McGuire served as its secretary and was its executive head. Gompers depended upon McGuire for counsel, and together they led the federation through a period of disinterest and inertia which threatened its life. They also resisted demands that the federation adopt more radical doctrines which might have repelled some of the unions. McGuire's support of Gompers was of great importance, for he commanded one of the great labor unions of the time. McGuire was a fine speaker and debater, and a militant and resourceful leader. He believed in the utility of the strike but opposed ill-prepared ventures. Several years before his death, he became involved in financial difficulties within his union. He was retired from office, and survived only three years.

Autonomy

The American Federation of Labor was on its way, but it did not have a smooth road ahead. Some of the sponsoring organizations were fearful that the new federation might take to itself powers reserved for the affiliates and encroach upon the rights of independent unions. Others complained of the expense of affiliation. But the federation was able to ride out the limited support of the first years. The autonomy of the national and international unions was secured by giving them representation at the conventions of the AFL on the basis of their membership, and while the complete freedom which these organizations enjoyed was frequently a restraint upon the federation, it was the only terms by which they would have agreed to join.

Gompers summarized very well the position of the federation when he stated it was essential for "workers to organize not only in a union but in a Federation."He claimed that previous efforts at unifying labor had failed because of "the non-recognition on the part of all who have hitherto attempted it of the principle of autonomy, or the right of the several bodies composing the organization to self-government. The American Federation of Labor avoids the fatal rock upon which all previous attempts to affect the unity of the working class have split, by leaving to each body or affiliated organizations the complete management of its own affairs, especially its own particular trade affairs."[29]

Support of Unions

A trades federation, even with this limitation, could still be a great advantage to the affiliated unions and labor in general. It could, on occasion, issue appeals for financial support of strikes or other needs facing unions, and it might establish a reservoir of experienced trade union negotiators who could be made available to assist locals and even internationals. The federation could be a clearinghouse for information to those seeking a union or trying to establish one. It was not easy to maintain the federation in the early years. Reluctantly, Gompers was forced by objections from several national unions to recommend a reduction in the per capita tax to the convention of 1887; the tax was cut to one-fourth of a cent. The same convention came out for the principle that only one union should be active in a trade, and called on the executive council to try to bring about amalgamations in instances where more than one existed. This was the theory of "exclusive jurisdiction" which became a basic principle of the AFL. In the meantime, efforts to find a working arrangement with the Knights went on.

The AFL refused to allow organizations not made up exclusively of trade unions to join. The credentials of E. W. Oyster and J. Harvey were rejected, and the delegates denied seats because they were sent by the Federation of Labor of Washington which "was not fully in sympathy with the trades-union movement, as it was overwhelmingly composed of Knights of Labor Assemblies."[30]

The Knights of Labor regarded any attempt to force all workers in a trade into a single craft organization as "puerile, narrow and . . . abortive."[31] At the same time, the Knights of Labor openly announced it would charter national trade assemblies whenever it regarded such a step as necessary. It obviously meant that dual unions would be formed, at least in some instances, and such activity ran directly counter to the desires of the trade unions affiliated with the AFL. The leaders of the Knights of Labor could see no reason for changing their customary methods of operation, nor could the AFL do much about conflicts between the Order and its affiliates. The Knights of Labor established a local assembly of steelworkers in Mingo Junction, West Virginia, which came into conflict with the Amalgamated Association of Iron and Steel Workers. W. H. Bailey, a member of the general executive board of the Knights of Labor, favored the formation of a National Trades District "which will solidify and unite all workers engaged in the iron industry to the Knights of Labor and bring them under one government."[32] All that Gompers could do, after he learned of the incident, was to write William Weihe, the head of the Amalgamated, and express an "earnest wish that you may be eminently successful in any conflict with these usurpers of the authority of the Trades Unions."[33]

In discussing proposals for a peace arrangement, Powderly wrote to Christopher Evans, treasurer of the AFL:

The General Assembly of the Knights of Labor in formulating the proposition which were, through you, presented to the convention of the American Federation of Labor were impressed with the belief that the said proposition could be acted on by the A.F. of L. Since each organization attached to the A.F. of L. is guaranteed freedom from dictation or interference, and since the A.F. of L. could only present the agreement of the Knights of Labor . . . as a "recommendation to its affiliated bodies," it would be useless to continue negotiations. The counter propositions, which have been placed before us by the A.F. of L. cannot be regarded by our Order in any light than the views of individuals who represent no constituencies over which they can exercise control. As the A.F. of L. could not act on the proposition of the Knights of Labor further attempts to make agreements with that body cannot but prove abortive, for an organization not vested with sufficient authority to receive and act on a proposition from a sister association, has no legal authority to make a counter proposition.[34]

Final efforts to reach an agreement were made in 1893 and 1894. Proposals for a discussion of differences were offered by the Knights of Labor, but Powderly showed some hesitancy when the AFL reacted favorably. At Gompers' suggestion, Joseph Buchanan called for a conference of organizations to bring about "a closer union of the labor forces of America."[35] The railroad, glass, and electrical workers also sent delegates to the St. Louis meeting which opened on July 11, 1894. The delegation from the Knights of Labor proposed annual meetings of the organizations of labor for the settlement of all differences. This would have meant the recognition of the status quo which the AFL affiliates had found intolerable, and would have recognized the "right" of more than one union to function in a trade or calling. Exclusive jurisdiction and trade autonomy were principles which the fledgling federation would not surrender. Nor would the AFL endorse the People's party. It was the last attempt by the AFL and the Knights of Labor to find a basis for a working agreement. After 1896, organizations affiliated with the Order could not join the AFL.

WHY WERE THE UNIONS ABLE TO SURVIVE

The failure of the Knights of Labor has been often attributed to the machinations of the skilled trades unions which, under the leadership of Gompers and McGuire, undermined it. This is a scarcely valid explanation. The Knights, at the time the trade unions launched the AFL, was a powerful body with a claimed membership of over 700,000. In contrast, the trade unions were divided and even when they established a federation, they endowed it with very few financial muscles. While Gompers proved in time to be a tenacious and resourceful leader, he was not in the front ranks when the AFL was launched. A leader with a steady job as head of a union, even a local union, would not have taken on the risky and uncertain business of piloting the federation through the shoals of suspicion that marked its first years.

Aside from issuing statements and writing letters, Gompers had no way of affecting the dispute between the Knights of Labor and the trade unions. Many internationals were unenthusiastic about engaging in a fight with the Knights. Single unions were not inclined then, any more than now, to become involved in the quarrels of other organizations, and many unions had few complaints against the Knights. The income of the AFL in its first year was $2,100.34, and while it more than doubled in 1888, despite the reduced per capita, it was only $4,538.50—certainly a modest sum with which to take on the swollen giant which had an income in 1886 and 1887, respectively, of over $197,000 and $267,348.90.[36] The income of the Knights of Labor in 1886 was almost eighty times as great as that of the AFL and in the next year, about sixty-five times higher.

It may be that the membership of the trade unions was larger than we have been led to believe. For example, an investigation by the Illinois Bureau of Labor Statistics in 1886 showed that there were a total of 634 labor organizations with 114,365 members. The largest number were distributed in 62 of 102 counties and 142 cities, towns, and villages—the greater part in Chicago. Trade unions were found in 80 industries, 46 of which had no Knights of Labor assemblies. The number of workers holding two cards—from the Knights and a trade union—was not large. In the year when the Order was at the peak of its power, there were in Illinois 328 local unions with over 61,000 members as compared to 326 local assemblies with over 54,000 members.[37] Nevertheless, the Knights of Labor was more cohesive than the separate and independent unions which made up the AFL. It is also likely that in the limited war the Knights waged against the unions at the place of employment, only assemblies operating as trade organizations could join in the contest. A mixed assembly had almost no opportunity to participate in the combat against a labor organization, for it usually was not a collective-bargaining agency. Consequently, a numerical comparison does not give the relative strength of the parties at the center of the dispute, the place of employment.

The Knights of Labor was not an organization which objected to the craft union, since trade assemblies were allowed to belong. It cannot be regarded as an organization which advocated an industrial type of labor formation. The Knights of Labor can best be regarded as a producers', and not specifically as a wage earners', organization. It had no program around which workers in industry could rally for a long campaign. The rush of members into its ranks in a short period has been duplicated by the Townsend movement in the 1930's and the Ku Klux Klan in the 1920's. Powderly knew that many of the recruits were not likely to remain a long time within the Knights of Labor. He warned that "men are misled by exaggerated newspaper reports, and join the Order only to be disappointed."[38] But the Knights could not prevent the inflow. The tactics of the Knights of Labor aroused the opposition of some trade unions and encouraged a number to join together in what appeared to be at first a defensive alliance. Only a minority of trade unions were involved in the campaign to set up a federation. As important as the sentiment for unity was the fear of usurpation of authority heightened by the experiences of some trade groups with the Knights of Labor. One can compare the history of the duel between the federation and the Knights of Labor with the struggle between the CIO and the AFL fifty years later. The Knights of Labor expired because it could not fulfill any function, and the AFL, despite the modest challenge of the ideological federations, had the field to itself.

At first the Knights of Labor was unaffected by the loss of two great strikes in 1886. Secretary Charles H. Litchman showed that the decrease in membership took place between July 1 and October 1, 1886, and claimed that the quarterly report of October 1, 1887, would "show an increase from initiations and reinstatements and the membership gained from new assemblies organized between July 1 and October 1, 1887."[39] Some of the losses were likely the result of lost strikes and black-listings, as well as the opposition of employers. Other losses could be attributed to disappointed expectations which generally accompanies massive membership increases. Considering the rapid climb of membership—almost half a million were gained in one year—the losses in 1886 seem rather moderate. The AFL suffered more severe losses in the first three years of the 1920's. The Knights of Labor performed only two significant functions for labor: political lobbying, and support and protection for weak unions. Almost from the beginning, these functions were more effectively performed by the AFL. In contrast to the AFL, which urged unions to accumulate strike funds to be used when necessary, the Knights' committee on strikes and boycotts believed that the "mere fact of an Assistance Fund being in possession of a District Assembly, for the purpose of assisting members who are on strike, is oftentimes an incentive to hasten or bring about a strike which might be avoided if there were no strike fund for that purpose."[40] The mixed districts, it was pointed out, complained of the use of the assistance fund to support labor disputes, and its abolition was recommended by the committee of the convention.

It does not appear correct to attribute the differences to the more radical views of the Knights. Many trade union leaders held similar opinions, and there is nowhere any intimation by the trade unions that they were opposed to the ideas of the Knights of Labor. On the contrary, the trade unions were ready to recommend to their members that they join the Order, providing the latter gave up dual organizations in the trades. In explaining his views on the matter, Gompers said that he had "joined the Knights of Labor for the purpose of confining the organization to theoretical educational work and to see that the Trade Unions were protected from being undermined or disrupted."[41] Gompers claimed that he, for the federation, had proposed that the Knights give up the idea of organizing trade locals and accept "the right of the Trade Unions to decide and dispose of all matters of difference between the employers and themselves and on the other hand we would surrender all mixed locals and recommend to the trade unions that they become members of the K. of L. as mixed locals."[42]

All unions could agree that it was essential for them to control their own affairs without the intervention of the general officers, who usually lacked knowledge and administrative ability to handle a vast number of local situations. The AFL hastened the decline of the Knights of Labor, but not through direct attack. It provided a home for the struggling union. Even though the AFL was in the first years much smaller and financially weaker, it was attuned to problems which faced workers at the place of employment. It warned against hasty strikes, but it favored those which were directed towards attainable objectives. It took a few years for its views to become accepted by organized workers and their unions, but every year the activities of the AFL became more important, and the Knights of Labor steadily declined.

CHAPTER 10

Shorter Hours

LEGISLATION

After the Civil War the eight-hour workday became one of the major objectives of the trade unions. In response to these demands, Congress adopted, on June 25, 1868, the simple statement that "eight hours shall constitute a day's work for all laborers, workmen and mechanics now employed or who may be employed by or on behalf of the Government of the United States."[1]

Attorney-General George F. Hoar interpreted the statute to mean that the pay of government workers could be cut by one-fifth as a result of the reduction of the hours of work from ten to eight. Labor refused to accept the view, and the issue appeared to be settled by the proclamation of President Ulysses S. Grant in May 1869. He directed that wages should be left unchanged when the hours were reduced. However, the proclamation was largely ineffective, and a second proclamation by President Grant in May 1872 reiterated his earlier position. Congress obviously approved of the President's attitude when it appropriated funds to compensate federal workers for wages lost. The U.S. Supreme Court nullified these good intentions when it held in *United States* v. *Martin,*[2] 1876, that the law was a directive to its agents and did not prohibit arrangements for longer than eight hours of work. The act was, thereby, not binding upon government officials who could decide on the hours of labor irrespective of legislative intent. Despite the proclamation of President Grant, the act was frequently violated by government supervisors. The enactment of improved eight-hour laws by Congress in 1888 was an attempt to overcome the court decisions. These applied only to the public printer and letter carriers and, in the latter case, it was specifically stated that the lowering of hours was not to be accompanied by reduced pay.

The Postmaster-General, however, interpreted the law to mean time spent in carrying mail and not all work performed by the mail carrier. While overthrown by the decision of the U.S. Supreme Court,[3] the views of the Postmaster-General revealed the difficulties of enforcing legislation lacking the wholehearted support of the administrators. An attempt to override the narrow interpretation was made by Congress in the law of 1892, which stated "That the service and employment of all laborers and mechanics who are now, or may hereafter be, employed by the Government of the United States, by the District of Columbia, or by any contractor or sub-contractor upon any of the public works of the United States, or of the said District, is hereby limited and restricted to eight hours in any one calendar day."[4] The Supreme Court found, however, that the statute did not apply to private shipyards engaged in government naval construction and was limited to workers employed directly by the United States government.[5] The difficulties of gaining reduced hours of labor for federal workers highlighted the problem of gaining relief through legislation.

DIRECT ACTION

The prolonged efforts to gain the reduced work hours through state and federal legislation led to a shift in emphasis by organized workers from dependence upon government to reliance upon their own economic strength. The escape clauses in the laws and their doubtful constitutionality made the legislative method questionable. Moreover, to gain the enactment of a law was a difficult process, while economic power could be applied to specific firms and places to achieve immediate reductions in work schedules, at least in those industries and firms in which workers were well organized and could exercise pressure upon their employers.

A General Strike

From the beginning of the Federation of Organized Trades and Labor Unions, methods for introducing a shorter workday occupied the attention of the delegates. In 1884, Secretary Frank Foster reported that no subject was more deserving of "the careful attention of the Congress."[6] Foster sought to gain the support of the national Democratic and Republican parties. The Republican chairman told him that no position had been taken, and the Democratic chairman failed to acknowledge his letter. Foster concluded that it was necessary for the federation to "assume the initiative in a national movement for the reduction of the hours of labor. Sporadic attempts of individual trades in certain localities have met with varying degrees of success, but there is little doubt that a universal, centrally directed advance would prove both practical and triumphant. . . . This much has been determined by the history of the national eight-hour law—it is useless to wait for legislation in this matter. In the world of economic reform the working class must depend upon themselves for the enforcement of measures as well as for their conception. A united demand for a shorter working day, backed by thorough organization, will prove more effective than the enactment of a thousand laws depending for enforcement upon the pleasure of aspiring politicians."[7]

Gabriel Edmonston, a delegate from Washington, D.C., proposed that the federation declare "that eight hours shall constitute a legal day's labor from and after May 1, 1886, and that we recommend to labor organizations throughout this jurisdiction that they so direct their laws as to conform to this resolution by the time named."[8] This action marked a turning point in the attitude of many trade unionists for, even though the movement was weak and the great industries unorganized, dependence was placed upon the power of workers on the job. Industries employing women and children, and government employees, or whose workers were subject to special hazards or disabilities might use the legislative method but, generally, the AFL believed that workers should use economic pressure for attaining this objective.

The Federation of Organized Trades and Labor Unions could not speak for the organized workers of the United States, since they were represented by unions and trade assemblies. Despite its unrepresentative character and lack of means, the federation made its greatest effort to bring about shorter hours. It urged unions to take action and seek reduced work schedules and in the event of failure to call strikes. The call brought responses and in some instances shorter hours were achieved.

The Knights of Labor did not join in the movement, and Powderly was rightfully convinced that those who had "passed the resolution did but little to secure its enforcement, and from the very first the movement, as far as its operations on May 1, 1886, were concerned, was doomed to defeat."[9] Gompers, on the other hand, thought that the movement to establish the eight-hour day was partially successful. He did not believe that a movement as extensive as the 1886 campaign could entirely succeed in the first effort. He pointed to the benefits gained by the strikes in 1886 and held that the results justified future campaigns to reduce the hours of work. He based his view on "the fact that as a result of the movement of 1886 there have been a number of trades that reduced the hours of labor from ten and twelve to eight; others again from twelve and fourteen to ten and nine, and many thousands of workingmen who before that time worked from fourteen to eighteen hours a day have had the hours of their labor reduced to twelve. It has been estimated that more than eight million hours of labor have been spared the toiler."[10]

Gompers strongly believed that a campaign for shorter hours would attract widespread attention in the ranks of labor to the work and leadership of the newly formed AFL. On the need for shorter hours of work all labor men could agree, and it was a cause which would unite the ranks and give the federation a significant role. He urged the convention not to be "content . . . with the passage of a resolution meaning nothing. If this convention should decide to engage the attention of the working people to the adoption of the 8-hour workday it should take such steps as would lead to practical action and results." It was voted to conduct meetings in favor of the eight-hour day in 1889 and to inaugurate the movement on May 1, 1890.[11]

The agitation for the eight-hour day placed the AFL before the workers of the country in a favorable light. Almost a thousand meetings extolling the virtues of the shorter hour movement were held by the AFL on legal holidays throughout 1889. In addition to Gompers and McGuire, these meetings were addressed by George E. McNeil, Frank K. Foster, and Henry George, among others. Pamphlets on the *Economic and Social Importance of the Eight-Hour Movement,* and *Eight Hour Primer* were widely distributed. Organizers toured the country in behalf of the shorter workday, and the aid of public officials and economists was solicited. Because the federation was in the center of these activities, it profited greatly from the shorter hour campaign. It was decided not to seek a reduction in the hours of labor for all workers simultaneously, but to concentrate efforts upon success in one trade which would be morally and financially supported by the rest of the labor movement.

The Knights of Labor was asked to cooperate, but again refused.[12] Powderly said that to "talk of reducing the hours of labor without reducing the power of machinery to oppress instead of benefit is a waste of energy. The advocates of the eight-hour system must go beyond a reduction of the number of hours a man must work and labor for the establishment of a just and humane system of land ownership, control of machinery, railroads and telegraphs, as well as an equitable currency system, before we will be able to retain the vantage-ground gained when the hours of labor are reduced to eight per day, as called for in the twenty-first resolution of the Preamble of the Knights of Labor."[13]

The Knights of Labor could not cooperate in a campaign for limited objectives, because its leaders did not believe that the methods pursued by the trade unions would succeed in permanently introducing reforms. But the federation did not believe that improvements in wages and in the hours of work had to wait for more fundamental changes in the economy. Instead, its leaders felt that it was feasible to introduce permanent and significant changes in the hours of work through the use of the power at the place of employment. In 1889, Gompers suggested that one or two trades be selected for carrying on the campaign for shorter hours and that the rest of organized labor support the particular trades financially. The scheme was adopted and an assessment upon all affiliates authorized by the convention.[14] The Carpenters' Union was selected to launch the campaign and its secretary, Peter J. McGuire, reported that it had been highly successful. The eight-hour workday was established, he claimed, in 137 cities and affected more than 46,000 carpenters and many other members of the building trades. This was the most successful campaign for shorter hours in which the federation played a dominant role. The objective and the method to be pursued were suggested to the federation, which raised $12,000 in support of the strikers. While Gompers was somewhat apologetic of the small size of the contribution, he believed "it materially aided" the movement for shorter hours.

The coal miners were selected in 1891 to continue the campaign. Economic conditions in the industry were, however, unpropitious, and the movement for shorters hours was deferred. Instead the heads of the United Mine Workers of America sought to use the funds accumulated for a jurisdiction-wide campaign in behalf of a local strike. The AFL Executive Council refused to provide the funds although it donated $2,000 for the miners' in Iowa. Actually, the Carpenters' Union was the only one which participated in the federation-inspired campaign. Although the federation continued to stress the shorter workday, preparations and the tactics were left largely to the decision of the various unions. With their growing memberships, the international unions did not all believe that the setting of a specific date for the inauguration of a shorter hour schedule in their jurisdictions was desirable, although the Granite Cutters' International Union followed this policy and was aided by the AFL in 1900. In the eight-hour campaign of the International Typographical Union, the AFL levied an assessment in its support and raised over $52,000, but it was a modest contribution when compared to the approximately $4,000,000 raised by a special assessment upon the members of the Typographical Union.[15] The federation increasingly took the view that the method by which shorter hours could be achieved was to be determined by the unions themselves. Unions were urged to make the reduction of hours of work a prime target, and the general inclination of the unions was to pursue this objective on a limited basis, in the sense that areas and firms which were most likely to introduce shorter hours were requested to do so and campaigns in entire jurisdictions avoided.

EUROPEAN RADICALISM

The eight-hour movement in 1886 was indirectly the cause of the Haymarket riot in Chicago, Illinois, which led to the death of a number of policemen and the trial and execution of several anarchists charged with being accessories to the murder of one of the policemen. The defendants in the Haymarket trial were all connected with the social revolutionary movement of their day. The movement itself was largely made up of European immigrants who had carried their ideas with them to their new homes in the United States. European radicalism was at the time dominated by two distinct tendencies: the socialist, expounded largely by the followers of Karl Marx and Frederick Engels or Ferdinand Lassalle; and the anarchist view whose chief spokesman was the Russian, Michael Bakunin. A union of all "advanced elements" on the European continent had taken place in 1864 with the formation of the International Workingmen's Association, or the First International, as it later became known. The International was a loose type of federation, and while it embraced the more revolutionary theorists and activists of the time it also contained within its ranks conservative English trade unionists.

The International was not a very radical group. It held a number of conferences on economic and political questions which were followed by the adoption of resolutions. Marx, the leading spokesman of the movement, was challenged in 1869 by Bakunin, who had organized the International Alliance of Social Democracy and sought admission to the International. Rejection of the application by the general council on the ground that its views were not in harmony with those of the International was the signal for a bitter feud which culminated in the expulsion of Bakunin and his followers by the 1872 convention at The Hague. Marx's disciples decided to transfer the weakened International to New York where it later expired.

Followers of the First International inaugurated the movement in New York in 1867 which led to the establishment of the Social party of New York and Vicinity. It nominated a ticket in the 1868 elections and polled a few votes. As a result of the poor showing, the party dissolved and some of its members formed the General German Labor Association. In the same year several small societies in New York, Chicago, and San Francisco, made up almost entirely of German immigrants, affiliated with the International. A provisional central committee was set up by the societies to coordinate their activities in accordance with the rules of the European International. By 1870 the International was making some progress in the United States and societies of Germans, French, Irish, Americans, Scandinavians, and Bohemians were now affiliated. The popularity of the movement was a signal to all kinds of reformers that the International was a favorable soil for their conflicting agitation.[16] It led to the formation of labor and Socialist political groups and parties which, despite the similarities of their principles, were in constant war with each other.

Socialist Labor Party

Several of the Socialist groups met in Philadelphia on July 19, 1876, and at the end of the meeting, on July 22, had formed the Working Men's party of the United States. Present at this meeting were F. A. Sorge, a close personal and political friend of Karl Marx, and Adolph Strasser and Peter J. McGuire, future leaders of the trade union movement. The name of the organization was changed to the Socialist Labor party at its second convention in 1877. The path of the new party was not easy. Aside from the usual difficulties encountered by reform and revolutionary organizations only about 10 per cent of its members were native Americans. "All the rest, including the most active and influential leaders of the party, were men of foreign birth, insufficiently acquainted with the institutions, customs, and habits of the country of their adoption, and frequently ignorant of its very language."[17]

Efforts to attract a native and an Americanized following were not very successful. Lack of progress aroused criticism; and a radical wing, influenced by anarchist doctrines, appeared toward the end of the 1870's. In 1877, Socialists in Chicago and Cincinnati had formed Educational and Defense societies *(Lehr und Wehr Vereine)* which were opposed by the heads of the party, who feared that the drilling with arms would create a false impression of the aims of the organization. The criticism led to a secession by some of the militant members. Even though the drilling with arms aroused fear, many of the members of these societies regarded them as sporting clubs. However, they also contained a number of hyperradicals and antisocial neurotics who hoped to revenge their frustrations.[18]

Rudolf Rocker, a leading anarchist and author, claims that the armed societies were playing at revolution and they, in fact, did little harm. The extremists, who withdrew from the Socialist Labor party, called themselves social revolutionaries to distinguish themselves from their moderate colleagues, the Social Democrats, and formed the Revolutionary Socialist Labor party. Gradually the social revolutionaries moved toward a pure anarchist position which not only repudiated political action but they also espoused "propaganda by the deed." This view was expressed in two forms: armed insurrection by small groups and acts of violence by single individuals against persons and property.[19]

Johann Most

Johann Most's arrival in the United States in 1882 gave the radicals an experienced agitator, who carried the prestige of exile and imprisonment in Austria, Germany, and England. Most had joined the German Social Democratic party as a young man and had been elected to the Reichstag in 1874. Forced to leave Germany after the enactment of the Anti-Socialist laws by Bismarck in 1878, he settled in London where he published the *Freiheit,* a radical journal. The views of the paper led to his exclusion from the Social Democratic party. When Most approved of the assassination of Alexander II by Russian terrorists in 1881, he was sentenced to sixteen months in prison. Upon his release, he departed for the United States. Most was an apostle of violence[20] and in a seventy-three page pamphlet he described the making and use of bombs and dynamite. He resumed his activity of editing and agitating, and his efforts were, at least partly, responsible for the calling of the Pittsburgh congress of revolutionary Socialists.

Twenty-six delegates were present at the opening of the convention on October 14, 1883, and they represented societies in eleven states. With the exception of two, the delegates were German, and the convention was carried on in that language and in English. A plan of organization was drawn up so as not to interfere with the autonomy of the separate groups, the name International Working People's Association was chosen, the use of armed force as a propaganda and defensive weapon was affirmed, and a set of principles was devised. In addition to advocating "energetic, relentless, revolutionary and international action," the program called for the establishment of a free society based upon cooperative production, and "free exchange of equivalent products by and between the productive organization without commerce and profit mongering."[21]

It is noteworthy that the conference which advocated the use of violence was composed mainly of foreigners who did not understand the problems of labor in the United States. The anarchist movement had its chief strength in Chicago, where the *Arbeiter Zeitung, Vorbote,* and the *Fackel,* as well as the English *Alarm,* were published. More conventional labor organizations were also well established in the city, and both groups heartily responded to the eight-hour agitation of the 1880's. The influence of the social revolutionaries among the organized workers of Chicago was very small, but, discontented with the conservative outlook of the Amalgamated Trades and Labor Assembly, the radicals seceded and set up the Central Labor Union with mostly German unions affiliated.[22]

THE HAYMARKET RIOT

Before the beginning of the general movement for the eight-hour workday, the lumber shovelers at the McCormick Reaper works had gone on strike on February 11, 1886, for reduced hours and higher wages. Temporarily settled, at the end of April, the strike was resumed when the company insisted upon employing strikebreakers who had been hired during the walkout; the plant was opened under police protection and operations were restored with nonunion workers. On May 3, 1886, a mass meeting of the striking lumber shovelers was held near the McCormick plant. August Spies, an editor of the anarchist *Arbeiter Zeitung,* came to the meeting "and mounted upon a car, and then the howls arose that he was a socialist, but when it appeared that he was a member of the Central Labor Union peace was restored and harmony prevailed."[23]

The meeting was peaceful, but at the changing of the shifts a number in the crowd began pelting the strikebreakers with fists, sticks, stones, and iron pipe. Responding to a riot call, the police used their clubs and guns to disperse the mob. It was reported that several had been killed and a larger number wounded. Outraged by the brutal assaults he witnessed, Spies returned to his editorial office and composed the "Revenge Circular" in which he called upon the workers "rise in your might . . . To Arms! We call you to arms."[24] About half of the 2,500 copies of the circular were distributed, and a protest meeting was later called at Haymarket Square for the night of May 4. In the announcement of the meeting were inserted the lines "Workingmen Arm Yourselves and Appear in Full Force," and Spies insisted that those be stricken from the announcement or he would not speak at the meeting.

When the audience assembled it was smaller than expected, and the meeting was shifted slightly to a private passageway down the street. Anticipating trouble, the police department had assembled a force of 180 men under the command of Inspector John Bonfield. August Spies opened the meeting at 8:30 P.M., spoke for a half an hour, and introduced Albert Parsons, editor of the *Alarm,* an English-language anarchist sheet. He was followed by Samuel Fielden, a teamster and a member of the English-speaking anarchist group in Chicago. Parsons and his wife and many others departed and only a small part of the initial crowd estimated to have been between 1,000 and 3,000 remained. Before Fielden could conclude his talk, Inspector Bonfield and Captain William Ward at the head of the police detachment marched toward the wagon on which Fielden was speaking. Captain Ward called for the meeting to disperse. Fielden protested the order and pointed to its peaceful character. As Fielden finished his remarks, a bomb was thrown among the police. It killed Policeman Mathias J. Degan instantly; six others died later.

The action of Inspector Bonfield, the officer in charge, has never been explained. No disorder had taken place at the meeting before the appearance of the police. Mayor Carter Harrison, who had been present for more than two hours, claimed that no untoward incidents had taken place, and he had suggested to Bonfield that the police on special duty be allowed to go home. A roundup of well-known anarchists began, and on June 3 indictments were returned against Albert Parsons, August Spies, Adolph Fischer, Michael Schwab, Samuel Fielden, Oscar Neebe, George Engel, Louis Lingg, Rudolph Schnaubelt (who was arrested and released but never found again), and William Seliger, who turned state's evidence. The indicted were charged with killing Policeman Degan, and each was charged with aiding, advising, and abetting an unknown person to commit the murder.

The defendants had been unmercifully attacked in the press and pulpit, and when the trial opened on June 21 public opinion was aroused against the defendants. The defense was convinced that the trial judge, Joseph E.

Gary, "absolutely ignored the constitutional right of trial by an *impartial jury* [italics in original]. . . . The Court held that jurors were competent who had *formed and expressed* an opinion of the guilt and innocence of the accused, based upon newspaper articles and rumors. . . . The Court carried his ruling to the extent of holding that even where the proposed juror stated that he had formed and expressed an opinion in reference to the guilt or innocence of the defendants, based upon what he had read, heard and believed to be true, and admitted that he had talked with parties who were present at the Haymarket riot, witnessing the occurrence there, and who detailed the same to the juror, and whose statements were believed by the juror to be true; still this did not disqualify the proposed juror."[25]

The defense lawyers also called the appellate court's "attention to the fact that we were subjected to most outrageous misconduct on the part of a special bailiff, who had charge of the summoning of the talesmen."[26] The defense was denied an opportunity to present evidence that the special bailiff had publicly stated: "I am managing this case and I know what I am about. These fellows will hang as certain as death."[27]

Of the ten indicted, Seliger testified for the state, and Schnaubelt was never apprehended. Parsons, who had not been arrested, surrendered voluntarily on the first day of the trial because he feared that his absence from the prisoners' dock might prejudice the jury against the other defendants.[28] By July 15 the jury had been completed; testimony began the following day and lasted until August 10. Nothing was proved against Oscar Neebe, and the defense argued "that there is no testimony that shows, or tends to show, that he advised, aided, or encouraged, abetted or assisted the throwing of a bomb. We find ourselves at a loss to argue the case of Mr. Neebe."[29] He owned two shares of stock in the *Arbeiter Zeitung.*

Testimony was given that Fischer and Engel were present at a meeting on May 3 at 54 West Lake Street. According to Godfried Waller, a police informer, who presided at the meeting, it was agreed that when the word "ruhe" or peace was published in the *Arbeiter Zeitung* under the heading "letter box" it was to be regarded as a signal for the armed men to meet. Police action was to be observed, and if a conflict should ensue, the armed men were to storm the police station and throw a bomb.[30]

The defense denied that such a plan had been contemplated. Moreover, the defense argued that only two, or at most, three of the defendants could have known of the plans made at the Lake Street meeting.[31]

The state failed to connect the defendants directly with the throwing of the bomb, or to establish that they had in any way approved or abetted this act. In his charge to the jury, the judge held that it was entirely competent for the state to prove that "these several defendants have advocated the use of deadly missiles against the police on occasions which they anticipated might arise in the future—that it is competent for them to show that they intended that the use should be made, not by an agreement beforehand as to the specific occasion when they should be used, but that they should be used when in the judgment of the person using them the time had come."[32]

Judge Gary furthermore instructed the jury if the defendants conspired with other persons to

excite the people or classes of people . . . to sedition, tumult and riot, to use deadly weapons against and take the lives of other persons, as a means to carry their designs and purposes into effect, and in pursuance of such conspiracy, and in furtherance of its objects, any of the persons so conspiring publicly by print or speech advised or encouraged the commission of murder without designating time, place or occasion at which it should be done, and in pursuance of, and induced by such advise or encouragement, murder was committed, then all of such conspirators are guilty of such murder, whether the person who perpetrated such a murder can be identified or not. . . . Nor does it matter, if there was such a conspiracy, how impracticable or impossible of success its end and aims were, nor how foolish or ill-arranged were the plans for its execution, except as bearing upon the question whether there was or was not such conspiracy.[33]

The defense claimed the doctrine means "the introduction, for the first time, into criminal jurisprudence, of the principle that a supposed or possible moral responsibility involves the penalty of legal offense."[34]

On August 19 the case was given to the jury, which returned a verdict of guilty against all eight defendants, condemning seven to death and Neebe to fifteen years in prison. The case was appealed to the Illinois Supreme Court and argued by Leonard Swett, an associate of Lincoln, and Captain Black and Sigmund Zeisler in the March 1887 term. Judgment was affirmed on September 14, and an appeal to the U.S. Supreme Court was denied on November 2. A movement for a pardon was then launched. A petition signed by thousands pleaded for amnesty, and leaders in the professions and business joined heads of labor unions in asking Governor Richard J. Oglesby for a pardon. A committee of leading men, including Samuel Gompers, traveled to Springfield to plead for mercy. Two of the defendants, Fielden and Schwab, petitioned the governor to spare their lives, and August Spies asked him to release the other defendants and execute him to satisfy the public lust for vengeance. Judge Gary and the prosecutor, Julius Grinnell, joined in asking for mercy for Fielden and Schwab, and the governor commuted their sentences. Engel, Fischer, Parsons, and Spies were hanged on the morning of November 11. Lingg cheated the hangman by exploding a bomb in his mouth a day before the execution date and died a painful death after six hours of suffering.[35]

The historian of the Haymarket affair tells us that the "American workingman was just as shocked and distressed by the bomb as anyone else. On the whole the American working class had no use for revolutionary 'isms.'

The disavowal of the bomb was, therefore, quite normal. Furthermore, the bomb was at least incidentally connected with the eight-hour movement. It was, therefore, necessary for labor to insist that the bomb and those responsible for it, were foreign to the eight-hour movement and inimical to the interests of the worker."[36]

Terence Powderly claimed he had "never felt called upon to say anything for it is none of my business."[37]

After the executions, anarchist agitation continued in Chicago and in the rest of the country as well. Doubts about the convictions were unresolved. When the fear and anger had receded, the belief that justice may not have been done on November 11, 1887, became more widespread. The dead could not be recalled, but the three imprisoned defendants could be released as a recognition of their innocence. Releasing anarchists adjudged guilty of murder was, however, not an easy political decision for a governor, and the amnesty committee, organized to effect the release of the imprisoned, found its pleas unanswered until the election of John Peter Altgeld as governor of Illinois in 1892. After assuming office in the following January, Altgeld informed the Amnesty Committee and the Trades and Labor Assembly of Chicago that an application for a pardon for the Chicago anarchists was not necessary. The governor had decided to study the record and make his decision on the basis of the evidence.[38]

In a statement accompanying the pardons he decided to grant, Altgeld severely upbraided the trial and prosecutor and declared that (1) the jury had been improperly drawn and was prejudiced against the defendants; (2) the jury was prejudiced and was therefore not competent to serve, "when . . . the trial judge ruled that these men were competent jurors, simply because they had, under his adroit manipulation, been led to say that they believed they could try the case fairly on the evidence, then the proceedings lost all semblance of a fair trial";[39] (3) the defendants were not proven guilty because the state "has never discovered who it was that threw the bomb which killed the policeman, and the evidence does not show any connection whatsoever between the defendants and the man who threw it." The governor found no law to sustain the rulings by Judge Gary and "in all the centuries during which government has been maintained among men, and crime has been punished, no judge in a civilized country has ever laid down such a rule." Finally, Altgeld condemned State Attorney Julius S. Grinnell for failing to ask for the dismissal of Neebe after he had declared that there was virtually no evidence against him.

The unanswered question in the tragedy has been, "Who threw the bomb?" Governor Altgeld believed that someone who had been manhandled by the Chicago police had taken the opportunity to revenge himself. Dr. David rejects this view. Frank Harris in his novel of the Haymarket tragedy, *The Bomb,* points the finger at the fugitive Schnaubelt, whose flight lent some credence to the view. During the life of the generation which witnessed the tragedy, claims and denials that Schnaubelt and others were guilty appeared periodically in the anarchist press. The son of one of the defense counsels has recently expressed the view that Schnaubelt was the bomb thrower. His opinion was based upon information he received from a physician whose father was close to the anarchist movement. The defendants do not appear to have known that a bomb was to be thrown, since they could not have expected the police to appear to suppress the meeting.[40]

The effect of the Haymarket tragedy on the labor movement was not great. The labor movement was not directly involved, although many organizations and leaders spoke out against the executions. Nor did the throwing of the bomb have any effect on the eight-hour movement. Even the campaign in one craft or industry was found to be inefficient because the position, stability, and bargaining power of all locals were not equal, and a jurisdiction-wide attempt to establish the shorter workday taxed the strength of the weaker locals and exposed them to reprisals by their employers which they could not meet.

CHAPTER 11

The Rise of Opposition to Labor
in the 1890's

The strikes in Homestead, Pennsylvania, in 1892 and in Pullman, Illinois, in 1894 revealed the growing hostility to unionism in American business. In Homestead an old established union which had negotiated with firms in the steel industry for years was forced to strike for its existence. Its members reacted with savage violence against those brought into the community to protect strikebreakers, but they were defeated. In contrast, the contest in Pullman initially involved unorganized workers who sought to establish a union in a model town so as to protect themselves against wage cuts and price rises at the company store or for services in the company-owned town. Supported in their contest by a recently formed and confident industrial union of railroad men, the Pullman workers were forced to surrender by the industrial might of the company supported by government.

Despite the differences in their origin, both strikes revealed the determination of the growing industrial giants to rid themselves of any second power in their plants and their willingness to use their full resources to effect their plans. The Homestead strike was supported by workers in other mills of the Carnegie Steel Company and the Pullman workers were aided by railroad men in and around Chicago.

THE TOWN OF HOMESTEAD

Homestead was in 1892 a relatively new community along the Monongahela River, lying six miles below its confluence with the Youghiogheny and seven miles above the point where it meets the Allegheny and forms the Ohio River. In 1871 the Homestead Bank and Life Insurance Company had purchased farms and divided them into building lots in hopes that a suburb of Pittsburgh would prosper. In the following year the Pittsburgh, Virginia and Charleston Railroad connected Homestead with Pittsburgh and commuting became an easy matter. A Lutheran church was built in 1874 and the launching of a glass factory two years later marked the industrial debut of the community. In 1881 the Klomans Company built a steel mill along the river banks; the mill later became a part of the Carnegie Brothers Company in 1886.[1]

THE UNION

The Amalgamated Association of Iron and Steel Workers of America was established in Philadelphia in 1876, through a merger of the Iron and Steel Roll Hands, the Associated Brotherhood of Iron and Steel Heaters, Rollers and Roughers, and the United Sons of Vulcan whose delegates met in Pittsburgh in August 1876 and set up the organization. Section 2 of the constitution announced that the objectives of the association "shall be to obtain by conciliation, or by other means that are fair and legal, a fair remuneration to the members for their labor; and to afford mutual protection to members against broken contracts, obnoxious rules, unlawful discharge, or other systems of injustice or oppression."[2] Before 1877 large classes of steelworkers were ineligible for membership in the union. Knoblers, turners, boiler-plate men, and sheet-iron shearmen were admitted in that year. At the suggestion of President William Weihe in 1887, the jurisdiction of the union was expanded and "all branches of labor directly interested in the manufacture of iron and steel should be made eligible to membership." The proposal was adopted in 1889, and "all men working in and around rolling mills, tin mills, steel works, nail, tack, spike, bolt and nut factories, and all works run in connection with the same, except laborers, were admitted, the latter to be admitted at the discretion of the subordinate lodge to which application is made for membership."[3] It faced continual internal dissension partly occasioned by differences in nationalities and also differences among the special crafts employed in the steel mills.[4] Like the preceding organizations in the iron and steel industry, the Amalgamated was not unwilling to engage in strikes. Jarrett claimed that between 1867 and 1875 the Sons of Vulcan had called eighty-seven authorized strikes within their jurisdiction, sixty-nine of them because of wage differences. The Amalgamated had few walkouts in its first two years, but in 1879 the union was attacked through the discharge of many of its active members, and strikes followed. Between 1876 and 1885, the Amalgamated authorized ninety-three strikes. Of the total number, twenty-eight were successful; sixty-one failed, and four were compromised.[5]

Members of the union opposed the reduction of working hours to eight because they found that working by the ton, they could not earn a proper day's pay. When some mills established the eight-hour system in 1885, President Weihe revoked the charters of the locals which accepted it. In the same year the union's convention voted to permit the establishment of eight-hour shifts in the steel mills. According to an early student of steel union-ism, the association officers favored the eight-hour workday while the rank and file did not. President Weihe noted in 1890 that "while the iron workers are not in a general way ready to go into a movement for the eight-hour system, the steel workers have a better opportunity and should not lose sight of a chance when it presents itself, to take the advantage and adopt it."[6] Despite the views of Weihe and other officers, a large number of heaters, rollers, roughers, and catchers "complained that their connection with the American Federation of Labor placed them in a false light in appearing to favor the eight-hour movement, 'which was not practicable for them as iron workers.' They suggested, therefore, that the Association sever its connection with the American Federation of Labor."[7] The petition was tabled at the 1890 convention.

H. C. Frick

Relations between Homestead management and the union were fairly satisfactory. Conditions were to change upon the emergence of Henry Clay Frick as an officer of the Carnegie Steel Company. Frick had been successful in the Connellsville mining district as a producer of coke. He was born in West Overton, Pennsylvania, in 1850. He began his business life as a clerk in a dry goods store and later became a bookeeper in his grandfather's dis-tillery. His great success, however, was achieved in the coke business. With E. M. Ferguson he organized the H. C. Frick and Company in 1877. He built the largest coke works in the area, and by 1882, Carnegie Brothers and Company were given representation on the board of directors. Frick was the personification of the ruthless business leader who would tolerate no opposition. His attitude toward labor was uncompromising. Once hav-ing decided to solve an issue by economic power, he crushed all who ques-tioned his decision, with the aid if necessary of the coal and iron police, the Pinkertons, and the state militia.

Early in 1887 the coke operators of the district offered a wage scale which was rejected by the miners. The differences were submitted to arbi-tration, but the local lodges refused to accept the award and went on strike. Frick favored an aggressive policy, and when the board of directors of the Frick Coke Company decided to yield, he resigned as president. He insisted that having persuaded the men to arbitrate and a "decision having been rendered in our favor, I think that, cost what it may, we should abide by it, and not start our works until our employees resume work at the old wages."[8]

Frick had his way, the union was broken, and his resignation was not accepted. In fact, Frick joined Carnegie Brothers and Company in January 1889 as a partner with the money loaned to him by Andrew Carnegie at 2 per cent interest. He became chairman of the firm, in charge of making and administering policy, with Carnegie as his only superior. Running true to form, Frick became embroiled in a dispute with the union less than six months after joining the firm. In proposing a renewal of the agreement in 1889, Frick suggested a reduction in tonnage rates for all except laborers, each employee to be required to sign the agreement individually, and finally, the expiration of the contract on January 1, 1892, instead of June 30, as was customary. Such an expiration date would give the company an advantage in bargaining.

The Homestead lodges refused to accept the new terms, and when the contract expired on July 1, a strike followed. An attempt was made to resume operations, and more than a hundred deputy sheriffs were assembled. No violence developed when the pickets did not allow the deputies to take possession of the plant, and the deputies refused to force passage through the pickets. At this point, the sheriff succeeded in bringing about a resumption of negotiations, and the strike was settled.[9]

Contract Renewal in 1892

With the approach of the expiration date of the contract with the Amalgamated, Frick became the head manager and chairman of the properties of the several Carnegie corporations which were merged and placed under the control of the Carnegie Steel Corporation, Limited. He sought to have the new scale considered in January 1892. Frick's desire for early negotiations was "to avoid being caught in the meshes of unpreparedness which might have placed the firm at the mercy of the union."[10] In March the union suggested a general raise in wages as the basis for a settlement. By the end of May, Frick proposed a downward revision of the scale for four departments employing 325 of the 3,800 men in the Homestead plant,[11] and lowering the minimum of the basic scale from $25.00 to $22.00 a ton. Under the old contract, wages in these departments depended upon the price of steel, and under the sliding scale, wages were unaffected if the price fell below $25.00. Frick proposed that the low point be dropped to $22.00. Failing to gain acceptance of his proposal, he notified J. A. Marshall, superintendent of the Homestead Steel Works, that the wage scales for open hearth and No. 32 and 119 inch mills be presented to the joint committee of the union, with the request that it give a decision not later than June 24. He directed that the committee be informed "that these scales are in all respects the most liberal that can be offered." He added that he did not care whether a man did or did not belong to a union, but believed that the employees at the Homestead Steel Works "would fare better working under the system in vogue at Edgar Thompson [where the company had defeated the Knights of Labor and established an open shop] Duquesne,"[12] which was manned by nonunion men.

Frick claimed that he could "place no reliance on the agreements [organized labor] made us, and we concluded that we would end the thing once and for all, and determine whether we had a right to employ whom we pleased and discharge whom we pleased. That strike [the 1891 coke strike] lasted . . . until the latter part of May of that year, at which time we succeeded in starting our works with what is called 'nonunion workers,' and from that time until the present we have had no trouble. Our men have been content and happy. We have not been bothered with the labor agitator and with committees asking all sorts of concessions."[13] A meeting of union men was held at Homestead on June 19, and the speakers exhorted the men to stand firm, but also urged moderation and respect for law.[14]

Frick's ultimatum called for a conference up to June 24, and the committee met him and the superintendent on June 23. At the conference the difference in the price of a ton of steel between the union committee and Frick was narrowed to $1.00; the union holding for $24.00 and Frick for $23.00. More important to the union was the company's insistence that the contract expire on January 1 instead of July 30. The men were adamant on this point, arguing that business was not as brisk in the winter as in the summer and that it was easier to be on strike in summer than in winter. In any event, negotiations were not resumed.[15] Frick had decided on other tactics. On June 25, F. T. F. Lovejoy, secretary of the Carnegie Company, announced that the rate would be $23.00 a ton on billets, irrespective of the views of the Amalgamated, and the date for fixing the scale would be shifted from June to January.[16]

Frick announced he would not deal with the Amalgamated, and in a press interview defined the issue as "whether the Carnegie Company or the Amalgamated Association shall have absolute control of our plant and business at Homestead."[17]

On June 29 a mass meeting of steel workers decided to strike on July 2. Without public announcement, the lodges elected an advisory committee of thirty-four members with Hugh O'Donnell as chairman. Special committees were appointed to patrol the riverfront and the river in skiffs, and the entrances to the city day and night.

In his negotiations Frick had the support of Andrew Carnegie, the principal owner of the Carnegie Brothers Company. In fact, Carnegie wanted to announce in April 1892 that the Homestead plant would go nonunion, but the announcement was withheld by Frick who believed it was inopportune.[18] Carnegie left for his customary vacation in Scotland, and on June 10 he wrote to Frick: "Of course, you will be asked to confer, and I know you will decline all conferences as you have taken your stand and have nothing more to say."[19] On June 28, Carnegie wrote: "Cables do not seem favorable to a settlement at Homestead. If these be correct, this is your chance to reorganize the whole affair, and some one over Potter [the superintendent] should exact good reasons for *employing every man* [italics in original]. Far too many men required by Amalgamated rules."[20]

Not unprepared, Frick had requested the Pinkerton Detective Agency to supply him with guards before he knew that his terms would be rejected. He "had the preliminary arrangements made for these men with an agent of Mr. Pinkerton, that is to say, an understanding we were to pay for these men. . . . Three hundred; that is to say, I didn't know how many we would want or whether we would want them at all when I had this preliminary talk, but after the 24th of June, when these workmen refused to make terms with us, we concluded it would be necessary to protect our own property and secure new workmen."[21]

Assembling and Transporting Guards

On June 25, Frick asked Robert Pinkerton to assemble 300 guards at Ashtabula, Ohio, not later than July 25, "when they may be taken by train to McKees Rocks, or some other point on the Ohio River below Pittsburgh, where they can be transferred to boats and landed within the inclosures of our premises at Homestead. We think absolute secrecy essential in the movement of these men so that no demonstration can be made while they are en route."[22]

The Battle

On July 4, the Carnegie Company called on the sheriff to provide protection for its property, and when he arrived in Homestead the next day, the advisory committee offered to maintain order and suggested he deputize a number of the strikers. He refused. During that night, more than three hundred Pinkertons were transferred to two barges and accompanied by a deputy sheriff were towed up the river from a point below Pittsburgh by the tugboat *Little Bill*. Plans were to land at Homestead before dawn. A scout of the advisory committee had noticed the suspicious movements of the boats along the Pittsburgh wharves and had wired O'Donnell: "Watch the river. Steamer with barges left here."[23] The town was alerted, and thousands rushed to the riverbanks to await the strangers. As the barges moved towards the Carnegie property, the wooden fence which had been erected at Frick's orders was torn down and part of the crowd moved toward the river to prevent a landing.

The Pinkertons pushed a gangplank ashore, and one of the crowd threw himself before them to prevent their passage. During the argument a shot was fired, followed by a volley from the crowd and general firing from the barges. Two strikers and two Pinkertons were killed, and a number of

Pinkertons wounded during the first skirmish. The strikers retreated behind steel and metal slabs so as not to expose themselves to fire; the Pinkertons temporarily abstained from trying to land.

Two hours later, another attempt at landing was made, and it was met by a fusillade from the strikers who were now partially protected by embankments of steel and iron. The Pinkertons again retreated to their boats and answered the strikers' fire through the windows and port holes. The tugboat *Little Bill,* which had carried the barges to their destination, now sought to bring them back. It was met by a volley of shot and finally escaped up the river to Pittsburgh, leaving the barges exposed. Oil was spread on the river in the hope of burning the barges, and dynamite was thrown at them, but these maneuvers failed. Finally, the Pinkertons raised a white flag as a token of surrender, but for a time it was ignored. By five o'clock in the evening, Hugh O'Donnell, the chairman of the advisory committee, agreed to the surrender of the Pinkertons and assured them safe passage. The crowd was of another mind; it swept over the barges and carried off the movable goods, and the Pinkertons fared badly as they ran through a gauntlet of men, women, and children who had seen some of their friends and relatives felled or killed.

Sheriff William H. McCleary called for troops and told Governor Robert E. Pattison that the Pinkerton guards were in the hands of the rioters and the plant had been taken over by the strikers. On July 10 the governor was informed that the "strikers are in control, and openly express to me and to the public their determination that the works will not be operated unless by themselves. After making all efforts in my power, I failed to secure a posse respectable enough in numbers to accomplish anything, and I am satisfied that no posse raised by the civil authority can do anything to change the condition of affairs, and consequent loss of life. Only a large military force will enable me to control matters."[24]

The governor ordered 7,000 troops to Homestead and the strikers were forced off the premises; the troops remained in Homestead until October 13. Hugh O'Donnell now decided to seek the intervention of Whitelaw Reid, the publisher of the *New York Tribune* and a leading Republican, in behalf of the ending of the strike. He told Reid that if the Carnegie Company would resume negotiations with the Amalgamated, the strike would be ended, and that there was "no disposition on the part of the employees to stand upon a question of scale, or wages, or hours or anything else."[25] Carnegie sought, after the strike was over, to pretend that he had wanted O'Donnell's offer considered, but he actually had cabled "nothing can be done."[26] Frick would not relent in his opposition to dealing with the Amalgamated, and Carnegie, locked away at his Rannoch Lodge in Scotland would not commit himself except to say that he had "implicit confidence in those who are managing the mills."[27] Carnegie's utterances, profoundly at variance with the sympathies he often expressed for trade unions, shocked many of his admirers. Carnegie later denied that he had approved of the hiring of Pinkertons. When they were hired in the 1887 strike at the Edgar Thompson plant, Carnegie claimed he did not know it was done. Of Homestead in 1892 he said that "to my best knowledge and belief, I never heard of such a thing. And of course I did not know they were employed at Homestead at the time."[28]

Assault on Frick

Frick, in the meantime, obtained unexpected sympathy from the foolish assault upon his life by a young anarchist, Alexander Berkman. Berkman had left New York with that purpose in mind and, in company with Henry Bauer and Carl Knold, two local anarchists, inspected the Pittsburgh building in which Frick had his office. The next day Berkman entered the office, fired and hit Frick twice, and although wounded by two bullets and thrusts from Berkman's stiletto, Frick grappled with his assailant until help came. Berkman was arrested. One man who did not respond to Frick's courage was W. L. Iams, a soldier in one of the regiments stationed at Homestead. He called for "three cheers for the man who shot Frick." He was strung up by his thumbs until he apologized. He refused, was cut down, court-martialed, and drummed out of camp. The torture turned out to be a serious error, for public sympathy was strongly against the officers, even among those who were sympathetic with Frick. Berkman was sentenced to twenty-five years in prison, of which he served fourteen; his accomplices were given five-year prison terms.[29]

Mills Reopened

Under the protection of the military, preparations for resuming operations began. Agents of the Carnegie Company scoured the cities for strike replacements, and despite the efforts of friendly labor groups alerted by the AFL, many recruits were obtained. On July 15 the furnaces were lit for the first time since the beginning of the strike. The following day the company announced that individual applications would be received until July 21, and all openings after that date would be filled with new men. A large force of nonunion men entered the plant at Homestead on July 22. In the meantime Frick had signed the union scale at the Pittsburgh and Beaver Falls mills, but the workers decided not to work until the trouble in Homestead was ended. Men employed in three other Carnegie mills, one of them unorganized, also joined the walkout.

Arrests

Action against the rioters followed charges by Chief Justice Edward Paxson of the Pennsylvania Supreme Court. He filed complaints of treason against a number of the strikers; others were indicted for murder. The law under which the charge was made had been passed in 1860, and the penalty had been fixed at $2,000 fine and imprisonment up to twelve years. The intervention of the Chief Justice, he claimed, "was due to the supreme importance of the cases and . . . he acted at the invitation of the county judges."[30] He declared that the action of the workers in Homestead violated the statute, and 167 were indicted under this and other laws. Gompers came to Homestead and in a speech assailed the Chief Justice. "I am not a lawyer," said Gompers, "but I don't think it necessary to be one to know what constitutes treason and what patriotism. Shall patriotism be measured by the yard stick of the Carnegie firm or be weighed as their pig iron. Is it because these men in those latter days like those in Boston harbor, declared they had some rights and dared to maintain them that they shall be called traitors? The men who lost their blood and limbs on the field of battle to maintain and preserve this country and knock off the shackles of milions can not be construed as traitors, Judge Paxson's charge notwithstanding."[31]

The American Federation of Labor

As soon as reports of the Homestead battle became known, Gompers wired to President William Weihe of the Amalgamated and asked what help the AFL could render. For a time Weihe did not want the executive council to meet in Pittsburgh, but on August 12 a meeting of the council assembled there. On Saturday, August 14, Gompers addressed 1,400 men in the Homestead rink. He was asked what he thought of the assault on Frick.

"I have been asked," said Gompers, "for my opinion of the attack on the life of Mr. Frick. I don't know why I should be asked to go out of my way to give Berkman an additional kick. I never heard of him until he made his attack. The laws of Pennsylvania will take care of him. I do know, however, that I have heard of thousands of men being shot down by day and by night, each and everyone of whom was a better man than this despot, Frick. Yet, I have never been asked for my opinion of any of these cases."[32]

The AFL issued an appeal for aid on August 13, and declared November 13 as Homestead Day, on which all workers were called on to aid in the defense of the workers indicted for murder and riot.[33] In addition, the AFL was active in the legal defense of the accused and tried to keep the strike going until a settlement could be obtained. "Sentiment at Homestead was kept warm by the unflagging efforts of the Amalgamated officials, and of President Gompers, of the Federation of Labor."[34] But the workers were fighting a losing battle. The mills were filled and the aid was not sufficient to prevent widespread suffering among the strikers and their families. At the time the "Federation officials sought to buoy the men up and revive the determined spirit which had been exhibited in the early stages of the conflict. Mr. Gompers taxed his powers of oratory to the utmost."[35] But the speeches could not halt the inevitable. On November 14 the men voted to return.

Trials

On November 18, Sylvester Critchlow was brought to trial on the charge of murder; he was acquitted. Jack Clifford was next, tried on the same charge, and was also acquitted. The same result followed the trial of Hugh O'Donnell. The state managed to have Robert J. Beatty, a cook in the mills, convicted on charges of assault and battery for administering poison to nonunion men in the mills. Hugh Dempsey, master workman of the District Assembly No. 3 of the Knights of Labor, was convicted on the same charge. The indictments against the other unionists were dismissed, as were those for riot and conspiracy against Frick, fifteen officers of the company, and two heads of the Pinkerton Detective Agency.

The Pinkerton National Detective Agency

The battle of Homestead brought on an investigation of the Pinkerton Detective Agency, the first time that organization came under public scrutiny.[36]

The Aftermath of the Strike

Hundreds of union men were locked out, and the Homestead plant was not to operate under a union agreement for forty-five years. Many were black-listed and were denied employment. The strike, according to the historian of the Carnegie Steel Company, became a national issue in the Presidential election of 1892, and "brought defeat to the Republican hosts. . . . Every inducement was made to bring Mr. Carnegie into the canvass, but he persistently declined to lend his influence or to pay one dollar to the campaign fund."[37] Carnegie returned to Pittsburgh in January 1893, and announced that he would not exchange Frick for any other manager.

The strike was a severe blow to the Amalgamated Association. It was also a vivid sign that the new generation of steelmakers were not inclined to tolerate a second power in their plants. The time was, however, not right for the complete ousting of the union from the industry, for there was at the time no single power in steel that could lay down the policy to be pursued in both labor and price matters. Nevertheless, the inability of the Amalgamated to resist a determined attack by a large company revealed its basic weakness, and although it remained an important force in the industry for more than a decade, Homestead revealed its vulnerable position.

THE PULLMAN PALACE CAR COMPANY

The Pullman Palace Car Company was organized by George Mortimer Pullman in 1867 with $1 million of capital. Its main object was the operation of parlor and sleeping cars under contract on the railroads. Soon after its organization the company began manufacturing cars for itself and for the general market. In 1880 the company decided "to build, in close proximity to the shops, homes for workingmen of such character and surroundings as would prove so attractive as to cause the best class of mechanics to seek that place for employment in preference to others. We also desired to establish the place on such a basis as would exclude all baneful influences, believing that such a policy would result in the greatest measure of success, both from a commercial point of view, and also, what was equally important, or perhaps of greater importance, in a tendency toward continued elevation and improvement of the conditions not only of the working people themselves, but of their children growing up about them. Accordingly, the present location of Pullman was selected."[38]

The company also erected stores, markets, a church, public schools, a public library, and halls for lectures and entertainment. Rents were fixed so as to earn 6 per cent on actual investment, with allowances for all buildings, and cost of city streets and other necessary improvements. Tenants were required to obey a list of rules, and the company retained the right to terminate the lease on ten days' notice; the tenants were given the same privilege. The paved streets were well laid out, and the town contained ample parks and playgrounds; saloons and brothels were not allowed, although such leisure-time activities might be easily found in the neighboring village of Hyde Park, outside of Chicago. "The Pullman Company deemed the environment of the town so wholesome that in 1893 it announced a superior type of laborer was being evolved in Pullman."[39]

In the plans for the ideal community, the profit motive was not given a subordinate place. Rents for company homes were 20 to 25 per cent higher than in Chicago and other neighboring communities; and workers, while not technically required to lease company houses, learned that those who did were assured steadier employment.

Pullman did not deem it necessary or desirable to establish a jail, hospital, orphanage, or public charity. While many of the public buildings were beautiful structures, "they often are not occupied because the rental required to be paid is higher than any church society is willing to pay to obtain the gospel privileges to be thereby secured. In the arcade is a tasteful library of books, carefully selected and cared for by the company. Three dollars per year is charged for its use. . . . the Company provides and pays a physician and surgeon by the year to furnish to injured employees necessary treatment and drugs. It is, however, also a part of his employment to secure from the injured party a statement as to the cause of the injury, and it is his custom to urge acceptance of any offered settlement. If suit follows, the doctor is usually a witness for the company."[40] The paternalism of the company was obviously directed at securing a docile and cooperative labor force stripped of many of the rights enjoyed by workers of other firms living in regular communities.

Shop abuses were not absent, and the U.S. Strike Commission heard charges that foremen were "arbitrary and oppressive." The company never recognized a labor organization.

THE RAILROAD UNIONS

The unions in the railroad industry were among the oldest in the country. The Brotherhood of Locomotive Engineers was founded in 1863, and by 1894 it had actually enrolled 32,033 members. The Brotherhood of Locomotive Firemen was formed in 1873, at Port Jervis, New York. Before its formation, the International Firemen's Union had been organized, with the function of protecting the rights of members against the encroachments of the employer. Absence of relief and insurance features tended to reduce the union's appeal, and it was absorbed by the brotherhood in 1878. The elevation of Eugene Victor Debs to leadership of the union in 1880 marked a turning point in its history. By July 1893 it had enrolled 28,681 members.

In 1883 the Brotherhood of Railroad Brakemen, called after 1890 the Brotherhood of Railroad Trainmen, was organized at Oneonta, New York, and it reached a membership of 8,540 by 1893. It has always maintained a beneficiary system which members were required to join. Organized in 1868 at Mendota, Illinois, the Conductors' Brotherhood, later known as the Order of Railway Conductors, did not at first sponsor or encourage strikes. It was a purely fraternal order, and in 1888 those favoring more aggressive policies withdrew and started the Brotherhood of Railway Conductors. Four years later the two organizations merged and adopted a protective policy. By 1893 the order had 20,356 members. The Switchmen's Union of North America was the last of the operating crafts to come upon the industrial scene. This union was the result of the reorganization of the defunct Switchmen's Mutual Aid Association, originally established locally in Chicago in 1877. Not until 1884 was the society able to make headway outside of its native habitat. The spread of local switchmen's unions led to the formation of the Switchmen's Mutual Aid Association in Chicago in 1886. Embezzlement of funds by the secretary-treasurer and the inroads of the American Railway Union undermined the position of this organization of over 10,000 railroad switchmen. It ceased to exist by 1895, and it was reorganized under another name in 1897.[41]

The main purposes of the brotherhoods were the promotion of the economic interests of their members, and their main tasks were given over to the negotiation of wage and hour schedules, lines of promotions, and other issues usually dealt with by the unions on the railroads. On the whole, the brotherhoods were not strike-minded, although they were ready to use this method to enforce demands they held just, and they maintained a strike fund to support those which were formally authorized by the leaders of their organizations.

The Strike on the Burlington

Cooperation between the Brotherhood of Locomotive Firemen and the Brotherhood of Locomotive Engineers in a common policy was the earliest joint effort by unions in the industry; it was initially started in 1887. Committees from the two unions met and worked out changes in classifications on three roads and were responsible for several improvements in the terms of employment. In January 1888 joint committees from the two unions were appointed to handle grievances that might arise and to submit proposals for changes in wages and working conditions to their respective carriers. When the Chicago, Burlington and Quincy Railroad refused to change the method of payment from the trip to the mileage basis, a strike was called. The boycott of Burlington rolling stock followed the demand of the two unions that connecting railroads not handle the cars of the striking carrier. As a result a suit was undertaken to compel the receiver of the Wabash, St. Louis and Pacific to handle the traffic of the struck line. In addition, a court order was sought to restrain P. M. Arthur, the head of the Brotherhood of Locomotive Engineers, from ordering the engineers on the Wabash not to haul the cars of the Burlington. Judge Walter Q. Gresham, before whom the case was tried, limited himself to ordering the receiver to exchange traffic with the Burlington on the ground the road was a common carrier.

Soon thereafter lawyers for the Burlington applied for an order to compel the Union Pacific to haul Burlington cars and to restrain the engineers from interfering. U.S. District Court Judge Elmer S. Dundy ordered "each and everyone . . . absolutely desist and refrain from striking, combining or confederating, for the purpose of organizing or assisting a strike, or from doing any other act or thing, and from refusing to perform any other act or thing in carrying out your unlawful, unjust and wicked purpose, through your unlawful, unjust and wicked combination, connivance, and conspiracy, either as individuals or as members of the Brotherhood of Locomotive Engineers."[42]

Judge Dundy further held that the engineers on the Union Pacific Railroad had a right to leave their jobs, "but they have not the right to enter in a conspiracy, and by concerted action suddenly leave the Union Pacific road without engineers, when the purpose of the conspiracy is to prevent the Union Pacific road from exchanging freight with the Burlington as by inter-state commerce law it is required to do. Against such action the court will enjoin."[43] The strike continued until December 1888. Although the men were defeated, the Burlington road agreed to provide recommendations for strikers it could not employ, and to rehire others whenever jobs were available. While no black-listing was to be practiced, the unions were clearly defeated.

THE AMERICAN RAILWAY UNION

Disenchantment with the activity and power of the separate unions spread among railway union members. The loss of the Burlington strike and the switchmen's strike in 1893 turned the thoughts of many active unionists to the need for a more inclusive organization. Among those sharing this view was Eugene Victor Debs, Grand Secretary-Treasurer of the Brotherhood of Locomotive Firemen.

Debs had been appointed to the office by Grand Master F. W. Arnold, who had removed his predecessor, W. N. Sayre, several weeks before the 1880 convention. Debs was re-elected that year and served until 1892. He favored a conciliatory policy and "had preached the doctrine of arbitration as early as the fifth convention" in 1878.[44]

Gradually Debs became disillusioned with the policies and practices of his own union as well as the other railway labor organizations. He came to the conclusion that only an inclusive organization of railwaymen could cope with the problems facing the workers in the industry. He informed the 1892 convention of his views, but the delegates would not listen to his declaration that he should no longer serve the Brotherhood of Locomotive Firemen as an officer. Despite the insistence of the delegates that he accept re-election, he refused, although for a time he remained editor of the *Locomotive Firemen's Magazine*.

On June 30, 1893, the American Railway Union was founded. Debs was elected president; George W. Howard, vice-president; and Sylvester Keliher, secretary. Organizing began on August 15, 1893, and the union enrolled between 125,000 and 140,000 railroad men before its first convention in June 1894, more than the combined membership of the four operating unions. It was a truly remarkable performance. According to its constitution, the American Railway Union includes "all railway employees *born of white parents* [italics in original]. . . . The protection of members in all matters relating to wages and their rights as employees is the principal purpose of the organization. Railway employees are entitled to a voice in fixing wages and in determining conditions of employment. Fair wages and proper treatment must be the return for efficient service faithfully performed. Such a policy insures harmonious relations and satisfactory results. The order, while pledged to conservative methods, will protect the humblest of its members in every right he can justly claim; but while the rights of members will be sacredly guarded, no intemperate demand or unreasonable proposition will be entertained."[45]

Strike on the Great Northern

The American Railway Union had its first encounter with a carrier when the Great Northern Railroad reduced wages which, according to

Debs, amounted to $146,500 a month. The union insisted that the cut be canceled, and when the road refused, a strike was called. It lasted eighteen days, and the dispute was submitted to a board of arbitration which restored the cut.[46] With confidence born of success, the American Railway Union planned its first convention in Chicago in June 1894. At the same time, dissatisfaction at the Pullman Company plant was coming to a head. According to union officers, about 4,000 of the employees of that company had been enrolled between March and May of that year, and the several wage reductions and short time work were a sore point.[47]

On May 7 a committee of forty-three, with representatives from all shops of the Pullman Company, met with Vice-President Thomas H. Wickes. Accompanied by Vice-President Howard, the committee requested the restoration of the 1893 wage cut and also complained of foremen's abusiveness. The committee was assured that an investigation of the complaints would be made and that no one would be penalized for being on the committee. On May 10 a meeting was held by the employees, and Howard persuaded the workers not to call a strike, although sentiment for a walkout was widespread. To the surprise of the union's chief officers, the men went out on June 11. Displeased by the action, Howard scolded the leaders. They "said that the members of this committee, although Mr. Pullman had personally promised that none of them would be discriminated against, were discharged the next morning."[48]

Debs visited the Pullman area, and was convinced the action was justified. He said:

. . . the wages and the expenses of the employees were so adjusted that every dollar the employees earned found its way back into the Pullman coffers; that they were not only not getting wages enough to live on, but that they were daily getting deeper and deeper into the debt of the Pullman Company; that it was impossible for many of them to leave there at all, even if they were disposed to quit to try and better their condition. Many of them told me personally that the conditions were very objectionable to them, but there was no escape for them. Wages had been reduced, but the expenses remained the same, and no matter how offensive conditions were they were compelled to submit to them. After I heard those statements I satisfied myself that they were true, and I made up my mind, as president of the American Railway Union, of which these employees were members, to do everything in my power that was within the law and within justice to right the wrongs of those employees.[49]

On June 1 the Civic Federation called upon Vice-President Wickes and urged him to consider conciliation and arbitration as a means for settling the strike; on the following day two other members of the Civic Federation made a similar plea. They were both rejected, because the company did not consider the issues in dispute as proper subjects for arbitration. On June 15 a committee of twelve from the union, then in session, called on Wickes and suggested the restoration of the 1893 wage cut. He replied that "as second vice-president of the Pullman Palace Car Company, he positively refused to entertain any proposition from the American Railway Union representing ex-members of the Pullman Palace Car Company."[50] A similar reply was given to a committee of strikers. Finally, on June 22, a union committee notified Wickes that the convention had voted that unless the strike was settled by June 26, a boycott against the Pullman Company would be called. Again the company refused to accept a communication from the American Railway Union.[51]

General Managers' Association

As soon as the union announced its boycott, the General Managers' Association countered with a declaration that it would be opposed. The association was a voluntary, unincorporated society made up of twenty-four railroads that served Chicago, and it was supported by assessments upon its members. Before the strike, the association had been concerned primarily with switching car service, loading and unloading cars, rates for services, and other such matters. In 1893 the association became involved in a wage matter when members of the Switchmen's Mutual Aid Association asked for pay increases, and arranged for the replacement of strikers. When the boycott threat of the American Railway Union became known, a special meeting of the Managers' Association declared that "the employees of . . . railway companies can not, nor can any of them with propriety embarrass said companies nor discommode the traveling public, because of their sympathy with the supposed wrongs of employees engaged in a wholly different class of labor. That we hereby declare it be the lawful right and duty of said railway companies to protest against said proposed boycott, to resist the same in the interest of their existing contracts, and for the benefit of the traveling public, and that we will act unitedly to that end."[52]

The Boycott

Pursuant to the decision of the convention, the boycott was instituted on June 26. A switchman refused to couple a Pullman to a train, and he was discharged; in answer, all switchmen quit. Following this procedure the railroads were entirely paralyzed at the end of the fifth day, July 1. Under the direction of John M. Egan of the General Managers' Association measures to counteract the boycott were instituted. Guards were sent to protect property. Egan also recommended the appointment of deputy marshals; he forwarded names of prospects to the U.S. marshal, who appointed between 1,500 and 2,000 deputies at his suggestion.[53] The marshals were paid by the roads. Replacements for strikers were also recruited, and the roads achieved a high degree of success.

Violence

At first the strike and boycott were generally peaceful. As it continued, violence and destruction of property increased and trains were stopped and delayed. Mayor John Hopkins, who had donated $1,500 to aid the strikers, described a mob of 3,000, composed largely of women and children. "On the main track of the Rock Island road . . . there were four trains standing, which had been there for some hours, and . . . there was an empty freight car turned over on its side lying across the track."[54] His views were supported by the chief deputy U.S. marshal for northern Illinois, who testified that the disorder was caused mainly by unruly boys and women, and he did not know of any violence being carried on by strikers.[55] Police Chief Michael Brennan testified "that in no case at any time during the strike were the police force insufficient wherever they went, to disperse any mob found. Only on one occasion was any resistance offered to the police force."[56] Brennan had many complaints from the railroad companies, especially from John Egan, who charged that the police were not acting forcefully enough. Some mail trains, however, were being delayed. Since interference with the mails involved the United States government, it became a basis for federal intervention.

Federal Intervention

The Post Office Department called the attention of the Department of Justice to the interference with the mails which it claimed was being obstructed in many parts of the country by the combined strike and boycott of the American Railway Union. Attorney-General Richard Olney was convinced "that the movement engineered by Mr. Debs was on an extraordinary scale and of a most threatening character, and might have to be dealt with by the Army of the United States." The Department of Justice took measures to put itself in the position "which had induced the President to authorize the use of troops. . . . That is to say, the Department of Justice instructed the District Attorney at Chicago, and afterwards other District Attorneys, to file bills in equity enjoining certain persons by name and all other persons cooperating with them from any interference with the mails or with interstate commerce—the bills being filed both on general grounds and under the express provisions of what is known as the Sherman Anti-Trust Law."[57]

Olney, formerly a railroad lawyer, as a first step, appointed Edwin Walker, a railroad lawyer, special counsel to Federal Attorney Thomas Milchrist, and on June 30, wrote to Walker:

It has seemed to me that if the rights of the United States were vigorously asserted in Chicago, the origin and center of the demonstration, the result would be to make it a failure everywhere else and to prevent its spread over the entire country.

In this connection it has seemed to me advisable not merely to rely on warrants against persons actually guilty of the offense of obstructing United States mails, but to go into a court of equity and secure restraining orders which shall have the effect of preventing any attempt to commit the offense.[58]

In accordance with Olney's plans and instructions, Walker and Milchrist applied for an injunction in the Federal Court for Northern Illinois, and on July 2, Circuit Judge William A. Woods and District Judge Peter S. Grosscup issued a sweeping order against Debs, other officials of the union, and against "all other persons combining and conspiring with them, and to all other persons whomsoever, absolutely to desist and refrain from in any way or manner interfering with, hindering, obstructing or stopping any of the business of any of the following named railroads."

On the next day, U.S. Marshal John W. Arnold wired that he was unable to enforce the writ of injunction, and that "reading of the writ met with no response except jeers and hoots. Shortly after that the mob threw a number of baggage cars across the track, since then no mail trains have been able to move. I am unable to disperse the mob, clear the tracks, or arrest the men who were engaged in the acts named, and I believe that no force less than the regular troops of the United States can procure the passage of the mail trains or enforce the orders of the Court."[59] The marshal's message was endorsed by the two government attorneys handling the case and by Judge Grosscup.

This was the signal awaited by Olney, who was now armed with the evidence needed to overcome the reluctance of President Grover Cleveland for the use of federal troops in Chicago.[60] Without consulting the governor of the state, President Cleveland ordered troops to the city; they arrived on July 4 and occupied positions in Blue Island and around the stockyards. Debs asked those who sympathized with the strike to wear white ribbons. After the arrival of the soldiers, violence increased. Newspaper reporters attributed a large part of the disorder to toughs and others looking for excitement and bent on destruction of property. Harold I. Cleveland, a *Chicago Herald* reporter who had covered the strike for his newspaper, testified "that in all the trouble that took place there was a very small percent of railroad men engaged in it; that it was the rough, vicious and lawless elements of those districts that produced the trouble."[61] Another reporter, Victor N. Harding of the *Chicago Times,* testified that the strikers had told him that they were opposed to the overturning of railroad cars then going on, and actually tried to prevent it.

W. C. Roberts, who attended the strikers' meetings as a reporter of the *Chicago Dispatch,* said that strikers were advised to "stay away from any excitement," and a reporter from the *Chicago Evening Mail* recalled that the speeches he had heard at Ulrich's Hall, where strike meetings were held, "counseled obedience to law and order, and my interview with Mr. Debs and Mr. Howard [was] all the same way."[62] On the other hand, N. D. Hutton, a reporter for the *Chicago Tribune,* believed that the majority of the crowds were railroad men.

Beginning on July 5 the riots spread, and property valued at hundreds of thousands of dollars was burned and pilfered. A number of buildings were destroyed, and in clashes between marshals and rioters several were killed and wounded. On July 8, President Cleveland ordered additional troops to Chicago and in a proclamation, ordered the rioting to cease.[63] The troops remained in Chicago for fifteen days, against the wishes of Mayor Hopkins. As a matter of fact, Hopkins had asked aid from Governor Altgeld, who had immediately sent National Guardsmen to Chicago on July 6 to assist the police.

Upon learning that federal troops were being sent to Chicago, Governor John P. Altgeld protested to the President and informed him that "the facts have not been correctly presented to you in this case, or you would not have taken the step, for it is entirely unnecessary and, as it seems to me unjustifiable."[64] Altgeld pointed to the ability of the state to handle any emergency and even offered to provide soldiers to the federal government. In a telegram Cleveland denied that troops had been sent in violation of the United States Constitution. Altgeld would not accept the answer, and in a long letter challenged the legality of the President's conduct. Cleveland refused to debate the issue and told Altgeld: "While I am still persuaded that I have neither transcended my authority nor duty in the emergency that confronts us, it seems to me that in the hour of danger and public distress, discussion may well give way to active efforts on the part of all in authority to restore obedience to law and to protect life and property."[65] Cleveland's answer won wide applause, and Altgeld faced the same kind of denunciation he had endured when he pardoned the Haymarket defendants. But the combination strike and boycott was not going well.

A Conference of Unions

On July 8 a conference of trade unions was held in Chicago at which aid to the railroad strikers was discussed and the advisability of calling a general strike in that city considered. A committee to confer with Mayor Hopkins on the tactics to be followed to settle the dispute was appointed. It was, however, agreed that if the Pullman strike were not settled by the afternoon of July 10, a general strike would be called. In trying to find a formula for ending the walkout, the various committees faced the insuperable difficulty that the General Managers' Association insisted that it had no authority over the Pullman Company and therefore it could do nothing to settle the dispute; the Pullman Company always announced that it had nothing to arbitrate. No basis for settlement having been found, the city-wide strike was called, but it met with little response. On the day of the calling of the abortive strike, Debs, Howard, Keliher, and L. W. Rodgers were arrested and placed under a joint bond of $10,000. Debs believed the arrest of the leaders demoralized the men, "and that ended the strike. It was not the soldiers that ended the strike; it was not the old brotherhoods that ended the strike; it was simply the United States courts that ended the strike."[66]

Gompers had considered going to Chicago, and the request from the mass meeting on July 8 induced him to call a meeting of the executive council and the heads of international unions for July 12. A delegation from the Cigarmakers' Union appeared, and Charles H. Dold, a leader of the Chicago labor movement, acted as spokesman; the delegation requested the calling of a general strike. The suggestion was considered and later rejected. Debs addressed the conference in the late afternoon, and Gompers described his talk as "calm" and "dispassionate." He asked that Gompers present to the Managers' Association his statement which proposed the rehiring of all strikers. The meeting of labor executives agreed to present Debs's statement, but asked that Debs come along. According to Debs, they "agreed to do it in consideration of my going with them, as president, but we did not see fit to accept that condition. So we declined the proposition. . . . We called upon Mr. Hopkins, who was then the chief magistrate of the city . . . and he said he would very willingly deliver the proposition to the managers."[67] Debs based his refusal to accompany Gompers on the antagonism of the railroad leaders to him, but the heads of the AFL and trade unions wanted Debs present to answer questions, if any were raised, and to have someone present who could speak for the employees on strike. "The executive council and the members participating in the conference believed it would be most unwise, as well as inexpedient, as well as detrimental to the interests of labor, to recommend a general strike in sympathy with the American Railway Union or the Pullman strikers."[68] Not only did the executive council lack such power, but the members of the conference believed that the willingness of the American Railway Union to end the boycott upon an agreement for the reinstatement of the railroad strikers was an admission that the strike had failed, "since the men who were engaged in the strike were asking to be permitted to return to work—of course, in a body, and that the question of the Pullman strike or the Pullman boycott was to be abandoned entirely."[69]

Expansion of the Struggle

The boycott against Pullman cars was fought by the railroads, and their insistence on attaching cars led to the spreading of the strike. Willingness of railroad men to handle mail cars without the offending Pullman cars coupled to the train was rejected by the carriers, who used the mail cars as a device through which they could force federal intervention by U.S. marshals and federal and state troops. Guards were mustered to protect trains, and injunctions against interference were pressed by the federal courts. The strike continued until August 2 and was called off by a conference of delegates. Soon thereafter the Pullman Company resumed operations.

Contempt of Court

The strike was to have indirect effects upon all labor. In the 1880's court-appointed railroad receivers had begun to sue for restraining employees on strike against commission of violence to railroad property or interfering with operations of trains. In the American Railway Union strike, injunctions had been procured in the federal courts against Debs and a number of other union officers, and on July 17 they were charged with contempt for disobeying court orders. Clarence Darrow took leave as counsel for the Chicago and Northwestern Railroad to join defense counsel. The defendants were found to have violated the injunction and were adjudged guilty of contempt of court. Debs was sentenced to six months in jail, and the three other defendants were each given three months. They began serving their sentences on January 8, 1895, at the McHenry County jail in Woodstock, Illinois.

An appeal was taken to the U.S. Supreme Court, and Lyman Trumbull appeared for the defense. In his decision for the Court, Justice David J. Brewer answered two questions raised in the affirmative: First, "Are the relations of the general government to interstate commerce and the transportation of the mails such as authorize a direct interference to prevent a forcible obstruction? Second, if authority exists, as authority in government affairs implies both power and duty, has a court of equity jurisdiction to issue an injunction in and of the performance of such duty?"

Justice Brewer replied that the power to regulate interstate commerce and the transportation of the mails is vested in the national government by the Constitution, and the government "may prevent any unlawful and forcible interference therewith." On the second point, the court declared: "injunctions are denied to those who have adequate remedy at law. . . . When the choice is between redress or prevention of injury by force and by peaceful process, the law is well pleased if the individual will consent to waive his right to the use of force and await its action. Therefore between the force and the extraordinary writ of injunction, the rule will permit the latter." On the basis of Debs's testimony, the Supreme Court, quoting the Circuit Court of Appeals, declared the "outcome, by the very testimony of the defendants, attests to the wisdom of the course pursued by the government," in securing the injunction. It held that the courts have jurisdiction to interfere in matters of obstruction of commerce by injunction; "that the proceedings in contempt . . . that under such complaint the Circuit Court has power to issue its process of injunction," and the defendants have been properly punished.[70]

Evaluating the Strike

The strike at Pullman came at a most inappropriate time for the American Railway Union. Having recruited almost 150,000 members, the union did not have sufficient time to weld its army together. The strike at Pullman presented the union with a serious dilemma—to repudiate its ideals or run the risk of arousing the full power of the railroad industry and the government. The union was only in its first year, and prudence called for the avoidance of a challenge to the combined forces of the industry.

The fact is that the strike was doomed from the beginning, and it was not because of lack of support. The American Railway Union's membership in 1894 was considerably larger than the combined memberships of all four brotherhoods. The ability of the union to tie up traffic demonstrated its influence, but neither a union nor any other institution can risk its existence on one throw of the dice. By ordering a boycott of the Pullman cars, it laid itself open to a campaign which led to its extinction. Whatever feeling the railroad unions may have had, they did not in their publications attack the ARU. The *Locomotive Engineers' Journal* charged in July 1894 that "George M. Pullman has acquired millions out of the product of his employees, aided by our Government's patent, which took his business out of the range of supply and demand, into which he proposes to plunge his laborers now and proposes to subject them to acceptance of that principle, and is willing to spend millions to do so rather than do what justice and common humanity demand."[71]

The AFL was not hostile to the American Railway Union; it donated $500 to the defense of the leaders and raised more. Much has been made of Gompers' refusal to carry Debs's message to the Managers' Association. It was not unreasonable to ask an officer of the American Railway Union to go along so that questions could be answered and negotiations, if possible, resumed. Gompers could not speak for the strikers, and any examination of Debs's statement shows that it might, if the carriers were willing to bargain, have required elaboration. As for the request to call a general strike, this would have been compounding the original act of folly. When the Chicago labor movement issued such a call to the workers of the city, the response was not favorable. Moreover, Debs in his statement to the Managers' Association had already admitted the strike was lost, for he and his coworkers were now ready to call off the walkout if the strikers were rehired. Gompers pointed out that this meant the strike had been lost, because the reinstatement of the Pullman workers was no longer mentioned. The American Railway Union had been beguiled by what appeared to be the illusion of large numbers, that is, that a large group is necessarily more powerful than a smaller one. The American Railway Union appeared to be a viable organization, and had it avoided the struggle in 1894, it might have survived and become a major power.

Even though public sentiment was aligned against the ARU, the railroads were by no means the favorite children of the public. The *Report of the Strike Commission* was critical of the railroads on many points, and the public image of the carriers had not yet been fully polished by public relations men. The Granger and Populist cries were still heard against the corporate monsters which spanned the country. The Erdman Act, a railroad regulatory statute which contained a clause against discriminating for union membership, was enacted in 1898. The American Railway Union made the decision to risk everything on the Pullman boycott. It did not go down because it lacked support. Gompers had no power to call a general strike even if he had favored such a step. Moreover, there was scant assurance that the heads of the affiliates would have followed him. In addition, with unemployment rampant, it is likely that the enlargement of the strike would have led only to increasing the size of the disaster.

CHAPTER 12

Expansion and its Limits

ARMIES OF UNEMPLOYED

The economic crisis that gripped the country in the early 1890's not only slowed the progress of organized labor but reversed it at many points. It was a decade in which farmers complained of low prices, businessmen of falling orders, and wage earners of wage cuts. Discontent with low returns and foreclosures led the farmers into independent political action in 1892, and about one million voters endorsed the Populist Presidential candidate, James B. Weaver. Conditions were even worse in the cities than on the farm. Unemployment was widespread, and the absence of social insurance or any efficient relief system compelled the unemployed to fend for themselves. Many, after exhausting their savings and credit, were forced to rely on the breadline and soup kitchen.

Armies of unemployed, their ranks augmented by tramps and professional beggars, swarmed over the countryside on foot, freight trains, or the front end of passenger trains. Hunger and fatigue compelled these wayfarers to interrupt their journeys in search of food and rest, and the towns were not overjoyed at their arrival. The hordes of drifters provided the armies of unemployed officered by General Jacob S. Coxey, Lewis C. Fry, and the lesser-known commanders.

Coxey favored a program of public works financed by noninterest bonds as a means of relieving unemployment. In behalf of his modest program, he led his "troops" on a march to Washington in the hope of convincing Congress. Leaving Massillon, Ohio, on March 25, 1894, he arrived, on schedule outside Washington on the first of April. About five hundred "Commonwealers," as they were called, marched to the Capital the next day in the hope of presenting a petition to Congress. The parade was allowed, but the meeting was prevented by the police. Coxey and some of his aides were arrested and later released. While Coxey's army was the best known, a number of others walked and rode through the country: Fry's industrial army through California and the Southwest, and General Charles T. Kelly's force was active in California.

In a large measure the armies of unemployed had no destination and were swelled by criminal elements. Nor were the railroads content to haul thousands of restless free riders, who in time became a threat to the safety of crews and property. Attempts to force the unwelcome hordes from the trains or to expel them from the towns led to clashes with which local communities could not cope. The towns enlisted their citizens and the railroads called on U.S. marshals and state and federal troops for assistance. Carriers in the hands of federal receivers began to rely on the federal courts to restrain the migrant armies from damaging railroad property by writs of injunction and punished violators of their orders by jail terms for contempt. It was the effective campaigns which inspired Attorney-General Richard Olney with the belief that the writ of injunction could also be used against the Pullman strikers in Chicago.[1]

Economic conditions improved following the election of William McKinley to the Presidency in 1896. It is unlikely, however, that the election played a dominant role in recovery. Although the business community feared and hated William Jennings Bryan, McKinley's Democratic rival, the evidence indicates that the depression had already run its course. The enactment of the Dingley Tariff gave added confidence as well as returns to protected industry which began expanding operations. Throughout the rest of the century the country enjoyed a satisfactory level of income and employment, and the favorable conditions continued well into the early years of the new century.[2]

CHANGES IN THE ECONOMY

The economic conditions facing the worker in the last year of the nineteenth century were considerably different from those surrounding his forebears a half-century ago. Important changes in organization and control had taken place which were to affect existence and functioning of his unions. The small shops and factories which dotted the countryside before the Civil War had given way in many industries to larger units. Equipping and provisioning of great armies had stimulated invention and accelerated growth in the size of business. The combination movement, the devising of the pool, and emergence of the trust had changed segments of the Amercan economy. Great railroad and communication networks, which speeded their cargo and messages, had been thrown across the country and the United States was now one economic unit, a market of tremendous size with opportunities to match. But not for all. The gifted, the long-armed, the shrewd, and the unscrupulous could amass great fortunes if luck played a supporting role. But there were also the protesting farmer, who believed himself oppressed by high charges and low prices, and the worker, who felt he shared in little of the flourishing prosperity.

Between 1850 and 1900, railroad mileage increased from 9,012 to 194,262 miles. Extension of telegraph lines and the invention and increase in the use of the telephone were also important in bringing distant parts of the country together. These changes helped to stimulate the growth of the large corporate enterprise which opposed union organization. An example is Charles Schwab, president of the U.S. Steel Corporation, who in testifying before the U.S. Industrial Commission in May 1901 refused to define the labor policy of his company, but explained that if he were a worker in a steel mill he would not want to belong to a union.[3]

Not all the leaders of large business organizations held the same view as Schwab, at least not publicly, and he may have been strongly influenced by his experience as an officer of the Carnegie Steel Company. Many large companies, however, were determined to limit the influence of organized labor and prevent the unions from gaining a foothold in their plants.

Leaders of many expanding corporations were unsentimental in their attitudes toward the worker. Many regarded labor as only another factor of production, not much different from a machine. In testifying against an eight-hour workday on government contracts, C. J. Harrah, president of the Midvale Steel Company, declared that "once a man passes inside the gate and gets inside the red fence, he stays there until his day's work is through." Men were fined for lying and insubordination, and Harrah testified "we have absolutely no regard for machinery or for men." To the surprise of Gompers, who was examining Harrah before a committee of Congress, Harrah announced: "Mr. Gompers, when you become better acquainted with me you will know there is nothing I hold back."[4]

UNION MEMBERSHIP

Membership of many unions sharply declined during the depression of the 1890's. Building tradesmen were then, as now, among the better organized workers and many of the unions in this industry suffered serious membership losses. Membership in the Bricklayers' Union fell from 27,000 to 19,000 between 1892 and 1894, and then partly recovered. The United Brotherhood of Carpenters and Joiners' membership went from 54,000 in 1893 to 28,000 in 1897.[5] Figures are not readily available for the experiences of other building trades' unions, but in view of the crucial role of the carpenters and bricklayers in the industry, it can be assumed that the experience of the other crafts was not likely to be different.

Railroad unions lost many members, a loss which must be attributed partly to the influence of the American Railway Union. The Brotherhood of Locomotive Engineers suffered a modest drop between 1894 and 1896, and then recovered; the Conductors had a similar experience. Membership in the Brotherhood of Railway Trainmen declined from 28,000 in 1893 to 19,000 in 1897 and then began to move upward. Both the Locomotive Firemen's Union and the Brotherhood of Railway Carmen suffered substantial losses, and the downslide of the latter was not reversed until 1899.[6]

Membership losses of the AFL were not large, perhaps the result of its modest size, and this organization merely marked time until the decline in business and employment ended. A change for the better began for the federation and the unaffiliated unions in 1897, and gains continued until 1904. Gains and losses in membership of the AFL may represent the movement of established unions into and out of the organization.

Climate of Opinion

Between 1897 and 1904 union membership climbed from 447,000 to 2,072,700 and substantial gains were made in every year.[7] In view of the growing power of large business and the determination of many of its leaders to expel trade unions from their establishments, the gains of organized labor in this period are truly impressive.

The increase in trade union membership, according to Professor Barnett, was greater than the increase in population or the gainfully employed. Trade union membership was heavily concentrated in 1897 in transportation, building, and metal and machinery, and by 1900, mining was in the third place as far as membership was concerned. Transportation, building construction, and mining formed until the 1930's, an important part of the trade union membership.[8]

The reaction of workers to unionism was obviously influenced by their experiences with the depression of the 1890's. Prolonged unemployment, with its accompanying destitution and suffering, tarnished the reputation of business, and the public regarded, at least for a time, the workers' quest for greater security and higher pay as justifiable. Exposures of corporate derelictions made the demands of labor for some countervailing power appear reasonable. The friendlier public attitude toward labor was written into federal and state legislation.

The coverage of federal legislation guaranteeing the right of workers to organize was narrower than in the 1930's. Federal authority to regulate was confined to the railroads, but the penalties for violations were more severe than those embodied in the Wagner Act, four decades later. Section

10 of the Erdman Act of 1898 provided that railroad carriers or any officers or agent of such corporation who shall require a worker, orally or in writing, to agree not to join a labor union, or "shall threaten any employee with loss of employment, or shall unjustly discriminate against any employee because of membership in such labor corporation, association, or organization . . . is hereby declared to be guilty of misdemeanor, and, upon conviction in any court of the United States of competent jurisdiction in the district in which such offense was committed, shall be punished for each offense by a fine of not less than one hundred dollars and not more than one thousand dollars."[9]

As has already been shown, the number of organized railroad workers was not very large and one cannot attribute the favorable congressional action entirely to their influence. In that it contained provisions to punish violators, this law was more stringent than the Wagner Act. Such legislation could not be enacted without widespread publlic support. Even more significant was the passage by seventeen states of laws prohibiting employers from discharging employees for belonging to or for joining labor unions, or from making it a condition of employment that they should not be members of such unions. Fifteen states passed such legislation in the 1890's and two states earlier.[10]

Typical of such laws is the Missouri statute enacted in 1893 which read as follows:

Protection of employees as members of trade unions. . . . Any person or persons, employer or employers of labor, and any person or persons of any corporation or corporations, on behalf of such corporation or corporations who shall hereafter coerce or compel any person or persons, employee or employees, laborer or mechanic to enter into an agreement, either written or verbal, from such person, persons, employees, laborer or mechanic, not to join or become a member of any labor organization, as a condition of such person or persons securing employment, or continuing in the employment of any such person or persons, employer or employers, corporation or corporations, shall be deemed guilty of a misdemeanor. The penalty for such misdemeanor shall be imprisonment in a penal institution for not more than six months, or by a fine of not more than two hundred dollars, or by both such fine and imprisonment.

A California statute enacted the same year reads:

Protection of employees as members of labor unions.—Sec. I. It shall be unlawful for any individual, or member of any firm, or agent, officer or employee of any company or corporation to prevent employees from forming, joining and belonging to any lawful labor organization, and any such individual, member, agent, officer or employee that coerces or attempts to coerce employees by discharging or threatening to discharge from their employ or the employ of any firm, company or corporation, because of their connection with such lawful labor organization, shall be guilty of a misdemeanor, and upon conviction thereof in any court of competent jurisdiction shall be fined in any sum not exceeding one hundred dollars or imprisoned for not more than six months, or both, in the discretion of the court.[11]

Although the laws could not stand up in the courts, they reflect public sentiment at the time of their enactment. Typical was the reaction of the Illinois Supreme Court. A statute forbidding discrimination against union members was enacted in 1893, and Charles Gillespie, a building contractor, discharged Reuben Gibbons, a carpenter in his employ, for joining a union. Gillespie was tried, convicted, and fined under the statute of June 17, 1893. He appealed to the Supreme Court which held in *Gillespie* v. *People,* 58 Northeastern Reporter, 1007 (1900), that the statute contravenes the Fourteenth Amendment of the federal Constitution, which provides that "no State shall make or enforce any law which shall abridge the privileges or immunities of citizens of the United States; nor shall any State deprive any person of life, liberty or property without due process of law, nor deny to any person within its jurisdiction the equal protection of the laws."

The court held that the

rights of liberty and property include the right to acquire property by labor and by contract. If an owner can not be deprived of his property without due process of law, he cannot be deprived of the essential attributes which belong to the right of property without due process of law. Labor is property. The laborer has the same right to sell his labor and to contract with reference thereto as any other property owner. The right of property involves as one of its essential attributes, the right not only to contract, but also to terminate contracts. In the case at bar the contract between plaintiff in error and Gibbons was not for any definite period of time, but Gibbons was employed by the day at so much per hour. In view of what has been said, it cannot be doubted that the plaintiff in error, Charles Gillespie, had a right to terminate his contract, if he had one, with Reuben Gibbons, subject to civil liability for any termination which should be unwarranted. One citizen can not be compelled to give employment to another citizen, nor can anyone be compelled to be employed against his will. The act of 1893, now under consideration, deprives the employer of the right to terminate his contract with his employee. The right to terminate such a contract is guaranteed by the organic law of the State. The legislature is forbidden to deprive the employer or employee of the exercise of that right. The legislature has no authority to pronounce the performance of an innocent act criminal when the public health, safety, comfort, or welfare is not interfered with. The statute in question says that if a man exercises his constitutional right to terminate a contract with his employee, he shall, without a hearing be punished as for the commission of a crime.

The court held that to refuse employment of union men was not a crime, but the exercise of a constitutional right to terminate employment, and the law contravenes the guarantee that no person shall be deprived of life, liberty, or property without due process of law.

The court also held that the law granted union members special privileges inasmuch as an employer was penalized for discharging a union man but not a nonunion man and was therefore unconstitutional under the state constitution.

Between 1897 and 1904 the net gains of organized labor were 1,625,-700, an annual average of 232,243, or 52 per cent. Considering that there are always some simultaneous losses, the net gains are even more impressive. Moreover, the advances were achieved without the direct assistance of government, since Section 10 of the Erdman Act did not provide any direct means for enforcement, and the state prohibitions upon interference with labor organization were in many instances set aside by the courts even before the decision invalidating Section 10 of the Erdman Act by the U.S. Supreme Court in *Adair* v. *United States*. Another impressive feature of the period was the ability of the unions to retain their membership, although they were simultaneously limited or ousted from some important industries.[12] But the increase in union membership was quite general and was shared by a large number of organizations. Actually, with the exception of spectacular strikes in the coal mines and the steel industry, the gains did not arouse a large amount of public interest, although employers and their organizations almost immediately after the turn of the century began to cry out against the growing power of unions. As Wolman has shown, the steadiest growth was experienced by the unions in the building construction, transportation, and printing industries. Membership in the building construction unions increased from 67,000 in 1897 to 391,600 in 1904. In the same periods, membership in the transportation unions moved from 116,000 to 446,300; and the printing trades' unions from 37,900 to 92,200. The most impressive gains were made in the mining industries, largely by the Coal Miners' Union. Membership in these industries rose from 20,900 in 1897 to 278,900 in 1904.[13]

The growth of membership created a number of problems for the organizations, but even more serious was the stimulus their expansion gave to employers who used the arts of both propaganda and economic power to reduce the influence of organized workers. In the plant, the picket line, and the courts, the labor movement faced the forces of hostile employers which in many instances were able to gain the day. Nevertheless, despite setbacks and inability to penetrate into or even to retain a large foothold in some industries, the unions in the period were able to establish themselves, and to ride out employer opposition and recessions in business.

CHAPTER **13**

Advances in Coal

In 1897 the United Mine Workers of America became the largest union in the United States, a position it retained for almost three decades. The United Mine Workers of America was itself the result of years of effort. After the collapse of the National Miners' Union in the 1870's, local unions continued to exist, but found themselves unable to solve the problems which confronted them or their employers. Mixed local assemblies of the Knights of Labor appeared in some of the Ohio coal areas, but Chris Evans, a leader of miners' unionism and the secretary of the AFL from 1889 to 1894, believed "there was always something lacking in the mixed local where the doctor, the grocer and the business man were called upon to act on questions in which the mine workers alone were directly interested."[1]

The 1880's witnessed the rapid growth of railroads throughout the northern coal districts. Producers from various fields started to compete for each other's markets, so that price changes tended to affect large producing areas and a greater number of producers. Interdependence of the separated coal producing areas was immediately recognized by operators and union leaders in the industry. For the union leaders, it clearly pointed to a national organization of miners working in every field regulating wages and, indirectly, influencing prices.[2]

Organization in the Hocking Valley was effected in the late 1870's, and beginning in 1880 an attempt was made to establish a statewide miners' union. The chief grievances at the time were the fluctuations in wages which usually followed changes in prices and the absence of a checkweighman at the mines to assure a proper weight. The Ohio Miners' Amalga-

166

mated Association was established in 1882; its "preamble" stated: "It is evident that some step should be taken to check the evils that were fast accruing from insane competition, the heavy foot of which always rests upon the wages of the producer. It was found that the lines of connection between the different mining districts of the State that were bound to be recognized or the utter ruin of the mining interests of the State would result, and complete degradation and misery of the miners would follow."[3] John McBride was elected president.

In the following year an interstate meeting of miners' delegates set up the Amalgamated Association of Miners of the United States; only Ohio and Pennsylvania sent large delegations, but Maryland and Illinois were unrepresented. In 1884 miners in the Hocking Valley refused to accept a wage cut proposed by the Columbus and Hocking Valley Coal and Iron Company. When attempts to find a basis for agreement failed, the operators announced that after June 27, 1884, mining rates would be reduced from 75 cents to 60 cents a ton. A district convention of miners at Straitsville decided to strike, and the Columbus and Hocking Valley Coal and Iron Company, the dominant firm, countered by discharging all strikers on July 11.[4] The strike lasted until March 18, 1885, involved 4,000 workers and caused much suffering. Appeals for assistance were sent out to labor groups throughout the country and $70,333.48 was collected in cash; food and clothing estimated at $26,740.67 were also collected.

All miners in the Hocking Valley returned, but the operators around Straitsville reduced tonnage rates ten cents below those prevailing in other areas. As a result the strike continued for two more months in this locality, and in the end the miners were forced to accept the operators' terms.

NATIONAL ORGANIZATION

As a result of correspondence among a number of local leaders, a national miners' convention was called in Indianapolis for September 9, 1885. Thirty delegates from seven states were in attendance, and the National Federation of Miners and Mine Laborers was launched. The "preamble to the constitution" declared that the troubles of miners and mine laborers were "everywhere the same. . . . The increased shipping facilities of the last few years have made all coal-producing districts competitors in the markets of this country. This has led to indiscriminate cutting of market prices and unnecessary reductions in our wages."[5]

Chris Evans was elected secretary of the union, and he was directed to invite the operators to a joint meeting to adjust prices and wages so as to avoid "strikes and lockouts and give to each party an increased profit from the sale of coal."[6] Only one operator, W. P. Rend, responded, but a second invitation brought operators from Illinois, Indiana, Ohio, and Pennsylvania to the meeting. A joint circular was issued at this time, since it was believed that greater attendance would help to inaugurate "a new era for the settlement of the industrial question in our mining regions in accordance with intelligent reasoning and based upon fair play and mutual justice."[7]

Representatives of miners and operators from five states—Illinois, Indiana, Ohio, Pennsylvania, and West Virginia—met in Pittsburgh and worked out the first interstate agreement in the bituminous coal industry. It was an important step in devising a method for settling on a scale of wages for large producing areas, and the method was, with interruptions, followed for almost half a century. No agreement was reached, but a joint meeting was called for Columbus, Ohio, on February 23, 1886.

At the second meeting, five states were represented at the opening session, and a Maryland delegation appeared later. A tonnage rate was agreed upon, and a joint committee to adjust differences was elected. The agreement was to run from May 1, 1886, to May 1, 1887. An attempt by the union representatives to reduce the hours of labor was unsuccessful.[8]

THE KNIGHTS OF LABOR IN THE COAL FIELDS

Mine and Mine Laborers National District Assembly No. 135, Knights of Labor, was established at St. Louis, Missouri, on May 20, 1886. It exacerbated the differences which had existed between local assemblies and unions in the coal fields. The Ohio Miners' State Convention in 1887 deplored the entrance of the Knights of Labor into the industry and announced that miners were themselves fitted to handle their affairs. The request of W. H. Bailey, the head of District Assembly No. 135, to be represented at the joint meetings in February 1887 was rejected. "because . . . further intercourse between the two boards would result in no good; we have therefore concluded not to meet National District Assembly No. 135."[9]

Sentiment for the formation of one miners' union, nevertheless, was widespread. Writing to General Master Workman T. V. Powderly, Secretary W. T. Lewis of District Assembly No. 135 informed him: "For nearly two years has District Assembly No. 135 tried to organize those men. . . . You know, or ought to know, that a trades district is nothing more or less than a trades union based on the principles of the Knights of Labor. . . . Today there are two rival organizations of miners in this country. . . . I do and will advise them to have but one organization, call it what they may."[10]

In response to the sentiment for unity of all coal miners, a joint convention of the two principal national organizations met at Columbus, Ohio, on December 5, 1888. Out of these deliberations, the National Progressive Union of Miners and Mine Laborers was formed. John McBride was chosen president and Patrick McBryd, secretary. The "preamble" observed that "there can be no protection or influence from individuals disunited or irresolute. The only safeguard to our craft is in the unity of its members, their intelligence and earnest cooperation. To protect ourselves from injustice and defend honest enterprise in mining business, it is necessary that we all stand on common ground and mutually defend our rights."[11]

The National Progressive Union failed to unify completely the coal miners, as District Assembly No. 135 continued to function. At the convention of the National Progressive Union in 1890, President John McBride took a strong position on the need for one organization. A joint convention of representatives of the two organizations formed the United Mine Workers of America, with John B. Rae as president and Robert Watchorn, secretary-treasurer. Both came from the Knights of Labor. The national executive board was given the power to direct the union between conventions and to settle differences with the operators. Ultimate power was lodged in the annual conventions. A per capita tax of twenty cents was imposed for financing the union. Provisions were at first made for dual affiliation: the members of the open branches with the AFL and the secret societies with the Knights of Labor. Opposition to the merger was expressed by Powderly and John W. Hayes, the secretary-treasurer of the Knights of Labor, but it was to no avail. The United Mine Workers of America remained united, although for a few years it continued to face opposition from some of the assemblies of the Knights of Labor.[12]

Joint Conference

The joint conference ended when some Illinois and Indiana operators withdrew in 1888. In 1891 the union sought unsuccessfully to revive the joint conference, but not enough operators' representatives attended. Local strikes were called in a number of fields. They were not generally successful. In the same year, the *United Mine Workers Journal* was launched. On April 24, 1894, the union, despite its depleted membership, called a strike and it was answered by over 125,000 miners, much to the surprise of the leaders. The strike affected the northern districts, and West Virginia coal mined by nonunion men found a favorable opportunity for entry into the western markets. The union was unable to supply many of the strikers with minimum necessities. Finally an agreement was patched up on June 9, when operators from several states agreed to a contract providing it could be enforced, presumably by the union. The contract was a nullity from the beginning. The lost strike brought the union to virtual bankruptcy, and it was not able to pay its per capita to the AFL.

The Strike of 1897

Tonnage rates for mining had fallen precipitously. With the union unable to resist, and demands for coal gradually declining as a result of the depression, prices of coal in the Pittsburgh district which had ranged from

69 cents in the thick vein to 79 cents in the thin vein in 1893, fell in 1897 to a low of 28 cents in the thick vein and to 47 cents in the thin vein. Other districts underwent similar experiences. A change in the labor force took place in many sections as a result of a substantial influx of Slavic and Italian immigrants, many of whom came from rural and nonindustrial sections of their own countries and were not accustomed to the discipline of labor organizations.[13] Membership had sunk from over 17,000 in 1894 to under 10,000 in 1897, but business conditions were more favorable in the latter year, because the business recovery had increased the demand for coal. The 1897 convention decided to demand an increase in tonnage rates and authorized the executive board to choose the time to enforce it upon the operators. Instead of increases, operators in the four principal northern coal fields announced a wage reduction.

A walkout was called for July 4, and all bituminous coal miners were invited to join. Over 100,000 miners responded, and the strike paralyzed the northern fields; the response was not favorable in West Virginia. The general labor movement, acting through the AFL, joined the struggle.

Gompers, President Ratchford, William Mahon of the Street Car Men, and Michael Carrick of the Painters' Union met in "conference in Pittsburgh . . . and there mapped out and planned out the strike of the miners in the bituminous fields. . . . We planned that out and thought it out, and when the strike was on we gave whatever was in us to help in that struggle until victory was perched upon your banner."[14]

Under the leadership of Gompers a meeting of nationally known labor officers first met in Pittsburgh to rally public sentiment and to call for financial aid for the strikers. Headquarters were established in Charleston, West Virginia, under President William D. Mahon of the Amalgamated Association of Railway Employees, to coordinate aid. Public support in the northern mining communities was with the strikers, but the situation was different in West Virginia, a crucial sector. The efforts of Eugene V. Debs and James R. Sovereign of the Knights of Labor, who sought to rally the strikers in that state, were largely to no avail. The courts intervened on the side of the operators with injunctions, and organizers were run out of many West Virginia communities, a pattern to be followed in that state for several decades. Although a special conference of labor leaders at Wheeling on July 27 protested the conduct of the authorities, it had no effect on their actions. Gompers, Sovereign, and Michael Ratchford protested to the governor, who expressed sympathy for the strikers but noted his inability to interfere with the courts.

Interstate Agreement

Negotiations for a settlement were begun in August, and after several sessions, an agreement was reached. It did not arouse universal approval among the miners, and the special convention to act upon the terms endorsed the contract by only a small vote. In January 1898 the Central Competitive Field Agreement was inaugurated. It was negotiated by the organized miners and operators in Pennsylvania, Ohio, Indiana, and Illinois. As explained by Herman Justi, Commissioner of the Illinois Coal Operators' Association, the "purpose of fixing the scale of wages, and the mining conditions in these States, was in order to bring them as nearly as possible upon a fair competitive basis. The idea of this interstate movement was to establish as far as possible uniformity not only in the scale of wages, but in the conditions of mining, and as a result it was applied also in the selling price of coal. Without any agreement being made as to what the price of coal should be, the fact that all the coal operators in those four States paid substantially the same scale of wages and were operating under the same conditions of mining made it possible for every operator to know approximately what the product of every coal mine cost every other operator."[15]

Every issue pertaining to the costs of mining was a proper subject of discussion. A fundamental principle of the interstate movement was that each district was to be allowed to produce coal at costs that were competitive and which would enable it to retain its share of the market. No attempt was made to make "wages uniform or the earning capacity of the men equal between the different districts, or within the districts themselves, the principal object being to so regulate the scale of mining as to make the cost of production practically the same in one district that it is in another, regardless of whether or not the earnings of the miners are equal."[16] The settlement introduced the eight-hour workday.

Conflict in Illinois

The settlement was not accepted by all operators in the four states. In the Pana and Virden area of Illinois, several large companies erected stockades and sought to import Negro strikebreakers from the southern states. On September 28 striking union miners and imported Negro strikebreakers fought a pitched battle on the streets of Pana, Illinois, with Winchesters and revolvers. Riots in other parts of the state followed. In Alabama the Afro-American Labor and Protective Association denounced "the action of the colored miners in going to Pana, remaining at Pana or participating in any manner in carrying out their tyrannical design against labor." An even worse clash, following an attempt to disembark strikebreakers, took place at Virden on October 12. In the clash seven miners and five guards were killed and about eight from each group wounded. Soldiers were sent by Governor John B. Tanner to take charge of the stockade with orders not to allow imported strikebreakers to land.[17] The strike at Virden was settled in November 1898 and in Pana almost one year later in October 1899. For the next two decades, no effort was made—until the attempt in the early 1920's at Herrin, Illinois—to operate a coal mine in Illinois with nonunion labor.

Significance of Victory

The victory of the United Mine Workers of America in the bituminous coal fields was one of the more important in the period. It brought thousands of workers into the union, and assured the predominance of the union for three decades. But the West Virginia operators refused the invitation to participate in the joint negotiations in 1898, and the combined efforts of the labor movement were unable to shut down production. West Virginia operators were determined to expand their markets, and their participation in the interstate agreement would have inevitably reduced their competitive advantage over those in several other states. The easier access to the seams, the thicker veins of coal, and the lack of organization of their labor which could be worked longer hours and paid lower rates gave West Virginia operators a position they were unwilling to surrender. President John Mitchell said in 1900: "The principal disturbing feature of the coal industry which in any degree threatens the perpetuity of the peaceful relalationship between operators and miners is the absence of organization or mutual understanding between the operators and miners of the State of West Virginia."[18]

THE ANTHRACITE DISTRICTS

In the 1880's the national character of the anthracite labor force began to change. Until the early 1880's the mining of hard coal was carried on largely by native Americans and Canadians, English, Welsh, Irish, Scotch, and German immigrants. Of the over 108,000 foreign born in the anthracite coal industry in 1880, over 102,000 were from English-speaking countries.[19] Fewer than 2,000 people of Slav origin were in the anthracite areas of Pennsylvania by 1880. Twenty years later the number had risen to over 89,000.[20]

For a time the differences in background and outlook of the English-speaking and the Slav groups were a barrier to unionization, but gradually organization sentiment spread through the anthracite fields. It was repressed by the severe regime which the coal companies had introduced. On September 10, 1897, the public became aware of the resentment against the company store in the anthracite areas. A group of miners, marching from Hazleton to Latimer to aid a strike against company prices which was going on, was gunned down by the sheriff and his deputies, who killed nineteen and seriously wounded forty. Ten members of a jury reported that the men had been "marching peacefully and unarmed on the public highway; that they were intercepted by said Sheriff Martin and his deputies and mercilessly shot to death, and wounded forty, we further find that the killing was unnecessary and could have been avoided without serious injury to either person or property, and we further find that the killing was wanton and unjustifiable."[21] Because the jury failed to agree, the sheriff and the others were freed.

THE STRIKE OF 1900

Once the coal miners gained a firm position, they were able to turn some of their energies to the anthracite districts, although the bituminous sector was not completely organized. National organizers of the United Mine Workers of America were sent into the anthracite coal fields, and the area was divided into District 1, composed of the Wyoming and Lackawanna fields; District 7, covering the Lehigh field; and District 9, the Schuylkill field. John Mitchell, president of the United Mine Workers of America, reported to the 1900 convention that progress in organizing the anthracite had been highly satisfactory.[22] President John Mitchell (1870–1919) was against hasty action.

Mitchell was born in Braidwood, Illinois, the son of a Scotch-Irish coal miner. Orphaned as a boy, he went to work in the mines at the age of twelve. In 1886 he left home and became an itinerant miner and worked in Colorado, New Mexico and Wyoming before he returned to his native community in 1888. He arrived in time to participate in the bitter lockout of the miners in his native area when they refused to accept a cut in pay. The miners were defeated. Two years later he joined a local of the newly formed United Mine Workers of America. He was successively a staff organizer, subdistrict secretary-treasurer, and by 1897, a member of the Illinois (Miners) State Executive Board. Sent as a delegate to the 1898 convention of his union, he was chosen vice-president. When President Michael Ratchford resigned to accept a place on the Industrial Commission, Mitchell became acting president. (The two outstanding leaders of the coal miners—Mitchell and John L. Lewis—first gained their top posts through resignations.)

In the anthracite disputes of 1900 and 1902, Mitchell showed himself to be a cool and shrewd tactician, ready to make concessions but not to surrender his main objective of union recognition. To compel recognition of the anthracite miners, he followed a cautious policy of reasonableness and avoiding words and actions which might lose him public support. He successfully opposed the calling of a symbolic bituminous general strike. Yet, he refused to yield when it meant surrender of his main objectives. Mitchell demonstrated that southern and eastern European workers were good union material, that these workers could be organized and withstand the pressures from employers and face hunger and privation in a long campaign.

Conservative in his political and social views and also in his public utterances, Mitchell was an exponent of industrial unionism. His views were based on his experiences in his own industry. He successfully insisted that the crafts yield their jurisdiction over members of their own trade and that the right of the United Mine Workers of America to enroll all workers in and around the mines be recognized by the AFL. He also had less fear of government than many craft unionists. In his personal and public utterances Mitchell was more conservative than Gompers. The latter enjoyed argument and debate, and would in fact bait his opponents so as to display his forensic gifts. Mitchell disliked controversy within his union and abhorred politics and intrigue which were inescapable in a large organization. He retired from his office in 1908 for a post with the National Civic Federation. After the United Mine Workers had given him a choice, in 1911, between resigning from the union or from his job, He severed his official connection with the National Civic Federation. He was appointed chairman of the New York Industrial Commission, a post he held until his death.

A convention of anthracite miners was called for Hazleton on August 13. The meeting directed the leaders to seek a conference with the coal operators, and drafted a list of twelve complaints to be presented. Among them were the charges that the system of dockage for impurities deprived the miners of a portion of their earned wages since they were not allowed a checkweighman; the tendency of the operators to increase the size of the carload without compensatory increase in pay; arbitrary fixing of rates by foremen and discrimination between persons in the setting of prices; arbitrary wage cutting so as to prevent more efficient workers from earning greater compensation; the fixing of a ton for purposes of compensation at arbitrary weights, some as high as 3,360 pounds; failure of many operators to make bimonthly wage payments required by law; charging higher than market prices for powder and for purchases at company stores; and compulsory payments for physicians' service to doctors selected by the companies.

The operators rejected the invitation to confer, and after some delay so that political pressures might force a settlement (Mark Hanna, the Republican "king maker," was anxious to prevent a strike), Mitchell proposed that the issues be submitted to arbitration. When this proposal was rejected, the strike was approved for September 17. A statement of the miners' demands and an appeal for sympathy and understanding were issued to the American people. The response to the call was unexpected by the operators and a pleasant surprise to the union leaders. Not all districts were equally affected by the walkout, but that the union made an excellent showing is attested by all contemporary observers.[23]

In general the walkout was not attended by violence. The most serious clashes took place at Shenandoah between foreign-speaking miners and company guards in which a spectator was killed, and another at Oneida where a special guard was wounded and later died. These clashes brought the National Guard into the area, but the strike was generally unaffected by the presence of troops.

In the meantime, the political effect of the strike became a concern to the Republican strategists, and they began to exert pressure upon the heads of the coal-carrying roads to settle. J. P. Morgan was brought in as an intermediary, and at a conference between Hanna and the heads of the coal-carrying roads, the possible harmful effect of the continuing strike on the fortunes of the Republican Presidential candidate was presented in forceful terms. But the operators were adamant against recognizing the United Mine Workers of America as the bargaining agent for their employees. To avoid what they apparently regarded as a humiliating concession, the operators began posting notices of 10 per cent wage increases and other changes, dependent, of course, upon the workers' return to employment.

The union called a convention of the three anthracite districts for October 12 at Scranton at which 857 delegates from every colliery in the anthracite fields were present. Sentiment to stay out until the union was recognized was expressed by a number of delegates, but Mitchell and the majority of the leaders favored a more conservative line. They were willing to accept the 10 per cent increase in rates, providing the operators agreed to retain this rate of payment until April 1, 1901. In addition, the convention insisted that the sliding scale in the Schuylkill and Lehigh regions be ended, and that grievance committees of the employees be recognized. The independent operators decided to accept the union's terms, providing the larger companies would follow. During October the dominant companies accepted the terms and the union ordered the miners back to the pits by October 29.[24]

The strike lasted from September 17 to October 29, and no serious breaks in the ranks took place. According to President Mitchell, the anthracite strike of 1900 "stands out in bold relief as the most remarkable contest between labor and capital in the industrial history of our nation; remarkable because it involved a greater number of persons than any other industrial contest; because of the entire absence of lawlessness on the part of those who engaged in the strike; and last, but not least, because it was the only great contest in which the workers came out entirely and absolutely victorious."[25]

While the last part of Mitchell's statement was more than a slight exaggeration, the outcome of the strike was a solid victory for the union. Nevertheless, a campaign for consolidation was necessary if the organization was not to be undermined. The miners wanted to be represented by a labor organization and they were willing to make substantial sacrifices to achieve this purpose. The union leaders were aware that their limited victory was, in part, the result of the political necessities facing the powerful industrial and financial interests.

When the agreement of 1900 expired on April 1, the union faced the problem of gaining a renewal. Mitchell sought a joint meeting, but his requests were rebuffed. A tridistrict convention in March 1901 made the same request, and again without success. Mitchell once more sought the aid of eminent outsiders. Ralph Easley of the National Civic Federation was asked to help; Hanna's assistance was requested, and J. P. Morgan was asked to intervene. In the end Mitchell was able to gain an extension of the contract to April 1, 1902, and an agreement that the anthracite companies would discuss employees' grievances with their committees.

THE STRIKE OF 1902

For the union the arrangements of 1901 could be regarded as only a holding operation. Moreover, the workers in some instances were losing patience with the Fabian tactics of the union. Wildcat strikes increased and the companies' insistence that grievance committees be made up exclusively of their own employees placed a strain upon the procedure. There were complaints that discrimination in work assignments was being practiced against more aggressive unionists. The anthracite question was discussed at the 1902 national convention of the United Mine Workers of America, and the customary resolution of support adopted. In March, 1902, Mitchell again invited the operators to a joint conference, but they rejected any meeting. The tridistrict convention at Shamokin on March 12, considered the operators' refusal, prepared a list of demands including the introduction of an eight-hour day without reduction in pay, and authorized the officers to call a strike if a satisfactory settlement was not reached.

Mitchell again enlisted the services of Easley and Hanna, but they were confronted by more serious obstacles. Neither side was happy with the agreement. Union members felt that the companies were not living up to their promises, and the companies believed the miners were indisciplined. The operators were convinced that the question of who was to be the "boss," the company foreman and superintendent or the union, had to be decided on the economic battlefield. Of course, they were confident of success.[26] Morgan declined to take action at the early stage of maneuvering. Mitchell then appealed to the National Civic Federation, and its leader, Senator Hanna, was instrumental in arranging a meeting between leading operators, Mitchell, and several of the leaders of the anthracite miners. The willingness of the anthracite railroad presidents to discuss what they regarded as exclusively their business with the union chiefs did not represent a change in their point of view; it was a concession to George W. Perkins, a leading Morgan partner who strongly favored a conciliatory policy.

The large coal companies were in no mood for concessions at the meeting. It was agreed, however, that the strike would not be called for thirty days, during which time efforts to work out an agreement were to be made. Meetings of representatives of the operators and miners took place, and a smaller joint subcommittee was appointed to seek a way out of the impasse. No agreement was reached at this point. Trying to prevent a strike, Mitchell proposed that the issue be submitted to a board of arbitration made up of Archbishop John Ireland, Bishop Henry C. Potter of the Episcopal church, and a third person selected by them. George F. Baer, the head of the Philadelphia and Reading Railroad, speaking for the operators, rejected these eminent outsiders and noted that the "laws organizing the companies I represent in express terms impose the business management on the president and directors. I could not if I would delegate this business management even to so highly respectable body as the Civic Federation, nor can I call to my aid as experts in the mixed problems of business and philanthropy the eminent prelates you have named."[27]

A temporary suspension was called on May 12, and a tridistrict convention summoned for May 14 to decide on policy. Mitchell spoke against continuing the walkout; he was convinced that the gains achieved by the anthracite miners in the last two years could be enlarged. He was fearful that the strike would expose the union to too many risks, but his advice was rejected by a relatively narrow vote. By a majority of 111½ votes, a strike was called upon which the fate of the union rested. Engineers, firemen, and pumpmen were allowed to remain in the mines, although they were later withdrawn when the companies refused to grant the eight-hour day. Mitchell urged that peaceful methods be followed.

The first month of the strike witnessed little violence. In the meantime, pressure for a national convention to decide on the shutting down of the bituminous mines presented Mitchell with a problem. Under the union's constitution, a special convention had to be called at the request of five districts. Mitchell was opposed to an enlargement of the strike. He strongly urged the convention on July 17 to obey its contracts. Instead of striking he argued for strong financial support. At Mitchell's recommendation, the International donated $50,000 to strike relief, voted varying assessments on the districts and imposed a 25 per cent assessment upon wages and salaries of all national and district officers. An appeal to the general public pointed to the desire of the union to secure "better treatment than we have received in the past and fair recompense for our labor. We have sought to accomplish this end by conciliatory methods. . . . We have faithfully lived up to the letter and spirit of every contract we have made, nor shall we violate them now."[28]

As the strike continued, destitution spread among the idle workers. The collections of the union were below the amounts needed to supply the strikers with a minimum payment, but such a "system of equality . . . would have required greater funds than were at the disposal of the union, since a per capita distribution would have resulted in intolerable suffering and uncontrollable discontent. . . . Funds received were therefore distributed according to the needs of applicants. The funds received by the national organization were divided among the three districts of the anthracite regions in proportion to the number of mine workers in each, but each of these districts distributed its quota according to the requirements of the various locals composing it. . . . In the distribution of relief, no discrimination has been made against non-union miners, who receive the same amount of aid as the union miners."[29]

Relief was conducted on an order basis. Strikers were given an order, not convertible to cash, upon a grocer and he was required to sign the order and itemize the goods purchased, to receive payment from the union. Need was reduced because many strikers obtained employment outside of the district, some in nonmining jobs within the strike area, and others were supported by friends and relatives. Only those in need were allowed relief.[30] About $1.5 million was distributed during the strike.

Neither side would yield on essentials, and the strike continued with a number of Republican politicians trying to find a formula for settlement. Some mines were reopened and violence increased. According to the *New York Tribune,* by the middle of September, fourteen persons had been killed and many more seriously wounded or mauled, and much property destroyed.[31] In the meantime, fears that the country would be short of coal in the coming winter appeared to be more than idle speculation. President Theodore Roosevelt had sought to intervene, but after considering a report by U.S. Commissioner of Labor Carroll D. Wright, the President decided for a time against intervention. The problem which faced President Roosevelt was the absence of authority to intervene in labor disputes. Heads of state and municipal governments could, like the President of the United States, use their moral authority, but they could be and were frequently overruled by the heads of corporations. Moreover, the government had to provide defense against violence to persons and property, and as a result its intervention was almost inevitably on the side of the employer. Had strikebreakers been available, the anthracite operators might have broken the strike, but they were unable to recruit a sufficient complement.

Roosevelt, however, continued to seek a settlement behind the scenes. The determination of the operators was reinforced by their moral convictions and George F. Baer was certain that "The rights and interests of the laboring man will be protected and cared for—not by the labor agitators, but by the Christian men to whom God in His infinite wisdom has given the control of property interests of the country, and upon the successful

Management of which so much depends."[32] Baer's prophesying did not meet with general approval, and to many it was but another sign of the self-righteous arrogance of the coal operators.

Finally deciding to intervene, Roosevelt invited leaders of the operators and miners to a White House conference on October 3. The heads of the coal-carrying roads and John Markle, an independent operator, represented the operators; Mitchell and the presidents of the three anthracite districts appeared for the miners. Attorney-General Philander C. Knox, Carroll D. Wright, and several other government officials were also present. Roosevelt expressed his reluctance to intervene as long as the possibility of a settlement existed, "but the urgency and terrible nature of the catastrophe impending over a large portion of our people in the shape of a winter fuel famine impel me, after much anxious thought, to believe that my duty requires me to use whatever influence I personally can to bring to an end a situation which has become literally intolerable."[33] Mitchell immediately expressed his willingness to have a tribunal named by the President arbitrate all differences, but Baer, speaking for the operators, denounced the violence of the union and demanded protection of mining properties by the state of Pennsylvania and by the federal government if necessary. Baer's view was supported by the other operators present.

An immediate result of the failure of the conference was the calling out of the National Guard, which failed to increase coal production. Moreover, the operators by their refusal to negotiate, coupled with the reasonableness of the union leaders, suffered a great loss of public support. President Roosevelt made another try at a settlement and suggested the miners return to work, after which he would appoint a commission to hear the evidence and recommend terms. Mitchell rejected this proposal.

Meantime, public pressure for a settlement mounted, and the obduracy of the operators aroused widespread resentment. In contrast, while Mitchell showed willingness to compromise, he wanted the union to be given some measure of security. Behind the scenes, influence and pressure were being exerted by leaders of the government from President Roosevelt to lesser officials. A proposal for arbitrating the differences by a board appointed by the President and an immediate return to work of the miners was made by President Roosevelt after a courtesy call at the White House by J. P. Morgan. Its basis had been worked out in a conference between Morgan and Elihu Root, Roosevelt's Secretary of War and an eminent corporation lawyer. The operators, while agreeing, laid down conditions which almost led to the aborting of the President's plan. A commission of seven with Edgar E. Clark, the head of the Order of Railway Conductors as a member, was in the end accepted by both sides. The operators had indicated opposition to the appointment of a labor leader, and Roosevelt described Clark as "an eminent sociologist." Mitchell recommended acceptance of the

President's proposals to the meeting of the tridistrict convention of October 21 and the miners were directed to return to their jobs.

The Commission

The commission of seven organized on October 14 and elected Judge George Gray of the Federal Court of Appeals as chairman, directed the parties to appear before it on October 27, and then adjourned until November 14 when hearings opened. The miners asked for a 20 per cent increase in rates for contract or piece work; a reduction of the hours of labor from ten to eight; a system of weighing coal so that 60 cents would be paid for each ton of 2,240 pounds; the incorporation in an agreement with the United Mine Workers of America and the coal companies of the terms agreed upon, including the method of settling differences.[34]

The operators rejected the demands. The commission heard 558 witnesses and issued its decision on March 18. It recommended an increase in wages of 10 per cent for tonnage miners and for all others; checkweighmen were to be allowed at the request of the majority of employees at a colliery; a board of conciliation was suggested for settling differences which arose during the contract; discrimination for belonging or not belonging to a labor union was condemned. In addition, the use of private guards was held to be against the public interest. The commission did not recommend the recognition of the union, but it did agree "that a plan, under which all questions of difference between the employer and his employees, shall first be considered in conference between the operator or his official representative, and a committee chosen by his employees from their own ranks, is most likely to produce satisfactory results and harmonious relations, and at such conference the employees would have the right to call to their assistance such representatives or agents as they may choose, and to have them recognized as such."[35]

While the issue of child labor was not directly submitted, the commission deplored the employment of male children as breaker boys, and noted that the statutory age of employment was not sufficiently high.[36]

The victory in the anthracite fields was one of the greatest in American labor history. It was gained against the formidable opposition of the operators in an industry dominated by the same financial groups which sought to limit the influence of unionism in other industries. By willingness to accept less than their demands, the mine workers, under the leadership of Mitchell, were able to force open a door to labor organizations that had been closed since the demise of the Workmen's Benevolent Association in the early 1870's. While the union did not gain all it asked for, nor did it manage to gain formal recognition, it was able to gain an impregnable place in the anthracite coal industry.

The victories in the bituminous and anthracite fields placed the United

Mine Workers of America at the head of the American labor movement. According to Mitchell, the union had grown from 11,000 in January 1898 to about 250,000 in July 1901.[37] Despite the fact that the bituminous coal areas were the earliest organized, they were over the years less stable than the anthracite sector. The competitive problem which faced the organized bituminous districts as a result of the expansion of the unorganized fields of West Virginia, and later Kentucky, and which posed insoluble difficulties for the union were absent in the anthracite sector. The inability of the union to organize West Virginia was not due to lack of effort, but to the armed and legal barriers successfully erected by the coal companies.

The United Mine Workers of America was not only an important source of new recruits for organized labor, but for the next twenty years it was to remain a stable support for other labor organizations and the entire labor movement.

CHAPTER 14

Gains and Losses in the Metal Trades

Union organizations and groups of employers in the stove industry, whose markets were not expanding rapidly and whose variety of products were limited, evolved a workable system of collective bargaining. In contrast, the expanding metal trades, producing a wide range of products, found labor organizations a hindrance to expansion and refused, after a short trial, to continue relations with organized labor.

STOVE FOUNDRIES

The stove foundry industry developed in the early nineteenth century, and by 1829 a successful plant devoted entirely to the manufacture of stoves was established in Taunton, Massachusetts. With improvements in transportation, other communities developed stove factories, and interlocal and regional competition steadily increased. In 1872 the National Association of Stove Manufacturers was organized, and it claimed that 2.1 million stoves had been produced in 1870. Employment in the industry was never large, and, perhaps because of its smaller size, a system of industrial relations which was developed in the 1890's lasted for more than fifty years. Moreover, while the stove founding industry maintained peaceful relations with the Iron Molders' Union of North America, the foundry employers and machine tool industry sought to expel their labor organizations from their industries and conducted formidable campaigns against them on both the industrial and propaganda fronts.

A factor contributing to peaceful relations over the years was the willingness of the organized molders to accept the piece-work system of wages. Consequently, the strikes in this industry seldom were disputes over the method of compensation, but involved percentages to be paid to particular groups of workers or the payment for the entire stove. The ratio of apprentices to be allowed was sometimes in question, and another source of friction was the treatment of the "bucks" or "berkshires." These men started as unskilled laborers in a foundry and learned the trade through experience rather than through apprenticeship courses. In contrast, the apprentice was guaranteed that upon the completion of his term he would automatically become a mechanic. During his apprenticeship he was paid by the employer. The "buck" had no such guarantee and was often paid by the molder.[1]

Strikes over the percentage were called in Philadelphia in 1855, and they resulted in the organization of an iron molders' local union which lasted until the next century. In the same year iron molders struck in Albany, New York. After the National Union organized in 1859, the number of disputes increased. In 1866 the Iron Founders' Association was organized by the employers, and a demand for a wage reduction followed by a lockout of union workers in eight cities by members of the Association followed. Efforts by Union President William H. Sylvis to confer with leading employers were rebuffed. Sylvis claimed that the International Union had spent $1,161,582 in support of strikes and lockouts since 1859. After a two-month strike, the employers withdrew their notices of wage reductions.

One of the sources of differences between the employers and the union was the failure of the union to raise prices in the eastern shops so as to equalize costs between eastern and western producers. While the union was able to fend off the attack in 1866, the employers in the western areas were not satisfied with the union's efforts to equalize prices between regions. The Stove and Hollow Ware Manufacturers' Association charged that "there is no reliance to be placed in the repeated promises made to us by the 'Molders' Union Association' for the regularization and equalization of prices East and West, and that certain rules adhered to by each section of said union are operating to the decided injury of both employers and employees in the West."[2]

The burden of the complaint of the western producers was that the union had allowed lower wages to prevail in the eastern shops with the result that the western manufacturers found themselves faced with the competition of low-wage products in their own markets. Sylvis denied the charges and claimed that the union had sought increases in the eastern shops but its efforts had been frustrated by the lockout in which the western producers cooperated. No agreement could be reached, and a long and—for the union—disastrous strike followed. It affected more areas than the strike in 1866, and the union lost almost half of its members. By 1870 it had only

3,860 members on its rolls. Strikes on a local basis continued, and in 1884 one of the larger local strikes of molders took place in Cincinnati. The International was unable to provide even a minimum of assistance, since the treasurer had absconded with $19,000.[3]

The relatively small local strikes culminated in 1887 in the largest one in the history of the iron molders' trade. Called the Bridge and Beach Strike, it was the result of the conviction of both industry and the union that a "showdown" fight was necessary. The employers had established in 1886 the Stove Founders' National Defense Association—an offshoot of the National Association of Stove Manufacturers that had functioned in nonlabor matters since 1872. The object of the Defense Association was to resist any unjust demand by the union. When the union struck for an increase in pay at the Bridge and Beach Company of St. Louis, the patterns, in accordance with the rules of the Defense Association, were sent to other firms. When union men refused to handle the struck patterns, a lockout followed. The patterns were continually transferred to shops in other communities, but the reaction of the union molders was the same. About 5,000 workers in fourteen towns and cities were affected by the strike and lockouts. The contest ended in the union's failure to win its demands, but it was able to survive the onslaught. On the other hand, the depletion of the supply of stoves enabled the manufacturers to recoup part of their strike losses by higher prices.

The Bridge and Beach Strike led to a reconsideration of tactics by both sides. Unofficial conferences between leaders of labor and management in the industry were followed by the approval by the convention of the Molders' Union for a conference with the Stove Manufacturers' Defense Association. On March 25, 1891, representatives of both associations met in Chicago, and the meeting adopted the principle of peaceful settlement of disputes between members of their respective organizations. Whenever differences arose in a plant, the union and the company were required to seek a settlement directly. If unable to do so, the issue was submitted to a conference committee, with equal representation from each organization. While a settlement was being considered, operation of the plant was to proceed in the ordinary manner. Wages were to be negotiated annually. The agreement did not provide for arbitration, because many employers in the industry would not accept third-party settlements.[4]

Under the rules adopted in 1891, each organization chose its representatives to the annual conferences and gave them full power to bind their organizations on wage rates to be paid for the coming year. The joint conferences were purely legislative bodies, and discussions of grievances were prohibited. Each organization enforced the agreement upon its members, and employers who refused to abide by the decisions of the joint conference committee were expelled from the association. The International Union insisted that locals abide by the accepted procedure, and violators were subject to discipline, including expulsion.

Similar agreements were worked out in 1903 by the Defense Association with the Metal Polishers, Buffers, Platers, Brass Molders and Brass Workers International Union, and with the Stove Mounters' International Union of North America. While the agreements did not cover as many workers or employers as those in the bituminous coal industry, the one in the stove molding industry represented an important attempt to eliminate strikes and lockouts which had plagued the industry over the years. Moreover, the agreement in the stove industry antedated the interstate agreement in the bituminous coal industry by several years. The pragmatic approach of the two organizations emphasized the necessity of devising workable agreements over issues which affected the parties rather than abstract principles. Because of the limited possibility for increasing rapidly the demand for the product, the agreements tended to act as a stabilizing force. While any single employer could increase his volume, the possibility for an over-all increase for the industry appeared to be limited approximately by net family formation. As a consequence, the arrangements worked effectively because the members of the industry were more anxious to have labor peace than risk a labor dispute with possible losses of business. While the experiment in industrial conciliation in the stove industry was a desirable step, the special characteristics of the industry eased some of the bargaining problems and made the introduction of similar programs in other branches of the metal and machinery industry more difficult.

The Stove Founders' National Defense Association had a membership of about sixty-five firms employing about 6,500 workers. Most of the firms confined themselves largely to the manufacture of stove plates, and while there were many kinds of products manufactured—coal stoves, hot-air ranges and parts of various kinds—the skill required of the journeyman was about the same. The relative uniformity of the product and the limited market made it desirable both for the union and for management to avoid excessive competition.

MACHINE AND JOBBING FOUNDRIES

In contrast to the relatively few products manufactured in stove foundries, the machine foundries produced "everything from a door key to a watch fob, weighing a few ounces, up to castings weighing hundreds of tons. We handled gray iron, malleable iron, steel bars, copper and aluminum, and almost anything you could think of; there were absolutely no combinations in any shape, manner, or form. . . . It was absolutely impossible to control the price."[5]

Despite the differences in the industrial make-up, the American Foundrymen's Association, organized in 1896, sought to follow the example of the Defense Association. In fact, the Molders' Union encouraged the machinery and jobbing foundrymen to organize, believing that an arrangement as satisfactory as the one in force in the stove molding industry could be established. Martin Fox, the head of the Molders' Union, urged a meeting of Detroit foundrymen in 1898 to establish a national organization with which his union could draw up an agreement. Pursuant in part to Fox's advice, the National Founders' Association was organized in January 1898 in New York. In February of 1899 the association and the Molders' Union signed the New York agreement, setting up machinery for the settlement of differences between an employer and his employees. Under the terms, disputes between members of the Founders' Association and the Molders' Union would, in the first instance, be dealt with by the parties themselves. In the event of failure, the issue would be submitted to the presidents of the two organizations and four other members, two from each group. "The finding of this committee of arbitration by a majority vote shall be considered final in so far as the future action of the respective organizations is concerned." A finding by a majority vote was binding, and no changes in the terms of employment were to be introduced pending the decision of the board. The committee of arbitration was to meet within two weeks after the submission of a grievance.[6]

Inability to settle deadlocked disputes put a strain on the system, because no provisions existed to arbitrate differences which the parties could not settle themselves. The system that had been established was actually conciliation, although it was called arbitration. According to Briggs, "we would exhaust every means at our command to agree by virtue of this conciliation, and then we would deadlock. Beyond that we could not go. This condition became so strained, the foundrymen feeling that at the expiration of about three or four years of this attempt that we were making no progress, that we decided to take some definite action. When I became an officer of the association, which by the way was in 1903, my directions from the council were to use every effort in the world that was at all consistent with business conditions to arrive at some method of settling these difficulties. We had had too many of them. We had become tired of chasing each other around the country holding conferences by virtue of that agreement. They urged that wherever I had an opportunity to do so I should request and urge to the best of my ability that we bring in the odd party and arbitrate."[7] The association was also dissatisfied with the number of local strikes that were called and the inability of the national union to prevent them.

The founders wanted some method to settle disputes and wanted such issues as the apprentice ratio and the use of machinery excluded from the union control. President Joseph Valentine of the Molders' Union testified that "the representatives of the National Founders' Association take a positive position on some questions which are involved; for instance, the making of castings by machines. The association's position on that question was this: That the machine was the product of the machine shop and they would not discuss with the representatives of the molders' union any price on those castings. They wanted to be free to operate the machines with whomsoever they pleased."[8] The union was not opposed to the introduction of machinery, but wanted to retain the jobs for its own members. In other words, the union sought the same daily pay for a molder as he had earned before. John Frey, an executive officer of the International Molders' Union, attributed the opposition of the members of his union to the machine to the fact that it was adopted by the industry to weaken the organization of labor. Frey contended that members of the union did work on the machine under satisfactory conditions.[9] However, satisfactory conditions would mean the placing of skilled craftsmen at customary wage rates on machines which could be operated by semi-skilled workers. The union only partially accepted the machine, for its insistence upon the retention of the skilled in jobs which did not require the services of such workers was an attempt to limit the use of machinery.

Apprentice ratios was another question which divided the parties. Strikes were not prevented by the agreement. A serious strike involving 600 molders in Cleveland over a wage increase in July 1900 was a danger signal that the conciliation system was not working. Although this strike was settled six months later, many smaller ones continued to break out and put a serious strain on the agreement system. Briggs estimated that about 150 strikes took place during the period the agreement was in effect, and that many foundrymen concluded it was a failure.

In February 1904 several heater shops in Utica, New York, asked for a 15 per cent reduction in molding prices. The union rejected the proposal. Instead of the employer appealing to the Founders' Association and retaining the status quo while the issue was being settled through the conciliation procedure, the employer put the reduction into effect. According to the union, the step was taken on the advice of the association on the theory that the union could present the issue as a grievance. But the union believed that the action violated its understanding with the association. For example, the union, if it asked for an increase of $2.00 a day, and the company refused, it could not insist that the raise be given in advance and then discussed as a grievance. No agreement could be reached in the dispute. An unsuccessful effort was made by the leaders to salvage the system, but it was only a symptom of its breakdown.[10]

In the spring of 1904 a meeting in Detroit was held with representatives of both organizations present. "It lasted four days and four nights. I think we had eight members of the Founders' Association there, various employers of laborers, and those who represented small foundries. We had an equal number from the iron molders' union as delegates, and also 28 business delegates of that union. . . . we devoted four days and four nights to an effort to arrive at an agreement, but after spending the two days we referred it to a subcommittee. That subcommittee devoted nearly two more days to it and reported they could not agree."[11] In November 1904 the association canceled the agreement.

The National Founders' Association became an opponent of labor organizations, although some of its members continued to deal with the Molders' Union. Members agreed to the following: "In consideration of fair dealing being a cardinal principle of this Association, we pledge ourselves to protect any of our fellow members who may require our support against any unjust demands of labor organizations and to endeavor to settle all disputes amicably."[12] The Founders' Association always argued that it had given collective bargaining a fair trial, and that during the seven years the New York agreement was in effect its members had met with representatives of the Molders' Union 2,500 times. It believed that the union had failed to recognize the changing character of the industry and the need to adopt labor policy to the demands of the times. The association also felt that President Joseph Valentine had less sympathy for the problems of the industry than his predecessor, Martin Fox. Another factor which led to the breakdown was the variety of products manufactured by the members and the difference in their market positions, as well as the contribution the union could make to their welfare. The members of the Founders' Association did not manufacture similar products, but used a broadly similar process—foundrying. In contrast, the members of the Defense Association produced stoves, and although their output was not uniform in kind, there was sufficient similarity in product and problems to make the desire for regulation desirable for many members. Numbers were another important difference. Unlike the stove industry, machinery foundrying was expanding in response to the great upsurge of industry in the early 1900's. The union with its restrictive policies, its bare tolerance of technical change, and its desire to limit apprentice ratios was interfering with industrial progress. It could not, as in the stove industry, be a regulator of competitive practice and act as a restraint upon competition through wage cutting. As a result, the Iron Molders' Union, which had been able to devise a workable program in the stove industry, failed in machinery and job founding. A contributing factor appears to be the failure of many locals to accept change, even though they were favored by the national officers.

UNIONS IN THE METAL AND MACHINERY INDUSTRY

Unions in the metal and machinery industry were formed before the Civil War. In addition to the Molders' Union, Knights of Labor assemblies were established in the railroad shops and some in machine shops. An international union, the International Union of Blacksmiths and Machinists, was established in 1859 and became a victim of the depression of 1877. The National Boilermakers' and Helpers Protective and Benevolent Union, established in 1881, failed to survive. It was followed by the Machinists National League in 1886, but it also quickly expired. During the same decade, the Pattern Makers' League of North America was organized and finally the United Machinists and Mechanical Engineers of North America in 1888, which became the National, and later the International, Association of Machinists of America. Organized by Thomas W. Talbot, a railroad machinist working on the Eastern Tennessee, Virginia and Georgia Railroad in Atlanta, Georgia, the union absorbed many associated with the National Trade Assembly 198 of the Knights of Labor.

Early in its history the union spread to the North and began recruiting members in the machine job shops. While it achieved some gains, its success was limited by the depression of the early 1890's. In 1893, James O'Connell was elected president and under his leadership the union pursued a militant trade union policy. He sought to develop the union into an effective instrument for negotiating agreements with employers in the trade. In 1895 the Machinists' Union joined the AFL, after it had omitted the white qualification from its constitution. The machinists, however, did not permit Negro workers to join until the 1940's.[13]

The 1897 convention of the AFL designated the International Association of Machinists as the union which would seek the establishment of the nine-hour workday. The decision to support the Machinists was an incident in a longer campaign for shorter hours which the federation had inaugurated during the year of its birth. The objective met the approval of the Machinists' Union and other labor organizations in the metal trades as well. A strike in the pattern shops in New York City in July 1899 led to an informal agreement among employers in that city that they would not make concessions, and the following month a more formal organization, the National Metal Trades Association, was established. Immediately, the National Metal Trades Association was confronted by a series of strikes in behalf of the nine-hour workday. Shops in Chicago, Cleveland, Detroit, Patterson, New Jersey, and Philadelphia were affected. D. D. Wilson, a vice-president of the International Association of Machinists, thought that the Chicago machinists acted too hastily in calling a strike. A demand for a reduction in hours had been made, and when the employers failed to agree, a strike which affected 3,500 workers was called.

The leaders of the National Metal Trades Association and President James O'Connell of the union tried to settle the Chicago walkout. At a meeting in Chicago on March 17, 1900, O'Connell rejected the Chicago agreement on the ground that he could not induce the members to accept it, although he himself approved it. Subsequently, the Chicago employers submitted a set of proposals including eventual reduction of the weekly hours of work to fifty-five, after twelve months, and for a system of disputes settlement through negotiation with ultimate appeal to the heads of both organizations. No strikes or lockouts were to be called "until every effort has been made to settle differences by negotiations or arbitration between the national organizations."[14]

The Chicago settlement was a forerunner of the Murray Hill agreement negotiated in New York on May 18, 1900, by committees from the two national organizations. It was agreed that existing strikes in Cleveland and Patterson would be ended. In "case of the refusal of any member of the respective organizations represented to observe and carry out in an honorable manner the findings and decisions of the board in regard to strikes and lockouts, based upon a fair, just, and liberal interpretation as to what is known as the Chicago agreement, we will report such member to our respective organization for discipline, suspension, or expulsion, as the merits of the case may justify."[15]

The Murray Hill agreement provided for a reduction of the weekly hours of labor to fifty-seven and within a year, to fifty-four, with the establishment of the nine-hour workday on May 20, 1901. A machinist was defined, time and one-quarter was allowed for overtime work, apprenticeship was regulated, and strikes and lockouts as well as discrimination against union members were forbidden. Differences over wage reduction to compensate for the reduced hours of work began as soon as the new schedules were put into effect. The union wanted the association to adopt a general policy, and the latter insisted the issue had to be settled on a local basis. Failure to agree led to the calling of a strike on May 20, which affected 58,000 machinists in the principal centers of the industry. As a result the association canceled its contract with the union on June 10, and eight days later it announced its open shop policy.

A "declaration of principles" announced that the members would "not admit of any interference with the management of our business." Strikes and lockouts were disapproved; the regulation of work, including decisions on the number of apprentices, helpers, and journeymen to perform a particular task was held to be the function of the employer. No negotiations over wages or other terms of employment with a union were allowed. Members were charged dues and assessments to support the activities of the organization. In case of strikes, the association assumed control. It disapproved "of strikes and lockouts in the settlement of industrial disputes. This association will not countenance a lockout, unless all reasonable means of adjustment have failed; neither will the members of this Association deal with striking employees."[16] The association established a strikebreaking service under which it maintained a card file of strikebreakers in different local offices. When a strike occurred, the association mobilized the strikebreakers available in different cities for service at the struck plant. In "many of its branches [it] maintained an extensive card catalogue of men skilled in metal trades. On the cards the union affiliations of the men were recorded for 'reference' by any of its members."[17]

The association also provided strike guards, called special service men, for members and nonmembers of the association. Nonmembers paid the guards themselves. These guards were recruited by the "grapevine" method in New York, Chicago, and Cleveland.[18] In addition, special contract operatives who were employed in shops were provided.

According to a Senate committee, from the time of its organization to 1937, the "National Metal Trades Association has used labor spies as a method of preventing the organization of workers in the metal trades' industry. For years workers in the plants of its members have been kept under surveillance by undercover men. Labor unions in the metal trades' industry have been infested with National Metal Trades Association spies, who have worked their way into positions of confidence in order to create discord."[19]

The National Metal Trades Association became a leading proponent of the anti-union forces in the country. It cooperated closely with other belligerent employers' associations, and sought to prevent the expansion of unions on the industrial plane and to reduce its influence in the halls of Congress and the state legislatures. The association changed its policies in 1937, giving up its strikebreaking activities.

Like the National Founders Association, the Metal Trades Association started as a conciliatory organization, one established to deal with organized labor. Its shift from conciliation to belligerency was influenced by the desire of labor organizations to control shop rules which would have restricted the authority of the employer. Moreover, the unions in the metal trades at the time were basically craft organizations whose members regarded with suspicion the introduction of technical changes which diluted their skill. Like the founders, the members of the National Metal Trades did not make the same products. They were, in fact, a group of heterogeneous producers, and the union could do little to regulate production or competition for the benefit of the entire group. Moreover, the metal trades were facing a time of great opportunity, and the restrictive practices of many of the crafts were regarded as barriers to expansion. Insistence upon limiting apprentices and opposition to piece work by the Machinists' Union were therefore found intolerable, and the inability of the union to compromise on these points strengthened those in the association who considered union policies as barriers to the progress of the industry.

CHAPTER 15

Anti-Unionism in the Steel Industry

CHANGES IN THE STEEL INDUSTRY

The defeat of the iron and steel workers' union in Homestead in 1892 was a serious blow. Even more important, it came at a time when the industry was undergoing rapid consolidation into larger units. Mergers and pools were followed by the formation of the U.S. Steel Corporation in 1901. The concentration movement in the steel industry had begun slowly in the 1880's and rose rapidly in the next two decades. Leaders of the industry were not anxious to operate in competitive markets and sought at first to use the pool for controlling prices and allocating production. Mergers, of which the Carnegie Steel Company was the prime example, began in the 1880's and were temporarily halted as a result of the depression of the 1890's.

In 1882, Carnegie, Phipps and Company (later the Carnegie Steel Company) inaugurated its policy of controlling the various steps in the making of steel by purchasing control of the H. C. Frick Coke Company, the largest owner of coal lands and largest producer of coke in the Connellsville region. Later the Carnegie Company leased almost 100,000 acres of natural gas land in western Pennsylvania and purchased important limestone quarries near Pittsburgh, thus acquiring independent sources of fuel and fluxing material. The company also acquired a large supply of iron ore and a fleet of steamers with which to transport it from the mines to the eastern ports of the Great Lakes. A controlling interest in the Pittsburgh, Bessemer and Lake Erie Railroad was secured to carry the ore from the port of Conneaut, Ohio, to the Carnegie mills at Duquesne, Pennsylvania. Many of these properties were improved, made more efficient, and their costs of production reduced. The "possession of these advantages along with the admirable equipment of its furnaces and mills, gave the Carnegie Company the foremost position in the iron and steel trade of the United States."[1]

As a leading contemporary student of corporate organization noted: "The lessons of this example were not lost upon the leaders in the iron and steel consolidation of 1898 and 1899. No sooner were the new companies fairly upon their feet, and had realized the necessity of greater economy, than they began a movement which looked toward the attainment of independence in raw materials similar to that which the Carnegie Company had already achieved."[2] The situation at the turn of the century was this: three great producers—the Carnegie Steel Company, the Federal Steel Company, and the National Steel Company—dominated the production of crude and semi-finished steel. Six other large concerns of secondary importance operated in various markets: the American Sheet Steel Company, the American Steel and Wire Company, the American Tin Plate Company, the American Steel Hoop Company, the American Bridge Company, and the National Tube Company.

Several of the secondary concerns, however, were seeking to free themselves from dependence upon the basic steel producers by building their own mills, and the latter planned to meet these threats by invading the markets of their customers. In January 1901 the Carnegie Company announced plans for building a tube mill at Conneaut, Ohio, on Lake Erie. The company also intimated that it would build sheet mills and it would invade other finished lines. Instead of the threatened war, the financiers restored peace; the Carnegie Company became part of the huge merger effected under the leadership of J. P. Morgan, whose firm handled the financing. The Carnegie Company, the Federal Steel Company, the National Steel Company, the American Sheet Steel Company, the American Steel Hoop Company, the American Tin Plate Company, and the National Tube Company became part of the great industrial and financial complex which at the time of the merger controlled 43 per cent of the pig iron production and 66 per cent of the steel ingot and castings production of the United States.[3]

THE STEEL UNION

Homestead was a serious blow to the Amalgamated Association, and membership fell from 20,975 in 1892 to 10,000 in 1894 and remained almost at that figure until 1900. The union was engaged in an uphill fight, and the steel mills in the Pittsburgh district were able to reduce steadily the power of the organization. Although it was stronger in the western mills, its failure to gain membership or even to retain those in its ranks for long periods was an ill omen. A reversal in the fortunes of the union appeared to take place in

1900, and the aggressiveness which had characterized the union's early years appeared to be returning. An important manifestation of the changed attitude was an amendment to the constitution adopted at the 1900 Amalgamated Association's convention: "Should one mill in a combine or trust have a difficulty, all mills in said combine or trust shall cease work until such grievance is settled."[4]

The resolution, passed at the height of the consolidation movement in the industry, was not given much consideration by the delegates. While such a policy might be difficult to enforce, it was based upon the experiences of the union in trying to maintain its position. In fact, the union found itself in constant difficulty because some of the steel companies would sign the scale only for union mills, and soon thereafter would shut down the organized plant and operate those which were outside of the union contract. Such a policy was not only regarded as unfair by the leaders, but embittered many of the idle unionists. Many of the delegates considered this policy as the only one that the union could follow, since the companies were not adverse to reopening the shut down plants without a union contract.

Attitude of the U.S. Steel Corporation

Almost immediately after its organization, the U.S. Steel Corporation considered the labor problem. On April 26, 1901, the executive committee decided that the "corporation as a whole would not deal in any way directly with labor organizations, but that each subsidiary company was responsible for the conduct of all negotiations and settlement with regard to labor conditions."[5] Opposition to the union was expressed, but the heads of the corporation wanted to avoid labor difficulties, at least for the present. The $1.4 million of securities, most of which had still to be marketed, would not be favorably affected by a long-drawn-out labor conflict. Despite these misgivings, the executive committee voted, on June 17: "That we are unalterably opposed to any extension of union labor and advise subsidiary companies to take a firm position when these questions come up, and say that they are not going to recognize it; that is, any extension of unions in mills where they do not now exist; that great care should be used to prevent trouble; and that they promptly report and confer with this corporation."[6]

The resolution, introduced by a member of J. P. Morgan and Company, was approved unanimously. Nevertheless, even the strongest opponent of union labor on the executive committee, Percival Roberts, believed it was best to postpone a contest. One of the firms in the merger, American Sheet Steel Company, had opposed the extension of union organization in its plants before it had become a subsidiary of the U.S. Steel Corporation. The union was mindful of this policy when it came time to renew the agreement in June 1901. Moreover, the constitutional requirement that all mills of a corporation were to be placed under the union contract gave the officers of the union little leeway. When no agreement was reached by July 1, strikes were called against the American Sheet Steel Company and the American Steel Hoop Company, two subsidiaries of U.S. Steel, both of which refused to accept the union terms on bargaining.[7] In the meantime, an agreement had been reached with the American Tin Plate Company for all mills except one.

President T. J. Shaffer notified the head of this company, Warner Ames, that inasmuch "as the American Sheet Steel and the American Steel Hoop Cos. have refused to sign the scale for their mills, and the American Tin Plate Co. is a part of the United States Steel Company, of which the above-named companies are also constituents, I hereby inform you that if this difficulty or agreement is not adjusted on or before Monday, July 8, it will be my very unpleasant duty to call from their work all of your workmen who are members of the Amalgamated Association."[8] President Ames objected to the union's decision. He told Shaffer that "the fact that your association has a grievance against any other company is no justification for a deliberate violation of its agreement with us."[9]

The U.S. Steel Corporation continued to seek a settlement and at a conference between officers of the three subsidiaries concerned and the officers of the union, the companies proposed that the American Tin Plate Company sign for all plants except one; that the American Steel Hoop Company sign for all mills under contract with the union the previous year; and that the American Sheet Steel Company sign for all of the mills under union agreements the preceding year, with the addition of four mills including one at Wellsville, Ohio (where twelve workers had been discharged for attempting to form a union). In all the association was offered six more mills under contract than had been suggested in the pre-strike negotiations. It was, from the point of view of the union, a very favorable offer, but it was rejected by Shaffer and John Williams, who was presumably the strong man in the Amalgamated.

The National Civic Federation, established for promoting the peaceful adjustment of labor disputes, entered the controversy through its conciliation committee, whose membership included Samuel Gompers, John Mitchell, and Senator Mark Hanna. A conference of strike leaders and J. P. Morgan, Charles M. Schwab, and Elbert Gary, heads of the U.S. Steel Corporation, was arranged through the offices of George Harvey, editor of *Harpers' Weekly,* on July 27. It was agreed that work would be resumed at the plants of the three companies and that the union would not seek to organize the nonunion properties.

In the conference, Morgan denied hostility to unions, and argued that it was not practicable for the corporation to recognize the unions for the unorganized mills. It was believed that some of the constituent companies would not have joined the merger unless they had been assured that they would not be compelled to recognize organized labor.[10] At another conference on July 29, Morgan made the same proposals and the union leaders rejected them again. Thereupon the companies began to replace the strikers.

Failure to reach an agreement led Shaffer to call out the workers in other plants of U.S. Steel on August 6. The workers answered on August 10 as requested. Employees in two plants of the National Steel Company and in two plants of the National Tube Company responded, employees in three mills of the Illinois Steel Company hesitated, and only a few came out under protest. Workers in the Chicago plants of the Illinois Steel Company positively refused to join the walkout. Whatever justification there may have been for calling strikes against the American Tin Plate Company, those called against the National Steel Company, the National Tube Company, and the Illinois Steel Company were in clear violation of contract, and "some of these scales, in fact, were signed during the progress of the strike."[11] In addition, the shutting down of these plants led to a loss of public sympathy which the Amalgamated had hoped would aid it in its fight against the newly formed corporation.

Senator Hanna arranged a meeting between the executives of the steel companies and a committee from the National Civic Federation made up of Mitchell, Gompers, Frank P. Sargent of the Trainmen's Union, Henry White of the Garment Workers' Union, and Ralph Easley and Professor J. W. Jenks. At this meeting, on September 4, Charles M. Schwab, speaking for the corporation, said that no opposition to unions existed, but since many mills had been started by nonunion labor, the companies would only sign for mills which had not started up. Moreover, the union was given only twenty-four hours to accept; otherwise all negotiations would be terminated. Gompers and Mitchell urged immediate acceptance, but Shaffer hesitated. Schwab, on the plea of the Civic Federation Committee, extended the time, but the union would not immediately accept. The strike dragged on until September 14, when it was settled on terms disastrous to the union.[12]

Under the agreement, the union lost fourteen mills, but it suffered much more. It could not, in fact, seek to organize any nonunion mill and had to agree not to issue any new charters or seek to organize any mills. The settlement aroused a wave of criticism within the union, and President Shaffer defended himself by an attack upon Gompers and Mitchell who, he claimed, had failed to provide the promised support. Shaffer's charges, in brief, were that Gompers had failed to give adequate support to the strike, and Mitchell had not come through with a strike in the coal mines nor had he used his influence in calling the railroad trainmen to the aid of the striking steel workers.

Several points are worth consideration. The first is the union's insistence upon signing all mills of a company. It was obviously ill-advised, since it could not be enforced. George W. Perkins, a power in the House of Morgan, expressed the view "that labor had a right to organize and that there should be no objection to their doing so."[13] One might, however, argue that the statement was disingenuous, in view of the unanimous adoption of the proposal, to prevent the extension of unionism, by the executive committee of the U.S. Steel Corporation.

Such an argument, however, is far from conclusive, for the directive embodied in that resolution was not followed in the offers made to the Amalgamated before the strike. The American Steel Hoop Company offered to sign for all four mills which had not been covered in the previous contract, indicating that the corporation was not completely bound by the earlier decision. Moreover, the union could have used the first contract to demonstrate its responsibility—a significant argument for those who were opposed to the anti-union policies of some of the members of the corporation. In fact, by extending the strike to the plants of U.S. Steel, operating under a valid contract, Shaffer and Williams were demonstrating the accuracy of the claims made by the enemies of unionism in the corporation.

It was plain that the Amalgamated had overestimated its strength, and that many steelworkers refused to follow its leadership. But Shaffer believed that the miners should have laid down their picks and rallied to the support of his union. Having just won a difficult strike in the anthracite fields, and facing a group of operators who were waiting for a chance to expel it from the pits, the calling of a strike in violation of contract would have forever sealed the fate of the union in these fields. The mobilization of public opinion, which Mitchell adroitly managed in the following year, would have been impossible if he had recklessly called out his members. The tactics of the steel companies in shutting down organized plants represented a problem to the union, but Shaffer's method of meeting it spelled defeat.

As for Gompers, he was opposed to general strikes on the principle that they could not achieve their purpose, and he recognized that they were not a legitimate tactic. Moreover, he had no power over international unions, which very likely would have ignored his call to arms. It is doubtful whether the executive council would have regarded favorably his usurpation of power to intervene in trade matters.

The calling of the 1901 strike appears in retrospect as a great act of folly which strengthened the enemies of organized labor in the greatest center of economic power. It weakened those, like George Perkins, who would have preferred a more moderate policy. Shaffer's tactics reinforced the opposition to unionism in the business world, revealed the weakness of the labor organization in the steel industry, and showed that the public would not inevitably take the side of labor.

Ousting of Amalgamated

After the defeat of 1901, the union steadily lost its strength. In the merger with the Carnegie Company, the union lost the mills of the American Steel Hoop Company in 1904. In addition, the puddlers, who became dissatisfied with the inclusion within the union of all classes of steel labor, seceded and formed the Sons of Vulcan in 1907. The results were a moderate loss of membership, the separation of a highly skilled group of workers, and an increase in jurisdictional difficulties between the seceding group and the Amalgamated. The final blow fell in 1909 when, at the expiration of the scale on June 30, the American Sheet and Tin Plate Company posted the following notice: "After a careful consideration of the interests of both the company and its employees, the American Sheet and Tin Plate Co. has decided that all its plants after June 30, 1909, will be operated as 'open' plants."[14] In addition, wages of several groups of skilled workers were reduced. The Amalgamated had no choice but to call a strike. The International Association of Tinplate Workers with about two thousand members in the tin mills joined the walkout. Not even an acknowledgment was given to the union's request for a conference. Finally, the company informed P. J. McArdle, president of the union, that the posted notices revealed the company's intention; Elbert Gray, the head of the U.S. Steel Corporation, refused to overrule his subordinate.

A special convention of the union appealed to the general labor movement for assistance. Differences between the two unions involved prevented an immediate mobilization of labor officers at Pittsburgh, as requested by McArdle, but the AFL convention denounced the U.S. Steel Corporation as "the most formidable and aggressive enemy the movement has had to contend with," and recommended a meeting of executive officers of the international unions and the AFL to consider aid to the beleaguered striking organizations and to devise a campaign of organization among the employees of the U.S. Steel Corporation.[15]

Thirty-six unions responded to the invitation and met in Pittsburgh on December 13, 1909. Each union was asked to assign one organizer who would work under McArdle's direction. In addition, a statement which charged the U.S. Steel Corporation with being an illegal combination in restraint of trade, excluding American workers from employment, degrading labor, and suppressing free speech and the right of assembly in company towns was presented to President William Howard Taft. It called for an impartial investigation by the federal government. Attorney-General George Wickersham did not believe the issues raised concerned violations of federal statutes. The AFL thereupon took their cause to the House of Representatives and was instrumental in bringing about an investigation by a committee of the House of Representatives under the chairmanship of Augustus Stanley—an investigation which revealed many of the business and labor practices of the U.S. Steel Corporation.

A number of unions sent organizers to aid the strike, and over $39,000 was donated by labor organizations to aid the strikers. But they were fighting a losing battle. On May 1, 1910, the company advanced its tonnage rates and on August 27, 1910, the union surrendered and called off the strike that had gone on for fourteen months. President McArdle claimed "the company hired a horde of inexperienced foreigners, Syrians, Poles, Hungarians and Italians who had no sheet or tin experience. These men were recruited in and about Pittsburgh by employment agencies or special agents of the company."[16] W. A. Irvin, a vice-president of the American Sheet and Tin Company, corroborated McArdle's charge by agreeing that in advertising for help during the strike, certain foreign nationalities were mentioned as desirable. "Based upon our experience in employing foreign labor for the tin houses, I [Irvin] gave him a list of those we preferred."[17] The losses marked the end of the union in the plants of the large steel companies. By 1911 membership in the Amalgamated had dropped to slightly above 4,300 and the total membership of the Amalgamated and the Sons of Vulcan was only 5,700.

The weakness of the Amalgamated in 1909 as compared to 1901 was also obvious in the rough treatment accorded its organizers in many steel communities. Not only was the Amalgamated subjected to restraining orders, but in many steel communities organizers were assaulted and ordered out of town.

LAKE SEAMEN

The U.S. Steel Corporation was also active in Great Lakes shipping, where it operated fleets of vessels carrying iron ore. Unionism had a long history among the sailors of the Great Lakes. The growth of grain traffic before the Civil War changed the character of shipping. Instead of ships moving with cargoes to the West, and the boats broken up for other purposes, the new traffic in grain created a demand for workers who depended upon sailing for their livelihood. It was this class of rough, hard-working men who organized the first union organization, the Seamen's Benevolent Union of Chicago, in August 1863 for "the moral, mental and mutual improvement of its members."[18]

In the 1870's ore carrying began to rival the lumber and grain trade as the chief source of employment. At the same time, the steamship began to displace the sailing vessel. The first union did not prosper, and it was reorganized in 1878. Soon thereafter, branches were established in a number of ports. Only those with a knowledge of practical seamanship were admitted. Employers made their first concerted effort to drive union men from the lake boats. At the same time, the union was faced with a problem that the branches tended, in favorable times, to revise the wage scale continually so that a ship might find, upon reaching port, that wages had been raised. The 1879 convention ruled that the scale would be set by the Chicago branch and no local could change it.

As a countermeasure, the owners set up the Cleveland Vessel Owners' Association in 1880. Recruiting offices were established in various lake ports. The Cleveland group also sought to enlist the vessel owners in other ports for a united attack upon the Seamen's Union. But the absence of a common interest among vessel owners—who were divided into those who hauled ore centering in Cleveland, the grain trade in Buffalo, and lumber in Chicago—made it difficult to set up a general association.

While the search for an effective seamen's labor organization was going on, the employers set up the Lake Carriers' Association in 1885. At first, the association was "to consider and take action upon all general questions relating to the navigation and carrying business of the Great Lakes and the waters tributary thereto."[19] The new association ran into the opposition of the Cleveland owners, but by 1891 a general amalgamation of all vessel owners on the Great Lakes took place. The revitalized association took over the shipping offices operated by earlier employers' groups and opened several others. A war of extermination was started against all unions, and its success led to another reorganization of the sailors' organization, under the name of the Lake Seamen's Union.

By 1896 the major source of freight traffic was iron ore, mainly because of the opening of the Mesabi Range in 1892 which soon became the main source of iron ore for the Pennsylvania steel mills. When the Rockefeller interests secured control of the Mesabi Range in 1895, a fleet of ore boats was organized. The Bessemer fleet, as it was called, introduced changes in labor relations. Because of greater capital investment, speed of loading and unloading was now emphasized. The severe weakening of the union and the business depression led to wage cutting during the early 1890's. Reversal of the downtrend in business made it possible for the union to gain an increase in wages in 1899.

The increase in steam vessels led to the formation of the first Firemen's Union in 1888, which affiliated with the Knights of Labor. Three years later, the Marine Firemen, Oilers and Water Tenders' Benevolent Association withdrew and became independent. Numerically weak, the leaders hoped to affiliate with the Seamen's Union, but the sailors would not allow deckhands or firemen to join their organization. As a result, the firemen affiliated with the International Longshoremen's Association, which had been formed on the Great Lakes in 1892 and exercised considerable power. In February 1902 the Marine Cooks' Association of the Great Lakes was formed, the last of the unlicensed crafts to form a union.

The engineers formed an organization quite early, in 1854, but it was, like the National Marine Engineers' Benevolent Association organized in 1875, mainly a fraternal group. Not until the turn of the century did this organization become a trade union. On the employer side, an important change took place in 1901 with the formation of the U.S. Steel Corporation, which took over the ore boats of the Pittsburgh Steamship Company and added new tonnage to the fleet. A successful strike following a demand for wage increases was carried out by the Marine Engineers' Benevolent Association in 1901. The following year, the firemen succeeded in gaining a wage increase. The growing strength of labor unions induced the owners to reorganize the Lake Carriers' Association as their labor relations agency, which in 1903 sponsored the Lake Carriers' Beneficial Association, a company union. The announced purposes of this group were "to establish and maintain, by contract or otherwise, such amicable relations between employer and employed as would avoid public injury that would result from lockouts or strikes in the lake carrying service; to provide, so far as may be, for the prompt and amicable adjustment of matters affecting shipping and the interests of vessel owners on the Great Lakes and their connecting and tributary waters."[20]

The idea of a trade agreement had been discussed by both the unions and employer groups before this time, and representatives of the seamen's and firemen's unions attended meetings of the Lake Carriers' Association. Moreover, the association had a contract with the grain scoopers at Buffalo. In 1903 the association signed a contract with all of the unions except the American Association of Masters and Pilots, which refused to agree to the terms offered. In 1904 the association ignored a request for a conference with the Masters and Pilots, basing its refusal on the ground that the master was the representative of the owner and in belonging to the same organization as his subordinate he could be outvoted. Agreements were, however, made with other seagoing unions. The resistance of the Masters and Pilots was broken by the middle of June 1904.

The association became more and more concerned with labor troubles. At its meeting in 1905 a minority favored a campaign to reduce the power of the labor organizations which had rapidly gained in membership and influence over wage negotiations. Complaints about the lack of discipline, especially of firemen, were also made. Firemen frequently deserted their ships, and their union resisted a proposal that their books be deposited with the captain for forfeiture in case of desertion. The union did seek to punish violators of agreements whenever complaints were made.

In the spring of 1908 it appeared that traffic on the lakes would be below the level of the preceding year, and that an attack upon the unions might succeed. Meeting in Cleveland on March 26, 1908, the association declared for the open shop. Only the owners of package freighters opposed the proposal. Requests by the unions for conferences were ignored; the published statements on the open shop were held to be adequate. On May 3 the association voted to deny union delegates access to ships, and an organized effort to deny union members employment followed.

The union fought back, but it was a losing battle. Not only were the shipping companies able to maintain traffic with replacements, but in the winter of 1908–1909, the association introduced its welfare plan. Under the plan, assembly rooms were established in the main lake ports for the use of the seamen who carried certificates issued by the association. A charge of $1.00 was made for the use of the facilities. In order to obtain a certificate, an officer or seaman had to agree "to discharge his lawful duties towards the ship . . . regardless of membership or affiliation on his part or that of any other member of the officers and crew with any union or association of any kind." Certificate holders were given continuous record discharge books which identified the vessel upon which the holder had been employed, the time he entered and left the employ of the particular company, and the quality of the service he rendered. Books were returned to the owner when the quality of the service was good or fair, "but when in the best judgment of the officer with whom the book is deposited, such entry cannot be made . . . the book shall be returned by the master to the secretary of the association together with a statement of explanation from the officer with whom the book was deposited. The association may thereupon take such action as it may deem wise and just after canceling . . . certificate."[21] Certificates had to be renewed annually. The books made blacklisting easier and more effective.

The strike continued with bloody clashes at a number of lake ports. The International Seamen's Union, to which the lake seamen were affiliated, levied two assessments in behalf of the strikers, and the general labor movement provided some assistance. But it was difficult to overcome the combined resources of the shippers. When the president of the association announced in the spring of 1912 that no discrimination would be directed against union members, the walkout was ended. It had lasted four years.

CHAPTER 16

Advances and Problems
in Building Construction

THE INDUSTRY

Unions in the building construction industry became the most stable labor organizations in the United States. From approximately 68,000 members, these organizations grew in numbers until by 1904, the total enrollment was over 391,000. Suffering a modest setback the following year, the building trades resumed their growth and achieved a membership of over 500,000 on the eve of World War I in 1916.[1]

Despite significant changes in technology and materials, the industry was dominated by the craftsmen, organized in almost two dozen unions each of which sought to expand the area in which its members were employed. The industry annually absorbed hundreds of millions of dollars of savings from commercial and home builders. Because of its role as a source of employment and investment, the industry has always been regarded as a barometer of, and even more an influence on, economic conditions. In contrast to many large-employment industries, building construction was mainly one of small employing units, and the ease of entry because of the low capital requirements needed, created many problems for contractors, material distributors and workers which only an effective union might cope with. The predominance of skilled workers has led to the evolution of rules, and the time limits on the completion of the product have given an effective union, and sometimes its officers, great influence in determining the prosperity of many firms. It has also led at times to serious abuses of trust.

The Bricklayers

By the middle 1890's national unions in the building trades were active in virtually every craft. The formation of the Bricklayers and Masons' International Union of America in 1865 marked the first successful attempt to set up a national union in the industry. Members in good standing were, from the beginning, entitled to a travel card good for thirty days from date of issue, and once renewable for the same period. The card had to be deposited in some local union before it expired. The national union sought to aid locals engaged in strikes, and the changes governing the strike provision indicate the increasing control exercised by the national union. At first, a local desiring to strike submitted a petition to the national union, which in turn automatically submitted it to the locals for approval. Two-thirds of the locals were needed for an endorsement of assistance. In 1883 the requirement was introduced that two-thirds of the members affected and voting had to approve a strike, and steps to settle the dispute by negotiation had to be made before the national officers were compelled to submit the assistance petition to the locals. After the enactment of this provision, national officers rejected strike petitions on various grounds—in 1891 six out of seven petitions were rejected—and in the seventh instance the local union decided not to submit the grievance to the membership.

The Carpenters

The carpenters made three fruitless efforts to establish national unions in 1835, 1854, and 1867. Not until 1881, as a viable national organization, was the Brotherhood of Carpenters and Joiners established. The brotherhood opposed piece work and established a national working card to control and assist the itinerant journeyman.[2] Organizations of local carpenters' unions existed in many communities; some of them were affiliated with the Amalgamated Society of Carpenters and Joiners, an English craft organization founded in England in 1860, whose members established branches in the United States. Another was the United Order of Carpenters made up of lodges generally around New York City, which had been organized in 1872. There were in addition, Knights of Labor assemblies of carpenters in some communities. Control of the New York market by the United posed a problem for the brotherhood, but it was solved by the merger of the two unions under the name of the United Brotherhood of Carpenters and Joiners of America. In Chicago, however, cooperation between local carpenter unions affiliated with the three different national organizations went on during the 1880's through a carpenters' council.[3]

At first the brotherhood maintained friendly relations with the Amalgamated, but with the steady rise in membership in the late 1890's conflicts between the two organizations increased. Acting upon complaints of the Buffalo local, the 1900 convention decided to support its members in that city in a conflict with the Amalgamated, and at the same time asked the AFL to recognize only the brotherhood as having jurisdiction in the carpenters' trade. The Carpenters' Union, despite its claim for jurisdiction over all woodworkers, consented in 1895 to the affiliation of the International Union of Machine Wood Workers with the AFL. Later, the Machine Wood Workers combined with the International Furniture Workers and the two formed the Amalgamated Wood Workers' International Union in 1895. Although an agreement on dividing jurisdiction had been made, the increase in factory-manufactured trim led the Carpenters' Union to annul the pact. Eventually the Wood Workers were compelled to join the Carpenters' Union.[4]

Other Unions

The Bricklayers and Carpenters' unions were the dominant labor organizations in the building construction industry. Unions in other trades were also established: the International Brotherhood of Electrical Workers in 1891; the Granite Cutters in 1877; the Brotherhood of Painters, Decorators and Paperhangers in 1887; the Operative Plasterers' Association of the United States and Canada in 1882; the United Association of Journeymen Plumbers, Gas Fitters, Steam Fitters, and Steam Fitters' Helpers of the United States and Canada in 1889; the National Association of Steam and Hot-Water Fitters and Helpers of America in 1888; the Journeymen Stone Cutters' Association in 1853; and the Mosaic and Encaustic Tile Layers and Helpers' International Union in 1898. All of these unions were craft organizations which are among the more stable unions in the United States. Their positions were naturally affected by the economic changes in general and by the problems facing their locals in their important markets.

TRADES COUNCILS

In the 1880's and 1890's, building trades' unions established trades councils made up of all or several crafts in the industry. One of the pioneer organizations, the Amalgamated Council of Building Trades was established in Chicago in April 1887. The stonecutters, painters, carpenters, plasterers, derrickmen, hod carriers, lathers, gasfitters, galvanized iron and cornice workers, slaters, and stairbuilders were the first to join, and other building trades followed. "When any branch represented desired to make a demand for an increase in wages or a decrease in hours, such demand could be submitted to the council, and, if approved by a two-thirds vote, it was binding."[5]

The spring of 1887 was marked by a serious struggle between the Chicago bricklayers and their contractors over the rather trivial issue of shifting pay day from Tuesday to Saturday. But another question in dispute was the right of the employers to hire unskilled labor at will. The strike lasted eleven weeks and was settled by arbitration. Judge Tulley, the umpire, rendered the following decision:

That recognizing the fact that organization of employees and employers, like these from which this committee originated, do exist and have become important factors in our industrial society, and that they will, in all probability, continue to exist, we do not attempt to determine whether the motive or basis of either organization was right or wrong. They appear to be a necessity arising out of the present conditions of society, and while such combinations keep "from violence," no great danger need be apprehended, nor do we attempt to determine which organization was to blame for the present paralyzed condition of the building industry of this city.[6]

A settlement of differences followed. The eight-hour workday was recognized, the foreman was to be a member of the union, "but he is restored to his position as the employee of the contractor, and, while so employed he is not subject to the rules of the union."[7] The arbitration agreement lasted until 1897, and the contractors' association insisted that the union compel all contractors in the trade to join the Chicago Mason Builders' Association. The union reluctantly agreed.[8]

The Amalgamated Council of Building Trades did not last for a long time. It was replaced by a new central body, the Building Trades Council, in 1891. The organization was sponsored by nine unions, and several others affiliated later. The object of the council was "to construct a central organization which shall subserve the interests of all the labor organizations engaged in the erection of buildings; for the purpose of assisting each other when necessary, thereby removing all unjust or injurious competition, and to secure unity of action for their mutual protection and support."[9]

Revenues of the council were derived from working cards sold to the affiliated unions, and an energetic effort was displayed in preventing non-card-holders from working in the Chicago industry. Working cards were issued quarterly. A rule of the Building Trades Council was: "All members of affiliated organizations are compelled to show their cards when requested by business agents, or to other members working on job, irrespective of trade, who is himself in possession of card."[10]

The power group in the council was the Board of Walking Delegates or business agents, since the large membership of the council prevented decisive action by the entire body. The Chicago Council evolved a series of rules which became a source of power: (1) nonunion men were to obey the rules of the union in the trade to which they worked. (2) Trades not represented in the council were not to be supported in disputes with the employer. (3) Seceding trades were not to be recognized by the council. (4) No trade was to work under police protection or use products of convict labor.[11]

The council became a powerful body in deciding jurisdictional disputes, and wage demands by unions had to be approved by two-thirds of the votes for them to be supported by the council. Under its sponsorship, the Building Materials Trades Council was organized by unions of brickmakers, planing mill workers, and others employed in material supply yards. The power of the Building Trades Council was used to prevent contractors from using nonunion manufactured building materials.

For several decades, employer associations had existed in the building construction industry. In fact, the National Association of Builders of the United States of America was organized in Chicago on March 29-31, 1887. The organization favored a uniform system of apprenticeship, and while affirming "the absolute personal independence of the individual to work or not to work . . . this association would appeal to employers in the building trades to recognize that there are many opportunities for good in associations of workmen; and, while condemning and opposing improper action on their part, they should aid and assist them in all just and honorable purposes."[12]

ULTIMATUM

For a number of years an inclusive building employers' organization did not exist in Chicago, but each group in a particular craft, such as the carpenters or bricklayers, had its own association. In 1897 the Employers' Conference Committee was formed, although no agreement on tactics to be pursued toward the organized craftsmen could be reached. A number of employers were for all-out war, and the advocates of a peaceful policy withdrew. The Conference Committee was reorganized in April 1899 under the name of Building Contractors Council. In August the contractors issued an ultimatum to the unions that after January 1900 the employers would not permit limitations upon the amount of work to be performed, restriction of machinery, interference with employees during working hours, sympathetic strikes, and the regulation of the number of apprentices. The statement was sent to the unions, and they took no action. To prevent a breakdown of operations, Martin B. Madden, a prominent materials dealer, intervened and negotiations between the parties were resumed. An agreement was reached and ratified by the Building Trades Council, but the single unions refused to accept the arrangements.

The contractors then announced that the "unions affiliated with the building trades council have absolutely ignored the joint agreement and failed to ratify the same. We hereby make the following rules to be enforced by the contractors of Chicago on and after February 5, 1900, and you will govern yourself accordingly."[13] The statement called for an eight-hour workday, time and one-half for overtime, and double time for Sundays and holidays. In addition, there was to be no limitation of output or restriction on the use of machinery, the foreman was to be the agent of the contractor, and the contractor would retain the right of hiring and discharge as well as determining the use of materials—irrespective of whether they were produced under union or nonunion conditions.

When Mayor Carter Harrison sought to bring about a settlement, the contractors denounced the building trades council as "unreliable, lawless, and corrupt," and declared that no possible benefit could come from such a meeting. They were, however, ready to advise the organization of specific groups to meet with their craftsmen, but not with the building trades council. Refusal to accept the ultimatum of the contractors led to a lockout on February 5, 1900, which ultimately affected between 50,000 and 60,000 workers. Attempts at mediation were made by the mayor and a number of others, but the contractors refused to deal with the Building Trades Council. Faced with no alternative, a number of unions, beginning with the Bricklayers', withdrew from the council and signed with the employer association in their crafts. By April 1, 1901, the contractors had their way. They were able to compel withdrawal from the council and compel acceptance of their terms.

It was a bitter and expensive struggle. An estimated $16 million in wages had been lost, and more than one hundred and fifty assaults took place, with four deaths. The council, bereft of supporting unions, dissolved. Among the charges made during the controversy was that business agents accepted bribes. Victor Falkenaux, a general contractor, testified that he knew from experience "that for a consideration you can settle a strike."[14] A claim was made that a strike of sheet metal workers had been settled by payments to union officers. Another contractor testified that money had been collected during a bricklayers' strike through payments. None of the contractors was willing to identify the culprits, and all denied that they themselves had paid bribes.

Corruption of labor union officers in the building construction industry was, in part, the result of the necessity for giving the business agent the power to call strikes. Building construction in the United States was carried on by contractors who generally put up the brick work, and then subcontracted the other work to as many specialty subcontractors as there were kinds of work. As subcontractors may have only a few days on the job, a violation of the union agreement or rules can only be handled by endowing the business agent with the power of calling a strike, for the job may be finished before a union meeting can be held. This power was necessary if the union was to enforce the agreement, but it also gave the business agent an opportunity for using the power for his own purposes.

NEW YORK CITY

Building construction employers in Chicago were in full control for the time being, but they did not solve the problems that beset their industry. Other markets complained of the same evils. In New York, the Board of Delegates began informally in 1884. It was largely a social gathering of the four business agents of the local building trades unions. Gradually, this informal board acquired considerable influence, and by 1890 it was the dominant power in the building trades. Personal rivalry led to a split in 1894, and two hostile groups, the Board of Delegates and the Building Trades Council, arose. Each group sought to dominate the local industry and supported rival unions in some trades. Jurisdictional wars were a constant threat, and in 1901 efforts were made to bring the two factions together. These efforts were successful, and in 1902 the groups amalgamated as the United Board of Building Trades. All the important unions except the Bricklayers joined. Delegates to the board were appointed by the locals, and unions failing to obey a decision on jurisdiction faced suspension. When a particular union sent a grievance to the board, all delegates having men on the job acted as an investigation committee, and a strike could be ordered by a majority of two-thirds of those voting. The sympathetic strike was used effectively, and unions that failed to retain the support of the board found it difficult to survive.

But in May 1903 the board was challenged from an unexpected quarter. Attempting to use a union of lumber and building drivers to extend its power over the building material yards, the building trades board was seriously threatened. When the drivers began pressing their demands upon single employers, the Association of Lumber Dealers and the Association of Brick and Material Handlers, which had been organized fifteen years earlier, closed down all their yards, and demanded that the United Board revoke its approval of the teamsters' tactics. When the demand was refused, the material yards were closed, causing a gradual suspension of building work and ultimately affecting about 70,000 workers.[15] The strike soon led to a division between the skilled and unskilled trades. Led by Sam Parks, the delegate from the Housesmiths' Union, a local of the International Association of Bridge and Structural Iron Workers, the unskilled organizations supported the teamsters, and the skilled groups seceded and set up the Board of Skilled Mechanics. The material yards reopened, and it was expected that work would be immediately resumed.

The building contractors, however, were unwilling to return to the system in force before the strike. Instead, they decided to insist upon the establishment of an arbitration system. Such a program could only be achieved by uniting the separate trades' associations into one Building Trades' Employers' Association with power "to determine, regulate and control the conduct of the members of this association and the employers' association represented on the Board in all matters pertaining to their employers."[16] Prices and competition were excluded from the subjects covered. The association sought to eliminate jurisdictional and sympathetic strikes, and to reduce the power of the business agent. General arbitration was suggested to the unions, under which each employers' organization, of which there were thirty-one, affiliated with the association would be represented by two members, and each union endorsing the plan by the same number. An executive committee of twelve, with six from each side was to decide all disputes unless overruled by the general board. The association sought the approval of the skilled trades, but it was rejected and the strike continued. After a deadlock of three weeks, the Civic Federation intervened and in lengthy conferences attended by sixty employers and the majority of unions helped to shape an agreement. It was decided that grievances would in the first instance be handled by the secretary of the union and if he failed, a written complaint would be submitted to the executive committee. If the latter failed to propose an acceptable solution, the matter would then be submitted to an arbitration board of four with an outside umpire if necessary. The power of the business agent was curtailed, and he was forbidden to call strikes. While the majority of the skilled unions accepted the plan, the unskilled unions under the leadership of Parks, held out but were eventually forced to surrender. Parks's local did not accept the terms until March 1904. The plan lasted until 1910, when it ended as a result of the refusal of the unions to discipline a local of steam fitters for striking in violation of the agreement.

During its existence 2,433 cases, 318 by employers, had been handled by the General Arbitration Board.[17] The plan suffered from several defects, and it was not re-established, although it represented the first extensive attempt at arbitration in the industry. Exclusion of the business agents from direct participation aroused the hostility of a powerful group of men in the unions. In addition, the union representatives on the board sometimes became rivals for union office, and consequently the exclusion of the business agent inevitably aroused opposition. Union and employer politics also reared its head, and with the passage of time issues were settled by political rather than industrial considerations. The national unions were not satisfied by some of the decisions on jurisdiction, arbitration took too much time, and inevitable delays led to dissatisfaction.[18]

Graft in New York

As in Chicago, rumors of graft in the building trades were current. In contrast to Chicago, evidence of the existence of corruption was demonstrated in the courts and one of the chief malefactors, Sam Parks, was convicted and sent to jail. Parks, a resourceful and tough organizer in a difficult union, boasted that he had raised the wages of his men from $2.50 to $4.00 a day. Despite his successes, an opposition faction bent on his defeat formed and almost succeeded. In the election for officers of the Housesmith's Union in January 1903, Parks was opposed by Robert Neidig, who was elected president of the local. Moreover, of the four posts as business agent, Parks was elected by the smallest margin. The opposition was confident that he would be defeated in the semi-annual election in July 1903. At this point several employers complained to District Attorney William Travers Jerome that Parks had compelled them to pay him strike insurance. Parks demonstrated, in this instance, that the money had been collected for waiting time and most of it had been paid to the members of the union. But Parks had accepted payments in other instances, and he was indicted and with two others sentenced to prison.[19] At the same time, the district attorney declared other union officers had accepted bribes and had been guilty of extortion. Jerome also claimed that Parks was on the payroll of the George A. Fuller Construction Company, and that some of the strikes called were designed to injure competitors of Parks's favorite contractor. These revelations in the two largest cities in the United States publicly revealed a problem which was to become more serious with time.

CHAPTER 17

Employers Take the Offensive

LOCAL GROUPS

Opposition to labor organizations had "expressed itself in local organizations of employers, manufacturers' associations, industrial associations, employers associations, citizens' alliances. The names have been different in different parts of the country, but they always had one common purpose, and that was organized resistance, either to some demand of organized labor or to some practice of organized labor, for the immediate purpose of protecting the individual interests of the members of such associations or employers or citizens against such encroachment."[1]

A call to arms was sounded by John Kirby, Jr., an industrialist operating in Dayton, Ohio. Unions had expanded in the metal trades of that city and under Kirby's inspiration, the Dayton Employers' Association was established in 1900. In St. Louis, James W. Van Cleave became the chief of the Citizens' Alliance, and under his aggressive leadership, the city became an important center of open-shop propaganda. The Chicago Employers' Association, organized by Frederick W. Job, was another active opponent of unionism. Made up of vigorous open shoppers, these organizations rallied employers against the closed shop and what they described as other evils of unionism.

CITIZENS' INDUSTRIAL ASSOCIATION

The diverse groups came together in the fall of 1903, and formed the Citizens' Industrial Association with David M. Parry of the National Association of Manufacturers as chairman of the executive committee. The 250 delegates from 124 organizations listened to warnings of the power of unions and called upon the employing interests to defend the true principles of the American government, free competition.

In February 1904 a constitution and by-laws were drawn up, and the Citizens' Industrial Association began its short and active existence.

It sought to assist the authorities of the state and nation "in maintaining and defending the supremacy of the law and the rights of citizens," to encourage harmonious relations between employer and employee, and to assist associations of employers "to establish and maintain industrial peace, and to create and direct a public sentiment in opposition to all forms of violence, coercion and intimidation." It also established a Bureau of Organization to assist in the formation of employers' groups, and a Bureau of Education for the publication and distribution of literature promoting its objectives.[2]

The association urged employers to organize in associations in their industries to forestall the spread of unionism. Under the leadership of C. W. Post, a wealthy dry cereal manufacturer, the Citizens' Industrial Association carried on propaganda through public meetings and in paid advertisements in the press. In some communities, the citizens' alliances resorted to stronger tactics in support of employers during strikes and lockouts. As a result, union organizing was impeded not only by the active support given to employers but by a community effort that was sometimes rallied to take action against organized labor. The Citizens' Industrial Association survived for three years.[3]

NATIONAL ASSOCIATION OF MANUFACTURERS

"It seemed to be the consensus of opinion of the organizations participating that it ought to concentrate more attention among the organizations on the effort being made through legislation to put the principles of the closed shop onto the statute books, and to make it difficult for those who undertook to run an open shop to secure protection for themselves and their workmen against the encroachments of organized labor."[4]

The chief promoter of the new alliance was the National Association of Manufacturers. Organized in 1895, its first years were devoted almost entirely to reform of the tariff and the promotion of foreign trade. Under the leadership of President David M. Parry, the association launched its campaign against unionism. In a bitter attack, Parry charged the unions with being socialistic and with countenancing violence, restriction of output, and the boycott. "Organized labor," he accused, ". . . does not place its reliance upon reason and justice, but on strikes, boycotts and coercion. It is, in all essential features, a mob knowing no master except its own will. Its history is stained with blood and ruin. . . . It denies to those outside its ranks the individual right to dispose of their labor as they see fit—a right that is one of the most sacred and fundamental of American liberty."[5]

National Council of Industrial Defense

The Manufacturers' Association conducted active campaigns against unionism among employers and developed effective propaganda materials against union labor and its activities. At the twelfth annual convention President Van Cleave called for the raising of a fund of $500,000 a year, for three years, to form a combination of employers' groups to combat organized labor.

At the second meeting, in New York, on October 28, 1907, James Van Cleave, the unanimously elected chairman, reported that "some cooperative action should be taken on the part of the Association of Manufacturers to keep themselves well informed and ready for prompt action where legislation is threatened contrary to their best interests."

Finally, on January 28, 1908, the National Council of Industrial Defense was established with Van Cleave as chairman. The council became the chief spokesman for the anti-union employing interests on legislative matters, and the National Manufacturers' Association and the Citizens' Industrial Association each "agreed to contribute for the prevention of the passage of injurious class legislation the sum of $500 a month for one year." National employers' associations were requested to contribute $50.00 a month.[6]

The council maintained divisions dealing with legislation, legal questions, and publicity and education.[7] Calling for joint effort among all employer groups, Van Cleave said that the council had been able to defeat the anti-injunction bill, the eight-hour bill, as well as other labor legislation. He claimed the Citizens' Industrial Association, the National Association of Manufacturers, and the American Anti-Boycott Association had "spent a lot of money" in these successful campaigns. He called for the establishment of a permanent bureau adequately financed in order to initiate similar campaigns in the state capitals. In Van Cleave's view, a single group of employers was powerless against the might of organized labor, but when all employer groups combine "to show [their] strength and . . . teeth if necessary" their power is immeasurably increased.[8]

The effective activities of the council were exposed by the investigation which followed the revelations of Colonel Martin Mulhall, who had been a principal go-between of the National Association of Manufacturers and politicians, members of Congress, and other public figures. It showed the effectiveness of the lobby in Washington, and of its ability to defeat legislation touching the vital interests of organized labor.[9] However, the investigation itself revealed that the power of the anti-employer combine was weakening, and that the rise of the Progressive movement under Theodore Roosevelt, as well as the election of Woodrow Wilson in 1912, were in part the result of the dissatisfaction with the labor policies of the Republican administration. Nevertheless, the council from its outset was extremely effective. Under the leadership of James A. Emery, counsel of the National Association of Manufacturers' and chief Washington lobbyist, the anti-union employers were able to delay the enactment of much legislation favorable to organized labor. Only with the Wilson administration was labor able to get long-sought relief.

THE AMERICAN ANTI-BOYCOTT ASSOCIATION

Steps to organize the American Anti-Boycott Association were the outgrowth of the campaign of the United Hatters of North America against manufacturers who refused to deal with it. Initiators of this project were Charles H. Merritt and Dietrich E. Loewe, who managed nonunion hat-making plants in Danbury, Connecticut. Both of them had operated under union agreements in the 1880's and early 1890's. During the severe decline in business in 1893, Danbury hat manufacturers requested the union to consent to a wage cut. The national officers of the Finishers' Union, with which the workers were affiliated, advised its members to agree. They refused. Thereupon, nineteen manufacturers, D. E. Loewe and Company and C. H. Merritt, among them, decided on a lockout.[10] The two firms were among those which broke the power of the Hatters Union. In 1901 the Hatters began an aggressive campaign to organize the plants outside of the union fold. Strikes and boycotts were used to bring unwilling employers to terms. A number of employers decided on counteraction. A meeting of open-shop firms in the hatmaking industry, held in New York in February 1902, decided to initiate the American Anti-Boycott Association and hired Daniel Davenport, a Bridgeport lawyer, as counsel and secretary. Organization was completed in December, and the preamble to the constitution declared: "The undersigned, aware of the far-reaching consequences and dangerous extent of the boycott, threatening capital by arbitrary proscription and labor by tyrannical persecution, form themselves into an association."[11]

Field men and solicitors were confidentially employed to recruit members "because men were afraid that the union machinery would be turned against them if their membership were disclosed. . . . Outspoken views, such as one hears today from businessmen on this subject, were exceptional in these early days."[12]

The association was endorsed by President Charles W. Eliot, president of Harvard University, who noted that it "has already proved to be an effective combatant, all people of good will may wisely wish it success in defeating and ultimately eliminating the boycott as conducted by the American Federation of Labor or other numerous bands of unionists."[13]

The Danbury Hatters' Case

Inevitably, the association played an important role in the Danbury Hatters' case. The Hatters' Union had sought for almost a decade to recoup the losses it suffered in the lockout of 1893, and it gradually succeeded in the Danbury area. In 1901 it tried to gain recognition from D. E. Loewe and Company, but the firm refused. The union waited until it had ended the successful boycott against Henry Roelf and Company, and then declared a strike against Loewe and Company on July 25, 1902. Almost all of the 230 employees left their jobs.[14]

A boycott on the products of the struck firm was imposed, and union agents toured the country to discourage purchases of Loewe's hats. The company took defensive measures and announced in a paid advertisement in the local newspapers, "that each and all the members of all labor unions, individually and collectively" would be held responsible for damages sustained by Loewe and Company."[15] The warning was unheeded. According to the attorneys, the boycott was effective and a profit of $27,000 in 1901 was turned into a loss of $17,000 in the next year, and a slightly smaller loss in 1903. In September 1903 a suit was begun against 248 members of the Danbury Hatters' Union in the federal court of Connecticut under the Sherman antitrust law for treble damages totaling $240,000. It was the first suit against a labor union under the Sherman law, and to protect themselves, Loewe's attorneys started a companion action in the Connecticut courts.

According to Loewe's attorneys, the boycott was part of a general scheme to unionize all hat factories and to prevent the interstate movement of nonunion goods in interstate commerce. The second contention of the lawyers was that union members as individuals were liable for the acts of their officers. In pursuance of the latter doctrine, the sheriff of Fairfield County, accompanied by the federal marshal attached the bank accounts of 248 union members. In defense, the Hatters' Union claimed that unions were not engaged in trade or commerce and were therefore not subject to the provisions of the Sherman law. The view was sustained by Federal District Judge James P. Platt, who dismissed the complaint. Thereupon, Loewe and Company was paid $20,000 by the hat manufacturers, and the Anti-Boycott Association took over the suit.

An appeal was immediately taken to the Court of Appeals, which referred the issue to the U.S. Supreme Court. In a lengthy decision by Chief Justice Melville W. Fuller, the court held that "Congress did not provide that one class in the community could combine to restrain interstate trade and another class could not." Justice Fuller stated that Congress had not exempted labor unions from the Sherman law as evident from the debates when the act was being considered, and he noted that a specific exemption of organized labor which had been voted by the Senate had been rejected by the conference committee of the two Houses.

Protest Meeting

It was a stunning blow to organized labor and a "Protest Conference" was called by the executive council for March 18, 1908. Representatives of many international unions, railway brotherhoods, and farmers organizations joined in demanding immediate amendment to the Sherman antitrust law. The Supreme Court decision applying the Sherman law to labor activities, according to the conference, "makes the crisis an especially grave one, for under that decision every normal, peaceful, and helpful activity of the workers whether exercised individually or in association may be construed as a 'conspiracy' or a combination in restraint of trade and commerce and punished by fine and imprisonment or both and damages may be inflicted to the extent of every individual's possessions."[16]

An appeal was presented to Congress which argued for an amendment to relieve organizations "not for profit and without capital stock and their members from the penalties of the Sherman law."[17] The Danbury Hatters' case was returned to the lower court, and the trial began on October 4, 1909. After eighteen weeks of testimony, the judge ordered a verdict for the plaintiffs, but left the decision on the fixing of damages to the jury. It brought in a verdict for the Loewe Company and assessed damages of $232,240.12 against the union. The verdict was reversed by the Circuit Court of Appeals, on the ground that the trial judge had improperly decided all issues except the amount of damages.

Another trial opened before Judge James L. Martin in August 1912. This time a verdict of $252,130.90, the full amount requested, was returned. An appeal was again taken to the Supreme Court, and the verdict was upheld, in a decision written by Justice Oliver Wendell Holmes, for a unanimous court. In January 1915, Gompers and Alton B. Parker, chief counsel for the union, petitioned Congress for the enactment of a deficiency bill for the payment of the judgment, but Congress refused. Loewe and his lawyers then took steps to collect the monies awarded them and the accrued interest. The AFL convention of 1910 had voted a two cents assessment for legal aid to the union which netted over $98,000. However, after the final decision, the executive council of the AFL decided that it did not have the means nor the authority to help the Hatters further.[18] The 186 defendants faced loss of their life savings and homes. The 1915 AFL convention considered the question, and voted to declare January 27, 1916, Hatters' Day, one in which every union member would be asked to donate one hour's pay to save the homes and savings of the Danbury Hatters. A total of $158,730.10 was raised in both appeals.[19] Added to the sums raised by the Hatters' Union, enough was collected to meet the judgment. Including costs of counsel and other legal fees, the Danbury Hatters' case cost the labor movement $421,477.[20]

The Bucks' Stove and Range Company Case

The outcome of the Danbury Hatters' suit was a great blow to organized labor's use of the secondary boycott, for the decision made unions liable for damage inflicted upon employers. The action by the Buck's Stove and Range Company was an attempt to hamper further the use of the boycott against unfair products. The company, located in St. Louis, was controlled by James Van Cleave, a militant anti-unionist and officer of several open-shop associations. Early in 1906, hours of labor were increased from nine to ten, and when the company refused to reinstate the earlier schedule, a strike was called in August 1906 by the three unions in the plant. At the request of the unions involved, the AFL placed a boycott on the company's products, which were placed on the "We don't patronize" list. Van Cleave, with the assistance of the Anti-Boycott Association, secured a temporary injunction on December 18, 1907; it was made permanent on March 23, 1908, restraining Gompers and other officers from continuing the boycott. Upon being served with the court order, Gompers secured the advice of counsel on the procedure to follow so that a test of the injunction in the higher court would be made. As a result, the AFL disregarded the order to abstain from publicizing the boycott. Contempt proceedings for violating the order were then instituted against Gompers, Frank Morrison, the secretary of the AFL, and John Mitchell, second vice-president; the defendants were respectively sentenced on December 23, 1908, to one year, nine months, and six months in jail. The case was appealed on the ground that it infringed the constitutional guarantees of freedom of press and speech.

The circuit court upheld the decision, but modified it in some respects. Both sides appealed to the U.S. Supreme Court. In the meantime, Van Cleave died, and the differences between the unions and the Buck's Stove and Range Company were amicably settled.[21] The Supreme Court "therefore, declined to further consider the case, which had become moot, and those two appeals were dismissed. When the main case was settled, every proceedings which was dependent on it, or a part of it, was also necessarily settled—of course, without prejudice to the power and right of the court to punish for contempt by proper proceedings."[22]

The defendants were again brought before Judge D. T. Wright, who had found them guilty in the first contempt trial. When they refused to apologize, the original sentences were reimposed. On appeal the U.S. Supreme Court found the statute of limitations had barred punishment, and the case was dismissed.

The defendants were displeased because the issues involved were not settled. On the other hand, C. W. Post, a leading opponent of organized labor and a stockholder in the corporation, tried to prevent a peaceful settlement of the original controversy between the unions and the company. When he failed, he brought an unsuccessful suit against the AFL and the new management.

The Danbury and the Buck's Stove and Range cases were serious defeats for organized labor. The AFL was forced to end the publication of the "unfair list." The two cases were evidence of the success of the offensive against organized labor, and raised the question whether the moderate policies of the AFL could ever succeed. In fact, the victories of business on the picket line and in the courts strengthened the hands of Gompers' opponents within the AFL.[23]

THE UNION

The International Association of Bridge and Structural Ironworkers was organized in 1896, at a convention in Pittsburgh, attended by thirteen delegates from five locals. Local unions of bridgemen existed in various communities before the introduction of steel skyscrapers. Bridgemen were first used to frame timbers, and they adapted themselves to the use of steel. Later, their jobs expanded to include work on steel buildings as well as bridges, and the first organization, the Bridge and Construction Men's Union, was established in Chicago in 1891. It became Local No. 1 in the International Association.

Erection of steel buildings was largely carried on by large construction companies. Workmen were either sent or came on their own from various points to the construction site. The work was among the more dangerous occupations in the industry, so that the typical structural iron worker was a man of more than usual courage.

The National Erectors' Association

The National Erectors' Association, first organized in 1903, under another name, became in 1906 a powerful and relentless foe of organized labor. Any firm or corporation engaged in the erection of iron and steel bridges or buildings was eligible for membership. Formed initially to deal with the Iron Workers' Union, the association was a loose group that had national agreements with the Iron Workers' Union until January 1, 1905, the expiration date. The agreements were not renewed.

Local agreements were, however, continued. The New York Iron Workers' Union had called a strike in the fall of 1905 against the American Bridge Company, the most powerful member of the association and followed this step by a walkout against subcontractors. In addition, the New York local called a strike for wage increases on January 1, 1906, involving many members of the association who had not been involved in the first dispute. It was this strike which brought a change in the attitude of the association. Its purposes were summarized in Article III of the short constitution: "The object of this Association shall be the institution and maintenance of the open-shop principle in the employment of labor in the erection of steel and iron bridges and other structural steel and iron work."[24]

In 1901, Frank Buchanan, a member of the Chicago local, was elected president, and he was anxious to develop policies which would have placed more power in the hands of the national officers and thereby curb some of the hasty actions of the locals. Buchanan was instrumental in working out an agreement with the American Bridge Company which would have given the Iron Workers' Union control of the company's jobs. Many locals, including the one under Parks's domination in New York, rejected the agreement.

Collective Bargaining

The International Association had made an agreement with the American Bridge Company, but there were complaints by the locals of the failure of the company to live up to its contract. A nationwide strike against the company had been started in March 1903, and after a three weeks' walkout, the Civic Federation arranged for a meeting between President Frank Buchanan and J. P. Morgan. Morgan, while declaring himself opposed to the closed shop announced that he favored organizations of labor in general and would try to help settle the matter. Several days later, a conference was arranged at which an agreement was reached between the American Bridge Company and the union.

Election of Frank M. Ryan as president of the union in 1905 seemed to change relations. In contrast to his predecessor, Ryan favored aggressive tactics, and he directed the strikes against the American Bridge Company with vigor. It appeared, however, that an agreement between the union and the company would be reached, but it ran aground on the refusal of the U.S. Steel Corporation, of which the American Bridge was a subsidiary, to consent to the unionizing of a tube mill under construction in McKeesport, Pennsylvania. Ryan himself favored accepting the offer of the company, but the Pittsburgh local would not agree to the proposal. The differences revolved around the organizing of about forty men on the McKeesport job.[25]

Ryan's conduct was similar to the tactics followed by the Amalgamated Association of Iron and Steel Workers in 1901. Instead of accepting a proposal which would have strengthened the position of the union, he decided on an all-or-nothing policy which ended in disaster. Both the heads of the company and the union agreed that:

in the conference with the officials of the U.S. Steel Corporation, the offer was made to employ union bridgemen on all erection work done by the American Bridge Company on a direct contract or through a sub-contractor. The company would not sign a written agreement embodying all the rules and regulations which ordinarily go with such contracts, but did offer to reduce to writing its proposition to employ union men exclusively, pay the recognized wages and work the uniform number of hours.

In agreeing to do that the company met substantially the demands which caused the strike and had the union representatives accepted the offer and waived their claim to the erection of the tube mill, they would have won every point for which they struck. In view of these admitted facts, it cannot be said that the company was at that time bent on destroying the structural iron workers' organization.[26]

But the union, intoxicated with its own power, turned down the proposal. Acceptance of the terms offered would have been against the directive of the union's convention, but a leader must attempt to carry out the dictates of his members and at the same time remain cognizant of the realities of the situation. In pursuing its campaign, the union called its members from the jobs of the American Bridge Company and subcontracting firms presumably working on its behalf. Local unions were advised that they were not to allow work to proceed "under the subterfuge that it had been taken away from the American Bridge Company."[27] It meant that a large number of jobs were struck on the assumption that they were controlled by the American Bridge Company.

Dynamite

In its fight against the Erectors' Association, the Iron Workers' Union turned to dynamite. Beginning in 1905, explosives were discovered on several nonunion jobs. The first record, according to *The Review,* a monthly of the Founders' Association, was the discovery of dynamite in the fire box of a hoisting engine on a job of the American Bridge Company. In all, ninety-five instances of dynamiting of property or of attempted dynamiting were made, presumably by agents of the union, from the summer of 1905 to the fall of 1911.[28] As the struggle continued, the American Bridge Company found that it could operate successfully without union iron workers.

THE OPEN SHOP IN LOS ANGELES

The open shop in that city was supported by the *Los Angeles Times* and its vigorous publisher, General Harrison Gray Otis. General Otis had taken over the newspaper in 1882 and had dealt with the local of the International Typographical Union, paying the union rates. But in 1890 a dispute started as a result of the request of the four newspapers of the city for a wage reduction. When it was refused by Los Angeles International Typographical Union No. 174, the workers were locked out and replaced by members of the Printers' Protective Fraternity. Otis established an effective nonunion shop, and he became a bitter enemy of unionism.

In the campaign to keep Los Angeles an open-shop city, the *Los Angeles Times* had the support of the majority of employers and the Merchants and Manufacturers' Association and its secretary, F. J. Zeehandelaar. Between 80 and 85 per cent of the firms in the city were members of the association, which had been established in 1894.[29] In strikes, the association provided and paid for guards, and financed recruiting campaigns for strikebreakers in other cities.[30] The effective employer campaign made Los Angeles one of the leading open-shop cities, and the success of the Merchants and Manufacturers' Association led the AFL to take the unusual step of levying an assessment upon the membership for aiding the weakened unions of Los Angeles; the appeal raised $16,617.72.[31] The Merchants and Manufacturers' Association countered these efforts by raising a counter fund of its own of $100,000.[32]

In the skirmishing between organized labor and open-shop employers, the latter was the more successful. In 1910, California unions embarked on a joint campaign to weaken the control of open-shop employers in their Los Angeles citadel. A dispute in the breweries found five unions aligned against the brewery owners, and the Merchants and Manufacturers' Association pledging support to the employers. But this dispute was only a prelude to the more extensive battle in the metal trades. Employers in the metal trades of Los Angeles fought occasional duels with the labor organizations in the industry, but in general they operated open shops; in some instances they denied employment to known union men. This state of affairs contrasted sharply with conditions in San Francisco where organized labor was a major force and the unions a power in industry and politics. In 1910 the San Francisco metal trades unions decided to combine their forces for an organizing drive upon the Los Angeles employers in their industry.

Some success was achieved, and on May 18 the metal trades of Los Angeles submitted a contract to the employers. Not a single acknowledgment was received, and the Willard and Wilson Company locked out thirty-four union metal tradesmen. This action was followed by lockouts by other firms in the industry. On June 1 a general strike in the trade was called, and after ten days, about 1,500 workers had left their jobs.[33] The general labor movement in California rallied to the cause of the metal workers, and a committee representing the state federation of labor, the San Francisco Labor Council, the state building trades' council, and several other central bodies was organized. Olaf Tveitmoe, a San Francisco building tradesman, was chosen chairman and Andrew Gallagher, active in labor and in politics, secretary. An assessment of twenty-five cents per member per week was levied and almost $300,000 was collected. But the anti-union employers were not without defenses. They possessed ample funds, as well as the support of the local government, which enacted an antipicketing ordinance.

Dynamiting of the Times Building

On October 1, 1910, the *Times* Building was destroyed by a bomb explosion and twenty persons lost their lives in the fire. General Harrison Gray Otis, the publisher, immediately charged that the explosion was the work of labor terrorists. The California State Federation of Labor, which convened its eleventh convention in Los Angeles on October 3, expressed its sympathy for the victims of the disaster and appointed a committee to investigate and report its conclusions. It charged the *Times* with laying the foundation for another Haymarket case, and denounced it "as a hostile and unscrupulous enemy, not only of unionism, but to progress generally."[34] Neither General Otis nor the members of the Merchants and Manufacturers' Association were convinced by these disclaimers. Investigations were started by the city and the Merchants and Manufacturers' Association, and after a time James B. McNamara and Ortie McManigal were arrested through the efforts of Detective William J. Burns, an owner of a private agency. The prisoners were indicted. Burns was also aware of the implication of John J. McNamara, the secretary-treasurer of the Iron Workers' Union, who was a leading promoter of the dynamiting policies and who had been secretly indicted by the Los Angeles grand jury. District Attorney John D. Fredricks was anxious to get John McNamara to California from Indiana without revealing his evidence. With the cooperation of Governor Hiram Johnson, a request for extradition was signed without public announcement.[35]

Armed with the necessary papers, a group of men, including Walter Drew of the National Erectors' Association, invaded the headquarters of the Iron Workers' Union while the executive board was in session, on April 22, 1911, and arrested John J. McNamara. The rest of those present were held prisoner while McNamara was brought before a court having no jurisdiction in such cases, given a perfunctory hearing, and secretly extradited to Los Angeles. Walter Drew, the counsel of the National Erectors' Association and a bitter foe of organized labor, was among those examining the files of Secretary McNamara, while these events transpired.[36]

Organized labor was shocked at the extra-legal methods used against an international union officer. A conference of labor officials in Indianapolis was called immediately for April 30. Gompers and William J. Spencer, secretary of the Building Trades Department, came from Washington to attend. Gompers informed the McNamaras of the meeting and told them that "renewed confidence in innocence of yourself and brother was unanimously and sincerely affirmed and indignant protest entered against outrageous kidnapping."[37]

Officers of nine international unions, including the Bricklayers' Union and the Brotherhood of Locomotive Firemen which were not affiliated with the AFL, issued a statement on May 10, in which they asked for a fair trial for the accused, and described John J. McNamara as "an industrious, reliable, painstaking and courageous gentleman."[38] At the request of the Iron Workers' Union, the AFL took over the defense. The Building Trades Department, the Label Trades Department, and the Metal Trades Department were asked to send representatives to a defense conference for the McNamaras. A permanent committee on ways and means was organized, consisting of Frank M. Ryan of the Iron Workers' Union, Gompers and Frank Morrison, secretary of the AFL, and the presidents and secretaries of each of the departments represented. International, local, and federal unions of the AFL were called upon to donate twenty-five cents per member to the defense.[39]

Gompers threw himself into the campaign for the McNamaras, and pleaded for a fair trial and for the funds to provide the accused with an adequate defense. A conference of officers of international unions in Indianapolis on June 29 endorsed the actions of the executive council.[40] Clarence Darrow, engaged as chief counsel, handled all monies for the legal defense. Funds were made available at the written order of Gompers to Morrison, who was secretary of the Ways and Means Committee. Money was never plentiful, and the AFL collected $236,105.25, and spent $227,-911.85; Darrow received $200,000.[41]

Gompers toured the Pacific Coast speaking on behalf of the McNamaras, visited them in prison, and reiterated his belief in their innocence.[42] In the meantime, conditions were worsening. Darrow complained of inadequate financial support, and the AFL made repeated appeals for aid. The selection of a jury began on October 11, 1911, and it proceeded slowly. On November 28 an investigator for the defense, Bert Franklin, was arrested and charged with attempting to bribe a juror. Three days later, the McNamaras pleaded guilty—James to murder and John J., the abducted union officer, to conspiracy in the dynamiting of the Llewellyn Iron Works.

Anton Johannsen, a member of the Carpenters' Union and active in the McNamara defense, told that Darrow and Lincoln Steffens had visited the newspaper publisher, Scripps Ray, to whom Darrow had expressed his serious misgivings about the outcome of the trial. Darrow believed the case should be settled if possible, for otherwise his clients might end up on the gallows. Lincoln Steffens, one of Darrow's confidants, then conferred with local businessmen and the district attorney and they agreed to accept a plea of guilty. The McNamaras, according to Johannsen, at first refused to consent, but after six hours of argument, they yielded.

After their plea of guilty, James McNamara was sentenced to life imprisonment, and John McNamara to fifteen years. The outcome of the trial distressed many unionists. On December 5 the conference of international officers reconvened, and in a statement declared that they had believed John J. McNamara was "the victim of as foul a conspiracy as was ever hatched. That belief was fostered . . . and grew into conviction largely because of the way in which McNamara was spirited from Indianapolis and hurried to a distant city, supposedly hostile to organized labor. In order that McNamara might be rushed from the city of his residence, private detectives, the Indianapolis police department, a judge of the police court, the mayor of the city and the governor of the state, all lent their aid in violation of law. . . ."[43]

The AFL did not criticize the plea of guilty. In a statement on December 7, it pointed to its belief, one held by many workers, that the explosion at the *Times* Building was caused by a gas leak. It reiterated its criticism of the manner in which the McNamaras had been arrested—"It was in Russian style, not American. Holding the members of the Executive Board of the Structural Iron Workers in confinement without warrant, hurrying J. J. McNamara away from Indianapolis in an automobile and by circuitous routes taken to California—what were those but features of high-handed irregularity, and tyrannical lawlessness, known in arrests in Russia." The statement also described J. J. McNamara "as a man of pleasing appearance and of mild manner."[44] The statement further declared that the labor movement was opposed to violence, expressed regrets at its use and appealed to the American public to judge the movement fairly upon its aims and not stigmatize it "because one or a few may be recreant to the good name and high ideals of labor."[45]

The dynamite cases were not over. A federal grand jury indicted fifty-one men, forty-seven members of the Iron Workers' Union, for conspiracy to transport dynamite and nitroglycerine. In addition, Darrow was indicted for conspiring to bribe two jurors. He appealed for aid to the AFL, but the executive council would not issue an appeal, and Gompers denied that there were funds available for that purpose. Darrow was acquitted in one trial, and in the second the jury failed to agree. With his spirit all but broken, he was finally allowed to return to his home in Chicago.

The Indianapolis Defendants

The defendants in the conspiracy trial were not to fare as well. Ortie E. McManigal, who confessed to dynamiting twenty-two jobs under the direction of John J. McNamara, was the chief witness. All defendants were convicted, and with the exception of five whose sentences were suspended, they received sentences ranging from seven years in federal prison given to President Ryan to one year and a day to seven defendants.[46] Meanwhile, William J. Burns, who had caught the dynamiters, was anxious to involve Gompers in the conspiracy. He failed. More success attended the efforts of Burns in his pursuit of Matthew Schmidt and David Caplan. A friend of anarchists, Caplan was turned in by the son of one of them who lived in the Home Colony outside of Tacoma, Washington. Schmidt went to trial in October 1915, and he was convicted of murder in January 1916. The jury recommended mercy, and he was sentenced to life imprisonment. Schmidt was paroled in 1939, after serving more than twenty-two years. Caplan was tried for manslaughter and was sentenced to ten years; he was released in 1923.

When the sixteenth annual convention of the Iron Workers' Union was called, the president of the union stood convicted of a conspiracy to transport dynamite. Addressing the delegates, Gompers said:

The Bridge and Structural Iron Workers of America are hard-working men, who are doing a wonderful service to society. . . . It behooves you to so meet the situation with which your organization is confronted that it will bring advantage to the men who are workng at their trade every day, and which will bring you honor and credit for having participated in this convention and taking the course and planning the policies for the future whch shall redound to the advantage of the craft of the organization of the men and women of labor throughout the American continent.[47]

Gompers urged the delegates to correct the mistakes of the past, to meet the "crisis as it confronts you men and you will come out of this crisis chastened, improved, stronger, more influential and powerful than ever before. . . . I can look back through the entire period and can look at no one instance or incident that I have cause to regret or to cause me to blush. We have done our level best to be of service to you. We propose to do our level best to be of some service to you as an International organization, to the local organizations, to the officers, to the members, to the great rank and file."[49]

COMMISSION ON INDUSTRIAL RELATIONS

Following the McNamara confession, a group of New York social workers sought a thorough and impartial investigation of industrial conditions. A committee of fifty-three, with Edward T. Devine as chairman, initiated the campaign, and a petition signed by, among others, Henry Morgenthau, Lillian Wald, Samuel McCune Lindsay, Stephen S. Wise, John H. Holmes, Louis Brandeis, Lyman D. Abbott, and Charles S. McFarland called for an investigation in industry and trade unions, the trend of law and court decisions on labor questions such as picketing the boycott, and the labor injunction, the economic cost of strikes, and the resources available to the state and federal governments for obtaining information of labor questions.[50] The petition was later endorsed by George E. Barnett, Thomas N. Carver, Irving Fisher, Ernest Freund, and Jane Addams, all of whom were acquainted with labor problems.

President Taft approved of the proposal on August 25, 1912, and legislation was enacted setting up a tripartite Commission on Industrial Relations of nine members with three each from the public, labor, and management. Soon after the enactment of the bill, Gompers proposed that James O'Connell and John B. Lennon be appointed as labor representatives, and that the third member come from the railroad brotherhoods. Taft favored John Mitchell and James Duncan as members, but he was persuaded against this step by Gompers. Among the public representatives was Ferdinand A. Schwedtman, an officer of the National Association of Manufacturers, who had been active in promoting industrial safety. Taft appointed the commission in December. The appointments were attacked in *The Survey* because a woman was not included and because Gompers' suggestions on labor members had been followed.[51] *The Survey* intimated that someone representing the industrial union viewpoint should be placed on the commission. The commission members were not confirmed by the U.S. Senate.

The task fell to President Wilson and he appointed John B. Lennon, James O'Connell, and Austin B. Garretson from labor. John R. Commons, Mrs. J. Borden Harriman, and the chairman, Frank P. Walsh, were selected as public members; and Frederick A. Delano, S. Thurston Ballard, and Harris Weinstock were named employers' members. The commission held hearings in many parts of the country, and looked into many of the "forgotten" corners of American industry. Its investigation of the Colorado coal strike and the Ludlow massacre focused public attention upon the anti-union policies of large corporations and the baleful consequences that sometimes followed.

THE NATIONAL CIVIC FEDERATION

Some employers did not regard organized labor as a social danger or a threat. The National Civic Federation sought to rally those who saw in the trade union movement a constructive force, and an institution devoted to promoting industrial justice which did not seek to subvert the economic basis of existing society. This federation was an outgrowth of the Chicago Civic Federation, which had been organized by Ralph Easley in 1894. In 1899, Gompers and Mitchell were asked to join the National Civic Federation, and they agreed to participate in the planned study of public questions.

After a short time, the National Civic Federation concentrated on promoting industrial peace, collective bargaining, and the trade agreement. The Civic Federation, emphasizing conciliation in labor disputes, sought to help the parties reach agreement. Gompers became the first vice-president, and he believed that by presenting the views of organized labor before assemblies which included distinguished educators, clergymen, and leaders of industry, a better understanding of the union movement and its aims would be achieved. Easley, Gompers, Mitchell, and Senator Mark Hanna, who began his association with the Civic Federation in the fall of 1901, were the leading members. At the December 1901 meeting, the Industrial Department with Hanna chairman, Gompers vice-chairman, and labor, public, and employer representatives was established.

The Civic Federation sought to settle some of the more important and difficult labor disputes of the first decade of the century. It made a major contribution to the settlement of the 1902 anthracite coal strike, and it brought the leaders of the union and the U.S. Steel Corporation together during the steel strike of 1901; it aided the union on the street railways. The federation brought the officers of the Iron Workers' Union and heads of the American Bridge Company together. Under the leadership of Hanna and with the support of many trade union leaders, the Civic Federation sought to convince business that the trade unions could be a constructive force and that their recognition was in the interest of all groups in the community. Hanna's death on February 15, 1904, left a serious gap. He was succeeded by August Belmont, a financier and politician, and in 1907, Seth Low a former mayor of New York replaced Belmont.

After the death of Hanna, the federation was reorganized, but its main effort was directed to promoting a better understanding between capital and labor. Both anti-union employers and the Socialists opposed it. The anti-union employers denounced members of the Civic Federation as "the facile instrument of the closed shop combine."[52] On the other hand, the Socialists regarded the Civic Federation as an agency which blunted the workers' hostility to capitalism and transformed the labor leader into an appeaser of big business. In 1905 a resolution expressing concern of the close liaison between labor leaders and capitalists as a result of the influence of the Civic Federation was introduced at the AFL convention by Victor Berger. It was overwhelmingly rejected. But such resolutions had a more hospitable reception in a number of unions, including the largest, the United Mine Workers of America.

When Mitchell retired from the presidency of the Miners' Union in 1908, he became head of the Trade Agreement Department of the Civic Federation. Two years later, he was given the choice by his union that he either withdraw from the Civic Federation or the United Mine Workers of America. Mitchell gave up his post with the Civic Federation.

In 1911 another assault upon the Civic Federation was unleashed at the AFL convention. Leading the attack were delegates from the United Mine Workers of America. It aroused a heated and bitter debate, with Gompers and Mitchell leading the defense. At the end, the assault was repulsed. Mitchell believed that the attacks upon the Civic Federation were unjust. Deriding the critics, Gompers pointed to the aid the Civic Federation had rendered to many unions. His argument was supported by many labor officials who had profited from the intervention of the Civic Federation. The resolution directing officers of the AFL to withdraw from the Civic Federation was defeated by a vote of 11,851 to 4,924. The opponents made a creditable showing, demonstrating the rising influence of the Socialists within the trade unions.

Many of the attacks on collaboration of organized labor and the employers seem to have been based upon prejudice rather than a careful appreciation of its true character. Leaders of unions who were Socialists were just as anxious to collaborate with employers in their industries as others. Their objections seem to have been against formal admission that a union and an employer had to cooperate on the job, that the avoidance of strikes and lockouts was desirable, and that the trade agreement was a proper objective of labor and management.

The National Civic Federation became increasingly concerned with the dangers of socialism, and after World War I, Ralph Easley was chiefly interested in fighting communism. The organization lost its original influence and purpose, and the 1935 AFL convention directed its officers to withdraw from it.[53]

CHAPTER 18

Organized Labor and Politics

From the beginning organized labor has been interested in politics, although sharp differences have arisen on the tactics to pursue and the policies to support.

THE POSITION OF THE AFL

At its first convention in Columbus, Ohio, in 1886, the AFL urged support "to the independent political movement of the workingmen." The next convention, in 1887, affirmed the "necessity of resorting to the use of the ballot and demanding of all candidates for public office a public pledge of support to the measures desired by them before voting for them."[1] This policy involved use of pressure politics and the endorsement of candidates who favored the legislation sponsored by the labor movement. In pursuance of this program, the federation in 1895 appointed Andrew Furuseth and Adolph Strasser as legislative committeemen charged with promoting bills favorable to labor before Congress. Members of the executive council resident in Washington also testified on bills affecting labor.

Socialism

A minority of union members were opposed to these tactics. They believed that the policy failed because it depended for its success upon the support of members of the Democratic and Republican parties who could never truly sympathize with the interests of labor.

The first skirmish over these differences took place at the 1890 convention when Lucien Sanial appeared as a delegate from the New York Central Labor Federation. As its name implies, the Central Federation was made up of unions in that city, and was engaged in a quarrel with a rival, the Central Labor Union, which performed similar functions. When the two central bodies came together in 1889, the charter of the Central Federation was surrendered to the AFL. The merger was of short duration and in 1890, the Central Labor Federation was reestablished. Its leaders, instead of requesting the AFL for a new charter, asked for the return of the old one. Gompers refused and claimed that the Central Labor Federation was no longer eligible to affiliate with the AFL because it had allowed the Socialist Labor party, a political organization, to join.

Angered by Gompers' attitude, the Socialists began a furious campaign against him and sent Lucien Sanial to the convention to contest the decision which in the meantime had been upheld by the executive council. Socialists took the position that their party was different from regular political organizations, since the latter were the creatures of the employing class. Consequently, they insisted that different criteria be applied in determining the eligibility of the Socialist Labor party to affiliate with a central body of trade unions. Gompers rejected the argument. The debate aroused a heated exchange, but the position of the executive council was overwhelmingly upheld.

Because of the criticism of the convention in refusing a seat to Sanial, Gompers denied that the vote bound any of the affiliates. "Our affiliates," Gompers said, "are guaranteed autonomy and independence. If they deem independent political action advisable, or if they desire to take political action by which to pledge candidates for public office, to stand by the advocates of labor measures and reward them, or to punish at the polls those who are inimical to their interests, these are matters entirely regelated to each organization, without dictation or hindrance."[2]

The Political Program

A critical debate on socialism and independent political action took place at the 1894 convention on the political program submitted the previous year by Thomas J. Morgan, a Socialist delegate from the International Machinists' Union. The preamble asserted that the "Trade Unionists of Great Britain, have by the light of experience and the logic of progress, adopted the principle of independent labor politics as an auxiliary to their economic action [which had] resulted in the most gratifying success." Except for one point in the program, the list of Socialist demands would almost automatically gain approval from a labor convention. Such proposals as compulsory education, direct legislation through the initiative and referendum, a legal workday of eight hours, sanitary inspection of workshop, mine and home, liability of employers for industrial accidents, the abolition of the contract system in public works, the abolition of the sweating system, and several similar proposals would normally call for little debate. However, the proposal endorsing "collective ownership by the people of the means of production and distribution" and the preamble obliquely endorsing independent political action were challenged by a number of delegates.

While approval of independent political action did not necessarily imply an endorsement of socialism, the two proposals were so regarded by many delegates. Some did not believe in socialism as a doctrine, and others disapproved of direct involvement in politics. Among the leaders of the opposition were several philosophical anarchists who were opposed to all kinds of politics. Peter J. McGuire, commenting in 1895 upon a resolution which declared "it is clearly the duty of union working men to organize a political party devoted exclusively to their interests as to organize in trades and labor unions," claimed he voted the independent ticket when possible and that he had supported the candidate of the Socialist Labor party in 1894. Nevertheless, he opposed the resolution because "so long as we have the red flag of socialism thrust upon us, we will have it combatted by philosophical anarchism. Let us drop them both."[3]

Philosophical anarchists and pure trade unionists both had a bias against independent party politics and political socialism, and many holders of these views were delegates to the early conventions of the AFL. At the time the issue of socialism and independent party politics was first debated, the leadership had not yet consolidated its position. Both Gompers and other members of the executive council were frequently challenged for re-election; and Gompers did not, in fact, have enough influence to win re-election in 1894.

To a query by Patrick McBryde, secretary-treasurer of the United Mine Workers of America, Gompers replied: "The American Federation of Labor is a voluntary organization. The resolutions or platform adopted by it at its conventions are expressive of the sentiments and demands of the majority of the organized workers affiliated with it. The resolutions and platforms adopted can not be imposed upon any affiliated organization against its wishes but the resolutions and platforms adopted are presumed to be observed by all organizations."[4] The 1895 convention declared "that party politics, whether they be democratic, republican, socialistic, populistic, prohibition or any other, should have no place in the convention."[5]

Local Issues and Central Bodies

The importance of state legislation and legislative bodies prevented the AFL from embarking upon a policy of independent political action, even if its leaders had approved of it. The leaders of the labor movement in the formative period of the AFL were not men with much formal education, but they had a deep appreciation of American institutions and locus of political power. One of the tasks delegated to the AFL by its founding fathers was establishing "State Trades Assemblies, or State Labor Congresses, to influence State Legislation in the interests of the working class." The state federations have been, from the beginning, the political arm of the organized workers whose interests they sought to promote before the legislature. While the state federations of labor, like the states themselves, have lost some of their authority because of the shift of power and influence to the federal government, they remain significant institutions today, and their importance was much greater in the early decades of the century.

The first state federation of labor was established in New York in 1865 following a series of protest meetings in New York City and Albany against an antistrike bill pending in the 1864 session of the legislature. At the meeting in Tompkins Square on April 1, 1864, Robert Crowe of the New York Tailors' Union suggested "that a state labor organization be formed to care for labor's legislative interests. A joint committee was organized to visit the capitol and see to it that the petitions reached the officers of the Senate and Assembly. . . . After the hearing, when organized labor's voice was for the first time heard in the halls of the State Legislature, the bill was pigeonholed and died in committee."[6] As a result of this experience, the labor unions of New York state organized the New York State Trades Assembly in February 1865. Henry Rockefeller, a printer, was elected president. The name was changed in the same year to Workingmen's Assembly of the State of New York. The state branch of the AFL was set up in 1888.

The Workingmen's Assembly carried on its political activity through its president and delegates to its annual conventions resident in the state capital, and a political branch was organized in 1882. In 1888 a legislative committee was established which cooperated with the AFL state branch. "The legislative agents of both state bodies usually worked together as the legislative programs of each were almost identical. In fact many of the labor unions of the state were represented in both state bodies; the point of difference being that the Workingmen's Assembly admitted Knights of Labor assemblies, while the State Branch of the A.F. of L. admitted only unions affiliated with the A.F. of L."[7] The two bodies were amalgamated in 1898 under the name of Workingmen's Federation of the State of New York and, with the disappearance of Knights of Labor assemblies, the organization became the New York State Federation of Labor in 1910.

The New York State Federation was followed by New Jersey and Massachusetts in 1879, Illinois in 1884, and Indiana in 1885. State federations more than doubled in the 1890's, and a large number were added between 1900 and 1904, and before World War I one was active in virtually every state. The rise of these labor bodies "helps to explain the truly remarkable spread of state labor and social legislation which got under way in the first decade of the present century."[8]

From 1870 the New York State Federation of Labor sponsored bills of interest to the working people of the state. In 1870 it won the enactment of an eight-hour law for all persons employed by a city, county, and state and in 1884 a prevailing wage law on all public works. Three years later it sponsored Saturday as a half-holiday with full pay for all employees of local, city, and state governments. It also gained a law in 1884 making employees preferred creditors; a mechanics' lien law in 1875; and an act to regulate private employment agencies in 1888. School age laws, sanitary regulation of factories and mercantile establishments, and workmen's compensation were among the laws sponsored by the New York State Federation of Labor.

Between 1894 and 1918 it supported laws requiring the closing of barber shops on Sunday, licensing, and sanitary standards. Thirty-four laws affecting building tradesmen were sponsored. Among them were those requiring enclosed elevator shafts in construction work, regulating apprentices, giving building mechanics and laborers preferred wage claims, compelling supervision of plastering by mechanics, and requiring thirty-four inch safety railings on scaffolds. Thirteen laws affecting metal tradesmen, foundry employees, molders, polishers, and blacksmiths were supported; twelve affecting hotels, liquor and brewery workers; seven requested by printing tradesmen; and twelve sought by employees in the retail trades. Some of them required inspection of premises, and Sunday and holiday closing laws requiring one day's rest in seven. Twenty laws were supported which regulated the employment conditions of stationary firemen, engineers, and electrical workers; twenty-nine laws, including full crew legislation for workers on steam and electric railroads; seven laws governing theatrical and motion picture establishments; and twenty-eight laws regulating mining, tunneling, subway and caisson workers. In addition, ninety-six laws affecting women and children in industry were sponsored.[9]

In addition the state federation supported legislation affecting the rights of the worker as a citizen, pension laws, and a variety of others.

In some states, state federations of labor were initiated by one or several large central bodies which had carried on lobbying in their state capitals. In its call for a convention, the Chicago Trade and Labor Assembly noted that, "we have various measures which we wish enacted into laws and several bad laws which should be repealed; and it is unnecessary to enumerate the benefits to be derived from holding a large and representative state convention of the organized labor element."[10] The Illinois State Labor Association, as the federation was first named, aimed to encourage the forming and securing of "legislation favorable to the interests of the industrial classes."[11]

Other state federations followed the same general course. After the formation of the California State Federation of Labor in 1901, it stationed a legislative agent in Sacramento, the state capital, to protect the interests of the workers of the state.[12] In West Virginia, the leaders believed "that unification of labor groups on a state-wide basis would provide the necessary strength to secure favorable legislation."[13]

The state federations of labor sought three types of legislative changes: those which concern a particular group of workers, the labor movement, and the public at large. At its first convention in 1884 the Illinois State Labor Association listed the following demands: abolition of convict labor, establishment of boards of arbitration for settling labor disputes, an eight-hour workday, except in agriculture, employer liability for industrial accidents, abolition of employment of children under fourteen years of age in factories and workshops, a compulsory education law, outlawing of iron-clad (yellow dog) contracts, weekly payment of wages and abolition of the "truck system." Abolition of land monopoly and more complete control of railroads and waterways in behalf of the common people was also requested.[14] Between 1884 and 1897 the Illinois federation sponsored Sunday closing laws on behalf of clerks, better protection of workers on railways, mines, and factories, equal pay for equal work for women, ballot reform, the initiative and referendum, and promotion of public works as a palliative to unemployment.[15] As the income of the Illinois federation increased, it expanded its legislative activity, and its leaders were instrumental in forming a joint legislative committee of the labor representatives from railroad unions and the United Mine Workers of America for common support of legislation.

In California, P. B. Preble, the first legislative agent of the California State Federation of Labor, appointed for the 1903 session, advised the leaders to improve their methods of drawing legislation, and to appoint representatives to watch all bills of interest to the workers of the state. He sponsored in 1903 a plumbing inspection bill, a seamen's bill, and the streetcar air brake bill—all of which were defeated.[16] Similarly, the West Virginia State Labor Federation devoted itself primarily to the promotion of labor legislation. Leaders of the federation prepared bills for the 1907 session of the legislature prohibiting the employment of children under the age of fifteen, improved safety appliances, sanitary standards in workshops, mines and factories, and improvement in the factory and mine inspection services. In subsequent sessions, the federation sponsored an employer liability bill, an anti-mine-guard bill so as to require mine guards and detectives to give bonds to protect citizens against unlawful acts, bills for boiler inspection and for greater safety of streetcar employees. "The first attempt to knock on the doors of the State Legislature did not meet with success. The Federation lobbyists were not too easily discouraged." As

Ned Sims, a leading labor lobbyist in the early years wrote: "Those law-makers did not take us very seriously at that time . . . but we kept hammering away. . . . They began to realize we were among those present."[17]

The state federation has the responsibility for drafting bills. Such bills may be furnished by the AFL, copied from other states, or drawn up by the state federation or attorneys for one of its constituent unions. The next task is to find a member of one or both legislative houses to introduce the bill. The next step is securing a hearing on the bill before a friendly committee if possible. The state federation must be prepared to meet opposition from chambers of commerce, industrial associations, insurance carriers, the medical or legal profession or any other group.

"After that comes the task of inducing a sufficient number of assembly-men to support the measure. . . . There are a thousand and one subtleties known to politicians by which a bill may be kept from coming to a vote or mysteriously sidetracked without any evidence of open opposition at all."[18] Similar tactics were followed by other state federations. "Much of the success of the Federation in its drive for labor legislation [in West Virginia] was due the technique the organization had developed. First of all, the responsibility of the president as chairman of the legislative committee to steer the desired bills through the State Legislature. . . . The secretary of the state labor body sent blank forms to every labor organization in the state, asking them to discuss the bills, giving their recommendations . . . and returning them to his office."[19]

An examination of the proceedings the different state federations of labor would show the same interest in similar legislation and the pursuit of the same methods for its adoption. The California State Federation of Labor, for example, sponsored mine inspection laws, inspection of scaffolding on buildings under construction, safety appliances on street cars, improved sanitary standards in bakeshops, electric headlights on locomotives, seats for elevator operators, requiring temporary floors for buildings in construction above two floors, protection for electrical workers against unnecessary hazards, licensing of plumbers, barbers, electricians prohibiting employers from ordering roofers to lift over one hundred pounds of materials, prescribing standards on trucks used primarily to transport workers, establishing sanitary facilities in foundries and work camps.[20]

The American Federation of Labor believed that the policies pursued by the state federations of labor were the desirable ones, but it never forbade a different course. When, after World War I, sentiment for independent political action rose among the rank and file, the AFL 1919 convention reported that the executive council had "not attempted to interfere with the attitude or inclination of any of its affiliated international unions either to encourage, limit, restrict or prohibit their membership in the [political] field of endeavor though it has counselled and advised that procedure which would permit the full development and uninterrupted advantages of economic trade union determinism. In that counsel and advice it has been followed by nearly all, if not all, of the international trade unions. . . . Insofar as Central Labor Unions are concerned, equal freedom is allowed and the same counsel and advice is extended."[21]

During this period a number of city central labor bodies and state federations of labor sponsored independent labor parties; others endorsed them. The Illinois Federation of Labor supported a farmer-labor party in 1919, and its leaders noted the "unfavorable reaction in the legislature the formation of a Labor Party was producing. The impression that it made no difference what a member might do for or against labor, since he would be opposed by a Labor Party anyway, was industriously fostered by the employers' lobby. In 1921 the Joint Labor Legislative Board found similar difficulties and . . . declared that the Labor Party venture had diminished its influence in the General Assembly." The Farmer-Labor party was responsible for the defeat of several of labor's friends in the legislature, and the legislative board urged "that more practical and sensible methods be used by labor in dealing with political matters than those which resulted in defeating the most capable and reliable representatives."[22]

Decisions on political tactics were always made on the local level, and maximum freedom existed for local unions to follow the policy they believed would serve the interests of the movement and its members. Like the AFL, the international unions normally followed a "hands-off" policy in political matters. The heads of internationals were not much concerned as long as the political policies of a chartered local did not create difficulties. This does not mean that support of an extreme party—a Communist party, for example—would have been accepted, but the Socialists and Labor parties were not so regarded. It is, therefore, noteworthy that the debates on ideology and the formation of third parties which usually stimulated eloquent discourses at AFL conventions were largely absent in the political discussions of the state federations of labor.

The behavior of workers and their organizations at the grass roots in their communities is a much better key to understanding American labor politics than the forensic efforts of Gompers and his close coworkers or of their ideological opponents. It cannot be overstressed that the decisions of the AFL and even the international unions on the political policies the workers of the United States should follow were not significant in shaping the decisions of the labor organizations in their own "backyards." Proponents of an independent labor party have customarily regarded the failure of American organized workers to embark upon such an enterprise as a sign of the social backwardness of the leadership. But American organized labor has been very active in politics since it was organized. It has been forced by necessity to direct its efforts to gaining relief from many evils to the legislature. The federations of labor concentrated their political efforts in the state capitols, where the remedies for existing evils were available, and they developed a method which has been eminently successful. The codes of labor and welfare legislation on the statute books of the State governments are largely, even if not wholly, attributable to the persistent efforts of the state federations of labor. The method gained results from the beginning and was effective despite the numerical weakness of organized labor. Labor's tactics were successful because its leaders recognized that legislators were more responsive to pressures from local and state sources than to the directives of their own party. The loose discipline and weak control by the party organization made labor's political tactics possible.

The state federations were needed for another equally important purpose, to watch and influence the enforcement of laws affecting the welfare of labor. Enactment of a specific piece of legislation is frequently only a first step. Effectiveness of legislation depends upon the willingness of police and other administrators to interpret enactments so that they serve the purposes intended by the legislature. The state federations served throughout their history as an agency which presented complaints against lax or incompetent enforcement of laws affecting labor's welfare, and was also the means by which complaints against harsh restrictions or burdensome rulings could be funneled to elected heads of the state. Union officers, accustomed to negotiating with employers, found it easy to negotiate with legislators over bills before them or for legislation to be sponsored and supported.

The federation leaders learned to know personally many legislators, their views, and the constraints under which they operated. They understood that in a democracy the legislator must return to his constituents for re-election. Consequently, they were aware that some could only support certain kinds of labor measures, but a legislator, especially an experienced one, might on occasion be able to provide assistance which might not always be obvious from the mere examination of the record. The criticism and contempt shown by ideologists for this process stem largely from a lack of appreciation of the manner in which legislative bodies operate in the United States. The support of legislators who voted against labor bills at times arouses the attacks of critics within and outside of the labor movement, but such support was frequently based on some service rendered.

The state federations of labor were effective because they avoided sponsoring issues upon which the membership was divided. If the leaders had sponsored programs at variance with the wishes of the majority of the members, or even a substantial minority, they would have been actively opposed or ignored. Because they limited themselves to supporting issues which had wide support or which could be justified on trade union grounds

—bills directly affecting a particular group of workers—the state federations could gain assistance from workers generally and from other sympathetic citizens. On the other hand, the federations could not sponsor legislation or programs upon which sharp differences existed. Because the membership, as well as other workers, faced different problems and needs, the federation always had to present a program to the legislature; they could not concentrate upon a single piece of legislation or waste their efforts in promoting noble but unattainable projects.

The state federations in all states supported measures in every session which directly affected the lives of thousands of workers. They cooperated in supporting measures which would rally the sympathy and support of a large majority of those affiliated with the federation and others as well. Their successes in repelling the "right-to-work" campaigns and other efforts to restrict union activity demonstrated the confidence of hundreds of thousands of workers and nonworkers.

Political Activity of the AFL

At the beginning the AFL hoped to avoid involvement in political activity. Secretary August McCraith was opposed to any emphasis upon political action, and in 1896 he proposed that the executive council prohibit AFL organizers from participating actively in support of the Presidential candidacy of William Jennings Bryan. He was overruled, since Gompers feared that if the prohibition were enforced, the AFL would be charged with being on Senator Mark Hanna's payroll.[23]

Despite such objections, the executive council in 1897 elected a committee to present a memorial to Congress requesting stricter enforcement of the eight-hour law on public works, amendment of the immigration laws to provide greater protection to American workers, reform of the currency system so as to secure the country against financial panics, and liberal appropriations for public works and rivers and harbors.[24] But the legislative interest of the AFL was increasingly centered upon gaining relief against the issuance of injunctions in labor disputes. The issue was first brought to the attention of the AFL in 1891 by an injunction against striking Pittsburgh printers issued by a Pennsylvania state court. The convention claimed the edict of the court to be "an unjustifiable and illegal interference with the liberties guaranteed in the bill of rights," and directed the executive council to "expend a sum not exceeding $3,000 in the prosecution of the case."[25] When the order was upheld by the State Supreme Court, Gompers' confidence remained unshaken, for he believed that if the issues were properly set forth before the appellate courts, the restraints placed upon labor by the restraining orders of the courts would be eliminated.

Gompers was in error because, at the same time that the injunction in

Pennsylvania was being contested, others of greater significance were being issued in the federal courts. Using the Interstate Commerce Act as a basis for relief, Judge William Howard Taft in 1893 directed P. M. Arthur, the head of the Brotherhood of Locomotive Engineers, to refrain from issuing, and withdrawing if already issued, an order to the engineers of the Pennsylvania Railroad not to handle the rolling stock of the Toledo, Ann Arbor and Michigan Railway Company, against which a strike was being conducted.[26] In addition to the Interstate Commerce Act, the courts, reinforced by the decision in the Debs case, began to rely also on the Sherman Act[27] for the issuance of labor injunctions. The proliferation of injunctions in labor disputes led Gompers to complain to President William McKinley about the use of "the judicial injunction restraining workmen from doing certain things recognized by the codes as perfectly within the lawful limit of their rights."[28]

Gompers was instructed to draw up a bill "to limit the meaning of the word 'conspiracy' and also the use of 'restraining orders and injunctions' as applied to disputes between employers and employees."[29] He and representatives of the railroad unions testified on this bill. Clarence Darrow also appeared and argued that violators of the law on the picket line should be subjected to criminal trials rather than punished for contempt as a result of violations of court orders. Gompers defended the right to strike, boycott, and picket. The proposal was amended so that it became unacceptable to labor and was defeated in the House. Restrictions upon the use of injunctions became the chief objective of the AFL's legislative activity. In 1902, Gompers, Mitchell, and Duncan drafted a statement denouncing the injunction and pointed to the inability of the labor movement "to persuade the Congress of the United States to enact a law that shall protect the rights and liberty of people engaged in industrial disputes, and many of the courts have interpreted this failure on the part of Congress to act, as a warrant and authority to extend the use, or more properly speaking, the abuse of the writ of injunction, so that the scope of each writ still further invades our constitutionally guaranteed rights."[30] The 1902 convention instructed the AFL to prepare bills on a number of subjects for submission to Congress.

The AFL's great concern with the writ of injunction was based on the fact that it directly affected the ability of unions to carry on their work effectively, but the federation also sought action on other legislation. Restriction of Oriental immigration, the eight-hour workday for federal government employees and on public works, and restrictions on child labor were demands made upon the Congress.

With the approval of the executive council, the heads of all affiliated unions were invited to meet the council on March 21, 1906. Fifty-one internationals and several state and city central bodies were represented and a "Bill of Grievances" declared that Congress had failed to deal adequately with legislation affecting the interests of labor. The bill charged that the eight-hour bill was defective, and a rider to an appropriation bill had been passed which nullified the eight-hour law in the construction of the Panama Canal, and that Congress had failed to handle the following issues of importance to organized labor: regulation of convict labor and immigration, adequate enforcement of Chinese exclusion, the establishment of seamen's rights equal to those enjoyed by other groups in the population, and especially the failure of Congress to enact legislation assuring safety of seamen at sea. The failure of Congress to grant relief to organized labor under the Sherman Act and to enact legislation freeing labor from the use of the injunction by federal courts in labor disputes were also emphasized. The charge was made that instead of "obtaining relief which labor has sought, it is seriously threatened with statutory authority for existing judicial usurpation."[31] A protest against the denial of the right of petition of government employees was entered.

The "Bill of Grievances" was presented to the President, the President Pro Tempore of the Senate, and the Speaker of the House of Representatives on March 21, and it aroused unfavorable comment among those who were targets of labor's political tactics. When Congress failed to heed the petition, the executive council appointed Gompers, Frank Morrison, and James O'Connell as the Labor Representation Committee and decided to actively enter the political arena. An appeal for funds was made on July 22, and $8,056.89 was collected; $7,834.11 was spent. Gompers entered the lists against Congressman Charles E. Littlefield of the Second Congressional District in Maine. A member of the Judiciary Committee, Littlefield was hostile to any proposal that would mitigate the effect of the injunctions in labor disputes. Gompers threw himself into the campaign with his usual energy, and for ten days spoke at nightly meetings; he was assisted by other labor officials. The campaign threw a scare into the Republican party and a number of national figures, including House Speaker Joseph Cannon, Secretary of War William Howard Taft and Senator Albert Beveridge, were rushed to Maine to salvage the Second District. President Theodore Roosevelt came forth with an endorsement.[32] Littlefield was elected by a sharply reduced majority, and the federation believed it was a worthwhile effort.

PARTY CONVENTIONS

In 1908, Gompers and several other members of the executive council attended the conventions of the Democratic and Republican parties. The Republicans refused to incorporate the demands of labor in its platform and indirectly endorsed the use of the injunction in labor disputes. In contrast, the Democrats adopted many of the suggestions of the labor committee. On the injunction issue, the Democratic platform stated that time "has proven the necessity of a modification of the present law relating to injunctions, and we reiterate the pledge of our national platforms of 1896 and 1904 in favor of the measure which passed the U.S. Senate in 1896, but which a Republican Congress has ever since refused to enact, relating to contempts in federal courts and providing for trial by jury in cases of indirect contempt."[33] Gompers, believing the workers would respond to the platform of the Democratic party by supporting it in the election, urged "workers and our friends throughout the country to support the party in the coming campaign which has shown its sympathy with our wrongs and its desire to remedy them and to see that the rights of the people are restored."[34] The executive council did not, however, go as far as Gompers in endorsing a political party. In a statement on August 1, 1908, the actions of the two parties were discussed, and workers were requested "to make the choice which is in accordance with the best interests of yourselves and of all the people."[35] When the campaign was over, Gompers was "somewhat disappointed with the immediate result." He was, however, certain there would be no loss of confidence on the part of labor.[36]

Organized labor fared better in the congressional elections of 1910. Fifteen trade unionists were elected to Congress, including Victor L. Berger, a Socialist from Milwaukee. Although Berger had crossed swords with Gompers at many AFL conventions, he was accepted as a representative of labor. What pleased the AFL leaders even more was the appointment of former Secretary-Treasurer William B. Wilson of the United Mine Workers of America as chairman of the labor committee. The experience of organized labor in 1912 was similar to other years; the Democratic party was more favorable to its requests than the Republican party. All trade unionists in Congress—eleven Democrats, three Republicans, and one Socialist—were endorsed for re-election.

The election of 1912 brought sixteen trade unionists into the House of Representatives and one to the U.S. Senate. The 1913 convention rejected an endorsement of a labor political party, but it expressed the hope "that a new political party will be formed which will express the reform and humanitarian impulses in society, and that it will be accompanied by greater efforts to organize the unorganized, so that with the more complete organization of labor in the economic field there will be safer and greater opportunities for the creation of a political labor party, or a party pledged to the conservation of human rights. . . . For the present we declare for a continuance and development of labor's nonpartisan political position."[37]

The AFL, continuing on its nonpartisan political course, pointed with pride in 1917 to its record of legislative accomplishments since it embarked upon active participation in elections in 1906. Its efforts, it claimed, were largely responsible for the enactment of legislation by Congress dealing with employers' liability, restriction of immigration, child labor laws for the District of Columbia, defeat of censorship in the Post Office Department, limiting the hours of labor of railroad employees, an eight-hour workday for postal clerks and letter carriers, laws governing appropriations for government activities, more generous vacation periods for government employees, and strengthening of the laws regulating hours of labor on government public works, prohibiting the transporting of articles made by children under fourteen years of age, and prohibition on the use of efficiency systems in government arsenals.

THE CLAYTON ACT

Restrictions upon the issuance of the injunction and relief from the onerous disabilities suffered by seamen were always at the top of the legislative agenda of the AFL. In 1901 a bill limiting the use of the injunction passed the House, and in the following two Congresses similar legislation was proposed but not passed. Following the submission of the "Bill of Grievances" by the AFL in 1906, nineteen bills dealing with the labor injunction were introduced in the House, the most important by Charles C. Pearre of Maryland which sought to define property so as to exclude labor disputes from the jurisdiction of equity courts. It failed to gain approval. A number of bills to regulate the issuance of injunctions were introduced in the first session of the Sixty-first Congress, but none was reported out of committee. In the Sixty-second Congress a drive to enact relief legislation got underway, and it was aided by the impending election. A bill satisfactory to labor passed the House, but it died in the Senate.

Finally in June 1914 the Clayton antitrust bill, H.R. 15657, went through the House and was described by Gompers in an editorial as "Labor's Magna Carta."[38] It passed the Senate on October 5 and was signed by President Wilson ten days later. Legislative "proposals to curb equity jurisdiction, from 1894 to 1914, [had] engaged the attention of every Congressional session but one."[39] Gompers believed the Clayton Act was "the most important and comprehensive measure ever enacted touching the freedom of the workers."[40]

Section 6 stated that "the labor of a human being is not a commodity or an article of commerce," and added that labor organizations were not to be construed as illegal combinations in restraint of trade under the Sherman law. It laid down procedure for the issuance of injunctions and limited the power of courts in contempt proceedings. The act further forbade the issuance of injunctions prohibiting workers singly or jointly from striking, peacefully assembling or performing other actions which were legal if done in the absence of a labor dispute.

The passage of the act reflected the increased political influence of organized labor as well as widespread conviction by lawyers that the writ of injunction had been misused in labor cases. Gompers felt the "labor sections of the Clayton Act are a great victory for organized labor."[41] Former President William Howard Taft, a Chief Justice of the United States in the 1920's, questioned these conclusions. In a speech to the American Bar Association, he claimed that Section 6 of the Clayton Act was "a mere declaratory statement of existing law," and argued that Section 20 allows the parties to a controversy to engage in conduct singly or jointly which does not constitute a crime as long as it does not affect those who have no interest in the dispute.[42] Organized labor had fought for this legislation for two decades. It is true that the law was rendered largely ineffective by the courts, but its enactment demonstrated the increased influence of labor in the halls of Congress.

THE SEAMEN'S ACT

A major legislative victory for organized labor was also achieved by the enactment of the La Follette seamen's bill. Seamen, over the years, had been subject to imprisonment for desertion of ships while under contract to start or complete a voyage and the law could be interpreted to make striking in port a felony. The Sailors' Union of the Pacific started the first campaign for legislative relief in 1892, and its efforts led to the enactment of a bill sponsored by Congressman James G. Maguire abolishing penalties for desertion on coastwise vessels. Assignment of wages on coastwise ships and the attachment of clothing of seamen were made illegal.

The U.S. Supreme Court soon nullified the effect of this legislation. It ruled that penalties for desertion could be imposed when it upheld the arrest of seamen on the *Arrago,* an American ship, for refusing to perform their duties. The arrested men had agreed to sail to Astoria, Oregon, then to Valparaiso, Chile, and return to San Francisco. When they left the vessel because of dissatisfaction at the first port, they were returned to the ship by the police. They refused to perform their duties and were arrested upon arrival in San Francisco. A writ of habeas corpus, on the ground that compulsory labor constituted a violation of the Thirteenth Amendment to the federal Constitution was denied by the Federal District Court. On appeal the U.S. Supreme Court upheld the denial of the writ.

The decision was denounced by organized labor, and efforts to mitigate its effects led to the enactment of a new law sponsored by Congressman Maguire and Senator Stephen M. White of California. Penalties for desertion in ports of the United States, Canada, Mexico, and the West Indies were limited to forfeiture of wages earned and clothing left on the vessel. The penalty for desertion in a foreign port was reduced to one month imprisonment, and assignments of wages was prohibited by seamen in the domestic trade. Wages could not be garnisheed or seized by a court.

The International Seamen's Union next sought to obtain complete exemption of workers aboard ships from special disabilities. Bills to meet special problems were also introduced in the first decade of the century, but none was enacted into law. Beginning in 1910, more comprehensive legislation was submitted to Congress by Senator Robert M. La Follette and Congressman William B. Wilson. After several efforts, the Seamen's bill was enacted in March 1915. The law abolished imprisonment for desertion and reduced penalties for disobedience aboard ship. Provisions for improved working conditions and safety were included, and seamen were granted the right to demand half of pay due in any port.[43] The AFL regarded the enactment of this legislation as one of its major legislative accomplishments, since it held that the restraints placed upon seafarers prevented them from utilizing effectively the trade union as a means for improving their conditions of employment.

19

Organization, Strife, and Militancy

Beginning in 1904, organized labor suffered some membership losses, and, even more important, its upward climb was halted through failure to maintain its momentum. Not until 1910 were the unions able to exceed permanently the membership figures of 1904.[1] After 1910 membership gains were continuous until 1920, with the exception of slight losses in 1914 and a sharper one in 1915. Many gains were made by old and established organizations, but one of the older ones, the United Mine Workers of America, was despite its growing membership unable to penetrate into a large part of West Virginia and Colorado. In contrast, the clothing workers after many trials and setbacks were able to build powerful and durable unions in their industries.

The Clothing Trades

Ready-made clothing for men was manufactured in New York City in the 1840's. The industry at the time was carried on partially in shops and in homes; the majority of workers were English, Scottish, and American. In the 1850's Irish and German tailors entered the industry, and the division of labor was first introduced in the men's branch of the clothing industry. Manufacture of ready-made clothing was not extensive until after the Civil War when the industry grew rapidly. In the middle 1870's, Hungarian, German, and Austrian Jewish immigrants flocked into the industry and they were joined in the 1880's by thousands of Russian and Polish Jewish workers.[2]

In the leading clothing centers in the 1890's—New York, Chicago, Philadelphia, and Boston—the labor force was dominated by immigrants. The sweating system under which merchants and manufacturers employed contractors and subcontractors to produce their merchandise was prevalent. Because their profits depended almost entirely upon the level of wages and the amount of work they could obtain, the sweating system became associated with harsh labor conditions, the speedup, and low wages.[3] Even without the introduction of machinery, it was found possible to utilize an advanced form of the division of labor, especially in the lower-priced grades of goods. Thousands of immigrants crowded into small shops provided the labor, since a little capital was all that was necessary for the thrifty and energetic to become contractors. Many subcontractors depended upon home work in which the entire family, including children, could be employed.

Organization

Organization of New York tailors in the ready-made clothing trade was first successful in 1877. Pants makers were organized, although not on a permanent basis until much later. In the most important branch of this industry, the ladies' cloak and suit trade, workers were generally drawn from the masses of Jewish and Italian immigrants who swarmed into the clothing markets. The contractor was the least important in this section of the industry which was dominated by the inside shop of more than average efficiency and consequently could compete with the contractor. Unions in this branch, however, were not more stable than in others. The first union in the trade was formed in 1888 as an assembly of the Knights of Labor. It did not last long; another formed in 1890 survived until 1894. The needle trades' unions, although not stable in many instances, were active in forming the United Hebrew Trades, a central body of unions affiliated with the AFL in 1888. This body was instrumental in spreading the doctrine of trade unionism among thousands of immigrant Jewish workers, but it was also a forum where such issues as socialism were often debated.

The First National Unions in the Garment Trades

Organizations of custom tailors in New York can be traced to 1862. Through the years, locals arose in several centers of the industry, and in April 1891 forty-seven delegates representing eighteen locals from four cities met in New York City and formed the United Garment Workers of America. This was the first national body in the ready-made garment industry; the United Tailors had been organized in New York in 1885 but only lasted a short time. It was destroyed in an ideological conflict.

The United Garment Workers of America, unlike many of the organizations in the garment trades, was officered by leaders of native or Anglo-Saxon origin. Uninterested and even hostile to the ideologies of socialism and anarchism, which were the intellectual staples of some of the immigrant leaders in the trade, this union frequently was out of sympathy with organized groups in New York City and other clothing markets. Nevertheless, the United Garment Workers of America was able to absorb District Assembly No. 231 of the Knights of Labor, which had functioned since 1873.

A national union of custom tailors, the Journeymen Tailors' National Trades Union, was founded in 1865 by delegates from seven cities. It lasted until 1876, but could not ride out the depression of the following year. Local unions continued to exist and by 1883, the Journeymen Tailors' National Union was established in the custom clothing trade. The union continued to represent the highly skilled tradesmen. Better paid, more highly skilled, this group was a typical craft organization whose chief officer, John B. Lennon, was the treasurer of the AFL for many years.[4] In 1916 it affiliated with the Amalgamated Clothing Workers of America.

Unions in the garment trades were, on the whole, not as stable as the skilled custom-order tailors. Factional fights (some of them without any relevance to the issues and problems of the workers), low incomes, continual floods of newcomers unaccustomed to the discipline of unionism seemed to make permanent organization a utopian dream. But there were a few tenacious believers who knew that the workers would learn to organize and to stay within the union. It was such a group which founded the International Ladies' Garment Workers' Union in 1900. Organized by eleven delegates representing seven locals in four cities, it appeared to be just one more futile effort to establish a viable union in the ladies' garment division of the clothing industry.[5]

For a time the new union was no more successful than the separate locals had been. Observers who examined the failure of the workers in the clothing trades to establish sound labor organizations tended to blame the leadership of the Jewish immigrants who now predominated. It was held that the conception of a labor organization shared by Jewish workers was that of a tradesman rather than that of a workman.

During a strike large numbers of them are to be found with almost nothing to live upon and their families suffering, still insisting, on the streets and in their halls, that their great cause must be won. But once the strike is settled, either in favor of or against the cause, they are contented, and that usually ends the union, since they do not see any practical use for a union when there is no cause to fight for.[6]

Commons found that Jewish workers were interested in abstract and metaphysical questions and prone to avoid the mundane activities vital to the union's survival. Of course, as unskilled and semi-skilled, easily replaceable workers with few resources and unused to the discipline of union organization, they like many other immigrants lacked staying power. But in this respect they were not much different from other semi-skilled and unskilled labor groups. In fact, a turning point in garment trade unionism came in both the mens' and women's division of the industry in 1909 and 1910. In New York City, Ladies' Waist Makers Union, Local No. 25, started a strike against the Triangle Waist Company in the last days of September 1909. A month later the local voted to call a general strike in the industry, a decision supported by the parent union, the International Garment Workers' Union. About 15,000 girls, most of them of Jewish and Italian origin, came out, and their number was later increased by an additional 5,000. Violence against pickets by police and private guards increased public sympathy for the strikers.

The Womens' Trade Union League, the Central Federated Union, and the United Hebrew Trades rallied and furnished financial aid and direction. Unable to get an industrywide settlement, the union was supported by a walkout in Philadelphia. No settlement on an over-all basis was made in either city. The union thereupon turned to single-firm agreements and managed to settle with almost 400 firms. By February 8, 1910, the strike ended in Philadelphia and a week later in New York.

The shirtwaist strike was only a prelude to the great effort to bring the strength of the ladies' garment trade, the cloak and suit shops, into the union fold. In 1910 over 1,500 shops, employing more than 50,000 workers, were operating in New York City. Like the rest of the industry, the workers were employed in inside and outside shops. The 1910 convention of the International Ladies' Garment Workers Union empowered the General Executive Board to call a strike if it became necessary. The New York Joint Board, made up of the locals in the trade in New York, began preparations for the walkout. On June 28, 1910, a mass meeting in Madison Square Garden, after hearing Samuel Gompers and others speak in English, Yiddish, and Italian, voted overwhelming approval for a strike. An estimated 50,000 answered the call, and the ranks were swelled by thousands of others as the strike continued.

A list of demands was formulated. They included abolition of payments for electricity, the forty-eight-hour week, union recognition, abolition of subcontracting, equal distribution of work, and the right of representation of the union in the shop by a delegate. The Cloak, Suit and Skirt Manufacturers' Protective Association demanded a list of written grievances. The union acceded to the request, and at the same time signed agreements with individual firms, many of which were smaller employers unable to afford a protracted contest. At the suggestion of A. Lincoln Filene, a Boston philanthropist, Louis Brandeis, then a Boston lawyer, intervened and after a number of conferences, was able to devise an agreement, the "Protocol of Peace." It was accepted by the parties on December 31, 1910. The agreement called for abolition of charges for electricity, no home work, the six-day workweek, with the option of Sunday employment instead of Saturday, weekly pay in cash, and the payment of piece workers as soon as work was approved by inspectors (piece rates to be fixed by joint committees of employer and union representatives), and regulation of overtime work so that it would not be performed in slack periods. The last point was designed as a work-sharing measure.

Inside subcontracting, allowing for contractors in large shops who were only "drivers" of labor, was abolished, and the preferential union shop recognized. The latter measure was suggested by Brandeis after employers refused on any terms to concede the closed shop. Union members were given preference in employment, but employers could hire nonunion workers if the union failed to supply personnel. To improve sanitary standards, a Board of Sanitary Control with union, employer, and public representatives was established, and a tripartite board of arbitration to settle all major differences and a committee on grievances to settle minor matters were established. The latter was staffed by representatives of industry and union.[7]

The first agreement, the so-called "Protocol," ran into difficulties. Unaccustomed to the slow and imperfect process of labor-management grievance settlement, the newly organized workers resorted to unauthorized strikes. At the beginning they had the sympathy of Abraham Bisno, the chief clerk, who was the central figure in the grievance procedure. Bisno was forced out of office by the objection of the employers. John A. Dyche, a relatively conservative trade unionist in an organization with many active Socialist members, ran into opposition from his own members. Dyche was succeeded by Isaac Hourwich, a writer and statistician more sympathetic to the rank and file. But the employers unequivocally rejected Hourwich, who was in the end forced to resign. Reorganization of the grievance procedure followed. The international officers who had opposed Hourwich's views and conduct lost their posts at the 1915 convention.

The "Protocol" was an important step towards "civilizing" a low-wage industry whose problems were complicated by the continual flood of immigrants who swelled the supply of labor. The union was, nevertheless, able to introduce many reforms and eliminate abuses that had plagued the industry over the years.

At times the history of the International Ladies' Garment Workers' Union has been a stormy one. But it has imposed upon parts of the industry standards of sanitation and safety and struggled against the corroding effects of racketeering and competition from unorganized markets.[8] The union has survived internal fights, a disastrous strike in the 1920's, Communist infiltration, and changes in the racial composition of the workers in its chief market in New York City. In the highly competitive ladies' garment industry, the union has never been able to relax its vigilance against the wage cutter or corrupt representative whose venality is a constant threat to union standards. The International Ladies' Garment Workers' Union has managed to remain one of the great labor organizations of the United States; its many contributions to the labor movement, as well as to its workers and industry, have justified its efforts and the sacrifices of the pioneers.

The Amalgamated Clothing Workers of America

Unlike the union in the ladies' garment section of the industry, the United Garment Workers of America was an old-line labor organization dominated by conservative trade unionists. The leaders were Americans, who had scant sympathy for the immigrant workers in their industry or faith in their ability to maintain stable unions. They were, moreover, deeply suspicious of the dramatic strikes which were endemic to the garment trades. They were also not inclined to give much attention to the problems and aspirations of the immigrant workers in the industry over which they held jurisdiction. The revolt of the men's garment workers was a two-stage affair: the first, against the employers in the Chicago market; the second, against the union at its 1914 convention.

In Chicago, where the first revolt flared in September 1910, the industry was divided into inside manufacturers, dominated by firms with substantial capital using advanced technologies, and the contracting shops depending upon a greater ratio of labor to capital. Staffed by immigrant workers, the Chicago industry, similar to those of other markets, frequently cut wage rates in an endeavor to gain business. On September 22, 1910, a foreman in one of the Hart, Schaffner and Marx shops reduced piece rates. Instead of supine acceptance, the wage cut sparked a revolt which spread through the entire industry of Chicago. The district council of the United Garment Workers took charge of the walkout and summoned the aid of the international officers. Headed by Thomas A. Rickert, the president of the union, a number appeared on the scene. Since they had witnessed similar demonstrations in the past, they remained skeptical of the possibility of founding a permanent union during a strike. In the meantime, demands for wage increases, abolition of payments for oil cans, bobbins and spools, premium payment for overtime, and more courteous treatment by foremen were made. They were entirely rejected.

As if to rid himself of an unwanted burden, President Rickert, without the consent of the strikers, made an agreement with Hart, Schaffner and Marx to arbitrate all differences, to re-employ strikers without discrimination, and to recognize the union. The agreement was repudiated by the workers. In the meantime, the desperate straits of the strikers had brought the Women's Trade Union League into the picture, and it played an important role in rallying public sentiment for the strikers. Crucial assistance was also given by the Chicago Federation of Labor and its chief officers, President John Fitzpatrick and Secretary Edward Nockles. Under their direction a system of commissaries was organized to provide food for the strikers. As the walkout continued, suffering among the strikers became more acute, but they did not yield. In fact, they repudiated a second agreement with Hart, Schaffner and Marx, calling for the rehiring of strikers not guilty of violence and for a board of arbitration to settle disputes involving union affiliation. This agreement was negotiated with the assistance of the mayor of Chicago. Not until the first two weeks in January 1911 were settlements made with Sturm and Mayer and Hart, Schaffner and Marx. These firms agreed to rehire members of the United Garment Workers Union without discrimination and to allow an arbitration board of three to settle all grievances. But the Wholesale Clothiers' Association would not deal with the union. On February 3 the 133-day strike was ended by the International; the local unions and the organizations cooperating were not consulted.

It was a bitter and bloody strike involving at one time as many as 40,000 workers; relief costs reached $200,000. During the walkout 874 arrests were made and 7 were killed during the bitter conflict.[9] But the union had gained an important toehold in the recognition afforded it by the major company in the Chicago clothing market. Under the initial agreement each side appointed an arbitrator and their inability to agree upon a third party led them to proceed to settle problems on their own. Clarence Darrow and Max Meyer, who represented the union and the employer, respectively, directed the improvement of sanitary conditions, a lengthened lunch period, and a more equal division of work. A grievance procedure was instituted with the right of the worker to appear in person or through a representative before the tribunal. Even more important, a wage increase of 10 per cent was allowed, minimum rates for piece workers introduced, and the workweek decreased to fifty-four hours with time and a half for work at additional hours. A complaint department headed by Earl Dean Howard, a professor at Northwestern University, was established. The flood of cases to the complaint department and the arbitration board threatened to break down the recently erected bargaining edifice. A number of short experiments were tried, and in the end a trade board with equal representation from each of the parties and a neutral was given original jurisdiction of all grievances. It appointed subordinates to handle all matters in the first instance with the right to appeal to the entire board. New issues for which no precedents existed were decided by the board of arbitration. In 1913 after the expiration of the original agreement, it was renewed after some effort and included a preferential shop.

The increase in membership did not quiet the dissatisfaction with the national leadership of the union. In 1911 and 1912 successful organizing drives were carried out in New York, and in December 1912 the New York tailors decided to strike to enforce a list of demands which they had submitted to their employers.

The demands called for the end of subcontracting and tenement house work, a forty-eight-hour week, time and a half for overtime, and 20 per cent wage increases. When the demands were rejected, a strike which eventually involved over 100,000 workers was called for December 30, 1912. The New York Clothing Trades Association suggested a settlement at the end of the third week, but the terms were rejected. Clashes between strikers and police led to court injunctions, but they did not affect the determination of the strikers. Individual settlements began during the latter part of February and on February 28, President T. A. Rickert decided to accept the offer of the manufacturers that the strikers return to work without prejudice and the issues in dispute be submitted to a committee of three distinguished citizens whose decision would be final and binding. The settlement was repudiated by the United Brotherhood of Tailors. The city authorities now took a more hostile attitude toward the strikers. In the end, more favorable terms were gained.

Rickert's conduct in New York heightened the ill feeling between the administration and its opponents. Before the 1914 convention, the New York locals sought its shift from Nashville, Tennessee, to Rochester, New York. On the ground that the locals seconding the proposals were in arrears in per capita taxes, the proposal was rejected without being put to a vote. When the convention opened on October 12, 1914, the New York delegation distributed a leaflet which stressed the support given to the organization of the New York market by the Joint Board of the United Brotherhood of Tailors. Moreover, since its formation in July 1913, the joint board had paid into the national treasury about $30,000 in per capita. This contribution was reflected in the surplus of over $72,000, the largest in the history of the United Garment Workers.[10]

In his report to the convention, President Rickert attacked "the abuse of your executive officers. . . . The statements that are made against the executive officers are not founded on truth. And those who make them know they are not."[11] In line with Rickert's sentiments, the credential committee refused to recognize the delegates from locals of the New York clothing workers. Thereupon the delegates who, although opposed to the administration, had been seated joined with those barred and withdrew from the convention to a hall of their own. The dissidents now claimed that they were the legitimate representatives of the United Garment Workers Union, since the national officers could only maintain control by disenfranchising delegates representing the majority of members.[12] The secessionists transacted their business and elected Sidney Hillman (1887–1946), president and Joseph Schlossberg, secretary.

A fight for possession of the United Garment Workers Union began, but the old officers were on strong legal ground, since they had retained control of the offices and funds. Moreover, the policy of the AFL automatically debarred secessionists from recognition. The argument that the AFL's support of the old officers was the result of bias against Jews, Italians, and Socialists is not only incorrect, but reveals ignorance of the AFL and its policies. The same principle was followed in the secession in the International Brotherhood of Electrical Workers as in the men's garment industry.

Suits and countersuits were started by each group and in the end, the secessionists agreed to give up their claim to the name and property of the old union and became the Amalgamated Clothing Workers of America. Denied affiliation with the AFL, the new leaders were able to organize the major section of the men's clothing industry. In the Chicago markets the Amalgamated had the sympathy and support of the local labor movement. The leadership rapidly learned to mobilize middle-class opinion in support of its organizing and other activities.

Hillman, the son of a flour merchant, was born in Zagare, a Lithuanian village, in 1887. He emigrated to England in 1906 and to Chicago in the following year. He became a clothing worker and eventually a cutter and participated in the 1910 strike, after which he became a business agent for a newly formed Chicago local of the United Garment Workers of America, chief clerk under the agreement in the ladies garment industry of New York City, and finally head of the Amalgamated Clothing Workers of America at its formation in 1914. He was a founder of the Committee for Industrial Organization, and participated in all of its important decisions. He was active in Labor's Nonpartisan League, the CIO Political Action Committee, and served the government during World War II as National Defense Advisory Commissioner, and Associate Director-General of the Office of Production Management.

Under his leadership, the Amalgamated established itself against the opposition of employers and retained its position as a major labor organization. Hillman was a shrewd leader, who knew how to utilize middle-class opinion and understood the needs of his industry. The ability of the union to prosper in the 1920's was an outstanding achievement. Throughout most of his career, the separation of the Amalgamated from the AFL limited Hillman's influence upon the general labor movement. His affiliation with the AFL in 1933 opened wider horizons. The Amalgamated sided with the CIO in the controversy over industrial unionism, and Hillman became from the beginning one of its more important leaders. He brought to its counsels a keen intelligence and shrewd judgment which was used to advantage by both John L. Lewis and Philip Murray. Hillman's role in supporting the Communists in the fight within the New York American Labor party did little credit to his judgment. Even less understandable was his role in postwar Germany and in the launching of the World Federation of Trade Unions, in which he played a major role.

There is little in the Amalgamated's history to indicate that it was a special kind of labor organization, or that its tactics and policies were of an order different from those of other unions. Hillman, the absolute master of the union throughout his life, was a resourceful general who utilized middle-class opinion to gain recognition and concessions from his industry. Considering the time, climate of opinion, and problems in his industry, they were perhaps the ideal tactics which could be pursued. But the same methods were not available to many other unions and leaders. Employers in mass-production industries, for example, would not have yielded to the same kind of pressure or have been impressed with the views of leaders in government and the professions. Business leaders who rejected the pleas of the President of the United States and the governors of their states would not be turned from their opposition to unions by the urging of a philanthropist.

CRISIS IN COPPER

The strike of copper miners in the upper peninsula of Michigan developed all the brutality, illegal suppression, heartache, and bitterness typical of the struggles in Colorado and Idaho. The introduction of a one-man drilling machine—the "water-Leyner"—transformed the smoldering discontent into an open strike. Demands for wage increases and the eight-hour workday were formulated, but as soon as the strike began on July 22, 1913, the companies appealed for troops. The entire National Guard was sent to the strike area. Thereupon, the Western Federation of Miners, directing the walkout, asked for mediation by the governor. The Calumet and Hecla Company, the chief producer in the area, hastily refused the offer of mediation.

For a time the strike was a peaceful affair, but the hiring of a large number of Waddell-Mahon Detective Agency guards was an unfavorable omen for continuing peace. The unorganized men drew up a set of demands, and with strict impartiality they were rejected by James McNaughton, the manager of the properties of the Calumet and Hecla Company. President Charles H. Moyer of the Western Federation of Miners proposed arbitration, and it was rejected by the companies. Meanwhile, violence began. Two strikers were killed, and three guards were convicted of manslaghter. The copper companies remained adamant in their refusal to deal with the union. In defense of their position they secured an injunction against the strikers. The companies also announced the establishment of the eight-hour day with no discrimination against any strikers in employment except those accused of violence.

The ranks of the strikers held, and a Citizens' Alliance made its appearance. Moyer, who was directing the walkout, was not intimidated; he expressed a desire for a peaceful settlement of differences. His plea was rebuffed. The strike had more than its share of tragedy. At a Christmas party given for strikers' children, someone shouted "Fire," and in the stampede, seventy-two people, the majority children, lost their lives. When Moyer refused to accept $25,000 offered by the Citizens' Alliance for the relief of the stricken families, his room was invaded by a mob. Beaten into insensibility, shot in the back, he was dragged before McNaughton, the manager of the Calumet and Hecla, and threatened with hanging if he did not leave the area. Moyer and a companion were then thrown on a Chicago-bound train, but Moyer returned as soon as the bullet was extracted from his back. Efforts to settle the strike were now made by the U.S. Department of Labor, but to no avail. It was called off after more than eight months with the union unrecognized.

The AFL was bitterly denounced by Moyer, who charged that the federation had failed in its duty to the metal miners. He insisted that an assessment should have been levied upon the constituent unions. The heads of the federation believed assessments were inadvisable and that many unions could not and would not pay them. Consequently, it would be necessary to suspend or make allowance for their failure, policies which always led to complaints and dissatisfaction among those who were able and willing to meet their obligations. In this assault upon the federation, especially Gompers, Moyer had the aid of the Socialist faction within the United Mine Workers of America.

The Western Federation of Miners was facing internal wars as well as the relentless opposition of its employers. Butte Miners' Union No. 1 was charged with subservience to the copper trust, and the opposition, seasoned by Socialists, fought a relentless battle against the local union as well as its national administration. Moyer's opponents organized a Central Committee for Industrial Union Organization and its leader, Thomas Campbell, ran for office against him. Defeated, Campbell charged fraud. He was expelled, but the fight against the Western Federation of Miners continued. Campbell's followers organized an independent union in Butte, and the relentless fight led to the dynamiting of the hall of the Butte Miners' Union on June 13, 1914. This was not the end of the warfare. The Butte Miners' Union No. 1 tried to enforce its job control, but the opposition resisted. Fighting went on with intervention by the governor, who sent troops to restore order, and the denunciation by Socialist Mayor Lewis Duncan of Moyer and his followers, who were blamed for the trouble. The companies, watching the fight between the two factions from the sidelines, were not displeased by events, for the bitterness generated by the internecine struggle gave the companies the opportunity to end union job control. Taking advantage of the division, the companies announced on September 8, 1914, that they would recognize neither union. Thus job control, which had existed in Butte for thirty-six years, came to an end. The Western Federation of Miners had lost the suffrage of the miners, and the new organization, the Butte Miners' Union, was unable to compel recognition.[13]

COAL MINING UNIONISM IN DIFFICULTY

While in general the United Mine Workers of America prospered, the organization was eventually to face serious difficulties because of its failure to organize the expanding fields of West Virginia. Compared to West Virginia, the unorganized coal fields of Colorado were a minor problem. The union, nevertheless, was to become engaged in a major and dramatic struggle in that area. In West Virginia, coal producers refused to surrender advantages they gained from not joining the Central Competitive Field, which the northern operators and the union regarded as a mechanism for introducing stable wages, prices, and costs. The special campaign directed by the United Mine Workers during the great strike of 1897 with the assistance of the AFL and other unions ended in failure, and the competitive problems worsened with time.

The union did not surrender, and almost annually it tried to penetrate the barriers erected by the West Virginia operators. In 1902 a more aggressive campaign was undertaken under the direction of Executive Board Member Thomas Haggerty. "Mother" Mary Jones, a colorful figure, and a squad of organizers tried to bring the Kanawah fields into the organization. A strike spread to the adjacent New River fields, and after several court injunctions and sporadic violence, an agreement was made with the operators in the Kanawah field in October 1902. The union, failing to gain a foothold in the New River District, called off the strike in July 1904.

Other attempts were made with as little success. The leaders of the union recognized that unless the West Virginia fields could be brought under an agreement, the structure of collective bargaining in the Central Competitive Field would be seriously weakened. In the meantime, the industry in West Virginia, partly because of its lower labor costs, was rapidly expanding. As John Mitchell noted in his report to the Miners' Union convention: "The strength of your union is not in the best organized districts. Unfortunately, and I say it regretfully, its strength is its least organized fields. You cannot be permanently safe, you cannot rest in security until West Virginia . . . [is] organized."[14]

At the expiration of the contract in 1912, the union demanded a raise of five cents per ton of screened coal, increases for day men, proportionate advances on narrow dead work, the eight-hour day, and the checkoff and no discrimination for union membership. The companies refused. A strike was called on April 20. On May 1, 1912, the companies announced: "We offer to you work at the scale of wages in effect on March 31, 1912. Any of our employees who do not wish to accept this offer and resume work will please vacate our houses at once."[15] The walkout affected the Paint Creek area, and in August the Cabin Creek & New River District became involved. Guards supplied by the Baldwin-Felts agency were brought in, and many striking miners were evicted from their homes. The union set up a tent colony at Holly Grove to house the families. As a result of the killing of a striker, nine guards, including the head of the Baldwin Felt agency, were indicted for murder.

Continued violence led to a request for troops by the sheriff, and after a pitched battle at Mucklow, Governor Glasscock sent three companies of National Guardsmen to the scene of the trouble. Colonel George C. Wallace, the officer in charge in the Cabin Creek area, organized on September 4, 1912, a military commission to try violators of orders and civil laws. Many of the arrested were sentenced to jail. Wallace "proceeded on the theory that a state of war existed, there, and we were exercising war powers."[16]

The restoration of more peaceful conditions led to a revoking of martial law by the governor on October 12, 1912, but less than a month later martial law was reinstated. It was removed on December 12. Miners complained that they were subject to a reign of terror carried on by the company guards. At the request of miners and other citizens, a commission to examine the conduct of the military and mine guards and the issues in the strike was appointed. Its report in November 1912 found that company guards had been guilty of "denials of the right of peaceable assembly and freedom of speech, many and grievous assaults on unarmed miners, and that their main purpose was to overawe the miners and their adherents, and if necessary beat and cudgel them into submission. We find the system employed was vicious, strife prompting and un-American."[17] The commission also accused the miners, holding their attempts to organize the state mines as one of the causes of the violence. Governor Glasscock tried to arbitrate the differences, but the operators refused on the ground that the union was attempting to wipe out the advantages of the West Virginia fields in favor of the northern mines.

Reopening of the mines was started in September 1912 and violence increased. A shocking attack upon the tent colony at Holly Grove was carried out on February 7, 1913, by an armored Chesapeake and Ohio train, the "Bull Moose" special. Armed men poured more than two hundred shots into the sleeping village. In retaliation armed miners assembled and marched towards Mucklow where they fought a battle with a platoon of mine guards. The governor thereupon ordered martial law for the third time.

Quin Morton, the general manager of the Imperial Coal Company, was charged with saying, "We will go back and give them another round." When testifying before a committee of the United States Senate, Morton was asked "whether . . . a cultured gentleman approves of the use of a machine gun in a populous village." Senator James E. Martine called Morton's conduct "appalling, horrible."[18] The Senate Committee condemned the military rule and the imprisonment of miners as a denial of constitutional rights. It, however, concluded that the union was not blameless and attributed its campaigns to a desire to organize the West Virginia fields. In April 1913 Governor Hatfield proposed settlement on the basis of no discrimination against union members, and some concessions in wages. Both sides accepted the compromise, but considerable resentment had been aroused among the miners.

Colorado

The violence in West Virginia was dwarfed by events in Colorado. The United Mine Workers of America had over the years attempted to organize the Colorado coal fields, but had failed to make substantial progress in the campaigns it conducted beginning in 1900. The companies led by the Colorado Fuel and Iron Company—a Rockefeller dominated concern—would not deal with the union. These companies dominated the Colorado mining areas "through the ruthless suppression of unionism, accomplished by the use of the power of summary discharge, the black list, armed guards, and spies, and by the active aid of venal state, county and town officials, who place the entire machinery of the law at the disposal of the companies in their persecution of organizers and union members."[19] Frank J. Hayes, vice-president of the United Mine Workers of America, was sent to Colorado. He informed Governor Elias M. Ammons that he wanted to adjust some difficulties between the miners and the operators in the southern coal field of the state, but when Hayes asked for a conference, the operators refused.[20]

The Wage Policy Committee of the district union requested the companies to work out an agreement. Only two operators replied to the request for a conference. On September 13 a second letter was sent but no answer was received by the union. Secretary of Labor William B. Wilson then sent Ethelbert Steward as an emissary to John D. Rockefeller, Jr., but he was told the matter was being handled by the officers in charge in Colorado. At the district convention in Trinidad on September 15, a strike was voted for September 23. Between 8,000 and 10,000 miners answered the call. Several hundred deputies were immediately commissioned; Sheriff Jefferson Farr of Huerfano County testified that he appointed 326 men. In preparation for the strike, the operators had brought in guns and ammunition. "Men were brought in from other States by car and train load and were delivered to the mining camps under guard of the militia, many of them being foreigners unacquainted with the work of mining coal."

The strikers moved from the company houses to the tent colonies established by the United Mine Workers of America. After the strike began, Governor Elias Ammons called a conference of the policy committee of the United Mine Workers of America which was attended by union president

John P. White. The policy committee was willing to accept a reasonable settlement, and an effort was made to draft a letter of agreement which both parties would sign. Secretary Wilson participated in these conferences, and the company "at the urgent request of the Governor and under some newspaper pressure" met a committee of its employees. According to President J. F. Welborn of the Colorado Fuel and Iron Company: "We reached no direct understanding; in fact we wanted none, as we were almost sure that had an understanding between the miners and ourselves been reached, it would have received the stamp of approval of the officers of the organization and in that way been twisted into an arrangement between us and the organization."[22]

Violence

Even before the strike began the coal companies engaged a large force of private watchmen who were deputized by the sheriffs of the two counties. Many of the guards were furnished by the Baldwin-Felts Detective Agency, known for its brutal conduct in the West Virginia coal fields. On September 24 a marshal employed by the Colorado Fuel and Iron Company was killed in Segundo, and a miner in the tent colony at Ludlow was shot down on October 9. In the meantime, the Colorado Fuel and Iron Company provided its guards with a specially built armored car, the "Death Special," which could be used to intimidate pickets and strikers. After a union miner was killed at the tent colony at Forbes and three others in Walsenburg, the miners began to arm. They looked upon the deputies as their enemies, and clashes between strikers and guards increased. Each side was capable of attacking in force, and men were killed on both sides. In the first month of the walkout, Governor Ammons tried to bring about an agreement and refused to send state troops. Toward the end of October he recognized that no agreement was possible and yielded to the companies' pressure. The National Guard was sent into the strike districts under the command of Adjutant General John C. Chase, who had commanded troops in the Cripple Creek troubles in 1903 and 1904.

At first the strikers welcomed the soldiers, who had been instructed to protect property and those willing to work, but not to assist imported strikebreakers by escorting them to the mines. The injunctions of the governor were soon disregarded, and the striking miners felt the same hatred for the National Guardsmen that they had for the deputies on the companies' payrolls. The behavior of the troops led to a protest convention of the Colorado State Federation of Labor on December 16, 1913. At the suggestion of the governor a committee of five, including James H. Brewster, a professor of law at the University of Colorado, was appointed to make an investigation. It found that General Chase's views of his duties were largely responsible for many of the difficulties.[23] The committee recommended that he be compelled to resign, that certain officers be removed, and that mine guards and private detectives be discharged from the militia. The recommendations were ignored.

The militiamen took the law into their own hands. When "Mother" Mary Jones, a union organizer, arrived in Trinidad on January 4, 1914, she was arrested and deported to Denver. She returned and was placed in a hospital where she was held incommunicado for nine weeks. General Chase also set up a military commission which arrested strikers and union officers without warrants. During February and March 1914 violence abated. A congressional committee was in Colorado investigating the dispute, and serious disturbances diminished, although minor clashes continued. Consequently, Governor Ammons withdrew most of the National Guard and left Company B, commanded by Lieutenant Karl E. Linderfelt (an officer whose removal had been recommended by the state investigating committee), on duty at Ludlow.

Ludlow

Deep hatred had developed between the strikers and the militia. Louis Tikas, the leader of the Greek strikers, had aroused the bitter enmity of the National Guardsmen. A demand for the release of a boy held in the Ludlow tent colony was made upon Tikas who answered that he was not there. Presumably to recover the boy, the militia attacked, looted and fired the tents, and murdered three captured miners, including Tikas and James Fyler, the local union secretary. Before shooting Tikas, Lieutenant Linderfelt had broken a Springfield rifle over Tikas' head. Two women and eleven children were smothered to death while seeking refuge in a hole in one of the tents.[24]

The murders of the women precipitated an armed rebellion against the National Guardsmen and private guards. President Wilson was notified by the heads of the Colorado labor movement that they had appealed to their members to arm themselves for defense. Workers were advised to "organize the men in your communities in companies of volunteers to protect the workers of Colorado. . . . gather together for defensive purposes all arms and ammunition legally available. . . ."[25]

Assistance was offered by many organizations of labor and even by those unaffiliated with the trade union movement. The militia at first claimed that the tents had been destroyed by the overturning of a stove, candle, or lamp, but this was immediately denied by John R. Lawson, an executive board member of the United Mine Workers of America and the *de facto* leader of the strike. The miners did not stop with denials, and more than one thousand workers belonging to a number of nationalities attacked the coal camps along a forty mile front.[26]

Armed miners took possession of the territory and seized mines in the area, killing guards and setting fire to buildings. "During the 10 days of fighting, more than fifty people, including those who died at Ludlow, were killed. On April 30th, in response to the request of Governor Ammons, federal troops arrived and the fighting ceased."[27]

Efforts to settle the dispute were renewed by Secretary of Labor Wilson after the Ludlow tragedy. Hywell Davies, a Kentucky coal operator, and W. B. Fairley, a former official of the United Mine Workers of America, offered proposals which served as a basis for the recommendations by President Wilson for settling the strike. The union was willing to accept, but it was rejected by the operators. The President made a second effort to bring about an agreement. He failed again when the operators refused to accept his conditions. A special convention ended the strike on December 10, 1914.[28]

Lawson and 162 miners were indicted for various offenses. Lawson was convicted of murder and sentenced to life imprisonment, but the Colorado Supreme Court overturned the verdict. To avoid a repetition of the Colorado incident, John D. Rockefeller, Jr., asked W. L. Mackenzie King, former Canadian Minister of Labor, to aid in "developing an organization in the mining camps which will assure to the employees an opportunity for collective bargaining, for easy and constant conferences with reference to any matters of difference or grievance which may come up, and any other advantages which can be derived from membership in a union. . . . I am wondering whether you can find the time to dictate, at your convenience, an outline of such an organization and send it to me for consideration."[29]

King drafted what became known as the Industrial Representation Plan, and Rockefeller and King visited the Colorado mines to explain it to the workers. Under the plan coal miners of the Colorado Fuel and Iron Company were divided into four districts, and employees with more than three months' tenure were allowed to vote for a representative, chosen by each 150 miners. Elections were held on a specific day in January. The elected representatives acted on behalf of the miners on wages and working conditions or other issues. Joint conferences were called every four months by the president of the company in every district, with each side equally represented.

In addition, permanent joint committees were established in each district to handle such matters as safety and sanitation, health, housing, and recreation. The joint committees also played a role in the adjustment of grievances, and a provision for arbitration was included in the plan. The costs were borne by the company and the president was chief administrator in fact.[30] The plan was an attempt to eliminate some of the abuses which the workers had charged were an integral part of the policies of the mining companies; however, it failed to prevent the strike of 1927 and, of course, became unviable after the enactment of the Wagner Act. It is, however, an example of an attempt to prevent the establishment of unionism by providing a forum for funneling of grievances.

CHAPTER 20

Militancy and Failure of Arbitration

The importance of railroad transportation to the economy led to the early seeking by Congress of methods of peaceful settlement of labor disputes on the railroads. After the Chicago, Burlington and Quincy strike, the first law dealing with the adjustment of differences between workers and carriers was enacted in 1888. It provided for voluntary arbitration and compulsory investigation, but it was never used. The strike also stimulated the first attempt to bring the unions into closer cooperation, although efforts to set up a formal plan of cooperation failed.[1]

The Erdman Act superseded the law of 1888. Enacted in 1898, it allowed either party to call upon the chairman of the Interstate Commerce Commission and the Commissioner of Labor for mediatory assistance in their dispute with the other party. When both sides agreed to mediation, the attempt was made, with the assistance of government officers, to find a basis of agreement. If mediation was unsuccessful, the mediators were obliged to seek to have the controversy submitted to arbitration. The next law, the Newlands Act of 1913, sought jointly by labor and the carriers, created a U.S. Board of Mediation and Conciliation. The law followed the Erdman Act in the matter of mediation, but it defined more specifically the method of choosing arbitrators. Forty-eight cases were settled under the Erdman law, twenty by mediation, eight by mediation and arbitration, and four by arbitration. In the remaining sixteen cases, one of the parties either refused the mediatory services or the issues were settled directly. Under the Newlands Act, fifty-six cases were settled: forty-five by mediation, and eleven by arbitration.[2]

CONCERTED MOVEMENTS

The first step of organized labor on the railroads was to standarize wages on a single carrier or system. When this was largely accomplished in the 1890's, the operating unions took the next step in unified action, the negotiation of the terms of employment over large geographical areas. This method was designed to circumvent the claim by carriers that they were paying competitive rates when demands for an increase were made. In 1902 the conductors and trainmen organized the Western Association with authority to negotiate in an area west of Chicago to Duluth and southwest from Chicago along a branch line of the Illinois Central Railway. Similar demands were made on the individual carriers in June 1902, and the roads, after negotiations, made concessions. Five years later the western carriers and the two unions dealt jointly through committees representing forty-two roads with a mileage of over 101,000 miles. These negotiations brought the intervention of the chairman of the Interstate Commerce Commission and the Commissioner of Labor, who were instrumental in bringing about a settlement.

The conductors and trainmen now divided the country into three districts—western, eastern, and southern—with clearly defined boundaries. The engineers and firemen followed suit. The engineers and firemen separately negotiated in 1907 with a Managers' Committee of the western roads. For a short time negotiations followed an established pattern. Failure of the parties to reach an agreement led to intervention by government mediators and the eventual settlement through their assistance or by arbitration. A request for a general wage increase by the Brotherhood of Locomotive Engineers on fifty-two eastern roads employing over 31,000 engineers, in 1912, led eventually to the submission of the issues to a board of arbitration of seven, two appointed by each of the parties and the remaining three by the arbitrators. When they failed to agree, the appointments of the three were made by the Chief Justice of the United States, the presiding judge of Commerce Court, and the Commissioner of Labor. It granted a smaller wage increase than had been expected, and P. H. Morrisey, who represented the men, disagreed with the majority decision. The union leaders were especially upset by the recommendations of the board for compulsory arbitration.

Morrisey, who was a former head of the Brotherhood of Railroad Trainmen, dissented sharply from this part of the report. "Regardless of any probable constitutional prohibition which might operate against it being adopted," wrote Morrisey, "it is wholly impracticable. The progress toward the settlement of disputes between the railways and their employees without recourse to industrial warfare has been marked. There is nothing under present conditions to prevent its continuance. It will never be perfect, but even so it will be immeasurably better than it would be under conditions such as the board proposes."[3]

The leaders of operating unions became disenchanted with arbitration and were unwilling to use this method. All the brotherhoods were at the same time drawing closer together. The trainmen and conductors had begun cooperating in negotiations in 1902, but the workers in front cabs—engineers and firemen—did not devise a joint program until 1913, when the Brotherhood of Locomotive Firemen and the Brotherhood of Locomotive Engineers made common wage demands on the western roads. Like many earlier ones, they ended in arbitration, although both parties had reservations about this method of settlement and only assented after President Wilson had intervened. A board of six heard testimony, and the result did not meet the expectations of the unions. President W. S. Carter of the Brotherhood of Firemen and Enginemen, declared that the "Western men did not get what they deserved. . . . For all these years I have been a strenuous advocate of arbitration for the adjustment of wage disputes between the railroads and their employees, but I am now reformed."[4]

A joint meeting of engineers and firemen representing workers on the Boston and Maine Railroad stated: "Our men on the Boston and Maine Railroad have profited little by arbitration, and they wish it clearly understood that no more wage controversies will be settled in the court of arbitration, if in their power to prevent."[5] Resolutions demanding the eight-hour day were also adopted. The feeling of disappointment was echoed by *The Railroad Trainman,* which observed: "There have been few arbitrations of a kind that have not brought their disappointments."[6] The brotherhood felt that the needs of their members were being neglected in favor of something called the public. *The Railroad Trainman* cited a number of cases in which the "public representatives with no knowledge of the subject to be decided did not in the least help out the arbitration."[7]

Dissatisfaction with the results of arbitration and the desire of the members of the unions for the establishment of an eight-hour workday in the operating service led to the joint movement of the four brotherhoods in 1916. As a preliminary step, meetings were held by the general chairman in the several regional associations of the Brotherhood of Locomotive Engineers, Brotherhood of Locomotive Firemen and Enginemen, Order of Railway Conductors, and the Brotherhood of Railroad Trainmen, which authorized the chief officers to meet and prepare a proposal to be submitted to the membership for approval. On December 15, 1915, the heads of these unions drew up a demand for the eight-hour workday in the road and yard freight service on runs of one hundred miles or less, and overtime after eight hours. On runs of over one hundred miles, overtime was to begin when the time duty exceeded the miles run by twelve and one-half miles per hour. All overtime was to be computed on a minute basis and was to be paid at time and one-half the pro rata rate.[8] Passenger service was not included in the demands.

The joint committee directed that the proposals be submitted to the members of each organization. The coalition of the four brotherhoods was the most powerful combination of labor ever devised in the United States. A publicity bureau was established in Cleveland by the four unions to present their case to the public. After the demands were approved by the membership, they were presented to the railroads on March 30 and were accepted by one employer, the Bush Terminal Company in Brooklyn, N.Y. At the request of the unions, it was agreed to bargain on a nationwide basis. Warren S. Stone of the Engineers, W. S. Carter of the Firemen, A. B. Garretson of the Conductors, and W. G. Lee of the Trainmen headed the brotherhood bargainers. The companies' case was presented by Elisha Lee. The negotiations opened in New York City on June 1 and closed on July 15 without an agreement.

In conclusion, the unions were informed: "The national conference committee of the railways has carefully considered your proposals and your explanations of their meaning and intended application. In our judgment, no reasons developed during our conferences to justify the extraordinary changes in operating methods and practices and the large expenditures for additional facilities which your proposals involve; nor was anything presented to justify your requested radical revision of the established basis of compensation for men in engine, train and yard service."[9] The carriers suggested that the issues in dispute be submitted for settlement to the Interstate Commerce Commission or to arbitration in accordance with the provisions of federal law.[10]

The unions would not consider arbitration. "It is impossible to secure men sufficiently familiar with railway operation fairly to decide all questions submitted to them. . . . There is no question but what the neutral arbitrators assume a task that carries so much responsibility that they really should not be called upon to assume, that it is unfair to ask them to sit in judgment on something we know they do not understand."[11]

Each organization in a separate ballot asked whether the demands should be enforced by a strike if necessary. The vote was as follows:[12]

Union	For	Against
Engineers	57,446	6,801
Firemen	69,570	1,204
Conductors	29,800	5,102
Trainmen	128,812	4,350

After the votes had been counted, the officers of the four brotherhoods and the general chairman on August 8 resumed their conference with the managers' committee, but no agreement was reached. The managers' committee requested the unions to join in a request for mediation. President Garretson of the Conductors, who acted as spokesman, replied that he did not believe that "mediation is better than negotiation between the parties directly in touch with each other. There is no necessity to go to a third party. Therefore we decline to join you in the request for mediation."[13] The applause from the 640 general chairmen of the four brotherhoods was proof that Garretson reflected their views.

Garretson announced that the brotherhoods "would accept the proffer of friendly offices" of the federal mediation board, "provided they were promptly exercised. Do not confuse arbitration and mediation. This means mediation. We are open to discussion, but not to arbitration."[14] When the mediation board asked for more time, Warren S. Stone, chief of the Engineers' organization, announced: "We do not intend to wait very long for the mediators to settle this controversy. The temper of the men is such they would not have waited a minute if we had not persuaded them to give the mediators a chance. . . . The men are restless already and something must be done to satisfy them."[15]

On August 12 the mediation board informed the union that the managers' committee would not yield but would agree to arbitrate. President Garretson replied: "Unless the managers are prepared to make some definite proposal we shall consider ourselves at liberty to proceed in accord with the methods of the brotherhoods to affect a settlement of the points of contention between us. That is to say, if need be we will withdraw our men from service."[16]

When it became clear that no agreement could be reached and that there was danger of a national tie-up of the railroad industry, Joseph P. Tumulty, secretary to President Wilson, came to New York with a message from the President inviting the parties to confer with him in Washington. On August 15, President Wilson held separate conferences with the representatives of labor and the Managers' Conference Committee. As the thirty-four labor representatives did not have full power to act, they requested the general chairmen to come to Washington from New York. They were addressed by the President on August 17 in the East Room of the White House. The President asked for the installation of the eight-hour day and the submission of all other issues to arbitration or to a commission of Congress. The union representatives accepted the President's proposals, but they were rejected by the carrier representatives.

Several conferences were held with each side by President Wilson between August 17 and 25. He also explored the possibility of getting legislation through Congress to meet the crisis. On August 28 the leaders of the brotherhood decided to end negotiations and issued an order, not publicly announced, for the beginning of the strike on September 4. The general chairmen left for their homes on August 28 with the strike plan. A vice-president and a committee were left behind in Washington. When the strike plans became known, President Wilson called the heads of the brotherhoods to the White House and appealed to them to cancel the strike order. Refusing, they argued that the matter was beyond their control. The President thereupon appeared before a joint session of Congress on August 28 and appealed for immediate action to prevent the walkout.

After summarizing the course of the dispute, President Wilson said:

It seemed to me, in considering the subject matter of the controversy, that the whole spirit of the time and the preponderant evidence of recent economic experience spoke for the eight-hour day. It has been adjudged by the thought and experience of recent years a thing which society is justified in insisting is in the interest of health, efficiency, contentment and a general increase of economic vigor. The whole presumption of modern experience would, it seemed to me, be in its favor, whether there was arbitration or not, and the debatable points to settle were those which arose out of the acceptance of the eight-hour day rather than those which affected its establishment.[17]

On September 1, H.R. 17,700, or the Adamson bill, was introduced. It provided that after January 1, 1917, eight hours should be deemed a day's work for purposes of reckoning compensation for service on the railroads. It passed the House after a discussion of an entire day; it passed the Senate the following day. After being assured that the President would sign the bill, the heads of the brotherhoods advised their members to cancel the order to leave their jobs.[18]

The question was now whether the law was constitutional. The railroads brought suit for restraining the enforcement of the law and were sustained in several U.S. district courts. On January 10, 1917, a meeting of general chairmen decided to postpone action for a reasonable time, but at a meeting in Cleveland on March 6 it was agreed that action to enforce the award would be taken.

Under the Adamson Act the President was authorized to appoint a commission to examine the effects of the eight-hour day upon the carriers. It had no power of subpoena, but the parties agreed to cooperate with it. In November and December 1916 the railroads instituted many suits to enjoin the enforcement of the law. It was agreed to use one as a test case and it was argued before the Supreme Court on January 8, 1917, while the others were continued. The brotherhoods, in the meantime, decided on more drastic action. The full general committee, consisting of the general chairmen of the four unions, met in Cleveland on March 10 and worked out a plan for gradual suspension of work on all railroads beginning on March 17 and ending on March 19. Each general chairman was given sealed orders to be opened on a specified day directing him to call out his members.

On March 15, the Managers' Conference Committee conferred with the labor chiefs who asked for the acceptance of President Wilson's proposals of August 16. The railroad group was willing to allow the Eight-Hour Commission to decide the application of the law if it were upheld by the Supreme Court, but if it were invalid the carriers wanted the controversy submitted to the Eight-Hour Commission. This meant arbitration, which the railroad unions strenuously opposed. They thereby notified their officers in the field that the strike would begin on schedule on March 15.

At this point, President Wilson intervened again by appointing a committee representing the Council of National Defense made up of Secretary of the Interior Franklin P. Lane, Secretary of Labor W. B. Wilson, Daniel Willard, president of the Baltimore and Ohio Railroad, and Samuel Gompers. According to Gompers:

> There was little or no effort made by the chiefs of the Brotherhoods and certainly not by me, as President of the American Federation of Labor, in urging enactment of the Adamson bill into law. We believed that the railroad presidents would concede the eight-hour day finally, if there was no other interference. As a matter of fact, the eight-hour day was inaugurated by agreement before the Supreme Court of the United States rendered its decision declaring the Adamson law constitutional. The chiefs of the Brotherhoods who are here, who were present in that long conference of probably forty-eight hours, when at the dawn of the early morning, the presidents of the railroads, the chiefs of the Brotherhoods and the commission appointed by the President . . . came to an agreement.[19]

Upon assurances that a satisfactory agreement would be worked out in forty-eight hours, the strike scheduled for March 17 and 18 was postponed until the evening of March 19. In a number of instances, the news of the postponement did not reach general chairmen and the strike went on according to the old schedule. On March 19 an agreement was worked out. On the same day, the U.S. Supreme Court in *243 Wilson* v. *New et al. U.S. 332 (1917),* upheld the law.[20]

The unions carried the day; it was a victory for the new militancy of the railroad workers, a militancy which was to carry into the postwar period of the 1920's. The reliance of the industry on arbitration was perhaps the chief reason for the growing militancy of railroad labor. These boards did not understand the problems of railroad labor, nor the pressures to which the leadership was subjected. Warnings against their failure to recognize the needs and aspirations of the worker were unheeded in their overriding concern for what they called the public interest. Moreover, the railroads were able to parry demands of their work force by suggesting arbitration, which increasingly failed to meet the expectations of the operating unions. The result was increased reliance upon direct negotiation, with the use of the strike weapon if necessary. The railroads had learned to depend upon arbitration to relieve them of hard decisions, and it was only through the unions' use of their economic power which finally compelled a temporary reversal of the use of this procedure.

CHAPTER 21

Jurisdictional Rights and Departments

Jurisdictional rights which affiliates claimed and the AFL recognized were a source of conflict. The second convention of the AFL "deemed it unwise for two local, national or international organizations of any one trade to exist in the same jurisdiction, and advised the amalgamation of trades in such instances. The Executive Council is instructed to use all means in its power to accomplish this end."[1] In the following year, the convention rejected an application for a charter by the Amalgamated Society of Carpenters on the ground that it was "detrimental to the interests of labor to have any more than one organization in any trade."[2] The principle of exclusive jurisdiction was therefore established in the first two conventions of the AFL, although the principle was violated in 1890, when the Amalgamated Society of Carpenters was allowed to join despite Gompers' conviction that "one organization of a trade is sufficient in any one country. That where more exist the *best results* are never attained."[3]

JURISDICTIONAL DISPUTES

Exclusive jurisdiction was not an inevitable principle in a Federation dominated by craft organizations, for it was possible for more than one union to operate in a trade or calling. Within narrow limits the boundaries of a trade could be ascertained but disputes could arise on the periphery of a jurisdiction over the assignment of jobs. It was natural that such disputes should be brought to the AFL, and the first jurisdictional complaint was made to the 1889 convention by the International Furniture Workers'

Union. The convention, seeking to avoid the issue, pointed to "the fact that the A.F. of L., is based on the principle which gives all organizations the right of self-government in trade matters; we, therefore, recommend that organizations affiliated with the A.F. of L., whose trades are so closely allied as are the furniture workers and the carpenters and joiners, should, in each district, adopt a code of working rules suitable to that particular district."[4]

In an effort to avoid the proliferation of jurisdictional difference, the federation provided in 1899 that an organization seeking to affiliate be required to specify its jurisdiction, and if it claimed branches of trades already covered by charters of other affiliated unions, its application would require approval of a regular convention of the AFL. If a charter were granted "to a distinct branch of a trade formerly part of another body, the parent body from that time forward shall be estopped from receiving into its ranks members of unions of the branch or trade when chartered."[5] Had the federation been able to enforce this clause, it would have prevented the long-drawn-out dispute between the Brewery Workers' Union and the crafts, because the former would not have been able to recruit craftsmen claimed by other affiliates.[6]

At the 1900 convention it was decided that a jurisdiction claimed by an existing affiliate could not without its written consent be trespassed upon. National and international unions were asked to define their jurisdictions so as to guide the federation in the future issuance of charters. The executive council pleaded for the maintenance of a fraternal spirit by its affiliates, and sought to back away from the duty continually thrust upon it by unions competing for the same jurisdiction. "For the Executive Council of the A.F. of L., itself, to determine a distinctive line might bring about the very reverse of the desire entertained by the disputants. After all, the best which can be done is to give an expression of opinion, depending upon the common sense and good will of the officers and members of affiliated organizations to yield a willing acquiescence."[7]

The Scranton Declaration

The AFL, despite its anxiety to avoid involvement, found itself continually confronted by the conflicting jurisdictional claims of its affiliates. It had no power to enforce its decisions, but in the absence of any other tribunal, the affiliated unions insisted upon bringing their differences to the AFL conventions. A serious dispute arose between the Miners' Union and several of the craft organizations over the organizing of certain workers in and around the mines. The International Blacksmiths' Union complained that members of its craft had been recruited into the United Mine Workers of America.[8] John Mitchell, president of the United Mine Workers, took notice of the complaints and reported to his organization:

The necessity of one organization having jurisdiction over all employees in or around coal mines has presented itself in such a manner during the past few years that I believe this convention should make provision for the organization of all outside workmen. At the present time the engineers, firemen and black-smiths in some localities are members of national unions representing their particular trade, and as a consequence strikes are engaged in which cause the enforced idleness of all members of our union. The fact that we represent such an overwhelming proportion of the employees in and about coal mines makes it imperative that our organization should be the sole judge of when strikes shall take effect. If these separate organizations are permitted or encouraged it places power in the hands of less than three percent of the employees of the coal mines in the country to cause a complete suspension of operations . . . these workmen should become members of our union and be permitted to organize in separate locals wherever deemed expedient, or there is a sufficient number of them to maintain a local union chartered by our national organization.[9]

In accordance with the recommendation, the officers were directed "to organize all engineers, firemen, blacksmiths, carpenters and others who may now be members of other trade organizations."[10]

It might be noted that the claim for an industrial union was not made upon the basis of a general principle, but solely on the ground that relatively few craftsmen could compel a much larger group of miners to strike. The position of the Miners' Union compelled the AFL at its 1901 convention to reconsider the question of jurisdictional rights. A special committee of five, with Gompers, Mitchell, and James Duncan as members, was appointed to wrestle with the problem. Its suggestions which became embodied in the Scranton Declaration recognized that organization on trade lines be continued. However,

owing to the isolation of some few industries from thickly populated centers where the overwhelming number follow one branch thereof, and owing to the fact that in some industries comparatively few workers are engaged over whom separate organizations claim jurisdiction; we believe that jurisdiction in such industries by the paramount organization would yield the best results to the workers therein. . . . We hold that the interests of the trade union movement will be promoted by closely allying the subdivided crafts, giving consideration to amalgamation and to the organization of district and national trade councils to which shall be referred questions in dispute, and which should be adjusted within allied craft lines.

The American Federation of Labor being a voluntary association can not direct and should not adopt methods antagonistic to or in conflict with established trade union laws, and in order to carry the above recommendations into effect, and in full recognition of its logical position the American Federation of Labor pledges its officers to aid and assist in the adjustment of such craft encroachments as disputants may be willing to submit to its arbitration.[11]

The Scranton Declaration was an attempt to meet a practical situation.

In view of the power of the United Mine Workers of America to enforce its jurisdiction upon all those who were employed in and around the mines, it would have been self-defeating folly for the AFL to insist upon a recognition of the crafts. However, in order to placate the latter, the recognition of the industrial character of the Miners' Union was implicitly defined as an exception. But the heart of the problem, as it came to the attention of the AFL, was its lack of power to enforce its decisions. This was clearly demonstrated in the dispute over jurisdiction in the brewery industry. The National Union of United Brewery Workmen was organized in 1886. It claimed jurisdiction over all workers in breweries, including brewers, maltsters, coopers, drivers, stablemen, engineers, firemen, and bottlers. Disputes had arisen between the Brewery Workers' Union and other organizations which claimed part of the above territory. The first controversy involved the coopers, and the AFL decided in 1898 that where there was enough coopers' work in a brewery to require the entire time of one cooper, he should belong to the Coopers' Union, but where only part time was required he should belong to the Brewery Workmen. The Brewery Workmen refused to obey the decree. It followed the same course in disputes with the Engineers', Stationary Firemen, and Teamsters' unions.

The tendency of unions to become engaged in jurisdictional disputes and to bring them to the AFL for settlement aroused Gompers' deep concern. He found it intolerable for an "organization to attempt to ride rough shod over and trample underfoot the rights and jurisdiction of a trade, the jurisdiction of which is already covered by an existing organization. This contention over jurisdiction has grown into such proportion and is fraught with such intensity as to arouse the most bitter feuds and trade wars. In most instances employers fairly inclined toward organized labor have been made innocently to suffer from causes entirely beyond their control."[12]

Despite the pleas of the AFL, jurisdictional disputes increased and unions frequently disregarded the views of federation conventions. For failure to obey a series of decisions, the Brewery Workers' Union was suspended, over the protests of Gompers, who announced publicly his opposition to the decision. Gompers' conduct was in violation of the rule of the executive council that members were not to reveal their votes on specific issues. Duncan upbraided Gompers and told him he was not the executive council, but Gompers insisted that the revocation of charter was a threat to the unity of the labor movement. In a letter defending his action, Gompers explained he was "more oppressed and depressed since the action of the Executive Council than I have ever felt in all my life. And yet my course in this matter is as undefined in my mind as it was upon what I regard as one, if not the most momentous days in my life, the day when the Executive Council pursued that course to revoke the charter of the Brewery Workers. No doubt you can imagine the position which I am placed in being required as President of the A.F. of L. to carry out a policy with which I am in essential variance and against the enforcement of which my judgment revolts. . . . I have repeatedly heard men resent the statement that the American Federation of Labor is the 'parent body' to the trade union movement, a statement with which you and I not only agree but affirm; and yet we see some of these men who stoutly resent the expression or the thought that the American Federation of Labor is the 'parent body' of trade unions, voted to revoke a charter of an international trade union, and who seriously proposed to dismember an international trade union. I am not only heart-sore; I am astounded."[13]

The federation was active in promoting mergers of unions occupying jurisdictions adjacent to each other. It refused to charter internationals with a too narrow base. It also compelled the Amalgamated Wood Workers' International Union to merge with the United Brotherhood of Carpenters and Joiners and the amalgamation of the Plumbers and Steamfitters' unions. It forced the Association of Railway Car Workers to leave when it would not merge with the unaffiliated Brotherhood of Railway Carmen. It made strong efforts to eliminate competing unions, and its labors were sometimes crowned with success. While the leaders of the federation accepted the fact that the skilled were more organizable than the unskilled, the leaders did not take the position that the latter would not organize.

Industrial Organization

In 1903 a more basic criticism of its structure was first presented to an AFL convention. A resolution was proposed to consider the regrouping of the trade unions along industrial lines. The proposal was rejected, but reappeared in different forms at subsequent conventions. In the meantime, the federation continued to try to bring about mergers of competing unions and to enlarge the jurisdiction by combining unions, the jobs of whose members were closely connected. In some instances other forms of cooperation were suggested. In the clothing industry, the executive council suggested in 1902 that the several unions set up federations of the clothing industry, with each union represented on an executive board.[14] The suggestion was not accepted. Gompers always argued that the AFL constantly sought amalgamation of related crafts. He pointed to the joining of the International Electrotype Plate Makers and the Stereotypers' and Electrotypers' Union after the AFL urged the merger, the joining of the Coppersmiths in the Sheet Metal Workers' Union, and other instances of the constructive role of the AFL in the area.[15]

COOPERATION AMONG TRADES

Closely related trades organized in different unions faced the necessity of devising some method of cooperation. Organizations in the same industry had devised informal and formal methods of cooperation in the trades' council. In his report to the 1888 convention, Gompers visualized the establishment of industrial divisions, made up of closely related unions, that would legislate on common problems. Nothing came of the suggestion, and in the meantime, closely related local unions began to form separate trades' councils. While such units were not formally recognized, they were not opposed by the AFL. A different view was taken of the National Building Trades' Council, established in December 1897, by a group of building trades' councils, a national union and local unions of the building trades which had no national organization. Always sensitive to the possibilities of a dual center of power developing, the AFL was not enthusiastic about the formation of the National Building Trades' Council. In fact, the federation wanted the trades' councils controlled by the AFL to be part of the general central bodies in the area. The local trades' councils would be authorized to deal with problems affecting common trade interests. The National Building Trades' Council, in contrast, sought the establishment of a national working card, the eight-hour day, equalization of wages of different trades in the building industry, and the securing of legislation in behalf of building construction workers. W. H. Steinbiss, the head of the national council, believed it was necessary "to form a national federation separate and distinct . . . to enact legislation for building trades councils and unions by building trades councils."[16]

In Gompers' opinion, there "was nothing for which a national building trades council can declare, which has not been more effectively emphasized and more nearly achieved by the American Federation of Labor; and that which has not been accomplished can be more readily attained by our Federation."[17] Gompers insisted that the AFL had sought to organize workers irrespective of trade or calling, and that the federation had organized metal and building trades' councils. He objected to their organizing separately and as rivals to the general labor movement. He pointed to the building trades' council sheltering a local expelled by an affiliate of the AFL and others which had never sought affiliation. Gompers said: "The organization of another body on other lines than are generally accepted by the whole labor movement, no matter how honestly conceived, is to be deprecated. There never yet existed, and never can possibly exist, two organizations or governments claiming jurisdiction over the same territory or peoples, endeavoring to administer to their welfare, without rivalry, antagonism and conflict arising therefrom . . . the very persistence of each authority endeavoring to advance the interests of its own organization makes the rivalry, bitterness and antagonism the more acute."[18]

Structural Building Trades Alliance

The opposition of the AFL did not prevent the national unions in the building trades from establishing a formal alliance. Since jurisdictional disputes and dual unions could be more efficiently handled on a national scale, the Structural Building Trades Alliance was established in 1903. Each international was given equal representation at conventions. Local alliances were to be established, and these bodies were to support the specific crafts in dispute if the alliance and the internationals involved approved. The promoters pointed to the interdependence of the building trades' unions as justification for their step.

Departments

The Structural Building Trades Alliance did not answer the need. The federation voted in 1903 to set up a convention committee to deal only with grievances arising among the building trades, but it rejected approval of a national council.[19] The alliance continued to operate and its secretary, William Spencer, informed the AFL Executive Council that the alliance would seek to eliminate sympathetic strikes, the majority of which he attributed to the unskilled.[20] Although the AFL did not regard the alliance favorably, the views and interests of the most powerful group of unions could not be ignored. President F. J. McNulty of the Electrical Workers' Union, urging the 1907 AFL convention to allow the building trades' unions to unite, stated: "In the past we have made enemies of our friends among employers through fighting over jurisdiction of work. We realize that unless the building trades can unite under one head, it will be impossible to eliminate these fights. The building trades have agreed among themselves to forget the jurisdictional quarrels, and with the assistance of the Executive Council try to create a Section that will eliminate those quarrels and protect our friends among the employers."[21]

The 1907 convention authorized the chartering of a Department to be composed of national and international unions in the building trades affiliated with the AFL. The department was authorized to issue charters to building trades' sections. Nineteen international unions met in the following year and organized the Building Trades Department, and as a concession to the power of the unaffiliated Bricklayers' Union, locals of that organization were allowed to join building trades' councils. Gompers, addressing the founding convention, expressed the hope that the department would "never weaken the bonds of union . . . with the trade unionists of other branches of labor."[22] Vice-President James Duncan of the AFL, also an officer of the building trades' union, believed that the power of the department to settle jurisdictional disputes would subordinate every national and international union to the department.[23]

The power of the department was almost immediately tested when the Carpenters' Union refused to accept its decision awarding certain work to the Sheet Metal Workers' organization. The department then asked the AFL to suspend the Carpenters' Union from the federation. The AFL

Executive Council refused, because it could only revoke a charter of an international when directed to do so by a two-thirds vote of a convention. Moreover, the council admonished the department to recognize that suspensions were likely to lead to bitterness—a poor method for welding the movement into a unified whole. The council recommended the reinstatement of the suspended union and the use of persuasion.[24] The Carpenters' Union rejoined the department the following year, but it soon became engaged in an even more serious dispute.

The cause of the new difficulty was an agreement signed by the carpenters with the unaffiliated Bricklayers' Union for a "general 'offensive and defensive' alliance."[25] No member of either union would accept employment if the other were not recognized. In the opinion of the unions in the department, the alliance was designed to destroy the Journeymen Stone Cutters' and the Marble Workers' unions. This charge was denied. The AFL intervened, and the Carpenters' Union was accepted in the following year. In 1916 the Bricklayers' Union became part of the AFL.

Other Departments

The Metal Trades Department of the AFL, organized in 1908, has functioned without much incident. It has chartered metal trades' councils, which have functioned in the shipyards, government installations, and the machine-tool industry; they have negotiated joint contracts and have conducted cooperative organizing campaigns. The Railway Employees' Department functions on behalf of the shopcrafts and conducts joint negotiations on behalf of its affiliates. In addition, the Union Label and Service Department promotes the union label and the purchase of union-made goods; the Food and Beverage Department and the Maritime Trades Department have developed a loose sort of cooperation among their affiliates. The Industrial Union Department unlike the above is not a department in the traditional AFL sense. Composed largely of former CIO unions, the department has been trying to develop cooperative organizing drives among its affiliates. It has held a number of conferences and published bulletins and pamphlets.

22

Dual Unionism

EARLY SOCIALIST GROUPS

Believers in dual unionism sought to build a labor federation which would compete successfully for the suffrage of the worker and destroy the influence and power of the AFL and the nonaffiliated railway brotherhoods whose jurisdiction the federation recognized. In contrast, a specific dual union might arise as a result of a secession or expulsion of a recalcitrant local from an existing union; the dual organization might share the philosophy and outlook of the organization from which it separated. Such an instance might only involve administrative or jurisdictional differences rather than differences of philosophy or doctrine.

Experience with the competition of the Knights of Labor sharpened the hostility of the AFL to dual organizations and even more to dual movements which sought to create another central power in the labor world. The fears of the AFL that dual movements tended to divide labor and to weaken its resistance in the face of the employer were naturally derided by those who believed that AFL policies were designed to strengthen the forces of capitalism and dilute labor's influence in the political and economic worlds.

The Socialist Labor party became in time the spokesman for a dual labor federation in the eastern part of the United States. Among its forerunners was the New York Communist Club, founded in 1857. Espousing the views of Karl Marx, it gained few members and was reorganized ten years later. The German General Union, organized in New York City in

1865, followed the views of German Socialist Ferdinand Lassalle and placed primary stress upon education and the establishment of producers' cooperatives financed by government. To a large extent these organizations reflected the conflicts and problems of Europe, mainly Germany, from where most of the members had immigrated. Largely through the influence of the New York Communist Club, the Social party was formed in 1867 as a result of a merger of the competing Socialist groups. The Social party advocated nationalization of industry and a number of immediate reforms. It advocated establishment of dual unions whenever existing organizations refused to affiliate with the party.[1] The party participated in the state elections in 1868, and its lack of success ended its existence.

The influence of German Socialists upon radical programs in the United States is also obvious from the formation of the Universal German Workingmen's Association in Chicago in 1869; it was the name of Lassalle's organization in Germany. The Labor party of Illinois, formed in 1874, was largely the work of the German group in Chicago. It advocated nationalization of banks and transportation, but the influence of Lassalle is evident in its sponsorship of government aid to producers' cooperatives. In the same year the Social Democratic Workingmen's party of North America was organized at a convention in New York City. A call for a national convention of all Socialist political groups appeared in the following year, sponsored by John M. Davis, editor of the *National Labor Tribune*. After rebuffing the believers in cheap money, a unity convention was called for Philadelphia in July 1876.

Socialist Labor Parley

The unity convention was made up largely of German-Americans who had affiliated earlier with one of the several radical or Socialist parties. Among the better known, or to become known, were Peter J. McGuire and Adolph Strasser, architects of the future AFL, and Otto Wedemeyer and Friedrich Sorge, friends and correspondents of Karl Marx. The convention formed the Workingmen's party of the United States. In the next year the name, Socialist Labor party, was adopted. Its new preamble declared that the "industrial emancipation of labor, must be achieved by the working classes themselves, independent of all political parties but their own."[2]

Friedrich Engels, Marx's collaborator and one sympathetic to the party's objectives, regarded the organization in 1887 as a political party in name only. It was made up predominantly of German immigrants who were not too well acquainted with the English language.[3] In 1890, Daniel De Leon, who was to dominate the Socialist Labor party until his death in 1914, became a member. De Leon was born on the island of Curaçao off the coast of Venezuela in 1852, and after studying in Germany, came to the

United States in the early 1870's. He became a lecturer in international law at Columbia University and in 1892, editor of *The People,* the official English organ of the party. Soon after becoming editor, De Leon began his attack upon pure trade unionism with its emphasis upon bread-and-butter issues. He regarded its advocates as betrayers of labor and as "labor fakers." For De Leon, "the labor leader . . . is nothing but a masked battery, from behind which the capitalist class can encompass what it could not without— the work of enslaving and slowly degrading the working class."[4]

The Socialist Labor party had captured District Assembly No. 49 of the Knights of Labor in New York City. Through control of this body, the party contributed to the defeat of Powderly in 1893, when it combined with the supporters of James R. Sovereign to oust him from the post of General Master Workman. Sovereign, however, was no more pliable than his predecessor. When the AFL, under the leadership of John McBride as much as under Gompers, failed to find approval, De Leon launched a dual labor federation, the Socialist Trade and Labor Alliance in December 1895. Added to the bitter attacks upon the leaders, the alliance widened differences between the Socialists and trade unionists.[5]

In addition to the several brands of European political socialism, a more indigenous type arose in the 1890's. It was mainly an offshoot of native radicalism which traditionally manifested itself in colonizing schemes, advocacy of cheap money, trust busting, and opposition to big business and monopoly. In the 1890's, J. A. Wayland established the *Coming Nation* and later the *Appeal to Reason,* both of which avoided traditional Socialist jargon with its antireligious overtones. Instead, the appeal was direct and in the customary language of American radicalism, easily grasped by the average man. Wayland, who had started at Greensburg, Indiana, tried a colonizing scheme in Tennessee, moved to Kansas City, and later to Girard, Kansas. A non-Marxist group of Socialists of German derivation functioned in Milwaukee. Its leader, Victor L. Berger, was at first active in the People's party and was instrumental in converting Eugene Victor Debs to socialism during the latter's imprisonment in the Woodstock jail. Debs participated in the launching of a scheme by the Brotherhood of the Cooperative Commonwealth and, when it failed, helped to launch the Social Democracy of America in 1897. But this organization became embroiled in differences over the respective merits of colonization and politics. It led to a split, with the anticolonizers forming the Social Democratic party of America. The party favored the cooperative commonwealth, public ownership of public and monopolistic industries, and sponsored a program of public works for supporting the unemployed. In contrast to the Socialist Labor party, it supported cooperation with the trade unions.

De Leon's insistence upon strict party discipline and his bias against the trade unions finally led to a split in his ranks. A group led by a young

New York lawyer, Morris Hillquit, seceded after an attempt to capture the party had failed. It made overtures to the Social Democratic party which, despite its suspicions, agreed to a common ticket of Eugene Debs for President and Job Harriman for Vice-President in the 1900 election. Debs polled over 98,000 votes. Unity under the name of the Socialist party was achieved at a convention in January 1901. The new party opposed the dual union policy of De Leon and believed that Socialists could win the approval of the trade union movement by example and education of non-Socialists.

ORGANIZED LABOR IN THE WEST

Dual unionism had an independent origin in the Rocky Mountain mining communities. Opposition to the AFL in this section was based upon experience rather than doctrine. Leaders of metal mining unions, accustomed to settling serious differences with the sword, were repelled by the cautious conservatism of their eastern coworkers. This attitude, born out of their experience, was reinforced by socialist ideas which many of the leaders accepted.

Labor organizations in the western part of the United States arose as local groups or as assemblies of the Knights of Labor. The largest and most militant groups were those organized in the metalliferous mines. A miners' union was established at Virginia City, Nevada, in 1863. Metalliferous miners' unions were formed in Colorado in 1878 and 1879.

Metalliferous miners lived and worked in a part of the country where differences were more likely to be settled by violence. An early strike in Leadville, Colorado, in 1880, showed all the characteristics of the Rocky Mountain labor wars. Begun as a result of the rejection of a demand for increased wages, it mushroomed when the miners compelled the hesitant carpenters to quit their jobs at the Crysolite mine. Under the leadership of Michael Mooney, 3,000 workers were involved.

A semi-military organization of citizens meanwhile was formed to preserve order. On June 11 a proclamation was issued by the Citizens' Committee of Five Hundred, announcing its readiness to protect miners willing to work. At the request of the sheriff, Governor Frederick W. Pitkin sent the National Guard to Leadville on June 14, and union men were forced to leave the camp. Upon assurance that union miners would suffer no discrimination, many were allowed to return. By June 22 all disorder had ended in Leadville.[7]

Coeur d'Alene

A more violent clash took place at Coeur d'Alene, Idaho, in 1892. It was the first serious dispute between miners and operators in the area; another was to erupt in 1899. Gold mining was begun in Idaho in the 1860's, but not until the 1870's, with the discovery of silver and lead around Wallace, did operation expand.

Several metalliferous miners' locals federated into the Coeur d'Alene Executive Miners' Union in 1889, the first central group in the industry. The operators followed by forming the Mine Owners Protective Association two years later. On January 1, 1892, the mines were closed, ostensibly to compel a reduction of freight rates by the railroads. When their reopening was announced in the latter part of March, the companies sought reductions of some daily rates from $3.50 to $3.00. To the objection of the union, the operators insisted that the step was necessary and permissible under the contract. The mines remained closed for two months longer, and the importation of replacements under guard began. Guards and strikers exchanged gunfire. Both a federal injunction and the governor's proclamation for avoidance of violence were ignored. On July 10, after a striker was killed, the miners took possession of the Frisco mine and forced the surrender of nonunion workers. Next, the Gem mine was overwhelmed, and finally, the Bunker Hill and Sullivan Company concentrator was seized. The strikers demanded the discharge of all workers. The governor declared martial law and sent troops to Wardner, Wallace, Burke, and Mullan on July 14. At the governor's request, federal troops arrived to assist in maintaining order.

General William P. Carlin, the officer in charge, directed a roundup of union men who, because of their large numbers, were detained in a hastily constructed prison, the bull pen. Local officials, unsympathetic with the military activities, were removed by the head of the state militia. Seventy-five strikers were lodged in the bull pen, among them the future head of the Western Federation of Miners, Edward Boyce. A number were tried for conspiracy and contempt of court, the latter charge for violating the injunction of Judge James H. Beatty. Several were convicted but were released by the U.S. Supreme Court when it overturned the indictments. Agreements were finally reached with all mining companies except the Bunker Hill and Sullivan which refused to recognize the union.[8]

WESTERN FEDERATION OF MINERS

The spread of unions of metalliferous miners led the Butte, Montana, Miners' Union to call for a convention of workers in the industry. Forty delegates representing fifteen locals met in Butte on May 15, 1893, and after five days established the Western Federation of Miners. John Gilligan was elected president; and W. J. Weeks, secretary-treasurer. The union, which was destined to lead some of the more violent labor battles in history, stated that "it is highly fitting and proper that the men who are engaged in the hazardous and unhealthy occupation of mining, milling, smelting, and the reduction of ores should receive a just compensation for their labors, which shall be proportionate to the dangers connected therewith, and such protection from law as will remove needless risk to life or health, and for the purpose of bringing about and promoting these and other proper and lawful ends, and for the general welfare of ourselves, families, and dependent ones, we deem it necessary and maintain the Western Federation of Miners."9

Cripple Creek

Gold mining began in and around Cripple Creek, Colorado, a district about twenty-five miles west of Colorado Springs, in 1891. About forty mines were active by 1893. Trouble started in the same summer when H. E. Locke, the superintendent of the Isabella mine, sought to lengthen the hours of labor. The threat of an increase in hours stimulated organization, and locals of the Western Federation of Miners were established in Altman, Cripple Creek, Victor, and Anaconda. The mine owners responded and formed an association to meet the presumed threat. In January 1894 the mine operators announced that hours of work would be lengthened to ten a day. The miners countered by demanding the establishment of the eight-hour workday in all mines.

Cripple Creek "was not an ordinary mining camp, but a newly settled, essentially frontier, district. The men were not of the mining population familiar to the coal fields—foreign born, ignorant, used to obedience, easily cowed—but of the characteristic frontiersman type, [they] came not so much to find work as to seek a fortune. Rough, ready, fearless, used to shifting for themselves. . . . Nor were the mine owners generally of the usual capitalistic type. The majority of them had gained their wealth by successful prospecting, or by lucky buying in the early days of the camp. It was Greek against Greek, similar ideas and strong methods on both sides."10 The other metalliferous mine communities were peopled by the same types and faced the same problems during disputes.

When compromise was impossible, a strike started. Injunctions against violence were issued, deputies were brought in from outside, and arrests were made. Conditions continued peaceful until the end of May when the strikers learned of plans to reopen the mines. Under the direction of J. J. Johnson, the miners established an armed camp on Bull Hill, a high bluff overlooking Altman. On May 24 a force of guards, recruited largely in Denver, arrived to protect the mining properties. To show their contempt, the miners blew up the Strong mine as trains carrying guards pulled into view.11

A movement for a compromise began, and the two sides exchanged prisoners they had captured in battle. "This is probably the only instance of a strike in which rights of belligerency were recognized, and a formal exchange of prisoners made."[12] Strict military discipline was followed in their camp, and a similar plan was pursued on Bull Hill where the miners were quartered. To prevent an outbreak, Governor Davis H. Waite intervened and ordered the militia to the scene. A conference between the opposing parties and militia officers reached an agreement for the withdrawal of the guards and the maintenance of order by the troops for thirty days. The mines were gradually reopened.[13]

Second Strike at Coeur d'Alene

Violence and armed clashes between strikers and guards reappeared in the Coeur d'Alene area in 1899. The Bunker Hill and Sullivan Company had managed, as was noted, to avoid dealing with the Western Federation of Miners after the strike of 1892.

On April 23 the Wardner union demanded $3.50 a day and recognition. Refusal led to a strike on April 26. The Bunker Hill and Sullivan Company raised wages, but would not recognize the union. Members were told they could leave their employment and some who failed to follow the suggestion were discharged. Reaction from the strikers was not long in coming. About one thousand armed men from Mullan, Burke, and Gem seized a train and ordered the engineer to proceed to Wardner where the Bunker Hill and Sullivan mine was dynamited. Upon learning of these events, Governor Frank Steunenberg declared martial law and requested the assistance of federal troops, since the National Guard had been mustered into service in the Spanish-American War.

Brigadier General H. C. Merriam and troops from Boise, Walla Walla, and Spokane were sent. Steunenberg appointed State Auditor Bartlett Sinclair to direct affairs in Shoshone County, the seat of the trouble. A roundup of miners began.[14] More than 700 suspects in the dynamiting were arrested and 528 were detained. The prisoners were given neither blankets nor bedding and were brutally treated in a bull pen. Sinclair sought to eliminate trouble makers and union men by denying them employment. He ordered those seeking work to secure a permit from Dr. Hugh France, who had been appointed to act as agent for the state. On May 20, Governor Steunenberg announced in a proclamation that all workers would be protected and that there "will, and is, no war upon organized labor as such, but certain so-called labor organizations, as they exist and have existed under various names and at various times in Shoshone County, are not to be considered with law respecting labor organizations."[15]

A number were brought to trial. Pat Corcoran, secretary of the Burke Miners' Union, was convicted of second-degree murder and sentenced to seventeen years' imprisonment in the state penitentiary; eight others escaped before the trial. Ten were convicted of interfering with the mails and sentenced to two-year terms in San Quentin prison in California. General

Merriam zealously pursued the innocent and the guilty alike. Protests against the conduct of troops led to an investigation by Congress, but the troops remained in the area until April 1901, after Steunenberg had left office. The imprisoned union leaders were pardoned in the same year. It was, however, in Cripple Creek that the union faced its greatest trial and experienced its most severe attack.

Cripple Creek Again

The eight-hour day had been a long-sought demand of the Western Federation of Miners. At first it was hoped that such a measure would be adopted by the Colorado legislature, but when such a bill was rejected in 1902, the federation decided to seek a reduced workday in the smelting and reduction plants through collective bargaining. Strikes for shorter hours took place early in 1903 at the Portland and Telluride reduction plants at Colorado City. When the walkout was settled and the reduced hours introduced on March 3, it was understood that it would be "enforced also in competing establishments. The Standard mill at Colorado City . . . continued to pay the old scale. . . . The inequality of wages caused dissatisfaction among the union employees of the Standard mill, and also caused the manager of the Portland and Telluride mills to be dissatisfied."[16] On July 3, 1903, the Mill and Smelter Men's Union struck against the U.S. Reduction and Refining Company.

On August 8 a committee from District 1 of the Western Federation of Miners sought to settle the walkout and when they failed, the miners, with a few exceptions, were ordered out on a sympathetic strike. On August 11, 3,552 miners answered the call. The Mine Owners' Association pointed in a statement to the harmony prevailing in the area since the strike of 1894. "No more arbitrary and unjustifiable action mars the annals of organized labor, and we denounce it as an outrage against both the employers and the employed. The fact that there are no grievances to adjust and no unsatisfactory conditions to remedy leaves the mine operators but one alternative, and that alternative they propose to adopt fearlessly."[17]

It was the beginning of a contest of unparalleled violence between the Western Federation of Miners and the operators, and it resulted in the virtual ousting of the union from the Colorado mining camps. Early in September the city authorities of Victor asked for troops. A commission sent to investigate by Governor James H. Peabody approved the request. The governor agreed, providing "the Miners' Association would provide funds for the necessary expenses of the soldiers while they should be in the strike district."[18] The need for troops was challenged by the county commissioners of Teller County and Sheriff H. M. Robertson, and mass meetings at both the cities of Cripple Creek and Victor expressed the same views.

But the arrival of 400 troops on September 4 led to the reopening of several mines the following week. Guards and soldiers surrounded every mine and patrolled the highways. From the beginning, General Sherman Bell took charge and began a series of daily arrests of union officers and active members. The military refused to obey the order for release of the petitioners on writs of habeas corpus; they were subsequently released on orders of the governor. An explosion in the Vindicator Mine wrecked the cage and killed the superintendent and a shift boss. The Mine Owners' Association charged that it was the work of the Western Federation. On December 4, Governor Peabody, after conferring with the Mine Owners' Association and officers of the Cripple Creek Citizens Alliance, declared Teller County, in which Cripple Creek was located, in a state of insurrection and rebellion. Sympathizers with, and members of, the union were disarmed. The writ of habeas corpus was suspended in the case of Victor Poole, and when the Colorado Supreme Court was asked to rule on the right of the governor to make such a decision, the defendant was released. "The men released under habeas proceedings were re-arrested at pleasure, and thus a heavy check kept upon the activity of the unions."[19]

Union men were arrested, meetings invaded, and visitors seized and deported. "It became a question whether one could go along the street without being molested. A drunken militiaman was a common sight."[20]

The union did not abjectly accept its fate. On June 4, 1904, a dynamite explosion wrecked the Independence railroad station, killing thirteen non-union miners who had just completed work at the Findley Mine and were waiting for a train. The Western Federation of Miners was immediately charged with the crime. The Mine Owners' Association forced the sheriff and other county officers to resign and had them replaced with others more willing to follow instructions. Clashes between union and nonunion forces went on, and the operators held the upper hand. Union men and sympathizers were driven out of town, and those who resisted were mobbed or killed. The *Victor Record,* a daily newspaper friendly to the unions, was sacked by a mob. The miners' unions were destroyed, and their active members scattered. A "rustling card" was introduced on which applicants for employment were required to answer if they had ever been members of the Western Federation of Miners. If the answer was in the affirmative, they had to state when they ended their connection with that organization. Applicants passing the tests were given a card entitling them to seek employment at the mines. After an applicant secured employment, the card was surrendered and returned to the secretary of the association. A new card was required if the worker sought a new position.[21]

Murder of Former Governor Frank Steunenberg

Former Governor Frank Steunenberg had directed the repression of the Coeur d'Alene miners during the 1899 strike. On December 30, 1905, as he was opening the gate of his home in Caldwell, Idaho, a bomb exploded and killed him instantly. A hunt for the murderer began, and a reward of $10,000 was offered by the state and $5,000 by his family for information leading to the arrest and conviction of the guilty. Harry Orchard, who was to confess to being a chief terrorist of the Western Federation of Miners, was arrested the following day. Two weeks later James McParlan, who had exposed and sent to death leaders of the Molly Maguires in the anthracite coal fields, took command of the case at the request of Governor Frank R. Gooding. McParlan was at first "not very sanguine" about a confession.[22]

Orchard claimed that he had been employed as an arsonist, dynamiter, and terrorist by the "inner circle" of the Western Federation. He revealed that his given name was Alfred Horsley and that he had deserted his wife, remarried without the benefit of divorce, and committed robbery, assault, and murder. He confessed to killing twenty-six men in dynamiting the Vindicator Mine and the railroad station at Independence. He claimed he had conferred with the heads of the Western Federation and George Pettibone, a Denver businessman and former union member, on the killing of the governor. Orchard claimed Steve Adams, a union terrorist, had aided in the bombing. McParlan believed that Orchard had been convinced to disclose the conspiracy after he had been told that 85 per cent of the members of the federation were innocent, and only the "inner circle" were guilty of the outrages.[23] Adams was arrested and confessed, but he repudiated his confession. He was then tried in February and in December 1907 at Wallace, Idaho, for murder and the juries disagreed both times. He was transferred to Telluride, Colorado, where he was tried for another murder and acquitted.

To avoid disclosure of his case, the attorney for Canyon County secretly filed a murder charge against William D. Haywood and Charles H. Moyer, respectively secretary-treasurer and president of the Western Federation of Miners, and George Pettibone, a Denver businessman who was presumably directing the campaign of terror. Warrants were issued, and the authorities decided to kidnap the accused from Denver, Colorado, where the defendants were living and thereby avoided a fight over extradition. Accordingly, the approval of the governor of Colorado was secured; the three defendants were arrested on Saturday, February 17, 1906, and brought to Idaho in a special train. Another member of the executive board of the Western Federation of Miners, L. J. Simkins, was also indicted, but was never found.

Attempts to gain the release of the accused through writs of habeas corpus failed when they were rejected by the U.S. Supreme Court. Although the Western Federation of Miners was unaffiliated with the AFL and was promoting a dual federation, the kidnapping of three union leaders aroused the entire labor movement. Led by Eugene V. Debs, the Socialists rallied to the accused, two of whom, Haywood and Moyer, were members of the Socialist party. The AFL supported the defendants. Haywood went to trial after he was denied a change of venue. On May 9, 1907, the case opened. The prosecution was led by former Governor James Hawley, who was assisted by Senator William Borah, the famous orator. Haywood's lawyers were led by E. F. Richardson of Denver, a noted western trial lawyer, and Clarence Darrow of Chicago, who had argued the contempt case for the defendants in the railway strike of 1894.

The case against Haywood rested on the evidence of Orchard. The defense convinced the jury that Orchard's action was motivated by personal vengeance and on July 28, Haywood was acquitted, Moyer was released on bail, and Pettibone, who, the state claimed, had been the link between the terrorists and the inner circle, was brought to trial on November 26, 1907, and acquitted on January 4, 1908.[24]

The Western Federation Turns to Dual Unionism

Three years after its formation, the Western Federation of Miners affiliated with the AFL. It was represented by two delegates at the 1896 convention, Patrick Clifford and Edward Boyce. Both were believers in direct action. Their views on tactics were based upon their experiences in industry and not upon philosophical reflection. Not impressed by what they saw at the AFL convention, they were also dissatisfied with the financial assistance given them during the Leadville, Colorado, strike of that year. In an effort to placate them, Gompers explained the financial limitations under which the AFL operated, the refusal of the unions to pay high per capita taxes, and the inability of the AFL to raise large funds. Gompers' fear of dual unionism and his belief in the unity of labor led him to plead with Boyce to remain within the AFL and fight for changes. Boyce was unconvinced.

In December 1897 the executive board polled its members on a plan for forming a united movement of western workers. The plan was approved, and a convention of 119 delegates, 77 from the metal miners, met in Salt Lake City on May 10, 1898, and organized the Western Labor Union. Gompers was concerned about the split along sectional lines, but was informed by Walter MacArthur, editor of the *Coast Seamen's Journal,* that the Western Labor Union was only the Western Federation of Miners under another name and that it would not amount to much. MacArthur was correct. In the next year the miners were embroiled in the Coeur d'Alene troubles, and Gompers assailed a statement of General H. C. Merriam, who had branded the Western Federation a criminal conspiracy. The AFL endorsed the fight of the Idaho miners, donated a modest sum for their relief, and demanded the withdrawal of federal troops.[25]

AMERICAN LABOR UNION

The Western Labor Union was not a great success. It recruited a few locals of service workers and building craftsmen in a number of metalliferous mining towns, but it never represented a serious threat to the AFL. Nevertheless, ever mindful of the danger of dual unions and hoping to heal the breach, Gompers sought to win the metal miners back to the fold. The 1902 convention of the Western Labor Union, after listening to Frank Morrison, secretary of the AFL, and Eugene V. Debs, who had become a leading Socialist, decided to change the name of the organization to the American Labor Union, shift its headquarters from Denver, Colorado, to Chicago, and inaugurate a general assault upon the AFL. The American Labor Union was, however, no more successful than its predecessor.

INDUSTRIAL UNIONISM

While the hegemony of the AFL was not seriously challenged by the existing dual labor federations, a number of labor leaders and writers were dissatisfied with its rate of progress and policies. In the fall of 1904, six persons active in the socialist and labor movements conferred in Chicago on steps that might be taken to launch a new labor center. These were William E. Trautman, editor of the *Brauer Zeitung;* George Estes, president of the United Brotherhood of Railway Employees; Isaac Cowen, American representative of the Amalgamated Society of Engineers of Great Britain, which had been expelled from the AFL; Clarence Smith, general secretary of the American Labor Union; and Thomas J. Haggerty, editor of the *Voice of Labor,* official organ of the American Labor Union.[26] Invitations for a conference were sent to a larger group. The accompanying letter explained the need for a "working-class political expression, through the Socialist ballot, in order to be sound, must have its counterpart in a labor organization builded as the structure of socialist society, embracing within itself the working-class in approximately the same groups and departments and industries that the workers would assume in the working-class administration of the Co-operative Commonwealth."[27] The recipients were invited to a secret conference at Chicago on January 2, 1905.

Victor Berger, the Socialist editor of Milwaukee, and Max Hayes, a Socialist and a leading member of the International Typographical Union, declined the invitation. Hayes criticized the venture, declaring he wanted to do his fighting within the general labor movement. Twenty persons were present at the secret conference in January where plans for a new labor federation were evolved and a "manifesto" was issued. It pointed out that machinery was wiping out the old skills and that "resistance to capitalist tyranny may be weakened by artificial distinctions."[28] Craft unionism was sharply attacked, and a movement, consisting "of one great industrial union embracing all industries, providing for craft autonomy locally, industrial autonomy internationally, and workingclass unity generally," was endorsed.[29]

THE INDUSTRIAL WORKERS OF THE WORLD

The American Federationist in its March 1905 issue sharply attacked the plan for a new labor federation and attributed the project to Socialists "out to smash the American trade-union movement." The industrial union convention met in Chicago on June 27, 1905. The Western Federation of Miners was the most important labor union represented, and many of the 203 delegates from the 43 organizations spoke only for themselves. Delegates with power to affiliate their unions represented a claimed 50,287 members. Among those was the Socialist Trade and Labor Alliance, which had sent 14 delegates.

The first convention was dominated by William D. Haywood, Debs, De Leon, and Father Thomas J. Haggerty, who was one of the authors of the Industrial Workers of the World preamble. Haggerty also drew the chart of the new organization, showing how workers were organized into industries and industries into departments. Its wheel-like appearance led Luke Grant, the leading labor reporter of the first decade of the century, to describe it as Haggerty's "Wheel of Fortune."[30]

Not many of the delegates could claim a large amount of trade union experience. Those from the Western Federation of Miners—Trautman, Clarence Sherman, and "Mother" Mary Jones of the United Mine Workers —had a fairly long history of participation in labor organizations. Debs had at one time been a trade union officer, and a number of delegates represented local unions. But editors and organizers of Socialist organizations were also delegates, and they represented no one but themselves.

The preamble was a class-war document. Its opening line stated: "The working class and the employing class have nothing in common." Political as well as industrial action was endorsed, although there were a number who wanted to exclude reference to politics. The convention lasted eleven days, named the new federation the Industrial Workers of the World, and elected C. O. Sherman, president; W. E. Trautman, secretary-treasurer; and an executive board of five, including Charles Moyer of the Western Federation of Miners.[31]

Three Stages of the IWW

The history of the IWW can be divided into three stages; the first stage ended in 1909. At the end of the first three years it sloughed off the political Socialists, both the reformers who supported President Sherman and later the verbal revolutionary De Leon and his followers. In the process it lost its most important source of support, the Western Federation of Miners. Moreover, the new organization could report in its first year few successes and many failures. The leaders admitted that IWW strikes were less successful than those conducted by unions of the AFL. In part, the results were due to the greater control exercised by AFL unions in their trades, their greater financial resources, and the experience of the leadership as well as the stability of the membership.

The second convention witnessed a fight to control the new organization, with President Sherman arrayed against Trautman and Vincent St. John, a metal miner and former officer of the Western Federation of Miners. The main charge against Sherman was financial extravagance, but the issues that divided the two factions are not clear. After the differences had been aired in the courts, as a result of the refusal of the Sherman faction to hand over the property, the Trautman-St. John group took control. Thereupon, the Western Federation of Miners, after a bitter debate at its convention, severed its connection with the IWW. But those in control, followers of De Leon and St. John, were temperamentally incompatible. De Leon and his followers were largely vocal revolutionaries, while St. John's legions were believers in and practitioners of direct action. St. John's followers were mainly migratory workers employed in the lumber, metal mining, and seagoing industries.

The 1908 convention witnessed the appearance of J. H. Walsh, a national organizer and head of the "Overalls Brigade," a group of propagandists and soap boxers who came on box cars from Portland, Oregon, to Chicago and held meetings along the way. De Leon's followers were outraged by the behavior of Walsh and his associates, who opened their meetings by singing "Hallelujah, I'm a Bum" and ended them by passing the hat for a collection to finance their journey to the next town. In addition to denying De Leon a seat, the 1908 convention excluded all reference to political action. De Leon and his followers withdrew and charged that the IWW had been captured by anarchists and labeled it as the "bummery," made up of the slum proletariat morally and intellectually unfit to lead labor. They organized the Detroit IWW, which changed its name in 1915 to the Worker's International Industrial Union.[32]

Free-Speech Fights

Free-speech fights and leadership in spontaneous strikes of unorganized workers were the primary activity of the IWW in the second stage of its existence. The first free-speech fight to attract national notice started in Spokane, Washington, in 1909, when the police interfered with the IWW soap boxers. The tactics followed by the IWW in this campaign were similar to those used in subsequent fights of this kind. The local members defied the police and were arrested. A call for the mobilizing of "footloose rebels" at the point of the trouble was issued. Hundreds of IWW members then converged on the community in question, mounted soap boxes, and courted arrest. The "beleaguered" communities, faced by an unexpected increase in their budgets for maintaining prisoners, would at the same time attract a considerable amount of attention. Uusually these tactics led to a compromise that was described as a victory for free speech.

San Diego, California, reacted differently. In that city the IWW campaign was met by a counterorganization of citizens and the imprisonment and manhandling of many of the free-speech fighters. Finally an investigation by Harris Weinstock at the orders of Governor Hiram Johnson castigated the abuses of the citizens' mobs which, through the use of vigilante tactics, not only assaulted members of the IWW engaged in a free speech fight, but also all who refused to approve of the illegal brutality and violations of law.[33]

Spontaneous Strikes

At the same time, the IWW was assuming leadership in spontaneous and unorganized strikes. Beginning with the walkout at the plant of the Pressed Steel Car Company at McKee's Rock, Pennsylvania, the IWW placed itself at the head of a number of desperation strikes in the eastern part of the country. In McKee's Rock, the walkout started over a reduction in pay and involved several thousand workers before it ended. Deputy sheriffs and armed guards surrounded the plant, and clashes between deputies and strikers, in which eleven pickets were killed, followed. Not until August did the IWW enter the dispute. Under the direction of Trautman, a local union was formed. After considerable violence, the management made concessions, and the strikers returned to work early in September. An impressive victory for the IWW, it was marred only by its failure to retain a local at the plant.

In more spectacular fashion, the same story was repeated in the textile industry. The legal reduction of weekly hours of labor of women and minors from fifty-six to fifty-four sparked the spectacular struggle in Lawrence, Massachusetts, in 1912. The strike began following the first pay period for time worked in January 1912. It listed fifty-seven days and involved from 14,000 to 23,000 workers at different times.

The IWW had organized a number of branches in Lawrence, but only the Italian local, established in 1911, managed to retain a few members.[34] The United Textile Workers of America had managed to organize a branch of 212 loom fixers, the most skilled workers in the industry, but the thousands of foreign-born, non-English speaking, semi-skilled, and unskilled workers were unorganized.

A committee from the Lawrence branch of the IWW sought a conference with the mill owners to determine the effect of the reduced schedule upon wages, but most mill owners refused to attend it. Strikes began the first days of January, but they did not become general until January 11. A sharp division existed between the skilled, who were members of the United Textile Workers, and the unskilled in the IWW. By January 14 delegates from English, French, Belgian, Italian, Polish, Lithuanian, and Syrian strikers elected Joseph J. Ettor, an organizer of the IWW, as chairman of the strike committee. Demands were formulated for a 15 per cent increase in wages, double pay for overtime, abolition of the bonus system, and no discrimination against strikers.

Troops appeared in Lawrence on Monday, January 15, and additional companies arrived later. On January 20 dynamite was discovered in a tenement, but it was proved to have been planted by John Breena, a local businessman, in order to discredit the strike. On January 19, President William M. Wood of the American Woolen Company, the largest employer of textile labor in the city, appealed to the workers to return to their jobs.[35]

Efforts to settle the dispute were continually made by city officials, by the State Board of Conciliation and Arbitration, and by distinguished Lawrence citizens. Officers of the American Woolen Company and other textile companies met with committees of strikers, including Ettor and William D. Haywood, who had come to the city to aid the strike. The early meetings failed.

On January 29 a clash between strikers and police resulted in the death of Anna Lo Pezzi, a picket killed by shots from a revolver. Ettor and Arturo Giovanitti, an Italian Socialist active in the strike, were arrested and charged with first-degree murder. To relieve some of the pressure, the strike committee decided to send the children of strikers to the homes of sympathizers in several eastern cities. On February 10 the first contingent of children left for New York City. Colonel E. L. Sweetser announced on February 17 that he would allow no further departure of children unless he was satisfied the consent of the parents had been obtained. On February 22 the marshal of Lawrence said that no more children would be allowed to leave the city. An attempt by the police to prevent the departure of a group of children on February 24 led to a riot in which thirty persons were arrested. Later, other children were allowed to leave without interference.

The action of the authorities aroused a storm of indignation, and resolutions to investigate the Lawrence strike were introduced in the House of Representatives. John Golden, head of the United Textile Workers, was so concerned with the possible effect the IWW might have upon his union that he justified the interference of the police.

Gompers apologized and attributed Golden's opinions to the serious strain under which he had labored. He regretted their affiliation. He, however, "disclaimed any desire to question their right to belong to any organization." He criticized the interference with the departure of the children, and defended the right of the strikers to "engage in the struggle, and as one of the means of aiding them in their struggle they determined to send their children away, and they had the right to do so."[36]

Early in March a number of plants began readjusting their wage scales. On March 19 the American Woolen Company presented a definite offer with specific raises for various jobs, and the strike committee recommended to several thousand strikers at a meeting on the commons that the offer be accepted. The strike was declared off in the mills which accepted the terms.[37]

During the period from January 12 to March 13, 296 persons were arrested on various charges, and since some had more than one charge and trial, 355 cases were tried. Of the total number of cases disposed of, 220 defendants were fined from $1.00 to $100.00. Of those fined, 40 were assessed more than $10.00. Fifty-four defendants were sentenced to prison, the severest sentences were of two years, and 27 received one year. The most serious was the charge of murder against the strike leaders, Ettor and Giovanitti; they were acquitted in November 1912.

The Lawrence strike was a dramatic struggle by thousands of workers, many of them of foreign origin, and their plight attracted nationwide attention. Despite the aid and dramatic leadership furnished by the IWW, the strike led to no permanent organization. Although textile workers had on the whole not been able to maintain stable organizations, the complete erasure of IWW influence raised the question whether the organization was a "revolutionary propaganda" league or a trade union organized on industrial lines. In fact, a small group led by William Z. Foster suggested that the IWW disband and form caucuses for "boring-from-within" the AFL. Foster later left the IWW and established the Syndicalist League of North America for this purpose.

Part of the problem facing the IWW was that its leaders looked upon strikes as propaganda devices. James P. Thompson, a founding member and leading propagandist, regarded the strike as "one big propaganda meeting. Every hour that the strike lasted the One Big Union was spreading like wildfire. The strikers of Lawrence were actually teaching the workers of the country how to fight."[38] The views of Thompson were held by a large number who were opposed to any type of centralized organization—the decentralizers—and wanted to carry the principle of local autonomy to a point where all issues would be decided on a local basis with the main office a center for exchanging information.

The ability of the IWW leaders to mobilize large unskilled masses, to display their poverty and suffering, was of a high order, but they failed in the elementary ability needed to build a permanent organization. This deficiency was also shown in the strike of textile workers in the silk plants of Paterson, New Jersey. A strike of silk workers had started in November 1912, and matters were patched up for a time. The Detroit IWW entered the field, but it was edged out by the more militant Chicago faction. In February 1913 a strike against the Henry Doherty mills was called, and it became general on February 25. Over 24,000 workers were affected. The usual problems confronted the strikers and the IWW leaders; an adamant refusal of the employers to bargain and lack of savings and resources made the strikers dependent upon support that could only be raised by appeals to labor groups and sympathizers. Interference with pickets and threats of violence and arrests were also problems. A bystander was killed in one of the clashes, and the grand jury returned indictments against Patrick Quinlan, a Socialist organizer, and Frederick S. Boyd, a writer; both were sentenced to prison.

Arrests of strikers were common; 2,338 were made. One of the reasons was the refusal of Recorder John F. Carroll to allow meetings. Over one hundred were sentenced to jail. One of the highlights of the strike was a pageant in Madison Square Garden, New York, arranged by writers and artists, including John Sloan, a well-known painter, and John Reed, the future historian of the first days of the October Revolution in Russia. Despite the resistance of the strikers, breaks in the ranks began in June, and by the middle of July, the strike of twenty-two weeks ended.

The IWW also became involved in its "native habitat" at the Durst Brothers ranch at Wheatland, California, in the summer of 1913. Almost 3,800 men, women and children answered the advertisements for hop pickers at the ranch, where they found miserable sanitary conditions, over-crowding, lack of drinking water, and low wages. A mass meeting elected a committee to ask for changes, and the owner slapped Richard Ford, one of the committeemen. The sheriff was sent for after a constable was unable to arrest Ford. The sheriff and several deputies arrived while a meeting was in progress, and during the attempt to arrest Ford, shots were fired. District Attorney Manwell, a deputy sheriff, and two pickets were killed. Ford, Herman Suhr, and two others were arrested and tried in Marysville in January 1914. The pickers were acquitted, and the two others were con-victed of second-degree murder and sentenced to life imprisonment. A campaign for their release was started, and the IWW Hop Pickers' Defense Committee threatened to destroy the crops unless Ford and Suhr were freed. This was one of the arguments Governor Johnson used when he refused to pardon the men. They were finally released after serving almost ten years in prison.

In 1914, William D. Haywood replaced Vincent St. John. In all of its activity, the IWW succeeded in building only two permanent locals with job control: Marine Transport Workers No. 8, with a membership of 3,800 Philadelphia longshoremen, and a small local of Italian bakers in New

York City. The Philadelphia longshoremen's local had been formed in 1913 during a strike on the sugar docks. It was largely the work of George Speed, a member of the IWW Executive Board, Joseph Schmidt, a Polish organizer, and Edward Lewis, one of the great radical soap boxers and mob orators of the time. But the success of these organizations was untypical. In 1914 less than 1,700 votes were cast in the election for the highest office in the organization, a reflection of the low membership.

It was at this point that the IWW embarked upon its third and most active stage which, if it had not been aborted by wartime and postwar prosecutions and persecutions, might have led to the establishment of permanent organizations in a number of industries employing large numbers of semi-skilled and unskilled workers. During a discussion on organizing at the 1914 convention, Frank Little, a member of the general executive board, suggested that the locals bordering on the middle western grain belt might cooperate in a concerted drive to organize the thousands of migratory workers annually employed in the harvesting of the grain crops. At the time, the IWW was mainly composed of local industrial unions directly attached to the central organization. Each local near the grain belt sought to organize the harvest hands who annually flocked to the area in search of temporary employment. Little's proposal, adopted by the convention, was that the efforts of the individual locals be combined.³⁹

A conference of nine locals established the Agricultural Workers Organization 400 in the spring of 1915. It was a centralized industrial union with a secretary and an organization committee responsible for agitation and recruiting. A set of demands was formulated, and a campaign against gamblers and high Jacks who rode the box cars on which the migrants normally traveled and lived in the "jungles" where they ate and spent their time between jobs was undertaken. The new departures were highly successful, and at the end of 1915 the new organization reported a surplus of more than $14,000 in its treasury. Such prosperity had never been achieved by any unit of the IWW. But this success was only a forerunner of things to come. In 1916 the organizers of the IWW embarked on more forcible tactics. Riders on freight cars entering the harvest belt had "to line up," join the IWW, or be unloaded from the trains. These tactics resulted in a large increase in income and members, and although some protesting voices were raised against the shock tactics, the leaders believed they had found a new and effective method of financing their organizing campaigns.⁴⁰

The success achieved by the Agricultural Workers led to the reorganizing of the structure of the IWW at the 1916 convention. Local and industrial unions were abolished and industrial unions with branches, administrative units with limited local autonomy, were established. In addition, mixed locals resembling the federal labor unions of the AFL were retained. Even more important were the funds provided to the general

IWW organization, along with the efforts of the Agricultural Workers Organization in other industries. Campaigns were launched in the lumber, metalliferous mining, and shipping industries. In the lumber industry, the IWW achieved a large measure of success and established the Lumber Workers Industrial Union No. 500.[41]

For the first time the IWW was functioning regularly as a labor organization, using its monies to organize slowly and systematically some of the industrial areas it had staked out for itself. The IWW publications began to stress the virtue of employment, improving conditions on the job, and the organization of the unorganized. The soap boxer lost his dominant position. The change in emphasis is clear from the views of Joseph Ettor, who refused to continue as a general organizer. Ettor believed that to be effective a general organizer would need a corps of assistants to direct. He argued that the IWW did not have the "funds to warrant undertaking any serious and extensive organizing campaigns."[42] Although Ettor's letter was written to the convention of 1916, when conditions he delineated had been drastically changed, his letter indicates the earlier problems of the IWW and the effect of the drives in the grain belt upon its activity.

The IWW made considerable gains in several industries employing a large complement of migratory workers. In the midwest grain belt, the Non-Partisan League, a farmers' political group influential in North Dakota, asked the Agricultural Workers Organization of the IWW to work out an agreement. Arthur Lesuer, a St. Paul attorney and counsel for the Non-Partisan League, addressed the 1917 spring meeting of the Agricultural Workers Industrial Union No. 400. A conference between Non-Partisan League representatives and the Agricultural Workers' leaders in Minneapolis devised a tentative agreement. Forrest Edwards, secretary of the Agricultural Workers Industrial Union No. 400, addressed a meeting of farmers at Minot, North Dakota, explaining the proposal.

The agreement provided for a wage of $4.00 a day for ten hours' work. The IWW agreed to supply workers pledged not to call strikes and to pay railroad fare instead of moving on freight trains.[43] The agreement was submitted to the membership in the bulletin of the Agricultural Workers Industrial Union No. 400 of June 25, 1917. Haywood objected and cited Article 3, paragraph 6 of the IWW constitution: "Any agreement entered into between the members of any union and their employers as a final settlement of any difficulty or trouble which may occur between them, shall not be considered valid or binding until the same shall have the approval of the General Executive Board of the Industrial Workers of the World."[44] Edwards assured Haywood that "it is nothing more or less than a verbal agreement. . . . It is one thing to have a theory and fine system of philosophy, but to apply that to conditions you are actually confronted with."[45]

The agreement was not enthusiastically received in many parts of the Non-Partisan League. Its members, far advanced politically in terms of their own problems and willing to support general labor measures, were not always ideal employers, and occasionally found members of the IWW difficult and undisciplined. The tentative wage agreement may also have appeared high in some sections of North Dakota, for normally rates were made on a local basis and were influenced by crop conditions. Even though the agreement was never finally consummated, its negotiation was sign of the changes taking place within the IWW and the effect of membership expansion upon the outlook of some of the leaders.

CHAPTER 23

Immigration and Organized Labor

At the beginning of its history the United States welcomed the immigrant. People were needed to fill the open spaces, till the soil, and provide labor for road and factory. A comparatively underdeveloped country, the youthful nation in the late eighteenth century was dependent upon the skills and know-how of Europe. The English prohibition against immigration of skilled craftsmen was frequently evaded before it was repealed by the British Parliament in 1824. Work skills had to be imported before they were "grown" at home, and many craftsmen were brought here in the first part of the nineteenth century on contract. Recruiting was usually carried on by the employer and his agent, and fares were advanced if necessary.[1]

Prior to 1820, the immigrant was allowed to finance his passage by means of an indenture under which he agreed to work a given period in return for the fare advanced to him. Immigration was largely left to individual decision.

Records of the number of immigrants coming to the United States were first established in 1820, and they show 8,326 new arrivals that year. Their numbers rose steadily reaching the high of 1,285,309 newcomers in 1907. The annual average of immigrants to the United States in the period of 1820 to 1830 was 13,802; for the decade 1900 to 1910, 879,539.[2] They declined to 782,870 in 1908, and reached another peak of 1,218,480 in 1914. World War I was a barrier, and the quota laws of the postwar period prevented the entrance of large numbers of new arrivals.

Up to the late 1880's the majority of immigrants came from the northern European countries—the British Isles, Germany, France, and the Scandinavian countries. Southern and eastern Europeans contributed few persons to the early immigrant stream; their proportion reached 25 per cent for the first time in 1887. In 1895 it had risen to 43.2 per cent and in the following year to 57 per cent. During the ten-year period between 1901 and 1910, 71.9 per cent of European immigrants came from southern and eastern Europe.[3]

Immigrants provided an almost inexhaustible supply of labor for the burgeoning economy of the late decades of the nineteenth century and the years before World War I. Inevitably, they found jobs in industries employing large numbers of native-born workers and earlier arrivals. During the last decades of the last century Slovaks and Magyars replaced native workers and those of German, Irish, and English origin in the iron and steel industry; in slaughtering and meat packing, German and Irish workers were ousted by Lithuanians, Bohemians, and Moravians. Native-born and German and English workers were replaced in the bituminous coal industry by Slovaks, Poles, and Italians; and Poles and Italians were substituted for English, French Canadians, and Irish workers in the woolen and worsted and other kinds of textile mills. Large numbers of southern and western European immigrants moved into the clothing industries and metalliferous mining. In many industries the native workers and earlier immigrants were pushed out of the semi-skilled and unskilled jobs, and they became concentrated in the skilled and supervisory positions. The influx of the "new" immigrants created widespread hostility against the invaders. It was widely held that they lowered wages, dragged down working conditions, and were not responsive to the appeal and discipline of labor organizations.

Such hostility was not much different from the kind encountered by the immigrants of the earlier periods. "In the decade, 1840–1850, the Irish immigrant girls were first employed in the New England cotton mills; the native women who had previously been the textile operatives protested; twenty years later the Irish girls, after they had become firmly fixed in the industry, rebelled because of the entrance of French Canadian girls into the spinning rooms, just as the French Canadian women are refusing to be brought into close working relations with the Polish and Italian females who are entering the cotton mills at the present time."[4]

The labor shortage occasioned by the withdrawal of manpower for the Civil War armies encouraged philanthropists and entrepreneurs to search for more immigrants. The Emigrant Aid Society was formed in Boston in 1863 by a number of businessmen interested in textile, machine and iron manufacturing, transportation, and shipping. The society hoped to raise a fund for financing immigration through gifts and loans. Its efforts were not immediately successful.

In the following year, the American Emigrant Company was organized as a private profit-making enterprise and was a merger of two established firms. The company sought to collect a million dollars from merchants and manufacturers to underwrite the immigration of workers from abroad. When it failed in its campaign for private support, it tried to gain subsidies for this purpose from the United States government. Although subsidies were denied, the government, because of labor shortages, encouraged the inflow of people from other lands. Lincoln, in a message to Congress in December 1863, urged enactment of a law to encourage immigration.

On July 4, 1864, the Act to Encourage Immigration was passed by Congress. Under its provisions immigrants were permitted to pledge wages for not exceeding twelve months to pay the expenses of passage. The debt could be enforced in the courts. Such a contract could not legally be considered as creating the condition for the existence of slavery or servitude. The immigrant whose passage was financed by an employer agreed to work for a maximum of twelve months under conditions lawfully presented for the regulation of his labor force. Agencies recruiting labor in Europe were paid fees by employers, and commissions from steamship and railroad companies added to the recruiter's income. The law was repealed in 1866, but the right to bring labor under contract to the United States was recognized.

CHINESE IMMIGRATION

Organized labor's attitude towards immigration was not always uniform. Eventually, it favored restriction, but its earliest opposition was directed against the Oriental.

In 1852, Governor Bigler of California recommended restrictive legislation against the Chinese. It did not arouse a popular response, but a law taxing foreign miners was passed the following year. A law placing a head tax upon Chinese immigrants, enacted by the California legislature in 1855, was declared unconstitutional by the California Supreme Court.

The Burlingame Treaty, signed by the United States and China in 1868, gave the same rights to Chinese nationals as were enjoyed by other foreigners in the United States. It led to an increase in the number of Chinese immigrating to the United States. Net immigration of Chinese, as shown by arrivals and departures to and from California by sea, increased sharply for three years after the signing of the Burlingame Treaty, receded for one year, and increased sharply again. By 1876 it was estimated that 93,000 Chinese lived in California.[5]

Even the bitterest opponents of Chinese immigration had to admit that the Chinese were useful and industrious. The Joint Special Committee of the United States, appointed in 1876 to investigate Chinese immigration, concluded "that the resources of California and the Pacific Coast have been more rapidly developed with the cheap and docile labor of Chinese than would have been without this element. So far as material prosperity is concerned, it cannot be doubted that the Pacific Coast has been a great gainer."[6] The committee found further "that many enterprising men find their profit in Chinese immigration, and the general resources of the Pacific are being rapidly developed by means of Chinese labor. Among those who testified were those who largely employ Chinese, or are interested in their transportation, and who find a profit therein. These testified that the results of Chinese immigration have been invariably beneficial in enhancing the material prosperity of the coast."[7]

Chinese workers were employed in a variety of trades and industries. Laundry work, cigar making, sewing machine work, and several other light industries were almost monopolized by Chinese labor. Woolen and silk manufacture, fruit picking, gardening, building levees for the restoration of tule lands, railroad building, placer mining, basket peddling of fruits and vegetables, fishing, and selling fish were among the activities employing Chinese labor. A representative of anti-Chinese societies testified that in these activities, the Chinese "have nearly driven out the entire white labor."[8]

Chinese competition with white labor generated a reaction and led to the forming of anti-coolie clubs in various parts of California. Their members pledged themselves not to employ Chinese workmen or purchase merchandise from those who employed Chinese. The clubs formed the Anti-Chinese Union, "composed, of course, of the working classes, the active members; in fact, being almost entirely workingmen, but they represent all nationalities. It may be that the Irish element predominates, because the Irish element predominates in the city [San Francisco], but there are Germans, Americans and all nationalities, and the membership is confined to no religion."[9]

The Sand Lots Riots

It was the fear of competition and unemployment which enabled the racist demagogue Dennis Kearney to transform a meeting on the sand lots of San Francisco, on July 23, 1877, demanding reform of labor conditions, into a howling anti-Chinese mob bent on the forcible expulsion of all Chinese workers from employment. The riots lasted for five days and only stern action by the police and citizen deputies prevented its spread through the city. The aim of the rioters was to force dismissal of all Chinese workers by their employers, an aim in many instances temporarily achieved, although most of the dismissed were rehired after order was restored.[10]

From the time of the sand lots riots, the California labor movement became an aggressive pleader for restrictions on Chinese and other types of Oriental immigration, regarding these workers as a threat to the wages, working conditions, and general welfare of all workers. California labor, because it needed support of its anti-Oriental policy before Congress, asked and received the assistance of organized labor in other parts of the country in this campaign.

C. F. Burgman, a cigarmaker and delegate from the Representative Assembly of Trade and Labor Unions of San Francisco to the founding meeting of the Federation of Organized Trades and Labor Unions of the United States and Canada, presented an anti-Chinese resolution in Pittsburgh, Pennsylvania, in 1881. The resolution called "for the use of our best efforts to get rid of this monstrous immigration." The convention, a direct predecessor of the AFL, adopted the resolution with one dissenting vote. Opposition to Chinese immigration became an article of faith of the AFL, in part because white labor leaders could sympathize with their fellow workers facing severe competition from a strange people, and partly because Samuel Gompers, also a cigarmaker by trade, was directly aware of the disastrous effect the competition of Chinese cigarmakers had upon the jobs and income of white members of the Cigar Makers' Union in San Francisco. The agitation of organized labor led to the enactment of the first Chinese exclusion law in 1882. It provided for the suspension of all Chinese immigration for ten years and was re-enacted in 1892. It should be noted that the AFL was not functioning in 1882. The Federation of Organized Trade and Labor Unions of the United States and Canada did not have enough funds to rent an office or employ a legislative representative to appear before Congress. Some historians persist mistakenly in attributing the anti-Chinese agitation within the labor movement to Gompers.

Soon after the establishment of the California State Federation of Labor in 1901 the renewal of the Chinese Exclusion law was placed before Congress, and the state federation spoke out strongly for its re-enactment. At its 1902 convention, the federation called for the re-enactment of the Chinese Exclusion Act by Congress, charged the Chinese immigrants with having been "detrimental to the general welfare of our country," and entered the lists against the Japanese immigrant who according to the convention was "a willing worker for wages less than a Chinese worker . . . and being more favored is a greater menace to our laboring population than the Chinese." The convention promised to "demand the enactment of legislation restricting immigration of that race to the United States."[11] Samuel Gompers was a leader in the campaign.[12]

The memorial calling upon Congress to re-enact the restrictions upon Chinese immigration in 1902 was approved by 149 California labor unions, 88 of them in San Francisco. The Santa Clara Socialist party also signed.[13] The law was extended in ten-year intervals until it was repealed in the 1940's.

Both the Knights of Labor and the National Labor Union had opposed Oriental immigration. The latter had in 1869 expressed its "unalterable opposition to the importation of a servile race for the sole and only purpose of tampering with the labor of the American workingmen."[14] The resolution, according to Powderly, was directed against Chinese labor. Three conventions of the Knights of Labor "had adopted resolutions unfavorable to the residence of the Chinese in America."[15]

The Union Label

The anti-Chinese legislation led to the appearance of the first union label. In 1872 a San Francisco cigarmaker hired a number of Chinese, and the "invasion" aroused the bitter opposition of white unionized cigarmakers of the city. Boycotts against the product of Chinese labor were instituted. To distinguish the product manufactured by Americans from those of the Chinese, a label was adopted in 1874. Thus, the first union label appeared as a weapon against the unorganized Oriental worker. It was white in color to indicate to the purchaser that he was buying a product manufactured by Caucasian workers. It appealed to the smoker: "Buy no cigars except from the box marked with the trade-union label, thus you help maintain the white as against the coolie standard of life and work."[16]

CONTRACT LABOR

Workers in the United States, many of whom had themselves come from other lands, opposed unrestricted movement from abroad because of its effect upon the supply of labor. Even when the opposition took on racial overtones, it was primarily based upon economic grounds, although leaders of labor did not at times hesitate to use the bias against the foreigner or special groups as an argument for restriction. As early as 1865, the Molders' Union and the Sons of Vulcan, a union of steelworkers, spoke out against imported strikebreakers. American unions sought to work out arrangements with the English-based Amalgamated Society of Engineers and the Amalgamated Society of Carpenters which would prevent the recruitment of strikebreakers for American firms.

Reaction of foreign workers depended upon their experiences at home. During a strike of bituminous coal miners in Pennsylvania and West Virginia against wage reductions, British miners were brought in to replace them. However, when the recruits came from areas in which unions were strong, they frequently refused to accept jobs during labor disputes. "On the other hand, immigrant miners imported from South Wales where strong trade unions had not developed up to this time sometimes behaved quite differently. . . . During 1865 many Welsh miners were said to have contributed to the successful cutting of wages."[17]

Immigration was stimulated by advertising campaigns abroad. According to the Immigration Commission, "Advertisements offering inducements to immigrants to proceed to the bituminous coal fields of western Pennsylvania were carried in New York newspapers [in 1869], and these announcements were frequently copied by European newspapers."[18]

Labor organizations did not at first oppose immigration, but with the growth in the number of annual arrivals fear that the flow of workers from abroad was adversely affecting the ability of labor in the United States to raise its wages were increasingly expressed. Land grant companies, steamship operators, and manufacturers sent agents to Europe to scour the countryside in search of labor for employment in the United States. In time, labor leaders, many of whom were born abroad, began to question the justice of imposing a tariff for the protection of manufactured goods in the United States while allowing the free entry of labor into the United States to compete with those employed. At the request of the Window Glass Workers' Union, the Knights of Labor drafted a bill forbidding the importation of foreign workmen; the bill was sponsored by Congressman Thomas Ferrel of New Jersey and Martin Foran of Pennsylvania. The general assembly of 1884 amended its preamble by adding: "That the importation of foreign labor under contract be prohibited."[19] In cooperation with Glass Bottle Blowers Assembly No. 300, the Knights of Labor succeeded in gaining the adoption of the Alien Contract Act by Congress in 1885.

It provided that "it shall be unlawful for any person, company, partnership or corporation in any manner to prepay the transportation or in any way assist or encourage the importation of any alien or aliens, and foreigners, into the United States . . . under contract or agreement."[20] It set a penalty of $1,000 for each violation. The act exempted from its restrictions skilled labor in short supply, members of the performing arts, and domestic servants. The law was amended several times, and the courts sought to give the law a liberal construction so that it would not "trespass upon the traditional American policy that extends welcome to all."[21]

The Alien Contract law differed from the earlier laws enacted by Congress—those of 1875 and 1882. The legislation of 1875 and 1882 sought to exclude the criminal and pauper, the ones who would or could not support themselves, but the alien anticontract labor laws of 1885, 1887, and 1888 tried to exclude those who had provided themselves with means of support in advance. The alien contract labor law was the first enactment to exclude able and industrious Europeans. Such a precedent had been established by the Chinese Exclusion Act of 1882 by excluding immigrants whose low standard of living and industriousness had enabled them to displace American workmen. It was, however, politically more difficult to exclude Europeans. "Any restriction which could hope for adoption must be a specific protection against a definite recognized evil. This evil existed and came prominently into view. It was the artificial immigration induced by employers for the purpose of breaking labor organizations."[22]

The most authoritative and detailed investigation on the subject expressed the view that the "extensive employment of southern and eastern European immigrants in manufacturing and mining has in many places resulted in the weakening of labor organizations or in their complete disruption. This condition has been due to the character of the recent immigrant labor supply and to the fact that such large numbers of recent immigrants found employment in American industry within a short period of time. On account of their lack of industrial training and experience before reaching this country, their low standards of living as compared with native American wage-earners, their necessitous condition on finding employment in this country, and their tractability, the southern and eastern Europeans, as already noted, have been willing to accept the rates of compensation and the working conditions as they have found them in the United States."[23]

In a report to the Industrial Commission, Professor John R. Commons noted that labor organizations were inclined to oppose the constant influx "of poor but hardworking people who are unfamiliar with the traditions and customs of organization, unaccustomed to the rules and the control which it imposes, incapable of learning the same through their ignorance of the language, and, moreover, forced by their poverty to work with docility and desperate energy for him who first gives him a job. . . . About 2 or 3 years after landing are enough to bring the immigrant to a realizing sense of the need of organization and to train him up to a certain ability in promoting it, but by that time a further crowd of inexperienced immigrants, who can not be reached by the organization, has gained a decisive influence in the trade."[24]

It is the adverse influence of the immigrant upon the labor market rather than opposition based on race or religion which accounts for the attitude of organized labor. Not until 1896 did the AFL endorse any restrictive measures, but it was moving gradually in that direction. The 1892 AFL convention endorsed a resolution of the United Garment Workers' of America denouncing the importing of workers presumably for agricultural settlement by the United Hebrew Charities of New York. The resolution noted that these immigrants were turned over to the "Sweater and so-called trade schools, are taught the rudiments of various sub-branches of the tailoring trade, and then cast upon the already demoralized and over-stocked labor markets."[25]

In his report to the convention of the same year, Gompers asserted that "unrestricted immigration is working a great injury to the people of our country." He decried the work of charitable groups which gathered hordes of people in Europe and dump them into the mines, railroads, and sweatshops. He expressed approval of restriction and regulation, a view which he had also favored at the 1891 convention.[26]

A proposal endorsing a bill in Congress to set up an educational test was endorsed by the resolutions' committee. The committee approved the "effort . . . in favor of the restriction of the artificial flow of immigration, encouraged as it is too often by avaricious steamship lines and corporations desirous of overcrowding the labor market with cheap foreign workers, in order to depreciate the price of labor . . . we nevertheless hold that extreme measures of restriction would be contrary to the spirit of our time, and the welfare of our country. And in doing so we do not share in the old Know-nothing sentiment which use the immigration question as a pretext to gloss over social wrongs."[27]

After a long debate, the resolution was referred to the executive council with instructions to report to the affiliates so that they would instruct their delegates on the action to be taken on this issue. At the next convention a mild educational test for immigrants seeking entry was endorsed. The federation always emphasized that its attitude toward restriction was not based upon any concept of racial superiority, but was designed to reduce the pressure upon the workers in the United States by continual increases in the labor supply.

The federation supported the quota laws limiting immigration to a percentage of nationals living in the United States. The law of 1924 was attacked as favoring immigrants from northern Europe at the expense of those from Italy and the Slavic nations, but to the federation these measures represented a means whereby the continual flow of immigration could be restricted.[28]

The federation, continuing to favor restricted immigration, relented only during World War II when it recognized the necessity for a more liberal policy on the admission of displaced persons. The 1946 AFL convention favored "the immediate entry of immigrants composed of displaced persons in Europe . . . which will permit the unfilled quotas of the war period to be completed by the entering into our country of the number of immigrants who otherwise would have been able to enter our ports if it had not been for the war, such action in no way modifying the existing immigration laws which have always had the support of the American Federation of Labor."[29] In subsequent conventions, the AFL favored more generous treatment of displaced persons. On immigration in general, the labor movement has favored restriction, although opposition to parts of the McCarren-Walter Act was registered by both the AFL and CIO. Some relaxation in views on restriction took place and the organizations of labor favored limited admission of refugees in the 1950's, and also of Hungarian nationals who had fought against their Communist government during the uprising in that city. In its long efforts to win and retain restrictions upon entry to the United States, the labor movement has been influenced by a desire to prevent increases in the supply of labor. Its fear of the immigrant was motivated by the effect of entry of large numbers upon the supply of labor and wages of those already in the United States. Labor organizations believed the worker was entitled to the same kind of protection as the manufacturer enjoyed through the tariff, elimination or reduction of competition in his home market. Leaders who were themselves of foreign origin did not see any contradiction in their espousal of limitation of the flow of workers into the United States. Like Socialist Congressman Victor Berger, they did not believe that because all workers were brothers, all had to assemble in Milwaukee. No matter how the fight for restriction is regarded, and it is a practice that extends beyond the United States, it should be recognized that the source for this agitation was fear of competition for a job and not fear of another race or religion.

CHAPTER 24

Defense and War

HISTORICAL POSITION

The American labor movement, like those of other countries, was opposed
to militarism and war. Fear that large armies might be used for suppression
of labor within the country and for adventures abroad dominated the minds
of leaders of labor in the nineteenth and early part of the present century.
The AFL expressed concern that the Spanish-American War might lead to
the establishment of an imperial republic, and that the maintenance of a
large standing army would become necessary if the United States were to
force its will upon foreign peoples. The 1899 AFL convention warned
against foreign entanglements in Europe and Asia, the failure to allow self-
rule for the Philippine Islands, and the raising of a standing army to more
than 25,000 men.[1]

EUROPEAN WAR

At the outbreak of war in Europe in 1914 the AFL repeated its historical
pacifist sentiments. It lamented the low value placed upon human life,
hoped that the decision on peace and war would be lodged directly in the
hands of the people, endorsed a league of nations for maintaining peace,
attacked militarism, and pointed to the danger of large standing armies.[2]

As war in Europe continued, concern that the United States might be
attacked or be compelled to intervene increased, at least in some sections of
public opinion. In August 1916, Congress created a Council of National

309

Defense composed of six members of the President's Cabinet. On October 30, Gompers was appointed as a member of the Advisory Committee of the Council of National Defense and chairman of the Committee on Labor, including conservation and welfare of workers. The job carried no salary, and its acceptance was approved by the AFL Executive Council. As war approached, Gompers was convinced that labor had to cooperate or lose the possibility of influencing decisions. In his view: "Either duties and service in connection with national defense will be imposed upon the workers without their advice when formulating these plans, or Labor must make this an opportunity for emphasizing the tremendous service that it has rendered to society, both in peace and in war, and for demanding that all plans be in harmony with the thought that human life and human welfare are the ultimate purpose which both peace and war serve. By following this constructive policy, Labor will be assuming toward this critical situation in which the nation now finds itself its rightful position towards all national problems and relations."[3] With the approval of the executive council, a meeting of the heads of affiliated national and international unions and the railway brotherhoods was called in Washington on March 12, 1917.

Present at this conference, in addition to the executive council, were 148 representatives of 79 affiliated organizations, 5 unaffiliated unions including representatives from the 4 railroad brotherhoods, and from 5 departments of the AFL. The statement, "American Labor's Position in Peace and in War," issued by the conference declared:

War has never put a stop to the necessity for struggle to establish and maintain industrial rights. Wage-earners in war time must, as has been said [,] keep one eye on the exploiters at home and the other upon the enemy threatening the national government. Such exploitation makes it impossible for a warring nation to mobilize effectively its full strength for outward defense.

We maintain that it is the fundamental step in preparedness for the nation to set its own house in order and to establish at home justice in relations between men. Previous wars, for whatever purpose waged, developed new opportunities for exploiting wage earner. . . . Labor was stripped of its means of defense against enemies at home and was robbed of the advantages, the protections, the guarantees of justice that had been achieved after ages of struggle. For these reasons workers have felt that no matter what the result of war, as wage-earners they generally lost.[4]

The statement noted that as "the representatives of the wage-earners we assert that conditions of work and pay in government employment and in all occupations should conform to principles of human welfare and justice. . . . The one agency which accomplishes this for the workers is the organized labor movement. The greatest step that can be made for national defense is not to bind and throttle the organized labor movement but to afford its greatest scope and opportunity for voluntary effective cooperation in spirit and action."[5]

As the next step, Gompers, as head of the Committee on Labor, called a meeting of representatives of labor, employers, and the public, and a statement was drawn up and submitted for approval by the Council of National Defense. A permanent organization was formed and an executive committee of eleven appointed. The following eight national committees, each headed by a chairman, were organized: wages and hours, mediation and conciliation, women and industry, welfare work, information and statistics, press, publicity and coordination of social agencies, and cost of living.

A proposed statement, which included the notice that "neither employers nor employees shall endeavor to take advantage of the country's necessities to change existing standards," aroused immediate opposition within the ranks of labor. Several union leaders protested the policy in letters to Gompers, who explained that neither he nor "any other representative of the American Federation of Labor has announced to the public or made any promise to any one in any form that 'there shall be no strikes of any kind during the war.' "6 Gompers explained that his agreement did not mean that there should not be any change in standards, since many workers would require a wage increase to maintain their existing real wage. He also assured President Daniel J. Tobin of the Teamsters' Union that the "resolutions in question clearly apply only to the large industries and the transportation systems whose operation are essential to the prosecution of the war. They are not intended to cover every petty labor difference in the country, though it is hoped that patriotic regard will be had by all citizens to the need of possible maximum of industrial peace everywhere."7

Special Labor Boards

At the outbreak of war, Secretary of War Newton D. Baker appointed Professor Felix Frankfurter special assistant to deal with labor problems. Frankfurter served until his appointment to the President's Mediation Commission and was succeeded by Walter Lippmann. When the latter was assigned to other war work, Stanley King was appointed. The War Department sought to handle labor matters through the U.S. Labor Department. To avoid differences, Secretary of War Baker entered on June 19, 1917, into an informal agreement with Gompers which "formed the basis of the [War] department's entire labor policy in its subsequent building program."8

Under this agreement, the Cantonment Adjustment Commission, the first of a number of boards and commissions was created to deal with labor relations. Members of this crucial commission were General E. H. Garlington, representing the Army; John R. Alpine, president of the Plumbers' Union, the labor member; and Walter Lippmann, who served for the public. On June 20, 1917, Louis B. Wehle, representing the Secretary of War, informed the AFL that "it must be clearly understood, as a basis for any labor adjustment machinery, that the government cannot commit itself in any way to the closed shop, and that the conditions in force on June 1, 1917, do not include any provisions which have reference to the employment of non-union labor." Gompers acknowledged that Wehle's view of the memorandum was correct, and that it "had referred only to union hours and wages. The question of union shop was not included."[9]

The failure to include the closed shop was protested by President William Hutcheson of the Carpenters' Union, who sharply criticized Gompers for agreeing to such terms. After an exchange between the two men, Hutcheson reluctantly conceded that it would have been difficult to impose the closed shop in government construction, but he continued to believe that Gompers had gone beyond his powers. The government was aware that the building trades were well organized and that they could, because of the tremendous volume of work and the importance of time, meet the needs of the government for construction workers. Union wages and hours were to be paid on the constructing of cantonments, and disputes were to be submitted to the Cantonment Adjustment Board. On July 27, 1917, the initial arrangement between the Secretary of War and Gompers was extended to cover other government construction work which might be carried on by the War Department.[10] With few exceptions, the commission settled all disputes, and virtually no serious interruption of building needed for war purposes took place.[11]

The Shipbuilding Labor Adjustment (Macy) Board

The attempt of Germany to blockade the Allied nations through the use of submarine warfare gave ship construction a crucial importance in the government's war program. The Shipping Labor Board on August 20, 1917, signed an agreement with the heads of the building and metal trades unions. W. L. Hutcheson of the Carpenters' Union would not sign because of the government's refusal to grant him the closed shop. Under the arrangement, all disputes concerning wages and working conditions in the repair or construction of ships would be settled by the Shipping Labor Adjustment Board headed by E. V. Macy, with L. A. Coolidge representing the government and A. J. Berres, the Metal Trades Department of the AFL. Hutcheson refused to appoint a representative. The board used the standards prevailing in the area for setting wages and working conditions which generally meant the use of union rates as a standard. At first the board ruled only in cases where disputes had arisen over the terms of employment. "Gradually, however, it began to feel its way toward legislating for all the manual trades in all the yards of a district irrespective of whether disputes had arisen."[12]

Eventually, board findings on wages and other conditions of employment were extended to all yards in a district. This approach was resented by the strong unions in Seattle and San Francisco, which believed their members had the power to gain higher wages if allowed to bargain freely with their employers.

Marine and Dock Industrial Relations Division

The Marine and Dock Industrial Relations Division was set up by the U.S. Shipping Board to handle wages and other issues affecting officers and crews on seagoing vessels. In May 1917 the Atlantic Agreement was worked out at a conference between the Shipping Board, the Shipping Committee of the Council of National Defense (on which shipowners were represented), and the International Seamen's Union. Wages and other standards were fixed under the agreement. Appeals were issued for seamen who had taken shore jobs to return to their former occupation and help relieve the labor shortage. The agreement was accepted by the unions and shipowners on the Pacific and Atlantic coasts.

In contrast, the shippers on the Great Lakes would not cooperate with the board or sign the call for the return of former seamen to the industry. Shipping on the Great Lakes was dominated by the large steel companies, which recruited their crews through the halls of the Lake Carriers' Association. Employees on the vessels of the Great Lakes were required to hold "continuous discharge books" without which employment could not be obtained. The certificate had to be deposited with the master and was returned with comments on the qualifications and character of the holder at the termination of his employment on the vessel. The union argued that the certificate was actually a device for black-listing active union men.

Representatives of the Lake Carriers' Association refused to attend meetings at which representatives of the International Seamen's Union were present. It was still possible to adjust wages, but no agreement on the use of discharge books or acceptance of the other features of the Atlantic Agreement could be reached. A strike of the Great Lakes shipping was scheduled for July 28, 1918. The strike was averted only by the intervention of the Shipping Board which compelled substantial compliance with the union demands.[13]

National Adjustment Commission

By agreement of the shipping operators, the AFL, and the International Longshoremen's Association, the National Adjustment Board was organized to adjust disputes between longshoremen and stevedores. Their authority was limited to the Atlantic and Gulf coasts because of opposition to the presence of union representatives by employers on the Great Lakes and the Pacific Coast. The National Adjustment Commission did not try to exercise authority in these areas except in special cases. Peace in the industry was generally maintained.

There was some hope that the system of peaceful settlements would be continued in the longshore industry after the war. In June 1919 the dock section of the National Adjustment Commission was able to obtain an agreement that the wartime truce would be made permanent. Although both the International Longshoremen's Association and Stevedores approved of the arrangement, it broke down in its first test in the New York harbor.[14]

Railroads

Shortly after the entry of the United States into World War I, the heads of the major railroads were called into conference by Daniel Willard, president of the Baltimore and Ohio Railroad Company and Chairman of the Advisory Commission's Committee on Transportation and Communication. At the meeting on April 11, 1917, the railroad executives pledged themselves to coordinate operations in a continental railway system and merge their operations. An executive committee, which became known as the Railroads' War Board, was appointed to direct the cooperative effort of the carriers with mileage of about 260,000 miles.[15]

The voluntary method seemed ineffective. "The labor situation was one of constantly growing menace with which the railroad companies were not able to deal, either acting individually or through the Railroads' War Board."[16] The railroads sought to hold off the extension of the shopcrafts' unions, which had won recognition on many roads but could not obtain a foothold on some of the more important carriers. As a result of pressure, the shopcrafts strengthened their positions on the railroads in the southeast and were able through the "Southeastern Agreement" of the winter of 1916–1917 to gain recognition from the principal roads in that territory. This successful campaign, added to the shortage of labor and the need for railroad service, created a favorable opportunity for the extension of the shopcraft unions. They now served notice that wages and working conditions would have to be standardized by January 1, 1918, or the roads would face a strike. In response to this threat, the railroads announced their willingness "unreservedly to place our interests in the hands of the President for protection, and for dispostion as he may determine is necessary in the public interest."[17]

Labor conditions, increasing costs of operation, and the belief that the carriers had not unified their operations adequately led the government to take over the railroads at the end of December 1917. The threat of a strike by the shopcrafts forced the government to transfer the controversy to the U.S. Secretary of Labor for settlement. The shopcrafts were granted full recognition on all roads. In February 1918 the Division of Transportation was created with W. S. Carter, the president of the Brotherhood of Firemen and Enginemen, as director. By a letter of February 14, 1918, the Director General of Railroads ordered the improvement of conditions in shopcraft labor. Later in the month, an order barring discrimination for membership or nonmembership in a union was issued. "As a result, the shopcrafts, the maintenance of way employees, the clerks, station men, freight-house men, *et cetera,* were organized promptly into local unions on the various railroads not already recognizing them and these local organizations became parts of the respective national labor organizations."[18]

Boards of adjustment of equal numbers from the unions and management were set up to settle grievances. Of the 5,000 to 6,000 cases considered by the three adjustment boards, only about ten cases were taken to the Director General of Railroads for determination; the others were settled by the boards. At about the same time, a Railroad Wage Commission, headed by Secretary of the Interior Franklin K. Lane, was appointed to recommend changes in compensation. A wage increase was recommended, and a Board of Railroad Wages and Working Conditions appointed to eliminate inequities between wages paid for similar work and to devise levels which would make remuneration of railroad men competitive with other industries, and thereby enable the roads to recruit labor. In July 1918 substantial changes in the wages of shopcrafts were made, and they were standardized on a national basis.

Increases in wages and working conditions were made to various classes of railroad labor during 1918. But inequities developed as a result of the timing of wage changes. The shopcraft unions insisted that they were entitled to a wage increase, and when the Board of Wages did not recommend what they regarded as adequate increases, unauthorized strikes of shopmen followed on many roads during the fall of 1919. Director General of Railroads Hines estimated that 200,000 shop craftsmen were out on unauthorized strikes during the fall of 1919.[19]

In the latter part of 1919 the Railroad Administration signed national agreements with the unions. They were made "in lieu of wage increases on the belief that they would impose on the transportation service a much less burden than would result if a wage increase were made. The agreements were signed in the latter part of 1919 to carry out in good faith commitments made earlier in the year to compose extremely difficult labor situations."[20]

Coal

The U.S. Fuel Administration was organized in August 1918 with Harry A. Garfield as fuel administrator. John P. White, president of the United Mine Workers of America, was appointed one of the labor advisers to the administrator. Under the Washington Agreement of October 6, 1917, wages were increased, and the contract made was to run to the end of the war or for two years after April 1918. In addition to these agencies, boards to oversee labor standards in firms manufacturing Army clothing, as well as the harness and saddlery industry, were established.

President's Mediation Commission

On September 19, 1917, President Wilson appointed the President's Mediation Commission to investigate labor conditions in the Rocky Mountain area, the Southwest, and the Pacific Coast. Made up of the Secretary of Labor, two representatives from employers, and two from employees, the commission was directed to "deal with employers and employees in a conciliatory spirit, seek to compose differences and to allay misunderstanding, and in any way that be open to them show the active interest of the government in furthering arrangements just to both sides. Wherever it is deemed advisable conferences of employers and employees should be called for the purpose of working out a mutual understanding between them which will insure a continued operation of the industry on conditions acceptable to both sides."[21]

The commission left for the Arizona copper fields on September 29, 1917, where serious labor difficulties had taken place. It was able to devise an arrangement whereby operations were restored. It also investigated disputes in the shipbuilding and telephone industries of the Pacific Coast and made an effort to settle the lumber strike there. It was not successful in this effort, and it refused to hear representatives of the Industrial Workers of the World, which was leading the walkout. But the Commission declared that "neither sinister influences nor the I.W.W. can account for the strikes. The explanation is to be found in unremedied and remediable industrial disorders."[22]

The commission was more successful in bringing about a truce of the threatened strike of 100,000 workers in the meat packing plants. The union in this industry had been virtually destroyed in 1903, and the companies were reluctant to make any concessions which might be interpreted as recognition. The meat packers continued to deal only with the Teamsters' Union. The President's Mediation Commission finally induced the packers and the union to arbitrate their differences and to accept permanent arbitration. John E. Williams was originally appointed, and after his withdrawal for ill-health, Judge Samuel Altschuler succeeded him. The agreement was not made between the employer and the union or with the employees, but because of the unwillingness of the packing companies to grant any kind of recognition to the union, was made between each party and the President's Mediation Commission. It worked during the war, and on March 30, 1918, Judge Altschuler directed the establishment of the eight-hour workday, and other changes in wages and working conditions.[23]

National Policy

On December 13, 1917, the Council of National Defense established the interdepartmental conference made up of representatives from the government production departments, with Franklin D. Roosevelt, Assistant Secretary of the Navy, one of the members. The committee presented a program which included (1) setting up machinery for adjusting labor disputes; (2) providing an adequate supply of labor through training and dilution of skills; (3) protecting labor through efficient safety; (4) safeguarding living conditions and providing decent housing; and (5) establishing an information agency and a publicity and educational division for the developing of a sound public opinion.[24] This group became the War Labor Policies Board with Felix Frankfurter, Assistant to the Secretary of Labor, as chairman.

Established in May 1918, the War Labor Policies Board functioned until the end of the war. Besides Labor, the War, Navy, and Agriculture departments, the U.S. Shipping Board, Emergency Fleet Corporation, the Fuel, Food and Railroad administrations, and the War Industries Board were represented. "The function of the board was to reconcile such differences so far as they referred to administration of labor matters and to recommend to the Secretary, who had been given over-all authority, unified labor policies to harmonize the industrial activities of separate branches of the government."[25]

The War Labor Policies Board sought to eliminate labor turnover, adopt uniform standards of employment in the different governmental agencies, develop a system of military exemptions for skilled workers, and devise methods for improving the living conditions of war workers employed in newly established war communities.

National War Labor Board

The need for devising a method of preventing disputes in war industry became more necessary as the conflict continued. On the recommendations of the Advisory Council, which had been appointed in 1917 to suggest policies to the secretary, six representatives were appointed by labor and six by management. The War Labor Conference Board, as it was called, recommended the appointment of a National War Labor Board which would, through conciliation and mediation, seek to settle labor-management differences in industries necessary for the effective prosecution of the war. Similar action was to be followed in industries which in the opinion of the board might affect national production. The board was authorized to appoint committees to hear controversies, and if no agreement was reached, appoint by unanimous vote of the board an arbitrator. In the event of failure to reach a unanimous decision upon an arbitrator, he was to be drawn from a list of ten nominated by the President of the United States.

The Board recommended that strikes and lockouts be avoided during the war and that the right to organize be recognized and not be denied or abridged by employers. Workers engaging in legitimate trade union activities were not to be discharged. In plants where the union shop existed it was to be continued and where the open shop was in effect, no attempt to displace it was to be made. The prevailing wages in an area were to govern wage setting, and the "right of all workers including common laborers, to a living wage is hereby declared."[26]

On April 8, 1918, the board began to function with Hutcheson, Victor Olander of the Seamen's Union, Frank J. Hayes of the Coal Miners' Union, T. A. Rickert of the United Garment Workers, and William H. Johnston of the International Association of Machinists as its labor members. During the war the decisions of the board were enforced by the President, but after the armistice the board announced it would consider only those controversies jointly submitted by the parties. In the sixteen months the board was active—it considered 1,251 controversies. "Of this number, 199 were submitted by both parties to the dispute. In 1,052 cases, one party refused to join the submission. Awards or recommendations were made in 490, or 39 per cent, of the cases submitted. In 34, or about 17 per cent of the cases jointly submitted the board was unable to agree, and the disputes were submitted to umpires for decision. Cases submitted by one party only were never referred to an umpire, such practice being construed as equivalent to compulsory arbitration."[27]

The three most important questions considered by the board were wages, hours, and discrimination for union membership. More than 150 disputes involved the right to organize. Collective bargaining was involved in 226 cases, and the board directed that collective bargaining be followed either with regularly established unions or with shop committees that had heretofore not existed. The latter part of the decision inadvertently caused a proliferation of organizations which later became company unions. In some instances the awards specified the methods to be followed in electing shop committees and the duties of the committees when elected. In some plants the parties were unacquainted with collective bargaining procedures and required considerable assistance from the staff of the board.

The board had no power of enforcement, and public opinion was largely depended upon to compel acceptance. However, when the Western Union Telegraph Company refused President Wilson's request to reinstate workers discharged for joining a union, its lines were taken over by the government. They were placed in the Post Office Department, headed by Postmaster-General Albert S. Burleson, scarcely a friend of organized labor.

The Commercial Telegraphers' Union insisted that discharges for union membership had been continued under government auspices. The dissatisfaction led to a strike on June 11, 1919, just prior to the return of the communication system to its private owners.

Workers in the telephone industry also found the Post Office Department a difficult employer. Failure to meet the demands for wage increases finally led to a strike by the New England telephone operators, who succeeded in compelling the Postmaster-General to bargain and to grant a substantial wage increase.[28]

President Wilson also commandeered the Smith and Wesson plant in Springfield, Massachusetts, when it refused to abide by a decision of the board. The company followed its prewar practice of discharging workers who joined unions and ignored a request from the War Labor Board that such employees be restored to their former positions. It was taken over by the War Department. In Bridgeport, Connecticut, members of the International Association of Machinists struck several ordnance plants on September 6, 1918. President Wilson asked the strikers to return immediately to their jobs and abide by the award of the board against which the men had struck. He informed the strikers that they would be barred from employment on war work or from utilizing the government employment service for procuring other jobs. In addition, strikers would be denied exemption from the draft. The men returned, whereupon the companies refused to rehire some of the strikers. In a letter to the companies, President Wilson said that since "the workmen have so promptly complied with my directions, I must insist upon the reinstatement of all these men."[29]

Effect of War Upon Organized Labor

During the war, organized labor increased its membership from 3,014,000 to 4,169,000 in 1919. The war momentum continued through the following year, and membership reached over 5,110,000, the highest in history. Labor's heightened importance was evident in other ways. Many leaders of labor served on government boards or in government missions. The increase in the influence of the political and economic movements of labor in Europe meant that spokesmen for workers in the United States could play a greater role, at least temporarily, in conferences abroad. The address of President Wilson to the 1917 AFL convention was another indication of the increased stature of labor. He pleaded for peaceful settlement of labor disputes so that production might not be impeded.[30]

American Alliance for Labor and Democracy

The AFL and the major part of the labor movement responded to the American war effort and supported the government throughout the hostilities with Germany. To counter the efforts of pacifist labor groups, the Central Federated Union of New York City established in June 1917 the American Alliance of Labor and Democracy. It called upon the workers to support loyally the government. From this body, a national organization with the same name was established at a conference at Minneapolis, Minnesota, in September 1917.

The conference announced "its unswerving adherence to the cause of democracy, now assailed by the forces of autocracy and militarism. As labor unionists, social reformers and socialists, we pledge our loyal support and service to the United States government and its allies in the present world conflict."[31] The declaration called for unity of action, denounced the enemies of the United States who spoke in the name of labor, and called for resistance to attempts to lower labor standards. It advocated conscription of wealth, as well as men, and protection of the right of workers to organize. Universal suffrage was endorsed.[32]

The alliance, with Gompers as chairman and Robert Maisel as director, established a news service and issued leaflets on labor and political topics. It went out of business at the end of the war, although the executive secretary sought its continuance.

Reconstruction

The 1919 AFL convention instructed the executive council to appoint a committee of five to draw up a program of reconstruction. Headed by John Frey, the committee called for recognition of the right of workers to collective bargaining. On unemployment, the document demanded just wages which "will create a market at home . . . and will lessen unemployment." Living wages and limitation of the hours of labor to eight a day were asked for all workers. Equal pay for women for equal work and the prohibition of employment of children under sixteen were other demands.

Labor's nonpartisan political policy was endorsed. "Public and semi-public utilities should be owned or operated and regulated by the government in the interest of the public." No position was taken upon the ownership of the railroads, but government ownership of wharves and docks was endorsed. "The American Merchant Marine should be encouraged and developed under government control and so manned as to insure successful operation and protect in full the beneficient laws now on the statute books for the rights and welfare of seamen."[33]

A demand was made that "all restrictions of freedom of speech, of the press, public assembly, association and travel be completely removed, individuals and groups being responsible for their utterances."[34] Restriction upon immigration was proposed. The statement opposed militarism or a large standing army, and charged that under militarism "a deceptive patriotism is established in the people's minds." It advocated a citizen army of moderate size, because the "history of every nation demonstrates that as standing armies are enlarged the rule of democracy is lessened or extinguished. Our experience has been that even this citizen soldiery, the militia of our states, has given cause at times for grave apprehension. Their ranks have not always been free from undesirable elements, particularly the tools of corporations involved in industrial disputes. . . . We insist that the militia of our several states should be wholly organized and controlled by democratic principles so that this voluntary force of soldiery may never jeopardize or infringe upon the rights and liberties of our people."[35]

Discharged soldiers and sailors should, in the opinion of the statement, be granted generous bonuses and paid up to a year's wages if unemployed.

In general, the statement contained few surprises but on several points, like ownership of the railroads, the position reflected the demands of special groups.

CHAPTER 25

Political Socialism and Government: Attacks on Radicalism

The AFL, despite criticism, remained satisfied with its political accomplishments. It pointed to the activity of the state federations, city central bodies, and national and international unions in the halls of Congress and before the state legislative bodies. But most of all, the federation believed that its legislative activity had brought many improvements to labor and the public interest. It not only fought for better terms of employment for the government worker, it also aided in the enactment of laws by the Sixty-fourth Congress granting citizenship rights to the people of Puerto Rico and creating a Federal Board of Vocational Education. The AFL held that its legislative agents had supported many bills that were of benefit to all the people. The feeling of satisfaction was not shared by all labor groups, for many believed that its political policies were stultifying and that only a party exclusively devoted to promoting the interests and destiny of labor could represent the needs of the worker. The most vigorous and persistent criticism of the federation's political program came from the socialists of all schools.

THE RISE OF SOCIALISM

In the public mind, the Socialist party became after 1901 the representative of socialism in the United States. Its members were active in politics and in the labor movement, and its rise since its formation in 1901, while not spectacular, was by 1912 fairly satisfactory. In 1912, Debs, as the party's candidate for President, polled 891,011 votes, or 5.9 per cent of the total. It was almost ten times as large as the 94,768 votes cast for Debs's first campaign for the Presidency in 1900. In 1910 the Socialist party elected its first congressman, Victor Berger—editor, trade unionist, and a persevering foe of the AFL hierarchy. Only one other Socialist, Meyer London, a labor lawyer from New York City, was elected to Congress for the first time in 1914.

Despite its emphasis on the wage earner and labor problems, and its attempt to speak for the workers in the mine, mill, and factory, the Socialist party achieved its greatest electoral successes in the agricultural states. The largest percentage of votes—16.6 per cent—cast for a Socialist Presidential candidate in any state was recorded in Oklahoma in 1912. Nevada, Montana, Washington, California, and Idaho were the other states in which the Socialist candidate polled more than 10 per cent of the vote in that year. In contrast, the Socialist vote in Ohio, the highest percentage polled in an industrial State, was 8.7 per cent. In Illinois the Socialist candidate polled 7.1 per cent; Pennsylvania, 6.9 per cent; New York, 4.0 per cent; and New Jersey, 3.9 per cent.[1] Occasionally, Socialists did much better in local elections than on state and national levels. Voters might vote for a local Socialist candidate as a protest against corruption or poor government or service. A number of communities elected Socialist municipal officers, but at the same time refused to give their votes to Socialist candidates for national or state offices.

Socialists were relatively more important in the trade union movement than in the political life of the country. While many active Socialists were business and professional men, others were wage earners who because of class consciousness or political and social awareness almost inevitably joined the unions in their trade or calling. Some Socialists, members of the Socialist Labor party and the Impossibilists, were enemies of the trade unions and were not adverse to scabbing.

The differences between Socialists and non-Socialist trade unionists concerned both political and economic issues. All Socialists were critical of the membership of the leaders of labor in the National Civic Federation, an organization promoting industrial peace and having among its members employers whose organizations were opposed to trade unions. The Civic Federation became a target of attack by all who did not approve its conciliatory policies. Morris Hillquit, a leading Socialist theoretician and himself a corporation lawyer, believed that the Civic Federation introduced into the labor movement a "subtle and insidious poison" which robbed the labor movement of independence and demoralized its leaders.[2] The leaders of the AFL were able to repel the attack.

The attack on the National Civic Federation, led by the delegates of the United Mine Workers of America, was mainly inspired by the leaders of that union who were also Socialists. It was also supported by a group hostile to John Mitchell, who had led the union for ten years. Mitchell piloted the United Mine Workers of America in its campaign to establish itself in the anthracite coal field. He was a leading spokesman for the traditional type of trade union policy. The vice-president of the United Mine Workers of America during Mitchell's tenure, Thomas L. Lewis, was generally conservative in his social and economic views. When defeated for re-election, Lewis found employment with an association of coal mine operators and was on opposite sides in negotiations with the Mine Workers. Lewis hated Mitchell and allied himself with the Socialists to embarrass him.

While the Socialists were unable to carry the day at AFL conventions, they were increasing their strength within many unions, where they either controlled the administration as in the Brewery and Bakery Workers, the Needle Trades, and the Mine, Mill and Smelter Workers, and Machinists, or were a powerful minority as in the Painters and Decorators, or exercised some influence as in the Typographical Union. In their trade union policies, the Socialists generally favored more active efforts to organize the unorganized, revision of the structure of the federation toward some type of industrialism, and an endorsement of independent political action.[3] Socialist activity within the trade unions was, however, dissimilar from the Communist tactics of infiltration and boring-from-within. No Socialist ever denied his affiliation or his cause on the floor of labor conventions.

The Socialists were not organized in a disciplined phalanx taking direction from a party secretary, nor did they always agree among themselves upon tactics and policies within their unions. For many years Max Hayes, who was the outstanding Socialist on the floor of the AFL conventions, annually clashed with Gompers. While speaking out against the policies of the AFL, Hayes was a leading member of the Wahnetas, the conservative faction within his own union and strongly supported the administration of its international president, James Lynch.

A high point in Socialist influence was reached in 1912 when the executive council of the AFL issued a defensive statement denying that unions cannot change their structure to meet the needs of an evolving technology. The statement was an attempt to meet the expected criticism of the industrialists. It pointed to the amalgamation of national and international unions, some of them aided by the AFL.[4] The statement denied that autonomy of a trade union meant that it could not expand its jurisdiction or amalgamate with other organizations.

The United Mine Workers' delegation, nevertheless, proposed "that this convention adopts and endorses the plan of organization by industries instead of by crafts which often divides the forces of labor, and that the officers of the A.F. of L. be instructed to use every effort to bring this about, and that they visit the different labor conventions and use their influence to mould sentiment along these lines."[5] The majority of the resolutions' committee recommended the reaffirmation of the Scranton Declaration, but a minority report approved the proposal of the United Mine Workers of America. On a roll call vote, the minority report, endorsing industrial unionism, was rejected by 10,934 to 5,929 votes, with 444 not voting.[6] Not all those who voted for industrialism were Socialists and not all opponents were craft unionists. Max S. Hayes, the most articulate of the Socialist delegates, recognized that:

at no time has the A.F. of L. prohibited international unions in a given industry from combining their forces. Indeed, the Federation has upon numerous occasions encouraged kindred organizations to unite, and has even gone to the extreme of expelling international unions for refusing to merge into larger organizations. Thus, the engineers in the mines were unseated because they declined to merge into the United Mine Workers, the car workers were expelled last year [1911] for refusing to join the larger body in that trade, and the Amalgamated Carpenters were ousted because they would not join the Brotherhood. This year the steamfitters had their charter revoked on account of their refusal to merge into the international union of plumbers, steamfitters, gasfitters, etc., who have been given complete jurisdiction over the pipefitting industry.

On the other hand there was but one industrial organization ousted for resisting the encroachments of craft unions, and that was the United Brewery Workers, who were readmitted at the succeeding convention, and the delegates virtually admitted their error in that instance by adopting a law that in future no organization can be expelled except by a two-thirds vote. The unions now classified as industrialist have fully that number of votes and can block any further attack upon their principles by a resort to such drastic methods. . . . At Rochester it was proposed that the pressure of compulsion be substituted for the voluntary plan, and the craft unionists rallied their followers by condemning the use of force to achieve industrial unionism.[7]

In addition to the Socialists, an opposition centering around the unions with headquarters in Indianapolis, Indiana, had developed. The Bricklayers', Carpenters', Hod Carriers', Coal Miners', Teamsters', and Typographical unions were among those which had their headquarters in that city. These organizations—the Bricklayers were not affiliated until 1916—were among the largest and most powerful in the AFL. Their officers were generally of a younger generation than Gompers and several other members of the executive council. In 1917, Daniel Tobin, the head of the Teamsters' Union, had the support of most of the Indianapolis unions in his successful challenge of John B. Lennon for the office of treasurer.[8] It appeared that the defeat of Lennon was only a beginning and that other members of the executive council would be challenged, but the war intervened and shifted loyalties.

St. Louis Declaration

World War I exercised a dramatic effect upon the fortunes of the labor movement and the Socialist party. Some of the leading Socialists were prosecuted for offenses against wartime laws. The party faced successive splits following the emergence of the Communist movement in the United States. Even before war actively touched the United States, the fortunes of the Socialist party appeared to be declining. The liberal policies of President Woodrow Wilson, his sponsorship of the Clayton and La Follette Seamens' acts, and the understanding he showed for the railroad workers inevitably reduced the protest ballots which were important components of the total Socialist vote. Wilson in 1916 also ran on a pacifist platform which inevitably attracted groups who might ordinarily provide a substantial vote for a Socialist office seeker. In addition, the best-known Socialist, Eugene Debs, refused to be a candidate and his place was taken by Allan L. Benson, a journalist and contributor to the *Appeal to Reason,* the Socialist journal with a mass circulation. Benson polled 590,294, or 3.2 per cent of the vote. As in 1912 the percentage vote in Oklahoma was the highest with 15.6, followed by Nevada with 13.1 per cent. Florida, Wisconsin, Idaho, Washington, and Arizona were next in line, but the party did not do well in the industrial states. In Ohio and Indiana, Benson polled 3.4 per cent of the vote in each state; Pennsylvania gave the Socialist candidate only 3.1 per cent; New York, 2.6 per cent; and the rest of the industrial states, a lower percentage.[9]

But the party faced a more serious crisis. Many Socialists were pacifists on religious or economic grounds, the latter group arguing that international solidarity of labor superseded national patriotism. On the entry of the United States into war, a special convention was called for April 1917 in St. Louis to decide upon the attitude to be taken. With a few protests from right-wing members of the party, largely writers, and a group of left wingers who wanted a more militant pronouncement, the party proclaimed its "unalterable opposition to the war just declared by the government of the United States."[10]

Equally as serious for the Socialist party was the emergence of a militant faction allied to the Communist or Bolshevik movement in the Soviet Union. At first this group merely expressed sympathy for the October Revolution and attacked the right-wing leaders of the party in the United States. The left-wing attacks were directed not only against the Socialist leadership but also against those who headed the unions and the AFL. As a consequence, the trade union Socialists gradually lessened their criticisms of the AFL administration and became, in many cases, closely attached to the leadership especially after the death of Gompers in 1924.

The Communist Splits

The Russian revolution of "October" (November 7, 1917) affected the left-wing movements of all countries of the world. A split within the Socialist party of the United States was almost immediately in the making and the left wing, always a minority, overnight gained thousands of adherents anxious to follow the road to revolution plotted by the master political strategist, Vladimir Lenin. An opposition group developed within the Socialist party which sought to transform the relatively moderate party into a Bolshevik conspiratorial organization. A national conference in New York during the spring of 1919 laid plans for capturing the Socialist party at the forthcoming convention in August 1919. The left wing, however, was split among itself; a group led by the Slavic Socialist Federation favored the formation of a Communist party without trying to capture the Socialist party. Another Communist group tried to capture the Socialist party at its August convention and, when they were repelled, they formed the Communist Labor party. At almost the same time, the more militant section dominated by the Slavic Socialist Federation set up the Communist party. Both parties claimed to be the true followers of the Russian Bolsheviks whom they hoped to imitate, at least in language. The Communist party, less circumspect in its pronouncements, advocated the whole gamut of Leninist principles, including the forceful overthrow of the government and its replacement by a dictatorship of the proletariat.[11] The Communists were soon driven underground; but the effect of the split, and the ones which followed later, had a disastrous effect upon the membership and activity of the Socialist party.

ANTI-RADICALISM DURING AND AFTER WORLD WAR I

Joe Hill

The periods before, during, and after World War I witnessed an aggressive drive against holders of heterodox and radical views. In 1915 the case of Joe Hill attracted national attention. Hill (or Hillstrom) had been a famous writer of IWW songs, but was otherwise not active in radical causes. He was convicted of the murder of a storekeeper and his son outside of Salt Lake City, Utah, during a robbery on January 9, 1914. It was claimed that he had been railroaded by the copper trust because of his radical ideas. At the time of his arrest, Hill had been wounded and claimed he had been shot in a quarrel over a woman. The case attracted widespread attention. After Hill was sentenced to die on July 6, 1915, a campaign, in which the AFL and Gompers joined, was undertaken. They appealed to President Woodrow Wilson for commutation of sentence. The governor and the Utah Pardon Board promised a reprieve if Hill would tell two of its members where he was the night of the shooting. He refused and was finally executed.[12]

Labor Tension in San Francisco

Much more important was the Mooney-Billings case which was an outgrowth of a bomb explosion during a preparedness parade in San Francisco in 1916.

The breach of contract by the San Francisco longshoremen had aroused considerable anger in the ranks of business, and Secretary of Labor William B. Wilson, a former executive officer of the United Mine Workers of America, protested the disregard of the agreement. Ostensibly angered by the irresponsible action of the longshoremen, the San Francisco Chamber of Commerce organized (on July 10, 1916) the Law and Order League not only to combat the irregular actions of unions, but also to fight all labor organizations. Using the excuse of the repudiated agreement by the Riggers and Stevedores, the board of directors, led by its president, Frank J. Koster, declared that to union members and their leaders, agreements were mere scraps of paper to be broken. Koster pledged a fund of a million dollars to finance a fight for the open shop.[13] Leaders of the State Federation of Labor regarded Koster's speech "as the keynote of the organized employers who recently raised a million dollars to establish 'Law and Order' and the so-called 'open shop,' etc."[14]

Feelings between organized labor and organized management in San Francisco became increasingly strained. Also, organized labor showed little enthusiasm for the preparedness propaganda. Many Americans, watching Belgium and France being overrun by the German imperial armies and the bitter stalemate which followed, became anxious about America's lack of military preparations and believed that if the Kaiser succeeded in conquering Europe, the United States would very soon be on his list. Committees to promote an expansion of the armed services were formed in many communities, and they sponsored parades in favor of military preparedness. San Francisco scheduled such a demonstration for July 22, 1916. While showing scant enthusiasm about the preparedness program, the local labor movement expressed no opposition to the plans. There was a division of sentiment when Andrew Gallagher, a San Francisco Labor Council leader, came out in favor of the parade. He was denounced by Thomas Mooney in *The Blast,* an anarchist monthly published in San Francisco under the direction of Alexander Berkman.[15]

Preparedness Day Bombing

As the preparedness parade reached Market and Steuart streets, at one-thirty in the afternoon, a suitcase containing a bomb, which had been left on the corner against a building, exploded and killed nine marchers and spectators. Thomas J. Mooney, his wife Rena, Edward D. Nolan, Israel Weinberg, and Warren K. Billings were arrested and charged with the crime. Billings was convicted and sentenced to life imprisonment; Mooney, in a separate trial, was found guilty and ordered to hang on May 17, 1917. The other three were subsequently released after a jury refused to convict them.

None of the arrested was an important leader of the San Francisco labor movement, although all of the five were active minor officers of labor unions.

From the beginning, Mooney's efforts to bring the street railway carmen on the United Railways into the union was given by his adherents as the reason he had been singled out for prosecution.[16] The carmen had organized a union in 1901, but the United Railroads resisted and sought to destroy it by refusing to negotiate. In the end, an agreement was reached that strikers would be rehired and no discrimination would be practiced by the company against them. Patrick Calhoun, one of the city's more colorful swashbuckling characters, took over the presidency of the United Railroad in 1902. His imperious temper did not easily tolerate another power, and constant attempts, obviously at his direction, were made to undermine the influence of the organization on the railways.[17]

In 1907 negotiations between the United Railroads and the union broke down and a strike was called on May 5. It was a bitter struggle; the San Francisco and California labor movements rallied to the strikers but the victory went to the company.[18]

In June 1916, Thomas J. Mooney sought support for a campaign to win 2,000 street carmen on the United Railroad for the union, and the San Francisco Labor Council was requested to give him "every assistance and encouragement . . . to accomplish the reorganization of the carmen on the United Railroads."[19]

Leaders of the San Francisco Labor Council were far from pleased when the walkout was called. First, Mooney had failed to ask the San Francisco Labor Council for permission to call the walkout—a practice customarily followed by the unions of the city. Secondly, Mooney obviously had not consulted the men who were to do the striking. The *Labor Clarion,* official organ of the council, called the strike "Mooney's Morbid Move." It charged he had been guilty of lack of preparation in calling a strike of unorganized workers, and that his faulty tactics were reflected in the response of only one carman to Mooney's call.[20]

According to President Wilson's Mediation Commission, "there can be no doubt that Mooney was regarded as a labor agitator of malevolence by the utilities of San Francisco, and he was the special object of their opposition. . . . The utilities against which Mooney directed his agitation, or who suspected him of mischievous activity, undoubtedly sought 'to get' Mooney. Their activity against him [was] directed by [Martin] Swanson, a private detective. It was Swanson who had engineered the investigation which had resulted in Mooney's prosecution."[21]

Mooney had aroused the suspicion of Swanson, who was convinced that Mooney had been guilty of dynamiting the towers of the Pacific Gas and Electric Company in 1913, for which Mooney had been tried three times in Contra Costa County. Swanson also held Mooney responsible for the dynamiting of a tower at San Bruno on July 11, 1916, and sought, according to Billings and Weinberg, to pay them $5,000 if they would identify

Mooney as the dynamiter. When they refused the offer, Swanson allegedly threatened to get them.[22]

Mooney had joined the Industrial Workers of the World, abandoned it for the Syndicalist League of San Francisco, became secretary of the International Workers' Defense League, and was active in the defense of Richard Ford and Herman Suhr. In 1916 he was closely associated, as a contributor, with the anarchist journal, *The Blast* of San Francisco. Attempts by the city newspapers to place the blame for the bomb throwing on radicals, nevertheless, were decried.[23]

Billings was tried in September 1916, convicted, and, because of an earlier felony conviction, sentenced to life imprisonment at Folsom Prison. In a letter to the San Francisco Labor Council, Billings claimed he had been convicted on perjured testimony and that the evidence presented by the state was contradictory. Billings believed that the request of the prosecutor for a sentence of life imprisonment was intended to encourage a confession in return for clemency.[24] Interest in the case began slowly to extend beyond the borders of California, and a National Defense Council was organized to aid the accused.

At first the California labor movement was not enthusiastic about being connected with the dynamiting case. The defendants were known as opponents of those who headed the movement. Consequently, when a resolution sponsored by District No. 68 of the International Association of Machinists at the 1916 convention of the state federation of labor charged that the prosecution of those arrested in the Preparedness Day dynamiting was "based entirely on conspiracy evidence of past labor wars centering in and about San Francisco, such as the Pacific General and Electric Strike, and an attempted strike on the United Railroad," it was challenged by the resolutions committee, which noted "that no one at this time is attempting to connect labor with the bomb outrage, and although statements were made in San Francisco . . . that the outrage 'was the culmination of a series of crimes by organized labor' so well was our position defined and our policies defended and explained that attacks on us along that line have ceased."[25] The report of the resolutions committee occasioned a long debate. Hugo Ernst, later the president of the Hotel and Restaurant Union and at the time a representative of the waiters of San Francisco, led the fight against the report. It was defended by Mike Casey of the San Francisco Teamsters, Thomas Tracy of the Printers, and Paul Scharrenberg, secretary of the state federation. The report of the committee was overwhelmingly adopted (38,196 to 4,226). The San Francisco Labor Council concluded that the testimony used to convict Billings and Mooney, in their separate trials, was contradictory and pledged its "aid in their efforts to secure justice."[26]

After Mooney's conviction, the *Labor Clarion* feared grave danger existed that innocent men might be sent to the gallows if something were not done to avoid the carrying out of the verdict returned by the jury in the Mooney case.

While the delegates felt that the defendants had no claim upon organized labor as such for assistance and that some of them had been a nuisance and hindrance to the advancement of the labor movement because of their foolish ideas and activities, still the interest of the movement in humanity and justice and civilization forbade it to remain silent even when the probability was so minute that human life might be wrongfully taken.[27]

Mooney was brought to trial on January 3, 1917, after his case had already attracted nationwide attention. He was convicted and sentenced to hang. Rena Mooney was acquitted, and Weinberg's trial followed; he was also acquitted—in November 1917—and released the following March. Nolan was released on bail and never brought to trial. The San Francisco Labor Council, which had been until then lukewarm on the Mooney case, charged that there were serious doubts of the fairness of the conviction of Mooney and Billings and called for an investigation.[28]

It became more and more widely felt that the men convicted had not received a fair trial; demands for a congressional investigation of the miscarriage of justice were made by their friends.[29]

President Daniel C. Murphy and Secretary Scharrenberg requested Congressman John I. Nolan from San Francisco, a trade unionist with a long record of activity in the San Francisco labor movement, to sponsor a resolution to that effect. Nolan, unimpressed with the plan, feared that an investigation might backfire "for the reasons we are all aware of that know Mooney's activities prior to the Preparedness Day explosion. I have reference to his radical action both in and out of the labor movement; also his trial at Martinez and Sacramento [for dynamiting, for which he was acquitted], as well as the conviction of Billings."[30] An appeal for funds to aid the defense was made by the state federation at about the same time.[31]

Failing to make any headway with their pleas for a new trial and for a reassessment of the evidence upon which Mooney and Billings had been convicted, Murphy and Scharrenberg sought the aid of the AFL.[32] At their request, Samuel Gompers appealed to President Woodrow Wilson for intervention in the Mooney case. To fortify the request, the issue was brought before the AFL convention, and a resolution requesting investigation by the federal government was unanimously approved. Upon the authorization of President Wilson, J. B. Densmore examined the evidence. At the same time, the council urged the governor of California to accept Densmore's report which concluded that Mooney had been a victim of perjured testimony. The executive council, and especially Gompers, were anxious that Mooney not be executed, because they had been convinced by leading California labor men that the evidence was perjured, and because they feared also the effect upon the opinion of European labor, then moving rapidly to the political left. The execution of Mooney, they were certain, would inevitably be used to poison the minds of the European wage earner against this country. Nor, in any sense, should injustice to innocent men be overlooked. The AFL hoped that Mooney and Billings would be pardoned, and then indicted and tried for the killing of one of the other victims. In the new trial, they believed the defense would be able to protect itself against the use of manufactured evidence. Their pleas came to naught.[33]

In the meantime, the mediation commission, appointed by President Wilson, investigated and expressed serious concern about the verdict. It found in "the atmosphere surrounding the prosecution and trial of the case ground for disquietude. . . . This feeling is reenforced by one factor of controlling importance. The most damaging testimony produced against Mooney came from a witness named Oxman. After Mooney's conviction there came to light letters confessedly written by Oxman prior to his having been called to testify. The plain import of these letters is an attempt by Oxman to suborn perjury in corroboration of the vital testimony which he was to give and which, in fact, he did give against Mooney." The commission did not regard Oxman's trial and acquittal of perjury as vitiating its opinion.[34]

Nevertheless, the state supreme court decided that it "cannot find that he [Mooney] was deprived of any right, constitutional or statutory, or that material error of law was committed calling for a reversal of judgment or an abrogation of the order denying his application for a new trial." The court's decision was unanimous, and it announced that its view was guided solely by the trial record made in the court below.[35]

When the California State Federation convention convened in October 1918, the leaders were convinced that another appeal to Governor William D. Stephens would be of no avail. He was "incomprehensibly obdurate," and, in self-respect, it would no longer appeal to him on the issue.[36]

Though California labor leaders were willing to fight for the release of men whose views and activities they opposed, but who, they believed, had been wrongfully convicted of crime, they would not participate in a Mooney Congress, sponsored by the Chicago Federation of Labor. The congress met in Chicago in January 1919 and turned out to be dominated by left-wing groups. Although the Mooney Congress adopted a number of stirring resolutions, no practical steps to release Mooney and Billings resulted, unless the call for a general strike for May 1 might be so defined. The executive council of the AFL was severely critical of this demonstration, feeling that not only would it accomplish nothing toward the release of the imprisoned, but the contrary, that it might actually hinder the campaign being waged for their freedom.[37]

Mooney was reprieved finally by Governor Stephens on July 27, 1918;

subsequently the reprieve was made permanent, with the sentence commuted to life imprisonment. Later, the governor explained that he commuted Mooney's sentence because he believed that both defendants should be "punished alike . . . and because I did not think Mooney should be hanged when there were a million or more people—good citizens—in the United States who sincerely but mistakenly believed him innocent."[38] An AFL committee sought to visit Governor Stephens, but he refused to see anyone on the case who did not have new evidence. "Of Mooney's guilt," Stephens declared, "there is in my mind no question. I am convinced he had part in one of the most atrocious crimes—involving treasonable purposes—ever perpetrated in our country. It is true that Mooney held membership in a local union in San Francisco and had attempted to organize the streetcar men of that city in a strike but he was never identified with the labor movement as a factor of influence or leadership. . . . Further clemency is not warranted by anything within my knowledge."[39] On May 20, 1920, E. D. Nolan, one of those arrested for the Preparedness Day bombing, resigned as secretary of the International Workers' Defense League and notified the California State Federation of Labor that the Defense League had been dissolved.[40]

The Mooney campaign was now taken over by several committees, most important of which was the Tom Mooney Molders' Defense Committee. Paul Scharrenberg, a delegate from the California State Federation of Labor to the convention of the 1923 AFL, attacked the loose methods of collecting funds followed by those working in behalf of Tom Mooney as well as the propaganda material being issued.[41]

In 1920, Samuel Gompers appointed a committee of five California trade unionists, to plead on behalf of the labor movement of the United States for the release of Mooney and Billings.[42]

Annually, the state federation demanded Mooney's release; regularly, this was refused. As Governor Stephens recognized, millions of people were convinced that Mooney and Billings were unjustly imprisoned. Unofficial efforts were made periodically by leaders of California labor to obtain Mooney's release, but labor could not neglect its other responsibilities. Mooney was never important in the California labor movement, his relation to it was always tenuous, and his case did not involve a clear-cut labor issue. Dastardly as the action of the McNamaras might have been—in the 1910 *Times* Building dynamiting (Chapter 17)—their criminal acts were actually, and mistakenly, carried out in behalf of a labor organization. Since he was innocent of the crime charged, Mooney was rightfully supported by the labor movement of California, but his demand that the movement give up all of its activities to concentrate upon his release was not reasonable.[43]

Mooney, upon learning of the resolution of the 1927 convention of the

California State Federation of Labor, wrote to William Green that he would "not under any circumstances accept a parole which precludes guilt in all cases. Parole to me would be far worse than imprisonment in San Quentin prison. I have not asked for a parole and would not accept one if it were tendered to me without asking."[44]

In the same letter, Mooney charged that "the Labor Leaders of California, with a few exceptions not only did not want us out, but secretly did everything in their power to bring about our downfall and now are hoping and working for our continual imprisonment."[45]

Paul Scharrenberg actually was active behind the scenes in behalf of Mooney's release and in July 1928 Governor C. C. Young wrote to him: "I feel decidedly that this is a matter which should go to the Parole Board in the ordinary course, rather than to come to myself. Of course, I realize that a great many feel that Mooney is entirely innocent of the offense for which he was convicted, but unfortunately, I do not feel that way, although I have given a good deal of study to the case."[46] Scharrenberg had urged the governor both publicly and privately to pardon Mooney. The governor always listened respectfully to the arguments and, just as regularly remained unconvinced.[47]

An appeal for a pardon to the California Supreme Court was rejected. The court reported that it had "examined the evidence and had reached the conclusion that both had been fairly convicted and did not deserve clemency."[48] Despite this, the California State Federation of Labor continued to press for a pardon for Mooney.[49]

With the election of Culbert L. Olson as governor, Mooney's appeal received sympathetic attention. After a hearing in January 1939, Governor Olson announced: "I now instruct Warden Smith to release you to freedom which I expect you to exercise with the high ideals I have tried to indicate."[50] Olson regretted his lack of authority to pardon Billings; approval of the state supreme court would be required in his case because of a previous felony conviction. At its 1939 convention, the state federation of labor went on record that the "fight to secure a pardon for Warren K. Billings is one in which every trade unionist should enlist."[51]

The federation was anxious to aid in gaining Billings' release but it saw no need of an elaborate organization. At the recommendation of the state supreme court in October 1939, Governor Olson commuted Billing's sentence to time served.

The Industrial Workers of the World (IWW)

Prosecution for violating wartime statutes fell heavily upon the Industrial Workers of the World. Strikes in the lumber and copper industries by members of the IWW led to severe attacks upon its members by citizens' groups and the federal government. In Bisbee, Arizona, a loyalty league whose members were deputized by the sheriff deported on July 12, 1917, more than 1,200 strikers. The President's Mediation Commission reported that "conditions in Bisbee were in fact peaceful and free from any manifestations of disorder or violence."[52]

Early on the morning of July 12, 1917, the sheriff and a large force of armed men "presuming to act as Deputies under the Sheriff's authority comprising about two thousand men, rounded up 1,186 men in the Warren District, put them aboard a train, and carried them to Columbus, New Mexico. The authorities at Columbus refused to permit those in charge of the deportation to leave them there, and the train carried them back to the desert town of Hermanas, New Mexico, a nearby station."[53] The deportees were without adequate food, water, or shelter for two days, and were then abandoned by the guards. On July 14, troops were directed by the War Department to escort the deportees to Columbus, New Mexico, where they were maintained by the federal government until the middle of September. The strikes around Bisbee and Jerome, Arizona, were ended as a result of the deportation. The President's Mediation Commission was able to bring about a settlement in other parts of the Arizona mining areas.

The responsibility of several of the large industrial groups around Bisbee for the deportations is clear from the report of a million-dollar settlement which the Phelps-Dodge Mercantile Corporation, the Calumet and Arizona Mining Company, the El Paso and Southwestern Railway, and other companies agreed to pay to the men deported from Bisbee. The companies paid married men with children $1,200, married men $1,000, and unmarried men $500 for the pain, inconvenience, and loss of income suffered. Absence of some of the deportees prevented the final signing of the agreement.[54]

The IWW was also active in the copper miners' strike in Butte, Montana. During the course of the walkout, a group of five men invaded the room of Frank H. Little, a member of the general executive board of the IWW, forced him to accompany them, and hanged him to a trestle. The strike of 1917 "in the lumber camps had been broken and the men went back beaten for the moment. There followed, however, the practice of 'conscious withdrawal of efficiency' and the so-called 'strike on the job.' "[55] The government, however, recognized that the IWW was filling a vacuum because the "operators manifested a bitter and uncompromising attitude towards any organization among their employees." An effort to meet it was made by the government, and Colonel Brisce P. Disque was sent in to find a remedy. He organized, with the approval of the Secretary of War, the Loyal Legion of Loggers and Lumber men. It was in effect "a Government union composed of workers in the lumber camps. . . . The membership rapidly grew until it included nearly 90,000 men."[56]

Although the IWW strikes in 1917 involved economic issues, the organization was believed to be engaged in a conscious policy of hampering the war effort. The belief was sufficiently widespread to induce President Wilson to appoint Justice J. Harry Covington of the Supreme Court of the District of Columbia to investigate. On the basis of his recommendations, raids were carried out on the IWW headquarters and forty-eight halls and offices of the organization. Materials were submitted to a federal grand jury in the United States District Court of Illinois, Northern District, and 165 officers and leaders were indicted for seeking to hamper the government's war effort through force, violence, and propaganda. After a long trial, 101 defendants were convicted and sentenced to prison, a number up to 20 years.

Indictments were also found against groups of IWW members in California, Kansas, and Oklahoma. They were convicted and sentenced to a federal prison; the group arrested in Kansas and Oklahoma was also charged with violating the Lever Act, forbidding interference with the production of food and fuel during the war.[57] The prosecutions of the IWW denuded the organization of its principal organizers, speakers, and writers. Nevertheless, there were some signs of renewed activity within the organization after World War I. A careful study of the activities and tactics of the IWW was undertaken by the Department of Justice. The Attorney-General of the United States was of the opinion in 1919 that "there is no Federal criminal law under which members of this organization can be proceeded against, and under rulings of the Department of Labor alien members of the organization cannot be deported merely for membership therein. In this connection it may be pointed out that certain States have seen fit to hold membership in the Industrial Workers of the World was sufficient to convict under their criminal syndicalism statutes."[58]

Criminal syndicalist statutes were enacted in the northwestern states, beginning with Idaho in 1917. They were usually defined as a "doctrine which advocates crime, violence, sabotage or other unlawful methods as a means of industrial or political reform."[59]

With the close of World War I, there was evidence of a relaxation by the authorities of the opposition to the IWW. In several instances juries refused to convict defendants who admitted membership for violating the criminal syndicalist statutes. The respite was only temporary. The shift to a moderate view was halted by the campaign against radicalism initiated by United States Attorney-General A. Mitchell Palmer in 1919. Even more important, at least in the Northwest, was the Armistice Day tragedy in Centralia, Washington, in 1919. In an attack on the IWW hall during the Armistice Day parade, four members of the American Legion were killed, and an IWW member, Wesley Everest, himself a war veteran, was lynched. As a result, members of the IWW were charged and convicted of second-degree murder and sentenced to long prison terms. A labor jury selected by the Pacific Coast labor movement, at the suggestion of the Seattle Metal Trades Council, found that a plan to raid and destroy the IWW hall had been made, that the defendants had acted in self-defense, and that they had not been given a fair trial. The clash in Centralia again ignited the hatred for the IWW which had lain dormant for a short period. Halls were shut or demolished, and members were picked up and imprisoned. The Attorney-General of Washington called the district attorneys together in order to devise methods by which the prosecutions of IWW members could be speeded.

Members were pursued in many of the states where they had attained their largest influence. The General Defense Committee reported that more than 2,000 were in jail in the early months of 1920. Many of those in the lumber areas of the Northwest were charged with vagrancy or criminal syndicalism. Beginning in 1922, the major area of prosecution shifted to California following a strike in 1922 on the Hetchy-Hetchy aqueduct. Soon thereafter, arrests under the criminal syndicalist laws began. John Dymond and Elmer Couts, professional witnesses, were the main source of evidence. Nevertheless, in the spring of 1923, the IWW tied up the docks at San Pedro, California, in a protest against the hiring hall ("Fink Hall") and at the same time demanded release of political prisoners. Several hundred were arrested, and a stockade was built to house the prisoners. An injunction enjoining membership in the IWW was issued by the Superior Court on December 1, 1923. In most areas the prosecutions abated by 1924, in part because of the lessened activity of the IWW and also because the change in public sentiment made such prosecutions less popular. According to Dr. Dowell, 31 men served in the Idaho penitentiary as a result of conviction, 52 in Washington, and 133 in California.[60]

Attack on Anarchists and Communists

The launching of the Communist parties in the United States coincided with a period of heightened labor militancy which was opposed by well-organized employer groups determined to make no concessions to organized labor and to strip it of some of its wartime gains. The rise of the Communist movement, with its revolutionary jargon, convinced many that this alien philosophy had inspired the discontent which had seized large sections of labor. Many others who knew better were not adverse to using the conveniently available revolutionary stick to beat newly formed unions in industry and to re-establish the prewar system of labor relations. New York, Illinois, and California criminal anarchy or criminal syndicalist laws were used to prosecute advocates of violent overthrow of government. Federal statutes adopted on February 3, 1917, and October 16, 1918, made aliens deportable if they were anarchists or believed in the overthrow of the government by force and violence.

Bombings

In April 1919, sixteen packages of bombs were seized at the New York Post Office. In addition, a bomb had been mailed to the home of former Senator Thomas W. Hardwick, who had been chairman of the Senate Committee on Immigration, and exploded while being opened by the maid, blowing off her hands. The sending of these bombs, on the eve of May Day, was interpreted as an anarchist warning and threat. Scarcely had the fears of May Day terror subsided when reports of bombings came from seven cities. On the night of June 2, 1919, the rectory of a Philadelphia Roman Catholic church and the house of a businessman were bombed. The residences of a judge and congressman in Boston were bombed; in Pittsburgh, the home of a federal judge; in Cleveland, the home of the mayor. No one was injured in these bombings. In New York, however, the home of Judge Charles C. Nott was wrecked and a watchman was killed by an explosion. Even more sensational was the bombing of the home of Attorney-General A. Mitchell Palmer.[61]

These bombings were largely responsible for the establishment of the General Intelligence Division within the Department of Justice on August 1, 1919, to "handle investigations connected with ultraradical activities in the United States. This division was formed with the purpose of collecting evidence and data upon the revolutionary and ultraradical movements for use in such proceedings as might be instituted against individual or organizations involved in the same."[62]

A series of blows were struck against foreign-born radicals by arrests on deportation warrants, beginning on November 7, 1919, and continuing on January 2 and February 14, 1920. The first group of 240 were deported on the Army transport *Buford* on December 21, 1919. Most of them were members of the Union of Russian Workers, an anarchist group, and some were members of other Russian radical organizations. Seven of the deportees were charged with nonpolitical offenses. The *Buford* arrived in Hangö, Finland, on January 7, 1920, and the deportees were conveyed to the Russian border under military escort two days later. Emma Goldman and Alexander Berkman, anarchist leaders, were among the deported.[63]

Roughly about 6,000 warrants for deportation were issued by the Secretary of Labor, but only half of them were served on those arrested in raids on January 2 and February 14, 1920. Approximately "4,000 arrests were made, the remainder of these warrants being 'thrown into the discard' by the detectives; that about 3,000 were cancelled after hearings, nearly if not quite all by myself [Louis F. Post, Assistant Secretary of Labor]; and that out of less than 1,000 deportations ordered after hearings, more than 500 were ordered by me."[64] Upon examination of constitutions of the IWW and the Communist and Communist Labor parties, the Secretary of

Labor found that the first two organizations "did not fall within the *inhibitions* of the immigration laws. He therefore held that an alien accused of membership in the IWW must be shown to have participated in or to have been sympathetically cognizant of the activities which the immigration laws condemn before a warrant of arrest could issue. The purport of this decision was that *mere* membership in an organization the constitution of which is lawful does not bring an alien within the proscription of the immigration statutes."[66] The same rule was applied to the Communist Labor party, but membership in the Communist party was held to warrant deportation. In 1920 314 persons were deported for falling within the prohibitions of the law. It was these raids and prosecutions which sent the Communists underground from which they emerged as the Workers' party in 1923.[66]

Effect of Prosecutions on IWW

The relentless campaign of suppression inevitably affected the ability of the IWW to function. Not only could it not carry on normal kinds of agitational and other activities but it was compelled to lead a virtual underground life in Idaho, Washington, and California. The effect of the constant pressure manifested itself in the decline in the level of experience of officers as well as the inability to recruit new members. The 1921 convention compounded the problem by a requirement that officers could only serve one term, after which they were not eligible for re-election until they had worked for an employer for a year. Such a rule expressed the anarchist belief in the primacy and wisdom of the rank and file, and the fear of bureaucracy prevented the development of an officer corps. The inexperience of the leadership is shown in the handling of the Marine Transport Workers Union No. 8 of Philadelphia longshoremen.

This union had functioned and supported the IWW since its formation in 1913. Its officers testified for the defense in the Chicago trial, and they supported the organization despite attacks upon it. Among migratory workers, there had always existed a suspicion that the Philadelphia longshoremen were not true IWW's. It was not at first based upon any specific actions or policies of the Philadelphia longshoremen but rather an expression of the resentment which the highly individualistic, undisciplined anarchistic migrant had against the settled, "respectable" steady worker. The former both envied the latter's good luck, and held his conservative cautiousness in contempt. Consequently, the migratory worker who placed little value on a steady job or income was not sympathetic to the Philadelphia members. As long as the IWW was dominated by men with some experience, the Philadelphia longshoremen were allowed to run their own affairs. The attack upon the only local with job control started on August 16, 1920, when the general executive board learned of a rumor that the longshoremen were loading ammunition to counterrevolutionaries in the Soviet Union. In any event, the local reprimanded the group who loaded ammunition and the issue appeared to be settled.

However, no sooner had this problem been settled when another was raised. At a meeting between representatives of the Philadelphia locals of grain scalers, checkers, and longshoremen and the general executive board, the Philadelphia members were informed that dues would have to be $1.00 a month and the initiation fee $2.00. This directive was rejected by the Philadelphia locals.[67]

E. E. Doree, a defendant in the Chicago trial and out on bail, explained the position of the longshoremen. "The IWW," he said, "has been notoriously unable to maintain shop control. . . . For brief periods, small groups in the IWW have maintained shop control, but it always slips. The only group to maintain shop control is the MTW in Philadelphia. Now, I think we should find the reason why. . . . To have shop control and a really powerful union industrially, it must be built upon a permanent membership who pay dues regularly, not upon a membership which merely pays dues through the busy seasons and, as well, a membership practically free from rejoiners."[68] Doree, insisting that the Philadelphia membership was stable, said that the "small initiation fee of the IWW is a failure. It neither furnishes financial resources to the IWW nor does it form an incentive to the member to keep his dues paid up."[69] He denied that a $25.00 initiation fee was prohibitive.

The executive board was adamant in its insistence that the Philadelphia longshoremen must reduce their initiation fee from $25.00 to $2.00 and attacked them for maintaining a large treasury. The local was suspended, reinstated, and finally expelled in 1922.[70]

CHAPTER 26

Postwar Radicalism and Reaction

With the end of the war, the organized labor movement faced a number of problems requiring almost immediate solutions. Organizing drives, while successful, as in the steel industry, had to be transformed into collective bargaining with union recognition if they were to bear permanent results. In addition, the increased memberships in many unions were impatient with cautious traditional tactics. A search for new policies and methods was underway. The belief that the heads of the movement were old and weary and that individual unions as well as the general labor movement were in need of new and more imaginative leadership was widespread.

Business leaders were also unhappy about the course of events during the war. In their view, organized labor had become too strong, and its improved bargaining position and the protection of the government had allowed unions to expand and gain a foothold in industries normally opposed to their recognition. The more aggressive opponents of organized labor began to urge business to organize so as to resist any further encroachments of labor organizations upon the rights of management. As a consequence, the immediate postwar period witnessed the greatest series of labor disputes in our history.

The number of strikes did not increase after the armistice; they reached a peak of 4,450 in 1917 and were not to be exceeded until 1937. But the number of workers affected in 1919 was about three and one-half times as large as in 1917. The steep rise in the number of strikes was due to the more aggressive mood of labor which encountered the heightened opposition of industry. Many of the strikes, even such apparently radical depar-

341

tures as the Seattle general strike, were defensive actions by unions seeking to hold established positions or an attempt to win some mete of recognition, as in the steel industry, by a bitterly resisting employer. Some of the strikes, like the one conducted by the Amalgamated Clothing Workers of America, sought and won the eight-hour workday. The independent Amalgamated Textile Workers of America, which sought the same objective in the New England textile mills, largely failed. This failure demonstrated again that insurgent or independent unions did not possess a sure-fire formula for success; it was easier to blame traditional unions for their failure than to improve upon their performance.

THE SEATTLE GENERAL STRIKE

The Seattle general strike was called in support of striking metal trades' workers in the shipyards. Dissatisfaction with wage setting had been widespread in this port because of the Shipbuilding Labor Adjustment Board's policy of equalizing wages on the Atlantic and Pacific coasts.

The Metal Trades Unions in Seattle had established a local Metal Trades Council, which reported for the seventeen unions in the ship yards. Demands for wage increases of $1.00 a day across the board were presented and denied by the Shipbuilding Labor Adjustment Board, or the Macy Board, as it was called. While some employers were willing to grant the demands, Charles H. Piez, the general manager of the Emergency Fleet Corporation, disapproved the concessions and they were withdrawn. The Metal Trades Council thereupon called for a strike vote by its affiliates. Approval was given by ten out of seventeen, although the strike call was rejected only by one; six others had failed to approve by the necessary majority under their constitutions.

On January 21, 1919, the metal tradesmen, as directed by the council, struck the shipyards of Seattle and Tacoma. An estimated 32,000 workers left their jobs. On the second day, an appeal for active assistance was made to the Central Labor Council, which polled its affiliated unions on calling a local general strike to support the metal tradesmen. When the general walkout was overwhelmingly approved, the council appointed a general strike committee. Too large and unwieldy, the General Strike Committee placed its authority in the hands of a smaller executive committee on February 2 for the duration of the general strike. The strike began on schedule on the morning of February 6 with an estimated 60,000 workers leaving their jobs. Food kitchens and milk stations were set up, and the people went about their affairs with few protests and little difficulty. The city's crime rate actually was below normal in this period.

On the second day of the strike, Mayor Ole Hanson issued a proclamation in which he guaranteed the people of Seattle "absolute and complete protection. . . . The anarchists in the community shall not rule its affairs. All persons violating the laws will be dealt with summarily."[1]

Officers of unions which had joined the walkout had begun to insist that their members live up to agreements and return to work. Moreover, there was nothing more the general strike could accomplish. It had demonstrated the unity of local labor, but such a demonstration could not compel the shipyards or the U.S. Shipping Board to give up their position. A few unions recognized the futility of continuing the strike on the fourth day and returned to work, but the majority held out until February 11.

As an aftermath, the editors of the Seattle *Union Record,* financed by local labor unions, were indicted for sedition but the case was dropped. It is always difficult to pinpoint the causes of complex events. Very likely the IWW agitation over the years was of some influence. Seattle had been an IWW stronghold, and members of that organization looked upon the city as their own. The city was not hostile to IWW's, and Hanson's predecessor, Mayor Hiram C. Gill, had befriended members of the organization.

Soon after the general strike, Hulet C. Wells was sent as a delegate to the Third International in Moscow. Wells returned in the fall of 1920 and issued a report denouncing the AFL. The meeting of the Central Labor Council greeted Wells's approval of the Soviet dictatorship and attack upon the AFL with loud applause and formal approval. The council was ordered to mend its ways and get into line with the views of the AFL.[2]

The General Strike in Winnipeg, Manitoba, Canada

Canadian labor was also in a militant mood in the postwar period. One of its manifestations was the One Big Union, established in Calgary, Alberta, in March 1919. The OBU resembled the IWW in outlook and program.[3]

The Winnipeg general strike followed the walkout of metal tradesmen and building tradesmen, and on May 6, 1919, the question of whether the strikers would be supported by all labor came before the Winnipeg Trades and Labor Council. Despite the warnings of moderate delegates, the meeting decided to take a strike vote of affiliates. According to the promoters of the inclusive walkout, seventy locals favored the general strike. On May 15, 1919, it began with a committee of five in charge. At first, deliveries of bread and milk were suspended but on the fourth day of the strike they were resumed with the approval of the strike managers. In the early days of the strike, a citizens' committee was organized to help restore vital services. Troops were sent to the city by the national government, and gradually workers in some trades began returning to their jobs.

Demobilized soldiers began parading in support of the strike or in opposition to its continuance. A force of special police was organized to aid in keeping order. It was their appearance on the principal streets which provoked a riot on June 19. Conditions appeared to be getting worse when the employers in the metal trades announced on June 16 that they would deal with members of unions through elected committees but would continue to refuse to recognize the Metal Trades Council. At the same time, the railroad carmen on both the Canadian Pacific and the Canadian Northern railroads voted to return to work.

As the general strike began showing signs of collapse, the government arrested eight strike leaders. On the same day a riot took place before the city hall in which two were killed and thirty injured. Faced by the resolute action of the authorities, the Trades and Labor Council ended the walkout on June 25, six weeks minus one day after the launching of the general strike.

Of the eight strike leaders tried, six were convicted of seditious conspiracy, five were sentenced to a year in prison, and one to six months. One of the accused, J. S. Woodsworth, was tried separately and acquitted.

The One Big Union did not seriously suffer from the lost strike. It gained members and by the end of 1919, it had over 41,000 recruits, 101 local unions and 8 central bodies. It continued its progress in the following year but at a slower rate. Gradually, conservative opinion reasserted itself. The One Big Union tried to invade the United States. Its agents were active in the textile mills of New England but made little impact upon the labor scene in the United States.[4]

THE NEW YORK WATERFRONT

A revolt against the officers of the unions developed on the New York waterfront as a result of dissatisfaction with the wage decisions of third parties. The Tidewater Boatmen's Union was organized in the Port of New York in 1902. Its members were employed on self-propelled coal boats, grain boats, scows, and dumpers. In 1917 the union enrolled harbor workers and lighter captains employed on lighters and barges; separate unions of stationary marine hoisting engineers, and railroad and terminal workers were organized about the same time. These unions, with the Marine Engineers Beneficial Association, established the Marine Workers' Affiliation in the Port of New York, as a central body for negotiating contracts with the employers.[5]

Wages of harbor workers and longshoremen were regulated during the war by the National Adjustment Commission set up by agreement between several government agencies, the AFL and the International Longshoremen's Association. No method for enforcement of awards had been devised, but the parties accepted the view that no interruption of work should take place. Local commissions were set up in twenty-four ports, and the national group acted as a board of appeal. At the expiration of the agreement at the close of the war, the parties reconstituted the National Adjustment Commission.

Employers in the Port of New York did not like to deal with the Marine Workers' Affiliation, and some ignored the award of the Harbor Board authorized to set wages in the Port by the National Adjustment Commission.

An appeal by President Wilson, who was attending the peace conference, led to arbitration. The decision was not accepted by the Marine Workers' Affiliation and a strike followed on March 4.[6]

President Thomas V. O'Connor of the Longshoremen's Union, in an attempt to settle the walkout, suggested that the strikers accept an increase in wages and return to work. Thomas L. Delehanty, president of the Marine Workers' Affiliation, charged O'Connor with being an "interloper."[7]

The April settlement, however, was reluctantly accepted. The peace was not long lasting, for a demand by the deep sea North Atlantic longshoremen for wage increases from 65 cents to $1.00 an hour and $2.00 an hour for overtime was placed before the National Adjustment Commission in September 1919. When the award of 5 cents an hour and 10 cents for overtime was announced, a strike on October 6, 1919 of 25,000 longshoremen completely paralyzed the port. Union officers tried to get the men back to work, and the charters of several of the locals supporting the walkout were revoked. In the meantime, William Z. Ripley, chairman of the National Adjustment Commission, announced that no increase would be granted to these workers on coastwise vessels, since it was necessary to maintain the historical differential between seagoing and coastwise work.

In contrast, all other North Atlantic ports, except for a short strike in Boston, accepted the award. In the Port of New York, the strike continued for four weeks and was a contest between President O'Connor and former vice-presidents of the International Longshoremen's Association. Richard J. Butler, who had been charged with operating a private detective agency to supply strikebreakers and had been denied a seat at the 1919 convention, and F. Paul Vaccarelli, who appeared to have had gangster connections. Both private stevedores and government agencies supported the international officers, and the AFL reiterated its views on the inviolability of contracts. On October 15 it was announced that locals with a membership of 15,000 had voted to return to work. This was a major break in the strike. By November 5 the men voted to return and ended the walkout.

In accordance with its original award, the issues were to be reopened on December 1, 1919, unless the cost of living showed a substantial decline. On that ground, the National Adjustment Commission reopened the wage issue on November 21, 1919, and increased the basic rate, effective

December 1, 1919, from 70 to 80 cents an hour and the overtime rate from $1.10 to $1.20.[8]

ACTORS

The widespread dissatisfaction among manual labor groups also affected the actors. The Actors Society had been organized in 1896, but it only tried to distinguish between bad and good managers. An attempt to broaden the organization into a trade union failed, but enough interest was aroused so that the Actors' Equity Association was founded in 1913. Equity sought affiliation with the AFL, but an actors' union, the Rats Actors Union of America had been formed in 1900. This group merged with the Actors International Union in 1910 and the White Rats Actors Union of America, an AFL affiliate was established in 1910. Its jurisdiction was ratified by the 1911 AFL convention.[9]

The Actors' Equity Association sought a standard contract which would protect its members against excessive rehearsal time, and limit the performances to eight per week unless additional compensation was paid, and some adjustment of the rules requiring purchase of costumes. Neither of the managers' associations would agree.[10] In the fall of 1917, the United Managers' Producers' Association signed a contract with Equity. Actors were assured a minimum of two weeks' employment after four weeks of rehearsal in dramatic shows and six weeks in musicals, a requirement of one week's notice before closing of a show, and two weeks' to an individual actor. Costumes were to be furnished to actresses earning less than $150 a week. Performances were limited to eight a week, except in shows where nine were established, and actors agreed to do unpaid extra performances on eleven designated holidays.[11]

The acceptance of Actors' Equity by the managing producers was only a temporary one. In May 1919 the Producing Managers' Association was formed. It rejected the contract submitted by Equity, and decided to fight on the issue of the closed shop. Lawrence L. Weber the secretary, announced the managers could not deal with an organization "which so far departs from its original ideals as to threaten the profession with what is known as a closed shop."[12]

While the dispute with the managers was going on, Actors' Equity was anxious to be affiliated with the AFL. The problem was that the White Rats had been given jurisdiction over "all parts of theatrical production occurring behind the footlights and in front of the scenery after the same has been placed in position by the stage mechanics . . . and any forms of entertainment known as either legitimate, variety or vaudeville. . . ."[13] Gompers was anxious to find a way to bring Actors' Equity into the federation, and he wrote that Equity "has grown to such proportions and exercises such powers and influence in the legitimate branch of the theatrical profession and dramatic art that its existence has not only been justified but its great beneficial work fully demonstrated."[14] He tried to find a basis for unifying the two actors' organizations and when the White Rats refused to make concessions the adjustment committee of the 1917 AFL convention recommended the cancellation of the White Rats' charter. Despite the claim of Vice-President Frank Duffy that "the White Rats Actors' Union was to all intents and purposes out of business," the convention refused to cancel the charter.[15] The White Rats Actors' Association turned in its charter, and a new one was issued on July 18, 1919, to Associated Actors and Artists of America (Four A's) of which Actors' Equity Association was a part.[16]

The Strike

After efforts to reach agreement failed, Equity called a strike on July 26, 1919, against *Chu Chin Chow,* a musical production. It was only partially successful. While discussions were going on, E. F. Albee, the head of the leading vaudeville chain, entered the controversy and advised an aggressive campaign against the leaders. He had used these tactics and the black list to break the White Rats Actors' Association, and he thought the same methods would yield favorable results for the managers. The actors decided to strike "until the Actors' Equity Association is recognized as the representative of the actor, and until a satisfactory arrangement is made with it governing the working conditions of the actor, we will not perform any service for any manager who is a member of the Producing Managers' Association, or who refuses to recognize our Association, or to issue its contracts, either in plays now being presented, or in plays which are now, or may hereafter be rehearsed."[17]

The strike started on August 7, 1919, spread to Chicago, Boston, and Los Angeles. The New York locals of the musicians' and stagehands' unions insisted that the actors must be recognized, and when the managers refused, they joined the strike. The strike aroused wide interest. It was not often that a Barrymore, an Eddie Cantor, or Ed Wynn was seen on a picket line or at a strike meeting. A few of the stars chose to support the managers; George M. Cohan was one who showed the most anger at the unionization of the actors and regarded it as a personal affront. But the majority of established actors sided with Equity, although a company union, the Actors' Fidelity League was established. The strike had the full support of the labor movement, and Gompers came to New York to speak to a strike meeting. After almost a month, a five-year contract, specifying rehearsal conditions, limiting performances to eight per week, and allowing for arbitration was signed.[18]

POLICE STRIKE

Policemen in many parts of the country were swept into the labor organizing campaigns in many communities. Boston, Los Angeles, Portland, Oregon, St. Paul, and Jersey City were among the thirty-seven cities in which policemen organized. Failure of money wages to keep pace with the rising cost of living was the chief cause for the change in the policemen's attitude towards labor organization. In Washington the policemen were ordered to resign from their union, and they contested the decision in the courts.[19] In Boston the members of the Policemen's Union refused to resign.[20] Police Commissioner Edwin U. Curtis thereupon announced a campaign to recruit a voluntary police force.

In a statement, officers of the union attempted to allay the fear that their affiliation with the AFL would deter members from doing their duty: "The members of the Boston Policemen's Union intend to do their full duty as police officers in the future as in the past, and retain their full membership in the American Federation of Labor."[21] In an effort to avert a walkout, a citizens' committee appointed by Mayor Andrew J. Peters and headed by James J. Storrow, recommended that the union disaffiliate from the AFL, and that a committee of three, one each appointed by the mayor, the union, and the police commissioner devise a plan for adjusting wages and working conditions. Commissioner Curtis rejected the recommendations. He also suspended nineteen officers of the union.

The suspensions were a signal for a strike of 1,500 policemen, on September 11, 1919, who made up about 85 per cent of the force. Absence of police was followed by twenty-four hours of rioting, looting, and violence. At the request of the city authorities, Governor Calvin Coolidge sent 5,000 militiamen to keep order. The governor was advised by the Massachusetts Federation of Labor that the removal of Commissioner Curtis and the reinstatement of the suspended policemen was necessary. The governor refused to overrule the commissioner, and expressed the "hope that circumstances may arise which will cause the police officers who have been suspended to be re-instated."[22] When the governor took command of the situation the following day, he described the strike of the policemen as "a desertion of duty."[23]

On September 10, a clash between soldiers and a mob resulted in the killing of two of the rioters, and the wounding of several others. Five more people were killed the next day, and one on September 13. The Central Labor Union called for a vote on the calling of a general strike, but the strike ended before action could be taken. President Woodrow Wilson, in a speech in Helena, Montana, denounced the strike as "a crime against humanity."[24] By September 14, order had been pretty well restored by the militia and voluntary police. Samuel Gompers sought an end of the dispute by a compromise. He suggested that the striking policemen return to work, and the suspensions be decided later. The Policemen's Union voted to accept. Commissioner Curtis, supported by the governor, found the proposal unacceptable, and Gompers then charged Curtis with responsibility for the strike. He said the AFL did not recruit policemen, but he described their organization as "a natural reflex of futile individual attempts to improve working conditions. . . . When men are underpaid or work under bad conditions, they seek redress."[25] Gompers said that policemen's unions were chartered by the AFL "with the distinct understanding that strike action will not be resorted to and no obligation is assumed which conflicts with their oaths of duty."[26]

Neither the commissioner nor the governor would allow rehiring of strikers. The Central Labor Union found the time inopportune for the calling of a general strike, and the policemen decided not to contest their dismissals in the courts. The calling of the Boston strike and its defeat halted the movement of policemen into unions, and many of those which existed were forced to dissolve on the threat of dismissal.

COAL

The Washington Agreement of October 6, 1917, regulated wages in the bituminous coal industry. According to Acting President John L. Lewis, the agreement was based upon an implicit assumption that the cost of living would be stabilized. Such expectations were not realized. An added complication was the bidding for workers by the operators; this was occasioned by shortages of coal miners resulting from voluntary enlistments and drafting into the armed services. To devise a policy to meet the situation, representatives of all districts met in Washington in August 1918, but the union representatives were informed by Fuel Administrator Harry A. Garfield that he would not permit any meeting of union and operator representatives for the purpose of adjusting wages.

Unrest spread through both the anthracite and bituminous coal fields. While Garfield was adamant against any wage increases, the strike of 20,000 anthracite miners in the Shamokin District caused him to reconsider. He sponsored an agreement which resulted in a wage increase from 90 cents to $1.10 a day.[27] In the bituminous coal fields, he would not allow a wage increase, and a dispute arose after the armistice as to whether the contract was still in existence in the bituminous fields. Under the Washington Agreement, the contract continued for the duration of the war but not later than April 1920. Many miners, not appreciating the subtleties of contract making, were convinced that the war had ended with the armistice. As a result, an insurgent movement of substantial proportions started in the Illinois District No. 12, the largest district in the union. It appeared for a short time that a fully developed secessionist movement had started. A convention of delegates from 141 locals with thousands of members protested the failure to raise wages. District President Frank Farrington, a power in the union, aided by the international headquarters, succeeded in suppressing the rebellion.

As a result of the wildcat strike, the penalty of $1.00 a day for time lost was imposed on all Illinois strikers. This penalty clause had been inserted in the contract at the insistence of Garfield, and the monies collected were turned over to the Red Cross. The penalties were a sore point with the men. Acting on the recommendations of the National Policy Committee made in March 1919, a convention of 2,044 delegates drew up a series of demands in September 1919 for a 60 per cent increase, the five-day week and the six-hour day, and the abolition of the penalty clause. Contracts were terminated effective on November 1, 1919.[28] When no progress was made in negotiations, the strike was called on schedule.

The government thereupon secured a restraining order in the U.S. District Court of Indiana on the ground that the strike was in violation of the Lever Food and Fuel Act. Judge Albert B. Anderson ordered the strike order canceled. A meeting of union officers voted to comply formally, and the U.S. Attorney, L. Bert Slack, assured Attorney-General A. Mitchell Palmer that the "withdrawal order duly signed in ink by the President and Secretary approved by Judge Anderson was mimeographed and sent also assured us that impression of seal not required by their laws and not customary or usual to affix seal in like cases we believe withdrawal order was prepared and sent out in good faith. [sic]"[29]

Acting President Lewis announced that "We cannot fight the government," but the miners did not heed his directive to return to work. It may be that the absence of a seal on the order was the reason for the disobedience, but no coal was produced in the union fields. When the strike continued, the federal government intervened again. Contempt proceedings were inaugurated against eighty-four officers of the United Mine Workers of America by the government before Judge Anderson. Subsequently, a federal grand jury indicted eighty-two operators and forty-three miners for violating the Lever Act. Former Supreme Court Justice Charles Evans Hughes was retained by the union as chief defense counsel, but the case was never brought to trial. A proposal by Fuel Administrator Garfield that wages be raised 14 per cent immediately and the other issues, including additional wage increases, be submitted to a board of arbitration was accepted. A board made up of John P. White, former president of the United Mine Workers of America; Rembrandt Peale, an operator; and W. M. Robinson, a California businessman, recommended with White dissenting a 27 per cent increase. It did not meet the expectations of the miners, but they accepted.

For the next decade the coal miners' union was to be wracked by opposition from the outside and factionalism from within. Historically, power in the United Mine Workers of America was centered mainly in the large organized districts. District leaders of the big districts were a force to reckon with. Moreover, differences between groups based either upon personal friendship, agreement on policy, or social views were not uncommon. Throughout most of his tenure in the national office, John Mitchell was opposed by Thomas L. Lewis, whose animus induced him after he had succeeded Mitchell to force him out of his post with the National Civic Federation.

John L. Lewis' rise to leadership within the Coal Miners' Union was not routine. He did hold a series of offices in his district, and after a stint as legislative agent for the Illinois District 12 in Springfield he became an organizer for the AFL. He was International Statistician in 1917 and later in the year, when President White took a post with the Fuel Administration, Vice-President Frank Hayes moved up to the presidency and appointed Lewis acting vice-president. Hayes resigned in the fall of 1919, and Lewis then became acting head of the largest union in the United States.

Lewis came into office at a time when the union faced the most difficult problems in its history. The growth of nonunion tonnage in West Virginia, Kentucky, and other states threatened the markets of the organized fields. The powerful opposition of the heads of several districts, including Frank Farrington, president of Illinois District No. 12, hampered the development of a flexible policy which might have solved some of the difficulties facing the union districts. While Farrington was the leader who supplied the votes and funds to Lewis' opponents, the nominal head of the opposition was Alexander Howat, president of Kansas District No. 14. The differences between the two men were complicated by Howat's opposition to the Kansas Court of Industrial Relations.

Kansas Court of Industrial Relations

Howat was a trade union militant and a recognized opponent of the international administration. Charged with accepting money from an operator, he had sued for vindication. He also claimed that the international officers had not shown sufficient confidence in his innocence, and several days were given over at the 1916 international convention to a debate on the innocence of Howat and the failure of the international officers to defend him. Since the presiding officer of the convention was involved in the issue, John L. Lewis, a delegate, was asked to act in his place. Lewis' demeanor as presiding officer did not please Howat.

The two men were political opponents within the union and they divided on another issue. The Kansas Court of Industrial Relations was established at the suggestion of Governor Henry J. Allen after the 1919 coal strike had caused a shutdown of virtually all coal mining in the state. Allen, who was not without national political ambitions, recommended compulsory arbitration of labor disputes in such public utilities as the fuel, food, and clothing industries. Wages and other conditions of employment were to be fixed, and penalties for violation of orders were defined. The Kansas labor movement protested the enactment, and the union miners refused to cooperate with the newly created court. In fact, the district convention voted to fine members cooperating with the tribunal. When Howat refused to obey the orders of the court, he was sentenced to jail for contempt. Protest strikes were called by a number of locals. The operators appealed to the international which revoked charters of locals refusing to order their members back to work. Howat supported the recalcitrant locals, and he was also suspended by the international union. Inevitably the AFL convention considered the Kansas law. It was denounced in the report of the executive council as "unjust, tyrannical and un-American. It was enacted during a time of great hysteria created through the propaganda of the governor of the State of Kansas. Bitter attacks were made on Labor. The law gives absolute protection to the public utilities owners."[30] A number of resolutions on the subject, including one from Alexander Howat were, also considered.

The convention instructed the executive council to cooperate with the organized labor groups in Kansas "to assist . . . in securing the relief they ask in bringing about the repeal of the laws involved."[31] A dispute soon arose between the United Mine Workers of America and the AFL over the support given the Kansas miners by state federations of labor and other central labor bodies. When Alexander Howat and Vice-President August Dorchy of District No. 14 of the United Mine Workers of America defied the Industrial Court law, they were imprisoned for contempt. Thousands of miners struck in protest. Lewis intervened and ordered their return. When they refused, their charters were lifted. The issue became intertwined with the factional dispute in the United Mine Workers of America, then at fever heat. Support of District No. 14 by state federations of labor led to the presenting of a request by the International Executive Board of the United Mine workers of America "that the President of the American Federation of Labor and the Executive Council declare themselves as in favor of collective bargaining, the observance of contracts voluntarily entered into and full compliance with the laws and decisions of affiliated unions by the membership over which they recognize jurisdiction."[32]

The executive council approved of the observance of contracts but refused to notify "State Federations, central bodies, local unions throughout the country . . . that they shall not in any way support the striking miners of Kansas who have gone on strike in protest against the imprisonment of Alexander Howat and Mr. August Dorchy."[33] It is, of course, difficult to determine to what extent the views of the executive council were colored by the campaign of John L. Lewis to unseat Gompers as president of the AFL. Since the Hearst chain of newspapers carried on a vigorous campaign against Gompers, it is possible that members of the council regarded Lewis' willingness to run under such circumstances as unfair. While this matter was not mentioned, the council pointed to the unanimous adoption of the following resolution by the AFL convention in June 1921:

Resolved, That we commend the organized workers of Kansas and particularly the mine workers and their officers of that state, upon whom the brunt of the battle has fallen, for so courageously opposing this law in the face of injunctions and threats of imprisonment by hostile judges; and thereby preventing this objectionable law becoming operative in the state selected for this legislative experiment and thus fighting the battle for the organized workers of the country.[34]

Gompers told Lewis that the executive council in view of the "emphatic instructions of the conventions of the A.F. of L. is to avoid any public statement which would certainly be interpreted and used to defeat the very purpose of these declarations. In addition, the Executive Council is fully persuaded that the effort to obtain a favorable decision from the judiciary as to the Kansas Industrial Court Law will prove futile and that the only hope for the repeal of that infamous statute lies in action by the organized workers of Kansas to demonstrate the utter futility of the attempt by law to prevent the strikes and to arouse the consciousness of the people of Kansas to that fact."[35]

War in West Virginia

The troubles of the Coal Miners' Union were not limited to internal differences although to a large extent they were accentuated by the problems facing the union. Since the first contract in the Central Competitive Field in 1898, the leaders were aware that their stabilizing program of prices and wages could not survive without the unionization of the West Virginia coal fields. Efforts to bring these into the union fold were continually made, but the opposition of the operators was too great. After World War I, another effort to reverse the situation was made, and the union succeeded in organizing about half of the 100,000 coal miners in West Virginia.[36]

It was difficult, however, to maintain the organization for in the non-union counties of Mingo, Logan, and McDowell, the operators refused to deal with the union. In May 1920 a strike was called in Mingo County, the main non-union area. Baldwin-Felts guards immediately appeared. When they evicted some miners from Mathewan, Chief of Police Sid Hatfield became embroiled in a dispute with Albert and Lee Felts and several others. The Felts brothers, four guards, the mayor, a small boy, and a miner were killed. Hatfield was tried for murder and acquitted. Later, accompanied by his wife and unarmed, he was shot down on the steps of the courthouse in Welch, McDowell County, where he had gone at the order of the court. His assassins pleaded self-defense and were acquitted. In the meantime, strikers were thrown out of the company-owned houses and tent colonies erected by the union for their shelter.

Repeated clashes brought federal troops into the area in August 1920. District President Frank Keeney denounced the move. The miners continued their strike, and in January 1921 reasonable quiet had returned and federal troops were withdrawn.

Warfare between miners and strike guards became serious again in May 1921. The miners decided on a large-scale action. In the Cabin and Paint Creek areas, the miners' forces were mobilized, in August 1921, and a plan was devised for invading Logan County, which was dominated by Sheriff Don Chafin, an enemy of the miners' organization. The sheriff organized a force of deputies to repel the invasion. At this point the governor appealed for troops. In the meantime, the miners' contingent had grown to several thousand. President Warren Harding ordered the armed strikers to disperse, but they refused and continued their advance. When fighting between armed miners and deputies seemed inevitable, President Harding ordered troops into Logan County. The miners offered no resistance, surrendered their arms, and dispersed. Officially, the strike continued, until October 1922, when it was terminated by the union. Many miners were indicted for various crimes but after the acquittal of William Blizzard, a union officer, the cases were dismissed.

The Herrin Massacre

The most serious violence to darken coal-mining history in the 1920's took place in Herrin, Illinois. It was an incident in the strike in the Central Competitive fields which began on April 1, 1922. The Southern Illinois Coal Company, controlled by William J. Lester, had opened a strip mine and employed union miners. During the strike he was allowed by the local union officials to uncover the dirt from the overlying coal on condition that no coal be shipped.[37] But guards from a private detective agency in Chicago were brought in to protect strikebreakers. They snarled and threatened those who came near the mine operations and aroused resentment among the strikers. Aware of the danger to the strikebreakers and property, the personnel officer of the Illinois National Guard urged Lester to close down operations, but he refused. The sheriff of Williamson County, in which Herrin was located, added his plea but Lester was adamant. On June 19, William J. Sneed, president of the subdistrict in which Williamson County was located, wired Lewis to determine the status of the Shovel Men's Union to which the strikebreakers claimed affiliation. Lewis replied that the particular union was an "outlaw" organization and that the members were scabs.[38] Shots had already been exchanged between guards and strikers; two union miners had been killed and one of the wounded died later. Miners attacked the mine. When the guards and strikebreakers surrendered they were beaten and shot, and mine buildings and cars were set on fire. Eighteen of the strikebreakers, including Superintendent C. K. McDowell, were killed. The gruesome slaying of men who had surrendered aroused the entire country.[39]

In September the grand jury of Williamson County indicted 214 men in connection with the Herrin massacre—44 for murder, 58 for conspiracy, 58 for rioting, and 54 for assault to murder. The grand jury also found that Sheriff Melvin Thaxton had failed to take adequate measures to preserve order. It upheld the right of the Southern Coal Company to operate, but noted that it "was either woefully ignorant of the danger of its operations or blindly determined to risk strife and conflict if profits could be made."[40] Five of the indicted went to trial for murder on November 8, 1922. On January 18, 1923, they were acquitted. Two of the acquitted, Otis Clark and Bert Grace, were joined by four other defendants in the second trial on charges of killing one of the other strikebreakers.

The second trial began on February 12, 1923, and on April 6 the second trial was over; the six defendants had been acquitted.[41]

THE STEEL CAMPAIGN

On April 7, 1918, William Z. Foster, a delegate from the Chicago local of the Brotherhood of Carmen, proposed that a joint organizing drive by the unions in the steel industry be undertaken. The proposal was approved, and Foster, who was elected a delegate to the 1918 convention of the AFL, proposed that the executive council call a meeting "of delegates of all international unions whose interests are involved in the steel industries and of all the State Federations and City Central bodies in the steel district, for the purpose of uniting all these organizations into one mighty drive to organize the steel plants of America."[42]

A preliminary conference was held during the convention and later, on August 1, 1918, the National Committee for Organizing the Iron and Steel Workers was formed with Gompers as chairman; John Fitzpatrick of the Chicago Federation of Labor, vice-chairman; and Foster, secretary. Each of the organizations represented donated $100 and also allocated organizers to the steel territories.[43]

The campaign opened on September 1, 1918, and the workers responded in large numbers to the appeal to organize. Thousands of workers paid an initiation fee and a month's dues. Large numbers joined the Union in Gary, Hammond, Indiana Harbor, and South Chicago, Indiana. By the end of September, the Amalgamated Association of Iron, Steel and Tin Workers was able to announce that the Calumet district around Chicago, one of the great steel-producing regions, was almost completely organized. The main thrust of the campaign was now directed to organizing the major steel centers in Pennsylvania, Ohio, and outlying plants.

The steel companies followed two kinds of tactics. In some communities organizers were harassed and meetings were suppressed. These methods were especially common in some important steel communities in Western Pennsylvania. On the other hand, successful meetings were held and members openly recruited in the Chicago area and in Gary, Indiana. "Spotters," operatives of private detective agencies, uncovered those who had affiliated and many were discharged, but it had no obvious effect upon organization. Actually, it spurred many of the newly organized to demand some kind of action, namely, a strike call.

On May 15, Michael F. Tighe, the head of the Amalgamated Association of Iron, Steel and Tin Workers, proposed a meeting to Elbert Gary, chairman of the board of the U.S. Steel Corporation. The action was taken on his own without consulting the National Committee for Organizing the Iron and Steel Workers. Tighe explained that this move was based on the view that his union and its members had a primary and predominant interest in the steel industry and that any attempt to reach a peaceable settlement was warranted. Although Gary acknowledged the letter, he would not negotiate.

Tighe's action was irregular in that he consulted neither his labor colleagues nor Fitzpatrick and Foster, who were the active heads of the National Committee, and for that omission he could be justifiably criticized. His position that he had a special interest in the industry and consequently was justified in seeking to protect it was not an unsupportable view. First of all, recognition of the paramount union in the industry, the one which controlled the men with the highest skill, would have broken down the barriers to all organization. It might also be argued that the individual approach was an open sign of weakness and lack of unity and could have encouraged the steel companies to greater resistance. There is, however, no evidence that the policies of the major companies were in any way influenced by Tighe's action. It certainly did not dent the unity of the steel worker. On May 25 a conference of 583 delegates from the unions in the industry directed that bargaining be sought with the major companies and elected a committee, including Fitzpatrick and Foster, to initiate efforts to that end. When Gary refused to acknowledge Gompers' request for a conference, the National Committee recommended that the twenty-four cooperating unions be advised to take a strike vote among members.

At a meeting in Pittsburgh on July 20, 1919, plans for a strike vote and the presentation of demands were made. The latter called for the establishment of the right to collective bargaining; reinstatement of those discharged for joining a union with pay for time lost; an eight-hour day and one day's rest in seven; abolition of the twenty-four-hour shift; establishment of standard scales of pay in all classifications; checkoff of dues; seniority to be used in layoffs and recalls to work; and abolition of physical examinations for applicants.[44]

The vote was overwhelming for a strike. Armed with this power, the committee appointed to negotiate called at the offices of the U.S. Steel Corporation and sought an interview with Gary. He refused to meet them, asked for their proposals in writing, and publicly announced that the committee had not been authorized to speak for the employees of the corporation. Accompanied by Gompers, the committee called on President Wilson, and although the President was sympathetic to the desire of the union representatives to establish collective bargaining, he was unable to change Gary's position. In the meantime, the steel workers were showing increasing signs of restiveness prompted by the discharge of active union members. On September 9 the heads of the twenty-four unions and the National Committee met in Washington to review the situation. They conferred for three days. President Wilson urged the postponement of the strike. The unions in a lengthy letter gave the President the reasons for their refusal. They pointed to Gary's statement that the steel workers had no need for "trained representation in their behalf in presenting grievances, the systematic persecution ever since the men started to organize, the denial of free speech by local officers encouraged by the steel companies," the planting "of guns and cannon" in the mills and the intimidation of workers by armed men, and the lack of "opposition to the men joining dual organizations." Finally, the letter concluded "delay is no longer possible. We have tried to find a way, but can not. We regret that for the first time your call upon organized labor can not meet with favorable response."[45] Gompers urged caution. He feared that the pressure for a walkout by the unorganized and newly unionized should be, at least temporarily, resisted. The overwhelming majority of the union heads were of a different opinion, although three union presidents voted for a strike postponement.

The strike was called for September 22, 1919, and was answered by the majority of steelworkers in every region. The National Committee claimed that 279,000 were out. Three days later it was reported that 340,-000 were out. On October 9 the strike, according to union sources, reached its greatest effectiveness, with 367,000 workers out. The companies questioned the figures and insisted that most of the strikers were unskilled workers who could be easily replaced.[46]

Clashes between strikers, deputized sheriffs, and private guards began at once. And the heads of the governments in the steel towns were not always neutral in the dispute. Meetings of strikers and their sympathizers were suppressed. William Z. Foster, who was a key figure in the organization campaign and in the strike, became a target of the press. His radical past was now resurrected, and the pamphlet on syndicalism which he and Earl Ford had authored was now dusted off to demonstrate that the steel strike was a radical conspiracy. Gompers defended Foster before a Senate Committee called to investigate the strike.[47]

The attitude of many local officials of western Pennsylvania communities was summed up by the mayor of Duquesne in denying a speaking permit to AFL Secretary Frank Morrison: "Jesus Christ himself could not hold a meeting in Duquesne."[48] In contrast to the behavior of Pennsylvania authorities, where the governor believed that suppression of free speech and assembly was purely a local matter, civil liberties in West Virginia were maintained throughout the strike. But the companies were determined to reopen their plants with strikebreakers. The Pennsylvania Federation of Labor held a conference on November 2 and called upon the governor and the United States government to restore civil rights to the workers in the state. The pleas went unheeded. Thousands of Negroes joined white strikebreakers in manning the plants. The Interchurch World Movement sought to effect a settlement, but it was no more successful than the government. In Gary, Indiana, a clash between strikers and strikebreakers resulted in the sending of the National Guard by the Indiana governor. Later he appealed for federal troops, and General Leonard Wood arrived with several companies. Martial law was established. An appeal for aid to the strikers was issued by the AFL on October 28. Although many of the strikers possessed few resources, the relief system instituted by the National Committee was effective in meeting every significant need. It was economically and efficiently managed.

The strike, while it succeeded in tying up the major plants in the steel industry, became increasingly ineffective as a result of the displacement of strikers. The repression and the success of the companies resulted in a proposal to end the walkout on December 13. It was supported only by the Amalgamated Association of Iron and Steel Workers and the Operating Engineers' Union. This gesture only postponed the inevitable, for on January 5, the executive board of the Amalgamated requested the end of the strike and the National Committee complied.[49] Twenty people, eighteen of them strikers, were killed. The most shocking was the brutal slaying of Mrs. Fanny Selins, a grandmother and strike organizer. Foster resigned at the end of January 1920 entirely on his own volition. He himself testified that the AFL and the international leaders stood by him during the time he was under attack for his former radical views.[50]

Inevitably, the failure of the strike was attributed, at least by some commentators, to the lack of unity, inadequate financial support, and the form of organization—a joint campaign by the twenty-four unions comprising the National Committee rather than a campaign by one industrial organization. But there never was before or since a more successful organizing campaign. The Report and Accounting of the National Committee for Organizing Iron and Steel Workers showed that organizers working under the direction of the committee recruited 156,702 members, who were distributed among the cooperating unions. The number allocated ranged from two for the Steam Shovel Men's Union to 70,026 for the Amalgamated Association of Iron, Steel and Tin Workers. "This detailed report includes only those signed up by the National Committee for Organizing Iron and Steel Workers and from whom initiation fees of $1.00 each was deducted and forwarded to the general office of the National Committee. It represents approximately 50 per cent to 60 per cent of the total number of steel workers organized during the campaign."[51]

The accounting did not include thousands of workers who joined but upon whose initiation fees no deduction was levied by the National Committee. In addition, "thousands more were signed up directly by the multitude of local unions in the steel industry that were not reported to the National Committee."[52] "It was reported that the financial cost of the year's work to one or two of the twenty-four unions of the Committee, in maintaining organizers, contributions, meetings, etc. approximated $200,000 a piece."[53]

Funds cannot be regarded as a limiting factor. The total receipts for strike relief reached $418,141.13, and at the end of the strike an unused $69,631.42 was turned over to the National Committee.

Did the workers in 1919 lack the will to stay organized? The evidence does not justify such a conclusion. Nor was the fact that they were organized in twenty-four separate unions a necessary weakness. It may be that the division of workers among so many organizations would have impeded the smooth functioning of collective bargaining and imposed severe strain upon the system. However, the steel workers were never able to reach that stage; they were overwhelmed by superior power. Workers in 1919 had no Labor Board to protect their right to organize and they could not, as did the Steel Workers Organizing Committee in the Little Steel Strike, retrieve a lost strike in the courts. Gary could freely say in 1919: it "has been my policy, the policy of our corporation, not to deal with labor leaders."[54]

In the Little Steel strike in 1937, the companies were no more squeamish about their tactics than Gary had been eighteen years earlier. Moreover, they were able to defeat the union and compel it to go back to the plants without a contract. The difference was that the union now turned to the National Labor Relations Board, which compelled the companies to recognize formally the Steel Workers Organizing Committee by signing a written agreement.

The loss of the steel strike was only one manifestation of the belligerency of employers in the period immediately following World War I. The steel strike must be regarded as a defensive action; for had the steel industry granted the unions even a modicum of recognition, the strike would never have been called. Employers, who in many instances had been compelled during wartime to recognize unions or deal with them, were anxious to throw off the shackles imposed by such organizations. The design of employers is evident in other industries and in their general attitude toward organized labor. In carrying out their plans they were aided greatly by the decisions of the U.S. Supreme Court and the conservative mood that took possession of the country.

CHAPTER **27**

Employer Attacks and
the American Plan

THE COURTS

The employer offensive in general, as well as in particular industries, was supported by the attitude of the courts and conservative opinion. In a series of decisions beginning with the Hitchman case, the U.S. Supreme Court made it more difficult for labor organizations to carry on defensive or offensive campaigns against employers.

The decision of the U.S. Supreme Court in *Hitchman Coal and Coke Company* v. *Mitchell,* 245 U.S. 229 (1917), was a severe blow to organized labor. A suit started in the U.S. District Court of West Virginia involved the right of a corporation to restrain a union from organizing its employees who had signed a yellow-dog contract not to join a labor organization during their tenure with the company. The United Mine Workers of America ignored the agreement between the individual employees and the company and launched an organizing drive to recruit them into the union. Thereupon, the company sought an injunction in the U.S. District Court to restrain the organization from carrying on its recruiting campaign. Ignoring the fact that such yellow-dog contracts were signed under economic duress and that their enforcement denied the workers an opportunity to join a union, the Supreme Court found that "the inducing of employees to unite with the union in an effort to subvert the system of employment at the mine by concerted breaches of the contracts of employment known to be in force there . . . [was an] unlawful and malicious method, and . . . [was] not to be justified as a fair exercise of the right to increase the membership of the Union." This decision made the yellow-dog contract a more effective instrument to inhibit unionization. Followed by *Duplex* v. *Deering,* 224 U.S. 443 (1921), *Truax* v. *Corrigan,* 257 U.S. 312 (1921), and *American Steel Foundries* v. *Tri-City Trades Council,* 251 U.S. 184 (1921), the U.S. Supreme Court stripped labor of the protection of the Clayton Act and upheld the right of the federal and state courts to restrict severely the activities of organized workers. In fact, under the theory that the carrying on of a business was a property right and therefore constitutionally protected, the court in *Truax* v. *Corrigan* forbade states to prohibit the issuance of injunctions in labor disputes on the ground that the failure to prevent mass picketing constituted a denial of protection to property.

Always alert to the effect of the acts of government and the courts upon the activities of organized labor, Gompers, on February 22, 1922, called the attention of the AFL Executive Council to "the rapidly growing abuse of the writ of injunction. . . . As you are aware, scarcely a day passes that does not witness the issuance of an injunction against workers somewhere in the country, either ordering them to do things which they have a lawful right not to do or ordering them not to do things which they have a lawful right to do."[1]

Alluding to the difficulties facing unions in making an effective legal defense against the increasing use of injunctions, he advised that it "should be our object to prevent the issuance of unlawful writs of injunction wherever possible; but where such injunctions are issued, the only course open to the workers is the course laid down in the declarations of our conventions. The unlawful injunction must be regarded by workers as non-existent and their conduct must be such as it would be if no such decree had been issued. The immediate consequences may be inconvenient but the ultimate result will be the retention of our freedom."[2]

INDUSTRIAL CONFERENCES

The attitude of business—especially large business—was also evident in the attitude of the employer members of the First Industrial Conference. In an effort to continue the wartime labor-management truce, at least in the formal sense, President Wilson called a meeting of labor, management, farmers, and the public to devise a policy to promote industrial peace. Gompers, who was charged with selecting the labor representatives, found himself criticized for not appointing the heads of the railroad brotherhoods as labor members. A number of other unions also complained of the failure to choose their officers as delegates. A system of representation was finally evolved which was acceptable to the majority of labor groups. Although

Gompers had no illusions on the importance of such a conference, he believed some good might come of it.

The conference opened on October 6 with fifty delegates present, including Elbert Gary and John D. Rockefeller, Jr., who attended as representatives of the public. Bert M. Jewell of the Railway Employees' Department was also a public representative, presumably to offset Gary and Rockefeller. Each of the three groups—labor, management, and the public—voted as a block and the unanimous approval of the three blocks was necessary for adoption of a proposal.

On October 14, Gompers, on behalf of the labor delegation, proposed the arbitration of the steel strike by a tripartite group of six to be drawn from the conference. Gary answered that he favored conciliation, arbitration, and cooperation whenever these laudable methods could be carried out without sacrificing principle. The laudatory methods could not be used in the pending steel strike, and he came out unequivocally for the open shop. Nor would Gary concede the right of organized labor to speak for the workers in the steel industry.[3]

Gary's adamant views reflected the opinion of many employers in and out of the conference. A split between the employer and labor delegations developed over an endorsement of collective bargaining. The labor representatives wanted an interpretation given which would recognize the right of the worker to join a union of his choice and bargain with his employer over the terms of employment through representatives of his own choosing, not necessarily on the company's payroll. The employer group favored a more restricted view which they believed would not encourage outside unions. When the employer contingent rejected a resolution endorsing "the right of wage earners to organize without discrimination, to bargain collectively, to be represented by representatives of their own choosing in negotiations, and adjustments with employers in respect to wages, hours of work, and relations and conditions of employment is recognized,"[4] the labor group withdrew, and the conference ended.

According to Henry S. Dennison, a member of the employer group, the "Employers Group stood very firmly against the necessity for any employer to meet with [a] representative of his workmen if that representative was not in his own employ. . . . Labor's special point was not so rigid but was a point which they pressed with vigor, although they couldn't press it as a general principle. It was that the Federation principle, the trades union principle, was the one principle of organization for employees which should be encouraged. . . . I put it that way because they could not and specifically did not stand against the work committee or shop unions as a principle. They simply said that they would be misused by employers and that there was no hope for the labor movement in any such form of organization; that the hope lay in their own form, the trades union."[5]

The Second Conference

Having failed to get agreement of the important labor and employer groups, the government called a second conference of public members only. In testifying before the meeting, Gompers doubted the effectiveness of solutions by tripartite boards. He believed that in a period of reaction, such as prevailed at the time, labor would fare poorly. He doubted the possibility of devising a simple formula for settling labor disputes. The conference itself did little but express the hope that friendlier feelings between the parties might develop. It advocated reliance on voluntary methods.[6]

The Open-Shop American Plan

Anti-union campaigns were normally part of the American economic and political landscape but "never before has America seen an open shop drive on a scale so vast as that which characterizes the drive now sweeping the country. Never before has an open-shop drive been so heavily financed, so efficiently organized, so skillfully generaled. The present drive flies all the flags of patriotic wartime propaganda. It advances in the name of democracy, freedom, human rights, Americanism."[7]

On January 21, 1921, a national conference of state Manufacturers' associations, meeting in Chicago, suggested that industry be run on the "American Plan," i.e., a shop which does not deal with the union.

Some employers were not satisfied with the definition and A. M. Glossbrenner of the Indiana Manufacturers' Association declared, "we will not employ an individual in any part of the plant that does not sign an individual contract in which it is expressed that he is not and will not become a member of a labor organization while in our employ."[8] The open-shop policy meant even more. Testifying before the Legislative (Lockwood) Committee of New York state investigating building costs, Eugene Grace, the head of the Bethlehem Steel Corporation, claimed his company would not sell fabricated steel to union builders and contractors in the New York and Philadelphia area.[9]

Grace admitted that the Structural Iron Workers' Union had not discriminated against nonunion products, but he nevertheless held his policy was in the public interest. According to President William H. Barr, in "1,300 cities of this country Chambers of Commerce have recommended the open shop."[10] Practically every industrial center developed an "American Plan" open-shop organization. In Seattle the Associated Industries was organized in March 1919 by open-shop employers desiring to spread the American Plan. In January of the following year, the Associated Industries of Detroit adopted the American Plan of Employment which declared for full discretion on the terms of employment by the employer.[11] The National Open Shop Association, which sought to establish local units, advised its potential members that the "work must be clothed with the utmost secrecy, as we have found that publicity usually beats our purpose. For this reason you can feel assured that we will treat the matter in strict confidence."[12]

The Associated Employers of Indianapolis initiated the movement to combine the loosely organized employer groups into a unified whole, and many employers' groups were induced to support the movement. Others were especially organized to promote it.

The propaganda materials of all the groups sponsoring the American Plan of Employment stressed the need for giving the employer full control in industry, decried the practices of organized labor, especially limitation of output and union security, and urged generally that employers eliminate the unions from their properties. Open-shop organizations were active in virtually every community.[13] The developing situation was regarded as sufficiently serious to cause the AFL Executive Council to call a conference of resident labor officials to decide on a program to be followed. On the advice of this group, a conference of national and international representatives was called for Washington on February 23, 1921.[14]

The purpose of the conference was to devise "ways and means of meeting the nation-wide attempt to destroy the American Labor Movement under the guise of an 'open shop' campaign—the question of an enlarged publicity campaign by organized labor to be made a special order of business of that meeting."[15]

Attended by representatives of ninety-seven national and international unions affiliated with the AFL and from three of the railway brotherhoods, the conference called for public support of collective bargaining, "removal by Congress of the usurped power of courts to declare unconstitutional laws enacted by Congress, election of judges, immediate restoration of exemption from or repeal of all anti-combination and so-called conspiracy laws, and repeal of all industrial court laws and other legislation which restricts the rights of workers to organize. The conference also called for an investigation of private detective agencies by Congress.[16]

The open-shop campaign under the slogan of the American Plan of Employment made serious inroads upon the organizations established during World War I. It strengthened employer resistance and expressed in vigorous form the decision of employers to roll back the advances in membership and control attained by unions during the war. The propaganda appeal was based on the restrictions and arbitrariness of union control and the desire of employers to treat the individual as a person.

The AFL believed that in 1922 there was "scarcely a trade in which there has not been conducted an organized campaign for the establishment of the so-called 'open shop.' Not only employers but big business and high finance through the country have contributed financially to this campaign and an enormous fund has been used in propaganda work."[17] The open-shop movement manifested itself in the resistance of the steel industry to unionization, the successful attempt by a large majority of Atlantic Coast shipowners to push the members of the International Seamen's Union off their boats, the expulsion of the union in the meatpacking houses from the plants of the large packers, and the resistance of long-organized employers in the building trades and the railroads to the demands of their workers. In fact, the industrial strife which followed World War I was the result mainly of the aggressiveness of employers.

The Seamen

Rejection of a proposal for a 25 per cent reduction in wage rates and abolition of overtime payments led in 1921 to the largest seamen's strike in American history. Over three hundred vessels were reported without crews in New York. All Atlantic Coast shipping was affected, and some in the Pacific Coast trade found it difficult to find adequate crews. Injunctions were issued by several judges, pickets were restrained, and many strikers were arrested for vagrancy and other crimes in the Atlantic and Gulf ports. At the end of fifty-two days, the strike was over and lost.

One of the consequences of the strike was an insurgent movement within the International Seamen's Union. A move to broaden the cooperation of seamen and longshoremen through a Transport Workers' Federation was begun and had the support of J. Vance Thompson, editor of the *Seamen's Journal*. The IWW also sought to use the current disaffection within the union for its own purposes. Andrew Furuseth, the venerable head of the Seamen's Union, regarded these maneuvers as danger signals threatening his organization. An attack upon the proponents of wider unity was launched; Thompson was removed and expelled from the union. The episode itself was the result of suspicion and disenchantment which followed defeat. The move for wider unity would have had tough sledding under more favorable circumstances. The sailors' suspicion of the shoreside worker is of long duration and is not altogether unjustified by experience. In theory, it might appear that wider unity was the answer, but neither the sailors on the Atlantic Coast nor the longshoremen on the Pacific could maintain their organizations in the postwar period of the 1920's. Moreover, unity, as far as mutual honoring of picket lines, could be more easily achieved because it does not require the sinking of the identity of the separate organizations within a single group and thereby minimizes fear and suspicion.

The Meatpacking Houses

A tenuous kind of union recognition was imposed upon the meatpacking industry as a result of the intervention of the President's Mediation

Commission. The Big Five Packers notified the Amalgamated Meat Cutters and Butcher Workmen in March 1921 of their intentions to cancel the agreement. Company unions were organized in a number of plants, and they challenged the right of the Amalgamated to speak for the workers in the industry. Despite the reluctance of the leaders and lack of enthusiasm of the rank and file, the Amalgamated was forced to call a strike on December 5, 1921. About 45,000 workers in thirteen cities joined in the walkout. The strike lasted until February 1922, when the industry returned to the open shop.

Printing and Clothing

Both the International Typographical Union and the Amalgamated Clothing Workers of America faced opposition. In the printing industry, the Closed Shop Division of the Joint Conference Council had agreed to the establishment of the forty-four hour week. As the time for this change approached, objections to the innovation were registered by influential members of the trade. The International Typographical Union refused to agree to a postponement and voted by an overwhelming majority to levy a 10 per cent assessment in support of a strike if that step became necessary to support the proposal. The International Printing Pressmen's Union was also a party to the forty-four hour agreement and joined the strike for its enforcement. The strike was called in February 1924 and continued through June of that year. As settlements were obtained, the assessment was reduced and finally canceled in June 1924. Between May 1921 and June 1924, the Typographical Union collected in strike assessments $17,-389,411.17 and spent in benefits $15,829,140.68. The Pressmen collected and spent close to a million dollars.

The Amalgamated Clothing Workers struck against attempts of employers in New York City to deny the union control over conditions in the shop. The contest lasted six months, but the union was able to ward off the attack.

Building Trades

The strength of the open-shop drive can perhaps be better gauged by the readiness of organized employers to attack well-established systems of union control in the building construction industry. The attack upon the unions in this industry came in Chicago and San Francisco, long-organized and powerful union centers. In San Francisco, the American Plan of Employment was introduced after the building trades unions had rejected an arbitration award reducing wages.

The Building Trades' Council under its leader P. H. McCarthy had maintained control of the building construction industry since 1900. Lumber and millwork had to bear the union stamp. The rule was not as stringently enforced in the use of other materials because the unions did not seek such protection. While changes in wages and working conditions were initiated by single unions, the council handled negotiations if it approved of the change.[18] As a result, the Building Trades' Council exercised almost complete dictatorial power in the San Francisco industry.

A change in the attitude of employers in San Francisco was clearly noticeable before World War I, although the aggression was mainly directed against unions in the culinary trades and on the docks, never among the better organized in the city. In 1920 the Builders' Exchange, a central organization of building contractors' associations formed chiefly for exchanging trade information, decided on a change of policy. Charles W. Gompertz was chosen president and William H. George, secretary. On September 20, 1920, it made its first move and directed that wages be rolled back to the levels of February 1920. The order was in violation of a pending contract and resulted in a strike of several crafts. The issue was temporarily settled by a conference between the city authorities, the unions, employers, and the Industrial Relations Committee of the Chamber of Commerce which decided to submit the dispute to arbitration.

The willingness of the leaders of the Building Trades' Council to accept arbitration was in itself unusual and a sign of uncertainty of the leadership and a clear indication that large employers and banks in San Francisco were ready to support the building trades contractors unless arbitration were accepted. Archbishop Edward J. Hanna, M. C. Schloss, a former member of the California Supreme Court, and George L. Bell were appointed; and after lengthy hearings, the arbitrators ruled that a 7.5 per cent decrease in wages across the board was warranted. A request for reconsideration was denied, and the arbitrators rejected the union argument that the submitted issue had been an increase in wages and consequently the board had exceeded its power. On May 3, 1921, the council announced their rejection of the award. Thereupon, the Builders' Exchange stated that the award would be enforced.

The Builders' Exchange ordered work to be started under open-shop conditions on June 13. The unions then accepted the award, but it was too late; the employers had decided on all-out war. The Builder's Exchange insisted that building contractors agree to an open shop before material would be furnished. The following items were placed under a permit system designed to compel obedience to the rule of the open shop: cement, lime, plaster, ready-mixed mortar, rock, sand and gravel, common brick, fire and face brick, terra cotta—all clay products. Contractors who refused to abide by the rules were denied the right to purchase materials.

In a letter to members, the secretary stated: "You are particularly requested to make sure before applying for a permit that your job is running on the American Plan. All jobs will be regularly inspected, permits will not be again granted to any member or non-member of the Builders' Exchange who secures a permit and then does not run his job on the American Plan and pay strictly the Builders' Exchange wage scale and no more in any way, shape or form."[19] A basis of agreement was submitted to the unions on July 21, 1921, but, since it required recognition of nonunion workers in the building construction industry, it was rejected by the members even though it had the endorsement of the leaders.

Growing dissatisfaction with the leaders followed the initial success of the employer offensive. A conference of building trades unions, on July 19, 1921, set up a dual organization to the Buildings Trades' Council. The Conference of Committee of Allied Building Trades Unions, as it was called, sought to negotiate with the Builders' Exchange, but it was not any more successful than the regular groups. It thereupon called for a general strike, but the call was vigorously attacked by the San Francisco Labor Council and gained little approval outside of the building trades. It started on August 3 and was called off on August 27.

Employer interests were well organized and financed. On August 28, 1921, the San Francisco building construction industry began operating on an open-shop basis. The crafts began drifting back to work, some sooner than others, but all were finally forced to accept the new regime. In the meantime, although rank and file revolts flared in a number of trades, they could not, any more than the regular organizations, stem the employer offensive. The chief target of the opposition, P. H. McCarthy, resigned as head of the council, and this was a signal for the end of the rank and file revolt but not for easing the employer opposition. McCarthy later resigned from his office in the State Building Trades' Council. The Industrial Association of San Francisco, a militant employer association, began to play a role in labor-management questions in the fall of 1921. The building construction industry was to operate on an open-shop basis for more than a decade. While the abuses of the unions undoubtedly helped to create the climate of opinion which made an attack upon them successful, the drive to disestablish unionism and curtail its power gained strength from the national open-shop drive of the postwar period.

The Landis Award

The open-shop drive also affected the Chicago building construction industry. As in San Francisco, the anti-union drive started as a result of a wage dispute in January 1921. The business agents of the thirty-two affiliated unions of the Building Trades Council of Chicago opposed a reduction of wages demanded by the contractors. At the contractors' request, the question was submitted to a referendum vote of the union membership and every building construction union rejected the proposal. A lockout followed on May 1, and it was lifted by an agreement to arbitrate. Judge

Kenesaw Landis, a federal district judge in Chicago, was finally selected arbitrator. Work resumed after his appointment. Judge Landis insisted that wages could only be settled by reviewing the working rules. "After a month's study, the arbitrator announced that there must be a radical revision of both the labor contracts and their appended working rules, and that all new agreements must incorporate a 'new uniform form' which would be approved by him."[20]

On September 21, Judge Landis issued his award, incorporating three principles with nineteen points. He said that the monopolies created by unions and employer associations were not tolerable unless the public interest is served; that qualified workers should be employed without discrimination; that no contractor should be denied competent help; that sufficient apprentices should be allowed; and that work rules should be devised to create efficiency, eliminate waste, and help preserve industrial peace. The closed shop was modified so that employers could hire on the market if the union could not supply competent help. In general, rules were drastically revised and wage rates reduced. In a concluding paragraph, Judge Landis denounced illicit combinations and urged action against them by the government.

The unions asked for a rehearing and some minor changes were allowed. On October 1, 1921, the Building Trades' Council accepted the award but seven unions, not parties to the arbitration, refused; they were joined in their opposition by four other unions. Many contractors showed no enthusiasm for the decision, but a new force, representing more militant employers, came on the scene to defend the award. The Citizens' Committee to Enforce the Landis Award, organized by the Association of Commerce, the Illinois Manufacturers' Association, the Chicago Employers' Association, and large employers and banks, took steps to recruit workers, train apprentices, and protect open-shop jobs against violence. Unions refusing to accept the award were denied security, and their crafts placed on an open-shop basis. Bombings of Landis Award jobs and harassment of unions took place. Since some unions favored the acceptance of the award, the Building Trades' Council was rent by dissensions; for a time the council was made up of unions that accepted the Landis Award. The head of the Building Trades' Department and officers of the international unions sought a settlement, but not until 1926 were the unions sufficiently united and able to bring return of the closed shop. The contracts of May 1926 ran until May 31, 1929, and restored the closed-shop agreement in all the trades.[21]

The influence of the nationwide open-shop events in the Chicago building construction industry is difficult to measure. Undoubtedly it contributed to the willingness of many employers to join in the open-shop crusade and made the raising of funds for an attack on the unions easier. On the other hand, the open-shop movement in Chicago, as in San Francisco, was based in part upon existing abuses in the building trades: abuses brought to light by legislative committees in New York and Illinois. Both investigations revealed widespread collusion, rigging and pooling of bids, and agreements to exclude nonunion and out-of-town materials. Graft was also evident.

Corruption was, if anything, conducted on a broader scale in New York, where Robert P. Brindell was the power. Brindell, who headed the Dock and Pier Carpenters' Union, dominated the building trades council, sold strike insurance, and supported a system of collusive bidding which became a source of gain for contractors, union leaders, and material dealers. The evidence assembled by the Lockwood Committee in New York showed that the unions were the strategic factor in regulating the illicit practices. Through his power to call strikes of the building trades' unions, Brindell could cripple a recalcitrant contractor. But in both New York and Chicago, the labor union officials were not the only profiteers from the corrupt bargain. Contractors and material dealers took their share. The derelictions of union representatives were inevitably exploited by the enemies of organized labor, and the exposure strengthened the opposition and helped the advocates of the open shop.

CHAPTER 28

Unions, Government, and Militancy
on the Railroads

In many respects the railroad industry was a microcosm of the crosscurrents and problems which labor and industry faced in the postwar period. Based on their experience during the war, the railroad unions were anxious for the government to continue its control over the properties. The aloofness of the operating unions from the general labor movement appeared to be breaking down. To some extent the enhanced spirit of fraternity was the result of the need of those and other railroad unions for general support, and in part it was a result of the desire of the leaders to play a more commanding role in shaping general labor policy. One sign of the new spirit was the invitation to Gompers and Frank Morrison, secretary of the AFL, to address the 1918 convention of the Brotherhood of Locomotive Engineers. Neither could accept, because the executive council was in session at the time of the convention, but the conventions showed their new attitude by unanimously endorsing affiliation with the AFL. This gesture was in part a mark of appreciation for the support of Gompers and the AFL in their fight for the eight-hour day.[1]

THE PLUMB PLAN

The disposition of the railroad properties following the end of World War I had to be decided by Congress. The question raised was whether the carriers, taken over during World War I, should be retained and operated by the government or returned to private management. The railway unions favored the Plumb Plan: a proposal devised by Glenn E. Plumb, an attorney, which called for the setting up of a government corporation to take over and operate the railroad properties "under the full regulatory power of the Government to whom it would account for its operations and expenditures."[2]

Management would be exercised by a board of directors of fifteen members, five of whom would be appointed by each of the following: the classified employees, the President of the United States, and all other officials of the railroads. Half of the net earnings at the end of the fiscal year would be divided among the classified employees and the other half would be used for investment and improvement of railroad properties. Leaders of the railroad unions were members of the Plumb Plan League formed to promote the program before Congress. The 1919 convention directed the executive council to cooperate with the railroad unions but did not endorse the Plumb Plan.[3]

Differences Between the AFL and Railway Brotherhoods

In June 1919 the four railway brotherhoods applied for affiliation with the AFL. Delay in accepting the application of these unions followed protests from William D. Mahon, head of the Amalgamated Association of Street and Electric Railways, who challenged the jurisdiction of the Brotherhood of Locomotive Engineers over employees of suburban electric railways. In May 1920 the railroad unions withdrew their application. Warren S. Stone, Grand Chief Engineer of the Brotherhood of Locomotive Engineers, speaking for the four unions, informed Gompers that the withdrawal was not based on jurisdictional differences, but on the constant disregard of the wishes of all railroad unions.[4]

Replying in detail, Gompers denied that the AFL had ever failed to support the railway unions on trade matters, although he admitted the AFL had not enforced the Plumb Plan. Gompers emphasized "that the Montreal Convention of the American Federation of Labor declared for Government ownership of railroads and democratic control and management of them."[5]

Gompers also pointed to the efforts of the AFL to modify the harsh restrictions upon labor in the Esch-Cummins (Railroad Transportation) Act of 1920 and asked Stone: "Can you point to any one instance in the entire history of the American Federation of Labor where it failed to support the Railroad Brotherhoods in any and all of their demands which were made upon Congress? You cannot point to one."[6] To the charge of domination by the executive council of the affiliates, Gompers replied that its members could not dominate:

The Council is directed to carry into effect with the limited powers placed in its hands, the decisions reached by the annual conventions of the American

Federation of Labor. There is a moral obligation that the organizations will aid in the conclusions reached but there is no power in the Executive Council or the convention of the A.F. of L. to dominate over the officers of an organization, or any national or international union.[7]

Nevertheless, Gompers was aware that the brotherhoods spoke for hundreds of thousands of organized railroad workers even though the brotherhoods insisted that they alone had a right to determine the railroad legislation to be supported before Congress. Such a view did not naturally sit well with the AFL railroad unions, which, through the Railway Employees' Department, sought to establish a legislative office of their own. Because he feared such a step would be an "affront to the four Brotherhoods and hurtful to the labor movement," Gompers was successful in squelching this move.[8]

For the period between 1920 to 1924, the railroad unions were the center of labor activity. Their novel and imaginative economic and political programs appeared to mark a new chapter in labor history.

TRANSPORTATION ACT OF 1920

The Transportation Act of 1920 returned the roads to their private owners. Section 3 established the U.S. Railroad Labor Board of nine members, three each from management, labor, and the public. The board was authorized to determine wages the parties themselves were unable to set. In determining the justness and reasonableness of wages and salaries or working conditions, the board was, so far as applicable, to take into consideration scales of wages paid for similar work in other industries, the relation between wages and the cost of living, training and skill required, the degree of responsibility, and the character and regularity of employment.

Some members of Congress, recalling the readiness of the the railroad unions to call a general strike in 1916, sought more drastic restraints upon their conduct. Senator Albert Cummins, chairman of the Interstate Commerce Commission, justified the imposition of criminal penalties for violation of the orders of the Railroad Labor Board:

The committee has substituted for the strike the justice which will be administered by the tribunals created in the bill for adjudging disputes which may hereafter arise. . . . From the public standpoint and in the interest of the people generally, it has become clear that in transportation, at least, both the strike and lockout must cease. . . . There is but one way by which this can be done: The Government must undertake to declare in any such case, what is justice, what is fair and right, then there must be no concerted rebellion or conspiracy among those whose rights have been adjudged for the purpose of coercing either of the parties to the dispute into another and different settlement.[9]

The particular provisions were opposed by the AFL and all railroad unions. Gompers claimed in a letter to Warren Stone that "as a result of the fight we put up that criminal labor features contained in the Cummins' Bill were killed and modified even unto its present unacceptable form."[10] The enactment of the Transportation Act did not allay the dissatisfaction. Even before the enactment of the law a strike had been planned by the Brotherhood of Railroad Trainmen and the Switchmen's Union of North America.

In January 1920 fourteen railway unions demanded a wage increase. The Brotherhood of Railroad Trainmen and the Switchmen's Union withdrew and presented separate proposals. They threatened to call a strike if a satisfactory increase was not granted. Gompers, induced to intervene, addressed a meeting of the executives of all railroad unions, including the brotherhoods. He reviewed events on the railroads involving labor beginning with the strike of 1877 and concluded that a strike of switchmen and trainmen would paralyze the entire railroad system. He pointed to the difficulties encountered by strikers in the coal fields and steel industry. As a result of the coal and steel strikes, he said that "the representatives in Congress and those in the Senate fell over each other in their eagerness to present bills to Congress directly and indirectly making strikes unlawful and punishable by huge fines and long terms of imprisonment—twenty years and ten thousand dollars." Gompers claimed the antisedition bills were "aimed at the organizations of the workers, the trade unions and even the unorganized, if they should organize temporarily."[11] Gompers warned that the injunction would be ruthlessly used against the strikers. He told them: "Nothing is more powerful than reserved power. If an organization shall throw all its power into a fight and the slightest set back is given it, it has nothing in reserve and goes to pieces."[12]

Outlaw Strike

While the Trainmen's and Switchmen's leaders called off their walkout, their decision was not universally approved by their members. The dissatisfaction of the members manifested itself in the "outlaw" switchmen's strike which began in the Chicago yards of the Chicago, Milwaukee and St. Paul Railroad on April 1, 1920. The unauthorized strike followed a dispute over the classification of John Grunau, who assumed leadership of the spontaneous walkout. In less than a week every road in Chicago was seriously affected, and the strike soon spread to many of the important railroad centers of the country. Leaders of the regular unions immediately recognized the insurgent movement as a threat to their organizations and sought to prevent its spread. For a time the strikers refused to return to their jobs and challenged the regular organizations by forming independent locals which united at the Montreal convention into the United Association of Railway

Employees of North America. But the strike gradually faded, and by September 20 it was formally ended. Strikers who had failed to return at a stipulated date lost their seniority, and the four brotherhoods took the view that "all positions made vacant by employees of our class engaging in such illegal action [outlaw strikes] were open to any and all who desired to accept service of that character, either temporary or permanent."[13]

Despite their readiness to take action against insurgents within their own ranks, the brotherhoods were for a time in agreement with the other railroad unions on political issues and tactics. The AFL railroad unions, with the support of the United Mine Workers of America and a number of others, were responsible for the endorsement of government ownership by the 1921 AFL convention. When the executive council was reviewing its report to the 1922 convention, William Green proposed an amendment that the AFL "will do what it can to bring about government ownership and democratic operation of the railroads."[14]

Green's more outspoken view was adopted by the council, but the brotherhoods were now of a different opinion. They found that their endorsement of government ownership was an embarrassment in their dealings with the carriers. In fact, a delegation from the brotherhoods called on Gompers and Frank Morrison and prevailed upon them "not to consider the question of the Montreal convention endorsement of government ownership of the railroad. . . . We were really stopped from saying anything about government ownership at their request."[15]

The Shopmen's Strike

The Railroad Labor Board had been authorized to set wages, and accordingly it issued a decision on May 1, 1920, raising rates of shopmen among other railroad workers. On the basis of a decline in the cost of living, the board on June 1, 1921 ordered a reduction in wages of shopmen ranging from five to eighteen cents an hour. A number of other changes affecting conditions of employment were ordered. Sentiment for striking was widespread, but the assurance to the operating crafts that their work rules would be considered by the board temporarily quenched the desire for a walkout in this branch of the service.

In March 1922 the railroads applied for another wage cut. On the ground that "employees on the railroads will be receiving, as a rule wages in excess of that paid to similar employees in other industries," the Board ordered a reduction for maintenance of waymen and shop employees effective on July 1, 1922.[16] The decision was greeted with widespread anger among the workers affected, and the convention of the Railway Employees' Department, in June 1922 authorized the issuance of a strike ballot. Overwhelmingly, the members of the several unions voted to authorize a strike.[17] Ben W. Hooper, chairman of the Railway Labor Board, justified the wage reductions and claimed the new schedules were higher from 100 to 169.9 per cent than those of the prewar period. He warned against a strike "that will surely prove disastrous to the organizations and unfortunate to the men composing them."[18]

Bert M. Jewell, the president of the Railway Employees' Department, appealed to the carriers directly, and told T. DeWitt Cuyler, chairman of the Association of Railway Executives, that the present impasse was caused by the refusal of the carriers to agree to the formation of the National Adjustment boards under the Transportation Act and on their unwillingness to engage in negotiations at the single carrier level.[19]

Cuyler rejected Jewell's charges, calling his attention to the willingness of the carriers to accept the wage increases ordered by the board on December 7, 1920, to the fact that contracting-out, a general complaint, was not a widespread practice, and that Jewell's other complaints had been rejected by the board.[20]

In an effort to avoid the strike, the Railroad Labor Board called a hearing for June 30. The union leaders refused to attend.[21] In view of the reported pessimism of many heads of the shopcraft unions about the outcome of the strike, their refusal to search for a compromise can only be explained by membership pressure and the fear of reprisals within their organizations. A confidential circular by an employer agent present at the executive meeting of the shopcraft union leaders at Cincinnati, Ohio, on June 23, 1922, noted the opinion of these officers that a "strike would fail."[22]

A strike for July 1 was nevertheless sanctioned by the Railway Employees' Department for "all shop craft employees below the rank of General Foremen." Of the 450,000 employees in these classifications, about 90 per cent answered the call. Boilermakers, blacksmiths, sheet metal workers, electricians, machinists, and carmen struck on July 1, and they were joined by the oilers and firemen ten days later. Two days after the strike had started, the majority on the Labor Board promulgated a resolution "outlawing" the striking shopmen and directing the employees who had remained on the job to replace the strikers' unions as bargaining agents under the Transportation Act. The resolution also contained a warning to several of the railroad organizations whose members had not left their jobs that they would suffer the same fate in the event of a walkout.[23]

Even before the strike had been called, the U.S. Attorney-General sought advice on the advisability of securing a restraining order against the strikers "on the ground it is a conspiracy and an interference with interstate commerce."[24] On June 27, W. H. Heron replied that "a proceeding involving bitterly contested questions of employer and employees should not be begun unless clear warrant of law for it exists. It is not enough that some authority or plausible reason may be found for it. There should be a preponderance of reason and authority as would compel the assent of all fairminded men."[25] So that there might be no doubt of his view, Heron added: "There can be no question that by common law as expounded by the courts, a mere strike, leaving out all elements of force, intimidation, secondary boycott, etc. is not illegal." Finally, he told the Attorney-General there was no provision in the law that the decision of the Labor Board "may be enforced by the courts, and it is well known that Congress definitely refused to set up in the Act compulsory arbitration."[26]

For a time the Attorney-General followed the advice given to him. On July 11, President Harding entered the dispute and declared that the strikers were in violation of the law and enjoined all from interfering with the operation of the railroads.[27] As anticipated by many of the leaders, the strike was not going well. The carriers were moving toward recognition of organizations established by workers who refused to strike or who had struck and returned to work. Anxious to end the walkout, the leaders in a conference with President Harding on July 27 agreed that the strike would be ended on condition that management and workers agreed to recognize the "validity of all decisions of the Railroad Labor Board," the carriers withdraw all law suits arising out of the walkout, and that all strikers would be returned to work in their former jobs with all their rights including seniority unimpaired. The railroads were willing to accept the first two points but would not guarantee seniority. President Harding expressed some disappointment at the rejection of the terms, and as a result of further conferences, the President was informed that the Association of Railway Executives had voted to accept his terms and allow seniority disputes to be settled by the U.S. Railroad Board. It appeared that a settlement would be made.[28]

Before an agreement could be reached formally, the attitude of the carriers and the government underwent a drastic change. The government had reported violence earlier, and by September 1, 1922, 3,250 deputy marshals had been appointed to protect railroad property.[29] Injunctions had been secured in fifteen districts. Daugherty expressed dissatisfaction with these local orders and on August 29 he instructed Assistant Solicitor Blackburn Esterlin: "Locate [Judge] Wilkerson and ascertain if he can come to Chicago . . . on very important business."[30] James H. Wilkerson had until recently been an assistant U.S. attorney and had been appointed to the U.S. District Court for the Northern District of Illinois, Eastern Division. Daugherty knew his man, for the unusually broad restraining order prohibited hindering, obstructing, or impeding the operation of trains and directed all parties not to in any manner, "by letters, printed or other circulars, telegrams, telephones, word of mouth, oral persuasion, or suggestion, or through interviews to be published in newspapers or otherwise . . . to abandon employment of said railway companies."[31] Officers of striking unions were enjoined from "issuing instructions, making public statements, suggestions to any officials or members of labor organizations constituting the said Federated Shop Crafts. . . ."

Judge Wilkerson's order proved ineffective from the beginning; and it angered the labor movement more than any other action in years. The breadth of the prohibitions, the actions restrained, and the conditions under which the order had been secured aroused serious doubts in the minds of many who were not normally friendly to organized labor. Gompers bitterly assailed it and said he would lay before the executive council a proposal for a general strike at its meeting the following week. Assistant Attorney-General Warren F. Warton informed Daugherty that the "whole tenor of statement [is] inflammatory and exciting."[32]

The question on how to proceed against Gompers was discussed by the Attorney-General's office. Assistant Attorney-General John W. H. Grim offered the view that since Gompers "is not a defendant [,] accordingly [he] has not been served with a copy of injunction and is not amenable to contempt."[33]

Gompers placed the general strike proposal before the executive council on September 7 and for the first time in the history of the AFL such a proposal was not rejected outright. In another resolution, the executive council, with James Duncan dissenting, called upon "the workers to resist the establishment of a practice that will destroy the very freedom and democracy and we call upon the people of America as a whole to protest against these abuses in the exercise of the injunction writ so clearly violative of the constitutional guarantees of the United States."[34]

But the resolutions did not deter the Attorney-General. Daugherty instructed U.S. Attorney Charles F. Clyne in Chicago to "serve on each and every counsel of the defendants in the case of *U.S.* v. *Railway Employees Department of AFL* to produce the respective clients who are leading officials of the shopcraft organizations with all their books, correspondence, financial accounts, check books and other documentary data."[35] In an effort to locate union officials, the Department of Justice had its agents follow attorneys who had no connection with the case, among them Clarence Darrow, who was shadowed by the Department of Justice while on the way from Chicago to New York.[36] In line with the efforts to prevent the unions from knowing its plans, Blackburn Esterlin, the assistant solicitor, informed Silas Strawn, a leading corporation lawyer in Chicago, that a party from the Department of Justice, including the Attorney-General, "desires to travel and sojourn at the Drake with as little publicity as possible. For that reason, I am asking you to undertake the arrangement for the aforesaid accommodations and that we may be allowed to go into them without stopping on the main floor to register."[37]

It is no wonder that Gompers charged that the Attorney-General "like a thief in the night, rushes from Washington . . . to a great metropolis; no public information given as to his errand or that he had gone at all . . . has applied for and obtained from a Judge, appointed recently and appointed upon his recommendation . . . and makes an application for an injunction, the features of which you all know and which are in direct conflict not only with the laws of the land but the Constitution of the United States."[38]

At the same time, Donald Richberg, counsel for the shopcraft unions, protested against the use of summary equity procedures "upon evidence found solely in an undigested mass of ex parte affidavits reeking with hearsay and perjury."[39]

The restraining order was modified on September 25, but the effect of the court orders and the militancy of the carriers affected the ranks of the strikers. On April 30, 1923, the attorneys for the unions were directed to withdraw from proceedings having to do with the injunction. Judge Wilkerson made the injunction permanent on July 12, 1923, but not a single person was brought to trial for violating it.[40]

The unions were, in the meantime, trying to find a basis for settling the strike and were aided by the heads of the Transportation Brotherhoods. A more conciliatory group of carriers led by S. Davies Warfield, president of the Seaboard Railroad, opened negotiations with the shopcraft unions. Daniel Willard of the Baltimore and Ohio Railroad, A. H. Smith of the New York Central, and Warfield, acting on behalf of eleven railroad systems, worked out a memorandum of agreement in conference at Baltimore with the heads of the shopcrafts. This was accepted by the General Conference Committee of the unions on September 13, 1922; it became known as the Baltimore Agreement.

Men not guilty of violence were to be returned at rates of pay existing on July 1, 1922; seniority of strikers was to be restored as of June 30, 1922; differences on this issue were to be settled in conference; and suits were to be withdrawn by both parties. The unions anticipated a greater acceptance of the agreement than followed. The strike had lasted seventy-five days and several organizations found their resources inadequate to meet the most pressing needs of their members. As a result, the unions sought to make the best possible terms they could. On 112 roads they were able to negotiate the Baltimore plan, 64 on a modification of the plan, but on 130 roads the strike was unconditionally declared off.[41]

It was a severe defeat for the unions, one from which they did not recover until the 1930's. The strike was precipitated by the rank and file who felt strongly that wage reductions had to be resisted. The leaders were pulled along; and if the confidential report of the undercover operator can be believed, they feared the outcome. The overwhelming vote to strike gave the leaders little choice but to carry out instructions. Not very hopeful to begin with, they soon recognized that their original appraisal had been only too correct. They had no choice but to accept terms which at best might be regarded as an orderly withdrawal.

Union-Management Cooperation

Union-management cooperation had been suggested to William Johnston, the head of the Machinists' Union, before the shopmen's strike. Although Johnston was a believer in socialism, he was also a trade unionist who believed that cooperation between the union and the employer was a prime necessity for the survival and prosperity of both. The opposition which such a program might have encountered earlier was severely reduced by the unfavorable outcome of the shopmen's strike. Aggressive voices, while not silenced, were not as loud and confident after defeat.

The principal inspirer of the program of the shopcraft unions was Otto Beyer, an engineer who was employed in the government arsenals. Beyer believed that cooperation between management and unions to reduce waste and increase output would make it possible to develop better relations between the parties and at the same time provide a fund of savings which could be shared between them. Prior to the shopmen's strike, in the spring of 1922, President Daniel Willard of the Baltimore and Ohio Railroad had agreed to try the experiment. William H. Johnston, president of the International Association of Machinists, was the chief sponsor on the union side. The necessities of the strike caused a postponement, but with its ending the experiment was introduced.

The Glenwood shops in the Pittsburgh area of the Baltimore and Ohio Railroad were selected for launching the program. The Machinists' effort was sufficiently successful to permit the agreement to be extended to all the shopcraft unions and later to all the shops on the Baltimore and Ohio Railroad. Through the efforts of Sir Henry Thornton and the leaders of the shopcrafts on the Canadian National Railway System, the union-management cooperative program was established on that railway.

The cooperative program operated through joint committees of equal numbers appointed by the unions and management on the railway system. These committees met periodically to discuss methods of improving production. At least once every three months, the Joint System Cooperative Committee met to review the work of the local joint groups.

Union-management cooperation was based upon seven basic principles: (1) recognition of the standard unions, (2) acceptance of unions as necessary and constructive, (3) development of written agreements governing wages and working conditions, (4) systematic cooperation between unions and management for the purpose of improving railroad service and eliminating waste, (5) stabilization of employment, (6) sharing the gains of cooperation, and (7) provision for the establishment of machinery to foster cooperation.[42] The program marked a new departure in labor-management relations, enabled the unions to strengthen their position on some of the roads, and gave the labor movement a new basis of appealing for public support. Whatever limits this program might have had, its aim was to promote efficiency and the best methods of work; it thereby softened the criticism that labor policy was inevitably directed towards restricting output.

CHAPTER 29

Independent Political Action

Pressure for independent political action in the early postwar period was greater than usual. More conscious political involvement by progressive farmers started even before the war when the Farmers' Non-Partisan League was organized by A. C. Townley in North Dakota. The league operated in the primaries of the old parties, and it was subsequently instrumental in forming the Minnesota Farmer-Labor party.[1] A contributing factor to the "political awakening" was the short-lived radicalism stirring some sections of the labor movement. The ranks of the old believers in independent politics were swelled by temporary recruits disenchanted with the old parties. The growing sentiment was recognized by the AFL leaders, and Samuel Gompers spoke out against an independent political policy before the New York Central Federated Union, one of the strongholds of third-party sentiment. His warnings did not halt the growing sentiment for a new political departure.[2]

Although sentiment for a labor party continued to rise, it gained few endorsements from union leaders and was opposed by the AFL leadership. It did win the support of central labor unions, state federations of labor, and many local unions. Not all internationals were opposed to the third party. The United Mine Workers of America, the Molders' Union, and several organizations on the railroads supported such a program. Both the Indiana and Illinois state federations of labor endorsed the formation of a third party by labor; and the Chicago Federation of Labor, one of the larger and most influential central bodies, sponsored the formation of a labor party in 1919. President John Fitzpatrick was nominated for mayor and polled more than 50,000 votes.

Promoters of the third-party movement were able to gain a sufficient following to organize a national labor party at a convention in Chicago on November 12, 1919. Most of the leaders of the venture were known proponents of third-party movements. In fact Max Hayes, for many years a leading Socialist and trade unionist, became its national chairman. There were, however, some new converts to the third-party movement, but at this stage they were in the minority.

Third-party sentiment was also on the rise in the ranks of the liberals. Under the leadership of J. A. Hopkins, an old Bull Moose Progressive from New Jersey, the Committee of Forty-eight was organized in an attempt to unify progressive sentiment in the Presidential campaign of 1920. Both the Labor party and the Committee of Forty-eight called simultaneous but separate meetings for Chicago in July 1920. It was hoped by leaders on both sides that a unified program could be worked out. Although discussions between the two groups failed to lead to a formal basis of unity, most of those present at the meeting of the Committee of Forty-eight finally moved over to the meeting of the Labor party, which became the Farmer-Labor party, and nominated a Presidential ticket of Parley Parker Christensen and Max Hayes. It polled about 300,000 votes in the 1920 election. The Farmer-Labor ticket did not do well in the large industrial states. Like the Socialist party before it, the Farmer-Labor party made its best showing in nonindustrial states, polling its largest vote in Washington.

THE FEDERATED FARMER-LABOR PARTY

The Farmer-Labor party did not attract many top labor or agriculture leaders. The Socialist party, facing a series of internal crises arising from the emergence of the Communists, did not endorse the new third-party movement. Nor would the Minnesota Farmer-Labor party, a successful third-party movement which had elected a United States senator, affiliate. As a result, the Farmer-Labor party was dependent upon leaders who had limited experience in politics and were not conversant with the significance of the developments then taking place in the extreme wing of social radicalism. Their inexperience showed itself clearly in the convention they called in Chicago in July 1923. Local unions, central federated bodies, farmer organizations, and political groups were asked to attend. Despite warnings from better informed sources, the sponsors invited the Workers' party, the legal arm of the Communist party then leading an underground existence, to send delegates. As a result, the sponsors of the conference found themselves in a minority while the followers of the Workers' party took over the meeting with the cold efficiency that has since become the hallmark of Communist tactics. Unmindful of the effect of this show of strength upon their positions within the trade unions, especially the Chicago Federation of Labor, the controlling group dominated the conference and established the Federated Farmer-Labor party.

The new party made little impression upon the general labor movement or even upon the groups seeking to form an effective third party. However, the Federated Farmer-Labor party, which became the instrument with which the Communists sought to intrude themselves into the third-party movement, was able to convince leaders of the Minnesota labor and farmer alliance to call a convention for the purpose of uniting all groups behind the candidacy of Senator Robert La Follette of Wisconsin. The Minnesota leaders were warned against this enterprise but they were not dissuaded. The convention met in St. Paul and nominated Duncan McDonald, an Illinois miner and Socialist, and William Boucks, who was active in farmers' movements. Before the campaign opened the Communists repudiated the ticket and nominated William Z. Foster and Benjamin Gitlow as candidates of the Workers' party. They polled few votes.[3]

The Conference for Progressive Political Action

Had the third-party movement been limited to the groups already mentioned, it would have made a small imprint upon American labor politics; for the Communists and other traditional sponsors of a third party were, at best, marking time. They were unable to attract many followers or to exercise any considerable influence upon organized labor. The shift in the political views of the railway unions after World War I was the principal reason for the increased strength which the movement for a more experimental political program gained. Enactment of the provisions of the Railroad Transportation Act of 1920 was a bitter blow to the railroad unions. The nonoperating railway organizations had greatly prospered during the war; their membership climbed from under 225,000 in 1914 to over 315,000 in 1920. But the railroad workers were bitterly dissatisfied with the decisions of the government and the attitude of the Railway Labor Board. A committee of railroad union executives made up of William H. Johnston of the machinists, Martin Ryan, a carman, E. J. Manion of the telegraphers, Timothy Healy of the stationary firemen and oilers, and L. E. Sheppard of the railway conductors invited labor and liberal organizations to a conference in Chicago on February 12, 1922. A number of unions outside of the railroad industry, the more important being the coal miners and needle trades as well as representatives of a group of liberal organizations including church groups and the Socialist party, were represented among the 124 delegates. Delegates from nine state federations also appeared.

Socialists and representatives of labor parties favored immediate commitment to independent political action, but the international unions were opposed to precipitous action. They, however, went along with it part of the way. It was decided that liberals and progressives would be supported on the old party tickets in the congressional elections of 1922 wherever such candidates were running for office. In districts where a candidate of the old parties could not be supported, the Conference for Progressive Political Action was to run a candidate of its own, if possible. The conference went a step further and recognized the Socialist party and elected its leader, Morris Hillquit, as a member of the national committee.

After the congressional elections of 1922, the Conference for Progressive Political Action met to evaluate its policies. The second conference met at Cleveland on December 11 and 12, 1922. Socialists and farmer-labor delegates again expressed the hope the Conference would embark immediately upon an independent labor party course, but the leaders of the large unions, exclusive of the needle trades, regarded politics from a perspective somewhat different from the Socialists. Their view of politics was more limited; they were more concerned with the daily acts of legislatures than were the adherents of independent politics. The independents were inclined to regard politics as a vehicle for reforming social and economic institutions. For the majority of trade unionists, politics was a means of gaining laws of immediate and direct benefit to workers and was, in fact, an extension of collective bargaining.

When the question of endorsement of a labor party was placed before the delegates, it was hotly debated and defeated by a vote of 64 to 52. The close vote did not accurately reflect the division, for the opponents of independent political action were mainly delegates from the large unions who represented thousands of members while the other group came from organizations of much more modest size. The conference called for the repeal of the Transportation Act, direct election of the President of the United States, endorsement of the farm products' financing bill, a soldiers bonus to be paid through an excess profits tax, amnesty for political prisoners, safeguarding of civil liberty, and government regulation of the coal industry.[4] The next meeting was held in St. Louis in February 1924 and a nationwide convention was called for St. Louis on July 4, 1924, presumably to nominate candidates.

The railroad unions that dominated the Committee for Progressive Political Action and that provided much of its finances could not immediately decide on the policy to be followed in the 1924 Presidential election. William G. McAdoo, who was a leading contender for the Democratic nomination that year, had during his tenure as Federal Railroad Administrator in World War I shown sympathy and consideration for the needs of the railroad worker and their unions. Labor did not expect much from President Calvin Coolidge, who was a candidate for re-election, and hoped that the Democrats would offer a more desirable alternative. The nomination of John W. Davis, a corporation lawyer with a "blue chip practice," gave the labor organization little choice. The convention at Cleveland was attended by over six hundred delegates from a variety of groups including the Socialist party. Power rested, however, in the hands of the railway unions that were anxious to demonstrate their dissatisfaction with the old political parties by nominating Senator Robert M. La Follette. Many of the influential delegates were little concerned with the present or future of the Committee for Progressive Political Action. Actually, a delegate from the Brotherhood of Locomotive Engineers was ready to nominate La Follette even before the convention had formally organized.

After the convention organized, President E. J. Manion of the Brotherhood of Railroad Telegraphers and chairman of the committee on organization suggested the nomination of Senator La Follette for President on his own platform and with the running mate selected by the national committee and La Follette. In addition, the executive was directed to call a conference in January 1925 for the purpose of drafting a plan for a permanent organization. The suggestions were accepted without dissent. La Follette favored a campaign with a fight against monopoly as the principal issue. His views were inevitably accepted without protest by the convention. In addition, the convention endorsed excess profits taxes and progressive taxes, lowering of the tariff, abolition of the "tyranny and usurpation of the courts, including the practice of nullifying legislation in conflict with the political, social or economic theories of the judges." It also favored abolition of the injunction in labor disputes and the right of a judge to punish for contempt in case of defiance of these orders and the election of federal judges without party designation for limited terms. The foreign policy of imperialism was denounced and a revision of the Treaty of Versailles in accordance "with the terms of the armistice and to promote firm treaty agreements with all nations to outlaw wars, abolish conscription, drastically reduce land, air and naval armaments and guarantee a public referendum on peace and war."[5]

Burton K. Wheeler, a progressive Democrat from Montana, was chosen to run for Vice-President and the campaign rallied many liberal groups behind it. The AFL, which had played no role in the launching of the candidacy of La Follette and Wheeler, faced the necessity for making an endorsement, although the federation normally had avoided taking sides openly on Presidential candidates. Despite the belief that the executive council was forced to take a position, the facts are otherwise. Gompers and Daniel Tobin were most anxious for an endorsement of La Follette and Wheeler, and only two members were opposed to this step. James Duncan favored La Follette personally but did not want the federation to shift from its historic policy of no endorsement. William Green of the Mine Workers, an active Ohio Democrat, wanted the federation to remain silent. Instead, the executive council endorsed La Follette and Wheeler by name.

At the same time, the AFL took pains to point out that the endorsement did not mean the abandonment of the nonpartisan policy in politics.

Considering the problems of launching a political campaign in a short time, the relatively small funds and manpower, and the absence of any patronage with which to encourage support, the La Follette-Wheeler ticket made a creditable showing. It only carried one state—Wisconsin—but in polling about five million votes, the Progressive candidates ran second in eleven others—the largest being California. As in the past, Progressive candidates made their best showing in the rural states. At the national committee meeting on December 12, 1924, the leaders of the railroad unions opposed the holding of a general meeting early in 1925. They were overruled, but the last meeting on February 21-22, 1925, voted to end the existence of the Conference for Progressive Political Action.

The ability of a group of unions to launch an independent political movement without the approval and even the tacit opposition of the AFL shows that Gompers and the other leaders close to his policies could never have forestalled a third-party movement if sentiment for such a step had existed on any scale. The unions were free to support any policy they believed would serve their aims; and in 1924 both John L. Lewis and William Hutcheson, the heads of the two largest organizations in the AFL, did not support La Follette and others followed the same policy. Even many central bodies, which were directly chartered by the AFL, would not endorse the La Follette-Wheeler ticket. The AFL never encouraged the formation of even the limited political activity which the railroad unions undertook. As a matter of fact, several times these unions contemplated setting up legislative committees to represent them before Congress and the federation, while quite concerned with the development of another power could do nothing to forestall such action.

Had the unions and their members believed that it was to their interest to continue the independent political movement, it would have been maintained. While the AFL believed a third party would not serve the interests of organized or unorganized labor, it could no nothing to change the decisions of the railroad unions. In the same manner, if the unions were convinced that a third party would have served their interest, they would have continued the organization. Obviously, they were not of that opinion. They realized, even while they were supporting the La Follette-Wheeler ticket, that it was essential to endorse congressional candidates of the old parties with a pro-labor record or at least one who would respond in a limited sense to the importunities of organized labor. Whatever limitations the nonpartisan political policy may have from the point of view of organized labor, it has shown itself to be a much more effective instrument than a third-party movement could have been. The fact is that the policy of the unions was designed like the unions themselves for a program of slow and steady change. It is not fitted to achieve grand programs of social reorganization or transference of productive enterprise from the private to the public sector. Time has vindicated the decisions of the labor movement in the past; for even with the vast changes that have taken place over the years in its numbers and policies, it has continued to espouse nonpartisanship in politics and it does not appear that it will change in the near future.

CHAPTER 30

Radical Opposition
in the Established Unions

Beginning with the denial of a seat to Lucien Sanial in 1890, a radical opposition to the leadership of the AFL arose within the ranks. Sometimes it represented no more than an annual objection at a convention, as when Victor Berger or J. Mahlon Barnes would protest the unanimous election of Gompers to his office. At other times the opposition would rally around some event or principle and challenge the position of the ruling group. Not all opponents of Gompers were in agreement. As already noted, a group of leaders, many of them heads of unions with headquarters in Indianapolis, were intent upon challenging the dominance of Gompers and his friends. It was they who rallied around the candidacy of Daniel Tobin and succeeded in removing John B. Lennon from his long-held post as treasurer of the AFL. Socialists also joined in the fight for industrial unionism at the 1912 convention.

In the postwar period, Socialists within the AFL supported resolutions for independent political action and other reforms, but the rise of communism as an issue within the AFL tended to bring many of them closer to the heads of the AFL. In fact, the majority of the delegation of the International Ladies' Garment Workers' Union supported Gompers in his race against John L. Lewis in 1921. There were, moreover, more persistent opponents of the official policy. In addition to the challenge of "progressive" unions comprising the railroad block and their allies, a more radical opposition also took form. Its leaders controlled few unions and, for a time, gained its chief strength in Chicago where it had the sympathetic support of President John Fitzpatrick and Secretary Edward Nockles of the Chicago Federation of Labor.

The leader of this challenge—to the continued dominance of Gompers and his associates over the AFL—was William Z. Foster. In 1915, Foster settled in Chicago, joined Local 453 of the Brotherhood of Railway Carmen, and was elected its business agent and delegate to the Chicago Federation of Labor. Under the benign and militant influence of Fitzpatrick, and the generalship of Nockles, Foster was given an opportunity to show his ability. He suggested the combining of the twelve craft unions in the Chicago stockyards for a common organizing campaign in 1916, and the Stockyards Labor Council was able to win recognition—a feat only the Teamsters' Union had been able to achieve prior to that time. (The Teamsters' Union had been recognized since 1904.) After his initial success, Foster suggested the promotion of a drive to organize the steel industry, and as a delegate from the Chicago Federation of Labor to the 1918 convention of the AFL, he sponsored this proposal. He was chosen secretary of the National Organizing Committee for the Organizing of the Iron and Steel Industry of which Gompers was honorary chairman and Fitzpatrick chairman. Its recruiting of several hundred thousand members for the twenty-four unions and its strike against the steel industry for recognition was a major, if unsuccessful, achievement of American labor.

With the ending of the steel strike, Foster faced a decision. He could have undoubtedly become an influential member of the trade union movement. His prestige was great, and his kind of talent was not overabundant within the trade union movement. He was, however, a man without a real base of power within an international union. Instead of continuing with his old tactics, he launched a new scheme for reorganizing the American labor movement.

THE TRADE UNION EDUCATIONAL LEAGUE

The Trade Union Educational League, created in Chicago in November 1920, was to be the battering ram with which Foster planned to break down the opposition to his program. The response to his message was at first reasonably favorable. Protected by the Chicago Federation of Labor, which endorsed the principal plank in the league's program, the amalgamation of trade unions operating in single industries into industrial organizations, it defied Gompers, who came to Chicago to plead for reconsideration of the heterodox doctrine.

The Profintern

Important changes, however, had taken place since Foster's departure from the radical movement in the period before World War I. The Russian revolution of October 1917 brought the Bolsheviks under Lenin's leadership to power and his concept of a centrally directed party of professional revolutionaries achieved an importance it had not held heretofore. Lenin's disillusionment with the traditional Socialist parties led him to initiate an effort to form an international organization based upon his own principles. With the prestige of a successful revolution behind him, obstacles were overcome and the Communist International was launched by a conference of revolutionary Socialists in Moscow in March 1919. The Communist International was a world party with the national units subordinate to it. In keeping with Lenin's concept of the role of the proletarian party, the Communist International defined its attitude toward other organizations of labor as "the creation of Communist nuclei everywhere they find proletarians, semi-proletarians." This meant subordination "of the factory committee and the unions to the Communist Party."[1]

A consummation of this policy was only possible through the capture of the moderate trade unions of the countries of the world and the expulsion of their leaders from the seats of power. An instrument for the achievement of this purpose was necessary, and in 1920 a Provisional Council of Labor Unions was established to carry out this campaign. As a first step, a congress to launch a permanent Red Labor Union International was called in Moscow for the fall of 1921. A delegation from the United States was recruited and among them was Foster, who agreed to attend the conclave in Moscow only as an observer.[2] He came back a fully convinced Communist with adequate support to launch The Labor Herald, which was to serve as the official organ of the Trade Union Educational League. The U.S. Department of State claimed that Foster had brought $40,000 back from the Soviet Union. In April 1923 the Trade Union Educational League received an additional $90,000 from the same source and a third donation of $40,000 at the meeting of Communist delegates in Bridgman, Michigan, in 1923.[3]

Activity

The Trade Union Educational League began its activity in February 1922, aided by its newly acquired funds. Branches were set up in many industrial centers. These groups were not unions in the ordinary sense, but collections of "militants" who were to oppose the policies of the conservative union officers. The league, which did not charge dues nor maintain formal membership lists, was presumably supported by the sale of literature and collections at meetings. Local groups were formed into industrial sections related to other industrial sections in the locality called general groups. Local industrial sections were combined into national industrial sections headed by a national industrial secretary. Sections were set up in the railroad industry, metal trades, needle trades, printing trades, coal industry, building construction, textile industry, marine transportation, and the tobacco industry.

The league favored the overthrow of capitalism, opposed class collaboration—which meant cooperation between labor and management—opposed dual unionism, advocated formation of a labor party, and affiliation with the Red International of Labor Unions. To carry out its policies, it favored the "creating of revolutionary cells and groups within the American Federation of Labor and the independent unions."[4]

In its first years, the league exercised some influence in a number of unions and central bodies. The International Molders' Union passed a pro-amalgamation resolution, but the issue was worded so as to take all effect out of the decision. In the United Mine Workers of America, the Trade Union Educational League lent its support to the dissidents who rallied around Alexander Howat and had some influence within that union. In the needle trades, the league made perhaps its greatest impression. Many of the members of these unions were Socialists, and a substantial minority were Russian born. The propaganda of the league set up no automatic adverse reaction. After a bitter struggle of several years, the league succeeded in capturing the New York Joint Board of the International Ladies' Garment Workers' Union in 1925. The next year, the perennial crisis in the cloak and suit industry came to a head. A commission appointed by Governor Alfred E. Smith made recommendations which the Communist leadership, anxious to direct a large strike, rejected. The strike lasted twenty weeks, drained the financial resources of the locals, and left the organization in a shambles. The strike committee, dominated by Communists, refused to accept the terms of the governor and other leading citizens who for years had been interested in the welfare of the industry, and even invited Arnold Rothstein, the chief organizer of the underworld, to mediate. The terms of settlement were less favorable than could have been obtained before the strike. In the end the union was broke financially and organizationally. The international officers finally intervened and took over the joint board and expelled some of the Communist strike leaders. The Communists joined with the Furriers' Union, which they controlled, and established the Needle Trades Workers' Industrial Union, a dual organization in the clothing industries.

Although the Communist organization failed to make substantial headway, it helped for a time to continue the demoralization of the New York clothing market. It disbanded in 1933 after its overtures for a formal merger were rejected by the leaders of the International Ladies' Garment Workers' Union.

The Amalgamated Clothing Workers of America at first favored the League, but changed its mind when Foster and his associates tried to inject themselves into the affairs of the union. President Sidney Hillman warned against these tactics and when his warnings were ignored, he took stern action against the invaders. The Communists succeeded in capturing the Furriers' Union, which they dominated for many years.[5]

The league suffered a sharp loss of prestige when it was revealed that William Z. Foster, who had heretofore denied his Communist affiliation, had been present at a secret meeting of Communist leaders in Bridgman, Michigan, in the spring of 1923. Perhaps a more decisive blow was the readiness of the league leaders to join with the Communist Workers' party to capture the Farmer-Labor convention, sponsored by the Chicago Federation of Labor, in July 1923. Foster immediately lost the support of his chief sponsors, Fitzpatrick and Nockles of the Chicago federation. But the league played an important role in gaining the endorsement of amalgamation of seventeen state federations of labor and about twenty internationals.[6]

In addition, the proposal was endorsed by numerous city central bodies and a large number of local unions. Inroads were also made in other organizations. Dissatisfaction was skillfully utilized to gain a foothold and to make alliances with groups hostile to the dominant administration. The league had sufficient influence in the Machinists' Union in 1925 so that its candidate polled a respectable vote against the incumbent international president, William Johnston. Nor was this the only union in which it exercised influence. In the Carpenters', the Jewelry Workers', the Textile Workers', the Men's Clothing Workers', the Tailors', the Bakery Workers', the Painter and Decorator's, and the Barbers' Unions, the league had adherents. In the United Mine Workers of America a relatively unknown candidate, supported by the Communists, George Voyzey, was able to poll 66,000 votes against the more than 166,000 votes of John L. Lewis for international president of the union in 1924. Much of this influence was gained by the expenditure of large subsidies sent by the Profintern, the trade union arm of the Communist International.[7] But aside from winning control of the Furriers' Union, accomplished in part with the aid of its Greek strong-arm men, the Communist campaign ended in failure. Moreover, not all the opposition groups were Communist-controlled or influenced. Some favored more militant policies, and some believed that a new day had dawned for labor. By 1924 the Communist thrust had been repelled in the majority of labor organizations, although the special circumstances in the coal mining industry and union, and in the New York clothing market, enabled them to continue their campaigns in these industries but eventually they also failed. It should also be noted that opponents of Lewis in the Miners' Union were willing to go along with the Communists for their own political advantage.

The AFL took steps against central labor bodies under the control of the dissidents. As for amalgamation, it was a useful propaganda device, and it showed that an outstanding organizer like Foster could succumb to a utopian program. Whatever merits industrial unionism had, it could only be brought into being on the plane of organization, as has since been demonstrated by the Congress of Industrial Organizations. As a practical matter few unions object to expanding their own jurisdictions; it is only when they are asked to give up rights that they come forth with objections. The amalgamation program could only be achieved by reorganizing the existing unions on a more "rational" basis. It took little account of the political and administrative problems that were involved in the practical realization of the program; and in its own way, it was just as visionary as the "wheel of fortune," which Father Thomas Haggerty had proposed for the Industrial Workers of the World. Adherents of the Trade Union Educational League soon faced stern action in a number of unions. In the United Mine Workers of America, they formed an International Committee which was immediately denounced as a dual union by the International Executive Board, and its followers were expelled. The Communists did capture District No. 26 in Nova Scotia, but when the officers approved of an unauthorized strike, its charter was revoked. The Communists also played a role in the anti-administration campaign to unseat Lewis as president of the union in 1926. John Brophy, a district president, ran against him, and he and his slate were defeated. Fraud was charged, but proof was not presented.[8]

In the coal industry, the Communists continued to be active. After the signing of the Jacksonville Agreement in 1924, the position of the union fields deteriorated. Increasing competitive pressure from the unorganized regions of West Virginia and Kentucky compelled the union to fight for survival. The inability of the United Mine Workers of America to devise a policy to meet the threat strengthened the position of the factions which had from the start fought Lewis' emergence as head of the union. Action against Alexander Howat for approving "outlaw" strikes against the industrial court law sharpened the animus that Howat had borne against Lewis over the years. He toured the mine fields denouncing Lewis on the grounds that he had betrayed the cause of coal mining unionism. Howat was not a Communist, nor were many of the others connected with the Save the Union Committee, which had Communist connections. But the Communists were influential and in strategic places. In fact, Pat Toohey, a Communist, was one of the sponsors of the Save the Miners' Union Conference called for Pittsburgh, Pennsylvania, on April 1, 1928.[9] Lewis expelled the leaders as secessionists, but the Communists in the committee were far from dismayed; they soon organized the National Miners' Union, a full-fledged dual organization.

The influence of the Communists in the Miners' and Garment Workers' Unions was largely due to the conditions in the industries at the time. The organized coal districts could do little to meet the growing competition of the southern nonunion fields. Influential persons in the union and regional leaders tried to use the difficulties as a lever to pry Lewis from the leadership of the United Mine Workers of America. The Communists were accepted, for they furnished financial and organizational sinews of war. The Save the Union Committee published the *Coal Miner* in Springfield, Massachusetts, under the nominal editorship of Frank Keeney of West Virginia, but Vernon Smith, who was on the staff of the *Daily Worker,* performed the actual chores. In part, the organized miners were willing to give critics of their international administration at least a hearing if not approval. It was a situation which was made to order for the Communists, but they reduced their influence by espousing a dual union. Much of the propaganda of the Communists and their associates has a strange sound, for it was built around the charge that John L. Lewis, the greatest organizer in the history of American labor and perhaps of world labor, did not want to and did not know how to organize.

The AFL could play only a subordinate role in the fight against the Communists. It attacked the Bolsheviks on political grounds and denounced their seizure of power and installation of a dictatorship of the proletariat. The Trade Union Educational League was sharply attacked, and a number of city central labor unions were sternly admonished to follow the principles and policies of the AFL or face a removal of their charters. The heads of the federation were especially irked when the Seattle Labor Council sent Hulet C. Wells to Moscow to attend the conference of the Red Labor Union International. It took several warnings before the council agreed to follow a more orthodox course. Somewhat similar situations developed in Detroit, Minneapolis, Tacoma, and Butte. Butte, Montana, had been over the years a center of militant labor activity by the IWW and insurgent-minded unionists affiliated with the AFL. William F. Dunne, later editor of the *Daily Worker,* was sent as a delegate to the Portland convention of the AFL. Because Dunne had sharply attacked the integrity of John L. Lewis in a newspaper, Philip Murray, a delegate and vice-president of the United Mine Workers of America, demanded that Dunne be ousted from the convention. The vote to expel Dunne passed by a vote of 27,837 to 108 with 643 not voting; Dunne was allowed to denounce his accusers in a vitriolic speech. The action of the convention was unusual, and Gompers explained that it was only the second time, the first in 1895, that credentials had been revoked.[10]

The Communists acknowledged defeat of their infiltration policy by organizing the Trade Union Unity League in Cleveland at a convention on August 31–September 1, 1928. It came on the eve of a depression, when the American labor movement was fighting what seemed like a hopeless battle to hold its own. The Communists formed a set of dual unions but like their IWW counterparts they exercised little influence, except in the training of staff, some of whom would be given an opportunity by the emergence of the Committee for Industrial Organization. Events shaping up during the paralysis of business and massive unemployment were to provide the Communists with many opportunities for entrenching themselves within the labor movement. For a time, it did indeed appear that Communist influence, if not a predominant one, was to be at least a force which all would have to take into account. But these events are related to the "revolution" of the 1930's rather than to the first phase of Communist infiltration.

Lewis Challenge to Gompers

John L. Lewis's attempt to send Gompers into retirement, in 1921, cannot be regarded as a struggle between the conservative and progressive forces within the AFL. It was only the second time that a serious rival contested the presidency; demonstration candidates can be disregarded. John McBride, another coal miner, defeated Gompers in 1894 and gave him his only sabbatical. All socialist delegates voted for McBride. It was somewhat different in 1921; the socialist vote was not on one side. Nor did the progressives vote as a solid phalanx. The contest itself aroused more than normal interest as a result of a vituperative campaign against Gompers by the Hearst press. He, nevertheless, won handily, polling 25,022 votes to 12,324 for Lewis, but 8,916 of the latter's came from three unions—the Machinists, Carpenters, and Lewis's own.

Had Lewis been chosen it might have changed quite a bit of history. Considering the erosion of his union's power in the 1920's, it is unlikely that he could have changed the drift of events in that decade. But with Lewis at the helm of the AFL in the early 1930's, the labor movement might have developed differently. Lewis might have prevented the split or compelled the skilled trades to defect, giving the industrial unions the name and property of the AFL.

CHAPTER 31

Unions in Retreat

The fears of the leaders of the coal miners that the central competitive field could not be maintained in the face of rising output in the nonunion areas became increasingly evident in the latter part of the 1920's. The Jacksonville Agreement signed in February 1924 at Jacksonville, Florida, was greeted by the union administration as a victory, but it only accentuated the problem of the organized fields. Inevitably, the difficulties faced by the union districts were exploited by the rivals of John L. Lewis and his administration. The gradual erosion of standards, the greater unwillingness of the operators in the union districts to make concessions, and their demand for wage revisions so as to meet the competition of the unorganized districts were factors in the political difficulties which faced the Lewis administration.

Throughout the entire decade of the 1920's, Lewis encountered the relentless opposition of powerful district leaders who were determined to use the union's misfortunes as a means of destroying an officer who had snatched the highest prize the organization offered. The inability of the union to hold its districts or to stamp out the advantages of the unorganized territories was adroitly used by the opposition to gain propaganda advantages. Lewis was charged with unwillingness and incapacity to bring the unorganized districts into the union field. In the elections for international president in 1926, the Save the Union Committee, an opposition group, nominated District President John Brophy of District 2, a bituminous field in Pennsylvania, as a candidate for international president. Brophy, scholarly and kindly, was a representative of the best type of unionist of the last generation. The Save the Union Committee had a number of proposals which were the staples of opposition groups within the Miners' Union at the time: union democracy; formation of a labor party; no wage cuts; short term contracts; and the insistence that union operators be required, as a condition for dealing with the union, to sign for all their mines the organized as well as those located in the nonunion territories. The last suggestion was the heart of the opposition program. Lewis derided this prescription as one that would result only in the de-unionization of the northern mines.[1] Brophy and the rest of the "Save the Union" contingent were defeated and immediately charged they had been counted out.

In retrospect, one must conclude that Lewis' presumed lack of knowledge and will to organize was part of the folklore of the 1920's. The charge that the failure of the union was the inevitable result of incompetence or venality of officials rather than the result of the lack of power of the union or its desire to organize must be put aside. Some of the charges were inspired by purely political reasons; others were made by persons who assumed that organization of workers was automatic and inevitable and that the inability of the union could be attributed to the incompetence of the leadership rather than the strength of the nonunion operators. The inability of the Miners' Union to retain its strength, let alone expand, under Lewis in the 1920's is the best gloss upon the problems faced by organized labor in the decade of the 1920's.[2]

The operators, on the offensive in 1927, demanded a competitive wage. Temporary agreements after a long suspension were made in some districts, but operators in Ohio and Pennsylvania refused. Union defeat after a long dispute was the result. The following year, the International Policy Committee allowed each district to settle on the best terms possible and ended the slogan of "No backward step." Wage cuts were accepted in Illinois and Indiana, but the Ohio and Pennsylvania operators would not bend. The ill-fortunes of the coal miners were attributed to the union heads, especially Lewis, and Save the Union committees emerged in many areas. Led by the more extreme of Lewis' opponents, including some Communists, these groups gained a following but not enough to loosen Lewis' grip. The insurgent movement spread to the anthracite region where it was also directed against Rinaldo Capellini, the head of District 7.

Stymied in their effort to gain control of the union by Lewis' ability to ward off the attacks, the insurgents sought to establish themselves by holding a convention of the Save the Union committee on April 1, 1928. In addition to Brophy, Powers Hapgood, a member of a distinguished literary family whose father had turned his firm, the Columbia Conserve Company, into a producers' cooperative, and Patrick Toohey, a Communist active in trade union matters, were prominent members at the Pittsburgh conference. The delegates issued a six-point program and thereby, according to Lewis, had set themselves up as a dual union; they were expelled. Brophy, who had gone along with the Save the Union Committee, found himself among the ousted. The Communists with whom the progressives had cooperated in an assault upon the United Mine Workers of America had by now shifted their policies from boring from within to dual unionism and launched a competing coal miners' organization: the National Miners' Union. Aside from the issuance of scurrilous propaganda, it played no role in subsequent developments in coal unionism.

In the campaign of suppression of the Save the Union Committee, Lewis had the support of the regular district officers, irrespective of their views or affiliations within the United Mine Workers of America. Virtually all regarded this group as a threat to the internal stability of the union and proceeded against its adherents. United action against the insurgents did not mean that a truce had been made on other issues. The center of the opposition to Lewis remained in the Illinois District No. 12. Lewis had scored a coup by producing evidence that Frank Farrington, president of District No. 12 and a leading opponent of Lewis, had accepted a large check from the Peabody Coal Company. Farrington, who was abroad representing the AFL denied that the check was a bribe; it was, he claimed, an advance on his salary as the labor advisor he intended to become. The removal of Farrington did not end the opposition to Lewis in District 12, and a dispute over the handling of finances finally led to challenge of the rights of the international officers to hold their posts.

Charges were made that several thousand dollars had been misappropriated by officers of Subdistrict 9 in Franklin County, Illinois. Officers of the subdistrict "admitted participation in the embezzlement of funds involved in the purchase of $50,000 worth of groceries by the subdistrict in 1927. They each admitted receiving in this deal the sum of $3,500 as a commission upon the purchases. This amount was deposited to the credit of each in a West Frankfort bank. . . ."[3] District officers were charged with knowing and abetting the irregular transaction. The district officers were ordered to remove the officers of Subdistrict 9, and, instead, parcelled out the locals in Subdistrict 9 among the contiguous subdistricts. "This action of the Executive Board of District 12 is in violation of the laws of the United Mine Workers of America and in defiance of the ruling of the International Executive Board."[4]

For refusing to carry out the directives of the international executive board, the officers of District 12 were removed and were replaced by a provisional group of officers headed by Frank Hefferly as district president. The members of District 12 were assured that the "creation of a Provisional District Union is an arrangement temporary in nature. When the affairs of the organization in Illinois again become normal and stability is restored to the structure of the District Union, the International Union guarantees to the membership of Provisional District 12 that an honest election will be held under the auspices of the International Union wherein the membership will be given opportunity to select officers of their own choice for the conduct of their affairs."[5]

The officers of District 12 decided not to submit to the directives and secured an injunction restraining the international officers from interfering with them. The *Illinois Miner,* edited by Oscar Ameringer, a veteran Socialist journalist, took up the fight in behalf of the district. *The United Mine Workers Journal* charged that the injunction was a plot engineered by Farrington to destroy the United Mine Workers of America.[6] One of the claims made by the opposition to Lewis was that the failure to hold a convention as provided in the constitution, in January 1929, meant that the international officers no longer could exercise their authority. The international officers answered that the convention had been postponed after such a step had been approved by the membership in a referendum vote, and moreover, the fact had been recognized by the officers of District 12 until charges had been made against them.[7]

Leaders of District 12, despite the silence of the court on this point, proceeded to call an international convention which was held in Springfield on March 10, 1930. Many of Lewis' opponents were there: John H. Walker, a candidate for the presidency of the union in 1908, a decade before Lewis was an important leader; Adolph Germer, Socialist and trade unionist, who was active in the Ludlow affair; and, of course, Alexander Howat of District 14. Lewis opened his own convention at Indianapolis on the same day. Claiming to be the rightful United Mine Workers of America, the insurgents elected Alexander Howat president, Adolph Germer vice-president, and John H. Walker secretary-treasurer. At the Lewis convention, he, Philip Murray, and Thomas Kennedy were re-elected. Leaders of the insurgents were expelled.

The "reorganized" United Mine Workers of America headed by Howat and Walker sought representation at the 1930 AFL convention, and Green quoted Section 5 of Article IV of the AFL constitution which prohibited recognition of groups seceding or suspended from a regular chartered union. Green also refused to allow the AFL to call a convention of representatives of all miners, and informed John H. Walker that "seceding groups which have withdrawn from a parent organization affiliated with the American Federation of Labor can only come back into affiliation with the parent organization through an agreement and understanding reached with the officers representing the national or international union affiliated with the American Federation of Labor from which the group had withdrawn."[8]

The internecine feud resulted in the control of the northern sections of District 12 by the Howat-Walker group, while the international under

Lewis dominated the southern areas. Each side was able to hold its own territory, and the disputes were finally settled in a decision by Judge Harry Edwards of Sangamon County before whom the issues were tried. He held that the constitution had not lapsed, that the Lewis' organization remained the United Mine Workers of America. He held, however, that Lewis had superseded his power when he removed the district officers without trial and that the district officers had been rightfully elected and were properly in command of their offices. Lewis was forbidden to interfere with the exercise of their authority.[9]

PROGRESSIVE MINERS OF AMERICA

While a truce was reached between the officers, the major problems facing the union were far from solved. The delegates to the District 12 convention in February 1932 drew up a set of demands. The operators countered with a request for a reduction of rates to the level of the recently adopted Indiana scale. John Walker, who had been elected district president, began fishing in troubled waters. Walker announced what might be called his "no backward step" policy and urged the miners in his district not to accept a pay reduction. In view of general economic and mining conditions, Walker's position was not tenable, but he and other district officers believed they might profit politically from embarrassing the international union. Failing to reach an agreement, a strike began on April 1, 1932, but by July an agreement accepting a substantial reduction in pay had been reached between the operators and the miners' leaders. The contract was, however, repudiated overwhelmingly on a referendum vote.

Lewis, whose displacement the district officers had actively sought in the preceding year, was now invited to assist in reaching an agreement. A contract substantially similar to the one repudiated was reached with Lewis' assistance, but the vote on its acceptance was lost. Thereupon, the district officers reached an agreement with the operators. It was for the shortest period in the history of the district and was to expire on March 31, 1933, less than a year from its inception.

The new agreement allowed for a substantial wage reduction of $1.10 a day and demonstrated that Lewis' opponents were also subject to economic constraints. But the miners in Illinois now believed that they had been betrayed, and the suspicion sown by the district officers bore fruit in a powerful insurgent movement which swept through District 12. A large measure of success was achieved; the failure to shut down the mines in Franklin County by the Progressives was perhaps the turning point in the attack against Lewis and his administration. The Progressives were, as a result, limited to the small mines, while the United Mine Workers of America was able to retain control of the large producers. When some of the operators tried to reopen their mines with contracts with the old union, armed clashes followed. Militia was sent into the area around Taylorville after several fatalities had resulted. Governor Henry Horner intervened and tried to find a basis of agreement but failed.

The Progressive Mine Workers of America was able to survive but the absence of experienced leaders doomed the organization to a parochial existence in the small mines in the northern part of the state. Fearful that its officers might develop too much power, the Progressives enacted a provision that the chief officers could not succeed themselves nor could any branch officer serve for more than two consecutive terms.[10] It meant that few were given an opportunity to develop experience or a rapport with the important groups in the industry. Moreover, because of its isolation from the general labor movement, the Progressive Mine Workers of America developed a suspicion and hatred of other labor groups, and were willing to use racial and anti-Semitic slogans. The Progressives, however, were a handy weapon that the AFL tried to use against Lewis and his union after they supported financially and organizationally the Committee for Industrial Organization. The Progressive Mine Workers of America was allowed in 1937 to affiliate with the AFL but little except a small per capita income was gained from the affiliation of this group. Nor did it prevent the indictment and prosecution of the leaders of the Progressive Mine Workers of America, thirty-six of whom were convicted of conspiracy in the federal courts. Each was sentenced to five years in prison and fined $20,000. The sentences were reduced. The Progressives became involved in a series of legal disputes which drained the union of its funds. By 1937 an estimated twenty-four miners had been killed in Illinois in the warfare between the two factions.[11]

The dissension which arose within the Miners' Union was primarily caused by the continual deterioration in the position of the union districts and the inability of the union to prevent the steady deflation of wages. A leadership, no matter how determined or adroit, cannot cope successfully with such conditions. In areas where the union was not facing opposition from within, it lost in many instances its members and the contracts it had held for three decades. Faced by these conditions, the union could only advocate the shorter work day and the Davis-Kelly bill, introduced by Senator James Davis and Congressman Clyde Kelly. It was a proposal to regulate the interstate commerce of bituminous coal through a system of licensing of producers with the aim of achieving some sort of stable production. The United Mine Workers of America opposed direct government intervention and favored regulation with the permission of the federal government by voluntary pools so that "coal companies may combine and agree upon production and prices under the approval of a governmental body representing the public interest, the price fixed to be sufficient to provide for adequate wages and a fair return on investment."[12] There was not much the union could do and the helplessness before the disaster that had overtaken the industry is clearly reflected in the grim editorials which appeared in the *United Mine Workers Journal* in this period. It must be reiterated that the failure cannot be attributed to the union leadership. In view of John L. Lewis' ability to ride out opposition, his resourcefulness and organizing ability, the comments of critics on his incapacity deserve little attention.

THE TEXTILE INDUSTRY

The AFL leaders were aware of the failure of the movement to expand in a generally favorable economic environment. Efforts to organize the automobile industry in 1926 through the cooperative action of metal trades and building trades unions ended in failure. The federation next inspired a plan to organize the southern textile industry. It may have been influenced by the strike of textile workers in Passaic, New Jersey, in 1926. Passaic was the center of a woolen industry employing more than 10,000 workers and dominated by the Botany Worsted Company. Because of depressed demands for the product, the workers were largely on short time. Against the advice of other woolen firms in the area, a 10 per cent reduction in wages was imposed in October 1925. Soon thereafter, Albert Weisbord, a graduate of City College in New York and the Harvard Law School, appeared. Weisbord, who admitted to his membership in the Communist party, began an active organizing campaign. By January 1926 a committee requested the restoration of the cut, and its members were discharged by Colonel F. H. Johnston, the head of Botany Worsted. A strike followed on January 26 and by February 23, a set of demands was announced.

The strikers demanded a 10 per cent wage increase over the old scale, a forty-four-hour work week, time and a half for overtime, improved sanitary conditions, and union recognition.[13] Employers rejected the demand and refused to deal with the United Front Committee which was headed by Weisbord. Gradually other producers were shut down, including the Furstman-Huffman mills, the second largest in the area. Mass picketing followed, and clashes between police and pickets became a common occurrence. Protests to the federal government were to no avail. The employers refused the slightest recognition to the United Front Committee on the ground that it was Communist dominated. Arrests and charges of illegal prosecution and violence were followed by the suggestion of Governor Harry Moore that the AFL intervene and take over the strike. Although the conditions of the strikers attracted a wave of sympathy, not until the strikers agreed to the withdrawal of Weisbord and the transfer of the strike leadership to the United Textile Workers of America, an AFL union, would the employers agree to negotiate. Finally, in December 1926, the Botany Worsted Company said that its workers would have the right to organize in "a legitimate association provided it is not of communist origin and purpose."[14] With the return of the workers to the Gena Worsted and the New Jersey Worsted mills in February 1926, the most dramatic strike of the latter part of the 1920's came to an end.[15]

The Southern Textile Drive

Frustrated by the failure of its campaign in the automobile industry to get started, the AFL leaders made a full-scale organizing effort in an even less promising industry—southern textiles. The first attempt was made in Elizabethton, Tennessee, in March 1929. An agreement, after a short strike, was reached with the American Bemberg and American Glanzstoff plants. But the union gained no real recognition. In fact, the truce was soon broken, and Edward McGrady, the AFL organizer, and Alfred Hoffman of the United Textile Workers were seized by a mob and deported from Elizabethton. This led to a public outcry and the intervention of Governor Henry Horton. Although another truce was reached, the union was not able to take hold.

The strikes in Tennessee and stirrings in other textile communities induced the 1929 AFL convention to undertake a more extensive campaign. A conference on January 6, 1930, of 229 delegates from 26 internationals and 7 state federations, as well as from a number of city central bodies and local unions in the region, launched the campaign. The finances were far from adequate, for the $14,000 donated by various unions was scarcely sufficient to launch an extensive drive. But in answer to the pleas of President William Green, 24 internationals assigned 38 organizers to work in the southern campaign. The federation allocated four additional ones to work under the direction of a committee of three—Francis Gorman of the United Textile Workers, W. C. Birthright of the Tennessee Federation of Labor, and Paul Smith of the AFL. In addition to the normal obstacles of worker apathy and employer opposition, the drive had to overcome declining employment and long lines of idle workers. The campaign continued. A strike of 4,000 operatives in the Riverside and Dan River cotton mills at Danville, Virginia, on September 29, 1930, was the last incident in the AFL southern drive.[16] This strike also failed.

The National Textile Workers' Union, a unit in the Trade Union Unity League, organized and controlled by the Communist party, became active in the southern textile areas at about the same time. A local union was launched in Gastonia, North Carolina, a community of 22,000 people and an important textile center about twenty miles west of Charlotte. By April 1, 1929, 1,700 of the 2,200 textile workers employed in the Manville-Jenckes Loray mill were out on strike. Demands for a forty-hour work week, a $20.00 weekly wage, reduced rents, and improved sanitary standards in the company houses were the main demands. One of the organizers sent down to Gastonia, George Pershing, announced that he was there "for the purpose of organizing the Young Communist Workers' League."[17] Pershing also informed reporters that the principal aim of the Communist party is control of industry by the workers and that is what would happen in Gastonia. The information was used effectively against the strikers who were trying to raise their wages. But other weapons were also used. A mob of 150 invaded the union headquarters and smashed furniture and destroyed food collected for the strikers.[18] Evicted from the company houses, the strikers organized a tent colony. On June 7 several officers including Chief of Police Aderholt came to the colony and demanded entrance. When union guards asked for a warrant, there was a short argument and finally shooting in which the chief was killed and two strikers wounded.

As a result, sixteen strikers and leaders, including Fred Beal, who was in charge of the walkout, were indicted for conspiracy to murder and secret assault with deadly weapons with intent to kill. Three of the indicted were women. The trial began on August 26, but because of illness of a juror a mistrial was ordered. In the second trial the number of defendants was reduced to seven; the others had been released. They were all found guilty of second-degree murder and sentenced to long terms in the penitentiary.[19] The convicted were released on $5,000 bail each and when their sentences were upheld by the North Carolina Supreme Court, they fled to the Soviet Union. Beal returned to the United States disillusioned. He published an autobiography in which he castigated North Carolina justice and exposed conditions in the Soviet Union where he had gone with hope and enthusiasm. He accepted imprisonment in the United States rather than remain in the workers' fatherland.

CONFERENCE FOR PROGRESSIVE LABOR ACTION

In May 1929 a group of trade unionists and sympathizers organized the Conference for Progressive Labor Action. Leaders in the project were the directors and teachers of Brookwood Labor College, a resident labor school in Katonah, New York. The charge was made that it was a radical institution and friendly to communism. After an investigation, the AFL Executive Council issued a statement criticizing Brookwood. Matthew Woll, who investigated the school for the council, claimed that no effort to censor had been made; the executive council was only providing information. This was not entirely true, since the adverse information would influence support. The issue came before the 1928 AFL convention, and the position of the council was unanimously endorsed.[20]

The Conference for Progressive Labor Action was organized around the *Labor Age,* which had since 1922 advocated more militant labor policies. The conference favored a broad program, including organization of the semi-skilled and unskilled, opposition to the National Civic Federation, open union membership to all workers irrespective of race, nationality, or religion, opposition to the labor injunction, and support of social insurance. In addition, union democracy and recognition of Soviet Russia were endorsed, a labor party was proposed, and a fight against war and imperialism was approved. Less than two years later, the conference shifted toward greater political activity and gradually faded from the labor scene.[21]

LEGISLATIVE ACTIVITIES

During the entire decade of the 1920's, organized labor made little progress. The first years were a time of enthusiasm and expanded horizons. More aggressive groups appeared to be coming to the fore, but much of the enthusiasm was rubbed out by the defeats administered upon new and old unions. In fact, such policies as government ownership of railroads were repudiated by their own sponsors.[22]

Labor banking also attracted the interest of many labor leaders, but it failed to gain enthusiastic endorsement from the AFL. Started in May 1920 by the International Association of Machinists as a means of aiding employers denied credit because they dealt with organized labor, the labor banking movement received a sharp impetus from the Brotherhood of Locomotive Engineers, which organized the Brotherhood of Locomotive Engineers National Cooperative Bank in November 1920. Under the leadership of Grand Chief Warren S. Stone, the financial operations of the union greatly expanded. For the next five years, labor banks increased in size and number; by 1926, thirty-six were operating.[23]

The number gradually declined, and the pioneer venture in labor-managed finance by the Brotherhood of Locomotive Engineers collapsed. The union and its members incurred serious losses. Only a bank with two branches operated by the Amalgamated Clothing Workers of America in New York and Chicago has survived as reminders of the financial experiments of the 1920's.

At no time was the AFL Executive Council enthusiastic about these financial experiments. In 1926 the council found that "there is inherent in the development of labor banks the potential and real danger that interests not concerned either in the welfare of employers or employees but prompted wholly for speculative gains will seek entrance into this field and by methods not beyond criticism attempt to mislead well-intentioned workers and unions into banking ventures and security or investment enterprise that will spell ruin to themselves and cast discredit and disaster upon the organized labor movement. The development of labor banks has given rise to other labor ventures in the investment, building and security field. We are prompted also to sound a note of warning against this increasing tendency to divert attention of the trade unionist from the more primary need of trade union organization and trade union functioning."[24]

Again in 1927, the federation warned that "great care and sound judgment should be exercised before labor unions and members of labor unions put their money into a new labor bank promotion or into investment companies stocks organized for the purpose of erecting and conducting such an enterprise."[25]

CHILD LABOR

The AFL was active in having the constitutional amendment outlawing child labor introduced in Congress. From the outset, the federation sought to have laws raising the school age or prohibiting the employment of children under the age of sixteen. The efforts of the federation were directed to securing laws in the state legislatures, and it aided the enactment of the law regulating child labor by the Sixty-fourth Congress in September 1916. The statute prohibited shipments in interstate or foreign commerce of articles or products of any mine or quarry on which children under sixteen years of age had been employed, or the product of any mill, cannery, workshop, factory, or manufacturing establishment in which children under the age of fourteen worked. It also included provisions governing the hours children between the age of fourteen and eighteen could work. The law was declared unconstitutional in *Hammer* v. *Dagenhart,* 251 U.S. 251 (1918).

Another law proposed to levy a 10 per cent excise tax on the products of any mill, cannery, workshop, factory, or manufacturing establishment in which children under fourteen were employed. Enacted in February 1919, it was also held unconstitutional in *Bailey* v. *Drexel Furniture Company,* 259 U.S. 20 (1922). Immediately after the decision, Gompers called a conference of men's and women's organizations concerned with abolishing child labor. A permanent committee was set up with Gompers as chairman. After concluding that the only remedy was through a constitutional amendment, the AFL had Senator Medill McCormick of Illinois introduce the amendment to the federal Constitution which gave Congress the power to prohibit the labor of persons under eighteen years of age.[26] A number of churchmen attacked the amendment after it passed the Congress and opposed its ratification by the legislatures. When ratification came before the voters of Massachusetts, Daniel Cardinal O'Connell and other high ranking prelates of the Roman Catholic church attacked the proposal and urged its defeat.

Gompers appealed to the voters of Massachusetts to support the amendment, and Secretary Frank Morrison wrote that "the American Labor movement is depending upon Massachusetts labor bodies to make an intensive campaign for ratification of child Labor Amendment and success of the referendum. Failure in Massachusetts may influence other states."[27] The AFL never slackened in its efforts to have the amendment ratified, but it had to wait for the adoption of the Fair Labor Standards Act in 1938 to end child labor outside of agriculture.

The federation was more successful in placing restrictions on the interstate movement of prison-made goods. This had been a demand of organized labor for many decades. Under the Hawes-Cooper Act, enacted in January 1929, states were allowed after January 19, 1934, to prohibit the importation of prison made goods.

A more important piece of legislation was the Railway Labor Act of 1926. The legislation was the result of the dissatisfaction of the railroads and the employees with the Railroad Labor Board. Efforts to have this Board abolished were made by the Howell-Barkley bill, which was drawn up by a committee from the AFL, the Railway Employees' Department, and the operating unions. Submitted to Congress in 1924, it failed to pass. Finally in 1925 committees from the carriers and the employee organizations jointly drew up a bill which was enacted by Congress and signed by President Calvin Coolidge on May 20, 1926.

The Railway Labor Act repealed Title III of the Transportation Act of 1920, the labor clauses of that law and the Newlands Act of 1913, and provided machinery for the settlement of disputes. In the event of a dispute between a carrier and its employees, the parties were required to confer and appeal to a board of adjustment if no settlement were reached. Recourse could also be had to a permanent board of mediation, and issues in dispute could be submitted to a temporary board of arbitration. If deemed necessary by the President of the United States, an emergency board to hear the dispute could be established. From the point of view of organized labor, Section 2 was of utmost importance. It provided that "representatives for the purpose of this Act, shall be designated by the representative parties in such manner as may be provided in their corporate organization or unincorporated association, or by other means of collective action, without interference, influence or coercion exercised by either party over the self-organization or designation of representatives by the other."

While recognizing the right of railway workers to organize, the law did not establish machinery for determining collective bargaining representatives or for enforcing the statute. The constitutionality of the provision was decided in *Brotherhood of Railway and Steamship Clerks* v. *Texas and New Orleans Railway Company,* 281 U.S. 548 (1930). The carrier had established a company union of clerks with which it negotiated terms of employment. The brotherhood brought suit in the U.S. district court, and the company was ordered to break up the company organization. The

Supreme Court, to which the case was brought on appeal, upheld the lower court decision. Speaking for a unanimous Court, Chief Justice Charles Evans Hughes found that workers had the right to safeguard their economic interests and that since "the carriers subject to the Act have no constitutional right to interfere with the freedom of employees to make their selections, they cannot complain of the statute on constitutional grounds."

This decision overruled the view expressed earlier that Congress could not prohibit interference with workers' organizations.

CHAPTER 32

The Depression and Continued Decline

The collapse of the stock market in October 1929 signaled the beginning of a severe decline in business and employment. Total gross product dropped from over $104 billion to a low point of slightly under $56 billion in 1933. National income in the same period dropped from $87 billion to $40 billion, and compensation of employees fell from $51 billion to $29 billion.[1]

The sharp decline in income was accompanied by continually increasing unemployment and part-time employment. The disastrous decline in building construction seriously affected the unions which were the most stable groups within the labor movement. Precise information on the number of idle was lacking, and the *American Federation of Labor Survey of Business,* which began publishing unemployment statistics of union members in September 1927, was one of the few public or private sources providing continual information on this important question. The AFL had been alerted to the possibilities of rising unemployment by a report from its research department in February 1928, which called attention to increasing unemployment among organized workers. This was a danger sign for union members who in the 1920's were predominantly made up of skilled workers and generally were not among the first laid off.

Neither the labor movement nor the government was prepared for the economic catastrophe which followed. The executive council of the AFL at its meeting in May 1929 suggested the establishment of a national employment service, a census to determine the number of unemployed, and regularization of employment. In November 1929, President Hoover asked

411

industry to avoid wage cuts and to speed investment. Standard suggestions, these were generally supported by the public. But the executive council would not in the first years of the depression of the 1930's support a system of unemployment insurance. The federation was hostile to such a program and did not endorse it until 1932. Up to that time, it had approved only one program of social insurance—workmen's compensation as a means of protecting loss of wages arising out of accidents in the course of employment. In 1913 the executive council declared that "injured workmen and their dependent families are immeasurably better protected and provided for under compensation laws than they were under the antiquated, cruel, and unjust common law as it related to an employer's liability."[2] But the measures advocated for the handling of the growing idleness were scarcely those which would inspire confidence in the appraisal of the situation. The federation also favored the time-honored device of reducing hours. In defense of its position, the council, in the face of swelling idleness, stressed that prevention is more desirable than relief or insurance. The unemployed reached, according to its own statistics, 4.7 million.[3] Nor was the federation ready to endorse unemployment insurance in the following year when its research staff estimated that more than 8 million workers were without jobs. Alarming reports were pouring in from cities whose relief budgets had doubled between January 1929 and 1930, and difficulties were being encountered in meeting rising welfare expenditures.[4] Breadlines were lengthening, and social workers reported that people unaccustomed to dependence were appealing for assistance.

Individuals and groups were urged, for example, in Wisconsin, "to get in touch with all the County Boards to urge them to increase their relief budgets at their October meetings. . . . As a result of these efforts, many Boards materially increased their budgets. Other Boards, which had intended to decrease their poor relief budgets, were persuaded to appropriate at least as much as they had in the past."[5] The fact is that, during 1930–1931, many welfare agencies received "a demand for relief greater than they had up to that time known. The communities were, however, still unwilling to acknowledge that they were face to face with disaster and the 'optimism' campaign being vigorously promoted by business at the time prevented any concerted action being taken in more than a few cities."[6]

The federation's opposition to unemployment insurance was not shared by all leaders of labor nor by all unions. At the 1931 convention Daniel Tobin of the Teamsters' and William Mahon of the Street Car Men's Unions spoke out against the views of the executive council. The federation urged appropriations for relief. The great problem was the absence of work, not unsatisfactory conditions of employment. In a number of communities the unemployed organized. The Unemployed Citizens' League of Seattle and the Unemployed Council of New York City, controlled by the Communists, were among the early organizations of unemployed. In addition to the Communists, Socialists and some close to the Committee for Progressive Labor Action organized unemployed groups. The latter committee was influential among the idle in Ohio, Pennsylvania, and West Virginia. A national organization of unemployed leagues was established in Cleveland in July 1933. The Chicago Workers' Committee on Unemployment, organized by the League for Industrial Democracy and headed by Karl Borders, a social worker, was one of the active local groups. It sought to bargain with the local relief authorities. The best known national group, the Workers Alliance of America, was established in Washington in March 1935. Led by David Lasser, it tried to arouse the communities to the plight of the unemployed.

On the whole, the unemployed groups were set up by persons and organizations with either communist or socialist views. The Unemployed Citizens' League of Seattle seems to have had leaders of more conservative outlook.[7] A resolution on organizing the unemployed was submitted to the 1935 AFL convention and was rejected. The federation believed that the unemployed should retain their membership in the unions of their craft or calling.[8]

The federation continued to press for reduction of the work week and supported public works. It did not neglect its normal activities, at least as they concerned holders of offices regarded by the federation as its own. William Green objected to the appointment of William Doak, a member of the Brotherhood of Railroad Trainmen, as Secretary of Labor. Members of the executive council approved Green's position, and Martin F. Ryan, the treasurer, even argued that Doak was not a member of organized labor.[9] In his protest, Green was following in the tradition set by Gompers, although Green's view was based on narrower grounds: the view that only a member of the AFL should be nominated. In protesting the appointment of James J. Davis as Secretary of Labor by President-elect Warren Harding in February 1921, Gompers reviewed the history of the Department of Labor and claimed "that in the President's Cabinet there should be not only a capable, faithful and loyal citizen but a man who has had the experience, the contact with the great mass of labor."[10]

The U.S. Department of Labor was established in 1914, achieving a demand of organized labor made since the 1860's. A bureau of labor had been established in the Department of the Interior in 1884, but it did not satisfy the workers' organizations. Four years later a Department of Labor without cabinet rank was established, but this agency was also deemed insufficient, as was the Department of Commerce and Labor of 1903. Organized labor wanted a department of cabinet rank so that someone acquainted with workers' problems would have direct access to the President of the United States. Finally, President William Howard Taft approved the measure creating the Department of Labor on March 4, 1913. It was designed to "foster, promote and develop the welfare of the wage earners of the United States, to improve their working conditions, and to advance their opportunities for profitable employment."

William B. Wilson (1862–1934) was its first secretary. A Scottish-born coal miner, he had held a number of offices of the United Mine Workers of America including that of secretary-treasurer. He was elected to Congress in 1906, and served until 1913, when he accepted the secretary's post.

The AFL, however, was facing more serious problems. In the fiscal year ending August 31, 1932, the federation showed a loss of 358,930 members. It was necessary to reduce expenses by $4,000 a month. The conditions were not improved in the seven months ending March 31, 1933. In that short period, the federation lost 428,607 members. For fiscal 1933, membership fell to an average of 2,126,796, the lowest since 1916. Green was given full power by the executive council to furlough employees and to draw the necessary sums from the defense fund and the building fund.[11] Total membership of trade unions fell steadily after 1927, and by 1933 it stood at 2,973,000, almost 575,000 below the 1927 enrollment.

The federation submitted an emergency program to meet the needs of the winter of 1931–1932. It included the maintenance of wages, recommendation for shorter hours, assurance of employment to a minimum work force, a request for each employer to hire additional labor, promotion of a program of public works, strengthening of public employment offices, keeping younger people in school, offering preference in employment to those with dependents, and providing relief to the needy unemployed from public and private funds.[12] Not until 1932, did the AFL endorse a compulsory unemployment insurance system, and there is evidence that the council took this step reluctantly. John Frey, a diehard, repeated his long-held opposition. Some objection was also made at the failure of the federation to support a national system, but this step was taken upon the assurrance of eminent constitutional lawyers that the courts would not uphold a national unemployment insurance law.[13]

Injunctions

The general labor movement gained an outstanding legislative victory with the passage of the Norris-LaGuardia Act regulating the issuance of injunctions in labor disputes by the federal courts. At the suggestion of the AFL, Senator Henrik Shipstead in December 1927 introduced a simple bill limiting the use of the injunction. After hearings by a subcommittee of the Senate Committee on the Judiciary, it submitted a bill in June 1928 which approached the question "from a new point of view, that of definitely specifying the procedure to be followed in labor cases. This was followed by the inclusion of planks in both the Republican and Democratic national platforms of 1928 pledging relief from the abuse of injunctions."[14]

Enactment of the bill failed, and it was sharply attacked by Andrew Furuseth on the floor of the 1929 AFL convention. Furuseth favored the Shipstead bill which, because of its generality, was believed to be an ineffective method of meeting the problem. He denounced the proposals of the executive council and sought to have its recommendations recommitted.[15]

During 1929 and 1930, the interest in the labor injunctions declined, but the AFL and others interested in this measure renewed their activity in the following year. In January 1931 the National Committee on Labor Injunctions, with former Federal District Judge Charles F. Amidon as chairman, was formed to promote the legislation. The committee had more than four hundred members, many of them distinguished lawyers and public men.[16] When the Seventy-second Congress met on December 7, 1931, the federation strongly urged adoption of an anti-injunction measure. It passed the House of Representatives by a vote of 363 to 13, the Senate by 75 to 5, and was signed by President Hoover on March 23, 1932. The final vote does not, however, reflect the strength of the opposition. It was no exaggeration when the executive council announced "that it really represents the outstanding legal accomplishment of the American Federation of Labor."[17] The law limited the issuance of injunctions in labor disputes by the federal courts, prohibited court injunctions against certain otherwise legal activities of unions, granted a jury trial to defendants in contempt cases committed outside of the court room, and compelled a change of venue when requested.

The Davis-Bacon Act

The Davis-Bacon Act does not affect as many workers as the Norris-LaGuardia Act, but it has been of considerable importance to the building trades unions, which are the oldest organized group of workers in the United States. The act, passed in 1931, provided that contracts of the United States or the District of Columbia for more than $5,000, involving the employment of workers in the construction, alteration, or repairing of public buildings, must contain a provision that the rate of wages should not be less than those prevailing in the area. The law was not effective until the amendments of 1935, but pressure for the legislation came predominantly from the AFL and the building trades unions.[18]

CHAPTER *33*

The National Industrial Recovery Act

The change in the fortune of organized labor which took place in 1933 was almost entirely due to the legislative measures enacted by the first administration of Franklin D. Roosevelt. By March 4, 1933, unemployment was conservatively estimated at more than twelve million workers. As a partial remedy, Senator Hugo Black and Representative William P. Connery introduced a bill for the establishment of the five-day and thirty-hour work week. This bill was favored by the labor movement, but opposed by the administration. It passed the Senate.

President Roosevelt believed the economy required more extensive treatment. In a message to Congress on May 17, 1933, he proposed a program for industrial recovery, the main objectives of which were the removal of obstructions to the free flow of commerce, the promotion of cooperative action among trade groups, and between labor and management, and the relief of unfair competition and unemployment. The bill, introduced in both houses of Congress, included Section 7(a) guaranteeing labor the right to organize, along the lines of a clause in the bankruptcy law of 1932: "that employees shall have the right to organize and bargain collectively through representatives of their own choosing." Appearing as the second witness before the House Committee on Ways and Means, President William Green of the AFL asked the addition of the following amendment: "And shall be free from the interference, restraint, or coercion of employers of labor, or their agents, in the designation of such representatives or in self-organization or in other concerted activities for the purpose of collective bargaining or other mutual aid and protection." Green defended his

416

proposal by the claim that it was a statement of declared public policy taken from the Norris-LaGuardia Act. Labor, he said, was not asking for new rights as this right was already "part of the law of the land."[1] Green claimed "workers are required, as a condition of employment, to join a company union. . . . If the workers are permitted to join a labor union it ought to be a free, independent labor union, and not a union, or so-called 'union' through which a corporation may exercise full and complete control, not only of its own industrial affairs, but of the economic life of the workers."[2]

The bill that passed the House on May 26 contained the above amendment and an additional one providing "that no employee and no one seeking employment shall be required as a condition of employment to join any company union or to refrain from joining a labor organization of his own choosing."[3]

When the House bill was considered by the Senate Finance Committee, it was attacked by the chief lobbyist for the National Association of Manufacturers, James A. Emery, who distinguished between trade unions and collective bargaining. He wanted company unions to have the same status as outside labor organizations. His views were supported by several other employer representatives. Finally, former Secretary of the Interior Robert P. Lamont opposed the guarantee of collective bargaining and urged modification. He observed that the iron and steel industry favored the open shop and opposed the closed shop. John L. Lewis appeared and pleaded for equal treatment of labor and industry. He argued that industry already enjoyed the right to bargain collectively, and consequently the same privilege should be accorded labor.

In reporting the measure, the Senate Finance Committee attached the following amendment:

That nothing in this title shall be construed to compel a change in existing satisfactory relationships between the employees and employers of any particular plant, firm or corporation, except that the employees of any particular plant, firm or corporation shall have the right to organize for the purpose of collective bargaining with the employer as to wages, hours of labor and other conditions of employment.

Senators George Norris and Burton K. Wheeler led the fight against the committee amendment on the floor of the Senate. They believed that it had the effect of nullifying any protection labor would receive under the section, and that it would protect the company union, an organization Wheeler claimed was dominated by fear. The amendment was stricken by a vote of 46 to 31 with 19 not voting.[4]

The law sought to stimulate employment and promote changes which would make unlikely another depression of the size and depth as the one affecting the country. In addition to providing aid for the needy and initiating a federally financed program of public works and work sharing, the law permitted industries to establish codes of fair practice and exempted them from the application of the federal antitrust laws. Representatives of industries or single trades through associations or groups could meet and arrange codes, which if they met specified standards and were approved by the President of the United States or his representative, became the standards for the industry or trade.

Every code of fair competition, agreement, and license approved, prescribed, or issued was required to include a clause recognizing the right of workers to bargain collectively through representatives of their own choosing and to be free of coercion from the employer or his agents in the designation of representatives for purposes of collective bargaining. No employee or one seeking employment was to be compelled to join a company union or to refrain from joining a labor union of his choice.

Employers were to comply with maximum hours of labor, minimum rates of pay, and other conditions of employment approved or prescribed by the President. Employers and employees were also afforded opportunities for establishing maximum hours of labor, minimum rates of pay, and other conditions of employment. "Approved codes were to become standards of fair competition for the entire industry within the meaning of the Federal Trade Commission Act, and enforceable by proceedings in equity in the Federal courts to restrain violations and by the imposition of a fine for any violation."[5] Hugh S. Johnson was appointed as administrator of the NIRA.

The first Cotton Textile Code was approved July 9, 1933. During its existence, the National Industrial Recovery Administrator approved 557 basic codes, and 181 supplementary codes. Labor boards made up of representatives of the industry, labor, and the administrator were appointed under most codes. From many points of view, the labor provisions embodied in Section 7 (a) were of much greater and lasting importance than the other sections of the law. William Green, in a letter to the national and international unions, said that "no legislative act so potential in consequence and far-reaching in scope, dealing directly with Labor and Industry, has heretofore been considered by the Congress of the United States. This measure can properly be regarded as novel in character and revolutionary in its relation to industry, industrial problems and labor." Green told the affiliates they "must be alert, prepared and ready to play [their] part and to take advantage of every opportunity which presents itself, through this legislative proposal, to organize, bargain collectively, increase wages and reduce the hours of employment. We must avail ourselves of the opportunity presented, through the enactment of this legislation, to reduce unemployment and to create work for all who are able and willing to work.

If the workers are to receive the full benefits of this proposed legislation they must organize and be prepared to act collectively and to bargain collectively. Only through organization can the workers make vital and operative the provisions of this legislation."[6]

A conference of international unions was called to discuss common problems by the AFL, and representatives of 106 internationals met in Washington to weigh the opportunities that had arisen as a result of the new legislation. The unions were urged to cooperate in organizing, and the AFL assured them it would assist in any program to recruit new members. After the adjournment of the meeting, Green informed the executive council that an "intensive organizing campaign will begin in Detroit. Organizer William Collins will be in charge of that campaign. . . . I have arranged for him to look over the ground and carry out the plan of organization in Detroit."[7] But the campaign was carried out on a moderate and desultory scale.

Enactment of the NIRA was, however, the beginning of the most extensive organization drive in the history of the American labor movement. Not only did the drive swell the ranks, but its extent and size posed a series of difficult problems. The most difficult one was the right of workers to organize industrial unions in the mass production industries and retain their affiliation with the AFL. While no centrally directed campaign was launched, a series of efforts on a small or large scale were carried out by local unions acting on their own or in cooperation with their international unions and more moderately by the AFL. The drive was not coordinated, and not all international unions were equally active in organizing.

Successful organizing campaigns were reported almost from the beginning of June 1933. According to the AFL, "hundreds of thousands of workers—more than 200,000 in the United Mine Workers of America alone—have been enrolled in the past two months in international unions and local unions directly affiliated with the American Federation of Labor. . . . Waiving the old requirement of organization along strictly craft lines, the Federation is meeting the emergency by enrolling the workers in entire industries in direct affiliation. . . . Ten thousand steel and glass workers in the New Kennsington, Pennsylvania neighborhood; another 10,000 in the Mine, Mill and Smelter Workers' Union; charter applications by rubber workers . . . and steel fabricators . . . gains reported by New England and West Virginia shoe workers, by Ohio boilermakers, leatherworkers, brickmakers and pressed steel fabricators, by the cleaners and dyers of New York, Youngstown, Ohio and San Francisco."[8] Because of the exemption and the ending of the fiscal year of many unions in months before the AFL convention, average membership of the AFL was underestimated. In view of the sharp increases in the months after July 1, 1933, this was obviously substantial; the Federation estimated its membership for October 1933 as 3,926,796.[9] The increase of almost 800,000 members in 1933 came in the months after June, and was greatly, if not entirely, influenced by the protection of the right to organize given in the NIRA.

Labor leaders were convinced that Section 7(a) had opened new opportunities for organizing. In a release to wage and salaried workers, the AFL informed workers: "For the first time in the history of the nation there has been written in a statute passed by the Congress of the United States a section according workers a legal right to organize and to be protected in the exercise of that right."[10] Industry was not, however, prepared to surrender its positions without a struggle. "Employers began to strengthen existing company unions, to revive company unions which had become moribund, and to organize entirely new ones."[11] The evidence shows in the months after the enactment of the NIRA, at least as many company unions were organized as those not controlled by the employer.[12]

The expansion of union organization took place at two levels. For a time the largest gains were made by established unions. The NIRA was the most potent instrument used by John L. Lewis and his organizers to rebuild the United Mine Workers of America, and the union was able to gain the acceptance of collective bargaining by the majority of southern bituminous coal operators, a feat never before achieved.

Opposition to Section 7(a) was manifested by the iron and steel industry, which sought to include a qualification that the plants of the industry were open to all capable workers irrespective of union membership. It also sought approval of employee representation plans and when the statement was withdrawn, an announcement that there would not be any change in labor policy was made. The industry demonstrated its views by refusing to meet with William Green as a labor advisor on the iron and steel code. Even more insistent was the automobile industry for modifying the collective bargaining provisions in the code. Finally, an "individual merit clause" was incorporated. It stated: "Without in any way attempting to qualify or modify, by interpretation the . . . requirements of the NRA, employers in this [automobile] industry may exercise their right to select, retain, or advance employees on the basis of individual merit, without regard to their membership or non-membership in any organization."

Employers in some industries were opposed to recognizing outsiders as representatives of their employees. As friction between labor and management mounted, the Labor and Industry Advisory Boards of the National Recovery Administration suggested the setting up of a national tribunal to settle differences between labor and management. In response to these pleas, President Roosevelt appointed on August 5, 1933, the National Labor Board to "pass promptly on any case of hardship or dispute that may arise from the interpretation or application of the President's Reemployment Program."[13]

The board with Senator Robert Wagner as chairman was made up of six additional members—three from management and three from labor. Its power was limited to conciliation and mediation. Since the suggestions of the board were frequently ignored, the President, by executive order on February 1, 1934, extended the board's power to hold elections to determine the employees' choice of representatives for collective bargaining, and in the event of interference by an employer or the refusal to comply otherwise with Section 7(a) to recommend action to the Attorney-General or the Compliance Division of the Recovery Administration. A clarifying statement was issued by President Roosevelt on October 19, 1933. He instructed:

Because it is evident that the insertion of any interpretation of Section 7(a) in a Code of Fair Competition leads only to further controversy and confusion, no such interpretation should be incorporated in any vote. While there is nothing in the provisions of Section 7(a) to interfere with the bona fide exercise of the right of an employer to select, retain or advance employees on the basis of individual merit, Section 7(a) does clearly prohibit the pretended exercise of this right by an employer simply as a device for compelling employees to refrain from exercising the rights of self-organization, designation of representatives and collective bargaining, which are guaranteed to all employees of said Section 7(a).[14]

Nevertheless, important firms refused to comply with orders of the board. The National Labor Board's lack of power induced Senator Wagner to introduce on March 1, 1934, the "Labor Disputes Act." Vigorously assailed by employer groups, the bill failed to gain approval. Congress instead enacted Public Resolution 44, conferring authority upon the President to appoint boards to investigate complaints and disputes of employees and employers under Section 7(a). It approved of the President's order of February 1, 1934, for the Labor Board to conduct bargaining elections. Under this authority, the President created on June 29, 1934, the National Labor Relations Board of three full-time members. The board was authorized to investigate differences arising out of Section 7(a) of the NIRA and to hold elections to determine representatives for collective bargaining. It could act as arbitrator at the request of the parties. Lloyd Garrison was appointed chairman, and Harry A. Millis and Edwin S. Smith were the other members. Upon the resignation of Garrison, Francis Biddle was appointed in his place.

This board, as much as its predecessor, faced the difficulty of acceptance by employers, especially the rule that the union receiving a majority is representative of all in the bargaining unit. Such a principle had been accepted by the War Labor Board and the Railroad Labor Board. The reasons for the majority rule was set out most cogently *In the Matter of*

Houde Engineering Corporation and UAW Federal Labor Union No. 18839, August 30, 1934, in which the board ruled "that the company's policy of dealing first with one group and then with the other resulted, whether intentionally or not, in defeating the objects of the statute. In the first place, the Company's policy inevitably produced a certain amount of rivalry, suspicion and friction between the leaders of the committees."

The Board concluded "that the only interpretation of Section 7(a) which can give effect to its purposes is that the representatives of the majority should constitute the exclusive agency for collective bargaining with the employer."

In 103 elections in 528 units held by the NLRB between July 10, 1935, and July 9, 1935, trade unions won 57 per cent of the contests and polled 20,682 votes or 59 per cent; company unions were first in 162 units and polled 12,207 or 34 per cent of the vote.[15] The fewer than 21,000 votes polled in the elections would indicate that the organization of workers, while substantial, was limited in extent.

Under Public Resolutions 44, eight special boards were established. Some, like the Automobile Labor Board and the National Steel Labor Board, played a role in the developing labor situations in their industries. The Textile Labor Relations Board was appointed to eliminate differences and dissatisfaction arising out of the textile strike in the fall of 1934. The National Bituminous Coal Board only met twice, and the National Longshoremen's Board was created to adjust the Pacific Coast longshoremen's strike. Most of the other boards set up under the NIRA to deal with labor problems did not play a significant role in labor management relations.

Throughout the existence of the NIRA the federation fought for a liberal interpretation of the labor clauses, truly regarding them as valid guarantees of the right to organize. Sometimes, the AFL feeling was shared by President Roosevelt, and at other times he showed irritation at its criticisms. On December 15, 1934, Roosevelt expressed his annoyance at the refusal of employers to agree to elections for determining collective bargaining representatives. At other times, he was irritated at the protests against some of the administrators of the NIRA.[16] The decision of the U.S. Supreme Court holding the NIRA unconstitutional—*A. L. Schechter Poultry Corp.* v. *United States*—on May 27, 1935, closed this chapter, but the labor movement had laid a firm basis for the expansion of organization in many industries and rebuilt its memberships in many others.

The AFL lamented the setting aside of that law. In a statement to the press, William Green emphasized the gains made under the NIRA in prohibiting child labor, raising minimum wages, and protecting the right to organize. He feared that workers would now be forced to depend upon sheer economic power for protection. "Reports reaching the American Federation of Labor headquarters show that immediately following the decision of the Supreme Court employers of labor began reducing wages, increasing hours and resorting to the old policy of the survival of the fittest as practiced before the inauguration of the New Deal."[17] Green called a meeting of the executive council for June 6 and submitted a statement which, after a long debate, was approved by a vote of 8 to 7. It urged workers "to meet the challenge offered . . . by organizing trade unions affiliated with the American Federation of Labor and fighting for higher wages, shorter hours, social justice, and improved conditions of employment.[18]

CHAPTER 34

Laying the Groundwork
for the Great Expansion

The regaining of control by the United Mine Workers of America over the major bituminous coal producing areas was the most important development in organization in a quarter of a century. For the coal industry it meant the beginning of a period of storm and stress, which was to last for more than a decade and finally lead to the stabilization of the industry under the joint auspices of labor and management. For the United Mine workers, it was the regaining of lost territory and extension into areas that had never been touched by successful union organization. For the labor movement, the revival of the Miners' Union gave John L. Lewis the financial and organizational base from which he could proceed to reorganize the labor movement and to embark upon the greatest campaign of unionization in labor history.

Between 1900 and 1927, the United Mine Workers of America was the largest union in the United States. It had always been a source of strength and stability, but its once far-flung domain had been sharply reduced. One of the major problems facing the union in the bituminous coal industry between 1897 and 1933 was the maintenance of stability in the great Appalachian Region and the Central Competitive field jointly comprising the coal producing areas of Pennsylvania, Ohio, Indiana, Illinois, Kentucky, and West Virginia. Since World War I this area has produced between 85 and 90 per cent of the total coal production in the United States.

Between 1924 and 1927, while the Jacksonville Agreement was in force in the organized districts, the producing areas of West Virginia, Virginia, and Kentucky made their great gains in output. Their nonunion policies enabled them to reduce prices and salvage the reductions by lowering wages. In 1928 the Pennsylvania mines joined the nonunion group.

The other union districts demanded revisions of their wage scales, and many formerly organized fields joined the nonunion group or were granted wage reductions. In this practice the southern operators had a decided advantage, for they could more easily undercut their northern competitors.[1] In the latter part of 1931 and 1932, the carnival of wage cutting reached an unparalleled intensity. In December 1931 the operators in the New River and Winding Gulf districts announced wage cuts effective December 28, 1931.[2] In February the operators in the Pocahontas district improved upon this measure by reducing wages 20 per cent. This was only one phase of the wage cutting cycle which the Pocahontas operators had initiated. Western Kentucky operators had reduced wages 10 per cent in January, and the Pittsburgh Terminal Company had instituted a similar cut on January 31, 1932.[3]

Sections of the Southwest, Illinois, and Indiana were all that was left of the once-proud union empire. In 1933 approximately 15 per cent of the total tonnage was produced under union conditions. Not since 1897 had the fortunes of the United Mine Workers been as low in the bituminous section of the industry.

The deunionization of the major portion of the bituminous coal industry was accomplished after a bitter struggle in Pennsylvania and Ohio. The defeat of the union was symptomatic of the difficulties facing all groups connected with the industry. The overexpansion of the war and postwar years led to a downward pull on prices after 1923 and forced many operators into bankruptcy or voluntary retirement. Since wages constituted between 60 and 65 per cent of costs, it was natural for operators to launch an attack upon them. Despite heroic efforts of the union to maintain the wage structure, it began crumbling under this relentless drive.[4] An attempt to bring about a stabilization of prices and production was made, and a sales agency, Appalachian Coals, was organized. This agency was designed to stabilize prices by limiting production and preventing ruinous competition.[5] The United Mine Workers of America had its own program of stabilization. This plan was presented in the Davis-Kelley bill, which proposed to set up a Bituminous Coal Commission with powers to license corporations engaged in mining coal for interstate commerce. Shippers and producers of coal would be allowed to enter into marketing pools, or joint selling associations if these arrangements were not against public interest. Companies receiving licenses were to exert every reasonable effort to maintain wage and working agreements and to settle disputes arising under them.

Employees were to be allowed to bargain collectively, and employers receiving a government license were to refrain from forcing their workers into a company union, or to resign their membership in a legitimate trade union.[6] This bill, which was a forerunner of the NRA, sought to bring about stabilization by protecting the wage structure.

The complete absence of standards is evident in the conditions in the once-organized District 2 of Pennsylvania. Checkweighmen were gone, miners were receiving a tonnage rate as low as 28 cents a ton, and were expected to produce anywhere from 2,600 to 3,000 pounds for a ton. In the fall of 1932, there was a clear revival of interest in the union in the Central Pennsylvania region, and it gradually increased in the spring of 1933.[7]

Even though the union had lost ground, it maintained a skeleton organization in most fields, and it had within its ranks skilled and resourceful organizers. Early in May 1933 the district leaders and executives were called into conference by President John L. Lewis, and the future strategy was devised. This meeting was attended by organizers from the union and unorganized districts, and they were advised on the tactics to be followed in the event the pending NRA bill was enacted into law.[8]

In June 1933 the labor situation in the industry was completely changed. Instead of wage reductions, several operators' associations were raising wages. In the Kanawah, Logan, and Williamson districts of West Virginia and the Harlan district of Kentucky, wages were increased between 10 and 18 per cent. Alabama operators followed suit, and the ones in central and western Pennsylvania kept in step with the trend. These wage increases were a recognition that the United Mine Workers of America had again become a factor in the industry. In Pennsylvania, operators tried to forestall organization by forming a company union, but desisted when a strike was threatened.[9]

An intensified organization campaign was launched immediately, the first fruit of which was the complete unionization of Western Pennsylvania. Delegates representing 40,000 miners of District 5 met on June 14 and informed the operators that they were ready to enter into collective bargaining relations on a district, competitive district, or national basis.[10] On June 15, Van A. Bittner, a trusted lieutenant of John L. Lewis, was placed in charge of organization work in West Virginia. A convention was immediately called, and miners from every county except McDowell were represented. Thousands of new members were recruited, and hundreds of locals sprang up overnight. Simultaneously, an organization drive was launched in Alabama under the direction of William Mitch.[11]

A tidal wave of union enthusiasm swept over the coal fields. Districts which had been bulwarks of anti-unionism were swept away while many others enlisted 100 per cent under the union banner. Pennsylvania, West

Virginia, Ohio, Maryland, Virginia, Kentucky, Tennessee, Alabama, Missouri, Colorado, Utah, Montana, Washington, Wyoming, New Mexico: all saw feverish organization activity going on. In Mingo, Logan, and McDowell counties, West Virginia, where organizers had formerly met terror and injunctions, they were now welcomed with open arms. Under the impact of the union, company organizations were disappearing, and district organizations were reviving.[12]

On July 23, 1933, 2,579 delegates, representing 160,000 newly organized southern miners, met in Charleston, West Virginia, and pledged their support to the union's demands for shorter hours and increased wages. Two months before that meeting barely a corporal's guard of union men could be found in this region. The delegates reported 728 new locals in four southern states and members in virtually every mining camp. This was undoubtedly the most important union meeting held south of the Ohio River. Van A. Bittner, who represented the international organization, urged the new unionists to cooperate with the employer and avoid wildcat strikes.[13]

Union operators from thirteen states presented a code, but it met the immediate opposition of the Smokeless and Appalachian Coal Association. They insisted that the pro-union operators only represented 25 per cent of the tonnage and that they would not be permitted to make terms for the industry.[14]

Other groups followed suit and demanded adjustments to meet their particular needs. Twenty-seven codes were finally submitted for approval, and almost every district and every interest made some special request. In the eyes of John L. Lewis, the demands of the different groups of operators were an attempt to continue the practices which had brought the industry to the brink of ruin. In Lewis' opinion, the industry was in need of regulation and a national code, and he counselled their adoption.[15]

The attempt to write a code for the industry struck another snag when the nonunion operators demanded that they be allowed to qualify Section 7(a). They wanted the right to limit collective bargaining to their own employees, or their representatives, but they were unwilling to meet other employers for common negotiations. It was evident that the union would not agree to these conditions, and that it had the power to force a strike in the entire bituminous coal industry. Negotiations were making no progress, because the nonunion operators refused to meet the leaders of the United Mine Workers in conference. It required the intervention of the President of the United States to bring the two groups together. Even then the nonunion operators attempted to exact an approval of the open shop as a condition of conferring. Pressure from Administrator Hugh S. Johnson forced them to concede. After the meeting of the full committees, the following sub-committee met: J. D. Morrow, Pittsburgh Coal Company; James

Francis, Island Creek Coal Company; Charles O'Neill, Peale, Peacock and Kerr; Ralph D. Taggert, Stonage Coke and Coal Company, representing the operators; and John L. Lewis, Thomas Kennedy, Phil Murray, Van A. Bittner, and Samuel Pascoe representing the miners.

After weeks of negotiation, the operators and miners on September 16 agreed on a code which was approved by President Roosevelt two days later. Immediately afterward, a conference representing 340,000 soft coal miners began under the direction of General Hugh Johnson. This was the first time that all of the leading operators of the Appalachian field were represented. After fourteen days of discussions, the first Appalachian agreement was signed. It was to run from October 2, 1933, to March 31, 1934, and affected an annual output of 350 million tons, and 340,000 miners employed in Ohio, Pennsylvania, West Virginia, Virginia, Maryland, eastern Kentucky, and northern Tennessee. The agreement marked the reestablishment of the United Mine Workers in its old districts and an extension of its control into the old nonunion strongholds. A joint statement signed by John L. Lewis and J. D. Morrow termed the agreement "the greatest in magnitude and scope" ever negotiated in the United States.[16]

It provided for an eight-hour day and forty-hour week, election of checkweighmen and pit committees, and created machinery for the settlement of disputes. Suspension of work during adjustments of disputes was forbidden, and operators were prohibited from discussing any grievance with workers engaged in an illegal strike. The basic ton was set at 2,000 pounds, and boys under seventeen could not be employed in a mine or in a hazardous occupation around a mine. The checkoff was recognized, and the yardage and dead-work rates were increased 20 per cent.[17]

The difficulties which faced the union in winning recognition in the southern bituminous area were repeated in the captive mines. Late in July miners in Fayette County, the center of the H. C. Frick Coke Company, went on strike after their demands for a checkweighman had been rejected by the company. After a dozen persons had been injured in clashes between strikers and deputies, Governor Pinchot ordered state police to patrol the roads in the strike area. The strike spread rapidly, and the sheriff of Fayette County forbade all picketing. He rejected the governor's plan to place state troops in charge and limit the number of pickets. The governor thereupon declared martial law, and dispatched three hundred troops to Fayette County. The governor, at the same time, charged the Frick Coal Company with "importing gunmen from New York." The troops were greeted upon their arrival in the strike region by enthusiastic crowds which looked upon the soldiers as deliverers from the abuses of the company guards.[18]

The strike originally directed mainly against the Frick Company mines in Fayette County spread to the captive mines owned by other companies in Westmoreland, Washington, Greene, and Allegheny counties. On August 1 the first serious clash between pickets and company guards ended with the wounding of eleven pickets. The deputies claimed that strikers had been on company property, and observers blamed the company guards for the outbreak. Following the clash, the Frick Company decided to close down all of its mines. The strike spread rapidly through Allegheny Valley and involved 60,000 miners. General Hugh Johnson intervened to prevent a spread of the strike to the commercial mines, but the captive mine operators rejected suggestions to confer with the officers of the United Mine Workers. Negotiations between the two groups were finally initiated by placing each in a separate room and carrying the proposals between them. Operators thereby were enabled to negotiate with the union without coming into physical contact with its representatives. The union adopted a conciliatory attitude, only insisting upon the right of the workers to appoint their own checkweighmen; but Thomas Moses, president of the Frick Company, would not agree.

After a breakdown of negotiations, President Roosevelt intervened and forced the operators to accept a truce. The strikers were to be reemployed without prejudice; checkweighmen, paid by the miners, were to be permitted; and a committee of three made up of George L. Berry, Gerard Swope, and Lewis Kirstein would consider all grievances until a code for the industry was adopted. The Frick Coke Company and the National Mining Company accepted those conditions, but the agreement was made with Administrator Johnson and not with the union. Upon the conclusion of the agreement, union leaders immediately ordered the strikers back to work.[19] Edward F. McGrady, labor advisor to General Johnson and an experienced labor leader, was dispatched to the troubled area. He assured the miners that their interests would be protected and urged them to return to work. The men returned to the pits and for a month only the contest over the election of Martin Ryan, the militant strike leader of the valley, disturbed the captive mine area.[20]

The captive miners were dissatisfied with the agreement, and on September 18 a new strike under the leadership of Martin Ryan began. William Feeney, the provisional district president, urged the men to remain in the pits, but his advice was unheeded. Two days after the first walkout, 35,000 miners were out on strike. An attempt of armed deputies to escort 100 strikebreakers through the picket line before the Gates mine, an H. C. Frick Company property, led to a clash in which seventeen pickets and one deputy were wounded. The deputies were held responsible for the clash, and an assistant mine superintendent and seven deputies were arrested and held on bonds of $2,000 on charges of felonious assault, rioting, and pointing firearms.[21]

Demands that the strikers return to their jobs were made by union and government officials. A meeting of delegates from sixty-seven locals met in Pricedale and decided to continue the walkout. At the height of the walkout almost 90,000 workers were involved. State troopers were sent into the strike area of the Allegheny Valley. Thomas Moses of the Frick Company and other owners of captive mines accepted the code, but the men refused to return until a contract had been made. At a meeting, Ryan demanded the signing of an agreement between the union and the operators as a condition of peace.[22]

The leaders of the steel companies were willing to accept the wage rates and working conditions of the coal code, but opposed the checkoff of union dues. Finally, a conditional checkoff was proposed under which operators would pay dues to any organization authorized by the individual worker. The owners reiterated their opposition to the union shop.[23]

A new problem developed when the Miners' Benevolent Association came on the scene as a representative of the miners. Union officers believed that this organization was fostered by the companies and that its purpose was to prevent a settlement. The owners now agreed to accept the union chosen by the workers as their representative in an election held under the direction of the National Labor Board. They also conceded the right of the workers to choose as their representatives officers of the United Mine Workers.[24]

The national organization was willing to accept this proposal, but it met with instant opposition among the thousands of strikers. Representatives of sixty-four locals of the United Mine Workers in the strike area met and appealed to President Roosevelt to meet with a committee of strikers. Led by District President Hynes, a committee of eight, comprising seven rank-and-filers from the pits, called on President Roosevelt. After a twenty-minute conference, they agreed to advise the strikers to return to work. The men were assured that representatives of the National Labor Board would proceed to the captive mine area to supervise an election for union representatives.[25]

In the elections held on November 22 and 23, the union slate was opposed by the Workers' Brotherhood and the Miners' Independent Brotherhood. Both of these organizations were charged with being company unions. The slate of the United Mine Workers carried twenty out of twenty-nine mines, the union losing nine out of fourteen in Fayette County. The officers of the union charged the company with practicing intimidation and fraud.[26] Of the total vote, 10,122 were cast for the United Mine Workers of America, and 4,403 for the company union. The union next proposed that negotiations between the captive mines and the United Mine Workers be opened. When the operators refused, the National Labor Board was called upon to decide the questions at issue.

The captive mine operators insisted that the union officers elected were chosen as individuals representing their workers and not as officers of the United Mine Workers. Moreover, the operators asked that mine committees be selected from the elected representatives. This would mean that the international officers of the United Mine Workers, who had been chosen representatives of the captive mines, would have to serve as committeemen in the adjustment of local disputes. Another question in dispute was the checkoff; the operators contending that the checkoff meant union recognition, which they had not accepted. Nathan Miller, counsel of the U.S. Steel Corporation, defended the position of the Frick Company before the National Labor Board on January 4, 1934.[27]

On January 19 the board ruled that John L. Lewis, Philip Murray, Thomas Kennedy, and three district officials represented the employees of the H. C. Frick Coke Company as their elected representatives. The checkoff was recognized, but allowed "any employee not a member of the United Mine Workers of America the right to make voluntary assignments of his wages for dues or payments to any organization of which he may be a member, or for any other purpose."[28] The agreement, though not recognizing the United Mine Workers, allowed union officers to act in their official capacity. Lewis and his coworkers did not make agreements as individuals but as officers of the union. On February 15, 1934, the H. C. Frick Company signed an agreement with the United Mine Workers of America. Wages and working conditions were the same as those in the Appalachian agreement, and the contract was to expire on the same date.

Another step toward complete unionization of the bituminous coal industry had been made in October 1933. The Colorado Fuel and Iron Company—the Rockefeller Corporation—which had established one of the pioneer company union arrangements, the Rockefeller Plan, after the Ludlow tragedy of the strike of 1912, agreed to disband the plan and recognize the United Mine Workers of America.[29] The union now controlled a greater percentage of production than ever in its history. (It did not control the tonnage produced in the mines controlled by the Progressive Miners of America, a dual organization.) There can be no question that the union's progress was in part due to the favorable conditions created by the National Recovery Administration. But the ability of the leadership to capitalize on opportunities must not be overlooked. If the efficiency of a leadership is to be judged by its ability to take advantage of opportunities, the leaders of the United Mine Workers must be recognized as among the most effective in the history of the American labor movement.[30]

The Miners' Union, which met for its thirty-third convention in Indianapolis, Indiana, on January 23, 1934, was a somewhat different organization which had gone through a decade of strife in the deflationary days of the 1920's.

For the first time in the entire history of the organization, delegates were present from every coal producing field on the American continent. They were there from all of the old-time union districts, and they were there also from Virginia, Utah, New Mexico, Logan county, McDowell county, Mingo county, Winding Gulf, the Pocahontas field and the sections of southern West Virginia that always were non-union up to the past year. They were there from Harlan county and all the other counties of eastern and southeastern Kentucky. . . . For many of these new delegates, it was the first time they ever had had the privilege of attending a convention of the United Mine Workers of America since their escape from economic and industrial bondage through the National Industrial Recovery Law and the gigantic organization drive of the United Mine Workers of America.[31]

The change in the composition of the membership and of the delegates was also shown by the absence from the convention of many of Lewis' former opponents. "Complete harmony prevailed in the convention. The old-time trouble makers were absent. Many of them are no longer members of the United Mine Workers of America, having lost their standing with the loyal members."[32] Lewis had now achieved an unchallenged position in his own union, since the base of the organization had been shifted from the long-organized districts of Illinois, Indiana, Ohio, and central Pennsylvania, to the southern areas of Virginia, West Virginia, Kentucky, and Tennessee. One of the centers of opposition to Lewis in the 1920's, the Illinois District 12, was not only bankrupt but the influx of thousands of miners from the nonunion areas reduced its political influence. The job, however, was only partially achieved. Hundreds of thousands of nonunion miners had been mustered into the United Mine Workers of America, but the work of consolidating the union's power, of organizing the remaining nonunion strongholds of Kentucky's Harlan and Bell counties, and of eliminating the southern wage differential remained to be done.

These tasks were later accomplished, but the victory of the United Mine Workers in its own jurisdiction and the establishment of a more powerful and viable union than ever in history were of greater significance than the winning of concessions for several hundred thousand miners. Lewis was now absolute master of his own house. His opponents were no longer a political factor in the organization. Lewis was free to use the organizational and financial resources of the United Mine Workers of America for unionization of other industries. He was released from the pinpricks and challenges of other leaders. No one would question his program nor cavil at his use of members' funds. With the checkoff and the miners behind him, he was free to use his great talents without danger of criticism. It can truly be said that the revival of the United Mine Workers of America was the greatest labor event in the short history of the National Recovery Administration, an event which was to make possible the forthcoming labor revolution in the late 1930's.

THE CLOTHING INDUSTRIES

The unions in the clothing industries also took advantage of the opportunities opened by the NIRA. While they faced determined opposition in many of their markets, the nonunion manufacturers were not as well organized nor did they possess the resources of those in the mass production or coal industries. It speaks highly for the leadership of both the International Ladies' Garment Workers' Union and the Amalgamated Clothing Workers of America that they were prepared to take advantage of the new opportunities.

Similarly, the International Ladies' Garment Workers' Union, which had suffered severely from internecine warfare and the assault of the Communists in the New York market, was able to regain its position in 1933 with an assist from the NIRA. More than 12,000 members joined the International Ladies' Garment Workers' Union in the summer of 1933 as a result of an agreement with the Cloak, Suit and Skirt Manufacturers' Protective Association in the New York market. But the union also expanded in other parts of the industry and into other markets. Not only did it bring thousands of dressmakers into the union, but the Philadelphia, St. Louis, and other markets established effective unions.

The Amalgamated Clothing Workers of America also increased its membership and expanded its jurisdiction into the shirt industry. Separated from the general labor movement by the refusal of the AFL to recognize a secessionist organization, it was able to join the AFL as a result of the pressure of John L. Lewis and George L. Berry of the Printing Pressmen's Union, after it agreed to purchase union labels from the United Garment Workers of America, recognized as the legitimate union in the industry by the AFL. Many other unions made less spectacular gains. The unions in the metal trades, shipbuilding, railroads, the service, and maritime trades began expanding. What is more, the labor movement regained its confidence, and a more militant note appears. The revival and expansion of unionism in the clothing industries were also of major importance in the shaping of labor developments of the future. These unions, under the leadership of Sidney Hillman and David Dubinsky, were more hospitable to innovation and changes within the labor movement. Over the years, they favored more aggressive organizing attempts and were sympathetic to structural changes within the labor movement. The Amalgamated Clothing Workers of America, as a recent affiliate of the AFL, did not have much influence within the federation, but its financial support and the aid it could provide through its organizers and leaders were to become of considerable importance in the oncoming organizational drives. The International Ladies' Garment Workers' Union was not as well situated, having suffered severely from communist factionalism which almost wrecked the organization, but it more than recouped its losses in the first year of the

NIRA. It was also able to give financial and organizational aid to the new organization drives. Moreover, David Dubinsky, a member of the executive council, could exercise a voice if not much influence on many questions which would soon press for solution.

But even more significant were the changes taking place in the heretofore unorganized sectors of the economy. Despite limited effort and inadequate support, the unions were progressing in the newer sections of the economy. In the rubber, automobile, steel, aluminum, glass, chemicals, metal mining, and other industries, dozens of local unions were functioning where few or none had existed before the NIRA.

CHAPTER 35

Strikes and Expansion in 1934

Organized labor continued to gain membership during 1934. In August enrollment was 697,983 greater than the same month of the preceding year. What is more, the federation reported the extension of its organization into new fields. Unions were established with and without the assistance of the AFL in the mass-production, service, textile, aluminum, and many other industries. The drives for membership did not go unimpeded. Company unions continued to prosper, and many employers refused either to deal with organized labor or granted the newly formed unions only grudging recognition. The refusal of employers to grant full recognition to newly organized unions led, in a number of instances during the year, to eruptions of violence and its bloody repression by the police and National Guard.

THE PACIFIC COAST LONGSHOREMEN'S AND SAN FRANCISCO GENERAL STRIKE

The strike of the Pacific Coast longshoremen was the most important labor walkout in 1934. As compared to the national textile strike, it did not affect large numbers of workers, but the shipping industry was vital to the economic and social life of the entire Pacific Coast. The strike, moreover, caused a general walkout in San Francisco, and the threat of one in Portland. In addition, the strikers gained a victory over some of the more militant anti-union employers, a victory which also provided an opportunity for Communist infiltration of the waterfront.

Unions of longshoremen were established on the Pacific Coast in the

1880's and 1890's. The position of these organizations was greatly influenced by events in the major ports. In 1899 the City Front Federation was organized in San Francisco, and included seamen, longshoremen, and teamsters in its membership. In 1901 it was successful in warding off an attack upon the organizations and compelling a compromise. It lasted, according to Andrew Furuseth, until 1906. A similar organization was set up in 1914, but did not survive.[1]

In June 1904 the locals of the International Longshoremen's Association, which had added temporarily "Marine and Transportation workers" to its name, held a convention in Everett, Washington, and established the Pacific Coast District. "The greater part of the time of the Convention [of 1905] was taken up in discussing the controversy now existing between our Association and the Sailors' Union of the Pacific."[2] The jurisdictional dispute between the two unions was settled in 1907 by Gompers, who had been chosen arbitrator. He held that the longshoremen would have to cease recruiting sailors into their organization.

Stevedoring employers on the Pacific Coast were an aggressive group, and they resisted organization by their employees. After a coastwise strike in 1916, the locals of the International Longshoremen's Union were seriously weakened. Hiring halls under employer sponsorship were established in a number of ports on that coast, but were discontinued at the orders of the United States Shipping Board during World War I. After the war, the Seattle stevedores introduced their first hiring hall, set up under the direction of Frank P. Foisie. Under this plan company gangs were continued, and the number of men hiring from the hall were reduced. Hours of work were regulated so as to equalize earnings among the regular men and those on call. The system worked well, and it was regarded as equitable. Nevertheless, a revival of organization took place in Seattle as well as in other Pacific Coast ports soon after the enactment of the National Industrial Recovery Act.[3]

The Longshoremen's Association of the Bay Area became the bargaining agent instead of the formerly recognized local of the International Longshoremen's Association. This independent organization, which had been formed during the 1919 strike, signed a five-year contract with the Waterfront Employers' Union. Known as the "blue book" union, it periodically renewed its agreement—the last time in 1933—and carried on without incident. The status of the "blue book" union was unclear, and for a time it was a member of the San Francisco Labor Council. A protest from the International Longshoremen's Association led to its ousting. A change in the situation took place immediately after the enactment of the National Recovery Act. Organizers of the International Longshoremen's Union were sent to the Pacific Coast, and they succeeded in reviving their organizations in all of the ports. San Francisco Local 38-79 was established with Lee J.

Holman as president; William J. Lewis became president of the Pacific Coast District. In September 1933 the local officials of the NIRA agreed that the "blue book" union was discriminating against members of the Longshoremen's Association in the allotment of jobs, but nothing else happened.

In the meantime, a revival of union organization was taking place among the seagoing workers on the Pacific Coast. On August 31, 1933, the Pacific Coast District International Seamens' Union, the union which represented seamen, deck crews, firemen, and others, as well as the employees of the stewards' department, sought to bargain for the unlicensed personnel, but the shipowners refused. In February 1934 the convention of the Pacific Coast Longshoremen's Association, representing the longshoremen, voted to take a strike vote in all its ports. When the vote was approved, the association prepared to call a walkout for February 25, 1934; this was halted, however, when President Roosevelt appointed a mediation board. The board was headed by Dr. Henry F. Grady, chairman; Judge Charles Reynolds and Dr. J. L. Leonard were the other members. Although a temporary agreement was reached and a strike was averted, the basic issues (wages and control of the hiring hall) were unresolved.[4] On May 9, the longshoremen left their jobs all along the Pacific Coast. Recruiting of strikebreakers began immediately, and the *San Francisco News* described the dispersal of two hundred longshoremen by the police "where shipowners were recruiting additional non-union workers to replace those on strike."[5] At first the teamsters agreed to haul merchandise to and from the piers, but later at a special meeting overruled the decision and decided instead not to haul. This was an important action—obviously taken against the desire of the leaders, who favored more modest assistance. On May 16 the seagoing licensed and unlicensed personnel joined the strike; later, a joint strike committee, on which all the unions involved were represented, was set up.

The seamen demanded recognition of the Pacific Coast District of the International Seamen's Union as their bargaining agent and submission to arbitration of all issues upon which no agreement could be reached. The ship operators were willing to bargain, but only on a company-by-company basis.[6] The Joint Strike Committee decided on June 19 that none of the organizations would return to work until settlements were reached with all the unions.

The strike was the first which involved the entire Pacific Coast and the shoreside, as well as the seagoing maritime unions. The crux of the dispute was control of hiring. Strike leaders claimed that employers maintained work on a casual basis, and that nearly twice as many men were on the lists as were needed. In addition, they charged foremen exercised arbitrary power. The union succeeded in closing down all the ports except Los Angeles. About 13,000 workers were involved. But the number affected is not a true index of the importance of the struggle that took place.

Soon after the beginning of the strike, shipowners in the port of Seattle described the police protection as inadequate. Mayor John F. Dore appealed to Governor Clarence D. Martin for troops. In San Pedro, California, a mob stormed a stockade sheltering strikebreakers, and in the riot which followed a striker was killed.[7]

Efforts to work out an agreement by Assistant Secretary of Labor Edward F. McGrady and President John P. Ryan of the International Longshoremen's Association failed. In mid-May, signs that some members of the business community of San Francisco were becoming restive and demanding a more aggressive policy began to appear. It was believed by some in the business community that the Waterfront Employers' Union was not showing sufficient militancy, and the Industrial Association, which had been organized in 1921 came into the picture and played a major role until the conclusion of the strike.[8] On June 1 and 5 the Industrial Association held meetings with leading businessmen during which plans for breaking the strike were laid out. The meeting on June 5 decided "to place full responsibility for the conduct of the waterfront strike in the hands of the Industrial Association in cooperation with the shipowners. This decision was not made public at this time as the plans which were later developed had not matured and the procedure for announcing those plans had not been decided upon."[9]

In the meantime, demands for opening the port increased among businessmen. An agreement had been reached by May 28, but the terms were not acceptable to longshoremen. Negotiated by Ryan and a committee from the Pacific Coast ports, the agreement failed to provide for the kind of union security the longshoremen demanded. Before the vote, the agreement was attacked by Harry Bridges, chairman of the strike committee in the Port of San Francisco.[10]

Under the Ryan agreement the hiring hall would be jointly managed, no discrimination against union members would be practiced, port committees for adjusting differences would be established, and wages would be negotiated after work had been resumed. The agreement was rejected in San Francisco, San Diego, Portland, and Tacoma. It was approved by longshoremen in Los Angeles, and those in Seattle did not vote.[11] One of the causes for the rejection was the failure to provide for the return of the seafaring trades.

An important turning point in the strike was the decision of the teamsters of San Francisco, against the desire of their older leaders, not to handle freight from cars loaded by nonunion stevedores. Paul Eliel, who was on the staff of the Industrial Association, was convinced that ships, after landing here, could be properly serviced. He claimed "that within two days after the time that the strike was called enough men had presented themselves for work at the current rates of wages to handle all of the cargo offered. . . . The action of the Teamsters' Union in May and the definite boycotting of the waterfront and final refusal by that organization in June to handle waterfront freight were the critical factors in the entire San Francisco strike situation."[12]

After the refusal of the longshoremen to accept the agreement of June 17, a trucking company was organized and, at a meeting on the following day, pledges of financial support were obtained. Reports of meetings of various groups of businessmen and government officials which discussed plans for opening of the port appeared in the press daily. In the meantime, in response to appeals from the business community, President Roosevelt appointed the National Longshoremen's Board to settle the dispute. Archbishop Edward J. Hanna headed the board and McGrady and A. K. Cushing served with him. At the same time, the Industrial Association notified the police it planned to begin trucking operations on July 2. The first offer by the Longshoremen's Board was rejected by the strikers, and plans for beginning trucking operations went on, although a postponement of three days was made. The employers were now ready to arbitrate all issues but, as the *Labor Clarion* observed, the "offer of the employers to arbitrate appears to have come too late. Had it been placed before a board a week ago, it is likely that it would have averted the impending enlargement of the strike."[13]

On July 3 trucking operations began. Five trucks loaded with merchandise were dispatched to the warehouse of the Atlas Trucking Company organized by the Industrial Association to combat the strike. On the next day, pickets attacked a train of cars on the Belt Line Railway, a state-owned operation, which was moving cars from the docks of the Matson Navigation Company to one of its ships. Learning of this, Governor Frank Merriam asked that trains be allowed to pass without interference—a demand refused by the strikers. Thereupon, the governor called out the National Guard.[14]

On July 5 the worst riot of the strike took place when masses of pickets fighting to prevent the movement of trucks from Pier 38 were attacked by the police. Two were killed and many injured. The *Labor Clarion* charged: "The Industrial Association deliberately precipitated the crisis by an insincere gesture to remove goods from docks to a warehouse a few blocks away, knowing in advance that the move would be countered by strikers and sympathizers and that bloodshed was inevitable. It savored of premeditation and deliberate and planned provocation of strife."[15]

The sending of troops into San Francisco—for the first time in thirty-five years—to quell a labor dispute and the provocative action of the Industrial Association missed their mark. Instead of terrorizing the strikers, these actions won them the almost united support of the city's labor movement. A resolution, framed by Edward Vandeleur, president, and John A.

O'Connell, secretary of the San Francisco Labor Council, denounced the Governor for sending troops and charged that the Governor's action had been responsible for bloodshed and rioting, and called for a resumption of negotiations "with a view of working out justice to all concerned."[16]

On the day following the riot, July 6, John A. O'Connell informed President William Green that the council had been "compelled to act on its own initiative, in order to prevent the breaking out of a disordered and disorganized general strike. If that eventually should be forced on us, it should be done on a unified and intelligent basis, instead of a haphazard and totally uncontrolled direction."[17] Green, too, denounced sending of troops, but told O'Connell also that the laws of the AFL forbade central bodies from calling general strikes. Such power, O'Connell was reminded, rested with the international and national unions.[18] Evidently, the leaders of the council were convinced that a general strike could not be avoided. They, therefore, sought to retain control of the movement even though their sponsorship violated the constitution and practices of the AFL.

Despite President Green's admonition, the labor organizations of San Francisco were preparing to call a general strike unless the waterfront employers gave up their positions. On July 11, 1934, the waterfront employers, in response to the pleas of the National Longshoremen's Board, announced that forty-two steamship companies had agreed to meet with representatives of their seafaring employees for the purpose of collective bargaining; such representatives were to be chosen in an election under the direction of the board.[19]

The most important step was the adoption by the council of a resolution of C. W. Deal of the Ferryboatmen's Union for the appointment of a Strike Strategy Committee of Seven "for the purpose of investigating in any manner deemed proper and expedient the status and general situation of the strike and further directed to consult and advise the responsible officers of the striking unions in order that such steps as it may deem proper and necessary to effectuate a joint program for the guidance and advice of the labor movement of San Francisco be formulated."[20]

Although the resolution was debated for some time, it passed by an overwhelming majority. Vandeleur, D. P. Haggerty, M. S. Maxwell, Frank Brown, J. A. O'Connell, George Kidwell, and Charles A. Deery were appointed, and they selected Vandeleur as chairman. In a statement he assured the community that the San Francisco labor movement wanted "to give the shipowners and the National Longshoremen's Board every chance to settle this crisis peacefully and we want to act peacefully and not violently. But we do not intend to yield one inch of the ground to which these men are justly entitled, and if their rights are overlooked we are ready to unleash the full strength of organized labor in San Francisco."[21] A reversal of the trend toward a general strike was now, of course, almost impossible, even if the leaders wanted to avoid such a step.

The stalemate could not be broken. The steamship companies were ready, in the first week of July, to meet with the representatives of the sea-faring employees; the unions requested, in the event direct negotiations failed, that the companies agree to submit the dispute to arbitration. The International Longshoremen's Association informed the National Longshoremen's Board that it would not submit the stevedores' offer to a referendum vote of its members until (1) agreement was reached on the management and administration of the hiring halls, and (2) the maritime unions and the shipowners had reached a satisfactory agreement. The strike strategy committee called a meeting to report on developments for July 13.[22]

Before the meeting Edward Vandeleur stated that "the general strike can still be avoided if the Waterfront Employees' Union will grant the Longshoremen's Union the right to conduct its own union headquarters in the same manner in which every other Union is conducting it, and if the shipowners will agree to submit to the President's Board all grievances in dispute for arbitration. If they refuse this [,] responsibility for a general strike will rest on their shoulders."[23] Each local union affiliated with the San Francisco Labor Council and the San Francisco Building Trades Council was asked to send five delegates to the special meeting.

As soon as the meeting convened, discussion began on the objectives which the strike should seek to attain. Harry Bridges, head of the San Francisco Longshoremen's strike committee, wanted no limit placed on the general walkout. C. W. Deal attacked Bridges' position, and was joined in his criticism by Hugo Ernst, of Waiters Union No. 30, who described Bridges as "an unknown doctor trying to treat a disease now running its course."[24]

Bridges, an Australian, had worked on the San Francisco docks during the 1920's and early 1930's. He did not belong to a union and joined in 1933. Bridges showed himself from the beginning to be forceful, courageous, and adroit. He favored more aggressive policies and was in the forefront of the movement for a general strike. He regarded the strike as a pause, as he was determined to give the union an impregnable position on the San Francisco and other Pacific Coast docks. He closely cooperated with left-wing groups, but his political views had not interfered with his trade union activities. He took over the hiring hall arrangement which the employers had introduced in the 1920's, and converted it into an instrument of union power. He ousted the more conservative officers, and became head of the Pacific Coast district of the International Longshoremen's Association, from which port he unsuccessfully tried to capture control of all American shipping. He took the locals out of the AFL and brought them into the CIO. He became the California district director of the CIO, but did not achieve spectacular successes in this office. Before, during, and after his stay in the CIO, Bridges followed the line of the Communist party, but he never neglected his trade union work; his members have the best conditions of any longshoremen in the world. The separation of his union from the general labor movement and the suspicion of his political views has limited the influence of one of the more able unionists of the last three decades.

At 2 A.M. on Sunday, July 15, the Market Street Railway workers left their jobs; they announced that their move was not an incident in the general strike, but was an attempt to settle numerous grievances of their own. Mayor Angelo Rossi of San Francisco declared an emergency and pleaded for the maintenance of peace and order. The General Strike Committee appointed a Permit Committee so that food trucks would be allowed to operate and food stores to continue in business. Governor Merriam, in turn, dispatched additional troops to the Bay Area. The strike continued with the National Longshoremen's Board trying to settle the issues so that a return to work would begin, or the parties could submit their differences to arbitration. Each day of the general strike some relaxation, in the form of allowing some operation to begin, was made. On July 19 the General Strike Committee voted by 191 to 174 to terminate the general walkout and asked all workers except those having specific grievances of their own, which included the longshoremen, the maritime unions, and the Market Street Railway workers, to return to their jobs. A minor incident was the address of NIRA Administrator Hugh S. Johnson, who in Berkeley denounced the general strike as a civil war, and urged labor to end the walkout and drive subversives from its ranks. The speech attracted attention, but did not affect events.[25] The closeness of the vote which was preceded by an angry debate reveals the confusion of mind and lack of unanimity within the committee.

In a statement, the General Strike Committee denied that the strike had been led by Communists; they insisted that at no time had the movement been out of control.[26]

Violence was not absent in several other Pacific Coast ports. In Seattle a policeman and a picket were killed on July 7. Four days later four pickets were wounded during an attack upon strikebreakers. On July 19, Governor Eugene L. Meier of Oregon threatened to use troops unless the strikers ceased interfering with trucks. Talk of a general strike began circulating in Portland labor circles.[27] At the same time, two hundred Seattle policemen, led by Mayor Charles L. Smith, were fighting a large force of strikers. The chief of police, opposing the mayor's drastic remedies, resigned. Only the port of Los Angeles functioned close to normal. Finally, the longshore employers agreed to arbitrate, and the proposal was approved by longshoremen voting in seventeen Pacific Coast ports, by a vote of 6,378 to 1,471.[28]

However, work could not be resumed until a settlement was reached with the seafaring unions. On July 30 the agreement between forty-two companies in the Shipowners Association of the Pacific and the International Seamen's Union was ratified by a vote of 4,305 to 509. The companies agreed to discharge any man who was employed after the strike was called on May 16 who prior to that date was not a regular employee or did not follow the sea as a regular occupation. These vacancies would not be available to those employed during the strike. No discrimination with regard to union membership was to be allowed, and the National Longshoremen's Board, which had aided in negotiating the agreement, was to be allowed to have an observer present in the hiring hall to prevent discrimination. The two unions of licensed officers also voted to return by the end of July. Strikers returned to their jobs on July 31.[29]

On October 12, 1934, the National Longshore Board handed down its decision: a thirty-hour and six-day work week, a standard wage rate of ninety-five cents an hour, and joint operation of hiring halls with nonmembers of the union using hiring hall paying a pro rata fee.[30] No agreement was reached on the wages and working conditions of seamen, and the issues were submitted to arbitration. On February 2, 1935, the board set up scales for workers in the three departments of the ship, recommended changes in other conditions, and set up a labor relations committee of six, three from the shipowners and three from the union side. The committee was to settle grievances arising under the contract. Members of the three Pacific Coast seafaring unions were given preference in employment. "All employment shall be direct from the offices of the union or from the docks."[31]

The unusual cooperation between the searfaring and shoreside unions was successful. In an effort to continue the unity between the several unions, the Maritime Federation of the Pacific was launched in April 1935. Harry Lundeberg was elected president. Differences among the affiliates arose almost immediately. Lundeberg, who was by temperament and outlook a syndicalist, did not wish to be a puppet of the left-wing political groups then seeking a foothold in the maritime industry. The historic differences between sailors and longshoremen over certain jobs also became an issue. By June 1938, Lundeberg took the Sailors' Union of the Pacific which he headed beginning in February 1936, out of the federation. Deprived of the support of the sailors, it ceased to exist. Lundeberg, a sailor of Norwegian origin, came from a family of union members and he was affiliated with the International Seamen's Union throughout the 1920's. He and a few coworkers were largely responsible for halting the Communist expansion on the Pacific Coast waterfront. His syndicalist views had put him on guard against Communist machinations to seize control of waterfront unions. Stubborn, shrewd, with a "strictly proletarian outlook," Lundeberg shared his members' fear and suspicion of the longshoremen, who were always trying to encroach on the work of the sailor. He cared little for the views of people outside his union, and the interests and welfare of his own members was his all-consuming concern. Greatly concerned with the union hiring hall, he was able to convince Senator Robert Taft of its necessity. He had an exaggerated notion of the power of "job action," which he picked up from members of the IWW on the waterfront. In his own union he held the unchallenged trust of his members. He was confident that he headed a great organization, which was increased when he, with the help of the AFL, launched the Seafarers International Union to challenge the CIO National Maritime Union on the east coast. As a means of showing his union's importance, he supported the purchase of an expensive building which, in view of the shrinking membership, turned out to be a white elephant. Lundeberg was an able but limited leader. Yet the general labor movement as well as the country owes a great debt to Lundeberg for his understanding of Communist purposes at a crucial period and for preventing them from controlling the seagoing vessels on the Pacific Coast.

The 1934 settlement was only a first step. Neither side was satisfied with the agreement. A period of strife followed before both the shoreside and seafaring organizations settled down. The Pacific Coast maritime strike was significant in showing the deep feeling of grievance held by thousands of workers as a result of their experience in the depression. Employers did not seem to be aware of the situation and appeared to yield at every point only after the propitious time for accepting such concessions by the strikers had already passed. The final act of folly, of course, was the attempt to open the port of San Francisco, although it was successfully achieved in Portland at about the same time. Running armed trucks through the picket line angered the entire San Francisco labor movement, and the killing of pickets undermined the last resistance to the general strike—which some had wanted and many had feared. The threat of a general strike against the calling of troops, however, did not materialize in Portland. Had concessions been made earlier, it is probable that moderate opinion among the strikers and especially among the teamsters, who were the strategic group in the situation, might have prevented the final act of the general strike.

The victory of the strikers immediately produced powerful and resourceful oppositions to the leaders of the unions to which the strikers were affiliated. It also encouraged more militant groups on the Atlantic and Gulf coasts to press for greater concessions than employers were willing to offer. Among the several violent and bloody strikes of that year, it may have had the most enduring and drastic effect upon employer-labor relations in a major industry and upon the labor movement in several sections of the country.

THE MINNEAPOLIS TRUCKERS STRIKE

On the Pacific Coast the radical leadership was able to entrench itself because of the existence of a vacuum, and has retained, because of its ability to represent the needs of the longshoremen, the loyalty of these workers. In Minneapolis, members of the Socialist Workers party, a group devoted to the brand of communism propagated by Leon Trotsky, gained a position of leadership in the Minneapolis truckers strike.

Local 574, the local union of truck drivers, was not making much progress, but in February 1934 a strike of coal drivers resulted in a compromise settlement. The union expanded its jurisdiction, and under the leadership of its president, William Brown, it began expanding its organizing to general cartage companies. Demands for changes in wages and working conditions were made, and their rejection led to a strike of about 5,000 truck drivers, helpers, and platform and inside men on May 15.

Rioting began almost immediately, and Governor Floyd Olson announced he would use the militia to suppress disorder. On May 21 a fight between several hundred special policemen and pickets in the "commission" area led to the injury of a score of strikers. The National Labor Board intervened and sought to end the strike, but it was not successful. On May 22 the most serious disorder of the strike began when a large mob of pickets attacked a force of special policemen in the "Battle of Deputies' Run." A. C. Lyman, vice-president of the American Ball Company and a special policeman himself, was felled by a club and died of a fractured skull. Several others were seriously injured. The specials retreated and were rescued by the regular police. A truce was called, and with pressure from the governor's office, an agreement to end the strike and negotiate a contract was reached on May 25.[32]

The agreement was overwhelmingly endorsed by the strikers, but the committee dealing for the employers had to receive the approval of the 160 firms it represented.

Negotiations were carried on for six weeks, but no agreement could be reached. The stumbling block was the refusal of the companies to recognize the union as the representative of inside workers. Finally, after its right to represent inside workers had been firmly rejected, Local 574 decided to strike again on July 16. On the second day of the renewed walkout, no trucks were moving. Clashes between strikers, guards, and company sympathizers took place, and on July 20, Henry Ness, a striker, was killed while doing picket duty in the wholesale grocery area.[33] The contest had reached a stalemate with neither side willing to make concessions. On July 23, Father Francis J. Haas and E. H. Dunnigan, federal conciliators, sought to bring about a settlement. Local 574 was willing to end the strike on condition that wages were raised and the order of the Regional Labor Board (of the NIRA) was carried out. This would have meant the full recognition of the union's right to represent inside workers.[34]

When no agreement was reached, Governor Olson called out the National Guard to keep order. The Central Labor Union protested, and Local 574 charged in a resolution that the presence of troops and the issuance of permits to truckers were imperiling the strike. The governor ignored the protests, because he sought to prevent violence and avoid favoring either party. Rigidly controlling the movement of commercial trucks, he prevented their movement through the streets except when engaged in interstate commerce or carrying breadstuffs, milk, rice, fuel, and grease. Local 574 appealed to the Central Labor Union to call a general strike as a protest, but that was not seriously considered. Olson was a member of the Farmer-Labor party to which most unions were affiliated, and nothing was done by the general labor movement to exacerbate the situation. When strike headquarters were raided, and the leaders, Miles and V. R. Dunne and others, were arrested, they were ordered released.

A second striker was killed, on August 2, by gunfire. In the end, the proposals of Father Haas and E. H. Dunnigan were accepted as the basis for an agreement. Strikers were to be rehired without prejudice, and employers, who reinstated all their employees within three days, were to submit a preferential hiring list to the Regional Labor Board. Such employers were to hire all workers from these preferential hiring lists. In the twenty-two firms known as market firms, the contract was to cover office workers and salesmen as well as drivers, helpers, and platform men. Office workers and salesmen, however, were to be excluded from the contract in 144 other firms. In addition, the companies agreed that a majority vote would decide representation for the entire unit, and that representation elections would be held within ten days, disputes would be arbitrated, and fifty cents an hour for drivers and forty cents for helpers, platform and inside men would be paid.[35]

The establishment of an active teamster organization was important for the subsequent expansion of the organization. It was from this center that the movement to expand the organization to over-the-road trucking in the Midwest was initiated, a movement which eventually led to the unionization of thousands of drivers and the establishment of collective bargaining in the central states area. Farrell Dobbs, a member of the Trotskyist faction and the dispatcher of pickets in the Minneapolis strike, was on the payroll of the Teamsters' Union as an organizer. He was eventually ousted and indicted with fifteen other leaders of the Socialist Workers party for violating the Smith Act. By that time, however, the Minneapolis local had played its major role, and the charges of President Daniel Tobin of the Teamsters' Union were obviously made when Local 574 was ready to switch to the Congress of Industrial Organizations, after its leaders were threatened with expulsion for espousing an antiwar policy.[36]

THE NATIONAL STRIKE IN THE COTTON
TEXTILE INDUSTRY

The approximately 1,200 firms in the cotton textile industry employed between 450,000 and 500,000 workers in 1933. About one-third of the employees were in northern mills and the others in the southern mills. Labor standards were below the average prevailing in the industry, and hours of work were long. The first code of fair competition was approved for the cotton textile industry on July 9, 1933. It provided for a maximum workweek of forty hours, abolition of child labor, continuance of wage differentials prevailing before the issuance of a code, and the payment of wages for forty hours at least equal to the amount which would be received for work at forty-eight hours before the code. Wages were raised from an average of eight to ten dollars a week to twelve and thirteen. Carrying out of these provisions led to some difficulties after May 1934. Increasing work loads, inadequate enforcement of the collective bargaining provisions embodied in Section 7(a) of the National Industrial Recovery Act, and the reduced workweek were all sources of dissatisfaction among the textile workers.

The approval of a curtailed workweek by the National Industrial Recovery Administration in May 1934 led to a threat by the United Textile Workers of America to call a general strike. Intervention by the government brought a cancellation of the strike order, after a conference attended by a representative of the Cotton Textile Institute in a personal capacity. This representative would not concede that the union could speak for the workers in the industry. The union was assured that representatives of employees in the industry would be appointed to several of the NIRA boards dealing with the industry, and that the Research and Planning Division of the NIRA would investigate the level of wages and worker productivity.[37] It subsequently found "no factual or statistical basis for any general increase in Cotton Textile wage rates."[38]

At the convention of the United Textile Workers in August 1934 a strong and widespread feeling of dissatisfaction existed. Although the union had increased its membership appreciably during the NIRA period, its numbers were not large and it did not possess many resources. A set of demands were made, including the establishment of a thirty-hour and five-day workweek, maximum workloads, recognition of the United Textile Workers as the bargaining agent in the industry, and signing of an agreement by various divisions of the textile industry with the international office of the union on issues affecting labor relations, and finally the setting up of an arbitration board to settle differences. The calling of a strike was authorized if the demands were not met, and a strike committee headed by Vice-President Francis J. Gorman was elected.

When the demands were announced, employers in the industry questioned the right of the United Textile Workers to speak for their employees.[39] When organizers were sent to the textile areas, Robert W. Bruere, chairman of the Cotton Textile Industrial Relations Board, sought to arrange discussions between the parties. Gorman rejected the suggestion and claimed that "experience in the operation of the board thus far gives us no confidence in its ability to adjust the issues now at stake in fairness to labor."[40] The strike began on August 31 in the cotton textile plants. According to George A. Sloan, chairman of the Cotton Textile Code Authority, only 31,000 out of 145,000 workers in the southern section of the industry had joined the walkout. At the beginning few mills in New England were affected.

In an attempt to settle the strike President Roosevelt on September 6 appointed a Textile Board of Inquiry headed by former Governor John Winant of New Hampshire. This, however, did not prevent serious violence caused in part by the flying squadrons who roamed the textile areas of the South in an effort to shut down plants. A gun battle in Trion, Georgia, resulted in the death of two strikers and injury to about fifteen others. Six were killed in a battle in Greenville, South Carolina, and another died as a result of gunshot wounds in Augusta, Georgia. In several southern states the militia was ordered to the strike zones, and the mills reopened behind the armed guards. At the end of the first week Gorman asked for the closing down of the textile mills and the arbitration of differences, a suggestion not taken seriously by the industry.

Violence on the picket line brought the National Guard to Danielson, Connecticut. Governor Theodore Francis Green sent the militia into the textile regions of Rhode Island. In Saylesville, Rhode Island, two were killed and four wounded on September 10 in a clash between pickets and National Guardsmen. The strike dragged on, but the textile employers showed no inclination to make any concessions. The Board of Inquiry reported on September 17 and recommended a more extensive investigation of conditions in the industry. It questioned the possibility of a national agreement vainly sought by the union. Strikers were facing not only the stern opposition of the police authorities, aided in many instances by militiamen, but their meager savings and credit were running low. Appeals brought some aid, but not in sufficient amounts to provide for minimum needs. On September 20, President Roosevelt called for the ending of the strike, and two days later the strike was called off. Gorman claimed that there were 10,000 troops protecting textile mills in Alabama, Georgia, and the Carolinas. The northern states of Connecticut and Rhode Island also used troops. It was a violent and bloody strike in which thirteen were killed and many others injured.

As far as one can judge, the walkout was one of the least excusable in history. The union claimed it was a victory, but its only effect was the appointment by President Roosevelt of the Textile Labor Relations Board with Chief Justice Walter P. Stacy of North Carolina as chairman. The board was authorized to investigate conditions in the industry and to recommend changes; it had no influence on future developments. The strike was called without adequate preparations and without a vote of the hundreds of thousands of workers who were called to join in the walkout. The United Textile Workers of America was a small union with almost no reserve funds. Yet its leaders blithely called out thousands, even though they knew that the union could provide little assistance. Strangely enough, the union, perhaps as a face-saving gesture, announced that the strike had won many concessions and virtual recognition for the United Textile Workers of America. There was little basis for the boast, as events were to demonstrate.

THE KOHLER COMPANY STRIKE

There were other violent strikes: some, like the Toledo Autolite walkout, leading to permanent unionization; others, typified by the violent encounter between the strikers and the Kohler Company, resulting in no organization. The Kohler Company, a manufacturer of plumbing fixtures, electric lights, and heating plants, was founded in 1873. Kohler Village, several miles from Sheboygan, Wisconsin, was established at the end of the 1890's. The company followed a paternalistic policy. It supported home ownership and paid wages higher than the prevailing rate in the area. Unionism did not attract Kohler workers until the NIRA days. Prior to that time no union organization was formed at the plant. After the enactment of the NIRA both a company union, the Kohler Workers' Association, and the Federal Labor Union No. 18545 were established.

Efforts to gain a contract were fruitless, and on July 16 a strike was called. Walter J. Kohler, the president of the company, announced he would not bargain with outsiders. Picketing started with the strikers trying to prevent the movement of fuel or raw materials into the plant. The company, on its side, hired a large force of deputies to protect its properties. On July 27 ill-feeling between deputies and strikers led to a clash before the American Club, housing some of the deputies, in which two strikers were killed and a number injured. The next day a regiment of National Guardsmen, dispatched by Governor Albert Schmedeman, arrived. The company agreed to an election under the direction of the National Labor Relations Board. It was won by the Kohler Workers' Association, although Federal Labor Union No. 18545 claimed that many of its members were laid off and that the board had allowed more than one hundred ineligible voters to participate.

Whatever may have been the reason, the strike demonstrated that a union could not stand up against an aggressive anti-union employer without the aid of the government. Section 7(a) gave only partial protection to the right to organize. It could be evaded by an employer determined to eliminate a union from his plant. It demonstrated the power of the employer and the weakness of a union, especially a newly organized one, to cope with a determined resourceful attack. The Kohler Company was to demonstrate two decades later that its success against the Federal Labor Union was no accident, nor the result of the inherent weakness or incapacity of the organization it faced in 1934.

CHAPTER 36

The National Labor Relations Act

The enactment of the National Labor Relations Act, introduced by Senator Robert F. Wagner and Representative William P. Connery, might rightfully be regarded as the greatest legislative victory gained by organized labor in American history. The law protected workers against discrimination for joining or belonging to a labor union and compelled employers to recognize and deal with representatives of their employees over the terms of employment.

The willingness of Congress to consider and enact this legislation was strongly influenced by the experience with Section 7(a) of the National Industrial Recovery Act. This provision, granting labor the right to organize and bargain collectively through representatives of its own choosing, did not contain any means of determining representation disputes or enforcement. It did not impose upon employers the duty to bargain or recognize the unions of their employees. As organization spread in various industries in which they were formerly weak or nonexistent, employers refused to recognize unions as proper and authorized spokesmen for their employees. Senator Wagner, who was the chairman of the National Labor Board, appointed under the National Recovery Administration, testified that the "Labor Board has sought to apply Section 7(a) by relying upon the prestige of its members and by appealing to public sentiment. During the summer [of 1933] these methods met with great success. But in recent months the Board has been confronted by some large employers who ignore public sentiment, who flaunt the clear intent of Congress, and who are a law unto themselves."[1]

The Labor Disputes bill, introduced by Senator Wagner on February 29, 1934, sought to prevent interference with workers' right to organize and bargain collectively through representatives of their own choosing, prohibited recognition of company-dominated unions by employers, and required employers to engage in collective bargaining. It also sought to place restrictions on employers encouraging or supporting company unions, authorized the board to mediate and conciliate labor disputes and to arbitrate differences at the joint request of the parties, to investigate and determine representation issues, and to issue cease and desist orders against employers engaging in prohibited acts. The decisions of the board were reviewable in the courts.

COMPANY UNIONS

Senator Wagner believed that the "greatest barrier to freedom [of choice by workers] is the employer-dominated union which has grown with amazing rapidity since the passage of the Recovery Act."[2] Company-dominated labor organizations arose in a few establishments at the turn of the century. One of the first was started by William Filene, a leading Boston merchant, who in 1898 transferred the management of the lunchroom and relief and entertainment activities of his employees to the Filene Cooperative Association. Five years later a more formal organization was established to allow employees a voice in the government of the association and to promote just relations between employees and management.[3]

Over the years other firms established "works' councils"—a term which describes all "forms of employee representation under which the employees of an individual establishment, through representatives chosen by and from among themselves, cooperate through conference in the consideration of employment conditions in that establishment."[4] One of the better-known of this type of company union was organized by the Nernst Lamp Company of Pittsburgh in 1904. Initially, the plan provided for each group—clerical, factory workers, and foremen—to select representatives with the factory superintendent as chairman.[5] The Industrial Relations Plan of the Colorado Iron and Fuel Company, launched after the bitter strike in 1913–1914, attracted attention because of the conditions and auspices under which it was introduced.[6] A few less well known were also established, but they did not catch on within American industry.

World War I

World War I was directly responsible for a sharp rise in the number of works' councils. Labor discontent in industries and plants producing war goods, which did not deal with outside unions, induced several of the war agencies to promote the establishment of works' councils as a means of achieving more stable labor relations. The Shipbuilding Labor Adjustment Board, the President's Mediation Commission, and the National War Labor Board all sought to have nonunionized employers facing labor difficulties establish shop committees, but the latter was the most important agency promoting these organizations.

Under the procedure of the National War Labor Board secret elections were held among employees of specific companies, who were allowed to choose one committeeman for each one hundred employees. Shop committees were installed in a number of plants, the first at the General Electric Company plant, in Pittsfield, Massachusetts. Plans were adopted to suit the needs of particular companies, and in general the committees were chosen either on a departmental or over-all basis. These shop committees were required to present grievances in writing. Of the 225 plans established in 1919, by 176 companies, 86 were created by the awards of the War Labor Board, 31 by the decisions of the Shipbuilding Labor Adjustment Board, 105 were set up by employers, and 3 were wartime committees.[7]

The Loyal Legion of Loggers and Lumbermen was a unique organization established as a result of the effort of the federal government. It was formed by Colonel Brice P. Disque, who had been sent to the Pacific Northwest in an attempt to settle labor difficulties arising out of general discontent with conditions of work as well as the agitation by the Industrial Workers of the World. Confronted by thousands of organized men who lacked spokesmen, he formed the Four L's with the approval of the War Department. The Portland convention, on March 4, 1918, pledged itself to abide by the decisions of Colonel Disque. He objected to both the IWW or the AFL organizing lumber workers. He, however, established an eight-hour day in the woods, with time and one-half for overtime, and the amounts to be paid for board and room. He also required improved sanitary conditions in the camps.[8]

The Four L's were influential in the lumber regions of Oregon, Washington, and Idaho, and to some extent in Montana until the 1930's. It was an intercompany-controlled union. After the war the Four L's reorganized in February 1919 on a fifty-fifty basis, which meant that employers and workers would be equally represented. Its object was to "provide an organization on the basic principle of the 'Square Deal' in which both employer and employee are eligible for membership and may meet on common ground."[9]

At first the AFL believed that company unions might serve as a first step in the organization of workers, that shop committees might mark "the beginning of industrial freedom."[10] The Federation, however, soon found that works' councils were a weapon against outside unions. The 1919 AFL convention, therefore, concluded "that company unions are unqualified to represent the interests of workers, and that they are a delusion and a snare set up by the companies for the express purpose of deluding the workers into the belief that they have some protection and thus have no need for trade union organization."[11] Employers were often dissatisfied with the plans, and many of those organized at the suggestion of a government body were later abandoned. Similar was the experience of many plans initiated by employers themselves. But the period between 1919 and 1924, nevertheless, witnessed the establishment of many works' councils. By 1924, 814 were reported in existence, of which 283 had been established since 1922. In the same period, plans in 194 companies had been abandoned. The number of employees covered had risen from 391,400 in 1919 to 690,000 in 1922 and 1,240,740 in 1924.[2] In contrast to the experience of the unions, employer representation plans gained through 1928 when they were in effect in 432 companies and had a membership of 1,547,766. The number of companies with plans declined in 1932 to 313 with an enrollment of 1,263,194 workers.[13]

The majority of members in these plans were employed in 1932 by firms with 15,000 or more workers on their payroll. In 1919, more than 48 per cent of the members of employee representation plans were in firms of that size and by 1932, the percentage had risen to 63 per cent. The enactment of the National Industrial Recovery Act with Section 7(a) guaranteeing the right to organize encouraged the establishment of many company unions. Of the 653 employee representation plans in existence in November 1933, 412 had been partially or entirely established after the enactment of the NIRA. Of the 1,164,294 members, 793,248 had been enrolled since 1933.[14] A study of 14,725 establishments in manufacturing, service, public utilities, mining and retail, and wholesale trade, employing 1,935,674 workers showed that more than 3 per cent dealt with company unions. These companies employed 385,954 or almost 20 per cent of all the workers covered.[15]

"Company unions were practically the only significant method of dealing in the [telephone and telegraph] industry."[16] In contrast, a survey of railroads employing 909,249 employees showed 646,169 or 71 per cent covered by agreements with outside unions, 218,885 or 24 per cent by agreements with system associations; the rest negotiated terms of employment on an individual basis.[17] Company unions established during the period of the NIRA were often organized to avert threatened strikes, counter the activity of outside unions, or as a means of allowing for employee representation believed necessary because of Section 7(a) of the NIRA.

These organizations were not always initiated by management, and frequently employees themselves took steps to prevent the forming of outside organizations. About two-thirds of the company unions studied in 1935, relied on the employer for financing and only 30 per cent set up regular systems of dues and initiation fees. As a rule companies operating such plans did not have the elaborate type of collective agreements usually made with outside unions. Less than one-fifth of 126 companies studied had any type of agreement, and 9 out of the 22 covered only procedural matters. Forty per cent provided for arbitration by some outside agency of differences between the parties.[18]

THE LABOR DISPUTES ACT

Whatever virtues these types of organizations had, they obviously did not perform the same services for the workers as did unions independent of direct or indirect employer control. In fact, these organizations were regarded as part of the armory of weapons the employer could use against outside unions. It was this view, supported by considerable historical evidence, which induced Senator Wagner and others to seek legislation preventing company-dominated organizations of labor from representing employees. Wagner believed that the "greatest barrier to collective bargaining [is] employer-dominated unions, which [have] grown with amazing rapidity since the passage of the Recovery Act. The employer-dominated union is initiated by the employer. He takes part in the determination of its rules, its procedure, and its policies. He can terminate it at will and he exercises absolute veto power over its suggestions. Certainly there is no real cooperation on an equal footing between employers and employees under such circumstances."[19]

Spokesmen for organized labor pointed to a body of principles and practices which had been developed by government bodies over time. Especially important were the decisions of the War Labor Board and those under the Railway Labor Acts of 1926 and 1934. The decisions of the Labor Boards under the National Industrial Recovery Act which had developed the principles of majority rule, good faith bargaining, the impropriety of company-dominated unions, as well as election procedures for determining bargaining representation also served as guidelines for those sponsoring the new labor law. William Green, president of the AFL, claimed that almost all company unions were organized to prevent the formation of labor unions affiliated with the AFL. Testifying on the same question, John L. Lewis observed: "If the Government is to encourage organization upon the part of employers who primarily are more able to protect themselves than are the workers, then it does seem to be entirely logical for the Government at least to give the workers the necessary degree of protection in the formation of their own voluntary forms of trade unions."[20]

Other labor union officials testified on behalf of the bill, and a number of students and arbitrators expressed general approval. The most detailed and vigorous criticism came from James A. Emery, chief counsel of the National Association of Manufacturers, who argued the bill was "invalid in law and unsound in policy. We will demonstrate it is not an exercise of the commerce power of Congress, but a deliberate and indefensible invasion of the right to regulate and even compel local employment relations, which the Supreme Court, without exception, has declared are exclusively a subject for State and not Federal control."[21] Even if the bill was constitutional, Emery believed it would lead to an unnecessary concentration of power in the hands of a government bureau, and he also criticized the rules of evidence which the board administering the law would be able to follow.

Arthur H. Young, a vice-president of the U.S. Steel Corporation and an expert on labor-management relations, objected to the philosophy as well as the purpose of the bill. He found it "both vicious and undesirable because of its fundamental philosophy as to the certain and complete clash of interest as between employer and employee. . . . This is in utter disregard of progress toward complete cooperation and the abolition of small remaining areas of conflict as between worker and his boss that has distinctly and uniquely characterized industrial relations in the United States of America."[22] The Labor Disputes bill was also opposed by William F. Dunne, who represented the Trade Union Unity League, a Communist-controlled labor federation. Dunne declared "we do not care to offer any amendments to this [Labor Disputes] bill. We are against it entirely."[23] A bill was reported favorably by the Senate Labor Committee. The bill that came out of committee represented the views of Senator David Walsh rather than those of Senator Wagner who planned to modify some of its provisions by amendments from the floor. While the bill was pending in the Senate, Senator Joseph Robinson and Congressman Joseph Byrnes introduced Public Resolution 44, which Congress hastily adopted. Public Resolution 44 was to expire on June 16, 1935, and gave the President power to establish boards to ascertain the facts in controversies arising out of the interpretation of Section 7(a) of the National Industrial Recovery Act. Such boards were authorized to conduct elections to determine representatives for collective bargaining and to investigate labor disputes. The board could not issue cease and desist orders, but might obtain compliance by requesting the removal of the Blue Eagle from an offender against Section 7(a) or by referring the issues to the Department of Justice for action by the courts.

The National Labor Relations Board, appointed under Public Resolution 44, found it difficult to enforce Section 7(a) because of the refusal of employers to attend hearings and the board had no power to subpoena witnesses or records. It was also unsatisfactory from the point of view of holding elections, the orders for which were frequently ignored or challenged in the courts.[24]

The National Labor Relations Act

The failure of Public Resolution 44 to meet the needs of organized labor stimulated a campaign for the enactment of legislation which would provide greater protection to union organization. On February 21, 1935, Senator Wagner introduced the "national labor relations bill" which was designed, according to the author, "to clarify the provisions of Section 7(a) of the National Industrial Recovery Act and to invest a permanent national labor relations board with adequate powers for their enforcement. It embodies, in perfect form, the labor disputes bill which I introduced last year."[25] The new bill was broader than the Labor Disputes bill, since the new one covered not only wages, hours, and conditions of employment, but also grievances. "The importance of this," according to Wagner, "is that an employer is not now permitted to organize a shop committee to present grievances on questions of safety and other minor matters even though he does not use such shop committee as a subterfuge for collective bargaining on the essential points of wages and hours. In other words, the present draft is intended to outlaw certain types of personal administration commonly used by employers and not hitherto felt to be obnoxious."[26]

The heart of the bill was the section dealing with unfair labor practices by employers. It was a principle used first in the 1914 Federal Trade Commission Act with the substitution of unfair labor practices for unfair trade practices. According to Wagner, the courts and administrative agencies have difficulties in enforcing "general declarations of rights in the absence of greater statutory particularity. Therefore, without in any way placing limitations upon the broadest reasonable interpretation of its omnibus guaranty of freedom, the bill refers in greater detail to a few of the practices which have proved the most fertile sources for evading or obstructing the purpose of the law."[27]

Wagner argued that the outlawing of discrimination by the employer for union membership was a logical and necessary extension of the provisions of the Norris-LaGuardia Act outlawing the yellow-dog contract. "If freedom of organization is to be preserved, employees must have more than the mere knowledge that the courts will not be used to confirm injustice. They need protection most in those cases where the employer is strong enough to impress his will without the aid of the law."[28] A major purpose of the law was to outlaw recognition of a company-dominated union.

A large number of government officials, including Secretary of Labor Frances Perkins, testified for the bill. Secretary Perkins wanted the agency placed under the jurisdiction of the Department of Labor, a proposal opposed by Senator Wagner and the members of the National Labor Relations Board. Roosevelt was cool, and a number of administration stalwarts opposed the bill. Sponsors of the legislation faced two problems: employer opposition and the fear by some who were favorable to the legislation that it could not pass the constitutional test before the U.S. Supreme Court. Questioned on the latter point by Senator William Borah, Wagner replied that "the courts have gone pretty far to hold that strikes seriously dry up trade channels and thus affect interstate commerce." Borah was not satisfied with the answer, and gave the example of a man working on a product which is finally shipped in interstate trade, but, he claimed, "his work had nothing to do with it at all, he is not engaged in the interstate part of it, but simply producing it, and you cannot deal with him if that work is not connected with interstate trade." Wagner, claiming there were precedents for the view held by him, cited *"the Bedford Stone Cutters case, . . .* the Supreme Court found justification for an injunction where workers refused to work upon stone which had been brought from another State, though their work was to be done within one particular State alone."[29]

Finally, it was Wagner's position that a strike in one state which affects enterprises, workers, or consumers in other states affects interstate commerce; "for we cannot regard State lines as economic barriers. It all depends, of course, upon the facts in each case."[30] More formidable opposition came from employers and their representatives. James A. Emery again made the most detailed criticism of the bill. He charged, first, that the bill sought to direct local employment, which is reserved to the states. He insisted that it was not a measure to regulate interstate commerce, but a subterfuge to allow federal intrusion in relationships within the province of the states. He also attacked the bill as an attempt to deny due process to employers charged with violating its provisions. Moreover, he held the bill violates the fourth amendment to the Constitution by permitting unreasonable searches and seizures, and by allowing the executive branch to assess damages, require restitution for lost pay, and make finding of facts.[31]

A number of other employer representatives also testified in opposition. They either argued against the bill on constitutional grounds, or questioned its necessity or the effects assumed by its sponsors. Instead of improving labor-management relations, employers saw in this legislation a device that would tend to divide employer from employee and increase rather than reduce industrial differences and strife. On May 2, Senator David I. Walsh reported the bill favorably on behalf of the Committee on Education and Labor. He noted that "the Government's promise in Section 7(a) stands largely unfilled. . . . In the committee's judgment, the present bill is a logical development of a philosophy and a consistent policy manifest in many acts of Congress dealing over a period of years with labor relations."[32] The report attributed at least 25 per cent of strikes to failure "to recognize and utilize the theory and practice of collective bargaining, under which are subsumed the rights of employees to organize freely and to deal with employers through representatives of their own choosing."[33]

The committee believed the bill sought to encourage by developing the procedure of collective bargaining, "that equality of bargaining power which is a prerequisite to equality of opportunity and freedom of contract." The committee found it necessary to state with a degree of particularity the kinds of practices which are forbidden, since it did not believe a general statement would serve the purpose of preventing unfair labor practices by the courts. The first unfair labor practice made it illegal for an employer "to interfere with, restrain, or coerce employees in the exercise of the rights guaranteed in Section 7." These are the right to organize and bargain collectively through representatives of their own choosing. "The four succeeding unfair-labor practices are not designed to impose limitations or restrictions upon the general guarantees of the first, but rather to spell out with particularity some of the practices that have been most prevalent and most troublesome."[34]

In attempting to outlaw company-dominated unions for the purpose of collective bargaining, the bill did "nothing to outlaw free and independent organizations of workers who by their own choice limit their cooperative action to the limits of one company. . . . The so-called 'company union' features of the bill are designed to prevent interference by employers with organizations of their workers that serve or might serve as collective bargaining agencies. Such interference exists when employers actively participate in framing the constitutions and by-laws of labor organizations; or when, by provisions in the constitution or by-laws, changes in the structure of the organization cannot be made without the consent of the employer."[35]

On the "duty to bargain collectively," the committee denied any desire "to compel agreements or to permit governmental supervision of their terms. It must be stressed that the duty to bargain does not carry with it the duty to reach an agreement because the essence of collective bargaining is that either party shall be free to decide whether proposals made to it are satisfactory."[36] The committee was, nevertheless, of the opinion "that a guarantee of the right of employees to bargain collectively through representatives of their own choosing is a mere delusion if it is not accompanied by the correlative duty on the part of the other party to recognize such representatives as they have been designated (whether as individuals or labor organizations) and to negotiate with them in bona fide effort to arrive at a collective bargaining agreement. Furthermore, the procedure of holding governmentally supervised elections to determine the choice of representatives of employees becomes of little worth if after the elections its results are for all practical purposes ignored."[37]

The principle of majority rule was incorporated in the bill, and the board was authorized to hold elections to determine the bargaining representative. In order to prevent interference with elections by the courts, as in a number of instances under Public Resolution 44, it was specified that no right to court review would be permitted anterior to the holding of an election. The committee, in discussing the constitutional issues raised by some witnesses, expressed the view that the regulations of employer-employee relationships contemplated does not violate due process of law, and based upon a number of decisions, especially in *Coronado Coal Company* v. *United Mine Workers of America,* 268 U.S. 295 and *Bedford Stone Co.* v. *Stone Cutters Association,* 274 U.S. 37, demonstrated according to the committee, that Congress has power to prevent burdens and restraints upon interstate commerce.

The debate on the bill in the Senate centered around the amendment of Senator Millard Tydings: "It shall be an unfair labor practice for any person, (a) to coerce employees in the exercise of the rights guaranteed in Section 7; (b) to interfere with, restrain, or coerce employees in their right to work and to join or not to join any labor organization."[38] This amendment aroused strong opposition of the proponents of the bill, for its adoption would have struck a blow at union security of all kinds and the exercise of pressure upon the unorganized for joining a union or even for withdrawal from work during a strike.

Senator Borah believed the legislation dealt with relations between employer and employee, and the amendment "introduces a wholly new field of legislation."[39] Senator James Couzens of Michigan supported the Tydings' amendment and argued that coercion from any source should be eliminated. Senator Walsh feared the amendment would lead to the filing of innumerable complaints by workers who claimed they were coerced and would transform the board into a police court. The Tydings' amendment was rejected.[40] Before the bill was passed, some questions arose among several leaders of the AFL on its effect upon the rights of craft unions; it was feared that it might strengthen the position of the industrial organizations on the eve of their great expansion. This position was not clarified, and some of the heads of unions were never satisfied. The subsequent division within the labor movement and the insistence of the board that AFL unions did not hold a preferential position angered many of its leaders who demanded that the craft unions be given greater consideration. During the dispute the AFL attacked the board as unfair, but its criticisms were undeserved.

In discussing the legislation, Senator Walsh explicitly stated: "The bill gives no legal sanction or approval to any labor organization whatever. It does not mention the name 'trade union' or any other national or local labor organization. It does not mention the name 'company union.' It does this, which some employers who have company unions resist; namely, it restricts somewhat the methods now pursued in financing company unions." The Senator pointed out that the company-dominated and not the company union was being outlawed by the legislation. The bill restricts contributions made to any union—the American Federation of Labor or the company unions." He emphasized that "if the American Federation of Labor or any other union is not honestly and sincerely and devotedly interested in the welfare of its members, we must recognize the fact that sooner or later the employees belonging to it will, in some election, move out of the American Federation of Labor and into an international union or other union of some kind, a different union of their own."[41]

In the House of Representatives, a bill following, in general, the Senate version was introduced by Congressman William P. Connery. Proponents and opponents reiterated their views before the House Labor Committee. The House bill was reported favorably, but Congressman Vito Marcantonio wanted the law to cover agricultural workers. The House enacted its own version and the differences were ironed out in conference. In signing the bill, President Roosevelt, on July 27, 1935, noted that by "defining rights, the enforcement of which is recognized by the Congress to be necessary as both an act of common justice and economic advance, must not be misinterpreted. It may eventually eliminate one major cause of labor disputes, but it will not stop all labor disputes. It does not cover all industry and labor, but is applicable only when violation of the legal right of independent self organization would burden interstate commerce. Accepted by management, labor, and the public with a sense of sober responsibility and of willing cooperation, however, it should serve as an important step towards the achievement of justice and peaceful labor relations in industry."[42]

The law was not immediately accepted; its constitutionality was doubted by eminent counsel. The National Lawyers Committee of the American Liberty League issued a 132-page legal argument that the act "constitutes an illegal interference with the individual freedom of employees" as guaranteed them by the Constitution. It decried the denial of rights to minority of employees, and unequal treatment of the employer by the statute. The committee concluded: "considering the Act in the light of our history, the established form of government, and the decisions of our highest court, we have no hesitancy in considering it is unconstitutional and that it constitutes a complete departure from constitutional and traditional theories of government."[43]

Twenty-five years later Judge J. Warren Madden, the first chairman of the National Labor Relations Board, observed: "I think that not many members of the committee would have in an advisory opinion to an important paying client said, 'I have no hesitancy in advising you the Act is a nullity and that you may disregard it, in complete confidence that any ensuing litigation will terminate in your favor.'"[44]

More serious were the injunctions against the hearings and other activities of the board by federal district courts. In a 5 to 4 decision, the law was upheld in *National Labor Relations Board* v. *Jones and Laughlin Steel*

Corporation, 301 U.S. 1 (1937). Chief Justice Charles Evans Hughes found the law does "not impose collective bargaining upon all industry regardless of effects upon interstate or foreign commerce. It purports to reach what may be deemed to burden or obstruct that commerce and, thus qualified, it must be construed as contemplating the exercise of control within constitutional bounds. It is a familiar principle that acts which directly burden or obstruct interstate or foreign commerce, or its free flow, are within the reach of the congressional power. Acts having that effect are not rendered immune because they grow out of labor disputes."

As to manufacturing of steel being a local industry outside of the flow of commerce and consequently immune from federal regulations, he did "not find it necessary to determine whether these features of defendant's business dispose of the asserted analogy to the 'stream of commerce' cases. The instance in which that metaphor has been used are but particular, and not exclusive, illustrations of the protective power which the Government invokes in support of the present Act. The congressional authority to protect interstate commerce from burdens and obstructions is not limited to transactions which can be deemed to be an essential part of a 'flow' of interstate or foreign commerce. Burdens and obstructions may be due to injurious action, springing from other sources. The fundamental principle is that the power to regulate commerce is the power to enact 'all appropriate legislation' for 'its protection and advancement.' "[45]

The Dispute Over Industrial Organization and the Emergence of the Committee for Industrial Organization

The establishment of federal labor unions in the hitherto unorganized mass-production industries created a series of jurisdictional problems which were not resolved by the normal methods used in such situations, and eventually led to a schism within the labor movement that lasted for twenty years. The AFL had over the years evolved the principle of exclusive jurisdiction, which meant that one union and one only would be authorized to recruit workers of a given craft or calling. In pursuance of this principle, the Woodworkers' and Amalgamated Carpenters and Joiners' Unions were compelled to merge with the United Brotherhood of Carpenters and Joiners of America, and the International Association of Railway Car Workers were ordered to join the Brotherhood of Railway Carmen. Similarly, a union of steam fitters was ordered into the Plumbers' Union. The organizations refusing to accept these directives were forced out of the federation.

Insistence by several unions upon their right to retain unions for craftsmen employed in and around the bituminous coal mines created a crisis in 1901. The United Mine Workers of America refused to relinquish these craftsmen and continued to recruit them into its own locals. The conflict was solved by the Scranton Declaration, which recognized that conditions

463

surrounding the coal communities warranted an exception to the principle of exclusive jurisdiction; the Mine Workers' Union was recognized as the proper agency for organizing all workers in and around the coal mines. Beginning in 1903, resolutions endorsing industrial unionism were introduced periodically at AFL conventions. In 1912 it was sponsored by the largest union, the United Mine Workers of America. The resolution aroused a long and at times acrimonious debate, and the sponsors were able to poll 35 per cent of the roll call vote. These resolutions were not significant, for they did not represent any differences over jurisdiction, but were merely an expression of opinion which could not have been enforced upon the affiliates.

The controversy which began in 1933 was of a different order. It is, nevertheless, necessary to recognize that the view of the unions objecting to industrial organization in the mass-production industries, which would include craftsmen belonging in their jurisdictions, were following a long established policy. For example, in 1929 the leaders of the unions in the Metal Trades Department discussed the problem of organizing a radio manufacturing plant in Chicago. Leaders of the local metal trades council asked to "be permitted to organize all workers in this particular radio factory into a federal labor union and after the organization was perfected, segregate, or transfer the mechanics into their respective unions."[1] The views of the heads of the international unions were solicited, and the majority did not oppose the organizing of the semi-skilled and unskilled into federal unions, directly affiliated with the AFL, but insisted upon tradesmen being placed in their own organizations. In the discussion, President James O'Connell of the department told the delegates that unless a plan for organizing the mass production industries was devised and accepted, it would be a waste of time and money to initiate such a campaign of organization.[2]

The difficulties anticipated by the 1929 convention of the Metal Trades Department made their appearance as soon as the AFL undertook to organize the employees in the mass-production industries. Arthur O. Wharton, the head of the International Association of Machinists, complained soon after the AFL had sent an organizer to Detroit to recruit employees in the automobile industry. Wharton, it may be noted, had been the author of the plan to unite the shopcraft unions in the railway industry so that while they remained in the organization of their crafts, they jointly negotiated grievances and conditions of employment. At the meeting of the executive council on September 7, 1933, three months after an AFL organizer had been stationed in Detroit, Wharton requested the issuance of a circular by the AFL to its voluntary and full-time organizers specifying precisely what kinds of workers were eligible for membership in federal labor unions.

William Green explained that the NIRA "aroused the spirit of organization . . . everywhere and came on us like a rising tide, appeals to come here, to come there. The United Mine Workers of America proceeded to organize the mine workers one hundred per cent in every state of the Union. Here comes a request from all these mass production industries. It was a problem we had to meet quickly and the matter of meeting it in a judicious way was apparent. We met here some time ago and we discussed the problem of organizing mass production industries particularly the automobile industry and I recall we agreed that we would proceed to organize these workers in Federal Labor Unions. . . . They are clamoring to come. If we raised the point 'you must go here, you must go there' we would never organize them. I have advised in every conversation with our organizers 'you respect the jurisdictional rights of the craft organizations and when you are confronted with a situation where they do not want a craft organization be patient with them.' When you belong to a craft organization we want you to go in. If it will mean the defeat of the organization of the workers then for the moment let us not make the division with the tide of organization running all over the country."[3]

Green pleaded for patience with the newly formed federal labor unions, but the heads of the unions affiliated with the Metal Trades Department were unwilling to show the same tolerance toward what they regarded as encroachments upon their jurisdictions. At the 1933 convention of the Metal Trades Department, a number of unions complained of the conduct of AFL organizers in placing metal trades craftsmen in federal labor unions. Wharton, who became one of the leading opponents of the tendency of AFL organizers to violate the jurisdictional rights of the crafts, complained that the joint organizing campaign of the Machinists' and Blacksmiths' Unions had been aborted in Pittsburgh, Pennsylvania, by an AFL organizer offering lower initiation fees and dues in a federal labor union. "What we want," said Wharton, "is to have positive instructions sent out by the American Federation of Labor which will prevent any poaching upon our International Unions. It is true that we were informed that eventually those members of Federal Unions who properly belong to our International Union will be transferred to us, but that transfer may be postponed for a long time, for mechanics properly belonging to us who begin their trade-union career on a basis of low initiation fees and low dues will not be enthusiastic over being transferred, and, in addition, under rulings which I understand have been made, it will be necessary for us to accept these members without their paying an additional initiation fee, so that our International Unions will be deprived of the necessary income through initiation. . . . The AFofL is maintained by our International Unions. It is supported by the per capita tax paid by our organizations, and it must not be permitted to interfere with our organizing campaign."[4]

Wharton's position was supported by the heads of the Sheet Metal Workers' and the Blacksmiths' and Metal Polishers' Unions; the resolution was unanimously adopted. In fact, John P. Frey, an officer of the department, brought his complaint to the AFL convention of that year. Frey asked the convention "to prevent the inclusion in Federal Labor Unions of any mechanic or laborer over whom the International Unions have jurisdiction through the charter rights given to them by the American Federation of Labor."[5] Frey was not the only delegate to present a resolution of the question to the 1933 convention. Suggestions were also made that the federal labor unions be treated more leniently than suggested by the metal trades unions. The resolutions' committee announced that there could "be no change in the structural form of organization of the affiliated national and international unions except by voluntary agreement." The committee recognized that developments in the mass production industries present new problems "which must be recognized and dealt with so that the rights and interests of affiliated national and international unions may be fully safeguarded and also that there be provided an immediate basis for the tentative organizing of these wage earners."

The committee argued "that the issuance of federal labor union charters may well serve this necessary temporary purpose, that is the organization of workers in mass production plants when the affiliated national and international unions give consent to the granting of such federal charters, and in plants of small communities where it may prove difficult for affiliated national and international unions to give the question of organizing their immediate attention."[6] President Charles P. Howard was not satisfied with the ambiguous pronouncement of the resolutions' committee. In a minority report Howard warned that it was necessary to develop policies to meet new conditions which require organizing on a different basis. He wanted the AFL to play a greater role in coordinating the organizing efforts that he believed now existed. Both the majority and minority reports were referred to the executive council.[7]

The executive council was directed to call a conference of national and international unions to discuss organizing work and problems. Meeting in Washington on January 24-25, 1934, delegates from seventy-five unions sought to find a basis for an amicable settlement of the differences over the form of organization to be permitted in the mass production industries. The conference directed that organizing be conducted with increased vigor, that the AFL call conferences of organizers of the different national and international unions for the purpose of eliminating conflict and promoting harmony, and that local unions be called upon to cooperate in the calling of mass meetings to spread the message of unionism among the unorganized.[8]

Considerable progress in organizing was made, but the craft unions were displeased by the encroachments by the federal labor unions upon their jurisdictions. In response to their complaints, President Green informed general and district organizers that it was "imperatively necessary that the jurisdictional rights of each national and international union affiliated with the American Federation of Labor be respected and observed. . . . It is especially important that this important rule be observed when *non-union* [italics in letter] workers are organized into federal labor unions. . . . Special emphasis should be put upon the necessity of organizing the unorganized workers into local unions where, according to their craft and calling, they properly belong. . . . Organizers of the American Federation of Labor should not under any circumstances seek to persuade and influence workers who are eligible to membership in national and international unions to join federal labor unions."[9]

Neither the old craft organizations, the newly established federal labor unions, nor their sponsors among the older affiliates were satisfied with the trend of events. Fourteen resolutions were submitted to the 1934 convention on this question and the resolutions' committee directed the executive council "to issue charters for National and International Unions in the automotive, cement, aluminum and such other mass production industries as in the judgment of the Executive Council may be necessary to meet the situation."[10]

In addition, the "Executive Council shall at the earliest practical date inaugurate, manage, promote and conduct a campaign of organization in the iron and steel industry."[11] As a concession to the existing organizations, the resolutions' committee recommended "that in order to protect and safeguard the members of such National and International Unions as are chartered, the American Federation of Labor shall for a provisional period direct the policies, administer the business and designate the administrative and financial officers of such newly organized unions."[12]

The report was a compromise hammered out after a six-day discussion in committee with John P. Frey and John L. Lewis occupying the "extreme ends of the battle that was waged."[13] In answer to the question raised by Wharton, Frey explained that automobile "repairs, automobile reconditioning, automobile accessories—the men engaged in these occupations are not engaged in mass production, and they are omitted from the report for that reason. The report deals only with what are generally accepted as the mass industries, the plants where a large number of workmen who are not craftsmen in the accepted sense of the word are employed on articles under mass methods."[14]

Even more specifically, the report of the resolutions' committee noted the desire of the AFL to meet the demand for organization among the workers in the mass production industries, but it explicitly stated: "We consider it our duty to formulate policies which will fully protect the jurisdictional rights of all trade unions organized upon craft lines and afford every opportunity for development and accession of those workers engaged upon work over which these organizations exercise jurisdiction."[15] The chairman of the resolutions' committee, Matthew Woll, cited this section of the report as proof of the desire to protect the jurisdictional rights of the craft unions.[16] After Joseph Franklin, the head of the Boilermakers' Union, had criticized the conduct of organizers of federal labor unions, he said: "With that understanding, that the rights of craft unions are to be fully protected in all of the plants, particularly outside of the generally recognized mass production plants, we favor the report of the committee."[17]

Lewis noted: "That is the understanding with which we signed that report, and we are going to have as many interpretations of these resolutions as there were conflicting viewpoints on the committee. . . . The resolution means what it says; it means the court and tribunal to determine its definition will be the Executive Council."[18] The report was unanimously adopted.

The 1934 resolution was a compromise. It placed the power of determining the kind of charters that would be issued to the workers in the mass production industries in the hands of the executive council. John P. Frey, the secretary of the resolutions' committee which brought in the 1934 compromise, stated the differences clearly in a letter:

At times I have found the policy of the chief executive officers of the A.F. of L. has run counter to my own trade union understanding. Fortunately, the views I held have received the unanimous support of my Executive Council and the officers of our affiliated unions. The issue is the form of organization, the apparent belief of leading officers of the A.F. of L. that the industrial form of organization should replace our craft structure. Some of my associates desire to make the open fight.[19]

The craft union leaders wanted to insist upon their view being accepted in the Washington meeting of January 1934, but Frey, fearing that it would mean "the washing of much dirty linen in open convention,"[20] dissuaded his colleagues from attacking. Again a fight on the industrial union issue seemed to be brewing at the 1934 AFL convention,

but at the last moment the opposition agreed to a report from the committee of which [Frey] was secretary, which was reasonably satisfactory.

Events since then have made it apparent that the understanding reached in San Francisco was not acceptable to those who wished to change our form of trade union structure, but that they believed in a construction of what was agreed upon which was at direct variance with its purpose and its definite and specific claims. Unless there is a change, the question must come up for discussion on the floor when we meet in convention this year. There must be a show down for it is becoming intolerable to have some International Unions determined that the other International Unions must change their form of organization against their desires.[21]

Frey's letter is important, for it reveals the state of mind of those who were determined to protect the jurisdiction of the craft unions. When the question of chartering unions in the automobile and rubber industries came before the executive council, the dispute which had been settled in San Francisco was renewed. Hutcheson insisted that the "declaration of the San Francisco convention clearly sets forth and maintains the jurisdiction of the craft organizations."[22] Lewis agreed and insisted that the report "sustains the efficiency and virtue of craft organizations. . . . In all my statements I sustain the right of craft organizations to live and render service." Lewis, pointing to the failure of past policies, argued that the San Francisco resolution authorized a change. Lewis charged: "There has been no execution of the San Francisco policy and under the principle laid down by Vice-president Wharton there will be no execution."[23] The craft unionists had the vote, and they decided to exclude maintenance workers and those engaged in installing machinery from the union of rubber workers. In the automobile industry, the pleas for an industrial union charter made by President William Green and John L. Lewis were overruled, and the union was denied the right to include in its ranks workers engaged in making tools and dies and those employed in and around automobile plants engaged in maintaining tools and buildings.[24]

As Frey had predicted, the issue was creating deep division in the ranks. At no time had the federation been confronted with such a situation. It was not a question of endorsing or rejecting a principle, but of determining the extent of the jurisdictions of a number of emerging unions, part of which would encroach upon the historical rights of long affiliated craft organizations. What the AFL was facing was a problem of jurisdictional adjustment of a magnitude and complexity without parallel in its history.

Twenty-one resolutions, dealing with some phase of industrial organization, were submitted to the Atlantic City convention of 1935. Majority and minority reports came out of the resolutions' committee, and of the six who signed the minority report, five were leaders of their unions. David Dubinsky, Charles P. Howard, and John L. Lewis already held reputations that reached beyond the labor movement, and the three others, A. A. Myrup of the Bakers', Frank B. Powers of the Telegraphers', and J. C. Lewis of the Iowa State Federation of Labor, were all known within the labor movement. The signatories of the majority report were not unknown. Woll had served on the executive council for two decades and had been mentioned as Gompers' heir apparent. Frey and Victor Olander were the scholars in an AFL convention, and several heads of the building trades' unions, as well as the secretary-treasurer of the Teamsters' Union, made up the majority.

The majority denied the charge of bad faith and claimed that their opponents "either misunderstood the Declaration adopted last year by the San Francisco Convention, or desire that the policy established in the

Declaration should be set aside and existing International Unions merged into industrial organizations organized for the several industries." After pointing to the failure of the labor movement to establish viable unions in the mass-production industries, the minority report stated:

In those industries where the work performed by a majority of the workers is of such nature that it might fall within the jurisdictional claim of more than one craft union, or no established craft union, it is declared that industrial organization is the only form that will be acceptable to the workers or adequately meet their needs. Jurisdictional claims over small groups of workers in these industries prevent organization by breeding a fear that when once organized the workers in these plants will be separated, union of action and their economic power destroyed by requiring various groups to transfer to National and International Unions organized upon craft lines.

To successfully organize the workers in industrial establishments where conditions outlined herein obtain there must be a clear declaration by the American Federation of Labor. It must recognize the right of these workers to organize into industrial unions and be granted unrestricted charters which guarantee the right to accept into membership all workers employed in the industry or establishment without fear of being compelled to destroy unity of action through recognition of jurisdictional claims made by National or International Unions.[25]

The debate that followed the submission of the reports to the convention showed that the differences had generated ill-feeling and bitterness among the proponents of conflicting views. The speeches of Howard, Lewis, and Murray arguing for experimentation with new forms of organization because the old ones had failed, and those of Woll, Wharton, and Frey pleading for tradition as well as the obligation of the AFL to sustain the jurisdictional rights of the craft unions were of an order seldom equalled and never excelled at AFL conventions. Frey paraphrased the Dartmouth College case by arguing that a charter was a contract and could not be suspended except by the consent of those who made it. He appealed to the sacredness of contracts made with the employer as proof that what is in fact a contract between an international and the AFL on jurisdiction could not be arbitrarily revised.[26]

Wharton's speech had an interest beyond the particular debate. As the author of the plan of cooperation among the railway shop crafts, he pointed to the existence of twenty-one unions on the railways. "So far as I am aware," he said, "it is the only industry that has gone through the six years of this industrial depression with its membership practically intact, maintaining all of its conditions of employment, maintaining its standards of wages and retaining its membership, in addition to which, through the active cooperation of these twenty-one organizations, we have eliminated in certain groups seventy-six company unions affecting some 200,000 workers in that industry."[27]

Wharton's argument could be directed against the ideological industrial unionists, who challenged the efficiency of the craft unions. However, that was not the position of the proponents of the industrial form of organization at the convention or within the executive council. Their argument was based upon the failure of the old methods of dividing workers in the mass production industries among several unions, and they pleaded for permission to allow those employed in mass production to form industrial organizations. Moreover, conditions in the railway industry, where jobs were more clearly defined and where organization had existed, in some instances for seventy years, were quite different from those prevailing in mass production.

When the debate ended, the report favoring industrial unions in the mass-production industries was defeated by a vote of 18,024 to 10,933.[28] The bitterness that the debate generated can be noted by the physical encounter between Lewis and Hutcheson, heads of the two largest unions in the federation. These two strong men of imperious temper had been powers in the federation for almost two decades. Until the split on industrial organization, their outlook on public issues was not dissimilar. Both were followers of the Republican party and were in general of conservative social and political outlook. However, Lewis recognized the opportunities and the need for expanding the organizations of labor, but Hutcheson seemed more anxious to continue the jurisdiction over maintenance men in the plants rather than to allow new methods. Their encounter came as a result of Lewis' criticism of Hutcheson's raising of a point of order against a delegate from a federal labor union. The clash of these two powerful men did not permanently disrupt their friendship or change their agreement on many issues. It was, however, a warning to the craft organizations that the industrial unionists would not accept the decision of the convention as the end of the battle.

THE COMMITTEE FOR INDUSTRIAL ORGANIZATION

Less than a month after the adjournment of the Atlantic City convention, a meeting of officers of eight unions was held in the headquarters of the United Mine Workers of America in Washington to organize the Committee for Industrial Organization. John L. Lewis was selected temporary chairman, and Charles P. Howard of the International Typographical Union, temporary secretary. Heads of eight organizations participated in the formation of the committee. The unions involved were the United Mine Workers of America; the International Typographical Union; Amalgamated Clothing Workers of America; International Ladies' Garment Workers' Union; United Textile Workers of America; Oil Field, Gas Well and Refinery Workers of America; United Hatters, Cap and Millinery

Workers' International Union; and International Union of Mine, Mill and Smelter Workers. Howard announced that the International Typographical Union was not a party and that he was acting as an individual.

The Committee for Industrial Organization, inviting other unions to affiliate, declared its purpose "to be encouragement and promotion of organization of the unorganized workers in mass production and other industries upon an industrial basis, as outlined in the minority report of the Resolutions Committee submitted to the convention of the American Federation of Labor at Atlantic City; to foster recognition and acceptance of collective bargaining in such industries; to counsel and advise unorganized and newly organized groups of workers; to bring them under the banner and in affiliation with the American Federation of Labor."[29]

The committee established a permanent office in Washington, D.C., and appointed John Brophy, a former district officer of the United Mine Workers of America and a candidate for the international presidency against Lewis in 1926, as director. Brophy was authorized to rent office space and receive and disburse monies. Several organizations pledged financial support. The first meeting did not define the scope of the committee's future activities, and it would appear that the organizers had no grandiose plans to challenge the established policies of the AFL. This view is supported by a letter from Howard to Max Zaritsky, the head of the United Hatters, Cap and Millinery Workers' Union, who was advised "that much can be accomplished in an educational way by having members of local unions and International representatives address Central Labor bodies upon the subject of industrial unionism. I am having my representatives report the names and addresses of members especially qualified as speakers who are in sympathy with our efforts."[30]

At least as far as Howard was concerned at the time, the committee had only modest objectives, but these were not so regarded by leaders of the craft unions. Although the announcement appeared in the daily press, Frank Duffy, secretary of the United Brotherhood of Carpenters and Joiners, sent Green a clipping from the *Daily Worker,* the official newspaper of the Communist party to inform him of the launching of the committee.[31] Green found the clippings interesting and of some importance.[32]

On November 23, 1935, Green made the fatal step which was to lead to the division of the American labor movement for twenty years. He reviewed the action of the 1935 convention and expressed "feelings of apprehension over the grave consequences which might follow from the formation of an organization within the American Federation of Labor even though it might be claimed that said organization is formed for the achievement of a laudable purpose."[33] Lewis resigned as vice-president of the AFL on the same date as Green's letter was sent, an indication that there would be no retreat from the committee. Lewis explained that he believed "that further membership would avail nothing in the form of con-structive action from the Executive Council."[34]

Replies were sent by the officers of the unions associated with the com-mittee. All insisted that the forming of the committee was proper and that the unions were loyal to the AFL. Thomas F. McMahon, replying on behalf of the United Textile Workers of America, could see no dual union policy and charged Green was "going far beyond what the law and practice of the American Federation has been since its inception."[35] Harvey Frem-ming of the Oil Field, Gas, Well and Refinery Workers of America, told Green that the dispute was between "groups which disagree as to policy [but] are equally loyal to the American Federation of Labor and equally determined that it shall grow and gain in strength to serve the wage earners."[36]

The most detailed reply came from Howard. It was a courteous and reasoned answer to the charges in Green's letter. Without asperity or sarcasm, he attempted to place the position of the committee in perspective. Written by the head of a craft union, a man of generally conservative temper who had opposed an endorsement of unemployment insurance on the floor of the 1932 AFL convention, the letter is perhaps the best state-ment for the Committee for Industrial Organization and is worth quoting at length.

Howard expressed a "high regard" for Green, "both personally and as President of the American Federation of Labor [and] respect [for his] opinions," but he was compelled to disagree with his conclusions "as to the propriety and ethics of the formation of the Committee for Industrial Or-ganization." Howard expressed his loyalty to the AFL and questioned Green's position on the rights of a minority within the federation. "It is not unethical or improper," said Howard, "for a minority to endeavor to have its proposals adopted by a majority through proper discussion of the issues and by effort to convert those whose interests are most affected—the rank and file of the workers." Howard disagreed that once a decision is made that a minority loses its rights to have it changed. He also charged that as a delegate to AFL conventions, he had observed the "strong cohesion of a controlling group for the purpose of determining every question from election of officers to selection of the city in which the convention is to meet the following year. . . . Much to our regret, some of us have had the conclusion forced upon us that the merits of proposals are not the deter-mining factor in rendering decisions."[37]

Howard insisted that the purpose of the committee was to encourage organization within the AFL and to organize the unorganized, "such an activity should cause no apprehension or concern. We propose to work for 'the recognition and acceptance of collective bargaining in such indus-tries' where collective bargaining does not now and has not existed. In this declared purpose, I find no logical reason for apprehension. If the workers in these industries are not organized for collective action they must continue to suffer from low wages and long hours and they will continue to constitute a menace to conditions established by organized workers."[38]

Howard then denied that the Committee of Industrial Organization intended to raid the membership of established unions, to attempt to influence any existing union, to change its form of organization, to use "unethical or coercive methods in conducting the educational campaign which has for its purpose organization upon an industrial basis," or "promote organization that in any way can be considered dual to the American Federation of Labor." Howard, who was the author of the 1934 report on industrial unions, claimed that the minority "had no thought that when charters were granted to the workers in those industries enumerated in the report they would be restricted. We believe the Executive Council failed to carry out the instructions of the convention. It is the condition thus created which makes necessary some agency within the Federation that has a sympathetic attitude toward organization of the workers in these industries upon the only basis that will be accepted by them or [be] effective for their protection."[39]

Green, in a letter of December 12, reiterated his fears that division and confusion would result from the formation of the Committee for Industrial Organization. He warned that reprisals by those opposed to the purposes of the committee would follow. It was evident that the CIO after less than a month's existence had reached "a point of no return." The insistence of Green that the committee dissolve would not be easily accepted by men of the caliber of those who were heading the CIO. Moreover, Lewis soon showed his unconcern with the views of Green or the AFL by charging in a publicly released letter to Green that he was secretly sympathetic to the objectives of the CIO. Lewis invited him to "return to your father's house."[40]

It was clear from the meeting of the Committee for Industrial Organization that its members had no intention of retreating. At its meeting, on December 9, 1935, reports were presented on a number of organizing projects. Adolph Germer described the outlook for organizing the automobile industry, and Brophy reported that requests for assistance had come from a large number of local unions.[41] "The heads of the international unions who make up the Committee emphasized that their sole aim was to strengthen the American Federation of Labor by activities looking to bringing the millions of unorganized in the mass production industries into the Federation."[42]

The executive council, at its first meeting since the formation of the CIO, directed that a circular be issued to directly chartered bodies notifying them that they "cannot give allegiance, assistance or support to the Committee for Industrial Organization or any other organization which attempts to usurp the functions of the American Federation of Labor."[43] The council then issued a declaration "that policies adopted at Conventions of the American Federation of Labor should be respected, observed and carried out. . . . It is the opinion of the Executive Council that the Committee for Industrial Organization should be immediately dissolved and that it should cease to function . . . and that the officers of the several organizations which constitute the Committee for Industrial Organization cooperate fully with the Executive Council in the application and execution of the organization policies adopted by an overwhelming majority of the duly accredited delegates."[44]

At the same meeting Green said that he had "searched the constitution of the American Federation of Labor, analyzed it, appraised it. I cannot find in this constitution where this Council is clothed with authority to suspend an International Union affiliated with the American Federation of Labor, but I do find that the convention is clothed with authority to revoke a charter of a National or International Union of the American Federation of Labor provided that it is ordered by a two-thirds vote of the convention."

Green went on to say that Gompers had held that a charter of an affiliated organization could be suspended by a majority vote of the delegates at the convention. "In conformity with that ruling International Unions affiliated with the American Federation of Labor have been suspended by a majority vote. But at no time can I find in the proceedings that the Executive Council has been clothed with the authority to suspend organizations affiliated with the American Federation of Labor."[45] A committee of three vice-presidents—George Harrison, chairman, G. M. Bugniazet, and Joseph Weber—were appointed to meet with the CIO unions and urge them to dissolve the Committee for Industrial Organization.

The leaders refused to dissolve the CIO and called attention to the failure of the council to "find that the C.I.O. had taken any action contrary to the constitution of the A.F. of L., or which went beyond our rights as representatives of over one-third of the members of the A.F. of L. The executive council expressed fears that the C.I.O. might become dual, though quoting no evidence to support those fears. We wish to emphasize again that we are trying to remove the roots of dualism by making it possible for the millions of mass-production workers now outside the A.F. of L. to enter on the only basis they will accept industrial unions." The committee denied it was attempting to win support from AFL central bodies, "since our efforts are directed towards increasing sentiment for industrial unionism in mass production industries, not to build any organization within the A.F. of L."[46]

At least two unions were anxious to avoid a split in the AFL. The Hatters' Union, after years of negotiations had just consummated a merger of the unions in the men's and women's division, and its severance from the AFL, it was feared, would restore the old division. The International Ladies' Garment Workers' Union recognized that its organizing campaigns in the small-town garment centers would be seriously hampered without the support of the local AFL organizations. David Dubinsky expressed the views of his general executive board "that under no circumstances shall we permit a split in the American Federation of Labor, even to the extent of complying with the decision of the A.F. of L. to dissolve the C.I.O., if need be, to avoid any suspension or expulsions."[47] At the same time Dubinsky sharply criticized the Harrison committee for not conferring with the representatives of the CIO unions for four months after its appointment and for giving the CIO organizations only one day's notice of a conference.[48]

The meeting between the AFL Harrison committee and Lewis, Philip Murray, Brophy, McMahon, and Glenn McCabe of the Glass Workers was held on May 19. Harrison explained that he could not discuss the merits of the dispute, but he could only propose abandonment of the CIO and "then we can get together and see if we can't find some solution."[49] At this two-hour meeting, Lewis again denied that the CIO "had any purpose to interfere with or obstruct the ordinary functions of the American Federation of Labor. . . . Finally he said he was under a mandate of his convention . . . and he did not intend to alter his course. He did not fear the execution of any decision that might be brought to him by the Council any more than he did the threat made if he persisted in carrying on the activities of the committee. He berated the Council for failure to carry on the organizing campaign in the steel industry."[50]

Green, in the meantime, changed his mind about the power of the executive council to suspend international unions. On the advice of his lawyer, he found that the council might act against recalcitrant unions under Article IX of the constitution.

The next step was a letter from George Harrison, chairman of the committee, to the executives of the ten unions—the Glass Workers' and Automobile Workers' Unions had affiliated with the CIO—to dissolve the organization which was described as a "rival organization within the American Federation of Labor."[51] Howard refused to comply with the directive and insisted:

This committee is just what the title implies—a committee to promote organization among the millions of unorganized industrial workers. That purpose is completely in harmony with what should be the aim and purpose of the American Federation of Labor. The work of this committee is educational and its purpose is to assist and inspire the unorganized. The Committee has not chartered, formed or attempted to form either a local, National or International

Union—or organization of any kind not affiliated with and under the jurisdiction of the American Federation of Labor.

In no instance has a provision of the Constitution of the American Federation of Labor been violated by the Committee. In the absence of such violation I challenge the authority of the Executive Council to pass judgment or attempt to apply a penalty.[52]

The answers to the Harrison letter did not satisfy the members of the executive council who were determined to take action against the unions belonging to the CIO. Several suggested the summoning of the heads of the unions before the executive council.[53] Accordingly, Green asked the CIO unions to meet with the executive council. The CIO questioned the procedure. Replying on behalf of Lewis, John Brophy informed Green:

If you are planning at the Executive Council meeting to make any charges against the U.M.W. or other unions in the C.I.O., I trust you will follow the usual union practice of putting such charges in writing so that we may be informed in advance of what, specifically, you wish to discuss. Nothing will be accomplished at the proposed conference unless the Executive Council is ready to stop hurling general, unsupported allegations, and is willing to examine the actual facts as to the C.I.O. activities and purposes. All the members of the C.I.O. have a right to know what reasons you think you have for considering the C.I.O. harmful to the American Federation of Labor. We have yet to hear of specific examples. For our part, we are ready to give evidence of the value of our activities in bringing thousands of new members into such A.F. of L. unions as the United Rubber Workers and the United Auto Workers.[54]

As noted, suspension of the CIO unions had been considered by Green. It had never been decided, although the AFL had taken a position on expulsion. In 1907 the executive council, over the protests of Gompers, had revoked the charter of the Brewery Workers' International Union because it had failed to carry out the decision of the preceding convention on the jurisdictional rights of coopers, firemen, and engineers employed in breweries.[55] When the issue came before the 1907 convention, Gompers criticized the action of the executive council and made the motion from the floor for restoring the charter of the Brewery Workers' Union.[56] Moreover, to prevent similar action by the council, a resolution introduced by the AFL Treasurer, John B. Lennon, was adopted: "The Executive Council of the American Federation of Labor shall only have power to revoke the charter of an affiliated national or international union when the revocation has been ordered by a two thirds majority of a regular convention of the American Federation of Labor, by a roll-call vote."[57] Charlton Ogburn, the general counsel of the AFL, thought, however, that he had found a way by which the Council could legally suspend the CIO unions.

Ogburn's advice, based upon Article IV, Section 5, of the AFL constitution, was: "No organization or person that has seceded or that has been suspended, which shows that the Constitution certainly contemplates the *suspension,* of an affiliated organization."[58] Since the power of suspension was not exclusively reserved to the convention, Ogburn claimed that it could be exercised by the executive council. In giving this mischievous advice, Ogburn was ignoring the entire history and practice of the AFL. For example, the chief argument against the CIO unions was that they were not following the decisions of the 1935 convention. In fact, it was recognized and stated many times that there was no more than a moral obligation for affiliates to obey the dictates of conventions. Several unions which were most insistent that sanctions be applied to the CIO unions were frequent violators of awards and decisions of AFL conventions. Moreover, the failure to specify complaints in the making of charges made the entire contemplated procedure a travesty on the historic outlook of the AFL, which was basically opposed to interference with the conduct of affiliates and was always slow to impose sanctions upon them.

Having, however, decided to proceed, the executive council allowed John P. Frey, head of the Metal Trades Department, to come before it on July 8, 1936, and demand the suspension of the CIO unions. George Harrison, a council member, doubted that the council had any such authority and observed that unions have a right "to band together to serve their needs." Harrison also pointed to the failure of the aggrieved unions to follow the customary procedure in charging violation of jurisdiction, and that the council had officially failed to propose a solution of the differences. Harrison went on to declare that the CIO unions "had a right to espouse the cause of industrial unionism within the limits of the constitution. If any organization has transgressed on the jurisdiction of any other union there is an established method of procedure. . . . I think we should proceed in the established way if we have any unions that have committed an offense under the constitution of the American Federation of Labor. I only question it because I do not think you have the power to carry it to a conclusion. Not having the power I question considering in the nature of charges."[59] In a private discussion, Lewis said he would dissolve the CIO if the AFL would commit itself to organizing the steel, rubber, automobile, and one other mass-production industry. Daniel Tobin asked that further efforts be made to ascertain what Lewis had in mind, but the executive council could not wait. It decided to accept the charges against the CIO unions and directed the unions affiliated with it to answer them.[60]

Lewis, speaking for the twelve unions—the Automobile, Flat Glass, Rubber Unions, and Amalgamated Association of Iron and Steel Workers had joined the CIO—claimed "the proceedings you contemplate are wholly unwarranted by the constitution of the A.F. of L."[61] He charged that suspension was a subterfuge to avoid the constitutional requirement of a two-thirds vote for expulsion. "Your rule," said Lewis, "undertakes to give the Council power to oust constitutional members of the Federation; it is in obvious conflict with the constitution; and has never been reported to any convention."[62] Actually, Charlton Ogburn informed Green that the courts would not allow "Suspension to be used as a subterfuge to evade the requirement of a two-thirds majority of the Convention for expulsion through depriving the suspended 'C.I.O.' unions of a vote on the question of their own expulsion."[63]

The CIO unions were of another view. They regarded the procedure as improper and violative of their rights. Consequently, they refused to answer the charges, attend the hearings, or challenge the suspension in the courts. In the meantime, Harrison urged "developing some mutually satisfactory basis of disposing of the pending controversy with the C.I.O., and I urge every possible effort be exerted in that direction. Further, I doubt the authority of the Executive Council to suspend an affiliated union without a direct mandate from the convention."[64] The hearings went on as scheduled, with David Dubinsky, a member of the council, arguing against suspension. Based upon the history of the AFL, the proceedings can only be described as farcical. Frey cited the efforts of the rubber workers to recruit craftsmen who were members of several unions. He compared the action of the CIO unions with the formation of minority groups within an international union, a completely improper comparison. As a student of the AFL, Frey must have known the AFL was always hesitant to expel.[65]

The executive council sustained the charges, and the character of the deliberations can be judged by the following exchanges. John Coefield, an officer of the Plumbers' Union and a council member, challenged the right of Dubinsky to sit on the council while charges were being presented against the CIO unions. In this view he was supported by William Hutcheson, but both Green and Tobin argued that Dubinsky had been elected by a convention and had a right to attend meetings of the council.[66] Green informed the CIO unions of the decision of the council that they must withdraw from the CIO by September 5, 1936. "Any union so announcing its withdrawal from the Committee for Industrial Organization or any organization substituted therefore . . . shall not thereafter be affected by this order but will be forgiven its breach of its contractual obligation as expressed in its charter."[67]

The CIO unions remained unconcerned with the suspension which became an obstacle to any discussion of the issues of organizing the mass production industries. Lewis insisted that rescinding the suspension would be necessary for any discussion, and the council appointed a committee to confer with the CIO.

The convention, meeting in Tampa, Florida, beginning on November 16, 1936, dutifully approved the suspensions and selected a committee of three vice-presidents to explore the basis for a settlement. The action of the executive council was endorsed, but the CIO was making the first successful inroads in its campaign to organize the mass-production industries. Already the suspensions must have appeared vain if not harmful. The restraints which affiliation with the AFL normally imposed upon affiliates were completely severed, and Green already in April 1937 complained of widespread encroachments of the jurisdiction of affiliates by CIO unions. "The country seems to be filled with C.I.O. organizers,"[68] he complained. The executive council, at the same meeting, noted that the situation was different from the one that faced the AFL in 1936. The CIO was now chartering dual unions and central bodies, but the suspension must be regarded as the primary cause of the new line. The council decided also to call a special conference of national and international unions to decide on a course of action.[69]

Several members of the council favored the immediate revocation of the charters of the CIO unions, but on the advice of Ogburn that such a step by a special convention could not be legally defended, it was avoided.[70] However, by a vote of 25,616 to 1,227, the 1937 convention voted to give the executive council full power to revoke the charters of all unions which refuse to return to the ranks. They were all eventually expelled.[71]

Meeting in Cincinnati, Ohio, for a two-day conference beginning on May 24, 1937, representatives from 103 national and international unions approved the suggestion of the executive council to undertake more extensive organizing campaigns and to cooperate with each other more closely. They also voted to support an increase of per capita of one cent per member per month at the next convention and advance the funds in the meantime. Approval of the expulsion of locals of CIO unions from AFL central bodies was also given. The International Typographical Union, whose president was secretary of the CIO, refused to endorse the decisions or pay the increased per capita.

During the AFL convention in October 1937, Harvey Fremming, secretary pro tem in the absence of the ailing Howard, suggested a conference of one hundred representatives of the CIO and AFL for the purpose of bringing about peace between the two organizations. After some verbal sparring, a committee of George Harrison, Matthew Woll, and G. M. Bugniazet of the AFL met with a special committee of eleven headed by Philip Murray of the CIO. Before the committees met, several leaders of the craft unionists privately expressed unwillingness to make serious concessions. Their confidence that they had ridden out the crisis was based upon the satisfactory showing of the AFL unions after the suspension of the CIO group. In his report to the executive council, Secretary-Treasurer Frank Morrison reported the federation had gained 485,000 members, exclusive of the suspended unions, in the last eight months.[72]

Conferences between the committees of the two organizations got underway and were held intermittently, beginning October 27, 1937, until December 21. It was finally agreed that the original CIO unions would not reaffiliate with the AFL, until differences between the twenty newly chartered CIO unions and the AFL organizations in the same jurisdictions were adjusted. All unions would then be simultaneously admitted. It was also agreed that the power of the executive council to suspend or expel an affiliate would be explicitly denied except by direct order of a convention.[73]

Lewis rejected the terms. He wanted all of the thirty-two CIO unions admitted immediately and differences discussed subsequent to admission. Lewis may have feared that peace would dull the edge of the organizing drives he planned in the nonunionized, as well as the organized, sectors of the economy, and he very likely underestimated the power and resiliency of the AFL unions. Instead of taking account of the defeat in the Little Steel strike in the summer of 1937 and seeking peace, he planned a series of challenges to the AFL, including the invasion of its long-organized bastion, the construction industry. Such campaigns taxed the financial resources and organizing staffs of the CIO and aroused the resentment of local and regional union officials, many of whom were at first sympathetic to the campaigns in the mass-production industries. In full control of his union's finances, Lewis was able to provide considerable sums, but he was forced to rely, in many instances, on organizers with Communist affiliations.

Dubinsky, a founding member, charged the CIO with the failure of peace negotiations. He claimed the AFL had made significant concessions on the issue of industrial unionism and denied the claim of Lewis that the AFL had wanted the ten original CIO unions to desert the other CIO units as a condition of peace. He warned against raiding of other organizations and asked the CIO to confine itself to organizing the unorganized. He also asked for a resumption of peace negotiations.[74] Dubinsky's views were ignored.

Born in Poland in 1892, Dubinsky, affiliated with the General Jewish Labor Union (Bund) in his native country and twice arrested by the Tsarist police, came to the United States in 1911. He settled in New York, found employment in a garment factory, and joined Cutters' Local No. 10 of the International Ladies' Garment Workers' Union. After participating in the cloakmakers' strike of 1916, he was successively elected a member of the local executive board, vice-president, president, and general manager. In 1921 he was chosen a member of the general executive board, and was a leader in repelling the attempt of the Communists to capture the union in the 1920's. He was chosen secretary-treasurer in 1929, and became international president in 1932.

Under Dubinsky's leadership, the union ousted the Communists from influence in the New York market and established control over the major markets of the industry. In recognition of his leadership and the growth of his union, Dubinsky was elected to the AFL Executive Council in 1934. He was a founding member of the Committee for Industrial Organization but refused to support a permanent split in the ranks and withdrew when a dual federation was established. His union rejoined the AFL in 1940, and he was reappointed to the executive council two years later. He supported the forming of the American Labor party and withdrew when it was captured by the Communists, and with Alex Rose of the Hatters, was the chief promoter of the Liberal party still functioning in New York City.

Endowed with restless energy and an unusual capacity for work, Dubinsky has recognized the problems of maintaining a union in an industry spread throughout most of the United States and in which thousands of employers operate. He has tried with some success to reduce the influence of nonunion highly mobile employers upon the organized portion of the industry. In his own union he has had to fight constantly the invasion of racketeers and he was among those who insisted that the general labor movement take a more forceful position in eliminating corruption from its ranks. Dubinsky, despite his fight against racketeers, is realistic and recognizes the limited power the labor movement can exercise in extirpating this evil. A believer in international labor cooperation, Dubinsky has been an opponent of the Communist trade union apparatus, and worked successfully for a more active anti-Communist policy by the American labor movement. As much as any other man, he was responsible for the failure of the Communist World Federation of Trade Unions to expand its power and the forming of the International Confederation of Free Trade Unions.

While not averse to public recognition, Dubinsky's primary interest is his own union. Widely informed and with years of activity on the political and international levels, no one is likely to refer to him as a "labor statesman," although it would not be an inappropriate designation. During the split, he was on good terms with many of the leaders in both the AFL and CIO. A strong believer in labor political action, the Liberal party despite its outward independence functions in the tradition of American labor politics. With Alex Rose he remains the chief tactician of the party. Interestingly enough, the chief support for the party comes from the middle class and not the blue collar worker. A powerful person and a difficult employer, Dubinsky can be friendly and understanding. His humor and his love of life save him from the pomposities and minor sins attached to labor leadership. He is a realistic progressive, who has achieved a place as one of the elder statesmen of the labor movement. Yet it would be an error to regard Dubinsky as old. He can outwork and outthink many younger men, and his influence is based upon hard work, a lively and imaginative mind, and great experience. His close personal and political friendship with George Meany does not diminish his influence among labor leaders. But his recognition has a solid basis in achievement and knowledge. Beginning with Joseph Barondess, many important leaders made their way to the top of the Jewish labor movement. Benjamin Schlessinger, Joseph Schlosberg, Morris Sigman, and Sidney Hillman, to mention a few. None, however, has exercised the influence and played as important a role within the labor movement as David Dubinsky.

Even though an honorable peace was not accepted, the CIO demonstrated that, under the protection of the right to organize, the mass production industries could be unionized. It also introduced new organizing methods more suitable for the campaigns in these industries than those which had been historically followed. But one of its major objectives, the reduction of the AFL to impotency, completely failed. In fact, the federation soon grew in membership at a much greater pace than its rival. This was no mere accident, for AFL unions were scattered through the economy and extended throughout the United States and Canada. Its success did not depend upon huge and highly financed drives, but upon thousands of established unions some of which might find their jurisdictions favorable for expansion.

Nevertheless, the CIO stimulated the greatest organizing campaigns in American history and compelled the junking of the principle of exclusive jurisdiction, which had been recognized as inapplicable to manufacturing industries early in the century.

It may be that 1938 was the optimum time for peace. It would certainly have reduced the Communist threat which grew to fairly substantial dimensions within the CIO and several of its unions. It would have also inhibited drives in organized industries which wasted the manpower and finances of both the AFL and CIO. But Lewis and others in the CIO were not ready to sacrifice their positions for an unknown and perhaps dubious truce.

It should be finally noted that the split over industrial organization followed a violation of the AFL's long-held policy of avoiding strong measures to enforce official dicta. The oft given advice of Gompers was that a voluntary federation must not attempt to dictate; its methods must be conciliation and discussion so that time might aid in solving differences. There are those who still believe a more powerful federation will be a force for progress and virtue. Aside from the absence of a mechanism which will enable the federation to impose its will, who can forecast with certainty that a powerful federation will not, like the executive council in the 1930's, use its office to thwart necessary adaptations.

CHAPTER 38

Organization in the Automobile Industry

One of the great achievements in the history of organized labor in the United States was the formation of the United Automobile Workers of America. The automobile industry is one of the youngest industries; between 1886 and 1898, about three hundred automobiles were produced in the United States.[1] Heavily concentrated in Michigan (about 60 per cent in 1937), the plants in that state employed about 63 per cent of all workers. From the time the industry left the homes and work shops of the founding inventors, it tended to depend upon a large supply of semi-skilled labor recruited from the small communities of Michigan and other midwestern and border states, as well as the influx of immigrants coming to the United States in the period between 1900 and World War I. By 1937 more than half a million workers were employed in the making of motor cars.

The industry experienced its first flush of real prosperity at the time when the open-shop gospel had been diligently spread among employers in the metal trades, many of whom became its suppliers. The Carriage and Wagon Workers International Union, an AFL affiliate since its founding in 1891, added "Automobile" to its name, but the change did not aid it in its organizing efforts in its expanded domain. Expelled from the AFL, it changed its name to Automobile, Aircraft and Vehicle Workers, and reached a peak of 40,000 members in 1920. Its membership, however, was largely concentrated in the parts plants.[2] A number of metal trades' unions complained to the AFL of the encroachment on their jurisdictions, and the refusal by the Carriage and Wagon Workers Union to mend its ways led to its expulsion.

ORGANIZING IN THE 1920's

The 1925 convention of the Metal Trades Department of the AFL directed its president to call a meeting of the affiliated unions with a view to launching a campaign to organize the workers in the industry. Accordingly, President James O'Connell invited the unions to meet with the officers of the Department to consider a plan. During the discussion, it was suggested "that if organization was attempted it would have to be along the line of mass organization."[3]

No steps were taken to initiate the campaign. Instead, a resolution by the delegate from the Metal Trades Department to the 1926 AFL convention asked the federation to undertake the task. It was approved and President William Green was entrusted with the job. He called several conferences of the unions having jurisdictions in the automobile industry, and it was agreed the AFL would be in charge and that initiation fees would be revised downward. Paul Smith, an AFL organizer, was made the director of the drive.[4]

"Workers in the automobile industry, except those engaged in the construction and maintenance of plants, equipment, parts or tools," were to "be organized into local unions directly affiliated with the A.F. of L. A local union shall include all workers employed in the plant unless the size of the plant requires division into smaller units, or unless it is desirable to combine workers in a number of plants into one local union."[5] Workers belonging to a directly affiliated automobile workers' union would also be given exchange privileges by national and international unions of the AFL, "and where possible membership in international unions without further cost, where such unions hold jurisdiction."[6]

Organizer Smith found many Detroit plants shut down and turnover high. He, therefore, shifted his base and tried to establish unions in Chicago and Milwaukee. Smith established several organizations, but he feared that an open campaign would only lead to the victimization of union members and wildcat strikes which might cause the discharge or other kinds of disciplining of those who joined.[7] That such fears were scarcely exaggerated can be noted by the experience of the International Association of Machinists, which established a local union at the General Motors Plant in St. Louis. "Eight men who had signed an application at our meeting Friday night were discharged Saturday morning. This was the second group which was discharged. It is evident the company has their stool pigeons in our meeting and the company is victimizing our most active workers."[8]

The over-all response was not favorable, and with the onset of the depression, the campaign was called off.

The National Industry Recovery Act

Soon after the adoption of the National Industrial Recovery Act, the AFL sent William Collins to Detroit as an organizer. A number of federal labor unions were established, but unaffiliated and company-dominated organizations were also organized. On August 18, 1933, William Green appeared before the National Recovery Administration considering the Code of Fair Competition in the automobile industry and submitted, on behalf of labor, a series of amendments. Green was especially concerned with the merit provision that had been suggested by the industry and accepted by the administrator of the NIRA. It allowed the automobile industry "to select, retain or advance employees on the basis of individual merit without regard to membership or nonmembership in any organization." The code was effective on September 5 and expired on December 31, 1933.

Organized labor believed the "merit clause" tended to weaken the protection of the right of workers to organize as guaranteed in Section 7(a) and protested to President Roosevelt. In a statement, the President asked that the qualifying provisions be avoided in the future.[9] Minimum wages and a maximum thirty-five-hour week were established. Without consulting the workers in the industry, the code was continued to September 15, 1934, by executive order. William Green was dissatisfied with the failure to hear the views of the employees, and he assured the automobile workers he would "make every effort to have the [merit] clause removed from the Automobile code."[10] In the meantime, organization in the industry was progressing. The National Automobile Chamber of Commerce, acting as the code authority, set up a bureau in Detroit for the adjustment of complaints of violation of the labor provisions of the code. Green informed the federal labor unions that the bureau could be recognized as an agency for adjusting labor differences.[11]

Green charged, in a letter to the unions in the industry, that discrimination "through refusal to rehire union men has been widespread in the automobile industry, and very difficult of proof."[12] He cited the decision of the Regional Labor Board of St. Louis in ordering reemployment of union members as a hopeful sign and urged patience. In the meantime, independent and company-dominated unions were spreading and challenging the federal labor unions at different points. But the companies were countering the organization of their workers by forming or encouraging the establishment of company unions and by discharging active unionists. Changes, however, were observable. When a strike in Detroit of the Hudson Motor Company and of Buick in Flint was threatened on March 6, 1934, William S. Knudsen, the executive vice-president of General Motors Corporation, and Alvan Maculey of the Hudson Company conferred with the leaders of the unions and the Regional Labor Board. The walkout was averted, but a more serious controversy erupted the following week.

Leaders of the AFL unions objected vigorously to discrimination against their members and the encouragement of company unions. Representatives of the unions of automobile workers of the General Motors and Hudson plants in the Detroit area, Lansing, Cleveland, and St. Louis came to Washington for a hearing on charges of discrimination against union members before the National Labor Board. The automobile manufacturers insisted their company unions met the requirements of Section 7(a) for collective bargaining. In view of the attitude of the automobile companies, the union representatives voted to strike the above plants on March 21.[13]

At the same time, the directors of the National Automobile Chamber of Commerce charged: "The American Federation of Labor seeks to make a union card, not merit, the sole condition of employment. They seek to control who shall be employed and what the output shall be. The aims are contrary to the principles on which the automobile industry has made its great contribution to industrial progress in this country."[14]

Having reached a stalemate and fearful that a widespread strike in the automobile industry would adversely affect the revival of industry, President Roosevelt requested Collins to withdraw the strike order. The President was told: "Power to act rests with officers' conference, which convenes at Pontiac, Michigan. Rest assured that we will urge them to meet the situation in the spirit you ask."[15] The President conferred with Green and later with heads of the major auto firms, after they had refused to accept the compromise suggested by Johnson. The leaders of the industry were adamant against allowing their employees to vote on a union, as Johnson had suggested. Following the employers' conference, the President met with Collins and a delegation of officers from federal local unions in the automobile industry. In the meantime, the fourteen firms belonging to the National Automobile Chamber of Commerce announced a readjustment of wages amounting to about a 10 per cent increase. The Ford Motor Company had taken this step previously.[16]

The strike was avoided by the settlement of March 25. Employers agreed to bargain collectively and not to discriminate against employees on the ground of union affiliation. "If there be more than one group, each bargaining committee shall have total membership pro rata to the number of men each member represents." An Automobile Labor Board of three, one from each side and an impartial chairman, was to pass on questions of representation, discharge, and discrimination. Decisions of the board were final and binding. Richard L. Byrd, a member of the Pontiac Labor Union 18941, was appointed to represent labor; Nicholas Kelley, chief counsel of the Chrysler Corporation, represented the industry, and Dr. Leo Wolman was the impartial member. In his announcement of the settlement, the

President stated: "The government makes it clear that it favors no particular union or particular form of employee organization. . . . In the settlement there is a framework for a new structure of industrial relations—a new basis of understanding between employers and employees. I would like you to know that in the settlement just reached in the automobile industry we have charted a new course in social engineering in the United States."[17]

The President's confidence in the settlement was not universally shared. Louis Stark, the leading labor reporter of the period, observed: "The lack of clarity in the language of several important sections of the document reached yesterday and prepared mainly by General Johnson and the manufacturers together with their counsel, has already given rise to certain questions that will have to be interpreted.

" 'Off the record' explanations by the disputants vary considerably. As a result of such variance a test of the principal provisions will probably be under way in a few days."[18] Stark also believed the settlement raised the prestige of the company unions.

At the beginning, the board devoted itself mainly to complaints of discrimination against union members and to the prevention and settlement of disputes. In December 1934 the board announced it would conduct elections in each plant on a two-stage basis—the first to nominate candidates, the second to elect representatives. A span of about a week would be allowed between the two. At the first or nominating election, the employees could choose any one to represent them irrespective of his employment or nonemployment with the company. A plant was divided into voting districts, each of which would choose a single representative. The two candidates receiving the highest votes would be placed on the ballot for the final election, and the one receiving the highest vote in the second or run-off election would become the representative of the district. The first group of elections was held at the plant of the Cadillac Motor Company, beginning on December 19, 1934, and others followed.

In reporting on the agreement to the executive council, Green explained "it would be far better to accept such a settlement than to run the risk of a strike in the automobile industry at the present time. We did not secure an ideal agreement or one that represents the full hopes and aspirations of the workers. The President intervened, urged acceptance of the settlement, and in order to avoid the conflict, the agreement proposed was adopted."[19]

Green went along with the request of President Roosevelt for extending the automobile code although there were in the words of the President a "number of matters connected with this Code with which I have never been fully satisfied."[20] The President wanted a number of things cleared up "and a number of other matters need immediate and intensive study."[21]

Green expressed his disappointment again at the failure to hold a public hearing on the renewal of the automobile code at which labor might have proposed changes, but he agreed with the President's request and asked for a study of labor conditions.[22] President Roosevelt asked S. Clay Williams, chairman of the National Industrial Recovery Board, to investigate "the possibilities of regularizing employment and otherwise improving the conditions of labor in this [automobile] industry."[23]

The settlement did not allay the discontent. Two months after the settlement, a serious strike took place at the plants of the Electric Auto Light Company, the Bingham Stamping and Tool Company, and the Logan Gear Company. The Toledo plants of the three companies were affected. Riots and assaults upon nonstrikers brought on a request for troops, and seven hundred National Guardsmen were sent to the city. In a clash between soldiers and strikers on May 25 two strikers were killed and twenty-five injured. Violence continued, about two hundred strikers and nonstrikers were hurt, and almost the same number arrested. Efforts to find a settlement succeeded with the help of Charles P. Taft. It came in time to halt a movement for the calling of a general strike. A 5 per cent wage raise was granted, and the union was given *de facto* but not formal recognition; the contract ran for six months and was to be continued unless abrogated by one of the parties.[24] The settlement was the first important gain made by the United Auto Workers. Over four thousand workers were employed by the three companies. Moreover, the parts industry had virtually no dealing with labor organizations, and like the major companies, the firms were anxious to avoid giving the unions the prestige of recognition.

Dissatisfaction was rising among auto workers. As a result, the AFL withdrew in September 1934 from participation in the elections slated by the Automobile Labor Board. Green informed President Roosevelt the "Board lost the confidence of labor very shortly after it was established in March 1934. The loss of confidence came because (1) the labor member of the Board completely failed to represent labor and became the center of agitation and discord within the unions. (2) The Chairman of the Board made it clear to the unions that he looked upon the functions of his Board as those of conciliation and mediation only. In no case has the Board ever actually ordered reinstated or rehired a man discriminated against for union membership, and in no case where reinstatement was recommended, was a time limit fixed for such reinstatement. Many whose reinstatement was recommended, were forced to return to work in inferior jobs. The Board's rules of seniority have not been satisfactorily enforced to protect workers in layoff and rehiring. (3) Subsequent to the settlement of March 25th there was enacted by Congress and approved by you Public Resolution No. 44 under which the National Labor Relations Board and the National Steel Labor Relations Board were created. Your executive orders establishing those Boards and the decisions of the National Labor Relations Board in the Houde and other cases have established the principle of majority representation, the automobile workers should not be denied that right. (4) Since the agreement of March 25th was for no fixed duration of time and since no plan of proportional representation had up to September 11, 1934, been announced by the Wolman Board, the American Federation of Labor upon that date notified you and the Manufacturers of their withdrawal from the Agreement. This we considered we had a legal and moral right to do."[25]

Green further charged that, despite the withdrawal of the AFL, the Automobile Labor Board continued to announce elections and that the election procedures were not designed to provide for free choice since they were conducted under the eyes of officials. Green also objected to the statements by members of the board on the strength of AFL unions in the industry. Under the attack of the AFL, the board discontinued its activities on June 16, 1935.[26]

TOWARD A NATIONAL UNION

The federal labor unions of the AFL were not the only organizations functioning in the industry. The Mechanics Educational Society with a following among tool and die makers tried to extend its jurisdiction to production workers. The Automotive Industrial Workers' Association, the Associated Automobile Workers, and a large number of company-dominated unions were vying for the suffrage of the workers in the industry. In June 1934, Collins called a conference of the 107 federal labor unions and a National Council of United Automobile Workers was appointed to advise the organizer in charge of the campaign in the industry. Francis Dillon replaced Collins in October 1934.[27]

At the meeting of the AFL Executive Council on February 1, 1935, the question of chartering an international union in the automobile industry was considered. Dillon did not think the time had yet arrived for such a step, but Green took a different tack. "The convention of the American Federation of Labor," he said, "directed that we proceed to organize an international union of automobile workers. That is the instruction of the convention to the Council. The Council listened with a great deal of interest to the statements made by the committee representing the National Council of Automobile Workers and Organizer Dillon, who is in charge of the organizing campaign in the automobile industry. You heard the different views that were expressed. We have organized 176 local unions of automobile workers. . . . In my opinion a fine nucleus for an international union has already been established, that a national union of automobile workers can be launched and if launched I have every reason to believe if officered properly and supervised and helped by the American Federation of Labor it can be a success."[28]

Lewis strongly supported Green's view. He noted that among the representatives of the automobile workers appearing before the council, "There is material there of men who have background, intelligence and who are ambitious and efficient." Lewis claimed that Dillon did not appear to oppose the formation of an international union, but he feared that a convention would provide an area for "the political skirmishing that would take place."[29] Arthur Wharton of the Machinists' Union objected and declared his union had 22,000 men organized in the automobile industry and was "not willing to relinquish jurisdiction over our men in the automobile plants and the automobile parts manufacturing plants. The skilled maintenance man . . . set up men, as they call them, under various names, belong to our organization."[30]

Green was sure "that it is absolutely impossible to organize these workers into unions where you draw the line of craft distinction. We cannot organize them that way. They are mass minded. They ask me over and over again. Are you going to divide us up? I cannot change that state of mind; it is there. We cannot organize them on any other basis."[31]

Lewis submitted a program which called for chartering an international union and for the temporary appointment of officers by the president of the AFL. It called for an organizing campaign under the direction of the AFL, with provisions being made for adequate publicity and financing. Finally, "all questions of overlapping jurisdiction in the automobile parts and special crafts organizations encountered in the administration of this policy be referred to the Executive Council for consideration at such time as the Council may elect to give these questions consideration."[32]

When Lewis' program was discussed eight days later, the council members representing several of the craft unions claiming jurisdictions in the automobile industry protested the invasions of these rights. Green insisted, however, "that if organization is to be established in the automobile industry it will be upon a basis that the workers employed in this mass production industry must join an organization en masse. We cannot separate them."[33] Green also expressed the view that automobile parts manufacturing is so closely related to auto production, "that a charter ought to cover both groups."[34]

Hutcheson claimed that the AFL had been brought to its present strength by the craft unions. While he felt the mass-production workers could be organized, he wanted the craftsmen's rights protected. However, he did "not believe we should give them a charter so broad that they could go out and claim any employee that might be employed by these automobile manufacturers." Lewis argued that his program provided for an appeal to the executive council after "we accomplished organization and not before, after the fact of organization has been accomplished not tie on reservations that will in themselves deter an effective campaign." Lewis was answered by Tobin, who cited the inability of the workers to establish industrial organizations outside of the mining areas. He did not believe it would work.[35]

Harrison then moved an amendment to Lewis' proposals which granted a charter to the automobile workers in the parts and assembly plants, but excluded tool and die makers essential to the making of these parts, and all others "employed in and around the plant who maintain machinery and buildings." Lewis again objected and asked that "caviling be deferred until we have some organization; that contention and dispute be deferred until in the light of what accomplishment is made in the objective we can take up the question of dividing the members, that contention over the fruits of victory be deferred until we have some of the fruits in our possession."[36] Green supported Lewis' position, and told the council "the moment you attempt to segregate them you will never get anywhere. If you tell them you go here, you go there you will never get anywhere. They are so closely related and inextricably interwoven they are mass minded. Whatever you do I will try to carry out but I will be a target of criticism and I know we will fail."[37]

Harrison's amendment was carried by a vote of 14 to 2, with Lewis and Dubinsky in the minority. As Green had predicted, the first convention assembled by the AFL, at which the international charter was presented, showed resentment at the restrictions imposed by the executive council. After a debate, although the charter was accepted, the criticism and hostility generated was an omen of difficulties to come.[38] The delegates also did not readily accept Green's temporary appointment of officers. On this issue, however, there was no division among the members of the executive council. Green, who was present at the convention, appointed Dillon president, Homer Martin vice-president, and Edward Hall secretary-treasurer. The eleven members of the national council were given posts on the executive board.[39]

Dillon was ousted at the 1936 convention, and Homer Martin replaced him as head of the union.

A watch on the developing situation was maintained by the Committee for Industrial Organization. A memorandum summarizing the situation in the automobile industry held that there was "renewed interest in organizing as a result of the Atlantic City Convention and the activities of the C.I.O., and some gains have been made by local unions. But the international union officers are doing nothing in the way of a general organization drive or adequately to resist the multplying cases of discrimination. The election of officers is essential to inspire necessary confidence on the part of the locals, the independent organizations, and the unorganized."[40] According to the memorandum, the "policy, as decided by the C.I.O. has been to work through the existing A.F. of L. unions. [Adolph] Germer's activities have been advisory, rather than organizational. He has everywhere stressed the importance of organization on an industrial basis within the A.F. of L. He has also influenced the members of and officers of the United Auto Workers in this direction."[41]

At the same time, Wharton was bitterly protesting the failure of Green to order craftsmen into the International Association of Machinists which he headed. A strike under the auspices of an independent union started on December 15, 1935, at the Detroit plant of the Motor Products Corporation. Subsequently, the AFL became involved. Union recognition was granted. In July 1936 the United Auto Workers Union joined the CIO, and Green expressed bitter disappointment at this step.[42] Between July 1, 1933, and April 1, 1936, the AFL locals in the automobile industry had paid in per capita $181,377.33, and the federation had spent on behalf of these groups $249,484.81.[43]

The Sit-down Strikes

Membership had not increased appreciably. Moreover, there were about as many workers belonging to unions not affiliated with the AFL as with the federation. In the middle of November 1936 there was a sudden stirring of activity among the auto workers. In imitation of the Akron rubber workers, a group of auto workers began a sit-down strike at the plant of the Bendix Products Company in South Bend, Indiana, on November 17, 1936. Claiming favoritism to nonunion workers, the union men demanded a closed shop. Negotiations were begun the day following the strike and continued until a settlement. After six days the strikers withdrew from the plants, and the dispute was settled at the end of ten days.[44]

The Bendix strike was a prelude to the wave of sit-down strikes that swept the automobile industry. Almost immediately afterwards, sit-downs took place at two Kelsey-Hayes plants in Detroit manufacturing automotive parts and were shut down by this maneuver. A plant of the Bohn Aluminum Company was subjected to the same procedure. In the meantime, Homer Martin, in an interview with William Knudsen, executive vice-president of the General Motors Corporation, requested nationwide negotiations of issues. He was told by Knudsen that grievances had to be taken up with plant managers. The same demand was then sent to Alfred P. Sloan, president of General Motors. He refused, and John L. Lewis charged that General Motors was evading its responsibility.[45]

Strikes in General Motors' plants in Atlanta and Cleveland followed disputes over union affiliation. December 28 witnessed the beginning of the major sit-down, affecting three plants in Flint—Fisher No. 1 and 2, and the Chevrolet plant. Approximately one thousand of seven thousand employees on strike decided to remain in the plants. Three days later, reports appeared that over 33,000 workers in seven plants were idle. On the last day of the year, Vice-President Knudsen declared: "General Motors

Corporation accepts the principle of collective bargaining and desires to maintain satisfactory relations with all its employees regardless of union or non-union affiliations."[46] He reiterated the position of the corporation that plant managers had power to make agreements.

Answering Knudsen's statement, Martin insisted that local bargaining was not satisfactory for reaching an agreement, and asked for industry-wide bargaining instead. The issue was now drawn between the parties. Steps to dislodge the sit-down strikers were initiated by the company on January 2, 1937. Circuit Judge Edward D. Black ordered the strikers to leave company property. A detachment of police was held in readiness to serve the order but was demobilized before carrying out the order.

On January 3, 1937, representatives from fifty locals in sixteen cities demanded the abolition of piece work, a thirty-hour workweek, reinstatement of all discharged for union activity, seniority to govern layoffs and rehiring, improved minimum wage scales, and conferences between the heads of the corporation and the union.[47] By January 5 the number idle had risen to over 43,000. The order of Judge Black was not carried out; he was an owner of a substantial amount of General Motors' stock.

President Alfred P. Sloan of the corporation announced on January 5 that "General Motors will not recognize a union as sole bargaining agency for its workers to the exclusion of all others. General Motors will continue to recognize for the purpose of collective bargaining, the representatives of its workers whether union or non-union."[48] "Work in General Motors will continue to depend on the ability and efficiency of the worker—not on the membership or non-membership in any labor organization whatsoever. This means that you do not have to pay tribute to any one for the right to work."[49] Since the parties were not making any progress, and the danger of violence persisted, Governor Frank Murphy sought a settlement. He conferred with the Union Strategy Board headed by Adolph Germer on January 9, but no progress was made.

By that time, the Flint Alliance, headed by former Mayor George Boysen, had entered the controversy. Knudsen said that "arbitrary action by the union barred talks. Acceptance of negotiations under the circumstances would have appeared as condoning of seizure."[50] By January 10, 93,000 workers were idle. As negotiations had reached a stalemate, the company decided to turn off heat and water at its occupied plants in Flint. A five-hour battle followed on January 12, in which twenty-four were hurt. Fearing the spread of violence, Governor Murphy ordered a National Guard regiment to duty, but it was instructed to remain outside of the strike zone. Municipal judges Edwin D. Mallory and Frank W. Cain issued about three hundred Joe Doe warrants against the sit-down strikers. At the same time, union members and sympathizers were arriving to aid the strikers if necessary.[51]

Governor Murphy was able to bring the parties together on January 14. For General Motors, it was a withdrawal from its position that negotiations had to be conducted on a local basis. In addition to Knudsen, the company was represented by its counsel, John Thomas Smith and Donaldson Brown, a vice-president and chairman of the finance committee. Martin and Vice-President Wyndham Mortimer, Germer, and John Brophy were among the union negotiators.

At three o'clock in the morning of January 15 the governor announced an agreement. The union was to withdraw the strikers from the plants; the company would begin bargaining and would not remove dies, tools, machinery, or any equipment affected by the strike except for export. In addition, the company promised not to discriminate against any of the strikers. Since the issue appeared to be settled, Boysen, speaking for the Flint Alliance, informed Knudsen that his members "do not want to be represented by the United Automobile Workers of America."[52] As a result of Boysen's intervention, the agreement became a dead letter and the strikers remained in the plants. Murphy now called upon Secretary of Labor Frances Perkins and President Roosevelt for aid. Murphy and Perkins conferred with Sloan, Knudsen, Smith, and Brown on January 20 but no agreement could be reached. The next day, Sloan left the conference and said that he did not "think at the moment anything can be accomplished."[53] He asked for the plants to be reopened.

At this point, Lewis entered the debate with a statement charging the "economic royalists represented by General Motors" had sought to drive the administration from power. "The administration," said Lewis, "asked labor help to repel this attack, and labor gave its help. The same economic royalists have their fangs in labor. The workers of this country expect the administration to help the workers in every legal way, and to support the workers in General Motors plants."[54]

President Roosevelt did not comment directly on Lewis' suggestion, but he remarked that "there are some moments when statements, conversation, and headlines are not in order."[55] A day later General Motors announced that 50 of its plants in 25 cities, employing 125,613 workers, had been forced to close as a result of the strike. Sloan, however, would not attend a conference called by Secretary Perkins to discover a formula for ending the deadlock. Sloan's refusal gave Roosevelt an opportunity for balancing the criticism of Lewis. He described Sloan's action "as a very unfortunate decision on his part."[56]

In a message to General Motors' employees, Sloan charged that the only issue was whether the union would "be given the exclusive privilege of acting as representatives of all our workers regardless of your desires." He declared that "we will negotiate with this group and will earnestly strive for an honorable settlement as soon as the illegal seizure of plants is terminated. . . . You will not have to pay tribute for the privilege of working in a General Motors plant."[57]

A rapid solution became increasingly imperative. An injunction ordering the sit-downers to cease their trespass on General Motors' property was issued by Judge Paul Gadola on January 28. The Flint Alliance asked Governor Murphy for protection in their attempt to go back to work. The request gave the governor an opportunity to reiterate his desire to find a settlement "without riot and bloodshed." He accused the Flint Alliance of contributing to the repudiation of the agreement which had been reached through the governor's efforts. Finally, he said: "Nothing in the world is going to get the Governor of Michigan off the position of working it out peacefully. All the power of General Motors or the Flint Alliance or Mr. Lewis' organization is insufficient to get the Governor of Michigan off that path."[58]

After the strike had continued for almost five weeks, John L. Lewis left for Detroit to try his hand at a settlement. Knudsen, Smith, and Donaldson Brown met with Lewis, Martin, and Mortimer on February 3, at the joint request of the governor and the President of the United States. General Motors denied the right of the union to exclusive bargaining rights "for all workers in the plants on strike, even those outside its membership. This position really means that if five hundred workers sit down and throw ten thousand other workers out of employment, this act of violence is sufficient authority to permit the union to speak exclusively for 10,000 employees thus deprived of work. . . . The C.I.O. unions have settled all their recent strikes such as Libby-Owens-Ford, Pittsburgh Plate Glass, Hercules Motors and others, on the basis of recognition for their members only as offered by the General Motors Corporation." The corporation was willing to allow a vote under the auspices of Governor Murphy to determine the number of workers who wanted to be represented by the Auto Workers' Union.[59]

Inability to reach an agreement resulted in the appointment of Knudsen and Lewis as a subcommittee to find an acceptable formula. It appeared several times that the conference would end without an agreement, but pressure from the governor and the President of the United States finally led to the ending of the strike on February 11. The agreement called for the company to recognize the union as bargaining agent for its members only, not to bargain on matters of general corporate policy with any other group from the twenty struck plants without Governor Murphy's sanction, to rehire without prejudice all strikers, and drop all court proceedings. In turn, the union agreed to call off the strike and evacuate the plants, refrain from intimidation and recruiting on company property, avoid striking and seek settlement of grievances by negotiation.[60]

The forty-four day strike ended in a victory for the strikers. It compelled the heads of the company to deal with the union, which they had stubbornly refused until the walkout. When the final arrangements were made, in the following month, it included a procedure for settling grievances and plans for layoffs and rehiring.[61] While the tenacity and courage of the union and its members should not be underrated, the victory of the sit-down strikers was clearly due to the insistence of the national administration and Governor Murphy that the dispute must be settled peacefully. There were enough troops, if Murphy had chosen to use them, to have driven the sit-downers out of the plants, and it is likely that such an act would have redounded to his political advantage. But Murphy was unwilling to take such drastic action, and the General Motors Corporation was compelled to make the first significant concession to the emerging new force. The victory, for such it must be regarded, demonstrated to the hesitant that the union was able to protect its members and that the motor companies would have to engage in collective bargaining.[62]

In a certain sense the sit-down strike at the plants of the Chrysler Corporation lacked the drama and excitement of the "battle of Flint." The new tactic spread like wildfire through Michigan industry and to other parts of the country and industries, until halted by stern action of the police and the courts.[63] In the Detroit plants of the Chrysler Corporation, an employee representation council was functioning but most of its members submitted their resignations through Richard Frankensteen, an officer of the United Automobile Workers of America. The council had originally been suggested by Walter P. Chrysler, and the defection took place in the midst of negotiations between the union and the company.[64]

During negotiations Frankensteen failed to obtain a satisfactory answer to a proposal. It was a signal for a sit-down strike, starting on March 8, 1937, in eight of the Detroit Chrysler plants employing over 60,000 workers. President Kent T. Keller and B. E. Hutchinson conferred on ending the demonstration with the union officers, but no agreement was reached. Governor Murphy arrived in Detroit on March 11 and said he would avoid intervening unless an emergency arose. At the same time a sit-down strike started in the Detroit Hudson plant. The Chrysler Company secured a writ from Circuit Judge Allan Campbell ordering the ouster of strikers, but this order was not enforced. On March 17, Murphy warned the strikers that court orders had to be obeyed, but neither he nor Sheriff Thomas Wilcox would enforce the court order; the sheriff claimed his force was inadequate.

Governor Murphy asked Walter Chrysler and Lewis to confer with him, on March 24. At the same time, the governor called for the evacuation of the plants and announced that troops would move into the city if the conference between the parties broke down. Lewis agreed that the sit-down strikers would leave the plants, and an agreement was reached on April 7. It recognized the union as bargaining agent for its members and stated that no coercion would be directed against nonunion men or prejudice against union members, that court proceedings would be canceled, and that the contract would continue until March 31, 1938. Negotiations on the details were to be resumed later. Walter Chrysler, who had negotiated the agreement on behalf of his company, thanked Murphy and James F. Dewey, a conciliator from the U.S. Department of Labor, for their assistance. He said that he "enjoyed meeting Mr. Lewis. He contributed a great deal to the successful outcome of the negotiations."[65]

While the strike was over, the taking of possession of plants was arousing grave concern among many who were not hostile to organized labor. Senator James Byrnes introduced an amendment to the Guffey-Vinson coal bill condemning the use of this tactic and declaring it illegal. It was defeated by a vote of 48 to 36. A proposal to investigate the sit-down strike failed in the House of Representatives the following day by a vote of 236 to 149.[66]

Almost immediately after its victories, the union faced the danger of a split in the ranks. Many of the 350,000 members who had joined the union had no previous experience with a labor organization. Although Detroit was a leading open-shop city up to the 1930's, an active radical movement had developed there through the years. In fact, a Socialist administration had governed Flint, the future center of the sit-down strike. While unionism was absent, a fairly large group of activists affiliated with various brands of radicalism developed in the stronghold of the industry.[67]

It is a minor irony that in one of the historic strongholds of the open shop, the stability of a union was imperiled by a split between the Progressives, or administration faction, and the Unity caucuses made up of Socialists and Communists. Because of differences among the disputants, David Dubinsky, attending the 1937 UAW convention as a representative of the CIO, told the delegates that if Communists were employed "in our industries, they are entitled to membership in the Union. And as long as they place the interests of their fellow members above the interests of a political party, they are entitled to participate in the Union's activities. As I say, whether workers are Republicans, Socialists, or Communists, they have their place within a trade union. Only when they abuse their membership, only when they become destructive, only when they serve a party first and the union next, my quarrel with them starts."[68] As a principle, the statement appears valid, but Dubinsky, who was a leader against the Communist assault upon his union, knew that the Communists were not likely to put the union first and the party next. His position was undoubtedly influenced by a desire to prevent a serious rupture within the youthful organization, and the hope that it would be able to throw off its infantile leftism in time.

Ora Gasaway, an international representative of the United Mine Workers of America, was also active in the promotion of peace. He told the delegates: "Your union has grown to a place where you are going to have to cut out all these factional fights in conventions and assemblies. . . . So I say when you speak about democracy for God's sake let us get down to business."[69] Lewis sounded the same note. The differences between the Progressives and the members of the Unity caucus did not impress him. As far as Lewis was concerned he "was for the officers of the United Automobile Workers because I think that they have covered themselves and your union with glory in the degree of their achievement." He compared the achievements of the union to the feat of the rope walker Blondin who carried a man on his back on a steel cable stretched across Niagara Falls. Lewis regarded the complaints of the leaders being radical or conservative as equivalent to the complaint that Blondin in the performance of his perilous feat leaned too far right or too far left.[70]

The achievements of the United Auto Workers, in terms of the situation in 1937, were best summed up by Dubinsky: "You are a young organization, built only through a miracle, I might say, and you are bound to become one of the most powerful, one of the largest organizations in our country. No other union, as wise or experienced as we may be, has been able to boast of building a union of three hundred and fifty thousand members within one year."[71] The representatives of the CIO were trying to keep the union together. The Progressives had a majority of the delegates and could control the convention, but the leaders of the CIO believed it would lead to a split. The two factions agreed, "to go along with the proposal of myself [Gasaway] representing Mr. Lewis and the proposal put to you this morning by Brother David Dubinsky."[72]

The compromise was approved by B. K. Gebert, the Communist "commissar" operating in the auto industry. Sixteen posts on the executive board were given to the Progressives and eight to the Unity caucus.[73] Although Martin was in the lead at the convention, he was unable to retain his position. In the shifting of alliances, politics was not without influence. Nevertheless, Martin lacked the political and leadership abilities to cope with the serious internal and external problems confronting the organization.

Before twelve months had passed, new and even more serious troubles were brewing. A sharp drop in membership necessitating reductions in staff accentuated the problems facing the United Auto Workers. Martin sought to solve his internal difficulties by suspending five members of the executive board for factionalism; all of them belonged to the opposition. The CIO intervened and Sidney Hillman and Philip Murray were able to gain a compromise. The expelled leaders were reinstated and Hillman, Murray, Martin, and R. J. Thomas, a vice-president of the union and a Martin supporter, were appointed as a coordinating committee to settle factional differences. But the committee was unable to maintain harmony, since Martin appeared to be losing influence. After the breakdown of Martin's efforts to gain an agreement with the Ford Company, Martin suspended fifteen of the twenty-four members of the executive board.

Martin charged his opponents with making false accusations and violating the Constitution. He, therefore, terminated the meeting, convened on January 10, 1939, to hear reports on the Ford Company negotiations.[74] Murray and Hillman tried once more to establish peaceful relations, but they failed. Martin charged the board with being dominated by Communists, and the board decided to remove him and proceed on its own. R. J. Thomas, a former Martin follower, was elected acting president by the Board.[75] There were now two rival organizations in the field, and each called a convention. In a statement, the CIO announced it "supports fully and completely the position of the international executive board."[76]

The statement of the CIO declared that Martin had agreed with the work of the coordinating committee appointed by John L. Lewis during the 1938 dispute. Since that time the committee had settled twenty-eight disputes referred to it by Martin, and he and others agreed to the settlements. The statement charged Martin had refused to consult with the board, to participate in its meetings, and to accept its decisions.[77]

The overwhelming majority of local unions and members decided to send delegates to the convention of the executive board. Meeting in Detroit on March 5, the Martin convention reported a minimum representation of under 63,000 members, about one-fourth subsequently represented at the Cleveland convention of his rivals. At his convention Martin attacked Lewis for having foisted Communist officers upon the union at the 1937 convention. He also charged Lewis with being a dictator.[78] In contrast, the Cleveland convention claimed to represent over three hundred thousand members; there can be no doubt it had by far the largest following among the automobile workers. The Communist party announced that it had "decided some time ago to abolish all Party fractions in the unions. . . . In order to remove any misunderstanding and to facilitate the above mentioned processes the Communist Party has decide to abolish all Communist papers now being issued within unions or shops. . . . The Communists will have no caucuses and will not act as an organized group. They are free to act on every question on the basis of their understanding and judgment. . . . Naturally we have some opinion on what would be best for the UAWA and for the labor movement. However, if Party members are influenced by our opinions, it will be of their own free will."[79] This statement is phrased in the Aesopian language which party followers well understand and, in fact, was a request that all except Communists refrain from forming factions. Walter Reuther, who emerged as the leader of the opposition to the Communists in the union, understood their signals and refused to be trapped.

Both Chrysler and the General Motors Corporation announced they would not deal with either faction. The CIO group, opening its convention on March 28, was addressed by Murray, Hillman, and Brophy. At the insistence of the CIO representatives, three CIO vice-presidents supported by the Communists agreed to withdraw as vice-presidents. Murray and Hillman advised that only one vice-president be retained, and it was finally accepted.[80] They also supported R. J. Thomas for president and George Addes for secretary-treasurer. Both were chosen. Thomas, an auto worker since 1923, had worked in the Cadillac and Chrysler plants in Detroit. He was a founder of the Automotive Industrial Workers Association made up of employees of Chrysler Corporation, and was elected its national president. After the merger of his union with the UAW, Thomas became president of Chrysler Local 7, Detroit.

The convention requested a continuation of the coordinating committee which had been meeting with the union officers since the fall of 1938 in an effort to prevent a split. However, the most important problem facing the CIO-Auto Union was the gaining of recognition by the major auto firms. The General Motors Corporation in letters to Thomas and Martin expressed a willingness to recognize bargaining committees in forty-six plants where there were no disputes over jurisdiction, but would not recognize either faction in plants where both were seeking to represent employees. Martin tried to call out the General Motors' workers in Flint and failed.[81]

A strike against the Briggs Corporation was settled. Action was also started against the General Motors Corporation after ten days by the CIO-UAW, which withdrew the skilled tool and die makers from plants during the crucial period of model changeover. This maneuver was effective, since it released the union from the possible burden of financially supporting a large body of strikers. The skilled men constituted only a small fraction of the total labor force. Employees idled, but not on strike, were able under the Michigan unemployment compensation act to draw benefits. The law was subsequently revised because of this experience. The tactic worked and the CIO-UAW was recognized.

The CIO Auto Workers' Union became in a short time the dominant organization in the industry, and the Martin organization affiliated with the AFL in 1939. With a grant of $50,000 from the CIO, a campaign to organize the Ford Company was begun in the fall of 1940. Michael F. Widman, a coal miner and staff member of the CIO, came to Detroit and assumed command. Richard T. Leonard, a regional director of the union, was the chief organizer from the Automobile Workers' Union. Sparring between the parties continued over a period of several months, but the union made considerable headway. When discharges of union activists began in the spring of 1941, a strike became inevitable. It was called on April 2, 1941. The entire force of 85,000 left the River Rouge plant in the suburban community near Detroit.

Crucial aid was supplied by a group of Negro leaders who sought to avoid a split between white and Negro workers. The Ford Company was a large employer of Negro labor, and its policies were more enlightened than those of many other employers in Michigan and elsewhere. Intervention by the state and federal governments led to a settlement ten days after the beginning of the strike. It called for no discrimination in rehiring, and the expediting of an election.

In the election for representatives for collective bargaining, the CIO union defeated its AFL rival by 51,866 to 20,364 votes in the Rouge plant, and 2,008 to 587 in the Lincoln plant. Slightly more than 2,000 votes were cast for no union.[82] The union now controlled the major producers in the automotive industries.

Factional divisions reappeared. A group centering around Walter Reuther was opposed by members of the executive board, including Secretary-Treasurer George F. Addes. President R. J. Thomas was a member of the latter group which had a number of Communists in its ranks. Several leaders shifted alliances from year to year; a number of non-Communists cooperated with the anti-Reuther group. Reuther's ambition to gain the chief post in the union was generally known. He achieved his aim in 1946 when he defeated Thomas by a narrow vote.[83]

With the Steel and Rubber Workers' Unions, the Auto Workers' organization represents the major achievements of the CIO. Under Reuther's leadership, the organization has shown imagination and drive. It is well managed, with a devoted staff, and without many traces of lethargy, complacency, or corruption. Nevertheless, like other organizations, it is hemmed in by its economic environment. Many members of the heroic generation are retired or old. For many newcomers, the days of the sit-down are only history, which they appreciate and admire, but it is an experience which they share only vicariously. The UAW is a great organization of labor, by the standards of the past or present. Yet, like others, it has had to adapt itself to the needs of its own members, for otherwise its *raison d'être* would be gone.

The gains under Reuther's imaginative leadership have been substantial, but there is a tendency to downgrade and even to avoid mentioning the names of a number of men who made major contributions to the unionization of the automobile worker. Perhaps, the outstanding example of this neglect is R. J. Thomas. He took over the union at the insistence of Murray and Hillman. Whatever limitations he may have had, he piloted the organization through one of its more difficult periods. He was president when the union achieved victory at Ford and when the AFL union was able to poll one-third of the vote. Undoubtedly, the ineffectiveness of the Martin leadership lightened the task of the UAW-CIO, but by 1946, when Thomas was defeated, the major organizing in the automobile industry had been accomplished. Reuther was necessary, if for no other reason than to end the factional bickering and to eliminate the split over an issue—Stalinism —which had no relevance to the union's activity or objectives. But the role of Thomas, Richard Leonard, and a number of others in the rise to power and prestige of the United Auto Workers' Union cannot be permanently suppressed.[84]

CHAPTER 39

Organizing the Steel Industry

The defeat of the twenty-four cooperating AFL unions in the 1919 steel strike put an end to organization campaigns in that industry for fifteen years. A Communist organization, the Steel and Metal Workers' Union, was established in 1929, and it made sporadic efforts to stir up interest. While it achieved little in the several strikes in which it was active, it gave a number of organizers to subsequent campaigns. The position of the industry on union organization was unambiguously stated by Robert P. Lamont. Testifying for the American Iron and Steel Institute, he told the Senate Finance Committee, considering legislation creating the NIRA, that the "industry stands positively for the open shop. It is unalterably opposed to the closed shop. . . . It is opposed to conducting negotiations regarding such matters otherwise than with its own employees; it is unwilling to conduct them with outside organizations of labor or with individuals not its employees. . . . If this position is not protected in the bill, the industry is positive in the belief that the intent and purpose of the bill cannot be accomplished."[1] The adoption of Section 7(a) did not meet with the approval of the steel industry.

The Steel Code was approved by President Franklin D. Roosevelt on August 19, 1933. After a ninety-day trial, it was extended until June 11, 1934. The board of directors of the American Iron and Steel Institute was appointed code authority. Under the provisions of the code, the workweek in the industry was limited to a maximum of forty-eight hours and to six days in any week, but the amount of work that could be performed in any six-month period was limited to an average of forty hours per week. Minimum rates for common labor were specified, and workers above that grade were to be paid a minimum of 15 per cent more than the rate prevailing on July 14, 1933.

Membership in the Amalgamated had steadily declined throughout the 1920's and by the first quarter of 1933, it had fallen to 4,800—under 2 per cent of production workers employed in the industry.[2]

The National Industrial Recovery Act stimulated the interest of steel workers in organization. A large number of company and noncompany unions were formed during the period in which the code was effective. According to Carroll Daugherty, there were only seven "formal employee representation plans operating in the [steel] industry in 1932. In addition, there were about ten companies that had informal arrangements for grievance presentation and adjustment through employee safety committees and through employee mutual benefit and relief associations. By the end of 1933, there were, according to the data supplied by the American Iron and Steel Institute, at least ninety-three formal plans in existence, including the pre-Code formal plans and the pre-Code informal arrangements which were formulated during the Code period."[3]

Many of the plans were organized by the companies or with their support. Daugherty was convinced "that the prospective and actual passage of the Recovery Act, together with the prospective and actual burst of outside union organizing activities, furnished the main stimulus to the establishment of employee representation plans. Neither can there be any question that the overwhelming majority of the plans were inaugurated by the companies themselves. In very few of the plans did the original suggestions for introduction come from the workers themselves."[4] Many of the plans in the large companies were established in June 1933, and the smaller companies introduced them in the period between June 1933 and January 1934.[5]

Expansion of outside unions in the industry manifested itself almost entirely in the establishment of new lodges of the Amalgamated Association of Iron, Steel and Tin Workers. By October 1933, the McKeesport district was about 85 per cent organized, and the closing down of headquarters, dismissing of organizers, and the refusal by the Amalgamated to request recognition of the companies led the McKeesport Pioneer Lodge to appeal to William Green for a federal charter. Green urged the lodge to remain in the Amalgamated and asked Michael Tighe president of the Amalgamated, to examine the complaints. Tighe replied that the Pioneer Lodge still owed the international per capita and the shortage of funds necessitated the closing of headquarters in the McKeesport area.[6]

Beginning in the third quarter of 1933, strikes in the industry increased. During the Code period, twenty-six strikes were called, twenty-one of them for union recognition. A major strike took place at the plants of the Weirton

Steel Company in Weirton and Clarksburg, West Virginia, and Steubenville, Ohio; it lasted from September 24 to October 18, 1934.[7] All of the strikes in the period involved the issues of discrimination or recognition. The walkouts failed to achieve their essential objectives of compelling a policy of toleration for the newly formed labor organizations.

The failure of the union to hold its membership gains or to compel the companies to grant it a modicum of recognition was in part responsible for the emergence of an insurgent group seeking a more aggressive policy. In April 1934 the special Amalgamated convention presented a seven-point program which called for recognition of the union and warned that a simultaneous or nationwide strike would be called by the middle of June if this demand was not met. The convention reconvened on June 15.

Pending consideration of its program of settlement, the convention suspended the strike. The industry suggested the appointment of an industrial relations board of three to hear differences between employers and employees and their organizations. Because the plan required that employers and company unions each be given one representative, the Amalgamated naturally concluded it would always be in a minority and opposed this solution. Addressing the convention, William Green urged the avoidance of a strike, if at all possible, and the presentation of a program of settlement which called for the appointment of an impartial board of three to adjust complaints, mediate disputes, and to arrange for collective bargaining conferences between employers and their unions.

A committee from the convention visited President Roosevelt, who expressed the "hope that some method will be found to adjust all the points that are in controversy and to preserve orderly relations without sacrificing any principle that is involved."[8] Secretary of Labor Frances Perkins was authorized to deal with the matter.

On June 28 the National Steel Labor Relations Board was appointed by Secretary Perkins under Public Resolution No. 44 with Judge Walter P. Stacy as chairman and Rear Admiral Henry A. Wiley and James A. Mullenbach as members. The companies, when requested, began to deal informally with the Amalgamated on conditions of employment and grievances. "By the end of October 1934, the Board had held three private unrecorded hearings or conferences and three public recorded hearings, each of which resulted in private agreements for the informal, open shop sort of dealings with Amalgamated lodges."[9] Various devices were introduced to make negotiations between the union and some employers easier; avoidance of explicit recognition was the reason for the use of these indirect methods. On October 15, 1934, the U.S. Steel Corporation proposed to the National Steel Labor Board that the "Carnegie Steel Company will receive and negotiate with members of any organization as such as representatives of the employees they represent irrespective of their number, and will undertake to adjust their complaints as to wages, discharges and similar items, but the Company does not engage to make any term contracts."[10] This proposal was rejected by the Amalgamated and the AFL because it did not contain a provision for majority rule. In the negotiations, the company improved its proposal slightly, but never to the point that it became satisfactory to organized labor.

Reporting on this matter to the executive council, Green said:

Our representatives were called in to meet Judge Stacy and Admiral Wiley (National Steel Labor Relations Board) and they presented a plan. They said "Would it not be better to accept this plan than run the risk of a fight with the Steel Corporation." Mr. Ogburn, the attorney representing the Steel workers, came to me and I told him under no circumstances would we agree to their proposals. It was a proportional representation plan. No self-respecting labor man could consider such a proposition. I was called in and met with them. I told them "never." I told the story of how I had gone to Pittsburgh and appealed to the delegates to refrain from striking, to trust the President and trust the Board he had set up. I said our organization could never live under that, negotiating with company unions, negotiating with independents. If they were willing to make concessions they would make it to the company union and we could never live under it any more than we could live under the automobile settlement. . . . The steel magnates came to Washington, then one day a call came to me to come to the White House. President Tighe was notified and he came. I went over and we met outside the room before going in, and who was there but Myron Taylor of the Steel Corporation, Grace of Bethlehem, Reed representing Mr. Weir, Jones and Laughlin and Girdler of Republic Steel. When I got in Stacy and Wiley handed me the sheet and it read as I told you except they had modified the second clause but it was the same old proposal. Miss Perkins was there, the Steel Board was there. I was there along with Tighe and Ogburn, who has been representing the Steel Workers and the American Federation of Labor before the National Steel Labor Relations Board, and these steel magnates. The President said he had called us in to see if we could not compose our differences. . . . The proposition was there—he thought it was worthy of consideration. He read it. "That may not be all that either side would like but I am just wondering whether it would not be better than getting into a conflict. I called upon labor and industry to establish a truce and this would be carrying out the spirit and letter of that truce." He read it over and emphasized it. "That gives labor representation and recognizes committees. They can speak for the workers they represent. It gives minority representation. That is right. Let workers decide what organization they want to be identified with. It would be in accordance with the spirit of Section 7(a), collective bargaining, and workers will be in the organization of their own choice." There was a bit of silence. I asked him if that had been sponsored by the Steel Board. They replied not exactly but it was a proposal they had considered and hoped it would be acceptable.

Then Mr. Taylor arose. "Mr. President, this is not entirely acceptable to us.

This provides for us going a long way. We want to treat with our men fairly and carry out the spirit of collective bargaining. In response to your request in furtherance of a truce in behalf of United States Steel Corporation, I accept." Grace got up and said the same thing, reluctantly. Great silence again. I had to rise and tell them that labor could not accept the proposal. It was not collective bargaining as we understand collective bargaining. No successful collective bargaining could be carried on except through one agency representing the workers and one representing the employers. We may theorize as much as we wish but collective bargaining cannot be carried on except through one agency representing the workers and one the employers and one agreement reached covering all groups. I said this was deceptive. With the fight that is made on trade unions we could not live under this proposal. After that the President said even though we had not gotten together he hoped we might try to reach an agreement.

After that was ended President Tighe went back to the Steel Board and objected in toto. The Board ordered an election, and the order was no more than issued than the order of the Court came out restraining the election.[11]

Factionalism

Dissatisfaction with the progress of organizing the industry was widespread among many of the newly recruited as well as some of those who had belonged to the Amalgamated for some time. In an effort to organize their forces, the insurgents met in Pittsburgh on February 3, 1935. Tighe thereupon suspended the lodges which had sent representatives to the meeting. A National Emergency Committee was formed with Clarence Irwin of Youngstown, chairman, and L. A. Morris, secretary-treasurer. A number of the suspended lodges protested to Green, who, while denying he could intervene in the affairs of an autonomous affiliate, sought a reconciliation.[12]

Green, disturbed by Tighe's suspension of seventy-four lodges, appointed James Wilson a former head of the Pattern Makers League of North America and a member of the AFL Executive Council, to mediate the dispute. Tighe soon informed Green "the International Executive Board of the Amalgamated Association of Iron, Steel and Tin Workers, were duly elected by referendum vote of the membership . . . [and] feel they are fully qualified and competent by the knowledge and experience they have acquired to deal with all questions that affect the Association welfare, without interference from outside sources, irrespective of what the good intentions of the sources may be."[13]

Despite opposition, Green was able to have Tighe accept Wilson as mediator. As a result, the international executive board rescinded, on July 25, 1935, its "former action in revoking the charters of those lodges who had attended the unauthorized and illegal meeting held in Pittsburgh, Pa., on February 3, 1935."[14] The agreement by no means ended the differences, but, largely through the efforts of Green's agent, Wilson, the split in the Amalgamated was ended in October 1935.[15]

The Dispute over Structure

During the fight between the locals and the International Union in the steel industry, the executive council of the AFL considered the assistance that might be provided by the AFL in organizing the steel industry. Green reported that the "Amalgamated is not functioning, [it is] weak, inefficient, losing ground . . . all the time and we must meet the situation just as it is, not in a theoretical way but in a practical way. There are a lot of young men there wishing to be organized, enthusiastic. Perhaps we can organize a staff and carry it along and we will have to supply the money and place someone in charge, and press into service a staff to carry on the organizing work. That is the fact that we must face."[16]

Daniel Tobin of the Teamsters' Union believed that although a union had rights to its jurisdiction, the mandate of the convention to organize the steel industry had to be considered. Tighe thought that a campaign to organize the industry would require at least $200,000 and he was "firmly convinced by the experience of the last eighteen months that to make any headway, plants must be organized industrially. The question of how to place them is one that can only be determined by the workers themselves."[17] In an answer to a question from Hutcheson, Green observed that the council should determine how the steel workers should be organized. This view brought an immediate protest from Wharton.

Lewis entered the discussion by declaring that the steel worker could not be organized except on an industrial basis. "If you believe otherwise," he said, "you may as well save your efforts, your trouble and your money." Answering Wharton directly, Lewis said:

The form of organization in the railroad industry which was the most remarkable character of cooperation ever manifested in the American Federation of Labor, had been brought about on a gradual basis starting with the most skilled men in the industry. You cannot do that in the steel industry. Unless the American Federation of Labor can arrange its affairs to do that we might as well save our money. We have been experimenting for a quarter of a century, as in the automobile and other modern mass production industries. The American Federation of labor is being threatened by its ineffectiveness. You have to utilize the services of these young men in the steel industry. They have no training, no background in trade unionism, no experience in the labor movement. They do not know what it is all about. . . . The steel workers originally were comprised of the skilled men and they refused to take in common labor in the plants. They were afraid of dragging down the skilled men to the status of common labor. The officers of the Amalgamated have been trained in that school. The world has gone by and left it sitting there, and the world will not go back. I do not know the cost. I only know it should be done whether we win or lose. The letter from the Amalgamated is full of advice but makes no suggestions as to what the Amalgamated is willing to do, stepping aside and permitting the Federation to follow its own policy.[18]

Lewis expressed the view that there would be little difficulty in organizing the steel workers, but it would be a problem to gain recognition. His view was shared by John A. Fitch, a leading student of the steel industry and its workers. Fitch informed Green that he believed "it is possible now to organize the steel workers, particularly in Steel Corporation mills, without danger of immediate reprisals on the part of the company . . . I wanted to put this before you while you and the Executive Council are considering the matter of organization in the steel industry. I do not believe there has been as propitious a time for organizing workers in the industry since the Homestead strike as there is now."[19] He felt difficulties would be compounded if the craft unions were to insist upon their rights to control in their jurisdictions in the industry. Instead, he wanted the AFL to take hold of the organizing drive, and he hoped that another international union could be formed. Hutcheson warned against interfering with another organization even if it were in bad straits. Green pointed to the directive of the 1934 convention to organize the steel industry. He was convinced that "the Amalgamated cannot organize these workers with their own resources or the set-up as it is, with the National organization based upon a philosophy upon which it rests or upon pursuing the policy which it is following. It may have been allright when the puddler and roller were the factor but the mechanical devices have made him a lesser factor than years ago. The puddler has completely gone. The change has been taking place but the Amalgamated has been standing committed to its old traditional policy. You cannot organize a great industry that way."[20]

After the discussion had gone on for more than a day, Thomas Rickert submitted the following proposal which was adopted: "That the President be instructed to inaugurate a joint organizing campaign of all unions in the steel industry; that he endeavor to secure the cooperation, financial and moral, of all existing organizations in and out of this industry in this campaign and that to him be left and delegated the planning and direction of this campaign."[21] The adoption of the resolution meant that the craft organizations would be allowed to recruit in the steel industry.

On October 20, 1935, the Amalgamated submitted a plan of organization to the executive council. It called for the AFL taking over the campaign, but the new recruits were to be mustered in lodges of the Amalgamated.[22] William D. Mahon, a member of the executive council and head of the Street Car Men's Union, thought that the plan of organization submitted by the Amalgamated was needlessly complicated and lacked understanding.[23]

The Committee for Industrial Organization

The formation of the Committee for Industrial Organization affected the position of the AFL and its affiliate in the steel industry. Lewis was convinced that organization of this crucial sector was possible if adequate finances and staff were provided by the general labor movement. On February 22, 1936, Lewis and Charles P. Howard, secretary of the CIO, proposed to the AFL that the eight unions affiliated with the CIO would "offer the services of trained organizers from our respective staffs for a properly planned campaign to organize steel."[24] They suggested the raising of a fund of $1.5 million "to launch the campaign on the requisite scale, and of this amount we pledge ourselves to raise the sum of $500,000 from our eight unions."[25]

The conditions for making this contribution were (1) the campaign of organization be conducted on industrial lines and (2) the leadership "be such as to inspire confidence of success. There must be placed in charge a responsible, energetic person, with a genuine understanding of the steel workers' problems, who will work in conjunction with an advisory committee representative of the unions supporting the drive."[26] Finally, Lewis and Howard suggested a conference to work out the details.

In accordance with the usual practice, the letter was submitted to all the members of the executive council for consideration.[27] The replies of a number of the members showed the reason why the AFL could not organize the industry. Harry Bates doubted "whether the $500,000, as offered by the Committee for Industrial Organization, would be forthcoming even if you were inclined to accept the strings that are tied to their offer."[28] Tobin regarded Lewis' letter as propaganda, opposed the invasion of the craft unions' jurisdictions, and believed "There isn't a chance in the world at this time to organize the steel workers. I make this statement after thirty-five years of following the history of that organization. It may be that if the Wagner Bill is sustained in court and other labor legislation is sustained, we may be able to get a foothold, but only after labor legislation allowing the workers to organize [will it be] possible to make any successful drive on organization."[29]

Other members of the council were either dubious of the good faith of the CIO, or did not want to embark upon any plan which would recognize industrial organization in the steel industry. On March 9, 1936, Green requested the International Union to aid financially in a vaguely planned campaign to organize the steel industry. Only 38 of the 110 affiliated international unions replied, 5 of which pledged $8,625 for the fund of $750,000 the AFL sought to raise.[30]

The convention of the Amalgamated Association in Cannonsburg, Pennsylvania, on May 8, 1936, became of crucial importance in the future plans of the AFL and its de facto rival, the CIO. Green, on behalf of the council promised an "organizing campaign will be launched and carried forward by the American Federation of Labor in cooperation with the Amalgamated Association of Iron, Steel and Tin Workers and the representatives of other organizations interested, affected and involved."[31] Lewis, after denouncing the proposal of the AFL, offered to "cooperate with your organization to the extent of the expenditure of a half million dollars."[32] Obviously both Green and Lewis were sufficiently concerned with maintaining "organizational" regularity to seek approval of the heads of a moribund union which had demonstrated its incapacity to meet the challenge of organizing the industry. The Amalgamated had a number of younger men in its ranks, and it may have been those who were the chief target of these rival leaders. Lewis may have also believed that he was on better ground to have the Amalgamated cooperating in his drive.

The sixty-first convention of the Amalgamated voted to conduct a campaign in the steel industry under its own auspices, requested other unions to waive their jurisdictional rights in the industry, and invited donations of organizers and funds by other unions. Explaining the action of the convention, Tighe told Green "that as a Sovereign Organization in itself, it intended to conduct its own business and affairs without interference or dictation from any source."[33]

Following the adjournment of the convention, the executive board secretly conferred with Green, who informed them of the organizing plans of the federation. They were found unsatisfactory by the board. Secretary Louis Leonard now sought a conference with John L. Lewis. The latter wired that "it would be a complete waste of time for all concerned for your committee to attend this meeting unless you are prepared to carry out the instructions imposed upon your officers by the recent Cannonsburg Convention. The policy of fluttering procrastination followed by your board is already responsible for the loss of some weeks of time and must be abandoned. I am fully advised concerning your secret conference with Green in Coshocton last week and know, as you must now know, that he has nothing to offer you except meaningless words and further delay."[34] Lewis further added that the Amalgamated "executive board must decide whether it will cooperate or obstruct. If you do not know your mind, please stay home. If you are prepared to accept the help of the Committee for Industrial Organization, which is the only agency which can or will aid your organization and the workers in the steel industry, you will be made welcome."[35]

A CIO committee, authorized by Lewis, met with Secretary-Treasurer Leonard but failed to reach an agreement. Lewis then told the Amalgamated Executive Board:

We have been trying for nearly two years to get action by the American Federation of Labor to organize steel, and we are naturally impatient with perfunctory actions that get nowhere. Delay on your part would be just as contrary to the mandate of your convention as has been the delay by the Executive Council in relation to the orders of the A.F. of L. delegates. The C.I.O. has stated its genuine desire to cooperate with your union in making good its chartered jurisdiction. But a right to jurisdiction ceases to have weight unless it is put into effect.[36]

At its meetings in Pittsburgh, in the last week of May, the executive board of the Amalgamated decided that the "A.F. of L. Executive Council is not ready to promote the campaign which the last two Federation conventions ordered. The Committee for Industrial Organization of which John L. Lewis is president renewed its offer to contribute funds and organizers from time to time if such a campaign as the 61st Convention ordered is sponsored at once by the Amalgamated Association. After a full week's session the Board . . . wired President Lewis for a conference to arrange such assistance and received his reply . . . setting Wednesday, June 3, at 8 P.M., in his Washington Office."[37]

Representatives of the International Executive Board met with the leaders of the CIO at the agreed time and signed the Memorandum of Agreement under which the Amalgamated joined the CIO, the Steel Workers' Organizing Committee was established, and the CIO agreed to donate $500,000 to finance the organizing campaign in the steel industry. It was also agreed that the Steel Workers' Organizing Committee was to "have power to grant dispensation from the payment of initiation fees to all persons joining the Amalgamated Association during such time as it deems advisable."[38]

The Steel Workers' Organizing Committee began to draw on the funds allocated to it by the CIO. At its first meeting on June 17, 1936, it reported that a general headquarters had immediately been established in the Grant Building in Pittsburgh, and that an executive committee with Philip Murray as chairman had been appointed. In addition to representatives from the Amalgamated, the Miners' Union, and the CIO, Julius Hochman of the Ladies' Garment Workers' Union and Leo Krzycki of the Amalgamated Clothing Workers Union were members. A publicity division, headed by J. B. S. Hardman, was engaged, and other staff people were appointed. The steel producing areas were divided into three regions with a director in each. Clinton S. Golden was in charge of District No. 1 with headquarters in Pittsburgh; Van A. Bittner, a district president of the Mine Workers' Union, was made director of District No. 2 centering in Chicago, and William Mitch, head of the Alabama Federation of Labor and a long-time official of the Mine Workers, headed District No. 3 with headquarters in Birmingham.

But the Steel Workers' Organizing Committee was convinced that only by a massive drive could the industry be organized. The committee therefore opened 42 additional subdistrict offices, and by the middle of July it had a staff of 284 employees, some of them on temporary loan from the

United Mine Workers of America or one of the other CIO unions.[39]

Iron Age noted: "The methods used by SWOC in its organization were far different from any used in the steel industry before. An elaborate and efficient headquarters in one of Pittsburgh's best buildings [has been established] and at least two hundred high pressure organizers were employed." After describing the methods of publicity and organizing, the magazine concluded that "SWOC has adopted the most up-to-date and efficient business methods in its organization drive."[40]

The American Iron and Steel Institute, speaking for the industry, announced in a series of advertisements that the purpose of the campaign was to impose the closed shop upon the steel worker. It stated that the "overwhelming majority of the employees of the steel industry recently participated in annual elections under their own collective bargaining plans and elected their representatives for collective bargaining. The elections were conducted by the employees themselves by secret ballot. One of the purposes of the announced campaign is to overthrow these plans and the representatives elected."[41] The institute warned that the organization drive threatened to interrupt the revival of employment that the industry had experienced.

Unmindful of the opposition, the committee went on with its campaign. In contrast to the 1919 effort, many of the workers recruited did not, in the early years, pay either an initiation fee or dues. Estimates have been made that in the first ten months of the organizing committee's existence "nearly $1,500,000" had been donated.[42] Another estimate was that by the summer of 1937, the United Mine Workers of America had contributed the great bulk of $2.5 million to the committee.[43]

The drive was novel in that its organizers not only sought to recruit single employees in the steel industry but tried to win over the company unions that had proliferated after the enactment of the National Industrial Recovery Act. The earliest and perhaps the most spectacular of the movements to undermine the dependence of the company on management was the convention attended by thirty-three delegates from eleven plants of the American Sheet and Tin Plate Company at New Castle, Pennsylvania, in November 1935.[44]

At the same time employees of the South Chicago plant of Carnegie-Illinois began pulling away from the company union and organized an independent: the Associated Employees. Three lodges of the Amalgamated in Indiana Harbor informed Green, in December 1935, that the company unions were on the verge of cracking.[45]

With the formation of the organizing committee, the employee representation plan was subjected to competition. The Associated Employees joined the committee in November 1935, and an attempt to halt the trend was made with the formation of a central joint conference of the several groups in the plants of the U.S. Steel Corporation. A tug-of-war started between the proponents of the company union and organizing committee, with the latter gradually carrying the day.

Early in November 1936 the U.S. Steel Corporation offered a 10 per cent increase in wages to its company unions. At the urging of leaders of the organizing committee, the majority of these organizations rejected the offer. Moreover, Secretary of Labor Frances Perkins, as the arbitrator under the contract, held that the company unions could not sign a wage agreement.[46] More than two hundred representatives of company unions from forty-two steel plants meeting in Pittsburgh on December 20, bolted to the organizing committee after hearing speeches by Arthur Young, in charge of employee relations for U.S. Steel, and Philip Murray. Resolutions drawn up by Elmer J. Maloy, a representative of the Duquesne plant of the Carnegie-Illinois plant, called for a national wage agreement, a minimum wage of five dollars a day.[47] The organizing committee had succeeded in breaking down the greatest obstacle to its advance.

Collective Bargaining in Big Steel

For twenty-eight years, the U.S. Steel Corporation had not bargained with a union it did not control. It had to decide whether it would meet the demands for recognition by resistance or make concessions. Beginning on January 9, 1937, John L. Lewis and Myron C. Taylor, chairman of the board of the U.S. Steel Corporation, discussed the recognition of the organizing committee. At the fourth meeting, Taylor came up with the formula of recognition for members of the union only; almost, but not quite the same one offered and rejected by the AFL in 1935. Accepted by Lewis, Murray, and the board of directors of the corporation, the limited recognition was sweetened by a wage increase of ten cents an hour and tonnage rates were increased so as to allow for eighty cents more a day in earnings. The work schedule was set at eight hours per day and forty hours per week, with time and one-half for work in excess of these amounts.[48] A contract was signed on March 17, 1937, with Benjamin Fairless heading the negotiators for the Carnegie-Steel Company and Philip Murray for the Steel Workers' Organizing Committee.

The signing of the contract could be regarded as a breach in the anti-union stronghold, but it was gained through personal and political influence and pressure. For all of its merits, the locals, the 134 established up to January 1, 1937, had not been tested in "battle." The committee met the first test at the Jones and Laughlin plant in Aliquippa, Pennsylvania. The Jones and Laughlin Company appeared to be one of a group of independents who wanted to avoid formal agreement with the organizing committee. Its attitude was unclear, because its officers negotiated with Murray soon after the agreement in Big Steel, but the terms offered were unsatisfactory. The company was willing to accept the same kind of contract as the U.S. Steel Corporation, but it wanted to retain the right to deal with other groups. It was also willing to grant the committee exclusive bargaining rights if it won an election conducted by the National Labor Relations Board within ten days. "There was doubt as to whether the union could win an election even if the company kept its hands off."[49] The committee therefore risked a strike, and the 25,000 workers employed in Aliquippa responded unanimously. The strike began on May 12, 1937, and ended in a preliminary agreement at the end of thirty-six hours.

Under the agreement, a collective bargaining election was held under the auspices of the National Labor Relations Board on May 20. The Steel Workers' Organizing Committee won by a vote of 17,028 to 7,207, a substantial but by no means overwhelming approval; the union was to gain later from various groups in the industry. An agreement following the pattern of Big Steel was negotiated, except that the committee gained exclusive bargaining rights.

The Little Steel Strike

The Little Steel Strike marked the temporary halt of the victorious march of the organizing committee. Despite employer success in this conflict, the Little Steel strike marked the end of the use, certainly on a large scale, of the time tested tactics of espionage, the use of armed guards, and the denial of constitutional and civic rights by local authorities to a labor organization seeking recognition. These tactics, exposed so thoroughly by the Subcommittee on Education and Labor of the United States Senate, headed by Senator Robert M. La Follette, were never to be used again successfully on an extensive scale in American labor warfare.[50]

Although the strike was lost, the union was able to pass through this trial to a more cohesive and stronger organization. Moreover, it marked the emergence of leadership from the steel workers' ranks, some of whom had come from the Amalgamated. The over-all influence of the Miners' leaders was reduced. In addition, the strike brought on the first rift between Roosevelt and Lewis, which was to fester into open opposition by 1940. The strike also marked the high tide of Communist influence within the Steel Workers' Union. Among the organizers listed by the Steel Workers' Organizing Committee for its own records, on July 19, 1936, seventy-five are identified as Communists. A number listed were well-known leaders of the Communist party, and several were active in trade-union work at the time. Communists provided the largest group except for the Amalgamated. Only one organizer from the Miners' Union was identified as a Communist, but a larger number from the Amalgamated Association of Iron, Steel and Tin Workers were thus described. Since the list was used for administrative purposes, its authenticity does not appear to be in question. Irrespective of Communist influence, the organizing committee was the one CIO union in which Communist influence was brief; Murray knew how to use Communists and at the same time prevent them from seizing control of the administrative machinery of the union. The large number of coal miners in official positions undoubtedly contributed to the result.

The Steel Workers' Organizing Committee attempted to negotiate agreements with the Republic Steel Corporation, the Youngstown Sheet and Tube Corporation, and the Inland Steel and the Bethlehem Companies; but none would sign an agreement. The companies were willing to bargain, but as expressed by the Republic Steel Corporation, they saw "no necessity for signing the C.I.O. contract."[51] When the companies refused to back away from their positions, a strike in twenty-seven plants of Republic Steel, Youngstown Sheet and Tube, and Inland Steel began on May 25. The chief strike zones centered around the Youngstown, Ohio, area where about 35,000 employees of Youngstown Sheet and Tube and Republic Steel were involved. Another crucial strike area was around Chicago, where the same two companies had plants and where Inland Steel had its major properties. The companies were ready to meet all conditions but refused to sign a contract with the committee. Violence began on the first day of the walkout and continued virtually to the effective ending of the strike. In Canton, Ohio, a picket was shot down by a company guard on the first day of the strike. Murray wired a protest to Girdler.[52]

A more serious riot took place in South Chicago on the third day of the strike. After a meeting at their headquarters at 113th Street and Green Bay Avenue, the gathering marched down "in the direction of the Republic Steel plant." It was dispersed by the police "before reaching its objective."[53] Nevertheless, limited picketing was allowed. On Sunday, May 30, the union called a protest meeting. Chairman of the meeting was Joe Weber, a union organizer and identified in the committee's list by the number 7, standing for Communist Party. Weber also used the pseudonyms of Roy Hudson and B. K. Gebert. Estimates of the audience ranged from one thousand persons to two and one-half times as many. When the meeting ended, it was suggested that the participants move toward the Republic Steel plant. On the way they met the police. The Senate Committee, investigating the Memorial Day incident, refused to accept the claim of the leaders of the demonstration that the march had been spontaneous, although it also rejected the police view that there was "a preconceived design to storm the plant. To this we cannot agree, but it is apparent that it was anticipated by many that some form of action would follow the meeting itself, and a further encounter with the police was not improbable."[54] Testimony indicated that the "meeting closed with a motion from someone in the crowd to establish a mass picket line in front of the Republic plant. The motion was carried by acclamation and the parade was formed. We think it is clear from all the evidence that nothing was said by the speakers at the meeting which could be even remotely construed as an incitement to assault police or to capture the plant."[55]

The brutal behavior of the Chicago police, the clubbing of helpless marchers, the wanton killing of ten men, the maiming of many others has seldom been equaled in the savage industrial conflicts of the past.[56]

Resumption of operations at the Republic mill in Warren, Ohio, brought with it a new problem. Mass picketing caused the U.S. Post Office Department to refuse mail deliveries. It brought an investigation by the U.S. Senate.

The sheriff of Mahoning County aided by forty-five deputies broke through the picket line and delivered a carload of food to the strikebreakers at the Youngstown Sheet and Tube plant in Warren. In Monroe, Michigan, the Republic Steel plant was opened by two hundred special police, after Governor Frank Murphy failed as a mediator.[57]

The strike at the Cambria plant of the Bethlehem Steel Corporation in Johnstown, Pennsylvania, began on June 11, after several fruitless attempts to have the company negotiate a contract. A strike of railroad employees employed by the corporation had begun on the preceding day. There were about fifteen thousand men involved. The Johnstown Citizens' Committee was organized three days later to fight the walkout. The citizens' committee played a role in preparing public sentiment against the strike. It organized a Steel Workers' Committee which promoted a "back-to-work" movement.[58] The citizens' committee, according to uncontroverted testimony, encouraged violence against pickets, sought to have leaders of Steel Workers' Organizing Committee expelled from the city, and, in general, tried to break the strike. The company, as did several of the other companies, supplied itself with a large amount of tear gas and munitions.[59] As soon as the strike started, Mayor Daniel J. Shields deputized several hundred special police.[60] Picketing was orderly, and there was little violence even after the reopening of the Cambria plant. Rumors of an invasion by thousands of members of the Miners' Union, on June 17, induced Sheriff Michael J. Boule to request Governor George H. Earle for troops. In compliance, the governor established martial law on June 21, and the troops remained in Johnstown for a week. He compelled a suspension of work. The closing of the plant was protested by the mayor whose role in the strike was subjected to examination by the Senate Sub-committee under the chairmanship of Senator Robert M. La Follette, Jr.[61]

On June 8, Governor Martin L. Davey of Ohio notified President Thomas M. Girdler, among others, that the "State of Ohio has done everything in its power to preserve law and order in the strike zones except the last resort of armed forces. The results are not satisfactory to either side in the industrial controversy."[62] To avoid bloodshed and rioting Girdler and others, including leaders of the union, were asked to meet with the governor.

Girdler refused to attend and sent John A. Voss, director of industrial relations, in his place. But Governor Davey was unable to effect an agreement. Republic announced on June 16 that it would no longer negotiate with Governor Davey.[63]

In Youngstown, Ohio, a "back-to-work" movement was started in the middle of June. Republic Steel declared its intentions to open its plants. The back-to-work efforts in Youngstown were led by the Independent Society of the Sheet and Tube Company. In an effort to find a basis for settlement, Secretary of Labor Frances Perkins appointed a Federal Mediation Board headed by Charles P. Taft with Lloyd K. Garrison, a former member of the National Labor Relations Board, and Edward F. McGrady, a former labor union officer, as members. It appeared that the appointment was the result of the request of Governor Davey, who had informed President Roosevelt that he was unable to make any progress towards a settlement.[64]

On the morning of June 21 the board met with Lewis, Murray, and several other leaders and proposed several methods for reaching an agreement with the companies. On the afternoon of the same day, the board met with representatives of the companies. President Eugene Grace of Bethlehem, Girdler, and Frank Purnell, President of Youngstown Sheet and Tube, were present, and Inland was represented by Wilfred Sykes, assistant to the president of the company. All four companies said that they "would not enter into an agreement with S.W.O.C."[65] The board also reported:

Mr. Girdler stated positively that he would not consent to a term contract because he believed it necessary for the proper operation of his company that they should be in a position to meet the fluctuating price of steel by wage variations if they became necessary. . . . The four companies, in addition, to their objection to the great amount of time which they stated would be consumed by grievance committees, insisted that the union would either immediately or at the end of the term in February, 1938, demand the closed shop and the check-off. They insisted also that the C.I.O. had proved its irresponsibility and cited specifically the automobile situation, but we pointed out that this case involved the S.W.O.C. and not any other union and that its leadership was largely recruited from the United Mine Workers Union, which we understood was thoroughly responsible and lived up to its agreement over a long period of years.[66]

Several additional meetings were held with representatives of the companies and with the leaders of Steel Workers' Organizing Committee, but no basis for a settlement could be found. The companies "refused to meet with Murray and the union representatives in a joint conference and maintained their position that they would not enter into any agreement, written or oral, with the S.W.O.C."[67] Even if the committee won an election held by the National Labor Relations Board, the companies insisted there would be no change in their positions.[68]

Refusal of the companies to accept any proposal that would give the union a modicum of recognition meant that the strike would continue. On June 19 a picket was killed before the Sheet and Tube plant at Youngstown, Ohio. On June 21, Governor Davey sent troops to Trumbull and Warren counties to keep mills closed that were not operating and to protect those that were. Several days later troops were sent to Youngstown, and the governor announced that all who wanted to work would be protected. Mills reopened in East Chicago on June 27, with the strike steadily losing its effectiveness. Having failed to find a basis for an acceptable agreement, Roosevelt announced that the country was tired of strikes and criticized both parties by invoking "A plague on both your houses." It was later explained that the houses were those of "extremists on both sides—those who want violence on one hand and those who will not negotiate on the other."[69]

Lewis waited until Labor Day to reply. In a speech over the Columbia Broadcasting System network, he declared: "Labor, like Israel, has many sorrows. Its women weep for the fallen and they lament for the future of the children of the race. It ill behooves one who has supped at labor's table and who has been sheltered in labor's house to curse with equal fervor and fine impartiality both labor and its adversaries when they become locked in deadly embrace."[70]

The strikes were ended in the plants of the Bethlehem, Republic, and Youngstown Sheet and Tube companies by back-to-work movements, protected by guards and militia men. Only Inland Steel made concessions. An agreement was reached through the efforts of Governor Clifford Townsend of Indiana. In a letter to the governor, the company agreed to recognize the Steel Workers' Organizing Committee for its members only, reinstate strikers without discrimination, and to virtually follow the contract of U.S. Steel on wages and grievance procedure. However, the company would not sign a written contract. The committee was less successful with the other companies. Few concessions were made by the Youngstown Sheet and Tube, Republic Steel, and Bethlehem Steel companies. While the strikes "phased out" in the three companies, the unions' position became easier in a number of the plants. Recognition of union officers for informal bargaining was granted in some instances.[71] The loss of the strike was by no means fatal; the National Labor Relations Act had been upheld, and even the intransigent Girdler had announced he would sign a contract if he were ordered to do so by the courts. In answering a question of Senator Allan Ellender, Girdler replied: "Whenever the law says I have to sign a contract and the law is properly upheld, then I'll have to sign a contract."[72]

It was a violent and costly strike in which 18 were killed and 168 injured.[73] Under earlier circumstances, the return without a contract after a lost strike would have meant the blacklisting of the leaders and the installation, at least temporarily, of draconian measures. Moreover, it would have revealed weaknesses which other employers could have noted and utilized. It was a defeat which revealed S.W.O.C.'s weakness and it affected staff and leaders. But the union had the protection of the Wagner Act, and a favorable climate of opinion, in part generated by the revelations of the La Follette Committee. The Steel Workers' Organizing Committee could report, by the end of 1937, the existence of 1,080 lodges and contracts with 445 firms covering about one half of a million workers. It employed a staff of 213 full-time field workers and 75 part-time workers. Eventually, the Little Steel companies were compelled to deal with the committee and sign written contracts. While the perseverance and heroism of the union and staff should not be underrated, the results followed largely from the decisions upholding the National Labor Relations Board. After orders to disestablish company unions and to sign written contracts were upheld, the companies could no longer resist. Agreements covering back-pay and reinstatement were negotiated following the refusal of the U.S. Supreme Court to review the decisions of the circuit court. Earlier, in *H. J. Heinz Co.* v. *NLRB,* the U.S. Supreme Court supported an order requiring a company to sign an agreement "as to wages, hours and working conditions . . . which serves both as recognition of the union with which the agreement is reached and as a permanent memorial of its terms."[74] This decision cut the ground from under the "no-signing" position of the Little Steel companies.

The Steel Workers' Organizing Committee, despite its setback, continued after a temporary lull to expand its membership, especially after the beginning of the defense boom in 1939. By 1942 the Amalgamated which had continued its nominal existence merged with the new union: the United Steelworkers of America established that year. At its first convention, the union announced that it had returned $601,000 borrowed from the "United Mine Workers of America which completely eliminates our financial indebtedness to that organization."

"In addition to the $601,000 borrowed from the United Mine Workers of America, SWOC received $960,000 from the CIO during 1936 and 1937. No payments were made on these contributions. The Committee for Industrial Organization pledged in 1935 and 1936, that it would give $500,000 to an appropriate agency which would undertake the organization campaign in steel. By arrangement with the Amalgamated Association, SWOC was established for this purpose. This pledged $500,000, was received by SWOC between June 1936 and January 1937. SWOC did not begin to collect dues from its members until April 1937."[75]

The Steel Workers' Union was able to ride out the defeat and the catastrophic drop in dues payments which followed the business decline of 1937. In assessing the power of the newly formed unions, the financial and organizational support it received from the United Mine Workers of America and other CIO unions should not be overlooked, nor the determination and sacrifice of thousands of steel workers.

The final outcome of the Little Steel strike clearly demonstrated the importance of the government in shaping labor relations and influencing the effectiveness of organizing and the character of the labor movement. Without the Wagner Act, it is more than likely that the Little Steel strike would have been one more heroic effort to impose organization upon the industrial leviathan, the steel industry. It is at least probable that the attempt of the union to enlarge its beachhead in the plants of the U.S. Steel Corporation so as to bargain for more than its own members would have been resisted and certainly, the steelworkers would have faced a different kind of opponent in the event of a strike in Big Steel. Nor would fabricating companies have "surrendered" so easily.

Whatever the reasons for the viability of the union, the United Steelworkers of America demonstrated its resilience, adaptability, and capacity to serve its members. It grew to be one of the three largest unions in the United States, a major source of strength and stability for the CIO, and the labor movement.

CHAPTER 40

The CIO Under Lewis

John L. Lewis could rightfully claim he was the promoter, and financier of the Committee for Industrial Organization. Through the United Mine Workers of America, Lewis provided, through nominal loans, 83.4 per cent of the total cost of the CIO in 1936 and 1937.[1] In terms of prior experience, or even today, it would be difficult to exaggerate the achievements of the CIO in the first two hectic years of its existence. Indirectly, the effects were much greater. The successful drives of the CIO forced the AFL to follow suit. The federation did not engage in dramatic large-scale campaigns, although its department of organization became more active. The greatest gains came from the stepped-up activity of the affiliates, which finally ceased quarreling over jurisdictional rights in the manufacturing industries.

By 1938 the major objectives of the original CIO had been achieved; the barriers of the mass production industries had been pierced, and effective unions established in these jurisdictions. Having rejected unity with the AFL, the CIO unions were compelled to create a new labor federation, since it was no longer possible to maintain the fiction that the CIO was only trying to strengthen the AFL. When the plan for setting up another federation was first announced, the International Ladies' Garment Workers' Union expressed its opposition to the project, because the 1937 convention of the union had directed the officers to "seek every means . . . to compose the rift in the ranks of organized labor."[2] When the CIO announced its intention of becoming a permanent federation, the general executive board rejected the invitation, and its action was subsequently endorsed by the twenty-fourth convention of the union.[3]

The Ladies' Garment Workers also had to consider the effect of its estrangement from the AFL upon the ability of the organization to organize shops in small nonindustrial communities in which "runaway" employers sought to operate. Such support was a problem for a number of unions and explained, in part, why a number originally sympathetic to the CIO refused to affiliate with it.[4]

With the withdrawal of the garment workers, the United Mine Workers and the Amalgamated Clothing Workers became the two most powerful organizations, in terms of members and in experienced leadership. The Mine, Mill and Smelter Workers' Union and the Oil Field Workers were original members of the CIO, but at this stage neither was numerically important nor did they contain within their ranks leaders who had already gained a national position. Behind these unions stood the recently formed organizations in the mass production industries. The Automobile Workers', Steel Workers', Radio and Electrical Workers', and Rubber Workers' unions which had been formed out of groups of federal locals and had grown to great size from the stimulus, financial and organizational, of the CIO.

THE RUBBER INDUSTRY

One of the more stable organizations in the CIO was the United Rubber Workers of America. In the 1930's the industry was concentrated in Ohio, where 68 per cent of the workers in the tire and tube plants were employed. Of the number employed in Ohio, 79 per cent worked in factories in Akron; California was next on the list with 6 per cent of the employees; and the remainder were scattered through the United States. Like other mass-production industries, the manufacture of rubber products was not unionized. Of the over 166,000 workers, 130,000 were male. Almost 97,000 of the males were native whites, under 31,000 foreign-born whites, and only 3,403 Negroes and 365 other races.[5]

The Amalgamated Rubber Workers' Union of North America, established in 1902, and affiliated with the AFL, had tried to function. The union lasted a couple of years. In 1913 leadership in a spontaneous strike was assumed by the Industrial Workers of the World, but this can only be regarded as a demonstration against poor working conditions and failure of the companies to handle grievances in a satisfactory manner. The strike called attention to abuses and brought an investigation by the committee of the Ohio state senate headed by William Green. It was, however, unable to settle the dispute.[6]

Organization in Rubber

In common with all industrial communities, the workers of Akron suffered severely from the effects of the decline in business and employment in the early 1930's. Soon after the passage of the National Industrial Recovery Act, local labor leaders began to organize the employees of the rubber plants in Akron. Simultaneously, rubber workers in other communities were heeding the call to unionize. On August 2, 1933, Coleman Claherty was sent as an organizer of the AFL to Akron.

At first Akron workers were recruited into federal labor unions of the AFL. At the same time, leaders of the craft unions protested against the practice of merging in federal labor unions craftsmen in their jurisdictions with the production workers in the rubber plants. While the dispute about the form of organization was going on, a number of company unions were established in Akron in the hope that the desire for unionization could be diverted into more pliable types of organizations. The companies also refused to bargain with the federal labor unions, but were forced by a threat of a general strike to withdraw from this position. In the spring of 1935, they agreed to bargain with the newly formed unions and assented to a representation election on condition that the Circuit Court of Appeals held such a step necessary.

During 1935 although membership in the Rubber Workers' unions declined, the leaders refused to accept the advice of President Green to elect Coleman Claherty as first president of the United Rubber Workers of America, established in September 1935. Nor would it agree to refrain from recruiting craftsmen claimed by organizations affiliated with the AFL.

In the early months of 1936 the union passed through a "trial by fire." In January a sit-down strike began in the plant of the Firestone Company over the disciplining of a shop steward and a failure to adjust piece rates. The company yielded. The strike at Goodyear, in February 1936, put the union to its greatest test. It started as a sit-down strike in protest against the layoff of 70 workers in the tire division, which was followed by their dismissal. The strike began on February 12, and by the middle of February, 14,000 employees were affected. The Industrial Assembly, a company union, tried a back-to-work movement, but it failed. Although the company secured a court injunction restricting picketing, it did not weaken the determination of the strikers. Nor could a law and order league, led by a former mayor, dent the spirit of the strikers. At the end of five weeks, on March 21, 1936, the strike was settled. Strikers were rehired without prejudice, and arrangements for negotiations provided. The six-hour day was conserved, and layoffs were regulated.

In July 1936 the Rubber Workers' Union joined the CIO. The union gained its first recognition from one of the Big Four firms in 1937. A contract with the Firestone Rubber Company was signed after a fifty-nine day walkout.[7]

THE NATIONAL MARITIME UNION

The National Maritime Union replaced the International Seamen's Union as the bargaining agent for seamen after a wildcat strike in the spring of 1936. It was able to compel and win elections on Atlantic and Gulf coast ships. It was formally organized, with CIO support, in May 1937. It was one of the unions controlled by the Communist party at the time, and it was to be a storm center for a number of years.[8] In September 1937 the National Labor Relations Board ordered elections to determine representatives for collective bargaining on 87 steamship lines, with 756 vessels operating on the Atlantic and Gulf coasts. The National Maritime Union won by a vote of 15, 754 to 3,250 and signed its first contract with the Black Diamond Steamship Company in November 1937.[9]

ELECTRICAL WORKERS

The United Electrical and Radio Workers of America, which started as a federal labor union in 1933, would not accept a restricted charter from the AFL. When the issue came before the executive council, in February 1935, Green argued for granting an industrial charter. Vice-President William Hutcheson said: "If that is the way we are going to go along we are going to run into a lot of trouble. I am perfectly willing to help organize any group of workers along reasonable lines so long as it does not infringe on our organization that has helped build up the labor movement to what it is today."[10] Green wanted to avoid any general discussion, and he urged that each case be settled on its merits. He argued that "in the development of organization we are big enough to know that while we shall protect and observe the autonomous rights and jurisdictional rights of each international union we will endeavor to meet extraordinary situations such as arise in mass production industries."[11]

Refusal of the AFL to grant an industrial charter led the federal locals "to go independent," and they affiliated with the CIO. In 1936 and 1937 the union won bargaining rights in a number of plants of the General Electric Company and gained a national contract in 1938. The union also established itself in the plants of the Westinghouse Electric and Manufacturing Company, the Radio Corporation of America, and most of the important radio and electrical manufacturing companies.[12]

ORGANIZING COMMITTEES

Several organizing committees were established. These were temporary arrangements for organizing a specific industry under the direction of a committee, especially appointed by the head of the CIO. The Steel Workers' Organizing Committee was the most important and successful in the use of this method, and the Textile Workers' Organizing Committee under the leadership of Sidney Hillman holds second rank. It was launched by agreement between the United Textile Workers of America and the CIO on March 9, 1937. The agreement provided for allowing the Textile Workers' Organizing Committee to administer the existing contracts of the United Textile Workers and to direct the organizing campaign in the textile industry, on condition that the CIO finance a drive in the industry.[13] Past efforts to organize textile workers had been seriously hampered by the lack of finances, but the CIO campaign was adequately financed. The latter donated $806,000 for the campaign, and the locals and joint boards, established by the Textile Workers' Organizing Committee, donated another $494,616.99 out of a total of $1,792,952.62.[14]

AMERICAN NEWSPAPER GUILD

The American Newspaper Guild was one of the more interesting unions formed during the depression of the 1930's. Efforts to establish locals of news writers by the International Typographical Union had not been successful. In part, newspaper editorial workers regarded themselves as professionals who could gain no advantage from joining a trade union. A change in attitude could be traced to the effect of the depression upon employment and earnings of editorial workers. Newspapers, faced with serious loss in advertising revenue and circulation, slashed costs, and among those affected were editorial workers. In many instances, they were less favorably treated than the organized printers and pressmen.

With the enactment of the National Industrial Recovery Act, in 1933, locals of editorial workers were formed in a number of cities. Publishers were not inclined to deal with them, but a combination of economic and governmental pressures forced a modicum of recognition. The largest local, in New York City, headed by Heywood Broun, the noted columnist, called a national convention in December 1933, which established the American Newspaper Guild. Although prejudice against the more blatant type of trade union tactics persisted, the aggressive opposition of the publishers turned the guild toward trade unionism at its second convention in June 1934. Gradually, the national organization obtained more power over bargaining and enlarged its jurisdiction to include noneditorial workers— those employed in the business office and in maintenance.

Resistance hardened attitudes, and the guild became a militant organization resorting to strikes when necessary or advantageous. The Guild affiliated with the AFL in 1936 and joined the CIO the following year.[15]

OTHER UNIONS

The Shoe Workers of America, Transport Workers of America, and the International Woodworkers of America were among the smaller unions formed by the CIO and were present at the founding convention. None of the three was alone in its fields. The Shoe Workers were operating in a jurisdiction which many unions had sought to organize; the Transport Workers of America gained its position by winning recognition in municipal transportation in New York City. The Woodworkers' were in competition with the Carpenters' Union for the lumberjack and sawmill worker, and were able to gain a foothold but not drive out its rival from its jurisdiction.

THE DEPRESSION OF 1937

The decision to transform the CIO from a temporary Committee into the permanent Congress of Industrial Organizations was taken at a time when the upward CIO thrust had largely been halted, and when it had suffered severe contraction in its dues receipts, following the serious decline in business and employment. According to the National Industrial Conference Board, unemployment rose from 5.1 million in September 1937 to 10.8 million in May 1938, one of the sharpest increases in history. The AFL claimed the low point for unemployment was 7.5 million in September 1937, which rose to 11.4 million in May 1938.[16]

The change in business was especially serious for newly organized groups, because the diminished flow of dues increased the problems of the new organizations and continued their dependence upon the largess of the older unions. With lengthening lines of the unemployed, it became more difficult to win concessions from newly organized employers whose normal opposition to the union's demands was now strengthened by the needs for increased economies. John L. Lewis, however, was convinced that the CIO had to move ahead, and he took steps to have the convention of the United Mine Workers of America authorize its officers to "offer whatever aid may be necessary, financial or otherwise, to the Committee for Industrial Organization."[17]

From November 1935 to June 1937, the CIO was supported by grants from its sponsoring unions. In June 1937 a voluntary system of per capita was introduced. For the three-year period in which the CIO functioned, the receipts were $3,540,385.62, and $3,510,954.93 were spent, $1,760,-838.65 on organizing.[18]

Founding Convention

Acting under a mandate from the conference of affiliated unions, Lewis summoned a convention for November 14, 1938, at Pittsburgh, Pennsylvania. The 476 delegates present represented 32 national and international unions, 9 organizing committees, 23 Industrial Union Councils, 115 city and county industrial councils, and 130 local industrial unions. In his opening address, Lewis called attention to the fact that 57 years ago, Gompers had founded in Pittsburgh, the convention city, the American Federation of Labor which had served its generation, but was no longer adequate for meeting the needs of the workers in the mass-production industries.[19]

The constitution adopted was a moderate document. It pointed to the "magnificient record of achievement," which, it held, justified the setting up of a permanent organization to serve the needs of labor. The committee was transformed into a permanent congress. Its objects were to organize effectively all workers regardless of race, creed, color, or nationality for their mutual aid and protection, extend the benefits of collective bargaining so as to secure for labor the means of dealing peacefully with employers, maintain all obligations under collective bargaining contracts, and promote legislation for greater protection of labor, civil rights, and democracy. National and international unions, organizing committees, local unions, and industrial union councils were eligible for membership. Local unions and industrial union councils were placed under the direct jurisdiction of the CIO.

National and international unions were given autonomous and independent status. The original member unions of the CIO would not have tolerated intrusion into their affairs, and the same principal of nonintervention was followed towards unions able to manage their political and financial affairs. Philip Murray answering a complaint against the head of the United Automobile Workers Union advised him "that the matter to which you refer is one that can only be taken care of through procedures provided in the constitution of the United Automobile Workers. It is not the business of the National CIO or of any of its subordinate branches including the Toledo Industrial Union Council to interfere with the internal matters of any international union. I would therefore suggest that you refrain from using your office as president of the Toledo Industrial Union Council to meddle with the affairs of the International Union of United Automobile Workers of America."[20]

No affiliate could be suspended or expelled except upon a two-thirds vote of the convention. The power over the organization was placed in the hands of the national and international unions and organizing committees, which like their counterparts in the AFL, could vote at conventions on the basis of membership; the industrial union councils were allowed one vote. A per capita tax upon national and international unions and organizing committees was imposed.

The president was the executive officer between conventions, with authority to interpret the constitution, appoint and suspend organizers subject to approval of the executive board. The executive board, made up of one member from each national and international union and organizing committee, was empowered to enforce the constitution and instructions of conventions, arrange for auditing finances, and consider differences between affiliates submitted to it. It also had the authority to investigate charges against affiliates and report its conclusions to the convention.

The resolutions covered largely the standard subjects considered at labor conventions: the union label, cooperatives, unity of white and Negro workers, a criticism of the decisions of the Supreme Court, national health, unemployment and social security, political action, education, antilynching, and a variety of other topics. The delegates elected John L. Lewis president, Philip Murray and Sidney Hillman vice-presidents, and James Carey secretary.

Second Convention

The second convention met in San Francisco in October 1939, the same city where the AFL five years before had enacted the resolution permitting industrial organization of the mass-production industries: a resolution that had never been carried out and had set off the struggle which ended in the forming of the CIO. Lewis was in a confident mood and before the warming applause of the delegates, he let his imagination soar. In 1934, he said, his was a "feeble voice," but now he came with "a mighty army of four million men and women." He promised to come back in five years "with at least ten million dues-paying members of the organization."[21] Such confidence was no idle boasting, even though the CIO had been stopped. Whatever one might think, the presence of delegates from thirty-five internationals, seven organizing committees, and a multitude of state and local industrial union councils and local industrial unions was striking testimony of the power of the organization. Lewis could also point to the substantial achievements of the Steel and Textile Organizing Committees, and the National Maritime Union, as well as others. In addition, the CIO was operating fifty regional and subregional offices.

But the sensational achievements of the first two years were already in the past. On the southern campaign, he reported special problems. Establishment of the United Construction Workers' for recruiting workers in and around the construction industry seemed like a waste of limited resources and perhaps designed to exacerbate further the bad feelings with the building trades' unions. Perhaps Lewis was also experiencing some "dizziness from success." Failure to make public a detailed financial report, as had been the practice of the AFL, cast some doubt upon CIO claims, but the organization nevertheless was making progress in important industries.

The resolutions of the second convention followed the pronouncements of the first except that the policies of the National Labor Relations Board were now under attack. What is even more noticeable was the failure to express a word of encouragement for the Allies then undergoing the first assaults of the German armies. Instead, the resolution on defense declared that the "C.I.O. will devote itself to continuing the organization of the unorganized American workers promoting genuine collective bargaining, for the welfare of American labor and the stabilization of industry, and, the preservation of peace, find a solution of the basic economic ills of this country and bring about a permanent prosperity."[22] The number of vice-presidents were increased to six, and only Reid Robinson of the Mine, Mill and Smelter Workers was close to the Communist party.

The war in Europe, which began in August 1939, strongly affected the course of events within the CIO. The organization was divided on the attitude to take. Lewis increasingly expressed an isolationist point of view, and while there were others within the CIO who were more friendly to England and France, the Communists were at the time strong exponents of a peaceful policy. At its meeting on June 3, 1940, the CIO Executive Board raised the question: "And after the current war-stimulated recovery has run its course, what then?"[23] Increasingly, Lewis took a position against the involvement of the United States in war. He attacked peacetime conscription in August, and in October 1940 the *United Mine Workers Journal* criticized government's failure to solve domestic problems and its concentration on war.[24]

Lewis' relations with President Roosevelt gradually deteriorated. Lewis' version of his break has been told by his admiring biographer and another by a harsh critic, but, given the temperament and aspirations of the leader of the CIO, it was inevitable that he would remain dissatisfied with the concessions and attention given him.[25] President Roosevelt's position was not an easy one. The CIO was not the only labor federation in the United States at the time. In fact, the AFL with its more than 4,200,000 members was very likely much larger; the CIO membership could not be verified, since it failed to publish a financial statement. Whatever may have been Roosevelt's sentiments or loyalties, he could not ignore the AFL, the dominant labor federation in the United States. Two members of the AFL Executive Council—George Harrison of the Brotherhood of Railway Clerks and Daniel Tobin of the Teamsters' Union—were influential in Democratic party politics. Other AFL leaders were too important for Roosevelt to ignore. Whatever may have been his motives, Lewis decided to oppose the third-term candidacy of Franklin Roosevelt in 1940.

There were other grounds of difference between Lewis and Roosevelt. Lewis, even before the beginning of World War II, complained that "corporations flagrantly violating the provisions of the National Labor Relations Board . . . are the very corporations receiving large government contracts." He wanted the President to issue an executive order that all bidders for government contracts be required to stipulate that they "are not and will not be, for the duration of the contract, in violation of the National Labor Relations Act."[26] President Roosevelt expressed concern, but he claimed that under the statute the government had to award its contracts to the lowest bidder, and the Comptroller General had held "that only an act of Congress could authorize a contracting agency to insert the stipulations in the specifications for a contract not authorized by statute."[27]

Lewis, in a longer second letter, repeated his request, and Roosevelt again told him "that the only unquestionable valid method of securing the objective proposed in the executive order which you suggest is by remedial legislation."[28] Unsatisfied, Lewis tried to get Sidney Hillman, who was serving as Commissioner of Defense, to have such an executive order issued. Of course, Hillman faced the same objections from the President.[29]

No one can question the right of Lewis to oppose a third term, intervention in Europe, or the failure of the two Roosevelt administrations to solve the more pressing domestic problems. To go beyond these facts is to engage in speculation on motives which can never be accurately discerned and which reveal the "analyst's" prejudice. On October 25, 1940, in a national radio address, which his biographer claims was heard by between twenty-five to thirty million people, Lewis made a slashing attack on Roosevelt's candidacy.[30] It was a powerful, emotion-charged assault upon Roosevelt's drift to war and his drive for personal power, including a pronouncement that his re-election for a third term "would be a national evil of the first magnitude."[31]

Had Lewis stopped at this point, the election of Roosevelt would simply have been a piece of bad political judgment. He was confident, however, that he was the spokesman not only for the members of the CIO but for all workers. He woefully failed to gauge his own position or labor's loyalty to Roosevelt when he declared that if Roosevelt were re-elected, "it will mean that members of the Congress of Industrial Organizations have rejected my advice and recommendations. I will accept the results as being the equivalent of a vote of no confidence, and will retire as President of the Congress of Industrial Organizations, at its convention in November."[32]

This was a fatal and unnecessary promise which Lewis must have believed would rally wavering followers behind him.[33] Lewis' reasons, aside from his differences over policy, show him not to have understood the Presidential office or the man who occupied it at the time. He was also exaggerating his strength and underestimating the power of the antilabor groups in Congress and the country. Most of all, he was forgetting that he was not the exclusive representative of organized labor in the United States.

Third Convention

Less than a month after Lewis' denunciation, the third convention of the CIO opened in Atlantic City, the same city where five years before Lewis had arraigned the leaders of the AFL for their failure to carry out the mandate of the 1935 convention to organize the mass-production industries. Lewis carried the fight to his open and concealed opponents. When George Baldanzi, a delegate from the Textile Workers', and Hyman Blumberg, from the Amalgamated Clothing Workers of America, criticized the failure of the CIO News to give any space to Roosevelt's election, Lewis took full responsibility for these omissions.[34]

But the 438 delegates assembled in Atlantic City had more serious business. In contrast to the AFL, which showed its sympathy for the heroic resistance of the Allies in the Battle of Britain and warned that if "Great Britain is defeated, then America and democracy are increasingly menaced and our peaceful pursuit of life is seriously threatened,"[35] the CIO resolution on national defense reiterated a series of demands for improvement in wages and enforcement of labor laws.[36] Walter Reuther and L. S. Buckmaster expressed reservations and pleaded for recognition of the dangers of aggression.

In contrast to the first two meetings, the third showed some differences of opinion. The resolution submitted by the Amalgamated Clothing Workers, a founding organization and an important source of funds, suggested labor unity. It led to a severe denunciation of Zaritsky and Dubinsky, who had withdrawn earlier from the CIO. The resolution was rejected.[37]

The crucial decision to be made by the 1940 convention was the election of a president. Lewis had promised to withdraw, but he was not enthusiastic about the outcome. There was a demonstration when he first appeared at the convention lasting one hour, according to his biographer, and according to a severe critic, forty-three minutes.[38] Signs and posters pleading with Lewis to revoke his promise were abundantly displayed. The Communists, who were then dutifully carrying out the Hitler-Stalin pact by opposing preparedness and Allied aid, were among the more anxious for a repudiation of the promise. No one in the convention had sufficient stature to insist upon another choice. Philip Murray was a vice-president of the United Mine Workers of America. The younger men present were too new and uncertain to throw down the gauntlet to one of the two or three ablest men thrown up by the American labor movement. Never known for his deep concern for the feelings of opponents, Lewis told the Amalgamated that if it "wants to take the easy way," it can "go on," which meant get out. Only one man, Sidney Hillman, had sufficient stature and could make demands upon the CIO leader. He was absent from the convention and engaged in government work.

Lewis had attacked Hillman by name and had repelled the criticisms of the delegates from the Amalgamated with characteristic disdain.

Hillman came to the convention, and in a reasoned speech he defended, among other things, his activity as a member of the National Defense Advisory Commission to which he had been appointed by President Roosevelt without clearance from either the CIO or AFL. It was Hillman who dared to say "that when John L. Lewis steps down there must be a demand for Phil Murray," although he formally regretted Lewis' departure.[39]

Murray was nominated in a gracious and laudatory speech by Lewis and unanimously elected. The reasons for Lewis' departure are less important than his surrender of the office. More than any other man by far, he was responsible for the successful organization of the mass-production industries. Shrewd, intelligent, eloquent, and courageous, Lewis was truly an unusual man in a time which saw Roosevelt, Churchill, and Stalin in power. It may have been that he wanted to pursue his campaign for labor unity, as he claimed. He may also have recognized that the great organizing drives were about finished, and that the unions, created largely by his energy and courage and the funds of the Miners' Union, would not show the kind of subservience he expected; or he may have believed he could run the CIO from the wings, with Murray as nominal head.

It was unfortunate that Lewis' position on many public issues, his insistence on parity with the President of the United States, as well as the fissure within the labor movement, made it impossible for the government to use his services in time of war. Had it been possible, the achievements of John L. Lewis might have matched those of Ernest Bevin in England. Lewis' performance at the labor-management conference called by President Roosevelt for the devising of a policy to govern labor relations during World War II, showed, according to all reports, that he had lost none of his tactical abilities or capacity to dominate.

Relations between Murray and Lewis began to cool almost before the former took over his new post. It appeared that Murray wanted to be his own man, and that Lewis was not completely happy at the new role of his subordinate, who was still vice-president of the United Mine Workers of America. In a characteristically bold move, Lewis presented his program for the "accouplement" of the AFL and CIO to Murray and Green without consulting either of them. According to a story by A. H. Raskin, a leading and reliable reporter in the New York Times, an agreement had been reached for the retirement of William Green and for the elevation of George Meany. At the same time the AFL and CIO would be merged and Murray would become secretary of the unified federation. Both Daniel Tobin and Green, who presumably were consulted on the proposal, denied knowledge. After publicly comparing Lewis' proposal to the Japanese assault on Pearl Harbor—an unfortunate comparison—Murray told Lewis he would submit his proposal to the executive board.

To Murray's complaint of not having been consulted, Lewis wrote an open letter in which he noted that he had been appointed chairman of the CIO Peace Negotiating Committee and that the 1939 meeting with representatives of the AFL had been adjourned pending a call from him. He claimed, therefore, that he was acting under the mandate of a convention which the executive board could not negate.[40] On the theory that Lewis' plan would weaken the administration's influence with organized labor, President Roosevelt intervened and conferred with Murray, on January 22. Instead of a merger, he recommended the setting up of a Labor Victory or Combined War Labor Board. This proposal was accepted, and at Murray's insistence, Lewis was kept off the board. Green, Meany, and Tobin represented the AFL; Murray, R. J. Thomas, and Julius Emspak, the CIO. According to a reliable informant, Green and other members of the AFL sharply criticized the selection of Emspak, who was an officer of a union recognized as a Communist party enclave.[41]

Lewis had worked with Murray almost from the beginning. Murray was able to support Roosevelt in 1932 and 1940 when Lewis favored a Republican candidate. But a public assault was something different, and Lewis was biding his time. In the meantime Hitler had invaded the Soviet Union, and Lewis' Communist supporters, those who staged the demonstrations in the days of the Hitler-Stalin pact, now became his cruelest and most vindictive critics. Lewis may have been wrong, but his was an honorable abhorrence of war shared by millions of his countrymen. He aligned himself with a group which would not only betray him, but would lead in spreading the most vicious calumnies against the man who created them as union officers. Without the funds and the protective shield that Lewis had held before them, the Communists could never have won a firm foothold in the CIO. But, opposed by the non-Communists, who favored a more active interventionist foreign policy, and by the opportunists, Lewis was now without important supporters in a federation he virtually had built single-handed.

After a short time Lewis moved to deprive Murray of his office in the Mine Workers' Union. The International Policy Board was called into session in Washington on May 25, 1942, to consider a number of issues, including Murray's absence from his post as vice-president. A request for a return of funds loaned to the CIO was made. The summary contributions of the United Mine Workers of America show that the miners carried the CIO for the first years. It was not unreasonable, therefore, for Lewis to ask for a major voice in its councils. Lewis estimated that the services of organizers, executives, and others provided by the Mine Workers equaled

$3,904,303.84. Loans of $1,665,000 were made of which $20,000 had been repaid. The total contributions equaled $5,569,303.84 in money and services, according to Lewis and Secretary-Treasurer Thomas Kennedy, not counting the cash loan of $601,000, made to the Steel Workers' Organizing Committee to finance the Little Steel strike, which had been repaid. Of the funds contributed, the greatest beneficiary was the Steel Workers' Organizing Committee, which had received $1,018,612.86 in loans that had not been repaid. Murray claimed he had always viewed the loans as contributions.

But the policy committee was summoned by Lewis to consider questions other than the monies owed to the union. The attacks on Lewis from groups within the CIO had been rising in intensity. Murray did not choose to stop the attacks, or perhaps was unable to do so, although he was obviously angry at Lewis, as his refusal to allow him on the Combined Labor War Board indicated. The announcement in the *United Mine Workers Journal* of Murray's removal from the vice-presidency by the executive board, which convened while the policy committee was in session, carried no stigma. It was noted that, in view of his duties as vice-president of the Mine Workers' Union, "under the necessary interpretation of the provisions of the UMWA constitution and the need at the present time for a working vice president there was nothing left to do but declare the office vacant, despite the ties of sentiment."[42] John O'Leary was appointed in his place.

Murray reacted, and before a meeting of the CIO Executive Board charged Lewis with being "hell bent on creating national confusion and national disunity" and that Lewis had proposed that Murray join him at the CIO 1941 convention in a fight against President Roosevelt's foreign policies. In addition he charged that Lewis had used his position as head of the Miners' Union to "hamper the nation's victory effort . . . both within and outside the labor movement."[43] Officers of all the mine workers' districts condemned the attack. It meant that Lewis and the United Mine Workers could not remain in the CIO. In October 1942 the convention of the United Mine Workers of America affirmed the decision to leave.[44] Lewis was now to devote himself mainly to the affairs of his own union. He returned to the AFL briefly, but left in 1947 over a disagreement on the attitude to be taken towards signing the non-Communist affidavit of the Taft-Hartley law.

The departure of Lewis from the CIO meant that the talents of the greatest labor leader of his generation were to be only partially used. Lewis could not remain in an organization whose leaders bitterly assailed him and questioned his motives and patriotism. He himself, however, had helped to create the "authoritarian" climate which dominated the CIO throughout its existence. He was the one who demanded that all who did not agree with his analysis or policies get out. He would still be heard from, and his statements and appearances before committees of Congress would continue to receive maximum newspaper coverage, but those were tributes to his gifts rather than an index of his importance in the general labor scene. The fact remained that after 1942 he could not seriously affect the general course of the labor movement, even though he has been regarded as a major contributor to the enactment of the Taft-Hartley Act.

CHAPTER 41

Defense Planning and Labor

The preparations for defense, followed by World War II, exercised a profound effect on the labor movement. They provided the organizations of labor, which for almost an entire decade had been operating under depressed economic conditions, a labor market in which workers were in some categories in short supply, made employers more willing to make wage and other concessions, and allowed the officers and staffs of the new unions an opportunity to gain experience in union administration and collective bargaining under more favorable economic conditions. Finally they brought leaders of organized labor and management closer together in efforts to solve the common national problems of training, procurement, and transfer of labor, settlement of differences, as well as such economic problems as price control. By the end of the war an entire corps of local, regional, and national labor officers had been trained and membership had been stabilized. Even limited membership security arrangements had been imposed with the aid of government, an arrangement that would have been much more vigorously resisted under normal conditions.

DEFENSE

As the war in Europe continued and the German armies overran Europe, the United States took the first steps to place itself in a more effective military position. The Advisory Commission to the Council of National Defense was appointed by President Franklin D. Roosevelt on May 29, 1940. William Knudsen was appointed for industrial production; Edward R.

Stettinius, Jr., industrial materials; Sidney Hillman, employment; Harriet Elliot, consumer protection; Chester C. Davis, farm production; Leon Henderson, price stabilization; and Ralph Budd, transportation. Each commissioner was allowed to engage a staff for carrying out his duties. Hillman's division subsequently became known as Labor Supply.[1]

Since President Roosevelt had failed to clear Hillman's appointment with the heads of the AFL or the CIO, both Lewis and Green were disappointed. Lewis regarded it as a slight and an insult, while Green, although disappointed that a member of the rival federation obtained the high post, conferred with Hillman and sought to discover the policies he would follow.[2] Green was assured that Hillman intended to use his position to advance the interests of the defense effort and that he would not follow a policy prejudicial to the unions in the AFL.

At no time did the President specify the functions of the Labor Division. Hillman, in the first months of his activity, sought to ease the problem of recruiting an adequate supply for the defense industries by coordinating the efforts of the U.S. Employment Service and the federal agencies involved in apprenticeship training, and at the same time to devise methods for settling disputes that might arise between labor and management in those industries.

To carry out these objectives (to forecast the labor needs of defense industries, the labor supply and training), he sought to coordinate the efforts of state and federal agencies engaged in training and distributing labor. Sections dealing with training-within-industry and labor relations were also set up. William Green, who favored the defense program and wanted organized labor actively participating in it, advised the President that it would be helpful if labor representatives were given an opportunity to advise on policy.[3] To bring the unions closer to the defense program, Hillman appointed a sixteen-man committee, made up of an equal number from the AFL and CIO.

Almost from the beginning Hillman was subjected to the criticism that defense contracts were being given to firms hostile to organized labor. Philip Murray demanded that the Bethlehem Steel Company be compelled to conform to the minimum wage requirements or be denied contracts.[4] Hillman was sympathetic, but he, of course, could not have his way on many labor issues. He was able to have adopted a "labor policy" that called for the absorption of the unemployed by avoiding wherever possible employment above forty hours a week, and stipulated that overtime should be paid for hours in excess of forty and for work on Saturdays, Sundays, and holidays. In addition, the statement called for obedience to all federal laws, including the National Labor Relations Act.

Lewis and some unions in the CIO were opposed to the defense program, even though disclaimers to that effect were issued. Others believed that the government was not taking adequate steps to bring violators of the labor laws to book by denying them contracts. Lewis charged that the labor policy enunciated by Hillman had never been carried out.

Defense Mediation Board

As the defense program expanded and more workers were employed in its behalf, strikes increased. Between December 1940 and March 1941 strikes rose from 147 to 316, and the number of workers involved from 458,314 to 1,543,803.[5] The figures by themselves do not show the seriousness of the increasing labor disputes. The strike at the Johnstown, Pennsylvania, plant of the Bethlehem Steel Company and the one at the McCormick works in Chicago were causing serious losses in defense production. The most damaging and, from a labor point of view, most unjustifiable strike took place at the Allis-Chalmers Plant in Milwaukee, Wisconsin. It started on January 22, 1941, and lasted until April 7. At the time the company held about $40 million in Navy contracts.

The Office of Production Management tried to settle the dispute, but no formula satisfactory to both sides could, for a time, be devised. Attempts to open the plant on March 28 led to serious violence, and Governor Julius Heil asked that work be temporarily suspended. An agreement was finally reached on April 6, 1941, under which provisions for disciplining would be appealed to a referee, all those who struck would be reinstated, wages would be negotiated, and final arbitration of unresolved differences would be utilized.[6]

Evidence that the strike vote was rigged was presented, and the leader of the walkout, Harold Christofel, was accused of using his position to interfere with the defense effort. Christofel was president of the Milwaukee Industrial Union Council, CIO, which ten days prior to the walkout had denounced the defense effort. Moreover, a committee from the Wisconsin legislature charged in a 6 to 1 vote that Christofel and other leaders were Communists. It was its length and unreasonableness, as well as the use of fraudulent methods, which led Green to denounce the strike as a conspiracy.[7]

Strikes in Defense Industries

In order to help the settlement of disputes between management and labor, President Roosevelt on March 19, 1941, appointed the National Defense Mediation Board composed of eleven members, three of whom represented the public and four each from labor and management. The board was to assist parties with an industrial dispute in adjusting their differences, to afford means of voluntary arbitration, to assist when desired by the parties in establishing methods for resolving future disputes, to investigate issues in dispute between employers and employees, and to take testimony and hold hearings on controversies certified to the board by the U.S. Secretary of Labor as one which "threatens to burden or obstruct the production or transportation of equipment or materials essential to national defense."[8]

Clarence A. Dykstra was appointed chairman; after several months he was succeeded by William H. Davis. The labor members were George Meany and George Harrison, who came from the AFL, and Philip Murray and Thomas Kennedy of the CIO. During its service, to January 12, 1942, the board handled 118 cases involving more than a million workers. In four instances the board's decisions were not carried out, and the President intervened. After having won a close election, the United Automobile Workers of America and the North American Aviation Company found it impossible to reach an agreement. Since the plant at Inglewood, California, produced about 25 per cent of the planes at the time, its continuing production was of major importance. The union insisted that the company must agree to a ten-cent an hour across the board increase in wages and a rise in the minimum from fifty to seventy-five cents an hour, and make agreed-upon wage increases retroactive to April 16. Through the efforts of the board, the walkout was postponed and the negotiations transferred to Washington. A hearing on the issues was started on June 2, but three days later, in violation of the interim arrangements, a strike was called.

The strike was denounced by Murray and by Richard T. Frankensteen, who charged it was caused by the "vicious underhanded maneuvering of the Communist Party."[9] Wyndham Mortimer, who had been a leader of the caucus dominated by the Communist party in the Automobile Workers' Union, was dismissed with four others. But the pleas of the national leaders were unheeded and President Roosevelt was forced to direct the Army to protect those who were willing to work. The next day, June 10, the mass pickets were dispersed and the strike ended. The issues were again submitted to the Defense Mediation Board, and the union won most of its demands.[10]

In the Federal Shipbuilding and Dry Dock Company case, the company employing almost three thousand shipyard workers refused to accept the following maintenance of membership clause:

In view of the joint responsibilities of the parties to the national defense, of their mutual obligations to maintain production during the present emergency, and of their reciprocal guarantees that there shall be no strikes or lock-outs for a period of two years from June 23, 1941, as set out in the "Atlantic Coast Zone Standards," incorporated herein and made a part hereof, the company engages on its part that any employee who is now a member of the union or who hereafter voluntarily becomes a member during the life of this agreement, shall, as a condition of continued employment, maintain membership in the union in good standing.[11]

L. H. Korndorff, president of the company, rejected this provision, and the union called a strike on August 7. When the company refused to withdraw from its position, the Kearney, New Jersey, shipyard was taken over by the Navy and the strike ended. It was returned to the company on January 7, 1942.

The most difficult controversy facing the board involved the demand for the union shop in the captive coal mines. It was one of a series of disputes involving the Mine Workers' Union, John L. Lewis, and the government. Because the captive mines controlled by the steel companies had refused to sign union-shop contracts, a strike was called on September 15, 1941. Hearings before the Defense Mediation Board opened on September 17 and ended five days later. An agreement was reached for the return to work for thirty days and thereafter until the expiration of a three-day notice, under the terms of the Appalachian Agreement governing the commercial part of the bituminous coal industry, except for the union-shop provisions. The companies had been dealing with the union since 1933 and checked off the dues of employees on a voluntary basis. On November 10 the board recommended that the parties agree to continue production on the existing terms and that the issue of the union shop be referred to arbitration. Murray and Thomas Kennedy dissented from the majority opinion.

The captive mine strike was resumed, and Roosevelt intervened. Replying to a letter from Roosevelt that he and Myron C. Taylor of the United States Steel Corporation work out a settlement, Lewis attacked Hillman as responsible and charged him with "vengeful and malignant opposition to the interests of the United Mine Workers of America." Lewis also declined to extend the contract.[12]

The strikes in the captive mines were arousing demands for anti-labor legislation, and Roosevelt felt the force of the intense pressure they generated in Congress and in the country. The strike, nevertheless, resumed on October 27, and Lewis wrote to the President telling him he would be glad to meet him and J. P. Morgan to discuss "the equities of the problems." In the entire history of labor relations there has seldom been such a calculated display of power. After a conference between Roosevelt, the chairman of the board, William H. Davis, and Myron C. Taylor, the parties agreed to submit the issue to the Defense Mediation Board, but without either party agreeing in advance to accept the award. The strike was ended on October 30, and the board considered the issue from October 31 until November 10, when it rejected by a vote of 9 to 2 the demand of the United Mine Workers of America. Murray and Kennedy thereupon resigned from the board.

On November 14, President Roosevelt held a conference at the White House with officials of the union and the steel companies. He warned that if legislation became necessary to keep the mines going, Congress would pass it. He suggested that they either work out some settlement or submit the issue in dispute to an arbitrator. He declared that the "Government of the United States will not order, nor will Congress pass legislation ordering a so-called closed shop."[13] Failure to bring about a settlement brought the resumption of the strike on November 17. Roosevelt asked again that the strike be ended, and Lewis, after a sharp and challenging letter, accepted arbitration. Benjamin Fairless represented the companies, Lewis, the miners, and John R. Steelman was the impartial member. On December 16 by a vote of 2 to 1, with Fairless dissenting, the union shop was granted. Lewis had won a public victory, largely the result of the unwillingness of Roosevelt to support antilabor legislation. It perhaps would have been unwise to enact laws limiting the rights of labor at a time when workers were being called upon to make sacrifices on behalf of defense and the war effort. There also may have been a desire on the part of Roosevelt not to punish labor organizations in general for the derelictions of a few.

Office of Production Management

The National Defense Advisory Commission was succeeded by the Office of Production Management in January 1941, with the same duties as in the Advisory Commission. William Knudsen was the director; Hillman, the associate director.

Stabilization Agreement in the Construction Industry

One of the more important agreements made was negotiated by Hillman with the building and construction trades. It was agreed that area rates would be influential in determining minimum wages to be paid on defense construction jobs. The hours to be worked on shifts were specified, and a uniform overtime rate of time and one-half was agreed upon. Other conditions, including a requirement that there be no stoppage of work, were accepted.[14] It meant, in fact, that the AFL unions would be given preference on defense construction work. Nineteen building construction unions accepted the agreement. Normally, such a policy would arouse only a minimum of difficulty or protest, but in July 1939, John L. Lewis had chartered the United Construction Workers' Organizing Committee, with his brother as head.

It is difficult to determine whether this venture was designed for spite, harassment, or for serious organizational purposes. It made little impression in the industry until October 1941. In that month, the Currier Lumber Company of Detroit, Michigan, was refused a contract to build 330 houses for the Federal Works Agency in Wayne, Michigan, although the firm was the lowest bidder by more than $200,000. The reason given for the exclusion was that the Currier Company dealt with the United Construction Workers' Organizing Committee. Hillman took responsibility for the rejection and cited a possible need for more than a million construction workers on defense projects. These, he insisted, could only be recruited with the aid of the 19 building trades' unions.[15] Hillman, who had opposed the forming of the United Construction Workers, charged it with raiding. The charge was denied by A. D. Lewis, who claimed his group was barred from bidding on government construction jobs. Hillman stuck to his position despite criticism. The building trades' unions cooperated with Hillman and appreciated his willingness to protect their interests; but William Hutcheson, the head of the Carpenters' Union, objected to Hillman addressing the 1941 convention of the Building Trades Department. Although Hillman had been invited by President John Coyne of the department, Hutcheson felt that a CIO man should not be allowed to address an AFL organization.[16]

The Shipbuilding Stabilization Committee

To eliminate pirating and labor turnover and to develop a more efficient program in the shipyards, the Shipbuilding Stabilization Committee was appointed on November 27, 1940. It was made up of representatives of private shipbuilders, the Maritime Commission, the U.S. Navy, the AFL, and the CIO unions with members employed in the industry. Morris L. Cooke was appointed chairman. At its first meeting, on December 5, 1940, it was agreed to avoid interrupting production until efforts by the National Defense Advisory Commission for adjusting differences had been exhausted.[17] Decisions of the committee were made by majority vote with each group voting as a unit.

In an effort to meet the problem of increasing labor shortages, a conference of representatives of the parties was held in San Francisco on February 3, 1941, at which time a tentative zone agreement was reached. It set forth a basic wage rate of $1.12 an hour for standard skilled mechanics for one year, subject to revision every six months thereafter. In addition, higher rates for premium mechanics, overtime payments, shift differentials, and other working conditions were determined. Similar zone agreements were negotiated in the Great Lakes and the Atlantic and Gulf coasts, with lower wages being established in the latter zones on the basis of historical differentials.[18]

No sooner had the majority of the Pacific Coast unions signed the agreement than it was broken by Machinists' Local 68 of the Bay Cities Metal Trades Council in the San Francisco area. A local of the Steel Workers' Organizing Committee was also involved. President Harvey Brown of the Machinists Union claimed that the Bethlehem Shipbuilding Corporation had refused to participate in the conference and had not signed the agreement. New demands for $1.15 an hour and double time for overtime were also presented. Although only 1,700 men were involved, the strike kept more than 15,000 men idle on naval work involving more than $342 million and affected "to a more or less extent 20,000 other shipyard workers employed on shipbuilding and repair contracts for the Navy Department and the Maritime Commission."[19] The strike was ended when the Office of Production Management insisted that the Bethlehem Shipbuilding Company sign the stabilization agreement, and when the Navy ordered the picket line abandoned and opened its rolls to machinists willing to accept employment.

FAIR EMPLOYMENT PRACTICES

Discrimination because of sex, color, nationality, and race prevented the utilization of many workers whose abilities could be effectively applied in defense industries. Robert C. Weaver was appointed to help develop training programs for Negro workers so that they would be used more extensively in defense plants. But training was purposeless unless employment was possible. Hillman issued a policy statement in September 1940 decrying discrimination, and President Roosevelt later in the same month made the same appeal. These statements were not effective. The President's Nondiscrimination Order of June 12, 1941, in which he advised industry "to take the initiative in opening the doors to all loyal and qualified workers regardless of race, national origin, religion or color," was a milestone.

Negro leaders remained dissatisfied with the results, and A. Philip Randolph, head of the Brotherhood of Sleeping Car Porters, urged a march on Washington as a protest against failure to provide employment opportunities. On July 25, 1941, President Roosevelt issued Executive Order No. 8802, under which a Committee of Fair Employment Practice was appointed to investigate discrimination in employment based upon race, creed, color, or national origin and to provide redress for valid grievances. Jurisdiction was limited to industries engaged in defense training. It was temporarily placed in the Office of Production Management. Irrespective of the achievements of this pioneer body, it introduced a new method for dealing with employment discrimination. While its effectiveness was limited, it was one of the more important actions in the defense period.

CHAPTER 42

Labor During the War

Soon after the attack on Pearl Harbor, President Roosevelt called a meeting of labor and management representatives to devise methods that would avoid interruptions of war work. Before the meeting, William Green, head of the AFL, called the executive council together, and the members pledged their cooperation in the war effort. The meeting of representatives of national unions endorsed the views of the council. With Murray in charge and the voices of the former critics of intervention and the Allied cause muted, the CIO favored all-out support of the program.[1]

The labor-management conference met in Washington on December 17, and the CIO and AFL submitted independent proposals. After their rejection, the delegates from both labor groups presented a program which called for the avoidance of strikes during the war and the establishment of a war labor board for the submission of all unsettled grievances that might lead to an interruption of work. The employer representatives sought to have requests for union security excluded from consideration by the board. The labor members, in turn, would not accept the limiting amendments and forced the President to intervene. Under Executive Order No. 9017 the National War Labor Board was established for "adjusting and settling labor disputes which might interrupt work which contributes to the effective prosecution of the war." This tripartite board, headed successively by William H. Davis, George Taylor, and Lloyd Garrison, was to fulfill one of the more difficult economic tasks of a wartime governmental agency and to resist, at the same time, political pressure and attacks from employer and labor. Roosevelt chose the route of agreement on a no-strike pledge rather than legislation, and by choosing the tripartite arrangement he rejected the experience of World War I and underrated the breakup of the Defense Mediation Board.

Later, the powers of the board were broadened to include the stabilization of wages. Although a board by the same name had been created to settle labor disputes in World War I, its authority was more restricted and its duties much more limited. Ultimately, the War Labor Board in World War II had the task of stabilizing wages in order to prevent a too-rapid expansion of purchasing power and to avoid upward pressure on prices. The diversion of economic resources to war purposes was much greater in the 1940's than in 1917–1918. When the United States began to prepare, in the fall of 1939, ample reserves of manpower and other productive capacity were idle. The more than 9 million unemployed appeared to offer an adequate reserve of labor, and there existed in 1939, the beginning of the defense period, unused capacity in steel and other industries vital to a war economy.

The existence of large unused resources made it easier to administer wage policy at the beginning of the war. Profit margins in many industries had been based upon low rates of operation and new business allowed for above break-even point returns. As a result the early wage increases put little pressure on established profit margins. The retention of time and one-half for overtime made it easier to impose the stabilization upon labor. Bringing idle resources into use had a stimulating effect upon economic activity, for the increased flow of income provided demand for consumer goods. As a result, the first year of the defense program witnessed an expansion of employment in the consumer-goods industries as well.

But the defense, and subsequent war program required expenditures on a massive scale, financed through credit creation by the banking system. The high personal and corporate taxes were not sufficiently steep to siphon off all income that could not be matched by added goods. In view of the failure of all belligerents to tax all surplus income, it can be assumed that a policy of this kind was spurned owing to the fear that it might have an adverse effect upon incentives to work. The magnitude of problems facing the economy becomes clear by noting the jump in employee compensation from under $65 billion in 1941 to almost $123 billion in 1945. In the same period disposable income rose from $92 to over $151.[2]

In the first months of the defense effort, some wholesale prices rose almost immediately, but a general upward movement was not observable until the early months of 1941. In December 1941 wholesale prices were more than 25 per cent above their August 1939 level. On the other hand, retail prices lagged and did not begin to move upward until the early months of 1941. By December 1941 the consumer price index was 12 per cent above the August 1939 level, with almost all the rise occurring during 1941.

Wage rates for the first year and a half after the beginning of the defense effort did not rise appreciably. In fact, they were, in January 1941, only 4.9 per cent above the level of August 1939 and exceeded this amount in April for the first time. From then until December 1941, the month of Pearl Harbor, wage rates rose steadily and reached 116.8 per cent of August 1939. Labor income, however, was much higher and was favorably affected by the increased overtime work at premium rates and the shifts of workers to higher-paying jobs and industries. Hourly earnings, which reflect total labor income better than wage rates, rose to 125.5 per cent in December 1941 from 100.0 in August 1939.[3]

The government, therefore, faced the need of recruiting and directing adequate labor supplies into industries producing war goods, preventing or slowing down price increases, and at the same time avoiding serious labor disputes.

There was, however, widespread objection in the ranks of labor to wage fixing. Philip Murray, head of the CIO, told the Senate Banking and Currency Committee that wage control was not necessary to control inflation, and he expressed the "firm and unqualified opposition of the C.I.O. to the inclusion of wage control in the price-control bill."[4] Senator Robert Taft did not see how price control, which Murray favored, could be enforced without some kind of restrictions on wages, but did not at the time urge it. The AFL wanted prompt action taken by Congress to stabilize the cost of living, but the executive council opposed attempts to stabilize production costs as contemplated by the bill on the ground they might lead to wage controls.[5]

The Emergency Price Control Act of January 30, 1942, did not direct the President to control wages, but did direct government departments "to work toward a policy of stabilizing costs of production including wages." For a time voluntary action or restraint was depended upon, but both were found ineffective. Before the War Labor Board had ended its first year of existence, it had to take more resolute action to control mounting wage income.

The board's authority was at first limited to dispute cases. Nevertheless, in the International Harvester Company case on April 15, 1942, the board, in approving a panel recommendation for 4.5 cents an hour wage increase, justified its decision by the claim that the new wage would not be higher than those paid by competitors and that upward "changes in the cost of living since the last wage adjustment in the industry justify the wage increase as granted by the Board."[6]

The following day William Green wrote President Roosevelt and advised against fixing wages by decree. He felt that freezing "or pegging wages would stunt the growth of our war production at the time when war industries are just beginning to grow." Green wanted wages left to voluntary bargaining, for, in his view, the "Government has already set up an agency which in the final settlement of wage disputes has applied a stringent check against wage increases. This agency, the National War Labor Board, has provided a check on wages which, because of the final authority of this Board in the settlement of wage disputes, is controlling. Any additional wage control would amount, in effect, to a double check on wages. Such a double check applies to no other group."[7] In his reply the President reviewed his anti-inflation proposals and told him: "The question of freezing of wages is a difficult one, and at this time I am not recommending it. . . . If voluntary methods fail, the freezing of wages will have to be reconsidered."[8] Green failed to realize that the "double check" applied to dispute cases and was in marked contrast to the absence of restraint in nonunion situations in the tight labor markets. In the latter, "voluntary" increases exceeded board allowances in dispute cases. The threat of wage inflation was greatest in the nonunion labor markets.

On July 16, 1942, the board, in the Little Steel case, laid down what became the guiding principles of wage regulation throughout the war. Although it was occasionally necessary to bend to the wind, the board did not retreat from its position. This step was taken after President Roosevelt, in a message to Congress on April 27, 1942, had outlined a seven-point program for stabilizing the cost of living. He proposed heavy taxation, ceilings on prices at all levels and on rents in areas affected by war plants, "stabilization of prices of farm products, encouragement of the purchases of War Bonds, rationing of scarce commodities, and discouragement of buying on installment, as well as encouragement of payment of debts, mortgages and other obligations, and the promotion of savings."[9]

Both Murray and Green opposed the President's views. Murray said that the "War Labor Board can no longer deal with cases on their merits."[10]

On July 16, 1942, the board decided the Little Steel case involving the Bethlehem Steel Corporation, Republic Steel Corporation, Youngstown Sheet and Tube Company, and Inland Steel Company. The Steel Workers' Union had requested an increase of $1.00 a day or 12.5 cents an hour which the board rejected. George Taylor, writing the opinion, based his argument on President Roosevelt's seven-point program: "The avoidance of another cycle of general wage increases as one item in a series of seven items conceived for the prevention of an upward spiral in the cost of living. The present decision meets this necessity by pointing the way in which wage inequalities may be eradicated without providing for a general wage increase which would feed an inflationary movement."[11]

The board then laid down five "guiding principles" to be applied in determining claims for wage increases. It found that the cost of living between January 1, 1941, and May 1942 had risen, after a period of stability, about 15 per cent. Consequently, workers who had not received a 15 per cent increase in hourly wage rates immediately before or after this period had their peacetime standards "broken" and were entitled "to have these standards re-established as a stabilization factor." Those who had received increases in hourly rates of 15 per cent or more and whose standards had been preserved could only have their wage claims considered on grounds of inequalities or substandards of living. This decision was based upon the anti-inflation program of the President.

The "catch up" provision was necessary because the relationship between wages and the cost of living depended upon the expiration date of the individual agreement. The relationship existing on January 1, 1941, was the basing point; none subsequent to that date was regarded as the "fair and equitable one." To the extent that wages had deteriorated since the last contract, a rollback in real wages took place. In other words, peacetime standards were not maintained.

The board believed, however, "that broadly speaking established peacetime labor standards should be reasonably maintained as a part of the process of ending the race between wages and prices. Such labor standards can be preserved without having any significant effect upon the broad inflation problem."[12]

The panel which heard the case of the steelworkers found that they had received between January 1, 1941, and May 1941 wage increases of 11.8 per cent. The board, therefore, allowed .032 cents per hour as "a stabilization factor under the National Economic Policy" and also 2.3 cents an hour to compensate for changes in the rules of wage settlement and the greater rise in the cost of living in the steel towns.[13] This decision, elaborating the Little Steel formula, became the basis for the wartime wage regulation.

Concern for the effect that the Little Steel decision would have on organized labor, especially the steelworkers, was expressed by the secretarial staff in the White House. Philip Murray was close to the administration, and the decision affected his position as head of the United Steelworkers of America. Fear existed that the members of the union would not stay in line. In a memorandum to Secretary Marvin McIntyre, Mrs. Anna Rosenberg told of a confidential report that the leaders of the union feared they could not hold their members in line.[14] The Wage Policy Board, nevertheless, accepted the decision and signed a contract with the steel companies on August 22, 1942.[15]

Although the AFL was not directly involved, Green regarded the wage dicta of the Little Steel case as a threat to collective bargaining. He wrote to the President on July 20, 1942, telling him that the AFL unions had agreed not to strike for the duration of the war and to submit differences to conciliation of the War Labor Board. "We did this with the definite understanding that collective bargaining was to remain fully operative. But the developments of the past week have convinced me that . . . I must speak plainly against proposed invasion of Labor's basic rights."[16] Green wanted wages set by collective bargaining and the board allowed to settle disputed cases.

Pressure on President Roosevelt for relaxing the principles of wage regulation expounded by the board was noted by its members, who expressed their "deep concern over reports that the procedures and authority of stabilizing wages by the War Labor Board machinery may be drastically modified." The members asked for an audience to discuss the issue.[17] In a separate letter Chairman Davis justified the "limit of wage increases which labor must accept." Davis feared that "the pressure of a competitive labor market might lead to voluntary wage increases of an amount and scope sufficient to break all effective wage stabilization. The War Labor Board had no control of these voluntary increases. The powers of the various government agencies concerned with wages have not been effectively used for lack of agreement, and in the absence of executive direction. This should be corrected by an Executive Order."[18]

Agitation for a "wage freeze" was increasing in intensity throughout the spring and summer of 1942. Murray, on occasion, and the CIO executive board decried such demands.[19] In September 1942 the President took a step towards tighter control of wage increases. In a message to Congress he called for amendments to the Emergency Price Control Act that would allow him to stabilize prices and wages. Accordingly, Congress voted the amendments of October 2, 1942, which directed the President to order, on or before November 1, 1942, the "stabilizing of prices, wages and salaries, affecting the cost of living . . . so far as practicable . . . on the basis of the levels which existed on September 15, 1942. The President may, except as otherwise provided in this Act, thereafter provide for making adjustments with respect to prices, wages, and salaries, to the extent that he finds necessary to aid in the effective prosecution of the war or to correct gross inequities."[20]

Soon thereafter the President issued Executive Order 9250, prohibiting wage changes without the approval of the War Labor Board. Whenever the board or the price administrator believed that a wage increase would necessitate a price increase, the approval of the Director of Economic Stabilization would be necessary. The latter was directed to formulate a comprehensive "national economic policy relating to the control of civilian purchasing power, rents, wages, salaries, profits, rationing, subsidies, and all related matters," for the purpose of preventing "avoidable increases in the cost of living."[21] Justice James F. Byrnes was appointed to the post.

For the first time in history, voluntary wage changes were brought under the control of the government, and the board was now given the herculean task of deciding all wage changes. On November 6, 1942, the board adopted four criteria as the basis for allowing a wage increase: (1) Maladjustments which referred to increases equaling 15 per cent in average straight time rates above the level prevailing on January 1, 1941. Only those groups whose increases were below the 15 per cent were eligible for wage rises under this criterion. (2) Inequalities and gross inequities referred to those rates which reflect "unusual and unreasonable differences in wage rates." (3) Substandards of living are those which the President in his message described as necessary to abolish. (4) Finally, wage rates might require increases to promote effective prosecution of the war. In addition, the board allowed merit increases or those based upon promotions and reclassifications.

Organized labor was highly critical of the President's order and the efforts of the War Labor Board to enforce it. In a meeting of the executive council of the AFL, William Hutcheson claimed that the no-strike pledge to the government was based implicitly upon its willingness to maintain the established conditions of labor.[22] Lewis put the matter more bluntly when he claimed "the Board breached the contract with labor when it set up in lieu of equity, the arbitrary Little Steel formula which attempted to freeze the wages of fifty million workers in America."[23] Lewis refused to say explicitly whether he would obey the no-strike pledge.

REGIONAL BOARDS

As a result of the much greater burden of work, the board was compelled to reorganize its activities in October 1942. Ten regional offices, each headed by a director, was appointed and tripartite advisory boards, which later became regional labor boards, were established. These boards were given authority, on November 6, 1942, to "make final decisions in wage adjustment cases where the requests were based on wage or salary inequalities or gross inequities"—providing price relief was not requested. The rise in dispute cases led the National War Labor Board to establish twelve regional labor boards vested with all the powers of the national board subject to review by the national board. The national board continued to handle cases of national importance and review decisions of the regional boards so that they conformed to national policy. The tripartite principle was followed in the appointment of members of the regional labor boards and the panels which initially held hearings on disputes.[24]

In addition, the board established a number of tripartite commissions or panels to handle problems of special industries. The West Coast Lumber Commission, the Wage Adjustment Board in the building construction industry, the Nonferrous Metals Commissions, Detroit Tool and Die Commissions, Shipbuilding Commission, Newspaper Printing and Publishing Commission, West Coast Aircraft Committee, the War Shipping Panel,

National Airframe Commission, Steel Commission, Telephone Panels, and the Northern and Southern Textile Commissions were appointed to handle special problems in the particular industries. Their decisions had to meet board criteria and could be set aside or amended by the board. Industry boards were needed to reflect labor cost competition in the product market; regional boards reflected competition for labor in local labor markets.

By March 1943 the maladjustment principle, the leading source for justifying wage increases, could no longer be effectively used. On April 8, 1943, President Roosevelt issued Executive Order 9328, the hold-the-line order, which limited wage increases to cases where they were necessary to correct substandards of living. This order did not affect wage changes attributable to promotions and reclassifications, or to cases where the increases were made to compensate for changes in the cost of living in accordance with the Little Steel formula. It limited adjustments that could be approved on the basis of inequalities and inequities. Convinced that these directives would not promote the war effort or lead to stabilization in the labor market, the board urged changes. As a result, the Economic Stabilization Director issued a clarifying directive which extended the board's authority to correct inequities.

Under the amended conditions, the board was authorized to establish wage brackets by occupational groups and labor market areas. These were to be regarded as "sound and tested" rates and not subject to change except in accordance with the Little Steel formula. Except under unusual conditions in "which the critical needs of war production require," wage rates more than 10 per cent below the average could be increased but not to a point nearer than ten per cent below the average. The board was able to utilize substandards of living, gross inequities, and successful prosecution of the war as criteria in wage setting.[25]

The labor movement was displeased with Executive Order 9328 and its modification. Meeting on May 20, 1943, the AFL Executive Council was "not satisfied that the workers of the country . . . will be given fair treatment under this modification."[26] The members of the council felt that a literal reading of the order would preclude wage adjustments.

STRIKES

Despite the no-strike pledge given by organized labor, labor disputes continued and after 1942 increased in every year of the war. Labor disputes had risen sharply with the advent of the New Deal; they reached a peak in 1937, with 4,700 involving 1.8 million workers, who lost 28.4 million mandays in idleness. The changes in business conditions led to an appreciable decline to a low point of 2,508 strikes in 1940. The defense boom stimulated demands for wage increases and other improvements, and the strike chart shot up to 4,288 in 1941. The effect of the war and the no-strike pledge may account for the decline of strikes in 1942.

YEAR	WORK STOPPAGES	NO. WORKERS INVOLVED (thousands)	MAN-DAYS LOST (thousands)
1941	4,288	2,360	23,000
1942	2,968	840	4,180
1943	3,752	1,980	13,500
1944	4,956	2,120	8,720
1945	4,750	3,470	38,000

They increased sharply in 1943, when they reached 3,752 involving 1,980 thousand workers and 13,500 thousand man-days lost. Strikes and workers involved mounted in 1944, but the strikes were of shorter duration. In the next year, the number of strikes dropped slightly, but the number of workers involved rose sharply. Man-days lost because of strikes were more than four times as great in 1945 as in the preceding year.

The Coal Strike

Demands for curbing strikes began almost with the start of the first defense activity. Congressmen and the press were severely critical of the continual work suspensions. The administration believed, however, that it was better to depend upon voluntary compliance than upon compulsion. The bituminous coal strike of 1943, with the miners leaving the pits on several occasions, and John L. Lewis' open attack on the principles used to regulate wages, increased the demand for government action against organized suspensions of work.

Announcing their refusal "to accept the 'Little Steel Formula' as a just measurement of wage rates,"[27] the policy committee of the United Mine Workers of America demanded a two-dollar-a-day wage increase for all classes of work in and around the mines. Negotiations with the northern operators were scheduled for March 10. In a four-hour address, Lewis denounced the effort to control wages while prices of necessities were rising.[28] Lewis declared that no war could be fought "without resultant inflation," and the increases secured by the mine workers "have been insufficient to put them on a parity with the earning standards of other classes of American citizens." The willingness of the AFL and CIO leaders to accept the stabilization program Lewis described as "cringing toadyism."[29]

As the end of the contract period approached, President Roosevelt requested the parties to continue producing coal, and the contract was extended from April 1 to May 1. A tripartite panel appointed by the board opened hearings on April 28, but miners' representatives failed to appear. A series of unauthorized strikes began at the same time; when they continued, the hearings were suspended in accordance with the board's rule of not considering cases during strikes or walkouts. The board also announced its decisions would have to conform with the stabilization orders and laws.

On May 1 a general strike in the bituminous fields began. Thereupon, the mines were taken over by the government and placed in charge of Secretary of the Interior Harold Ickes. President Roosevelt appealed to the miners to return to work and assured them of his desire that they should receive fair treatment. He also announced that work would be carried on under protection of troops, if necessary. The strike was called off and the miners began returning on May 3. Hearings on the case were resumed by the panel on May 6. On May 25 the board's decision rejected the request for a two-dollar-a-day increase but allowed an increase in vacation payments and other minor concessions. The final order in this phase of the case was issued on June 18, 1943. It rejected the demand for portal-to-portal pay. The demand itself arose as a result of a ruling by the U.S. Circuit Court of Appeals for the Fifth Circuit, in a case involving the Tennessee Coal, Iron and Railroad Company, on August 13, 1941, that time spent in the iron mines was working time and should be included in the employees' workweek under the Fair Labor Standards Act.

Issuance of the board directive order on May 25 was followed by widespread strikes in the mines. President Roosevelt again intervened and requested the miners to return. Lewis recommended that the strike be ended on June 7, and work was resumed. A final directive order was issued on June 18 which confirmed, in general, the earlier views. The miners began a strike three days later. On June 23 the President denounced the action of the miners' leaders as an "intolerable [one that has] highly stirred the anger and disapproval of the overwhelming mass of the American people."[30] He stated, moreover, that the government would deny draft exemption to miners on strike under forty-five years of age, and he subsequently requested the right to draft men up to sixty-five years of age for non-military service (it was denied by Congress). Lewis ordered the men back to work until October 31.

Another stage of the general coal miners' controversy began when the union and the Illinois Coal Operators Association requested approval of a new contract which included provisions for an eight-hour day with time and one-half for the eighth hour, a forty-hour week with time and one-half for the sixth day, and a general increase of $1.25 a day to cover portal-to-portal travel time.

The board refused to approve the agreement, and declared on August 24 that the $1.25 a day increase was not "a genuine settlement of alleged claims arising under the Fair Labor Standards Act," because the increase included all workers, those employed inside the mine as well as outside. A second contract was submitted on September 23, and the board now found that travel time was adequately calculated. It found, however, that the base rate of $8.50 provided in the Illinois agreement was 37.5 cents above the allowable wage increases under the rules. The labor members bitterly assailed the reasoning of the majority decision which allowed $8.125 instead of the $8.50 agreed upon by the parties.[31]

Following the decision, strikes again started, and the mines, which had been returned to private operation on October 12, were again seized by the government on November 1. An agreement was finally made between the union and the government represented by Secretary Ickes. Travel time was calculated at forty-five minutes and was paid for. Miners agreed to cut their lunch period from thirty minutes to fifteen and would therefore increase their productive labor by fifteen minutes which would be paid for at 37.5 cents, thus allowing for a base rate of $8.50 without piercing the wage stabilization program. Because of differences in travel time between mines, payment for it would have changed the established competitive relations between the mines. By compensating all miners for travel time, a general wage increase was provided; there was no compensation for travel time as such.

The contract was approved by the board with one public member dissenting because he believed Secretary Ickes should not have negotiated while the miners were on strike. The three other public members, in an opinion, insisted "the wage stabilization line had been held despite a batering-ram assault."[32] The decision pointed out that the miners demand for a $2.00 a day increase for seven hours of productive work had been rejected, and they were allowed $1.50 for an extra hour of full work a day.

Lewis' behavior, his unrestrained assaults on the board (especially the chairman), and its decisions contributed to the enactment of the War Labor Disputes bill. It was the first anti-labor measure enacted by Congress and brought a move to deny unions failing to obey a directive of the War Labor Board the checkoff and closed shop. The penalty recommended by Chairman Davis was that "all those benefits which accrue to the union under the terms and conditions laid down in the Board's order" be denied to a disobedient union. "But," said Ickes, "the check-off and closed shop are not benefits accruing under the Board's order. In coal, they are established by custom and provision of pre-existing contracts."[33] Ickes also argued against the proposal in a letter to the President, in which he told him that the proposed remedy was unjustified and that it might also cause difficulties in the coal fields.[34] Dues checked off were withheld temporarily but given to the union when it obeyed the directives of the board.

The coal mines were returned to the operators on December 17, 1943. Since the Southern Coal Producers' Association refused to subscribe to the agreement until June 1944, the mines were not completely returned until June 21, 1944.

The War Labor Disputes Act

The rise in strikes finally had its effect upon Congress. The Smith-Connally bill, the first antilabor measure to pass Congress in a generation, was enacted over President Roosevelt's veto on June 25, 1943, two days after Lewis had called the bituminous miners out on strike for the second time in two months. Roosevelt's suggestion for raising the age for non-combatant military service to sixty-five years was rejected. The President was authorized to take over any plant producing war material threatened with suspension by a labor dispute and to maintain existing conditions of employment unless advised to do otherwise by the National War Labor Board after an investigation. Interference with government-operated plants through strikes, lockouts, or slowdowns was made illegal and violators were subject to fines and imprisonment. The powers of the War Labor Board, granted under executive orders and in the Emergency Price Control Act of 1942, were affirmed. The board was given power to require attendance of witnesses and production of documents and allowed to apply to federal courts for an order to obey its subpoena.

Thirty days' notice of a pending dispute had to be given to the Secretary of Labor and the War Labor Board and the National Labor Relations Board. Failure to agree within thirty days required a strike vote under the auspices of the National Labor Relations Board. Labor unions were forbidden to contribute to candidates running for office in national elections.[35] Inferentially the law approved strikes called by majority vote.

Both Murray and Green denounced the bill and urged its veto. The President complied with their request, but his veto was overridden.[36]

THE COST OF LIVING

As the allowances under the Little Steel formula and the other criteria were exhausted, the organizations of labor were faced with the need for finding some basis for justifying their demands for wage changes and other improvements. Almost from the beginning they believed that the government was more severe in its restrictions of wage increases than of price increases. The labor organizations advocated rises in tax rates on corporations and high-income receivers, favored control of prices on cost-of-living items, and food subsidies so that prices of necessities would remain stable and would not be allowed to rise.[37]

Whatever merits such demands might have, they were matters which were within the authority of Congress and which the President could not completely determine. The AFL and CIO thereupon attacked the reliability of the cost-of-living index upon which the entire wage-stabilization program was based. Complaints by labor led Roosevelt to request Chairman Davis to appoint several board members to investigate the index and make clear how the "figure is arrived at, whether changes should be made in its component parts, or other improvements." The President believed if the "committee could agree . . . it would have a salutary effect all over the country, because today all kinds of exaggerated statements are made."[38]

No agreement was reached by the board committee. The 1943 CIO convention criticized the use of "government-fixed wage formulas."[39] Green wrote to President Roosevelt asking him to cancel the power of the Director of Economic Stabilization over wages. President Roosevelt assured him that he desired to maintain the independent position of the War Labor Board and that he had given the Economic Stabilization Director only the "minimum control that is necessary to carry out the responsibility imposed upon me with respect to the stabilization of the cost of living under the Act of October 2, 1942."[40]

During most of 1944 leaders of the AFL and CIO continued to attack the War Labor Board's views on wage stabilization and the Little Steel formula. Murray criticized, on January 25, 1944, the reliability of the U.S. Bureau of Labor Statistics' cost-of-living index before the Senate Committee on Education and Labor. On the same day George Meany and R. J. Thomas, president of the United Automobile Workers Union, both members of the War Labor Board, charged that the index was inaccurate and that it understated the rise in the cost of living between January 1941 and December 1943 by 20 per cent. U.S. Commissioner of Labor A. F. Hinrichs denied the charge. The Meany-Thomas argument was that there had been large shifts of population to war-production centers not covered by the bureau index, that the increased employment of women meant a substantial rise in restaurant eating by wage earners and rising prices of meals were not measured, that quality deterioration had not been considered, that periodic sales which allowed the workers' family to purchase many goods at reduced prices had ceased, and that the index failed to consider black-market prices.[41]

Finally the President was forced to appoint a committee of three experts, headed by Professor Wesley Mitchell, to investigate. The committee supported the accuracy of the index, but conceded that as a result of quality deterioration, disappearance of cheaper grades, absence of sales, and underreporting of prices actually charged, there would be an underestimate of from 3-4 per cent.[42]

At the same time, a drive for what George Meany called "a realistic modification in the Little Steel Formula because the formula has become a thumbscrew with which to torment the working people of America and their families"[43] continued. He charged that the Little Steel formula was designed to maintain the peacetime standards of living of the worker and that it had failed in this task. He claimed, moreover, that the economic policy presented to Congress in the President's message of April 27, 1943, had only been carried out as far as stabilizing wages was concerned. Congress, he claimed, had failed to tax the rich sufficiently, the cost of living had not been stabilized, farm prices had been stabilized at 10 per cent above parity, rationing had not been effective, and black markets had proliferated.[44]

The 1944 conventions of the AFL and the CIO both condemned the refusal of the War Labor Board to recommend the modification of the Little Steel formula.[45]

FRINGE BENEFITS

While the board continued to enforce its principles of wage stabilization, it faced the practical need for meeting some of the complaints of organized labor. The board well knew that some flexibility was needed if widespread worker protests were to be avoided. It therefore allowed firms to adopt certain kinds of fringe benefits. Consequently, when President Harry Truman issued Executive Order 9599 on August 14, 1945 (V-J Day), abolishing control of wages, if offsetting price increases were not requested, the board had approved a number of changes in industrial practice which were to influence labor-management negotiations in the future. In fact, the unions, having exhausted their ability to gain wage increases because of the limiting criteria, turned to other methods of gaining benefits for their members.

The board supported the principle of equal pay for equal work for men and women. This principle was embodied in official policy by the adoption of General Order No. 16, on November 24, 1942, which allowed such equalization without approval, although the board retained the right to review. Such changes could not be the basis of a request for price increases. Unions brought requests for annual vacations with pay for production workers in the early months of the war. Board policy from the beginning was to allow such requests, providing they met certain standards and were not a subterfuge for a wage raise. Various acceptable methods for computing were approved.

Payment of shift premiums to compensate for work on less desirable shifts was approved under certain conditions. With mounting war orders, firms increased their operations from one to two or three shifts. In view of the lesser attractiveness of these added work periods, an amount above the standard rate was added to the going hourly rate. The board recognized these payments as proper and as costs which could be offset by savings on unit overhead which was now spread over a larger volume of output. However, industries normally operating around the clock because of the nature of the product manufactured—as in many chemical plants or as a result of custom as in some textile operations—did not normally pay shift differentials. Consequently, approval of such payments would mean both an increase in wages and in costs. The board thereupon differentiated between firms which normally operated single and those which operated more than one shift in allowing shift differentials.

The unions pushed for a variety of other fringe benefits which have since become normal provisions of labor-management contracts. Unions sought approval of holidays with pay, and the board allowed such payments where it found they were common in the industry or locality. Reasonable sick leave plans were also approved, as were insurance and hospitalization plans. These benefits had frequently been denied to production workers.

Unions asked for severance pay for employees entering the armed services. The board approved such payments but usually would not order them in dispute cases. Unions also began making demands for severance pay; and voluntary plans were approved, although the board would not order incorporation of such provisions in contracts.[46]

COMPLIANCE WITH BOARD ORDERS

Despite criticisms from the labor and employer sides, the performance of the War Labor Board was one of the more notable accomplishments of a government agency dealing with economic problems during World War II. Its ability to gain compliance of decisions, which were frequently objectionable to one of the parties, is one of the remarkable examples of "voluntarism" in our history. "Between January 12, 1942 and August 18, 1945, the National War Labor Board closed 17,650 dispute cases involving approximately 12.2 million workers. In over 95 per cent of these cases, the decision of the Board and its agents resolved the dispute without further threat to production."[47] The board followed a pragmatic policy; if a dispute did not interfere with the war program, it was allowed to stay in mediation.

Nevertheless, some unions and employers refused to accept board determinations. In many instances noncompliers reversed their position, but in forty-six cases or three-thousandth of 1 per cent of the disputes closed by the board, one of the parties remained adamant. Such cases were referred to the President, who could order seizure of the plant. His authority was based upon his constitutional power as commander-in-chief of the armed services, and after June 1943 upon the War Labor Disputes Act.

Seizure of the bituminous coal mines attracted the most attention because of the dramatizing of the dispute by John L. Lewis and the readiness of the miners to shut down needed production. The dispute between the United Mail Order, Warehouse, and Retail Employees' Union and Montgomery Ward and Company attracted a great deal of attention because of the stubborn opposition of Sewell Avery, the company's president, in obeying an order of the War Labor Board. The union was certified as the exclusive bargaining agent on February 28, 1942. On June 2, 1942, the dispute was sent to the War Labor Board. The board directed that a maintenance of membership provision be written into the contract; the company refused to accept it on the ground it was not engaged in war production and the board had no authority over it. A strike at Montgomery Ward would not affect war production, but a prolonged walkout might raise the question of the right of workers in defense plants to strike. When the President directed the Army to take over the properties in Chicago, on April 26, 1944, Sewell Avery refused to leave the premises or to acknowledge possession. He was carried out by several soldiers. Under-Secretary of Commerce Wayne C. Taylor took over the establishment.[48]

The company carried its plea to the U.S. district court, which upheld its contention. It was reversed, however, by the Circuit Court of Appeals of the Seventh Circuit. During the meeting of the executive council of the AFL, a statement declaring that "regardless of the material facts or of the union . . . in the controversy with the Montgomery-Ward Company, the Executive Council is primarily concerned in upholding the power and authority of the National War Labor Board. This is the issue which transcends all other considerations in the Montgomery-Ward case."[49] Hutcheson threatened to oppose the statement publicly if it were issued.

MANPOWER

The manpower reserves that had existed at the end of 1939 were slowly exhausted. Utilization of the unemployed and the millions of women entrants into the labor market eased the manpower problems, although shortages of specific skills were apparent by the middle of 1941. As the war continued, it became increasingly difficult to obtain workers for some industries. The need to concentrate defense orders in certain areas where housing, schools, and other facilities were in short supply intensified the problem. High turnover rates complicated the problem. In order to plan the distribution and use of labor more effectively, the President on April 18, 1942, created the War Manpower Commission. Paul V. McNutt was appointed chairman and several cabinet officers were members. The commission was given broad powers with the task to estimate labor needs and coordinate federal policies on recruitment, training, and placement.[50]

As the war continued, the problem of labor pirating appeared, and Executive Order 9279 was designed to prevent unhealthy competition for labor. Under its authority, the Manpower Commission directed hiring and recruitment of workers for specified employments to be conducted through the U.S. Employment Service or in accordance with the rules of the regional manpower director. The purpose was to prevent the high turnover of labor, reduce unnecessary migration, and distribute needed help to war industries, where it could be used to maximum advantage. A system of priorities for directing workers into essential industries was also established.[51] The CIO suggested that the available manpower could be more effectively used if discrimination against Negroes and women workers were eliminated.[52]

Green proposed a more elaborate program. He opposed freezing of workers into jobs, and advocated a provision of occupational deferment from military service, adequate housing facilities for those sent to work in remote sections, and financing of the cost of transportation by the employer.[53]

As demands for a labor draft mounted, a joint committee made up of labor, industry, and agricultural representatives expressed opposition to such a step. The declaration recognized that manpower was being wasted through ineffective uses and excessive labor turnover, and failure of workers to transfer to essential employments. The statement called attention to the large reservoir of employable women remaining outside of the labor force and claimed that the American people would do better under a voluntary system than under a compulsory one.[54]

President Roosevelt believed, however, that the voluntary system was not completely effective in providing the needed manpower, and in January 1944 he recommended to Congress the enactment of a National Service law under which workers could be compelled to accept employment in war industries. It drew an immediate objection from William Green, who, in a letter to members of Congress, claimed "we have fought and won the battle of production, [and] such legislation at this time is highly unnecessary."[55] Claiming that such legislation would not prevent strikes, he pointed to the experience of Great Britain as proof that it would not solve manpower problems and would undermine the principles and practices of democracy.

Senator Truman, in answering Green's letter, told him the President's suggestion was two years too late, since the "peak of the manpower problem has been reached and we are on the down grade now so far as employment is concerned. . . . If the National Service Law had been set up at the same time the Military Draft Act was passed there would have been a good reason for it and it would have been a successful arrangement. Now it would only cause widespread dissatisfaction and will accomplish nothing so far as I can see."[56] This bill, as well as the May bill introduced in 1945, which had similar aims, was defeated by Congress. No real compulsory manpower program was used in the United States. In fact, beginning with the end of World War II, the labor movement began worrying about the ability of the American economy to provide ample employment rather than shortages of labor.

CHAPTER 43

Storm and Strife in Reconversion

FEAR OF UNEMPLOYMENT

Even at the height of the war, labor leaders feared that the ending of hostilities would be accompanied by a return to large-scale unemployment. Donald Nelson, the head of the War Production Board, was one of the first high officials in a wartime agency to recognize the need for preparing for peace before hostilities ended. Believing that governmental controls would be needed to prevent economic disorganization, he urged the establishment of an agency of the government vested with authority to direct industry during the reconversion period.[1]

In the plans for reconversion, the problems of demobilizing millions of workers and of shifting millions more from industries and areas producing war materials to those engaged in civilian tasks were not given major attention by the governmental authorities. In a joint letter the AFL, CIO, and Railway Labor Executives Association regretted that the Senate Military Affairs Committee had considered bills for contract termination "divorced from legislation dealing with the human side of demobilization. . . . Emergency unemployment compensation for demobilized workers is an indispensable part of any overall legislation and should not be sidetracked . . . for separate consideration."[2] The letter, in addition, advocated an orderly program of reconversion to civilian production and special unemployment benefits for unemployed workers as well as servicemen.

The concern of the labor organizations was that a sudden ending of the war in Europe would catch the country unprepared and would lead to unemployment on a scale equal to the 1930's.[3] In January 1944 the CIO urged that transition problems in key industries be handled by an industrial council of representatives from labor, business, and government.[4]

Leaders in both federations sought policies that would foster the maintenance of income. Increases in minimum wages, lowering the age of retirement, and raising old age and survivors' benefits were some of the proposals that both the CIO and AFL endorsed. The federation, however, was more anxious about the abolition of government controls. Both organizations wanted the return to free collective bargaining, and they differed only on the degree of control to be exercised in the economy.[5] In general, the organizations of labor were dissatisfied with the reconversion legislation. Murray denounced the bill of Senator Walter George, which passed Congress in the summer of 1944, describing it as "inadequate," and pointed "scornfully at a Congress with no more imagination than to believe that deep trouble and unemployment can be avoided only because the nation still has a war to carry on against Japan."[6]

The same fear seemed to dominate the executive council of the AFL. In August 1945 it charged that the country was getting "too little reconversion. Unless preparations for resumption of peacetime production are speeded up, it may be too late to avoid a major post-war depression. Unless more adequate provision is promptly made for human needs during reconversion, peace may bring economic disaster to the American people. Our country is less prepared for peace today than it was for war at the time of Pearl Harbor."[7] The council wanted the war effort scaled down to a one-front basis, a peacetime production program initiated, and controls over the economy dropped as quickly as possible. It also called for a restoration of collective bargaining, higher minimum wage standards, the enactment of the Kilgore bill—which sought to supplement state unemployment benefits by the federal government—and the enactment of the Wagner Postwar Housing bill.[8]

WAGE POLICY AFTER V-E DAY AND V-J DAY

Following the surrender of Germany, the National War Labor Board decided to continue wage controls without basic changes. After V-E Day it laid down general guidelines for the maintenance of wages in plants converted to civilian production. Following the Japanese surrender, Executive Order 9599 allowed voluntary wage increases as long as they were not used as an application for price increases or for raising costs to the government. Price or cost increases to the government were not to be considered in wage increases to correct inequities. The relaxation of wage controls were, in part, a response to the pressure of organized labor, but a conviction was also widespread that the unemployed, who, it was believed, would increase in large numbers, would be a check upon excessive wage rates.[9]

On January 1, 1946, the War Labor Board was succeeded by the National Wage Stabilization Board, a tripartite agency. Its principal function was to "exercise indirect controls over wage or salary increases, that is, to rule upon applications for approval of voluntary increases which might be used as a basis for increasing prices or rent ceilings or which might result in higher costs to the Government. The Board determined whether such wage increases could be used in whole or in part for these purposes."[10]

Williard Wirtz was appointed chairman, and the other public member, Sylvester Garrett, was appointed vice-chairman. Labor and industry each appointed two representatives. Irrespective of the wishes or even the desirability of controls upon some economic activities, the public demand— as shown by the actions of large groups of workers and employers—was for ending all wartime regulation of economic activity. On November 9, 1946, President Truman announced the removal of controls on wages and salaries. The board thereupon took steps to end its activities.

Toward the end of March 1945 the AFL, CIO, and the U.S. Chamber of Commerce approved a code of principles to promote maximum industrial peace. The National Association of Manufacturers would not sign the conference report, although it had been represented at the joint meetings.[11] When Green reported this matter to the executive council, Hutcheson announced that he could sit down with the Chamber of Commerce and the NAM, but that he found it difficult to meet with the CIO. Obviously his views were shared by other members of the council. A resolution that representatives of the AFL meet with the employers and not with the CIO was carried, with William C. Doherty and George Meany opposed.[12]

Meeting immediately after V-J Day, the AFL Executive Council rejected a proposal for the extension of the no-strike pledge for six months. Hutcheson "thought the time had come when the war is over [and] that we should get back our rights as Americans."[13] Meany believed that such a pledge would not represent the entire membership. The CIO unions showed immediately by their actions that they did not believe it was feasible to extend this policy beyond the active period of the war.

Labor-Management Conference

The labor-management conference called by President Truman for November 5 opened on schedule. Addressing the delegates, the President told them they were appointed by their organizations and not selected by the government. He outlined the seriousness of the problems, and alluded to the number of bills for restricting labor before Congress. He urged the delegates to find a solution to the vexing problems facing both industry and the worker.[14]

As soon as the conference got under way, a dispute on the make-up of the executive committee started. John L. Lewis' efforts to gain membership was described by Philip Murray as "a veritable blitz." Lewis insisted that the United Mine Workers of America was entitled to representation and that he did not "like Mr. Murray's unique and despicable German terminology."[15] Murray then joined in welcoming Lewis to the executive committee. When this issue was settled, a round of speeches by the Secretaries of Labor and Commerce and the heads of the labor and industry organizations followed.[16]

A resolution on wages by Murray, as well as amendments by William Green and Ira Mosher, an employer delegate, were defeated.[17] While little was accomplished, the conference did not end on any note of disappointment. A consensus on less important issues was reached: Voluntary arbitration, initial steps in the writing of contracts, and on methods of improving the Conciliation Service. Lewis took the floor and praised the unity of the employers which he contrasted with the division in the labor delegation. He ended with the hope "that those same people, the same management and the same principles of free enterprise and the same spirit of democracy that prevails under our flag will carry us through whatever may betide tomorrow."[18] His speech drew the "only round of applause given for a farewell address. The applause came from the management side. The few delegates left on the labor side of the room sat on their hands."[19]

STRIKES

Following the victory over Japan the country faced the task of demobilizing its armed services and shifting its war workers. The labor force had grown from 51 million in 1940, with only 500,000 in the armed services, to 63 million in 1944, with 11 million in the armed services. Three million of the increase came from normal growth, and the remainder from increased entrance of women and others in the non-working population. Growth in the number of the employed was accompanied by increased hours of work, and estimates were made that the longer hours of labor added the equivalent of 5 million to the labor force. Millions of workers also had been upgraded by the changing demand for labor.[20]

With vivid memories of the depression of the 1930's, union leaders and members were concerned over the possibilities of loss of income from the end of overtime work, downgrading, and the reappearance of large-scale unemployment. These fears, among other considerations, stimulated demands on industry that in many instances could not be entirely met except by concomitant price increases. Strikes, as was noted above, were by no means absent during the war, but in most instances they were different in aim from those which began after V-J Day. In the entire wartime period, 14,731 strikes involving 6,744,000 workers, with man-day losses of 36.3 million, took place.[21]

The wartime strikes, however, were sporadic, usually unauthorized by leaders. There was also the public opposition and the pressure of the War Labor Board for their termination. The strikes that followed V-J Day were more stubborn and long-lasting. However, in contrast to those in the period after World War I, they were virtually free of violence. Approximately 4,600 strikes involving 3.3 million workers and adding up to almost 35 million man-days took place in 1945. The months following V-J Day accounted for 37 per cent of the stoppages, and they included 47 per cent of the workers on strike during the year and accounted for three-fourths of the lost time. During the war months of 1945, time lost by strikes equaled 0.17 per cent of the annual working time, in the postwar months the percentage of lost time rose 0.93 per cent. The average time lost by each worker on strike was 5.3 days before, and 16.3 days after, V-J Day.[22]

The 1945 strike wave began on September 17 with a walkout of 43,000 refinery workers in twenty states. The Oil Workers International Union (CIO) demanded fifty-two hours' pay for a forty hour workweek, or about a 30 per cent increase. Intervention by the government failed, and, on October 4, President Truman ordered the Navy Department to take over and operate the struck refineries. A fact-finding panel was appointed by the Secretary of Labor, and the walkout in the end was settled by a wage increase of 18.5 cents an hour. This was the beginning of a twelve-month series of labor-management conflicts unmatched for their "scope and intensity" in any comparable period in American history. In the period between August 15, 1945, and August 14, 1946, 4,630 work stoppages took place. They involved 4.9 million workers, who lost 119.8 million man-days of work, or 1.62 per cent of all work time in the period.[23]

Estimates were made that 213,000 workers were on strike on September 15, and the number was to rise every month until the first months of 1946.[24] The number of monthly strikes in 1945 reached a high point in September with 550, and the number of workers involved were highest in the following month with 560,000. Days lost as a result of strikes were also highest in October 1945, with 7,800,000, but although they receded somewhat the following month they were again at 7,500,000 in December. The number of days-lost almost tripled in January when 19,700,000 man-days were lost. The crest of the strike wave was reached in the following month with 22,900,000 man-days lost. It then dropped sharply to more than 13 million man-days in May, to 4,580,000 in June, and fluctuated around that figure, declining again to 3,100,000 man-days lost in December.

Although the strike wave involved virtually all industries—automobile, agricultural implements, coal, electrical manufacturing, meat-packing, oil refining, longshoremen, railroad and steel workers—the more significant contests were in the coal and railroad industries, where the government took firm steps to suppress the walkouts; in the automobile industry, where the United Automobile Workers of America sought an increase and insisted that the General Motors Corporation had to agree not to increase its prices; and the steel industry, where the employers were willing to make wage concessions providing the government would grant them offsetting price increases. Price rises were also a consideration in the meat packing, agricultural implement, and electrical manufacturing industries.

GENERAL MOTORS STRIKE

Soon after V-J Day the executive board of the United Automobile Workers expressed preference for industrywide wage negotiations. However, if they were not acceptable to the companies, the executive board decided to negotiate with single firms in the industry. It also hoped to avoid "strikes outside the test corporation, if such strikes shall in any way tie up automobile manufacturing competitors of that corporation."[25] The idea was to strike one company at a time, on the theory that in this fashion more pressure would be exerted since each would fear loss of its markets to its competitors.

The General Motors Corporation, the super-giant in the industry, was selected for the testing. In addition to the demand for a 30 per cent wage increase, Vice-President Walter Reuther, who headed the union in the plants of the corporation, presented the novel proposal that wage increases were to be granted without accompanying price increase.[26] The terms were rejected, and a vote, under the terms of the War Labor Disputes Act, showed a substantial majority favoring the use of the strike to enforce the demands.

General Motors offered a 10 per cent increase, which Reuther rejected as a "bribe"; he charged that the refusal of the corporation to discuss ability to pay was an unfair labor practice.[27] On November 19 the General Motors Council, representing all the unionized plants of the company suggested arbitration by a board of three, which "will have full access to books, records, and any 'other documents' of both sides which the board may consider essential to intelligent and factual solution."[28] A strike was voted, but the date was not announced. It was called on November 21 and led to a strike of 180,000 workers, who walked off their jobs in more than ninety plants. H. W. Anderson, a vice-president in charge of labor relations, declared that the union had sought in its proposal for arbitration to compel the company to "relinquish its right to manage its business. This was not an offer of arbitration but a demand for abdication. Actually your proposal means that an arbitration board would assume the responsibilities of management; that it would assume responsibility for determining what is sound financial and economic policy for General Motors."[29] Anderson also charged that the union was hasty in calling the strike and in not waiting for a reply to its letter.

Sparring through the public press began before the strike and continued up to the settlement. Reuther evidently believed that the insistence upon a wage increase without a price increase would attract public support. On December 10, General Motors canceled the agreement with the union. President Charles Wilson denied that the company was anti-union. In an attempt to exercise pressure of its own, General Motors announced its reluctance to continue its maintenance of union membership provisions in its future contracts.[30]

When the strike went on without prospect of settlement, John L. Lewis injected himself into the controversy. While testifying before a congressional committee, he noted that General Motors was making more money by keeping its plants closed than it would be by operating. Presumably this conclusion was based upon tax refunds that would cover its losses. He also observed gratuitously that "dishonesty of the company is equalled only by the stupidity of that labor organization," presumably the United Automobile Workers.[31] President Truman, in an effort to bring about a settlement, appointed a committee of three—Lloyd Garrison (chairman), Milton Eisenhower, and Judge Walter P. Stacy—to investigate the dispute and make recommendations.[32]

When the board was organized, Truman expressed the view that, since ability to pay is always a question, a board should be allowed to examine a company's books and records but keep its knowledge confidential. When the board requested confidential records, the company declined to participate in the proceedings in which ability to pay was treated as an issue. It stated that it had not applied for price relief, and prices and profit margins were not proper questions for discussion and it therefore withdrew from the proceedings.[33] The board recommended a wage increase of 19.5 cents an hour, but the suggestions did not serve as a basis for settlement. The company instead offered 13 cents an hour increase, or 12 per cent above existing rates. In rejecting the recommendations, President Charles E. Wilson said that the board's recommendations were based on the "unsound principle" that a specific company should have to pay higher wages than its competitors because it is more prosperous.[34]

The strike dragged on without signs of settlement. Early in January a citizens' committee, headed by former Director of the Office of Price Administration Leon Henderson, appealed for contributions to assist the strikers. In the last days of January, the United Automobile Workers settled with two other major automotive companies. The union accepted a raise of 18 cents an hour from the Ford Company, and 18.5 cents from the Chrysler Corporation. Instead of the 30 per cent demanded from General Motors, these raises equaled, respectively, 15.1 per cent and 16.7 per cent.[35]

While the strike was on, a settlement in the steel industry dispute on the basis of an 18.5-cents-an-hour increase created a pattern followed by most of the large employers that year. It was the amount which the United

Electrical, Radio and Machine Workers Union accepted for the General Motors plants in which it bargained. R. J. Thomas, the head of the Auto Workers' Union, attacked the settlement.[36]

The same offer was rejected by the Auto Workers, and in a private conference, Wilson informed the union's three top leaders, "this is our last offer. Take it or leave it."[37] But the delegates to the General Motors Council rejected 18.5 cents an hour. The union repeated its request for arbitration but it was still unacceptable to the corporation. In turn, the company asked the union for a referendum on the acceptance of the settlement among the strikers. The union agreed with reservations, and no satisfactory statement for submission to a vote could be devised.[38]

The long strike continued without any significant differences separating the parties. Reuther's demand for holding the price line had been relegated to the depository of forgotten slogans, but the union wanted the company to accept the recommendations of the fact-finding commission for 19.5 cents an hour increase. In the end, at negotiations attended by Murray and Wilson, the strike was settled on March 13, after 113 days, with a raise of 18.5 cents an hour.[39]

Candidacy and Election of Reuther

Before the strike had ended, Reuther announced his candidacy for the presidency of the United Automobile Workers Union.[40] It brought the General Motors strike into the center of union politics. R. J. Thomas, the incumbent president, charged that the strike was called too soon, and he criticized the injection of the price issue into wage negotiations. Aside from the political nature of the criticism, it had considerable merit. Raising the price question and demanding books for public examination obviously stiffened the resistance of the company and prolonged the strike. Such issues may have an appeal to certain groups, but they have never gained extensive public support. Nevertheless, Reuther was able to win election in 1946 by a narrow vote of 4,226 to 4,108 for Thomas. Reuther's victory gave the union a resourceful and adroit leader and a master in the political and public relations arts. Reuther was not, however, in full control as his opponents won control of the executive board. In his report to the 1947 convention Reuther attacked them and they fought back.[41] But they were fighting a vain battle. George Addes, the secretary-treasurer of the union, made the signing of the non-Communist affidavits, required by the Taft-Hartley Act, a leading issue. But so strongly had Reuther solidified his position in this faction-ridden organization that the opposition would not even run a candidate against him. At the 1947 convention the Reuther forces were able to take full control of the union. Swept out of office, among others, was Addes, who had held office for eleven years and was one of the pioneers in the union.

Reuther's victory in 1947 was of utmost importance to the trade-union movement and to the American people. It placed the United Automobile Workers' Union solidly in the anti-Communist camp. Men like Thomas, Addes, and Richard Leonard were always anti-Communists, but they, because of the Reuther group's position and strength, were forced by necessity to compromise on this issue. With Reuther and his associates in full control, no weasling on the Marshall Plan or failure to support the program of the free world would be possible. Reuther was the one man who could reduce the significance of Stalinism, which by a freak of historical circumstances held an important place in the organization. Reuther's victory was a sign of the union's coming of age; the victory of his group was a good day for the free world.

STEEL INDUSTRY

The issue in the steel industry was completely different. Instead of the United Steelworkers of America demanding that wages be increased and prices kept at the existing level, industry called attention to the linkage of wages and prices. Even before the union in the industry could formally transmit its demands for a $2.00-a-day increase in wages, Benjamin Fairless, the head of the U.S. Steel Corporation, noted that such an increase amounted to a 32 per cent rise in the basic labor rate and 21 per cent in the average over-all straight-time rate of his company's operations. "Wages," said Fairless, "cannot be considered separate and apart from steel prices. . . . The Office of Price Administration now has data from steel companies making eighty-five per cent of the country's steel which show that on an average basis these companies are losing money on two-thirds of the tonnage they produce."[42]

While the situations in the steel and automobile industries may appear similar, they are basically different. Fairless insisted that unless his company were allowed to raise prices, which were then controlled by the government, it could not grant any wage increases, because its margin of profit was too low or nonexistent. General Motors did not raise the question of its ability to pay; it simply argued that its profit rate was not bargainable with the union. Fairless was unwilling to undertake any negotiations while the price question was unsettled, but Philip Murray, the chief negotiator for the union, claimed that the company was obligated to bargain. As a result, a strike vote was taken, and approval by 409,977 to 83,990 given.[43] On December 11 the National Policy Committee of the United Steelworkers announced that a strike in the industry would begin on January 14, 1946. On December 30, President Truman appointed a three-member fact-finding board headed by Nathan P. Feinsinger, a professor of law.

Negotiations started on January 10, 1946, and the union was ready to accept a raise of 19.5 cents an hour, the amount the fact-finding board had recommended in the General Motors dispute. President Truman, at a conference with the parties, suggested 18.5 cents an hour increase as a fair amount. It was accepted by the steel union but rejected by the industry. The strike, therefore, started on January 21 and affected about 750,000 workers and 85 per cent of the industry.

The central issue in the dispute involved prices. Irving S. Olds, chairman of the board of directors of the U.S. Steel Corporation, said that a price rise of $6.25 would be needed to compensate for the 18.5-cents-an-hour rise in wages suggested by President Truman. A considerable amount of jockeying over price went on, and by February 15 the union and the corporation had agreed, after the company was granted a $5.00-a-ton price increase, to a raise of 18.5 cents an hour. The other companies followed.[44]

TRAIN SERVICE

The greatest strike in the history of the railroads came about as a result of a wage dispute between the carriers and the Brotherhood of Railroad Trainmen and the Brotherhood of Locomotive Engineers. All of the unions —operating and nonoperating unions—filed requests for wage increases and changes in work rules on July 24, 1945. Following the usual procedure, the parties invoked the services of the National Mediation Board. The carriers requested that the unions withdraw the request for rules' changes; and of the twenty unions, only the Trainmen and Engineers refused.[45] They insisted that rules were part of the controversy and that the negotiators on the union side had "no authority to reject or to assume a position by making a recommendation that we defer this issue."[46] The unions took strike votes of their members, and they were approved. The nonoperating unions and three operating unions—the Order of Railroad Conductors, the Brotherhood of Locomotive Firemen and Enginemen, and the Switchmen's Union—accepted arbitration. An emergency board was appointed in the Trainmen's and Engineer's case on March 8. The arbitration board after a hearing recommended 16 cents an hour increase, and the emergency board recommended the same amount for the Trainmen and Engineers. A joint meeting of general chairmen at Cleveland on April 25, 1946, voted to "reject said recommendations that are not consistent with our demands, and that we authorize the President and the Wage Committee to set a time for the men to leave the service if a satisfactory settlement cannot be effected with the carriers in the meantime."[47]

In a joint statement Presidents A. F. Whitney and Alvanley Johnston charged that the emergency board had followed a standard of 16 cents an hour set by the arbitration board deciding the claims of other railroad workers. The emergency board, they claimed, had not given adequate attention to the request for revisions of rules. "The time has come," they declared, "when all American labor must defend itself against any such a ruthless principle that once a certain group of labor agrees to arbitrate, all other groups of labor in the same or related industries should be bound by awards growing out of agreements to which they were bound."[48]

Negotiations with the carriers were terminated on May 2, and the strike date was set for May 18. President Truman stepped into the controversy in an attempt to avert a walkout and invited the heads of the Trainmen and Engineers to a conference at the White House on May 14. Conferences were held for the next three days, and the union heads informed the President that the failure of the carriers to offer more than 16 cents an hour increase would lead to a strike. The President took the roads over on May 17, expressing the hope the "engineers and trainmen involved would cooperate in preserving and continuing rail service."[49]

The Office of Defense Transportation was placed in charge. Discussions continued, and President Truman submitted a final offer of an additional 2.5 cents increase per hour in lieu of working rules. When this offer was rejected by the two unions, the railroads of the United States were completely halted at 4 P.M. on May 23 by the withdrawal from service of the trainmen and engineers. President Truman went before Congress on the next day and asked for stringent legislation that would authorize him to seize properties in the event of strikes and lockouts endangering the public safety or welfare. Walkouts would be made illegal during government operations, and the terms of employment would be frozen. The strike was called off in its third day.

Congress rejected the proposals, but the strike was settled on the President's terms in what Whitney described as "The Duress Agreement."[50] Perhaps more than any of the other postwar strikes, the one which paralyzed the railroads of the country and affected every town and hamlet stimulated widespread sentiment for curbing the power of organized labor. Whitney could speak of "duress" and declare that there existed a "determined program to eliminate Harry S. Truman from political life," but his arrogant conduct gave the President no choice. Whitney subsequently denied that he had made political threats.[51] No government can stand idly by while a union or employer paralyzes the economic and social life of the country over a wage difference.

THE STRIKE IN COAL

Almost equally effective in arousing anti-labor sentiment was the tie-up in the bituminous coal industry that led to government seizure and the punishment of the union and its leader, John L. Lewis, for refusing to obey a court order.

The bituminous coal contract was to expire on March 31, 1946, and the United Mine Workers of America submitted a list of proposals including the establishment of a health and welfare fund, adjustment of the controversy governing supervisory employees, increases in wages and reductions in working hours, and adjustment of vacation, holiday, and severance pay.[52] After receiving authorization from the members in accordance with the War Labor Disputes Act, the miners went on strike on April 1, after a thirty-day postponement in compliance with a request from President Truman. Except for a twelve-day truce, the strike lasted through May 29. As the coal stocks were worked down, and no agreement was in sight, the government took over the mines on May 22, 1946. Conferences were then begun between Secretary of Interior Julius Krug, who had been placed in charge of the mines, and union negotiators. The contract between Krug and Lewis was signed in the office of President Truman. It represented, according to the *United Mine Workers Journal*, "the greatest economic and social gains registered by the U.M.W.A. in a single wage agreement since the birth of the union in 1890. . . . The agreement and understanding reached give promise of promoting a new social order in the coal fields of America."[53]

The contract called for an increase of the basic hourly wage of 18.5 cents, introduced a number of other improvements, and established a health and welfare fund financed by 5 cents a ton royalty for each ton of coal mined. Later the Secretary of Interior signed an agreement for supervisors, a sore point with the private coal operators, who were not in control of the mines at the time.[54] After making the agreements, the government wanted to return the mines to the private owners. A conference was called on September 11 by Admiral Benjamin Moreell, coal mines administrator, in the hope that an agreement could be reached for returning the mines.

Before satisfactory arrangements could be devised, a dispute involving monthly vacation payments to miners began. Another difference was whether railroad weights or tipple weights should be accepted as a basis for computing the contributions to the welfare fund. When Secretary Krug refused to modify his original decision, Lewis said that the contract had been breached. He demanded, therefore, the attendance of government representatives at a joint conference "for the purpose of negotiating new arrangements affecting wages, hours, rules, practices, differentials, inequalities and all other pertinent matters affecting or appertaining to the national bituminous coal industry."[55] When the request for a conference was rejected, Lewis announced that the miners would go on strike on November 20.

The government denied that the agreement had been breached and rejected Lewis' demand that the contract could unilaterally be reopened. In brief, Krug told Lewis that he had no power to annul the contract that covered the period of government possession of the mines. He also notified him that the U.S. Attorney-General in a formal opinion had held that Lewis was without power to terminate this contract with the government. Krug urged Lewis "to reconsider the position . . . and to enter into conference with the bituminous coal operators negotiating committee without loss of the coal production which is so critically needed at this time."[56]

When Lewis refused to cancel the strike call, the government on November 18, 1946, applied to the Federal District Court in the District of Columbia for a "judgment to the effect that the defendants had no power unilaterally to terminate the Krug-Lewis agreement."[57] Lewis had not issued a formal strike notice, but he had informed the miners of his unsuccessful negotiations with Krug. Holding that this notice was in fact a strike notice, the government, pending a final determination, requested a "temporary restraining order and preliminary injunctive relief." The court directed the defendants from "continuing the notice of November 15th, from encouraging the mine workers from seeking to interfere with the operation of the mines by strike or cessation of work." The order was to expire by November 27. However, the walkout began on November 18 and continued until the majority of bituminous mines were shut down.

The government on November 27 brought an action before Judge T. Allan Goldsborough, who had issued the original order, to hold the defendants, the union and Lewis, in contempt of court. After dismissing the challenge to its jurisdiction, a hearing was held and a verdict of guilty given on December 3, 1946. The union and Lewis were found guilty of civil and criminal contempt. Goldsborough fined the union $3.5 million and Lewis $10,000. Philip Murray, William Green, and the Railway Labor Executives Association denounced the verdict. Lewis called off the strike on December 7. By agreement, the case was appealed directly to the U.S. Supreme Court.

The decision was sustained by a divided court. On the question whether the Norris-LaGuardia Act applied to the United States as an employer, and thereby barred issuance of an injunction by the district court, the Supreme Court divided five to four. The government was sustained in its contention that the district court had a right to issue a restraining order to preserve existing conditions while it considered its own authority. It ruled that the miners working were government employees and that "in seizing and operating the mines the Government was exercising a sovereign function." Finally, the Supreme Court approved the merging of the civil and criminal contempt into one case. The fine against Lewis was affirmed, but the Court found the union's fine too severe and it was reduced to $700,000 conditional upon the union withdrawing its contract termination notice, and thereby purging itself of contempt, within five days after issuance of the Supreme Court mandate. Failure to comply was to reimpose automatically the initial fine of $3.5 million.[58] Lewis complied.

OTHER SETTLEMENTS

The settlement in steel served as a pattern of wage increases that was used in some of the larger and more stubborn walkouts in the first year and a half after V-J Day. The United Electrical, Radio and Machinery Workers Union led almost 200,000 workers on strike in the plants of General Electric, General Motors, and the Westinghouse Corporations. The union asked for a $2.00-a-day increase, and President Charles E. Wilson of General Electric linked wage increases to prices.[59] The strike started on January 15, 1946. On March 14 a settlement for 18.5 cents was reached with General Electric, and two months later—May 10—with Westinghouse Electric and Manufacturing Company on the same terms.

The 25,000 employees who went on strike on January 21 in the plants of the International Harvester Company did not return for 86 days. The settlement was for 18 cents an hour. In the strike against the plants of the large packers, both the CIO and AFL unions cooperated. Walkouts in the plants of Swift, Armour, Wilson, Cudahy, and the Morrell companies followed refusal of a 25-cent-an-hour increase. The companies clamed that under existing price limits they could only grant 7 cents. The strike started on January 16, 1946, was followed by the appointment of a fact-finding board and seizure of the striking plants on January 26. Settlements started on February 7 on the basis of the recommendations of the panel that wages be increased 16 cents an hour. In compensation for the increased costs, prices of dressed beef were raised, and Swift and Company regarded this as demonstrating that its insistence that wage raises had to be followed by price raises had been vindicated.[60] Strikes on the Greyhound buses, the tugs in New York Harbor, and a variety of other industries were eventually settled by an increase in wages close to the amounts granted in the steel industry.

Fact-Finding Board

In a number of the postwar disputes the President or the Secretary of Labor appointed fact-finding boards to examine the issues and recommend settlements. As already noted, recommendations of a panel served as a basis of settlement in the steel industry. Fact-finding boards were also appointed in the petroleum refining, automobile, meat-packing, interstate bus transportation, and the farm-machinery manufacturing disputes.[61]

General Strikes

During 1946 two sympathy strikes took place in widely separated parts of the United States—Rochester, New York, and Oakland, California. They developed under different circumstances. In Rochester the strike started as a result of the city administration's seeking to prevent employees in the Division of Public Works from joining a union. On May 15, 1946, the city manager abolished several hundred jobs in that department, and union leaders charged that it was an attempt to abort a campaign to organize. The AFL Central Labor Council and the CIO each named three members of a strategy board and, when a number of garbage collectors ceased work and were dismissed, the strategy committee called a general walkout on May 28. When the city administration agreed the next day to allow unionization, the strike was ended.[62]

As in Rochester, the dispute in Oakland involved recognition of the union, although the employer was a private party and not the government. The dispute involved Department and Specialty Store Employees Local Union 2165, which had organized and sought bargaining rights at two stores—Kahn's and Hastings. Both claimed that their labor negotiations were in the hands of the Retail Merchants' Association. The association represented 27 stores with about 7,500 employees, and recognition would be determined upon winning a majority in all the enterprises.

Unable to reach an agreement, strikes were called at both stores in October 1946. They were supported by the teamsters' locals in Alameda County.[63] On November 30, 1946, the leaders of the local labor movement were informed that deliveries would be made at 2 A.M. the following day. Police surrounded the area at the stipulated time and allowed only loaded trucks to enter. The use of large squads of police to protect strikebreakers led the Central Labor and Building Trades Councils of Alameda County on December 2, 1946, to call a general labor holiday for the next day.[64] Economic activity in Alameda County was completely paralyzed, and interurban transportation between the East Bay communities suspended. No newspapers were published in the two days the demonstration lasted.[65]

The strike was ended when the city authorities promised not to use its police to escort professional strikebreakers in and out of the city. The strikes against the stores which originally precipitated the general walkout were not settled for several months—five for Hastings and seven months for Kahn's.[66]

The postwar strike wave lost much of its force. Although the number of walkouts tended to remain high, the man-days lost in 1947 through work stoppages was less than a third of the number in the preceding year. The grim forecasts that the country faced mass unemployment were fortunately proved to have been exaggerated. In fact, the enactment of the Employment Act of 1946, designed to promote conditions favorable to full or high-level employment, was both the result of fear of rising idleness coupled to a desire to promote government policies that would aid in achieving high levels of employment.

The misgivings of the pessimistic forecasters were not realized. "During the fall and winter of 1945–1946, men were released from the armed forces at a rate of more than a million a month. After brief periods of rest most of them entered the civilian labor market."[67] In the first months of 1947 the armed forces had been reduced to 1.5 million members. Of the total number of 13.5 million veterans demobilized, 12 million were in the labor force, and reabsorption of former servicemen proceeded without much difficulty, although unemployment was greater than among other parts of the working population. Two years after V-J Day, the level of unemployment was 3.5 per cent, the lowest, except for wartime, in several decades.[68]

44

The Taft-Hartley Act

The expansion of union membership inevitably brought with it new problems. Moreover, abuses of stewardship, jurisdictional strikes and the use of the secondary boycott, refusal of some unions to bargain in good faith, as well as the sharp rise in labor disputes in the immediate postwar period, created a widespread public demand for remedial action. The Case bill, which had passed both houses of Congress during the strike wave of 1946, barely failed enactment over the veto of President Harry Truman. The Eightieth Congress, elected in the fall of 1946, believed that it had a mandate to pass legislation reforming the federal labor laws.

President Harry Truman recognized the existing sentiment for change, and in his State of the Union message to Congress, on January 6, 1947, suggested action be taken to prohibit jurisdictional strikes and certain kinds of secondary boycotts. He also asked for the creation of more efficient machinery for the avoidance of strikes and lockouts. Finally, he recommended the appointment of a temporary joint commission to inquire into the entire field of labor-management relations and report back to Congress not later than March 15, 1947.[1]

From the beginning of the session it was evident that a split existed among Republican legislative leaders, who in the Eightieth Congress, which began in January 1947, represented the majority party. Senator Robert A. Taft claimed that the "Republican Party has frequently declared its belief that the solution of employer-employee relationships rests on a sound system of collective bargaining . . . it means that the Wagner Act should be retained."[2]

However, leaders of the majority in the House of Representatives expressed opposition to Taft's position and favored stiffer restrictions.[3] The differences between leaders of both the House and Senate are evident in their respective hearings as well as in their reports and the bills they initially passed. The witnesses before the House Committee on Education and Labor were almost all hostile to organized labor. Many favored the repeal of the Wagner Act, the application of the antitrust laws to labor organizations, and restrictions on industrywide bargaining and union security. The few labor representatives who attended the hearings held by the House committee were sharply questioned by its members.[4]

In contrast, the hearings before the Senate Committee on Labor and Public Welfare, presided over by Senator Taft, heard almost an equal number of representatives from each side. Taft and other members of the Senate committee showed a readiness to listen and consider the arguments presented by both labor and employer witnesses. Senator Allen J. Ellender told Green, when the latter objected to restrictions on jurisdictional strikes, that "Congress is going to do something to stop jurisdictional strikes and secondary boycotts and we want your assistance."[5]

After about six weeks of testimony by 126 witnesses before the House committee, and 98 before the Senate, bills were reported to both chambers. The difference between the respective committees is obvious in both their attitudes and their recommendations. The House committee found that "as a result of labor laws ill-conceived and disastrously executed, the American workingman has been deprived of his dignity as an individual. He has been cajoled, coerced, intimidated, and on many occasions beaten up, in the name of the splendid aims set forth in section 1 of the National Labor Relations Act."[6] After enumerating the abuses suffered by the workers, the report declared that the worker's "mind, his soul, and his very life have been subjected to a tyranny more despotic than any one could think possible in a free country."[7]

The temper of the House committee is evident in its failure to discuss the provisions of the bill with the minority that held other views. The latter were given copies of the bill on April 10, 1947, and asked to submit its opinions two days later. The minority believed that the committee recommendations, if enacted into law, would repeal the National Labor Relations Act, make virtually all strikes illegal, and make trade unions liable for treble damages under the Sherman law. "The bill," the minority claimed, "does not merely wipe out labor's gains under the beneficient administration of President Roosevelt; it turns the clock of history back at least a century and a half and eliminates safeguards and protections which both Republican and Democratic Congresses have sponsored for generations."[8]

The House bill abolished the National Labor Relations Board, denied the protection of the statute to foremen, eliminated the requirement of good faith in collective bargaining, and established a cumbersome procedure ending finally in a strike vote of the workers involved. Only if a majority approved could a strike be called. Secondary boycotts were outlawed, as were featherbedding and industrywide bargaining. The functions of the board were separated: the board was authorized to make decisions in cases, and an administrator was given the investigatory and prosecuting functions. Internal affairs of unions were subjected to regulation, and the checkoff was made voluntary and had to be authorized by the individual employee who could revoke such authorization upon thirty days' notice. The closed shop was outlawed, and the union shop could be introduced if authorized by a majority of employees in the bargaining unit. A series of unfair labor practices by employees was included, and the law listed the subject matter of collective bargaining and excluded a number of subjects that historically had been proper matters for negotiation. The law denied employees the right to strike over matters not listed.[9]

The bill changed the rules of evidence the board was to follow. It forbade contributions by unions to candidates for political office, applied the antitrust laws to labor organizations, made unions suable for breaches of contracts, and set up an independent federal conciliation agency.

In contrast, the Senate Committee on Labor and Public Welfare did not believe that the "social gains which industrial employees have received by reason of these statutes"—the Norris-LaGuardia Act of 1932 and the National Labor Relations Act of 1935—"should be impaired in any degree[;] we do feel that to the extent that such statutes, together with the regulations issued under them, and decisions regarding them, have produced specific types of injustice, or clear inequities between employers and employees, Congress should remedy the situation by precise and carefully drawn legislation."[10]

The Senate bill also eliminated the supervisor from coverage of the act as an employee. It abolished the closed shop but allowed the other forms of union security, provided a majority of employees in bargaining authorized such a provision. Employers and individual employees could invoke the processes of the board against unions engaged in enumerated unfair labor practices, including jurisdictional strikes and secondary boycotts, and the government was given power to suppress such activities through the injunction. The bill also would have reorganized the board and made unions suable for contract violations. The conciliation service was established as an independent agency.[11] What strikes a reader of the Senate report is its reasonableness and absence of the malevolent anti-union prejudice that permeates the House document. In a supplemental report, Senator Taft and three other colleagues suggested several other changes involving welfare funds and secondary boycotts, as well as jurisdictional disputes.

The labor movement was deeply concerned by the possible effect of the legislation. Union leaders opposed the bills before congressional committees and sought to rally public sentiment against them.

But one passed the House on April 18 by a vote of 308 to 107, with 17 not voting. At its meeting on April 22, 1947, the AFL Executive Council charged that the legislation in Congress would destroy the labor movement. Joseph Padway, counsel for the AFL, called the bill enacted by the House, the "most vicious and malicious anti-labor bill ever enacted in this or any other country."[12] In his view, the House bill "effectively destroys every constitutional right of workers such as the right to organize, the right to be free from employer domination, the right to bargain collectively for improved working conditions."[13]

The Senate bill was much milder. A provision that would have placed restrictions on industrywide bargaining by requiring that local groups could withdraw from a national contract and negotiate for themselves was defeated by a vote of 44 to 43. Taft claimed that industrywide bargaining, under his amendment, "could continue exactly as it is today, but would have to be with the voluntary consent of the unions who bargain together. Today it must be with the voluntary consent of their employers, any employer can withdraw today, but not any union. . . . This amendment permits a union, if it does not approve the proceedings of the national bargaining, to withdraw and make its own responsible contract with its responsible employer."[14]

On May 13 the Senate passed the act "to amend the National Labor Relations Act . . ." by a vote of 68 to 24, with 3 not voting. The Senate bill was essentially the Wagner Act; it did not rescind any significant union rights. By no interpretation could the final product be described as a "slave bill," although such a designation might with some accuracy be applied to the House bill.[15] Since the bills passed by the two houses were different, conference committees were appointed. The belief held by leading Senators that only the milder Senate version could be passed over a Presidential veto was one of the reasons for its more moderate provisions.[16] Taft announced that he was not inclined to yield to the House and that he would not go along in the effort to restrict industrywide bargaining.[17] Fred Hartley, chairman of the House Committee on Education and Labor, thereupon stated the House conferees would not insist upon the outlawing of industrywide collective bargaining and would also accept the Senate's refusal to allow private parties to sue for injunctions in certain kinds of labor disputes as approved by the House.[18]

Virtually all of the severe restrictions sponsored by Hartley and passed by the House were eliminated in conference. The threat of a veto forced the retreat of the House. The attitude of those who had hoped for a stronger measure was perhaps expressed by Congressman Clare E. Hoffman, who said that the labor leaders "should write letters of commendation to those who engineered its adoption,"[19] meaning the conference report. The bill passed the Senate by a vote of 54 to 17, and the House by 320 to 79.

On June 20, 1947, the bill was vetoed by President Truman and returned to the House. In his message the President set up four standards for reform legislation, none of which the bill, in his opinion, met. (1) Would the bill lead to more or less government intervention in economic life? Truman answered the question affirmatively and objected because "political power would supplant economic power as the critical factor in labor relations." This he held to be undesirable. (2) The President's message also claimed that Congress was influenced too much by the troubles and tensions of the reconversion period and ignored the evidence that difficulties were receding and labor-management relations were improving. (3) Truman did not believe the bill was workable. (4) He thought that it was unfair and discriminatory against labor.[20]

Without debate, the House overrode the veto by a vote of 331 to 83. The Senate allowed debate, and Taft defended his bill as fair and denied it was punitive or weak. Taft claimed that the vetoed bill was based "on the theory of the Wagner Act. It is based on the theory that the solution of the labor problem in the United States is free, collective bargaining—a contract between one employer and all of his men acting as one man. That is the theory of the Wagner Act, that they shall be free to make the contract they wish."[21] The veto was overridden by a vote of 68 to 25 with 2 not voting.

The law introduced changes in administration, retained the unfair labor practices of employers from the Wagner Act, and introduced several regulations governing the conduct of unions. The unions were forbidden to coerce employees in the choice of collective bargaining representatives, discriminate or cause employers to discriminate against employees, cause payment for services not performed, or engage in jurisdictional strikes or secondary boycotts. The latter two activities could be enjoined by the board, which was required to apply for injunctive relief to a U.S. district court upon complaint by an employer that he was being subjected to either or both of these practices. The closed shop was outlawed, and the union shop allowed, if approved by a majority in the bargaining unit. Thirty per cent of workers in a bargaining unit could petition the Labor Board for a decertification election, and if a majority of the voters approved, the union forfeited the right to act as bargaining representative. Damage suits against employers and unions were permitted for violation of contracts. A procedure to be used in emergency strikes was established, and the government was given the right to seek a postponement or suspension of such walkouts for a limited period through an injunction in the U.S. district courts. Unions and corporations were forbidden to contribute to candidates for federal political office. Supervisory employees were denied protection under the statute. The Federal Conciliation Service was made into an independent agency, unions seeking the service of the National Relations Board were required to file their constitutions, by-laws and financial statements with the U.S. Department of Labor, and their officers had to file an affidavit declaring they were not members of the Communist party or any organization supporting it.

Philip Murray suggested that the AFL, CIO, and the Railroad Brotherhoods meet at an early date to devise a common policy for meeting the threat he believed faced the unions as a result of the passage of the law.[22] The AFL refused to join in a common program of protest. Instead, at the suggestion of the resident members of the council, Green called a meeting of international unions to consider the problems raised by the new labor legislation. Meeting in Washington, representatives of 105 internationals denounced the Taft-Hartley law as introducing uncertainty and confusion, and re-establishing "the abhorrent principle of government by injunction."[23] The meeting planned to challenge the law in the courts, seek its repeal by Congress, and protect the unions against possible suits. The CIO was equally vehement in its denunciation of the law, and a resolution at the 1947 convention pledged itself "not to permit this Act to destroy either the economic or the political rights of the people. . . . We hereby dedicate our organizations and the entire membership to work unceasingly in the political field in complete unity with all labor organizations and other progressive groups to insure the political repudiation of those reactionaries who are responsible for the Taft-Hartley Act."[24]

In addition, there were a number of protest strikes in the coal mines and mass meetings decrying the passage of the act. The labor movement was faced with the need of defining its position on the signing of the non-Communist affidavits. Those unions refusing to sign would be denied the right to utilize the services of the National Labor Relations Act. The United Steelworkers of America, the United Electrical and Machinery Workers Union, the International Typographical Union, and the United Mine Workers of America were among a number of other organizations which refused to sign the non-Communist disclaimer. The first two later receded from their opposition; the common course, however, was for unions to sign the non-Communist disclaimer.

Autonomous unions could decide their position for themselves, but the attitude of the AFL and CIO became important after Robert Denham, the attorney for the board, held that officers of these organizations had to file a non-Communist affidavit for their affiliates to become eligible for the services of the board. At the meeting of the executive council, of which John L. Lewis had become a member in 1946, the question was discussed. Lewis opposed signing and sharply criticized the contemplated changes in the AFL constitution necessary to conform with the Taft-Hartley law. He regarded such a step "as a shameful humiliation,"[25] but he was the lone dissenter.

Lewis carried his fight into the 1947 AFL convention, but he failed to rally much support for his point of view. Several weeks after the convention, Lewis disaffiliated from the AFL in a two-word telegram to President William Green.[26] The latter regretted the withdrawal of his old union for the second time and pointed to the democratic manner in which the decision has been made.[27]

A more direct challenge to the Taft-Hartley Act was made by the International Typographical Union whose officers believed that the law would interfere with its ability to bargain effectively with employers in the printing trades. The 1947 convention, thereupon, declared that the Labor-Management Relations Act did not compel the union to sign a contract "and refraining from doing so is not a violation or evasion of the law."[28] The convention directed its locals that upon the expiration of existing contracts, "and until the laws [Taft-Hartley] are amended and free collective bargaining is again recognized, our members may accept employment only from employers who are willing to employ them under the 'Conditions of Employment' which the several unions adopt, after approval by the Executive Council of the I.T.U."[29] The union announced that it would comply with all legal requirements, but it did not favor its local unions qualifying as representatives "under the Labor-Management Relations Act, except in special cases."[30]

The enactment of the resolution was the result of growing hostility towards the American Newspaper Publishers Association, generated in part by the attacks of the leaders of the Typographical Union. G. N. Dale, chairman of the association's Special Standing Committee, complained on behalf of its board of directors of the criticisms made by President Woodruff Randolph and others. In an attempt to prevent further misunderstanding, Dale assured the International Typographical Union that the American Newspaper Publishers Association desired "amicable relations with employees, stability in labor-management relations, and mutual respect." He suggested a meeting of representatives of the two organizations for the purposes of working out an understanding on common problems. Randolph alluded to the support given to the enactment of the Taft-Hartley law by the majority of newspapers, and informed the publishers that the union would not sign contracts "under present conditions created by the Taft-Hartley law."[31]

Representatives of the union and publishers met in Indianapolis, Indiana, on September 25. In brief, the union believed it could not enter into a contract with the publishers because the Taft-Hartley law forbade the closed shop; it was, however, willing to enter into an understanding without a written contract.[32] It is obvious that the leaders of the Typographical

Union, especially President Randolph, misjudged the possible effect of the Taft-Hartley law upon the position of their organization. Moreover, in view of the Supreme Court's decision in the H. J. Heinz and Company case, the refusal to sign a contract agreed to with an employer could not be sustained.

The union justified its position on the ground that the collective bargaining agreement was a development of the 1880's, and that prior to that time the employer, in recognizing a labor organization, accepted "the union rules covering wages, hours and working conditions without a written memorial of these terms—which were to be found in the union's rules and laws. Even in 1947, almost a quarter of the I.T.U.'s 850 locals had no written agreements, the same remains true for many other craft unions."[33]

Whatever may have been the history of the written agreement, it was obviously irrelevant in the face of a precedent requiring the employer to sign a contract if he reaches an agreement. Since the Taft-Hartley law extended the requirement to bargain with organizations of labor, it was an obvious corollary that a union could not refuse to accept a written contract.[34] The policy of no written contract was largely responsible for the strike against the Chicago newspapers which began on November 24, 1947. Another effect of the policy was the filing of charges by a number of printing firms and printing employer groups, beginning with an action against the local union in Baltimore, Maryland, which was followed by suits in other communities and finally by the filing of charges by the American Newspaper Association against the international that it had restrained and coerced its locals into refusal to bargain.[35] A temporary injunction restraining the ITU from refusing to bargain in good faith was issued by Judge Luther M. Swygert of the Federal District Court of Indiana. It was dissolved on November 2, 1949.[36]

To finance the Chicago and other strikes, the membership approved a 4.5 per cent assessment on all wages earned in the printing trade. The strike dragged on for almost twenty-two months and was finally ended on September 18, 1949. The Chicago Typographical Union No. 16 voted to accept the contract "in accord with its own laws and the Taft-Hartley Act and the injunction issued against it."[37] However, whatever may have been gained by the strike, the terms did not include the closed shop or the "Conditions of Employment" which the union wished to substitute for the written agreement. The economic demands were certainly not the main cause of the Chicago dispute.

A joint committee was appointed, under the Taft-Hartley Act, to observe the administration and prevent the "sabotage" of the law. It also sought to ascertain if the statute was effective and what changes might be introduced if such were found necessary.[38] The testimony before the joint committee showed the same difference of opinions as existed before the passage of the act. Labor spokesmen asked for repeal, and employers sought to have some of the provisions governing the secondary boycott, industrywide bargaining, and other clauses made more stringent.

One of the surprises for those who opposed union security was the overwhelming affirmative vote for the union shop. Testifying before the joint committee, Paul Herzog, chairman of the National Labor Relations Board, reported that of the over 900,000 ballots cast in union-shop elections up to May 1, 1948, "95 per cent were cast in the affirmative."[39] In the first ten months, 19,520 union-shop elections were held, and only 352 voted to reject.

The joint committee split on the steps to be taken to improve the law. Senator Taft and two other senators submitted amendments that they claimed would embody the "best features of all past labor laws."[40]

The labor movement was confident after the re-election of President Truman that it had a chance to gain a repeal of the Taft-Hartley Act and its replacement with minor amendments to the Wagner Act. In his state of the Union message to Congress, the President requested repeal which was favorable to the demands of labor. At the beginning of the session of the Eighty-first Congress, a bill embodying the views of the labor organizations, H.R. 3032, was offered. It failed to rally substantial support. Instead, two bills by Congressman John S. Wood appeared to be favored despite opposition from the AFL and CIO.[41]

A substitute supported by the House leadership, including Speaker Sam Rayburn, was offered by Congressman Sims. It was also opposed by the labor movement. The House adopted the Wood bill by 217 to 203, and by a herculean effort of the House leaders, and the labor movement, the amendments were recommitted by a vote of 212 to 209.[42]

The fight for amendment shifted to the Senate. Senator Robert Taft had submitted a list of changes designed to meet some of the objections of organized labor. Senator Elbert Thomas presented a bill for outright repeal.[43]

The Taft amendments were adopted. They made the general counsel subject to the board, made the injunction in certain cases discretionary rather than mandatory, abolished elections for determining the union shop, lessened the penalty on featherbedding, but retained seizure in emergency disputes and gave the government the power of enjoining such disputes for a limited time. When the amendment to strike the injunction from the bill offered by Senator Scott Lucas was defeated by 46 to 44, Green wrote the majority leader that "amendments designed to make the Taft Bill more palatable would be useless and a waste of time, as the action yesterday in the Senate [retention of the seizure provision and government injunction] makes it absolutely unacceptable."[44] Thus ended the most favorable opportunity for revising the law.

The dire consequences forecast by the labor movements were scarcely realized. Unions continued to gain members through 1952. The enactment of the Labor-Management Relations Act stimulated and tended to expand the political activities of the AFL and many of its affiliates and also of the CIO. Section 304 prohibited political contributions by corporations and labor unions; it subjected labor unions found guilty of violations to a fine up to $5,000 and a union official up to $1,000 and imprisonment for one year for a violation. Philip Murray tested this provision by distributing a copy of the *CIO News* that endorsed the candidacy of Edward Damartz for representative from the third Maryland district. The Supreme Court upheld the dismissal of the indictment—*U.S. v. CIO,* 335 U.S. 106 (1948). Almost ten years later an indictment against the United Automobile Workers was sustained when it allowed a candidate to appear on a television program which the union financed—*U.S. v. U. A. W.,* 352 U.S. 567 (1959). The indictment was, however, dismissed by the lower court.

FOREMEN'S ASSOCIATION

The definition of employee in Section 2 (3) of the Taft-Hartley Act, which excluded supervisors from coverage had a catastrophic effect on the Foremen's Association of America. Formed in 1941 in the Detroit plant of the Ford Motor Company, the association at its first convention in November 1941 elected Robert H. Keys president. After the board in the Packard Motor Company case had ordered the company to bargain, the association was able to win contracts from a number of large firms. In 1945 it claimed 245 chapters and a membership of 28,000.[45]

The U.S. Supreme Court, in *Packard Motor Company* v. *National Labor Relations Board,* 330 U.S. 485 (1947), supported the board's view that supervisors were employees under the National Labor Relations Act, but their exclusion from coverage under the Taft-Hartley amendments doomed the association.[46] As soon as the clause became effective, employers refused to bargain with the Foremen's Association of America, and it lost the economic power it had exercised in the preceding eight years. William T. Gossett, vice-president and general counsel of the Ford Motor Company, claimed that between 1941 and 1948, foremen had called fourteen strikes in the plants of the company but none had taken place after the protection of the law had been withdrawn.[47] The experience of the foremen is another demonstration of the importance of the labor relations' law for the continuing prosperity of the unions of the United States.

LABOR ORGANIZING

The Taft-Hartley law did not seriously affect union membership or the functioning of labor organizations. As noted above, the United Mine Workers of America withdrew from the AFL because the executive council would not refuse to sign the non-Communist disclaimer. However, the independent Communications Workers Association joined the CIO after the members voted approval by 71, 312 to 34, 419.[48]

Southern Campaign

Both the AFL and the CIO launched organizing drives in the South in 1946; these continued into 1947 and then quietly expired. In May 1946 the CIO set up a special committee to organize the South. These plans had been approved on March 15-16, 1946, by the executive board, and $1 million was pledged by CIO affiliates, the largest amounts—$200,000— each by the United Steelworkers of America and Amalgamated Clothing Workers of America. Van A. Bittner was appointed director; George Baldanzi and Jack Kroll, his assistants; and Sherman Dalrymple, secretary-treasurer.

Bittner announced that the CIO drive would concentrate on the oil, chemical, lumber, and textile industries.[49] Directors were appointed for each of the southern states. Some gains were reported in the first months of the campaign. Through the months of July and August 1946, the CIO reported victories in a number of National Labor Relations Board elections.[50] According to the report of the officers to the 1947 convention, the CIO had increased its membership by 28,000 in the South.[51]

With the death of Bittner in 1946, the CIO campaign passed to other hands. On the basis of their experience, the leaders believed that new methods would be needed. They felt that the "Taft-Hartley Act had stimulated open, violent resistance to peaceful, legal union activities," and that these had multiplied the difficulties of organizing the South.[52]

The AFL announced on March 29, 1946, that it was reviving its southern drive that had been postponed by war conditions. A conference was called for May 11 and 12 in Asheville, North Carolina, and President Green appointed George L. Googe, chairman of the southern campaign and policy board, as the directing authority. A plan for organizing in the fourteen southern states was devised and twelve additional organizers were sent into the southern areas. "The total manpower of the A.F. of L. and its State Federations and local bodies is 117. This is the over-all figure counting every head. Twelve of these organizers are negroes."[53]

The policy board believed that special attention should be given to organizing Negro workers and called for the "elimination of what few remaining handicaps and discriminations still exist against negro workers in the A.F. of L. unions in the South."[54] In its report to the 1947 convention, the executive council claimed that it had organized 330,000 workers in new shops, new locals, or new bargaining units, and approximately 130,000 members had joined existing unions.[55] The figures were based on the reports of George L. Googe, who was in charge. After July 1947 the southern campaign tapered off.

For reasons known to us all, these difficulties of new organization have been greatly increased by the unfavorable political and legislative atmosphere. More and more time of the representatives and organizers have been taken up in negotiations due to the employer tactics of postponement and stalling. The concentration of officers of local and central bodies and of State Federations has been increasingly directed to the effects of the new State and Federal labor laws. . . . It has seemed sensible and expedient to substantially reduce the direct organization activities and institute gradual retrenchment over the whole field with the intent of consolidating our position in the South. This procedure would seem to be a logical one even if the dilemmas and problems presented by the Taft-Hartley regime did not exist.[56]

Although the Taft-Hartley law does not appear, on the basis of the evidence, to have been decisive, it made organizing more difficult by allowing the use of dilatory tactics by employer lawyers. Senator Taft planned in 1950 to offer twenty-eight amendments and was anxious to obtain some concessions from the spokesmen of organized labor. They could only suggest outright repeal, a course that could not succeed with the composition of Congress. Moreover, it would have meant the complete repudiation of his own work and a confession of complete failure by Taft. In a discussion with two of the legislative representatives of the AFL, Taft alluded to the conservative members of the House of Representatives and said that he "did not want to get into a fight with these members and 'then to have to fight the Unions, as well.' "[57] Taft wanted to reach an understanding with his colleagues in Congress, but he also needed support from organized labor if his amendments were to have a chance of enactment. The labor leaders who had convinced themselves and their members that the Taft-Hartley Act was a "slave law" were in no position to negotiate changes which would have eliminated some of the undesirable provisions. By their intransigent attitude, they had lost the power of maneuver. Their overreaction to the Taft-Hartley law tied their hands and they found themselves in a position where they could accept nothing but repeal. They never appreciated Taft's real point of view, and the contribution he made towards the enactment of a nonpunitive law which scarcely affected the position of organized labor.

CHAPTER 45

International Policy

From the beginning, organized labor in the United States was sympathetic to the efforts of workers in other countries to liberate themselves from oppression. Fraternal relations with the labor movements in other countries were developed, beginning with England in 1894.

In keeping with its belief in the international cooperation of workers' organizations, the AFL Executive Council greeted the International Labor Congress meeting in London in the fall of 1888. In the same message, the council presented its view that "the trade union is the historic and natural form of working class organization. . . . The late war of slave emancipation has added to the ranks of our class more than four million people who stand in direct necessity of organization and education."[1] The message concluded with a defense of trade-union organization and the necessity of developing cooperation among workers.

Gompers reluctantly rejected the invitation of Wilhelm Leibknecht, in 1888, and one from Andre Gily, the following year, to attend international labor conferences. Leibknecht was told that the AFL took the view that the movement in the United States was not sufficiently advanced to be represented by a delegate.[2] Gompers assured André Gily that it was "not through want of a fraternal feeling and a recognition of the identity of interest of the workmen of all countries that we are not represented."[3]

Gompers always showed a lively interest in international labor affairs. He greeted the International Labor Congress in Brussels in 1891; and in 1892 he first advocated an exchange of union cards among unions of the same trade in different countries.

John Burns and David Holmes were appointed to represent the British

Trades Union Congress at the 1894 AFL convention, and the long relationship between the two federations was inaugurated. It marked the beginning of an exchange of fraternal delegates that has continued until the present day. Gompers was hopeful that contacts with British trade unionists could be enlarged by establishing relations with the labor movements of other countries. In September 1896 he requested the executive council to allow the fraternal delegates from the AFL to the Trades Union Congress to urge the calling of a meeting of the national federations for the purpose of setting up an International Trades Union Federation. The executive council rejected the proposal.[4]

Concerned with movements of other countries, Gompers in 1905 declared that the American labor movement could not be indifferent to the struggles of "peoples of all countries for justice and right."[5] Some other members of the executive council were not eager to become involved with problems outside of the United States. Nevertheless, the 1905 convention directed the council to examine the sentiment of the international unions on exchanging cards with organized workers from other countries.

INTERNATIONAL FEDERATION OF TRADE UNIONS

On the whole, the movement in the United States kept aloof from "entangling alliances." When an issue involving human rights or aid for striking workers abroad came before a convention, sympathy or limited financial support was usually given. Thus, the executive council voted to ask President Theodore Roosevelt to end the extradition treaty with Tsarist Russia.[6] In the same year, the convention approved the issuance of an appeal in behalf of Swedish workers who were locked out by the organized employers of that country.[7]

Trade Union Secretariats

A first step in international labor cooperation was the formation of trade union secretariats by unions of several countries in a particular craft or calling. The Tobacco Workers' International, established in 1889, was the first one of these efforts to survive, and it was followed in the same year by similar organizations in the hat and shoemaking trades. Leather workers, miners, printers, metal workers, textile workers, and those employed in transport were among those who established international secretariats. They sought to work out common policies and to support each other in cases of need or attack, and unions in the United States joined in these endeavors.

International Trade Union Unity

Leaders of labor believed that a more inclusive organization was needed to promote international cooperation and understanding among workers and unions of different countries. One of the obstacles to the setting up of an international trade-union movement was the belief among some of the leaders that general, social, political, and economic questions fell within the province of the Second (Socialist) International. This body had been set up in 1889 as the successor to the First International—the International Workingmen's Association which functioned from 1864 to 1872.

Through the efforts of the Danish trade unions and the British Trades Union Congress, an international trade union conference was called in Copenhagen, Denmark, for August 21, 1901. In addition to the Scandinavian countries, Great Britain, France, Germany, Finland, and Belgium were represented. The delegates agreed to hold an annual conference at which reports on labor conditions in affiliated countries would be given, and policies of mutual interest to the workers of the world would be devised.[8]

The AFL did not join until 1911. In 1909 it instructed representatives to the British Trades Union Congress to participate in the International Trade Union Conference as fraternal delegates. The 1910 AFL convention authorized the sending of a delegate to the Budapest conference in August 1911. The right of the AFL representative, James Duncan, to a seat was challenged by William Z. Foster, who was in Budapest representing the Industrial Workers of the World. His position was supported by the French Federation of Labor, but after a heated debate the charges were dismissed and Duncan was seated.

The AFL recommended the formation of an International Federation of Trade Unions, with each national center guaranteed its autonomy. In a statement, the AFL announced that it did not favor antimilitarist propaganda and antipatriotism, in the sense proposed by the French Générale Confédération du Travail. The AFL suggested that the labor movement of each country seek to prevent the transfer of strikebreakers across national borders wherever a strike existed or is contemplated. It also favored more uniform legislation governing the hours of labor of men and women in dangerous trades, the restriction of the labor of children to at least fourteen years or older, and the publication of an official journal in several languages for disseminating information on labor conditions in various countries.[9]

The International Secretariat became the International Federation of Trade Unions, and the AFL affiliated with it. In 1913, Carl Legien, the head of the German Federation of Labor, was chosen international president, and it was voted to hold the next conference in San Francisco during the World's Fair in 1915.

World War I

The International Federation of Trade Unions was inevitably divided by World War I. In a letter to Gompers, Legien blamed the war on Russia.[10] English and French labor leaders in turn objected to the German control of the IFTU headquarters and urged its removal from Germany to a neutral center, preferably Switzerland. The AFL executive council did not, at first, want to become involved in a dispute, but it did vote, with one member dissenting, to withhold per capita payments.[11] Legien was willing to make concessions and authorized the establishment of a sub-office in a neutral country, but the suggestion did not meet with the approval of the leaders of the labor movements in the Allied countries. They, therefore, decided to set up a central office in Paris headed by Léon Jouhaux.

The London meeting of Socialist and labor groups on February 14, 1915, had favored transfer of the headquarters, and Gompers wrote Legien that "in the best interests of the continuity and usefulness of the international trade union movement," the headquarters should be shifted from Germany to a neutral country. Legien regarded the request as unfair and harmful.[12]

One of the first actions of the Paris central office was to call a conference of the national trade union leaders of the Entente countries at Leeds, England, on July 6, 1916. Representatives from England, France, Belgium, and Italy drew up a program calling for a guarantee of the right to organize by law; free movement of labor between countries, except during serious economic crises; restriction of the hours of labor of women and minors; and the regulation of health and safety in industry.

An international trade union conference was called in Stockholm, Sweden, for June 1917, but the labor movements of the majority of Allied countries refused to send representatives. Gompers wrote Jan Oudegest, the head of the Dutch trade unions, who had called the conference, that he could not "see any good could come from our participation."[13] The meeting was held, and another conference was scheduled for Berne, Switzerland, on October 1, 1917, to which the AFL was invited to send delegates. The executive council rejected the invitation, but asked that one be called at a more opportune time.[14] A number of countries refused to attend and others were denied visas by their governments.[15]

Despite failure, trade union leaders were anxious to restore their relations broken by the war. As soon as the fighting ended, the trade unions of different countries sought an immediate meeting to prepare for resumption of formal cooperation. With the United States and Belgium refusing to participate, delegates from fifteen countries met on February 6 and 7, 1919, at Berne, Switzerland, and called an international trade union meeting in Amsterdam for July 1919. At the latter meeting the Belgians protested the actions of the German military during the occupation of their country and the failure of the German trade unions to protest. A conciliatory statement in behalf of the German delegation was issued by John Sassenbach. "The German trade unions have always recognized that a great injustice has been done to Belgium. The Germans always condemned the atrocities which occurred during the occupation."[16] The German delegation later repudiated the declaration. Legien explained that they did not object "to the spirit of the statement but to the wording."[17]

The dispute provoked a long and bitter discussion, with Gompers sharply criticizing the views of the German delegates. This issue was settled, but the AFL delegates remained uneasy. During the meeting, the International Federation of Trade Unions was reorganized. At the insistence of the United States, each national federation was given complete autonomy, and in accordance with a principle of the AFL, only one national organization was declared eligible for affiliation. The convention decided that the international would gather and exchange information for the various national federations, appeal for assistance for national organizations, and study economic and social problems including labor migration. The blockade of Russia was condemned and socialization of industry approved. The approval of these proposals did not sit well with the American delegation, but they were, in fact, a reflection of the more moderate views prevalent within European labor at the time. A number of members of the executive council were strongly opposed to trafficking with organizations tinged with socialism; and others, afflicted with a bad case of xenophobia, were not enthusiastic about cooperating with foreign labor groups. The executive council and the convention of 1920 refused to affiliate.[18]

The withdrawal of the AFL from "foreign entanglements" reflected the general desire of the people of the United States to isolate themselves from the problems and wars of Europe. Gompers was among those who favored cooperation, but he was overruled. The convention of 1920 objected to failure to grant each national federation "complete autonomy." Pronouncements by the IFTU which the AFL regarded as revolutionary were also a source for dissatisfaction, nor could endorsement of the principle of socialization of industry, which the AFL opposed, be accepted.[19] Jan Oudegest, the secretary of the IFTU, wanted to avoid mutual recrimination and mutual criticism. He told Gompers that in its manifestoes the IFTU had used the language "current in Europe and which is used by the trade union movement in all countries."[20]

These explanations were rejected. The isolationist temper of the members of the council is also evident in the strong opposition against issuing an appeal for aid to the German Trade Union Federation in December 1923. When Gompers asked for a vote on this question, three members of the council disapproved and two others were unenthusiastic but yielded to the entreaties of Gompers that the German unions should be given assistance. But more active participation in conferences or other affairs of Europe was rejected.[21]

INTERNATIONAL LABOR ORGANIZATION

During the early years of the war, the AFL urged that a labor assembly or conference be called at the time and place of the meeting of the peace conference so that the workers of the world would have a voice in the determining of the conditions of peace. These views had been considered and approved by the labor movements of other countries. Gompers headed a labor delegation to the peace conference, which included James Duncan, John R. Alpine, Frank Duffy, and William Green. As a result of the demands of labor groups, a Commission on International Labor Legislation was appointed by the Paris Peace Conference on January 31, 1919. It was directed to investigate the international conditions affecting employment, to consider international policies needed to secure common action on them, and to recommend the kind of permanent agency needed to continue investigations and cooperation with and under the direction of the League of Nations.[22] The resolution provided for two representatives from each of the five great powers and five representatives from the other powers represented at the Peace Conference. Gompers was elected president of the commission.

At its meetings, from February 1 to March 24, 1919, the commission had drawn up a labor charter of nineteen points to be incorporated into the peace treaty. Among them were proposals to limit work hours to eight a day and forty-eight a week, and the abolition of child labor for those under fourteen years of age. The right of association for employers and workers was recognized, and the principles of a living wage and one day's rest in seven were endorsed. Equal pay for equal work, inspection of factories, free migration of people, provisions for prevention of unemployment, and the right of seamen in the merchant marine to leave vessels while in port were approved.

As a participant noted, Gompers had misgivings about the International Labor Office which was to be established under the charter. Nevertheless, he fought for its endorsement by the 1919 convention of the AFL. It was overwhelmingly approved, but American labor was not represented at the International Labor Office until the United States government accepted membership in 1934.[23]

Rise of Hitler

Throughout the 1920's the AFL continued a desultory correspondence with the head of the IFTU and reasons for not affiliating were always found. With the rise of Hitler, William Green and some other leaders became more concerned with events in Europe. The 1933 convention voted to boycott German-made goods, and a Chest for the Liberation of the Workers of Europe, a fund to aid victims of Hitlerism and fascism, was endorsed by the 1935 convention. Leading labor officials accepted membership on this committee. These were signs of increased interest and concern with foreign affairs.

Events abroad made the AFL more sympathetic to the International Federation of Trade Unions. The British Trades Union Congress, with which the AFL had maintained amicable relations over the years, was interested in bringing the AFL into the IFTU. Negotiations were begun in 1935, and the AFL accepted an invitation to send a delegate to the Warsaw conference in August 1937. Matthew Woll, its representative, found his position challenged, as a result of the influence of John L. Lewis and Sidney Hillman with some of the continental delegations. In the end, the federation was accepted as a member. It soon appeared that the AFL's venture into international trade union relations would be short-lived. The IFTU, in response to the sentiment of a "united front" against fascism rampant among some of its affiliates, approached the Soviet trade unions with a suggestion for affiliating. At first rejected, the issue was again considered as a result of pressure exercised by some of the British unions upon the leaders of the British Trades Union Congress; the latter were very influential within the IFTU. Green informed Walter Citrine, secretary of the British Trades Union Congress, that the "Council of Trade Unions of the Soviet Government of Russia does not represent a democratic trade union movement free from government domination and control. In this respect, we cannot distinguish any difference between the Central Council of Trade Unions of the Soviet Government of Russia and the Nazi and Fascist-controlled labor front movements of Germany and Italy."[24]

Moreover, Green told Citrine that the affiliation of the Soviet unions would lead to disunity and perhaps the ultimate destruction of the IFTU.

After the Soviet-Nazi pact and the declaration of war, the affiliation of the Soviet trade unions ceased to be a question for the IFTU. But its leaders were driven from the continent, killed, and imprisoned in concentration camps. The AFL appealed for assistance to the exiled German trade unionists and intervened with the State Department on behalf of a number of fleeing leaders of the IFTU, asking the department to grant them entering visas.[25]

Anglo-Soviet Trade Union Committee

After the Nazi attack on the Soviet Union in June 1941, the position of the British Trades Union Congress on cooperating with the Soviet labor organizations underwent a radical change. British organized labor, anxious to cooperate with the spokesmen for Soviet workers, sought to draw the American labor organizations into this venture. Citrine, acting under a mandate of the 1941 British Trades Union Congress, was instrumental in setting up the Anglo-Soviet Trade Union Committee in October 1941. A program of cooperation of the labor movements of the two countries was agreed upon, and a plan for broadening the committee to include representatives of the AFL endorsed. "The matter," Citrine informed Green, "is regarded by our General Council and the All-Union Central Council of Trade Unions of the U.S.S.R., as one of very great importance, and it is because it is felt it would assist your Council to reach a decision on the merits of the proposal, that I was deputed to travel to the United States on hearing from you as to a suitable date when I could meet the Executive of the A.F. of L."[26]

The AFL was willing to develop closer relations with the British Trades Union Congress, but it rejected formal cooperation with the Soviet trade unions.[27] A complicating factor was introduced into the negotiations when Citrine requested the AFL executive council to include representatives of the CIO and the Railroad Brotherhoods in the projected Anglo-American Trade Union Committee.[28] The CIO executive board, at its meeting in September 1942, directed its officers to seek closer unity of the organized workers in the United States with those of the countries in the United Nations.[29] Green and other members of the AFL executive council were opposed to cooperating with the CIO in international matters and objected to "the sudden interest" of the brotherhoods in international labor activities. Green told A. F. Whitney, head of the Brotherhood of Railway Trainmen, that he could not recall where one of the brotherhoods had ever been concerned with the relationship to the British Trades Union Congress which the AFL had carried on for several decades.[30]

Citrine and a committe from the Trades Union Congress came to Washington and sought to have the AFL change its policy of excluding the CIO from the projected Anglo-American committee. Political pressure was exercised, and Citrine, in his plea for allowing the CIO to join, explained that Prime Minister Winston Churchill and Foreign Secretary Anthony Eden had intervened and emphasized the importance of having the CIO affiliate with the Anglo-American Trade Union Committee. Green told Citrine that the AFL would not retreat from its position. He expressed the belief, while pointedly excluding Murray and John L. Lewis, that many officers and staff members of the CIO were Communists, who tried to sabotage the war effort before the attack on the Soviet Union. He contrasted their attitude with the support of the Allies given by the AFL.[31]

The problem facing the leaders of the English trade union movement was a difficult one. Since 1894 they had had friendly relations with the AFL, but now a competing federation was demanding recognition on the international plane. Moreover, the Southport Congress in September 1943 directed the calling of an international labor conference and included the CIO among organizations to be invited. In turn, the CIO was anxious to branch out into the area of international labor relations. At its convention in 1942 it had expressed the belief in the necessity of cooperation of all free people in the struggle against fascism. In the following year the convention directed its officers to announce the urgent desire of the CIO to join in "convening an international trade union conference of the labor centers of all the United Nations."[32]

President Murray accepted the invitation of the British Trades Union Congress to attend the preliminary conference in London in 1944. His conduct was unanimously approved by the 1944 CIO convention, and he appointed Sidney Hillman, president of the Amalgamated Clothing Workers of America, R. J. Thomas, president of the United Automobile Workers, and Emil Rieve, president of the Textile Workers Union of America, as delegates to attend. An agenda for the future World Trade Union Conference was worked out and a list of subjects to be discussed, including the anticipated peace settlement, organization of world peace, Allied occupation, representation of labor at the peace conference, relief, rehabilitation, and postwar construction, was accepted.

WORLD TRADE UNION CONFERENCE

At the world trade union conference which met in London during February 6-17, 1945, the CIO was represented by twelve delegates headed by Hillman; the British delegation comprised fifteen and the Soviet Union, thirty-five. Representation from other countries was substantial. A total of forty-nine national labor centers, some still under Axis domination, sent delegates. Committees on the peace settlement, the Allied war effort, and postwar reconstruction brought in resolutions. All of the declarations were unanimously adopted, and committees appointed to draft a constitution to be submitted to the meeting of the World Trade Union Conference in Paris in October 1945.

The Paris meeting endorsed the actions of the London conference, approved the constitution and resolutions, and elected Louis Saillant, a French Communist, general secretary. "The aims and objectives of the newly-born World Federation of Trade Unions," was, according to the CIO, "so clearly recognized that within a year the only large trade union center not included in membership was the American Federation of Labor."[33] The 1946 CIO convention commended the efforts of Murray and other officers for their efforts in the establishment of the WFTU and their participation in its councils.[34] Over the protests of the AFL, the International Federation of Trade Unions was liquidated. It is not easy to know the reasons why eminent trade union leaders of the free world were willing to walk into a Communist trap. Only the pressure from the unions dominated by the left wing can account for the willingness of a man with the keen intelligence and unsurpassed experience of Walter Citrine to go along with the plan for the

World Federation of Trade Unions. It is true that Citrine voiced his misgivings during the Paris sessions, and even warned against the use of political trickery and paper organizations for promoting factional ends. Nevertheless, he understood as well as any other man the protean forms of the Communist International apparatus, its ruthless and all-consuming purpose to destroy all labor organizations that would not bend to the needs of Soviet policy.

The CIO was in a different position. Not only were the Communists a powerful minority, but they occupied a number of strategic posts in the organization. Leaders of the CIO had also resented their exclusion from international labor affairs. The AFL leaders still regarded the CIO as a secessionist group, and they refused to share certain prerogatives—such as representation at the Britsh Trades Union Congress. Murray, always seeking parity with the AFL, whose opposition was strengthened by its suspicions of the many Communists in important places in the CIO, saw in the creation of the WFTU an opportunity for asserting international equality with the AFL. Murray, however, was inexperienced on the international level, was overworked, and had too many responsibilities. Sidney Hillman was ready to take on the role of international statesman. He knew and understood Communist tactics; his attack on the Communists at the 1940 CIO convention reflected a determination to prevent victory of the party line in the CIO. Perhaps the valor of the Soviet armies, as well as ambition and dislike of the AFL, spurred him to new adventures. He was quite content to allow the CIO to become the American representative of the Communist-dominated World Federation of Trade Unions.

THE MARSHALL PLAN

From the beginning the WFTU came under the control of the Communists. It was clear that the controlling group regarded the organization as a political instrument and that Saillant and his supporters did not believe in the principle of autonomy of the national federations. Differences would be tolerated as long as they were not significant. The 1947 CIO convention endorsed the WFTU and called upon the American delegates to the Security Council and the General Assembly of the United Nations to support a proposal that it be given representation on the Economic and Social Council of the United Nations.[35]

Divisions between the free and Communist-controlled affiliates soon made their appearance, but for the first eighteen months they were not allowed to create a gulf between the two viewpoints. The differences between the Soviet government and the Western powers over policies to be followed in occupied Germany and Austria, as well as the methods to be pursued in the promotion of recovery, soon created an unreconcilable conflict in the WFTU. The differences centered ultimately around the "Plan for European Recovery" presented by General George Marshall on June 7, 1947.

The WFTU constituted a danger to the free world because it could be used as an instrument of foreign policy by the Soviet government and the world Communist apparatus. The affiliation of the majority of trade union federations of the free world, especially the British Trades Union Congress and the CIO, gave WFTU decisions the appearance of impartiality which made resistance to them more difficult. The AFL had recognized the growing importance of foreign relations, and, in 1944, established the Free Trade Union Committee with Jay Lovestone as its secretary. Lovestone had been a founding member of the American Communist party, but he had broken with communism and had become a dedicated defender of democratic principles and one of the more knowledgeable students of world communism, especially of its relations to the labor movements of the world. As soon as the war ended, the AFL fought for the right of German workers to form trade unions. Two representatives, Irving Brown and Henry Rutz, were sent to open offices in Europe. The fight of the AFL in behalf of the nascent German trade unions and its efforts to prevent its repression by the occupation authorities and at the same time defend them against Communist infiltration and control form one of the brilliant chapters in the history of American labor. The free world owes a great deal to Matthew Woll, George Harrison, David Dubinsky, William Green, and George Meany. Their understanding, courage, and willingness to espouse what seemed, at the time, an unpopular cause was of inestimable service to the labor movements and to all of the people of the free world. In 1945 the AFL was alone; the Trades Union Congress and the CIO were captives of the WFTU.[36] Nevertheless, it continued to demand rights for German labor and occupation policies which would allow for the emerging growth and prosperity in Western Germany.

On October 5, 1947, the Cominform—the international arm of world communism—denounced the program for aiding the economic recovery program of Europe by the United States as an imperialist plot to dominate the world in behalf of monopoly capitalism. The CIO inferentially rejected these views. Secretary of State George Marshall was invited to address the 1947 convention, and a resolution endorsing the European Recovery Plan was passed.[37] A number of delegates challenged the position of the Communists, and Reuther called for a stand against all forms of totalitarianism.

Soon after the issuance of the Cominform statement attacking the Marshall Plan, the majority of the executive bureau of the WFTU voted to exclude the CIO proposal for a discussion of American aid to Europe from the agenda of its meeting. The official *Information Bulletin* opened an attack on the Marshall Plan, and the CIO and British Trades Union Congress began to resist what they regarded as improper uses of official publications. In fact, Philip Murray endorsed the Marshall Plan in testifying before the Senate Foreign Relations Committee. Dissent was registered by Howard McKenzie, a vice-president of the then Communist-dominated National Maritime Union affiliated with the CIO.[38]

At the same time, the AFL Executive Council called on Congress to approve the Marshall Plan, and William Green testified on its behalf. Both major labor groups in the United States were united on this issue.[39]

The free trade unions were anxious to promote European recovery and make a contribution to the economic revival of their countries. In addition, they believed it was essential that the trade unions play a role in the Marshall Plan in order to protect the interests of labor so that the workers might share in the economic progress the plan would make possible.

To devise a common policy, the British Trades Union Congress and the free unions of the Benelux countries called a conference in London for March 9-10, 1948, for the purpose of devising a common policy on the European Recovery Program. Both the AFL and the CIO were invited.

Twenty-six organizations in fifteen countries appointed forty-eight representatives. Several organizations which had been invited refused to participate—the most important being the Confederation Générale du Travail and the Generale Italiana del Lavoro of Italy. Frank Fenton, Irving Brown, and Henry Rutz represented the AFL; James B. Carey, Michael Ross, and Elmer Cope, the CIO; and Bert M. Jewell, the Railway Labor Executives Association. The conference found no unacceptable conditions attached to the proposals of the American government, and there would be no interference in the internal affairs of European countries by the United States. It also decided to make the ERP Trade Union Advisory Committee open to all bona fide trade union organizations desiring to participate. The conference advised close collaboration with the governments carrying out the program by the union of each country.[40]

Similar views were expressed at the July Trade Union Conference. The organizations involved sought to work out cooperation along trade union lines on problems arising out of the European Recovery Program. The conference understood the basic purpose of the program as the encouragement and "the provision of means for European countries to ascertain and coordinate their resources as a whole and to enable them to make up deficits which become apparent, from American sources."[41]

The International Confederation of Free Trade Unions

Once the Cominform denounced the European Recovery Program, or the Marshall Plan, the free trade unions found themselves in an impossible position. They either had to oppose the aid offered by the United States, in accordance with the will of world communism and thereby allow the World Federation of Trade Unions to use its resources and name to undermine the program, or withdraw. Inevitably, efforts at compromise failed, and the CIO representatives described the meeting of the WFTU on September 17-21, 1948, as a "wrangle between communists and trade unionists."[42]

The 1948 CIO convention authorized the officers and executive board, "in consultation with the British TUC and other free trade union centers, to take whatever action in relation to the WFTU and the international labor movement as will best accomplish CIO policies and objectives."[43] On January 18, 1949, the CIO withdrew from the WFTU. With the departure of major non-Communist trade union federations, the WFTU lost much of its propaganda power as the spokesman for labor. It also made possible the rallying of the free trade unions into a federation of their own and gave them an opportunity to present the views of the free world and counter the attacks of the Communists and the WFTU. The AFL applauded the severance of relations by the free trade unions and called for the formation of a genuine free international trade union organization "dedicated to the principles of freedom, justice and lasting peace."[44] The federation recognized that CIO participation would be necessary if a free international trade union federation was to be established. As the representative of millions of American workers, the CIO was given equal status in the plan, although the AFL was convinced that the 6 million members claimed by the CIO as a basis for voting in the projected international federation was excessive.[45]

In a sense the partial retreat by the AFL from its historic position that it was the exclusive representative of American labor in international affairs was an act of realism and belated justice. The AFL was ready to make concessions, but its suspicion of the CIO was not completely abated. Part of this attitude was influenced by rivalry, but it feared that the CIO was not experienced in the international area and was prone to support doubtful causes. At the same time, the AFL recognized that the CIO could not be excluded; its strength and support were needed and the British and other free trade unions would not have agreed to keeping the CIO out of any international labor body.

After consulting representatives of trade union national centers in the United States and Europe, Vincent Tewson, general secretary of the British Trades Union Congress, called a conference to discuss the possibility of developing closer cooperation among the unions of the free world. Both the AFL and the CIO were represented at the first conference in Geneva on June 25-26, 1949. The preparatory conference appointed a committee to draft a constitution and program for the "international trade union organization which will embrace all free and democratic trade union organizations throughout the world, and which will aim at the closest possible consultation and collaboration with the International Trade Union Secretariats."[46]

Conferences and discussions continued, and on November 28 the Free Labor Conference met in London. The CIO sent delegates, with Walter Reuther, David McDonald, and Allan Haywood among them. In addition to William Green and George Meany, the AFL delegation included Matthew Woll, George M. Harrison, David Dubinksy, Charles M. McGowan, and William Doherty. Fifty-six national centers in 50 countries were represented by 162 delegates from more than 48 million trade unionists.[47] The meeting established the International Confederation of Free Trade Unions. In a statement, "For Bread, Freedom and Peace," the confederation welcomed the labor movements of all free nations, and called upon them to unite for freedom and abundance. It rejected "the false theory that workers must sacrifice political and spiritual freedom to obtain economic security and social justice."[48]

Latin America

The American Federation of Labor supported the Mexican revolution of 1912. The 1912 convention demanded that the United States government avoid hostile acts against the movement to displace the ruthless and bloody tyrant, Porfirio Diaz. In the succession of revolts and counterrevolts that followed, the AFL supported the forces of democracy and freedom against efforts of the reactionaries and adventurers to reimpose a dictatorial regime upon the Mexican people. The federation was also active publicly and behind the scenes against the efforts of American interests to encourage intervention by the United States. Out of these activities came the first Pan American labor conference in November 1918. The conference laid plans for periodic meetings. The Mexican representatives attacked the treatment of Mexican nationals living in the United States by unions and employers and demanded that the United States political prisoners convicted during the war be released. The Pan American Federation of Labor functioned for a decade and used its influence to improve relations between the labor movements of North and South American countries. Gompers regarded the movement as an example of international labor cooperation. He insisted on attending its meeting in Mexico City during his illness in December 1924. He opened the conference on December 4, 1924. He became seriously ill, and was rushed to Laredo, Texas, where he died on December 13, 1924.

The Pan American Federation of Labor continued to function throughout the 1920's, and the complaints against the actions of the American government and corporations by Latin American labor officials were carried by AFL leaders to the United States government. Relations between the AFL and later the CIO and Latin American labor movements continued throughout the 1930's and 1940's. With the formation of the International Confederation of Trade Unions, a Latin American division in which the American labor movement had participated was set up. The aim of the unions of the United States has been to help Latin American workers create a democratic and effective trade union movement able and willing to improve the lot of its members.[49]

CHAPTER 46

Political Activity of Organized Labor

LEGISLATIVE COMMITTEE

After the 1924 La Follette-Wheeler campaign, the labor movement returned to its older and long-tried policy of endorsing candidates of either political party favorable to its program. Beginning with Andrew Furuseth and Adolph Strasser in 1895, the AFL maintained a legislative committee in Washington to keep a check on legislation before Congress and to rally votes for or against bills in accordance with the policy of the federation expressed at conventions or at meetings of the executive council. It was the job of the legislative committee to analyze virtually every bill introduced and favor or oppose it in accordance with the position of the AFL. This did not mean a merely passive registering of views, but rather an active effort to rally congressional support for the position of the labor movement. The legislative committee also compiled the voting records of all members of Congress at the end of the congressional sessions. Matters concerning labor handled by government departments were also within the province of the legislative committee, and unions and central bodies could call upon it for assistance.

Every state federation of labor and many city central bodies have maintained legislative committees in their respective state capitals, and internationals have increasingly stationed representatives in Washington. The Railway Labor Executives' Association, organized in 1926, made up of the unions in the AFL and the independent brotherhoods, was the first group of unions to set up a separate legislative body. The RLEA has been a policy making body on legislative and other matters for its affiliates, and it has been very effective in gaining concessions. Congress guaranteed the right to organize and established a system of old-age benefits for railroad workers before it granted these benefits to other employers. The RLEA has published *Labor,* a weekly largely devoted to economic, political, and social questions. The effectiveness of the political methods devised by the AFL is shown by their adoption by the CIO. A legislative committee headed by Lewis functioned during his term in office. The CIO established a legislative department headed by Nathan Cowan to promote the interests of its unions before Congress. Voting records of congressmen and senators were distributed among national and local unions.[1]

Representatives from the labor movement have usually appeared before the conventions of the two major political parties to ask for incorporation of their legislative proposals in their respective platforms. The federation did not endorse candidates for the Presidency until 1952, although discussions and the observations might indicate the candidates favored. During congressional elections, the voting records of candidates were distributed, and endorsements in accordance with the wishes of the local labor movement in the candidate's district made. The federation biennially selected a Nonpartisan Political Compaign Committee to circulate the information and present its demands to the political parties. In 1928 it was dissatisfied with the platform of both parties, but Daniel Tobin, the treasurer of the federation, resigned from the executive council after it rejected his motion that the Presidential candidacy of Alfred E. Smith be endorsed.[2]

LABOR'S NONPARTISAN LEAGUE

While to some extent the formation of the CIO presented the AFL with a rival on the political as well as the economic front, the two organizations frequently supported the same bills before Congress and the legislatures. With a long record of activity and considerable achievement, the federation was inclined to be more cautious and less eager to enlist in behalf of "large" causes. As with its industrial policies, the federation was more concerned, at least theoretically, with the possible.

In keeping with its policy, the executive council recommended the continuance of nonpartisanship in the campaign of 1936. There was, however, widespread sentiment in the ranks of organized labor for a more forthright and active policy in this Presidential campaign. In April 1936, Labor's Nonpartisan League was organized with George L. Berry, the head of the Pressman's Union, as chairman. John L. Lewis and Sidney Hillman occupied prominent positions in the league. A permanent organization was established on August 10.[3] As usual, the AFL appointed a committee to examine the records of congressmen and make endorsements, but even though the overwhelming majority of labor officers and their members favored the re-election of Franklin D. Roosevelt, the AFL would not formally endorse him.

The continuance of the historic program was justified by the success gained by the federation in blending "into a common brotherhood and . . . in a strong organization men and women of differing political opinions and beliefs."[4] Labor's Nonpartisan League was very active in the 1936 Presidential campaign. The United Mine Workers of America, the chief supporter of the league, contributed $486,288.55 to the campaign.[5] Its president, John L. Lewis, contributed more than finances; he toured the coal areas and other sections of the country extolling the virtues of the Democratic ticket. Labor's Nonpartisan League undoubtedly made a contribution to the overwhelming victory scored by Roosevelt.

In 1938 the AFL came out against Labor's Nonpartisan League as an organization that was now entirely controlled by the CIO. It cited the withdrawal of George Berrry, who had been succeeded by Lewis as chairman. Sidney Hillman became vice-chairman. The AFL, in March 1938, castigated the league as a CIO agency opposed to the interests of the federation and called upon its members to withdraw.[6]

The federation, in the following year, ordered its affiliated central bodies to withdraw from Labor's Nonpartisan League.[7] The AFL convention branded the league as "an accessory to the CIO and antagonistic to the American Federation of Labor."[8]

The view of the AFL that Labor's Nonpartisan League was entirely controlled by John L. Lewis was to be confirmed by the 1940 Presidential campaign. In keeping with its past policy, the AFL refused to give a blanket endorsement to any political party. Its representatives appeared before the platform committees of both parties. The federation summarized its political position as "a strict adherence to a non-partisan political policy. This procedure requires that the platforms of the political parties must be compared and the records of candidates for office must be carefully scrutinized."[9] Information on the candidates and the action of the parties on labor planks were submitted to all affiliates.

The CIO was silent on its political plans for the 1940 campaign. Its leader had not decided on the policy Labor's Nonpartisan League would pursue. Addressing, in July 1940, a meeting of the Townsend Clubs—an organization seeking a pension of $200 a month for every person over sixty years of age—John L. Lewis predicted "that if Franklin Delano Roosevelt will run for a third term that Mr. Willkie will defeat him ignominiously."[10] Lewis offered Senator Burton K. Wheeler, a pro-labor isolationist, as the one man who could carry the Democratic standard to victory. Lewis' advice was not taken, and he decided to support the Republican candidate, Wendell Willkie. Lewis refused to continue as head of the CIO in accordance with his promise not to seek re-election if Roosevelt were elected to a third term.

Philip Murray, who became head of the CIO on Lewis' retirement in 1940, was closer to the New Deal and to Roosevelt than his predecessor had been. Murray's political policies were not far from those espoused by the AFL, although the CIO was inclined to take more aggressive political positions. It lacked under Murray and, for a short period of his leadership, under Reuther, the suspicion and even fear of government which over the years had been characteristic of the AFL.

POLITICAL ACTION COMMITTEE (PAC)

A new departure in American labor politics was the formation of the political Action Committee by the CIO Executive Board on July 7, 1943. Sidney Hillman was appointed chairman, Van A. Bittner vice-chairman, and R. J. Thomas secretary. The committee was authorized to conduct a campaign for mobilizing the members of the CIO and other organized workers and their families "for effective action on the political front."[11] After a series of regional meetings, the CIO established a national headquarters in New York City and fourteen regional offices, each in charge of a regional director to organize the political campaign. The CIO unions contributed $631,-214.11. Up to July 23, PAC received $671,214.11, spent $371,086.56, and froze the remainder until November 7. The voluntary contributions financed PAC's election activities.[12]

In a statement the CIO called for a strong home front through the maintenance of "economic, social and legislative standards as a guarantee of wholesome living standards for our people and the protection of the highest possible morale among our millions of workers."[13] The CIO also established the National Citizens Political Action Committee made up largely of artists, writers, and other professionals, with a generous sprinkling of Communist fellow-travelers and political innocents.

As a first step, Hillman called on William Green to join in working out a common political program. Green brought the question before the executive council, which reaffirmed its traditional "nonpartisan political policy and that we will continue to support our friends and oppose our enemies, and in order to do that effectively . . . we cannot join with any other group in the formulation of a political policy."[14] Hillman was not only active in PAC, but he attempted to mediate in the dispute between the Stalinist Communists and anti-Communists, made up of progressive trade unionists and Social Democrats, for the control of the American Labor party, which had been formed in New York state during the Presidential campaign in 1936. This party was the creation of the New York leaders of the garment trades, who hoped that the thousands of New York

Socialists would be willing to vote for Roosevelt and Garner, an action they would find distasteful if they had to cast their vote for the Democratic ticket.

Hillman had never played an important role in the American Labor party and the Communists, then soaring on the wave of extreme patriotism, sought to capture the party. During the dispute Hillman intervened and offered a compromise which would have placed the party in control of the Communists. This is precisely what happened, for, rather than accept the Hillman compromise, the Socialists and non-Communist progressives withdrew and formed the Liberal party. The American Labor party gradually declined and finally was not able to gain sufficient votes in the elections to qualify for a place on the ballot. Thus ended one of Hillman's less successful efforts at settling disputes.

Hillman was too knowledgeable not to have been aware of the significance of his action. According to his biographer, Hillman "used to say that he was very well aware of who was a communist and who was not."[15] Hillman had a position of "realistic detachment" toward extremists from the right and left. His alliance with the New York Communists is compared to his cooperation during his government service with Secretary of the Navy James Forrestal and William Knudsen, who headed defense and procurement. Even more ludicrous is the author's equating Hillman's actions with Winston Churchill's cooperation with the Soviet Union during World War II.[16] As a government officer, Hillman had no choice but to cooperate with leading government officials. As for Churchill, the Soviet Union was at the time holding in check the bulk of the German armies. What type of force or influence did the American Communists dispose of to warrant Hillman's cooperation?

Congressman Howard K. Smith thought that the CIO unions were guilty of violating the War Labor Disputes Act, which he had authored, by contributing funds to influence the elections of 1944. Smith called upon Attorney-General Francis Biddle to prosecute the officers who had contributed union funds for this purpose under Section 9 of the law.[17] The demand was rejected, as was a subsequent one by Oklahoma Senator E. H. Moore. Biddle denied that the Corrupt Practices Act applied to primaries. As the activities of the CIO, PAC, and NCPAC, were financed by individual contributions, Biddle could find no basis for prosecution.[18] This view was supported by an investigation of campaign expenditures by the special Senate committee which "found no clear-cut violation of the Corrupt Practices Act on the part of the Political Action Committee."[19]

Hillman became a center of political attack. His Jewish origin and a report that Roosevelt had asked James F. Byrnes, who was to be nominated for vice-president, to "clear it with Sidney" were used to paint Hillman as a future dictator.[20]

In March 1944 PAC started a drive to register the voters and began issuing a tabloid *Political Action News*. In the midst of the campaign Murray announced that PAC would serve as a permanent political arm of the CIO. The AFL refused to diverge from its traditional views and established its customary Nonpartisan Campaign Committee. The executive council also directed "that under no circumstances" were directly chartered central bodies or affiliated unions to "collaborate with representatives of dual organizations or allow representatives of dual organizations to participate in the formation and execution of the non-partisan political policy of the American Federation of Labor."[21] George L. Berry, the president of the Printing Pressman's Union, protested the statement, as he had a "grave doubt as to the authority of the Executive Council of the A.F. of L. to proceed on its political basis—that is the responsibility of the International Unions as they elect, and beyond that the question as to what party they may wish to join and the parties they support seems to me to be one to be determined by the individual, and we shall not interfere with that prerogative."[22]

The 1944 CIO convention praised the wisdom and foresight of Murray and the executive board, and pointed to the election of Roosevelt and Truman as proof of the "correctness of our decision to abstain from and discourage any move in the direction of a third party. We reaffirm that decision and reject any and all proposals for a third party."[23] The convention voted to continue the Political Action Committee and placed the work of political action and education under its direction. Hillman continued as chairman, but he resigned as directing head of the National Citizens Political Action Committee. He was replaced by Elmer Benson, who had been governor of Minnesota.[24]

From the point of view of financial expenditures, the 1944 campaign by PAC was the greatest effort ever made by a labor organization. The organization received $647,903.26 from the trade unions, $376,910.77 from individual contributions, and spent $948,351.14.[25] In addition, National Citizens PAC received $380,306.45, and spent all but slightly more than $1,100 of it.

The death of Hillman led to the appointment of Jack Kroll, who had served as Hillman's assistant as director of CIO PAC. The federation followed its usual nonpartisan policy, and PAC was less active in the 1946 congressional campaign than it had been in the Presidential contest of 1944. Interestingly enough, Kroll announced that PAC had not participated in the Wisconsin senatorial primary in which Joseph McCarthy defeated Senator Robert M. La Follette, Jr. for the senatorial nomination.[26] In view of Senator La Follette's services to progressive causes, his support of virtually all the legislation sponsored by organized labor during his senatorial tenure, and the yeoman service he performed on the committee investigating employer-directed espionage in unions and other forms of denial and interference with the rights of labor, the failure is an eloquent commentary on the source of political decision-making in CIO PAC. La Follette, like his father who proceeded him in the Senate, was suspicious of entangling alliances and had a clear understanding of the nature and the intentions of the Soviet Union. These views made him unacceptable to the Communist "apparatchics," who controlled PAC endorsements in Wisconsin.

THIRD PARTY

In an effort to keep its factions united, the CIO Executive Board voted against its officers affiliating with Americans for Democratic Action, a liberal group sponsored by Mrs. Eleanor Roosevelt among others. The same rule was applied to the Progressive Citizen's Committee, which was an outgrowth of the National Citizen's Political Action Committee originally formed by Sidney Hillman. The National Citizens PAC was showing increasingly its "party colors" and was following the Communist line on important issues.[27] A more serious problem confronted the CIO when Henry Wallace announced his candidacy for the Presidency on a third party ticket. Reactions to the announcement differed. *The Daily Worker,* the journalistic spokesman for the Communist party, headlined it as "A Historic Candidacy," while Jack Kroll declared: "It has been the policy of the C.I.O. Political Action Committee not to support a third party."[28]

Unions controlled by the Communists and front organizations quickly fell in line. Sidney Hillman's intervention in the affairs of the American Labor party was revealed as a serious error in judgment. Officers of the Amalgamated Clothing Workers resigned from New York's American Labor party, and one of its leaders declared that "a third party must inevitably play into the hands of labor's enemies."[29] The CIO Executive Board by a vote of 33 to 11 decided "it was politically unwise to inject a third party into the political scene of 1948." The CIO Political Action Committee voted by 9 to 2 against a policy of partisanship.[30] One of the minor consequences of the anti-third party position of the CIO was the resignation of Lee Pressman as counsel for the Steelworkers' Union and of the CIO. He had, in addition to his other duties, served as secretary of the convention's resolution's committee, an unusual post for a non-wage working attorney.[31]

In 1948, Van A. Bittner and Green testified on behalf of their respective organizations before the Republican and Democratic parties. Both labor programs were in essential agreement. Their most important plank was the repeal of the Taft-Hartley Act. In addition, they called for higher minimum wages, improvements in social security, fair employment practice legislation, and tax revision. It was a clear indication that those who controlled official CIO policy at this time were in close agreement with the AFL on political, economic, and social questions.[32] However, the AFL and CIO differed on endorsing candidates for the Presidency. The AFL reiterated its traditional nonpartisan position, although George Harrison, a member of the executive council, headed labor for Truman and Barkley. Daniel Tobin, who had served three times as the head of the Democratic party's labor committee, belatedly and unenthusiastically endorsed Thomas Dewey for the Presidency.[33]

The CIO Executive Board, by a vote of 35 to 12, on August 21, 1948, endorsed Truman and Barkley. The issue split the organization and was the forerunner of action against the Communists. The opponents clothed their arguments with references to Truman's antilabor actions, but it was the Marshall Plan, bitterly opposed by the Cominform, which was the true cause for the opposition. It should be recalled that the attacks of the Communist-controlled unions on Roosevelt during the Hitler-Stalin pact were also usually explained by reference to domestic issues.[34]

LABOR'S LEAGUE FOR POLITICAL EDUCATION

Until 1947 the AFL had followed its traditional political policies; it published and distributed the voting records of members of Congress and periodically elected a Nonpartisan Campaign Committee, made up of the permanent officers of the AFL and several members of the executive council, to influence the election of labor's friends and defeat its enemies in the congressional elections. It maintained no permanent political department, nor was this task entrusted to a member of the staff. In fact, the AFL devoted only a minor fraction of its energies and resources to political activity. Largely as a result of the passage of the Taft-Hartley Act, the sixty-sixth convention of the AFL recommended the "immediate establishment of 'Labor's Educational and Political League.' "[35]

The league was directed to acquaint the workers of the country with the economic and political views of the AFL, to prepare and disseminate information on the attitude of candidates for nomination or election to federal office, raise funds, and employ a staff for carrying out its duties. A conference of international presidents was called on December 5 and 6, 1947, to make final plans for launching the league. Vice-President Matthew Woll, George Harrison, and Charles McGowan prepared a program.[36]

In explaining the need for an intensified political program by the AFL, President Green informed the conference of international presidents that he had been surprised by the strength of antilabor feeling in Congress and by the overriding of President Truman's veto of the Taft-Hartley Act.[37] Vice-President Daniel Tobin stressed that suggestions and amendments were welcome. The executive council recommended that Labor's League for Political Education be governed by a national committee consisting of the members of the AFL Executive Council and all national unions affiliated with the AFL. The national committee was to choose its officers annually. An administrative committee was appointed and authorized to select a national director and the necessary staff. Secretary-Treasurer George Meany assured the delegates that the league was "by no means a departure from the old political philosophy of the A.F. of L. of 'defeating your enemies and rewarding your friends' . . . that policy is just as valid today as when it was initiated many years ago by Samuel Gompers and those associated with him in the founding of this Federation."[38] Meany added that the formation of the league was an "attempt to give effect to that philosophy in line with present conditions."[39] In his view, it was no longer sufficient "to send Central Labor Unions and Local Unions the voting records of Congressmen or representatives in the various State Legislatures. He declared we have gotten beyond that point. He stated we have got to do something more than that; we have got to make our people politically conscious; develop them politically in their own self-interest, not for the purpose of attempting to run the country but for the purpose of protecting ourselves."[40]

The administrative committee tentatively selected Senator Burton K. Wheeler as director, but objections by some members, as well as newspaper reports that Wheeler had reservations on the Marshall Plan and that he regarded his office as a policy-making one, put an end to his consideration. After going over a long list of names, Joseph Keenan, secretary of the Chicago Federation of Labor, was appointed.[41] The Department of Political Education, under the chairmanship of George Harrison, was in charge of endorsements. Other committees dealt with finances and public relations; one was also established to mobilize women voters. Counsel advised that union-contributed funds could be used for education but not for political campaigning. Later, a League for Political Education was established in every state. A news service was supplied, and voting records of candidates were circulated. In 1948 more than $115,000 was donated by the unions for the educational funds, and a larger sum for political action was raised by voluntary contributions of individuals. Expenditures for political education by unions were held proper. Educational work by the league was financed after 1951 by the AFL. Neither the AFL nor the league endorsed Presidential candidates in 1948, although George Harrison, chairman of the Department of Political Direction, was active in behalf of the Truman-Barkley ticket.

As the campaign rolled on, John L. Lewis sought to settle an old score with President Truman. He denounced him as "totally unfit . . . careless with the truth, elastic in his principles . . . a malignant scheming sort of an individual who is dangerous to the United Mine Workers of America and dangerous to the United States of America."[42] George Harrison described

Lewis's statement as designed to aid the election of Thomas Dewey. Undaunted by Lewis' opposition and the defection of several labor leaders to the Republican party, Jack Kroll, the director of the CIO Political Action Committee, forecast on the basis of spot polls in factories a victory for Truman.[43] Following the 1948 election, Labor's League for Political Education was voted permanent status.

On the basis of data reported to the Clerk of the House of Representatives, national labor organizations spent $1,291,343 in the 1948 Presidential campaign, but the total does not include the funds raised by local groups. The largest amount, $513,003, was spent by the CIO Political Action Committee. Labor's League for Political Education was second, with an expenditure of $343,293. Of the political committees sponsored by each of eleven unions, the largest expenditure—$240,532—was reported by the International Ladies' Garment Workers' Union.[44]

Labor's League for Political Education raised over $600,000 for its educational fund in 1948–1949, and under $500,000 in 1950–1951. These funds were used for writing and circulating printed material, for radio and television programs, and for organizing state and local groups.[45] Both PAC and LLPE continued their activities after the 1948 campaign. The CIO pointed to the broad character of PAC's program. "Stress has been laid during the work of your Political Action Committee, on the inclusive nature of the CIO program which embraces matters of broad concern such as valley authorities, aid to education, housing, health, farm programs, civil rights, and other subjects."[46] A similar view was voiced by the LLPE Department of Political Education. It believed that labor had to support candidates who were concerned with and would support programs to increase the incomes of farmers and low-paid wage earners, as well as development programs for the western states which could be "the greatest single bulwark against unemployment."[47]

Leaders of organized labor were anxious to find a candidate in Ohio who could defeat Senator Robert Taft for re-election in 1950. Regarded as the author of the "slave" Taft-Hartley law and the leader of the conservative coalition in Congress, his defeat could be used as a lesson and a warning to antilabor legislators. When the issue was raised at the meeting of the LLPE Administrative Committee, George Harrison, a resident of Ohio and a shrewd judge of the politically possible, "stated that Taft cannot be defeated by a two by four candidate as he is . . . well-informed on the political and economic questions of our country and he has an unlimited amount of resources. . . . He stated that Mr. Joe Ferguson, the City Auditor, would like to run but he doesn't have what it takes to defeat Taft."[48]

Joe Ferguson, the chosen candidate against Taft, was overwhelmingly defeated. In a statement, Taft claimed his victory demonstrated that the voters would not accept dictation from the CIO Political Action Committee.[49] The reason for the senator's statement was the Ohio CIO *PAC*'s *Speaker's Handbook on Robert Alphonso Taft* linking the senator with Fascists and their causes. It was a work of guilt by insinuation.

Representatives from both the AFL and CIO appeared before the platform committees of the Democratic and Republican parties in 1952 and presented their views. According to the CIO, 107 of its members attended as delegates to the Democratic convention.

AFL and CIO delegates worked closely together. A joint coordinating committee was organized with George Harrison, James McDevit, director of Labor's League for Political Education, Jack Kroll, director of PAC as members. Vice-President Alben Barkley, who sought the Presidential nomination, withdrew after the coordinating committee refused to support him.

Not all labor officers were happy at the display of power politics. AFL Vice-President Charles Macgowan described the rejection of Barkley "as a tragedy." John L. Lewis wired Sam Caddy, a district officer of the Miners' Union and a delegate from Kentucky, that Barkley should be placed in nomination. The *United Mine Workers Journal* noted that no "one familiar with the tactless political leadership of the CIO is ever surprised over their foolhardy movements and endorsements. The CIO has demonstrated over and over again its lack of gratitude in making political choice. The CIO's dirty political campaign brought about the defeat of Senator Wheeler . . . plus their 'commie' wing vote against La Follette . . . for re-election to the Senate—simply because they would not champion 'commie' sponsored legislation—is a lasting stigma that the CIO can never live down.

"For the AFL to sit idly by and let their own George Harrison, representing and publicly speaking for the AFL, join with Kroll and Reuther in turning thumbs down on Barkley is indeed a mighty despicable performance."[50] The AFL renounced tradition and endorsed the Democratic Stevenson-Sparkman ticket.[51]

The 1952 campaign demonstrated more clearly the increased fragmentation of labor's political effort. Thirty-five political labor organizations reported to the Clerk of the House of Representatives that they had spent a total of $2,070,350.19 in the campaign, the largest sum by the CIO PAC, which spent $505,721.70; the International Ladies' Garment Workers' Union, $265,345.10; and Labor's League for Political Education, $249,-257.92.[52]

Committee for Political Education

At the merger of the AFL and CIO in 1955, the Committee on Political Education was "vested with the duty and responsibility to assist the Executive Council in meeting the need for sound political education . . . encouraging workers to register and vote, to exercise their full responsibility of citizenship and to perform their rightful part in the political life of the city, state, and national communities."[53] The committee is a permanent division and carries on the functions of PAC and LLPE. It is a commentary on the wisdom of the political policy followed over the years by the American labor movement that the merger convention affirmed the "need for a continuing and expanding nonpartisan program of political education" and "labor's traditional policy of avoiding entangling alliances with any other group and of supporting worthy candidates regardless of their party affiliation."[54]

CHAPTER 47

Communist Activity in Organized Labor

BASIS OF EXPULSION POLICY

The expulsion of a number of unions by the CIO for continually following the line of the Communist party marked a new departure in American labor. From the beginning of its history, the labor movement had within its ranks members and leaders critical of the private-enterprise system who favored its reorganization on a collectivist basis. Anarchists and Socialists played a role in many unions, and were seldom restrained in presenting their views at labor gatherings. Debates at AFL conventions on collectivism and political tactics, which were closely linked, were often vigorous and sometimes bitter. Even in the midst of sharp exchanges, the loyalty of Socialists and Anarchists to the trade-union movement was never questioned, although espousal of dual unionism by some Socialists made them a target for attack. Leaders of the AFL were proud of the freedom of speech which prevailed at their annual sessions, and Gompers appeared a bit embarrassed at the expulsion of William Dunne, a future editor of the *Daily Worker,* from the 1923 convention. The basis for this decision was, however, the impugning of the integrity of John L. Lewis rather than Dunne's political views.

The appearance of the Communists on the world labor scene after World War I created a new series of problems for the democratic union organizations. In line with Lenin's doctrine of party organization, attempts to dominate the trade unions were made by Communist party activists. The United States was no exception, and a campaign to capture the trade unions and subordinate them to party rule was undertaken in the early 1920's. The campaign failed, and in response to a directive from the Moscow headquarters of the Red Trade Union International, the boring-from-within policy was abandoned. Instead, a dual labor federation was launched. A reversal to the initial policy followed the changed conditions of the first New Deal. While leaders of organized labor were generally opposed to Communist doctrine and philosophy, their objections to Communist-led unions were founded on different grounds. The undeviating support of Soviet policy by followers and open and concealed members of the Communist party, the disregard of the interests of American workers or the United States when such interests did not coincide with those of the Soviet government became intolerable. The move to expel was not based upon an issue of personal belief, but upon the unwillingness of the CIO leaders to allow an organized group directed by a political organization devoted to the interests of the Soviet government to influence its policies.

The Trade Union Unity League set up by the Communist apparatus in 1928 functioned roughly until 1935. A number of industrial unions were established, but these were mainly paper organizations whose leaders could occasionally lead a strike or a demonstration but they were unable to gain a place for themselves among the workers of the country. As organization picked up, beginning in 1933, the leaders of such Communist organizations as the Needle Trades Workers Industrial Union attempted to merge with regular AFL organizations, but this attempt failed.

By the end of 1934 the Communist party trade union policy was changing again to "boring-from-within" the established unions. A confidential document reported that party members had begun to move into the Textile Workers' Union, the Amalgamated Association of Iron, Steel and Tin Workers, and a number of others.[1] Communist infiltration brought with them countermeasures from experienced trade union officers, many of whom had resisted the first infiltrating assault upon the trade unions in the 1920's.

The formation of the CIO and the large demands its successes imposed upon the relatively few experienced leaders provided the Communists with an extremely favorable opportunity. Absence of trained staff and the lower level of trade union sophistication among the large masses of newly organized, gave Communist activists a fine opportunity to gain a following in the ranks of organized workers who had almost unanimously rejected their appeal. The Communists did not, however, turn to the CIO as soon as it was formed. Having recently abandoned dual unionism, the leaders did not readily evaluate the significance and permanence of the movement for industrial organization. For a time the Communists continued to support the policy of infiltrating the AFL unions, and the Waterfront Section of the Communist party as late as July 1936 advised "that we Communists say that the struggle of the workers to organize must be carried on within the A.F. of L. regardless of its reactionary leadership for it is here that the great mass of organized workers are to be found."[2] But the Communists were not able to make much headway within the older established labor unions.

In 1937, William Z. Foster clearly indicated that the time had come for a shift in the party trade union line, and the movement of Communists into the CIO began.[3] Lewis, who then headed the CIO, and Murray, after him, chose to forget the assault upon the United Mine Workers of America in the 1920's and welcomed their effort. The viciousness of the Communist assault upon Lewis and his union in the 1920's can be recalled by the demand made by Murray that William Dunne, a Communist editor and a delegate to the 1923 AFL convention, be excluded from the floor. The convention agreed, but now it was reported that the purge by union leaders "of radical trouble makers was not directed at Communists as such."[4] Help was accepted, according to this gospel, from any source including the Communist party. More than five dozen Communists were known to have been on the staff of the Steel Workers' Organizing Committee.

A number of warning voices were raised, but by 1938 the Communists were in major strategic positions in the CIO. They were influential, if not in control of the legal and publicity departments, and were either a strong minority or in full control of more than a dozen unions. Roadblocks were appearing; the Communists did not have it all their way. Roy Hudson, who under the name of Joe Weber played a provocative role in the Memorial Day riot before the South Chicago Republic Steel plant, was a leading spokesman for Communist trade union policy. He attacked those who "fight to prevent maritime workers from uniting around a correct policy in their relationship to the C.I.O. developed along a number of fronts. The main opposition came from forces led by Lundeberg, head of the Sailors' Union of the Pacific, a syndicalist strongly under the influences of Trotskyites, whose policies brought him more and more into alliance with the most reactionary elements in the labor movement."[5]

Through the first years of the CIO's existence, the Communists were pursuing a "People's Front" policy, instituted in 1935 because of the Soviet Union's fear of the resurgence of Hitler Germany. The policy was directed toward organizing groups along a wide political spectrum against the threat of Nazi aggression. This policy required the drawing into a common anti-Fascist campaign of progressives, labor people, and even those conservatives who were opposed to fascism. In this period, which spanned the years between mid-1935 and the Nazi-Soviet pact of August 1939, the Communist line emphasized that opposition to fascism was a defense of the United States and its institutions. "Communism as Twentieth-Century Americanism" was one of many patriotic themes of this period.

A sharp break in Communist policy took place with the beginning of World War II in Europe. The Communist view was stated by its general secretary to the Eleventh National Convention of the Communist party in New York in 1940. "Under the slogan of National Unity, the economic royalists . . . are splitting the nation into two camps. . . . President Roosevelt, assuming leadership of the war party, has also assumed the leadership of domestic reaction."[6] The "Report" then says: "Fifty thousand airplanes is the slogan which opened up the 1940 Presidential campaign. For what?" The answer given by the "Report" was the planes which became the shield of the Allies were to be used in a campaign of conquest in Latin America.[7]

The Communist party fractions in the trade unions immediately changed their political direction. The New York Seamen's and Harbor Workers Branch of the Communist party described the second world war, prior to Hitler's attack on the Soviet Union, as "an imperialist war for profits, markets and colonies. The American working people have nothing to gain and everything to lose by American participation in this War."[8] Similarly the *Pilot,* the official organ of the National Maritime Union— then under Communist domination—reported that President Joseph Curran had testified before the Senate Foreign Relations Committee on behalf of the union in February 1941 against the Lend-Lease bill.[9] A similar policy was pursued by all the Communist-dominated unions. All of the unions fell into line. The Food, Tobacco, Agricultural and Allied Workers immediately attacked the war in Europe as an imperialist war, opposed Roosevelt's Lend-Lease program to England, and selective service legislation.[10]

Similar evidence was presented against the Marine Cooks and Stewards. Its policies on national and international issues synchronized perfectly with changes in the Communist party line. During the period of the Popular Front, this union was hot for international action against Fascist aggression. It changed its policies completely when the Soviet Union and Nazi Germany signed a pact. In June 1940 this organization sponsored at the convention of the Maritime Federation of the Pacific, a Communist-dominated central body of Pacific Coast maritime unions, a resolution which asserted the war in Europe "is not a war for the advancement of democracy in any part of the world, but a war whose sole purpose is the further enrichment of the few who would gain new and profitable economic positions from such a war."[11]

There were, of course, millions of pacifists and believers in isolation in the United States who opposed American involvement, but their views were not controlled by the needs and position of a foreign power. Whether pacifists or isolationists were correct is immaterial; they were people of good faith who believed their policies would serve the interests of the United States.

In addition, the Communists had substantial minorities in a number of unions they did not control. The changes in the views of the Communist party in the United States synchronized with Hitler's attack on the Soviet Union on June 22, 1941. The organizations which had supported Lewis' assault upon the Roosevelt defense program, which had promoted strikes in defense plants—the Allis-Chalmers and North American Aviation Co. being the outstanding examples—again reversed their policies.

ATTACK ON THE SOVIET UNION

In unison, all the Communist-dominated unions changed their policy on the war. Instead of the war now being described as an imperialist venture, it was called "a vital concern to the labor movement."[12] Harry Bridges, head of the International Longshoremen's and Warehousemen's Union, in an article in October 1941 questioned whether his union would have "to start making motions or passing resolutions as to whether we shall not only support the President in an actual declaration of war to stop Hitler but as to whether we will insist that such declaration be made."[13] This statement demanding a war declaration contrasted sharply with Bridges' report to the Longshoremen's and Warehousemen's Union District 1, in April 1940.

In the earlier report Bridges warned: "It [is] generally recognized that the present administration's policies in regard to the international situation, its pro-allied sympathizers, the endorsement of millions of dollars being sent abroad while millions of Americans suffer unemployment and poverty can result in the embroiling of America into a foreign war in which she can have no concern except the protection of the investments of the large bankers and industrial interests of the country."[14]

From bitter opponents seeking to sabotage the defense effort and aid to beleaguered England, the Communists and their trade union satellites became temporarily super-patriots who bitterly assailed honest critics of the war effort. In addition, the Communists began to agitate for the "second front," presumably needed for American defense. Thus John L. Lewis fell a victim to the virulent mendacity of the Communist unions within the CIO. On May 9, 1943, William Z. Foster, head of the Communist party, "attacked John L. Lewis, he attacked the miners' union. He attacked them because the miners are not willing to forget wage increases and decent working conditions. And of course this behind the lines 'skulk' said that he was doing this stuff 'for the war.' "[15] Before the meeting the *Chicago Times* printed an ad, paid for by the Communist party, attacking Lewis and the Miners' Union.

In their report to the 1943 convention, the officers of the Communist-dominated International Longshoremen's and Warehousemen's Union described Lewis "as the single most effective agent of the Fascist powers within the ranks of labor."[16] Never to do things by halves, the Bridges' union favored a National Service Act—a form of labor conscription— uncompromisingly opposed by the heads of the AFL and CIO.

The conciliatory policy of the Communist party of the United States did not survive the end of World War II. The change in the line was signaled by Jacques Duclos, a leader of the French Communist party, who with the ending of the war in Europe attacked what he described as "revisionism" in the Communist party of the United States.[17] Duclos denounced the moderate policies that had been followed by American Communists and called upon them to extirpate fascism which he said had many concealed supporters in the United States. With military regularity, the Communist-dominated unions again reversed themselves. Attacks on the labor movement, the American government, and the democratic countries of the free world began as expected.

POSTWAR

The CIO faced a serious dilemma. A special report of the Research Institute of America listed eighteen unions—with the United Electrical, Radio and Machine Workers of America, the largest of the group—as Communist controlled.[18] A number of these organizations had few members. Several others ousted their Communist officers in the next several years and changed their policies. Communist strength in the CIO began to decline as a result. In July 1946, President Morris Muster of the Furniture Workers resigned his post and charged his union was Communist-dominated.[19] The National Maritime Union pried itself loose from the Communist orbit after seven maritime unions set up the Committee for Maritime Unity in February 1946, with Joseph Curran and Harry Bridges as co-chairmen. Communist backers of the united maritime front hoped to forge a weapon that could be used to expel the AFL unions from the waterfront, and thereby give the Communists complete control of American shipping as well as of the longshoremen on the Pacific Coast. The Pacific Marine Firemen, Oilers and Watertenders and Helpers Association withdrew soon after the first meeting of the Committee for Maritime Unity, since it did not wish to engage in interunion warfare.

Joseph Curran and several other officers of the National Maritime Union withdrew from the committee in January 1947, despite the opposition of the Communist blocs in his organization. The withdrawal ended the Committee for Maritime Unity and the possibility of a successful *Putsch* against the non-Communist organizations on the waterfront.[20] Another Communist-controlled union, the Transport Workers Union of America, also changed its course as a result of the shift in the party line on domestic and international issues. Under the leadership of Michael J. Quill, the union had been a stalwart party-line organization until 1948. A split over policy, early in 1948, led to a fight for control. The union's convention in December 1948 ousted the followers of the Communist party from the International Executive Board, elected Quill (now an anti-Communist leader), and condemned "the Soviet Union's abuses in the exercise of the veto power which have frustrated the Security Council from achieving the lofty purpose for which it was created . . . and . . . the organized opposition to the European Recovery Program by the Soviet Union and its satellites and the method by which the Economic misery of Europe is used for political advantage and to promote chaos and confusion."[21] Transport Workers Union of America (CIO) became a staunch member of the anti-Communist camp in the CIO. A fight within the Industrial Union of Marine and Shipbuilding Workers Association also took place with the Communists losing the contest.[22]

In some of the Communist-dominated unions secessions took place. Raids by other CIO organizations were also effective. Forty-two locals representing about 26,000 workers with bargaining rights in Connecticut left the International Union of Mine Mill and Smelter Workers. The United Electrical, Radio and Machine Workers complained to Philip Murray about the raids carried out by the United Automobile Workers.[23]

Revolts were loosening the control of the Communists within a number of unions, but they retained the protection which their affiliation with the CIO gave them. Neither Lewis nor Murray would move firmly against them. In fairness, one might note that it was a difficult decision for the head of a labor federation to open an attack upon a large number of the affiliates on issues which were primarily political. Within the labor movement the right of unions to pursue their own policies and present their own views has always been recognized. The attacks on Socialists and other dissidents ended at the conventions and were never in the entire history of the AFL carried on beyond that point. Nor was the loyalty of Socialists to the labor movement ever questioned.

The Communists, as has already been noted, presented a different issue. Following the dictates of an international conspiratorial apparatus in the service of a foreign power, the Communists had been shown to be ready to sacrifice the interests of their own members and the country and its people when it suited the ends of the Soviet Union. A labor movement must allow for wide differences of opinion, but can it tolerate an organized phalanx controlled by the conspiratorial and espionage apparatus of a foreign power? At one time, it was a question whether the anti-Communists in the CIO, could muster a majority. The victory of Walter Reuther in the 1946 convention of the Auto Workers' Union was of great importance, as was the realignment of a number of unions.

As a first step, the CIO Executive Board voted on November 15, 1946, authority to President Murray to take over the funds and property of local and state Industrial Union Councils which failed to conform to CIO policy. These central bodies were directly chartered by the CIO and were not autonomous units.[24] Murray had brought the subject of Communism in the CIO before the executive board, and because of disagreement he had appointed a committee of six—three from each side—to draw up a statement, later adopted unanimously by the board. Murray announced that "the statement of policy determines and sets up certain guideposts that necessarily must be followed by each of our International affiliates, including our state and city industrial union councils. It is a statement of policy designed to chart a course for the overall conduct of our International Unions and all of our subsidiary affiliates."[25]

Following Murray's statement a "Declaration of Policy" was adopted which rejected the "efforts of the Communist Party or other political parties and their adherents to interfere in the affairs of the CIO."[26] Only two delegates, Howard McKenzie and Joseph Stack from the National Maritime Union—soon to free itself from Communist domination—voted against the statement; they later changed their vote.[27] The AFL taunted its rival for evading a fight on the Communist issue at its convention by the use of "weasel worded" pronouncements.[28] Nevertheless, the action of the CIO convention represented a giant step against the Communist caucus and it was the first time the issue had openly been faced. It is of some significance that the Communist activists present at the 1946 convention felt no hesitancy in voting for a statement which castigated their tactics. The two less experienced, and more "honest," delegates who had refused to denounce their own program and conduct were soon set on the right path by the commissars who were always present to instruct the brethren on the true course and to bring the deviators into line. There was other evidence of tension between the Communist and anti-Communist blocs at the convention but, for the moment, they decided to maintain an uneasy truce.

In March 1947 Murray was given approval to appoint a committee to investigate the dispute within the International Union of Mine, Mill and Smelter Workers. Jacob S. Potofsky of the Amalgamated Clothing Workers; Van A. Bittner, United Steelworkers; and L. S. Buckmaster of the United Rubber Workers were appointed. The committee recommended that the Provisional Metal Workers Council, headed by John J. Driscoll, should be disbanded and the members returned to the Mine, Mill and Smelter Workers. The committee also found that Maurice Travis, who was serving as head of the Mine, Mill and Smelter Workers, had been expelled for disruption from Local Union 1440 of the United Steelworkers of America. The committee also disapproved of the chartering of the forty-two unions in the Provisional Metal Workers Council by the Industrial Union of Marine and Shipbuilding Workers of America.[29]

The lines within the CIO were being drawn. The Communists had no intention of giving up their positions. One important issue confronting the labor movement in the late 1940's was its attitude toward European aid and the Marshall Plan. The entrance of Henry Wallace as a third-party candidate for President raised the question of political tactics the CIO would follow, and caused serious differences within the leadership.[30]

Steps were taken by Murray and the executive board to compel local and state Industrial Union Councils to adhere to CIO policies. In February 1948, Murray notified Harry Bridges that as regional director of northern California for the CIO, he must either carry out the program of the CIO or resign his post as director. Bridges refused to follow either course and was removed.[31] John Brophy, director of the CIO Local and State Industrial Union Councils, insisted that these organizations would have to follow CIO policy on the Marshall Plan and also reject the third-party candidacy of Henry Wallace.[32] Refusing to comply, a number of Industrial Union Councils had their charters lifted in 1948, and the central bodies were reorganized.[33]

Because of differences over politics, the representatives of Communist-dominated unions began to resign from CIO PAC.[34] Even more important was the aggressive assault upon Communist policies by other leaders of CIO unions. In April 1948, Walter Reuther announced that the United Automobile Workers' Union would admit rank and file members of Communist-dominated unions seeking a new home.[35] The United Steelworkers of America, Murray's union, decided that members of the Communist party, Fascist, or other totalitarian organizations would be ineligible to hold membership in the union. A similar prohibition was adopted by the CIO Glass, Ceramic and Silica Sand Workers.[36]

At the 1948 convention of the CIO, the Communist-dominated unions were under assault. Their representatives refused to retreat. In fact, three representatives from Communist unions signed a minority report attacking the Marshall Plan and charged that "huge sums of the Marshall Plan are being given to these Nazis to rebuild the German cartels and trusts in heavy industry."[37] The anti-Communist bloc had been strongly reinforced by the accessions of many who had once cooperated with the party. Even more important was the open enrollment of Philip Murray with his tremendous prestige in the anti-Communist camp.

But the Communists were not inclined to surrender. The 1949 convention of the International Longshoremen's and Warehousemen's Union reasserted its right to follow its own views on policy issues. It also demanded a report on the expenditure of per capita and on the actions of the executive board. The resolutions angered Murray, who sharply criticized the head of the union, Harry Bridges.[38] At a meeting of the CIO Executive Board, the Mine, Mill and Smelter Workers, a leading Communist union, was attacked for "besmirching the name of Murray."[39] The Communist bloc also opposed giving the United Steelworkers of America jurisdiction over iron ore miners who supplied the basic raw material to the steel industry. At the end of the sessions of the Board, Murray told the Communists to conform to policy or resign. He also announced: "This is a Communist situation which must be dealt with at the . . . convention."[40]

The Communist-dominated unions fought back. The largest of the group, the United Electrical Workers, demanded as a condition for continuing its per capita payments that the CIO direct its affiliates to cease raiding its membership, that Secretary-Treasurer James Carey be ordered to end his activities against the UE, and that the CIO give assurance that there would be no interference with its internal affairs or with its right to designate its own representatives.[41] This demand was rejected, as was the proposal of the UE delegation which sought a compromise on October 26, 1949.[42]

Murray had crossed the Rubicon. Once having decided that the Communist unions could no longer be tolerated within the CIO, all possibilities for compromise were gone. At the 1949 convention, a resolution was introduced: "We can no longer tolerate within the family of CIO the Communist Party masquerading as a labor union." This was the opening statement of a scathing catalogue of the misdeeds of the leadership of the United Electrical, Radio and Machine Workers of America and a call for the expulsion of the organization from the ranks. The resolution charged that the UERMWA "has been selected by the Communist Party as its labor base from which it can operate to betray the economic, political and social welfare of the CIO, its affiliates and general membership. The program of the UERMWA leadership that has gradually unfolded is but an echo of the Cominform."[43]

Harry Bridges, whose organization was still an affiliate of the CIO, disdained to answer the charges, but argued that the UERMWA was being expelled without trial and that his union stood for the same program. Walter Reuther defended the procedure and denied Bridges' charges that the UERMWA had been denied due process. Instead, he pointed to the failure of the organization to appear to answer charges on several occasions. He also dealt with the attacks upon Murray and the CIO made in the official newspaper of the union on trial, as well as in pamphlets published by the organization. According to Reuther, the United Electrical Workers had charged that the CIO stood for "Cain and Abel unionism, gangsterism and terror; selling out labor's political freedom by hog-tying it to a single reactionary political party; dictatorship; no choice for the rank and file; the use of Ku Klux Klan and race baiting tactics; the chartering of stool-pigeons and company agents."[44]

Murray's speech was not only a bitter attack upon the Communist leadership, but he also revealed that he had tried to get the leaders of the United Electrical Workers to change their Communist-oriented policies as early as 1946. Murray claimed that he had directed the attention of President Albert J. Fitzgerald, Secretary-Treasurer Julius Emspak, and Director of Organization James Matles to the fact that "the payroll of the United Electrical Workers was virtually padded by and through the employment of many Communist agents."[45] Murray's claim has been substantiated by the list of the UE's top officials and ninety-three others, among them regional directors, business agents, editors, and staff members, who have expressed friendship and support for Communist causes.[46]

Murray did not question the right of any union to attack the Marshall Plan, but he charged that it was merely a pretense for undermining the trade union movement and the government of the United States. "I have asked," said Murray, "these so-called apostles of democracy to stand somewhere, sometime upon the floor of a national convention of the CIO and to criticize the Cominform, or criticize Russia's policy of expansionism, to criticize any of the policies of Russia, and these hypocrites run from me. They dare not stand upon their dirty feet and give any expression of opposition to anything the Soviets are doing. They are inbred with a feeling of hatred against democratic institutions and democratic countries. They lend assistance to every satellite of Communist dictated Russia. . . . Their allegiances are pledged to a foreign government."[47]

The UERMWA was expelled, and even more important was the addition of a new section to the CIO constitution: "No individual shall be eligible to serve either as an officer or as a member of the Executive Board who is a member of the Communist Party, any fascist organization, or other totalitarian movement, or who consistently pursues policies and activities directed toward the achievement of the program of the Communist Party, any fascist organization, or other totalitarian movement, rather than the objectives and policies set forth in the Constitution of the CIO."[48] A resolution was passed authorizing the executive board "to take appropriate action to protect the CIO" from "those who have consistently directed their policies and activities toward the achievement of the program or purposes of the Communist Party."[49]

In accordance with this provision, President William Steinberg of the American Radio Association and member of the CIO Executive Board, brought charges on November 5, 1949, against ten affiliated unions. Murray appointed committees to hear the charges, but the accused refused to present testimony. Aside from denouncing the proceedings they made no defense. In each instance, the record of the union under charges was examined, and its adherence to Communist policy traced. The similarity of behavior of these unions, their changes in attitude, and their support of the views of world communism were amply demonstrated. The committees recommended expulsion, and the CIO Executive Board, acting under its mandate, complied with the recommendations, except with regard to the United Furniture Workers of America.[50] A revolt led by President Morris Pizer was successful in ousting the party-line administration in this union.

An attempt to prevent the ouster in the courts failed when Judge Simon Rifkind in the U.S. District Court for the Southern New York District denied the request of the United Office and Professional Workers and the Food, Tobacco and Agricultural Workers a declaratory judgment that the 1949 amendments to the CIO constitution were invalid and the expulsions illegal. In denying the petition the judge held that in dealing with a "confederation of national unions in its relations to one of constituent unions, I [Judge Rifkind] begin that such a confederation, democratically organized, and prima facie acting within the scope of its constitution, ought to have its way until it is demonstrated that in having its way it has unlawfully trespassed upon the rights of its members."[51] He also held that a federation of unions has the right to compel those with whom it is at variance to conform, as for example, a group of craft unions could expel those who advocate industrial unionism. There was no matter of public policy involved, as no one's livelihood was endangered by the refusal of a federation to allow membership by a particular union.

The importance of the CIO action can scarcely be underestimated, for in a relatively short period, a number of the Communist-dominated unions ceased to exist—among them the government unions, office workers, food and tobacco, fisheries, and farm equipment. The protective cover given to them by the CIO had enabled these organizations to survive and prosper. Moreover, as long as they were affiliated they could not be raided. (Actually, in preparation for subsequent expulsion, raiding was permitted by the CIO.) Moreover, the CIO provided a respectable cover against attack. In a sense, as long as Communist unions retained their affiliation with the CIO, Murray, Emil Rieve, Reuther, and others acted as a shield for them with both their own members and the public at large.

This is evident from the experience of the expelled organizations. Only one, the International Longshoremen's and Warehousemen's Union, has been able to retain the membership it had when expelled. The International Union of Mine, Mill and Smelter Workers has been able to continue, but its membership has been sharply reduced. It is at least probable that had the CIO chartered a competing union in the metalliferous mines, this Communist front would have been further reduced in size.

Following the expulsion of the UE, the CIO chartered the International Union of Electrical, Radio and Machine Workers. Even though the UE had functioned for fifteen years, had held bargaining rights with major companies in its industry, and had on the day-to-day basis performed effectively as a trade union, the great majority of its members chose to leave it and join its newly formed rival. Nor can the attitude of the chief companies dealing with those unions be completely exempted for the ability of the UE to survive.[52]

While the Communists sought to penetrate into places of influence and power in unions of the AFL, the important difference was that they seldom were able to seize the control of an international. As a result a possibility always existed that the international would intervene and oust the Communists from control over a local or district council. The story of the operations of such Communist fronts as the Conference of Studio Unions, set up under the leadership of Herbert K. Sorrell in Hollywood, has been documented by a special subcommittee of the House of Representatives Committee on Education and Labor.[53] But they were ousted because they did not control the administration of an international union. The latter could always intervene and compel a subordinate unit to conform to general policy, although the Labor-Management Reporting (Landrum-Griffin) law may make such steps more difficult. This is obvious from the experiences of several unions in which the Communists established fairly effective enclaves. In each they were ousted after the international officers believed themselves strong enough to intervene.[54]

The capture of an international union by the Communists makes their ousting extremely difficult. It is analogous to the capture of a government of an area by the Communists. Only revolt of large groups of members, always difficult, or an assault by a rival union can then oust the Communists. This was the experience in the CIO. The revolts led by Curran and Quill were of great importance and contributed greatly to weakening Communist control and influence within the CIO. The formation of the IUE by the CIO made it possible for an organization to challenge the jurisdiction of the UE. Control of a local, while serious, is similar to a Communist organization operating within a democratic country. It presents a danger to the union, but the situation is not irretrievable.

CHAPTER 48

The Korean War

FRINGE BENEFITS

In the period between 1946 and 1950, union membership did not change significantly. Exclusive of Canadian unions, membership of those with headquarters in the United States approached 15 million. A number of labor organizations attempted to retain and extend the pension rights they had gained during World War II, or to establish these rights in firms where they were not in effect and make them a condition of collective bargaining. Some concerns resisted these efforts, and they were the cause of major strikes in the coal and steel industries.

John L. Lewis was not happy with the course of events in the bituminous coal industry. He had cause for complaint; a mine disaster in Centralia, Illinois, snuffed out the lives of 111 miners. Calling a six-day mourning period, he started a campaign to oust Secretary of the Interior Julius Krug from the cabinet. He also asked Congress to remit the fine imposed upon the union for violating the order of Judge Allan T. Goldsborough for ending the 1946 strike. Striking out against Krug, Lewis charged him with responsibility for the existence of unsafe mines, and Krug answered that the government had received little cooperation from the United Mine Workers of America in its campaign to devise an effective mine safety program.[1]

When the request was made for the return of the amount of the union's fine reduced by the U.S. Supreme Court, Goldsborough noted that the refund was based upon compliance with the court order. He did not doubt the genuineness of the miners' grief, but he noted that the suspension of mining coincided with the planned strike for April 1. This matter was worked out, but the Miners' Union became embroiled in another dispute. The Southern Coal Producers' Association, which had not entirely accepted the union, announced its opposition to industrywide bargaining. Moreover, the southern operators wanted to eliminate paid travel time and to re-establish the southern differential. In view of the union's and Lewis' attitude on these questions, their sponsorship by the southern operators could not be regarded as good faith bargaining. The southerners also wanted to explore the need for a welfare fund, they opposed federal control of safety rules, and they sought complete exemption of supervisors from union control.

While the conference was going on, the southern operators announced they were going to explain their position to the newspapers. The union delegation, objecting to a public discussion of proposals made in executive session, warned that negotiations would not be continued in the event the operators went through with their plans. Disregarding the warning, the operators publicly discussed the demands and counterdemands made by the parties. The union charged that this was an attempt to deceive the public that "a legitimate wage proposal" had been made.[2] The union refused to continue the conference.

A more serious dispute between northern operators and the United Mine Workers of America arose after the termination of the War Labor Disputes Act on June 30, 1947. The mines were returned to the private operators. The union was able—two weeks after the passage of the Taft-Hartley Act—to make the best contract in the history of the industry. From nine hours, portal to portal, and a fifteen-minute lunch period the workday was reduced to eight hours a day and a thirty-minute lunch period, which meant that an average of six and one-half hours of productive labor would be performed. A significant change in the contract was the elimination of all penalties for work stoppages so as to avoid any liability of the union to penalties under the Taft-Hartley law. Royalties for the health and welfare fund were raised to ten cents a ton, wages were increased $1.20 a day to $13.05, and the mine safety code which Lewis had negotiated with Julius Krug was retained.[3]

Differences over payments of pensions soon appeared; Ezra Van Horn, the operators' trustee, refused to approve any pension program, although the fund had accumulated more than $29 million. The differences involved actuarial soundness, with Lewis advocating a policy of pay as you go. After eight months of negotiation, Lewis informed the miners that "no payments of any character have been made to any beneficiary or to anyone else from the Welfare Fund set up under the 1947 Agreement."[4] Since a strike was threatened, President Harry Truman appointed a three-man board of inquiry, under the emergency dispute provisions of the Taft-Hartley Act, to examine the issues and report.

At first Lewis refused to attend the hearings, and in a letter to the chairman of the Board of Inquiry, Judge Sherman Minton of the Circuit Court of Appeals, charged the other two members with prejudice against the miners. He testified, however, when the board secured a court order directing him to appear. He insisted that pensions should be based upon a pay-as-you-go principle and that he was concerned with payments to those in need and not with actuarial problems. At the end of the hearings, the Attorney-General secured a restraining order. On April 3, 1948, Judge Matthew McGuire of the U.S. district court directed the union and its officers to instruct members to discontinue the strike, return immediately to their jobs, and refrain from further interference with work in the mines. Judge McGuire also directed the miners and operators to carry out their agreement so that pensions would be paid. This was the first injunction under the Taft-Hartley law.[5]

When the miners failed to obey the order, the government began contempt proceedings against the union and Lewis. Before the contempt charge was tried, Lewis and Van Horn agreed to the appointment of Senator Styles Bridges as the third trustee. In an emergency session, the Bridges' compromise was accepted. It called for the payment of $100 a month pension to miners with twenty years work in the mines who had reached the age of sixty-two years.[6] Proceedings for contempt of the restraining order were not suspended. Judge Goldsborough, before whom the issue was tried, found that Lewis had signaled to the miners to strike by the letter of March 12, 1948, which claimed the operators had "dishonored" their contract. The judge denied that the use of the word "strike" was necessary, holding that a walkout could be called by "a nod, wink or code." For failing to obey the injunction, the union was fined $1.2 million and Lewis, $20,000.[7] Subsequently, the operators tried to prevent payment of pensions, but Judge Goldsborough ruled that they were payable to members of the union and were not limited by the Taft-Hartley Act or the employees of signatory employers.[8]

The fines were later upheld by the Circuit Court of Appeals on the ground that the union and Lewis were obliged to obey the order of the court. Differences between the operators and the union continued. Another attempt by the Justice Department to bring the United Mine Workers of America to trial for contempt failed. The miners had refused to obey a court order against striking, but Judge Richmond B. Keech held that the Department of Justice had not presented clear and convincing evidence that the court order had been disobeyed.[9] This was the last encounter between a major group of bituminous coal operators and the union.

After the agreement of 1950 had been signed, Harry Moses, chief negotiator for the industry, called for divorcing "future labor relations from the government and court control which has been exercised over them; each side of the table must accept its full share of our social responsibilities."[10] It was to carry out these suggestions that the northern operators established the Bituminous Operators Association with Moses as president.[11] The Southern Coal Producers Association was later organized to represent the southern operators. As an indication of the changed spirit in the industry, the contract raising the basic daily wage from $14.75 to $16.35 a day was signed in Lewis' office on January 18, 1951, by Harry Moses and Joseph E. Moody representing the southern producers.[12]

The fight in the bituminous coal industry established the principle that the union could demand and exercise a voice over pensions and other welfare payments, subjects not widely regarded as falling within the boundaries of collective bargaining. Lewis compelled the coal industry to accept the pension plan he favored. He was also successful in eliminating strikes and stabilizing the industry for a decade.

The same issue appeared in the steel industry. But problems were to reappear; and they were to become more serious after Lewis withdrew from active service. As a first step the United Steelworkers of America sought to bargain with the Inland Steel Company over pensions and retirements, but the company claimed that these issues were not matters for collective bargaining. The union thereupon filed a complaint, charging refusal to bargain with the National Labor Relations Board. Its contention was upheld by the board, and the company appealed the decision.

In its ruling the Circuit Court of Appeals of the Seventh Circuit found that pensions and age of retirement were encompassed in conditions of employment and were properly subjects of collective bargaining; the court denied the company's petition to review the order of the board.[13] The Supreme Court denied certiorari, and thereby the union could insist that the companies agree to bargain over pensions. But, of course, employers were not obliged to grant such demands.

It was obvious as soon as the Wage Policy Committee of the United Steelworkers of America had met that an open conflict in the steel industry was likely. The union was determined to gain pensions for its members, while the leading firms in the industry were equally determined to deny them. On July 6, 1949, the union's demands on the U.S. Steel Corporation were rejected on the ground that pensions were not bargainable items included in the contract reopening clause under which negotiations were carried out. The request that life, accident, health, medical, and hospital insurance be financed exclusively by management was also refused.[14]

When the union announced it planned to strike if no agreement were reached by July 15, President Harry Truman suggested a sixty-day postponement, pending investigation by a board of inquiry which he promised to appoint. The industry at first rejected the proposal on the ground that the board would not function under the emergency provisions of the Taft-Hartley law and would therefore make recommendations. The union threatened to strike, and Truman refused to act under the Taft-Hartley provisions, claiming no emergency existed. Upon assurance that the panel's views were not binding on the parties, the industry changed its position. Carroll B. Daugherty was appointed head of a three-men panel. The union asked for an increase of 30 cents an hour, with 12.5 cents to be used for wage increases, 11.23 for pensions, and 6.27 for a broad social insurance program. The industry reiterated its objections to the pension and insurance program, but it was informed by the board that the matter could be presented and if the issues were found nonbargainable under the reopening clause, the board would make such findings.[15]

The union's request for a wage increase was rejected by the board, but it recommended that six cents an hour be allowed for financing pensions and another four cents an hour for employer-paid social insurance. The union accepted the recommendations, but the companies refused to go along. They were willing to set aside ten cents an hour for pensions and welfare providing employees were willing to share the cost and the union extended the contract beyond April 30, 1951.[16]

Negotiations led to a stalemate, and the union called a strike on October 1, 1949. Murray claimed that the failure of the steel companies to accept the recommendations of the board caused the tie-up. Benjamin Fairless, the head of the U.S. Steel Corporation, answered that acceptance would be equivalent to compulsory arbitration.[17] On October 17, John L. Lewis, whose union was engaged in a walkout in the bituminous mines, suggested in letters to Murray and William Green that the two striking unions and eight others each donate a quarter of a million dollars to a general strike fund that would be controlled and allocated through the headquarters of the AFL to the striking unions. The suggestion was approved by all, but no steps were taken to put his suggestion into effect. It was a publicity device which achieved its purpose.[18]

A break in the strike came when the Bethlehem Steel Company signed an agreement for noncontributory pensions and for contributory insurance.[19] It was followed by similar agreements with other firms in the industry. The agreements in the coal and steel industries made these programs matters of negotiation between management and their employees. It meant that the organizations of labor would have some voice in influencing the size and conditions of benefit payments, recognized that the benefits were paid in lieu of wages, and that workers had a right to a voice in determining programs and their administration.

KOREA

The assault upon South Korea by the Communist government of North Korea on June 25, 1950, found both the AFL and the CIO united in support of the American government. In a statement, Murray hailed the response to aggression and favored the increase in the defense budget requested by the President.[20] The CIO Executive Board in August 1950 approved the anti-aggression campaign of the United Nations in Korea and called for "complete and unhesitating cooperation of every individual in America." At the same time, the CIO attacked the Communist-promoted Stockholm "peace petition." To finance the expanded military effort, the CIO favored an excess profits tax, selective price control, scarce material allocation, wage adjustments, and the strengthening of manpower resources.[21]

In a statement on August 10, 1950, the executive council of the AFL endorsed pegging of prices at levels in effect during June preceding the outbreak of the Korean War, called for increase in taxes on incomes and estates, but opposed wage controls. Instead, the council proposed that wages "be permitted to rise through the process of collective bargaining and otherwise."[22] The statement also opposed manpower controls.

Under the Defense Production Act of 1950, the President was given authority to impose selected wage and price controls and to impose a general freeze on wages and prices if such a step became necessary.[23] The emphasis, however, was upon voluntary restraint. The confidence that inflationary price and wage movements might be voluntarily restrained was not warranted by events. Pressures for price and wage rises spread through the economy in the summer of 1950, and the hope that government controls over the economy would be held to a minimum were undermined by the large-scale intervention of the Red Chinese armies into the Korean War during November 1950. It became necessary to divert greater resources into the defense area, and with it the danger of inflation became greater.[24] The board was given power to recommend to the economic stabilization director, under whose authority it operated, wage policies that would promote stable wages and prices. A dispute over policy led to the resignation of Economic Stabilization Administrator Allan Valentine on January 19, 1951. He was succeeded by Eric Johnston.

The United Labor Policy Committee

In the first months of the Korean War, W. Stuart Symington, chairman of the National Security Resources Board, was authorized to coordinate the activities of government agencies working on defense matters. In order to encourage labor participation, an informal committee was established with three members from the AFL, three from the CIO, and three from several unaffiliated unions. Out of the informal cooperation, the United

Labor Policy Committee was established on December 20, 1950.[25] The committee was to "have no direct relationship to any government agency. It shall meet independently, holding itself in readiness to make representations to the President of the United States and government agencies having to do with mobilization problems."[26] All decisions required unanimous approval, and the issues to be considered related to problems of mobilization and utilization of manpower. The committee was to meet biweekly with no alternates for the members allowed. Subcommittees on manpower, production, wages, and prices were established.

By then the country faced a much more serious task. The assault upon South Korea by the Communist North Korean armies on November 25, 1950, changed the magnitude of the task facing the economy of the United States. On December 16, 1950, President Harry Truman proclaimed the existence of a national emergency and appointed Charles E. Wilson, the president of the General Electric Company, director of a newly established Office of Defense Mobilization with wide authority to direct the defense program. A committee of eight members from the United Labor Policy Committee met with President Truman on December 20, 1950, and outlined the economic policies it favored.

The committee called for control of prices of goods. The United Labor Policy Committee wanted changes in wage administration; objected to allowing the overruling of the decisions of the Wage Stabilization Board; and demanded wage increases be allowed to compensate for rises in the cost of living and productivity. The committee also wanted premium overtime payments retained in existing agreements or in law, and recognition of existing collective bargaining continued. Finally, the committee called for enlarging of the labor force and avoidance of compulsion in the labor market.[27]

Wage Stabilization

Executive Order 10161 created a tripartite Wage Stabilization Board within the Economic Stabilization Agency. The board was in charge of planning policies to encourage the stabilizing of wages. Cyrus Ching of the Federal Mediation and Conciliation Board was appointed chairman on October 30, 1950, and representatives of labor, management, and the public were appointed later. The first job facing the board was to work out a program to handle wage changes during the emergency. It was granted authority to proceed by Economic Stabilization Administrator Eric Johnston.

On January 26, 1951, the freezing of labor at levels existing as of January 25, 1951, was introduced. Wages were defined to include "all forms of remuneration to employees by their employers for personal services, including, but not limited to, vacations, night shift and other bonuses, incentive payments, year-end bonuses, employer contributions to or payments of insurance or welfare benefits, employer contributions to a pension fund or annuity, payments in kind, and premium overtime payments."[28] Modifications were made to allow wage increases based upon agreements entered into prior to the date of the wage freeze.

The freeze was a temporary device until such time as a principle for regulating wages could be devised. After debate and revisions, the Wage Stabilization Board voted, with the labor members dissenting, for a formula that allowed an increase in wages up to 10 per cent above the straight-time hourly rates prevailing on January 15, 1950. When this plan was adopted, the labor members withdrew from the Wage Stabilization Board and protested "against an attempt to do a grave injustice to all Americans who work for wages and salaries. We are acting on the instructions of the United Labor Policy Committee. . . . As their representatives, we cannot give our approval or be a party to the unfair and unworkable formula adopted by the industry and public members of this Board."[29] Nevertheless, Economic Stabilization Administrator Eric Johnston put the majority plan into effect.

The wage question was only one of the issues that aroused the dissatisfaction of the United Labor Policy Committee. Leaders of organized labor were especially incensed at Director of the Office of Defense Mobilization Charles E. Wilson, who was charged with carrying over into government "his private philosophy of 'Big Business.' The Committee found that Mr. Wilson was simply not interested in trying to work out arrangements under which labor could contribute to the defense program."[30]

The committee claimed it had recommended a trade union representative for a top policy staff in the Office of Defense Mobilization, but Wilson was unwilling to appoint him. The committee regarded the appointment as a test of whether labor would be given full recognition in the mobilization program. Wilson was told that millions of workers were increasingly disturbed by the evidence that the defense mobilization program "reflects only the philosophy of big business. . . . Developments in wage policy, price policy, taxes, rent control, small business participation, and the general management of defense mobilization have shocked all Americans who work for wages and salaries."[31] Wilson denied the charges, claimed that the United Labor Policy Committee had failed to nominate a trade union representative to the top staff of the Office of Defense Mobilization, and suggested that the "points raised in your letter can more appropriately be discussed with other representatives of labor at the meeting of the Labor Advisory Committee of the Office of Defense Mobilization." Finally, Wilson stated: "Decisions on specific problems must, of course, give due consideration not only to the interests of labor but also to those of agriculture, industry, and the American people."[32]

Wilson's letter, in fact, ignored the complaints, and as a result all labor representatives serving on existing defense organizations resigned on February 28, 1951. The labor groups were convinced that to continue to serve on defense agencies would bring about "no constructive results and merely delude the public and wage earners we represent into believing that labor acquiesces in what is being done."[33] Outlining the list of charges, the labor group claimed that the wage order adopted by Economic Stabilizer Eric Johnston was "unfair, unworkable and unjust." The committee charged that the director of economic stabilization had allowed retail stores an increase in ceilings prices. It noted that "wages are frozen. Nothing else in the economy is frozen."[34]

The sharpest criticism, however, was reserved for the manpower policies and their controls, which Wilson was charged with seizing "without ever discussing the matter with his labor advisory committee. Both by correspondence and by several hours of discussion, we have sought to show Mr. Wilson that manpower policies would best be formulated in the Department of Labor . . . we asked Mr. Wilson to reconsider that decision. He refused flatly and finally, and without attempting to offer any logical reasons for his refusal."[35] Finally, the committee charged that Wilson treated the Office of Defense Mobilization as his "private preserve" and denied labor an opportunity to "participate at the top policy level of the ODM."[36]

The walkout lasted for two months; on April 30, 1951, the United Labor Policy Committee announced the immediate return of labor representatives to all defense agencies. This step had been foreshadowed when members of the United Labor Policy Committee agreed, in a conference with President Truman on April 5, to participate in a new seventeen-member National Advisory Board on Mobilization Policy. Labor, management, farmers, and the public were each allowed four members and Wilson was chairman. The board reported directly to the President.

On April 16 the National Advisory Board on Mobilization Policy recommended by a vote of 12 to 4, with the industry members dissenting, to recommend to the President the re-establishment of the Wage Stabilization Board. It was made up of eighteen members and was granted power to assume jurisdiction of any labor dispute not resolved by collective bargaining or by conciliation and mediation which threatened an interruption of work affecting the national defense where the parties agreed to accept the board's decision, or when the President believed that the dispute affected substantially the progress of national defense.[37] The change was a necessary concession to gain the cooperation of organized labor. Changes in the handling of manpower questions were also made to meet the criticisms of the United Labor Policy Committee. The walkout ended on April 30, 1951, and the President appointed the eighteen members of the Wage Stabilization Board on May 30, 1951, with George Taylor, chairman.[38]

The National Manufacturer's Association believed that the Defense Production Act had been evaded by the President's order. Congress, the association claimed, sought to encourage voluntary settlements. The insistence by labor upon granting the board authority in dispute cases, the association charged, was based upon a belief that exercise of such power would aid the recruitment drives of organized labor. Instead of the President using his emergency powers under the Taft-Hartley Act in labor disputes affecting defense work, which the unions bitterly opposed, he would rely on the board's authority for a settlement. The NAM thought that such a policy was improper and contravened the intent of Congress.[39] Congress heeded the criticism; for the amendments of June 28, 1952, which created a statutory Wage Stabilization Board, also denied the board authority in dispute cases.

Labor won its demand for places on the major staffs of defense agencies. George M. Harrison of the Brotherhood of Railway Clerks was appointed assistant to Defense Mobilizer Wilson; David J. McDonald, assistant to Economic Stabilizer Johnston; and several others were given high posts in other government agencies. However, the labor movement—both the AFL and CIO—continued to be critical of the government's efforts to halt inflation, especially Defense Production Act amendments of 1952. Labor criticized the limited extension of the stabilization program for only ten months and federal rent control until September 30, 1952. It was also displeased by the denial of authority to the Wage Stabilization Board to recommend settlement of labor disputes, as well as the exclusion from coverage of agricultural workers, employees of establishments with fewer than eight employees, and those working in bowling alleys. Nor did labor take kindly to the exemption of all fruits and vegetables, representing about 20 per cent of the food dollar, from controls, and extension of the Capehart amendments which allowed manufacturers to pass on to consumers all cost increases up to July 26, 1951.

In its decisions the Wage Stabilization Board allowed for maintenance of real wages by permitting compensatory increases for changes in the cost of living since January 15, 1951. Adjustments were allowed, after December 15, 1951, for intraplant inequities, but no more than 30 per cent of the rates could be changed and straight-time hourly wage rates in the unit affected could not rise more than 1 per cent and no employee could receive more than a fifteen cents an hour increase. Wages below one dollar an hour were not subject to control. Rare and unusual cases could be handled outside of the provisions of the standards set up by the board. A variety of welfare programs—pensions, disability, paid sick leave, and medical expenses—were allowed.

The Steel Dispute

One of the more significant labor disputes during the Korean War involved the workers and firms in the steel industry. It also raised the question of the President's power to act in emergencies. In November 1951 the United Steelworkers of America served a list of twenty-two demands on members of the industry as of the date of the expiration of the contract. The demands included wage increases totaling eighteen cents an hour, time and one-half for Saturday and double-time for Sunday work, improvement in holiday payments, and liberalization of vacations, higher shift premiums, improved seniority provisions, a new incentive system, and a revision of grievance procedure. At the first meeting of the parties, Benjamin Fairless, the head of the U.S. Steel Corporation, rejected the proposals and urged holding the dikes against inflation.[40]

Since President Truman did not believe that the stalemate could be broken by further negotiations, and because he was anxious to avert a strike, he intervened on December 22, 1951, and referred the issues to the Wage Stabilization Board. He also announced that later the Office of Price Stabilization would determine whether the wage increase justified a price increase. The union postponed its strike for forty-five days.[41] On January 2, 1952, a panel of six headed by Harry Shulman, professor of law at Yale University, was selected to hear the case and make recommendations. On the basis of the panel report, the board on March 20, 1952, recommended an increase of 12.5 cents an hour immediately and additional increases of 2.5 cents effective July 1, 1952, and 2.5 cents effective January 1953. Improvements in shift differentials, holiday pay, and Saturday and Sunday premium pay were also recommended. The companies criticized the recommendations, while the union accepted them with minor complaints.[42]

Negotiations were resumed, but no agreement was reached. The stumbling block seemed to be the amount of price relief that would be granted the industry. When 600,000 steelworkers walked off the job on April 8, 1952, President Truman seized the mills, which were placed under the direction of Secretary of Commerce Charles Sawyer. The strike was canceled. A bitter attack on the President followed in and out of Congress. Clarence R. Randall of the Inland Steel Company, charged that Truman's action was an "evil deed without precedent in history, discharges a political debt to the C.I.O.," and that "Phil Murray now gives Harry S. Truman a receipt marked 'Paid in Full.' "[43] The companies appealed to the courts against the seizure order and were at first denied a temporary restraining order by Federal District Judge Alexander Holtzoff. Judge David Pine, however, found on April 30, 1952, that there was "utter and complete lack of support" in law or in the Constitution for the President's action. The decision was followed immediately by the resumption of the strike, which ended after a request for a return to work by President Truman. The U.S. Circuit Court of Appeals stayed the decision pending its rveiew by the U.S. Supreme Court.

By a vote of 6 to 3, the Supreme Court denied on June 2, 1952, that the President held authority to seize an industry. Justice Hugo Black, speaking for the court, claimed that seizure would inflict present and future damage upon the properties of the companies, and he could not find a specific grant of authority for the President's action.[44] The decision was again followed by the withdrawal of the men from the mills. On June 18 the United Mine Workers of America offered the strikers a loan of $10 million, subject to Murray's "draft and order, as your need and circumstances require."[45] The strike continued for fifty-three days and was settled at a conference between Fairless and Murray after a meeting with President Truman. The agreement called for an increase in hour rates equaling 16 cents an hour with an additional 5.4 cents an hour for fringe benefits. A modified union shop was granted. Compensatory price increases were allowed by the stabilization authorities.[46] Work was resumed, after the ratification of the agreement, on August 2.

The Bituminous Coal Case

The steel case created widespread criticism of the Wage Stabilization Board. Its refusal to approve a settlement reached between the United Mine Workers of America and the bituminous coal operators virtually ended its existence. The union and the Bituminous Coal Operators Association reached an agreement on September 29, 1952, for an increase of wages of $1.90 a day with an added 10-cents-a-ton royalty for the Welfare and Retirement Fund. A similar agreement was signed with the Southern Coal Producers Association. Effective October 1, 1952, the across-the-board wage increase raised the basic day rate in northern bituminous fields to $18.25 and the adjustment in royalty brought it to 40 cents a ton on coal mined for sale or use.

Harry Moses, the chief negotiator for the industry, was "gratified to be able to inform the American people that they will have an uninterrupted supply of bituminous coal this fall and winter."[47] In accordance with the law, the contract was submitted for approval to the Wage Stabilization Board, headed at the time by Archibald Cox, professor of law at Harvard University. By a vote of 8 to 4, with the labor members dissenting, the board approved a $1.50-a-day increase, allowing $1.05 a day to offset the 5.9 per cent increase in the cost of living, and another 45 cents under the "Board's responsibility to maintain proper wage relationships and prevent hardships and inequities." This was 40 cents less than the operators were willing to grant. By October 20, 1952, two days after the board's decision, 300,000 miners had left the pits in protest. Following a conference between

Moses, Lewis, and President Truman at the White House, Lewis asked the miners to return to work pending a review of the decision.

At the hearings before the board on November 14, 1952, Moses defended the contract and said it represented a "constructive contribution to the stabilization of the coal industry."[48] Lewis forecast "unrest and confusion" unless the $1.90 was restored. When Economic Stabilizer Roger L. Putnam failed to act, President Truman intervened. Recognizing the importance of wage stabilization, President Truman stressed other considerations. He told Putnam that the decision in the "coal case must not only recognize the importance of continuing stabilization as an effective program, but must face up to problems completely apart from stabilization which are involved in the transition from this Administration to its successor. In view of my concern on this point, and in view of the fact that the decision you had planned to make would not, in my opinion, have met the requirements of this unique situation, I feel it necessary for me to exercise the final authority in the coal case."[49] The President pointed to the difficulties of the miners' lives and expressed regret at the necessity for overruling the Wage Stabilization Board and allowing the full increase of $1.90 a day. He declared: "The ultimate responsibility is mine in any event."

Following the President's decision, Chairman Cox and the industry members resigned from the board. On December 13 Economic Stabilizer Putnam was authorized to administer wage control, and he appointed the four public members of the board as the Wage Stabilization Committee to administer the program. By executive order, wage and salary controls were suspended early in February. The AFL Executive Council immediately called upon its affiliates to demand higher wages in contract renewals in 1953, and the CIO did the same.[50]

Between January 1951 and February 6, 1953, when the wage freeze was ended, the Wage Stabilization Board received 169,943 petitions, 128,810 of them for wage and salary adjustments. The others were requests for approval of a health and welfare, or of pension and profit-sharing plans. During its existence, the board decided 110,000 wage and salary cases; the remainder were withdrawn or transferred for decision to other government agencies. Eighty-two per cent of the wage and salary requests were approved; 12 per cent modified, and 6 per cent rejected. Because of the absence of many dispute cases—only twenty-seven were handled—a large proportion of the cases (78 per cent) were decided by unanimous vote. Industry was outvoted by a combination of labor and public members in 7 per cent of the cases; and labor by industry and the public in 10 per cent.

Disbanding of the United Labor Policy Committee

Although the AFL and CIO had earlier cooperated informally on some issues, and even closer relationships among members and officers of the two federations existed on the local and regional level, the United Labor Policy Committee was the AFL's first formal recognition of its rival. The committee waged a successful campaign for greater recognition of organized labor in defense agencies. The similarity of views of the two groups and their ability to cooperate convinced many that the committee was the first step towards a reunion of the labor federations.

Dissatisfaction with the operation of the committee arose within the AFL. It appeared that it was too successful. Some within the federation began to resent and fear the influence of the CIO leaders in the government; others argued that the committeee was an obstacle to formal unity of the two labor organizations. Another complaint was that the CIO had followed an independent policy at the meeting of the International Confederation of Free Trade Unions during its 1951 meetings at Milan. There were also rivalries and differences between several leaders of the respective organizations. George Meany voiced the complaints at the meeting of the executive council. The council voted to withdraw from the committee. In the announcement, the AFL noted that the committee had been organized to meet an emergency situation and it had served that purpose well. Since further changes in defense policies could only be obtained in Congress, the federation did not want the committee to act as a joint legislative representative.[51] Murray regretted the action, pointed to the success of the committee, and pledged himself to continue to seek labor unity.[52]

CHAPTER 49

Reunification

The ending of peace negotiations between the AFL and the CIO in 1937, and the transformation of the CIO into a permanent federation, established a serious rival to the AFL. From the beginning, the AFL believed that a reunification of the labor movement was essential, but it was not at first ready to allow the new CIO organizations to enter as independent units.

Right from the beginning the structural differences between the unions of the two federations were not as great as might appear from the slogans and shibboleths publicly expounded by each. The CIO was not made up of exclusively industrial unions. In fact, ten of the twenty-nine unions in the CIO in 1939 were craft organizations.[1]

Industrial organizations were not numerous in the AFL, but the United Mine Workers of America, which had held affiliation for forty-eight years, the International Ladies' Garment Workers' Union, and the United Textile Workers of America had functioned as industrial organizations. In addition, there was a wide variety of hybrid organizations which have been classified under the catch-all title of "Amalgamated." The system of government adopted by the CIO unions was similar to those found within the AFL. In fact, the United Steelworkers of America, formed in 1942, was in some respects more centralized than many of the organizations of the AFL. CIO unions were also autonomous, and over a period of time the executive boards began insisting that locals conform to national policy. Administrators of CIO locals have been appointed by the internationals, and they have been compelled to conform to general rules and practices.

A cardinal principle of the AFL—the autonomy of the internationals —became a cornerstone of CIO government. Lewis for a time and Murray after him exercised a great deal of influence within the councils of the CIO unions. However, this power was not a prerogative of the president, but a tribute to the trust of the members and their leaders and a recognition of Murray's superior experience and ability in negotiations with employers. It should be noted that the United Electrical, Machine and Radio Workers of America refused to postpone their contract with the General Motors Corporation in 1946, pending the company's settlement with the United Automobile Workers, even though this was requested by Murray. The autonomy of the CIO unions is best illustrated by the refusal of ten affiliates to cease following the political policies of the Communist party, which were opposed by the majority of the leaders of the general organization. It is clear, therefore, that the governmental forms adopted by the CIO were similar to those of the AFL and were unlike those of such centralized organizations as the Industrial Workers of the World and the Knights of Labor.

Most of the CIO unions demonstrated in the first years of their existence an ability to survive. They showed a capacity for meeting employer attacks, overcoming declines in membership and income occasioned by business depression, training a staff of officers and executives at regional and local levels, creating a disciplined membership willing to run the risks and losses necessary to preserve the union and to repel raids by the AFL. It was clear in 1939 that the reunification of the labor movement would present serious structural problems if the AFL refused to relax the principle of exclusive jurisdiction. As long as AFL organizations regarded particular jurisdictions as their own and insisted upon the absorption of CIO rivals, a merger would be difficult, if not impossible. In time, the unification of the labor movement became entangled in labor and governmental politics; the distribution of posts in a merged federation became a vexing question; loyalties to specific organizations were fostered; and suspicions and fears hardened so that it became increasingly difficult to devise acceptable formulas for a merger. The leaders of the AFL admired and feared John L. Lewis, and always had respect for the character and abilities of Philip Murray. It is notable that at no time did the leaders of the AFL question the basic trade union loyalties of Lewis and Murray. They did not regard all other CIO officers and staff members in the same light, and they were openly hostile to those they suspected of being Communists and fellow-travelers.

Nevertheless, unity efforts were faintly restarted in 1939 when President Franklin D. Roosevelt in letters to the heads of the rival federations expressed the hope "that a constructive negotiated peace with honor may come about between the American Federation of Labor and the Congress of Industrial Organizations within the early months of the new year."[2] Green accepted the invitation the day following receipt of the President's letter and appointed Harry Bates, Matthew Woll, and Daniel J. Tobin, all members of the executive council, to meet with the representatives of the CIO. Lewis headed the CIO delegation.

The conference of representatives of the two organizations was opened in Washington, and Roosevelt expressed his satisfaction at the conference "for the purpose of beginning negotiations for the settlement of these differences in good faith, and with honor and for the best interests of labor and the country generally."[3] Lewis was not ready for serious negotiations. First he requested the calling of special conventions by the AFL, the CIO, and the four Railway Brotherhoods. The latter had not been affiliated with either federation and had not expressed any interest in an inclusive labor federation. Lewis also outlined other conditions, including a stipulation that neither he nor William Green was to serve as president of the unified body. (Of course, Lewis would continue as head of the United Mine Workers of America, the source of his livelihood and power.) The presidential office would, under Lewis' proposal, be reserved for a member of the Railway Brotherhoods. The conference was adjourned pending resumption of negotiations upon the call of Lewis.[4]

Lewis had failed to call any conferences, and when questioned, claimed prior engagements.[5] Roosevelt, in anticipation of his candidacy in 1940, was anxious to restore peace in the labor movement. He suggested negotiations to the two federations at their respective conventions in November 1939. The AFL accepted the proposal, but the President's letter received a curt answer from Lewis. Roosevelt conferred several times with Green and with Lewis, but Lewis submitted the same proposal he had offered at the peace meeting in March which the AFL had found unsatisfactory. The AFL Executive Council wanted Lewis to carry the blame for failure to achieve labor peace and requested the President to issue a statement "so that the responsibility for the continuation of the division which exists in the ranks of labor can be placed where it properly belongs."[6]

Lewis was replaced as head of the CIO at the 1940 convention. No steps to restore unity were taken in the first year of Murray's tenure. On January 17, 1942, Lewis addressed a letter, in his capacity "as a member of the standing negotiating committee of the Congress of Industrial Organizations," to Green and Murray calling for the "accouplement" of the two federations.[7] Although Green expressed the readiness of the AFL committee to meet, Murray, who was now in charge at CIO headquarters, was incensed at Lewis' action, which had been made without consulting him.

Lewis explained that, as chairman of the CIO committee for negotiating with the AFL, he was empowered to initiate negotiations, and he was anxious to bring about unity in the ranks of labor. Lewis' actions, however, appear to have been induced by less idealistic considerations. He had surrendered the office of CIO president after the workers of the country had refused to follow his political advice in the campaign of 1940. His long-time subordinate, Murray, insisted upon being his own man and refused to allow Lewis to run the organization by proxy. Normally, Lewis could depend upon his great abilities and resources to regain control of the CIO, but his allies, the Communists, had more important business on hand—the defense of the Soviet Union. Now they deserted him and circulated wicked calumnies against his person and intentions. Aside from the unquestioned loyalty of the Mine Workers, Lewis could not now count on other unions in the CIO. Had Hitler not launched his attack on the Soviet Union, Lewis could have bided his time and might have been able to drive Murray from the presidency and replace him with a more pliable instrument. There were a number of Mine Workers members available for such an office. As his immediate chances for a successful coup in the CIO did not exist, Lewis, who retained friends and admirers in the AFL, believed he could exercise more influence in a united labor movement.

In this regard, Lewis appears not to have been in error. Within the AFL, performance as a leader of a union was the chief index of prestige, and on that score Lewis had earned an extremely high mark. Unity negotiations, however, were soon entangled in party politics. William Hutcheson, the head of the Carpenters' Union, was anxious to proceed with peace negotiations, but George Harrison and William Green wanted to follow a more cautious policy. In fact, Harrison asked for the appointment of nonbuilding tradesmen on the AFL peace committee—Bates, Hutcheson, and Tobin, the peace negotiators, were all in the Building Trades Department—but his request was overruled.[8]

Instead of taking steps to revive negotiations, Green wanted President Roosevelt to call the peace meeting for the amalgamation and solidification of the labor movement.[9]

After Green informed Duffy on March 3, 1942, that he had not had an opportunity to discuss the issue with the President, Hutcheson tartly told Green, "you were able to contact the President on various matters and not have to wait for what might be considered by you some opportune time. Therefore, I would request . . . that you give this matter attention."[10] But neither Roosevelt nor Murray was inclined to encourage peace negotiations at this time. Murray had gained complete control over the CIO; coal miners favoring Lewis remained in the United Mine Workers of America.

Green requested President Roosevelt on March 13, 1942, to issue an invitation to the AFL and the CIO to resume their suspended peace negotiations. Roosevelt stated that he hoped the periodic meetings of the Combined Labor War Board would serve this purpose. Hutcheson was irritated at what he regarded as the usurpation of the functions of the peace committee of which he was a member and asked Green his views of the matter.

Green then denied that Roosevelt had given consideration to the make-up of the AFL peace committee and averred "that at no time did the President ever suggest who the committee should be, how said committee should be constituted or how they should be selected as representatives of the American Federation of Labor and the CIO."[11]

The executive council at its meeting in May reiterated its desire for a unified labor movement, announced that its committee to negotiate a settlement with the CIO was made up of Harry Bates, William Hutcheson, and Daniel Tobin, and instructed Green to invite Murray to appoint a committee to confer.[12] Green immediately called on Murray to appoint a committee so that a joint exploration of "the possibilities of labor peace and the establishment of unity and solidarity within the ranks of labor" might be undertaken.[13] The CIO under the leadership of Murray was also unwilling to embark upon serious efforts to achieve labor unity. The AFL was concerned and had been forced to recognize industrial organization in the mass-production industries and virtually all the leaders saw no need for two federations; their strong distaste for dual unionism was at the time the chief reason for their desire for unity.

Instead of accepting Green's invitation, the CIO Executive Board suggested the calling of a conference of national and international unions from both federations to consider "increased production, political support to those candidates in support of the President of the United States and the war effort, and increased labor participation in the executive and administrative branches of the government."[14] The resolution suggested the forming of a United National Labor Council of representatives from both groups which would formulate a program to "aid the cause of labor and the war program."[15]

The members of the AFL Executive Council almost unanimously shied away from this proposal. Most of them did not believe that anything could be accomplished by a meeting of the kind suggested by Murray.[16] Green rejected the proposals and denied that conferences seeking organic unity would in any way interfere with cooperation in behalf of the war effort or the Combined Labor War Board. Green regarded these questions as separate and urged resumption of negotiations. On August 1, 1942, Murray replied that he had been deeply concerned by jurisdictional disputes and suggested that a committee from the two organizations seek a solution to this problem.[17]

On December 2, 1942, the joint AFL and CIO Peace Committee agreed, as a means of promoting peace and cooperation between the two federations, to establish a joint committee to hear and decide jurisdictional differences that might arise between their organizations: "If the joint committee fails to agree upon a complaint lodged with the committee it shall select a distinterested arbiter to render a decision on the dispute in question. The arbiter's decision shall be final and binding. In the event an arbiter cannot be agreed upon by the committee within five days, the President of the United States shall be requested to name an arbiter."[18]

Director of Economic Stabilization James F. Byrnes sought to have the AFL Metal Trades Department and a group of CIO unions operating in the same area approve of a no-raiding agreement in their jurisdictions. Harvey Brown, president of the International Association of Machinists, refused and claimed the "no-raiding agreements" had not been effective in the metal trades. The AFL metal trades' organizations were especially critical of the attempt of the Industrial Union of Marine and Shipbuilding Workers to have their agreement with the Kaiser shipyards canceled.[19] The no-raiding pact was nevertheless approved by the AFL Executive Council, and a motion by George Harrison unanimously adopted "that it be the policy of the A.F. of L. not to undertake to raid C.I.O. unions where they hold bargaining rights."[20] But this action was far from final.

At the meeting of the joint committee on April 1, 1942, complaints of continued raiding were made by the AFL.[21] While no progress in bringing the CIO unions back to the AFL was made, John L. Lewis wanted to reaffiliate with the latter, and applied on May 3, 1943. The AFL was not in any haste to accept the offer. It appointed a committee of three members of the executive council to negotiate terms of admission.[22]

Murray was obviously not interested in peace negotiations. He was the head of an independent labor movement, and he could speak for several million workers. He was on friendly terms with President Roosevelt, to whom he could present his views on labor and other public issues. Instead of unity, Murray wanted cooperation between the two federations so as to "forge a broad program of action which could be accepted by all members of the labor movement, honestly interested in the welfare of the American worker, regardless of what that affiliation might be."[23] The AFL, interpreting Murray's invitation as a refusal to resume conferences for uniting the labor movement, issued a statement to that effect.[24] The federation finally, in January 1946, allowed the United Mine Workers of America to affiliate. Lewis described it as a "pooling of collective strength," and an "object lesson which will be approved by the workers throughout the country and sustained by every thoughtful citizen."[25]

On December 6, 1946, Murray reopened unity negotiations, and suggested to the AFL and the Railway Brotherhoods united action against the contemplated antilabor legislation by the newly elected, Republican-dominated Eightieth Congress.[26] Green, after consulting with the executive council, told Murray that protection could be obtained only by the "establishment of organic unity and solidarity within the ranks of labor."[27] Green appointed himself, George Meany, William L. Hutcheson, and John L. Lewis as the committee from the AFL and called for a meeting as soon as practicable.[28]

The AFL committee, and CIO representatives Murray, Walter Reuther, Jacob S. Potofsky, Emil Rieve, and Albert J. Fitzgerald met on May 12, 1947, at Washington, D.C. The CIO made the following proposals: (1) Emergency joint action against anti-union legislation. (2) Proposals for an AFL-CIO agreement "to eliminate jurisdictional disputes" and prevent inter-union boycotts and raiding. (3) Recognition in the unified labor movement of the principles of the industrial organization autonomous rights of international unions and creation of effective labor political machinery. (4) Exploration by AFL-CIO unions in each field of the possibility of eliminating jurisdictional strife and seeking common programs.[29]

The federation, in contrast, had never accepted the existence of two federations vying for support among workers, Congress, and the legislatures. Slowly the leaders of the federation recognized that concessions had to be made if the division was to be ended. The federation's proposals in 1947 show the leaders' flexibility and pragmatism. The AFL peace negotiators asked that the unions of the CIO simply affiliate with the AFL; this policy was followed by the United Mine Workers of America, which included District 50 with its heterogeneous memberships that overlapped the jurisdictions of a number of AFL unions. The "jointure" was to be completed by the October 1947 convention of the AFL to which meeting the CIO unions were to send delegates. Joint committees would continue to work out details of the merger and to cooperate on the economic and legislative fields. The conferees parted on good terms and expressed the conviction "that the economic, social and industrial interest of labor can be best served through the establishment of a united labor movement."[30]

The AFL negotiators were not enthusiastic about the setting up of a political division, and some of the leaders believed it tended to give left-wing groups too much influence. Differences over the name also appeared. The CIO's insistence upon protection of the rights of autonomous unions drew objections from some of the metal trades. Nevertheless, the AFL suggestions were the only ones that might have provided for merger and were actually the basis for ultimate unification. The federation feared that cooperation would hinder rather than promote merger. Murray tried to reopen the question on July 2, 1947, by asking for cooperation in a common program against the Taft-Hartley law. The suggestion was, after consultation with members of the executive council, politely rejected.[31]

Murray again appealed for united action in a letter to Green and the Railway Brotherhoods on December 15, 1948, but the offer was declined. Green repeated that organic unity was the prime requisite for cooperation.[32] In the meantime, cooperation between organizations in the AFL and CIO was increasing. The two federations cooperated in the forming of the International Confederation of Trade Unions in 1949. On April 4, 1950, Murray again addressed a letter to Green, the heads of the Railway Brotherhoods, and the president of the International Association of Machinists (which was temporarily independent) calling for unification of the labor movement. Murray wanted the establishment of a joint committee of the organizations involved to "coordinate our efforts in the economic, legislative and political spheres. It should also seek to achieve the organic unity of all of American labor."[33]

Committees to confer were appointed, and Green and Murray discussed the issues by themselves. Murray wanted the United Mine Workers of America included in the unity negotiations, but the AFL insisted that the conference be limited to the two federations. A subcommittee of Charles MacGowan of the International Brotherhood of Boilermakers, Iron Ship Builders and Helpers of America and a vice-president of the AFL and Allan Haywood, executive vice-president of the CIO were appointed to draw up an agenda. According to Haywood, Murray regarded it as a serious mistake to exclude Lewis from the unity negotiations. In this discussion, MacGowan argued that the AFL Executive Council "had no objections to meeting with the CIO, which is another federated body, but that it did object to meeting with individual International Unions, who would have the same voting power in such a conference as the eight million members of the American Federation of Labor."[34]

The conference, nevertheless, was able to work out a statement, the first formal one issued jointly by the AFL and CIO, which announced that the two federations would continue to work together in the field of foreign relations, in legislation and political action, and also seek to develop a broader program of cooperation.[35] At the suggestion of MacGowan, the AFL committee was enlarged, and the result of the negotiations of 1950 was the forming of the United Labor Policy Committee.[36]

After its suspension in August 1951, no further meetings were held by the representatives of the two federations. Lewis sought to revive a general peace meeting, but the executive council pointed to its long-held views, and expressed its readiness to reopen "negotiations for full organic unity of American labor when the C.I.O. is ready to resume the deliberations."[37]

DEATHS OF MURRAY AND GREEN

Murray and Green, who came out of the same United Mine Workers of America which they had both served as international officers, died in 1952 eleven days apart—Murray on November 9 and Green on November 21. The task of unifying the labor movement fell to others.

Murray was born in New Glasgow, Scotland, on May 25, 1886. His family had emigrated from Ireland, and his father worked in the mines of Lanarkshire, where his son joined him at the age of ten. The family came to the United States in 1902, and father and son found work in the coal mines in the Pittsburgh, Pennsylvania, area. At the age of eighteen Murray accused a weighman of cheating him, and the fight that followed led to his dismissal. Six hundred miners struck for his reinstatement.

During the strike he was elected president of the local union of United Mine Workers of America. The strike was lost, but Murray's career as a labor leader was started. He was elected eight years later to the international executive board, president of District 5, in 1916, and vice-president of the United Mine Workers of America in 1920. He served through one of the more stormy periods of the union's history, saw its control eroded in the 1920's and re-established to an unprecedented level in the 1930's and 1940's. Murray served on the Regional War Labor Board in Pennsylvania during World War I, on the Labor and Industry Board of the National Recovery Administration in the early 1930's, and on the Board of Education in his home city, Pittsburgh.

Murray worked side by side with John L. Lewis for two decades and played a key role in contract negotiations and in policy decisions. He became the chief assistant to Lewis in the early years of the CIO and was active in smoothing the factional divisions which developed in a number of its unions, including the United Automobile Workers. Placed in charge of the drive to organize the steel industry by the CIO as chairman of the Steel Workers' Organizing Committee, he became president of the United Steelworkers of America when that organization was established in 1942. He also replaced Lewis as head of the CIO when the latter failed to stand for re-election in 1940, and served in that capacity until his death.

Murray was among the three or four outstanding leaders produced by the American labor movement. For a time overshadowed by John L. Lewis, his talent for analysis, negotiation, and conciliation fitted him more than his chief for the headship of a federation of autonomous unions. Possessed of a simple eloquence which could move audiences, he was personally more approachable and popular than Lewis. His talent for compromise stood him in good stead in his early years as head of the CIO.

To have transformed the heterogeneous and discordant locals and internationals into a movement required talent of the highest order, and while he could not compete with Lewis on the hustings or in the public prints, Murray always controlled and dominated the movement he led. Not easy to anger, Murray, when aroused against injustice or personal disloyalty, was ready to destroy his opponents. During World War II, Murray cooperated closely with the government, but he also sought to gain concessions for the steelworkers he led. As a member of the Combined Labor War Board, he met frequently with President Roosevelt. For years, he believed it necessary to tolerate the Communists in the CIO, but when he decided that their presence created a danger to the labor movement and the country, he led the fight for their expulsion. Through most of his years as head of the CIO, he enjoyed the trust and confidence of virtually all of its leaders.

He was always ready to assist in the solution of internal differences or in employer negotiations. Murray was not sparing of his time or energy in behalf of other unions. The confidence shown him was earned and deserved.

William Green was born at Coshocton, Ohio, on March 3, 1873, the son of an English coal miner who had emigrated to the United States from Wales. He became a miner at the age of sixteen and a charter member of the United Mine Workers of America at its founding in 1890. He served as a local union officer, subdistrict president and president of the Ohio District of the United Mine Workers of America in 1906.

From 1911 to 1913 he served in the Ohio Senate, where he sponsored the Workmen's Compensation law, the coal screening law for miners, and other social and labor legislation. While in the Senate, Green was appointed statistician by International President John P. White of his union. He was elected secretary-treasurer of the Miners' Union in 1912 and held the office from 1913 to his election as president of the AFL in 1924. He retained the office until his death on November 21, 1952.

Green succeeded Gompers at a time when the attack upon the labor movement, initiated and carried through under the American Plan of Employment, had spent its force, and when the first assault of the Communists upon the American labor movement had partially subsided. During the first five years of his tenure as president of the AFL, the movement suffered from the conservative reaction, the loss of control in some of the older organized areas, and the hostility of government and the courts. The AFL made few advances, but it did not lose any ground. The Depression affected the labor movement adversely, and Green followed the views of the majority of the members of the executive council in opposing unemployment insurance until 1932, although he had earlier approved such proposals.

Green favored industrial unionism for the mass-production industries and supported the views of John L. Lewis in the sessions of the executive council. When overruled, he believed he had to conform to the majority view. When the CIO was established, he believed it would lead to a division in the ranks. When its unions refused to disband the CIO, he went along with the movement to expel the recalcitrant unions. In the early drives of the CIO, it fell to Green to lead the defense of the AFL against its inroads, and perhaps more than those of any other man his efforts prevented the expansion of the CIO beyond the mass-production industries. While not a great leader, it can be truly said he held the federation together in one of the more serious crises of its history. Green was an internationalist, a forceful opponent of communism which he well understood. He was among those in the AFL who refused to go along with the forming of the Communist World Federation of Trade Unions and helped to save the unions of the free world from a disastrous trap. A forceful and tireless speaker, he was able to see the AFL stronger and more virile at the time of his death than when he first took over the reins.

NEW FACES AT THE HELM

Green was succeeded by George Meany, who had served as secretary-treasurer of the AFL since 1940. Meany was born in New York City on August 16, 1894, the son of Michael Meany, the president of a local plumbers' union. At the age of twenty-eight, George Meany became a business agent and was elected successively vice-president and president of the New York State Federation of Labor. In the latter position he achieved a reputation as a successful legislative agent. Meany is a man of strong views and forceful expression. Not normally an eloquent speaker, he can rise to great oratorical heights when aroused by an issue or personal arrogance. His denunciation of the posturing of John L. Lewis during the debate on the non-Communist Taft-Hartley affidavit at the 1947 AFL convention won him the esteem of the high officials of the federation and cleared his way for uncontested election to the presidency of the federation. Meany has a sharp, tenacious, uncluttered mind. Not at home on the platform, he is likely to be underrated by those who equate eloquence and mental capacity. Meany knows the limitations that surround the office of president of a labor federation of autonomous unions, and he is not likely to engage in adventures; he is a traditionalist.

The CIO had two candidates for Murray's office. Walter Reuther was nominated by O. A. Knight of the Oil Workers' Union, and Allan S. Haywood by David J. McDonald. Reuther polled 3,078,181 votes to Haywood's 2,613,103, and Reuther became the third president of the CIO.[38]

Walter Philip Reuther, born in Wheeling, West Virginia, on September 1, 1907, came from a family of union members; his father Valentine was president of the Ohio Valley Trades and Labor Assembly. Reuther was an apprentice tool and die maker; he also studied at Wayne University. He worked in the factories around Detroit, and in the early 1930's visited Europe and the Soviet Union, where he was employed at his trade. He joined the United Automobile Workers Union in 1935, upon his return to the United States. He became active in his local and was elected president of the West Side Local 174. In the factional battle in the early years, Reuther was a member of the unity caucus, and he was one of the vice-presidents removed by President Homer Martin in 1939. He was a member of the executive board, a vice-president, and after 1946, president of the union. He was chosen director of the General Motors Division in 1939 and participated in the drive to organize the Ford Company.

Reuther can be regarded as one of the more eminent leaders of the labor movement during its stormy history. Imaginative and articulate, he is anxious to break out of the narrow confines of trade union activity into the more challenging fields of domestic and international politics. Nevertheless, Reuther does not neglect his union business and well realizes that the organization is the basis of his power from which all of his influence flows. While solving the problems of a war economy or underdevelopment, Reuther has also to his credit the supplementary unemployment benefit program, one of the more imaginative proposals to come out in recent collective bargaining history. Reuther is a superb union leader, who has been tested as an organizer, on the picket line, and in negotiations. While he is an eloquent expounder of social unionism, there is no more effective business unionist practicing in the United States.

Because of his early flirtation with socialism, Reuther is likely to place more stress upon the opinions of intellectuals, and his great concern with the views of this group encourages him to espouse public relations devices like the Public Review Board. Reuther is more complicated and perhaps more ambitious than most trade union leaders of this or other times. He is a tireless worker, completely devoted to his union.

During his life Murray was in a position to decide whether peace negotiations would be carried on with the AFL, and the terms upon which they would be conducted. No one could challenge him as the spokesman for the CIO, for he had guided a number of unions, including Reuther's own, through dangerous periods when dissension or external attack threatened their existence. He advised and aided others, and he led a great union as large as any in the United States. Reuther was in a different position. At best he could only claim to be first among equals, and some within the CIO might even contest that claim. Nor could he, like John L. Lewis, dominate through the charisma that enshrouds great men and powerful personalities. In fact, Reuther's "social engineering" could be a weakness in a labor leader.

The Turn to Unity

The meeting of the executive council which chose Meany president appointed the standing committee on organic unity. Reuther followed suit and announced that he wanted Communists and racketeers ousted from organized labor. Labor unity met his approval providing it did not result in a sacrifice of principles.[39] At its first meeting since 1950, on April 7, 1953, the conferees recognized that raiding was the chief obstacle to organic unity. A subcommittee of Meany, Secretary William Schnitzler, and Matthew Woll from the AFL, and Reuther, James Carey, and David J. McDonald from the CIO were appointed to seek a solution.

The first meeting of the subcommittee considered a study of the records of the National Labor Relations Board and found, according to George Meany, "that raiding is not a profitable business either for the A.F. of L. or C.I.O."[40] In the two-year period between January 1, 1951, to December 31, 1952, 1,246 bargaining elections involving 366,470 workers held by the board could be defined as raids. A CIO union instigated the petition in 700 instances and an AFL union in about 550. Only 62,504 workers of the 366,470, or 17 per cent, voted to change unions. Out of these elections, AFL unions gained about 35,000 workers and CIO unions approximately 17,000 workers. Considered from the point of view of the two federations, the net shift was about 7,000 workers, scarcely an impressive number.[41]

Nor was raiding an efficient device for fattening membership by individual unions. It is likely that funds spent on organizing the unorganized could have yielded greater returns. Following the report of the subcommittee, a no-raiding agreement was drafted and announced jointly by Meany and Reuther on June 2, 1953. It was only binding upon particular affiliates of the respective federations who signed the no-raiding pact. It was approved by the 1953 convention of the AFL and CIO and signed by the two chief officers of each organization on December 16, 1953.

The no-raiding agreement recommended that no "union affiliated with either federation shall attempt to organize or to represent employees to whom an established bargaining relationship exists between their employer and a union in the other federation." A procedure for settling differences, including arbitration by an umpire, was incorporated in the agreement. The agreement was of limited duration. On a trial basis it was to remain effective from January 1, 1954, until December 31, 1955.[42]

One of the chief advocates of unity—John L. Lewis—was missing from the negotiations. The AFL would not allow him to participate in 1950, the time that the United Labor Policy Committee was formed, and Meany, who was in full command on the AFL side in 1952, would not allow him to participate in the current negotiations. In an interview, Meany said: "Good Lord, he's the fellow that split the AFL. He's the fellow who tried to split the CIO after he got tired of that. He's the fellow who came to the AFL in 1947 and tried to split it again."[43]

The way was not clear for the merger. William Hutcheson, who had given up his post as head of the Carpenters' Union and remained on the AFL Executive Council, raised some objection and threatened to disaffiliate. The challenge was accepted, and after a short stay on the outside, the Carpenters returned to the AFL.[44] The net result of the Carpenters' maneuver was the resignation of Hutcheson from the executive council and his replacement by Dave Beck, who had been elected president of the Teamsters' Union. Beck was not enthusiastic about the merger, but he did not attempt to prevent its consummation. He did, however, raise jurisdictional questions.

Failure of adherence to the no-raiding agreement by many AFL unions induced the CIO Executive Board to postpone its operative date. Meany took steps to prevent a breakdown and argued that there had been no understanding that a minimum number of unions had to approve before the no-raiding pact was effective. He also called attention to the provision that the no-raiding pact only governed the conduct and relations of those who signed the pact. Meany insisted that the AFL was acting in good faith. On the basis of this assurance, the CIO reversed its position and decided to go ahead with unity negotiations. As a result the two federations on June 9, 1954, exchanged the ratifications of the no-raiding pact by their affiliated organizations; 65 out of 110 AFL unions and 29 out of 32 CIO organizations had signed.[45]

On June 24, 1954, a joint statement by Meany and Reuther announced that invitations had been sent to officers of unions of the two federations to dine together on June 29. "The signing and ratification of the No-Raiding Agreement between our two organizations," they said, "is an historic step. We are confident that the achievement of the No-Raiding Agreement may function in a spirit of understanding and fraternal friendship."[46]

While the two federations were closer to unity than they had been since the initial rupture in 1935, several powerful organizations—the AFL Carpenters' and Teamsters' unions, and the CIO Steelworkers' union refused to sign the no-raiding agreement. David J. McDonald, who succeeded Murray as head of the Steelworkers' union, wanted to follow an independent policy or at least show his influence. Addressing the convention of his organization on September 23, 1954, McDonald asked that immediate steps be taken to achieve organic unity. He held the time was ripe for merger of the AFL and CIO as the "idea of industrial unionism has been accepted . . . and there are millions of workers working in industrial unions who are members of the American Federation of Labor."[47] Lewis encouraged McDonald's independence in a telegram in which he told him "you are unfortunate in your affiliation with a federated group, dominated by intellectual inebriates in frantic pursuit of butterflies of their delusions."[48] On a more serious note, McDonald was assured that the "affinity between members of the Steelworkers and Mineworkers is basic and more than a fraternal relationship. . . . The strength of these two great organizations and the material well being of their members, and of the population dependent thereon, will be augmented and the security of the nation enhanced by future cooperation and concert of action."[49]

McDonald was not flattered or charmed sufficiently to accept Lewis' bait. He also lacked Lewis' freedom of maneuver and was very likely indulging in a harmless flirtation with Lewis. He emphasized that his union would remain in the CIO but asked for more expeditious action on unity.

Whatever McDonald's intentions might have been, his independent posture underlined the difference in the positions of Reuther and Murray. No one, even Hillman, who was the strongest man in the CIO exclusive of its chief, would have publicly rebuked Murray on matters of basic policy. Reuther, however, for all his virtues and capacities, could not command the undeviating loyalty of the heads of the CIO unions on issues on which the latter had independent views, nor did he have the general prestige or power to impose his views upon them. He was in a position with respect to the CIO unions similar to the one held by Meany in his federation. Whatever McDonald's intentions might have been, his public pronouncements were a signal that the organizations in the CIO were becoming restive and that some might withdraw, if not immediately, at least sometime in the future, if unity with the AFL was not achieved. A three-hour session of the Joint Unity Committee on October 15, 1954, decided "to create a single trade union center in America through the process of merger which will preserve the integrity of each affiliated national and international union."[50] The full committee met again in Washington on January 4, 1955, and after reviewing results, directed the subcommitee—Reuther, Carey, and McDonald of the CIO and Meany, Bates, and William Schnitzler of the AFL —to draft a merger agreement. The respective conventions of each organization approved the trend of negotiations. By February 8, 1955, the merger agreement was ready, and it was approved by the full joint committee meeting in Miami, Florida. The two federations agreed to create a single trade union center in which "each national and international union, federal labor union, local industrial union and organizing committee . . . holding a charter or certificate of affiliation granted by either federation shall retain its charter or certificate of affiliation and become, by virtue of the merger, an affiliate of the merged federation."[51] The integrity of each affiliated union was recognized and each was allowed to retain the same jurisdiction it had held "in its respective prior federation." Affiliates occupying conflicting and duplicating jurisdictions were to be encouraged to merge. Craft and industrial unions were recognized as necessary methods of trade union organization, and the right of all workers, irrespective of race, creed, color, or national origin to belong was explicitly declared. American trade unions were to be protected from corrupt influences and from infiltration by Communist activists.

The government and structure outlined for the new federation contained few surprises. An Industrial Union Department with status comparable to the departments of the AFL was to be established and open to all industrial unions. A similar request by Lewis in 1937 proved to be the chief stumbling block to unity that year. Arrangements for pooling property, and the appointment of the heads of staff were made. It was agreed that initially the president and secretary-treasurer of the merged federation would be elected from the unions of the AFL. It is not likely that Murray, with an unmatchable record of achievement, would have been willing to make such a concession.

In a joint statement, Meany and Reuther assured their affiliates the agreement would preserve "the identity and integrity of the more than 140 trade unions now affiliated with the AFL and CIO. They will continue, under this plan, to conduct their own individual collective bargaining with employers as in the past. The agreement provides a mechanism for voluntary—not compulsory—merger of individual trade unions in the same field."[52] The AFL Executive Council and CIO Executive Board approved the agreement and directed the drafting of a constitution.

A prepared constitution was submitted to the full Joint Unity Committee at its Washington meeting on May 2, 1955. With Vice-President Michael Quill of the CIO dissenting, the document was sent to the AFL Executive Council and the CIO Executive Board for approval. The meeting recommended that the federations hold parallel conventions in New York beginning on December 1, 1955, and that the merged convention be opened on December 5, 1955. The full unity committee met once more on July 20, 1955, and finally agreed that the name of the merged federation would be the American Federation of Labor–Congress of Industrial Organizations.[53]

THE MERGER

As a first step, members of the subcommittee signed the merger agreement and the "Implementation Agreement," on November 30, 1955, under which the transfer of property was arranged and the rights of the unions and members in the merger were formally recognized. At the convention of the AFL, Woodruff Randolph of the International Typographical Union wanted a clearer statement of the rights of unions to their jurisdictions. He also objected to the grant of more power to the merged federation than the AFL had enjoyed. Meany disagreed and cited a number of instances in which the AFL compelled international unions to follow a specific policy or face expulsion. Consequently, he did not believe that the dangers to affiliates envisaged by Randolph existed. The merger agreement was adopted with a delegate from the Painters and Decorators dissenting.[54]

The seventeenth and last convention of the CIO was opened in New York City on December 1, 1955. A bill from John Owens, secretary-treasurer of the United Mine Workers of America, for $1,665,000 still owed to the union was received. Owen claimed that the Mine Workers had extended in cash and service approximately $7,250,000 "in the campaigns to organize the men and women into most of the national organizations affiliated with the Congress of Industrial Organizations." The amount did not include cash loans of $601,000 to the Steel Workers' Organizing Committee for the conduct of the Little Steel strike, which had been repaid nor amounts repaid or donated directly to organizations in the CIO. Before the CIO was liquidated, Owens asked that the loan be honored for the sake of the "millions of men and women who are the beneficiaries of the contributions the United Mine Workers of America have made." The letter was unanswered.[55]

President Walter Reuther refreshed the "memories of the warmth and friendship that we had for our great and beloved leaders, Philip Murray, Sidney Hillman, Allan Haywood, and Van Bittner."[56] Even when President

Reuther recited the coal miners' song, "Sixteen Tons," made famous by Tennessee Ernie Ford, the name of the miners' leader was not mentioned. John L. Lewis had no place in the Parthenon inhabited by the great who founded the CIO.

The discussion of the merger brought an objection from Michael Quill, who spoke with his usual asperity. He did not like the proposed constitution, the lack of real protection against racial discrimination, and the weak prohibition on raiding. Quill was answered by Reuther, who charged that his methods of argumentation had been learned in the Communist party where Quill had done service. David McDonald supported the merger, and in a nostalgic note, recalled the launching of the CIO in mid-November 1935, and remembered that John L. Lewis had been there. But none among the delegates, whose many unions had been founded and succored by the largess of the Coal Miners, could find a word of praise in this final hour for this organization or its embattled leader.[57]

The first convention of the AFL and CIO assembled on schedule on December 5, 1955. Whatever differences may have existed with regard to CIO membership, they were not sufficient to prevent the working out of an acceptable formula. During the unity negotiations, the AFL submitted its financial report, but the CIO refused. Instead, the latter claimed a "voting membership" of 5,692,000, which Meany estimated as "a little less than 4,000,000."[58] The discrepancy was not made an issue, and David McDonald reporting for the Joint AFL-CIO Unity Committee, moved that the "initial constitutional convention of the American Federation of Labor-Congress of Industrial Organizations confirms and ratifies the action of the separate conventions of the American Federation of Labor and of the Congress of Industrial Organizations in ratifying, approving and adopting the Resolution on the Achievement of Labor Unity, the Agreement for the Merger of the American Federation of Labor and the Congress of Industrial Organizations, the Implementation Agreement and the Constitution of the American Federation of Labor and Congress of Industrial Organizations."[59]

The membership of 15 million affiliated with the merged federation made it the largest labor group in the history of the United States and the free world. President George Meany and Secretary-Treasurer William Schnitzler, in accordance with the merger agreement, were elected to the same posts in the merged organization. The resolutions adopted followed the pattern which have annually appeared at labor conventions in the last decade. The "preamble" to the constitution expressed the attitude of the labor movement of the time. It emphasized the fulfillment of the hopes and aspirations of the working people through collective bargaining and "the exercise of the rights and responsibilities of citizenship." The class struggle declaration of the original AFL constitution and the emphasis upon industrial organization found in the CIO constitution are absent.

The twelve objectives and principles are in line with traditional aspirations of organized labor in the United States: The federation aimed to aid workers to secure improved wages, hours and conditions of employment; assist affiliated unions; encourage affiliation of national and international unions with the federation; help workers irrespective of race, creed, or color to share in the benefits of organization; seek to secure beneficial legislation for all the people and oppose such as is harmful; protect democratic institutions; promote the cause of peace and freedom; cooperate with and assist free and democratic labor movements in other countries; preserve and protect the autonomy of affiliates so that each abstains from raiding; encourage the sale of union made goods; safeguard the democratic charter of the labor movement and protect the autonomy of each affiliated national and international union; and finally, encourage workers to register and vote so as to exercise their duties of citizenship.[60]

All of these objectives could be approved by every trade unionist in the United States. Aside from greater emphasis upon political action, which both federations had adopted independently, and the explicit opposition to communism and corruption, the constitution of the merged federation contained no surprises. Like its ancestor federations, unions are autonomous, and the power of the federation is strictly limited. In line with precedent, the convention was made the highest authority; the executive council of twenty-seven vice-presidents plus the president and secretary-treasurer —the two executive officers—became the ruling body between conventions. Eighteen vice-presidents plus the two executive officers came from the AFL, and ten vice-presidents from the CIO. In addition, an executive committee made up of the president, secretary-treasurer, and six vice-presidents were to be chosen, and the committee was required to meet every two months to advise the executive officers.

In addition, the general board made up of members of the executive council and the president or other principal officer of each affiliated national or international union, and trade and industrial department was established. It was required to meet at least once a year or at the call of the president to decide questions submitted to it.[61] The subordinate state and local central bodies of the two federations were absorbed, and a system of per capita payments was devised for meeting the expenses.

In its first years, the merged federation fulfilled all reasonable expectations. It did not possess magic formulae for solving jurisdictional strife and for devising invincible organizing techniques. Inevitably a federation made up of 135 national and international unions, 5 departments, 93 state branches, 490 central bodies and industrial union councils, 148 local unions and local industrial union councils would have its share of problems.[62] One of the more serious differences arose over the jurisdiction of maintenance work in large mass-production plants. Throughout its history, the AFL found that problems involving jurisdictional claims were the most difficult to solve. The pleas and complaints of Gompers are found in the convention proceedings, and he was more outspoken in his correspondence about this issue. Disputes over work assignments have always been a problem, and the one between the industrial unions in the building trades is basically similar to the earlier ones. Because it involved a group of CIO unions and a number of old AFL craft organizations, the dispute appeared to be a renewal of the Civil War over structure. Strong feeling was expressed on both sides, but one must remember that such disputes have sometimes led to strikes, violence, and boycotts of unions against each other. A serious aspect of the current dispute was the danger that the contest would be transformed into a difference of principles rather than over assignments. As has happened in the past, when possibilities of compromise seemed least favorable, a formula was found for allaying the struggle.

There have been no sensational changes in organizing, partly because a federation is not the most effective instrument for such tasks. It can mobilize organizers and other resources for a specific campaign which individual unions cannot finance or manage, but a federation cannot do much organizing en masse on a day-to-day basis. It can assist particular organizations with limited help and funds. All and all, the federation has achieved its objectives. It has not been able because of the autonomy of international unions to do as much in eliminating racial discrimination as some of the leaders had hoped. The federation, and even an international, has little coercive power that it can employ against a union located in the south. It took more than one regiment of troops and several million dollars to get James Meredith into the University of Mississippi; the federation has neither funds nor power to compel obedience to its *humane dicta* on civil rights.

50

Organized Labor and the Negro

Free Negro wage earners were members of the labor force before the Civil War. In the South employers regarded some white labor as inferior to Negro workers. Employers in ante-bellum Virginia complained that white workers were lazy and did not like to work with slaves. In addition, white men would leave their jobs for the midwestern states of Illinois and Wisconsin to become independent farmers as soon as they had accumulated a few dollars.[1] The "whites who possessed political and economic powers were inclined to side with such labor against their own race."[2]

Although the industrial experience of Negro slaves was generally limited, they were employed in a number of manufacturing industries and in the coal and iron mines. Negro workmen showed a large measure of adaptability, industriousness, and fortitude. Even though the typical Negro slave was a field hand, considerable evidence is found that he was capable of learning the manual skills of the artisan.[3]

Even before emancipation, the free Negro faced the opposition and prejudice of the white man. Ill-feeling between free Negroes and foreign workmen in the North was not uncommon before the Civil War. As the Negro artisan and the unskilled moved into the towns after the end of the Civil War, hostility toward the newcomer was engendered by the fear of competition.

NATIONAL LABOR UNION

The National Labor Union was an attempt to establish a nationwide central labor federation after the Civil War, and at its first convention in 1866, it took note of the Negro question. It called on "every union to help inculcate the grand, enobling idea that the interests of labor are one; that there should be no distinction of race or nationality."[4] The reasons for the policy of nondiscrimination were practical, for workers had a special interest in their cooperation. Negroes, it noted, were being educated and their numbers were increasing. Consequently, the interests of labor required that they be encouraged to form unions, labor leagues, and other kinds of workers' organizations. Nevertheless, the 1867 convention would take no position on the Negro question because of "diversity of opinion amongst our members."[5] The 1868 convention of the National Labor Union urged Negroes to form organizations and send delegates to the next convention, but no special steps were taken to recruit them into labor organizations.[6]

It should be noted that the views of the National Labor Union were not binding upon any of its affiliates. Since the central body did not engage in bargaining with employers, its attitude was a noble but not necessarily a significant expression of good will.

THE KNIGHTS OF LABOR

As the inclusive organization of the wage earners of the United States, the Noble Order of the Knights of Labor did not discriminate against workers on the grounds of race, creed, color, or nationality. The Knights welcomed all workers, and Powderly advised an officer "to organize a Colored Assembly in your city and turn all applicants of that kind over to them."[7] Nevertheless, Negroes in the Knights of Labor were usually granted equality. Whatever views might have been held by a particular group, the prevalent attitude in the order was that the Negro was to be treated on par with other members. This feeling was illustrated by an episode at the special convention in Richmond, Virginia, in the spring of 1886. Governor Fitzhugh Lee had agreed to address the convention. J. E. Quinn, the Master Workman of New York City, wanted the governor introduced by Frank J. Ferrell, a Negro delegate from that city. Powderly demurred, for he believed it would be disrespectful to allow a Negro to introduce a southern governor. He compromised by allowing Ferrell to introduce the Grand Master Workman, who in turn introduced Governor Lee.[8] Conventions of the Knights of Labor were attended by Negro delegates who were treated courteously and enjoyed the same rights as other delegates.

THE AFL

The labor unions that began to dominate the labor scene in the 1870's were, in the main, craft organizations, many of which carried on fraternal as well as protective activities. Moreover, these unions normally required a period of apprenticeship and attempted to restrict entry by various devices, including the closing of books. As the authors of an early and major study of the Negro in unions noted, more than thirty years ago: "While race prejudice is a very fundamental fact in the exclusion of the Negro, the desire to restrict competition so as to safeguard job monopoly and control wages is extricably interwoven with it."[9] These facts are important in accounting for the differences in the attitudes of some unions in the AFL and the Knights of Labor. From the beginning the AFL "looked with disfavor upon trade unions having provisions in their constitutions excluding from membership persons on account of race and color and they requested they be expunged."[10]

Gompers visited the convention of the International Association of Machinists, which had sought affiliation with the AFL, and asked it to eliminate discrimination on the basis of color from its laws. He was assured that such action would be taken by the next convention.[11] During 1891, Gompers said that the federation had resolved "to call a convention of all machinists' unions for the purpose of forming a national union which shall recognize no color line."[12] Gompers also told the head of the National Association of Machinists that the AFL had authorized "calling a convention of machinists' unions opposed to the narrow policy of race prejudice and for the formation of a National Union upon a broad comprehensive basis and principle."[13] Gompers wanted to combine the existing machinists' unions in one organization affiliated with the AFL. He pleaded with the National Association of Machinists to "strike out the clause, which though in itself is so objectionable and unmanly, accomplishes no good."[14]

The Machinists would not eliminate "white only" from their constitution. Gompers described the action as one of "unseemly haste" and explained that "a feeling prevails among the delegates that since the organization originated in the South and the race prejudice existed to a large degree there, the local unions would secede from the International Association should the word 'white' be stricken out."[15] Elaborating his view to the head of the Machinists' Association, Gompers recognized that the AFL was formed "upon the idea that to the union of the trade belongs absolute jurisdiction on all matters connected with that trade. . . . The recognition of this cardinal principle, however, did not deny us the right of expressing the sentiments of trade unionism against any matter involving the general interest of the labor movement."[16]

Gompers was defeated for re-election in 1894, and during the illness of his successor, John McBride, James Duncan acted as president. Duncan suggested that the Machinists eliminate "white only" from their constitution, but "the Southern lodges could act as they do now with a provision in your constitution leaving it a question of local option and thereby retaining the same feeling that exists in that section at the present time without dismembering your National Body."[17]

When a protest against granting a charter to the International Association of Machinists was received, McBride wrote that "for several years efforts have been made by our Executive Council, and President Gompers to have that organization eliminate the color line from their constitution and affiliate with the A.F. of L. . . . Having complied with the requests made by the A.F. of L. officials by removing the objectionable clauses from their constitution, and applied for a charter of affiliation, the members of our Council granted a charter conditioned upon the final endorsement by the next convention of the A.F. of L."[18]

After Gompers was returned to office, he reiterated the older view to the Brotherhood of Locomotive Firemen. He told the latter organization that the AFL does not compel any of "its affiliated organizations to accept the colored workman. . . . No more than it compels organizations to accept Americans, Germans, Frenchmen, Englishmen, Irishmen, or even Hottentots. What the American Federation of Labor declares by its policy, that organizations should not declare against accepting the colored man because he is colored. . . . It should be a wrong-doer against labor; it should not be a nationality or race against whom the doors are barred."[19]

While the AFL favored equal treatment of workers irrespective of race, the affiliated unions were, in some instances, pursuing a different policy. Discrimination against Negro workers led to a criticism of organized labor by Booker T. Washington, the head of the Tuskegee Institute. The 1897 convention of the AFL denounced the charges and appealed to the records of the federation as proof that the Negro suffered from no discrimination. During the debate on the resolution, L. C. Jones, a delegate from Federal Labor Union 6877 in Columbus, Georgia, declared that his union did not admit Negroes. "Delegate Gompers said that a union affiliated with the American Federation of Labor had no right to debar a Negro from membership."[20] Nevertheless, the particular union continued to retain its affiliation with the AFL, although a majority of the speakers on this question expressed opposition to discrimination.

Whatever sentiments were held by the AFL, the leaders faced strong opposition to the mixing of white and colored workers in the same organization. A policy of separation was regarded as the only one which would make possible the retention of unions in the South. In a letter to James E. Porter, Gompers said:

I would of course prefer unity of organization as well as unity of purpose; but, if it be the desire of the organizations of the colored workers as represented by you, and it is also the desire of the Central Labor Union already in existence in New Orleans, that a separate charter be issued to a C.L.U. representing the colored workers, then as previously stated in my letter to you I have no hesitation in saying that the A.F. of L. may grant a charter, after the matter has been determined by the A.F. of L. at the coming convention.[21]

In his report to the 1900 AFL convention Gompers dealt with the problems of organizing the Negro worker at some length. He called attention to the refusal of local unions in the South to accept colored workers. A similar policy had been followed by AFL central bodies in that section. Gompers faced the following dilemma: "To insist upon a delegation from unions of colored workers being accorded representation in a central body would have meant the dissolution of that organization; and thus neither the desired purpose nor any good would have been accomplished."[22] Gompers reiterated that unions "should open their portals to all wage workers irrespective of creed, color, nationality, sex, or politics. Nothing has transpired in recent years which has called for a change of policy on this question."[23] He ended his report with a warning that unless the Negro worker is allowed to organize, and the white worker shows him his friendship, there could "be no question but that they will not only be forced down in the economic scale and used against any effort made by us for our economic and social advancement, but race prejudice will be made more bitter and the injury of all."[24]

The 1900 convention concluded that in trying to extend unionization to the South, the "difficulties increase by reason of the race struggle, and, while we do not in any way abate the policy laid down by the American Federation of Labor, namely, that the trade union is open to all regardless of race, sex, nationality, creed or color, we recommend that the laws be so amended as to permit of charters being granted to separate local unions and central bodies composed of colored workers."[25]

The problem of organizing Negro workers came up at the same time. George L. Norton had been appointed organizer for New Orleans and protests against the appointment of a Negro were received. Gompers was apologetic and told Norton "it hurts me very much to be compelled to ask you to exercise greater discretion and not run counter to the men who have these prejudices, and possibly in that way obviate rather than intensify the feeling of bitterness."[26] At the same time, Gompers wrote to John M. Callahan, a white organizer also stationed in New Orleans, asking him to confer with Norton.

There is no necessity to run counter to social distinctions, but the wage workers ought to bear in mind that unless they help to organize the colored men, they will of necessity compete with the white workmen and be antagonistic to them and their interests. The employers will certainly take advantage of this condition and will do all they can to even stimulate race prejudice. . . . As a man whom I have every reason to believe you are, serious, earnest and honest in the desire to see our fellow wage-workers improve their condition, I ask you to examine into this question more closely and to see whether I am not right. View it in a common sense manner. Start out the investigation not with the old prejudices that you have heard from infancy, but study it in the light of the historical struggles of the people of all nations, and you will find I am right.[27]

One should remember that this letter was written less than thirty years after the issuance of the Emancipation Proclamation by President Lincoln. Gompers had only persuasion and appeals to labor ideals, sentiment, and interest to break down prejudice. It took the entire power of the federal government to compel the city of New Orleans to open the public schools to a Negro child. It is easy to understand why Gompers, without power, could do little and, as the federation grew in size and numbers, his moral authority on an issue which aroused deep and bitter feelings was lessened.

In 1901, Gompers refused to grant an organizer's commission to a Negro when objections were raised by David Kreyling, secretary of the St. Louis Trades and Labor Council. This decision carried out a policy that the recommendation of a central body in the locality was required for the granting of a commission.[28] Gompers was interested in the organizing of colored workers and told P. F. Sargent, the head of the Brotherhood of Firemen, that he hoped the convention of the Firemen's Union would take "some action . . . for the interests of the colored firemen."[29]

In view of the federation's position that all wage workers should be organized, it faced the necessity of providing a place for colored workers employed in crafts or industries in which unions would not admit colored workers. The authority was given to the executive council in 1902 to issue charters to central labor unions, local unions, or federal labor unions composed exclusively of Negro workers.[30] This provision was an attempt to meet a situation, but the fact that the federation stood ready to organize Negro workers into separate federal labor and trade unions whenever internationals rejected Negro workers, meant that the federation had retreated from its earlier position. In fact, Gompers in 1902 refused to request admission of a Negro to the Barbers' Union because "each affiliated organization is in entire control over the affairs of its local unions and adopts such rules and regulations governing the same as it may be deemed advisable, insofar as such regulations do not conflict with the Constitution of the A.F. of L."[31] The AFL actually allowed unions to amend their constitutions, specifically excluding Negroes from membership—the first instance being the Stationary Engineers in 1902.[32] An early student noted that of the unions containing 1.2 million members in 1902, those which contained 500,000 included 40,000 Negroes; another group of 200,000 members had 1,000 Negro members in its ranks; and a third group of 500,000 members included no Negroes.[33]

As noted by Dubois, white workers in the South and also to a large extent in the North did not favor the organizing of Negroes. It placed both unions and the federation in a serious dilemma. For example, the appointment of a colored organizer for the southern states by the Carpenters' Union "aroused considerable uneasiness among some of our local unions in the South, and numerous communications have recently reached the General Office either cautioning against any attempt to organize the colored men of our craft or opposition to the appointment altogether on racial grounds. . . . Prejudice on these lines has no standing in the labor movement, and we cannot consistently deny admittance in our organization to any man because he belongs to the African race."[34] Yet, Negro workers were being systematically excluded from locals of the Carpenters' Union at the time the head of the international strongly opposed the policy of discrimination.

As its numbers and organizations increased, the principle of autonomy became the shield which protected the internationals following an exclusionary policy against Negroes. The federation felt itself powerless to compel changes in the racial policy of affiliated Internationals. The operating crafts on the railroads never admitted Negroes and were not members of the federation, and fear that attempts at compulsion might force a large number of organizations outside the AFL was ever present. Not being able to compel, the federation believed that it would be better to organize excluded Negro workers into directly chartered organizations until a change in racial policy by particular internationals took place.

The internationals faced the same problem with their locals. The Secretary-treasurer of the Painters' Union told Gompers that a union of white men in Augusta, Georgia, wanted the international to compel a Negro local to surrender its charter, and that such trouble had existed in that city for some time, although "the negro is the best union man."[35]

The labor movement was not only neglecting to organize Negro workers, but it was following a deliberate policy of exclusion of Negroes from many jobs.[36] Booker T. Washington expressed resentment at the practices of organized labor, and Gompers again explained the necessity for the organization of Negro and white workers. But the Negro frequently was unable to follow such logic. No one could pry open the doors of the internationals practicing a "white only" policy.[37]

NORTHWARD MIGRATION

In the three-year period following the outbreak of World War I in Europe, more than 400,000 Negroes left the South for jobs in northern industry. One of the reasons which made the migration possible was the shortage of labor after the virtual shutdown of immigration as a result of the efforts of European governments to retain their potential soldiers and workers within their own boundaries.[38] Movement was inspired by more attractive wages and working conditions prevailing in the North. Labor agents who had gone South found the area at first indifferent to the labor losses, but this attitude gave way to deep concern. Licenses for labor recruiters became difficult to obtain, and labor agents were harassed and prevented from carrying on their tasks. Several southern states tried complete suppression of labor agents. Thousands of Negroes entered the steel mills, meat-packing plants, found work on railroad right-of-ways, and in many other industries. Resentment against the migrants aroused by fear that they would "seize" jobs belonging to the white men was not long in making its appearance.[39]

Requests for Organizing

The influx of thousands of Negro workers into northern industrial areas created many problems for the new arrivals. Coming usually from an agricultural background, the Negro carried the feeling of indifference or hostility, shared by his white counterpart, against organized labor. In addition, he was more easily intimidated, possessed fewer resources, was more dependent upon the white employer, had virtually no knowledge or contact with union organizations, and was finally a victim of discrimination by white unionists. All of these factors made the Negro more susceptible to strikebreaking than white workers. Such an attitude was not, as has been proven, a permanent one, but the employment of large numbers of Negro strikebreakers in the wave of post-World War I labor disputes exacerbated the feeling of hostility between the races. John Fitzpatrick, chairman of the National Committee for Organizing Iron and Steel Workers, made up of twenty-four AFL unions, estimated that approximately 30,000 Negro strikebreakers worked in the 1919 steel strike. He feared that if this continued, the industrial centers "are bound to be paralyzed by race riots. . . . As I find it the Northern Negro is alive to the situation and cannot be used to any great extent, but the Southern Negro is brutally exploited and has no real knowledge of the situation in which he is being used."[40]

But Negroes interpreted events to mean that greater effort to organize colored workers had to be made by the labor movement. The 1917 convention referred such a resolution to Gompers and Secretary Frank Morrison for action, but nothing came of it.[41] More important was the meeting of a group of distinguished Negro workers headed by R. R. Morton of the Tuskegee Institute and members of the executive council. Gompers denied that discrimination was practiced against any group of workers by the AFL. Technically the statement was true, but it begged the real issue. Gompers did not regard the issuance of separate charters as a sign of discrimination, but a method forced upon the federation by the necessities of establishing some kind of organization among southern colored workers. He said that he had never liked this method and conceded it was not desirable, but he insisted that unless separate charters were given to colored trade and federal labor unions and to city central bodies, there would not be any unions in the South. He described some of the problems of maintaining a voluntary federation and said it could not get too far ahead of its member unions.[42]

The exchange of views did not lead to much progress, and at the next convention several resolutions calling for more vigorous efforts to organize colored workers were introduced. A complaint of the lack of representation given colored freight handlers by the Brotherhood of Railway Clerks was also made. An even more significant resolution called for the chartering of an international to organize colored labor "or to use its influence to have them chartered from the International Union having jurisdiction over them."[43]

At the 1920 AFL convention the question of exclusion of Negro workers by a constitutional prohibition against their admittance by an international union was raised by a resolution. An attempt was made to have the Brotherhood of Railway Clerks eliminate a "white only" clause from its constitution. Gompers and Morrison had participated at a meeting with the union and urged a change. But none was made. The resolutions' committee did not show much sympathy with compelling affiliates to change their racial clauses. The delegates were told:

The resolution asks that we decide who is eligible to admission to a national organization affiliated with the A.F. of L. The committee has not that authority, the Executive Council has not that authority, and the convention has not that authority. That authority rests only with the national and international unions. The committee and the Executive Council wish to see the colored men organized. We reaffirm the action taken at the last convention, that if a national or international refuses to accept colored workers the American Federation of Labor will grant them charters.[44]

The resolutions' committee was overruled, and an amendment that the Brotherhood of Railway Clerks remove the "white only" clause be stricken from its constitution was adopted. The convention also directed the calling of a conference of unions with jurisdictions employing Negro workers for the purpose of devising an organizing program.

Efforts were made by Gompers to have the resolutions of the conventions carried out. He wrote to the unions having clauses in their constitutions, conferred with their officers, and addressed their conventions. The view of Martin F. Ryan, the general president of the Brotherhood of Railway Carmen, a union excluding Negroes from membership, clearly indicates the dilemma of the leaders of the movement. Gompers wrote three letters to the Brotherhood of Railway Carmen on the subject of discrimination against the Negro and the action of the AFL before he received an answer. Ryan was "very much in favor of the adoption by our Brotherhood of some plan or scheme that would admit the negro to membership."[45]

He submitted a strong recommendation to the union's convention for opening the rolls to Negro workers, and the issue occupied more time of the delegates than any other. Ryan went on to say "that it matters not what views I or others may hold concerning the question of admitting negroes to membership . . . the members of the Brotherhood of Railway Carmen of America will not under any circumstances agree to organize them except under certain conditions, and that by barely a constitutional vote."[46] The clause adopted after so much effort, including a personal plea to the delegates from Gompers, was one permitting the organizing of colored workers into separate lodges which were to be under "the jurisdiction of the nearest white local."[47]

A considerable increase in the employment of Negro workers took place on the railroads during the strike of shopmen in 1922.

The six railway shopcrafts agreed with the AFL Executive Council that colored mechanics, helpers, and laborers would be allowed to become members of the International Brotherhood of Firemen and Oilers, and the respective crafts would negotiate for the colored workers in their trade. The federation was requested to transfer federal labor unions of Negro railroad workers in the mechanical trades to the Firemen and Oilers. Both Bert M. Jewell, head of the Railway Employees' Department, and Gompers stressed the temporary character of the arrangement and asked that whenever unions changed their policies with regard to admitting Negro workers they be allowed to claim members of their craft in the Firemen's and Oilers' Union.[48]

Resolutions requesting greater emphasis upon the organization of Negro workers were introduced annually at AFL conventions in the 1920's. In March 1926, T. Arnold Hill of the Department of Industrial Relations of the National Urban League and Rienzi B. Lemus, the head of the Grand Council of Dining Car Employees, requested the executive council to show more energy in organizing Negro workers. Appointment of a Negro, preferably one affiliated with the trade union movement as a special organizer to head the program, was suggested. The council referred the matter to President William Green.[49] The Trade Union Committee for Organizing Negro Workers was formed at this time in New York City, with Frank R. Crosswaith as chairman, but it died after a short existence for lack of support.

PULLMAN PORTERS

A small group of Negro employees of the Pullman Company established the Brotherhood of Sleeping Car Porters in New York City on August 25, 1925. A. Philip Randolph was invited to address the group, and he became its first organizer.[50] In Randolph, the Porters' Union selected a man of unusual eloquence, one who was to devote almost forty years to eliminating overt and tacit discrimination by unions against Negro workers and to enlarging Negro employment opportunities in industry. Randolph was born in Florida, in 1889, and was educated at City College of New York. He had worked in his native state, and he well knew the problems and aspirations of Negro labor. A founder with Chandler Owen of the *Messenger,* a magazine promoting socialism and trade unionism, Randolph became after a few years the leading spokesman on trade union matters among the Negro people. Courageous and tenacious, he did not allow the fact that his organization was small in numbers to stifle his annual demands at AFL conventions for the abolition of unfairness against Negro workers. His fine presence, courtesy, and loyalty to the AFL, as well as his moving eloquence, gave Randolph great moral power. More than any single man he has been responsible for the formal ending of discrimination by a number of unions. Randolph followed the Gompers' tradition of always demanding "more and more" equality for the Negro worker, and he will never be satisfied until it is completely achieved. Despite occasional public criticism of his demands by white trade unionists, Randolph has the respect of the entire labor movement, and he and Willard Townsend were the first Negroes to serve on the highest body of the labor movement, when they were elected to the executive council of the AFL-CIO at the merger convention in 1955.

After some difficulty over the claims of the Hotel and Restaurant Workers' Union, the executive council decided to allow Pullman porters to join federal labor unions. There were some mild objections from Edward Flore, the president of the Hotel and Restaurant Employees' Union, but the convention approved their admission.[51] In 1936 a national charter was given to the Brotherhood of Sleeping Car Porters.

DISCRIMINATION

The issue of discrimination which had first arisen at the conventions in the period during and after World War I became more important with time. The discussions at AFL conventions might be divided into three periods. In the early years of the AFL, the opposition to this practice came from those white delegates who believed that trade union membership should be opened to all wage earners. Beginning in the years of World War I, resolutions critical of discrimination were introduced by delegates from federal labor unions. But a more aggressive note is struck in the resolutions on the subject at the 1934 convention, and it marked a new phase of the struggle for equal treatment by Negro labor. A resolution demanded that the AFL expel international unions guilty of practicing discrimination. It was not adopted but the convention authorized for the first time the appointment of a committee by the president to investigate and report to the next convention on the issue.[52]

A committee of five was appointed and held meetings, but its majority report was not adopted by the AFL. One member, Jerry Hanks of the Barber's Union, opposed any action, on the ground that the problem antedated the forming of the AFL.[53] Thomas C. Carroll of the Brotherhood of Maintenance of Way Employees and another member of the committee believed that discrimination was a problem of educating the trade unionist. He was opposed to any action that would compel international unions to change their practices, for it would "first be necessary to amend the constitution and by-laws of the A.F. of L. and take from its component organizations the self-autonomy guaranteed them."[54]

John Brophy, who was chairman of the committee, was dissatisfied with the attitude of the executive council. He claimed that the formal presentation of the committee was suppressed and that "in denying us the opportunity to report completely nullified the committee's work."[55] Brophy charged that the committee was merely a "face-saving" device used by the executive council to hide its own desire for maintenance of the status quo on race matters.

Four members of the committee urged the elimination of bars against Negro members by affiliated unions, and those who refused were to be denied representation at AFL conventions. Newly chartered unions would be forbidden to include racially discriminating clauses in their constitutions and would be required to conform to "oft-repeated declarations of A.F. of L. conventions on equality of treatment of all races within the trade union movement."[56] The executive council did not publish or approve the above views. It merely noted that the "report of the Committee indicates that there are a few National and International Unions that deny membership to Negroes."[57] Since every union is autonomous, the council argued, "the welfare of the negro worker will be best served by a campaign of education of white workers to bring to them the necessity of solidarity in the ranks of the workers and the voluntary elimination of all restrictions against full rights of membership to the negro."[58]

The issue was discussed by a number of delegates. The principle of autonomy was invoked, and the AFL's powerlessness to compel changes asserted.

It was undoubtedly true the federation could not compel internationals to change their constitutions, but the affiliates were not completely oblivious to persuasion and pressure. Randolph, by publicly revealing the prejudice of organizations which were themselves suppliants for rights, not only showed their contradictory and unconscionable conduct, but compelled the leaders of the federation as well as the heads of the unions to seek changes. Organizing Negro workers, denied membership by an international, into an AFL federal labor union was not a satisfactory method. The fact that grievances would be handled by white locals meant there was no direct way for Negro workers to ask for rectification of anomalies or injustice. Moreover, the federation did not organize a particular group of workers into federal labor unions without clearing the matter with the international union; this policy was followed even when the matter concerned an unaffiliated organization whose jurisdiction the AFL recognized. Negro railroad firemen, denied admission by the Brotherhood of Railroad Firemen and Enginemen, sought an AFL charter. President D. H. Robertson of the Firemen's Union refused to approve. He blandly claimed that the brotherhood protected the "interests of colored firemen. . . . These men are not promoted to positions of locomotive engineers, with the result that as time goes on they become senior firemen and in order that there may be no discrimination against white men, agreements have ben negotiated to limit the exercise of rights by colored firemen." This arrangement, Robertson claimed, "is not always satisfactory to the negroes and we have experienced some difficulty as a result of their efforts to have these agreements set aside by the courts. Our difficulties in this respect will increase if the A.F. of L. follows the organizing plan outlined in your communication. I hope, therefore, that the charters will not be granted."[59]

The letter is perhaps the best criticism of the policy of organizing separate federal locals. Robertson's objection is, moreover, that the AFL would make possible more effective protection of the Negro workers' jobs. The U.S. Supreme Court in *Steele* v. *Louisville and Nashville R.R.*, 323 U.S. 192 (1944), found the practice of the Firemen's Union improper.

The CIO

The formation of the CIO as a permanent federation in 1938 created a labor center where formal discrimination by the international unions was absent. No affiliate of the CIO excluded Negroes or other minorities by constitutional provision, tacit consent of locals, or established segregated local unions of minorities. Among the unions using the above devices to exclude Negroes from membership in 1940 not one was affiliated with the CIO.[60]

The CIO was created largely by the funds and leadership of unions that had no racial provisions in their constitutions. Negroes have been members of the United Mine Workers of America since its inception. The International Ladies' Garment Workers' Union and the Amalgamated Clothing Workers of America, the other two major organizations which launched the CIO, had many Negro members in their ranks.

The CIO unions as a rule were not made up of large numbers of skilled workers who underwent a relatively long apprenticeship training. Unions in the mass-production industries, to be effective, had to welcome all workers. The automobile and steel industries, for example, employed large numbers of Negro workers and attempts to exclude them from union membership would have been fatal to successful organizing campaigns. The workers in the industries that the CIO sought to organize had worked alongside Negro workers. Another factor was the spirit of the times and the leadership of the CIO.

The CIO unions did not close their books or restrict members by other means. Nor did they exercise the kind of monopoly in their labor markets enjoyed by some of the craft organizations. Consequently, exclusion would not be an effective method for gaining more employment for white members, and the industries had already decided the question of employment of Negroes before the unionization campaigns began.

AFL affiliates gradually removed their racial clauses, but complaints against discrimination by locals continued to be charged at conventions of the federation. Leading the fight for action, Randolph declared he was aware that the AFL as such did not discriminate and that his attacks were leveled at a number of affiliated unions.[61]

Fair Employment Practice

As a result of the increased demand for equal employment opportunities, and the threat of a march upon Washington, led by A. Philip Randolph, more attention was given to fair employment opportunities by government. The President's Committee on Fair Employment Practices (FEPC) was created in 1941, with representatives of the AFL and CIO on the committee. Addressing the 1941 convention, when fair employment practice was discussed, Milton P. Webster of the Brotherhood of Sleeping Car Porters, denied that AFL unions were the only ones guilty of racial discrimination. "We have found," he said, "as much discrimination in fact more, in those that are not American Federation of Labor Unions. As a matter of fact, the question of discrimination against Negroes, and that is the largest problem the committee has to deal with, is no respector of organization. Even those company unions have taken the same attitude; so have some of the CIO Unions and some of the American Federation of Labor Unions, and probably the greatest offender is the Railroad Brotherhoods."[62]

The CIO repeatedly condemned racial discrimination, and it also set up the CIO Committee To Abolish Racial Discrimination with James Carey as chairman and Willard S. Townsend as secretary. In its first two years of operation, the committee organized seventy-one local committees dealing with this question. It also published a considerable amount of literature and sought to develop acceptance of an enlightened racial policy.[63] In addition, a number of the CIO unions established departments dealing with fair employment practices and antidiscrimination. One of the more active was the one operated by the United Automobile Workers, headed by Walter Reuther and William H. Oliver.[64] Both the AFL and the CIO supported fair employment practices legislation before Congress and tried to rally their locals behind it.[65]

The Merged Federation

The merged federation declared that among its purposes was one "to encourage all workers without regard to race, creed, color, national origin or ancestry to share equally in the full benefits of union organization."[66] The Standing Committee on Civil Rights was vested "with the duty and responsibility to assist the Executive Council to bring about at the earliest date the effective implementation of the principle . . . of non-discrimination."[67] The issue came to the surface again when a resolution was presented asking the expulsion of the Brotherhood of Railroad Trainmen and the Brotherhood of Locomotive Firemen and Enginemen because they "exclude Negroes from Membership in their constitutions which constitute a violation of the letter and spirit of the Constitution of the American Federation of Labor and Congress of Industrial Organizations."[68] The resolutions' committee recommended that the AFL-CIO Executive Council seek compliance at the earliest date with the AFL-CIO constitution.

Randolph sharply criticized the practices of these two unions and rightfully claimed that Negro railroad workers were subject to severe discrimination. Agreeing with many of Randolph's criticisms, Meany pointed to the fact that the present officers of the two unions, in contrast to their predecessors, were opposed to the color bar and were seeking its removal from their unions' constitutions. Meany insisted that progress had been made. When he "became Secretary-Treasurer of the AFL on January 1, 1940, there were more than 20 unions in the AFL at that time that had a color bar in their constitutions. By constant work, year in and year out, led mainly by President Bill Green—and he never let up on this issue, he never let up on a union that had the color bar in its constitution, and he never advocated throwing it out to compel them to eliminate the color bar."[69] All of the unions referred to by Meany had removed the color bar, for the organizations against which the complaint had been filed were not members of the AFL in 1940.

At the 1961 AFL-CIO convention Randolph demanded that steps be taken to abolish racial discrimination in unions whether it be by constitutional exclusion, ritual or tacit agreement, the abolition of racially segregated locals irrespective of the wishes of the members and wipe out barriers to the Negroes' participation in apprenticeship training programs. Randolph also called for desegregation of southern city central labor bodies and integration of Negro trade unionists in departments and staffs of the federation, international unions, and other central bodies. He asked for greater representation of Negroes on committees dealing with civil rights, and the adoption of a Code of Fair Trade Union Racial Practices.[70] A comprehensive resolution urging equal treatment of minorities was adopted. Randolph claimed that it did not go far enough, but that he would accept the statement as the best one that can be obtained. He expressed the view that if earnest and vigorous efforts were made to carry out the resolves, progress in equal treatment would be made under the steps outlined in Resolution No. 143.[71]

Most Negro trade unionists wanted a more forceful policy against unions which practiced discrimination, and leaders of the federation found no way in which they could eliminate, at once, separate racial locals, especially in those instances where such a policy was favored by Negro workers. In fact, to some extent, the present federation faces the dilemma of the old AFL: how to compel autonomous unions to adopt an enlightened racial policy. The attitude of the federation is that this type of question cannot be solved by the use of compulsion, for many unions would rather disaffiliate than give up their southern members. This issue involves more than a loss of per capita income because the expulsion of southern memberships, for many unions, would be a serious weakening of their bargaining power. While the federation cannot basically compel, it can use its influence, persuasion, and pressure to gain more equal treatment for the Negro.

Charges of bad faith or failure to carry out instructions of conventions are likely to lead to explosive situations, and in the discussion on segregated locals at the 1959 convention, Meany told Randolph he was not the only representative of Negro labor.[72] This statement was blown up quite beyond its significance. Meany had the right to express his views, for he more than anyone else was the spokesman for American trade unionists. He had never been guilty of advocating or practicing discrimination.[73]

Negro American Labor Council

In an attempt to promote elimination of racial discrimination within the labor movement and elsewhere, almost one thousand delegates established the Negro American Labor Council at the first convention in Detroit, May 28-31, 1960. A. Philip Randolph was named chairman, and an executive board and other officers were chosen.[74]

Some of the leaders pointed out the United Hebrew Trades, organized in 1888 in New York City, as a model. It was largely interested, however, in bringing the Jewish immigrant workers into the trade union movement so that they might develop an instrument for improving conditions of work.[75] Many trade unions were grateful for the assistance rendered by the United Hebrew Trades in organizing the immigrant Jewish workers, but others were indifferent. The United Hebrew Trades organized locals of Jewish building tradesmen, bakery workers, shoemakers, and other trades. Eventually, the locals were turned over to the International unions having jurisdiction in the particular crafts, many of which displayed little enthusiasm for the new recruits.[76]

The problem facing the Negro American Labor Council is not the organizing of Negro workers, but compelling unions to eliminate discrimination in entry, employment, and promotion of Negro workers in as far as they are controlled by the organizations of labor. While Jewish and other immigrant workers also faced prejudice and suspicion within the trade union movement, it was likely to be of more temporary duration.

One of the interesting by-products of this controversy is the charge that the International Ladies' Garment Workers' Union and the United Steelworkers of America are guilty of racial bias and discrimination. It would require considerable evidence, in view of the past attitude of these organizations, to prove such charges. The manner and the conditions under which the charges were published raises questions of their credibility. The charge against the Steelworkers involved a local union in Atlanta, Georgia, and the general counsel of the National Labor Relations Board found "far from encouraging or even tolerating discriminatory working conditions, had in fact utilized its bargaining strength to the end of eliminating existing disparity." A specific charge against the Garment Workers' Local 10 of cutters was dismissed, on May 17, 1963.[77]

The other charges against the Ladies' Garment Workers' Union are not based upon specific practices or actual evidence, but upon the constitutional requirements for holding office within that union. According to the testimony of Mr. Herbert Hill before the House Labor and Education Committee, on August 17, 1962, a business agent was sent to Puerto Rico in order to deprive the union members of the island of the opportunity to represent themselves. But this is a common practice in the union and is not used against any group. Business agents are sent to communities on the mainland. Mr. Hill objects to limiting political caucuses to three months before conventions. This rule applies to all groups in the union, and why it is a device to disenfranchise on racial grounds is not at all clear. Mr. Hill calls this an "incredible denial of democratic rights." It is no such thing, and if Mr. Hill were acquainted with the subject he would know that this provision is more liberal than those found in most unions. Even if this limitation is unfair or improper, it has no reference to racial discrimination. By the way, it was first included as a check upon Communist caucuses. Virtually all labor organizations discourage the existence of factions and caucuses, and it has no relationship to racial questions. Nor is the objection to the qualifications needed for election to the office of vice-president valid. Such an officer is responsible for managing locals and joint boards with thousands of members and administering contracts involving millions of dollars in wage payment. No effort was made to examine the duties of the office and evaluate the qualifications on that basis. It is especially unfortunate that the charges were made against a union and labor officials who have sought greater opportunities and rights for Negro workers.

Even when international officers are opposed, racial discrimination is likely to be practiced on a local level. Complaints against the discriminatory practices of some unions—mainly in the skilled trades—are undoubtedly valid. The Negro has been the chief sufferer from such policies. Many of these organizations are highly selective and admit only a small percentage of white applicants. Usually successful applicants are related to members or are recommended by clergymen, politicians, or others of influence. As a result, Negroes and other racial minorities are likely to be excluded, or at least few will be admitted. The skilled unions control, to a large degree, the apprenticed trades and the Negro has difficulty in being accepted for training.[78] Whatever may be the reason, the creation of a barrier to training means that the Negro will be permanently debarred, or at least impeded, in moving up the occupational ladder. As many Negro families cannot afford protracted and expensive higher education for their children, the denial of an opportunity to learn a trade means permanent consignment to the unskilled and semi-skilled labor categories, with the resultant loss of income to the individual and society. The limited control which even the best-intentioned union officers can exercise in eliminating discrimination, especially in trades which are not expanding or in areas where jobs are in short supply, means that discrimination can only be handled through fair employment practices legislation. Even with such a law on the statute books, effective enforcement is exceedingly difficult. The labor movement and its constituent unions can make a contribution to a fair and equal job policy, but pressure by government is needed to support the efforts of the leaders of labor. Those who place the blame on the leadership and exculpate the rank and file are not facing up to the realities. The members rather than the leaders, as was shown at the 1963 convention of the Brotherhood of Firemen and Enginemen and in many others in the past, are the most guilty of discrimination and anxious to continue such a policy. A fair employment practice act will help to make discrimination less effective and make it easier for the enlightened members and leaders to succeed. It would be an illusion to believe that fair employment practice can be established overnight. The Negroes' plea is just and the remedies are long overdue, but discriminatory job practices require long and patient effort. Demonstrations may be effective in calling attention to inequality and "triggering" remedial action, but the establishment of more just and humane standards requires a long, stubborn, detailed campaign. When picketing becomes a way of life, the objectives are sometimes lost in the emotional satisfaction of engaging in a noble enterprise. The just demands of the Negro can be attained much easier with the support of the labor movement, for Negro workers also need the protection of organized labor. Access to union hiring halls would mean that Negro craftsmen would have equal opportunity for employment, but in many skilled crafts the employer has the unquestioned right to discharge. In seeking to widen the opportunities for Negro workers, the problems facing the unions and particular industries will have to be given consideration.

CHAPTER 51

Violence and Improper Activities

THE LOUISVILLE AND NASHVILLE STRIKE

The strike on the Louisville and Nashville Railroad and seven allied lines was the largest railroad walkout since the shopmen's strike of 1922; it involved 24,000 workers in the thirteen-state railway system. On May 22, 1953, the nonoperating organizations served notice under Section 6 of the Railway Labor Act, proposing improved vacations, paid holidays, premium pay for Sunday work, group life insurance, hospitalization, and surgical and medical payments for employees and their families financed by the carriers. The demands moved through the normal routines provided under the Railway Labor Act, including the emergency board procedures. When the unions found the recommendations of the emergency board unsatisfactory, conferences were initiated on May 14, 1954, to work out more acceptable arrangements. An agreement was reached on August 21, 1954, but several railroads withdrew from the Southeastern Conference Committee and refused to accept the terms agreed upon by the remainder of the carriers.

The Louisville and Nashville Railroad and its affiliated roads rejected the proposed contributory health and welfare arrangement under which each employee would contribute $3.40 a month and the carrier an equal amount. They also would not accept the plan to purchase a life insurance policy equal to the annual earnings of each employee with a minimum of $3,500, and a third week's vacation for employees with at least fifteen years of service.

Failure to find an acceptable formula led to a strike. It began on the Louisville and Nashville, the North Carolina and St. Louis, and the Clinchfield Railroad on March 14 and was extended two days later to the Atlanta Joint Terminals, Atlanta and West Point Railroad, Western Railroad of Alabama, Augusta Union Station, and the Georgia Railroad. Operating unions honored the picket lines. The carriers announced that unless the engineers, firemen, brakemen, conductors, and switchmen returned to their jobs by March 23, they would be dismissed. Injunctions were sought in the state courts; strikebreakers were hired in an effort to operate the roads; and a considerable amount of violence took place. One picket was killed, and a number of other pickets were seriously injured. The governors of the states in the affected areas, meeting on April 19, urged arbitration. The National Mediation Board was active in trying to find a basis for settlement.

The company charged widespread vandalism, arson, and destruction of property; and the unions countered by pointing to assaults and the running down of pickets by strikebreakers in automobiles and other threats against the unions. Finally, through the efforts of the National Mediation Board, the fifty-seven-day strike was ended on May 9. Striking employees were to return to work, without discrimination; the conditions governing holiday pay and vacations accepted by other carriers were to be effective on the Louisville and Nashville Railroad; and Francis J. Robertson, an attorney with a practice in Washington, D.C., was appointed neutral referee to decide all unsettled issues. Each side was given two days to present its evidence, and the decision was rendered on May 19.

The award, released through the National Mediation Board, required the Louisville and Nashville Railroad and its subsidiaries to pay the full-cost hospital, medical, and surgical benefits. The referee justified the decision on the grounds that the earnings of the carriers involved were better than they had been on May 15, 1954, when the emergency board recommended fifty-fifty sharing of costs of the above benefits. He also claimed that the placing of the entire costs upon the employer was in harmony with the growing practice in industry. The unalterable opposition of the carrier to a compulsory plan requiring deductions of wages left the referee no alternative.[1]

SOUTHERN BELL TELEPHONE STRIKE

The violence that surrounded the Louisville and Nashville Railroad strike was in many respects a throwback to an earlier period. Prior to the New Deal, telephone workers had a spotty history of organization. Local and regional organizations of telephone workers were founded, but not until the late 1940's was a national organization, the Communications Workers of America, founded. Initially, the association was organized into thirty-nine divisions, and President Joseph Beirne wanted a more unified organization. The telephone company refused to bargain on a countrywide basis.[2]

In 1953 the Communications Workers of America faced a serious and successful test. It conducted a fifty-nine-day strike against the Indiana Bell Telephone Company that cost the union $450,000. At the same time, a six-week strike against the Western Electric Company cost $215,000.[3] An even more stubborn dispute took place at the Buffalo plant of the Western Electric Company in the following year. The strike over seniority started on June 17 and lasted for 146 days. The Communications Workers Association announced that only about one-half of the striking members drew on the strike fund. Estimates were that the strike cost about $145,000.[4]

These bitterly contested walkouts were only a curtain raiser for the most extensive labor dispute in the history of the telephone industry. Started on March 14, 1955, against the Southern Bell Telephone Company, the strike affected 45,000 workers in nine southeastern states. The CIO Executive Board pledged $1,250,000 for aid.[5] The main issue in dispute was a no-strike, no-lockout clause, as well as the exclusion of certain issues from arbitration. On April 15, 22,000 steelworkers in Birmingham, Alabama, went out on a one-day sympathy strike. After 72 days the strike was settled.

While the strikers gained a weekly wage increase from $1.00 to $4.00, the company succeeded in gaining final authority on disputes over benefit plans, leaves of absence, compliance with health and safety measures, and demotions during the trial period. Legitimate picket lines could be recognized by employees of the company without penalty.[6] It was the longest strike in any operating company of the Bell system. Beirne credited the favorable outcome to the support of members of the union in the Western Electric plants for respecting the picket lines and to the financial assistance given by AFL and CIO affiliates.

Although the strikers began returning to work on May 24, the company charged the members of the Communications Workers of America with being guilty of gross vandalism and sued for $5 million. W. A. Smallwood, the union's southern director, denied the charges and claimed that the suit was a violation of the "back-to-work" agreement between the parties. "The company," he claimed, "is trying to harass and punish striking workers who had the courage to stand up for their convictions."[7]

The agreement brought with it one of the largest arbitrations in the history of American labor disputes. Involved were the jobs of 245 workers who had been discharged for misconduct during the walkout. Four arbitrators had been selected, and they met as a group (en banc) and decided on procedural rules after which single arbitrators held hearings in the localities where the misconduct took place. Arbitrators were empowered to sustain, set aside, or modify the penalty and to order back pay. On May

18, 1956, the company announced that in the 200 out of 245 cases that had gone to arbitration, 43 discharges had been upheld and another 18 had not been contested by the union. Among the remaining 139 cases, 52 had been reinstated with full back pay and 86 suffered some loss of pay and were reinstated by the company without arbitration.[8] About $200,000 in back pay was granted. Four members of the union were also convicted of conspiracy to destroy company property. Finally, the union settled the company's suit for $5 million by paying $315,000, presumably to compensate for the physical damage during the strike.[9]

IMPROPER ACTIVITIES

The investigation by the Select Committee on Improper Activities in the Labor Management Field called attention to corruption and malfeasance by officers of a number of unions. The committee, under the chairmanship of Senator John L. McLellan, functioned from February 1957 until September 1959 and publicized the misdeeds of a number of labor organizations and their officers. From the point of view of its effect upon the views of the public and legislation by Congress, the investigation may be regarded as the most important labor event, aside from the merger of the AFL and the CIO, in the 1950's.

Although the committee called attention to the existence of unconscionable abuses of power, its revelations touched relatively few labor organizations. Even those unions that were shown to have abused their obligations and trust could claim that only a few of the subordinate units were affected; and where the top officers appeared to be or were proven guilty of malfeasance, many locals could claim they were innocent of the slightest wrongdoing. The revelations themselves, while they demonstrated serious violations of members' rights and fiduciary trust, did not provide many new insights into the nature and causes of labor racketeering. The voluminous evidence confirmed that corruption tended to be largely confined to industries where it had existed over the years. Building construction, the service trades, longshoring, the clothing industries, trucking, and a number of others remained, as they had before the 1950's, the centers of the disease.

Complaints of improper dealing and extortion by union officers, mainly in the building trades, were made before the U.S. Industrial Commission at the turn of the century. The activities of Sam Parks, Martin (Skinny) Madden, Robert Brindell, Louis Lepke, George Scalise, Joseph Fay, Willie Bioff, George Browne, and a host of others have been documented by a number of writers.[10] Early in the history of the AFL the problem was recognized. Gompers warned against corrupt individuals, and the 1898 convention of the AFL considered charges against the officers of the Hotel and Restaurant Employees' International Union and Bartenders' International League. Complaints were also received against the officers of the Retail Clerks' National Protective Association, and the federation appointed committees to seek to eliminate the conditions in these organizations.[11] But the AFL was unable to intervene in the internal affairs of its affiliates, especially against the more powerful ones. In fact, the leaders knew no way they could impose standards of rectitude, and they thereby took the position that nothing could be done about such matters. Such an attitude came from a recognition of the realities of the situation. Most of the time, corruption affected a particular local, and even the heads of the international might refuse to intervene if they believed that interference might cause internal friction. As for the AFL, its attitude of nonintervention, which was largely the result of lack of power, was subsequently supported by the principle of trade autonomy.

The attitude of the AFL is illustrated by the testimony of Gompers before the New York Joint Legislative Committee to investigate building construction costs after World War I. The committee headed by Senator George P. Lockwood found that the head of the Building Trades Council of New York City, Robert R. Brindell, was guilty of extortion and of selling strike insurance.[12] The investigation showed that labor was only one group mulcting the public through a series of carefully designed monopoly practices. According to the Lockwood investigation, there were "combinations between the manufacturers and the dealers; between producers and manufacturers; between dealers and unions of workingmen, so that the whole industrial and commercial system in the industries connected with building construction is riveted in an interwoven criss-cross . . . under the incubus of a pyramid of combinations extending from the workingmen and retailers and reaching its apex in the original producer."[13]

The committee also noted that some unions had gone to the "extreme length of agreeing not to furnish union labor to any employer who [was] not [a] member of the association and [were] permitting the members of the Employers' Associations to charge exorbitant profits."[14] Although the unions were a strategic factor in the monopoly, for their power to withhold labor was a powerful weapon against recalcitrants, it nevertheless remains true that labor was only one part of a larger conspiracy. Nor were the practices in New York unique. A legislative committee looking into the Illinois building construction industry during the same period described the object of a number of employer associations as "the regulation of prices and their apportionment of orders."[15] Commenting on the power of the contractors' associations, the report noted: "In most instances the combines exercised complete control over the line of work, even to the extent of designating a contractor who should do the work. A member about to bid upon a particular piece of work was required to report that fact to the Association. . . . In this connection the agreements with the different labor organizations resulted in the virtual exclusion of any contractor not a member of the Association, from doing work in Chicago. Business agents of the labor organizations enforced a fulfillment of the agreement upon members of their organizations," who were not allowed to work for anyone not belonging to the contractors' association.[16]

It is obvious that in these situations the unions are only part of a larger conspiracy. There are, however, instances where the corrupt business agent performs no illicit service for the employer; he uses the union as an instrument of self-enrichment by illicit acts. Since the amounts paid to a corrupt union official are regarded as a cost of doing business, the union member foregoes the sum paid to his officer, or he is likely to obtain a lower amount of employment. Consequently, there can be no defense of corruption even from the narrow point of view of the worker's self interest. Yet the situations in which the union officer is part of a larger combination and where he merely uses the union's power for extortion must be distinguished. Although the latter practice is also observable in the building construction industry, it is more clearly revealed in the activities of William Bioff and George E. Browne of the International Alliance of Theatrical Employees, who were engaged on behalf of themselves and the Criminal Capone syndicate of Chicago in large-scale extortion which netted them millions of dollars.[17]

The AFL took note of public outcries against misuse of union office, and the 1932 convention recognized that there was ground for improvement within the labor movement. It noted that criminals had invaded some organizations of labor. The convention protested this intrusion, but suggested no steps for expulsion.[18] Even though the federation failed to denounce corruption within the labor movement, President William Green tried to prod the heads of unions into action. Green called the attention of President P. J. Morrin of the Iron Workers' Union to the acceptance by the union's New Jersey representative, Theodore L. Brandle, of $10,000 from the Iron League of New Jersey. He asked Morrin to take action "to safeguard the integrity, the good name and standing of your own International Union, as well as the organized labor movement."[19] Later, Green again asked for action against Brandle, although he noted that "you have the power to deal with this case of Brother Brandle to which I am calling your attention, and neither the Executive Council nor any other International Union has any authority to do so. It is clearly a matter of your meeting responsibility and exercising authority conferred upon you."[20] Eventually, Brandle and four others were expelled from the International Association.[21]

The AFL also deputized Edward McGrady to investigate the activities of Sam Kaplan, the head of the Motion Picture Operators in New York. Edward McGrady found that Kaplan was an employer who manufactured moving picture machine supplies and who employed labor, that his salary had been increased from $250 in 1926 to $21,800 in 1928. McGrady further found that Kaplan received, in addition, presents from Motion Picture Local No. 306 of $10,000 and $20,000 during this two-year period. Another charge was that he ran his business on a nonunion basis. In asking for action against Kaplan, Green recognized that the federation lacked "authority to interfere in the internal affairs of a local union or an international or national organization. On the other hand, the Council is clothed with authority to administer and direct the affairs of the American Federation of Labor between conventions and to guard jealously the welfare of labor. The good name, the honor and the integrity of the organized labor movement must be protected and preserved if our organization is to live."[22]

Kaplan was eventually eliminated, but the International Alliance of State Employees and Moving Picture Operators of the United States and Canada became involved in a much greater scandal when the union was seized in 1933 by gangsters acting through a group of faithless officers. Nor could the problem of racketeering within the labor movement be exorcised by fair words and good intentions. It must be recognized, however, that organizations were sometimes themselves victims of criminal elements. The cry of alarm of the Illinois Federation of Labor emphasized the dangers the labor movement of that state faced in the early 1930's. Gangsters, deprived of their chief source of income by the repeal of the prohibition upon the manufacture and sale of alcoholic beverages, turned to the labor unions to recoup their losses. The labor movement pleaded for assistance against this menace and explained:

The gangster menace particularly in the metropolitan area of Cook County, has reached a stage which seriously endangers the future of some of the organizations connected with the Illinois Federation of Labor and which calls for defensive action on the part of the trade union movement of the entire state. In the past year, a vice-president of the Illinois Federation of Labor was actually kidnapped and held in captivity while gangsters forced the local union of which he was head to pay a ransom for his safe return. Shortly afterwards a vice-president of the international union with which that local was affiliated met his death by gun shot at the hands of gangster assassins. There have been cases where men, without a shadow of legal right, have threatened to "muscle in" to local unions of which they have never even been members. Others have masqueraded under organization names which, to the general public, seem to connect them with locals affiliated with the American Federation of Labor, although no such connection existed. The effect of this has been to seriously endanger the progress of the trade union movement by retarding legitimate and highly essential organization activities and by damaging the general reputation of the trade union movement.[23]

In 1933 the AFL reiterated its opposition to "racketeering and gangsterism of all forms."[24] These views were repeated by different conventions but by themselves could do little to eliminate or lessen the problem. In 1933 a committee to investigate racketeering was appointed by the U.S. Senate. As a result of the investigations, Senate 2248, which had the support of the U.S. Department of Justice, was introduced. It was initially opposed by the AFL, but amendments to the bill finally made it acceptable.[25] The law made acts of violence, intimidation, and extortion in interstate commerce punishable. The statute was found not to apply to labor unions whose agents required over-the-road truckers to pay the local a day's wages or hire a local driver to guide the trucks from the city limits to their destination. The U.S. Supreme Court found that such practices were traditional union activities and not prohibited. The amendment in 1946 prohibited a demand for money for the unloading of goods of an interstate vehicle and imposed severe penalties for violation. These practices had been used by some teamster locals.[26]

Always alert to possibilities that investigations of wrongdoing might involve traditional union activities, the federation sent a committee of vice-presidents to confer with District Attorney Thomas E. Dewey in October 1935 when the latter was appointed to investigate organized criminal activities.[27] Dewey assured the committee he was not concerned with occasional violence arising in the course of labor disputes. The committee and Dewey were "in complete accord that racketeering in the labor unions . . . must be stamped out."[28]

The annual passage by AFL conventions of resolutions deploring misuse of union office and pleading for greater rectitude had little effect on malefactors. In 1940 the delegation from the International Ladies' Garment Workers' Union to the AFL convention sought to strengthen the power of the federation to impose standards upon the affiliates. The resolution proposed that the executive council or an agency acting on its behalf be granted "summary power to order the removal by any national or international union affiliated with it or federal local chartered by it, of any officer or officers convicted of any offiense involving moral turpitude or convicted of using their official positions in their unions for personal gain."[29] The resolution also sought to have national and international unions adopt procedures for punishing members who use their office for personal gain. While the resolutions' committee was considering the proposal, David Dubinsky, the head of the Ladies' Garment Workers' Union, was attacked by Joseph S. Fay, a vice-president of the International Union of Operating Engineers, who objected to the Garment Workers' Union suggestion.[30]

The resolutions' committee found the proposal too drastic. It argued that the AFL "is a federation of self-governing national and international unions who have been guaranteed their right to self-government, which includes their election and selection of officers and control over their con-duct."[31] In discussing the question, President William Green challenged critics to show "any racketeering in the American Federation of Labor. . . . Our national and international unions are autonomous bodies, chartered by the American Federation of Labor, governed by their own laws and administered by the officers of said organizations. . . . We have never as-sumed and never will assume dictatorial policies toward national and in-ternational unions affiliated with the American Federation of Labor, but with all the power we possess we appeal to the membership of every Inter-national Union affiliated with the American Federation of Labor to keep the American labor movement clean, maintain it on a high plane, and if there is any attempt on the part of wrongdoers to seek to secure control of their movement, to deal with them vigorously at once."[32]

A small step towards intervention was nevertheless taken; for when-ever the executive council believed that an international union was not fulfilling its responsibility in acting against corrupt officers serving it or its subordinate units, the council was authorized to "apply all of its influence to secure such action as will correct the situation."[33] The resolution was unanimously adopted, and among those who voted for it were Fay and George E. Browne.

On the following day George E. Browne, who was soon to be charged with extortion on a giant scale, was elected twelfth vice-president with only the delegation from the International Ladies' Garment Workers' Union ab-staining.[34]

Soon after the convention the executive council had the first opportu-nity of acting under this provision. A complaint was made to Green that the Painters' Union had refused to remove a convicted bribe taker, Jacob Wellner, from the office of business agent of a local in Brooklyn, New York. On the motion of Vice-President William Hutcheson, the AFL Ex-ecutive Council decided to "ascertain whether the Brotherhood of Painters, Decorators and Paperhangers of America is endeavoring to evade or is evading its responsibility."[35] Accordingly, Vice-President Matthew Woll was asked to investigate. After discussing whether Wellner was guilty or innocent—he had been convicted in the courts—Woll found the AFL could only use its influence but could not compel obedience to its orders. As a result, the 1940 resolution became a dead letter at its first use.[36]

In the meantime, attacks by Westbrook Pegler, a widely syndicated newspaper columnist, on improper labor practices attracted widespread at-tention. Pegler had hit pay dirt in his exposure that George Scalise, head of the Building Service Employees' International Union, had been con-victed of white slavery. At its 1941 convention the AFL directed all central bodies to refuse to seat delegates who have been convicted of "serious wrongdoing which reflects dishonor on the trade union movement; and such delegate, if convicted after being seated, shall be unseated by such central labor body."[37] While the AFL was finding itself in public difficulty because of its constitutional inability to repress the derelictions of union officers on the staffs of affiliates, the CIO was virtually free of the problems of dishonesty and racketeering. The occasional charge against an officer of a CIO union was expeditiously handled. Although the CIO could not underwrite the integrity of all who held office, neither the economies of the industries in which the unions operated nor the established practices allowed for the organized kinds of corruption. Racketeering all through this period, therefore, continued, as in the past, to be largely a problem of the unions in the AFL, although the actual number of officers and organizations exposed for wrongdoing was never large.

Congress showed increasing concern with certain union practices, and a committee of the House of Representatives found in 1953 "a gigantic, wicked conspiracy to, through the use of force, threats of force, and economic pressure, extort and collect millions of dollars not only from unorganized workers but from members of unions who are in good standing, from independent businessmen, and, on occasion, from the Federal Government itself."[38] Serious charges were made against Local 985 of the Teamsters' Union, which operated in the coin-machine industry in Detroit and whose president was charged with "gangsterism, extortion and violence."

The AFL was in continual difficulties as a result of the conduct of a few labor organizations. In May 1952, Dubinsky, who was a member of the executive council, complained that there were a number of gangster-infested unions in New York City, that charters were being given to questionable persons, and that his organization was having difficulty with corrupt elements. An investigation was ordered, and it was found that the Distillery, Rectifying and Wine Workers International Union was distributing charters outside of its industry; that the International Jewelry Workers had put an organizer on its payroll who had a criminal record; and that the AFL Automobile Workers Union was engaged in malodorous practices. Although Meany recognized the lack of power of the federation, he wanted the council to insist that the charters given outside of a particular industry be revoked. Meany also asked the council to direct the Automobile Workers Union to withdraw a charter given to John Dio.[39]

Finally, the federation broke with tradition when it intervened in the affairs of the International Longshoremen's Union. Dissatisfaction with the union had been mounting in the Port of New York, and it burst out in a wildcat protest strike by five out of thirty-seven local unions in the Port of New York against a recently negotiated Atlantic Coast wage agreement. The strike began on October 18, 1951, and finally engulfed the entire port. The walkout was ended on November 9, 1951, after New York State Labor

Commissioner Edward Corsi appointed a three-man Board of Inquiry to investigate the dispute.

The board headed by Dean M. P. Catherwood found that the collective agreement had been validly ratified, although some of the delegates to the wage-scale conference had not been properly chosen, that the conference had been dominated by the International president of the union, and that some locals resorted to ballot stuffing. Nevertheless, the board recommended that the contract remain in full force and effect. To consider employee grievances properly, it recommended an appointment of a full time permanent arbitrator for the Port of New York. It also recommended a tribunal to which complaints against officers of the union could be made, introduction of reforms to allow employers greater freedom to choose foremen stevedores, and abolition of the public loading system, regarded as a source of evil and corruption on the waterfront.[40]

The charges were vehemently denied by the International Longshoremen's Association and the "Report" was attacked as an intrusion into the internal affairs of the labor movement. The ILA called upon the AFL to investigate what it described as a threat to organized labor.[41] A committee appointed by William Green found that the commissioner of labor had the authority to assign a board of inquiry to investigate strikes. It was not certain, however, whether such authority extended to unauthorized walkouts. It also saw a danger in the implied promise of the board to the strikers "to reform the ILA." On the whole the committee appointed by the AFL supported the criticisms of the board voiced by the Longshoremen's Union.[42]

Less than six months after the report of the AFL committee, Dubinsky called George Meany's attention to the disclosures of waterfront conditions by the New York State Crime Commission. Dubinsky pointed to a resolution adopted by the 1940 convention of the AFL which requested all national and international unions "to adopt rules or amendments to their constitution or where no provision . . . prevails embodying appropriate provisions for adequate disciplinary action against any of their officers and/or members who may have been found guilty of betraying the trust reposed to them, or having used their official position for personal and illegal gain, who have been or may be convicted of such acts which cast discredit upon the labor movement."[43] This was one of the most important letters written by a labor leader in the 1950's, for it raised the question whether the resolutions of AFL conventions on racketeering would be evaded on technical grounds or an effort would be made despite the presumed lack of power to carry them out.

George Meany, who had succeeded Green as president, believed "that the Council has the power now to apply all of its influence in order to correct a situation such as the press reports indicate exist in the New York waterfront."[44] Meany informed the executive council on February 2, 1953, "that the AFL must do something in this matter [the New York water-front]." He did not think that the federation should set up a police agency; instead the situation should be regarded from a trade union angle. It was not, in his opinion, the job of the labor movement to catch criminals, "but it is our business," he said, "to see that the union protects its members. Mr. Meany stated that we ought to tell the union that it is not protecting its members and we would like to have them let us know within a reasonable time what they have done about it."[45] Vice-Presidents George Harrison, Charles MacGowan, and Daniel Tracy were appointed to study the situation and suggest action.

The following day the AFL informed the Longshoremen's Union that the New York investigation had "reported widespread alleged crime, dishonesty, racketeering and other highly irregular practices in which it's reported that the officers of your International and Local Unions had been and are involved. . . . Your relationship with the American Federation of Labor demands that the democratic ideals, clean and wholesome free trade unionism must be immediately restored within your organization and all semblance of crime, dishonesty and racketeering be forthwith eliminated."[46]

The letter demanded immediate reforms, including the removal of men with criminal records from union office, reform of the shape-up method of hiring, restoration of democratic procedures in the union, and removal of all officials tainted with corruption or guilty of wrongdoing. In reply, the officers of the ILA were willing to suggest to the New York locals the abolition of the shape up, but the long discussion of what constituted a criminal record indicated an unwillingness to eliminate such persons from the union payroll. The ILA cited the case of indictments against leaders during strikes as evidence that the term "criminal" could be loosely used. Steps to improve democratic procedures in the local unions were, according to the letter, contemplated.[47] Meany told the heads of the ILA: "Your report cannot be accepted as indicating compliance with our directive of February 3, 1953."[48]

Conferences and exchanges of letters went on without any agreement being reached. Acting upon the direction of the executive council, Meany advised the officers and members of the ILA on August 11, 1953, that "the Executive Council will recommend to the 72nd Annual Convention . . . that the International Longshoremen's Association be suspended from affiliation until such time as the Executive Council of the American Federation of Labor is satisfied that the International Longshoremen's Association has taken the necessary action to comply in good faith with our request of February 3, 1953."[49]

Last-minute efforts to meet the request of the AFL were made. Promises of reform were given, but were later repudiated. The charter was revoked, upon the recommendation of the executive, by the 1953 AFL convention by a vote of 79,079 to 736.[50] The long-followed policy of the federation was to avoid chartering another union in a jurisdiction occupied by a suspended organization, and a similar policy was usually followed in cases where the charter was revoked. As a rule, a challenge to an existing union involves large expenditures of funds and energy. In addition, the suspended organization might in the future be willing to make amends and be able to return to the fold in the future. In any event, the executive council decided to charter a competing organization, the International Brotherhood of Longshoremen. A. M. Keeny of the International Association of Machinists was chosen to head the campaign to displace the ILA on the New York waterfront.[51]

A board of trustees headed by Meany was appointed to supervise the new organization's campaign. Ten ILA locals in Manhattan and Brooklyn immediately switched to the new union, and the number of cards were sufficiently large for the brotherhood to request a representation election by the National Labor Relations Board. Over the protests of the AFL, an election was ordered for December 22 and 23, 1953. The first election won by the ILA was set aside, and the New York Shipping Association, the National Maritime Union (CIO), the Communists, and underworld elements supported the ILA. But the brotherhood was not alone. The AFL threw in almost one million dollars in organizing expenses. The drive for a clean union was also supported by all New York newspapers except the *Daily Worker,* the official spokesman of the Communist party. In the second election the ILA won by a vote of 9,407 to 9,144, and was certified as the bargaining agent.[52] To finance its campaign, John L. Lewis loaned the ILA a large sum of money, and lauded the gaining of a two-year contract by the ILA as "the victorious culmination of a two-year fight against a sinister combination of labor, political, and financial interests."[53] It was a unique and earnest effort by the federation to oust a corrupt union from its control over the employment of more than 24,000 workers. It was also a warning to the AFL leadership that campaigns to oust a long and well-entrenched union should not be undertaken lightly. The clamor of outsiders for campaigns to purify various sections of labor and the economy does not involve the purists in risks or costs, and the federation, as the campaign on the New York waterfront demonstrated, could not embark upon a reform crusade too lightly. Ethics also requires some regard for the funds of the honest members who are supporting the federation.

HEALTH AND WELFARE PLANS

Unparalleled growth of welfare and pension programs created another source of corruption within the labor movement. Plans of this kind had their beginning in the late nineteenth century, but their greatest growth occurred in the 1940's and after. Stimulated by the control over wages during World War II, the decisions of the courts that health and welfare programs were bargainable issues, and the high corporation taxes, these plans mushroomed without regulation or control. They stimulated the creation of pure racket organizations which had no concern for the interests of their members.[54]

Current welfare programs provide health and death benefits, disability, hospital, medical, and surgical insurance. Self-insurance, Blue Cross and Blue Shield, or commercial insurance policies may be used for making benefits available for claimants. Many companies also provide pensions, benefits upon the permanent withdrawal from the labor market because of age or permanent disability. Various plans in operation affect more than 75 million workers. An investigation by a committee of the U.S. Senate found that the "great majority" of these plans are honestly and efficiently administered, but it also noted the existence of grave abuses which it was convinced would not be "self-correcting."[55] Abuses were by no means limited to the union-administered plans; some were managed by corporations.

Among abuses were the failure of employers to make contributions, favored treatment of certain employers, payment of high commissions and service and administration fees, and outright embezzlement.[56] The findings did not surprise the AFL Executive Council which had found "there are instances where it is charged that local unions have permitted administrative costs to go too high and where abuses have been charged in the distribution of commissions by agents of insurance companies."[57] David Beck, the head of the Teamsters' Union and a member of the council, objected to the statement and complained it was directed at his organization.

Ethical Practices

Public concern with improper labor activities mounted after the blinding of Victor Riesel, a newspaper columnist specializing in labor news, by alleged labor racketeers.[58] Under Article II, Section 10, of the AFL-CIO constitution, the object of the federation was "to protect the labor movement from any and all corrupt influences. . . ."[59] The constitution (Article VIII, Section 7) allowed the president or any other member of the executive council of the AFL-CIO "to request appointment of a committee to investigate reports that an affiliate was dominated by corrupt influences, and upon a two-thirds vote of its members the Council could make recommendations or give directions to the affiliate involved and shall have further authority, upon a two-thirds vote, to suspend any affiliate found guilty of this section."[60]

The first constitutional convention of the AFL-CIO in December 1955 took note of the problem of maintaining a labor movement that was above suspicion. It called upon its affiliates to maintain the high ethical standards set forth in the constitution of the federation and established the Committee on Ethical Practices "vested with the duty and responsibility to assist the Executive Council in carrying out the constitutional determination of the Federation to keep the Federation free from any taint of corruption . . . in accordance with the provisions of the constitution."[61]

In June 1956 the executive council of the AFL-CIO voted authority to the Committee on Ethical Practices to conduct hearings on behalf of the council into situations "in which there is reason to believe an affiliate is dominated, controlled or substantially influenced in the conduct of its affairs by any corrupt influence and in which such formal investigation is requested by the President or any members of the Executive Council." The committee was also asked to develop a set of principles for the guidance of the AFL-CIO which will aid in maintaining the AFL-CIO free from corrupt influences.[62]

Noting a reluctance of some union officers to discuss some of their financial dealings, the AFL-CIO Executive Council in June 1956 called for cooperation of labor officials with public agencies investigating racketeering and declared that if a "trade union official decides to invoke the Fifth Amendment for his personal protection and to avoid scrutiny by proper legislative committees, law enforcement agencies or other public bodies into alleged corruption on his part, he has no right to continue to hold office in his union."[63]

Six codes of ethical practices were approved by the executive council. The first one noted that local union charters had in a few instances fallen into the hands of corrupt groups who have used them for their "own illicit purposes instead of legitimate trade union objectives."[64] Possession of charters covering paper locals had "enabled such racketeers to victimize individual workers, employers and the general public, while giving a black eye to the labor movement."[65] The committee called upon the federation and the national and international affiliates to require the application by "a group of bona fide employees eligible for membership in the union, within the jurisdiction covered by the charter, for the issuance of a charter for a local union." Moreover, the purpose of the issuance of such charter ought to be the promotion of the welfare of the workers and not to be used as a device for the enrichment of a corrupt group.

Code 2 prescribed standards for administering health and welfare funds. It asked that union officials, who serve as trustees and who receive a full-time salary from an organization of labor, not accept another salary for serving as trustee. The code also called for avoidance by trustees of direct or indirect benefits from their office, maintenance of complete financial records, and full disclosure and reports to beneficiaries at least once a year. The council recommended that commercial carriers should be selected through competitive bids, and the reasons for their selection should be given to the membership.[66]

The third code recommended that persons who constitute corrupt influences should be denied the right to hold office or to dominate labor organizations. Code 4 found it was "too plain for extended discussion that a basic ethical principle in the conduct of trade union affairs is that no responsible trade union official should have a personal financial interest which conflicts with the full performance of his fiduciary duties as a workers' representative."[67] While Code 4 recognized that American labor union officials have never been denied an opportunity for owning property, it emphasized that "the nature of the trade union movement and the responsibilities which necessarily must be accepted by its leaders, make the strictest standards with respect to any possible conflict of interest properly applicable."[68]

The code also urged trade union officials to avoid personal financial interests that conflict with the performance of their duties and advised union officers against holding a substantial interest in a business with which they bargain collectively. Of course, no union officer, the code declared, could accept kickbacks or under-the-table payments.[69]

Ethical Practices Code 5 called for careful handling of union funds, regular auditing of accounts, and the placing of such information before the membership. The purpose of investment of union funds was not obtaining maximum profits, but using funds in an ethical manner so as to promote the objectives of the union, the interests of the members, and the purposes of the labor movement. The code suggested that affiliates comply with minimum accounting standards, conduct "their proprietary functions, including all contracts for purchase or sale for the rendition of housekeeping services in accordance with the practices of well-run institutions, including the securing of competitive bids for all major contracts."[70] It advised against allowing officers to borrow or invest funds for personal gain or the entering into contracts for goods and services which would redound to the personal profit of a union officer.

Finally, Code 6 dealt with union democratic processes. It recommended protection of the right of each member to participate fully in the affairs of his union, to fair treatment in the application of union rules and law, and in the exercise of rights as a member. The Ethical Practices Committee urged the holding of regular conventions at least once every four years with free and fair elections. The code urged that local union officers be chosen democratically, that the rights of members be protected, and that national and international unions take steps to institute corrective measures whenever necessary.[71]

The adoption of the codes represented a departure in the practices of the general labor movement. Heretofore, the affiliated national and international unions jealously guarded their autonomy and would not permit the federation to place any limitation upon their freedom. Even though the ethical practices code was not completely effective, the affiliated organizations admitted the right of the AFL-CIO to investigate their activities and behavior. The federation was also granted the right to expel a union if its standards were below those regarded as necessary and desirable.

McLellan Committee

The McLellan Committee of the U.S. Senate was appointed after the Senate Permanent Subcommittee on Investigations had found "collusion between certain dishonest management and union officials that had the effect of increasing the cost to the Government of goods and commodities it purchased and the supplying of inferior quality."[72] Einar Mohn, vice-president of the Teamsters' Union, acting for the absent President David Beck, advised all officers of his organization to challenge the power of the committee to inquire into their actions.[73]

The attitude of teamster officers and the preliminary disclosures led to the introduction of separate resolutions calling for an inquiry. Senator Wayne Morse suggested a select committee, and the Senate approved a bipartisan committee made up initially of Senator John McLellan, chairman; Senator Irving Ives, vice-chairman, and Senators John F. Kennedy, Sam J. Ervin, and Pat McNamara, Democrats; and Joseph R. McCarthy, Karl E. Mundt, and Barry Goldwater, Republicans. This group formed the Select Committee on Improper Activities in the Labor or Management Field under Senate Resolution 74, on January 30, 1957. The select committee was authorized "to conduct an investigation and study of the extent to which criminal or other improper practices or activities are, or have been, engaged in the field of labor-management relations or in groups or organizations of employees or employers to the detriment of the interests of the public, employers or employees."[74] The committee's first hearing centered around an attempt to control vice operations in Portland, Oregon. The hearings began with the testimony of Wallace Turner and William Lambert, reporters on the Portland *Oregonian*. They testified that they had secured information from James B. Elkins, a professional gambler, of a conspiracy to control gambling operations involving officials of Multnomah County and officers of the Teamsters' Union, including Frank Brewster, a vice-president of the international and head of the Western Conference of Teamsters.[75]

As indicated, the committee did not discover very much new information with regard to conditions in Portland, Oregon, but it did show the borrowing of union funds by Brewster and Dave Beck,[76] the president of the Teamsters' Union, and the purchase of securities with union funds which were to be returned by the beneficiaries of these transactions. An even more sordid story centered around Dave Beck, who in 1952 "had supplanted the aging Dan Tobin, who had ruled the union with an iron hand for forty-five years—virtually from the birth of the organization at Niagara Falls, New York in 1903."[77] Of course, Tobin never ruled the

International Brotherhood of Teamsters, Chauffeurs, Warehousemen and Helpers of America with an iron hand. The union was a congeries of local baronies that no man ruled. Tobin was elected, moreover, as a reform candidate against Cornelius P. Shea, who was defeated in 1907.

Beck "viciously abused the trust of the union's 1½ million members" and "shamefully enriched himself at their expense."[78] Beck borrowed several hundred thousands from the Western Conference of Teamsters, received kickbacks from a number of enterprises, including some from Nathan Shefferman, a labor consultant and Beck's special friend.[79]

It was the opinion of the committee that officers of "the teamsters' union have . . . shamefully betrayed their own members."[80] The heads of the union were charged with cooperating with underworld characters. "James R. Hoffa used his official teamster position to break the strike of teamster members against the Commercial Carrier Corporation in Flint, Michigan, and his wife and the wife of his first lieutenant, Owen Bert Brennan, secretly went into the trucking business under the sponsorship of Commercial Carriers and with the financial and legal help of the company."[81] Teamster officials were charged with entering into business relations with firms with which they bargained. Beck borrowed money from companies employing members of the union he headed, and Hoffa was a business partner of the broker handling the health and welfare account for the Central Conference of Teamsters which Hoffa headed at the time. The committee also listed a large number of convicted felons who were close to the power sources within the Teamsters' Union.[82]

One of the more brazen operations involved Philadelphia Local 107, which Raymond Cohen took over. The treasury was looted, and sweetheart agreements were made with certain companies, while others were denied the same concessions.[83]

Bakery and Confectionery Workers International Union

One of the more flagrant examples of bribery and corruption involved James G. Cross, president of the Bakery and Confectionery Workers International Union, one of the older organizations of labor and one which had an unsullied reputation for internal democracy and honest administration. A Socialist, Cross had been a student at Brookwood, a left-wing resident labor college. He and George Stuart, a vice-president, were guilty of gross violation of the rights of members; they robbed a local union under trusteeship and both were the beneficiaries of kickbacks. The debauching of one of the finer labor organizations is a sordid episode in American labor history.[84]

The McLellan Committee found the financial activities of President Anthony Valente and Secretary-Treasurer Lloyd Klenert of the United Textile Workers of America, "an unblushing exercise in avarice [which] can scarcely be matched." These two worthies misappropriated $178,000, or about 18 per cent of the union's income for 1957. The money was used to purchase clandestinely homes for the two officers. Equally as shocking, was the approval given to these peculations by the union's executive board.[85]

Teamsters' Union

The committee threw light on the activities of John Dioguardi (Dio) and Anthony (Ducks) Corallo, two notorious gangsters and racketeers operating in the New York City area. Their operations must be regarded as part of the criminal world rather than labor crime. The union organizations established by these two and their coadjutors were engines of extortion and embezzlement; they were not essentially instruments of collective bargaining used for the personal aggrandizement of the officers. The racket union which Dio, Corallo, and others organized preyed largely upon the low-paid unorganized worker. The committee "pointed out that the contract signed by . . . employers with these racket-controlled unions had the effect of preventing legitimate union organization in these plants. The advantage to the employer was that he could wave a contract in the face of any union organizer and declare he was already signed up. The fact that these contracts were substandard also resulted in financial gain for the employers involved."[86]

It is interesting to review the summary of the behavior of a typical racket union. Either the union approaches the employer or the latter gets in touch with a racket organization to ward off genuine unionization. A contract is signed which usually has the following characteristics: A wage scale with a few cents above the legal minimum; with substandard provisions on holidays with pay, vacations, and welfare benefits. Seniority is usually ignored, a grievance procedure is absent, and the enforcement of the meager terms is not considered. As for the union, no meetings are ever held, and the members have no knowledge of their officers. Complaints are likely to be grounds for immediate dismissal without appeal. For being denied the slightest protection, the racket union exacts regular dues.[87] What seems even more reprehensible was that charters for these criminal activities were given by the Teamsters' Union and the Allied Industrial Union, both affiliates of the AFL-CIO at that time.

The committee investigated some of James Hoffa's business activity and found that he had borrowed money from a number of people with whom he dealt as a union officer. The committee reported that Hoffa "repeatedly betrayed the members of his own union by entering into a number of business relationships with employers with whom his union negotiated. He also entered into business relationships with insurance carriers and banks which handled millions of dollars in teamster union funds."[88] Many of Hoffa's business ventures were in the trucking field in which he also exercised great power as negotiator on behalf of members of his union. The committee found that all "of Hoffa's businesses . . . were not in the trucking field. He associated with . . . a company set up for the purpose of making investment loans; joined with Allen Dorfman, general agent of the Union Casualty Co., which handles the health and welfare funds of the Central Conference of Teamsters, in the purchase of a summer camp in Wisconsin; and joined the same Mr. Dorfman and others in a North Dakota land venture."[89]

Nathan W. Shefferman

The McLellan Committee also brought to public attention the new type of middleman in labor relations. Nathan W. Shefferman, a Chicago labor relations consultant, with a list of important clients headed by Sears, Roebuck and Company was an ideal representative of this new type. He was the chief of Labor Relations Associates of Chicago, founded in 1939, with original working capital furnished by Sears, Roebuck and Company. Shefferman was on the staff of the National Industrial Recovery Board labor division, and later became a highly paid authority on the use of devices to abort union organizing drives. According to the committee, Shefferman was an expert in forming "spontaneous" anti-union employee committees during union organizing drives. This method, as revealed before the committee, consisted of the setting up by the employer or a representative of Shefferman's firm of an anti-union committee made up of certain selected employees, "some of whom received financial and other consideration for their participation in these activities."[90]

Substituting a friendly for a militant union was another technique developed by Shefferman and his associates. Shefferman's acquaintance with many labor leaders enabled him to carry out his assignments more effectively. We have here the anomaly of labor leaders serving the anti-union purposes of a paid employer agent.

International Union of Engineers

The committee found the International Union of Operating Engineers guilty of denying a substantial part of the membership a voice in the affairs of the organization. William E. Maloney, who served as president from 1940 to 1958 (he resigned when the McLellan Committee began investigating his activities), used his power ruthlessly to install trusteeships over local unions that were reluctant to accept his policies. He favored certain contractors and insisted that locals overlook their failure to make payments into the union's welfare fund as required by the collective bargaining agreement. Evidence was adduced that Maloney had purchased a yacht with union funds, that he had taken almost $200,000 for which no accounting was made. Maloney was not the only one in the union guilty of peculations.

"While indisputably the past master of the art of using the union as the vehicle of his own selfish aims, he voiced no objections to similar or somewhat smaller-scale activities by . . . loyal lieutenants."[91]

Several were, however, not as fortunate as their chief. Victor S. Swanson, the business manager of San Francisco Local No. 3, and several other local officers of the 24,000-member union were convicted of stealing thousands of dollars from the local by real estate manipulations and sentenced to prison. They were also removed from office by Maloney's successors.

Equally damaging evidence was compiled by the committee against Local 138 headed by William DeKoning and, after his retirement, by his son. Both maintained a brutal autocracy over the members and the craft in their jurisdiction. Local 825 of Newark, New Jersey, was another local dominated by an extortioner and thug, Joseph S. Fay, who was convicted in 1948, with Joseph Bove of the Hod Carriers' Union, of extortion. But as great an evil within the Operating Engineers' Organization was the misuse of the power to impose trusteeships upon locals. These trusteeships were imposed for an unspecified time and lasted in some instances more than a generation. In the view of the committee, "the International Union of Operating Engineers stands out as an ugly example of ruthless domination of working men and women through violence, intimidation and other dictatorial practices. . . ."[92]

Among the charges made against the union was the absence of democracy and the disenfranchisement of thousands, the imposition of trusteeships as a means "of continuing domination and looting of locals under these regimes, collusion with favored contractors, conflict of interests, misuse and diversion of union funds for personal purposes.[93]

Carpenters' Union

The committee found grave misuse of his position by Charles Johnson, Jr., a member of the executive board of the United Brotherhood of Carpenters and Joiners of America, whom it charged was guilty of a gross conflict of interest. The committee found that President Maurice Hutcheson had allowed misuse of the union's funds, and that he had overpaid Maxwell C. Raddock, who ran *The Trade Union Currier* as an advertising medium under the guise of a labor paper. This biweekly newspaper had been investigated in 1948 by AFL Vice-President Matthew Woll, who declared that the paper wrongfully claimed to be endorsed by the AFL, that its advertising solicitors usually insinuated that unless space was purchased by the employer "he might be in 'labor trouble,' " that employers were intimidated, billed for advertisements they had not authorized, and that advertisements had been solicited over long distance telephone in cities a long way from New York where the publication has its headquarters. The executive council of the AFL disclaimed connection with it, and urged all unions to disassociate themselves from the publication.[94]

Nevertheless, Maurice Hutcheson paid hundreds of thousands of dollars to Raddock for editorial services and for the writing of a biography of his father.[95]

Other Unions

A Chicago local of the Hotel, Restaurant Employees and Bartenders International Union was found to be dominated by Capone gangsters. On the management side, the Chicago Restaurant Association employed underworld characters and was guilty of improper methods in its labor relations.[96] Evidence also showed that the Amalgamated Meat Cutters and Butcher Workmen on North America made a questionable contract with the Great Atlantic and Pacific Tea Company extending the forty-five-hour week for thirty-three months without any prior notification to the membership. As a *quid pro quo* the welfare fund was turned over to the union for administration. Patrick Gorman, the secretary-treasurer, and Harry Block, a vice-president, had signed the agreement. Charles A. Schimmat, the national director of warehousing for the A & P, "was asked by Mr. Block to keep it quiet, not to publicize it."[97] Initially, about ten thousand workers in the New York area were organized without opposition from the company, a rather unusual procedure and obviously designed to frustrate the organizing campaign of a union the company regarded as less desirable.[98]

Up to 1952, the company in the eastern division opposed unionization of the employees, but Vice-President Block made suggestions which were "attractive" to the A. & P.[99] Louis Block, his brother, and two other relatives received, over a period of three years—1955, 1956, 1957[100]—a total of $241,605.

A vice-president of the Sheet Metal Workers International Association and head of Chicago Local 73 was accused of accepting payoffs. It was denied by the officer in question, Arthur H. Cronin.[101]

Testimony was also presented to show that the International Brotherhood of Boilermakers, Iron Ship Builders, Blacksmiths, Forgers and Helpers of America Hamilton Lodge 74 of Houston, Texas, suffered discrimination in the allocation of work, and that it had to pay a large fraction of the dues to the international. Most of the testimony, however, shows a factional division, but scarcely any kind of racketeering.[102]

In the 270 days of testimony, more than 1,520 witnesses were heard. If violence in labor disputes is disregarded, charges of racketeering were made against local or international officers of ten unions that were affiliated with the AFL. Evidence against officers of the following international unions was presented: the Teamsters', Bakery and Confectionery Workers', Meat Cutters', Operating Engineers', and Carpenters' unions, and the United Textile Workers of America. Local officers of the Hotel and Restaurant Employees' and Boilermakers' unions were charged with improper activities. Even in the Teamsters' Union, which occupied a large part of the committee's attention—34 of the 58 volumes are devoted to it—only relatively few locals were accused of wrongdoing, although the charges against the heads of this union and several of its vice-presidents were of a serious character.

Expulsion

Although the number of organizations that were exposed for improper activity was not large, the revelations that grave abuses were possible stimulated the movement to compel reform of improper practices. The ethical practices committee considered charges against six unions—Allied Industrial Workers, Bakery, Distillery, Laundry Workers International, Textile, and Teamsters' unions. Three—Textile, Distillery, and Allied Industrial Workers—agreed to mend their ways. The United Textile Workers of America approved the appointment of a special representative by President Meany. It agreed, moreover, to eliminate corrupt elements from its roster of officers and to call a special convention to cancel the financial arrangement with President Anthony Valente and Secretary-Treasurer Lloyd Klenert under which they would have received $104,000 for withdrawing from office. Valente and Klenert were to be barred from holding office.[103]

The Distillery, Rectifying and Wine Workers' International Union and the Allied Industrial Workers also escaped expulsion by accepting probation and the appointment of a monitor by President Meany.[104]

Three unions—the Teamsters', Bakery and Confectionery, and Laundry Workers' organizations—refused to meet the terms laid down by the federation as conditions for continuing affiliation. They were expelled by the 1957 convention.[105] New international unions were chartered to replace the expelled Bakery and Confectionery and the Laundry Workers' unions, but no rival to the Teamsters' Union was found in the trucking industry. In the bakery and laundry industries, strong opposition to the improper conduct of the officers of the respective unions existed, and the organizations encouraged by the federation were able to make substantial inroads upon the memberships of the expelled organizations. Such possibilities did not exist in the trucking industry, and the federation gave encouragement but not much financial or organizational support to raids on the Teamsters' Union. The feeling that the existing leadership was too strongly entrenched and that the federation could not mobilize sufficient finances or manpower for a successful campaign to oust the Teamsters' Union in its principal centers seems to have been demonstrated by time. The Teamsters' Union is not only large numerically, but its strategic position plus the prestige of local and regional leaders in their areas, the relations with employers, and the loyalty of thousands of members would make a campaign to replace it in its main jurisdictions difficult, expensive, and hazardous. Moreover, in many sections of the country the local labor movements would scarcely support such a campaign. Whatever conclusion is reached on the integrity of the national leadership, many regional and local teamster chiefs are men of integrity who are able and devoted to their organization and its members. Many of these men have cooperated with other local and regional labor organizations and have frequently aided other workers on the picket line.

The federation can expel but cannot basically eliminate racketeering. The federation has demonstrated that it will intervene in cases of flagrant corruption; but its willingness to allow the International Longshoremen's Association to rejoin demonstrates that the standards of ethical practice are not exeremely high.

The Landrum-Griffin Act

Recognition by Congress that the federation was powerless to prevent improper practices was to some degree responsible for the enactment of the Labor-Management Reporting (Landrum-Griffin) Act. It required filing of financial statements by all unions, including income, expenditures, and salaries, and forbade conflicts of interest, borrowing of union funds by officers or members of more than $2,000, and required bonding of officers and staff members. The law also regulated trusteeships imposed by internationals on its locals and limited the duration of trusteeship. A bill of rights specified the rights of members to free speech, assembly, and trial. The holding of elections and the time span between them are specified. The Secretary of Labor is given power to ask remedies in the courts for denial of rights to members, and misuse of funds are made offenses under federal law.

The Landrum-Griffin Act marked another important step in the intervention of government in the affairs of labor organizations. As in the preceding labor legislation, most of the fears were not realized. Neither did the extensive reporting and complaints show widespread misuse of funds or violation of the rights of members.

In fiscal year 1960, 52,278 reports were filed, 93 per cent local unions, 1 per cent national unions, and the rest intermediate bodies.[106] Financial reports were supplied by 39,080 organizations.

The Labor-Management Reporting and Disclosure Act gave the Secretary of Labor broad powers to investigate violations or contemplated violations of the statute. During fiscal year 1960, 2,041 alleged violations involving 1,445 cases were investigated. Many were found without merit. The U.S Bureau of Labor Statistics estimated that the 184 national and international unions reporting had 78,110 local unions, which do not include the single plant organizations. With almost 80,000 local unions, and several hundred more intermediate bodies and international organizations with over 18 million members the number of complaints seem few indeed.[107]

Moreover, many were technical in character and made out of ignorance; others were trivial and would scarcely arouse concern in other types of organizations, let alone government intervention. If all legislative bodies in the United States were held to the same requirements as the unions, they would find it difficult to enact legislation. Many of the complaints were made by chronic oppositionists, and others out of malice. Labor unions of the United States did little to adjust their methods of conducting their affairs, which is an eloquent commentary upon the basic democratic procedures of the trade union movement.

An even more startling statistic is contained in the "Summary of Operations" for fiscal year 1962. During this period, the bureau conducted 5,448 investigations on the basis of complaints or "spot checks." Of the 3,174 closed during the year, 1,263 indicated no violation, while 1,911 (or 60 per cent) disclosed some defficiency in the reports or other violation of the act. However, 96 per cent of these violations were found to be technical or without criminal intent, in which case, the BLMR took the necessary action to have the violation corrected and to prevent its recurrence. In only 76 cases, where criminal intent was uncovered or where the union was unwilling to comply voluntarily, was prosecutive action initiated.[108]

The majority of the complaints—3,953—concerned inadequate reporting. Of the 603 complaints of breach of fiduciary responsibilities, 337 involved embezzlement. However, only 48 were found to be actionable. There was one case of illegal discipline of a union member which was closed and 52 instances in which members charged they were deprived of rights through violence. In the latter group, 38 cases were closed during the fiscal year, and only one was legally actionable.[109]

Salutary results are likely to follow from the financial reporting requirements and the penalizing of embezzlement and violation of fiduciary trust. In a number of the cases reported the officials found guilty were allowed to make restitution as a condition for suspension of the penalty by the court. In several instances the money misappropriated from the union was substantial, but in many others the amount was relatively small. Up to now, the Landrum-Griffin Act has inflicted no harm upon the labor movement. The results must have disappointed those whom Gompers called "labor's fool friends," the liberals, ex-Trotskyists, and left-wing Socialists, who have convinced themselves that only a conspiracy of the leaders of labor has prevented the rank and file from espousing their particular programs, and that the labor organizations were cesspools of venality and corruption. One of the great contributions of the Landrum-Griffin law is to demonstrate the basic falsehood of such beliefs, and to show that for probity and integrity the labor movement compares favorably with other American institutions.

CHAPTER **52**

Some Closing Observations

Organized labor in the United States today has been shaped by social, economic, and political conditions existing throughout its history. Its lack of interest in abstract and long-range reform programs, its pragmatism, its limited political interests reflect the practical outlook of the American community. Within a broad pattern, unions of the United States also show considerable diversity. The industry, labor force, problems facing workers, opposition encountered, and the kind of business organization affect the character of particular unions. However, despite these differences, the majority of unions in the United States still concentrate most of their activities upon protecting the members in the place of employment.

As a result of the efforts of organized labor, American workers enjoy rights at the place of employment equal or superior to those of workers in any other country. The exercise of rights by unions may sometimes appear arbitrary as, for example, in opposition to unilateral changes in working rules by the employer, but in itself it reflects the greater liberty enjoyed by the individual. If liberty means limitation upon the exercise of power over persons, the unions have been one of the great forces in the modern world for its extension.

Unions have continued to follow the policy of "more and more" in matters of wages, and like the rest of the community labor believes that continual improvement is the right and destiny of all Americans. The exhortations of sales managers for exceeding last year's records and the constant quest for greater productivity by industrial managers and greater profit by heads of enterprises reflect a similar hope that the future must be better than the present. The labor movement in its eternal quest for higher real wages recognizes that if the American economy is to achieve the hoped for $4\%_{10}$ per cent annual growth in productivity, labor will be at least entitled to its proportionate share of this rise. The assumption of continuous improvement is deeply ingrained in the outlook of organized labor in the United States. As the ability of firms and industries to make wage concessions is not, at any one time, the same, it would be difficult for unions to accept any formal limit on their demands, although in practice they must take cognizance of ability to pay and other considerations. Generally unions oppose a centrally formulated wage policy. They believe it would be inequitable and unenforceable, and they would be reluctant to give up their power to determine this question in the light of prevailing circumstances. The principle of autonomy, which is a cardinal principle of the merged federation as it was of the AFL and CIO, gives to each affiliate the right to determine the question in accordance with its interests, and it is doubtful if this power would ever be surrendered to another authority, even one in their own ranks.

Autonomy of each organization makes it difficult for the federation to impose standards in jurisdictional disputes as well as in matters of ethical practice. It does not possess the power to investigate behavior except under limited conditions, and even if it discovers derelictions, it can only suspend or expel if the affiliate is unwilling to accept its advice or directives. However, the federation wields considerable influence in these areas despite its lack of power. Unions can reject, and do, the jurisdictional awards of federation-appointed arbitrators without running the risk of sanctions. Yet, because of the absence of any other tribunal, the federation is almost inevitably the institution to which the most stubborn jurisdictional disputes are directed. As such differences are a threat to the unity of labor, the federation has only the interest of finding a solution. The merged federation was able to devise a formula which ended the threat of open civil war between the industrial unions and the building trades.

The labor movement of today is much different from the one that existed in the early 1930's. Its numbers are about six times as great, and the level upon which it operates its legal, political, and research activities has been greatly expanded. It shows a much greater and continuing interest in foreign affairs and international labor. It is concerned with a greater variety of legislative problems and public issues. But despite the great changes, it shows clearly the influence of the labor movement of the past. Its major interest remains improvement in the conditions of employment within the established institutional framework. As in the past, unions remain largely powerless, except for delaying actions, against the erosions of their positions by technical innovations (automation). Relieving unemployment generated by such changes has always been and remains beyond the power of labor unions, although they have made some contribution in this area by labor-management arrangements. Yet like the level of employment in general, the reabsorption of the technically displaced, their retraining, and offsets to wage loss must be the primary responsibility of government.

The existence of the labor movement with its great concern for the individual worker has reduced greatly the appeal of collectivist doctrines among labor. It has given the worker in the United States a mechanism for eliminating discrimination and injustice at the place of employment unmatched in the world. Serious weakening of organized labor would create a vacuum which might be filled by organizations more concerned with basically changing the economy than with serving the workers of the country.

At no time has the American labor movement failed to support the government in conflicts with foreign powers. It gave up its long-held pacifism to support the United States in the first world war, and it has since sought to defend and promote democratic principles and policies throughout the world. The American labor movement has always regarded the government as the representative of all the people including the working population. Even when it has been highly critical of particular policies, it has not regarded the government as an alien and hostile force. Organized labor has always regarded itself as part of the larger American community with a right and duty to participate in shaping the institutions under which it lives. It is not without faults, but it has represented in the past as it does today the only agency in this society which can prevent the growth of absolutism in industry which inevitably spreads when power is unrestrained.

Notes

INTRODUCTION

1. The ingenious comparisons of growth rates between a free and controlled economy miss the point. They are meaningless except that they demonstrate that if more resources are diverted towards investment, an economy will tend to grow more rapidly. In a free society, trade unions and other private groups are in a position to insist that some of the productivity gains be paid out in current consumption.

CHAPTER 1. THE FIRST ORGANIZED ACTION

1. Carl Bridenbaugh, *The Colonial Craftsman* (New York: New York University Press, 1950), p. 76.
2. William B. Weeden, *Economic and Social History of New England* (Boston: Houghton Mifflin Co., 1801), I, 82.
3. Thomas Wertenbaker, *The First Americans, 1617–1690* (New York: Macmillan Co., 1927), p. 69.
4. Bridenbaugh, *op. cit.*, p. 126.
5. Victor S. Clark, *History of Manufactures in the United States, 1607–1860* (Washington: Carnegie Institution of Washington, 1916), pp. 146-148; Charles M. Andrews, *Our Earliest Colonial Settlements* (New York: New York University Press, 1933), p. 42.
6. Clark, *op. cit.*, p. 161.
7. Carl Bridenbaugh, *Cities in Revolt* (New York: Alfred A. Knopf, 1955), p. 86.
8. *Ibid.*, pp. 145-146, 285.
9. Melvin Thomas Copeland, *The Cotton Manufacturing Industry of the United States* (Cambridge, Mass.: Harvard University Press, 1923), p. 4.

10. *Ibid.*, p. 5.

11. Clark, *op. cit.*, p. 443.

12. John R. Commons and associates, *History of Labour in the United States* (New York: Macmillan Co., 1918), I, place the first strike of wage earners in the United States in 1786, when the printers of Philadelphia struck for a minimum wage of six dollars a week. Richard B. Morris, *Government and Labor in Early America* (New York: Columbia University Press, 1946), p. 196, claims that a strike of journeymen tailors in New York took place in 1768.

13. *Ibid.*, p. 28; see Rola L. Tryon, *Household Manufacturers in the United States, 1640–1860* (Chicago: University of Chicago Press, 1917).

14. *Ibid.*, p. 32.

15. William A. Sullivan, *The Industrial Worker in Pennsylvania, 1800–1840* (Harrisburg, Pa.: Historical and Museum Commission, 1935), p. 87.

16. John R. Commons and associates (eds.), *A Documentary History of American Industrial Society* (Cleveland: Arthur H. Clark Co., 1910), III, 62.

17. *Ibid.*, II, 104-105.

18. *Ibid.*, III, 93.

19. *Ibid.*, pp. 93-94; quote on p. 119.

20. Ethelbert Stewart, "A Documentary History of Early Organization of Printers," *Bulletin of the Department of Labor,* November 1905, p. 856.

21. *Ibid.*, p. 863.

22. *Ibid.*, p. 867.

23. John Bach McMaster, *The Acquisition of Political Social and Industrial Rights of Man in America* (Cleveland: Imperial Press, 1903), p. 56.

24. *Ibid.*, pp. 61-62; Commons, *A Documentary History*, III, 62-63

25. Sullivan, *op. cit.*, p. 97.

26. Quoted from "To the Master Printers of the City of New York, July 13, 1811, signed by D. H. Reins, W. Burbridge, and S. Johnston, Committee," in George A. Stevens, *New York Typographical Union No. 6* (Albany, N.Y., Annual Report of the [New York] Bureau of Labor Statistics, 1912), pp. 67-68.

27. Commons, *A Documentary History*, I, 12.

28. *Ibid.*, I, p. 124.

29. Commons, *History of Labour*, I, 127, 129.

30. Stewart, *op. cit.*, p. 877. See also Commons, *A Documentary History,* Vols. III, IV, and Supp. IV.

31. Stevens, *op. cit.*, p. 36; Barnett, *op. cit.*, p. 11.

32. Barnett, *op. cit.*, p. 9.

33. Stevens, *op. cit.*, pp. 75-81; Barnett, *op. cit.*, pp. 12-13.

34. The resolution is reproduced in Seth Luther, *An Address to the Workingmen of New England on the State of Education and The Condition of the Producing Classes in Europe and America* (Boston: Published by the author, 1832), Appendix B, p. 34.

35. Commons, *A Documentary History*, III, 64-65.

36. *Ibid.*, p. 68.

37. *Ibid.*, p. 81.

38. *Ibid.*, p. 236. An analysis of this case is found in Walter Nelles, "The First American Labor Case," *Yale Law Journal,* December 1931, pp. 165-200; Richard Morris, "Criminal Conspiracy and Early Labor Combinations in New York," *Political Science Quarterly,* March 1937, pp. 51-85, discusses the prosecution of the New York cordwainers case in 1809–1810, and a host of

earlier ones which Commons and others regarded as combinations of non-wage-earner producers.

39. Commons, *A Documentary History,* III, 253-255, 366.

40. *Ibid.,* p. 369.

41. *Ibid.,* p. 385.

42. *Ibid.,* p. 106.

43. *Ibid.,* p. 200.

44. *Ibid.,* p. 264.

45. Massachusetts, p. 111.

CHAPTER 2. THE FIRST LABOR MOVEMENT

1. Evans Wooden, "Labor Troubles Between 1834 and 1837," *Yale Review,* May 1892, pp. 90-92.

2. George E. Barnett, *The Printers* (Cambridge, Mass.: American Economic Association, 1909), reproduces the letter answering the appeal on pp. 359-360.

3. Ethelbert Stewart, "Two Forgotten Decades in the History of Labor Organizations, 1820–1840," *American Federationist,* July 1913, pp. 518-524.

4. From the *Democratic Press* (Philadelphia), June 14, 1827, in John R. Commons and associates (eds.), *A Documentary History of American Industrial Society* (Cleveland: Arthur H. Clark Co., 1910), V, 80.

5. From Poulson's *American Daily Advertiser* (Philadelphia), June 18, 1827, in *ibid.,* p. 81.

6. From *Freeman's Journal* (Philadelphia), June 15, 1827, in *ibid.,* p. 83.

7. Commons, *A Documentary History,* V, 84.

8. John R. Commons and associates, *History of Labor in the United States* (New York: Macmillan Co., 1935), I, 188-189.

9. Commons, *A Documentary History,* V, 86-87.

10. Preamble was taken from *Mechanics Free Press,* October 25, 1828, in *ibid.,* pp. 89-90. For the last quote, see statement of William English in *ibid.,* p. 215.

11. *Ibid.,* VI, 216.

12. *Mechanics Free Press,* July 5, 1828, in *ibid.,* p. 20.

13. *Mechanics Free Press,* August 16, 1828, in *ibid.,* pp. 91–92.

14. Commons, *A Documentary History,* I, 198.

15. "Report of the Working Men's Committee," *Working Men's Advocate* (New York), March 6, 1830, in Commons, *A Documentary History,* VI, 95-96.

16. "Report of the Working Men's Committee," in *ibid.,* pp. 97-100.

17. *National Gazette* (Philadelphia), July and August 1830, in *ibid.,* pp. 107-108.

18. From the *Mechanics Free Press,* July 10, 1830, in *ibid.,* V; quotes are on pp. 119, 121.

19. From the *Morning Courier* (New York), April 25 and 28, 1829, in *ibid.,* pp. 146-148.

20. "The Report and Resolutions of the Committee of Fifty," in *Workingmen's Advocate,* October 31, 1829, reprinted in *ibid.,* pp. 149-150.

21. *Ibid.,* p. 157.

22. "Address and Resolutions of the Conference Committee of the Wards," from a pamphlet, *Proceedings of a Meeting of Mechanics and Other Working*

Men, which appeared in the *Working Men's Advocate,* December 29, 1829, and later in *ibid.,* p. 158.

23. *Ibid.,* pp. 160-164.

24. *Ibid.,* p. 169.

25. Richard William Leopold, *Robert Dale Owen* (Cambridge, Mass.: Harvard University Press, 1940).

26. Frank T. Carelton, "The Working Men's Party of New York City," *Political Science Quarterly,* September 1902, p. 415.

27. From *Columbian Centennial* (Boston), February 15, 1832, in Commons, *A Documentary History,* V. 192.

28. "The Constitution," *ibid.,* pp. 192-193; "The Labor Movement in America To 1861," in George McNeil (ed.) *The Labor Movement: The Problem of To-Day* (Boston: A. M. Bridgman Co., 1887), p. 79.

29. Commons, *History of Labor,* I, 320.

30. Walter Hugins, *Jacksonian Democracy and the Working Class* (Stanford, Calif.: Stanford University Press, 1960), p. 51.

31. George Barnett, *op. cit.,* p. 13.

32. Stewart, *op. cit.,* pp. 520-521.

33. *Ibid.,* p. 532.

34. Circular presented by John Finch, president of the Typographical Association, before his union on June 22, 1833, and issued as a circular by the Typographical Association. It is printed in Commons, *A Documentary History,* V, 212; and Stevens, *op cit.,* pp. 162-163.

35. Commons, *ibid.,* pp. 212-213.

36. *Ibid.,* p. 213.

37. Constitution is in *ibid.,* p. 218.

38. *Ibid.,* p. 219.

39. From the *National Trades' Union,* in *ibid.,* p. 245.

40. From the *National Trades' Union,* August 15, 1836, in *ibid.,* p. 257, 259.

41. From the *National Trades' Union,* Ooctober 17, 1835, in *ibid.,* p. 267.

42. *Ibid.,* pp. 279-281.

43. Quoted from *Man,* June 16, 1834, in *ibid.,* p. 308.

44. *National Trades' Union,* March 12, 1836, in *ibid.,* pp. 295-296.

45. *Ibid.,* p. 308.

46. *The Morning Courier and New York Enquirer,* March 26 and April 11, 1836, in *ibid.,* pp. 309-315.

47. *Register of Pennsylvania,* November 30, 1833, in *ibid.,* p. 338.

48. *Pennsylvanian,* January 9, 1833, in *ibid.,* p. 339.

49. *Ibid.,* p. 341.

50. Constitution, in *ibid.,* p. 347.

51. *Pennsylvanian,* March 12, 1836, in *ibid.,* p. 349.

52. *National Laborer,* May 14 and 21, 1836, in *ibid.,* pp. 357-359.

53. *Pennsylvanian,* February 9, 1836, in *ibid.,* p. 389.

54. *Pennsylvanian,* March 28, 1836, in *ibid.,* VI, 33.

55. *Ibid.,* p. 118.

56. *Ibid.,* V, 203.

57. *Ibid.*

58. Quote from the constitution was published in *Man,* September 2, 1834, in *ibid.,* VI, 225.

59. *Ibid.,* pp. 213-214.
60. *Ibid.,* V, 214.
61. *Ibid.,* VI, 215.
62. *Ibid.,* for quote, p. 216.
63. From the *National Trades' Union,* October 10, 1835, in *ibid.,* p. 234.
64. The memorial was given to Ely Moore, who had been elected president of the National Trades' Union and who was a member of Congress. *Ibid.,* 246.
65. *Ibid.,* p. 241.
66. *Ibid.,* p. 281.
67. *Ibid.,* p. 288.
68. *Ibid.,* quote on p. 295; also see p. 296.
69. *Ibid.,* pp. 298, 301 for the quotations.
70. *Ibid.,* p. 304.
71. From the *National Trades' Union,* April 25, 1836, in *ibid.,* p. 314.
72. From the *National Trades' Union,* October 10, 1835, in *ibid.,* p. 315.
73. *Ibid.,* p. 320.
74. *Ibid.,* pp. 327-328.
75. *Ibid.,* p. 326.
76. *Ibid.,* p. 323.
77. *Ibid.,* p. 339.
78. *Ibid.*
79. *Ibid.,* pp. 341-342.
80. Barnett, *op. cit.,* p. 16.
81. Ethelbert Stewart, "A Documentary History of Early Organization of Printers," *Bulletin of the Department of Labor,* Nov. 1905, p. 873.
82. Stewart, *ibid.,* p. 891.
83. Quoted in Barnett, *op. cit.,* pp. 21-22.
84. *Ibid.,* p. 22.
85. The pamphlet is reprinted as Appendix A, No. 12, in Stewart, *op. cit.,* p. 989.
86. Stewart, *ibid.,* pp. 907-908.
87. *Ibid.,* p. 908.
88. *Ibid.,* p. 909.
89. The last two quotes are from "Address to Local Societies by the Convention of the National Typographical Society in 1836," reprinted in *ibid.,* pp. 977-978.
90. George McNeil (ed.), *op cit.,* pp. 85-86.
91. For a discussion of the causes of the panic of 1837, see Reginald Charles, *The Panic of 1837* (Chicago: University of Chicago Press, 1924), Chapters 1 and 2.

CHAPTER 3. SETBACKS AND SURVIVAL

1. The question has been dealt with extensively and adequately by Lloyd Ulman, *The Rise of the National Trade Union* (Cambridge, Mass.: Harvard University Press, 1956).
2. Jesse R. Robinson, *The Amalgamated Association of Iron, Steel and Tin Workers* (Baltimore: Johns Hopkins Press, 1920), p. 14.
3. Ethelbert Stewart, "A Documentary History of Early Organization of Printers," *Bulletin of the Department of Labor,* Nov. 1905, pp. 915-932.

4. *Ibid.,* p. 934.

5. Appendix A, No. 10, in *ibid.,* p. 982, contains the appeal.

6. *Ibid.,* p. 983.

7. *Ibid.*

8. John Jarrett, "The Story of the Iron Workers," in George McNeil (ed.), *The Labor Movement: The Problem of To-Day* (Boston: A. W. Bridgman, 1887), p. 269.

9. *Twelfth Annual Report of the [Massachusetts] Bureau of Statistics of Labor* (Boston, 1881), pp. 8-10

10. Frank T. Stockton, *The International Molders' Union of North America* (Baltimore: Johns Hopkins University, 1921), p. 11.

11. Henry E. Hoagland, "The Rise of the Iron Molders' International Union," *American Economic Review,* June 1913, p. 297.

12. *Ibid.,* pp. 298-299.

13. *Ibid.,* p. 300.

14. *Ibid.*

15. *Ibid.,* p. 302.

16. Quoted in *ibid.,* p. 305.

17. See *ibid.,* p. 307; Jonathan Grossman, *William Sylvis, Pioneer of American Labor* (New York: Columbia University Press, 1945), Chapter IX.

18. The changes in views of individuals do not always give a clue to the nature of their activities. For example, William D. Haywood was a trade unionist, albeit a militant one, before he become a Socialist lecturer and then an IWW leader. William Z. Foster was, for a time, a successful trade union organizer. None of their subsequent radical activity casts any light upon the trade union movement, except that they, along with Debs, found it wanting.

19. Charles H. Green, *The Headwear Worker,* (New York: United Hatters, Cap and Millinery Workers International Union, n.d.) p. 21.

20. Quoted from the rules and regulations, in Donald B. Robinson. *Spotlight on a Union* (New York: Dial Press, 1948), p. 39.

21. Quoted in Robinson, *op. cit.,* p. 44.

22. Quoted in *ibid.,* p. 45.

23. *Ibid.*

24. *Third Annual Report of the [U.S.] Commissioner of Labor,* 1887 (Washington: Government Printing Office, 1888), p. 1038.

25. William A. Sullivan, *The Industrial Worker in Pennsylvania, 1800–1840* (Harrisburg, Pa.: Historical and Museum Commission, 1958), found 138 strikes had taken place in Pennsylvania between 1800 and 1840, a much larger number than had previously been identified.

26. *Ibid.,* pp. 1037-1040.

27. John R. Commons and associates (eds.), *A Documentary History of American Industrial Society* (Cleveland: Arthur A. Clark Co., 1910), VIII, 240.

28. The table devised by Professor Slichter is reproduced in Ulman, *op. cit.,* p. 4.

29. *Eleventh Annual Report of the [Massachusetts] Bureau of Statistics of Labor, January 1880* (Boston: Rand, Avery, and Company, Printers to the Commonwealth, 1880), pp. 8-9.

30. *Third Annual Report of the [U.S.] Commissioner of Labor,* p. 1041.

31. George McNeil (ed.), *op. cit.,* pp. 118-119.

CHAPTER 4. IN SEARCH OF SHORTER HOURS

1. Hannah Josephson, *The Golden Threads* (New York: Duell, Sloan and Pearce, 1949), Chapter 4, describes the Waltham system of employing young women.

2. Norman Ware, *The Industrial Worker* (Boston: Houghton Mifflin Co., 1924), p. 125.

3. *Ibid.*, p. 132.

4. John R. Commons and associates (eds.), *A Documentary History of American Industrial Society* (Cleveland: Arthur H. Clark Co., 1910), p. 81. The quote is from Massachusetts House (1842), No. 4.

5. *Working Men's Advocate*, October 19, 1844, in Commons, *A Documentary History*, VIII, 97.

6. *Ibid.*, p. 99.

7. Quoted in Charles Sotheran, *Horace Greeley and Other Pioneers of American Socialism* (New York: Humboldt Publishing Co., 1892), p. 125.

8. Ware, *op. cit.*, pp. 190-193.

9. John R. Commons and associates, *History of Labor in the United States* (New York: Macmillian Co., 1918), I, 512-514.

10. Helene Zara Zahler, *Eastern Workingmen and National Land Policy, 1829–1862* (New York: Columbia University Press, 1941), p. 33.

11. *The Awl*, April 5, 1845, in Commons, *A Documentary History*, VIII, 104-105.

12. *Voice of Industry*, June 12, 1845; last two quotes from *ibid.*, July 13, 1845.

13. Massachusetts House Legislative Document 50 (March 1845), in Commons, *A Documentary History*, VIII, 133-135.

14. Quotes are from Massachusetts House Legislative Document 50, in *ibid.*, p. 150. The report was signed by William Schouler, chairman.

15. New York *Weekly Tribune*, April 22, 1848, in *ibid.*, p. 200 for quote.

16. From *Pittsburgh Daily Commercial Journal*, August 3, 1848, in *ibid.*, p. 202, which reproduces statement of manufacturers.

17. *Ibid.*, p. 204.

CHAPTER 5. THE LABOR MOVEMENT IN THE 1860's

1. Emerson David Fite, *Social and Industrial Conditions in the North During the Civil War* (New York: Macmillian Co., 1910), p. 24.

2. *Ibid.*, Chapter 4; Melvin Thomas Copeland, *The Cotton Manufacturing Industry* (Cambridge, Mass.: Harvard University Press, 1923), pp. 11-16.

3. Fite, *op. cit.*, p. 190.

4. Edward A. Wieck, *The American Miners' Union* (New York: Russell Sage Foundation, 1940), p. 63. Andrew Roy, *A History of the Coal Miners of the United States* (Columbus, Ohio: J. L. Trauger Printing Co., 1903), p. 75, claims the Bates Union was formed in 1849.

5. Wieck, *op. cit.*, p. 63; Roy, *op. cit.*, p. 75.

6. Wieck, *op. cit.*, pp. 218-219, gives the entire statement; Roy, *op. cit.*, p. 65, quotes extracts.

7. Quoted in Wieck, *op. cit.*, p. 91.

8. See John McBride, "Coal Miners," in George McNeil (ed.), *The Labor*

Movement: The Problem of To-Day (Boston: A. W. Bridgman Co., 1887), pp. 248-249.

9. Quoted from *New York Tribune,* August 6, 1850, in Harry C. Bates, *Bricklayers' Century of Craftsmanship* (Washington: Bricklayers, Masons and Plasterers International Union of America, 1955), p. 15.

10. Quote from *New York Tribune,* May 23, 1850, in *ibid.,* p. 13.

11. *Fincher's Trade Review,* October 4, 1864, in *ibid.,* pp. 17-18.

12. *Convention Proceedings, 1865–1866* (typewritten) p. 11; in *ibid.,* p. 21.

13. *Ibid.,* pp. 27-29.

14. *Eighth Annual Report of the [Massachusetts] Bureau of Statistics of Labor,* 1877, pp. 18-19.

15. Don D. Lescohier, *The Knights of St. Crispin: A Study in Industrial Causes of Trade Unionism,* University of Wisconsin Bulletin No. 355 (Madison, Wisc., 1910), pp. 7-8.

16. *Report of the [Massachusetts] Bureau of Statistics of Labor Embracing the Account of its Operations and Inquiries from March 1, 1870, to March 1, 1871,* p. 117.

17. *Ibid.,* pp. 127-128.

18. Lescohier, *op. cit.,* p. 217.

19. A number of articles of the Crispin constitution are printed in *Eighth Annual Report of the [Massachusetts] Bureau of Statistics of Labor,* 1877, pp. 22-23.

20. P. M. Arthur, "The Rise of Railroad Organization," in George McNeil (ed.), *op. cit.,* pp. 312-313.

21. *Ibid.,* pp. 315-316.

22. *Ibid.,* p. 323.

23. John R. Commons and associates (eds.), *A Documentary History of American Industrial Society* (Cleveland: Arthur H. Clark Co., 1910), IX, 126.

24. Eugene Staley, *History of the Illinois State Federation of Labor* (Chicago: University of Chicago Press, 1930), p. 69.

25. John R. Commons and associates, *History of Labour in the United States* (New York: Macmillan Co., 1918), I, pp. 86-97.

26. Commons, *A Documentary History,* I, 130.

27. *Ibid.,* p. 132.

28. *Ibid.,* pp. 135-138, quote on p. 135.

29. *The Address of the National Labor Congress to the Workingmen of the United States,* in *ibid.,* p. 141. The address was the work of a committee headed by A. C. Cameron, and it was authorized by the 1866 convention but not issued until the following year.

30. *Ibid.,* p. 148.

31. *Ibid.,* p. 153.

32. *Ibid.*

33. *Ibid.,* pp. 163-165.

34. *Ibid.,* p. 171.

35. *Ibid.,* pp. 174, 175.

36. Quotes are from *ibid.,* p. 187; Jonathan Grossman, *William Sylvis, Pioneer of American Labor* (New York: Columbia University Press, 1945), p. 191.

37. Commons, *A Documentary History,* IX, 207-208.

38. *Ibid.,* pp. 229-231.

39. *Ibid.*, pp. 239-240.

40. *Twenty-first Annual Session of the International Typographical Union,* 1871, p. 13.

41. *Coopers' Journal,* February 1872, p. 599.

42. *First Annual Report of the [Ohio] Bureau of Labor Statistics,* 1878, p. 35.

43. *Coopers' Journal,* October 1872, p. 599.

44. Commons, *A Documentary History,* II, 158; *Constitution and Rules of Order of Industrial Brotherhood of the United States* (no date or place).

45. *Twenty-third Annual Session of the International Typographical Union,* 1875, pp. 48-49.

CHAPTER 6. THE ERUPTION OF VIOLENCE

1. Joseph D. Weeks, *Report on Trades Societies in the United States,* a monograph issued by the Census Office, Department of Interior, and part of *Report on the Statistics of Wages in Manufacturing Industries with a Report on the Average Retail Prices of Necessaries of Life and on Trades Societies and Strikes and Lockouts* (Washington: Government Printing Office, 1886), p. 1.

2. Joseph D. Weeks, *Report on Strikes and Lockouts Occurring Within the United States During the Calendar Year 1880,* monograph issued by the Census Office, Department of the Interior (Washington: Government Printing Office, 1886), p. 3.

3. *Ibid.*, p. 6.

4. George O. Virtue, *The Anthracite Mine Laborers,* Bulletin of Department of Labor (Washington, November 1897), pp. 729-30; Peter Roberts, *The Anthracite Coal Industry* (New York: Macmillan Co., 1901), pp. 1-82, deals with the growth of the industry.

5. Charles Edward Killeen, *John Siney: The Pioneer in Industrial Unionism and Industrial Government,* an unpublished manuscript in the Library of the University of Wisconsin.

6. *Twelfth Annual Report of the [Massachusetts] Bureau of Statistics of Labor,* January 1881, p. 84. *First Annual Report of the [Pennsylvania] Bureau of Labor and Agriculture,* 1872–1873, pp. 331-336.

7. Quote in *Twelfth Annual Report of the [Massachusetts] Bureau of Statistics of Labor,* p. 25; also in Virtue, *op. cit.,* p. 734.

8. *Ibid.*, pp. 29-31; Marvin W. Schlegel, *Ruler of Reading: The Life of Franklin B. Gowen* (Harrisburg, Pa.: Archives Publishing Co. of Pa., Inc., 1947), pp.19-21.

9. *Twelfth Annual Report of the [Massachusetts] Bureau of Statistics of Labor,* p. 86.

10. Schlegel, *op. cit.,* pp. 62-76.

11. *History of Schuylkill County, Pennsylvania* (New York: W. W. Munsell and Co., 1881), p. 16.

12. George Potter, *To the Golden Door* (Boston: Little, Brown and Co., 1960), p. 328.

13. A description of the methods of the Molly Maguires in the files of the Pinkerton's National Detective Agency, Inc., in New York City.

14. J. Walter Coleman, *Labor Disturbances in Pennsylvania* (Washington: The Catholic University of America, 1936), pp. 40-69.

15. Allan Pinkerton, *The Molly Maguires and the Detective* (New York: G. W. Carleton and Co., 1877), describes the work of the agent and many of the acts of violence. The author was convinced that the Mollies were a secret and criminal band.

16. The information is taken from notes and reports in the archives of Pinkerton's National Detective Agency, Inc.

17. Report of James McParlan, December 10, 1875.

18. From the archives of Pinkerton's National Detective Agency, Inc.

19. Schlegel, *op. cit.*, p. 144.

20. The study of the Molly Maguires by Wayne G. Broehl, Jr., to be published by Harvard University Press, re-examines the question and presents a great deal of new information.

21. Clifton K. Yearley, Jr., "The Baltimore and Ohio Railroad Strike of 1877," *Maryland Historical Magazine*, September 6, 1956, p. 188.

22. Robert V. Bruce, *1877: The Year of Violence* (Indianapolis: Bobbs-Merrill Co., 1959), pp. 34-42.

23. Yearley, *op. cit.*, pp. 31-32.

24. *Ibid.*, p. 200.

25. Telegram to President Hayes from Governor Henry M. Mathews, July 17, 1877, in Edward Winslow Martin (pseudonym of James Dabney McCabe), *The History of the Great Riots* (Philadelphia: National Publishing Co., 1877), pp. 24-25.

26. The telegrams exchanged between Governor Mathews, President Hayes, and Secretary McCrary are given in *ibid.*

27. Telegram from W. H. French to Major General Hancock, July 23, 1877, in *ibid.*, p. 42.

28. J. A. Dacus, *Annals of the Great Strikes* (St. Louis: Scammell and Co., 1877), pp. 102-103.

29. Telegram of sheriff to governor, July 19, 1877, in Martin, *op. cit.*, p. 78.

30. In *ibid.*, pp. 93, 114.

31. *Ibid.*, p. 179.

32. The complete report of the coroner's jury is in *ibid*, pp. 185-188.

33. *Ibid.*, pp. 254-258.

34. To the Committee of Employees of the New York Central and Hudson River Railroad Company from William H. Vanderbilt, July 24, 1877, in *ibid.*, p. 264.

35. Letter to the employees of the New York Central and Hudson River Railroad from William H. Vanderbilt, August 1, 1877, in *ibid.*, pp. 278-279.

36. Resolution of the meeting in *ibid.*, pp. 309-310.

37. Letter issued on July 24 by Charles Paine, general superintendent, in *ibid.*, p. 345.

38. *Ibid.*, pp. 354-358.

39. Proclamation of Governor Shelby M. Cullom, July 27, 1877, in *ibid.*, pp. 393-394.

40. In *ibid.*, pp. 395-419.

CHAPTER 7. THE KNIGHTS OF LABOR

1. Terence V. Powderly, *Thirty Years of Labor* (Philadelphia: T. V. Powderly, 1890), p. 74.

2. *Ibid.*, p. 77.

3. *Ibid.*, p. 78.

4. *Ibid.*

5. *Ibid.*, p. 81.

6. Uriah S. Stephens to W. Albin, March 13, 1879; to John M. Cooper, June 5, 1879. The letters of officers of the Knights of Labor are in the archives of The Catholic University, Washington, D.C.

7. Powderly, *op. cit.*, p. 83.

8. Stephens to James S. Sullivan, August 19, 1879.

9. Powderly, *op. cit.*, p. 97.

10. Statement of Grand Secretary Robert D. Layton, in *Report of the Committee of the [U.S.] Senate Upon Relations Between Labor and Capital*, (Washington: Government Printing Office, 1885), I, 2-3.

11. Powderly, *op. cit.*, pp. 99-101.

12. Quote is from the convention proceedings of the Philadelphia convention, in *ibid.*, pp. 120-121.

13. *Ibid.*, p. 128.

14. The "preamble" is reprinted in *ibid.*, pp. 129-130; it is also found in *Report of the Committee of the [U.S.] Senate . . . ,* p. 2.

15. Quote in Powderly, *op. cit.*, p. 130.

16. *Ibid.*, p. 146.

17. *Record of the Proceedings of the Second Regular Session of the General Assembly,* January 1879, p. 75; secrecy and the reaction of the Catholic hierarchy is treated in detail by Henry J. Browne, *The Catholic Church and the Knights of Labor* (Washington: Catholic University Press, 1949).

18. Quoted in Browne, *op. cit.*, p. 324; see also Terence V. Powderly, *The Path I Trod* (New York: Columbia University Press, 1940), pp. 317-382, for his role in the efforts to avoid condemnation of the Knights of Labor by the Vatican.

19. Cardinal Gibbon's statement to the Prefect of the Sacred Congregation of the Propaganda is reprinted as Appendix III in Browne, *op cit.*

20. *Record of the Proceedings of the Second Regular Session of the General Assembly . . . ,* p. 54.

21. *Ibid.*

22. *Ibid.*, p. 55.

23. *Ibid.*, pp. 69, 72.

24. Powderly, *op. cit.*, pp. 236-237.

25. See Norman J. Ware, *The Labor Movement in the United States, 1860–1895* (New York: D. Appleton Co., 1929), pp. 320-333, for an appraisal. Ware's book is the standard work on the subject. See also *Report of the Committee of the [U.S.] Senate on the Relations Between Capital and Labor,* 1885, I, 4-6.

26. *Record of Proceedings of the Third Regular Session of the General Assembly,* September 1879, pp. 120, 130.

27. *Record of the Proceedings of the Fourth Regular Session of the General Assembly,* 1880, p. 171.

28. *Ibid.*, p. 172.

29. *Ibid.*, p. 181.

30. *Ibid.*, p. 225.

31. Article VIII of the constitution in *ibid.*, p. 247.

32. *Record of the Proceedings of the Fifth Regular Session of the General Assembly,* 1881, p. 281.

33. Powderly to L. J. Mooney, March 30, 1880.

34. Powderly to Brother Lawler, October 11, 1881.

35. *Record of the Proceedings of the Sixth Regular Session of the General Assembly,* 1882, p. 279.

36. *Record of the Proceedings of the Seventh Regular Session of the General Assembly,* 1883, p. 405.

37. Powderly to W. A. Vanner, February 8, 1883.

38. *Record of Proceedings of the Seventh Regular Assembly . . . ,* pp. 493, 502.

39. *Iron Molders' Journal,* November 10, 1878, p. 15; *Proceedings of the Fourteenth Session of the Iron Molders' Union, 1878,* p. 35.

40. *Twenty-seventh Annual Session of the International Typographical Union,* 1879, pp. 39-40; *Twenty-eighth Annual Session of the International Typographical Union,* 1880, p. 61.

41. Ware, *op. cit.,* p. 66.

42. Testimony of Samuel Gompers in *Report of the Committee of the [U.S.] Senate . . . ,* p. 270.

43. *Terre Haute Press,* August 3, 1881.

44. *Report of the First Annual Convention of the Federation of Organized Trades and Labor Unions of the United States and Canada,* 1881, p. 7.

45. *Ibid.*

46. *Ibid.,* pp. 14-15.

47. Terence V. Powderly to A. M. Owens, October 22, 1881, in archives of the Catholic University, Washington, D.C.

48. *Report of the First Annual Convention of the Federation of Organized Trades and Labor Unions . . . ,* p. 15.

49. *Thirty-first Annual Session of the International Typographical Union,* 1883, p. 11.

50. *Report of the Annual Session of the Federation of Organized Trades and Labor Unions of the United States and Canada,* 1884, p. 17.

51. *Ibid.,* pp. 24-25.

CHAPTER 8. STRIKES OF THE KNIGHTS OF LABOR

1. *Report of the Committee of the [U.S.] Senate Upon the Conditions of Capital and Labor* (Washington: Government Printing Office, 1885), I, 115.

2. *Ibid.,* p. 116, for quote.

3. *Ibid.,* p. 1084.

4. *Ibid.,* p. 1092.

5. Norman Ware, *The Labor Movement in the United States, 1860–1895* (New York: D. Appleton and Co., 1929), pp. 128-129; George E. McNeil (ed.), *The Labor Movement: The Problem of To-Day* (Boston: A. M. Bridgman Co., 1887), pp. 391-392.

6. Resolution quoted in Joseph R. Buchanan, *The Story of a Labor Agitator* (New York: Outlook Co., 1903), p. 74.

7. Buchanan, *op. cit.,* pp. 76-98.

8. *Investigation of Labor Troubles in Missouri, Arkansas, Kansas, Texas, and Illinois,* 49th Cong., 2d sess., House of Representatives Report 4714, (Washington: Government Printing Office, 1887), p. i.

9. *Ibid.,* p. ii.

10. Request to Captain R. S. Hayes, first vice-president and executive officer of the Missouri Pacific Railway Company and associated roads, in *ibid.,* p. iii.

11. Quote is from *ibid.,* p. v; see also Buchanan, *op. cit.,* pp. 214-216; Ware, *op. cit.,* pp. 140-141.

12. *Investigation of Labor Troubles;* H. Rept. 4174, Part I, p. vi.

13. *Ibid.,* p. x; Buchanan, *op. cit.,* p. 239.

14. Ruth Allen, *The Great Southwest Strike* (Austin, Texas: University of Texas, 1942), pp. 44-45.

15. *Ibid.,* p. 46.

16. *Labor Troubles in the South and West,* Part I, p. xii.

17. *Ibid.,* p. xiii.

18. *Record of Proceedings of the General Assembly of the Knights of Labor Commencing With Session at Richmond, Virginia, October 4 to 20, 1886,* IV, 137.

19. Bureau of Labor Statistics and Inspection of Missouri, *The Official History of the Great Strike of 1886 of the Southwestern System,* 1887, p. 17.

20. *Labor Troubles in the South and West,* p. xviii.

21. Terence V. Powderly, *The Path I Trod,* (New York: Columbia University Press, 1940), pp. 121-123.

22. Powderly to Gould, April 12, 1886, in *Labor Troubles in the South and West,* p. 42.

23. Powderly to McDowell, April 8, 1886, in *ibid.,* p. 19.

24. Testimony of McDowell, in *ibid.,* p. 19.

25. Powderly, *op. cit.,* pp. 121-123.

26. T. B. Barry, a member of the general executive board to the general assembly, November 22, 1886, in *Proceedings of the General Assembly of the Knights of Labor Eleventh Session,* 1887, p. 1419.

27. P. M. Flannagan to Powderly, November 7, 1886, in *ibid.,* p. 1419.

28. *Ibid.,* p. 1421.

29. Powderly to Barry, November 10, 1886, in *ibid.,* p. 1421.

30. Barry and Albert A. Carlton to Powderly, November 11 and 12, 1886; Powderly to Barry and Albert A. Carlton, November 11, 1886, in *ibid.,* p. 1482.

31. *Ibid.,* pp. 1775-1776.

32. G. O. Virtue, "The Anthracite Mine Laborers," *Bulletin of the Department of Labor,* November 1897, pp. 728-774.

33. *Labor Troubles in the Anthracite Regions of Pennsylvania, 1887–1888,* H. Rept. 4147, 50th Cong., 2d sess., pp. lxxxv-cxiii, 136-137, 148.

34. *Ibid.,* pp. viii-xi.

CHAPTER 9. THE AMERICAN FEDERATION OF LABOR

1. Powderly to J. P. McDonnell, September 24, 1882.

2. *Record of Proceedings of the Eighth Regular Session of the General Assembly* 1884, pp. 704, 764.

3. Powderly to John F. Grosscup, June 23, 1880.

4. *Thirty-second Annual Session of the International Typographical Union,* 1884, p. 12.

5. *Twenty-first Annual Convention of the Bricklayers, and Masons' International Union,* 1886, pp. 62-63.

6. *Fifteenth Annual Session of the Cigar Makers' International Union,* 1883, pp. 2-8.

7. *Ibid.*

8. *Thirty-first Annual Session of the International Typographical Union,* 1886, p. 24.

9. *Report of the Committee of the [U.S.] Senate on the Relations Between Labor and Capital and Testimony Taken by the Committee,* 1885, I, 322.

10. *Ibid.,* p. 328.

11. Powderly to Fred Turner, May 1, 1886.

12. *Record of Proceedings of the General Assembly of the Knights of Labor, Richmond, Virginia,* October 1886, pp. 137-138.

13. *Proceedings of the Bricklayers' and Masons' International Union,* 1887, p. 63.

14. *Ibid.,* p. 64.

15. *Record of Proceedings of the Second General Session of the General Assembly,* January 1879, p. 62.

16. *Record of Proceedings of the Eighth General Session of the General Assembly,* 1884, p. 572.

17. *Record of Proceedings of the Ninth General Session of the General Assembly,* 1885, p. 25.

18. Powderly to L. Steenback, May 1, 1886.

19. *Record of Proceedings, October 1886,* p. 200; *Proceedings of the General Assembly of the Knights of Labor Eleventh Session,* 1887, pp. 1528-1531.

20. Buchanan, *op. cit.,* pp. 314-315.

21. *Record of Proceedings,* 1887, p. 1528.

22. *Record of Proceedings,* October 1886, pp. 154-156; Gompers regarded T. B. McGuire, a member of the K. C. general executive board and the Home Club, as a leader of the anti-trade-union faction. Gompers to Robert A. Mullen, February 10, 1896.

23. *First Annual Convention of the American Federation of Labor,* 1886, p. 18.

24. *Ibid.,* p. 18.

25. The last statement, up to the word "occupation," was made by John Howes; the rest, by A. G. Denny, another member of the Knights' committee, in *ibid.*

26. *Record of Proceedings of the Regular Session of the General Assembly,* 1887, p. 1447.

27. *First Annual Convention of the American Federation of Labor,* 1886, pp. 19-20.

28. *Ibid.,* p. 19.

29. Gompers to Web Weavers Amalgamated Association, March 5, 1888.

30. *Official Report of Proceedings of the Second Annual Convention* (AFL), 1887, p. 8.

31. Philip Taft, *The A. F. of L. in the Time of Gompers* (New York: Harper and Brothers, 1957), p. 87. The quote is from the *Journal of the Knights of Labor,* October 22, 1888.

32. W. H. Bailey to the General Executive Board, March 3, 1887, in *Record of Proceedings,* 1887, p. 1370.

33. Gompers to William Weihe, February 25, 1887.

34. Powderly to Christopher Evans, February 8, 1892.

35 From the circular calling the conference of July 1894 by Joseph H. Buchanan.

36. The finances are taken from the convention reports of the particular years.

37. *Fourth Annual Report of the [Illinois] Bureau of Labor Statistics*, 1886, p. 169.

38. *Record of the Proceedings of the Seventh Regular Session*, p. 410.

39. *Record of Proceedings*, 1887, p. 1547.

40. *Ibid.*, p. 1765.

41. Gompers to N. E. Mathewson, October 10, 1890, in AFL-CIO archives.

42. *Ibid.*

CHAPTER 10. SHORTER HOURS

1. *U.S. Statutes at Large*, XV, 77.

2. *United States* v. *Martin*, 94 U.S. 400 (1876).

3. *United States* v. *Post*, 148 U.S. 124 (1893).

4. *27 U.S. Statutes at Large*, 340.

5. *Ellis* v. *U.S.*, 206 U.S. 246 (1907).

6. *Report of Proceedings of the Federation of Organized Trades and Labor Unions of the United States and Canada*, 1884, p. 10.

7. *Ibid.*, p. 11.

8. *Ibid.*, p. 14.

9. Terence V. Powderly, *Thirty Years of Labor* (T. V. Powderly, 1890), p. 252.

10. *Report of Proceedings of the Third Annual Convention* (AFL), 1888, p. 9. Quote from Gompers' report.

11. *Ibid.*, pp. 9-10, 25.

12. *Report of Proceedings of the Ninth Annual Convention* (AFL), 1889, p. 14.

13. Powderly, *op. cit.*, pp. 263-264.

14. *Report of the Proceedings of the Ninth Annual Convention . . .*, p. 30.

15. *Report of Proceedings of the Twenty-seventh Annual Convention* (AFL), 1907, p. 66.

16. Morris Hillquit, *History of Socialism in the United States* (New York: Funk and Wagnalls Co., 1903), pp. 175-196.

17. Hillquit, op. *cit.*, pp. 213-214.

18. Rudolf Rocker, *Johann Most Das Leben Eines Rebellen* (Berlin: "Der Syndikalist," 1924), p. 160.

19. Henry David, *History of the Haymarket Affair* (New York: Farrar and Rinehart, 1936), pp. 54-68.

20. *Revolutionäre Kriegswissenschaft* (New York: Druck and Verlag des Internationalen Zeitungs, n.d.), A typical statement: "Dynamit han durch eine Lunte, einen glimmenden Schwamm oder eine in Brand gestecket Zunderschnür zur Explosion kommen," p. 7.

21. David, *op. cit.*, pp. 99-100, for quotes.

22. John R. Commons and associates, *History of Labour in the United States* (New York: Macmillan Co., 1918), II, 386-387.

23. *The Lives, Crimes and Conviction of the Eight Chicago Anarchists* (Chicago: G. S. Baldwin, 1886), p. 36.

24. The "Revenge Circular" is reproduced in David, *op. cit.*, p. 192.

25. *August Spies et al.* v. *The People of the State of Illinois.* Brief and Argument for Plaintiffs in Error. In the Supreme Court of Illinois, Northern Grand Division, March Term A.D. 1877, p. 333.

26. *Ibid.*, p. 391.

27. Quoted in *ibid.*, pp. 391-392.

28. Ernest Bloomfield Zeisler, *The Haymarket Riot* (Chicago: Alexander J. Isaacs, 1958), p. 29.

29. *August Spies et al.* v. *The People of the State of Illinois*, pp. 2-3.

30. *Ibid.*, pp. 85-86.

31. *Ibid.*, p. 109.

32. *Ibid.*, pp. 152-153.

33. Quoted from judge's charge in *ibid.*, pp. 256-257.

34. *Ibid.*, p. 269.

35. Zeisler, *op. cit.*, pp. 78-79.

36. David, *op. cit.*, p. 406.

37. *Record of Proceedings of the General Assembly of the Knights of Labor*, 1887, pp. 1499-1500.

38. Harry Barnard *"Eagle Forgotten": The Life of John Peter Altgeld* (Indianapolis: Bobbs-Merrill Co., 1938), p. 188.

39. Henry M. Christman (ed.), "Reasons for Pardoning Fielden, Neebe, and Schwab, the So-Called Anarchists," in *The Mind and Spirit of John Peter Altgeld* (Urbana, Ill.: University of Illinois Press, 1960), p. 84.

40. Zeisler, *op. cit.*, pp. 115-116.

CHAPTER 11. THE RISE OF OPPOSITION TO LABOR IN THE 1890's

1. Margaret T. Byington, *Homestead, the Households of a Mill Town* (New York: Charities Publication Society, 1910), pp. 3-6.

2. John Jarrett, "The Story of the Iron Workers," in George McNeil (ed.), *The Labor Movement: The Problem of To-Day* (Boston: A. W. Bridgman Co., 1887), pp. 285-286.

3. Constitution and General Laws of the National Amalgamated Association of Iron and Steel Workers of the United States, adopted as amended by the national convention at Pittsburgh, June 1890, Art. I, Sec. I; see Jesse S. Robinson, *The Amalgamated Association of Iron, Steel and Tin Workers* (Baltimore: Johns Hopkins Press, 1920), for the policies of the Amalgamated.

4. John A. Fitch, *The Steel Workers* (New York: Charities Publication Society, 1910), p. 98.

5. Jarrett, *op. cit.*, p. 308.

6. Fitch, *op. cit.*, p. 96.

7. *Ibid.*

8. H. C. Frick to Henry Phipps, Jr., John Walker and others, May 13, 1887, in George Harvey, *Henry Clay Frick: The Man* (New York: Charles Scribner's Sons, 1928), p. 85.

9. Fitch, *op. cit.*, p. 120.

10. Harvey, *op. cit.*, p. 109.

11. *Employment of Pinkerton Detectives*, House of Representatives Report 2447, 52d Cong., 2d sess., pp. 19-22.

12. *Ibid.*, p. 23.

13. *Investigation of Labor Troubles,* U.S. Senate Report 1280, 52d Cong., 2d sess., p. 159. Testimony of H. C. Frick.

14. Arthur G. Burgoyne, *Homestead* (Pittsburgh: D. S. Mitchell, 1893), p. 24.

15. Testimony of President William Weihe in S. Rept. 1280, pp. 196-198.

16. Burgoyne, *op. cit.,* p. 32.

17. H. Rept. 2447, p. 30.

18. James Howard Bridge, *The History of the Carnegie Steel Company* (New York: Aldine Book Co., 1903), p. 204, gives the notice sent by Carnegie.

19. Excerpts from Carnegie's letter are in *ibid.,* p. 205.

20. Excerpts from letter in *ibid.,* p. 206.

21. Testimony of H. C. Frick, in H. Rept. 2447, p. 33.

22. *Ibid.*, p. 34.

23. Burgoyne, *op. cit.,* p. 54.

24. Sheriff W. H. McCleary to Governor Robert E. Pattison, July 10, 1892, in *ibid.,* p. 58.

25. Hugh O'Donnell to Whitelaw Reid, July 16, 1892, in Edward Bemis, "The Homestead Strike," *Journal of Political Economy,* June 1894, p. 385.

26. Quoted in *op. cit.,* p. 231.

27. Quoted in *ibid.,* p. 233.

28. House of Representatives, *Hearings Before the Committee on Investigation of the U.S. Corporation* (Washington: Government Printing Office, 1912), IV, 2528.

29. Emma Goldman, *Living My Life* (New York: Alfred A. Knopf, 1931), p. 98.

30. Burgoyne, *op. cit.,* p. 203, for the quote.

31. Quoted in Burgoyne, *op. cit.,* p. 216.

32. Quoted in Burgoyne, *op. cit.,* p. 168.

33. Burgoyne claimed that reports of the receipts for Homestead Day were about $40,000. Burgoyne, *op. cit.,* p. 220.

34. *Ibid.,* p. 177.

35. *Ibid.,* p. 221.

36. Statement of William A. and Robert A. Pinkerton, in S. Rept. 1280, p. 242.

37. Bridge, *op. cit.,* p. 248.

38. Statement of George M. Pullman, *Report on the Chicago Strike of June–July, 1894 by the U.S. Strike Commission* (appointed by the President, July 26, 1894, under the Provisions of Sec. 6 of Chap. 1063 of the Laws of the United States Passed October 1, 1888 [Washington: Government Printing Office, 1895]), p. 529.

39. Alden Lindsey, *The Pullman Strike* (Chicago: University of Chicago Press, 1942), p. 49.

40. *Report of the U.S. Strike Commission,* p. xxii.

41. C. H. Salmon, *The Burlington Strike: Its Motives and Methods Including the Causes of the Strike* (Aurora, Ill.: Bunnell and Ward, 1889), pp. 23-32; Emory R. Johnson, "Brotherhood Relief and Insurance of Rail Employees," *Bulletin of the Department of Labor,* July 1898, pp. 555-561; *Reports of the [U.S.] Industrial Commission,* 1901, Vol. xvii; Part 10.

42. Salmon, *op. cit.,* pp. 127-129, 174, 321-322; quote on 322.

43. Quoted from decision in *ibid.*, p. 323.

44. Quoted from an address of Debs in *Locomotive Firemen's Magazine*, September 1896, p. 178.

45. From the "Constitution of the American Railway Union," in *Report of the U.S. Strike Commission*, p. 58.

46. Testimony of Eugene V. Debs, in *ibid.*, pp. 134-135.

47. Testimony of George W. Howard, in *ibid.*, p. 6.

48. Testimony of Secretary Sylvester Keliher, in *ibid.*, p. 79.

49. Statement of Debs, in *ibid.*, p. 130.

50. *Report of the Special Committee*, in *ibid.*, p. 80.

51. Statement of Thomas H. Wickes, in *ibid.*, p. 590. The record of the convention dealing with the Pullman Affair is in *ibid.*, pp. 87-94.

52. Resolution of General Managers' Association, in *ibid.*, p. 250.

53. Testimony of John M. Eagan, in *ibid.*, p. 271.

54. Testimony of Mayor Hopkins, in *ibid.*, p. 345.

55. Testimony in *ibid.*, pp. 341-342.

56. *Ibid.*, p. 354.

57. Henry James, *Richard Olney and His Public Service* (Boston: Houghton Mifflin Co., 1923), p. 201, contains extracts from Olney's memorandum on the Chicago strike, and the quote is from there.

58. Quoted in *ibid.*, p. 48.

59. Telegram in *ibid.*, p. 49.

60. Allan Nevins, *Grover Cleveland, A Study in Courage* (New York: Dodd, Mead and Co., 1932), pp. 622-623.

61. Testimony in *Report of U.S. Strike Commission*, p. 373.

62. *Ibid.*, p. 384, for quote, and p. 400.

63. Lindsey, *op. cit.*, p. 214.

64. John P. Altgeld to President Grover Cleveland, July 5, 1894, Harry Barnard, *"Eagle Forgotten": The Life of John P. Altgeld* (Indianapolis: Bobbs-Merrill Co., 1938), pp. 295, 310.

65. Cleveland to Altgeld, July 6, 1894, in *ibid.*, pp. 306-307.

66. Testimony of Debs, in *Report of U.S. Strike Commission*, p. 143.

67. Testimony of Debs, in *ibid.*, p. 146.

68. Quote from Gompers' testimony, in *ibid.*, p. 191.

69. *Ibid.*

70. *In re Debs, Petitioner for habeas corpus*, 158 U.S. 564 (1895).

71. *Locomotive Engineers' Journal*, July 1894, p. 634.

CHAPTER 12. EXPANSION AND ITS LIMITS

1. The armies of the unemployed of the 1890's are fully treated in Donald D. McMurray, *Coxey's Army* (Boston: Little, Brown and Co., 1929).

2. Victor S. Clark, *History of Manufactures in the United States, 1860–1914* (Washington: Carnegie Institution of Washington, 1928), pp. 544-546.

3. *Report of the Industrial Commission on Trusts and Industrial Combinations*, 1901, XIII, 461.

4. *Report of the Hearings on Hours of Labor for Workmen, Mechanics, etc. Employed Upon Public Works of the United States Before the Committee Relative to H.R. 6882*, 1900, p. 82.

5. *Report of the Industrial Commission*, XVII, 118, 129.

6. *Ibid.*, 824, 826, 832, 845.

7. Leo Wolman, *Growth of American Trade Unions, 1880–1923* (New York: National Bureau of Economic Research, 1924), pp. 22-23. George E. Barnett, "Growth of Labor Organization in the United States, 1897-1914," in *Quarterly Journal of Economics,* August 16, p. 788.

8. See Barnett, *op. cit.,* p. 789, for earlier periods to 1914.

9. An act concerning carriers engaged in interstate commerce and their employees, approved June 1, 1898.

10. Massachusetts, Connecticut, New York, Pennsylvania, New Jersey, Ohio, Indiana, Illinois, Wisconsin, Minnesota, Kansas, Missouri, California, Colorado, Idaho, and Georgia. The Pennsylvania statute applied only to employees of corporation.

11. *The Corporations Auxiliary Bulletin,* April 1902, pp. 209-210.

12. Wolman, *op. cit.,* p. 34.

13. *Ibid.,* Appendix.

CHAPTER 13. ADVANCES IN COAL

1. Chris Evans, *History of United Mine Workers of America from the Year 1860 to 1890* (Indianapolis: United Mine Workers of America, 1919), I, 87.

2. Frank Julian Warne, "The Union Movement Among Coal-Miners," *Bulletin of the Department of Labor,* March, 1904, pp. 384-385.

3. "Constitution and By-Laws of the Ohio Miners' Amalgamated Association," in *ibid.,* p. 97.

4. Edward W. Bemis, "Mine Labor in the Hocking Valley," *Publications of the American Economic Association,* July 1886, pp. 27-28.

5. "Preamble and Constitution of the National Federation of Miners and Mine Laborers of the United States and Territories, Adopted at Indianapolis, Indiana, September 12, 1885," in Evans, *op. cit.,* I, 139.

6. The letter is reproduced in Evans, *ibid.,* p. 145.

7. The circular is reproduced in *ibid.,* pp. 147-151.

8. *Minutes of the Joint Conference,* in *ibid.,* pp. 175-188.

9. Correspondence between the two organizations is in *ibid.,* II, 224-225.

10. From W. T. Lewis to T. V. Powderly, October 30, 1888, in *ibid.,* pp. 385-386.

11. "Preamble," in *ibid.,* p. 403.

12. *Ibid.,* pp. 323-324.

13. Arthur E. Suffern, *Conciliation and Arbitration in the Coal Industry of America* (Boston: Houghton Mifflin Co., 1915), pp. 33-38.

14. Statement is from a speech by Gompers to the 1914 convention of the United Mine Workers of America, in *American Federationist,* March 1914, p. 205.

15. *Report of the Industrial Commission on the Relations of Capital and Labor Employed in the Mining Industry* (Washington: Government Printing Office, 1901), XII, 677-678.

16. Statement of John Mitchell, president of the United Mine Workers of America, in *ibid.,* p. 698.

17. Evans, *op. cit.,* II, 609.

18. *Report of the Industrial Commission . . . ,* XII, p. 699.

19. Frank J. Warne, *The Slav Invasion and the Mine Workers* (Philadelphia: J. B. Lippincott Co., 1904), p. 52.

20. *Ibid.*, p. 58.

21. Evans, *op. cit.*, II, 611.

22. Robert J. Cornell, *The Anthracite Coal Strike of 1902* (Washington: Catholic University Press, 1957), p. 38.

23. *Ibid.*, pp. 43-45.

24. Selig Perlman and Philip Taft, *History of Labor in the United States, 1896–1932* (New York: Macmillan Co., 1935), IV, p. 46.

25. *Minutes of the Twelfth Annual Convention of the United Mine Workers of America*, 1901, p. 28.

26. Cornell, *op. cit.*, p. 41.

27. Baer to Mitchell, May 9, 1902, quoted in *ibid.*, p. 90.

28. Quoted from *Minutes of Special Convention of United Mine Workers of America*, 1902.

29. Walter E. Weyl, "The Relief System of the Mine Workers," *Charities*, September 6, 1902, p. 243.

30. Cornell, *op. cit.*, p. 121.

31. *New York Tribune*, September 30, 1902.

32. *Cleveland Citizen*, August 26, 1902.

33. Quoted in Cornell, *op. cit.*, p. 182.

34. *Report to the President on the Anthracite Coal Strike of May-October 1902 By the Anthracite Strike Commission* (Washington: Government Printing Office, 1903), pp. 39-41.

35. *Ibid.*, p. 64.

36. *Ibid.*, p. 84.

37. Testimony of John Mitchell, in *Report of Industrial Commission . . . ,* XII, 699.

CHAPTER 14. GAINS AND LOSSES IN THE METAL TRADES

1. John P. Frey and John R. Commons, "Conciliation in the Stove Industry," *Bulletin of the Department of Labor*, January 1906, pp. 125-128.

2. Notice signed by W. R. Ressor and S. R. Burton, in *ibid.*, p. 135.

3. *Ibid.*, pp. 141-142.

4. *Ibid.*, p. 153.

5. Testimony of O. P. Briggs, former president of the National Founders' Association, in *Final Report and Testimony Submitted to Congress by the Commission on Industrial Relations* (Washington: Government Printing Office, 1916), I, 461.

6. *Ibid.*, p. 457.

7. *Ibid.*, pp. 456, 458.

8. Testimony of Valentine, in *ibid.*, p. 484.

9. Testimony of John P. Frey, in *ibid.*, p. 531.

10. Testimony of O. P. Briggs, in *ibid.*, p. 458.

11. Testimony of O. P. Briggs, in *ibid.*

12. Quoted in Clarence E. Bonnett, *Employers' Associations in the United States* (New York: Macmillan Co., 1922), p. 65.

13. Mark Perlman, *The Machinists* (Cambridge, Mass.: Harvard University Press, 1961), pp. 1-24.

14. *Report of the Industrial Commission on the Chicago Labor Disputes of*

1900, VIII, 502. The agreement was presented by Henry Franklin Devens, assistant secretary of the National Metal Trades Association.

15. *Ibid.,* p. 505.

16. *National Metal Trades Association Constitution, Bylaws, Declaration of Principles,* in "Violations of Free Speech and Rights of Labor," *Report of the Committee on Education and Labor, Pursuant to S. Res. 266* (Washington: Government Printing Office, 1939), Part I, p. 25.

17. *Ibid.,* p. 110.

18. *Ibid.,* p. 112.

19. *Ibid.,* p. 70.

CHAPTER 15. ANTI-UNIONISM IN THE STEEL INDUSTRY

1. Edward Sherwood Meade, "The Genesis of the United States Steel Corporation," *Quarterly Journal of Economics,* August 1901, pp. 533-534.

2. *Ibid.,* p. 534.

3. U.S. Commissioner of Corporations, *Report on the Steel Industry* (Washington: Government Printing Office, 1911), I, p. 12; Charles A. Gulick, *Labor Policy of the United States Steel Corporation* (New York: Columbia University Press, 1924), p. 20.

4. Art. 17, Sec. 2, of Constitution of Amalgamated Association of Iron, Steel and Tin Workers, in *Report on Conditions of Employment in the Iron and Steel Industry* (Washington: Government Printing Office, 1913), III, 116.

5. *Report on the Steel Industry,* III, 117.

6. *Hearings Before the Committee on Investigation of U.S. Steel Corporation* (Washington: Government Printing Office, 1912), II, 1558.

7. The letter signed by President T. J. Shaffer of the Amalgamated Association calling the strike is in *Report on Conditions of Employment in the Iron and Steel Industry,* III, 123-124.

8. T. J. Shaffer to Warner Ames, July 1, 1901, in *ibid.,* p. 124.

9. Ames to Shaffer, in *ibid.,* p. 124.

10. Philip Taft, *The A. F. of L. in the Time of Gompers* (New York: Harper and Brothers, 1957), p. 239.

11. *Report on Conditions of Employment in the Iron and Steel Industry,* III, 127.

12. Marguerite Green, *The National Civic Federation and the American Labor Movement* (Washington: Catholic University Press, 1956), pp. 26-29.

13. *Hearings Before the Committee on Investigation of U.S. Steel Corporation,* II, p. 1558.

14. *Report on Conditions of Employment in the Iron and Steel Industry,* III, 131.

15. Circular issued by the American Federation of Labor, November 27, 1909.

16. *Hearings Before the Committee on Investigation of U.S. Steel Corporation,* IV, 3120.

17. *Ibid.,* p. 3062.

18. Quoted from an old seal and miscellaneous records of the Lake Seamen's Union, in E. Hoagland, *Wage Bargaining on the Vessels of the Great Lakes* (Urbana, Ill.: University of Illinois Press, 1917), p. 10.

19. Quoted in *ibid.,* p. 19.

20. Art. III of the *Articles of the Lake Carriers' Association*, 1903, quoted in *ibid.*, p. 50.

21. *Hearings Before the Committee on Investigation of U.S. Steel Corporation*, IV, 2996, for above quotes.

CHAPTER 16. ADVANCES AND PROBLEMS IN BUILDING CONSTRUCTION

1. Leo Wolman, *Growth of American Trade Unions, 1880–1923* (New York: National Bureau of Economic Research 1924), Appendix.

2. Robert A. Christie, *Empire in Wood–A History of the Carpenters' Union* (Ithaca, N.Y.: New York State School of Industrial Labor Relations, 1956), pp. 29-40.

3. *Industrial Chicago–The Building Interests* (Chicago: Goodspeed Publishing Co., 1891), p. 544.

4. Frederick S. Deibler, *The Amalgamated Wood Workers International Union* (Madison, Wisc.: University of Wisconsin Press, 1912), pp. 64-77.

5. *Industrial Chicago*, p. 560.

6. *Ibid.*, p. 576.

7. *Ibid.*, p. 579.

8. Testimony of Thomas Preece, business agent of the Chicago Bricklayers' Union, in *Report of Industrial Commission*, VIII, 476-477.

9. The quote is from Art. XVI of Book of Rules of the Building Trades Council, J. A. Miller, "Coercive Trade-Unionism as Illustrated by the Chicago Building-Trades Conflict," *Journal of Political Economy*, June 1901, p. 321; see also, S. V. Lindholm, "Analysis of the Building Trades Conflict, from the Trade Union Standpoint," *Journal of Political Economy*, June 1900, pp. 327-333.

10. Miller, *ibid.*, p. 323.

11. J. E. George, "The Chicago Building Trades Conflict," *Quarterly Journal of Economics*, May 1901, p. 352; Royal E. Montgomery, *Industrial Relations in the Chicago Building Trades* (Chicago: University of Chicago Press, 1927), p. 23.

12. Quoted from proceedings of convention, 1887, by George C. Sikes, "The Apprentice System in the Building Trades," *Journal of Political Economy*, June 1894, p. 399.

13. *Report of Industrial Commission Chicago Labor Dispute*, VIII, 39.

14. *Iibid.*, pp. 325-326.

15. John R. Commons, "The New York Building Trades," *Quarterly Journal of Economics*, May 1904, pp. 409-416; Charles H. Winslow, *Conciliation and Arbitration in the Building Trades of New York*, U.S. Bureau of Labor Statistics Bulletin No. 124, pp. 5-7.

16. Quote in Commons, *op. cit.*, p. 418.

17. Winslow, *op. cit.*, p. 17; *Final Report and Testimony Submitted to Congress by the Commission on Industrial Relations* (Washington: Government Printing Office, 1916), I, 1583-1591.

18. William Haber, *Industrial Relations in the Building Industry* (Cambridge, Harvard University Press, 1930), pp. 48-91.

19. Commons, *op. cit.*, p. 432.

CHAPTER 17. EMPLOYERS TAKE THE OFFENSIVE

1. Statement of James A. Emery, "Maintenance of a Lobby," in *Hearings Before a Subcommittee of the Senate Committee on the Judiciary on S. Res. 92,* 63d Cong., 1st sess., 1913, IV, p. 3715.

2. *Violations of Free Speech and Rights of Labor,* Senate Report 6, Part 6, 76th Cong., 1st sess., Pursuant to S. Res. 266 (74th Cong.), pp. 7-8.

3. Selig Perlman and Philip Taft, *History of Labor in the United States, 1896–1932* (New York: Macmillan Co., 1935), IV, pp. 129-137.

4. Testimony of James A. Emery, in *Hearings Before a Subcommittee . . . ,* p. 5720.

5. Quoted from the speech of President David M. Parry to the New Orleans Convention in 1903 in Albion. Guilford Taylor, *Labor Policies of the National Association of Manufacturers* (Urbana, Ill.: University of Illinois, 1928), pp. 35-36.

6. *Hearings Before a Subcommittee . . . on S. Res. 92,* p. 3736.

7. *Ibid.,* p. 3737.

8. *Ibid.,* p. 3733.

9. *Ibid.,* pp. 3762-3816, contains a list of documents and letters connected with these activities.

10. Donald B. Robinson, *Spotlight on a Union* (New York: Dial Press, 1948), pp. 74-75.

11. Walter Gordon Merritt, *History of the League for Industrial Rights* (New York: League for Industrial Rights, 1925), p. 11.

12. *Ibid.,* p. 14.

13. Quoted in *ibid.,* p. 14.

14. Robinson, *op. cit.,* pp. 86-87.

15. Walter Gordon Merritt, *Destination Unknown* (New York: Prentice-Hall, Inc., 1951), pp. 15-16.

16. *American Federationist,* April 1908, p. 268.

17. *Ibid.,* p. 262.

18. *American Federationist,* February 1915, p. 116.

19. *Report of the Proceedings of the Thirty-sixth Annual Convention of the American Federation of Labor,* 1916, p. 78.

20. Robinson, *op. cit.,* p. 94.

21. *American Federationist,* September 1910, pp. 807-808.

22. *Samuel Gompers, et. al. v. The Buck's Stove and Range Company.* On writ of certiorari to the Court of Appeals of the District of Columbia (May 15, 1911). Opinion of Mr. Justice Lamar, Senate Document 33, 62d Cong., 1st sess., p. 16.

23. Philip Taft, *The A. F. of L. in the Time of Gompers* (New York: Harper and Brothers, 1957), pp. 262-271.

24. Luke Grant, *The National Erectors' Association and the International Association of Bridge and Structural Ironworkers* (Washington: Commission on Industrial Relations, 1915), p. 13.

25. *Ibid.,* pp. 40-45.

26. *Ibid.,* pp. 50-51.

27. Quote from Circular No. 30 issued by the union, in Grant, *ibid.,* p. 66.

28. *The Review,* January 1913, pp. 28-34.

29. Testimony of F. J. Zeehandelaar, in *Final Report and Testimony Submitted to the Congress by the Commission on Industrial Relations,* VI, 5493.

30. *Ibid.,* p. 5499.

31. Philip Taft, *op. cit.,* p. 277.

32. Grace Heilman Stimson, *Rise of the Labor Movement in Los Angeles* (Los Angeles: University of California Press, 1955), pp. 312-313.

33. Stimson, *op. cit.,* pp. 340-341; testimony of C. F. Grow, business agent of the Machinists' Union, in *Final Report and Testimony of Commission on Industrial Relations,* VI, 5549-5551.

34. "Final Report of Special Investigating Committee on 'Times' Explosion," *Report of Proceedings of the Eleventh Annual Convention of the California State Federation of Labor,* 1910, p. 91.

35. John D. Fredericks to Governor Hiram Johnson, October 4, 1911, in Johnson papers at the Bancroft Library of the University of California at Berkeley.

36. "President Ryan's Report," *The Bridgemen's Magazine,* May 1911, p. 263.

37. Gompers to J. J. McNamara, June 29, 1911.

38. *The Bridgemen's Magazine,* June 1911, p. 326.

39. *American Federationist,* July 1911, pp. 536-537.

40. *The Bridgemen's Magazine,* July 1911, p. 404.

41. *Financial Report of the McNamara Defense Fund* (Washington: American Federation of Labor, 1912).

42. *Los Angeles Record,* September 18, 1911.

43. *The Bridgemen's Magazine,* January 1912, pp. 4-5.

44. Statement issued by the Ways and Means Committee, in *ibid.,* p. 8.

45. *Ibid.,* p. 10.

46. *The Bridgemen's Magazine,* January 1913, p. 16.

47. *Ibid.,* March 1913, p. 148.

48. *Ibid.,* p. 149.

49. *Ibid.,* p. 150.

50. *The Survey,* December 30, 1911, p. 1563.

51. *Ibid.,* December 28, 1912, p. 386.

52. Quoted from the *Square Deal,* January 1906, in Marguerite Green, *The National Civic Federation and the American Labor Movement 1900–1925* (Washington: Catholic University Press, 1956, p. 114. Mother Green's study is the authoritative examination of the National Civic Federation, and many of the facts are drawn from it.

53. See Philip Taft, *op. cit.,* pp. 225-231.

CHAPTER 18. ORGANIZED LABOR AND POLITICS

1. *Official Report of Proceedings of the Second Annual Convention of the American Federation of Labor,* 1887, p. 26.

2. *Report of Proceedings of the Eleventh Annual Convention* (AFL), 1891, p. 15.

3. *Report of Proceedings of the Fifteenth Annual Convention* (AFL), 1895, p. 79.

4. *Report of Proceedings of the Fourteenth Annual Convention* (AFL), 1894, p. 38.

5. *Report of Proceedings of the Fifteenth Annual Convention* (AFL), 1895, Art. VIII, Sec. 6, p. 6.

6. John M. O'Hanlon, "History of The New York State Federation of Labor," in *Annual of the Rochester, N.Y. Trades and Labor Assembly*, 1927, p. 17.

7. *Ibid.*, p. 23.

8. Eugene Staley, *History of the Illinois State Federation of Labor* (Chicago: University of Chicago Press, 1930), p. 562.

9. *Achievements of the New York State Federation of Labor*, pamphlet issued in 1918.

10. Quoted from the Chicago *Inter-Ocean*, December 13, 1883, in Staley, *op. cit.*, p. 18.

11. Quotation from constitution, in *ibid.*, p. 47.

12. *The California State Federation of Labor*, unpublished manuscript by Philip Taft.

13. Evelyn L. K. Harris and Frank J. Krebs, *From Humble Beginnings: West Virginia State Federation of Labor* (Charleston, W. Va.: West Virginia Labor History Publishing Committee, 1960), p. xvl.

14. Staley, *op. cit.*, pp. 33-34.

15. *Ibid.*, p. 140-175.

16. "Report of Legislative Agent," in San Francisco *Labor Clarion*, October 23, 1903.

17. Harris and Krebs, *op. cit.*, p. 33.

18. Staley, *op. cit.*, pp. 411-412.

19. Harris and Krebs, *op. cit.*, p. 134.

20. From the manuscript on the *California State Federation of Labor*. Similar laws have been supported by state federations of labor of many states. Numerous legislative reports of the state federations of labor have been examined. A short and excellent statement is James H. Maurer, "State Federations as Movement Centers," in J. B. Hardman, *American Labor Dynamics* (New York: Harcourt, Brace and Howe, 1928), 357-359. Maurer was president of the Pennsylvania State Federation of Labor and a Socialist candidate for Vice-President in 1932.

21. *Report of the Proceedings of the Thirty-ninth Annual Convention of the American Federation of Labor*, 1919, p. 374.

22. Staley, *op. cit.*, pp. 379-380.

23. *Minutes of Executive Council*, March 20, 1896.

24. *Ibid.*, April 21, 1897.

25. *Report of Proceedings of the Eleventh Annual Convention of the American Federation of Labor*, 1891, p. 27.

26. *Toledo, Ann Arbor and Michigan Railway Co.* v. *The Pennsylvania Co.*, 54 Fed. Rep. 730.

27. *In re Debs, Petitioner*, 158 U.S. 564 (1895); see Felix Frankfurter and Nathan Greene, *The Labor Injunction* (New York: Macmillan Co., 1930), pp. 5-10.

28. Gompers to President William McKinley, November 18, 1897.

29. *Report of a Hearing Before the Committee on the Judiciary of the House of Representatives, March 23, 1900, on the Bill to Limit the Meaning of the Word "Conspiracy" and also the Use of "Restraining Orders Injunctions" as Applied to Disputes Between Employers and Employees, etc.*, 1900.

30. Statement issued on April 19, 1902, by executive council.

31. *American Federationist,* May 1906, p. 295.

32. *Ibid.,* October 1906, pp. 795-810.

33. *Ibid.,* August 1908, p. 603.

34. *Ibid.*

35. *Ibid.,* September 1908, p. 746.

36. *Ibid.,* p. 1064.

37. *Report of Proceedings of the Thirty-third Annual Convention of the American Federation of Labor,* 1913, pp. 314-315.

38. *American Federationist,* July 1914, p. 553.

39. Frankfurter and Greene, *op. cit.,* p. 163.

40. Samuel Gompers, "The Charter of Industrial Freedom," *The American Federationist,* November 1914, p. 970.

41. *Ibid.,* p. 971.

42. "Recent Antitrust and Labor Injunction Legislation: An Address by William Howard Taft," Senate Document No. 614, 63d Cong., 2d sess., pp. 16-17.

43. Arthur Emil Albrecht, *International Seamen's Union of America: A Study of Its History and Problems,* U.S. Bureau of Labor Statistics Bulletin No. 342, pp. 34-39.

CHAPTER 19. ORGANIZATION, STRIFE, AND MILITANCY

1. In 1907 and 1908 membership was larger than in 1904, but the losses of the following year dropped enrollment below 1904 again.

2. John R. Commons, "Immigration and Its Economic Effects," *Reports of the Industrial Commission,* 1901, XV, 322.

3. Henry White, *The Sweating System,* Department of Labor Bulletin, May 1896, pp. 360-361.

4. Charles Jacob Stowell, *The Journeymen Tailors' Union of America: A Study in Trade Union Policy* (Urbana, Ill.: University of Illinois, 1918), pp. 9-12.

5. Louis Levine, *The Women's Garment Workers* (New York: B. W. Huebsch, 1924), p. 103.

6. Commons, *op. cit.,* p. 327.

7. Mary B. Sumner, "The Settlement of the Cloakmakers' Strike," *Survey,* September 17, 1910, pp. 847-850.

8. Leo Stein, *The Triangle Fire* (Philadelphia: J. B. Lippincott Co., 1962), deals with one of the great tragedies in the garment trades, when 146 workers were burned in a fire in a shirtwaist factory in New York City.

9. *The Clothing Workers of Chicago* (Chicago: Amalgamated Clothing of America, 1922), pp. 44-50.

10. *The Garment Worker,* October 16, 1914; *Documentary History of the Amalgamated Clothing Workers of America, 1914–1916,* pp. 4-5.

11. *The Garment Worker,* October 16, 1914.

12. *Documentary History of the Amalgamated Clothing Workers . . . ,* *op. cit.,* pp. 7-11.

13. Selig Perlman and Philip Taft, *History of Labor in the United States, 1896–1932* (New York: Macmillan Co., 1935), IV, pp. 248-261.

14. Quoted from *United Mine Workers of America* v. *Coronado Coal Co.*

Brief for Defendant in Error, p. 41, in A. F. Hinrichs, *The United Mine Workers of America and the Non-Union Coal Fields* (New York: Columbia University Press, 1919), p. 119.

15. *Investigation of Conditions in Paint Creek Coal Fields of West Virginia in Pursuance of S. Res. 37*, Senate Report. 321, 63d Cong., 2d sess., I, 953.

16. *Ibid.*, p. 238.

17. "Report to Governor W. E. Glasscock by Commissioners," in *ibid.*, pp. 370-371.

18. *S. Rept. 321*, 63 Cong., 2d sess., I, 946; II, 1735.

19. George P. West, *Report on the Colorado Strike* (Washington: U.S. Commission on Industrial Relations, 1915), p. 15.

20. *Final Report and Testimony Submitted to Congress by the Commission on Industrial Relations*, VII, 7190; *United Mine Workers' Journal*, September 11, 1914, p. 1.

21. *Report on the Colorado Strike Investigation Made Under H. Res. 387*, Doc. 1630, 63d Cong., 3d sess., p. 32.

22. Letter from J. F. Welborn, president of the Colorado Fuel and Iron Company to Mr. McClement, December 4, 1913, in West, *op. cit.*, p. 91; The United Mine Workers of America at the time, was not seeking to establish the closed shop in the Colorado mines. It would have accepted the smallest crumb of recognition. Allan Nevins, *John Rockefeller* (New York: Charles Scribner's Sons, 1940), II, 671, intimates that this demand was crucial, but the Colorado Fuel and Iron Company would not deal with the union on any terms.

23. Testimony of James H. Brewster, in *Final Report and Testimony, op. cit.*, VII, pp. 6644-6645.

24. Barron B. Beshoar, *Out of the Depths* (Denver, Colo.: Golden Bell Press, n.d.), p. 182. Testimony of Lieut. K. E. Linderfelt in *Final Report and Testimony, op. cit.*, p. 6895.

25. *Final Report and Testimony, op. cit.*, p. 6985.

26. Beshoar, *op. cit.*, p. 189.

27. West, *op. cit.*, pp. 107-318, for quote; see also Beshoar, *op. cit.*, pp. 180-194.

28. *Final Report and Testimony of U.S. Commission on Industrial Relations*, VIII, 7070-7083.

29. John D. Rockefeller, Jr., to W. L. Mackenzie King, August 1, 1914, in West, *op. cit.*, p. 158.

30. Ben M. Selekman and Mary Van Kleeck, *Employes' Representation Plan* (New York: Russell Sage Foundation, 1924), pp. 12-27, 59-72.

CHAPTER 20. MILITANCY AND FAILURE OF ARBITRATION

1. *Report of the United States Board of Mediation and Conciliation on the Effects of Arbitration Proceedings Upon Rates of Pay and Working Conditions of Railroad Employees* (Washington: Government Printing Office, 1916), p. 8.

2. *Ibid.*, p. 12.

3. Quote is from Morrisey's dissent in *American Federationist*, January 1913, pp. 22-23.

4. *Locomotive Firemen and Enginemen's Magazine*, August 1915, p. 220.

5. *Ibid.*, September 1915, p. 355.

6. *The Railroad Trainman*, January 1916, p. 91.

7. *Ibid.*, p. 92.

8. *Ibid.*, February 1916, p. 152.

9. *Ibid.*, July 1916, p. 634.

10. *Ibid.*

11. *Ibid.*, p. 635; the same views were expressed by President W. S. Carter, in the *Locomotive Firemen and Enginemen's Magazine*, June 1916, p. 639.

12. *The Railroad Trainman*, October 1916, p. 901.

13. *Locomotive Firemen and Enginemen's Magazine*, September 1916, p. 290.

14. *Ibid.*

15. *Ibid.*, p. 291.

16. *Ibid.*

17. Speech in *Locomotive Firemen and Enginemen's Magazine*, October 1916, p. 382.

18. *The Railroad Trainmen*, October 1916, p. 905.

19. *Remarks of Samuel Gompers Before Conference of the Executives of the Railroad Organizations Affiliated with the A. F. of L. and the Four Brotherhoods*, February 10, 1920, in the archives of the AFL-CIO.

20. *Report of the Eight-Hour Commission to the President and Congress of the United States, 1917; Cooperative Movement Brotherhood of Locomotive Engineers, Brotherhood of Locomotive Firemen and Enginemen, Order of Railway Conductors, Brotherhood of Railroad Trainmen* (no place or date), gives a summary of the joint movement; *The Railroad Trainman*, April 1917, pp. 282-283.

CHAPTER 21. JURISDICTIONAL RIGHTS AND DEPARTMENTS

1. *Official Report of Proceedings of the Second Annual Convention of the American Federation of Labor*, 1887, p. 29.

2. *Report of Proceedings of the Third Annual Convention* (AFL), 1888, p. 19.

3. Gompers to Julius Rush, December 24, 1888.

4. *Report of Proceedings of the Ninth Annual Convention* (AFL), 1889, p. 34.

5. *Report of Proceedings of the Nineteenth Annual Convention* (AFL), 1889, p. 156.

6. Philip Taft, *The A. F. of L. in the Time of Gompers* (New York: Harper and Brothers, 1957), pp. 192-194.

7. *Report of Proceedings of the Twentieth Annual Convention* (AFL), 1900, p. 69.

8. *Minutes of Executive Council of the American Federation of Labor,* July 18, 1900.

9. *Minutes of the Twelfth Convention of the United Mine Workers of America*, 1901, p. 49.

10. *Ibid.*, p. 90.

11. *Report of Proceedings of the Twenty-First Annual Convention* (AFL), 1901, p. 240.

12. *American Federationist*, December 1902, p. 931.

13. Gompers to John B. Lennon, May 8, 1907.

14. *Minutes of Executive Council of the American Federation of Labor,* April 15, 1902.

15. *American Federationist,* December 1905, pp. 940-941.

16. W. H. Steinbiss to Gompers, January 23, 1901.

17. *Report of Proceedings of the Twenty-first Annual Convention* (AFL), 1901, p. 18.

18. *Ibid.,* p. 18.

19. *Report of Proceedings of the Twenty-third Annual Convention* (AFL), 1903, pp. 212-213.

20. *Minutes of Executive Council of the American Federation of Labor,* September 14, 1904; William J. Spencer, "Structural Building Trades Alliance," *The Carpenter,* March 1905, p. 5.

21. *Official Report of Fifth General Conference Structural Building Trades Alliance,* p. 6.

22. *First Annual Convention of the Building Trades Department of the American Federation of Labor,* 1908, p. 2.

23. James Duncan to executive council of AFL, February 19, 1908.

24. *Report of Proceedings of the Thirty-first Annual Convention* (AFL), 1911, p. 111.

25. Frank Duffy to Gompers, June 8, 1914.

CHAPTER 22. DUAL UNIONISM

1. Herman Schlüter, *Die Internationale in Amerika* (Chicago: Deutsche Sprachgruppe der Sozialist Partei der Vern. Staaten, 1918), pp. 87-88. "Neue Trade Unions sollen geschaft werden, wenn die bestehenden Unions es ablehnen, dieser Organization (der Partei) beizutreten," p. 88.

2. Quoted in Nathan Fine, *Labor and Farmer Parties in the United States,* 1828–1928 (New York: Rand School of Social Science, 1928), p. 104.

3. Friedrich Engels, *Die Arbeiterbewegung in Amerika* (New York: Verlag von Louis Weiss, 1887), p. 6. "Sie ist eine Partei nur dem Namen nach denn nirgendwo mit Amerika ist sie, bis jetzt, wirklich im Stand gewesen, als politische Partei handlen aufzutreten . . . sie hat bis ganz neurdings fast auschliesslich aus eingewanderten Deutschen befonden, die sie ihrer eignen Sprache bedienen and mit der englischer Landessprache nur wengi vertraut sind."

4. Quoted in Fine, *op. cit.,* p. 153.

5. *Report of Proceedings of the Fifteenth Annual Convention of the American Federation of Labor,* 1895, p. 65. Gompers, who was a delegate from his union, charged that delegates to the AFL, "Were treacherous enough to support it [the Alliance]."

6. *A Report on Labor Disturbances in the State of Colorado from 1880 to 1904, Inclusive,* Senate Document 122, 58th Cong., 3d sess., 1905, p. 35; Vernon H. Jensen, *Heritage of Conflict* (Ithaca, N.Y.: Cornell University Press, 1950), p. 13.

7. S. Doc. 122, 58th Cong., 3d sess., pp. 69-74.

8. *Reports of the Industrial Commission,* XII, 491; Jensen, *op. cit.,* pp. 24-37.

9. From the "preamble" to the constitution of the Western Federation of Miners, reprinted in Senate Document 122, 58th Cong., 3d sess., pp. 36-37.

10. Benjamin McKie Rastall, *The Labor History of the Cripple Creek District,* University of Wisconsin Bulletin, No. 198 (Madison, Wisc., 1908), p. 23.

11. *Ibid.*, p. 33.

12. *Ibid.*, p. 40.

13. *Ibid.*, pp. 47-51.

14. *Coeur d'Alene Mining Troubles,* S. Doc. 142, 56th Cong., 1st sess., p. 31.

15. *Ibid.*, p. 37.

16. S. Doc. 122, 58th Cong., 3d sess., p. 160.

17. Statement in *ibid.*, p. 162.

18. *Ibid.*, p. 175.

19. Rastall, *op. cit.*, pp. 114-115.

20. *Ibid.*, p. 115.

21. *Ibid.*, p. 142.

22. James McParlan to J. C. Fraser (assistant manager of Eastern Division of Pinkerton's National Detective Agency), January 15, 1906, in files of Pinkerton's National Detective Agency.

23. McParlan to Governor Frank R. Gooding, January 22, 1906, in files Pinkerton's National Detective Agency.

24. From the documents in Archives of Pinkerton's National Detective Agency.

25. Philip Taft, *The A. F. of L. in the Time of Gompers* (New York: Harper and Brothers, 1957), pp. 155-156.

26. Vincent St. John, *The I.W.W.: History, Structure and Methods* (Chicago: I.W.W. Publishing Bureau, 1917), gives the information on the origin of the movement. St. John held a number of offices, including that of secretary-treasurer, from 1905 to 1914.

27. Quoted in Paul Brissenden, *The I.W.W.: A Study of American Syndicalism* (New York: Columbia University Press, 1919), p. 59.

28. Quoted in *ibid.*, p. 62.

29. *Ibid.*, p. 63.

30. The article from the *Chicago Inter-Ocean* was reprinted in the *San Francisco Labor Chronicle,* June 2, 1905. The term was used in a letter to Gompers by an unnamed correspondent, and Gompers popularized it.

31. See preamble in Brissenden, *op. cit.*, Appendix I.

32. Don K. McKee, "Daniel De Leon: "A Reappraisal," *Labor History,* Fall 1960, deals with the views and activities of De Leon.

33. Brissenden, *op. cit.*, 264.

34. *The Strike at Lawrence, Massachusetts, Hearings* Before the Committee on Rules of the House of Representatives on H. Res. 409 and 433, H. Doc. 671, 62d Cong., 2d sess., 1912, p. 85.

35. *Report on Strike of Textile Workers in Lawrence, Mass.* in 1912, S. Doc. 870, 62d Cong., 2d sess., 1912, p. 40.

36. H. Doc. 671, 62d Cong., 1st sess., pp. 128-129.

37. *Ibid.*, pp. 57-59.

38. *Solidarity,* October 19, 1912.

39. *Ibid.*, October 10 and November 28, 1914.

40. See Philip Taft, "The I.W.W. in the Grain Belt," *Labor History,* Winter 1960, pp. 53-67.

41. James Rowan, *The I.W.W. in the Lumber Industry* (no place or publisher), p. 25.

42. Joseph J. Ettor to W. D. Haywood, in *Proceedings of the Tenth IWW Convention,* 1916, pp. 63-64.

43. Robert L. Morlan, *Political Prairie Fire, the Non-Partisan League, 1915–1922* (Mineapolis: University of Minnesota Press, 1955), p. 135.

44. In the Supreme Court of United States, October Term 1920, *Haywood* v. *U.S. On Petition for a Writ of Certiorari to the U.S. Circuit Court of Appeals for the Seventh Circuit,* p. 1538.

45. *Ibid.*

CHAPTER 23. IMMIGRATION AND ORGANIZED LABOR

1. Charlotte Erickson, *American Industry and the European Immigrant* (Cambridge, Mass.: Harvard University Press, 1957), pp. 3-6.

2. *Abstracts of Reports of Immigration Commission,* Senate Document 747, 61st Cong., 3d sess., 1911, I, 56-57.

3. *Ibid.,* pp. 60-65.

4. *Ibid.,* pp. 501-502.

5. *Report of the Joint Special Committee to Investigate Chinese Immigration,* Senate Report 689, 44th Cong., 2d sess. (Washington: Government Printing Office, 1877), p. 1196. The estimates were made by Alfred Wheeler, an attorney, from the Custom House records of the Port of San Francisco.

6. *Ibid.,* p. ii.

7. *Ibid.,* p. iv.

8. Testimony of Cameron H. King, attorney for anti-Chinese societies and "the labor interests of the state," in *ibid.,* p. 33.

9. Testimony of Cameron H. King, in *ibid.,* p. 263.

10. Ira B. Cross, *A History of the Labor Movement in California* (Berkeley, Calif.: University of California Press, 1935), pp. 88-93.

11. *Proceedings of the California State Federation of Labor,* 1902, p. 74.

12. *Chinese Exclusion Testimony Taken Before the Committee on Immigration,* S. Rept. 776, Part 2, 57th Cong., 1st sess.

13. *For the Re-enactment of the Chinese Exclusion Law, California's Memorial to the President and the Congress of the U.S.,* S. Doc. 191, 87th Cong., 1st sess. (Washington: Government Printing Office, 1902).

14. Quoted in Terence V. Powderly, *Thirty Years of Labor* (T. V. Powderly, 1890), p. 210.

15. *Ibid.,* p. 220.

16. John Graham Brooks, *The Trade Union Label,* Department of Labor Bulletin, March 1898, pp. 197-198, for quote. See also Walter MacArthur, *The Union Label, Its History and Aims* (Washington: American Federation of Labor, n.d.).

17. Erickson, *op. cit.,* pp. 50-51.

18. *Reports of the Immigration Commission,* S. Doc. 768, 61st Cong., 3d sess., 1911, I, 28.

19. Powderly, *op. cit.,* pp. 225-227.

20. *U.S. Statutes at Large,* XXIII, 332.

21. Samuel P. Orth, "The Alien Contract and Labor Law," *Political Science Quarterly,* March 1907, p. 60.

22. *Reports of the Industrial Commission on Immigration and on Education,* XV, 647.

23. *Abstracts of Reports of Immigration Commission,* I, 531.

24. John R. Commons, "Immigration and Its Economic Effects," *ibid.*, p. 312.

25. *Report of Proceedings of Twelfth Annual Convention of the American Federation of Labor*, 1892, p. 38.

26. *Ibid.*, p. 14.

27. *Report of the Proceedings of the Sixteenth Annual Convention* (AFL), 1896, p. 81.

28. Philip Taft, *The A.F. of L. in the Time of Gompers* (New York: Harper and Brothers, 1957), pp. 302-308.

29. *Report of the Proceedings of the Sixty-fifth Convention* (AFL), 1946, pp. 520-521.

CHAPTER 24. DEFENSE AND WAR

1. *Report of Proceedings of the Nineteenth Annual Convention of the American Federation of Labor*, 1899, pp. 148-149.

2. *Report of Proceedings of the Thirty-fourth Annual Convention* (AFL), 1914, pp. 48-49.

3. Circular letter from Gompers to the heads of national and international unions and the railway brotherhoods, March 12, 1917.

4. "American Labor's Position in Peace or in War," statement issued by American Federation of Labor, March 12, 1917.

5. *Ibid.*

6. Samuel Gompers to Daniel J. Tobin, April 17, 1917.

7. *Ibid.*

8. *Report of the Activities of the War Department in the Field of Industrial Relations During the War* (Washington: Government Printing Office, 1919), p. 10.

9. Louis B. Wehle to Frank Morrison, June 20, 1917; Gompers to Wehle, June 22, 1917; in AFL-CIO archives.

10. Louis B. Wehle, "The Adjustment of Labor Disputes Incident to Production For War in the United States," *Quarterly Journal of Economics*, November 1917, pp. 125-126.

11. Alexander M. Bing, *War-Time Strikes and Their Adjustment* (New York: E. P. Dutton and Co., 1921), pp. 18-19.

12. P. H. Douglas and F. E. Wolfe, "Labor Administration in Shipbuilding Administration During War Time," *Journal of Political Economy*, March 1919, p. 162.

13. Bing, *op. cit.*, pp. 33-38.

14. *Ibid.*, pp. 42-43.

15. *Thirty-first Annual Report of the U.S. Interstate Commerce Commission*, 1917, pp. 64-65.

16. Walker D. Hines, *War History of American Railroads* (New Haven: Yale University, 1928), p. 19.

17. Quotation is from a communication from the Railroads' War Board to the Federal Commissioner of Mediation and Conciliation, in *ibid.*, p. 19.

18. Hines, *ibid.*, p. 155.

19. *Ibid.*, p. 173.

20. *Ibid.*, p. 175.

21. Louis B. Wehle, "Labor problems in the United States During the War," *Quarterly Journal of Economics*, February 1918, p. 368.

22. *Report of President's Mediation Commission to the President of the United States* (no place or date), p. 6.

23. Bing, *op. cit.,* p. 54; Wehle, "Labor Problems," pp. 390-392; *Monthly Labor Review,* May 1918, pp. 115-126.

24. Memorandum by Gompers in the archives of AFL-CIO, dated January 4, 1918.

25. *Reports of the Department of Labor,* 1919, p. 136.

26. U.S. Bureau of Labor Statistics, *National War Labor Board,* Bulletin No. 287, p. 33, also pp. 9, 17, 34.

27. *Ibid.,* p. 20.

28. Bing, *op. cit.,* pp. 112-115; Selig Perlman and Philip Taft, *History of Labor in the United States, 1896–1932* (New York: Macmillan Co., 1935), IV, pp. 443-444.

29. The letters of President Wilson to the strikers and the companies are in *National War Labor Board,* pp. 36-37.

30. *Report of Proceedings of the Thirty-seventh Annual Convention of the American Federation of Labor,* 1917, pp. 2-4.

31. *Ibid.,* p. 98.

32. *Ibid.,* p. 99.

33. *American Federation of Labor Reconstruction Program* (Washington: American Federation of Labor, 1918), p. 8.

34. *Ibid.,* p. 10.

35. *Ibid.,* p. 14.

CHAPTER 25. POLITICAL SOCIALISM AND GOVERNMENT

1. William English Walling, "Socialist Gains and Losses in Recent Elections," *New Review,* February 6, 1913.

2. Quoted in Philip Taft, *The A.F. of L. in the Time of Gompers* (New York: Harper and Brothers, 1957), p. 228.

3. David J. Saposs, *Left Wing Unionism* (New York: International Publishers, 1926), pp. 37-40.

4. *Industrial Unionism in Its Relation to Trade Unionism, Report of the Executive Council of the American Federation of Labor to the Rochester, N.Y. Convention,* 1912.

5. *Report of Proceedings of the Thirty-second Annual Convention of the American Federation of Labor* 1912, p. 243.

6. *Ibid.,* pp. 311-312.

7. Max S. Hayes, "The Rochester Convention of the A.F. of L.," *New Review,* January 4, 1913, pp. 20-21.

8. *Report of Proceedings of the Thirty-seventh Annual Convention* (AFL), 1917, pp. 423-428.

9. Alexander Trachtenberg (ed.), *The American Labor Year Book, 1917– 1918* (New York: Rand School of Social Science, 1918), pp. 336-337.

10. Nathan Fine, *Labor and Farmer Parties in the United States, 1828– 1928;* (New York: Rand School of Social Science, 1928), pp. 310-315.

11. Theodore Draper, *The Roots of American Communism* (New York: Viking Press, 1960), pp. 121-175.

12. Wallace Stegner, "Joe Hill: The Wobblies' Troubadour," *New Republic,* January 5 and February 9, 1948, expresses the view that Joe Hill was guilty.

See also Wallace Stegner, *The Preacher and the Slave* (Boston: Houghton Mifflin Co., 1950), a novel based on the life of Hill.

13. *Law and Order in San Francisco: A Beginning* (San Francisco: Law and Order League, 1916), pp. 19, 25.

14. *Report of Proceedings of the Seventeenth Annual Convention of the California State Federation of Labor*, 1916.

15. *The Blast*, April 1, 1916.

16. Robert Minor, *The Frame-Up System: Story of the San Francisco Bomb* (San Francisco: International Workers' Defense League, 1916).

17. *Labor Clarion*, April 1 and 15, 1904, deals with Calhoun and his hostility to labor.

18. *Report of Proceedings of the Ninth Annual Convention of the California State Federation of Labor*, 1908, pp. 67-68.

19. Resolution submitted by Division 518 of the Amalgamated Association of Street and Electric Railway Employees of America, signed by Edward D. Vandeleur, president, and John J. Dyer, secretary, in archives of San Francisco Labor Council.

20. *Labor Clarion*, July 21, 1917.

21. "Report on the Mooney Dynamite Cases in San Francisco submitted by President Wilson's Mediation Commission," *Official Bulletin*, January 28, 1918, p. 14.

22. *The Mooney-Billings Report: Suppressed by the Wickersham Committee* (New York: Gotham House, 1932), pp. 37-41.

23. *Labor Clarion*, July 28, 1916.

24. Warren K. Billings to San Francisco Labor Council, October 1, 1916.

25. *Report of Proceedings of the Seventeenth Annual Convention of the California State Federation of Labor*, 1916, pp. 34-36.

26. *The* [Oakland] *World*, February 23, 1917.

27. *Labor Clarion*, February 23, 1917.

28. *Coast Seamen's Journal*, April 25, 1917.

29. Edward Nockles and Andrew Furuseth to Fremont Older, May 30, 1917.

30. John I. Nolan to Murphy, June 4, 1917.

31. Daniel C. Murphy and Paul Scharrenberg to organized labor, July 9, 1917.

32. Daniel C. Murphy to Samuel Gompers, September 19, 1917.

33. Philip Taft, *The A.F. of L. in the Time of Gompers* (New York: Harper and Brothers, 1957), pp. 377-379.

34. *Report of President Wilson's Mediation Commission*, p. 15.

35. *The Sacramento Bee*, March 1, 1918.

36. *Report of Proceedings of the Nineteenth Annual Convention of the California State Federation of Labor*, 1918, pp. 35-37.

37. Taft, *op. cit.*, p. 377; *Minutes of Executive Council of the California State Federation of Labor*, January 12, 1919.

38. William D. Stephens in a letter to the *Sacramento Bee*, May 27, 1931.

39. Governor W. D. Stephens of California to Paul Scharrenberg, November 29, 1919.

40. This information was given to William Green by Paul Scharrenberg, in a letter, June 10, 1931. *Proceedings of Twenty-first Annual Convention of California State Federation of Labor*, 1920.

41. Remarks of Paul Scharrenberg are in the files of the California State Federation of Labor.

42. *Tri-County Labor News,* October 8, 1920.

43. *Report of Proceedings of the Forty-seventh Annual Convention of the American Federation of Labor,* 1927, p. 364.

44. Tom Mooney to William Green, January 2, 1928.

45. *Ibid.*

46. Governor C. C. Young to Scharrenberg, July 13, 1928.

47. Scharrenberg also discussed the Mooney case with me.

48. *In the Matter of Application Made in Behalf of Thomas J. Mooney for a Pardon* (Sacramento: California State Printing Office, 1930).

49. Scharrenberg to Governor James Rolph, June 10, 1931.

50. *California Labor,* January 15, 1939.

51. *Report of Proceedings of the Fortieth Annual Convention of the California State Federation of Labor,* 1939, pp. 75, 135, 145.

52. *Report on the Bisbee Deportations Made by the President's Mediation Commission to the President of the United States,* November 6, 1917.

53. *Ibid.*

54. *The Survey,* June 2, 1919, p. 451.

55. *Report of the Activities of the War Department in the Field of Industrial Relations During the War* (Washington: Government Printing Office, 1919), p. 44.

56. *Ibid.,* p. 45.

57. Philip Taft, "The Federal Trials of the I.W.W.," *Labor History,* Winter 1962, pp. 57-92.

58. *Report of the Attorney-General of the United States for the Year 1920,* p. 177.

59. Quoted in Eldridge Foster Dowell, *A History of Criminal Syndicalism* (Baltimore: Johns Hopkins Press, 1939), p. 17.

60. *Dowell, op. cit.,* p. 139.

61. Louis F. Post, *The Deportations Delirium* (Chicago: Charles H. Kerr, 1923).

62. *Report of the Attorney-General of the United States for the Year 1920,* p. 173.

63. *Report of the U.S. Department of Labor,* 1920, p. 171.

64. Post, *op. cit.,* p. 167.

65. *Ibid.,* p. 79

66. *Ibid.,* p. 167.

67. W. T. Neff to Secretary-Treasurer George Hardy, November 12 and December 4, 1920, in *Solidarity,* December 7, 1920.

68. *Solidarity,* November 13, 1920.

69. *Ibid.*

70. *Ibid.,* December 18, 1920.

CHAPTER 26. POSTWAR RADICALISM AND REACTION

1. Proclamation is reprinted in Murray Morgan, *Skid Row: An Informal Portrait of Seattle* (New York: Viking Press, 1951), p. 213.

2. Philip Taft, *The A.F. of L. in the Time of Gompers* (New York: Harper and Brothers, 1957), pp. 456-457.

3. D. C. Masters, *The Winnipeg General Strike* (Toronto: University of Toronto Press, 1950), pp. 19-39.

4. The facts on the Winnipeg general strike are from Masters, *op. cit.,* pp. 41-144.

5. Benjamin M. Squires, "The Marine Affiliation of the Port of New York: An Experiment in Industrial Unionism," *Journal of Political Economy,* December 1919, pp. 849-856.

6. Squires, *op. cit.,* pp. 860-871; Alexander Bing, *War-Time Strikes and Their Adjustment* (New York: E. P. Dutton and Company, 1921), pp. 47-48.

7. *Proceedings of the Twenty-fifth Convention of the International Longshoremen's Association,* 1919, pp. 318-319.

8. Benjamin M. Squires, "The Strike of Longshoremen at the Port of New York," *Monthly Labor Review,* December, 1919, pp. 95-115, is the source of much of the information on the outlaw strike.

9. *Report of Proceedings of the Thirty-first Annual Convention of the American Federation of Labor,* 1911, p. 320.

10. Alfred Harding, *The Revolt of the Actors* (New York: William Morrow and Co., 1929), pp. 22-24.

11. *Ibid.,* p. 41.

12. Quoted in *ibid.,* p. 57.

13. *Report of Proceedings of the Thirty-first Annual Convention* (AFL), p. 320.

14. Gompers to Hugh Frayne, May 22, 1916.

15. *Report of Proceedings of the Thirty-seventh Annual Convention of the American Federation of Labor,* 1917, pp. 376-377.

16. *Minutes of the Meeting of the Executive Council of the American Federation of Labor,* August 10, 1919.

17. Quoted in Harding, *op. cit.,* p. 80.

18. *Ibid.,* pp. 173-178.

19. *New York Times,* September 14, 1919.

20. *Boston Herald,* August 2-22 and 27, 1919.

21. *Ibid.,* August 27, 1919.

22. *Providence Journal,* September 11, 1919.

23. *Ibid.,* September 13, 1913.

24. *New York Times,* September 12, 1919.

25. *Ibid.,* September 14, 1919.

26. *Ibid.*

27. *Report of Acting President John L. Lewis to the Twenty-seventh Consecutive and Fourth Biennial Convention of the United Mine Workers of America,* 1919, pp. 4-7.

28. *Minutes of the Twenty-seventh Consecutive and Fourth Biennial Convention of the United Mine Workers of America* (12th day session), pp. 55-56.

29. U.S. Attorney L. Bert Slack to U.S. Attorney-General, November 15, 1919, in National Archives.

30. *Report of Proceedings of the Fortieth Annual Convention* (AFL), 1920, p. 90.

31. *Ibid.,* p. 380.

32. Committee of International Executive Board of the United Mine Workers of America to Samuel Gompers, December 9, 1921.

33. Gompers to Lewis, December 13, 1921.

34. *Report of Proceedings of the Forty-first Annual Convention* (AFL), 1921, p. 379.

35. Gompers to Lewis, December 3, 1921.

36. Winthrop D. Lane, *Civil War in West Virginia* (New York: B. W. Huebsch, Inc., 1921), pp. 43-55; McAllister Coleman, *Men and Coal* (New York: Farrar and Rinehart, Inc., 1921), pp. 94-104.

37. Lester began mining coal on June 13 with nonunion men and shipping three days later. A Chicago steamshovel men's union was supposed to be the organization to which the new employees belonged.

38. Paul M. Angle, *Bloody Williamson* (New York: Alfred A. Knopf, 1952), pp. 14-19.

39. *Ibid.,* p. 10.

40. *Ibid.,* p. 40, for quote. See also p. 41.

41. *Ibid.,* pp. 60-62.

42. *Report of Proceedings of the Thirty-eight Annual Convention* (AFL), 1918, p. 207.

43. For example, the United Mine Workers of America appointed sixteen organizers who were directed to report to Foster. *Twenty-seventh Consecutive and Fourth Biennial Convention of the United Mine Workers of America* (12th day session), p. 3.

44. Philip Taft, *The A.F. of L. in the Time of Gompers* (New York: Harper and Brothers, 1957), p. 388.

45. The quotes are from the letter to President Wilson from the national meeting of trade unionists, in the *Monthly Labor Review,* December 1919, pp. 83-84; Gary presented his views on unions and strikes in a speech to the American Iron and Steel Institute in which he charged the strike was radically inspired and aimed to take over the properties of the companies. The speech is reprinted in *The Survey,* November 8, 1919, p. 53.

46. *Monthly Labor Review,* December 1919, p. 84.

47. U.S. Senate Committee on Education and Labor, *Investigation of Strike in Steel Industry,* 66th Cong., 1st sess., Part I, pp. 112-113.

48. *Public Opinion and the Steel Strike* (New York: Harcourt, Brace and Co., 1921), p. 169. This document contained the supplementary reports of the investigators to the Commission of Inquiry, the Interchurch World Movement. See also S. Adele Shaw, "Closed Towns," *The Survey,* November 8, 1919, p. 62. Marshall Olds, *Analysis of the Interchurch World Movement Report on the Steel Strike* (New York: G. P. Putnam's Sons, 1923), is a criticism of the "Interchurch Report."

49. *Minutes of the National Committee for Organizing Iron and Steel Workers,* December 13 and 14, 1919; *Amalgamated Journal,* January 15, 1920.

50. William Z. Foster, *The Great Steel Strike* (New York: B. W. Huebsch, 1920), p. 243.

51. Excerpts from the report of the National Committee for Organizing Iron and Steel Workers in the Commission of Inquiry. The Interchurch World Movement, *Report on the Steel Strike,* p. 194.

52. *Report on the Steel Strike,* p. 194.

53. *Ibid.,* p. 196.

54. *Investigation of the Strike in the Steel Industry,* I. 163.

CHAPTER 27. EMPLOYER ATTACKS AND THE AMERICAN PLAN

1. Gompers to executive council, February 22, 1922.

2. *Ibid.*

3. *Proceedings of the First Industrial Conference* (Washington: Government Printing Office, 1920), pp. 220-221.

4. *Ibid.,* p. 275.

5. Henry S. Dennison, "The President's Industrial Conference of October," *Bulletin of the Taylor Society,* April 1920, pp. 80-81.

6. Philip Taft, *The A.F. of L. in the Time of Gompers* (New York: Harper and Brothers, 1957), pp. 400-401.

7. Savel Zimand, *The Open Shop Drive* (New York: Bureau of Industrial Research, 1921), p. 5.

8. Quoted from the *Proceedings of the Convention of the National Conference of State Manufacturers' Associations,* 1921, p. 70, in *ibid.,* p. 6.

9. *New York Times,* December 16, 1920.

10. *The Open Shop Review,* January 1921, p. 29.

11. Zimand, *op. cit.,* pp. 18-20.

12. The letter was signed by James L. Glass, secretary of the National Open Shop Association, and appeared in *American Federationist,* October 1922, p. 733.

13. Samuel Gompers, "The Conspiracy Against Labor," *American Federationist,* October 1922, pp. 734-735; Selig Perlman and Philip Taft, *History of Labor in the United States, 1896–1932* (New York: Macmillan Co., 1935), IV, pp. 491-494.

14. Executive Council Document No. 22, from Samuel Gompers, December 30, 1920.

15. *Ibid.*

16. *American Federationist,* April 1921, pp. 296-297.

17. *Report of Proceedings of the Forty-second Annual Convention of the American Federation of Labor,* 1922, p. 71.

18. Frederick L. Ryan, *Industrial Relations in the San Francisco Building Trades* (Norman, Okla.: University of Oklahoma Press, 1935), pp. 107-110.

19. W. H. George to members of the Builders' Exchange, April 13, 1921, in *American Federationist,* October 1922, pp. 734-735; also Ryan, *op. cit.,* pp. 149-153.

20. Royall E. Montgomery, *Industrial Relations in the Chicago Building Trades* (Chicago: University of Chicago Press, 1927), p. 245.

21. *Ibid.,* pp. 270-309.

CHAPTER 28. UNIONS, GOVERNMENT, AND MILITANCY ON THE RAILROADS

1. *Memorandum of Gompers to Executive Council of the American Federation of Labor,* May 16, 1918.

2. Statement of Glenn E. Plumb before the Senate Interstate Commerce Committee, reprinted in *The Railway Carmen's Journal,* May 1918, p. 1,058.

3. *Report of Proceedings of the Thirty-ninth Annual Convention of the American Federation of Labor,* 1919, p. 391.

4. Warren S. Stone to Gompers, June 4, 1920.

5. Gompers to Stone, July 13, 1920.

6. *Ibid.*

7. *Ibid.*

8. *Minutes of the Executive Council of the American Federation of Labor,* June 6, 1921.

9. *Government Control of Railroads,* Senate Report 304, 66th Cong., 1st sess., pp. 21-22. Harry D. Wolf, *The Railroad Labor Board* (Chicago: University of Chicago Press, 1927), deals with this subject.

10. Gompers to Stone, July 13, 1920.

11. *Speech of Samuel Gompers to the Executives of the Railroad Organizations Affiliated with the A.F. of L. and the Four Brotherhoods,* in the archives of the AFL-CIO, February 10, 1920, p. 7.

12. *Ibid.,* p. 12.

13. "Final Decision on Seniority Rights of the Outlaw Strikers," *Locomotive Engineer's Journal,* October 1920, p. 946. The article was signed by the heads of the four brotherhoods.

14. *Minutes of the Executive Council of the American Federation of Labor,* May 9, 1921.

15. *Ibid.,* June 1, 1922.

16. "Decision No. 1036," *Decisions of U.S. Railroad Labor Board with Addenda and Interpretations,* 1923, III, 423-438.

17. *Official Proceedings Seventh Convention Railway Employees' Department, A.F. of L.,* 1922, pp. 10-12; Wolf, op. cit., pp. 214-265.

18. Hooper to Bert M. Jewell, June 20, 1922, *Official Proceedings Seventh Convention Railway Employees' Department,* p. 14.

19. T. DeWitt Cuyler to Bert M. Jewell, June 20, 1922, in *ibid.,* pp. 15-16.

20. Cuyler to Jewell, June 29, 1922, in *ibid.,* p. 18.

21. *Ibid.,* p. 39.

22. Memorandum in the National Archives (n.d.), Attorney-General's Division, Shopmen's Strike of 1922, File 16-150.

23. Resolution in *ibid.,* p. 39.

24. Memorandum from Attorney-General H. M. Daugherty to W. H. Heron, June 24, 1922, in National Archives, Attorney-General's Division, Shopmen's Strike of 1922, File 16-150-100. This memorandum does not appear in *Appendix to the Annual Report of the United States for the Fiscal Year 1922,* which includes the correspondence on the strike (Washington: Government Printing Office, 1924).

25. Memorandum of W. H. Heron to Attorney-General H. M. Daugherty, June 27, 1922, in *ibid.*

26. The last two quotes are from Heron's memorandum.

27. *Official Proceedings Seventh Convention Railway Employees' Department—American Federation of Labor,* 1926, pp. 43-44.

28. For the exchange of letters between the carriers, the unions, and President Harding, see *ibid.,* pp. 44-55.

29. *Appendix to the Annual Report of the Attorney-General of the United States For the Fiscal Year 1922,* p. 23.

30. Daugherty to Esterlin, August 29, 1922; Esterlin to Daugherty, August 29, 1922, in National Archives, Attorney-General's Division, Shopmen's Strike of 1922, File No. 66-150. This letter is not reprinted in *Appendix to Annual Report of Attorney-General, 1922.*

31. From the restraining order, see *Proceedings Seventh Convention Railway Employees' Department,* pp. 57-58.

32. Special Assistant Attorney-General Warren F. Warton to Attorney-General H. M. Daugherty, September 1, 1922.

33. W. F. Warton to Daugherty, September 2, 1922, in National Archives, Attorney-General's Division, Shopmen's Strike of 1922, File No. 16-150-sub 100.

34. *Minutes of the Executive Council of the American Federation of Labor,* September 7, 1922.

35. Daugherty to Charles F. Clyne, September 6, 1922, in National Archives, Attorney-General's Division, Shopcraft Strike of 1922, File No. 66-150-sub 100.

36. Holland to Daugherty, September 7, 1922, in National Archives, Attorney-General's Division, Shopmen's Strike of 1922, File No. 66-150-sub 100. This telegram does not appear in *Appendix to Annual Report of Attorney-General, 1922.*

37. Blackburn Esterlin to Silas Strawn, September 6, 1922, in National Archives, Attorney-General's Division, Shopmen's Strike of 1922, File No. 66-150-sub 100. The telegram and answers do not appear in *Appendix to Annual Report of Attorney-General, 1922.*

38. The quote is from an address of Gompers at a mass meeting in Beethoven Hall, New York, October 5, 1922, in National Archives, Attorney-General's Division, Shopmen's Strike of 1922, File No. 66-150-sub 100.

39. Donald Richberg to Solicitor General James M. Beck, October 5, 1922. The memorandum in which Solicitor James Beck is told not to answer the issues raised in Richberg's letter but merely acknowledge its receipt does not appear in the *Appendix to Annual Report of Attorney-General, 1922,* pp. 53-54. A memorandum to Attorney-General Daugherty protesting the tone of Richberg's letter appears in the *Appendix,* p. 56.

40. *Official Proceedings Seventh Convention Railway Employees Department,* 1926, pp. 58-60.

41. *Ibid.,* pp. 64-69. With regular organizations virtually destroyed on many roads, company unions with or without the direct encouragement of management were initiated on many of the railway systems. According to the Railway Employees Department, 61 company unions were established on the railroads between 1922 and 1926.

42. Louis A. Wood, *Union-Management Cooperation on the Railroads* (New Haven: Yale University Press, 1931), pp. 62-121.

CHAPTER 29. INDEPENDENT POLITICAL ACTION

1. Robert L. Morlan, *Political Prairie Fire: The Non-Partisan League, 1915–1922* (Minneapolis: University of Minnesota Press 1955), pp. 22-56.

2. Samuel Gompers, *Should a Labor Party Be Formed* (Washington: American Federation of Labor, 1918).

3. Theodore Draper, *The Roots of American Communism* (New York: Viking Press, 1960), pp. 90-95, deals with this episode.

4. Nathan Fine, *Labor and Farmer Parties in the United States, 1828–1928* (New York: Rand School of Social Science, 1928), pp. 398-406; Selig

Perlman and Philip Taft, *History of Labor in the United States, 1896–1932* (New York: Macmillan Co., 1935), IV, 532-534).

5. The last two quotations are from the platform in Fine, *op. cit.,* p. 410.

CHAPTER 30. RADICAL OPPOSITION IN THE ESTABLISHED UNIONS

1. *Theses and Statutes of the Third (Communist) International,* adopted by the Second Congress, July 17–August 7, 1920 (Moscow: Communist International, 1920), p. 35.

2. Theodore Draper, *American Communism and Soviet Russia* (New York: Viking Press, 1960), pp. 66-69.

3. U.S. Senate Committee on Foreign Relations, *Recognition of Russia,* Hearings Before a Subcommittee Pursuant to S. Res. 50, 66th Cong., 1st sess., 1924, p. 152.

4. William Z. Foster, *The Bankruptcy of the American Labor Movement* (Chicago: *The Labor Herald,* 1923), p. 45.

5. Selig Perlman and Philip Taft, *History of Labor in the United States, 1896–1932* (New York: Macmillan Co., 1935), IV, 538-561. An excellent description of the Trade Union Educational League is Earl R. Beckner, "The Trade Union Educational League," *Journal of Political Economy,* August 1925, pp. 410-431.

6. Beckner, *op. cit.,* p. 427.

7. Benjamin Gitlow, *The Whole of Their Lives* (New York: Charles Scribner's Sons, 1948), p. 123. Gitlow was a high officer in the Communist party and its candidate for Vice-President of the United States in 1924. He served a prison term for conviction of criminal anarchy in New York City in 1921. He broke with the party in 1929.

8. Perlman and Taft, *op. cit.,* pp. 563-565. Brophy later wrote: "The economic conditions following the War that led to the decline of the United Mine Workers are not explained at all adequately and then putting blame on Lewis is distorted." Brophy to John K. Jessup, August 22, 1936, in AFL-CIO archives.

9. Draper, *op. cit.,* p. 290; Perlman and Taft, *op. cit.,* pp. 566-567.

10. Philip Taft, *The A.F. of L. in the Time of Gompers* (New York: Harper and Brothers, 1957), pp. 457-460.

CHAPTER 31. UNIONS IN RETREAT

1. *Proceedings of the United Mine Workers of America,* 1927, I, 436-460.

2. For another view see Irving Bernstein, *The Lean Years* (Boston: Houghton Mifflin Co., 1960), pp. 87-134.

3. *United Mine Workers Journal,* October 1, 1929, p. 3.

4. *Ibid.,* October 15, 1929, p. 3.

5. *Ibid.,* p. 5.

6. *Ibid.,* December 15, 1929, p. 6.

7. *Ibid.,* November 15, 1929, p. 4.

8. William Green to John H. Walker, October 13, 1930.

9. *United Mine Workers Journal,* March 15, 1931, pp. 8-9.

10. Harriet D. Hudson, *The Progressive Mine Workers of America: A*

Study in Rival Unionism (Urbana, Ill.: University of Illinois, 1952), pp. 119-120.

11. McAlister Coleman, *Men and Coal* (New York: Farrar and Rinehart, 1943), p. 177: Selig Perlman and Philip Taft, *History of Labor in the United States, 1896–1932* (New York: Macmillan Co., 1935), IV, pp. 612-614.

12. The quotation is from the report of Senator Davis on the Davis-Kelly bill and appeared in the *United Mine Workers Journal*, August 1, 1932, p. 9.

13. Beulah Amidon, "An Old Fashioned Strike," *The Survey*, April 1, 1926, pp. 10-11.

14. Quote from statement of Colonel Johnston in *The Survey*, January 1, 1927, p. 468.

15. *Ibid.*, March 15, 1926, p. 620.

16. Philip Taft, *The A.F. of L. from the Death of Gompers to the Merger* (New York: Harper and Brothers, 1959), pp. 9-11; Perlman and Taft, *op. cit.*, pp. 603-605.

17. Quoted in Fred Beal, *Proletarian Journey* (New York: Hillman-Curl, Inc., 1937), p. 137.

18. Mary Heaton Vorse, "Gastonia," *Harper's Magazine*, November 1929, p. 702.

19. The information is from Beal, *op. cit.*, pp. 164-208. Beal was the leader of the strike.

20. *Report of Proceedings of the Forty-eighth Annual Convention of the American Federation of Labor*, 1928, p. 339.

21. *The American Labor Year Book, 1930* (New York: Rand School of Social Science, n.d.), pp. 86-93; *ibid.*, 1932, p. 71.

22. In his report to the executive council in August 1921, Gompers suggested the appointment of a committee of six, three from the executive council and the others from the railway unions. He also asked that a conference of railroad unions be called to devise a program. No steps were taken because the railway unions found their advocacy of government ownership an impediment in their negotiations with the carriers. *Minutes of the Executive Council of the American Federation of Labor*, August 22, 1921.

23. *The Labor Banking Movement in the United States* (Princeton: Industrial Relations Section, Princeton University, 1929), p. 110.

24. *Report of Proceedings of the Forty-sixth Annual Convention* (AFL), 1926, p. 49.

25. *Report of the Forty-seventh Annual Convention* (AFL), 1927, p. 62.

26. Release from AFL, June 1, 1922, and December 4, 1922.

27. Frank Morrison to Frank H. McCarthy, October 10, 1924, in archives of AFL-CIO.

CHAPTER 32. THE DEPRESSION AND CONTINUED DECLINE

1. Figures are from U.S. Bureau of the Census, *Statistical Abstract of the United States* (Washington: Government Printing Office, 1962), p. 312.

2. *Report of Proceedings of the Thirty-third Annual Convention of the American Federation of Labor*, 1913, p. 51.

3. *American Federationist*, August 1941, p. 25.

4. Helen Hall, "When Detroit's Out of Gear," *The Survey*, April 1, 1930, p. 11; *American Federationist*, April 15, 1930, p. 93.

5. Don D. Lescohier and Florence Peterson, *The Alleviation of Unemployment in Wisconsin* (Madison, Wisc.: Industrial Commission of Wisconsin, 1931), p. 193.

6. Joanna C. Colcord, assisted by William C. Koplovitz and Russell H. Kurtz, *Emergency Work Relief* (New York: Russell Sage Foundation, 1932), pp. 13-14.

7. See Arthur Hillman, *The Unemployed Citizens' League of Seattle* (Seattle, Wash.: University of Washington Press, 1934). Bernard Karsh and Phillips L. Garman, "The Impact of the Political Left," in Milton Derber and Edwin Young, *Labor and the New Deal* (Madison, Wisc., University of Wisconsin Press, 1957), pp. 71-115.

8. *Report of Proceedings of the Fifty-fifth Annual Convention* (AFL), 1935, pp. 677-678.

9. Comments in file of AFL-CIO.

10. Gompers to President Warren G. Harding, February 7, 1921, in archives of AFL-CIO.

11. *Minutes of the Executive Council of the American Federation of Labor,* October 27, 1932; May 1, 1933.

12. *Report of Proceedings of the Fifty-first Annual Convention* (AFL), 1931, p. 78.

13. *Report of Proceedings of the Fifty-second Annual Convention* (AFL), 1932, pp. 344-360. See also Philip Taft, *The A.F. of L. from the Death of Gompers to the Merger* (New York: Harper and Brothers, 1959), pp. 35-36.

14. Edwin E. Witte, "New Developments in Labor Injunctions," *American Labor Legislation Review,* September 1929, p. 308.

15. *Report of Proceedings of the Forty-ninth Annual Convention* (AFL), 1929, pp. 317-334, 340-352.

16. *New York Times,* January 5, 1931.

17. *Report of Proceedings of the Fifty-second Annual Convention* (AFL), 1932, p. 65.

18. House Committee on Education and Labor, *Legislative History of the Davis-Bacon Act* (Washington: Government Printing Office, 1962).

CHAPTER 33. THE NATIONAL INDUSTRIAL RECOVERY ACT

1. *National Industrial Recovery, Hearings* on H.R. 5664, House Committee on Ways and Means, 73d Congr., 1st sess., pp. 16-22.

2. *Ibid.*

3. *Congressional Record,* May 26, 1933, Part 4, p. 4360.

4. *Congressional Record,* June 8, 1933, p. 5279; see also Paul Brissenden, "Genesis and Import of the Collective Bargaining Provisions of the Recovery Act," *Essay in Honor of Wesley Clair Mitchell* (New York: Columbia University Press, 1935), pp. 27-62. Louis Lorwin and Arthur Wubnig, *Labor Relations Board* (Washington: Brookings Institution, 1935), pp. 26-49. Raymond S. Rubinow, *Section 7 (a): Its History and Administration* (Washington: Office of National Recovery Administration, Division of Review Labor Studies Section), Work Materials No. 45, Part E.

5. *The National Recovery Administration: A Message from the President of the United States Transmitting a Report on the Operation of the National Recovery Administration,* Prepared by Those Members of the Committee of

Industrial Analysis Who Have No Official Relationship to the Government (Washington: Government Printing Office, 1937), p. 8.

6. Circular letter signed by William Green, May 27, 1933, addressed to all national and international unions.

7. Green to members of executive council, June 21, 1933, in AFL-CIO archives.

8. *American Federation of Labor Weekly News Service,* July 22, 1933.

9. *United Mine Workers Journal,* October 1933.

10. *Attention: Wage and Salaried Workers Everywhere,* a leaflet issued by the American Federation of Labor, June 17, 1933.

11. William H. Spencer, "Collective Bargaining under Section 7 (a) of the National Industrial Recovery Act," *Journal of Business,* April 1935.

12. *Individual and Collective Bargaining Under the N.I.R.A.* (New York: National Industrial Conference Board, 1938), pp. 35-37.

13. Quoted in Spencer, *op. cit.,* p. 8.

14. "The Text of President Roosevelt's Clarification of Section 7 (a) of the National Industrial Recovery Act, September 19, 1933," issued by the National Industrial Recovery Administration.

15. Lorwin and Wubnig, *op. cit.,* 309-310.

16. Memorandum to Donald Richberg from President Roosevelt, December 15, 1934, in Franklin Delano Roosevelt Library at Hyde Park, N.Y. *Minutes of the Executive Council of the American Federation of Labor,* January 14, 1934.

17. Statement to the press by William Green, president of the American Federation of Labor, June 3, 1935.

18. *Statement of Executive Council of the American Federation of Labor,* June 6, 1935.

CHAPTER 34. LAYING THE GROUNDWORK FOR THE GREAT EX-
PANSION

1. E. Berquist and associates, *Economic Survey of the Bituminous Coal Industry Under Free Competition and Regulation* (Washington: Office of National Recovery Administration, March 1936), Work Materials No. 69, I, pp. 60-72.

2. *Coal Age,* January 1932, p. 35.

3. *Ibid.,* February 1932, p. 87.

4. Berquist, *op. cit.,* pp. 59-64.

5. *Coal Age,* February 1932, p. 43; June 1932, p. 36.

6. *Ibid.,* February 1932, p. 83.

7. *United Mine Workers Journal,* May 15, 1933, p. 5.

8. *Ibid.,* May 15, 1933, pp. 1-2: Louis Stark in *New York Times,* September 23, 1933.

9. *Coal Age,* July 1933, p. 249.

10. *Ibid.,* July 1, 1933, pp. 12-13.

11. *Ibid.,* June 15, 1933, pp. 6, 9, 11.

12. *Ibid.,* July 1, 1933, pp. 3-4.

13. *United Mine Workers Journal,* August 1, 1933, p. 8; *New York Times,* July 24, 1933.

14. *New York Times,* July 15, 16, 19, and August 10, 1933.

15. *Ibid.,* August 9, 11, 1933.

16. *Coal Age*, October 1933, pp. 354-358.

17. *United Mine Workers Journal*, October 1, 1933, p. 4; October 15, 1933, pp. 11-12.

18. *Pittsburgh Press*, July 26-30, 1933.

19. *Ibid.*, August 2-6, 1933.

20. *Ibid.*, August 9-12, 1933.

21. *Ibid.*, September 12, 14, 17, 1933.

22. *Ibid.*, September 19 and October 1, 1933.

23. *Ibid.*, October 11-13, 1933; *United Mine Workers Journal*, October 15, 1933, p. 4.

24. *United Mine Workers Journal*, November 1, 1933, p. 5; *Coal Age*, November 1933, pp. 387-388; *Pittsburgh Press*, October 21-30, 1933.

25. *Pittsburgh Press*, November 1-5, 1933.

26. *United Mine Workers Journal*, December 15, 1933, p. 3; *Pittsburgh Press*, November 22-25, 1933.

27. *Coal Age*, January 1934, p. 35.

28. *Ibid.*, February 1934, p. 82.

29. *Ibid.*, November 1933, p. 387.

30. See Walter Galenson, *The CIO Challenge to the AFL* (Cambridge: Harvard University Press, 1960), Chapter 4. Waldo B. Fisher "Bituminous Coal," in Harry A. Millis (ed.), *How Collective Bargaining Works* (New York: Twentieth Century Fund, 1942).

31. *United Mine Workers Journal*, February 1, 1934, p. 3.

32. *Ibid.*

CHAPTER 35. STRIKES AND EXPANSION IN 1934

1. International Longshoremen's Association, *Proceedings of the Twenty-third Convention*, 1915, p. 108.

2. International Longshoremen, Marine and Transportation Workers' Association, *Proceedings of the Fourteenth Annual Convention*, 1905, p. 144.

3. Charles P. Larrowe, *Shape Up and Hiring Hall* (Berkeley and Los Angeles: University of California Press, 1955), pp. 92-93.

4. Paul Eliel, *The Waterfront and General Strikes, San Francisco, 1934* (San Francisco: Industrial Association of San Francisco 1934), gives a step-by-step report of developments in the strike. Mr. Eliel was on the staff of the Industrial Association which participated on the employer side in the controversy. When checked against the San Francisco newspapers of the period, his narrative is reliable, although inevitably he shows lack of sympathy for the strikers and some bias against them.

5. *San Francisco News*, May 8-10, 1934.

6. *Report of the National Longshoremen's Board*, pp. 4-5, in the Franklin Delano Roosevelt Library, Hyde Park, N.Y.

7. *New York Times*, May 14, 15, 1934.

8. Quote from Eliel, *op. cit.*, p. 43; *San Francisco News*, July 1-4, 1934.

9. Eliel, *op. cit.*, p. 43-44, quotes from the files of the Industrial Association.

10. *Ibid.*, p. 33.

11. *Ibid.*, pp. 75-76.

12. *Ibid.*, p. 50.

13. *Labor Clarion*, July 13, 1934.

14. *San Francisco Examiner*, July 5, 1934.

15. *Labor Clarion*, July 13, 1934; *San Francisco News*, July 5, 1934.

16. Resolution adopted by San Francisco Labor Council, July 6, 1934, in archives of council.

17. John A. O'Connell to William Green, July 7, 1934.

18. Telegram from William Green to John O'Connell, July 9, 1934, and letter from Green to O'Connell of the same date; in archives of San Francisco Labor Council.

19. *Report of the National Longshoremen's Board*, p. 10; *The Seamen's Journal*, August 1, 1934, p. 1.

20. *The Seamen's Journal*, July 13, 1934.

21. *Ibid.*

22. "To all Unions Affiliated with the San Francisco Labor Council and Building Trades Council from Strike Strategy Committee." July 12, 1934, in archives of San Francisco Labor Council.

23. Statement, undated, in archives of San Francisco Labor Council.

24. Minutes of Special Meeting, July 13, 1934, in archives of San Francisco Labor Council.

25. *New York Times*, July 18, 1934.

26. *Labor Clarion,* July 20, 1934.

27. *New York Times,* July 20-29, 1934.

28. San Francisco approved by 2,014 to 722, but Portland voted in favor by 795 to 33. *New York Times*, July 26, 1934.

29. *The Seamen's Journal*, August 1, 1934, pp. 113-114.

30. *Ibid.,* November 1, 1934, p. 162.

31. Quotation is from arbitration decision in *ibid.*, February 1, 1935, p. 19.

32. *New York Times*, May 22, 23, 1934; *The Organizer*, July 16, 1934 (a paper published by Local 574 during the strike).

33. *The Organizer,* July 17-22, 1934.

34. *Ibid.,* July 24, 1934.

35. *The Organizer*, August 22, 1934. Charles R. Walker, *American City* (New York: Farrar and Rinehart, 1937), deals with this episode at length.

36. Daniel Tobin to Stephen T. Early, July 12, 1941, in Franklin Delano Roosevelt Library, Hyde Park, N.Y., Box 2978.

37. *Report of Board of Inquiry for the Cotton Textile Industry,* September 17, 1934. The "report" appeared in *The Textile Worker*, September 1934.

38. *Ibid.,* p. 379.

39. *Ibid.,* p. 382. *Providence Journal*, August 17, 1934.

40. *Providence Journal*, August 25, 1934.

CHAPTER 36. THE NATIONAL LABOR RELATIONS ACT

1. Testimony of Senator Robert F. Wagner on S. 2926, *To Create a National Labor Board, Hearings Before the Committee on Education and Labor, U.S. Senate,* 73d Cong., 2d sess., Part I, p. 10.

2. *Ibid.,* p. 91.

3. Mary LaDame, *The Filene Store* (New York: Russell Sage Foundation, 1930), pp. 119-120.

4. National Industrial Conference Board, *The Growth of Works Councils in the United States: Special Report No. 32,* 1925.

5. National Industrial Conference Boards, *Works Councils in the United States: Research Report No. 21,* December 1919.

6. *Ibid.,* p. 00

7. *Ibid.,* p. 13.

8. U.S. War Department, *A Report of the Activities of the War Department in the Field of Industrial Relations During the War,* September 15, 1919, pp. 46-47.

9. *The Bulletin Loyal Legion of Loggers and Lumbermen,* March 1919.

10. *American Federationist,* September 1918, p. 810.

11. *Report of Proceedings of the Thirty-nine Annual Convention of the American Federation of Labor,* 1919, p. 303.

12. National Industrial Conference Board, *Special Report No. 32,* 1925, pp. 4-5.

13. *Collective Bargaining Through Employee Representation* (New York: National Industrial Conference Board, 1933), p. 16.

14. *Individual and Collective Bargaining Under the N.I.R.A.* (New York: National Industrial Conference Board, 1933), p. 24.

15. U.S. Bureau of Labor Statistics, *Characteristics of Company Unions,* Bulletin No. 634, 1938, pp. 35-37.

16. *Ibid.,* p. 57.

17. *Ibid.,* p. 58.

18. *Ibid.,* pp. 114-157.

19. *National Labor Relations Board Legislative History of the National Labor Relations Act 1935* (Washington: Government Printing Office, 1949), p. 39; contains a record of the hearings, testimony, reports of congressional committees, and the debates in Congress.

20. *Ibid.,* p. 170.

21. *Ibid.,* p. 375.

22. *Ibid.,* p. 760.

23. *Ibid.,* p. 1023.

24. Testimony of Francis Biddle, chairman of the National Labor Relations Board, in *ibid.,* pp. 1468-1474.

25. *Ibid.,* p. 2368; Leon Keyserling, "The Wagner Act: Its Origin and Current Significance," *The George Washington Law Review,* December 1960, p. 208.

26. National Labor Relations Board, *Legislative History,* p. 1320.

27. *Ibid.,* p. 1414.

28. *Ibid.,* p. 1414. Senator Walsh, the chairman of the Labor Committee, completely abdicated the control and direction of the bill to Senator Wagner who wrote the bill, testified in both houses on its behalf, led the debates and wrote the Senate Committee report. Keyserling, *op. cit.,* p. 208.

29. The colloquy between the senators is in NLRB *Legislative History,* pp. 1421-1422.

30. *Ibid.,* p. 1422.

31. *Ibid.,* p. 1630.

32. *Ibid.,* p. 2301.

33. *Ibid.*

34. *Ibid.,* p. 2309.

35. *Ibid.*

36. *Ibid.,* p. 2312.

37. *Ibid.*
38. *Ibid.*, p. 2348.
39. *Ibid.*, p. 2349.
40. *Ibid.*, pp. 2399-2400.
41. *Ibid.*, p. 2375.
42. *Ibid.*, p. 3269.
43. National Lawyers Committee of American Liberty League, *Report on the Constitutionality of the National Labor Relations Act* (Pittsburgh: Smith Brothers Co., 1935), pp. 104, 128.
44. J. Warren Madden, "The Origin and Early History of the National Labor Relations Board," *George Washington Law Review,* December 1960, p. 237, for the last two quotes.
45. See Irving Bernstein, *The New Deal Collective Bargaining Policy,* (Berkeley, Calif.: University of California Press, 1950).

CHAPTER 37. THE DISPUTE OVER INDUSTRIAL ORGANIZATION AND THE EMERGENCE OF THE COMMITTEE FOR INDUSTRIAL ORGANIZATION

1. *Proceedings of the Twenty-first Annual Convention of the Metal Trades Department,* 1929, p. 27.
2. *Ibid.*, p. 65.
3. *Minutes of the Meeting of the Executive Council of the American Federation of Labor,* September 7, 1933, in archives of AFL-CIO.
4. *Report of Proceedings of the Twenty-fifth annual Convention of the Metal Trades Department of the American Federation of Labor,* 1933, pp. 43-45.
5. *Report of Proceedings of the Fifty-third Annual Convention of the American Federation of Labor,* 1933, p. 500 .
6. The last three quotations are from *ibid.,* p. 501.
7. *Ibid.*, pp. 503-504.
8. *Report of Proceedings of the Fifty-fourth Annual Convention* (AFL), 1934, pp. 41-42.
9. William Green to the general and district organizers of the American Federation of Labor, February 19, 1934.
10. *Ibid.*, pp. 587, 590.
11. *Ibid.*, p. 587.
12. *Ibid.*
13. Quote from Frey's remarks in *ibid.,* p. 590.
14. *Ibid.*, p. 590.
15. *Ibid.*, pp. 590-591.
16. *Ibid.*, p. 593.
17. *Ibid.*, p. 594.
18. *Ibid.*
19. John P. Frey to W. A. Appleton, March 21, 1935, in folder 6 of the papers of Frey at the manuscript collection of the Library of Congress.
20. *Ibid.*
21. *Ibid.*
22. Quote from remarks of Hutcheson at meeting of executive council, May

5, 1935, in Philip Taft, *The A.F. of L. from the Death of Gompers to the Merger* (New York: Harper and Brothers, 1959), p. 90.

23. The last two quotations are from *ibid.,* p. 89.

24. *Ibid.,* pp. 104-107.

25. *Report of Proceedings of the Fifty-fifth Annual Convention* (AFL) 1935, pp. 522-524, for the last two quotations.

26. *Ibid.,* 524-564, for the speeches. Frey's contract arguments on p. 558.

27. *Ibid.,* p. 569.

28. *Ibid.*

29. *Minutes of Committee for Industrial Organization,* Washington, D.C., November 9, 1935. This was a three-page typewritten report.

30. Charles P. Howard to Max Zaritsky, November 11, 1935.

31. Frank Duffy to William Green, November 14, 1935, in archives of AFL-CIO.

32. Green to Duffy, November 19, 1945.

33. William Green to John L. Lewis, November 23, 1935, in archives of AFL-CIO. Similar letters were sent to the other participants in the formation of the committee.

34. Lewis to Zaritsky, November 25, 1935, in headquarters of the United Hatters, Cap and Millinery Workers Union.

35. Thomas F. McMahon to William Green, November 26, 1935, in archives of AFL-CIO.

36. Harvey C. Fremming to Green, November 27, 1935, in archives of AFL-CIO.

37. The last four quotations are from Charles P. Howard to William Green, December 2, 1935, in archives of AFL-CIO.

38. *Ibid.*

39. *Ibid.*

40. Lewis to Green, December 7, 1935.

41. *Agenda for Committee Meeting of Committee for Industrial Organizations,* December 9, 1935.

42. Press release from the Committee for Industrial Organizations, December 10, 1935.

43. *Minutes of the Executive Council of the American Federation of Labor,* January 20, 1936.

44. *Ibid.*

45. *Ibid.*

46. Lewis, Howard, Sidney Hillman, Dubinsky, Fremming, Thomas F. McMahon, and Max Zaritsky to Green, February 21, 1936.

47. David Dubinsky to John Brophy, June 1, 1936.

48. Dubinsky to George M. Harrison, June 1, 1936.

49. *Summary of Meeting Between C.I.O. and Subcommittee of the A. F. of L. Executive Council,* held at United Mine Workers of America headquarters, May 19, 1936.

50. *Minutes of the Meeting of the Executive Council of the American Federation of Labor,* May 19, 1936.

51. George Harrison to Max Zaritsky, May 20, 1936, in headquarters of United Hatters, Cap and Millinery Workers.

52. Charles P. Howard to George M. Harrison, June 2, 1936, in headquar-

ters of United Hatters, Cap and Millinery Workers Union. A copy of the letter was sent to Zaritsky, a member of the committee.

53. G. M. Bugniazet to Green, June 16, 1936; Frank Duffy to Green, June 15, 1936; William L. Hutcheson to Green, June 18, 1936; and Harry Bates to Green, June 10, 1936, all contain suggestions for taking actions against the CIO unions.

54. John Brophy to William Green, June 23, 1936.

55. *Report of Proceedings of the Twenty-seventh Annual Convention* (AFL), 1907, pp. 81-83.

56. *Ibid.*, p. 277.

57. *Ibid.*, p. 234.

58. Charlton Ogburn to William Green, May 1, 1936.

59. Statement of Harrison is in *Minutes of the Executive Council of the American Federation of Labor,* July 14, 1936.

60. *Ibid.*, July 15, 1936.

61. Lewis to Green, July 21, 1936.

62. *Ibid.*

63. Ogburn to Green, July 22, 1936.

64. Harrison to Green, July 31, 1936.

65. *Proceedings of the Executive Council in the Matter of Charges Filed By the Metal Trades Department Against the Committee for Industrial Organization and National and International Unions Holding Membership Thereon,* pp. 153-319.

66. *Minutes of the Executive Council of the American Federation of Labor,* August 5, 1936.

67. Green to Lewis, August 6, 1936. Similar letters were sent to the heads of all CIO unions.

68. *Minutes of the Executive Council of the American Federation of Labor,* April 20, 1937.

69. *Ibid.*, April 22, 1937.

70. Charlton Ogburn to William Green, April 21, 1937. William Green to William L. Hutcheson, April 23, 1937, in files of AFL-CIO.

71. *Report of Proceedings of the Fifty-seventh Annual Convention* (AFL), 1937, pp. 416-417.

72. *Minutes of the Meeting of the Executive Council of the American Federation of Labor,* May 25, 1937.

73. Taft, *op. cit.*, pp. 195-197.

74. *New York Times,* January 12, 1938.

CHAPTER 38. ORGANIZATION IN THE AUTOMOBILE INDUSTRY

1. Ralph C. Epstein, *The Automobile Industry* (New York: A. W. Shaw, 1928), pp. 23-30.

2. William H. McPherson, *Labor Relations in the Automobile Industry* (Washington: Brookings Institution, 1940), p. 17.

3. *Minutes of the Executive Council of the Metal Trades Department of the American Federation of Labor,* January 25, 1925, in office of Metal Trades' Department.

4. *Conference of Building and Metal Trades Unions on Automobile Work-*

ers Campaign, held in the Executive Council Room of the American Federation of Labor Building, Washington, D.C., June 24, 1927.

5. *Minutes of Executive Council of the American Federation of Labor,* May 10, 1927.

6. *Ibid.*

7. Paul Smith to William Green, February 27, 1928.

8. T. J. Conboy to William Green, January 29, 1927, in AFL-CIO archives.

9. *American Federation of Labor Weekly News Service,* December 9, 1933.

10. Circular Letter to All Automobile Workers Local Unions, from William Green, December 23, 1933.

11. Circular Letter to All Automobile Workers Federal Labor Unions, from William Green, February 13, 1934.

12. To All Automobile Workers Federal Labor Unions, from William Green, February 20, 1934.

13. William Green to Automobile Workers Local Unions, March 21, 1934.

14. *New York Times,* March 19, 1934.

15. The telegram to President Roosevelt appeared in *ibid.,* March 21, 1934.

16. *Ibid.,* March 24, 1934.

17. *Ibid.,* March 26, 1934.

18. *Ibid.,* March 27, 1934.

19. William Green to executive council, March 27, 1934.

20. Franklin D. Roosevelt to William Green, November 2, 1934.

21. *Ibid.*

22. Green to President Franklin D. Roosevelt, November 10, 1934.

23. Franklin D. Roosevelt to S. Clay Williams, November 21, 1934.

24. *New York Times,* May 24–June 3, 1934.

25. William Green to President Franklin D. Roosevelt, February 2, 1935, in Franklin Delano Roosevelt Library, Hyde Park, N.Y.

26. *Final Report of the Automobile Labor Board* (unpublished), October 22, 1953, in National Archives.

27. *Op. cit.,* pp. 16-18; *Proceedings of the First Constitutional Convention of the International Union United Automobile Workers of America Convened by Authority of American Federation of Labor,* 1935, p. 23.

28. *Minutes of the Executive Council of the American Federation of Labor,* February 4, 1935. On this and other issues see Walter Galenson, *The C.I.O. Challenge to the A.F.L.* (Cambridge, Mass.: Harvard University Press, 1960), pp. 123-192.

29. The last two quotations are from *ibid.*

30. *Ibid.*

31. *Ibid.*

32. *Ibid.*

33. *Ibid.,* February 12, 1935.

34. *Ibid.*

35. *Ibid.*

36. The last three quotations are from *ibid.*

37. *Ibid.*

38. See *First Constitutional Convention of the United Automobile Workers of America,* p. 66.

39. *Minutes of the Executive Council of the American Federation of Labor,* October 6, 1935.

40. *Summary of Auto Situation,* issued by CIO, January 9, 1936, in the files of United Hatters, Cap and Millinery Workers Union.

41. *Ibid.*

42. Green to Homer Martin, July 13, 1936.

43. Memorandum in the files of the AFL-CIO.

44. *New York Times,* December 18-28, 1936.

45. *Ibid.,* December 23-25, 1936.

46. *Ibid.,* January 1, 1936.

47. *Ibid.,* January 4, 1937.

48. Statement of Sloan in *ibid.,* January 5, 1937

49. Alfred P. Sloan, Jr., *General Motors and Its Labor Policy,* January 5, 1937. A statement issued to all employees of General Motors.

50. *New York Times,* January 7, 1937.

51. *Ibid.,* January 12-13, 1937.

52. Letter from Boysen to Knudsen, January 15, 1937, appeared in *ibid.,* January 17, 1937.

53. *Ibid.,* January 22, 1937.

54. *Ibid.,* January 22, 1937, contains Lewis' statement.

55. *Ibid.,* January 23, 1937.

56. *Ibid.,* January 27, 1937.

57. Alfred P. Sloan, Jr., *A Message to Our Employees on Progress of the Strike Situation,* January 27, 1937.

58. Statement of governor in *New York Times,* January 29, 1937.

59. *General Motors and the Strike Conference,* issued on behalf of General Motors Corporation, Messrs. William S. Knudsen, Donaldson Brown, and John Thomas Smith, in Detroit on February 8, 1937.

60. Alfred P. Sloan, Jr., *A Message to General Motors Employees,* March 1, 1937.

61. *New York Times,* March 13, 1937.

62. See J. Woodford Howard, Jr., "Frank Murphy and the Sit-Down Strikes of 1937," *Labor History,* Spring 1960.

63. *Fansteel Metallurgical Corp.* v. *N.L.R.B.,* 306 U.S. 242 (1939).

64. *New York Times,* March 4, 1937.

65. *Ibid.,* March 25 and April 7, 1937.

66. *Ibid.,* April 6, 7, 1937.

67. Philip Taft, *The Structure and Government of Labor Unions* (Cambridge, Mass.: Harvard University Press, 1956), pp. 213-226.

68. *Second Annual Convention of the United Automobile Workers of America,* 1937, p. 131.

69. *Ibid.,* p. 33.

70. *Ibid.,* p. 165.

71. *Ibid.,* p. 135.

72. *Ibid.,* p. 206.

73. B. K. Gebert, "The Convention of the 400,000," *The Communist,* November 1937, p. 902.

74. *New York Post,* January 20, 1939; *Daily Worker,* January 15, 1939; McPherson, *op. cit.,* p. 20.

75. *Daily Worker,* January 23, 1939; *New York Times,* January 16, 1939.

76. *New York Times,* January 25, 1939.

77. *Ibid.*

78. *Ibid.*, March 6, 1939.

79. "Communist Party Defines Position as Auto Union Convention Opens," *Daily Worker*, March 27, 1939.

80. *New York Times*, April 2, 1939.

81. *Daily Worker*, June 15, 1939.

82. R. J. Thomas, *Automobile Unionism: A Report Submitted to the 1941 Convention of the UAW-CIO, convened in Buffalo, New York, August 4, 1941*, pp. 10-28.

83. *Proceedings of the Tenth Convention of the United Automobile, Aircraft and Agricultural Implement Workers*, 1946, p. 231.

84. For a description of the factional rivalries within the union, the anti-Reuther position is given by Benjamin Stolberg, *The Story of the C.I.O.* (New York: Viking Press, 1938), pp. 156-186. Stolberg is both colorful and prejudiced, but he knew the general lineup in the union. Irving Howe and B. J. Widick, *The UAW and Walter Reuther* (New York: Random House, 1949), pp. 107-171, also deals with the factional struggle. It is written from the Socialist and anti-Communist point of view, and exhibits little sympathy for the purely trade union activities of the union. It is especially incapable of understanding a man like Thomas or his significant contribution to the prosperity of the Auto Workers' Union.

CHAPTER 39. ORGANIZING THE STEEL INDUSTRY

1. Statement in the files of the AFL-CIO.

2. Carroll R. Daugherty, Melvin G. deChazeau, and Samuel S. Stratton, *The Economics of the Iron and Steel Industry* (New York: McGraw Hill Book Co., 1937), II, 944-953.

3. *Ibid.*, p. 1005.

4. *Ibid.*, p. 1008.

5. *Ibid.*

6. Earl J. Forbeck to Green, December 27, 1933; Green to Forbeck, January 12, 1934; Green to Michael Tighe, January 12, 1934; Tighe to Green, January 15, 1934.

7. Daugherty, *op. cit.*, pp. 935, 1056-1057.

8. Statement of President Roosevelt, June 19, 1934, in Franklin Delano Roosevelt Library, Hyde Park, N.Y.

9. Daugherty, *op. cit.*, p. 1040.

10. The proposals are in the *Annual Reports of International Officers to Sixtieth Annual Convention of the Amalgamated Association of Iron, Steel and Tin Workers*, pp. 70-82, in *ibid.*, p. 1042.

11. Statement of William Green in *Minutes of Executive Council of the American Federation of Labor*, February 4, 1935.

12. Joseph J. Clair to Green, April 13, 1935.

13. Tighe to Green, April 17, 1935.

14. To the officers and members of Blue Eagle Lodge No. 151, Ohio, from Michael F. Tighe, president, and Louis Leonard, secretary-treasurer, August 5, 1935.

15. James A. Wilson to Clarence Irwin, September 30, 1935; Clarence Irwin to suspended lodges, October 7, 1935.

16. Green's statement in *Minutes of Executive Council of the American Federation of Labor,* February 11, 1935.

17. Tighe to Green, January 15, 1935.

18. Lewis' statement in *Minutes of Executive Council of the American Federation of Labor,* February 11, 1935.

19. John A. Fitch to William Green, January 15, 1936.

20. Green's remarks are in *Minutes of Executive Council of the American Federation of Labor,* February 12, 1935.

21. *Ibid.*

22. *Suggested Plan to Organize the Steel Industry submitted to Executive Council of the American Federation of Labor by the International Executive Board Amalgamated Association of Iron, Steel and Tin Workers of North America,* October 20, 1935.

23. William D. Mahon to Green, November 25, 1935.

24. John L. Lewis, chairman and Charles P. Howard, secretary, Committee for Industrial Organization, to William Green, February 22, 1936.

25. *Ibid.*

26. *Ibid.*

27. Green to Lewis, February 28, 1936.

28. Harry Bates to Green, February 25, 1936.

29. Daniel J. Tobin to Green, February 26, 1936.

30. *Minutes of Executive Council of the American Federation of Labor,* March 9, 1936.

31. William Green to the officers and delegates in attendance at the convention of the Amalgamated Association of Iron, Steel and Tin Workers, May 8, 1936.

32. Lewis to the officers and delegates in attendance at the convention of the Amalgamated Association of Iron, Steel and Tin Workers, May 8, 1936.

33. Tighe to Green, May 15, 1936.

34. John L. Lewis to Louis Leonard, undated, in files of AFL-CIO.

35. *Ibid.*

36. Lewis to International Executive Board; Amalgamated Association of Iron, Steel and Tin Workers, May 21, 1936.

37. Statement from the International Executive Board in *Amalgamated Journal,* June 4, 1936.

38. "Memorandum of Agreement," *First Wage and Policy Convention of the Steel Workers' Organizing Committee,* 1937.

39. The information on staff and district and subdistrict officers is from a list of staff members and the organizations with which they were affiliated issued by the Steel Workers' Organizing Committee, July 19, 1936. See also Robert R. Brooks, *As Steel Goes* (New Haven: Yale University Press, 1940), pp. 153-158.

40. *Iron Age,* January 7, 1937, pp. 70, 77.

41. *New York Times,* June 29, 1936, contained the advertisement which appeared in a large number of other daily papers.

42. Brooks, *op. cit.,* p. 150.

43. Walter Galenson, *The CIO Challenge to the AFL* (Cambridge, Mass.: Harvard University Press, 1960), p. 110; also Brooks, *op. cit.,* pp. 159-160.

44. From a memorandum, *Summary of Situation in Steel,* January 23, 1936, in files of AFL-CIO.

45. Resolution sent to Green by E. Anderson Lodge No. 42, December 6, 1935, in files of AFL-CIO.

46. Steel Workers' Organizing Committee, *Reports of Officers To the Wage and Policy Convention in Pittsburgh,* 1937, p. 9.

47. *New York Times,* December 20, 21, 1936; see also Brooks, *op. cit.,* pp. 75-106.

48. Brooks, *op. cit.,* pp. 107-108; *New York Times,* March 3, 1937.

49. Brooks, *op. cit.,* p. 123.

50. The work of this committee has not always received sufficient credit for its exposure of the malodorous practices of some sections of American industry. It played a major role in shaping public opinion of the time toward a more favorable appraisal of the activity of organized labor.

51. "Violations of Free Speech and Rights of Labor," *Hearings Before a Subcommittee of the Committee on Education and Labor, U.S. Senate,* August 11, 1938, Part 34, p. 13797.

52. *New York Times,* May 27, 1937.

53. "Violations of Free Speech and Rights of Labor," *Report of the Committee on Education and Labor Pursuant to S. Res. 266,* July 22, 1937, p. 6.

54. *Report of the Committee on Education and Labor Pursuant to S. Res. 266,* July 27, 1937, pp. 9-10.

55. *Ibid.,* p. 11.

56. Meyer Levin was present at the riot and testified before the La Follette Committee. In his novel, *Citizens,* he attributes the clash to the incitement of a Trotskyist who was an active union leader in the strike. It is obviously an apologia, since it was known that the Communists prepared for an encounter between the police and marchers. Of course, no one anticipated the tragic results, but a person present has informed the writer that the role of the Communists in provoking the riot was not contestable. At any rate, the conduct of the police was inexcusable and in violation of every principle of decency and humanity.

57. "Violations of Free Speech and Rights of Labor," *Hearings Before a Subcommittee on Education and Labor, 75th Cong., 3d sess., Pursuant to S. Res. 22, Part 39,* August 2, 3, and 4, 1938, pp. 12057-12058.

58. *Ibid.,* Part 19, pp. 8266-8278.

59. *Ibid.,* pp. 8344-8345.

60. Mayor Shields testified the number were between 500 and 700 in *ibid.,* Part 19, March 10-12, 18 and 19, 1938, p. 8398.

61. *Ibid.,* p. 8641.

62. "Violations of Free Speech and Rights of Labor," *Hearings Before a Subcommittee of the Committee on Education and Labor, U.S. Senate 75th Cong., 3d sess., Pursuant to S. Res. 266* (74th Cong.), Part 34, pp. 13934-13935. Davey's letter to Girdler and the latter's answer.

63. *New York Times,* June 16-17, 1937.

64. Davey's letter is in *ibid.,* June 17, 1937.

65. *Hearings,* Part 34, p. 13939.

66. The quote is from the report of the board to Secretary of Labor Frances Perkins, June 30, 1937, in *ibid.,* p. 13938-13939.

67. *Ibid.,* p. 13941.

68. Both Girdler, Vice-President C. M. White, and the director of indus-

trial relations of Republic Steel Corporation took this position. *Ibid.*, pp. 13874-13879.

69. The quote is from *New York Times,* June 30, 1937. See also *ibid.*, June 21-30, 1937, for events leading up to the statement.

70. *The United Mine Workers Journal,* September 15, 1937, p. 4.

71. See *New York Times,* July 1, 1937; Brooks, *op. cit.,* pp. 137-152; Galenson, *op. cit.,* 103-114.

72. *Hearings Before the U.S. Senate Committee on Post Offices and Post Roads,* 75th Cong. 1st sess., on S. Res 1.40, 1937, p. 243.

73. Steel Workers' Organizing Committee, *Reports of Officers To the Wage and Policy Committee,* 1937, p. 12.

74. 311 U.S. 514 (1941).

75. *Proceedings of the First Constitutional Convention of the United Steelworkers of America,* 1942, I, 42. See Galenson, *op. cit.,* for developments in collective bargaining.

CHAPTER 40. THE CIO UNDER LEWIS

1. Saul Alinsky, *John L. Lewis* (New York: G. P. Putnam's Sons, 1949), pp. 263-264.

2. *Report of Proceedings of the Twenty-third Convention of the International Ladies' Garment Workers' Union,* 1937, p. 446.

3. *Report of Proceedings of the Twenty-fourth Convention,* 1940, p. 453.

4. On the importance of the AFL in small communities, see Green to Jennie Matyas, December 22, 1938. This is one of several letters in which Green urged support of ILGW efforts to organize while it was unaffiliated with the AFL. Letters are in the files of AFL-CIO.

5. Harold S. Roberts, *The Rubber Workers* (New York: Harper and Brothers, 1944), pp. 18-19.

6. See Roberts, *op. cit.,* pp. 38-78; Selig Perlman and Philip Taft, *History of Labor in the United States, 1896–1932* (New York: Macmillan Co., 1935), IV, pp. 277-278.

7. Roberts, *op. cit.,* pp. 136-172.

8. Joseph P. Goldberg, *The Maritime Story* (Cambridge, Mass.: Harvard University Press), 1958, pp. 150-166.

9. Philip Taft, "The Unlicensed Seafaring Unions," *Industrial and Labor Relations Review,* January 1950, pp. 199-200.

10. *Minutes of the Executive Council of the American Federation of Labor,* February 12, 1935.

11. *Ibid.*

12. For the early history of unionism and collective bargaining, see Milton Derber, "Electrical Products," *How Collective Bargaining Works* (New York: Twentieth Century Fund, 1942), pp. 744-805.

13. *Building a Union of Textile Workers Report of Two Years Progress to the Convention of the United Textile Workers of America and the Textile Workers' Organizing Committee Affiliated with the Congress of Industrial Organizations,* 1929, pp. 10-11.

14. *Ibid.*, pp. 64-65.

15. Robert K. Burns, "Daily Newspapers," *How Collective Bargaining Works* (New York: Twentieth Century Fund, 1942), pp. 108-117.

16. Kenneth D. Roose, *The Economics of Recession and Revival* (New Haven, Conn.: Yale University Press, 1954), pp. 41-42.

17. *United Mine Workers Journal,* February 15, 1938.

18. *Proceedings of the First Constitutional Convention of the Congress of Industrial Organizations,* 1938, pp. 38-40.

19. *Ibid.,* p. 9.

20. Telegram from Philip Murray to Richard L. Lazette, May 22, 1950, in Murray Papers of Catholic University, Washington, D.C.

21. *Daily Proceedings of the Second Constitutional Convention of the Congress of Industrial Organizations,* 1939, p. 80.

22. *Ibid.,* p. 107.

23. *United Mine Workers Journal,* June 15, 1940.

24. *Ibid.,* September 1 and October 15, 1940.

25. Alinsky, *op. cit.,* pp. 181-191. For another version, see James A. Wechsler, *Labor Baron* (New York: William Morrow and Co., 1944), pp. 93-121.

26. John L. Lewis to President Franklin D. Roosevelt, January 18, 1939.

27. Franklin D. Roosevelt to Lewis, January 30, 1939.

28. Quotation is from Roosevelt to Lewis, March 20, 1939, in reply to Lewis to Roosevelt, February 21, 1939.

29. Lewis to Hillman, July 15, 1940.

30. Alinsky, *op. cit.,* p. 188.

31. Lewis' speech appears in full in the *United Mine Workers Journal,* November 1940, p. 6.

32. *Ibid.*

33. See Alinsky, *op. cit.,* pp. 207-208.

34. *Daily Proceedings of Third Constitutional Convention of the Congress of Industrial Organizations,* 1940, pp. 121-125.

35. "Report of Executive Council," *Report of the Proceedings of the Sixtieth Annual Convention of the American Federation of Labor,* 1940, p. 203.

36. *Daily Proceedings of the Third Constitutional Convention . . .* pp. 129-130.

37. *Ibid.,* pp. 158-165.

38. Alinsky, *op. cit.,* p. 213; Wechsler, *op. cit.,* p. 127.

39. *Proceedings of the Third Constitution of CIO,* p. 192.

40. The issue is covered in a series of reports from A. H. Raskin in the *New York Times,* January 18 to 25, 1942.

41. See Philip Taft, *The A.F. of L. from the Death of Gompers to the Merger* (New York: Harper and Brothers, 1959), pp. 222-223.

42. *United Mine Workers Journal,* June 1, 1942, p. 8.

43. The quotations in this paragraph are from *ibid.,* June 15, 1942, p. 17. See also *The CIO News* magazine II, June 8, 1942.

44. *Ibid.,* November 1, 1942, p. 5.

CHAPTER 41. DEFENSE PLANNING AND LABOR

1. Richard J. Purcell, *Labor Policies of the National Defense Advisory Commission and The Office of Production Management* (Washington: Civilian Production Administration, 1946), p. 1. *Defense,* August 30, 1940, p. 3.

2. Saul Alinsky, *John L. Lewis* (New York: G. P. Putnam's Sons, 1949),

pp. 181-182; *Minutes of Executive Council of the American Federation of Labor,* October 2, 1940.

3. William Green to the President of the United States, May 17, 1940, in files of AFL-CIO.

4. Letter from Murray to Hillman, August 14, 1940, quoted in Purcell, *op. cit.,* p. 35.

5. *Report on the Work of the National Defense Mediation Board,* March 19, 1941-January 12, 1942 (Washington: Government Printing Office, 1942), U.S. Bureau of Labor Statistics Bulletin No. 714, p. 1.

6. *New York Times,* March 1, 8, 27, 28, and April 7, 1941.

7. *Ibid.,* April 7-10, 1941. *Amendments to the National Labor Relation Act, Hearings Before Committee on Education and Labor,* 80th Cong., 1st sess., IV, 2130-2133.

8. Press Release from the White House, issued on March 19, 1941.

9. *New York Times,* June 10, 1941.

10. *Ibid.,* June 6-11, 1941; U.S. Bureau of Labor Statistics Bulletin No. 714, pp. 156-160.

11. Bulletin No. 714, p. 186.

12. The letters of Lewis to Roosevelt, October 26, 1941, are in the *United Mine Workers Journal,* November 1, 1941, p. 414.

13. Transcript of speech in Bulletin No. 714, p. 268.

14. *Memorandum of Agreement Between the Representatives of Government Agencies Engaged in Defense Construction and the Building and Construction Trades Department of the American Federation of Labor,* undated, in the files of the AFL-CIO.

15. Testimony of Sidney Hillman, in *Hearings Before a Special Committee Investigating the National Defense Program, U.S. Senate, 77th Cong., 1st sess., Pursuant to S. Res. 71,* Part 8, pp. 2511-2513.

16. *Report of Proceedings of the Thirty-fifth Annual Convention of the Building Trades Department, American Federation of Labor,* 1941, p. 136.

17. *Defense,* March 18, 1940, p. 5.

18. Purcell, *op. cit.,* pp. 223-225.

19. Testimony of Assistant Secretary of the Navy Ralph A. Bard in *Hearings Before a Special Committee Investigating the National Defense Program, U.S. Senate, 77th Cong., 1st sess., Pursuant to S. Res. 71,* Part 4, Testimony of Harvey Brown, *ibid.,* p. 1174.

CHAPTER 42. LABOR DURING THE WAR

1. *Daily Proceedings of the Fifth Constitutional Convention of the Congress of Industrial Organizations,* 1942, pp. 41-42, *Minutes of the Executive Council of the American Federation of Labor,* December 15, 1941, January 16, 1942.

2. Harold M. Douty, *Problems of Dispute Settlement and Wage Stabilization During World War II,* U.S. Bureau of Labor Bulletin No. 1009, pp. 108-109.

3. *Ibid.,* p. 114.

4. Statement of Philip Murray read by Ralph Hetzel in *Hearings Before the Committee on Banking and Currency, U.S. Senate, 77th Cong., 1st sess., on H.R. 5990,* 1941, p. 30.

5. *Minutes of the Meeting of the Executive Council of the American Federation of Labor,* January 15, 1942.

6. From the decision in *Termination Report, National War Labor Board* (Washington: Government Printing Office, n.d.), II, 286.

7. William Green to Franklin D. Roosevelt, April 16, 1942.

8. Franklin D. Roosevelt to William Green, April 23, 1942, in files of AFL-CIO.

9. The seven points and other parts of the message are in *Termination Report, National War Labor Board,* I, 178-179.

10. Wayne Coy reported his conversation with Murray in a memorandum to President Roosevelt, April 28, 1942, in Official 2546, Box 3, Franklin Delano Roosevelt Library, Hyde Park, N. Y.

11. The Little Steel decision is in *Termination Report of National War Labor Board,* II, 288-299.

12. Quotation is from decision in *ibid.,* p. 297.

13. *Ibid.,* p. 299.

14. From Anna Rosenberg to Mr. McIntyre, July 14, 1942, in files of the Franklin Delano Roosevelt Library, Hyde Park, N. Y.

15. *The CIO News,* August 24, 1942.

16. William Green to Franklin D. Roosevelt, July 20, 1942, in files of AFL-CIO.

17. The letter was signed by all members of the board, July 29, 1942, in files of AFL-CIO.

18. William H. Davis to the President, July 29, 1942.

19. *The CIO News,* August 31 and September 7, 1942.

20. Act of October 2, 1942, in *Termination Report of National War Labor Board,* II, 63.

21. Executive Order No. 9250, in *ibid.,* p. 73.

22. *Minutes of the Executive Council of the American Federation of Labor,* January 17, 1943.

23. *Hearings Before a Special Committee Investigating the National Defense,* U.S. Senate, 78th Cong., 1st sess., Pursuant to S. Res. 6, Part 18, pp. 7429-7430.

24. For a discussion of these changes, see Allan B. Richards, *War Labor Boards in the Field* (Chapel, N.C.: University of North Carolina Press, 1953).

25. *Termination Report of National War Labor Board,* I., 189-190.

26. *Minutes of the Meeting of the Executive Council of the American Federation of Labor,* May 21, 1943.

27. *United Mine Workers Journal,* February 15, 1943, p. 3.

28. *Ibid.,* March 15, 1943, pp. 9, 17-20.

29. *Ibid.,* April 15, 1943, pp. 11, 15.

30. Quoted in Arthur Suffern, "The National War Labor Board and Coal," *Termination Report of National War Labor Board,* I, 1099.

31. *Washington Daily Labor Report,* October 27, 1943, pp. G3-G4.

32. Quoted in *Termination Report of National War Labor Board,* I., 1109.

33. The first quote is from Davis' letter to Ickes, and the second is from Harold L. Ickes to William H. Davis, July 27, 1943, in Franklin Delano Roosevelt Library, Official File 407B, Hyde Park, N. Y.

34. Ickes to the President, July 28, 1943, in *Termination Report of National War Labor Board,* II, 84-85.

35. Law is in *Termination Report of National War Labor Board*, II, 80-84; see also David Suskind, "Labor Legislation," *Yearbook of American Labor*, pp. 69-71.

36. *The CIO News*, July 19, 1943; *American Federation of Labor Weekly News Service*, June 15, 1943.

37. *American Federation of Labor Weekly News Service*, November 23, 1943.

38. Roosevelt to Davis, October 22, 1943; copy in files of AFL-CIO.

39. *Report of Proceedings of the Forty-third Annual Convention of the American Federation of Labor*, 1943, p. 505, for quote. See also *The CIO News*, November 8, 1943.

40. Green to Roosevelt, December 8, 1943; Roosevelt to Green, December 28, 1943.

41. George Meany and R. J. Thomas, *The Cost of Living Index*, a pamphlet of more than 100 pages, was presented to substantiate the charge.

42. "Report of President's Cost of Living Committee," *Daily Labor Report*, November 17, 1944.

43. *Statement of George Meany, Secretary-Treasurer of the American Federation of Labor, to The Special Panel of the National War Labor Board, on the Little Steel Formula*, April 14, 1944, in the files of the AFL-CIO.

44. *Ibid*.

45. *Final Proceedings of the Seventh Constitutional Convention of the Congress of Industrial Organizations*, 1944, pp. 317-318; *Report of Proceedings of the Sixty-fourth Annual Convention of the American Federation of Labor*, 1944, pp. 510-512.

46. The views of the board on fringe benefits are covered in *Termination Report of National War Labor Board*, I, Section V.

47. *Ibid.*, p. 415.

48. *The CIO News*, May 1, 15, 1944.

49. *Minutes of the Meeting of the Executive Council of the American Federation of Labor*, May 3, 1944. See H. Rept. 104, Pursuant to H. Res. 521, 78th Cong., 2d sess.

50. *Monthly Labor* Review, June 1942, pp. 1325-1326.

51. *Ibid.*, March 1943, p. 470.

52. *The CIO News*, December 21, 1942.

53. *American Federation of Labor Weekly News Service*, October 27, 1942.

54. *Ibid.*, November 9, 1943.

55. William Green to members of the U.S. Senate and House of Representatives, January 13, 1944.

56. Harry S. Truman to William Green, January 21, 1944, in AFL-CIO files.

CHAPTER 43. STORM AND STRIFE IN RECONVERSION

1. J. Carlyle Sitterson, *Development of the Reconversion Policies of War Production Board April 1943 to January 1945*, issued by Bureau of Demobilization, Civilian Production Administration, *Historical Reports on War Administration, War Production Board;* Special Study No. 15, p. 13.

2. Letter sent to each member of the U.S. Senate, May 1, 1944, signed by William Green, Philip Murray, and Julius Luhrsen, in files of AFL-CIO.

3. See testimony of Matthew Woll, in *Hearings Before the Special Com-*

mittee on Post-War Economic Planning, U.S. Senate, 78th Cong., 2d sess., Part 3, pp. 737-749.

4. *Daily Labor Report,* January 10, 1944.

5. *American Federation of Labor Weekly News Service,* February 13, 1945: *Daily Labor Report,* March 9, 1945.

6. *Daily Labor Report,* September 20, 1944, p. A-5.

7. *Minutes of the Meeting of the Executive Council of the American Federation of Labor,* August 6, 1945.

8. *Ibid.,* August 7, 1945.

9. *The Termination Report of the National War Labor Board* (Washington: Government Printing Office, n.d.), pp. 443-458.

10. *The National Wage Stabilization Board* (Washington: Government Printing Office, n.d.), pp. 6-7.

11. Letter signed by Eric Johnston, William Green, and Philip Murray, to President Roosevelt, March 28, 1945, in AFL-CIO files.

12. *Minutes of the Executive Council of the American Federation of Labor,* May 4, 1945.

13. *Ibid.,* August 16, 1945.

14. *President's National Labor-Management Conference General Plenary Sessions,* II, 5-9. These were mimeographed records of the conference and did not give any information on place, name of publisher, or date issued.

15. *Ibid.,* p. 30.

16. *Ibid.,* pp. 66-74.

17. *Ibid.,* pp. 114-138.

18. *Ibid.,* p. 158.

19. *Daily Labor Report,* November 30, 1945, p. AA-5.

20. *Economic Problems of the Reconversion Period, Fourth Report of the House Special Committee on Post-War Economic Policy and Planning, Pursuant to H. Res. 408,* 1944, pp. 16-17.

21. *Monthly Labor Review,* May 1946, p. 723.

22. *Ibid.,* February 1946, pp. 245-246.

23. *Ibid.,* p. 883.

24. *New York Times,* September 16, 1945.

25. *United Automobile Worker,* October 1, 1945.

26. *Daily Labor Report,* October 3, 1945.

27. *New York Times,* November 8, 1945.

28. *Daily Labor Report,* November 19, 1945, p. A-12.

29. *New York Times,* November 24, 1945, for Anderson's statement.

30. *Daily Labor Report,* December 12, 1945.

31. *Ibid.,* December 10, 1945.

32. *New York Times,* December 13, 1945.

33. *Ibid.,* December 29, 1945.

34. *Daily Labor Report,* January 11, 1946, p. AA-3.

35. *New York Times,* January 27, 1946.

36. *Ibid.,* February 13, 23, 1946.

37. *Ibid.,* March 1, 1946, for quote.

38. *Ibid.,* March 1-5, 1946.

39. *The CIO News,* March 18, 1946.

40. *New York Times,* March 11, 1946.

41. Reuther's full report is in *Daily Labor Report,* September 10, 1947, pp. E-1-13.

42. Statement in *Daily Labor Report,* September 9, 1945. See also "United States Steel Replies to the Union Demand for a $2 Wage Increase"; this was a letter from John A. Stephens, Vice-President Industrial Relations, to Philip Murray, October 25, 1946.

43. *Ibid.,* November 30, 1945.

44. *Ibid.,* February 18, 1946; *Monthly Labor Review,* March 1946, pp. 426-427.

45. *The Railroad Trainmen,* January 1946, pp. 3-5.

46. *Ibid.,* p. 43.

47. *Ibid.,* May 1946, p. 155.

48. Statement of A. F. Whitney and Alvanley Johnston in *ibid.,* p. 155.

49. *Locomotive Engineers Journal,* June 1946, p. 379.

50. *Ibid.,* June 1946, pp. 195-197.

51. In a speech in Providence, Rhode Island, November 19, 1947.

52. *United Mine Workers Journal,* March 15, 1946, p. 5.

53. *Ibid.,* June 1, 1946, p. 3.

54. *Ibid.,* August 1, 1946, pp. 6-7.

55. John L. Lewis to Honorable J. A. Krug, October 21, 1946, in *ibid.,* November 1, 1946, pp. 3-4.

56. The quotes are from a letter from Krug to Lewis, in *Daily Labor Report,* November 15, 1946, p. F1.

57. *United States* v. *United Mine Workers of America,* 330 U.S. 266, 1948.

58. *United States* v. *United Mine Workers of America,* 330 U.S. 261, 1948.

59. *New York Times,* February 11, 1946.

60. *Daily Labor Report,* January 16, 18, and February 7, 27, 1946.

61. *Monthly Labor Review,* April 1946, p. 548.

62. *Ibid.,* July 1946, p. 87.

63. *East Bay Labor Journal,* October 26, and November 1, 1946.

64. *Ibid.,* December 6, 1946.

65. *Contra-Costa Labor Journal,* December 6, 1946.

66. *Ibid.,* August 29, 1947.

67. Harold Wool, "Recent Trends in the Labor Force," *Monthly Labor Review,* December 1947, p. 642.

68. *Ibid.,* p. 642. See Joel Seidman, *American Labor from Defense to Reconstruction* (Chicago: University of Chicago Press, 1953).

CHAPTER 44. THE TAFT-HARTLEY ACT

1. National Labor Relations Board, *Legislature History of the Labor-Management Relations Act, 1947* (Washington: Government Printing Office, 1948), I, 851-852, contains the section dealing with labor legislation suggested by President Truman in his message.

2. *Daily Labor Report,* January 9, 1947.

3. *New York Times,* January 16, 1947.

4. *Amendments to the National Labor Relations Act, Hearings Before the Committee on Education and Labor, U.S. House of Representatives, 8th Cong., 1st sess.,* II, 636-638. See examination of Van A. Bittner, representing the CIO, in *ibid.*

5. *Labor Relations Program, Hearings Before the Committee on Labor and Public Welfare, U.S. Senate, 8th Cong., 1st sess., on S. 55 and S.J. Res. 22,* II, p. 993.

6. *Legislative History of the Labor-Management Relations Act*, p. 295.

7. *Ibid.*

8. "Minority Report," in *ibid.*, p. 355.

9. *Ibid.*, p. 386.

10. "Federal Labor Relations Act of 1947," in *ibid.*, p. 407.

11. *Ibid.*, pp. 407-436.

12. *Daily Labor Report*, April 23, 1947, p. A-6.

13. *Ibid.*

14. *Legislative History of the Labor-Management Relations Act*, II, 1300.

15. *Ibid.*, p. 1522.

16. *New York Times*, May 15, 1947.

17. *Ibid.*, May 14, 1947.

18. *Ibid.*, May 16, 1947.

19. *Ibid.*, May 30, 1947.

20. The veto message is in *Legislative History of the Labor-Management Relations Act*, II, 915-921.

21. *Ibid.*, p. 1653.

22. Philip Murray to William Green, July 2, 1947.

23. *American Federation of Labor Weekly News Service*, July 11, 1947.

24. *Daily Proceedings of the Ninth Constitutional Convention of the Congress of Industrial Organizations*, October 14, 1947, p. 41.

25. *Minutes of the Meeting of the Executive Council of the American Federation of Labor*, October 9, 1947.

26. Lewis to Green, December 12, 1947.

27. *Daily Labor Report*, December 15, 1947.

28. *Proceedings of the Eighty-ninth Session of the International Typographical Union*, 1947, p. 80.

29. *Ibid.*

30. *Ibid.*

31. G. N. Dale to Woodruff Randolph, September 9, 1947; Randolph to Dale, September 10, 1947, in *The Typographical Journal*, October 1947, pp. 292-293.

32. *Ibid.*, pp. 296-297.

33. *Taft-Hartley and the International Typographical Union* (Indianapolis, Ind.: International Typographical Union, 1949), p. 2.

34. *The Typographical Journal*, December 1947, p. 432.

35. *National Labor Relations Act of 1949, Hearings Before a Special Committee of the Committee on Education and Labor, U.S. House of Representatives, 81st Cong., 1st sess., on H.R. 2032.*

36. Injunction is printed in *The Typographical Journal*, April 1948, pp. 248-249.

37. Woodruff Randolph, "Victory in Chicago Strike Greatest in History of International Union," in *ibid.*, October 1949, p. 238.

38. *Labor-Management Relations, Hearings Before the Joint Committee on Labor-Management Relations Congress of the U.S. 80th Cong., 2d sess., on the Operation of the Labor-Management Relations Act of 1947*, p. 3.

39. *Ibid.*, p. 50.

40. Senate Report 99, 81st Cong., 1st sess., Part 2, p. 2.

41. *Appendix to Congressional Record*, 81st Cong., 1st sess., XCV, Part 3, 2382-2383, for AFL and CIO statements.

42. *Congressional Record*, XCV, Part 4, 5543.

43. *Ibid.*, Part 6, pp. 726-7230.

44. Green to Scott W. Lucas, June 29, 1949, in files of AFL-CIO. The views of the CIO were the same as the AFL. See *Proceedings of the Eleventh Constitutional Convention Congress of Industrial Organizations,* 1949, pp. 101-104.

45. *Monthly Labor Review,* February 1946, pp. 241-243.

46. *Daily Labor Report,* July 22, 1948, p. A-17.

47. S. Rept. 99, *op. cit.,* p. 19.

48. *Daily Labor Report,* May 9, 1949.

49. Memorandum for the press, issued by the CIO, May 3, 1946.

50. *Daily Labor Report,* July 12, and August 6, 14, 16, 1946; January 23, and February 6, 1947. *The CIO News,* May 13; June 3; September 2, 1946.

51. *Daily Proceedings of the Ninth Constitutional Convention* (CIO), October 14, 1947, p. 7.

52. *Proceedings of the Eleventh Constitutional Convention* (CIO), 1949, pp. 92-94.

53. Report to Executive Council, American Federation of Labor, on the Southern Campaign, undated, in files of AFL-CIO.

54. *Ibid.* The policy board was made up of southern union officials.

55. *Report of the Proceedings of the Sixty-sixth Annual Convention of the American Federation of Labor,* 1947, pp. 173-175.

56. *Report to Executive Council, American Federation of Labor,* on the Southern Campaign, July 31, 1947.

57. Memorandum from W. G. Husing and George D. Riley, National Legislative Committee, AFL, on *Talk with Senator Taft on reported proposed Amendments to the Taft-Hartley Act,* December 15, 1950.

CHAPTER 45. INTERNATIONAL POLICY

1. Samuel Gompers, Daniel McLaughlin, William Martin, G. Edmonston, and P. J. McGuire to the Officers and Delegates of the Federational Trade Union Congress in London assembled, October 27, 1888.

2. Samuel Gompers to Wilhelm Leibknecht, November 22, 1888, in AFL-CIO archives.

3. Gompers to André Gily, May 20, 1889.

4. *Vote Book of the Executive Council of the American Federation of Labor,* September 8, 1896.

5. *American Federationist,* December 1905, p. 938.

6. *Vote Book . . . ,* January 11, 1909.

7. *Report of Proceedings of the Thirtieth Annual Convention of the American Federation of Labor,* 1909, pp. 256-257; also "Appeal for Swedish Workers," executive council of American Federation of Labor, December 3, 1909.

8. Walter Schevenels, *Forty-five years, 1901–1945; International Federation of Trade Unions* (Brussels: M. Leemonnier, 1955), pp. 20-26.

9. *Minutes of the Executive Council of the American Federation of Labor,* February 20, 1911.

10. Legien to Gompers, August 27, 1914.

11. *Vote Book . . . ,* April 26, 1915. W. A. Appleton, Léon Jouhaux to Gompers, February 16, 1915.

12. Gompers to Legien, March 4, 1915; Legien to Gompers, April 12, 1915.

13. Gompers to J. Oudegest, May 24, 1917.

14. Cablegram from Gompers to Lindquist in Stockholm, June 27, 1919, in archives of AFL-CIO.

15. Schevenels, *op. cit.,* pp. 71-78.

16. *Preliminary Conference of International Federation of Trade Unions,* July 25, 1919, p. 15.

17. Carl Legien to E. Fimmen, September 20, 1919.

18. Philip Taft, *The A.F. of L. in the Time of Gompers* (New York: Harper and Brothers, 1957), pp. 431-438.

19. *Minutes of the Meeting of the Executive Council of the American Federation of Labor,* March 3, 1921.

20. J. Oudegest to Samuel Gompers, September 29, 1919.

21. Document 6, March 6, 1923, and Document 134, December 11, 1923, *Vote Book of . . . ,* December 11, 1923.

22. International Labor Office, Official Bulletin, I. April 1919–August 1920, p. 1; Carol Riegelman, "War-Time Trade Union and Socialist Proposals," in James T. Shotwell (ed.), *The Origins of the International Labor Organization* (New York: Columbia University Press, 1934), pp. 55-78.

23. Philip Taft, *The A.F. of L. from the Death of Gompers to the Merger* (New York: Harper and Brothers, 1959), pp. 234-235.

24. William Green to Sir Walter Citrine, June 15, 1939.

25. A request for aid was issued under the signatures of William Green and George Meany, February 28, 1940; Green appealed for visas to the State Department on February 7, 1941.

26. Walter Citrine to William Green, March 20, 1942.

27. *Minutes of the Executive Council American Federation of Labor,* May 20, 1942.

28. Citrine to Green, July 23, 1942.

29. *Daily Proceedings of the Fifth Constitutional Convention Congress of Industrial Organizations,* 1942, p. 117.

30. Green to A. F. Whitney, September 22, 1942.

31. *Minutes of the Meeting of the Executive Council of the American Federation of Labor,* January 27, 1943.

32. The quotation is from a *Report on WFTU, 1945–1949* to the CIO executive board, May 17, 1949 (mimeographed), p. 2.

33. *Ibid.,* p. 8.

34. *Eighth Constitutional Convention of the Congress of Industrial Organizations,* 1946, p. 175.

35. *Daily Proceedings of the Ninth Constitutional Convention* (CIO), October 16, 1947, p. 12.

36. Philip Taft, *op. cit.,* pp. 342-359.

37. *Daily Proceedings of the Ninth Constitutional Convention* (CIO), October 15, 1947, pp. 59-76.

38. *Daily Labor Report,* February 3, 1948.

39. *Minutes of the Executive Council of the American Federation of Labor,* January 26, 1948; statement of William Green before the Senate Foreign Relations Committee, February 23, 1948 in AFL-CIO archives.

40. *European Recovery Program Report of the International Trade Union Conference,* March 9, and 10, 1948 (London: Trades Union Congress, 1948), pp. 45-46.

41. *European Recovery Program—Second International Trade Union Conference Declaration,* July 30, 1948 (mimeo.).

42. *Report of the WFT, 1945–1949, to the C.I.O. Executive Board,* p. 18.

43. *Daily Proceedings of the Tenth Constitutional Convention* (CIO), 1948, pp. 119-120.

44. *Minutes of Executive Council of the American Federation of Labor,* February 6, 1949.

45. *Ibid.,* May 16, 1949.

46. Preparatory International Trade Union Conference, *First Report of Drafting Committee,* Geneva, July 25-26, 1949.

47. *Daily Proceedings of the Eleventh Constitutional Convention* (CIO), 1950, p. 187.

48. *Free Trade Unions Form the I.C.F.T.U.* (mimeo.), p. 20.

49. Philip Taft, *The A.F. of L. in the Time of Gompers* (New York: Harper and Brothers, 1957), pp. 320-332, deals with the activity of the AFL and Latin America.

CHAPTER 46. POLITICAL ACTIVITY OF ORGANIZED LABOR

1. *Final Proceedings of the Seventh Constitutional Convention of the Congress of Industrial Organizations,* 1944, p. 76.

2. *Minutes of Meeting of the Executive Council of the American Federation of Labor,* August 1, 1928.

3. *New York Times,* August 11, 1936.

4. *American Federation of Labor Weekly News Service,* May 2, 1936.

5. Saul Alinsky, *John L. Lewis* (New York: G. P. Putnam's Sons, 1949), p. 163.

6. "To Officers of National and International Unions, State Federations of Labor and City Central Bodies," March 21, 1938.

7. William Green to the Marin County Central Labor Council, San Rafael, California, March 1, 1939.

8. Green to National and International Unions, State Federations of Labor, City Central Bodies and Directly Chartered Unions, December 11, 1939.

9. *Report of the National Nonpartisan Political Committee of the American Federation of Labor,* September 30, 1940.

10. *The CIO News,* July 1940.

11. Quote is from the *Sixth Constitutional Convention of the Congress of Industrial Organizations,* 1943, in Joseph Gaer, *The First Round* (New York: Duell, Sloan and Pearce, 1944), p. 60.

12. *Ibid.,* pp. 176-180.

13. *Daily Labor Report,* November 11, 1943.

14. *Minutes of the Meeting of the Executive Council, American Federation of Labor,* August 12, 1943.

15. Matthew Josephson, *Sidney Hillman, Statesman of American Labor* (New York: Doubleday and Co., 1952), p. 605.

16. *Ibid.*

17. *Daily Labor Report,* January 13, 1944.

18. Biddle's letter, in *ibid.,* September 25, 1944.

19. U.S. Senate Report 101, 79th Cong., 1st sess., p. 23.

20. See Josephson, *op. cit.,* pp. 619-635.

21. Letter from William Green to affiliated unions and central bodies, February 23, 1944, in files of AFL-CIO.

22. George Berry to Green, March 17, 1944, in files of AFL-CIO.

23. *Seventh Constitutional Convention of the Congress of Industrial Organizations,* 1944, p. 210.

24. *Daily Labor Report,* May 23, 1944.

25. *Report of the Special Committee to Investigate Presidential, Vice-Presidential and Senatorial Expenditures in 1944,* p. 23.

26. *Daily Labor Report,* August 14, 1946.

27. *Ibid.,* March 14, 1947.

28. *Ibid.,* December 30, 1947.

29. *Ibid.,* January 7, 1947.

30. *Ibid.,* January 22, 23, 1947; *The CIO News,* January 28, 1947.

31. Pressman's letter of resignation and Murray's reply are in *Daily Labor Report,* February 6, 1948.

32. For the planks presented by the two federations see *ibid.,* June 17, 18, and July 9, 1948.

33. *Ibid.,* August 25, and November 3, 1948.

34. *Ibid.,* August 31, 1948, for the speech of Donald Henderson, head of the Food and Tobacco Workers' Union, subsequently expelled from the CIO for being Communist-dominated.

35. *Report of Proceedings of the Sixty-sixth Annual Convention of the American Federation of Labor,* p. 607.

36. *Minutes of the Meeting of Executive Council, American Federation of Labor,* October 7, 1947.

37. *Conference of Officers of National and International Unions,* Washington, D.C., December 5, 1947 (typewritten), in files of AFL-CIO, p. 3.

38. *Ibid.,* p. 13.

39. *Ibid.*

40. *Ibid.,* p. 15.

41. *Minutes of the Meeting of the Administrative Committee, Labor's League for Political Education,* February 4, 1947, pp. 9-11; February 5, 1947, pp. 12-16.

42. *Daily Labor Report,* October 6 and 8, 1948.

43. *Ibid.,* October 27, 1947.

44. *Congressional Quarterly,* 81st Cong., 1st sess., V, 82-83.

45. *Educational Fund Receipts,* in LLPE office in Washington.

46. *Proceedings of the Eleventh Constitutional Convention of the Congress of Industrial Organizations,* 1949, p. 184.

47. Labor's League for Political Education, *Report to the Administrative Committee,* May 17, 1949.

48. *Minutes of the Administrative Committee of Labor's League for Political Education,* August 16, 1949. Mr. Ferguson was state auditor.

49. *Daily Labor Report,* November 13, 1950.

50. *United Mine Workers Journal,* August 1, 1952, p. 8.

51. *Ibid.,* September 23, 1952.

52. *Congressional Quarterly,* IX (1953), 54.

53. "Article XIII (c)," Constitution of the American Federation of Labor and Congress of Industrial Organizations, 1955.

54. *Report of the First Constitutional Convention Proceedings, American Federation of Labor-Congress of Industrial Organizations,* 1955, pp. 158-159.

CHAPTER 47. COMMUNIST ACTIVITY IN ORGANIZED LABOR

1. *Confidential Report on Communists and Communist Activities Within the Trade Union Movement, submitted to President Green,* February 11, 1935. This analysis was a copy on Trade Union Work, December 11, 1934 (mimeo., no date or place).

2. *Maritime Worker,* July 20, 1936.

3. Max M. Kampelman, *The Communist Party and the C.I.O.* (New York: Frederick A. Praeger, 1957), p. 15.

4. *New York Times,* April 3, 1937.

5. Roy Hudson, "New Developments in Organizing the Marine Industry," *The Communist,* November 1937, p. 1017.

6. Earl Browder, *The People's Road to Peace* (New York: Workers Library, 1940), pp. 26-27.

7. *Ibid.,* p. 29.

8. Branch Resolution 1940 carried unanimously with no abstentions on May 14, 1940.

9. Kampelman, *op. cit.,* p. 20.

10. *Communist Domination of Certain Unions,* Senate Document 89, *Report of the Subcommittee on Labor and Labor-management Relations of the Committee on Labor and Public Welfare, U.S. Senate, 82d Cong., 1st sess., on Communist Domination of Certain Unions.* These are the reports of a number of committees which heard charges against Communist-dominated unions in the CIO.

11. Kampelman, *op. cit.,* pp. 35-36.

12. *Ibid.,* p. 87.

13. This article appeared in the union paper, October 1941, and was quoted in *ibid.,* p. 87.

14. Quoted in *ibid.,* p. 87.

15. *United Mine Workers Journal,* June 1, 1943, p. 13.

16. *Communist Domination of Certain Unions,* S. Doc. 89, p. 88.

17. "On the Dissolution of the Communist Party in the United States," *Daily Worker,* May 27, 1945, Section 3.

18. *Communists in Labor Unions,* special report prepared for members of the research Institute of America, April 4, 1946.

19. *Daily Labor Report,* July 1, 1946.

20. Philip Taft, *The Structure and Government of Labor Unions* (Cambridge, Mass.: Harvard University Press, 1956), pp. 199-205.

21. *TWU Express,* December 1948, p. 14.

22. *Daily Labor Report,* January 10, 1946.

23. *Ibid.,* May 16, 1947, and April 2, 1948.

24. *Ibid.,* November 15, 1946.

25. *Final Proceedings of the Eighth Constitutional Convention of the Congress of Industrial Organizations,* 1946, p. 112.

26. *Ibid.,* p. 114.

27. *Ibid.;* Kampelman, *op. cit.,* pp. 49-50.

28. *Daily Labor Report,* November 21, 1946.

29. *Report to President Philip Murray, Congress of Industrial Organization by Committee Appointed to Investigate Breach within the International Union of Mine, Mill and Smelter Workers,* May 16-17, 1947.

30. See *supra.*

31. Allan S. Haywood to Harry Bridges, February 18, 1948, in *Daily Labor Report,* February 20, and March 19, 1948.

32. John Brophy to Local and State Industrial Union Councils, *ibid.,* March 10, 1948.

33. Kampelman, *op. cit.,* pp. 156-158.

34. Officers of the UE resigned on March 19, 1948.

35. *Daily Labor Report,* April 13, 1948.

36. *Ibid.,* August 30; *Steel Labor,* June 1948.

37. *Proceedings of the Tenth Constitutional Convention of the Congress of Industrial Organizations,* 1948, p. 158.

38. *Daily Labor Report,* April 8, 1949.

39. *Ibid.,* May 17, 1949.

40. *Ibid.,* May 19, 1949.

41. *Ibid.,* September 21, 1949.

42. *Ibid.,* October 26, 1949.

43. *Proceedings of the Eleventh Constitutional Convention* (CIO), 1949, pp. 302-303.

44. *Ibid.,* p. 315.

45. *Ibid.,* p. 320.

46. *Hearings Regarding Communist Infiltration of Labor Unions,* Hearings Before the Committee on Un-American Activities, House of Representatives, 81st Cong., 1st sess., 1949, Part I, pp. 651-681.

47. *Ibid.,* p. 325.

48. *Ibid.,* p. 240.

49. *Ibid.,* p. 336.

50. For a detailed discussion of the trials, see Kampelman, *op. cit.,* pp. 167-224.

51. *Daily Labor Report,* April 20, 1950.

52. See the testimony of Lemuel R. Boulware in *Communist Domination of Unions and National Security,* in *Hearings Before a Subcommittee of the Committee on Labor and Public Welfare,* 82d Cong., 2d sess., 1952, especially pp. 450-464; *Proceedings of the Twelfth Constitutional Convention of the Congress of Industrial Organizations,* 1950, pp. 99-100.

53. *Jurisdictional Disputes in the Motion-Picture Industry, Hearings Before a Special Committee of the Committee on Education and Labor, House of Representatives,* 80th Cong., 2d sess. See especially testimony of Roy M. Brewer, Matthew M. Levy, and Herbert K. Sorrell, president of the Conference of Studio Unions. Sorrell's Communist connections are listed on pp. 2365-2370.

54. David J. Saposs, *Communism in American Unions* (New York: McGraw-Hill Book Co., 1959), pp. 15-118.

CHAPTER 48. THE KOREAN WAR

1. *Daily Labor Report,* March 31 and April 1, 3, 8, 10, 1948.

2. *Ibid.,* June 3, 1947. Quote is from *ibid.,* June 4, 1948.

3. *Ibid.,* July 3, 8, 1947.

4. John L. Lewis to the Officers and Members of all Local Unions in all Bituminous Districts of the United States, March 12, 1948, in *United Mine Workers Journal,* April 1, 1948, p. 5.

5. *Ibid.,* April 15, 1948, pp. 2-3.

6. *Ibid.*, p. 3.

7. *Daily Labor Report,* April 20, 1948.

8. *Ibid.*, June 14, 1948.

9. *Ibid.*, March 2, 1950.

10. *Ibid.*, May 25, 1950.

11. *Ibid.*, October 13, 1950.

12. *Ibid.*, January 18, 1951.

13. *Inland Steel Company* v. *National Labor Relations Board,* 15 Labor Cases, Par. 16, 737 (Chicago: Commerce Clearing House, 1949).

14. *Daily Labor Report,* July 6, 1949.

15. *Ibid.*, July 28, 1949.

16. *Ibid.*, September 12, 28, 1949.

17. *New York Times,* October 1, 1949.

18. The exchange of letters between Lewis and Green and Murray is in *Daily Labor Report,* October 14, 17, 1949.

19. *Ibid.*, October 31, 1949.

20. *The CIO News,* July 24, 1950.

21. *Ibid.*, September 4, 1950.

22. *Statement of the Executive Council of the American Federation of Labor,* August 10, 1950.

23. *Wage Stabilization Program, 1950–1953* (Washington: Wage Stabilization Board Economic Stabilization Agency, 1953), I, 1-2.

24. *Daily Labor Report,* October 10, 1950.

25. *Report by William Green, President, to State Federations of Labor and Central Labor Unions on Defense Mobilization Problems,* March 20, 1951, p. 5.

26. Statement by the meeting of representatives from the AFL, CIO, Railway Brotherhoods, and IAM, at the Statler Hotel in Washington, December 15, 1950.

27. *Statement to the President of the United States Submitted by the United Labor Policy Committee,* December 20, 1950.

28. *Wage Stabilization Program, op. cit.,* p. 78.

29. *Minutes of United Labor Policy Committee,* February 16, 1951.

30. *Report of William Green, op. cit.,* p. 8.

31. William Green, George E. Leighty, Philip Murray, and A. J. Hayes to Charles E. Wilson, February 20, 1951, in files of Industrial Union Department.

32. The last two quotes are from Charles E. Wilson to United Labor Policy Committee, February 20, 1951.

33. *Statement of United Labor Policy Committee,* February 28, 1951, p. 1.

34. *Ibid.*, p. 2.

35. *Ibid.*, p. 3.

36. *Ibid.*

37. *Wage Stabilization Program, op. cit.,* II, 5.

38. *Statement of the United Labor Policy Committee,* April 30, 1951; *Daily Labor Report,* April 17, and May 3, 1951.

39. *Daily Labor Report,* May 4, 1951.

40. *Ibid.*, November 15, 1951.

41. Statement of President Truman in *Wage Stabilization Program, op. cit.,* III, 356-358.

42. Special supplement of *Daily Labor Report,* March 22, 1952, contains the board's decision.

43. For Randall's speech, see *Daily Labor Report,* April 10, 1952; *New York Times,* April 10, 1952.

44. *Daily Labor Report,* June 6, 1952.

45. John L. Lewis, Thomas Kennedy, and John Owens to Philip Murray, June 18, 1952, in *United Mine Workers Journal,* July 1, 1952, p. 8.

46. *Daily Labor Report,* July 25, 1952.

47. *United Mine Workers Journal,* October 1, 1952, p. 3.

48. *Ibid.,* November 1, 1952, p. 3.

49. *Ibid.,* December 15, 1952, p. 5, for the President's letter to Roger L. Putnam.

50. *Monthly Labor Review,* April 1953, pp. 420-421.

51. Statement of William Green, August 28, 1951.

52. Statement by Philip Murray on United Labor Policy Committee, August 28, 1952.

CHAPTER 49. REUNIFICATION

1. Among them were (1) Marine Engineers' Benevolent Association; (2) American Communications Associations; (3) National Maritime Union—a compound of seagoing crafts; (4) Longshoremen's & Warehousemen's Union; (5) Federation of Architects, Engineers, Chemists and Technicians; (6) American Newspaper Guild; (7) Office and Professional Workers; (8) Federal Employees; (9) Retail Clerks; and (10) State, County and Municipal Workers.

2. Franklin D. Roosevelt to William Green, February 23, 1939.

3. Statement in the files of the AFL-CIO, issued March 7, 1939.

4. William Green to the Officers of National and International Unions, State Federations of Labor, City Central Labor Unions, and Local Trade Federal Labor Unions, March 20, 1939, for the views of the AFL.

5. Memorandum of Matthew Woll, March 13, 1939, and of William Green, April 5, 1939, in files of AFL-CIO.

6. *Statement of the Executive Council of the American Federation of Labor,* February 8, 1940.

7. John L. Lewis to William Green, January 17, 1942.

8. *Minutes of the Meeting of the Executive Council of the American Federation of Labor,* January 17, 1942.

9. Frank Duffy to William Green, February 25, 1942. Duffy was repeating a view expressed by Green to the executive board of the Carpenters' Union, of which he was secretary.

10. William Hutcheson to Green, March 9, 1942. Hutcheson, who headed the Carpenters' Union, prodded Green after the latter told Duffy he had an opportunity to discuss resumption of peace negotiations with the President.

11. Green to Hutcheson, March 28, 1942, in reply to Hutcheson to Green, March 20, 1942.

12. *Minutes of the Meeting of the Executive Council of the American Federation of Labor,* May 14, 1942.

13. William Green to Philip Murray, May 23, 1942.

14. Resolution of the CIO Executive Board, adopted June 3, 1942, in files of AFL-CIO.

15. *Ibid.*

16. The views of members of the council were given in the following letters: Edward Flore to Green, June 9, 1942; G. M. Bugniazet to Green, June 10,

1942; Daniel Tobin to Green, June 10, 1942; Harvey Brown to Green, June 10, 1942; William Birthright to Green, June 11, 1942; William D. Mahon to Green, June 11, 1942; William Hutcheson to Green, June 15, 1942; Felix H. Knight to Green, June 18, 1942.

17. Green to Murray, June 23, August 4, 1942; Murray to Green, August 1, 1942.

18. The agreement of December 2, 1942, was signed by Harry Bates, Daniel J. Tobin, and William L. Hutcheson for the AFL, and by Philip Murray, R. J. Thomas, and Julius Emspak for the CIO.

19. *Minutes of the Executive Council of the Metal Trades Department of the American Federation of Labor,* December 7, 1942, and May 10, 1943.

20. *Minutes of the Meeting of the Executive Council of the American Federation of Labor,* January 19, 1942.

21. Memorandum of AFL Committee to Negotiate Peace with CIO, April 1, 1943.

22. *Report of the Proceedings of the Sixty-third Annual Convention of the American Federation of Labor,* 1943, pp. 41-42.

23. Murray to Green, December 18, 1944.

24. Statement by William Green, December 18, 1944.

25. *Daily Labor Report,* January 29, 1946.

26. Murray to Green, December 5, 1946.

27. Green to Murray, January 31, 1947.

28. Murray to Green, January 31, 1947.

29. Congress of Industrial Organizations, *Fact Sheet on Labor Unity,* July 6, 1950.

30. A note from statement issued on May 2, 1947, and Murray to Green, July 31, 1947.

31. Murray to Green, July 2, 1947; Green to Murray, July 16, 1947.

32. Murray to Green, December 15, 1948; Green to Murray, December 22, 1948; February 28, 1949.

33. Murray to Green, April 4, 1950.

34. Quote is from a memorandum from Charles J. MacGowan to Daniel J. Tobin, D. W. Tracy, members of the AFL peace negotiating committee, July 31, 1950; *Minutes of the Meeting of the Executive Council of the American Federation of Labor,* May 11, and August 8, 1950.

35. *Daily Labor Report,* July 25, 1950.

36. *Ibid.*

37. *Minutes of the Meeting of the Executive Council of the American Federation of Labor,* September 29, 1952.

38. The Automobile, Brewery, Amalgamated Clothing Workers, Electrical, Radio and Machine Workers, Maritime, Oil Workers Retail, Wholesale and Department Store Employees, Rubber Workers, Textile, and Transport Service Workers gave their votes to Reuther. Haywood was supported by the Broadcast, Engineers and Technicians, Communications, Glass, Ceramic and Silica Sand, Government and Civic, Insurance and Allied, Lithographers, Marine and Shipbuilding, Optical and Instrument, Packinghouse, Paperworkers, Playthings, Jewelry and Novelty, Railroad, Steel, Transport, Utility, and eight out of nine delegates from the Woodworkers, unions. *Proceedings of the Fourteenth Constitutional Convention of the Congress of Industrial Organizations,* 1952, pp. 466-472, 491-511.

39. *Daily Labor Report,* February 5, 1953.

40. *Minutes of the Meeting of the Executive Council of the American Federation of Labor,* May 21, 1953.

41. Arthur Goldberg, *AFL-CIO Labor United* (New York: McGraw-Hill Book Co., 1956), p. 76.

42. Appendix D, in *ibid.,* p. 273.

43. Quoted in *ibid.,* p. 79.

44. *Daily Labor Report,* August 20, and September 8, 1953.

45. Goldberg, *op. cit.,* p. 83.

46. *Daily Labor Report,* June 24, 1954.

47. *Ibid.,* September 23, 1954.

48. Lewis to McDonald, in *ibid.*

49. *Ibid.*

50. *Proceedings of the Sixteenth Constitutional Convention of the Congress of Industrial Organizations,* 1954, p. 64.

51. "Agreement for the Merger of the American Federation of Labor and the Congress of Industrial Organizations," *Proceedings of the Seventeenth Constitutional Convention of the Congress of Industrial Organizations,* 1955, p. 75.

52. *Report of the Proceedings of the Seventy-fourth Annual Convention of the American Federation of Labor,* 1955, p. 50.

53. *Ibid.,* pp. 52-53.

54. *Ibid.,* pp. 354-364.

55. John Owens to James Carey, November 30, 1955, in *United Mine Workers Journal,* December 1, 1955, p. 2.

56. *Proceedings of the Seventeenth Constitutional Convention* (CIO), 1955, p. 9.

57. *Ibid.,* pp. 301-313.

58. *Minutes of the Executive Council of the American Federation of Labor,* May 21, 1953.

59. *American Federation of Labor and Congress of Industrial Organizations, First Constitutional Convention Proceedings,* 1955, p. 22.

60. Article II, Constitution of the American Federation of Labor and Congress of Industrial Organizations.

61. Articles VII, X, in *ibid.*

62. These figures underestimate the number of local central bodies and local unions and local industrial unions, some of which were not represented at the convention.

CHAPTER 50. ORGANIZED LABOR AND THE NEGRO

1. Luther Porton Jackson, *Free Negro Labor and Property Holding in Virginia, 1830–1860* (New York: D. Appleton-Century Co., 1942), p. 39.

2. *Ibid.*

3. Charles H. Wesley, *Negro Labor in the United States* (New York: Vanguard Press, 1927), pp. 15-17.

4. John R. Commons and associates (eds.), *A Documentary History of American Industrial Society* (Cleveland: Arthur H. Clark Co., 1910), IX, 159.

5. *Ibid.,* p. 185.

6. *Ibid.,* p. 239.

7. Terence V. Powderly to W. M. Pattill, May 15, 1883, in Library of the Catholic University, Washington, D.C.

8. Terence V. Powderly, *Thirty Years of Labor* (Scranton, Pa.: Terence V. Powderly, 1889), p. 348.

9. Sterling S. Spero and Abram L. Harris, *The Black Worker* (New York: Columbia University Press, 1931), p. 55.

10. *Report of the Proceedings of the Tenth Annual Convention of the American Federation of Labor,* 1890, p. 31.

11. *Report of the Proceedings of the Eleventh Annual Convention* (AFL), 1891, p. 12.

12. Samuel Gompers to R. T. Coles, April 28, 1891, in files of AFL-CIO.

13. Gompers to Harry E. Easton, April 30, 1891.

14. *Ibid.*

15. Gompers to executive council, May 17, 1893, in files of AFL-CIO.

16. Gompers to James O'Connell, November 3, 1893.

17. James Duncan to James O'Connell, undated, in files of AFL-CIO, signed by Duncan as acting president.

18. John McBride to Thomas Morgan, July 16, 1895.

19. Samuel Gompers, "Why Affiliate with the Federation," *American Federationist,* July 1896, p. 103.

20. *Report of the Proceedings of the Seventeenth Annual Convention* (AFL), 1897, p. 78.

21. Gompers to James E. Porter, June 18, 1900, in files of AFL-CIO.

22. *Report of the Proceedings of the Twentieth Annual Convention* (AFL), 1900, p. 22.

23. *Ibid.,* p. 23.

24. *Ibid.*

25. *Ibid.,* p. 112.

26. Gompers to George L. Norton, May 17, 1892.

27. Gompers to John M. Callahan, May 17, 1892.

28. Gompers to J. B. Powell, February 12, 1901; Gompers to David Kreyling, August 3, 1901. In a letter to Chris Evans, Gompers said: "You understand that in the appointment of volunteer organizers for any locality, the recommendation should always be endorsed by the Central body of such place." Chris Evans had recommended an appointment which Gompers had cleared with the Central Labor Union of Saginaw, Michigan.

29. Gompers to P. F. Sargent, May 17, 1902.

30. Article XI, Section VI, AFL Constitution.

31. Gompers to W. Boyd Greene, December 19, 1902.

32. W. E. Burghardt Du Bois (ed.), *The Negro Artisan* (Atlanta: Atlanta University Press, 1902), in John R. Commons, *Trade Unionism and Labor Problems* (New York: Ginn and Co., 1905), pp. 362-368.

33. *Ibid.,* p. 367.

34. This appeared in the President's Page of *The Carpenter,* January 1903, p. 3.

35. M. P. Carrick to Gompers, March 5, 1903.

36. Gompers to Booker T. Washington, February 16, 1912.

37. Samuel R. Spencer, *Booker T. Washington and the Negro's Place in American Life* (Boston: Little, Brown and Co., 1955), pp. 117-118.

38. Emmett J. Scott, *Negro Migration During the War* (New York: Oxford University Press, 1920), pp. 3-19.

39. *Ibid.,* pp. 95-133.

40. John Fitzpatrick to Gompers, March 29, 1920, in files of AFL-CIO; Spero & Harris, *op. cit.*, pp. 129-131.

41. *Report of the Proceedings of the Thirty-seventh Annual Convention* (AFL), 1917, pp. 349-350.

42. Memorandum of meeting between members of executive council and a committee of Negro leaders at the Federation Building in Washington, D.C., April 22, 1918.

43. *Report of the Proceedings of the Thirty-ninth Annual Convention* (AFL), 1919, pp. 304-305.

44. *Report of the Proceedings of the Fortieth Annual Convention* (AFL), 1920, p. 311.

45. Martin F. Ryan to Gompers, December 10, 1921, in files of AFL-CIO.

46. *Ibid.*

47. Constitution of the Brotherhood of Railway Carmen of America, 1921, Clause C, Section 6.

48. *Minutes of the Meeting of Executive Council of the American Federation of Labor,* February 14, 1924.

49. *Minutes of the Meeting of the Executive Council of the American Federation of Labor,* March 25, 1925.

50. Brailsford R. Brazeal, *The Brotherhood of Sleeping Car Porters* (New York: Harper and Brothers, 1946), pp. 16-17.

51. *Report of the Proceedings of the Forty-ninth Annual Convention* (AFL), 1929, pp. 384-385.

52. *Report of the Proceedings of the Fifty-fourth Annual Convention* (AFL), 1934, pp. 333-334.

53. Jerry Hanks to Green, December 4, 1935.

54. T. C. Carroll to Green, November 21, 1935.

55. John Brophy to William Green, November 6, 1935.

56. *Report of the Proceedings of the Fifty-fifth Annual Convention* (AFL), 1935, p. 809.

57. *Ibid.,* p. 808.

58. *Ibid.*

59. D. S. Robertson to Green, February 25, 1938.

60. Herbert R. Northrup, *Organized Labor and the Negro* (New York: Harper and Brothers, 1944), pp. 2-7, *The CIO and the Negro Worker* (Washington: n.d.), gives the views of the CIO.

61. *Report of the Proceedings of the Sixty-first Annual Convention* (AFL), 1941, p. 492; *Report of the National CIO Committee to Abolish Discrimination,* September 1945 (pamphlet).

62. *Report of the Proceedings of the Sixty-fourth Annual Convention* (AFL), 1944, p. 594.

63. *Seventh Constitutional Convention of the Congress of Industrial Organizations,* 1944, pp. 93-94.

64. Report of Walter P. Reuther to the Seventeenth Constitutional Convention, UAW, 1959, p. 95D.

65. *Statement Presented by William Green on the Ives-Chavez Anti-Discrimination Bill, S. 984, Before the Senate Committee on Labor and Public Welfare,* June 20, 1947.

66. *Constitution of the AFL-CIO and Other Official Documents Relating to the Achievements of Labor Unity* (Washington: AFL-CIO, 1956), Article II (4), p. 4.

67. *Ibid.*, Article XIX, (b).

68. *Proceedings of the AFL-CIO Third Constitutional Convention*, 1959, I, 479.

69. *Ibid.*, p. 487.

70. *Proceedings of the AFL-CIO Fourth Constitutional Convention*, 1961, I, 463-470.

71. *Ibid.*, pp. 475-516.

72. Meany's actual statement was: "Who the hell appointed you as guardian of all the Negroes in America?"

73. See Herbert Hill, "Has Organized Labor Failed the Negro?" *Negro Digest*, May 1962.

74. *New York Times*, May 28-31, 1960.

75. Melech Epstein, *Jewish Labor in U.S.A.* (New York: Trade Union Sponsoring Committee, 1950), p. 169.

76. *Ibid.*, p. 190.

77. Quote from decision in *i.u.d. fact sheet*, April 1963, p. 4.

78. *The Negro Wage-Earner and Apprenticeship Training* (New York: Labor Division National Association for the Advancement of Colored People, n.d.) discusses the problem of discrimination in training.

CHAPTER 51. VIOLENCE AND IMPROPER ACTIVITIES

1. *The Railway Clerk*, June 1, 1955, pp. 27-28; *Daily Labor Report*, April 19, and May 9, 1955.

2. *Daily Labor Report*, May 12, 1947, and June 26, 1950.

3. *Ibid.*, October 20, 1953.

4. *Ibid.*, November 12, 1954.

5. *Ibid.*, April 6, 8, 1955.

6. *Monthly Labor Review*, July 1955, p. 813.

7. *Daily Labor Report*, May 31, 1955.

8. *Ibid.*, May 18, 1956.

9. *Ibid.*, February 7, 1957.

10. Malcolm Johnson, *Crime on the Labor Front* (New York: McGraw-Hill Book Co., 1950), is one of the better volumes on the subject.

11. *Report of the Proceedings of the Eighteenth Annual Convention of the American Federation of Labor*, 1898, p. 55; *ibid.*, 1899, pp. 57, 155.

12. *State of New York, Intermediate Report of the Joint Legislative Committee on Housing* (Albany: J. B. Lyon Co., 1922), pp. 36-48.

13. *Ibid.*, pp. 65-66.

14. *Ibid.*, p. 55.

15. *Report of Illinois-Building Investigation Commission to His Excellency Len Small, Governor and the Fifty-third General Assembly*, 1919, pp. 34-35.

16. *Ibid.*, p. 35.

17. Johnson, *op. cit.*, 15-33; *Jurisdictional Disputes in the Motion Picture Industry, Hearings Before a Special Subcommittee of the Committee on Education and Labor, House of Representatives*, 80th Cong., 1st sess., especially testimony of Herbert Sorrell, Mathew Levy, and Richard Walsh. Bioff and Browne were convicted with several members of the Capone syndicate for extorting $3 million from the five major Hollywood moving picture studios for strike insurance between 1935 and 1940.

18. *Report of the Proceedings of the Fifty-second Annual Convention of the American Federation of Labor,* 1932, pp. 297-298.

19. William Green to P. J. Morrin, June 19, 1931.

20. Green to Morrin, July 27, 1932.

21. P. J. Morrin to Green, June 23, 1933.

22. Green to William C. Elliott, July 27, 1932.

23. To trade unionists and all other interested citizens in Illinois, from the Illinois Federation of Labor, Reuben Soderstrom, president; Victor Olander, secretary-treasurer, January 9, 1933.

24. To the officers and members of all organizations of labor, from William Green and Frank Morrison, November 15, 1933.

25. Memorandum to President William Green from George Roberts, chief of the AFL, Legislative Committee, November 18, 1934; William Green to Attorney-General Homer Cummings, in House Report 1833, 73d Cong., 2d sess., on S. 2248, 1934.

26. *U.S.* v. *Local 807 of the International Brotherhood of Teamsters, Chauffeurs, Stablemen and Helpers of America,* 315, U.S. 521 ((1942); Title 18, U.S. Code, Act of July 3, 1946, c. 537, 79th Cong., 60 Statute 420.

27. *Minutes of the Meeting of the Executive Council of the American Federation of Labor,* October 6, 1935.

28. *Ibid.*

29. *Report of the Proceedings of the Sixtieth Annual Convention* (AFL), 1940, p. 504.

30. Fay was soon to be convicted with Thomas Bove, a vice-president of the Laborers' Union, of a giant shakedown and was sentenced to prison. *New York Times,* November 21, 1940.

31. *Report of the Proceedings of the Sixtieth Annual Convention* (AFL), 1940, p. 505.

32. *Ibid.,* pp. 505-506.

33. *Ibid.,* 505.

34. *Ibid.,* p. 630.

35. *Minutes of the Meeting of the Executive Council of the American Federation of Labor,* February 13, 1941.

36. *Report of Vice-President Matthew Woll on the case of Jake Wellner,* May, 1941.

37. *Report of the Proceedings of the Sixty-first Annual Convention* (AFL), 1941, p. 543.

38. *Investigation of Racketeering in the Detroit Area,* Ninth Intermediate Report of the Committee on Government Operations, 83d Cong., 2d sess., p. 2.

39. *Minutes of the Meeting of the Executive Council of the American Federation of Labor,* May 21 and August 14, 1952; February 2 and May 22, 1953.

40. *Final Report to the Industrial Commissioner from Board of Inquiry on Longshore Industry Work Stoppage, October–November, 1951, Port of New York,* January 1952.

41. *Statement of the International Longshoremen's Association, AFL, on the Report, Dated January 22, 1952, of Industrial Commissioner Corsi's Board of Inquiry,* no date or place.

42. Matthew Woll, William S. Collins, Martin Lacey, Marx Lewis, and Thomas Murray to William Green, August 7, 1952.

43. David Dubinsky to George Meany, December 30, 1952.

44. George Meany to David Dubinsky, January 15, 1953, in files of AFL-CIO.

45. *Minutes of the Meeting of the Executive Council of the American Federation of Labor,* February 2, 1953.

46. George Meany and William F. Schnitzler to the officers and members of the International Longshoremen's Association, February 3, 1953.

47. Joseph P. Ryan, president, Harry R. Hasselgren, secretary-treasurer, and the Executive Council International Longshoremen's Association to George Meany, May 15, 1953.

48. George Meany to Joseph P. Ryan and Harry R. Hasselgren, May 26, 1953.

49. George Meany to the officers and members of the International Longshoremen's Association, August 11, 1953.

50. *Report of the Proceedings of the Seventy-second Annual Convention* (AFL), 1953, pp. 492-493.

51. *Minutes of the Meeting of the Executive Council of the American Federation of Labor,* September 22, October 11, 1953.

52. *Daily Labor Report,* August 27, 1954.

53. *Ibid.,* November 26, 1954.

54. See *In the Matter of Helsid Realty Corporation and Organized Building and Factory Service Employees Union, Local 21, 22, New York State Labor Relations Board No. 61, Case No. SE-31461, 1959.* Jay Kramer, chairman of the New York State Labor Relations Board, noted that there were 227 unaffiliated self-chartered locals and internationals. He was convinced that the problem of racketeering "in its most acute form, concerns self-chartered locals, such as the one at bar, which are not bound by codes of ethics, which have no tradition of good faith collective bargaining with employers and no history of service to employees." *Ibid.*

55. *Welfare and Pension Plans Investigation, Final Report of the Committee on Labor and Public Welfare, Submitted by its Subcommittee on Welfare and Pension Funds, Pursuant to S. Res. 225,* 1956, p. 17.

56. *Ibid.,* pp. 18-40.

57. *Minutes of the Meeting of the Executive Council of the American Federation of Labor,* February 9, 1954.

58. *Daily Labor Report,* June 6, 1956.

59. *Constitution of AFL-CIO,* 1955.

60. *Ibid.,* Art. VIII, Sec. 7.

61. *First Constitutional Convention Proceedings of the American Federation of Labor-Congress of Industrial Organizations,* 1955, p. 98.

62. Quote from *AFL-CIO Codes of Ethical Practices* (Washington: American Federation of Labor-Congress of Industrial Organizations, 1957), p. 9.

63. *Ibid.,* p. 12.

64. *Ibid.,* p. 14.

65. *Ibid.*

66. *Ibid.,* pp. 18-23.

67. *Ibid.,* p. 26.

68. *Ibid.,* p. 28.

69. *Ibid.,* p. 30.

70. *Proceedings of the AFL-CIO Constitutional Convention,* 1957, II, 88.

71. *Ibid.,* pp. 91-93.

72. *Violation or Nonenforcement of Government Laws and Regulations in*

the Labor Union Field, Hearings Before the Permanent Subcommittee on Investigations of the Committee on Government Operations, U.S. Senate, 85th Cong., 1st sess., Pursuant to S. Res. 188 (84th Cong.), 1957, p. 1.

73. *Daily Labor Report,* January 7, 1957.

74. *Investigation of Improper Activities in the Labor or Management Field, Hearings Before the Select Committee on Improper Activities in the Labor or Management Field, 85th Cong., 1st sess., Pursuant to S. Res. 74* (85th Cong.), Part I, p. 1.

75. *Ibid.,* pp. 3-15.

76. *Ibid.,* Part 4, is given over to the testimony of Frank W. Brewster and by staff members of the committee on his activities.

77. *Interim Report of the Select Committee on Improper Activities in the Labor or Management Field, Pursuant to S. Res. 74 and 221, 85th Cong., 1958, 2d sess.,* Senate Report 1417, p. 60.

78. *Ibid.,* p. 85.

79. *Ibid.,* p. 86.

80. *Ibid.,* p. 443.

81. *Ibid.,* p. 444.

82. *Ibid.,* pp. 448-450.

83. *Second Interim Report,* pp. 513-516.

84. *Investigation of Improper Activities in the Labor or Management Field, op. cit.,* Part 8, especially the testimony of James G. Cross, Joseph G. Kane, George Stuart, and Elsie K. Lower.

85. *Ibid., Interim Report,* pp. 131-162.

86. *Second Interim Report,* p. 183.

87. *Ibid.,* pp. 183-184.

88. *Ibid.,* p. 250.

89. *Ibid.*

90. *Ibid.,* p. 256.

91. *Ibid.,* p. 384.

92. *Ibid.,* p. 437.

93. *Ibid.,* pp. 437-438.

94. From an undated memorandum in the files of AFL-CIO.

95. *Second Interim Report,* pp. 591-592.

96. *Ibid.,* pp. 592-670.

97. *Investigation of Improper Activities in the Labor or Management Field, Hearings Before the Select Committee on Improper Activities in the Labor and Management Field, 85th Cong., 2d sess., Pursuant to S. Res. 74 and 221* (85th Cong.), Part 29, p. 11,328.

98. See testimony of Patrick E. Gorman, secretary-treasurer of the union, in *ibid.,* pp. 11,334-11,360.

99. *Ibid.,* p. 11,398.

100. *Ibid.,* Part 30, p. 11,659. Testimony of Vice-President Max Block.

101. See *ibid.,* Part 42, for testimony of contractors and union.

102. See *ibid.,* Part 52.

103. *Proceedings of the AFL-CIO Constitutional Convention 1957,* I, 456-461.

104. *Ibid.,* II, 467-468.

105. *Ibid.,* I, 55-105, 206-253, 518-544.

106. U.S. Department of Labor, Bureau of Labor-Management Reports, *A Report of the Bureau of Labor-Management Reports, Fiscal Year 1960,* p. 22.

107. U.S. Department of Labor, *Directory of National and International Unions in the United States,* 1959, Bureau of Labor Statistics Bulletin No. 1267, p. 15.

108. U.S. Department of Labor, *Summary of Operations, Bureau of Labor-Management Reports, Fiscal Year 1962,* p. 3.

109. *Ibid.,* p. 4.

Index

791

Green, General Duff, 31
Green, Marguerite, 731 *n.* 12, 734 *n.* 52
Green, Governor Theodore Francis, 448
Green, William, 537, 604, 673, 744 *n.* 40, 745 *nn.* 44-45, 751 *n.* 8, 754 *nn.* 6-7, 17, 756 *nn.* 17-18; AFL presidency, 654; AFL testimony (1948) before Republican and Democratic parties, 612-613; Amalgamated Association of Iron, Steel and Tin Workers, 506, 508, 510, 511-512; on anti-labor feeling in Congress, 613; Automobile Workers and, 469, 485, 486, 487, 488-489, 491, 492, 654, 761 *nn.* 7-8, 10-13, 19-22, 25, 762 *n.* 42; CIO expulsions and, 475, 479; CIO peace negotiations, 646, 647-648, 650-651; Committee for Industrial Organization and, 472, 477, 758 *nn.* 9-18, 759 *nn.* 31-33, 35-40, 46, 760 *nn.* 53-54, 58, 61-64, 67, 70; on company unions, 455; death of, 654-655; Doak and, 413; federal labor unions and, 465; general strikes and, 440; German free trade unions and, 601; on government ownership of railroads, 376; iron and steel code and, 420; international conference on labor legislation, 584; on jurisdictional rights of craft unions, 467; LaFollette and, 387; Lewis and, 492, 575, 585, 635, 647, 654, 766 *n.* 4; Marshall Plan and, 602; on mass production industrialism, 654; Mooney and, 334; National Industrial Recovery Act and, 418-419, 422; National Service Law and, 562; on new unions, 464; New York Port inquiry and, 692; in Ohio Senate, 654; as peace conference delegate, 596; political influence of, 775 *nn.* 24-26, 28, 30, 39, 776 *nn.* 7-8, 21-22; racial policy and, 785 *nn.* 53-55, 59, 65; racketeering and, 687-688, 690; reunification and, 781 *nn.* 51, 2, 4-5, 7, 9-11, 13, 16, 782 *nn.* 17, 23-24, 26-28, 30-33; rubber industry and, 469, 520, 524; southern campaign (1946), 589; Soviet trade unions and, 597; steel industry organization and, 507-508, 510, 763 *nn.* 6, 11-13, 764 *nn.* 16-17, 19-21, 23-29, 31, 33, 765 *n.* 45; on suspension powers, 476, 508; on Taft-Hartley, 773 *nn.* 22, 26, 774 *n.* 44; on violence, 787 *nn.* 19-22, 24-25, 42; on wage controls, 548-549, 550-551, 771 *n.* 11; war policies and, 539, 546, 557, 768 *n.* 3, 769 *nn.* 7-8, 16, 770 *nn.* 18, 40, 56, 2, 780 *nn.* 18, 25, 30-31; World Federation of Trade Unions and, 654
Greenback-Labor ticket (1878), 84

Greene, Nathan, 735 *n.* 27
Greene, W. Boyd, 784 *n.* 31
Gresham, Walter Q., 148
Greyhound Bus Company, strike, 576
Griffiths, Richard, 89
Grim, John W. H., 379
Grinnell, Julius S., 133-134
Grosscup, John F., 723 *n.* 3
Grosscup, Peter S., 153
Grossman, Jonathan, 716 *n.* 17, 718 *n.* 36
Growth of American Trade Unions (Wolman), 732 *n.* 1
Growth of Works Councils in the United States: Special Report No. 32, The (National Industrial Conference Board), 756 *n.* 4
Gulick, Charles A., 731 *n.* 3

Haas, Father Francis J., 445-446
Haber, William, 732 *n.* 18
Haggerty, D. P., 440
Haggerty, Thomas J., 257, 289, 290, 395
Hall, C. A., 100
Hall, Helen, 752 *n.* 4
Hammer v. Dagenhart, 408
Hammond, William J., 65
Hancock, General W. S., 79, 720 *n.* 27
Hand-Loom Weavers, New York, 30
Hanks, Jerry, 675, 785 *n.* 53
Hanna, Edward J., Archbishop, 368, 439
Hanna, Mark, 174-176, 195-196
Hanson, Ole, 342, 343
Hapgood, Powers, 399
Harding, Alfred, 646, 746 *n.* 17, 749 *n.* 28
Harding, Victor N., 153
Harding, Warren G., President, 354, 378, 753 *n.* 10
Harding, William, 60
Hardman, J. B., 513, 735 *n.* 20
Hardwick, Thomas W., house bombed, 338
Hardy, George, 745 *n.* 67
Harper's Magazine, 752 *n.* 18
Harper's Weekly, 195
Harrah, C. J., 161
Harriman, Mrs. J. Borden, 227
Harriman, Job, 281
Harris, Abraham L., 784 *n.* 9
Harris, Evelyn L. K., 735 *nn.* 13, 17, 19
Harris, Frank, 134
Harris, George, 115
Harrison, Carter, 131, 208
Harrison Committee, 476
Harrison, George M., 53, 480, 492, 531, 604, 759 *nn.* 48, 51-52, 760 *nn.* 59, 64; CIO peace negotiations, 647; Committee for Industrial Organization and, 475-478; defense mobilization and, 640; German free trade unions and, 601; National Defense Mediation Board, 540; New York Port inquiry, 693; Truman-Barkley ticket, 613-616

Hart, Schaffner and Marx, 250-251, 252
Hartley, Fred, 582
Hartranft, Governor John F., 77-78
Harvey, George, 195, 726 *nn.* 8, 9
Harvey, J., 118
Hasselgren, Harry R., 788 *nn.* 47-48
Hatfield, Sid, 353-354
Hatters Unions, 40-41; *see also under* United Hatters
Hawes-Cooper Act, 409
Hawley, Governor James, 288
Hawthorne, Nathaniel, 47
Hayes, A. J., 780 *n.* 31
Hayes, Frank J., 260, 318, 351
Hayes, John W., 169
Hayes, Max S., 289, 324, 325, 384, 743 *n.* 9
Hayes, Rutherford B., President, 77, 720 *nn.* 25-26
Haymarket riot, 127-128, 130-131, 135; trial of rioters, 132-134
Haymarket Riot, The (Zeisler), 726 *n.* 28
Haywood, Allan S., 604, 652, 655, 779 *n.* 31
Haywood, William D., 290, 293-294, 297, 741 *n.* 42; IWW head, 295, 716 *n.* 18; murder indictment, 287
Haywood v. U.S. On Petition for a Writ of Certiorari to the U.S. Circuit Court of Appeals for the Seventh Circuit, 741 *nn.* 44-45
Headwear Worker, The (Green), 716 *n.* 19
Head Tax, 301
Health and Welfare Plans, 694-695
Hearings Before the Committee on Banking and Currency, U.S. Senate, 77th Cong., 1st Sess., on H. R. 5990, 768 *n.* 4
Hearings Before the Committee on Education and Labor, U.S. Senate, To Create a National Labor Board, 756 *nn.* 1-2
Hearings Before the Committee on Investigation of U.S. Steel Corporation, 727 *n.* 28, 731 *nn.* 6, 16-17
Hearings Before the Senate Committee on Post Offices and Post Roads, 766 *n.* 72
Hearings Before a Special Committee Investigating the National Defense Program, U.S. Senate, 77th Cong., 1st Sess., Pursuant to S. Res. 71, 768 *n.* 15, 769 *n.* 23
Hearings Before the Special Committee on Post-War Economic Planning, U.S. Senate, 78th Cong., 2d Sess., 770 *n.* 3
Hearings Before a Subcommittee on Education and Labor, U.S. Senate, 75th Cong., 3rd Sess., Pursuant to S. Res. 266, 765 *nn.* 62, 65-67

Railroad Unions. *See specific groups*, e.g., Brotherhood of Railway Carmen

Railroad Wage Commission in World War I, 315

Railway Carmen's Journal, The, 748 n. 2

Railway Clerk, The, 786 n. 1

Railway Employees' Department, AFL, 363, 377, 409, 673; seventh convention, 749 nn. 18-21, 27-28, 750 nn. 31, 40-42

Railway Labor Act (1926), 409

Railway Labor Board, 385

Railway Labor Executives' Association, 563, 575, 606-607

Railway and Steamship Clerks, Brotherhood of, v. Texas and New Orleans Railway Company, 409-410

Randall, Clarence R., 641

Randolph, A. Philip, 673-674, 675; Code of Fair Trade Union Racial Practices, 678-679; march on Washington threat, 345, 677; Negro American Labor Council and, 669

Randolph, Woodruff, 585, 660, 773

Raskin, A. H., 534, 767 n. 40

Rastall, Benjamin, 739 nn. 10, 19

Rat circulars in printing industry, 30-32

"Rat" lists, 32, 36

Ratchford, Michael, 170, 173

Ray, Scripps, 224-225

Rayburn, Sam, 587

Recognition of Russia, Hearings (U.S. Senate Committee on Foreign Relations), 751 n. 3

Recommendations of the Anthracite Coal Commission of 1902, 180

Reconstruction program of AFL, 320-321

Record of the Proceedings of the Fourth Regular Session of the General Assembly, 721 nn. 27-31

Record of the Proceedings of the General Assembly of the Knights of Labor Commencing with a Session at Richmond, Virginia, 723 n. 18

Record of the Proceedings of the Ninth General Session of the General Assembly, 724 n. 17

Record of the Proceedings of the Second Regular Session of the General Assembly, 721 n. 17, 724 n. 15

Record of the Proceedings of the Seventh Regular Session of the General Assembly, 722 nn. 36, 38

Record of the Proceedings of the Sixth General Session of the General Assembly, 722 n. 35

Record of Proceedings of the Third Regular Session of the General Assembly, 721 n. 26

Red Labor Union International, 392, 619

Reed, John, 60, 295

Re-enactment of the Chinese Exclusion Law, California's Memorial to the President and the Congress of the United States, For the, 741 n. 13

Reform political movements, 19-20; convention of 1845, 49

Regional Labor Board, 552-553

Reid, Whitelaw, 142, 727 n. 25

Reins, D. H., 712 n. 26

Remarks of Samuel Gompers Before Conference of the Executives of the Railroad Organizations Affiliated with the A.F. of L. and the Four Brotherhoods, 738 n. 19

Rend, W. P., 167-168

Report of Acting President John L. Lewis to the Twenty-seventh Consecutive and Fourth Biennial Convention of the United Mine Workers of America, 746 n. 27

Report of the Activities of the War Department in the Field of Industrial Relations During the War (U.S. War Dept.), 742 n. 8, 745 nn. 55-56, 757 n. 8

Report of the Attorney-General of the United States for the Year 1920, 745 n. 58

Report on the Bisbee Deportations Made by the President's Mediation Commission, 745 nn. 52-53

Report of Board of Inquiry for the Cotton Textile Industry, 756 nn. 37-39

Report of the Bureau of Labor-Management Reports, Fiscal Year 1960, 789 n. 106

Report on the Chicago strike of June–July, 1894, by the U.S. Strike Commission, 727 n. 38

Report on the Colorado Strike (West), 737 n. 19

Report on the Colorado Strike Investigation Under H. Res. 387, 737 n. 21

Report of the Committee on Education and Labor Pursuant to S. Res. 266, 765 nn. 53-55

Report of the Committee of [U.S.] Senate Upon Relations Between Capital and Labor, 721 n. 25, 722 nn. 1-4, 724 nn. 9-10

Report on the Constitutionality of the National Labor Relations Act, 758 n. 43

Report of the Eight-Hour Commission to the President and Congress of the United States, 1917; Cooperative Movement Brotherhood of Locomotive Engineers, Brotherhood of Locomotive Firemen and Enginemen, Order of Railway Conductors, Brotherhood of Railroad Trainmen, 738 n. 20

Report of a Hearing Before the Committee on the Judiciary of the House of Representatives, March 23, 1900, on the Bill to Limit the Meaning of the Word "Conspiracy" and also the Use of "Restraining Orders Injunctions" as Applied to Disputes Between Employer and Employees, etc., 735 n. 29

Report of the Hearings on Hours of Labor for Workmen, etc., Mechanics Employed Upon Public Works Before Committee Relative to H.R. 6882, 728 nn. 4-5

Report of the Industrial Commission on the Relations of Capital and Labor Employed in the Mining Industry, 729 n. 15

Report of the Industrial Commission on Trusts and Industrial Combinations, 728 n. 3

Report of the Joint Special Committee to Investigate Chinese Immigration, 741 nn. 5-9

Report on Labor Disturbances in the State of Colorado from 1880 to 1904, Inclusive, A, 739 n. 6

Report of the National Longshoremen's Board, 755 n. 6, 756 n. 19

Report to the President on the Anthracite Coal Strike of May-October 1902, 730 n. 34-36

Report of President Wilson's Mediation Commission, 743 n. 22, 744 n. 34

"Report and Resolutions of the Committee of Fifty," 17

Report of the Special Committee to Investigate Presidential, Vice Presidential and Senatorial Expenditures, 777 n. 25

Report on the Steel Strike (Interchurch World-Movement), 747 nn. 51-53

Report of the Strike Commission, 158

Report on Strike of Textile Workers in Lawrence, Massachusetts (Sen. Doc.), 740 n. 35

Report on Strikes and Lockouts Occurring in the United States During the Calendar Year 1880 (Weeks), 719 nn. 2-3

Report of the Subcommittee on Labor and Labor-Management Relations of the Committee on Labor and Public Welfare, U.S. Senate, 82nd Cong., 1st Sess. on Communist Domination of Certain Unions, 778 n. 10

Report on Trade Societies in the United States (Weeks), 719 n. 1

Report of the United States Board of Mediation and Conciliation on the Effects of Arbitration Proceedings Upon Rates of Pay and Working Conditions of Railroad Employees, 737 nn. 1-2

About the Author

Born in Syracuse, New York, PHILIP TAFT was gradu-
ated from the University of Wisconsin where he received
his B.A. and Ph.D. degrees. While a graduate student at
Wisconsin he collaborated with Professor Selig Perlman
on the fourth volume of John R. Commons's classic
History of Labor in the United States.

After working for a year with the Social Security
Board in Washington, D.C., Mr. Taft went to Brown
University as an assistant professor in the Department
of Economics, and is currently a full professor there. He
has also taught at Wesleyan University, Columbia University, the universities of Michigan, Wisconsin, California at Berkeley, and at Harvard.

During and after World War II, Professor Taft
worked as a labor arbitrator and was a member of the
New England Regional Panel of the War Labor Board.
For a number of years he has served as consultant on
the staff of the Rhode Island Department of Employment Security. He is a former chairman of a Rhode
Island Commission on Workmen's Compensation. In
1961 he was a member of the Labor Study Group of
the Committee for Economic Development.

Philip Taft is also author of *Structure and Government of Labor Unions, Movements for Economic Reform, Economics and Problems of Labor,* as well as two
volumes on the American Federation of Labor.

Format by Sidney Feinberg
Set in Linotype Times Roman
Composed, printed and bound by American Book–Stratford Press, Inc.
HARPER & ROW, PUBLISHERS, INCORPORATED